# Psychology in Action

12th Edition

**KAREN HUFFMAN**

Palomar College

**KATHERINE DOWDELL**

Des Moines Area Community College

**CATHERINE A. SANDERSON**

Amherst College

| | |
|---|---|
| VICE PRESIDENT AND EXECUTIVE PUBLISHER | George Hoffman |
| EXECUTIVE EDITOR | Veronica Visentin—Editorial Director |
| DIRECTOR OF DEVELOPMENT | Barbara Heaney |
| PRODUCT DESIGNER | Wendy Ashenberg |
| SENIOR MARKETING MANAGER | Glenn Wilson |
| SENIOR CONTENT MANAGER | Dorothy Sinclair |
| SENIOR PRODUCTION EDITOR | Sandra Rigby |
| CREATIVE DIRECTOR | Jon Boylan |
| SENIOR DESIGNER | Wendy Lai |
| PHOTO DEPARTMENT MANAGER | Melinda Patelli |
| SENIOR PHOTO EDITOR | Mary Ann Price |
| PRODUCTION SERVICES | Furino Production |

Cover photo: © vernonwiley/Getty Images
Study Tip and Test Yourself icon photos: Billy Ray/Wiley
Chapter Opener tennis shoes photo: © alexxl66/iStockphoto

This book was typeset in 9.5/11.5 Source Sans Pro at Aptara and printed and bound by Quad/Graphics. The cover was printed by Quad/Graphics.

Founded in 1807, John Wiley & Sons, Inc. has been a valued source of knowledge and understanding for more than 200 years, helping people around the world meet their needs and fulfill their aspirations. Our company is built on a foundation of principles that include responsibility to the communities we serve and where we live and work. In 2008, we launched a Corporate Citizenship Initiative, a global effort to address the environmental, social, economic, and ethical challenges we face in our business. Among the issues we are addressing are carbon impact, paper specifications and procurement, ethical conduct within our business and among our vendors, and community and charitable support. For more information, please visit our website: www.wiley.com/go/citizenship.

This book is printed on acid-free paper.

Enhanced EPUB ISBN: 978-1-119-39483-9

The inside back cover will contain printing identification and country of origin if omitted from this page. In addition, if the ISBN on the cover differs from the ISBN on this page, the one on the cover is correct.

Printed in the United States of America.

V10014982_102319

# About the Authors

Courtesy of Karen Huffman

**KAREN HUFFMAN** is an emeritus professor of psychology at Palomar College, San Marcos, California, where she taught full time until 2011 and served as the Psychology Student Advisor and Co-Coordinator for psychology faculty. Professor Huffman received the National Teaching Award for Excellence in Community/ Junior College Teaching given by Division Two of the American Psychological Association (APA), along with many other awards and accolades. She's also the author and co-author of several textbooks, including *Psychology in Action, Psychology,* and *Real World Psychology*. Professor Huffman's special research and presentation focus is on active learning and critical thinking. She has been the invited speaker and conducted numerous presentations, online web seminars, and teaching workshops throughout the United States, Spain, Canada, and Puerto Rico.

Courtesy of Katherine Dowdell

**KATHERINE DOWDELL** is a professor of psychology at Des Moines Area Community College in Iowa, where she teaches courses in introduction to psychology, abnormal psychology, lifespan development and social psychology. She also currently serves as District Chair of Behavioral Sciences. Professor Dowdell received her BA in Psychology from the University of Pennsylvania, and her MS in Clinical Psychology from the University of Pittsburgh.

Professor Dowdell began working with Karen Huffman and the Wiley Psychology team as a Wiley Faculty Network mentor in 2007. She has taught and mentored faculty on best practices and the use of technology in teaching. She has conducted numerous online presentations and live workshops. As a decade-long user of WileyPLUS, Professor Dowdell has served as a development consultant on everything from WileyPLUS functionality, to video content, instructional design, user-experience and faculty training.

Courtesy of Catherine Sanderson

**CATHERINE A. SANDERSON** is the Manwell Family Professor of Life Sciences (Psychology) at Amherst College. She received a bachelor's degree in psychology, with a specialization in health and development, from Stanford University, and received both masters and doctoral degrees in psychology from Princeton University. Professor Sanderson's research examines how personality and social variables influence health related behaviors such as safer sex and disordered eating, the development of persuasive messages and interventions to prevent unhealthy behavior, and the predictors of relationship satisfaction. This research has received grant funding from the National Science Foundation and the National Institute of Health. Professor Sanderson has published over 25 journal articles and book chapters in addition to five college textbooks, a high school health textbook, and a popular press book on parenting. In 2012, she was named one of the country's top 300 professors by the Princeton Review.

# Brief Contents

# Contents

© vernonwiley/Getty Images

What do you think about the death-defying mountain climber on the cover of this text? Most readers don't recognize the time and thought authors and publishers commit to visually capturing the essential message of their work. In our case, we've always chosen activity-oriented images for all twelve editions of *Psychology in Action* because, as its name implies, our textbook has earned its reputation as a leader in *active learning.*

Beginning with our first edition, we were the first to include *Try This Yourself* activities, *Study Tips, Research Challenges,* and other "hands on" demonstrations (e.g., *Critical Thinking Exercises* and *Media Challenges* that are available as graded assignments in the WileyPlus program). Why? We've always believed that student success is best assured through active learning, which encourages students to think critically and engage with

the material—thus leading to deeper levels of processing. Our enduring foundation in active learning continues in this twelfth edition—as shown in the following examples.

What's **NEW** in *Psychology in Action* 12e? Given our commitment to active learning and evidence-based research, we've chosen to make the development of a *growth mindset* and *grit* as the central goals and theme of this edition. As you may know, studies find that these two factors may be the most significant factors in determining career and academic success. In fact, some research suggests that they may be even more important than IQ (Datu et al., 2016; Dweck, 2007, 2012; Suzuk et al., 2015).

With this focus on a growth mindset and grit in mind, we start each chapter with a NEW *Psychology and a Classic* (or *Contemporary*) *Success* feature, which offers a brief description of a famous figure who exemplifies both qualities. (See the following example of J. K. Rowling.) The stories are then embedded throughout each chapter to illustrate core concepts. We believe offering these repeated success stories will reassure our readers that achievement is largely under their control,

---

## Try This Yourself

### Testing for Reflexes

If you have a newborn or young infant in your home, you can easily (and safely) test for these simple reflexes. (Most infant reflexes disappear within the first year of life. If they reappear in later life, it generally indicates damage to the central nervous system.)

### Test Your Critical Thinking

1. What might happen if infants lacked these reflexes?
2. Can you explain why most infant reflexes disappear within the first year?

photos by Linnea Leaver Mavrides/Courtesy Catherine Sanderson

**A Rooting reflex**
Lightly stroke the cheek or side of the mouth, and watch how the infant automatically (reflexively) turns toward the stimulation and attempts to suck.

photos by Linnea Leaver Mavrides/Courtesy Catherine Sanderson

**B Grasping reflex**
Place your finger or an object in the infant's palm and note his or her automatic grasping reflex.

photos by Linnea Leaver Mavrides/Courtesy Catherine Sanderson

**C Babinski reflex**
Lightly stroke the sole of the infant's foot, and the big toe will move toward the top of the foot, while the other toes fan out.

---

## Research Challenge

### Why Do Men and Women Lie About Sex?

The *social desirability bias* is of particular concern when we study sexual behaviors. A fascinating example comes from a study that asked college students to complete a questionnaire regarding how often they engaged in 124 different gender-typical behaviors (Fisher, 2013). Some of these behaviors were considered more typical of men (such as wearing dirty clothes and telling obscene jokes), whereas other behaviors were more common among women (such as writing poetry and lying about their weight). Half of the participants completed these questionnaires while attached to what they were told was a polygraph machine (or lie detector), although in reality this machine was not working. The other half completed the questionnaires without being attached to such a machine.

Can you predict how students' answers differed as a function of their gender and whether they were (or were NOT) attached to the supposed lie detector? Among those who were attached to a supposed lie detector and who believed that it could reliably detect their lies, men were more likely to admit that they sometimes engaged in behaviors seen as more appropriate for women, such as writing poetry. In contrast, women were more likely to admit that they sometimes engaged in behaviors judged more appropriate for men, such as telling obscene jokes. Even more interesting, men reported having had more sexual partners when they weren't hooked up to the lie detector than when they were. The reverse was true for women! They reported fewer partners when they were not hooked up to the lie detector than when they were.

How does the *social desirability response* help explain these differences? We're all socialized from birth to conform to norms (unwritten rules) for our culturally approved male and female behaviors. Therefore, participants who were NOT attached to the supposed lie detector provided more "gender appropriate" responses. Men admitted telling obscene jokes and reported having more sexual partners, whereas women admitted lying about their weight and reported having fewer sexual partners.

These findings were virtually reversed when participants believed they were connected to a machine that could detect their

lies. This fact provides a strong example of the dangers of the social desirability response. It also reminds us, as either researchers or consumers, to be very careful when interpreting findings regarding sexual attitudes and behaviors. Gender roles may lead to inaccurate reporting and exaggerated gender differences.

Inti St Clair/Getty Images

### Test Yourself

1. Based on the information provided, did this study (Fisher, 2013) use descriptive, correlational, and/or experimental research?
2. If you chose:
   - *descriptive research*, is this a naturalistic observation, survey/interview, case study, and/or archival research?
   - *correlational research*, is this a positive, negative, or zero correlation?
   - *experimental research*, label the IV, DV, experimental group(s), and control group. (Note: If participants were not randomly assigned to groups, list it as a *quasi-experimental design*.)
   - both *descriptive* and *correlational*, answer the corresponding questions for both.

Check your answers by clicking on the answer button or by looking in Appendix B.

**Note:** The information provided in this study is admittedly limited, but the level of detail is similar to what is presented in most textbooks and public reports of research findings. Answering these questions, and then comparing your answers to those provided, will help you become a better critical thinker and consumer of scientific research.

---

### Study Tip

*One way to differentiate the two subdivisions of the ANS is to imagine skydiving out of an airplane. When you initially jump, your sympathetic nervous system has "sympathy" for your stressful situation. It alerts and prepares you for immediate action. Once your "para" chute opens, your "para" sympathetic nervous system takes over, and you can relax as you float safely to earth.*

❖ Psychology and a Contemporary Success | J. K. Rowling

PA Images/Alamy Stock Photo

Joanne Rowling, best known as J. K. Rowling (1965–), is a British novelist, screenwriter, and film producer famous for her authorship of the *Harry Potter* series of fantasy novels (see photo). Rowling (pronounced *rolling*) was born in Yate, England, to parents who, as she says, "came from impoverished backgrounds and neither of whom had been to college." They did, however, love to read, and Rowling grew up surrounded by books to become the classic "bookworm." After graduating from Exeter University, Rowling moved to Portugal, where she met and married a Portuguese journalist. The marriage soon ended in divorce, and Rowling moved with her daughter to live near her sister in Edinburgh, Scotland. Struggling to support herself and her young daughter, she reluctantly signed up for welfare benefits, saying that she was "as poor as it is possible to be . . . without being homeless." Rowling sold her first novel in the Harry Potter series for only $4,000. Since then, though, this series of books has sold over 450 million copies (McClurg, 2017; Rowling, n.d.).

Despite her apparently wildly successful life, Rowling has endured numerous hardships. She reports that her teenage years were very unhappy due to her mother's protracted illness and a strained relationship with her father. The period after her divorce and her mother's painful death from multiple sclerosis was a particularly difficult time for Rowling. She saw herself as such a dismal failure that she even contemplated suicide. Fortunately, therapy helped her climb out of her diagnosed clinical depression, and she later reported that it was her experiences with such deep despair that led her to create the *Dementors*—the soul-sucking monsters found in the *Harry Potter* series (Bennett, 2012; Oppenheim, 2016; Rowling, n.d.).

and thereby inspire them to use grit and a growth mindset to achieve their own personal dreams and aspirations. As shown in **Table 1**, we also include two additional NEW features— *Psychology and Your Personal Success* and *Psychology and Your Professional Success*—to further demonstrate how the content of each chapter, along with a growth mindset and grit, can help them succeed in the real world.

Given that our gracious and loyal previous adopters may be interested in what changes we've made and/or the updating we've added in this 12th edition (i.e., to the basic content, key terms, and continued features), we've created a handy summary of these changes in **Table 2**. This table also summarizes the key assets for each chapter provided in WileyPLUS.

# Additional Resources

## WileyPlus with ORION

Given that students obviously don't all learn and achieve at the same rate, WileyPLUS with ORION provides adaptive practice in a digital tutorial, homework, and assessment platform that significantly improves individual student performance and success rates.

- Identify their personal strengths and weaknesses through adaptive, 24/7, robust self-testing with immediate, personalized feedback

- Save time by making study time and practice testing more efficient
- Better prepare for both online and in-class quizzes and exams
- Create a focused and personalized study plan that reflects their individual learning needs
- Truly engage with course content—resulting in deeper levels of processing, higher performance, and overall achievement in the course
- Improve their individual, academic success skills and transfer them to all other college courses
- Quickly assess individual and class activity and track student progress using real time data and analytics, and then adjust lectures and testing material appropriately
- Create meaningful assignments and additional resources with personalized feedback for each student
- Save preparation and grading time with high-quality instructor resources and automated grading of assignments, practice tests, and exams
- Enhance lectures and create a focused and personalized course that reflects their individual teaching style
- Quickly identify and understand student learning trends to improve classroom engagement
- Improve their course year after year using WileyPLUS data

## Wiley E-Textbook

E-Textbooks are complete digital versions of the text that help students study more efficiently as they:

- Access content online and off line on a desktop, laptop, or mobile device
- Search across the entire book content
- Take notes and highlight
- Copy and paste or print key sections

Wiley E-Text: Powered by Vitalsource® allows student access to course content anytime and anywhere. With the Wiley E-Text, students can:

- Create a personalized study plan
- Easily search content and make notes
- Share insights and questions with peers

## Wiley Custom

This group's services provide the freedom and flexibility for instructors to:

- Adapt existing Wiley content and combine texts
- Incorporate and publish personal instructional materials
- Collaborate with Wiley's team to ensure both instructor and student satisfaction and success

## Wiley Custom Select

Wiley Custom Select allows instructors to build their own course materials using selected chapters of any Wiley text and their own material if desired. For more information, contact Wiley sales representatives and/or visit http://customselect.wiley.com/.

# Acknowledgments

**Reviewers:** To the professors who reviewed material and gave their time and constructive criticism, we offer our sincere appreciation. This text is much stronger, clearer, and concise thanks to their efforts. We are deeply indebted to the following individuals, and trust that they will recognize their contributions throughout the text.

Mary Beth Ahlum, *Nebraska Wesleyan University*; Kathryn Alves-Labore, *Forsyth Technical Community College*; Roxanna Anderson, *Palm Beach State College*; Susan Antaramian, *Christopher Newport University*; Darin Baskin, *Lone Star College*; Matthew Bell, *Santa Clara University*; Barbara Boccaccio, *Tunxis Community College*; Amy Bradshaw Hoppock, *Embry-Riddle Aeronautical University*; Courtney Brewer, *Suffolk County Community College*; Melissa Brown, *State University of New York,* College at Brockport; Michael Cassens, *Irvine Valley College*; Sky Chafin, *Grossmont College*; Charlene Chester, *Morgan State University*; Wanda Clark, *South Plains College*; Herb Coleman, *Austin Community College*; Lorry Cology, *Owens Community College*; Rosalyn Davis, *Indiana University, Kokomo*; Ben Denkinger, *Augsburg College*; Michael Dudley, *Southern Illinois University, Edwardsville*; Sylvia Edwards-Borens, *Texas State Technical College, Waco*; Daniella Errett, *Pennsylvania Highlands Community College*; Rebecca Ewing, *Central Georgia Technical College*; Linda Fayard, *Mississippi Gulf Coast Community College*; Johnathan Forbey, *Ball State University*; Jamie Franco-Zamudio, *Spring Hill College*; Audrey Fresques, *Paradise Valley Community College*; William Fry, *Youngstown State University*; Perry Fuchs, *The University of Texas at Arlington*; Janet Gebelt, *Westfield State University*; William Goggin, *University of Southern Mississippi*; Kate Guts, *Seattle University*; Jill Haasch, *Elizabeth City State University*; Barbara Hall, *Iowa Valley Community College*; Kate Halverson, *Des Moines Area Community College*; Andrew Herst, *Montgomery College*; Becky Howell, *Forsyth Technical Community College*; Vivian Hsu, *Rutgers, The State University of New Jersey*; Dominique Hubbard, *Northern Virginia Community College, Alexandria*; Jeannie Hudspeth, *Ozarka College*; Sierra Iwanicki, *Eastern Michigan University*; Alisha Janowsky, *University of Central Florida*; Joan Jensen, *Central Piedmont Community College*; Robert Rex Johnson, *Delaware County Community College*; Karen Jolley, *Central Georgia Technical College*; Deana Julka, *University of Portland*; Kristina Klassen, *North Idaho College*; Jim Koopman, *Des Moines Area Community College*; Monica Lackups-Fuentes, *Eastern Michigan University*; Julie Learn, *Indiana University of Pennsylvania*; James Leone, *Bridgewater State University*; Bernard Levin, *Blue Ridge Community College*; Carolyn Lorente, *Northern Virginia Community College*; Karen Markowitz, *Grossmont College*; Alex Marvin, *Seminole State College of Florida*; Daniel McConnell, *University of Central Florida*; Mark McKellop, *Juniata College*; Ticily Medley, *Tarrant County Community College, South Campus*; Amy Meeks, *Texas State University*; Elisabeth Morray, *Boston College*; Gabe Mydland, *Dakota State University*; Ronn Newby, *Des Moines Area Community College*; Mason Niblack, *Salish-Kootenai College*; Caroline Olko, *Nassau Community College*; Mary-Ellen O'Sullivan-Vollemans, *Housatonic Community College and Southern Connecticut University*; Alison Pepper, *University of Montana, Missoula College*; Doug Peterson, *University of South Dakota*; Susan Poulin, *Central Main Medical Center College of Nursing and Health Professions*; Chris K. Randall, *Kennesaw State University; Matthew Rhoads, Arkansas State University*; Nicole Rodiles, *Imperial Valley College*; Theresa Rufrano-Ruffner, *Indiana University of Pennsylvania*; Sharon Sanders, *University of Cincinnati, Clermont College*; Hildur Schilling, *Fitchburg State University*; Sharon Sexton, *Texas States Technical College*; David Shepard, *South Texas College*; Jessica Siegel, *University of the South*; Stuart Silverberg, *Westmoreland County Community College*; Amy Skinner, *Central Alabama Community College*; Sherry Span, *California State University, Long Beach*; Nelly Sta Maria, *Suffolk County Community College*; Cari Stevenson, *Kankakee Community College*; John Story, *Bluegrass Community and Technical College*; Eva Szeli, *Arizona State University*; Rachelle Tannenbaum, *Anne Arundel Community College*; Kim Taylor, *Spokane Falls Community College*; Jane Theriault, *University of Massachusetts, Lowell*; Tiffany Thomas, *Des Moines Area Community College*; Sherri Toman, *United Tribes Technical College*; Katie Townsend-Merino, *Palomar College*; Alicia Trotman, *Mercy College*; Victoria Van Wie, *Lone Star College, CyFair*; Catherine Wehlburg, *Texas Christian University*; John Wright, *Washington State University*; Jason Young, *Hunter College*.

## Special Thanks from the Authors

We'd like to offer our very special thank you to the superb editorial and production teams at John Wiley & Sons. Like any cooperative effort, writing a book requires a strong and professional support team, and we are deeply grateful to this remarkable group of people: Mary Ann Price, Senior Photo Editor; Maureen Eide, Senior Designer; Sandra Rigby, Senior Production Editor; and a host of others. Each of these individuals helped enormously in the production of this text. Without them, this program would not have been possible.

- This twelfth edition particularly benefited from the incredible patience, wisdom, and insight of Emma Townsend-Merino. Her title, Assistant Development Editor, does not reflect the true scope of her responsibilities and contributions. Emma's patience, wisdom, and professionalism inspire all who know her. As Jason Spiegelman (our incredible Test Bank author) noted, "she's awesome!"

- Our personal appreciation and gratitude also goes out to Veronica Visentin, our Executive Editor, who recently took over responsibility for the psychology team at Wiley and added her energy and personal touch to this Twelfth Edition. We're similarly thankful and beholden to Glenn Wilson, who also recently joined us as the Senior Market Development Manager. He handled all the ins and outs of marketing and was instrumental in the creative ideas for this edition.

- *Psychology in Action* also could not exist without a great team of contributors. We gratefully acknowledge the expertise and immense talents of Beverly Peavler, whose careful guidance and editing greatly improved this edition. In addition, we offer a big, heartfelt thank you to our team of fabulous ancillary authors: Jason Spiegelman (The Community College of Baltimore County) Test Bank and PowerPoint; Ronn Newby (Des Moines Area Community College) Instructor's Resource Guide; Melissa Patton (Eastern Florida State College) Instructor Demonstration Videos; and Kate Halverson (Des Moines Area Community College) Practice Tests. We love and appreciate each and every one of you!

- The staff at Furino Production deserves a special note of thanks –especially, Jeanine Furino. Their careful and professional approach was critical to the successful production of this edition. Jeanine supervised this project from manuscript through final text, with great patience and incredible grace.

- We'd also like to express our heartfelt appreciation to the hundreds of faculty across the country who contributed their constructive ideas to *Psychology in Action* 12e, and to our many students over all the years. They've taught us what students want to know, and inspired us to write this book.

- Finally, all the hard work of the entire staff, and months of writing, producing, and marketing of this book, would be wasted without an energetic and dedicated sales staff. We wish to sincerely thank all the publishing representatives for their tireless efforts and good humor. It's a true pleasure to work with such a remarkable group of people.

## Personal Acknowledgments from the Authors

- **From Karen Huffman:** Katherine Dowdell and I warmly welcome Catherine Sanderson to the shared authorship of the twelfth edition, and sincerely thank her for her timely research and invaluable contributions. Working with both of my co-authors has been a great and rewarding experience! In truth, the writing of this (and all editions of *Psychology in Action*) has been a group effort involving the input and unflagging support of my co-authors, along with all of my wonderful friends, family, and valued colleagues. To each person, I offer my most sincere thanks: Amy Beeman, Joline Bourdages, Sky Chafin, Haydn Davis, Mike Garza, Teresa Jacob, Jim Matiya, Lou Milstein, Kandis Mutter, Tyler Mutter, Roger Morrissette, Katie Townsend-Merino, Maria Pok, Fred Rose, Kathy Young. They and many others provided personal friendship, feedback, careful editing, library research, and a unique sense of what should and should not go into an introduction to psychology text.

  A special note of appreciation goes to my dear friend and colleague, Tom Frangicetto at Northampton Community College. His co-authoring of the critical thinking Prologue, and full authorship of most of the critical thinking exercises for each chapter, provided invaluable, "hands on" opportunities for our students to practice and develop their critical thinking skills.

  Finally, I send a big hug and continuing appreciation to Richard Hosey. His careful editing, constructive feedback, professional research skills, and shared commitment to excellence were essential to this revision. Last, and definitely not least, I thank my beloved husband, Bill Barnard. My professional life and personal happiness are in your loving hands.

- **From Katherine Dowdell:** Many thanks to my co-authors, Karen and Catherine, for their dedication, scholarship, and enthusiasm throughout this journey. I'd also like to express my deep appreciation to Tiffany Thomas, Kate Halverson and our colleagues at DMACC for their input, insight, and advice on the text and WileyPLUS. And finally, my love and gratitude to my family, Mark, Jane and Vaughn Hommerding, for their unfailing love and support for all that I am and do.

- **From Catherine Sanderson:** I am thrilled to be joining the author team for *Psychology in Action*, and appreciate the warm welcome from Karen and Katherine. I'd also like to thank my fabulous research assistant, Chris Roll, for all of his work on gathering and checking references. Last, but certainly not least, I owe a big thanks to my family (Bart, Andrew, Robert, and Caroline) for supporting yet another writing endeavor … and all the resulting take-out dinners!

# TABLE 1  New Special Features in *Psychology in Action*, 12e

| Chapter Title | Psychology and a Classic/Contemporary Success | Psychology and Your Professional Success | Psychology and Your Personal Success | WileyPLUS Assets : Animations(A), Mini Courses(MC), and Interactives(I) |
|---|---|---|---|---|
| **1**<br>**Introduction and Research Methods** | Michael Jordan | Would You Like a Career in Psychology? | Why Are a Growth Mindset and Grit Important? | • Correlation does not mean causation (A)<br>• Components of an experiment (A)<br>• Research methods (MC)<br>• The scientific method (I) |
| **2**<br>**Neuroscience and Biological Foundations** | Adele Diamond | | How to Train Your Brain | • Sympathetic and parasympathetic nervous systems (A)<br>• Peripheral and central nervous systems (A)<br>• Lateralization of the brain (A)<br>• The human brain (MC)<br>• Key parts of the neuron (I)<br>• Communication between neurons (I) |
| **3**<br>**Stress and Health Psychology** | Marcus Luttrell | How Well Do You Cope with Job Stress? | Can Mindfulness Improve Your GPA? | • Three types of conflict (A)<br>• The HPA axis and General Adaptation Syndrome (A)<br>• Physical response to stress (MC) |
| **4**<br>**Sensation and Perception** | Helen Keller | | Helen Keller's Inspiring Advice | • Sensation vs. perception (A)<br>• The body senses (A)<br>• Understanding perception: Selection and interpretation (A) |
| **5**<br>**States of Consciousness** | Albert Einstein | Potential Career Costs of Addiction | Can Maximizing Your Consciousness Save Lives? | • Inattentional blindness, selective attention, automatic vs. controlled processes (A)<br>• Sleep deprivation (A)<br>• Why we sleep: Four theories (A)<br>• Agonist and antagonist drugs: How do they produce their effects? (I) |
| **6**<br>**Learning** | Cesar Millan | Why Can't We Get Anything Done Around Here? | Can Learning Principles Help You Succeed in College? | • Reinforcement vs. punishment (A)<br>• Effective use of reinforcement and punishment (A)<br>• Six principles of operant conditioning (A)<br>• Schedules of reinforcement (A)<br>• Classical conditioning (MC) |
| **7**<br>**Memory** | Elizabeth Loftus | | Can Memory Improvement Increase Success? | • ESR memory model (A)<br>• Factors in forgetting (A)<br>• Memory distortions (A)<br>• Memory tools for student success (A) |
| **8**<br>**Thinking, Language, and Intelligence** | Bill Gates | Is a High IQ Essential to High Achievement? | Strategies for Better Problem Solving | • Problem solving (A)<br>• Barriers to problem solving (A)<br>• Issues in measuring intelligence (A)<br>• Language and the brain (I)<br>• Language acquisition (I) |

| Chapter Title | Psychology and a Classic/ Contemporary Success | Psychology and Your Professional Success | Psychology and Your Personal Success | WileyPLUS Assets : Animations(A), Mini Courses(MC), and Interactives(I) |
|---|---|---|---|---|
| 9 **Life Span Development I** | Oprah Winfrey | Does Ageism Matter? | The Power of Touch | • Research methods in development: Cross-sectional vs. longitudinal design (I)<br>• Cognitive development (A)<br>• Styles of attachment (A)<br>• Parenting styles (I) |
| 10 **Life Span Development II** | Nelson Mandela | | What Are the Secrets to Enduring Love? | • Moral development (A)<br>• Erikson's psychosocial theory (MC) |
| 11 **Gender and Human Sexuality** | Ellen DeGeneres | | Are Your Conflicts Constructive or Destructive? | • Cognitive factors influencing arousal (A) |
| 12 **Motivation and Emotion** | Malala Yousafzai | What Are the Best Ways to Increase Motivation? | Are There Research-Based Secrets for Happiness? | • Environmental factors in eating and obesity (A)<br>• Persistence and grit (A)<br>• Theories of motivation (MC)<br>• Symptoms of anorexia and bulimia (I) |
| 13 **Personality** | Abraham Lincoln | Should You Match Your Personality With Your Career? | Can (and Should) We Improve Our Personalities?<br><br>Could You Pass the Marshmallow Test? | • Trait theories (A)<br>• Unconditional love (A)<br>• Reciprocal determinism (A)<br>• Freud's personality structure (I) |
| 14 **Psychological Disorders** | Jennifer Lawrence | | Can Resilience Promote Mental Health in Children and Adults? | • How phobias are created (A)<br>• Learned helplessness (A)<br>• Gender differences in managing depression (A)<br>• Biopsychosocial model of schizophrenia (MC)<br>• Anxiety disorders (I) |
| 15 **Therapy** | J. K. Rowling | | What Are the Keys to Good Mental Health? | • Systematic desensitization (A)<br>• Operant conditioning (A)<br>• Group therapy (A)<br>• Cognitive behavioral therapy (MC)<br>• Three major approaches to therapy (I)<br>• Five common goals of therapy (I) |
| 16 **Social Psychology** | Sonia Sotomayor | How Can We Reduce Attributional Biases?<br><br>Can Prejudice Affect Your Career Success? | Using Psychology to Increase Your Dating Appeal | • Attribution (A)<br>• Groupthink (A)<br>• Altruism: Why do we help? (A)<br>• Cognitive dissonance (MC)<br>• Prejudice and discrimination (I) |

**TABLE 2    Continuing** Special Features in *Psychology in Action*, 12e

| Chapter Title | Research Challenges (RC)/ Gender and Cultural (G&C) Diversity | Significantly Revised Topics (RT)/Added New Topics (ANT) | Deleted Key Terms (DKT)/ New Key Terms (NKT) | NOW in Wiley-Plus Critical Thinking Exercises (CT)/ Media Challenges (MC) | *Sample* WileyPlus Assets: Videos (V), Animations (A), Virtual Field Trips (VFT) |
|---|---|---|---|---|---|
| **1** **Introduction and Research Methods** | (RC) Why Do Men and Women Lie About Sex? (G&C) Psychology's History of Diversity | (RT) Moved research ethics to the Science of Psychology section, updated and revised correlational research (ANT) New connections of famous figure (Michael Jordan) with key chapter topics. Added discussion of quasi-experimental designs, growth mindset, and grit | (DKT) The term "survey" replaced with survey/interview (NKT) Functionalism, grit, growth mindset, natural selection, representative sample, structuralism | (CT) How to Think Critically About Psychological Science (MC) Is College Worth It? | Applying Research Methods (V) The Experiment (V) The Art of Prediction (A) Yerkes Primate Center (VFT) |
| **2** **Neuroscience and Biological Foundations** | (RC) Does Lying Lead to More Lies? (RC) Phineas Gage—Myths versus Facts (G&C) Are Male and Female Brains Different? (G&C) Culture and Job Stress | (RT) Moved Genetic Inheritance to Ch. 9, expanded discussion of frontal lobes (ANT) New connections of famous figure (Adele Diamond) with key chapter topics. Added discussion of executive functions and positive effects of simple mental skills training and physical exercise on brain functioning | (DKT) Moved key terms related to genetics to Chapter 9 (NKT) All-or-nothing principle, executive functions, fight-flight-freeze response, motor cortex, nervous system, somatosensory cortex | (CT) DNA Testing: Changing Lives, Saving Lives (MC) The (Invisible) Plague of Concussion | Dissecting the Brain (V) Interaction of Genes and Environment (V) Drawing and Building A Brain (V) The Brain (A) Alcohol, Neurotransmitters and Your Brain (A) Neuroimaging (VFT) Reading Your DNA (VFT) |
| **3** **Stress and Health Psychology** | (RC) What are the Hidden Benefits of Practice Testing? (RC) When Do Losers Actually Win? (G&C) What are the Problems with Acculturative Stress? | (RT) Updated and revised the benefits of stress, social media's negative effects, and PTSD with a focus on veterans (ANT) New connections of famous figure (Marcus Luttrell) with key chapter topics. Added discussion of acculturative stress, chronic pain, and cognitive appraisal. Moved table and major discussion of defense mechanisms from Chapter 13 to this chapter | (DKT) Type A and Type B (NKT) Acculturative stress, chronic pain, fight-flight-freeze response (versus fight or flight) | (CT) Perils of Procrastination (MC) Are We Denying the Dangers of Stress? | Sources of Stress (V) Coping with Stress (V) Positive Psychology (V) Biofeedback (VFT) Managing Stress Improves Health (A) |

| Chapter Title | Research Challenges (RC)/ Gender and Cultural (G&C) Diversity | Significantly Revised Topics (RT)/Added New Topics (ANT) | Deleted Key Terms (DKT)/ New Key Terms (NKT) | NOW in WileyPlus Critical Thinking Exercises (CT)/ Media Challenges (MC) | *Sample* WileyPlus Assets: Videos (V), Animations (A), Virtual Field Trips (VFT) |
|---|---|---|---|---|---|
| 4 **Sensation and Perception** | (RC) Can Music Improve the Taste of Beer? (RC) Does Wearing Red Increase Your Sex Appeal? (G&C) Are the Gestalt Laws Universally True? | (ANT) New connections of famous figure (Helen Keller) with key chapter topics. Added discussion and new figure on feature detectors in the brain, new figure and research on depth perception | (NKT) Gestalt psychology, parapsychology, priming, volley principle for hearing | (CT) Why Do So Many People Believe in ESP? (MC) Astrology and Crime | Seeing and Hearing (V) A World Turned Upside Down: Visual Processing (V) Perception (A) How We See and Hear (A) 3-D Media (VFT) |
| 5 **States of Consciousness** | (RC) What's Wrong with Distracted Driving? (G&C) Are There Differences in Dreams? | (RT) Significantly updated and revised text on sleep deprivation, opioids, LSD, Ketamine, and marijuana (ANT) New connections of famous figure (Albert Einstein) with key chapter topics. Added discussion of effects of multitasking on learning, new figure on sleep deprivation, emotionality and impulse control | (NKT) Inattentional blindness, suprachiasmatic nucleus | (CT) The Spectacular Now (MC) Teen Night Owls | Automatic Processing and Multitasking (V) Myths about Sleep, Dreaming and Drugs (V) Diagnosing Sleep Disorders (VFT) |
| 6 **Learning** | (RC) Do Dogs Prefer Food or Praise? (RC) Does the Media Impact Our Body Size Preferences? | (RT) Expanded discussion of Skinner's response to Thorndike and his definition of reinforcement and punishment (ANT) New connections of famous figure (Cesar Millan) with key chapter topics, added discussion of classical conditioning and emotional eating | (DKT) Removed conditioning as a key term, and the word "stimulus" from key terms of generalization and discrimination | (CT) What Kind of Name Is Ryan For a Girl? (MC) The Return of the Working Class Hero | Classical and Operant Conditioning in Action (V) Understanding Reinforcement and Punishment (V) Classical Conditioning (A) The Search Dog Foundation (VFT) |
| 7 **Memory** | (RC) Can Taking Photos Impair Our Memories? (G&C) Does Culture Affect Memory? | (RT) Updated and expanded discussion of infant memories, working memory with new figure, traumatic brain injury, eyewitness testimony, and repressed memories (ANT) New connections of famous figure (Elizabeth Loftus) with key chapter topics. Added discussion and new figure of the four major models of memory | (DKT) Sleeper effect (NKT) Parallel distributed processing, repression | (CT) Critical Thinking Is No Laughing Matter . . . Or Is It? (MC) How Memoirists Mold the Truth | Constructing Memory (V) Organizing Long-Term Memories (V) How Could I Forget That? (V) Eyewitness Memory (V) Enhancing Your Memory (A) USA Memory Championships (VFT) Alzheimer's Treatment Center (VFT) |

| Chapter Title | Research Challenges (RC)/ Gender and Cultural (G&C) Diversity | Significantly Revised Topics (RT)/Added New Topics (ANT) | Deleted Key Terms (DKT)/ New Key Terms (NKT) | NOW in Wiley-Plus Critical Thinking Exercises (CT)/ Media Challenges (MC) | *Sample* WileyPlus Assets: Videos (V), Animations (A), Virtual Field Trips (VFT) |
|---|---|---|---|---|---|
| **8 Thinking, Language, and Intelligence** | (RC) Is creativity Linked with Psychological Disorders? <br><br>(G&C) Can Your Nonverbal Language Reveal Your Roots? | (RT) Updated discussion on the value of play and creativity, expanded and updated research on controversies surrounding racial/ethnic differences <br><br>(ANT) New connections of famous figure (Bill Gates) with key chapter topics and added new discussion of artificial intelligence | (DKT) Babbling, cooing, overextension, over-generalization, savant syndrome, telegraphic speech <br><br>(NKT) Artificial intelligence, cognitive offloading, convergent thinking, embodied cognition, mental age, triarchic theory of intelligence | (CT) 12 Years A Slave <br><br>(MC) How Social Media Is Ruining Our Minds | Barriers to Problem Solving (V) <br><br>Understanding IQ (V) <br><br>Standards for Psychological Tests (V) <br><br>Problem Solving (A) <br><br>Baby Sign Language (VFT) <br><br>High IQ Society (VFT) <br><br>Down Syndrome Connection (VFT) |
| **9 Life Span Development I** | (RC) Deprivation and Development <br><br>(G&C) Should Diversity Affect Research? | (RT) Expanded discussion of cultural effects on developmental research. Added new research on prenatal exposure to smoke and later obesity and how taking "selfies" relates to narcissism <br><br>(ANT) New connections of famous figure (Oprah Winfrey) with key chapter topics. Added discussion of imprinting, along with new figure and section on genetics and theory of mind | (DKT) Moved age-related positivity effect to Chapter 10 <br><br>(NKT) Behavioral genetics, chromosomes, DNA, epigenetics, gene, temperament, theory of mind | (CT) Overcoming Egocentric Thinking <br><br>(MC) Older and Slower? | Understanding Development in Context (V) <br><br>The Strange Situation (V) <br><br>Attachment Through the Lifespan (V) <br><br>A Guide to Parenting (VFT) <br><br>Piaget and Cognitive Development (A) |
| **10 Life Span Development II** | (RC) Are Brain Differences Associated with Age-Related Happiness? <br><br>(G&C) Effects on Moral Development | (RT) New section on how to increase your positivity and how traveling may increase immoral behavior <br><br>(ANT) New connections of famous figure (Nelson Mandela) with key chapter topics. Added discussion of connection of theory of mind with autism, along with the age-related positivity effect | (DKT) Moved resiliency to Chapter 14 <br><br>(NKT) Age-related positivity effect | (CT) Morality and Academic Cheating <br><br>(MC) Millennials: Not the Marrying Kind | Kohlberg's Stages of Moral Reasoning (A) <br><br>Erikson's Psychosocial Theory (V) <br><br>Factors in Marital Satisfaction (V) <br><br>Attitudes Toward Aging (V) <br><br>Dying with Dignity: Hospice (VFT) |

| Chapter Title | Research Challenges (RC)/ Gender and Cultural (G&C) Diversity | Significantly Revised Topics (RT)/Added New Topics (ANT) | Deleted Key Terms (DKT)/ New Key Terms (NKT) | NOW in Wiley-Plus Critical Thinking Exercises (CT)/ Media Challenges (MC) | *Sample* WileyPlus Assets: Videos (V), Animations (A), Virtual Field Trips (VFT) |
|---|---|---|---|---|---|
| **11 Gender and Human Sexuality** | (RC) Is Gender Income Inequality Real? <br><br>(RC) Does Political Affiliation Reflect Sexual Behavior? <br><br>(G&C) Sexuality Across Cultures | (RT) Expanded discussion of sexual prejudice and sexual orientation, including LGBTQ <br><br>(ANT) New connections of famous figure (Ellen DeGeneres) with key chapter topics. Added new discussion on gender and income inequality, the double standard, pair bonding, the fallacy of "stranger danger," and child sexual abuse | (NKT) Double standard, gender stereotypes, pair bonding, sexuality, sexually transmitted infection | (CT) The Scarlet Letter <br><br>(MC) Scarcity of Women in Science? | Clearing Up the Confusion: Gender Roles, Gender Identity and Sexual Orientation (V) <br><br>Gender (A) <br><br>The Sexual Response Cycle (V) <br><br>Healthy Sexuality (V) <br><br>Sexual Communication (V) <br><br>Planned Parenthood (VFT) |
| **12 Motivation and Emotion** | (RC) Does Wearing "Sexy" Clothing Signal Sexual Interest? <br><br>(G&C) Are Emotions Affected by Culture and Evolution? | (RT) Revised discussion and figure on intrinsic vs. extrinsic motivation, and updated and expanded theories on basic emotions <br><br>(ANT) New connections of famous figure (Malala Yousafzai) with key chapter topics. Added new table and research: <br><br>• Emotions <br>• Psychology of happiness <br>• Botox injections and the link to decreased empathy <br>• How expectancies increase alcohol consumption <br>• How sleep deprivation, photos of food, and processed foods increase eating | (NKT) Adaptation-level phenomenon, display rules | (CT) The New Psychology of Success <br><br>(MC) Mirror, Mirror on The Wall? | Get Motivated (V) <br><br>Hormones and Hunger (V) <br><br>Emotional Intelligence (V) <br><br>The Polygraph (A) <br><br>Surgical Weight Loss Center (VFT) |
| **13 Personality** | (RC) Do Nonhuman Animals Have Unique Personalities? | (RT) Revised levels of consciousness figure, updated step-by-step diagram on psychosexual stages, moved defense mechanisms table to Ch. 3, revised five-factor model and self-concept figures | (DKT) Morality principle, pleasure principle, reality principle <br><br>(NKT) Behavioral genetics, character, temperament | (CT) Maslow Revisited <br><br>(MC) Can Personality Predict Health? | Applying Rogerian Techniques (V) <br><br>Exploring Your Personality (V) <br><br>Measuring Personality (V) <br><br>Freud's Defense Mechanisms (A) <br><br>Personality Research (VFT) |

**xvii**

**TABLE 2  Continuing Special Features in *Psychology in Action*, 12e** *(continued)*

| Chapter Title | Research Challenges (RC)/ Gender and Cultural (G&C) Diversity | Significantly Revised Topics (RT)/Added New Topics (ANT) | Deleted Key Terms (DKT)/ New Key Terms (NKT) | NOW in Wiley-Plus Critical Thinking Exercises (CT)/ Media Challenges (MC) | *Sample* WileyPlus Assets: Videos (V), Animations (A), Virtual Field Trips (VFT) |
|---|---|---|---|---|---|
| | | (ANT) New connections of famous figure (Abraham Lincoln) with key chapter topics. Added discussion and figures:<br>• Freud and modern western culture<br>• Mischel's marshmallow test<br>• Personality and behavioral genetics<br>• Identical vs. fraternal twins and adoption studies<br>• Introversion and extraversion misconceptions | | | |
| **14 Psychological Disorders** | (RC) Are Head Injuries Related to Depressive and Other Psychological Disorders?<br><br>(RC) Does Unequal Pay for Equal Work Increase Female Anxiety and Depression? | (RT) Moved and expanded discussion of the stigma of mental illness, suicide and other general terms to front of chapter to better apply to all disorders, expanded discussion of gender strategies for managing depression<br><br>(ANT) New connections of famous figure (Jennifer Lawrence) with key chapter topics. Added discussion and new figures:<br>• OCD<br>• Antisocial and borderline personality disorders<br>• Nonsuicidal self-injury<br>• Psychology student syndrome<br>• Resilience | (NKT) Mania, major depressive disorder, nonsuicidal self-injury, psychological disorder, psychology student syndrome, resilience | (CT) How Your Thoughts Can Make You Depressed<br><br>(MC) Lefties and Psychotic Disorders | Myths About Mental Illness (V)<br>Signs of Suicide (V)<br>OCD (VFT)<br>Bipolar Disorder (VFT)<br>Schizophrenia (A) |
| **15 Therapy** | (RC) Can Watching Movies Prevent Divorce?<br><br>(G&C) Therapy in Action | (RT) Moved evaluation of psychoanalysis to include psychoanalytic therapies, significantly revised figures for systematic desensitization and aversion therapy | (DKT) Antianxiety drugs, antidepressant drugs, mood-stabilizer drugs | CT) Cinema Therapy<br><br>(MC) Finding Treatment Grows Harder | A Guide to Psychotherapy (V)<br>Myths About Therapy (V)<br>CBT (A)<br>ECT Treatment Center (VFT)<br>Kicking the Habit: Drug Treatment (VFT) |

| Chapter Title | Research Challenges (RC)/ Gender and Cultural (G&C) Diversity | Significantly Revised Topics (RT)/Added New Topics (ANT) | Deleted Key Terms (DKT)/ New Key Terms (NKT) | NOW in WileyPlus Critical Thinking Exercises (CT)/ Media Challenges (MC) | *Sample* WileyPlus Assets: Videos (V), Animations (A), Virtual Field Trips (VFT) |
|---|---|---|---|---|---|
|  |  | (ANT) New connections of famous figure (J. K. Rowling) with key chapter topics. Added new discussion, figures and/or tables:<br><br>• Cognitive triad and depression<br>• Token economy<br>• Evidence-based practice in psychology (EBPP)<br>• Side-by-side comparison of treatments for psychological disorders<br>• Psychedelic drugs and psychosis<br>• Evidence-based practice in psychology (EBPP)<br>• Metacognitive therapy<br>• Mindfulness-based cognitive therapy (MBCT) Therapeutic alliance<br>• Well-being therapy (WBT) | (NKT) Evidence-based practice in psychology (EBPP), metacognitive therapy, mindfulness-based cognitive therapy (MBCT), therapeutic alliance, well-being therapy (WBT) |  |  |
| 16 **Social Psychology** | (RC) Can a 10-Minute Conversation Reduce Prejudice?<br><br>(G&C) How Does Culture Affect Personal Space?<br><br>(RC) Can Long-Distance Relationships Survive? | (RT) Moved prejudice to social cognition section, expanded discussion on flirting, deleted female named hurricanes<br><br>(ANT) New connections of famous figure (Sonia Sotomayor) with key chapter topics. Added new discussions and/or new figures:<br><br>• Prefrontal cortex and relation to social behavior<br>• How taking pain pills can change attitudes<br>• Implicit biases<br>• Saving your own life<br>• Social facilitation<br>• Social loafing | (DKT) Frustration-aggression hypothesis, mere-exposure effect<br><br>(NKT) social facilitation, social loafing, changed triarchic theory of love to triangular theory of love | (CT) To Kill A Mockingbird<br><br>(MC) When Science Becomes News | Implicit Attitudes (V)<br><br>Bystander Effect (V)<br><br>Attitudes and Cognitive Dissonance (A)<br><br>Internet Dating (VFT) |

## Successful Living Through Critical Thinking

*Co-authored with Thomas Frangicetto (and generous contributions from his students at Northampton Community College, Bethlehem, PA)*

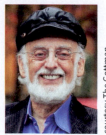

**Benedict Cumberbatch as Sherlock**

> "Sherlock Holmes is not a cold, calculating, self-gratifying machine. He cares for Watson. . . and for Mrs. Hudson. He has a conscience . . . In other words, Holmes has emotions—and attachments—like the rest of us. What he's better at is controlling them and only letting them show under very specific circumstances."
>
> Maria Konnikova (2012), "Stop Calling Sherlock Holmes A Sociopath!"

Psychologist Maria Konnikova also could have said that Sherlock Holmes – the famous fictional detective created by Sir Arthur Conan Doyle and popularized in numerous movies, books, and TV shows – is an excellent *critical thinker*. In applying fundamental, psychological principles of deduction, perception, skepticism, and logic, Holmes realized that emotions could be the enemy of sound reasoning (Kellogg, 1986). Even the most sublime emotion of all, *love*, is not to be trusted. In one story, Holmes says to his best friend and crime-solving companion, Dr. John Watson, "Love is an emotional thing, and whatever is emotional is opposed to that cold reason which I place above all things."

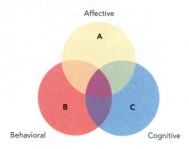

**John Gottman as John Gottman**

Why are we opening this Prologue on Critical Thinking with a discussion of emotions? We believe, as Sherlock Holmes did, that our capacity for objective reason is compromised when we are highly emotional (Halpern, 2014; Paul & Elder, 2002). What about Sherlock Holmes' love life? Although he "cared deeply" about special people in his life, he apparently never experienced *romantic love*. Had Holmes been a real person working with Dr. John Gottman (a preeminent authority on romantic relationships—see Chapter 10), and had he applied his critical thinking skills to his love life, he may have been more successful. Effective critical thinking is the best route to finding lasting love, as well as the best antidote to self-defeating, repetitive thoughts, feelings and actions. Unlike the common use of "critical" as a negative type of criticism and fault finding, critical thinking is a positive, life-enhancing process and key to success in all parts of our lives.

What exactly is critical thinking? We define it as: *Thinking about our feelings, actions, and thoughts so we can clarify and improve them* (adapted from Chaffee, 1988, p. 29). As you can see in **Figure 1**, there are 3 main categories of critical thinking, with at least 15 overlapping **critical thinking components (CTCs):** Affective (feelings/emotions), Behavioral (actions), and Cognitive (thoughts).

Affective

A

Behavioral    Cognitive

B        C

**FIGURE 1** ABCs of Critical Thinking

# Critical Thinking Components (CTCs)

*(Note: Most CTCs include personal examples generously provided by students at Northampton Community College.)*

**Affective Components** (Emotional foundation for critical thinking)

1. **Empathize and Demonstrate Altruism:** Critical thinkers are empathic. They try to understand others' feelings, thoughts, and behaviors. Noncritical thinkers view everything in relation to themselves, which is known as "egocentrism" (Chapter 13). The ability to consider the perspective of another person is the most effective antidote to egocentric thinking. *There are children who lag behind in language development. It's best to empathize. When I am a teacher, there are going to be many times where I need to know that differences are "okay."* Kayla Ann Felten

   Can you see how empathy would naturally lead to altruism—*actions designed to help others with no obvious benefit to the helper* (Chapter 16)? Once we stand in another's shoes and mirror their emotions, we naturally want to help them.

2. **Welcome Divergent Views and Critical Dialogue:** Critical thinkers examine issues from every angle, especially opposing viewpoints. This quality is especially valuable in decision-making and avoiding groupthink (Chapter 16). *Most Americans don't try to understand the sociocultural influences of suicide bombers. They believe that martyrs are crazy, while Palestinians believe that martyrdom is to be idolized. My decision to believe that martyrdom is a form of self-expression may clash with the views of many, but as an American, I have the right to believe what I want.*

   Sophia Blanchet

   Critical thinkers also actively question others, challenge opinions, and welcome questions and challenges in return. Socratic questioning is an important type of critical dialogue, which deeply probes the meaning, justification, or logical strength of an argument (Elder & Paul, 2007). It is easy to avoid such time-consuming dialogues, but they are a vital part of intellectually healthy relationships. *My mother has been calling me for the last year because she is dying. It has taken a long time to warm up to her because of the past. After many years, we are finally expressing our feelings with each other. This has been gratifying because we have become friends. My hope is that when the end comes, we will know that, despite our faults, we really loved each other.* Tim Walker

3. **Tolerate Ambiguity, but not Magical Thinking:** Formal education often trains us to look for a single "right" answer (aka *convergent thinking*—Chapter 8). But critical thinkers know that many issues are too complex to have one right answer. They value qualifiers such as "probably" and "not very likely." *A big difference between high school and college level thinking is tolerating ambiguity. In high school, we were often taught there was one right answer. In college, we learn that things are more complex. We also learn that some questions do not even have an "answer" or may have multiple answers.* Chereen Nawrocki

   Tolerating ambiguity does not mean that all beliefs and opinions are equally valid. Despite scientific consensus on many issues, noncritical thinkers often resort to magical thinking, which makes unwarranted links between one event—some action we've taken—and some unconnected result (Riggio, 2014). Consider superstitious behaviors, the belief in supernatural forces—such as ghosts, alien abductions, possession by spiritual entities—or even winning big one time at gambling and expecting to win repeatedly (Sagan, 1996; Shermer & Gould, 2007). *The problem with magical thinking is that we can believe that our actions are caused by the magical force instead of being due to us or the social environment. Reliance on magical thinking to explain things leads to self-deception and a lack of insight.* Ronald Riggio

4. **Appreciate Eclecticism and Synthesize:** Critical thinkers are not bound to one way of thinking. They appreciate and select what appears to be the best or most useful option when faced with competing ideas and approaches. For example, a psychotherapist might have training in one theoretical perspective, but also use techniques from other perspectives when more appropriate for the problems presented. This CTC goes beyond *welcoming divergent views*; it also involves analyzing all potential sources for value and content.

   Critical thinkers are also able to combine or "synthesize" various elements into a useful composite. *Understanding a suicidal person is the key to saving them. Critical thinkers "recognize that comprehension comes from combining various elements into a useful composite." By seeing patterns or "warning signs"—such as different symptoms of depression and changes in behavior—you can recognize suicidal thinking.* Micelle Pascoe

5. **Value Emotional Intelligence (EI):** Defined as "the ability to know and manage one's emotions, empathize with others, and maintain satisfying relationships," emotional intelligence (Chapter 12) can serve as the bridge between our intelligence and emotional reactions. *I think increasing children's emotional intelligence is a superb idea—especially a focus on managing aggressive impulses. The ability to manage aggressiveness means you are well on your way toward learning to control your feelings and recognizing the feelings of others too.* Amy Harding

**Behavioral Components** (Actions necessary for critical thinking)

6. **Listen Actively and Cultivate Trust:** Critical thinkers fully engage their thoughts, feelings, and actions when listening to another person. They ask questions, nonverbally affirm what they hear, and request clarification. *My brother was diagnosed with a rare kidney disease, and I tried my hardest to communicate with him and appreciate his thoughts and feelings. When he would try to talk about his feelings, I would often interrupt or tell him what he should think or feel. I was trying to focus on my need to control my own feelings when I should have been doing what he needed the most from me: active listening.* Toni Snead

   In addition to active listening, being both trusting and trustworthy are essential qualities to bring to all meaningful relationships. One caution: Not everyone is worthy of your total trust. It is a privilege that must be earned over time and trial. For Gottman, trust is not something that just "grows" between people; rather, it is the "specific state that exists when you are both willing to change your own behavior to benefit your partner"—in other words, "you have each other's back" (Gottman, 2012).

7. **Employ Precise Terms and Define Problems Accurately:** Precise terms help critical thinkers identify issues clearly so they can be objectively defined and empirically tested. When two people argue about an issue, they are often defining it differently without even knowing it. *I have had a Japanese girlfriend for the last year and a half. Our cultures are very different and at times we do not understand each other. But, if we remain open and help each other appreciate what words like "love" and "commitment" mean to us, we can learn how to understand each other better.* Anar Akhundov

   A critical thinker also tries to frame the issues as accurately as possible to prevent confusion and to lay the foundation for gathering relevant information (see CTC #8). This CTC appears to contradict *tolerating ambiguity* (see CTC #3), but critical thinkers are able to tolerate ambiguity until it is possible to *define problems accurately.*

8. **Gather Information and Delay Judgment until Adequate Data are Available:** Impulsivity is a major obstacle to good critical thinking. Rash judgments about others, impulse purchases of a new car or home, uninformed choices for political candidates, or "falling in love at first sight" can all be costly mistakes that we may regret for many years. A critical thinker does not make snap judgments. Instead, he or she collects up-to-date, relevant information on all sides of an issue and delays decisions or judgment until adequate information is available. *I am a white male. I have met African Americans I don't like, I have met Asians I don't like, I have met Hispanics I don't like, and yes, I have met whites I don't like. So if I don't like an entire race of people because I don't like certain people of that race, then I shouldn't like my own race either, because there are people of my race I don't like. You cannot judge a race by its worst representatives. I know I would not want my whole race judged by "White Power," KKK members. Maybe someday we will just have one race—the human race.* Ryan Umholtz

9. **Cultivate Open-Mindedness and Modify Judgments in Light of New Information:** Critical thinkers are willing to examine their own thinking and abandon or *modify their judgments* if compelling evidence contradicts them. Non-critical thinkers stubbornly stick to their beliefs and often *value self-interest above the truth*. The ability to say, "I'm rethinking my opinion," reflects the open-minded flexibility of a good critical thinker. *For much of high school, I procrastinated. However, I procrastinate less now that I am in college. I know now that these assignments are for my benefit and that a certain level of self-motivation is required in order to succeed in life. I am paying for my education, so I may as well get as much out of it as I can.* Tom Shimer

10. **Accept Change:** Critical thinkers remain open to the need for adjustment throughout our life cycle. Because critical thinkers fully trust the processes of reasoned inquiry, they are willing to use these skills to examine even their most deeply held beliefs, and to modify these beliefs when evidence and experience contradict them. *It's easy to tell a woman to get out of a bad relationship because she doesn't deserve to be abused. It's much harder when you're the one in the relationship. It's important for the abused woman to stop trying to "change" the man, thinking the situation will get better. It's vital not to be stuck in a toxic situation and accepting change is the first step.* Katrina Kelly

**Cognitive Components** (Thought processes required for critical thinking)

11. **Recognize Personal Biases and Value Truth above Self-Interest:** Being an effective critical thinker does not mean the absence of bias, but rather the willingness to recognize and correct it. *We may think we are hitting the benchmarks on social issues when we drop a "bill or two in the bucket" and consider our job done. Some of us view the suffering of others as the result of their own actions. Over-generalizing that all "purple people" are lazy and all "orange people" are uncivilized reflects bias . . . [where] there is no room for empathy or simple kindness. Unless we recognize our personal biases, instead of hiding behind them as a cover for a lack of humanness, we will never witness another's oppression and "feel their pain."* Mary Ellen Allen

   Critical thinkers also avoid the tendency to cater to our self-interests, while ignoring conflicting information. We must recognize that, even when it appears otherwise, the "truth" is always in our self-interest. *No matter what my interest was in watching my friends do drugs, I valued the truth against their reasons for why I should begin to smoke with them. Anytime I felt tempted, I valued what my mother told me. The truth was in front of my eyes. Family members that were homeless, indulging in illegal drugs, were the truth for me. I valued my life more than I wanted to fit in.*                                                        Nicole Bouvet

12. **Recognize Fact versus Opinion and Resist Overgeneralization:** *Facts* are statements that are supported by objective evidence. *Opinions* are statements that express how a person feels about an issue or what someone *believes* to be true. It is easy to have an uninformed opinion about any subject, but critical thinkers seek out and evaluate facts before forming their opinions.

    Overgeneralization is applying an experience to other situations that are only superficially similar. It's also a form of "tunnel vision"—failing to see the bigger picture because you see just a small sample of the whole. *While watching a rerun of "Jersey Shore," I made an over-generalization about "Jersey guys"! The show convinced me that every Jersey boy in his twenties was a meathead without moral values and who only cared about his looks. I met a Jersey boy and automatically thought he was like one of the guys from the show. Turns out he was an educated man who happened to come from New Jersey.*        Caitie Stoneback

13. **Analyze Data for Value and Content and Apply Knowledge to New Situations:** By evaluating the nature of evidence and the credibility of sources, critical thinkers recognize blatant appeals to emotion, unsupported claims, and faulty logic. They also can spot sources that contradict themselves, or have a vested interest in selling a product, idea, or viewpoint that is only partially accurate (a "half-truth"). *This is an important CTC when it comes to choosing a religion because it takes a full analysis of a religious system in order to make the right choice. If I break down all of a religion's content for its inherent value, I will be making a well-informed decision.*        Ali Nabavian

    Noncritical thinkers can often provide correct answers, repeat definitions, and carry out calculations, yet they are unable to transfer their knowledge to new situations because of an inability to "synthesize" seemingly unrelated content (see #4). *History teaches that war rarely puts an end to a conflict. America's experience in Iraq argues that military action against Iran means inviting more trouble. Iran would retaliate, inviting a tit-for-tat escalation, putting American interests in great danger. Polls tell us most Americans prefer diplomatic options.*

Nivedita "Minu" Mahato

14. **Independent Thinking:** Rather than passively accepting the beliefs of others or being easily manipulated, critical thinkers are independent. They hold firm to their own values, while recognizing the difference between being independent and just being stubborn (Sagan, 1996; Shermer & Gould, 2007). *All my life, I was a follower. I did what everyone else did—the designer clothes, the makeup, the highlights, etc. Instead of thinking independently, I went with the crowd. And that was one of my greatest downfalls.*

Courtney Fisher

15. **Metacognition** (aka *reflective thinking*) involves analyzing your mental processes—*thinking about your own thinking*. Critical thinkers who are motivated to examine and trace the origin of their beliefs can often be heard saying things like: "What was I thinking?" or "I don't know why I believe that, I'll have to think about it." *My dad and I had a torn relationship following my parents' divorce. I couldn't live with my mother anymore, so I thought about living with my dad. I began employing meta-cognition. I wanted to understand my anger toward him. I realized when we fought, it was just frustration. I decided to move in with my dad, and I'm happy to say our relationship has changed dramatically for the better. Using critical thinking made a huge difference.*

Laura Markley

© alexxl66/iStockphoto

# Introduction and Research Methods

## LEARNING OBJECTIVES

**Summarize psychology's past, modern perspectives, and what psychologists do.**

• **Define** psychology, critical thinking, and pseudopsychologies.
• **Review** structuralism, functionalism, and the psychoanalytic perspectives.
• **Discuss** modern psychology's seven major perspectives and the contributions of women and people of color.
• **Describe** the biopsychosocial model, along with individualistic and collectivistic cultures.
• **Summarize** psychology's major career options and specialties.

**Discuss the key principles underlying the science of psychology.**

• **Compare and contrast** the fundamental goals of basic and applied research.
• **Describe** the scientific method, its key terms, and its six steps.
• **Review** psychology's four main goals.
• **Discuss** the ethical concerns and guidelines for psychological research.

**Summarize psychology's three major research methods.**

• **Review** descriptive research and its four key methods.
• **Discuss** correlational research and its limits and value.
• **Identify** the key terms and components of experimental research.

**Review the key strategies for student success.**

• **Describe** the four steps important to improving your study habits.
• **Discuss** ways to improve your time management.
• **Identify** the key factors in grade improvement.
• **Summarize** why attitude adjustment is key to student success.

Leigh Vogel/Contributor/Getty Images

### ❖ Psychology and a Contemporary Success | Michael Jordan

Who comes to your mind when someone mentions the best ever basketball player? For most of us, and even according to the official NBA website, Michael Jordan (1963–) is judged to be "the greatest basketball player of all time." Born into a family of five children, Jordan always loved sports and played with an unusual passion, yet he failed to make his high school basketball team in his sophomore year. He overcame this early setback and made the team the following year, later earning a scholarship to play for the University of North Carolina—thanks to his perseverance and intensive practice. Even more impressive, Jordan went on to play professionally for the Chicago Bulls, where he led the team to six NBA championships and won the Most Valuable Player Award five times. In 2016, Barack Obama presented Jordan with one of the nation's highest honors—the Presidential Medal of Freedom. (See the photo.)

How do psychologists explain this incredible level of achievement? Researcher Carol Dweck believes Jordan reflects a **growth mindset**, the self-perception that one's abilities can change and improve with effort (Dweck, 2007, 2012). Other psychologists have emphasized his **grit**, which includes perseverance and passion in the pursuit of long-term goals (Datu et al., 2016; Yeager et al., 2016). We'll discuss these very important traits in more detail at the end of this chapter and throughout this text.

**Growth mindset** A psychological term referring to a self-perception or a set of beliefs about one's personal abilities and the potential for change and improvement with effort.

**Grit** A psychological term referring to perseverance and passion in the pursuit of long-term goals.

## Chapter Overview

Welcome to the exciting world of **Psychology in Action**. As the story of Michael Jordan and the name of this text imply, psychology is an *active*, dynamic field that affects every part of our lives—our relationships at home, college, and work, as well as in sports, politics, television, movies, newspapers, and the Internet. And psychology encompasses not only humankind but our nonhuman compatriots as well—from rats and pigeons to cats and chimps.

Given that this first chapter is an overview of the entire field of psychology, we begin with a formal definition of psychology, followed by its brief history as a scientific discipline. Next, we discuss the seven major perspectives of modern psychology, as well as its many different specialties and career options. Then, we explore the science of psychology, including basic and applied research, the scientific method, the four major goals of psychology, and its research ethics. Next, we discuss the three major research methods. We close with a section, called *Tools for Student Success*, that provides proven, research-based techniques for improving your study habits, time management, and grades, as well as showing you how psychology can contribute to your attitude adjustment and personal success. This section will help you enjoy and master the material in this and all your other college textbooks and courses. Be sure to study it carefully. We care about you and want you to succeed!

As further evidence of our commitment to your achievement, we've included numerous study tips throughout each chapter, along with a special feature (called *Psychology and a Contemporary Success*, shown above). These stories of real-life classic and contemporary figures who have prospered despite incredible obstacles have been shown to increase overall motivation and achievement. We also provide two additional sections—*Psychology and Your Professional Success* and *Psychology and Your Personal Success*, which highlight how psychology applies to your career and personal life. We believe this focus on success will not only help you master the content of the course, but will also inspire your own personal efforts and ultimate life success.

Finally, we invite you to let us know how your study of psychology (and this text) affects you and your life. You can reach us at khuffman@palomar.edu, kdowdell@dmacc.edu, and casanderson@amherst.edu. We look forward to hearing from you.

Warmest regards,

Courtesy of Karen Huffman

Courtesy of Katherine Dowdell

courtesy of Catherine Sanderson

*Karen R. Huffman*    *Katherine L. Dowdell*    *Cathie A. Sanderson*

## Why Study Psychology?

### Did you know that the study of psychology

- ... will increase your chances for personal, academic, and professional success? Our major goal for this edition of *Psychology in Action* is to help maximize your overall success and ability to persist during difficult and challenging times through a repeated focus on a *growth mindset* and on *grit*, which includes both passion and perseverance in the pursuit of long-term goals.

- ... will deepen your understanding of yourself and others? The Greek philosopher Socrates admonished us long ago to, "Know thyself." Studying psychology will greatly contribute to your understanding (and appreciation) of yourself and others. Knowing thyself and others, along with psychology's scientifically based guidelines and techniques, will also improve your relationships with friends, family, and coworkers.

- ... will broaden your general education and success as a global citizen? Psychology is an integral part of today's political, social, and economic world. Understanding its principles and concepts is essential to becoming an educated, well-informed person who can contribute to society and succeed in our global economy.

Paul Bradbury/ OJO Images/ Getty Images

- ... will improve your critical thinking? Would you like to become a more independent thinker, a better decision maker, and a more effective problem solver? These are only a few of the many critical thinking skills that are enhanced through a study of psychology.

## 1.1 | Introducing Psychology

### LEARNING OBJECTIVES

**Retrieval Practice** While reading the upcoming sections, respond to each Learning Objective in your own words.

**Summarize psychology's past, modern perspectives, and what psychologists do.**

- **Define** psychology, critical thinking, and pseudopsychologies.
- **Review** structuralism, functionalism, and the psychoanalytic perspectives.

- **Discuss** modern psychology's seven major perspectives and the contributions of women and people of color.
- **Describe** the biopsychosocial model, along with individualistic and collectivistic cultures.
- **Summarize** psychology's major career options and specialties.

**Psychology** The scientific study of behavior and mental processes.

The term **psychology** derives from the roots *psyche*, meaning "mind," and *logos*, meaning "word." Modern psychology is most commonly defined as the *scientific study of behavior and mental processes. Scientific* is a key feature of the definition because psychologists follow strict scientific procedures to collect and analyze their data. *Behavior* (such as crying, hitting, and sleeping) can be directly observed. *Mental processes* are private, internal experiences that cannot be directly observed (like feelings, thoughts, and memories). As you can see in the photo, psychologists study not only behavior and mental processes, but also the application of that knowledge to marketing, health management, and many other aspects of our everyday life.

**Critical thinking** The process of objectively evaluating, comparing, analyzing, and synthesizing information.

Psychology also places high value on *empirical evidence* that can be objectively tested and evaluated. In addition, psychologists emphasize **critical thinking**, *the process of objectively evaluating, comparing, analyzing, and synthesizing information* (Caine et al., 2016; Halpern, 2014). Unfortunately, a recent study revealed that high school and college students can't tell the difference between factual information presented by a reputable newspaper and that presented online by fringe activist groups (Wineberg & McGrew, 2016). In this study, college students were given 10 minutes to review two different websites: one belonged to the American Academy of Pediatrics (a reputable organization nearly 100 years in existence and with over 65,000 members) and the other belonged to the American College of Pediatricians (a group that has only about 200 members and has been classified as a hate group for claiming homosexuality is linked with pedophilia). Yet college students generally saw information presented by both groups as reliable. Does this help explain why the need to critically evaluate the information we receive, and its source, is particularly important during these times of heated political debates and growing reliance on social media outlets for news?

As part of your critical thinking, be careful not to confuse psychology, which is founded on the scientific method, with *pseudopsychologies*, which are based on false or unfounded common beliefs, folk wisdom, or superstitions. (*Pseudo* means "false.") These sometimes give the appearance of science, but they do not follow the basics of the scientific method. Examples include purported psychic powers, horoscopes, mediums, and self-help and "pop psych" statements such as "I'm mostly right brained" or "We use only 10% of our brains." For some, horoscopes or palmists are simple entertainment. Unfortunately, some true believers seek guidance and waste large sums of money on charlatans purporting to know the future or to speak with the deceased (e.g., Wilson, 2015b). Broken-hearted families also have lost valuable time and emotional energy on psychics claiming they could locate their missing children. As you can see, distinguishing scientific psychology from pseudopsychology is vitally important (Lilienfeld et al., 2010, 2015; Loftus, 2010). Given the popularity of these misleading beliefs, be sure to test your own possible myths in the following **Myth Busters** section.

Jeff Morgan 01/Alamy Stock Photo

**Psychology in action!** One of the many benefits you'll receive from studying psychology is that you'll soon be able to easily recognize the psychological principles used in this ad that have been carefully designed to influence you as a prospective customer.

## Myth Busters

**True or False?**

_____ **1.** The best way to learn and remember information is to "cram," or study it intensively during one concentrated period.

_____ **2.** Advertisers and politicians often use subliminal persuasion to influence our behavior.

_____ **3.** Most brain activity stops when we're asleep.

_____ **4.** Punishment is the most effective way to permanently change behavior.

_____ **5.** Eyewitness testimony is often unreliable.

_____ **6.** Polygraph ("lie detector") tests can accurately and reliably reveal whether a person is lying.

_____ **7.** Behaviors that are unusual or violate social norms may indicate a psychological disorder.

_____ **8.** People with schizophrenia have multiple personalities.

_____ **9.** Similarity is one of the best predictors of satisfaction in long-term relationships.

_____ **10.** In an emergency, as the number of bystanders increases, your chance of getting help decreases.

The magician James Randi has dedicated his life to educating the public about fraudulent pseudopsychologists. Along with the prestigious MacArthur Foundation, Randi has offered $1 million to "anyone who proves a genuine psychic power under proper observing conditions" (Randi, 2014; The Amazing Meeting, 2011). Even after many

Henry Groskinsky/Time Life Pictures/Getty Images

years, the money has never been collected, and the challenge has been terminated. For details, please see http://web.randi.org/home/jref-status

**Answers: 1.** False (Chapter 1), **2.** False (Chapter 4), **3.** False (Chapter 5), **4.** False (Chapter 6), **5.** True (Chapter 7), **6.** False (Chapter 12), **7.** True (Chapter 14), **8.** False (Chapter 14), **9.** True (Chapter 16), **10.** True (Chapter 16)

## Psychology's Past

Although people have long been interested in human nature, it was not until the first psychological laboratory was founded in 1879 that psychology as a science officially began. As interest in the new field grew, psychologists adopted various perspectives on the "appropriate" topics for psychological research and the "proper" research methods. These diverse viewpoints and subsequent debates molded and shaped modern psychological science.

Psychology's history as a science began in 1879, when Wilhelm Wundt [VILL-helm Voont], generally acknowledged as the "father of psychology," established the first psychological laboratory in Leipzig, Germany. Wundt and his followers were primarily interested in how we form sensations, images, and feelings. Their chief methodology was termed "introspection," and it relied on participants' self-monitoring and reporting on conscious experiences (Freedheim & Weiner, 2013; Goodwin, 2012).

A student of Wundt's, Edward Titchener, brought his ideas to the United States. Titchener's approach, now known as **structuralism**, sought to identify the basic elements, or "structures," of mental life through introspection and then to determine how these elements combine to form the whole of experience. Because introspection could not be used to study animals, children, or more complex mental disorders, however, structuralism failed as a working psychological approach. Although short-lived, it did establish a model for studying mental processes scientifically.

Structuralism's intellectual successor, **functionalism**, studied the way the mind functions to enable humans and other animals to adapt to their environment. William James was the leading force in the functionalist school (**Figure 1.1**). Although functionalism also eventually declined, it expanded the scope of psychology to include research on emotions and observable behaviors, initiated the psychological testing movement, and influenced modern education and industry. Today, James is widely considered the "father" of American psychology.

**Structuralism** Early psychological approach promoted by Wundt and Titchener that used introspection to study the basic elements (or structures) of the mind.

**Functionalism** Early psychological approach associated with William James that explored how the mind functions to enable organisms to adapt to their environment.

Bettmann/Getty Images

**FIGURE 1.1** **William James (1842–1910)** William James founded the perspective known as functionalism and established the first psychology laboratory in the United States, at Harvard University. In modern times, he is commonly referred to as the "father" of American psychology, whereas Wundt is considered the "father" of all psychology.

**Psychoanalytic perspective** An earlier approach to psychology developed by Sigmund Freud, which focuses on unconscious processes, unresolved conflicts, and past experiences.

**Psychodynamic perspective** A modern approach to psychology that emphasizes unconscious dynamics, motives, conflicts, and past experiences; based on the psychoanalytic approach, but focuses more on social and cultural factors, and less on sexual drives.

**Behavioral perspective** A modern approach to psychology that emphasizes objective, observable, environmental influences on overt behavior.

**Humanistic perspective** A modern approach to psychology that perceives human nature as naturally positive and growth seeking; it emphasizes free will and self-actualization.

**FIGURE 1.2** **B. F. Skinner (1904–1990)** B. F. Skinner was one of the most influential psychologists of the twentieth century. Here he uses the so-called "Skinner box" to train a rat to press a lever for a reward.

During the late 1800s and early 1900s, while functionalism was prominent in the United States, the **psychoanalytic perspective** was forming in Europe. Its founder, Austrian physician Sigmund Freud, believed that a part of the human mind, the unconscious, contains thoughts, memories, and desires that lie outside personal awareness yet still exert great influence. For example, according to Freud, a man who is cheating on his wife might slip up and say, "I wish you were her," when he consciously planned to say, "I wish you were here." Such seemingly meaningless, so-called "Freudian slips" supposedly reveal a person's true unconscious desires and motives.

Freud also believed many psychological problems are caused by unconscious sexual or aggressive motives and conflicts between "acceptable" and "unacceptable" behaviors (Chapter 13). His theory led to a system of therapy known as *psychoanalysis* (Chapter 15).

*Freud: If it's not one thing, it's your mother.* —Robin Williams (Comedian, Actor)

## Modern Psychology

As summarized in **Table 1.1**, contemporary psychology reflects seven major perspectives: *psychodynamic*, *behavioral*, *humanistic*, *cognitive*, *biological*, *evolutionary*, and *sociocultural*. Although there are numerous differences among these seven perspectives, most psychologists recognize the value of each orientation and agree that no one view has all the answers.

Freud's nonscientific approach and emphasis on sexual and aggressive impulses have long been controversial, and today there are few strictly Freudian psychoanalysts left. However, the broad features of his theory remain in the modern **psychodynamic perspective**. The general goal of psychodynamic psychologists is to explore unconscious *dynamics*—internal motives, conflicts, and past experiences.

In the early 1900s, another major perspective appeared that dramatically shaped the course of modern psychology. Unlike earlier approaches, the **behavioral perspective** emphasizes objective, observable environmental influences on overt behavior. Behaviorism's founder, John B. Watson (1913), rejected the practice of introspection and the influence of unconscious forces. Instead, Watson adopted Russian physiologist Ivan Pavlov's concept of *conditioning* (Chapter 6) to explain behavior as a result of observable stimuli (in the environment) and observable tight line responses (behavioral actions).

Most early behaviorist research was focused on learning; nonhuman animals were ideal participants for this research. One of the best-known behaviorists, B. F. Skinner, was convinced that behaviorist approaches could be used to "shape" human behavior (**Figure 1.2**). As you'll discover in Chapters 6 and 15, therapeutic techniques rooted in the behavioristic perspective have been most successful in treating observable behavioral problems, such as those related to phobias and alcoholism (Cheng et al., 2017; El-Bar et al., 2017; Tyner et al., 2016).

Although the psychoanalytic and behavioral perspectives dominated psychology for some time, in the 1950s a new approach emerged—the **humanistic perspective**, which stresses *free will* (voluntarily chosen behavior) and *self-actualization* (an inborn drive to develop all one's talents and capabilities). According to Carl Rogers and Abraham Maslow, two central figures with this perspective, all individuals

Nina Leen/Time & Life Pictures/Getty Images

**TABLE 1.1**   **Modern Psychology's Seven Major Perspectives**

| Perspectives | Major Emphases | Sample Research Questions | |
|---|---|---|---|
| **Psychodynamic** | Unconscious dynamics, motives, conflicts, and past experiences | How do adult personality traits or psychological problems reflect unconscious processes and early childhood experiences? | |
| **Behavioral** | Objective, observable, environmental influences on overt behavior; stimulus–response (S-R) relationships and consequences for behavior | How do reinforcement and punishment affect behavior? How can we increase desirable behaviors and decrease undesirable ones? | |
| **Humanistic** | Free will, self-actualization, and human nature as naturally positive and growth seeking | How can we promote a client's capacity for self-actualization and understanding of his or her own development? How can we promote international peace and reduce violence? | |
| **Cognitive** | Mental processes used in thinking, knowing, remembering, and communicating | How do our thoughts and interpretations affect how we respond in certain situations? How can we improve how we process, store, and retrieve information? | |
| **Biological** | Genetic and biological processes in the brain and other parts of the nervous system | How might changes in neurotransmitters or damage to parts of the brain lead to psychological problems and changes in behavior and mental processes? | |
| **Evolutionary** | Natural selection, adaptation, and reproduction | How does natural selection help explain why we love and help certain people, but hurt others? Do we have specific genes for aggression and altruism? | |
| **Sociocultural** | Social interaction and the cultural determinants of behavior and mental processes | How do the values and beliefs transmitted from our social and cultural environments affect our everyday psychological processes? | |

| | |
|---|---|
| **Study Tip**<br><br>**Illustrations**<br><br>*Do not skip over photos, figures, and tables. They visually reinforce important concepts and often contain material that may appear on exams.* | **Why do we need seven perspectives?** What do you see in this figure? Is it two profiles facing each other, a white vase, or both? Your ability to see both figures is similar to a psychologist's ability to study behavior and mental processes from a number of different perspectives.  |

Makc/Shutterstock

naturally strive to develop and move toward self-actualization. Like psychoanalysis, humanistic psychology developed an influential theory of personality and its own form of psychotherapy (Chapters 12 and 15).

The humanistic approach also led the way to a contemporary research specialty known as **positive psychology**—the study of optimal human functioning (Diener, 2016; Diener & Tay, 2015; Seligman, 2003, 2015). For many years, psychology understandably focused on negative states, such as aggression, depression, and prejudice. In recent years, leaders in the

**Positive psychology** The study of optimal human functioning; emphasizes positive emotions, traits, and institutions.

positive psychology movement, such as Ed Diener, Martin Seligman, and Shelly Taylor, have pushed for a broader study of human experiences, with an emphasis on: (1) *positive emotions* (like hope, love, and happiness), (2) *positive traits* (such as altruism, courage, and compassion), and (3) *positive institutions* that help promote better lives (such as improved schools and healthier families) (Seligman, 2003). Thanks to its scientific methodology and broader focus on optimal functioning, *positive psychology* has provided a wealth of new research found throughout this text.

One of the most influential modern approaches, the **cognitive perspective**, emphasizes the mental processes we use in thinking, knowing, remembering, and communicating (Goldstein, 2015; Greene, 2016). These mental processes include perception, memory, imagery, concept formation, problem solving, reasoning, decision making, and language. Many cognitive psychologists also use an *information-processing approach*, likening the mind to a computer that sequentially takes in information, processes it, and then produces a response.

During the past few decades, scientists have explored the role of biological factors in almost every area of psychology. Using sophisticated tools and technologies, scientists who adopt this **biological perspective** examine behavior through the lens of genetics and biological processes in the brain and other parts of the nervous system. For example, research shows that genes influence many aspects of our behavior, including how kind we are to other people, whom we vote for in elections, and even whether or not we decide to purchase a handgun (Barnes et al., 2014; Ksiazkiewicz et al., 2016; Wilson, 2015a).

The **evolutionary perspective** stresses natural selection, adaptation, and reproduction (Buss, 2011, 2015; Dawkins, 2016; Goldfinch, 2015). This perspective stems from the writings of Charles Darwin (1859), who suggested that natural forces select traits that aid an organism's survival. This process of **natural selection** occurs when a particular genetic trait gives an organism a reproductive advantage over others. Because of natural selection, the fastest, strongest, smartest, or otherwise most fit organisms are most likely to live long enough to reproduce and thereby pass on their genes to the next generation. According to the evolutionary perspective, there's even an evolutionary explanation for the longevity of humans over other primates–it's grandmothers! Without them, a mother who has a two-year-old and then gives birth would have to devote her time and resources to the newborn at the expense of the older child. Grandmothers act as supplemental caregivers.

Finally, the **sociocultural perspective** emphasizes social interactions and cultural determinants of behavior and mental processes (**Figure 1.3**). Although we are often unaware of their influence, factors such as ethnicity, religion, occupation, and socioeconomic class have an enormous psychological impact on our mental processes and behavior.

For instance, researchers recently found that a 10-minute conversation with a random stranger led to significant decreases in *transphobia* (an irrational fear of transgender people) and that these effects lasted at least three months (Broockman & Kalla, 2016). What caused such a dramatic change? Rather than just presenting facts and talking "to" participants, the researchers asked them to recall and discuss their own personal experiences with judgment or prejudice. Afterward, they were encouraged to think about how their story related to the experiences of transgender people. Do you see how this type of *empathy induction*—encouraging someone to actively take the perspective of another—would lead to reduced prejudice? Or why this research was so widely cited in scientific journals and the mass media (Bohannon, 2016; Resnick, 2016)? It's due in part to the fact that deeply held attitudes, like prejudice, are so notoriously difficult to change. For more information on this study, see Chapter 16.

**Cognitive perspective**    A modern approach to psychology that focuses on the mental processes used in thinking, knowing, remembering, and communicating.

**Biological perspective**    A modern approach to psychology that focuses on genetics and biological processes.

**Evolutionary perspective**    A modern approach to psychology that stresses natural selection, adaptation, and reproduction.

**Natural selection**    Darwin's principle of an evolutionary process in which heritable traits that increase an organism's chances of survival or reproduction are more likely to be passed on to succeeding generations.

**Sociocultural perspective**    A modern approach to psychology that emphasizes social interaction and the cultural determinants of behavior and mental processes.

©AP/Wide World Photos

**FIGURE 1.3   Psychology in a global economy**   Technological advances allow instant communication for people who not long ago were isolated from events in the rest of the world. How do you think these changes affect these men from Enaotai Island in West Papua, New Guinea?

## Gender and Cultural Diversity

### Psychology's History of Diversity

During the late 1800s and early 1900s, most colleges and universities provided little opportunity for women and people of color, either as students or as faculty members. One of the first women to be recognized in the field of psychology was Mary Calkins. Her achievements are particularly noteworthy, considering the significant discrimination that she overcame. For example, married women could not be teachers or professors in co-educational settings during this time in history. In Mary Calkins' case, even after she completed all the requirements for a Ph.D. at Harvard University in 1895, and was described by William James as his brightest student, the university refused to grant the degree to a woman. Nevertheless, Calkins went on to perform valuable research on memory, and in 1905 served as the first female president of the American Psychological Association (APA). The first woman to receive her Ph.D. in psychology was Margaret Floy Washburn from Cornell University in 1894. She also wrote several influential books and served as the second female president of the APA.

Francis Cecil Sumner became the first Black person to earn a Ph.D. in psychology (Clark University, 1920). Dr. Sumner later chaired one of the country's leading psychology departments, at Howard University. In 1971, one of Sumner's students, Kenneth B. Clark, became the first person of color to be elected APA president. Clark's research with his wife, Mamie Clark, documented the harmful effects of prejudice and directly influenced the Supreme Court's landmark 1954 ruling against racial segregation in schools, *Brown v. Board of Education* (**Figure 1.4**).

Calkins, Washburn, Sumner, and Clark, along with other important people of color and women, made significant and lasting contributions to psychology's development. Today, women earning advanced degrees in psychology greatly outnumber men, but, unfortunately, people of color are still underrepresented (Graduate Study in Psychology, 2017; Willyard, 2011).

Library of Congress Prints and Photographs Division

**FIGURE 1.4    Kenneth Clark (1914–2005) and Mamie Phipps Clark (1917–1985)**    Kenneth Clark and Mamie Phipps Clark conducted experiments with Black and White dolls to study children's attitudes about race. This research and their expert testimony contributed to the U.S. Supreme Court's ruling that racial segregation in public schools was unconstitutional.

### Culture and the Biopsychosocial Model

The seven major perspectives have all made significant contributions to modern psychology. This explains why most contemporary psychologists do not adhere to one single intellectual perspective. Instead, a more integrative, unifying theme—the **biopsychosocial model**—has gained wide acceptance. This model views biological processes (genetics, neurotransmitters, evolution), psychological factors (learning, personality, motivation), and social forces (family, culture, gender, ethnicity) as interrelated. It also sees all three factors as influences inseparable from the seven major perspectives (**Figure 1.5**).

Why is the biopsychosocial model so essential? As the old saying goes, "A fish doesn't know it's in water." Similarly, as individuals living alone inside our own heads, we're often unaware of the numerous, interacting factors that affect us—particularly cultural forces. For example, most North Americans and Western Europeans are raised to be very individualistic and are surprised to learn that over 70% of the world's population live in collectivistic cultures. As you can see in **Table 1.2**, in *individualistic cultures*, the needs and goals of the individual are emphasized over the needs and goals of the group. When asked to complete the statement "I am . . . ," people from individualistic cultures tend to respond with personality traits ("I am shy"; "I am outgoing") or their occupation ("I am a teacher"; "I am a student").

In *collectivistic cultures*, however, the person is defined and understood primarily by looking at his or her place in the social unit (Fang et al., 2016; Moleiro et al., 2017; Saucier et al., 2015) (see **Study Tip**). Relatedness, connectedness, and interdependence are valued, as opposed to separateness, independence, and individualism. When asked to complete the statement "I am . . . ," people from collectivistic cultures tend to mention their families or nationality ("I am a daughter";

**Biopsychosocial model**    An integrative, unifying theme of modern psychology that sees biological, psychological, and social processes as interrelated and interacting influences.

**Study Tip**

**Reference Citations**
*Throughout this text, you will see citations to publications at the ends of many sentences. These citations—such as (Johnson, 2016)—give authors' names and the dates of their publications. Instructors rarely expect you to memorize the names and dates in parentheses. They are provided as a starting point for research projects, for additional information on a topic of interest, and to double-check the research sources. Complete publication information (title of article or chapter, author, journal name or book title, date, and page numbers) can be found in the References section provided with this text.*

**FIGURE 1.5** **The biopsychosocial model** When we consider people as individuals (**Figure a**), we don't always get a complete picture of their emotions and motivations. Stepping back to see the same individuals in a broader context (**Figure b**) can provide new insights. With this "bigger picture" (the child's immediate surroundings and his or her group's behavior) in mind, can you better understand why each child might be feeling and acting as he or she is? The biopsychosocial model recognizes that there is usually no single cause for our behavior or our mental states (**Figure c**). For example, our moods and feelings are often influenced by genetics and neurotransmitters (biological), our learned responses and patterns of thinking (psychological), and our socioeconomic status and cultural views of emotion (sociocultural).

a.

c.

b.

"I am Chinese"). Keep in mind, however, that these sample countries and their sample values exist on a continuum, and that within each country there is a wide range of individual differences.

Looking again at the photos from the cultures in Figure 1.5, do you recognize how learning more about the biopsychosocial model offers increased understanding of ourselves, our

**TABLE 1.2** **A Comparison Between Individualistic and Collectivistic Cultures**

| Sample Individualistic Countries | Sample Collectivistic Cultures |
| --- | --- |
| United States | Korea |
| Australia | China |
| Great Britain | India |
| Canada | Japan |
| The Netherlands | West Africa region |
| Germany | Thailand |
| New Zealand | Taiwan |

| Sample Individualistic Values | Sample Collectivistic Values |
| --- | --- |
| Independence | Interdependence |
| Individual rights | Obligations to others |
| Self-sufficiency | Reliance on group |
| Individual achievement | Group achievement |
| Independent living | Living with kin |
| Personal failure leads to shame and guilt | Failing the group leads to shame and guilt |

## Try This Yourself

### Are You an Individualist or a Collectivist?

If asked to draw a circle with yourself in the center, and the people in your life as separate circles surrounding you, which of the two diagrams comes closest to your personal view?

If you chose (a), you probably have an *individualistic* orientation, seeing yourself as an independent, separate self. However, if you chose (b), you're more closely aligned with a *collectivist* culture, seeing yourself as interdependent and interconnected with others.

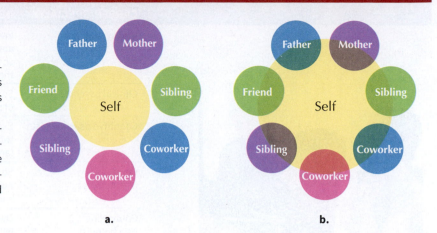

a.                b.

friends, and our families, and how it may improve our understanding and sensitivity to other cultures? For example, Americans generally define *sincerity* as behaving in accordance with our inner feelings, whereas people from collectivist cultures tend to see their equivalent word for sincerity as behavior that conforms to a person's role expectations and duties (Yamada, 1997). This explains why collectivistic behaviors might appear insincere to Americans.

## ❖ Psychology and Your Professional Success | Would You Like a Career in Psychology?

Many people think of psychologists only as therapists, and it's true that the fields of clinical and counseling psychology do make up the largest specialty areas. However, many psychologists have no connection with therapy. Instead, we work as researchers, teachers, or consultants in academic, business, industry, and government settings, or in a combination of settings (e.g., Roediger, 2017; Silvia et al., 2017; Sternberg, 2017). As you can see in **Table 1.3**, there are several career paths and valuable life skills associated with a bachelor's degree in psychology. Of course, your options are even greater if you go beyond the bachelor's degree and earn your master's degree, Ph.D., or Psy.D.—see **Table 1.4**. For more information about what psychologists do—and how to pursue a career in psychology—check out the websites of the American Psychological Association (APA) and the Association for Psychological Science (APS).

| TABLE 1.3    What Can I Do with a Bachelor's Degree in Psychology? |
| --- |
| **Top Careers with a Bachelor's Degree in Psychology** |
| Management and administration |
| Sales |
| Social work |
| Labor relations, personnel, and training |
| Real estate, business services, insurance |
| **Sample Skills Gained from a Psychology Major** |
| Improved ability to predict and understand behavior |
| Better understanding of how to use and interpret data |
| Increased communication and interpersonal skills |
| Increased ability to manage difficult situations and high-stress environments |
| Enhanced insight into problem behavior |

Note that the U.S. Department of Labor predicts only an average rate of growth for psychologists in the next decade. However, the good news is that a degree in our field, and this course in general psychology, will provide you with invaluable lifetime skills.

**TABLE 1.4**   **Sample Careers and Specialties in Psychology**

| CAREER/SPECIALTY | DESCRIPTION |
|---|---|
| Biopsychologist/neuroscientist | Investigates the relationship between biology, behavior, and mental processes, including how physical and chemical processes affect the structure and function of the brain and nervous system |
| Clinical psychologist | Specializes in the evaluation, diagnosis, and treatment of psychological disorders |
| Cognitive psychologist | Examines "higher" mental processes, including thought, memory, intelligence, creativity, and language |
| Comparative psychologist | Studies the behavior and mental processes of non-human animals; emphasizes evolution and cross-species comparisons |
| Counseling psychologist | Overlaps with clinical psychology, but generally works with less seriously disordered individuals and focuses more on social, educational, and career adjustment |
| Cross-cultural psychologist/psychological anthropologist | Studies similarities and differences in and across various cultures and ethnic groups |
| Developmental psychologist | Studies the course of human growth and development from conception to death |
| Educational psychologist | Studies the processes of education and works to promote the academic, intellectual, social, and emotional development of children in the school environment |
| Environmental psychologist | Investigates how people affect and are affected by the physical environment |
| Experimental psychologist | Examines processes such as learning, conditioning, motivation, emotion, sensation, and perception in humans and other animals (Note that psychologists working in almost all other areas of specialization also conduct research.) |
| Forensic psychologist | Applies principles of psychology to the legal system, including jury selection, psychological profiling, assessment, and treatment of offenders |
| Gender and/or cultural psychologist | Investigates how men and women and different cultures vary from one another and how they are similar |
| Health psychologist | Studies how biological, psychological, and social factors affect health, illness, and health-related behaviors |
| Industrial/organizational psychologist | Applies principles of psychology to the workplace, including personnel selection and evaluation, leadership, job satisfaction, employee motivation, and group processes within the organization |
| Personality psychologist | Studies the unique and relatively stable patterns in a person's thoughts, feelings, and actions |
| Positive psychologist | Examines factors related to optimal human functioning |
| School psychologist | Collaborates with teachers, parents, and students within the educational system to help children with special needs related to a disability and/or their academic and social progress; also provides evaluation and assessment of a student's functioning and eligibility for special services |
| Social psychologist | Investigates the role of social forces in interpersonal behavior, including aggression, prejudice, love, helping, conformity, and attitudes |
| Sport psychologist | Applies principles of psychology to enhance physical performance |

Rob Marmion/Shutterstock

**Clinical and counseling psychology**   For most people, this is the role most commonly associated with psychology.

Jeffrey L. Rotman/Getty Images

**Comparative and experimental psychology** Research with human and nonhuman animals has provided valuable insights into behavior and mental processes.

Courtesy of Katherine Dowdell

**Psychologists often wear many hats**   Professor Katherine Dowdell teaches full time at Des Moines Area Community College, serves as a department chair, and is a co-author of this text.

© Billy R. Ray/Wiley

## Retrieval Practice 1.1 | Introducing Psychology

Completing this self-test and connections section, and then checking your answers by clicking on the answer button or by looking in Appendix B, will provide immediate feedback and helpful practice for exams.

**Self-Test**

1. Psychology is defined as the _____.
   a. science of conscious and unconscious forces
   b. empirical study of the mind and behavior
   c. scientific study of the mind
   d. scientific study of behavior and mental processes

2. Define *critical thinking*.

3. _____ is generally acknowledged to be the father of psychology.
   a. Sigmund Freud          b. B. F. Skinner
   c. Wilhelm Wundt          d. William Tell

4. Which of the following terms do not belong together?
   a. structuralism, unconscious behavior
   b. behaviorism, observable behavior
   c. psychoanalytic, unconscious conflict
   d. humanism, free will

5. The _____ views biological processes, psychological factors, and social forces as interrelated influences, and it is one of the most widely accepted themes of modern psychology.
   a. eclectic perspective          b. nature-nurture model
   c. interactionist position       d. biopsychosocial model

**Connections—Chapter to Chapter**

Answering the following questions will help you "look back and look ahead" to see the important connections among the various subfields of psychology and chapters within this text.

1. In the Prologue to this textbook, you learned about Critical Thinking Components (CTCs). Among these are distinguishing fact from opinion (behavioral), welcoming divergent views (affective), and synthesizing information (cognitive). Discuss how each of these CTCs is relevant to the study of psychology.

2. In Chapter 16 (Social Psychology), you'll discover some of the reasons why people choose to help each other. Using at least three of the seven modern perspectives of psychology, explain why a person might choose to help (or not to help) a person in need.

> **Study Tip**
>
> *Each major topic concludes with Self-Test questions that allow you to stop and check your understanding of the key concepts just discussed. Our students have found that completing these questions greatly improves their test scores. Be sure to also provide your own answers to the Connections questions, and then compare all your answers with those provided in Appendix B provided with this text.*

---

## 1.2 | The Science of Psychology

### LEARNING OBJECTIVES

**Retrieval Practice** While reading the upcoming sections, respond to each Learning Objective in your own words.

**Discuss the key principles underlying the science of psychology.**

- **Compare and contrast** the fundamental goals of basic and applied research.

- **Describe** the scientific method, its key terms, and its six steps.

- **Review** psychology's four main goals.

- **Discuss** the ethical concerns and guidelines for psychological research.

---

## Basic and Applied Research

In science, research strategies are generally categorized as either *basic* or *applied*. **Basic research** is most often conducted to advance core scientific knowledge, whereas **applied research** is generally designed to solve practical ("real-world") problems (**Figure 1.6**). As you'll see in Chapter 6, classical and operant conditioning principles evolved from numerous *basic research* studies designed to advance the general understanding of how human and nonhuman animals learn. In Chapters 14 and 15, you'll also discover how *applied research* based on these principles has been used to successfully treat psychological disorders, such as phobias.

**Basic research** A type of research primarily conducted to advance core scientific knowledge; most often conducted in universities and research laboratories.

**Applied research** A type of research primarily conducted to solve practical, real-world problems; generally conducted outside the laboratory.

**FIGURE 1.6** **Applied research in psychology** Note how psychological research has helped design safer and more reliable appliances, machinery, and instrument controls (*Psychology Matters*, 2006).

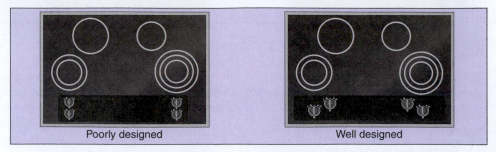

Poorly designed | Well designed

**a. Spatial correspondence** Controls for stovetops should be arranged in a pattern that corresponds to the placement of the burners.

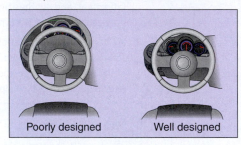

Poorly designed | Well designed

Poorly designed | Well designed

© studio9400/iStockphoto

© pictafolio/iStockphoto

**b. Visibility** Automobile gauges for fuel, temperature, and speed should be easily visible to the driver.

**c. Arrangement of numbers** A top-down arrangement of numbers on a cell phone is more efficient than the bottom-up arrangement on a computer's keyboard.

Similarly, in Chapter 7, you'll see how basic research on how we create, store, and retrieve our memories has led to practical applications in the legal field, such as a greater appreciation for the fallibility of eyewitness testimony.

Remember that basic and applied research approaches are not polar opposites. Instead, they frequently share similar goals, and their outcomes interact, with one building on the other.

## The Scientific Method

While conducting either basic or applied research, psychologists follow strict, standardized procedures so that others can understand, interpret, and repeat or test their findings. Most scientific investigations consist of six basic steps, collectively based on the **scientific method** (**Step-by-Step Diagram 1.1**). For example, are you wondering whether completing the *Retrieval Practice* exercises sprinkled throughout each chapter of this text, including those at the ends of sections and those within the Learning Objectives and Key Terms, is worth your time? Or if it will help you do better on exams?

Let's see how we might use the scientific method to answer these questions. Starting with Step 1, you would first *identify the question of interest*, which in this case is: "How might retrieval practice exercises affect exam grades?" As part of this identification, you need to clarify the specific factors your research will need to observe and measure—in this case, retrieval practice exercises and exam grades. Note that these specific factors are officially referred to as *variables*, which are simply any traits or conditions that can vary or change. After completing this first part of Step 1, you would perform a literature review, which involves consulting professional journals and studying previous research findings on retrieval practice and exam grades.

To complete Step 2, you would need to form an educated guess based on your literature review in Step 1. You would then turn this guess into a statement, called a **hypothesis**, which provides predictions that can be tested in some way. You would need to explicitly state how each of the variables in your hypothesis will be **operationally defined** (observed and measured). For example, a

**Scientific method** The cyclical and cumulative research process used for gathering and interpreting objective information in a way that minimizes error and yields dependable results.

**Hypothesis** A tentative and testable explanation (or "educated guess") about the relationship between two or more variables; a testable prediction or question.

**Operational definition** A precise description of how the variables in a study will be observed and measured.

| STEP-BY-STEP DIAGRAM 1.1 | The Scientific Method |

**STOP!** This Step-by-Step Diagram contains essential information NOT found elsewhere in the text, which is likely to appear on quizzes and exams. Be sure to study it CAREFULLY!

**Study Tip**

*Research has shown that having access to diagrams showing how a process works results in higher performance on tests than having no diagrams at all, or just a text outline of the process (Bui & McDaniel, 2015). This and other research, along with our own experiences as educators, explains why we've included numerous step-by-step diagrams throughout this text.*

Scientific knowledge is constantly evolving and self-correcting through application of the scientific method. As soon as one research study is published, the cycle almost always begins again.

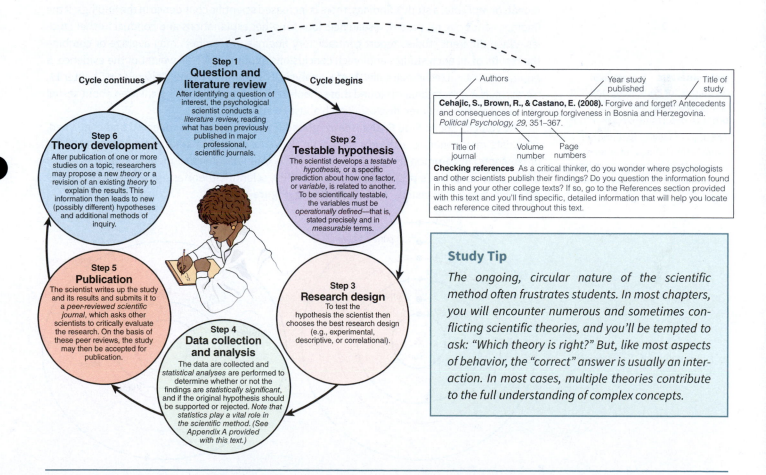

**Step 1**
**Question and literature review**
After identifying a question of interest, the psychological scientist conducts a *literature review,* reading what has been previously published in major professional, scientific journals.

**Cycle continues**    **Cycle begins**

**Step 6**
**Theory development**
After publication of one or more studies on a topic, researchers may propose a new *theory* or a revision of an existing *theory* to explain the results. This information then leads to new (possibly different) hypotheses and additional methods of inquiry.

**Step 2**
**Testable hypothesis**
The scientist develops a *testable hypothesis,* or a specific prediction about how one factor, or *variable,* is related to another. To be scientifically testable, the variables must be *operationally defined*—that is, stated precisely and in *measurable* terms.

**Step 5**
**Publication**
The scientist writes up the study and its results and submits it to a *peer-reviewed scientific journal,* which asks other scientists to critically evaluate the research. On the basis of these peer reviews, the study may then be accepted for publication.

**Step 4**
**Data collection and analysis**
The data are collected and *statistical analyses* are performed to determine whether or not the findings are *statistically significant,* and if the original hypothesis should be supported or rejected. *Note that statistics play a vital role in the scientific method. (See Appendix A provided with this text.)*

**Step 3**
**Research design**
To test the hypothesis the scientist then chooses the best research design (e.g., experimental, descriptive, or correlational).

Authors      Year study published      Title of study

**Cehajic, S., Brown, R., & Castano, E. (2008).** Forgive and forget? Antecedents and consequences of intergroup forgiveness in Bosnia and Herzegovina. *Political Psychology, 29,* 351–367.

Title of journal      Volume number      Page numbers

**Checking references**   As a critical thinker, do you wonder where psychologists and other scientists publish their findings? Do you question the information found in this and your other college texts? If so, go to the References section provided with this text and you'll find specific, detailed information that will help you locate each reference cited throughout this text.

**Study Tip**

*The ongoing, circular nature of the scientific method often frustrates students. In most chapters, you will encounter numerous and sometimes conflicting scientific theories, and you'll be tempted to ask: "Which theory is right?" But, like most aspects of behavior, the "correct" answer is usually an interaction. In most cases, multiple theories contribute to the full understanding of complex concepts.*

better grade on your exams might be operationally defined as earning one letter grade higher than the letter grade on your previous exam. Using your initial question about the value of the Retrieval Practice exercises, your hypothesis and operational definitions might be: "Students who spend two hours studying Chapter 1 in this text and one hour completing the Retrieval Practice exercises will earn higher scores on a standard academic exam than students who spend three hours studying Chapter 1 without completing the Retrieval Practice exercises."

For Step 3, you would most likely choose an experimental research design and solicit volunteers for your experiment. For instance, you might recruit 100 volunteers from various classes. Of these, you could randomly assign 50 to Group 1 (Retrieval Practice) and the other 50 to Group 2 (no Retrieval Practice). After having both groups study for three hours, you could present and score a 20-point quiz, followed by a statistical analysis (Step 4) to determine whether the difference in test scores between the two groups is **statistically significant**. To be statistically significant, the difference between the groups must be large enough that the result is probably not due to chance.

In Step 5, you could publish your research, and then you could go on to further investigate additional study techniques that might contribute to theory development on the most effective study methods, Step 6. [You'll be interested to know that research does exist on the superiority of retrieval practice in improving retention of material and exam scores (Carpenter & Yeung, 2017; Trumbo et al., 2016; Weinstein et al., 2016), which is why self-testing is so often emphasized throughout this text. As you'll see in Chapter 3, practice testing can even reduce the negative effects of stress (Smith et al., 2016)!]

Note also in Step-by-Step Diagram 1.1 that the scientific method is cyclical and cumulative. Scientific progress comes from repeatedly challenging and revising existing theories and building new ones. If numerous scientists, using different procedures or participants in varied settings, can repeat, or *replicate*, a study's findings, there is increased scientific confidence in the findings. If the findings cannot be replicated, researchers look for other explanations and conduct further studies. When different studies report contradictory findings, researchers may average or combine the results of all such studies and reach conclusions about the overall weight of the evidence, a popular statistical technique called **meta-analysis**. For example, as you'll discover in Chapter 11, a cross-cultural meta-analysis found that school-based programs teaching children about sexual abuse led to more children disclosing such abuse (Walsh et al., 2015).

As you can see in Step 6, after many related findings have been collected and confirmed, scientists may generate a **theory** to explain the data through a systematic, interrelated set of concepts. In common usage, the term *theory* is often assumed to mean something is only a hunch or someone's personal opinion. In reality, scientific theories are based on empirical evidence, rigorously tested, and self-correcting (**Figure 1.7**).

**Statistical significance**  A statistical statement of how likely it is that a study's result occurred merely by chance.

**Meta-analysis**  A statistical technique for combining and analyzing data from many studies in order to determine overall trends.

**Theory**  A well-substantiated explanation for a phenomenon or a group of facts that have been repeatedly confirmed by previous research.

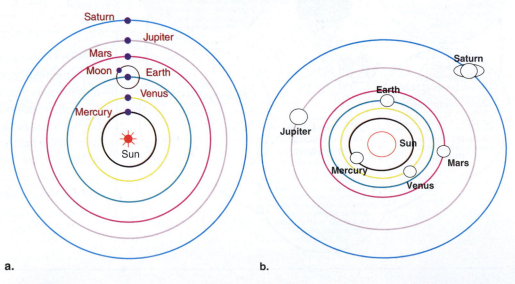

**FIGURE 1.7**  **Opinions versus facts—science to the rescue!**  Early experiments, conducted primarily by Nicolaus Copernicus (1473–1543), led to a collection of facts and the ultimate theory that the Earth was not the center of the universe (as generally assumed at the time) **(Figure a)**. Instead, it rotated around the sun with the other planets in concentric circles. Later scientists (astronomers Johannes Kepler and Tycho Brahe) built on this Copernican (heliocentric) theory with additional experiments that led to a revised theory, in which the orbits were not circular, but rather elliptical **(Figure b)**. Today, researchers have expanded the theory even further by demonstrating that our sun is not the center of the universe, but only a part of a galaxy that in turn is only one of many billions. Can you see how these incremental changes illustrate the value of scientific theories and their ever-changing and self-correcting nature?

## Psychology's Four Main Goals

In contrast to *pseudopsychologies*, which we discussed earlier and which rely on unsubstantiated beliefs and opinions, psychology is based on rigorous scientific methods. When conducting their research, psychologists have four major goals—to *describe*, *explain*, *predict*, and *change* behavior and mental processes:

1. **Description**   Description tells what occurred. In some studies, psychologists attempt to *describe*, or name and classify, particular behaviors by making careful scientific observations. Description is usually the first step in understanding behavior. For example, if someone says, "Boys are more aggressive than girls," what does that mean? The speaker's definition of aggression may differ from yours. Science requires specificity.

2. **Explanation**   An explanation tells why a behavior or mental process occurred. *Explaining* a behavior or mental process requires us to discover and understand its causes. One of the most enduring debates in science is the **nature–nurture controversy**. Are we controlled by biological and genetic factors (the nature side) or by the environment and learning (the nurture side)? As you will see throughout the text, psychology (like all other sciences) generally avoids "either/or" positions and focuses instead on *interactions*. Today, almost all scientists agree that most psychological, and even physical, traits reflect an interaction between nature and nurture. For example, research suggests numerous interacting causes or explanations for aggression, including culture, learning, genes, brain damage, and testosterone (Bushman, 2016; Gerring & Vasa, 2016; Lippa, 2016).

   **Nature–nurture controversy** An ongoing dispute about the relative contributions of nature (heredity) and nurture (environment) in determining the development of behavior and mental processes.

3. **Prediction**   Psychologists generally begin with description and explanation (answering the "whats" and "whys"). Then they move on to the higher-level goal of *prediction*, identifying "when" and under what conditions a future behavior or mental process is likely to occur. For instance, knowing that alcohol is linked with aggression (e.g., Buchholz et al., 2017; Crane et al., 2016), we can predict that more fights will erupt in places where alcohol is consumed than in places where it isn't.

4. **Change**   For some people, change as a goal of psychology brings to mind evil politicians or cult leaders brainwashing unknowing victims. However, to psychologists, *change* means applying psychological knowledge to prevent unwanted outcomes or bring about desired goals. In almost all cases, change as a goal of psychology is positive. Psychologists help people improve their work environments, stop addictive behaviors, become less depressed, improve their family relationships, and so on. Furthermore, as you may know from personal experience, it is very difficult (if not impossible) to change someone's attitude or behavior against her or his will. (*Here is an old joke*: Do you know how many psychologists it takes to change a light bulb? *Answer*: None. The light bulb has to want to change.)

## Psychology's Research Ethics

So far, we've discussed applied versus basic research, the scientific method, and the four basic goals of psychology. Now we need to examine the general ethics that guide psychological research. The two largest professional organizations of psychologists, the American Psychological Association (APA) and the Association for Psychological Science (APS), both recognize the importance of maintaining high ethical standards in research, therapy, and all other areas of professional psychology. The preamble to the APA's publication *Ethical Principles of Psychologists and Code of Conduct* (2016) requires psychologists to maintain their competence, to retain objectivity in applying their skills, and to preserve the dignity and best interests of their clients, colleagues, students, research participants, and society. In addition, colleges and universities today have institutional review boards (IRBs) that carefully evaluate the ethics and methods of research conducted at their institutions.

## Respecting the Rights of Human Participants

The APA and APS have developed rigorous guidelines regulating research with human participants, including:

- **Informed consent** Researchers must obtain **informed consent** from all participants *before* initiating an experiment. Participants are made aware of the nature of the study, what to expect, and significant factors that might influence their willingness to participate, including all physical risks, discomfort, and possibly unpleasant emotional experiences.

- **Voluntary participation** Participants must be told that they're free to decline to participate or to withdraw from the research at any time.

- **Restricted use of deception, followed by debriefing.** If participants knew the true purpose behind certain studies, they might not respond naturally. In one of psychology's most famous, and controversial, studies (Milgram, 1963), researchers ordered participants to give electric shocks to another participant (who was really a confederate of the researchers and was not receiving any shocks). Although this study was testing participants' willingness to follow orders, they were told that the study was examining the use of shocks to assist with learning. Obviously, in this case, participants' behavior could not be accurately measured if they were told the real focus of the study. Therefore, researchers occasionally need to temporarily deceive participants about the actual reason for the experiment.

  However, when deception is necessary, ethical guidelines and restrictions still apply. One of the most important is **debriefing**, which is conducted once the data collection has been completed. The researchers provide a full explanation of the research, including its design and purpose and any deception used, and then address participants' misconceptions, questions, or concerns.

- **Confidentiality** Whenever possible, participants are provided anonymity. All personal information acquired during a study must be kept private and not published in such a way that an individual's right to privacy is compromised.

## Respecting the Rights of Nonhuman Animals

Nonhuman animals have long played an essential role in scientific research (**Figure 1.8**). Without nonhuman animals in *medical research*, how would we test new drugs, surgical procedures, and methods for relieving pain? In *psychological research*, nonhuman animals (mostly rats and mice) are used in only 7 to 8% of studies (APA, 2009; ILAR, 2009; MORI, 2005). Nevertheless, they have made significant contributions to almost every area of psychology—the brain and nervous system, health and stress, sensation and perception, sleep, learning, memory, motivation, and emotion. For example, an experiment with rats found that those who are fed a diet high in fats and sugars show impairment in their learning and memory (Tran & Westbrook, 2015). This study could have critical real-world implications for people, but do you see why this type of research would be unethical and impossible to conduct using human subjects?

Nonhuman animal research has also produced significant gains for some animal populations. Examples include the development of more natural environments for zoo animals and more successful breeding techniques for endangered species.

Despite the advantages, using nonhuman animals in psychological research remains controversial. While debate continues about ethical issues in such research, psychologists take great care in handling research animals. Researchers also actively search for new and better ways to minimize any harm to the animals (APA Congressional Briefing, 2015; Morling, 2015; Pope & Vasquez, 2011).

Jonathan Selig/Getty Images

**FIGURE 1.8** **Test your critical thinking**
1. Nonhuman animals, like the mice in this photo, are sometimes used in psychological research when it would be impractical or unethical to use human participants. Do you believe nonhuman animal research is ethical? Why or why not?

2. What research questions might require the use of nonhuman animals? How would you ensure the proper treatment of these animals?

## Respecting the Rights of Psychotherapy Clients

Professional organizations, such as the APA and APS, as well as academic institutions and state and local agencies, all require that therapists, like researchers, maintain the highest ethical standards (Ethical Principles of Psychologists, 2016; Knapp et al., 2017). Therapists must also honor their clients' trust. All personal information and therapy records must be kept confidential. Furthermore, client records are only made available to authorized persons, and with the client's permission. However, therapists are legally required to break confidentiality if a client threatens violence to him or herself or to others, if a client is suspected of abusing a child or an elderly person, and in other limited situations (Fisher, 2016; Gebhardt, 2016).

### A Final Note on Ethical Issues

What about ethics and beginning psychology students? Once friends and acquaintances know you're taking a course in psychology, they may ask you to interpret their dreams, help them discipline their children, or even ask your opinion on whether they should start or end their relationships. Although you will learn a great deal about psychological functioning in this text, and in your psychology class, take care that you do not overestimate your expertise. Also remember that the theories and findings of psychological science are cumulative and continually being revised.

David L. Cole, a recipient of the APA Distinguished Teaching in Psychology Award, reminds us that, "Undergraduate psychology can, and I believe should, seek to liberate the student from ignorance, but also the arrogance of believing we know more about ourselves and others than we really do" (Cole, 1982, p. 24).

---

## Try This Yourself

### Want to Participate in Psychological Research?

If you'd like more information about psychological research—or if you'd like to try participating in some research studies yourself—go to https://www.mturk.com/mturk/welcome. Through Amazon's *Mechanical Turk (MTurk)* online service, researchers all over the world post studies that need participants. You may get paid for participating, but more importantly, you'll be making a valuable contribution to psychological science!

---

© Billy R. Ray/Wiley

## Retrieval Practice 1.2 | The Science of Psychology

Completing this self-test and the connections section, and then checking your answers by clicking on the answer button or by looking in Appendix B, will provide immediate feedback and helpful practice for exams.

### Self-Test

1. Label the six steps in the scientific method.

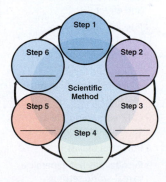

Step 1
Step 6
Step 2
Scientific Method
Step 5
Step 3
Step 4

2. A(n) _____ provides a precise definition of how the variables in a study will be observed and measured.

   a. meta-analysis
   b. theory
   c. independent observation
   d. operational definition

3. The goal of _____ is to tell what occurred, whereas the goal of _____ is to tell when.

   a. health psychologists; biological psychologists
   b. description; prediction
   c. psychologists; psychiatrists
   d. pseudopsychologists; clinical psychologists

4. Briefly explain the difference between a scientific theory, an opinion, and a hunch.

5. A participant's agreement to take part in a study after being told what to expect is known as _____.

   a. psychological standards       b. an experimental contract
   c. debriefing                    d. informed consent

### Connections—Chapter to Chapter

Answering the following question will help you "look back and look ahead" to see the important connections among the various subfields of psychology and chapters within this text.

In the Prologue to this textbook, you learned about Critical Thinking Components (CTCs). For each of the six steps of the scientific method, list at least one CTC used in or demonstrated by that step.

## 1.3 | Research Methods

### LEARNING OBJECTIVES

**Retrieval Practice**   While reading the upcoming sections, respond to each Learning Objective in your own words.

**Summarize psychology's three major research methods.**

• **Review** descriptive research and its four key methods.

• **Discuss** correlational research and its limits and value.
• **Identify** the key terms and components of experimental research.

Having studied the scientific method and psychology's four main goals, we can now examine how psychologists conduct their research. Psychologists generally draw on three major research methods—*descriptive*, *correlational*, and *experimental*. Bear in mind that these major research methods all share several common goals: to gather information, generate research ideas, provide data for current and further studies, and communicate results. But, as you can see in **Table 1.5**, each of these approaches has advantages and disadvantages, and psychologists often use variations of all three methods to study a single problem. In fact, when multiple approaches lead to similar conclusions, scientists have an especially strong foundation for concluding that one variable does affect another in a particular way.

**TABLE 1.5   Psychology's Three Major Research Methods**

| Method | Purpose | Advantages | Disadvantages |
|---|---|---|---|
| **Descriptive**<br>• Naturalistic observation<br>• Survey/interview<br>• Case study<br>• Archival research | To observe and record behavior and mental processes | • Allows studies in real-world settings with real-world applications<br>• Provides in-depth information on individuals and/or large groups<br>• Offers data and ideas for future research<br>• Meets psychology's goal of *description* | • Little or no control over variables<br>• Potential biases<br>• Cannot specify cause and effect<br>• Single cases or large surveys may be misleading<br>• Ethical and legal concerns over collection and use of data |
| **Correlational**<br>Statistical analyses of relationships between variables | To detect if two or more variables are related | • Allows studies in real-world settings with real-world applications<br>• Identifies strength and direction of relationships<br>• Offers data and ideas for future research<br>• Meets psychology's goal of *prediction* | • Little or no control over variables<br>• Potential biases<br>• Cannot specify cause and effect<br>• Possible illusory correlations and third-variable problems<br>• Ethical and legal concerns over collection and use of data |
| **Experimental**<br>Manipulation and control of variables | To determine potential cause and effect | • Allows more precise control over variables<br>• Permits causal explanation of behavior and mental processes<br>• Meets psychology's goal of *explanation* | • Cannot manipulate or control certain variables<br>• Potential biases<br>• Results may not generalize to real-world settings<br>• Ethical and legal concerns over use of data and manipulation of participants and certain variables |

Note that the three methods are not mutually exclusive. Researchers may use one, two, or all three methods to explore the same topic.

# Descriptive Research

Almost everyone observes and describes others in an attempt to understand them, but in conducting **descriptive research**, psychologists do so systematically and scientifically. The key types of descriptive research are *naturalistic observation*, *survey/ interview*, *case study*, and *archival research*.

**Naturalistic Observation**   As the name implies, **naturalistic observation** involves systematic observation and recording of participants in their natural setting—without interference by the researchers. Such observations can be conducted in a wide variety of settings, from supermarkets to airports to outdoors. Their major function is to gather descriptive information about the typical behavior of people and non-human animals. For example, Jane Goodall's classic naturalistic observations of wild chimpanzees provided invaluable insights into their everyday lives, such as their use of tools, their acts of aggression, their demonstrations of affection, and, sadly, even their killing of other chimps' babies (infanticide). A recent observational study of humans examined whether Uber and Lyft drivers take longer to respond to ride requests from Black travelers than from White travelers (Ge et al., 2016). Can you guess what they found? See Chapter 16 for the full story.

The chief advantage of naturalistic observation is that researchers can obtain data about natural behavior in a real-world setting, rather than in an artificial experimental situation. But naturalistic observation can be difficult and time-consuming, and the lack of control by the researcher makes it difficult to conduct observations for behavior that occurs infrequently.

For a researcher who wants to observe behavior in a more controlled setting, *laboratory observation* has many of the advantages of naturalistic observation, but with greater control over the variables (**Figure 1.9**).

**Survey/Interview**   Psychologists use **surveys/ interviews** to ask people to report their behaviors, opinions, and attitudes (see cartoon). In Chapter 3, you'll read about survey research showing that even a single close childhood friendship can protect vulnerable children in lower socioeconomic circumstances from several psychological risk factors (Graber et al., 2016).

One key advantage of this approach is that researchers can gather data from many more people than is generally possible with other research designs. Unfortunately, most surveys/interviews rely on self-reported data, and not all participants are honest. As you might imagine, people are especially motivated to give less-than-truthful answers when asked about highly sensitive topics, such as infidelity, drug use, and pornography.

**Case Study**   What if a researcher wants to investigate photophobia (fear of light)? In such a case, it would be difficult to find enough participants to conduct an experiment or to use surveys/interviews or naturalistic observation. For rare disorders or phenomena, researchers

Jeffrey Greenberg/Photo Researchers

**FIGURE 1.9   Laboratory observation**   In this type of observation, the researcher brings participants into a specially prepared room, with one-way mirrors or hidden cameras and microphones. Using such methods, the researcher can observe school children at work, families interacting, or other individuals and groups in various settings.

**Descriptive research**   A type of research that systematically observes and records behavior and mental processes without manipulating variables; designed to meet the goal of *description*.

**Naturalistic observation**   A descriptive research technique that observes and records behavior and mental processes in a natural, real-world setting.

**Survey/interview**   A descriptive research technique that questions a large sample of people to assess their behaviors and mental processes.

**"The good news is we had a 100% reader response."**

Cartoon Resource/Shutterstock

**Case study** A descriptive research technique involving an in-depth study of a single research participant or a small group of individuals.

try to find someone who has the problem and study him or her intensively. This type of in-depth study of a single research participant, or a small group of individuals, is called a **case study**. In Chapter 2, we'll discuss the fascinating case study of Phineas Gage, who suffered a horrific brain injury, and in Chapter 9 we'll share a disturbing case study examining the effects of extreme childhood neglect and abuse. Such studies obviously could not be conducted using another method, for ethical reasons and because of the rarity of the conditions being studied.

**Archival research** A descriptive research technique that studies existing data to find answers to research questions.

**Archival Research** The fourth type of descriptive research is **archival research**, in which researchers study previously recorded data. For example, archival data from 30,625 Himalayan mountain climbers from 56 countries found that expeditions from countries with hierarchical cultures, which believe that power should be concentrated at the top and followers should obey leaders without question, had more climbers reach the summit than did climbers from more egalitarian cultures (Anicich et al., 2015). Sadly, they also had more climbers die along the way. The researchers concluded that hierarchical values impaired performance by preventing low-ranking team members from sharing their valuable insights and perspectives. (If you're wondering about how America ranked, we're a little below midpoint in hierarchical values.)

Interestingly, the new "digital democracy," based on spontaneous comments on Twitter or Facebook, may turn out to be an even better method of research than the traditional random sampling of adults. Researchers who used a massive archive of billions of stored data from Twitter found "tweet share" predicted the winner in 404 out of 435 competitive races in the U.S. House elections in 2010 (DiGrazia et al., 2013). Apparently, just the total amount of discussion—good or bad—is a very good predictor of votes.

## Correlational Research

As you've just seen, data collected from descriptive research provides invaluable information on behavior and mental processes. The findings typically describe the dimensions of a phenomenon or behavior in terms of who was involved, what happened, and when and where it occurred. However, if we want to know *whether* and *how* two or more variables change together, we need **correlational research**. As the name implies, the purpose of this approach is to determine whether any two variables are *co-related*, meaning a change in one is accompanied by a change in the other. If one variable increases, how does the other variable change? Does it increase or decrease?

**Correlational research** A type of research that examines whether and how two or more variables change together; designed to meet the goal of *prediction*.

For example, a recent study found that as we get older, our job satisfaction tends to increase—yet over time within a given organization we become less satisfied (Dobrow et al., 2016). How can we explain this odd finding? Our job satisfaction apparently follows a cyclical pattern. When first employed, we go through a "honeymoon period," but our satisfaction tends to decline the longer we stay in that particular job. However, when we move on to another organization, with generally higher wages, our satisfaction increases.

As you can see, correlational research allows us to make *predictions* about one variable based on knowledge of another. Suppose scientists noted a relationship between hours of studying and performance on exams. The researchers could then predict exam grades based on amount of studying. The researchers also could determine the direction and strength of the relationship using a statistical formula that gives a **correlation coefficient**, which is a number from −1.00 to + 1.00 (see **Concept Organizer 1.1**).

**Correlation coefficient** A number from −1.00 to +1.00 that indicates the direction and strength of the relationship between two variables.

---

**CONCEPT ORGANIZER 1.1**  **Understanding the Role of Correlation Coefficients in Correlational Research**

**STOP!** This Concept Organizer contains essential information NOT found elsewhere in the text, which is likely to appear on quizzes and exams. Be sure to study it CAREFULLY!

As mentioned, *correlational research* examines whether and how two or more variables change together. Once researchers have collected measures on a group under study, they calculate a statistic known as a *correlation coefficient*. This number ranges from −1.00 to +1.00 and is commonly represented by the letter r, as in r = +.54 or r = −.32. As you'll see below, the + or − sign indicates the *direction* of the correlation, whereas the number (.54 or .32) indicates the *strength* of the correlation between two variables. Understanding what all of this means is crucial to becoming an educated consumer of research.

- **Direction of the correlation**    Correlational research can produce three types of correlations that vary in different directions. As shown in **Figure 1.10** below, when two factors vary in the same direction (**Figure a**), meaning they increase or decrease together, it's called a *positive correlation*. When two factors vary in opposite directions (**Figure b**), with one increasing as the other decreases, it's known as a *negative correlation*. When there is NO relation between the two variables (**Figure c**), it's a *zero correlation*. The *plus* or *minus* sign in a correlation coefficient indicates the *direction* of the correlation, with plus indicating a positive correlation (as in +.07) and minus indicating a negative correlation (as in −.07). For a zero correlation, no sign is used (as in .00).

  Correlation coefficients are often depicted in graphs called *scatterplots*, a type of graph in which two variables are plotted along two axes (see again Figure 1.10). Note that each dot in a scatterplot represents the values of two variables for one participant. The pattern (or "scattering") of the plots reveals the direction of the correlation (positive, negative, or zero).

- **Strength of the correlation**    Look again at the scatterplots in Figure 1.10, and note how the various dots cluster around the three solid dark lines. The closer the dots are together, the stronger the relationship—little scatter (more clustering) indicates a high correlation. Note in **Figure 1.11** (shown on the right) that as the number of the correlational coefficient decreases and gets closer to 0.00, the relationship weakens. In comparison, a correlation of +1.00 or −1.00 indicates the strongest possible relationship. And, once again, we interpret correlations close to zero as representing no relationship between the two variables.

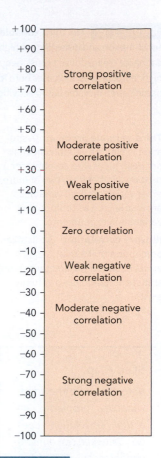

**FIGURE 1.11**    **Interpreting the strength of various correlation coefficients**

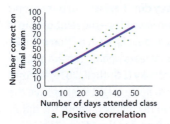
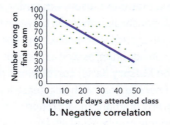
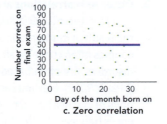

**FIGURE 1.10**    **Three types of correlation**    Note that these are hypothetical graphs, but the results in **Figure a** and **Figure b** are consistent with research findings on the importance of class attendance (e.g., Putnam et al., 2016). For more details, see the *Tools for Student Success* section at the end of this chapter.

## Try This Yourself

### Test Your Understanding of Correlations

Can you identify whether each of the following pairs most likely has a positive, negative, or zero correlation?

1. Health and exercise
2. Hours of TV viewing and student grades
3. Happiness and helpfulness
4. Hours of sleep and number of friends
5. Extraversion and loneliness

**Answers:** 1. positive, 2. negative, 3. positive, 4. zero, 5. negative

## The Limits of Correlations
Correlations are sometimes misleading, confusing, or not particularly useful. In addition, the observation, recording, and data analyses from both descriptive and correlational studies can lead to ethical and legal concerns. For example, surveying or observing survivors after a terrorist attack and then using their data to make generalized predictions may lead to further trauma for the victims. Therefore, it's very important to note two major cautions concerning correlations.

1. **Correlation does NOT prove causation!**    Correlational studies can detect whether or not two variables are related. However, they cannot tell us which variable is the cause or

**FIGURE 1.12** **The third-variable problem** Ice cream consumption and drowning are highly correlated. Obviously, eating ice cream doesn't cause people to drown. A third factor, high temperatures, increases both ice cream consumption and participation in water-based activities.

**Third-variable problem** A situation in which a variable that has not been measured accounts for a relationship between two or more other variables; third variables are also known as confounding variables in experiments.

**Illusory correlation** A mistaken perception that a relationship exists between variables when no statistical relationship actually exists.

which is the effect—or whether other known or unknown factors may explain the relationship (**Figure 1.12**).

Consider this surprising positive correlation: Cities with a higher number of churches have a higher crime rate. Does this mean that an increase in churches leads to more crime? Of course not! Instead, a *third variable* (increased population) is the real source of the link between more churches and more crime.

This mistake of confusing correlation with causation is referred to as the **third-variable problem**, which refers to a situation in which a variable that has not been measured accounts for a relationship between two or more other variables. Would you like a less obvious and more commonly confused example? See **Figure 1.13**.

2. **Observed correlations are sometimes illusory—meaning they don't exist!** In this second problem, there is NO factual, statistical connection between two variables—the relationship is the result of random coincidence and/or misperception. Popular beliefs, such as that infertile couples often conceive after an adoption, as well as the irrational fears behind certain anxiety disorders, are often based on **illusory** (false) **correlations** (Brodsky & Gutheil, 2016; Wiemer & Pauli, 2016). Can you see how someone with an intense fear of flying might misperceive the odds of crashes based on overly dramatic media reports? If you're confused about the differences between the third-variable problem and illusory correlations, see the **Study Tip**.

**Study Tip**

*Note that with the* third-variable problem, *an actual correlation does exist between two or more variables, but a third factor might be responsible for their connection. In contrast, with an* illusory correlation *there is NO measurable connection between two variables— the apparent connection is totally FALSE.*

Interestingly, superstitions, such as breaking a mirror supposedly leading to seven years of bad luck or sports fans wearing their lucky team sports jackets because they believe it will bring the team good luck, are additional examples of illusory correlations. We mistakenly perceive an association that factually does not exist. Unfortunately, these and other well-known superstitions (**Table 1.6**) persist despite logical reasoning and scientific evidence to the contrary.

Why are beliefs in illusory correlations so common? As you'll discover in upcoming chapters, we tend to focus on the most noticeable (salient) factors when explaining the causes of behavior. Paying undue attention to the dramatic (but very rare) instance when an infertile couple conceives after adoption or when a gambler wins a large payout on one specific slot machine is an example of the *saliency bias* (see Chapter 16). In addition to this saliency bias, we also more often note and remember events that confirm our expectations and ignore the "misses." This is known as the *confirmation bias*.

**FIGURE 1.13** **Correlation versus causation** Research has found a strong correlation between stress and cancer (Chapter 3). Just as we can't tell whether the chicken or the egg came first, the correlation in this case does not tell us whether stress causes cancer, whether cancer causes stress, or whether other known and unknown factors, such as smoking, drinking, or pesticides, could contribute to both stress and cancer. Can you think of a way to study the effects of stress on cancer that is not correlational—and is still ethical?

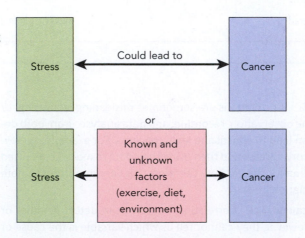

The key thing to remember while reading research reports in this or any textbook, or reports in the popular media, is that observed correlations may be illusory and that correlational research can NEVER provide a clear cause and effect relationship between variables. Always consider that a third factor might be a better explanation for a perceived correlation. To find causation, we need the experimental method.

**TABLE 1.6**   **Superstitions as Illusory Correlations**

| | Behavior | Superstition |
|---|---|---|
| | **Wedding plans:**<br>*Why do brides wear something old and something borrowed?* | The something old is usually clothing that belongs to an older woman who is happily married. Thus, the bride will supposedly transfer that good fortune to herself. Something borrowed is often a relative's jewelry. This item should be golden, because gold represents the sun, which was once thought to be the source of life. |
| | **Spilling salt:**<br>*Why do some people throw a pinch of salt over their left shoulder?* | Years ago, people believed good spirits lived on the right side of the body, and bad spirits on the left. If someone spilled salt, it supposedly meant that a guardian spirit had caused the accident to warn him or her of evil nearby. At the time, salt was scarce and precious. Therefore, the person was advised to bribe the bad spirits with a pinch of salt thrown over his or her left shoulder. |
| | **Knocking on wood:**<br>*Why do some people knock on wood when they're speaking of good fortune or making predictions?* | Down through the ages, people have believed that trees were homes of gods, who were kind and generous if approached in the right way. A person who wanted to ask a favor of the tree god would touch the bark. After the favor was granted, the person would return to knock on the tree as a sign of thanks. |

**The Value of Correlations**   After discussing all the limits of correlational research, we need to emphasize that it's still an incredibly valuable research method, offering at least three major contributions:

1. **Prediction**   A correlation can tell us if a relationship exists between two variables, which allows us to use one variable to predict scores on another. Consider a recent study that found a positive correlation between years of education and physical health. This correlation means that we can predict that as your educational level increases, your overall health will also increase. In fact, the age-adjusted mortality rate of high school dropouts (ages 25–64) is more than twice that of those with some college (Cutler & Lleras-Muney, 2006; Picker, 2016). This large and persistent correlation between education and health has been repeatedly observed over many years and in many countries. Although there are several possible explanations for this finding, researchers in this area suggest the results are most likely due to healthier behaviors among the more highly educated, along with different thinking and decision-making patterns. If you'd like to explore how increased education might also affect your overall lifetime income, check out the "Media Challenge" for Chapter 1 located within the WileyPlus/Learning Space program.

2. **Real-world settings**   A second value to correlational studies is that, like descriptive studies, they can be conducted in real-world settings that would otherwise be impossible or unethical to study. For example, smoking cigarettes and drinking alcohol while pregnant are highly correlated with birth defects (Doulatram et al., 2015; Mason & Zhou, 2015; Roozen et al., 2016). Conducting experiments on pregnant women would obviously be immoral and illegal. However, evidence from this strong correlation, along with other research, has helped convince many women to avoid these drugs while pregnant—likely preventing many birth defects. On a lighter note, research described in Chapter 3 reports a long-suspected link between high stress levels and reduced odds of conception (Akhter et al., 2016). Do you recognize how this type of correlational data offers encouraging news and pleasant options for those trying to conceive—like taking a vacation?

   These real-world settings also often have practical applications. For example, many parents and professionals have repeatedly expressed concerns about the potential ill effects of Facebook and other social media sites on young people. In fact, a recent study compared 12 million Facebook users with nonusers and found that people with moderate levels of online social interaction and high levels of offline social interaction actually have a lower short-term mortality risk (Hobbs et al., 2016). Research has long showed that people who have strong social networks live longer, but this is the first large-scale study showing that online relationships may also be good for our mental and physical health. Similarly, correlational findings that drunk driving and distracted driving are highly linked with serious and fatal car accidents have led to strict laws that have reduced these practices.

3. **Future research** Finally, correlational research, like descriptive studies, offers data and ideas for future research. Even though correlation does NOT prove causation, it can point to *possible* causation, which can then be followed up with later experiments—the topic of our next section.

## Experimental Research

**Experimental research** A type of research that involves the manipulation and control of variables to determine cause and effect; designed to meet the goal of *explanation*.

**Experiment** A careful manipulation of one or more variables (independent variables) to measure the effect on some behaviors or mental processes (dependent variables).

**Independent variable (IV)** The variable that is manipulated by the experimenter to determine its causal effect on the dependent variable; also called the treatment variable.

**Dependent variable (DV)** The variable that is observed and measured for possible change; the factor that is affected by (or dependent on) the independent variable.

**Experimental group** Participants in an experiment who receive the treatment under study—that is, those who are exposed to the independent variable (IV).

**Control group** Participants in an experiment who do NOT receive the treatment under study—that is, those who are NOT exposed to the independent variable (IV).

**Random assignment** A research technique for assigning participants to experimental or control conditions so that each participant has an equal chance of being in either group; minimizes the possibility of biases or preexisting differences within or between the groups.

As you've just seen, both descriptive and correlational studies are essential because they provide valuable data, insights, and practical applications. However, to determine *causation* (what causes what), we need **experimental research**. This research method is considered the "gold standard" for empirical science because only through an **experiment** can researchers manipulate and control variables to determine cause and effect (Cohen, 2014; Goodwin & Goodwin, 2013; Morling, 2015).

To understand the important key terms and the general setup for an experiment, imagine that you're a psychologist who wants to investigate how texting while driving affects the incidence of traffic accidents. To set up your imaginary experiment, carefully study **Step-by-Step Diagram 1.2**. Step 1 begins with the creation of a testable *hypothesis*, which we defined earlier as a tentative and testable explanation (or "educated guess") about the relationship between two or more variables. As part of this hypothesis, you need to note the specific factors (or variables) that will be observed and measured in your potential experiment. Experiments have two kinds of variables: *independent* and *dependent*. The factor, or *variable*, you manipulate (or change) is called the **independent variable (IV)**. The variable you plan to measure and examine for possible change is known as the **dependent variable (DV)**. In this case, the variable you manipulate (the IV) will be texting versus not texting, and the variable you measure for possible change (the DV) will be the number of traffic accidents.

For Step 2, you assign your research participants to either the **experimental group**, participants who receive the treatment under study, or the **control group**, participants who do NOT receive the treatment under study. Note that having two groups allows the performance of one group to be compared with that of the other. To minimize potentially critical differences between the two groups, you need to *randomly assign* participants to either the experimental group or the control group. **Random assignment** refers to the use of chance procedures (such as a coin toss or a random numbers table) to ensure that all participants have an equal opportunity to be in either group.

For Steps 3 and 4, you—the experimenter—will ask all participants to drive for a given amount of time (e.g., 30 minutes) in a driving simulator. While they're driving, you will record the number of simulated traffic accidents (the DV). [Note: The goal of any experiment is to learn how the dependent variable is *affected by* (depends on) the independent variable.]

During Step 5, you'll compare the results from both groups and report your findings to a peer-reviewed scientific journal like the ones found in the References section provided with this text. Keep in mind that because the control group was treated exactly like the experimental group, except for the IV, any significant difference in the number of traffic accidents (the DV) between the two groups would be the result of the IV. In contrast, if you found little or no difference between the groups, you would conclude that texting does not affect traffic accidents.

Before going on, note that actual research does find that cell phone use, particularly texting, while driving definitely leads to increased accidents and potentially serious or fatal consequences (e.g., Carney et al., 2016; Yannis et al., 2016). In other words: "Let's all just put down the phone and drive."

## Research Problems and Safeguards

As you've seen, descriptive, correlational, and experimental research methods all have serious limits and potential biases. To offset these problems, researchers must establish several safeguards to protect against potential sources of error from both the researcher and the participant.

| STEP-BY-STEP DIAGRAM 1.2 | **Experimental research design** |

**STOP!** This Step-by-Step Diagram contains essential information NOT found elsewhere in the text, which is likely to appear on quizzes and exams. Be sure to study it CAREFULLY!

**Study Tip**

*To help you remember the independent and dependent variables (IV and DV), note that the IV is called independent because it is controlled and manipulated by the experimenter. The DV is called dependent because the behavior (or outcome) exhibited by the participants is assumed to depend on manipulations of the IV. You might find it helpful to carefully study these drawings and create a visual picture in your own mind of how:*

 *the experimenter "manipulates" the IV to determine its causal effect on the DV,*

 *and then the experimenter "measures" the DV, which "depends" on the IV.*

When designing an experiment, researchers must follow certain steps to ensure that their results are scientifically meaningful. In this example, researchers want to test whether people texting on cell phones while driving have more traffic accidents than those who don't text while driving.

**Step** ❶ After identifying the IV and DV and reviewing the literature, the experimenter develops a testable hypothesis.

**Step** ❷ Next, the experimenter randomly assigns participants to one of two different groups—*experimental* or *control*. Having an experimental group, which receives the treatment, and a control group, which does not receive the treatment, allows a baseline comparison of responses between the two groups.

**Step** ❸ Next, both the experimental and control groups are assigned to a driving simulator. The experimental group then texts while driving, whereas the control group does not text. Texting or not texting is the independent variable (IV). And the number of simulated traffic accidents is the dependent variable (DV).

**Step** ❹ The experimenter counts the number of simulated traffic accidents for each group and then analyzes the data.

**Step** ❺ The experimenter compares the results from both groups, writes up his or her report, and submits it to scientific journals for possible publication.

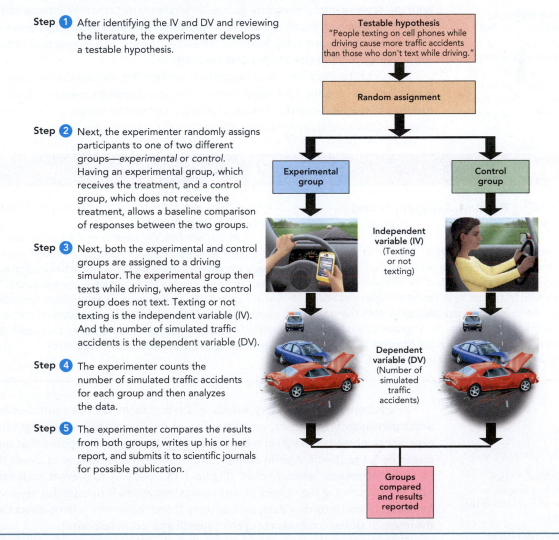

**Testable hypothesis**
"People texting on cell phones while driving cause more traffic accidents than those who don't text while driving."

**Random assignment**

**Experimental group**

**Control group**

**Independent variable (IV)** (Texting or not texting)

**Dependent variable (DV)** (Number of simulated traffic accidents)

**Groups compared and results reported**

## Potential Researcher Issues
Let's start with **sample bias**, which occurs when the researcher recruits and/or selects participants who do not accurately reflect the composition of the larger population from which they are drawn. For example, some critics suggest that

**Sample bias** A bias that may occur when research participants are unrepresentative of the larger population.

**FIGURE 1.14**  **Controlling for confounding variables**  Recognizing that certain outside variables may affect their experimental findings, researchers strive for balance between the experimental and control groups, making sure the variables are the same for both. Once balance is achieved, and the independent variable (IV) is added to the experimental group, the experimenters check to see if the scale's balance is significantly disrupted. If so, they can then say that the IV *caused* the change. However, if the IV is not "heavy" enough to make a significant difference, then the experiment "failed," and experimenters go back to further refine their approach, start over, or go on to a new project.

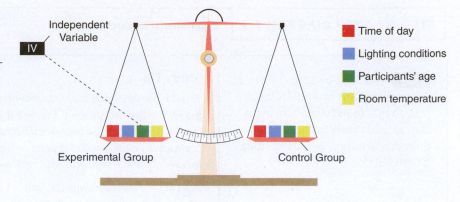

Independent Variable

IV

- 🟥 Time of day
- 🟦 Lighting conditions
- 🟩 Participants' age
- 🟨 Room temperature

Experimental Group          Control Group

**Representative sample**  A selected sample of participants whose demographics and characteristics accurately reflect the entire population of interest.

**Confounding variable**  An extraneous factor or variable that, if not controlled, could confuse, or *confound*, the effects of the independent variable (IV) and contaminate the results of an experiment; also known as the third-variable problem in correlational research.

psychological literature is biased because it too often uses college students as participants. We can counteract potential sample bias by selecting participants who constitute a **representative sample** of the entire population of interest.

It's also critical to control for extraneous, **confounding variables** (such as time of day, lighting conditions, and room temperature). These variables must be held constant across both the experimental and control groups. Otherwise, if not controlled, these variables might confuse, or *confound*, the effects of the independent variable (IV)—thereby contaminating your research results (**Figure 1.14**). As discussed earlier, *random assignment* also helps control for confounding variables (see the **Try This Yourself**).

As a critical thinker, do you recognize how confounding variables in an experiment are essentially the same as the third-variable problem associated with correlational research? Whenever we observe a relationship between variables, we need to recognize the possibility that an unwanted, third variable might have affected (confounded) the results.

## Try This Yourself

### Understanding Random Assignment and Confounding Variables

Have you wondered if the decoration and overall ambiance of a restaurant could affect your eating behavior? To answer this question, a group of researchers modified the environment in one section of a fast food restaurant by dimming the lights and adding relaxing music, plants, candles, and tablecloths. They then randomly assigned customers to sit in either the original section of the restaurant or this new section (Wansink & Van Ittersum, 2012). All participants freely ordered whatever food they preferred, but those in the

more relaxing part of the restaurant took longer to eat their meal and ate 18% fewer calories.

Can you see how the *random assignment* of the customers controlled for any potential *confounding variables*? All participants freely entered the same restaurant, and each individual was equally likely to be assigned to either section in the restaurant. Thanks to these controls, the researchers can legitimately conclude that the *independent variable* (IV) (relaxing versus standard restaurant condition) caused the change in the *dependent variables* (DVs) (time spent eating and number of calories consumed).

**Experimenter bias**  A bias that occurs when a researcher influences research results in the expected direction.

**Ethnocentrism**  The belief that one's culture is typical of all cultures; also, viewing one's own ethnic group (or culture) as central and "correct" and judging others according to this standard.

In addition, if experimenters' beliefs and expectations are not controlled for, they can affect participants' responses, producing flawed results. Imagine what might happen if an experimenter breathed a sigh of relief when a participant gave a response that supported the researcher's hypothesis. A good example of this comes from the case of *Clever Hans*, the famous mathematical "wonder horse" (**Figure 1.15**). One way to prevent such **experimenter bias** from destroying the validity of participants' responses is to establish objective methods for collecting and recording data, such as using "blind" observers with no direct connection to the research and/or computers to present stimuli and record responses.

Experimenters also can skew their results if they assume that behaviors typical in their own culture are typical in all cultures—a bias known as **ethnocentrism**. One way to avoid this problem is to have researchers from two cultures each conduct the same study twice, once with their own culture and once with at least one other culture. This kind of *cross-cultural sampling* isolates group differences in behavior that might stem from any researcher's ethnocentrism.

## Potential Participant Issues

We've seen that researchers can inadvertently introduce error (the experimenter bias). Unfortunately, participants can produce a similar error, called **participant bias**. For example, researchers often use surveys as their main research method or as part of an experiment. And, as you might expect, when participants are asked to self-report on sensitive topics, such as their sexual behaviors or drug and alcohol consumption, they often attempt to present themselves in a favorable way, rather than giving true accounts. This tendency to over-report "good behaviors" and to under-report "bad behaviors" is aptly named the *social desirability* response (see the following **Research Challenge**).

vikarus/Getty Images

**FIGURE 1.15** **Can a horse add, multiply, and divide?** Clever Hans and his owner, Mr. Von Osten, convinced many people that this was indeed the case (Rosenthal, 1965). When asked to multiply 6 times 8, minus 42, Hans would tap his hoof 6 times. Or if asked to divide 48 by 12, add 6, and take away 6, he would tap 4 times. Even when Hans's owner was out of the room and others asked the question, he was still able to answer correctly. How did he do it? Researchers eventually discovered that all questioners naturally lowered their heads to look at Hans's hoof at the end of their question. And Hans had learned that this was a signal to start tapping. When the correct answer was approaching, the questioners also naturally looked up, which signaled Hans to stop. Do you see how this provided an early example of experimenter bias?

**Participant bias** A bias that occurs when a research participant contaminates research results.

---

## Research Challenge

### Why Do Men and Women Lie About Sex?

The *social desirability bias* is of particular concern when we study sexual behaviors. A fascinating example comes from a study that asked college students to complete a questionnaire regarding how often they engaged in 124 different gender-typical behaviors (Fisher, 2013). Some of these behaviors were considered more typical of men (such as wearing dirty clothes and telling obscene jokes), whereas other behaviors were more common among women (such as writing poetry and lying about their weight). Half of the participants completed these questionnaires while attached to what they were told was a polygraph machine (or lie detector), although in reality this machine was not working. The other half completed the questionnaires without being attached to such a machine.

Can you predict how students' answers differed as a function of their gender and whether they were (or were NOT) attached to the supposed lie detector? Among those who were attached to a supposed lie detector and who believed that it could reliably detect their lies, men were more likely to admit that they sometimes engaged in behaviors seen as more appropriate for women, such as writing poetry. In contrast, women were more likely to admit that they sometimes engaged in behaviors judged more appropriate for men, such as telling obscene jokes. Even more interesting, men reported having had more sexual partners when they weren't hooked up to the lie detector than when they were. The reverse was true for women! They reported fewer partners when they were not hooked up to the lie detector than when they were.

How does the *social desirability response* help explain these differences? We're all socialized from birth to conform to norms (unwritten rules) for our culturally approved male and female behaviors. Therefore, participants who were NOT attached to the supposed lie detector provided more "gender appropriate" responses. Men admitted telling obscene jokes and reported having more sexual partners, whereas women admitted lying about their weight and reported having fewer sexual partners.

These findings were virtually reversed when participants believed they were connected to a machine that could detect their lies. This fact provides a strong example of the dangers of the social desirability response. It also reminds us, as either researchers or consumers, to be very careful when interpreting findings regarding sexual attitudes and behaviors. Gender roles may lead to inaccurate reporting and exaggerated gender differences.

Inti St Clair/Getty Images

#### Test Yourself

1. Based on the information provided, did this study (Fisher, 2013) use descriptive, correlational, and/or experimental research?

2. If you chose:
   ○ *descriptive research*, is this a naturalistic observation, survey/interview, case study, and/or archival research?
   ○ *correlational research*, is this a positive, negative, or zero correlation?
   ○ *experimental research*, label the IV, DV, experimental group(s), and control group. (Note: If participants were not randomly assigned to groups, list it as a *quasi-experimental design*.)
   ○ both *descriptive* and *correlational*, answer the corresponding questions for both.

Check your answers by clicking on the answer button or by looking in Appendix B.

**Note:** The information provided in this study is admittedly limited, but the level of detail is similar to what is presented in most textbooks and public reports of research findings. Answering these questions, and then comparing your answers to those provided, will help you become a better critical thinker and consumer of scientific research.

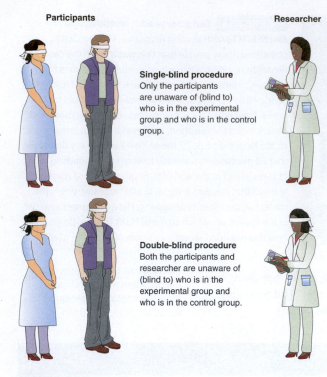

**Participants**

**Researcher**

**Single-blind procedure**
Only the participants are unaware of (blind to) who is in the experimental group and who is in the control group.

**Double-blind procedure**
Both the participants and researcher are unaware of (blind to) who is in the experimental group and who is in the control group.

**FIGURE 1.16** **A single- or double-blind experimental design** In an experiment to test a new drug, the participants taking the drug, and possibly the researchers as well, must be unaware of (or "blind" to) who is receiving a *placebo* (a fake pill) and who is receiving the drug itself. This is necessary because researchers know that participants' beliefs and expectations can change their responses and the experimental outcome—the so-called "placebo effect" (Brown, 2013; Draganich & Erdal, 2014).

**Single-blind study** An experimental technique in which only the participants are unaware of (blind to) who is in the experimental group and who is in the control group.

**Double-blind study** An experimental technique in which both the researcher and the participants are unaware of (blind to) who is in the experimental group and who is in the control group.

**Placebo** An inactive substance or fake treatment used as a control technique in experiments; often used in drug research.

**Placebo effect** A change that occurs when a participant's expectations or beliefs, rather than the actual drug or treatment, cause a particular experimental outcome.

**Additional Research Safeguards** Scientists attempting to minimize both experimenter and participant bias often use **single-blind** and **double-blind studies**. As you can see in **Figure 1.16**, this approach requires that participants, and sometimes also experimenters, be unaware of (or "blind" to) the treatment or condition to which the participants have been assigned.

Imagine you are in an eight-week experiment and are told that you will be taking a pill that will stop your headaches. Can you see how it's critical that you, as a participant, and possibly the experimenter who collects your data, should be blind as to whether you are in the control or experimental group? In this example, that means you won't know if you are being given the actual experimental drug or a harmless **placebo** pill that has no physiological effect. Researchers do this because your expectations or beliefs, rather than the experimental treatment, can produce a particular outcome, called a **placebo effect**. Giving members of the control group a placebo, while giving the experimental group a pill with the active ingredients, allows researchers to determine whether changes are due to the pill that's being tested or simply to the participants' expectations.

Also, as you discovered in the previous section on ethical guidelines, researchers attempt to control for participant bias by offering anonymous participation, along with guarantees of privacy and confidentiality. In addition, one of the most effective (and controversial) ways of preventing participant bias is to temporarily deceive participants about the true nature of the research project. For example, in studies examining when and how people help others, participants may not be told the true goal of the study because they might try to present themselves as more helpful than they actually would be in real life—another example of the social desirability response.

## Quasi-Experimental Designs

Given the numerous limits and problems with the experimental method we've just described, some researchers turn to alternative methods called *quasi-experimental designs*. The prefix *quasi-* means "sort of," and in this case the research looks "sort of" like a true experiment. But it lacks a key ingredient—*random assignment to groups*—because in many situations random assignment is impossible or unethical. For example, imagine that you wanted to study how a father's later attachment to his child was affected by his presence or absence at that child's birth. You obviously can't randomly assign fathers to either the present-at-birth condition or the absent-at-birth condition. Recognizing that assessing the differences between the two groups still might provide important information, experimenters can compare the two groups without random assignment, and it would then be officially called a quasi-experimental design. Why can't quasi-experimental designs make the same strong claims for causation that could be made based on true experiments? Without random assignment, uncontrolled third variables might skew the results.

## Take-Home Message

We've just presented a large number of research problems and safeguards associated with the various research methods (descriptive, correlational, and experimental), and we've gathered them all into **Figure 1.17**. Be sure to study it carefully.

Given all these problems, should we simply pack our bags and go home? Of course not! Psychological research does have its limits, but having a general understanding of research methods will help guide you through the often conflicting claims made in newspapers, in television ads, and by our friends and neighbors. Research findings have also offered solutions to practical problems, led us to significant improvements in our personal and interpersonal lives, and provided invaluable guidelines that will help us make more informed decisions. If you'd like further information about research methods and statistical analyses, see Appendix A.

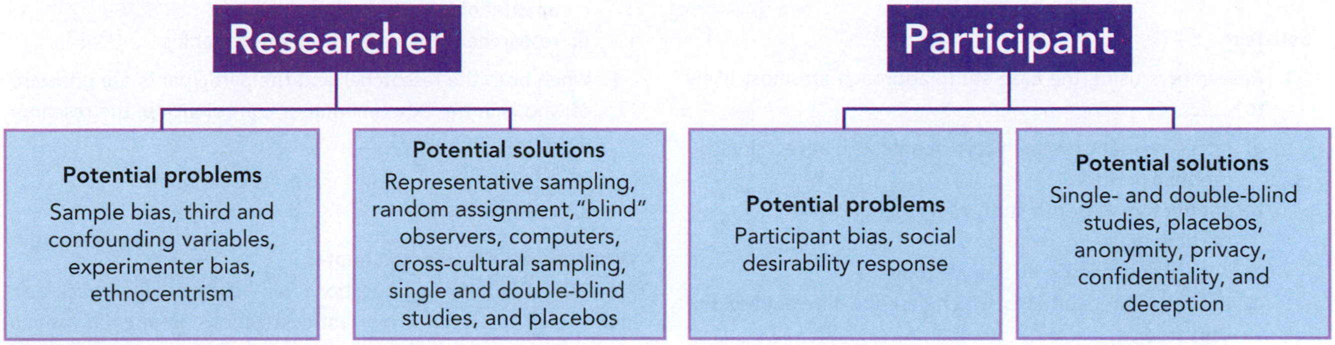

**FIGURE 1.17** **Potential research problems and solutions**

## Try This Yourself

### Want to Be a Better Consumer of Scientific Research?

The news media, advertisers, politicians, teachers, close friends, and other individuals frequently use research findings in their attempts to change your attitudes and behavior. How can you tell whether their information is accurate and worthwhile? The previous discussion of psychological research methods will help you identify the primary problem with each of the following sample research reports:

- CC = Report is misleading because correlation data are used to suggest causation.
- CG = Report is inconclusive because there was no control group.
- EB = Results of the research were unfairly influenced by experimenter bias.
- SB = Results of the research are questionable because of sample bias.

___**1.** A clinical psychologist strongly believes that touching is a valuable adjunct to successful therapy. For two months, he touches half his patients (group A) and refrains from touching the other half (group B). He then reports a noticeable improvement in group A.

___**2.** A newspaper reports that violent crime corresponds to phases of the moon. The reporter concludes that the gravitational pull of the moon controls human behavior.

___**3.** A researcher interested in women's attitudes toward premarital sex sends out a lengthy survey to subscribers of *Vogue* and *Cosmopolitan* magazines.

___**4.** An experimenter is interested in studying the effects of alcohol on driving ability. Before being tested on an experimental driving course, group A consumes 2 ounces of alcohol, group B consumes 4 ounces of alcohol, and group C consumes 6 ounces of alcohol. After the test drive, the researcher reports that alcohol consumption adversely affects driving ability.

___**5.** After reading a scientific journal that reports higher divorce rates among couples living together before marriage, a college student decides to move out of the apartment she shares with her boyfriend.

___**6.** A theater owner reports increased beverage sales following the brief flashing of a subliminal message to "Drink Coca-Cola" during the film showing.

**Answers: 1. EB; 2. CC; 3. SB; 4. CG; 5. CC; 6. CG**

© Billy R. Ray/Wiley

## Retrieval Practice 1.3 | Research Methods

Completing this self-test and the connections section, and then checking your answers by clicking on the answer button or by looking in Appendix B, will provide immediate feedback and helpful practice for exams.

### Self-Test

1. Researchers using the case study approach are most likely to _____ .
   a. interview many research participants who have a single problem or disorder
   b. conduct an in-depth study of a single research participant
   c. choose and investigate a single topic
   d. use any of these options, which describe different types of case studies

2. When a researcher observes or measures two or more variables to find relationships between them, without directly manipulating them or implying a causal relationship, he or she is conducting _____ .
   a. experimental research    b. a correlational study
   c. non-causal metrics       d. a meta-analysis

3. Which of the following correlation coefficients indicates the strongest relationship?
   a. +.43                     b. −.64
   c. −.72                     d. .00

4. If researchers gave participants varying amounts of a new memory drug and then gave them a story to read and measured their scores on a quiz, the _____ would be the IV, and the _____ would be the DV.
   a. response to the drug; amount of the drug
   b. experimental group; control group
   c. amount of the drug; quiz scores
   d. researcher variables; extraneous variables

5. When both the researcher and the participants are unaware of who is in the experimental or control group, the research design can be called _____ .
   a. reliable                 b. double-blind
   c. valid                    d. deceptive

### Connections—Chapter to Chapter

Answering the following questions will help you "look back and look ahead" to see the important connections among the various subfields of psychology and chapters within this text.

1. In Chapter 2 (Neuroscience and Biological Foundations), you'll learn about the structures and functions of the nervous system and the brain. Using the terms *naturalistic observation, case study, correlational research*, and *experiment* (from this chapter), describe how scientists could use each of these different research methods to study the brain.

2. In Chapter 3 (Stress and Health Psychology), you'll discover what scientists have learned about an experience common to us all: stress. Think about a stressor in your life. Using psychology's four main goals, *describe* your stressor, *explain* how it affects you, *predict* when and how it might affect you in the future, and discuss what you can do to *change* it.

# 1.4   Tools for Student Success

## LEARNING OBJECTIVES

**Retrieval Practice**   While reading the upcoming sections, respond to each Learning Objective in your own words.

**Review the key strategies for student success.**

• **Describe** the four steps important to improving your study habits.

• **Discuss** ways to improve your time management.
• **Identify** the key factors in grade improvement.
• **Summarize** why attitude adjustment is key to student success.

> **Study Tip**
>
> **Tools for Student Success**
>
> *This special section includes tips for success in this and all your other college courses. In addition, watch for these "Study Tip" boxes throughout this text.*

In this section, you will find several well-documented tools and techniques guaranteed to make you a more efficient and successful college student In fact, a recent experiment with randomly assigned college students found that the group of students who were asked to self-reflect and to identify and use learning resources wisely improved their class performance by an average of one-third of a letter grade compared to the group that did not self-reflect (Chen et al., 2017). For an example of this type of self-reflection, and an overview of the major topics in this section, be sure to complete the following **Try This Yourself**.

## Try This Yourself

### Skills for Student Success Checklist

Answer true or false to each item. Then, for each item that you answered "True," pay particular attention to the corresponding headings in this *Tools for Student Success* section.

### Study Habits

____ **1.** While reading, I often get lost in all the details and can't pick out the most important points.

____ **2.** When I finish studying a chapter, I frequently can't remember what I've just read.

____ **3.** I generally study with either the TV or music playing in the background.

____ **4.** I tend to read each section of a chapter at the same speed, instead of slowing down on the difficult sections.

### Time Management

____ **5.** I can't keep up with my reading assignments given all the other demands on my time.

____ **6.** I typically wait to study and then "cram" right before a test.

____ **7.** I go to almost all my classes, but I generally don't take notes, and I often find myself texting, playing games on my computer, or daydreaming.

### Grade Improvement

____ **8.** I study and read ahead of time, but during a test I frequently find that my mind goes blank.

____ **9.** Although I study and read before tests, and think I'll do well, I often find that the exam questions are much harder than I expected.

____ **10.** I wish I could perform better on tests and could read faster or more efficiently.

### Attitude Adjustment

____ **11.** Going to class is a waste of time.

____ **12.** I just can't do well on tests.

## Study Habits

If you sometimes read a paragraph many times, yet remember nothing from it, try these four ways to successfully read (and remember) information in this and most other texts:

1. **Familiarization**   The first step to good study habits is to familiarize yourself with the general text so that you can take full advantage of its contents. Scanning through the Table of Contents will help give you a bird's-eye view of the overall text. In addition, as you're familiarizing yourself with these features, be sure to also note the various tables, figures, photographs, and special feature boxes, all of which will enhance your understanding of the subject.

2. **Active Reading**   The next step is to make a conscious decision to *actively* read and learn the material (Putnam et al., 2016). Reading a text is *not* like reading a novel or fun articles on the Internet! You must tell your brain to slow down, focus on details, and save the material for future recall (see the following **Try This Yourself**).

## Try This Yourself

### Demonstrating the Importance of Active Reading

(a) Using a stopwatch, test to see how fast you can name the color of each rectangular box.

| | | | |
|---|---|---|---|
| GREEN | RED | BROWN | RED |
| BROWN | GREEN | GREEN | BLUE |
| GREEN | BROWN | RED | BLUE |

(b) Now, time yourself to see how fast you can state the color of ink used to print each word, ignoring what each word says.

How did you do? Interestingly, young children who have learned their colors, but have not yet learned to read, easily name the colors in both sections in about the same amount of time. However, virtually every adult takes more time, and makes more errors, on (b) than on (a). This is because, over time, our well-learned ability to read words overrides the less common task of naming the colors. We include this demonstration, known as the *Stroop effect*, here because it helps illustrate the importance of active reading. If you passively read a chapter in a text once, or even several times, you'll still do poorly on an exam. Just as it takes more time to state the color in part (b), it will take you more time to override your well-learned passive reading and focus on the details to truly learn and master the material.

**SQ4R method** A study technique based on six steps: Survey, Question, Read, Recite, Review, and wRite.

Note taking while reading is one of the most effective ways to actively read. Ask yourself, "What is the main idea?" Then write down key ideas and supporting details and examples. Another way to read actively is to use the **SQ4R method**, which was developed by Francis Robinson (1970). The initials stand for six steps in effective reading: Survey, Question, Read, Recite, Review, and wRite. As you might have guessed, this text was designed to incorporate each of these steps (**Step-by-Step Diagram 1.3**).

3. **Avoid highlighting and rereading**   Marking with a yellow highlighter or underlining key points, as well as rereading text material after initial reading, are common techniques students use while studying. Unfortunately, they're essentially a waste of time! Research clearly shows that highlighting and rereading are among the LEAST effective of all the major study techniques, whereas *distributed practice* and *practice testing* (explained later in the grade improvement section) are the MOST effective (Dunlosky et al., 2013). As previously discussed, you need to actively focus on your reading. Highlighting and rereading generally encourage passive reading.

4. **Overlearn**   Many students tend to study new material just to the point where they can recite the information, but they do not attempt to understand it more deeply.

**STEP-BY-STEP DIAGRAM 1.3** | **Using the SQ4R Method**   Follow these steps to improve your reading efficiency.

**STOP!**   This Step-by-Step Diagram contains essential information NOT found elsewhere in the text, which is likely to appear on quizzes and exams. Be sure to study it CAREFULLY!

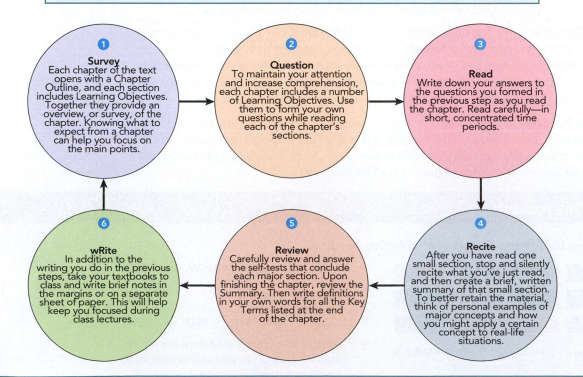

**1 Survey**
Each chapter of the text opens with a Chapter Outline, and each section includes Learning Objectives. Together they provide an overview, or survey, of the chapter. Knowing what to expect from a chapter can help you focus on the main points.

**2 Question**
To maintain your attention and increase comprehension, each chapter includes a number of Learning Objectives. Use them to form your own questions while reading each of the chapter's sections.

**3 Read**
Write down your answers to the questions you formed in the previous step as you read the chapter. Read carefully—in short, concentrated time periods.

**4 Recite**
After you have read one small section, stop and silently recite what you've just read, and then create a brief, written summary of that small section. To better retain the material, think of personal examples of major concepts and how you might apply a certain concept to real-life situations.

**5 Review**
Carefully review and answer the self-tests that conclude each major section. Upon finishing the chapter, review the Summary. Then write definitions in your own words for all the Key Terms listed at the end of the chapter.

**6 wRite**
In addition to the writing you do in the previous steps, take your textbooks to class and write brief notes in the margins or on a separate sheet of paper. This will help keep you focused during class lectures.

For best results, however, you should overlearn. In other words, be sure you fully understand how key terms and concepts are related to one another and can generate examples other than the ones in the text. In addition, you should repeatedly review the material (by visualizing the phenomena that are described and explained in the text and by rehearsing what you have learned) until the information is firmly locked in place. This is particularly important if you suffer from test anxiety. Would you like a quick demonstration of why we sometimes need to overlearn? See the following **Try This Yourself**.

## Try This Yourself

### Demonstrating the Importance of Overlearning

Can you identify which one of these 10 pennies is an exact duplicate of a real U.S. penny? Unless you're a coin collector, you probably can't easily choose the correct one without comparing it to a real coin—despite having seen thousands of pennies. Why? As you will discover later in the text (Chapter 7), you must encode (or process) the information in some way before it will be successfully stored in your long-term memory. Most of us don't need to carefully study and overlearn the details of what a penny looks like, because we can function in our everyday world with a superficial glance at the coin. So why are we providing this demo? The point is that if you're going to take a test on pennies, or any material, you need to carefully study to the point of overlearning in order to do well.

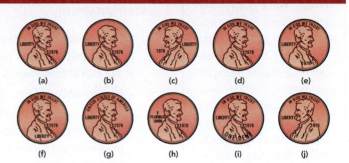

Nickerson, R. S., & Adams, M. J. (1979)

**Answers:** Coin a is the duplicate of a real

## Time Management

If you find that you can't always strike a good balance between work, study, and social activities, or that you aren't always good at budgeting your time, here are four basic time-management strategies:

- **Establish a baseline.** Before attempting any changes, simply record your day-to-day activities for one to two weeks (see the sample in **Figure 1.18**). You may be surprised at how you spend your time.

- **Set up a realistic schedule.** Make a daily and weekly "to do" list, including all required activities, basic maintenance tasks (like laundry, cooking, child care, and eating), and a reasonable amount of down time. Then create a daily schedule of activities that includes time for each of these. To make permanent time-management changes, shape your behavior, starting with small changes and building on them.

- **Reward yourself.** Give yourself immediate, tangible rewards for sticking with your daily schedule, such as calling a friend, getting a snack, or checking social media.

- **Maximize your time.** To increase your efficiency, begin by paying close attention to the amount of time you spend on true, focused studying versus the time you waste worrying, complaining, and/or fiddling around getting ready to study ("fretting and prepping").

|  | Sunday | Monday | Tuesday | Wednesday | Thursday | Friday | Saturday |
|---|---|---|---|---|---|---|---|
| 7:00 |  | Breakfast |  | Breakfast |  | Breakfast |  |
| 8:00 |  | History | Breakfast | History | Breakfast | History |  |
| 9:00 |  | Psychology | Statistics | Psychology | Statistics | Psychology |  |
| 10:00 |  | Review History & Psychology | Campus Job | Review History & Psychology | Statistics Lab | Review History & Psychology |  |
| 11:00 |  | Biology |  | Biology |  | Biology |  |
| 12:00 |  | Lunch / Study |  | Exercise | Lunch | Exercise |  |
| 1:00 |  | Bio Lab | Lunch | Lunch | Study | Lunch |  |
| 2:00 |  |  | Study | Study |  |  |  |

**FIGURE 1.18    Sample record of daily activities**   To help manage your time, draw a grid similar to this, and record your daily activities in appropriate boxes. Then fill in other necessities, such as daily maintenance tasks and "downtime."

> **Study Tip**
>
> **Is Class Attendance a Waste of Time?**
>
> *Unfortunately, some students believe this to be true. They think they can pass college courses by simply doing the basic assignments, taking exams, and/or making up lost points with extra credit. While some college professors may not notice or penalize you for missing class, they often do test over material covered in their lectures. Similarly, many professors don't assign homework or offer extra credit. They assume students are independent, self-motivated adult learners and that grades for their course should reflect each student's knowledge and performance, which is typically measured by scores on quizzes and exams.*

Time experts also point out that people often overlook significant *time opportunities*—spare moments that normally go to waste that you might use productively. When you use public transportation, review your notes or read your textbook. While waiting for doctor or dental appointments, or to pick up your kids after school, take out your text and study for 10 to 20 minutes. Hidden moments count!

## Grade Improvement

Here are five essential tools for grade improvement and overall test-taking skills. Each of these strategies will have a direct impact on your overall grade point average (GPA) in all your college classes, as well as your mastery of the material. However, research has clearly shown that the last two techniques—*distributed practice* and *practice testing*—are the MOST important keys to grade improvement.

1. **Maximize each class session.** As you know, the authors of this text are all college professors, and this advice may sound biased. However, solid psychological research (Putnam et al., 2016) recommends that all students should:
   - *Prepare ahead of time*. Be sure to study the assigned material ahead of each class.
   - *Attend every class*. Most instructors teach many ideas and offer personal examples that are not in the text. And even if they do repeat what is covered in the text, we all need to have multiple exposures to new material. Think of your professor's lecture as if your employer is going out of his or her way to tell you what you need to know to maximize your paycheck or to advance in the company (see the **Study Tip**).
   - *Stay focused*. Students often mistakenly believe that they can absorb information, and do well on exams, by simply going to class. Paying full attention by taking detailed notes by hand versus a laptop (Mueller & Oppenheimer, 2014) during each class session is one of the most efficient and profitable uses of your time.

     In contrast, casually listening to the professor, while also texting, playing computer games, or talking to other classmates, is largely a waste of time. In fact, a recent study in an introductory psychology class found that Internet use during lectures was *negatively correlated* with student performance, which as you know means that as Internet usage went up performance went down (Ravizza et al., 2017). A good rule to remember is that one hour of full attention in class is generally worth about four hours on your own. Why? Professors generally lecture on what they consider most difficult or valuable, and this material more often appears on exams!
2. **Improve your test-taking skills.** Expect a bit of stress but don't panic. Pace yourself but don't rush. Focus on what you know. Skip over questions when you don't know the answers, and then go back if time allows. On multiple-choice exams, carefully read each question, and all the alternative answers, before responding. Answer all questions and make sure you have recorded your answers correctly.

   Also, bear in mind that information relevant to one question is often found in another test question. Do not hesitate to change an answer if you get more information—or even if you simply have a better guess about an answer. Contrary to the popular myth widely held by many students (and faculty) that "your first hunch is your best guess," research suggests this is NOT the case (Benjamin et al., 1984; Lilienfeld et al., 2010, 2015). Changing answers is far more likely to result in a higher score (**Figure 1.19**).

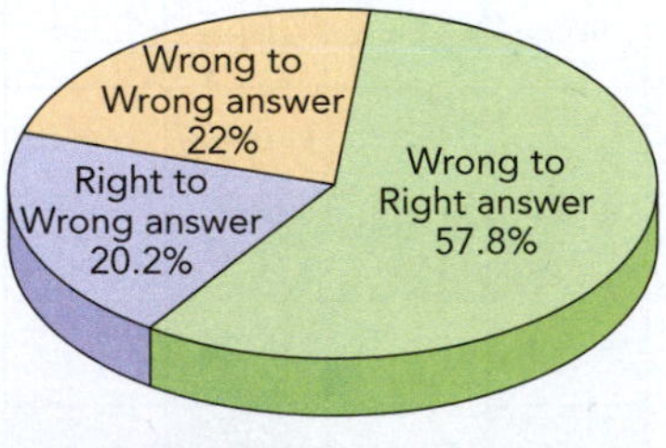


**FIGURE 1.19 Should you change your answers?** Yes! Research clearly shows that answer changes that go from a wrong to a right answer (57.8 percent) greatly outnumber those that go from a right to a wrong answer (20.2 percent). *Source:* Benjamin et al., 1984.

3. **Take study skills courses.** Improve your reading speed and comprehension, and your word-processing/typing skills, by taking additional courses designed to develop these specific abilities. In addition, instructors, roommates, classmates, friends, and family members can often provide useful tips and encouragement.
4. **Distribute your practice.** Spreading your study sessions out over time (distributed practice) is far more efficient than waiting until right before an exam and cramming in all the information at once (massed practice) (Chapter 7). If you were a basketball player, you wouldn't wait until the night before a big play-off game to practice. The same is true for

exam preparation. Keep in mind that distributed practice is NOT simply rereading the chapter several times over a few days. As mentioned earlier, you need to actively focus and study what you're reading.

5. **Practice your test taking.**   For most of us, taking tests is NOT one of our favorite activities. However, it's important to note that, as we have mentioned several times, research has clearly shown that practice test taking and distributed practice are two of the most efficient ways to study and learn—and thereby improve your exam performance (Carpenter & Yeung, 2017; Putnam et al., 2016; Trumbo et al., 2016). Just as you need to repeatedly practice your free-throw shot to become a good basketball player, you need to repeatedly practice your test-taking skills.

If you can easily see how distributing your practice and practice testing apply to sports but have trouble seeing their value in academics, consider this study conducted in actual introduction to psychology courses. Researchers (who were psych professors doing this study in their own classes) compared students who took brief, multiple-choice quizzes at the start of each class, which made up the bulk of their final grade, to those in a typical class with final grades based entirely on four big exams (Pennebaker et al., 2013). The researchers found that this type of frequent testing led to higher grades (on average a half a letter grade increase) not only in this psychology class, but also in the students' subsequent college classes. Beyond the value of practice testing itself, how would you explain this grade increase? Students in the daily quiz condition showed higher class attendance, which included lectures over the material included on quizzes and exams. In addition, the researchers discovered that frequent testing required students to diligently keep up with the material, which led to better study skills and time management.

Based on this growing body of research, and our own teaching success with frequent testing, we've designed this text to include numerous opportunities for practice testing sprinkled throughout each chapter. As you're actively reading and studying each chapter, be sure to complete all these self-tests. When you miss a question, try to immediately go back and reread the sections of the text that correspond to your incorrect response. You also can easily access the free flashcards and other forms of self-testing in your WileyPlus/Learning Space course.

## Attitude Adjustment

As you recall, psychology has four major goals—to *describe*, *explain*, *predict*, and *change* behavior and mental processes. Regarding the goal of change, we included a joke—"How many psychologists does it take to change a light bulb?" The answer was "none," because the light bulb has to want to change itself. Although it's an admittedly corny joke, it still reflects an essential truth— *change comes from within*. We're all heavily influenced by interacting biological, psychological, and social forces (the *biopsychosocial model*), but if we want to change things (like becoming a more successful student), psychological forces are where we have the greatest personal control.

Can you see, then, why *attitude adjustment* is so important? You have the power to decide that you can, and will, improve your academic skills! Instead of focusing on negative thoughts like, "I can't go to the party because I have to study," or, "Going to class feels like a waste of time," try counter statements such as, "I'm going to learn how to study and make better use of my class time, so that I can have more free time." Similarly, rather than thinking or saying, "I never do well on tests," do something constructive like taking study skills and/or test preparation courses at your college.

> *I hope the millions of people I've touched have the optimism and desire to share their goals and hard work and persevere with a positive attitude.* —Michael Jordan

## Psychology and Your Personal Success | Why Are a Growth Mindset and Grit Important?

If you'd like more evidence concerning the power of personal attitudes, think back to our opening story of Michael Jordan. How would you explain his personal life success? Some might say that he

**FIGURE 1.20**   **Dweck's growth mindset versus fixed mindset**   Do you see how a growth mindset is basically just having a "can do" attitude?

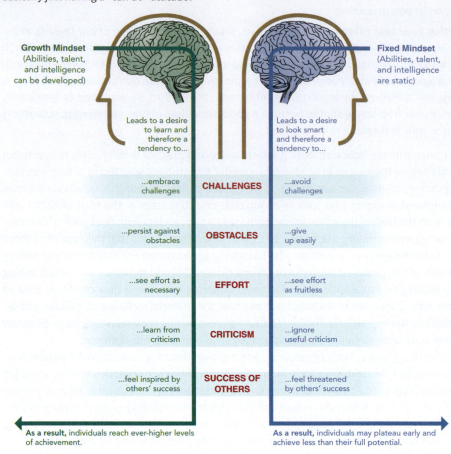

Growth Mindset
(Abilities, talent, and intelligence can be developed)

Fixed Mindset
(Abilities, talent, and intelligence are static)

Leads to a desire to learn and therefore a tendency to...

Leads to a desire to look smart and therefore a tendency to...

| ...embrace challenges | **CHALLENGES** | ...avoid challenges |
| ...persist against obstacles | **OBSTACLES** | ...give up easily |
| ...see effort as necessary | **EFFORT** | ...see effort as fruitless |
| ...learn from criticism | **CRITICISM** | ...ignore useful criticism |
| ...feel inspired by others' success | **SUCCESS OF OTHERS** | ...feel threatened by others' success |

**As a result,** individuals reach ever-higher levels of achievement.

**As a result,** individuals may plateau early and achieve less than their full potential.

Based on Dweck, 2007, 2012.

was just lucky, that he had devoted parents, or that he inherited great natural talent. While all of this is true, psychologists have discovered that a *growth mindset* and *grit* are generally the most significant factors in success in both work and academic settings (Datu et al., 2016; Dweck, 2007, 2012; Yeager et al., 2016). Why? People with a *growth mindset* believe their abilities, talents, and even intelligence can change and grow through their own effort. In contrast, those with a *fixed mindset* believe the opposite—that these same traits are fixed and set in stone! As you can see in **Figure 1.20**, having a growth mindset leads to higher achievement as a result of an individual's attitude and response to challenges, obstacles, effort, criticism, and the success of others.

In addition to a growth mindset, having a history of *grit* (which includes both perseverance and passion in the pursuit of long-term goals) sets most high achievers apart from the competition. Psychologist Carol Dweck says Jordan is "perhaps the *hardest working athlete* in the history of sport. If anyone has reason to think of himself as special, it's he." But, Dweck writes, "Jordan knew how hard he had worked to develop his abilities. He was a person who had struggled and grown, not a person who was inherently better than others." Through hard work and determination, Michael Jordan just "stretched" himself beyond the competition.

Bear in mind that no one is born with a growth mindset and grit. You can decide to develop and perfect these skills on your own. As the study of psychology teaches us, humans have a great capacity to change, adapt, and grow. That's why we include an inspiring story of success, like that of Michael Jordan, at the start of each chapter. Research shows that such stories and even just talking to friends and mentors about what they had to do to succeed helps increase our own growth mindset and grit. We also include this special "Tools for Student Success" section at the end of this first chapter because we want to share the best tips from psychology to improve your academic success in this and all your college courses. Throughout this text, we'll also share psychology's exciting discoveries about achievement in all parts of your life. Stay tuned!

© Billy R. Ray/Wiley

## Retrieval Practice 1.4 | Tools for Student Success

Completing this self-test and the connections section, and then checking your answers by clicking on the answer button or by looking in Appendix B, will provide immediate feedback and helpful practice for exams.

### Self-Test

1. Which of the following is NOT one of the recommended study habits?

   a. active reading      b. familiarization
   c. highlighting        d. note taking

2. List the six steps in the SQ4R method.

3. One of the clearest findings in psychology is that _____ practice is a much more efficient way to study and learn than _____ practice.

   a. spaced (distributed); massed
   b. active; passive

   c. applied; basic
   d. none of these options

4. _____ is particularly important if you suffer from test anxiety.

   a. Overlearning
   b. Hyper-soma control
   c. Active studying
   d. Passive listening

5. Research suggests that _____ might be two of the most efficient ways to study and thereby improve your grades.

   a. highlighting and rereading
   b. personal control and better time management
   c. active studying and the SQ4R method
   d. distributed practice and practice testing

### Connections—Chapter to Chapter

Answering the following question will help you "look back and look ahead" to see the important connections among the subfields of psychology and chapters within this text.

In Chapter 6 (Learning), you'll explore how almost all significant human behavior is learned. Explain how the common experience of test anxiety might be learned.

---

### Study Tip

*The WileyPlus program that accompanies this text provides for each chapter a* Media Challenge, Critical Thinking Exercise, *and* Application Quiz. *This set of study materials provides additional, invaluable study opportunities. Be sure to check it out!*

# Chapter Summary

## 1.1 Introducing Psychology   3

- **Psychology** is the scientific study of *behavior* and *mental processes*. The discipline places high value on *empirical evidence* and **critical thinking**. *Pseudopsychologies*, such as belief in psychic powers, are not based on scientific evidence.

- Wilhelm Wundt, considered the father of psychology, and his followers were interested in studying conscious experience. Their approach, **structuralism**, sought to identify the basic structures of mental life through introspection.

- The **functionalist** approach, led by William James, considered the father of American psychology, studied the way the mind functions to enable humans and nonhuman animals to adapt to their environment.

- The **psychoanalytic perspective**, founded by Sigmund Freud, emphasized the influence of the unconscious mind, which lies outside personal awareness.

- Contemporary psychology reflects the ideas of seven major perspectives: **psychodynamic**, **behavioral**, **humanistic**, **cognitive**, **biological**, **evolutionary**, and **sociocultural**.

- Despite early societal limitations, women and people of color have made important contributions to psychology. Pioneers include Mary Calkins, Margaret Floy Washburn, Francis Cecil Sumner, and Kenneth and Mamie Clark.

- Most contemporary psychologists embrace a unifying perspective known as the **biopsychosocial model**.

- Psychologists work as therapists, researchers, teachers, and consultants, in a wide range of settings.

**Test Your Critical Thinking**

**1.** Psychologists are among the least likely to believe in psychics, palmistry, astrology, and other paranormal phenomena. Why might that be?

**2.** Which of the seven modern perspectives of psychology do you most agree with? Why?

**3.** How might the biopsychosocial model explain the major difficulties or achievements in your own life?

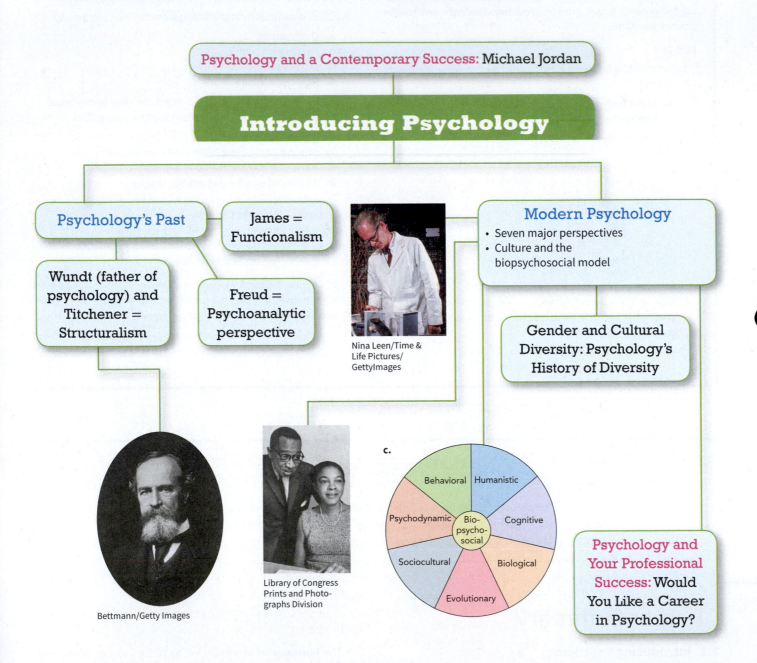

**Psychology and a Contemporary Success:** Michael Jordan

# Introducing Psychology

**Psychology's Past**

James = Functionalism

Wundt (father of psychology) and Titchener = Structuralism

Freud = Psychoanalytic perspective

Nina Leen/Time & Life Pictures/ GettyImages

**Modern Psychology**
- Seven major perspectives
- Culture and the biopsychosocial model

**Gender and Cultural Diversity:** Psychology's History of Diversity

Bettmann/Getty Images

Library of Congress Prints and Photographs Division

c.

Behavioral    Humanistic
Psychodynamic    Bio-psycho-social    Cognitive
Sociocultural    Biological
Evolutionary

**Psychology and Your Professional Success:** Would You Like a Career in Psychology?

## 1.2  The Science of Psychology    13

- **Basic research** is conducted to advance core scientific knowledge, whereas **applied research** works to address practical, real-world problems.

- Most scientific investigations consist of six basic steps, collectively known as the **scientific method**. Scientific progress comes

from developing a hypothesis and an operational definition and testing for **statistical significance**. It also involves repeatedly challenging and revising existing **theories** and building new ones.

- Psychology's four basic goals are to *describe, explain, predict*, and *change* behavior and mental processes through the use of the scientific method. One of psychology's most enduring debates is the **nature–nurture controversy**.

• Psychologists must maintain high ethical standards, including respecting the rights of therapy clients and research participants (both human and nonhuman). **Informed consent**, voluntary participation, restricted deception (followed by **debriefing**), and confidentiality are critical elements of research using human participants. Psychologists also take care to protect research animals. U.S. researchers and clinicians are held professionally responsible by the APA and APS, their research institutions, and local and state agencies.

**Test Your Critical Thinking**

**1.** If you had a million dollars to contribute to either basic or applied research, which one would you choose? Why?

**2.** Which group's rights—human participants, nonhuman animals, or psychotherapy clients—are the most important to protect? Why?

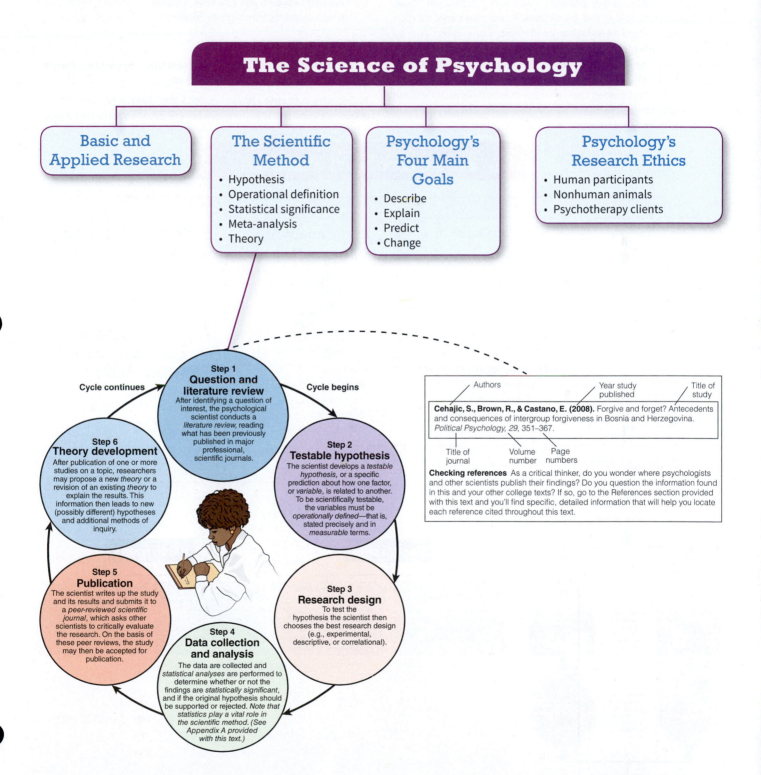

# The Science of Psychology

**Basic and Applied Research**

**The Scientific Method**
• Hypothesis
• Operational definition
• Statistical significance
• Meta-analysis
• Theory

**Psychology's Four Main Goals**
• Describe
• Explain
• Predict
• Change

**Psychology's Research Ethics**
• Human participants
• Nonhuman animals
• Psychotherapy clients

Cycle continues

**Step 1**
**Question and literature review**
After identifying a question of interest, the psychological scientist conducts a *literature review*, reading what has been previously published in major professional, scientific journals.

Cycle begins

**Step 6**
**Theory development**
After publication of one or more studies on a topic, researchers may propose a new *theory* or a revision of an existing *theory* to explain the results. This information then leads to new (possibly different) hypotheses and additional methods of inquiry.

**Step 2**
**Testable hypothesis**
The scientist develops a *testable hypothesis*, or a specific prediction about how one factor, or *variable*, is related to another. To be scientifically testable, the variables must be *operationally defined*—that is, stated precisely and in *measurable* terms.

**Step 5**
**Publication**
The scientist writes up the study and its results and submits it to a *peer-reviewed scientific journal*, which asks other scientists to critically evaluate the research. On the basis of these peer reviews, the study may then be accepted for publication.

**Step 3**
**Research design**
To test the hypothesis the scientist then chooses the best research design (e.g., experimental, descriptive, or correlational).

**Step 4**
**Data collection and analysis**
The data are collected and *statistical analyses* are performed to determine whether or not the findings are *statistically significant*, and if the original hypothesis should be supported or rejected. *Note that statistics play a vital role in the scientific method. (See Appendix A provided with this text.)*

Authors | Year study published | Title of study

**Cehajic, S., Brown, R., & Castano, E. (2008).** Forgive and forget? Antecedents and consequences of intergroup forgiveness in Bosnia and Herzegovina. *Political Psychology, 29*, 351–367.

Title of journal | Volume number | Page numbers

**Checking references** As a critical thinker, do you wonder where psychologists and other scientists publish their findings? Do you question the information found in this and your other college texts? If so, go to the References section provided with this text and you'll find specific, detailed information that will help you locate each reference cited throughout this text.

## 1.3  Research Methods    20

- **Descriptive research** systematically observes and records behavior and mental processes to meet the goal of *description*, without manipulating variables. The four major types of descriptive research are **naturalistic observation**, **survey/interview**, **case study**, and **archival research**.

- **Correlational research** measures the relationship between two variables, and it provides important information about those relationships and predictions. Researchers analyze their results using a **correlation coefficient**. Correlations can be *positive,* meaning they vary in the same direction, or *negative,* meaning they vary in opposite directions. A *zero* correlation occurs when there is no relationship between the variables. A correlation between two variables does not necessarily mean that one causes the other. It could be a **third-variable problem** or an **illusory correlation**.

- **Experimental research** manipulates and controls variables to determine cause and effect. An **experiment** has several critical components, including **independent** and **dependent variables**, and **experimental** and **control groups**. In addition, researchers avoid **experimenter bias** and **participant bias**. There are also errors caused by **sample bias, third variables, confounding variables**, and **ethnocentrism**. Methods of protection include representative sampling, **random assignment**, the use of **single-** and **double-blind studies**, and **placebos**. experiment protects against potential problems from both the researcher and the participants.

### Test Your Critical Thinking

1. Which form of research would you most trust—descriptive, correlational, experimental, or meta-analysis? Why?

2. Cigarette companies have suggested that there is no scientific evidence that smoking causes lung cancer. How would you refute this claim?

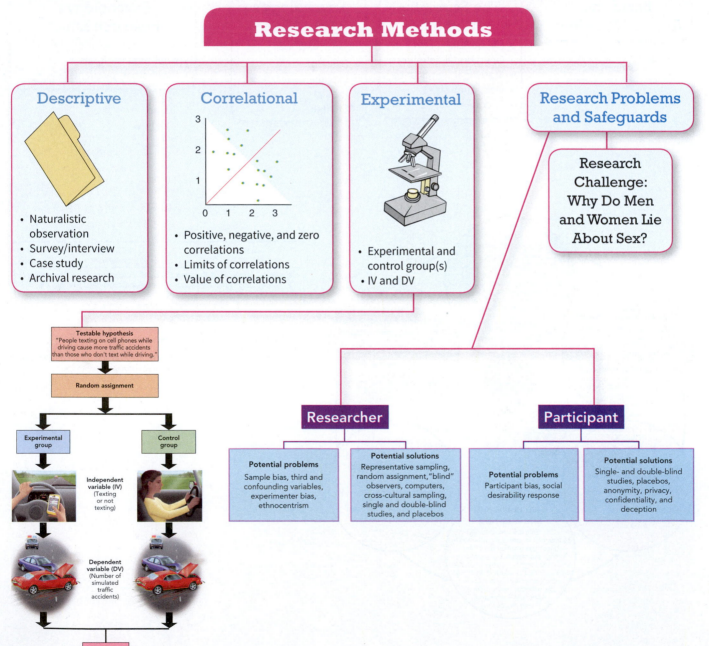

# Research Methods

## Descriptive
- Naturalistic observation
- Survey/interview
- Case study
- Archival research

## Correlational
3
2
1
0  1  2  3
- Positive, negative, and zero correlations
- Limits of correlations
- Value of correlations

## Experimental
- Experimental and control group(s)
- IV and DV

## Research Problems and Safeguards

Research Challenge: Why Do Men and Women Lie About Sex?

**Testable hypothesis**
"People texting on cell phones while driving cause more traffic accidents than those who don't text while driving."

**Random assignment**

Experimental group

Control group

Independent variable (IV)
(Texting or not texting)

Dependent variable (DV)
(Number of simulated traffic accidents)

Groups compared and results reported

### Researcher

**Potential problems**
Sample bias, third and confounding variables, experimenter bias, ethnocentrism

**Potential solutions**
Representative sampling, random assignment, "blind" observers, computers, cross-cultural sampling, single and double-blind studies, and placebos

### Participant

**Potential problems**
Participant bias, social desirability response

**Potential solutions**
Single- and double-blind studies, placebos, anonymity, privacy, confidentiality, and deception

### 1.4 Tools for Student Success   32

- To improve your study habits, try familiarization, active reading (including note taking and the SQ4R method), and avoiding highlighting and rereading. While studying, also be sure to go beyond simple recitation and overlearn.
- For better time management, you can establish a baseline, set up a realistic schedule, reward yourself, and maximize your time.
- To improve your grades, maximize each class session, improve your general test-taking skills, and take study skills courses. The two most efficient keys to grade improvement are distributed practice and practice testing.
- Attitude adjustment is important to your personal success, and two of the key components are a growth mindset and grit, which includes perseverance and passion in pursuit of long-term goals.

**Test Your Critical Thinking**

**1.** What topic or tip for student success do you consider most valuable? Why?

**2.** What prevents you, or other students you know, from fully employing the strategies for student success presented in this section?

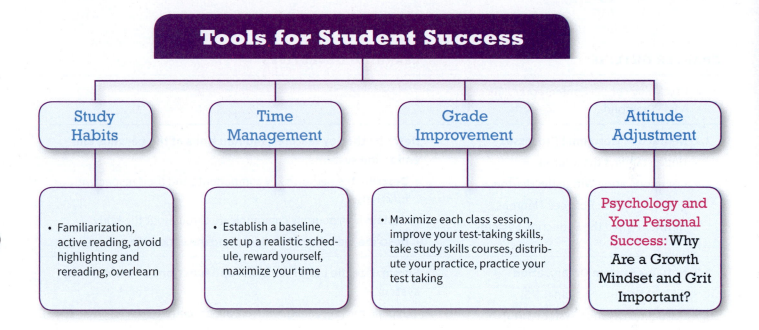

# Key Terms

**Retrieval Practice**   *Write your own definition for each term before turning back to the referenced page to check your answer.*

- applied research   13
- archival research   22
- basic research   13
- behavioral perspective   6
- biological perspective   8
- biopsychosocial model   9
- case study   22
- cognitive perspective   8
- confounding variable   28
- control group   26
- correlation coefficient   22
- correlational research   22
- critical thinking   4
- debriefing   18
- dependent variable (DV)   26
- descriptive research   21
- double-blind study   30
- ethnocentrism   28
- evolutionary perspective   8

- experiment   26
- experimental group   26
- experimental research   26
- experimenter bias   28
- functionalism   5
- grit   2
- growth mindset   2
- humanistic perspective   6
- hypothesis   14
- illusory correlation   24
- independent variable (IV)   26
- informed consent   18
- meta-analysis   16
- natural selection   8
- naturalistic observation   21
- nature–nurture controversy   17
- operational definition   14
- participant bias   29

- placebo   30
- placebo effect   30
- positive psychology   7
- psychoanalytic perspective   6
- psychodynamic perspective   6
- psychology   4
- random assignment   26
- representative sample   27
- sample bias   26
- scientific method   14
- single-blind study   30
- sociocultural perspective   8
- SQ4R method   34
- statistical significance   16
- structuralism   5
- survey/interview   21
- theory   16
- third-variable problem   24

© alexxl66/iStockphoto

# CHAPTER 2

# Neuroscience and Biological Foundations

| CHAPTER OUTLINE | LEARNING OBJECTIVES |
|---|---|
| ❖ **Psychology and a Contemporary Success** Adele Diamond | |
| **2.1 Neural and Hormonal Processes** <br> • Understanding the Neuron <br> • Communication Within the Neuron <br> • Communication Between Neurons <br> • Hormones and the Endocrine System | **Describe the key features and functions of the nervous and endocrine systems.** <br> • **Describe** the neuron's key components and their respective functions. <br> • **Explain** how neurons communicate throughout the body. <br> • **Describe** the roles of hormones and the endocrine system. |
| **2.2 Nervous System Organization** <br> • Central Nervous System (CNS) <br> • Peripheral Nervous System (PNS) | **Summarize the major divisions and functions of our nervous system.** <br> • **Explain** the key features and role of our central nervous system (CNS). <br> • **Define** neuroplasticity and neurogenesis. <br> • **Describe** the key components and role of our peripheral nervous system (PNS). |
| **2.3 A Tour Through the Brain** <br> • Biological Tools for Research <br> **GCD Gender and Cultural Diversity** <br> Are Male and Female Brains Different? <br> • Brain Organization <br> **RC Research Challenge** <br> Does Lying Lead to More Lies? | **Review the tools used in biological research, along with the brain's key structures and functions.** <br> • **Identify** the tools neuroscientists use to study the brain and nervous system. <br> • **Describe** the major structures of the hindbrain, midbrain, and forebrain, as well as their respective functions. |
| **2.4 The Cerebral Cortex** <br> • Lobes of the Brain <br> **RC Research Challenge** <br> Phineas Gage—Myths Versus Facts <br> ❖ **Psychology and Your Personal Success** <br> How to Train Your Brain <br> • Two Brains in One? | **Summarize the key features and major divisions of the cerebral cortex.** <br> • **Discuss** the location and functions of the eight lobes of the cerebral cortex. <br> • **Describe** the brain's two specialized hemispheres and split-brain research. |

### ❖ Psychology and a Contemporary Success | Adele Diamond

Courtesy Adele Diamond

Adele Diamond's father grew up in the Catskills of New York attending a one-room schoolhouse. Unfortunately, his education soon ended when he was forced to drop out and work to help support his family. As part of the first Jewish family in his neighborhood, the Diamond family also suffered intense anti-Semitism, with signs everywhere such as, "No Jews and dogs allowed." Adele's mother was from New York City and would have attended college if not for the Great Depression. Adele herself grew up in New York City, where her father died while she was in high school. Despite this hardship, Adele graduated as valedictorian and went on to earn high academic honors from Swarthmore College and a PhD from Harvard and to pursue postdoctoral studies at Yale.

Today, Adele Diamond (see photo) is the Canada Research Chair Professor of Developmental Neuroscience at the University of British Columbia. She's been recognized as one of the 15 most influential neuroscientists alive today and was named one of the "2,000 Outstanding Women of the 20th Century." Her research on the region of the brain known as the prefrontal cortex has changed medical practice around the world. And, as you'll see later in this chapter, her discoveries of the brain's *executive functions (EFs)* have improved the lives of millions of children (Adele Diamond, n.d.; Developmental Cognitive Neuroscience, n.d.). This is how Professor Diamond explains her life's work: "We know that the prefrontal cortex is not fully developed until the 20s, and some people will ask, 'Why are you trying to improve prefrontal abilities when the biological substrate is not there yet?' I tell them that 2-year-olds have legs, too, which will not reach full length for 10 years or more—but they can still walk and run and benefit from exercise" (Carey, 2008).

# Chapter Overview

Does the story of Adele Diamond inspire you? Are you, like many of our students, surprised that neuroscience and the study of the brain are even a part of psychology? As discussed in Chapter 1, the biological approach is one of seven major perspectives in modern psychology. This area of research is often called *biopsychology, psychobiology, behavioral neuroscience,* or *neuroscience*. All four terms focus on the scientific study of the biology of behavior and mental processes—the subject of this chapter.

## Why Study Psychology?

### Did you know that

- . . . moving, dancing, or singing in synchrony with others can raise your pain threshold and increase your feelings of closeness?

- . . . the belief that some people are "left-brained" and others are "right-brained" is largely a myth?

- . . . all your thoughts, feelings, and actions result from neurotransmitter messages flashing between billions of tiny nerve cells? Or that organisms from lizards to elephants all depend on much the same neurotransmitters that our own brains use?

- . . . scientists have established a link between repeated concussions and permanent (and possibly fatal) brain damage?

- . . . cells in our brains die and regenerate throughout our lifetime? Or that they are also physically shaped and changed by learning and from experiences we have with our environment?

FatCamera/Getty Images

- . . . scientists have created human embryos through cloning? Or that extracted stem cells can be used for diseases like cancer, Parkinson's disease, and diabetes?

**Sources:** Ascherio & Schwarzschild, 2016; Bilder, 2016; Carlson & Birkett, 2017; Eyo et al., 2017; Freberg, 2016; Garnier et al., 2017; Nelsen et al., 2014; Nitschke et al., 2017.

We begin with a look at the neuron, which is the foundation of the brain and nervous system. Next, we explore how neurons communicate and how their chemicals (called neurotransmitters) affect us. Then, we examine the importance of hormones and our endocrine system. Following this, we discuss the overall organization of our nervous system—the central and peripheral systems. We conclude with a brief tour of the tools used in biological research and the major structures and functions of our mysterious and magical human brain.

> **Study Tip**
>
> *Be aware that this chapter does contain a high number of new biological terms, which some students find a bit overwhelming. However, it's essential to master this material because it provides the foundation for topics we'll cover throughout this text. More importantly, knowing the proper terms and functions of your own brain and nervous system will help you understand and make better choices about the care of these vital structures. Just as we routinely wear shoes to protect our feet, we need seat belts and helmets to protect our far more fragile brains and nervous systems!*

## 2.1 | Neural and Hormonal Processes

**LEARNING OBJECTIVES**

**Retrieval Practice**  While reading the upcoming sections, respond to each Learning Objective in your own words.

**Describe the key features and functions of the nervous and endocrine systems.**

- **Describe** the neuron's key components and their respective functions.
- **Explain** how neurons communicate throughout the body.
- **Describe** the roles of hormones and the endocrine system.

**Neuron**  The basic building block (nerve cell) of the nervous system; responsible for receiving, processing, and transmitting electrochemical information.

**Glial cells**  The cells that provide structural, nutritional, and other functions for neurons; also called glia or neuroglia.

**Dendrites**  The branching fibers of neurons that receive neural impulses from other neurons and convey impulses toward the cell body.

**Cell body**  The part of a neuron that contains the cell nucleus and other structures that help the neuron carry out its functions; also known as the soma.

**Axon**  A long, tube-like structure that conveys impulses away from a neuron's cell body toward other neurons or to muscles or glands.

Stop for a moment and consider your full human body. Did you know that your brain and nervous system are responsible for receiving, transmitting, and interpreting all the sensory information from your internal and the external environment? Are you surprised to learn that your body is composed of about 10 trillion cells divided into about 200 different types—muscle cells, heart cells, etc.? For psychologists, the microscopic nerve cells, called **neurons**, are the key figures because they are essential to understanding who we are as individuals and how we behave. In other words, our every thought, mood, or action is a biological experience. To fully appreciate these neural bases of behavior, we must start with the *neuron*.

### Understanding the Neuron

Each neuron is a tiny information-processing system with thousands of connections for receiving and sending electrochemical signals to other neurons. Each human body may have as many as 1 *trillion* neurons.

Neurons are held in place and supported by **glial cells**, which make up about 90% of the brain's total cells. Glial cells also supply nutrients and oxygen, perform cleanup tasks, and insulate one neuron from another so that their neural messages are not scrambled. In addition, they play a direct role in nervous system communication and our immune system (Dan, 2017; Eyo et al., 2017; Sénécal et al., 2016). In short, our neurons simply could not function without glial cells. However, the "star" of the communication show is still the neuron.

Note that there are different types of neurons, but they generally share three basic features: **dendrites**, the **cell body**, and an **axon** (**Figure 2.1**). *Dendrites* look like leafless branches of a tree. In fact, the word *dendrite* means "little tree" in Greek. Each neuron may have hundreds or thousands of dendrites, which act like antennas to receive electrochemical information from

**FIGURE 2.1** **Key parts and functions of a neuron**   Red arrows in the figure on the left indicate direction of information flow: dendrites → cell body → axon → terminal buttons of axon.

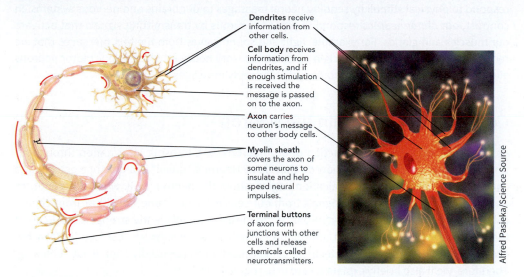

**Dendrites** receive information from other cells.

**Cell body** receives information from dendrites, and if enough stimulation is received the message is passed on to the axon.

**Axon** carries neuron's message to other body cells.

**Myelin sheath** covers the axon of some neurons to insulate and help speed neural impulses.

**Terminal buttons** of axon form junctions with other cells and release chemicals called neurotransmitters.

Alfred Pasieka/Science Source

**Study Tip**

*To remember the three key parts of a neuron, picture your hand and arm as:*

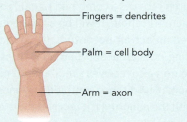

Fingers = dendrites

Palm = cell body

Arm = axon

*To understand how information travels through the neuron, think of the three key parts in reverse alphabetical order:* Dendrite → Cell Body → Axon (D, C, B, A).

other nearby neurons. The information then flows into the *cell body*, or *soma* (Greek for "body"). If the cell body receives enough information/stimulation from its dendrites, it will pass the message on to a long, tube-like structure, called the *axon* (from the Greek word for "axle"). The axon then carries information away from the cell body to the *terminal buttons*.

The **myelin sheath**, a white, fatty coating around the axons of some neurons, is not considered one of the three key features of a neuron, but it plays the essential roles of insulating and speeding neural impulses. As you'll discover in the next section, our human body is essentially an information-processing system dependent upon electrical impulses and chemical messengers. Just as the wires in data cables are insulated from one another by plastic, the myelin sheath provides insulation and separation for the numerous axons that travel throughout our bodies. And just as the data cable wires are bundled together into larger cables, our myelin-coated axons are bundled together into "cables" called *nerves*.

The importance of myelin sheaths becomes readily apparent in certain diseases, such as *multiple sclerosis,* in which myelin progressively deteriorates and the person gradually loses muscular coordination. Although the disease often goes into remission, it can be fatal if it strikes the neurons that control basic life-support processes, such as breathing or heartbeat. Myelin is also critical in the first few weeks and months of life. Research shows that social isolation during these critical periods (as occurs for babies who are neglected in some orphanages) prevents cells from producing the right amount of myelin. Sadly, this loss of normal levels of myelin leads to long-term problems in cognitive functioning (Makinodan et al., 2012).

**Myelin sheath**   The layer of fatty insulation wrapped around the axons of some neurons that increases the rate at which neural impulses travel along the axon.

Having described the structure, function, and importance of the neuron itself, we also need to explain that we have two general types of neurons—sensory and motor. Our *sensory neurons* respond to physical stimuli by sending neural messages to our brains and nervous systems. In contrast, our *motor neurons* respond to sensory neurons by transmitting signals that activate our muscles and glands. For example, light and sound waves from the text messages that we receive on our cell phones are picked up by our sensory neurons, whereas our motor neurons allow our fingers to almost instantaneously type reply messages.

## Communication Within the Neuron

As we've just seen, the basic function of our neurons is to transmit information throughout the nervous system. But exactly how do they do it? Neurons "speak" in a type of electrical and chemical language. The communication begins within the neuron itself, when the dendrites and cell body receive electrical signals from our senses (sight, sound, touch) or from chemical messages from other nearby neurons. If the message is sufficiently strong, it will instruct the neuron to "fire"—to transmit information to other neurons. As you can see in **Step-by-Step Diagram 2.1**, this type of electrical communication is admittedly somewhat confusing. Therefore, we'll also briefly explain it here in narrative form:

**Step 1**  Neurons are normally at rest and ready to be activated, which explains why this resting stage is called the "resting potential."

**Step 2**  If a resting neuron receives a combined signal (from the senses or other neurons) that exceeds the minimum threshold, it will be activated and "fire," thus transmitting an electrical impulse (called an **action potential**). (Note that in Step-by-Step Diagram 2.1, we're only demonstrating how an action potential "fires"—also known as "excitation." However, this resting neuron also receives simultaneous messages telling it NOT to fire—a process called "inhibition." Given these contradictory messages, the neuron does something simple—it goes with the majority! If it receives more excitatory messages than inhibitory, it fires—and vice versa.)

**Step 3**  The beginning action potential then spreads and travels down the axon. As the action potential moves toward the terminal buttons, the areas on the axon left behind return to their resting state. Note that this firing of an action potential is similar to a light switch, where once you apply the minimum amount of pressure needed to flip the switch, the light comes on. There is no "partial firing" of a neuron. It's either on or off. This neural reaction of firing either with a full-strength response or not at all is known as the **all-or-nothing principle**. But if this is true, how do we detect the intensity of a stimulus, such as the difference between a rock and a butterfly landing on our hand? A strong stimulus (like the rock) causes more neurons to fire and to fire more often than does a butterfly.

Now that we understand how communication occurs within the neuron, we need to explain how it works between neurons.

**Action potential**  A neural impulse, or brief electrical charge, that carries information along the axon of a neuron; movement is generated when positively charged ions move in and out through channels in the axon's membrane.

**All-or-nothing principle**  The principle that a neuron's response to a stimulus is either to fire with a full-strength response or not to fire at all; also known as the all-or-none law.

---

**STEP-BY-STEP DIAGRAM 2.1** | **Communication *Within* the Neuron**

**STOP!**  This Step-by-Step Diagram contains essential information NOT found elsewhere in the text, which is likely to appear on quizzes and exams. Be sure to study it CAREFULLY!

The process of neural communication begins within the neuron itself, when the dendrites and cell body receive information and conduct it toward the axon. From there, the information moves down the entire length of the axon via a brief, traveling electrical charge called an action potential, which can be described in the following three steps:

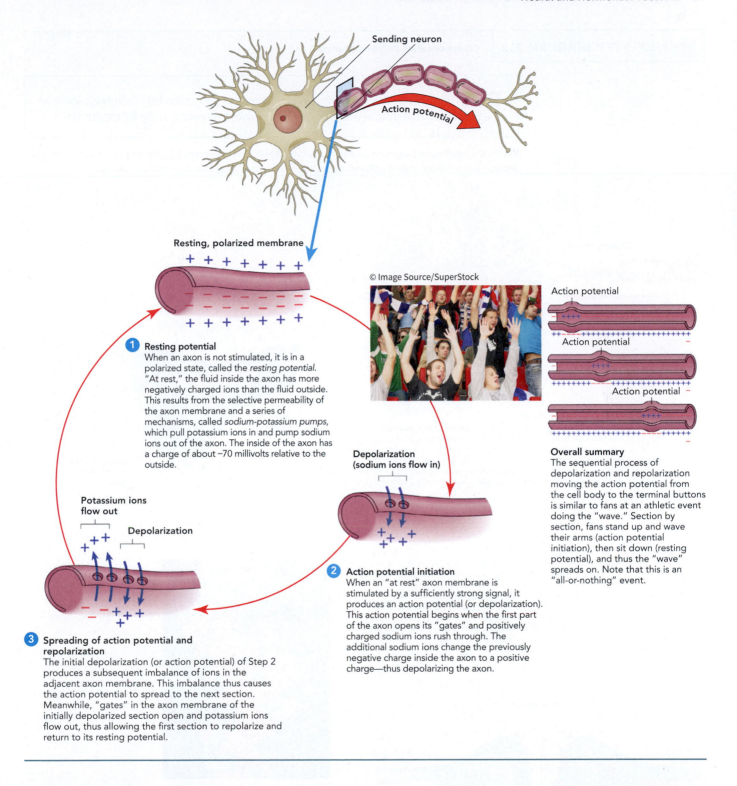

Sending neuron

Action potential

Resting, polarized membrane

+ + + + + + +

− − − − − −

+ + + + + +

© Image Source/SuperStock

**1** **Resting potential**
When an axon is not stimulated, it is in a polarized state, called the *resting potential.* "At rest," the fluid inside the axon has more negatively charged ions than the fluid outside. This results from the selective permeability of the axon membrane and a series of mechanisms, called *sodium-potassium pumps,* which pull potassium ions in and pump sodium ions out of the axon. The inside of the axon has a charge of about −70 millivolts relative to the outside.

**Depolarization**
(sodium ions flow in)

**Potassium ions flow out**

**Depolarization**

+ + +
⊕ ⊕ ⊕ ⊕
− − + +
+ +

**3** **Spreading of action potential and repolarization**
The initial depolarization (or action potential) of Step 2 produces a subsequent imbalance of ions in the adjacent axon membrane. This imbalance thus causes the action potential to spread to the next section. Meanwhile, "gates" in the axon membrane of the initially depolarized section open and potassium ions flow out, thus allowing the first section to repolarize and return to its resting potential.

**2** **Action potential initiation**
When an "at rest" axon membrane is stimulated by a sufficiently strong signal, it produces an action potential (or depolarization). This action potential begins when the first part of the axon opens its "gates" and positively charged sodium ions rush through. The additional sodium ions change the previously negative charge inside the axon to a positive charge—thus depolarizing the axon.

Action potential

Action potential

Action potential

**Overall summary**
The sequential process of depolarization and repolarization moving the action potential from the cell body to the terminal buttons is similar to fans at an athletic event doing the "wave." Section by section, fans stand up and wave their arms (action potential initiation), then sit down (resting potential), and thus the "wave" spreads on. Note that this is an "all-or-nothing" event.

# Communication Between Neurons

As you discovered in Step-by-Step Diagram 2.1, neural transmission (via *action potentials*) within the neuron can be compared to a crowd's behavior doing the "wave" in a stadium. The analogy helps explain how the action potential travels down the axon in a "wave-like" motion. However, the comparison breaks down when we want to know how the message moves from one neuron to another—or how the "wave" in a stadium gets across the aisles. The answer is that within the neuron, messages travel electrically, whereas between neurons the messages are carried across the **synapse** via chemicals called **neurotransmitters**— see **Step-by-Step Diagram 2.2.**

**Synapse**  The gap between the axon tip of the sending neuron and the dendrite and/or cell body of the receiving neuron; during an action potential, neurotransmitters are released and flow across the synapse.

**Neurotransmitter**  A chemical messenger released by neurons that travels across the synapse and allows neurons to communicate with one another.

## STEP-BY-STEP DIAGRAM 2.2 | Communication *Between* Neurons

**STOP!** This Step-by-Step Diagram contains essential information NOT found elsewhere in the text, which is likely to appear on quizzes and exams. Be sure to study it CAREFULLY!

Within the neuron, messages travel electrically (see Step-by-Step Diagram 2.1). Between neurons, messages are transmitted chemically. The three steps shown here summarize this chemical transmission.

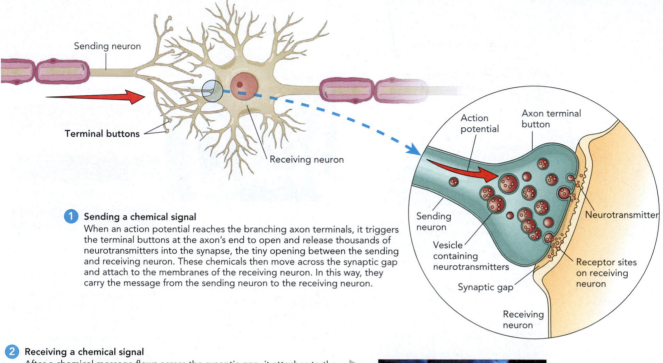

**1 Sending a chemical signal**

When an action potential reaches the branching axon terminals, it triggers the terminal buttons at the axon's end to open and release thousands of neurotransmitters into the synapse, the tiny opening between the sending and receiving neuron. These chemicals then move across the synaptic gap and attach to the membranes of the receiving neuron. In this way, they carry the message from the sending neuron to the receiving neuron.

**2 Receiving a chemical signal**

After a chemical message flows across the synaptic gap, it attaches to the receiving neuron. Keep in mind that each receiving neuron gets multiple neurotransmitter messages. As you can see in this close-up photo, the axon terminals from thousands of other nearby neurons almost completely cover the cell body of the receiving neuron. It's also important to understand that neurotransmitters deliver either excitatory ("fire") or inhibitory ("don't fire") messages. The receiving neurons will only produce an action potential and pass along the message if the number of excitatory messages outweigh the inhibitory messages.

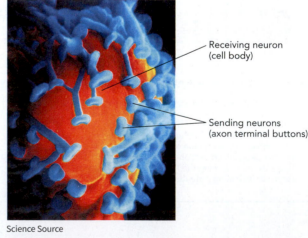

Science Source

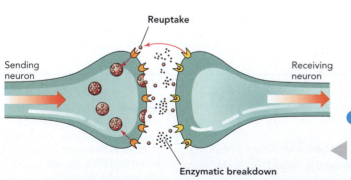

**3 Dealing with leftovers**

Given that some neurons have thousands of receptors, which are only responsive to specific neurotransmitters, what happens to excess neurotransmitters or to those that do not "fit" into the adjacent receptor sites? The sending neuron normally reabsorbs the excess (called "reuptake"), or they are broken down by special enzymes.

Like Step-by-Step Diagram 2.1, this procedure is complicated, so we'll also briefly summarize it in narrative form here.

Beginning with Step 1, note how the *action potential* travels down the axon and on to the knob-like terminal buttons. These buttons contain small tiny vesicles (sacs) that store the neurotransmitters. These neurotransmitters then travel across the *synapse*, or gap between neurons, to bind to receptor sites on the nearby receiving neurons. (The neuron that delivers the neurotransmitter to the synapse is called a *pre-synaptic neuron*.)

Now, in Step 2, like a key fitting into a lock, the neurotransmitters unlock tiny channels in the receiving neuron and send either excitatory ("fire") or inhibitory ("don't fire") messages. (The receiving neuron is called a *post-synaptic neuron*.)

Finally, in Step 3, after delivering their message, the neurotransmitters must be removed from the receptor sites before the next neural transmission can occur. Note how some of the neurotransmitters are used up in the transmission of the message. However, most of the "left-overs" are reabsorbed by the axon and stored until the next neural impulse—a process known as *reuptake*. In other cases, the "leftovers" are dealt with via enzymes that break apart the neurotransmitters to clean up the synapse.

### Appreciating Neurotransmitters

While researching how neurons communicate, scientists have discovered numerous neurotransmitters with differing effects that will be discussed here and in later chapters. For instance, we now know that certain neurotransmitters play significant roles in various medical problems. Decreased levels of the neurotransmitter dopamine are associated with Parkinson's disease (PD), whereas excessively high levels of dopamine appear to contribute to some forms of schizophrenia. **Table 2.1** presents additional examples of how some of the most common neurotransmitters affect us. Scientists have also found that some **agonist** drugs enhance or "mimic" the action of particular neurotransmitters, whereas **antagonist** drugs block or inhibit the effects (**Figure 2.2**).

Perhaps the best-known neurotransmitters are the endogenous opioid peptides, commonly known as **endorphins** (a contraction of *endogenous* [self-produced] and *morphine*). These chemicals mimic the effects of opium-based drugs such as morphine: They elevate mood and reduce pain (Antunes et al., 2016; Fan et al., 2016). In fact, drinking alcohol causes endorphins to be released in parts of the brain that are responsible for feelings of reward and pleasure (Mitchell et al., 2012).

Surprisingly, researchers have even found that when we sing in choirs and/or move in synchrony with others our pain thresholds are higher and we tend to feel closer to others—even if the other singers and dancers are strangers (Tarr et al., 2016; Weinstein et al., 2016). The researchers attributed these findings to the release of endorphins. They also hypothesized that singing and dancing may have evolved over time because they encourage social bonding with strangers!

**Agonist** A molecule that binds to a receptor and triggers a response that mimics or enhances a neurotransmitter's effect.

**Antagonist** A molecule that binds to a receptor and triggers a response that blocks a neurotransmitter's effect.

**Endorphin** A chemical substance in the nervous system similar in structure and action to opiates; involved in pain control, pleasure, and memory.

**FIGURE 2.2** **How poisons and drugs affect neural transmission** Foreign chemicals, like poisons and drugs, can mimic or block ongoing actions of neurotransmitters, thus interfering with normal functions.

Most snake venom and some poisons, like *botulinum* toxin (Botox®), seriously affect normal muscle contraction. Ironically, these same poisons are sometimes used to treat certain medical conditions involving abnormal muscle contraction. As shown in the photo, the Botox poison is used for cosmetic purposes to reduce frown lines.

Altrendo Images/Stockbyte/Getty Images

**Normal neurotransmission**

Postsynaptic receptor site

Neural impulse

Somewhat like a key fitting into a lock, receptor sites on receiving neurons' dendrites recognize neurotransmitters by their particular shape. When the shape of the neurotransmitter matches the shape of the receptor site, a message is sent.

Neurotransmitters without the correct shape won't fit the receptors, so they cannot stimulate the dendrite, and that neurotransmitter's message is blocked.

**a.** Normal neurotransmitter activation

**b.** Blocked neurotransmitter activation

**How poisons and drugs affect neurotransmission**

Some *agonist drugs*, like the nicotine in cigarettes (and the poison from a black widow spider bite), are similar enough in structure to a specific neurotransmitter (in this case, acetylcholine) that they mimic its effects on the receiving neuron, and a message is sent.

Some *antagonist drugs or poisons* (*like curare*) block neurotransmitters like acetylcholine, which is vital in muscle action. Blocking it paralyzes muscles, including those involved in breathing, which can be fatal.

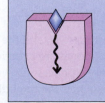

**c.** Agonist drug "mimics" neurotransmitter

**d.** Antagonist drug fills receptor space and blocks neurotransmitter

**TABLE 2.1   How Neurotransmitters Affect Us**

| Neurotransmitter | Sample Agonist/ Antagonist Acting Drugs | Known or Suspected Effects |
|---|---|---|
| Acetylcholine (ACh) | Nicotine, amphetamines, LSD, PCP, marijuana | Muscle action, learning, attention, memory, REM (rapid-eye-movement) sleep, emotion; decreased ACh may play a role in Alzheimer's disease |
| Dopamine (DA) | Cocaine, methamphetamine, LSD, GHB, PCP, marijuana, Ecstasy (MDMA), L-Dopa (treatment for Parkinson's disease), chlorpromazine (treatment for schizophrenia) | Movement, attention, memory, learning, emotion; excess DA associated with schizophrenia; too little DA linked with Parkinson's disease; key role in addiction and the reward system |
| Endorphins | Heroin, morphine and oxycodone (treatments for pain) | Mood, pain, memory, learning, blood pressure, appetite, sexual activity |
| Epinephrine (or adrenaline) | Amphetamines, ecstasy (MDMA), cocaine | Emotional arousal, memory storage, metabolism of glucose necessary for energy release |
| GABA (gamma-aminobutyric acid) | Alcohol, GHB, rohypnol, valium (treatment for anxiety) | Learning, anxiety regulation; key role in neural inhibition in the central nervous system; tranquilizing drugs, like Valium, increase GABA's inhibitory effects and thereby decrease anxiety |
| Glutamate | Alcohol, phencyclidine, PCP, ketamine (an anesthetic) | Learning, movement, memory; key role in neural excitation in the central nervous system; factor in migraines, anxiety, depression |
| Norepinephrine (NE) [or noradrenaline (NA)] | Cocaine, methamphetamine, amphetamine, ecstasy (MDMA), Adderall (treatment for ADHD) | Attention, arousal learning, memory, dreaming, emotion, stress; low levels of NE associated with depression; high levels of NE linked with agitated, manic states |
| Serotonin | Ecstasy (MDMA), LSD, cocaine, selective serotonin uptake inhibitors (SSRIs—Prozac, used to treat depression, is an SSRI) | Mood, sleep, appetite, sensory perception, arousal, temperature regulation, pain suppression, impulsivity; low levels of serotonin associated with depression |

Tim Clayton-Corbis/Contributor/Getty Images

Which neurotransmitters best explain the skills of the winner of four gold medals for gymnastics in the 2016 Olympics, Simone Biles (pictured here), or those involved in your own athletic abilities?

Endorphins also affect memory, learning, blood pressure, appetite, and sexual activity. For example, rats injected with an endorphin-like chemical eat considerably more M&Ms than they would under normal conditions, even consuming as much as 17 grams (more than 5% of their body weight; DiFeliceantonio et al., 2012). Although this may not seem like a lot of chocolate to you, it is the equivalent of a normal-sized adult eating 7.5 pounds of M&Ms in a single session!

## Hormones and the Endocrine System

We've just seen how the nervous system uses neurons and neurotransmitters to transmit messages. We also have a second type of communication system made up of a network of glands, called the **endocrine system** (**Figure 2.3**). In contrast to the nervous system, the endocrine system uses **hormones** (from the Greek *horman*, meaning "stimulate" or "excite") to carry its messages (**Figure 2.4**).

Why is the endocrine system important? Without the hypothalamus and pituitary, the testes in men would not produce *testosterone*, and the ovaries in women would not produce *estrogen*. As you may know, these hormones are of critical importance to sexual behavior and reproduction. In addition, the pituitary produces its own hormone that controls body growth. Too much of this hormone results in *gigantism*; too little will make a person far smaller than average, a *hypopituitary dwarf*.

**Endocrine system**   A network of glands located throughout the body that manufacture and secrete hormones into the bloodstream.

**Hormone**   Chemical messengers manufactured and secreted by the endocrine glands, which circulate in the bloodstream to produce bodily changes or maintain normal bodily functions.

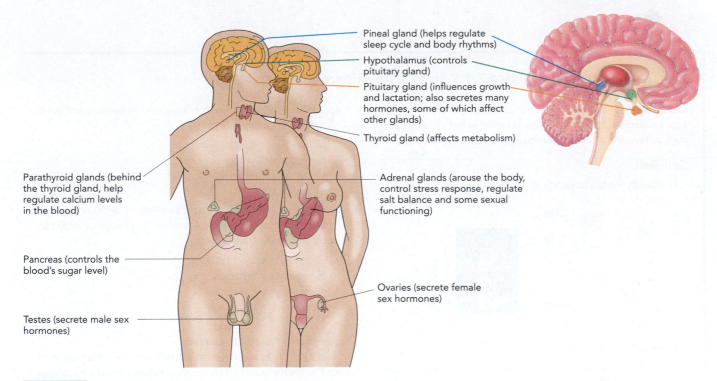

Pineal gland (helps regulate sleep cycle and body rhythms)

Hypothalamus (controls pituitary gland)

Pituitary gland (influences growth and lactation; also secretes many hormones, some of which affect other glands)

Thyroid gland (affects metabolism)

Adrenal glands (arouse the body, control stress response, regulate salt balance and some sexual functioning)

Parathyroid glands (behind the thyroid gland, help regulate calcium levels in the blood)

Pancreas (controls the blood's sugar level)

Ovaries (secrete female sex hormones)

Testes (secrete male sex hormones)

**FIGURE 2.3    The endocrine system**    This figure shows the major endocrine glands, along with some internal organs to help you locate the glands.

Other hormones released by the endocrine system help maintain our body's normal functioning. For example, hormones released by the kidneys help regulate blood pressure. The pancreatic hormone (insulin) allows cells to use sugar from the blood. Stomach and intestinal hormones help control digestion and elimination.

Before going on, note that in spite of the previously mentioned differences between the nervous system and the endocrine system, they're actually close relatives that are intricately interconnected. In times of crisis, the hypothalamus sends messages through two pathways—the neural system and the endocrine system (primarily the pituitary gland). The pituitary sends hormonal messages to the adrenal glands (located right above the kidneys). As you'll discover in Chapter 3, the adrenal glands then release *cortisol*, a stress hormone that boosts energy and blood sugar levels, *epinephrine* (commonly called adrenaline), and *norepinephrine* (or nonadrenaline). (Remember that these same chemicals also can serve as neurotransmitters.)

The pituitary gland also releases another important hormone, *oxytocin*, which plays a very interesting role in love, attachment, and social bonding. In addition, oxytocin enables contractions during birth, nursing, and sexual orgasm, and high oxytocin levels are also found during hugging, cuddling, and emotional bonding with romantic partners. One study even discovered that men who receive a spray of the hormone oxytocin rate their female partners as more attractive than unfamiliar women—thus suggesting oxytocin may increase faithfulness (Scheele et al., 2013). Perhaps even more intriguing is the research showing that dogs who stare at their owners show elevated levels of oxytocin. And, after receiving these dog gazes, the human's level of oxytocin also increases (Nagasawa et al., 2015)! Can you see why this might explain why we feel so good after sharing eye contact with our dogs?

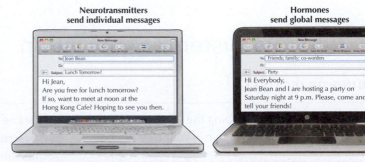

**Neurotransmitters send individual messages**

To: Jean Bean
Cc:
Subject: Lunch Tomorrow?

Hi Jean,
Are you free for lunch tomorrow? If so, want to meet at noon at the Hong Kong Cafe? Hoping to see you then.

**Hormones send global messages**

To: Friends; family; co-workers
Cc:
Subject: Party

Hi Everybody,
Jean Bean and I are hosting a party on Saturday night at 9 p.m. Please, come and tell your friends!

**FIGURE 2.4    Why do we need two communication systems?**    Just as some e-mail messages are only sent to certain people, neurotransmitters only deliver messages to specific receptors, which other neurons nearby probably don't "overhear." Hormones, in contrast, are like a global e-mail message that you send to everyone in your address book. Endocrine glands release these hormones directly into the bloodstream. The hormones then travel throughout the body, carrying messages to any cell that will listen. Hormones also function like global e-mail recipients forwarding your message to yet more people. For example, a small part of the brain called the hypothalamus releases hormones that signal the pituitary (another small brain structure), which stimulates or inhibits the release of other hormones.

© Billy R. Ray/Wiley

## Retrieval Practice 2.1 | Neural and Hormonal Processes

Completing this self-test and connections section, and then checking your answers by clicking on the answer button or by looking in Appendix B, will provide immediate feedback and helpful practice for exams.

### Self-Test

1. Identify the five key parts of a neuron.

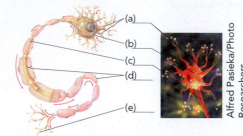
(a)
(b)
(c)
(d)
(e)

Alfred Pasieka/Photo Researchers

2. An action potential is _____.
   a. the likelihood that a neuron will take action when stimulated
   b. the tendency for a neuron to be potentiated by neurotransmitters
   c. the firing of a nerve, either toward or away from the brain
   d. a neural impulse that carries information along the axon of a neuron

3. According to the all-or-nothing principle, _____.
   a. a neuron cannot fire again during the refractory period
   b. a neurotransmitter either attaches to a receptor site or is destroyed in the synapse
   c. a neuron either fires completely or not at all
   d. none of these options is correct

4. Chemical messengers that are released by neurons and travel across the synapse are called _____.
   a. chemical agonists
   b. neurotransmitters
   c. synaptic transmitter
   d. neuroactivists

5. Chemicals manufactured and secreted by endocrine glands and circulated in the bloodstream to change or maintain bodily functions are called _____.
   a. vasopressors
   b. neurotransmitters
   c. hormones
   d. chemical antagonists

### Connections—Chapter to Chapter

Answering the following question will help you "look back and look ahead" to see the important connections among the various subfields of psychology and chapters within this text.

In Chapter 15 (Therapy), you'll learn that mental illness is often treated with the use of drugs, such as antidepressants. One commonly prescribed type of antidepressant is known as a *selective serotonin reuptake inhibitor (SSRI)*, which is designed to increase levels of serotonin, a neurotransmitter related to depression. Using what you have learned in this chapter about communication between neurons, explain how an SSRI could result in an increase in the amount of serotonin available in the brain.

---

## 2.2 | Nervous System Organization

### LEARNING OBJECTIVES

**Retrieval Practice** While reading the upcoming sections, respond to each Learning Objective in your own words.

**Summarize the major divisions and functions of our nervous system.**

- **Explain** the key features and role of our central nervous system (CNS).

- **Define** neuroplasticity and neurogenesis.
- **Describe** the key components and role of our peripheral nervous system (PNS).

---

**Nervous system** The electro-chemical communication system that carries information to and from all parts of the body.

Have you heard the expression "Information is power"? Nowhere is this truer than in the human body. Without information, we could not survive. Neurons within our **nervous system** must take in sensory information from the outside world and then pass it along to our entire body. Just as the circulatory system handles blood, which conveys chemicals and oxygen, the nervous system uses chemicals and electrical processes to convey information.

The nervous system is divided and subdivided into several branches (**Figure 2.5**). The main branch includes the brain and a bundle of nerves that form the *spinal cord*. Because this system is located in the center of the body (within the skull and spine), it is called the **central nervous system (CNS)**. The CNS is primarily responsible for processing and organizing information.

The second major branch of the nervous system includes all the nerves outside the brain and spinal cord. This **peripheral nervous system (PNS)** carries messages (action potentials) to and from the CNS to the periphery of the body. Now, let's take a closer look at the CNS and the PNS.

**Central nervous system (CNS)**
The part of the nervous system consisting of the brain and spinal cord.

**Peripheral nervous system (PNS)**
The part of the nervous system composed of the nerves and neurons connecting the central nervous system (CNS) to the rest of the body.

**Study Tip**

*When attempting to learn and memorize a large set of new terms and concepts, like those in this chapter, organization is the best way to master the material and get it "permanently" stored in long-term memory (Chapter 7). A broad overview showing the "big picture" helps you organize and file specific details. Just as you need to see a globe of the world showing all the continents to easily place individual countries, you need a "map" of the entire nervous system to effectively study the individual parts.*

**FIGURE 2.5**  **Major divisions of our nervous system**

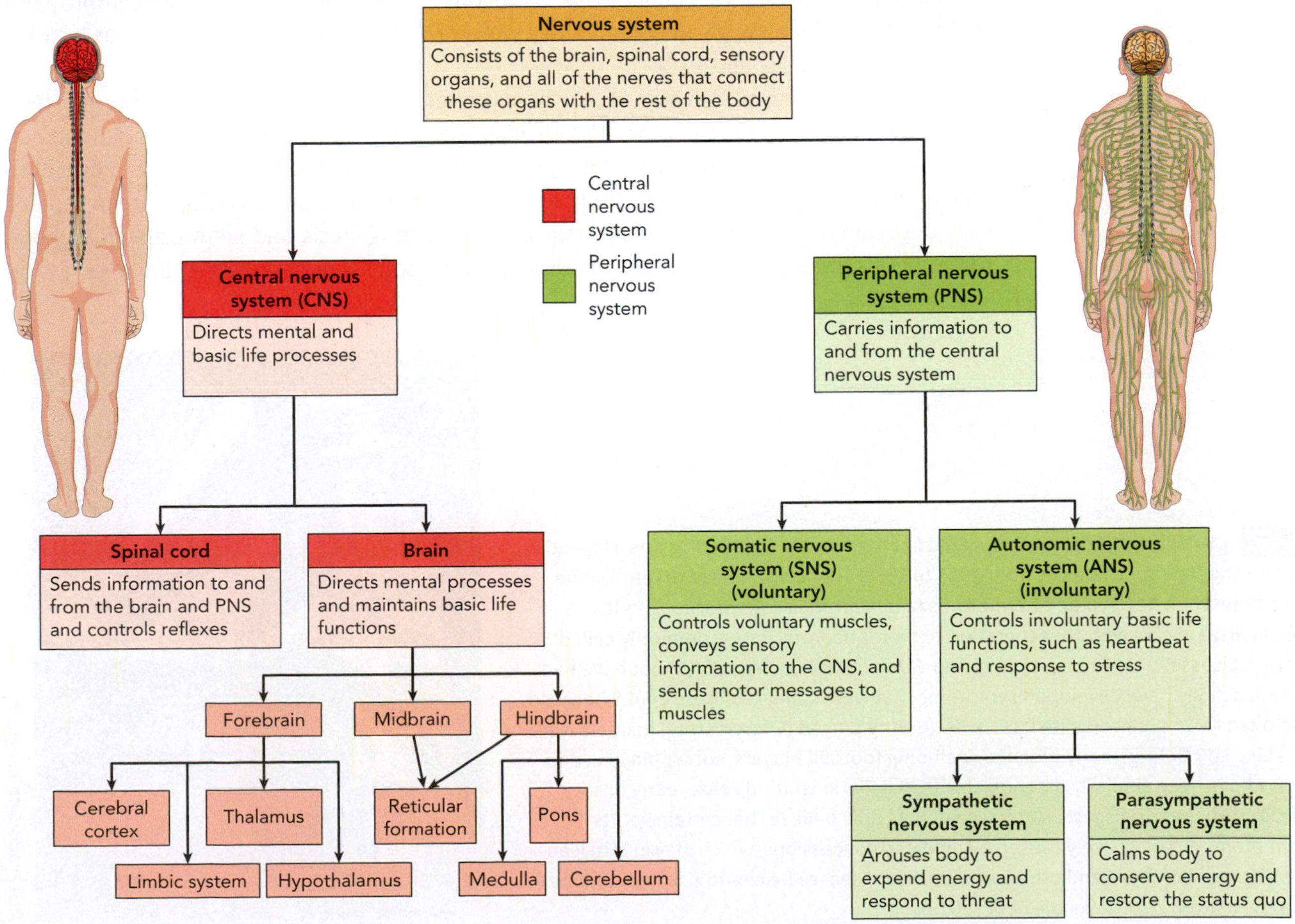

# Central Nervous System (CNS)

The central nervous system (CNS) is the branch of the nervous system that makes us unique. Most other animals can smell, run, see, and hear far better than we can. But thanks to our CNS, we can process information and adapt to our environment in ways that no other animal can. Unfortunately, our CNS is also incredibly fragile. Unlike neurons in the PNS, which often are able to regenerate, neurons in the CNS can suffer serious and permanent damage. As we'll see later in this chapter, repeated head trauma, particularly when associated with loss of consciousness, can lead to debilitating and potentially fatal illnesses (**Figure 2.6**).

Note, though, that the brain may not be as "hardwired" and fragile as we once thought. In the past, scientists believed that after the first two or three years of life, damaged neurons within the brain or spinal cord of most animals, including humans, were impossible to repair or replace. However, we now know that the brain is capable of lifelong *neuroplasticity* and *neurogenesis*.

### Neuroplasticity

**Neuroplasticity** The brain's lifelong ability to reorganize and change its structure and function by forming new neural connections.

Rather than being a fixed, solid organ, the brain is capable of changing its structure and function as a result of usage and experience (Garnier et al., 2017; Månsson et al., 2017; Presti, 2016). This "rewiring," officially known as **neuroplasticity**, is what makes our brains so wonderfully adaptive. In later chapters, we'll discuss how neuroplasticity remodels our brains after learning and experience. But here we'll look at how it helps the brain modify itself after damage. For example, when infants suffer damage to the speech area of their left hemisphere, the right hemisphere can reorganize and pick up some language abilities. Remarkably, this rewiring has even helped "remodel" the adult brain following strokes. Psychologist Edward Taub and his colleagues (2004, 2014) have had notable success working with stroke patients (**Figure 2.7**).

### Neurogenesis

**Neurogenesis** The formation (generation) of new neurons.

Whereas *neuroplasticity* refers to the brain's ability to reorganize and restructure itself, **neurogenesis** is achieved through the formation (generation) of new neurons in the brain. It's important and encouraging to know that accumulating research finds regular, moderate physical exercise can increase neurogenesis, particularly in the hippocampus, and thereby improve memory function and help prevent cognitive decline (Ma et al., 2017; Nokia et al., 2016; Suwabe et al., 2017).

**Stem cells** Immature (uncommitted) cells that have the potential to develop into almost any type of cell, depending on the chemical signals they receive.

What actually causes neurogenesis? The source of these newly created cells is **stem cells**—rare, immature cells that can grow and develop into any type of cell. Their fate depends on the chemical signals they receive. Experiments and clinical trials on both human and nonhuman animals have used stem cells for bone marrow transplants and to repopulate or replace cells devastated by injury or disease. Research on neurogenesis and stem cells offers hope to patients suffering from strokes, Alzheimer's, Parkinson's, epilepsy, stress, and depression

**FIGURE 2.6** **Lou Gehrig's disease or repeated head trauma?** Lou Gehrig was a legendary player for the New York Yankees from 1925 to 1939. Tragically, he had to retire while still in his prime when he developed symptoms of *amyotrophic lateral sclerosis (ALS)*, a neurological disease caused by degeneration of motor neurons (later commonly called "Lou Gehrig's disease"). However, scientists now think that Lou Gehrig may not have had ALS. Instead, he may have developed symptoms that were similar to those of ALS because he was so often hit in the head with baseballs. (Gehrig played before batting helmets were required.) Like Lou Gehrig, many athletes, including football players, soccer players, and boxers, may have been similarly diagnosed with ALS, Parkinson's disease, early onset dementia, or Alzheimer's disease. Many researchers now believe that certain sports-related symptoms are most likely caused by repeated concussions, which may in turn lead to the development of these and other serious brain diseases (Ascherio & Schwarzschild, 2016; Eade & Heaton, 2016; Tweedie et al., 2016).

MLB Photos/Getty Images, Inc.

(Belkind-Gerson et al., 2016; Eyo et al., 2017; Khan & He, 2017). In addition, stem cell injections into the eyes of patients with untreatable eye diseases and severe visual problems have led to dramatic improvements in vision (Fahnehjelm et al., 2016; Song & Bharti, 2016).

Could stem cell transplants allow people paralyzed from spinal cord injuries to walk again? Scientists have had some success transplanting stem cells into spinal cord–injured nonhuman animals (Gao et al., 2016; Raynald et al., 2016; Sandner et al., 2015). When the damaged spinal cord was viewed several weeks later, the implanted cells had survived and spread throughout the injured area. Even more encouraging, the transplant animals also showed some improvement in previously paralyzed parts of their bodies. Medical researchers are also testing the safety of embryonic stem cell therapy for human paralysis patients, and future trials may determine whether these cells will repair damaged spinal cords and/or improve sensation and movement in paralyzed areas (Granger et al., 2014; Presti, 2016; Robbins, 2013).

Before going on, it's important to note that neuroplasticity and neurogenesis are NOT the same as *neuroregeneration*, which refers to the regrowth or repair of neurons, glia, or synapses. This process is fairly common within the peripheral nervous system. You've undoubtedly watched a cut heal on your skin and/or known of someone who slowly regained his or her feeling and function after a serious motor vehicle accident or severe fall. In contrast, regeneration after damage within the central nervous system is far less common. However, scientists have made significant advances in promoting axon growth, preventing scar formation, and enhancing compensatory growth on uninjured neurons. In addition, you'll be happy to know that relatively simple mental skills training and physical exercise have significant benefits for our brains, including increasing neurogenesis and helping to prevent the cognitive declines associated with disorders such as Alzheimer's disease and Parkinson's disease (DiFeo & Shors, 2017; Jang et al., 2016; Ma et al., 2017).

Now that we've discussed neuroplasticity and neurogenesis within the central nervous system, let's take a closer look at the spinal cord. Because of its central importance for psychology and behavior, we'll discuss the brain in more detail in the next major section.

Courtesy Taub Therapy Clinc/UAB Media Relations

**FIGURE 2.7**   **A breakthrough in neuroscience**   By immobilizing the unaffected arm or leg and requiring rigorous and repetitive exercise of the affected limb, psychologist Edward Taub and colleagues "recruit" stroke patients' intact brain cells to take over for damaged cells (Taub et al., 2004, 2014). The therapy has restored function in some patients as long as 21 years after their strokes.

### Spinal Cord

**Spinal Cord**   Beginning at the base of our brains and continuing down our backs, the spinal cord carries vital information from the rest of the body into and out of the brain. But the spinal cord doesn't simply relay messages. It can also initiate certain automatic behaviors on its own. We call these involuntary, automatic behaviors **reflexes**, or *reflex arcs*, because the response to the incoming stimuli is automatically sent to the spinal cord and then "reflected" back to the appropriate muscles. This allows an immediate action response without the delay of routing signals first to the brain.

As you can see in the simple reflex arc depicted in **Step-by-Step Diagram 2.3**, a sensory receptor first responds to stimulation and initiates a neural impulse that travels to the spinal cord. This signal then travels back to the appropriate muscle, which reflexively contracts. The response is automatic and immediate in a reflex because the signal travels only as far as the spinal cord before action is initiated, not all the way to the brain. The brain is later "notified" of the action when the spinal cord sends along the message.

**Reflex**   An innate, automatic response to a stimulus that has biological relevance for an organism (e.g., the knee-jerk reflex).

---

**STEP-BY-STEP DIAGRAM 2.3**   **How the Spinal Reflex Operates**

**STOP!** This Step-by-Step Diagram contains essential information NOT found elsewhere in the text, which is likely to appear on quizzes and exams. Be sure to study it CAREFULLY!

In a simple reflex arc, a sensory receptor responds to stimulation and initiates a neural impulse that travels to the spinal cord. This signal then travels back to the appropriate muscle, which reflexively contracts. Note that the reflex response is automatic and immediate because the signal only travels as far as the spinal cord before action is initiated, not all the way to the brain. The brain is later "notified" when the spinal cord sends along the message, which, in this case of the hot pan, leads to a perception of pain. What might be the evolutionary advantages of the reflex arc?

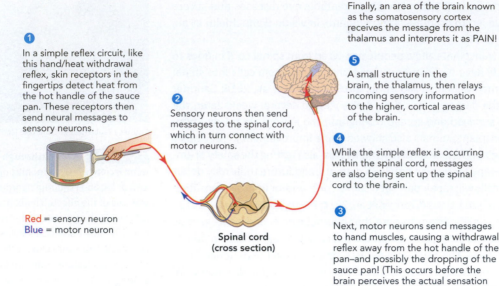

**1** In a simple reflex circuit, like this hand/heat withdrawal reflex, skin receptors in the fingertips detect heat from the hot handle of the sauce pan. These receptors then send neural messages to sensory neurons.

**2** Sensory neurons then send messages to the spinal cord, which in turn connect with motor neurons.

**6** Finally, an area of the brain known as the somatosensory cortex receives the message from the thalamus and interprets it as PAIN!

**5** A small structure in the brain, the thalamus, then relays incoming sensory information to the higher, cortical areas of the brain.

**4** While the simple reflex is occurring within the spinal cord, messages are also being sent up the spinal cord to the brain.

**3** Next, motor neurons send messages to hand muscles, causing a withdrawal reflex away from the hot handle of the pan—and possibly the dropping of the sauce pan! (This occurs before the brain perceives the actual sensation of pain.)

Red = sensory neuron
Blue = motor neuron

**Spinal cord (cross section)**

We're all born with numerous reflexes, many of which fade over time (see the **Try This Yourself**). But even as adults, we still blink in response to a puff of air in our eyes, gag when something touches the back of the throat, and urinate and defecate in response to pressure in the bladder and rectum.

Reflexes even influence our sexual responses. Certain stimuli, such as the stroking of the genitals, can lead to arousal and the reflexive muscle contractions of orgasm in both men and women. However, in order for us to have the passion, thoughts, and emotion we normally associate with sex, the sensory information from the stroking and orgasm must be carried on to the appropriate areas of the brain that receive and interpret these specific sensory messages.

## Try This Yourself

### Testing for Reflexes

If you have a newborn or young infant in your home, you can easily (and safely) test for these simple reflexes. (Most infant reflexes disappear within the first year of life. If they reappear in later life, it generally indicates damage to the central nervous system.)

### Test Your Critical Thinking

1. What might happen if infants lacked these reflexes?

2. Can you explain why most infant reflexes disappear within the first year?

photos by Linnea Leaver Mavrides/Courtesy Catherine Sanderson

**Ⓐ Rooting reflex**
Lightly stroke the cheek or side of the mouth, and watch how the infant automatically (reflexively) turns toward the stimulation and attempts to suck.

photos by Linnea Leaver Mavrides/Courtesy Catherine Sanderson

**Ⓑ Grasping reflex**
Place your finger or an object in the infant's palm and note his or her automatic grasping reflex.

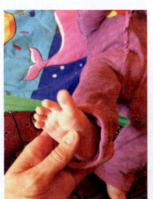

photos by Linnea Leaver Mavrides/Courtesy Catherine Sanderson

**Ⓒ Babinski reflex**
Lightly stroke the sole of the infant's foot, and the big toe will move toward the top of the foot, while the other toes fan out.

# Peripheral Nervous System (PNS)

The peripheral nervous system (PNS) is just what it sounds like—the part that involves nerves *peripheral* to (or outside) the brain and spinal cord. The chief function of the PNS is to carry information to and from the central nervous system (CNS). It links the brain and spinal cord to the body's sense receptors, muscles, and glands.

Looking back at Figure 2.5, note that the PNS consists of two separate subdivisions. The first, the **somatic nervous system (SNS)**, consists of all the nerves that connect to sensory receptors and skeletal muscles. The name comes from the term *soma*, which means "body," and the SNS plays a key role in communication throughout the entire body. As you recall from Step-by-Step Diagram 2.3, the SNS (also called the skeletal nervous system) first carries sensory information to the brain and spinal cord (CNS) and then carries messages from the CNS to skeletal muscles.

The other subdivision of the PNS is the **autonomic nervous system (ANS)**. The ANS is responsible for involuntary tasks, such as heart rate, digestion, pupil dilation, and breathing. Like an automatic pilot, the ANS can sometimes be consciously overridden. But as its name implies, the autonomic system normally operates on its own (autonomously).

The ANS is further divided into two branches, the sympathetic and parasympathetic, which tend to work in opposition to each other to regulate the functioning of such target organs as the heart, the intestines, and the lungs (**Figure 2.8**). Like two children on a teeter-totter, one will be up while the other is down, but they essentially balance each other out.

**Somatic nervous system (SNS)**
The subdivision of the peripheral nervous system (PNS) that connects the central nervous system (CNS) to sensory receptors and controls skeletal muscles.

**Autonomic nervous system (ANS)**
The subdivision of the peripheral nervous system (PNS) that controls the body's involuntary motor responses; it connects the sensory receptors to the central nervous system (CNS) and the CNS to the smooth muscle, cardiac muscle, and glands.

**FIGURE 2.8** **Actions of the autonomic nervous system (ANS)** The ANS is responsible for a variety of independent (autonomous) activities, such as salivation and digestion. It exercises this control through its two divisions—the sympathetic and parasympathetic branches.

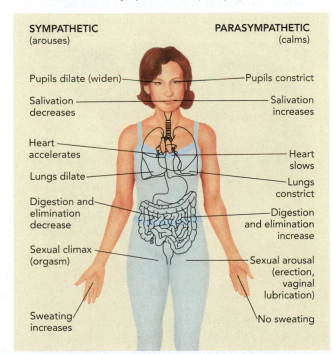

SYMPATHETIC (arouses)          PARASYMPATHETIC (calms)

Pupils dilate (widen) — Pupils constrict
Salivation decreases — Salivation increases
Heart accelerates — Heart slows
Lungs dilate — Lungs constrict
Digestion and elimination decrease — Digestion and elimination increase
Sexual climax (orgasm) — Sexual arousal (erection, vaginal lubrication)
Sweating increases — No sweating

Parasympathetic dominance

Geri Lavrov/Photographer's Choice/Getty Images, In

Sympathetic dominance

Beto Hacker/Getty Images, Inc.

## Study Tip

*One way to differentiate the two subdivisions of the ANS is to imagine skydiving out of an airplane. When you initially jump, your sympathetic nervous system has "sympathy" for your stressful situation. It alerts and prepares you for immediate action. Once your "para" chute opens, your "para" sympathetic nervous system takes over, and you can relax as you float safely to earth.*

**Sympathetic nervous system**
The subdivision of the autonomic nervous system (ANS) that is responsible for arousing the body and mobilizing its energy during times of stress; also called the "fight-flight-freeze" system.

**Parasympathetic nervous system** The subdivision of the autonomic nervous system (ANS) that is responsible for calming the body and conserving energy.

During stressful times, either mental or physical, the **sympathetic nervous system** arouses and mobilizes bodily resources to respond to the stressor. This emergency response is often called the "fight or flight" response. (Note this response has recently been expanded and relabeled as the "fight-flight-freeze" response, which will be fully discussed in Chapter 3.) If you noticed a dangerous snake coiled and ready to strike, your sympathetic nervous system would increase your heart rate, respiration, and blood pressure; stop your digestive and eliminative processes; and release hormones, such as cortisol, into the bloodstream. The net result of sympathetic activation is to get more oxygenated blood and energy to the skeletal muscles, thus allowing you to cope with the stress—to either fight or flee.

In contrast to the sympathetic nervous system, the **parasympathetic nervous system** is responsible for calming our bodies and conserving energy. It returns our normal bodily functions by slowing our heart rate, lowering our blood pressure, and increasing our digestive and eliminative processes.

The sympathetic nervous system provides an adaptive, evolutionary advantage. At the beginning of human evolution, when we faced a dangerous bear or an aggressive human attacker, there were only three reasonable responses—fight, flight, or freeze. The automatic mobilization of bodily resources can still be critical, even in modern times. However, less life-threatening events, such as traffic jams, also activate our sympathetic nervous system. As the next chapter discusses, ongoing sympathetic system response to such chronic, daily stress can become detrimental to our health. For a look at how the autonomic nervous system affects our sexual lives, see **Figure 2.9**.

**FIGURE 2.9** **Autonomic nervous system and sexual arousal** The complexities of sexual interaction—and, in particular, the difficulties couples sometimes have in achieving sexual arousal or orgasm—illustrate the balancing act between the sympathetic and parasympathetic nervous systems.

Piotr Marcinski/Shutterstock

© 4774344sean/iStockphoto

**a. Parasympathetic dominance** Sexual arousal and excitement require that the body be relaxed enough to allow increased blood flow to the genitals—in other words, the nervous system must be in *parasympathetic dominance*. Parasympathetic nerves carry messages from the central nervous system directly to the sexual organs, allowing for a localized response (increased blood flow and genital arousal).

**b. Sympathetic dominance** During strong emotions, such as anger, anxiety, or fear, the body shifts to *sympathetic dominance*, which causes blood flow to the genitals and other organs to decrease because the body is preparing for "fight, flight, or freeze." As a result, the person is unable (or less likely) to become sexually aroused. Any number of circumstances—performance anxiety, fear of unwanted pregnancy or disease, or tensions between partners—can trigger sympathetic dominance.

© Billy R. Ray/Wiley

## Retrieval Practice 2.2 | Nervous System Organization

Completing this self-test and connections section, and then checking your answers by clicking on the answer button or by looking in Appendix B, will provide immediate feedback and helpful practice for exams.

### Self-Test

1. Fill in the blank lines.

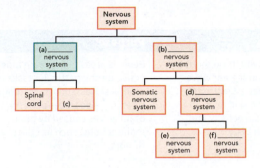

2. The central nervous system _____.

   a. consists of the brain and spinal cord
   b. is responsible for the fight-flight-freeze response
   c. includes the automatic and somatic nervous systems
   d. has all these characteristics

3. The peripheral nervous system is _____.

   a. composed of the spinal cord and peripheral nerves
   b. less important than the central nervous system
   c. contained within the skull and spinal column
   d. a combination of all the nerves and neurons outside the brain and spinal cord

4. The _____ nervous system is responsible for the fight-flight-freeze response, whereas the _____ nervous system is responsible for maintaining or restoring calm.

   a. central; peripheral
   b. parasympathetic; sympathetic
   c. sympathetic; parasympathetic
   d. autonomic; somatic

5. If you are startled by the sound of a loud explosion, the _____ nervous system will become dominant.

   a. semiautomatic       b. afferent
   c. parasympathetic     d. sympathetic

### Connections—Chapter to Chapter

Answering the following question will help you "look back and look ahead" to see the important connections among the various subfields of psychology and chapters within this text.

In Chapter 1 (Introduction and Research Methods), you discovered that psychologists are very concerned with following strict ethical guidelines in conducting research. In this chapter, you have learned that damage to neurons in the CNS can lead to serious and permanent damage. Consider the ethical guidelines requiring *informed consent* and *voluntary participation*. Can individuals with impaired memory or serious brain injury understand their rights as research participants? Discuss how psychologists studying these conditions might address possible ethical concerns.

---

## 2.3 | A Tour Through the Brain

### LEARNING OBJECTIVES

**Retrieval Practice**   While reading the upcoming sections, respond to each Learning Objective in your own words.

**Review the tools used in biological research, along with the brain's key structures and functions.**

- **Identify** the tools neuroscientists use to study the brain and nervous system.
- **Describe** the major structures of the hindbrain, midbrain, and forebrain, as well as their respective functions.

---

*The brain is the last and grandest biological frontier, the most complex thing we have yet discovered in our universe. It contains hundreds of billions of cells interlinked through trillions of connections. The brain boggles the mind.*                    —James Watson
(American Biologist, Geneticist, Co-discoverer of DNA's Structure)

Ancient cultures, including those of the Egyptians, Indians, and Chinese, believed the heart was the center of all thoughts and emotions. Today, we know that the brain and the rest of the nervous system are the center of virtually all parts of our life.

We begin our exploration of the brain with a discussion of the tools that neuroscientists use to study it. Then we offer a quick tour of the brain, beginning at its lower end, where the spinal cord joins the base of the brain, and then moving upward, all the way to the top of the skull. As we move from bottom to top, "lower," basic processes, such as breathing, generally give way to more complex mental processes.

## Biological Tools for Research

How do we know how the brain and nervous system work? We use a variety of tools, including those shown in **Table 2.2**. Interestingly, scientists in early times sought answers by *dissecting* the brains and other body parts of human and nonhuman animals. They also used *lesioning* techniques (systematically destroying bodily tissue to study the effects on behavior and mental processes). By the mid-1800s, this research had produced a basic map of the nervous system, including some

**TABLE 2.2    Sample Tools for Biological Research**

| | Tool | Description | Purpose |
|---|---|---|---|
| Larry Mulvehill/Science Source | **EEG (electroencephalogram)** | Electrical activity throughout the brain sweeps in regular waves across its surface. Electrodes attached to the skin or scalp detect this brain activity and record it on an EEG. | Reveals areas of the brain most active during particular tasks or mental states, such as reading or sleeping; also traces abnormal brain waves caused by brain malfunctions, such as epilepsy or tumors. |
| Mehau Kulyk/Science Source | **CT (computed tomography) scan** | Computer-created cross-sectional X-rays of the brain or other parts of the body produce 3-D images. Least expensive type of imaging and widely used in research. | Reveals the effects of strokes, injuries, tumors, and other brain disorders. The CT scan shown on the left used X-rays to locate a brain tumor, which is the deep purple mass at the top left. |
| N.I. H/Science Source | **PET (positron emission tomography) scan** | A radioactive form of glucose is injected into the bloodstream; a scanner records the amount of glucose used in particularly active areas of the brain and produces a computer-constructed picture of the brain like the one on the left. | Originally designed to detect abnormalities, now used to identify brain areas active during ordinary activities (such as reading or singing). |
| Scott Camazine/Science Source | **MRI (magnetic resonance imaging)** | Using a powerful magnet and radio waves linked to a computer, a scanner creates detailed, cross-sectional images. Note the fissures and internal structures of the brain shown on the left. The throat, nasal airways, and fluid surrounding the brain are dark. | Produces high-resolution 3-D pictures of the brain useful for identifying abnormalities and mapping brain structures and function. |
| Science Photo Library/ Science Source | **fMRI (functional magnetic resonance imaging)** | Newer, faster version of MRI that detects blood flow by picking up magnetic signals from blood that has given up its oxygen to activate brain cells, shown on the left. The yellow-highlighted areas in this fMRI are "lit up," which tells us that oxygen from the blood is being heavily used in these regions. | Measures blood flow, which indicates areas of the brain that are active and inactive during ordinary behaviors or responses (like reading or talking); also shows changes associated with various disorders. |
| | **Other methods**<br>(a) Cell body or tract (myelin) staining<br>(b) Microinjections<br>(c) Intrabrain electrical recordings | (a) Colors/stains selected neurons or nerve fibers.<br>(b) Injects chemicals into specific areas of the brain.<br>(c) Records activity of one or a group of neurons inside the brain. | Increase overall information of structure and function through direct observation and measurement. Intrabrain wire probes allow scientists to "see" individual neuron activity. |

areas of the brain. Early researchers also relied on clinical observations and case studies of living people who had experienced injuries, diseases, or disorders that affected brain functioning.

Modern researchers still use such methods, but they also employ other techniques that allow them to "look inside" the healthy human brain while it's at work (see again Table 2.2). Most of these methods are relatively *noninvasive*—that is, their use does not involve breaking the skin or entering the body. Why are these modern techniques so important? Neuroscientists have likened their potential transformative effects to those of the telescope for astronomy and the microscope for biology. Thanks to fMRI brain scans, for example, we can now identify which of our brain areas are most active when we're listening to music, feeling angry or sad, or even thinking and planning ahead. We also can gain insights and potential answers to popular questions such as: "Does stress change our brains?" (See Chapter 3.) "Can we train our brains?" (Check out the *Psychology and Your Personal Success* at the end of this chapter.) And perhaps one of the most controversial questions of all, "Are male and female brains different"? (See the following **Gender and Cultural Diversity**.)

## Gender and Cultural Diversity

### Are Male and Female Brains Different?

Over the years, numerous physical differences have been reported between the brains of men and women. And, as you might imagine, the interpretations of these differences and of their significance are highly controversial. What are the facts? Research using brain scans, autopsies, and volumetric measurements has identified several structural and functional differences in the brains of men and women (e.g., Gur & Gur, 2016). For example, several studies have revealed sex differences in the hippocampus, which is critical to the formation and retrieval of memories (Duarte-Guterman et al., 2015; Scharfman & MacLusky, 2017). In addition, the corpus callosum, a band of tissue connecting the brain's two hemispheres, is correlated with manipulating spatial relationships, and there is a size differential here between men and women (Garrett, 2015; Newman, 2016). **Table 2.3** illustrates samples of the type of tasks researchers have used to demonstrate these and other reported sex differences.

Many scientists strongly support such studies of brain differences, saying that they greatly increase our understanding of both normal and pathological brain functioning and development (e.g., Biasibetti et al., 2017; Macey et al., 2016; McCarthy et al., 2012). Some critics, however, emphasize that sex differences in the brain are generally small, that there is considerable variation within groups of men and women, and that gender should not be seen as a strict, binary difference—either male or female (Hyde, 2016; Miller & Halpern, 2014; Richardson, 2015).

Unfortunately, studies of brain sex differences do lead some people to mistakenly believe that differences between men and women are *hardwired* and immutable to change. Can you see how this might increase prejudice and discrimination? And how a focus on brain differences might dissuade people from fighting to improve opportunities for women and men alike? Bear in mind that meta-analyses show that the two sexes are quite similar on most psychological variables (Hyde, 2016). And there is simply no scientific basis for believing that all, or even most, brain differences are hardwired. As you'll discover throughout this text, our brains are remarkably adaptive, and biological and environmental variables interact and influence one another throughout our lifespan—the *biopsychosocial model*.

**TABLE 2.3**  **Problem-Solving Tasks Reportedly Favoring Women and Men**

| Tasks Favoring Women | Tasks Favoring Men |
|---|---|
| **Perceptual speed:** As quickly as possible, identify matching items. | **Spatial tasks:** Mentally rotate the 3-D object to identify its match. |
| **Displaced objects:** After looking at the middle picture, tell which item is missing from the picture on the right. | **Spatial tasks:** Mentally manipulate the folded paper to tell where the holes will falls when it is unfolded. |
| **Verbal fluency:** List words that begin with the same letter. | **Target-directed motor skills:** Hit the bull's eye. |
| **Precision manual tasks:** Place the pegs in the holes as quickly as possible. | **Disembedding tests:** Find the simple shape on the left in the more complex figures. |

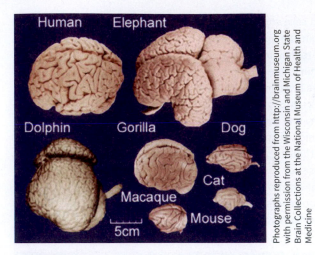

Photographs reproduced from http://brainmuseum.org with permission from the Wisconsin and Michigan State Brain Collections at the National Museum of Health and Medicine

**FIGURE 2.10** **Brain comparisons** In general, lower species (such as fish and reptiles) have smaller, less complex brains. The most complex brains belong to dolphins, whales, and higher primates (such as gorillas, chimps, and humans).

# Brain Organization

Having studied the tools scientists use for exploring the brain, we can now begin our tour. Let's talk first about brain size and complexity, which vary significantly from species to species (**Figure 2.10**). As in the brains of other animals, the billions of neurons that make up the human brain control much of what we think, feel, and do. Certain brain structures are specialized to perform certain tasks, a process known as *localization of function*. However, most parts of the brain perform integrating, overlapping functions.

As you can see in **Figure 2.11**, scientists typically divide and label the human brain into three major sections: the *hindbrain*, *midbrain*, and *forebrain*.

## Hindbrain
Picture this: You're asleep and in the middle of a frightening nightmare. Your heart is racing, your breathing is rapid, and you're attempting to run away but find you can't move! Suddenly, your nightmare is shattered by a buzzing alarm clock. All your automatic behaviors and survival responses in this scenario

**FIGURE 2.11** **The human brain** Note on the left side of this figure how the forebrain, midbrain, and hindbrain radically change in their size and placement during prenatal development. The profile drawing in the middle highlights key structures and functions of the right half of the adult brain. As you read about each of these structures, keep this drawing in mind and refer to it as necessary. (The diagram shows the brain structures as if the brain were split vertically down the center and the left hemisphere were removed.)

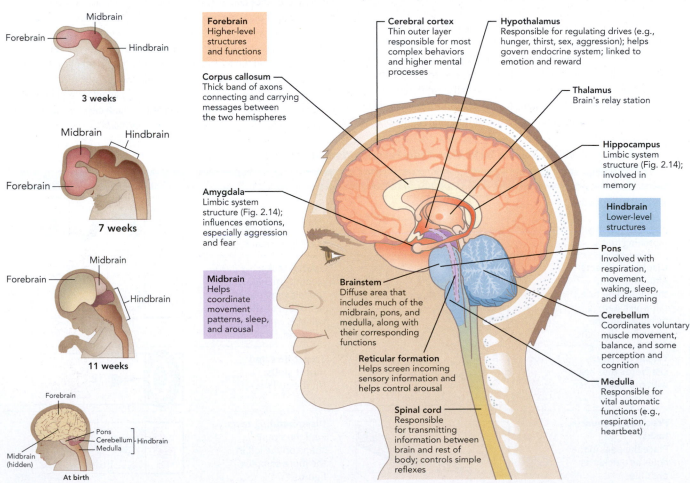

are controlled or influenced by parts of the hindbrain. The **hindbrain** includes the medulla, pons, and cerebellum.

The **medulla** is essentially an extension of the spinal cord, with many neural fibers passing through it carrying information to and from the brain. Because the medulla controls many essential automatic bodily functions, such as respiration and heart rate, serious damage to this area is most often fatal.

The **pons** is involved in respiration, movement, sleeping, waking, and dreaming (among other things). It also contains axons that cross from one side of the brain to the other (*pons* is Latin for "bridge").

The cauliflower-shaped **cerebellum** (Latin for "little brain") is, evolutionarily, a very old structure. It coordinates fine muscle movement and balance (**Figure 2.12**). Researchers using functional magnetic resonance imaging (fMRI) have shown that parts of the cerebellum also are important for memory, sensation, perception, cognition, language, learning, and even "multitasking" (Garrett, 2015; Ng et al., 2016; Presti, 2016). Interestingly, researchers have found that people who play video games for 30 minutes a day for two months show increases in gray matter in the cerebellum, right hippocampus, and right prefrontal cortex (Kühn et al., 2014). Gray matter is critical for higher cognitive functioning, and we'll describe these brain areas in more detail in the next section. For now it's enough to know that these brain sections are largely responsible for spatial navigation, strategic planning, and fine motor skills in the hands. In short, research suggests that playing video games may actually be good for your brain!

### Midbrain

The **midbrain** helps us orient our eye and body movements to visual and auditory stimuli, and it works with the pons to help control sleep and level of arousal. It also contains a small structure, the *substantia nigra*, that secretes the neurotransmitter dopamine. Parkinson's disease, an age-related degenerative condition, is related to the deterioration of neurons in the substantia nigra and the subsequent loss of dopamine.

Running through the core of the hindbrain and midbrain is the **reticular formation (RF)**. This diffuse, finger-shaped network of neurons helps screen incoming sensory information and alert the higher brain centers to critical events. Without our reticular formation, we would not be alert or perhaps even conscious.

Before going on, note that the reticular formation passes through the **brainstem**, a diffuse, stem-shaped area that includes much of the midbrain as well as the pons and medulla in the hindbrain (see again Figure 2.11). At its lower end, the brainstem connects with the spinal cord, and at its upper end it attaches to the thalamus.

### Forebrain

The **forebrain** is the largest and most prominent part of the human brain. It includes the cerebral cortex, limbic system, thalamus, and hypothalamus (**Figure 2.13**). The last three are located near the top of the brainstem. The cerebral cortex (discussed separately, in the next section) is wrapped above and around them. (*Cerebrum* is Latin for "brain," and *cortex* is Latin for "covering" or "bark.")

An interconnected group of forebrain structures, known as the **limbic system**, is located roughly along the border between the cerebral cortex and the lower-level brain structures (**Figure 2.14**). Although opinion is divided upon whether other structures, such as the hypothalamus and thalamus, should be included as part of the limbic system, its two most important structures are the hippocampus and amygdala. The limbic system is generally responsible for emotions, drives, and memory. In Chapter 7, you'll discover how the **hippocampus**, a key part of the limbic system, is involved in forming and retrieving our memories. However, the limbic system's major focus of interest is the **amygdala**, which is linked to the production and regulation of emotions—especially aggression and fear (Cohen et al., 2016; LeDoux, 1998, 2007; Månsson et al., 2017). Ironically, researchers have found supportive evidence within the amygdala

**FIGURE 2.12** **Walk the line** Asking drivers to perform tasks like walking the white line is a common part of a field sobriety test for possible intoxication. Why? The cerebellum, responsible for smooth and precise movements, is one of the first areas of the brain to be affected by alcohol.

*Getty Images, Inc.*

**Hindbrain** The lower or hind region of the brain; collection of structures including the medulla, pons, and cerebellum.

**Medulla** The hindbrain structure responsible for vital, automatic functions, such as respiration and heartbeat.

**Pons** The hindbrain structure involved in respiration, movement, waking, sleep, and dreaming.

**Cerebellum** The hindbrain structure responsible for coordinating fine muscle movement, balance, and some perception and cognition.

**Midbrain** The collection of structures in the middle of the brain responsible for coordinating movement patterns, sleep, and arousal.

**Reticular formation (RF)** A diffuse set of neurons that helps screen incoming information and helps control arousal.

**Brainstem** A diffuse, stem-shaped area of the brain, including much of the midbrain, pons, and medulla; responsible for automatic survival functions, such as respiration and heartbeat.

**Forebrain** A collection of upper-level brain structures including the cerebral cortex, limbic system, thalamus, and hypothalamus.

**Limbic system** The interconnected group of forebrain structures involved with emotions, drives, and memory; its two most important structures are the hippocampus and amygdala.

**Hippocampus** The seahorse-shaped part of the limbic system involved in forming and retrieving memories.

**Amygdala** A part of the limbic system linked to the production and regulation of emotions—especially aggression and fear.

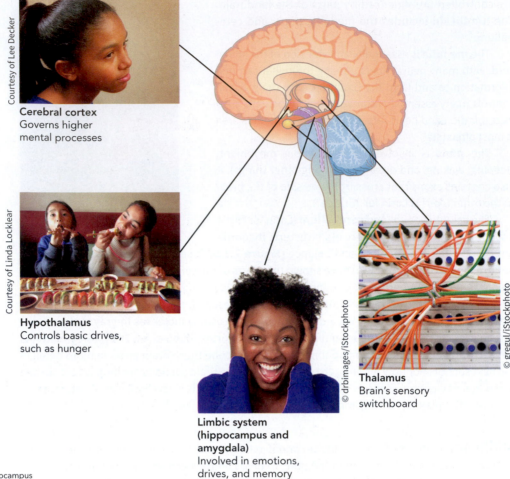

**FIGURE 2.13** Major structures of the forebrain

**Cerebral cortex**
Governs higher mental processes

Courtesy of Lee Decker

Courtesy of Linda Locklear

**Hypothalamus**
Controls basic drives, such as hunger

© drbimages/iStockphoto

**Limbic system (hippocampus and amygdala)**
Involved in emotions, drives, and memory

© gregul/iStockphoto

**Thalamus**
Brain's sensory switchboard

**Thalamus** The forebrain structure at the top of the brainstem that relays sensory messages to and from the cerebral cortex.

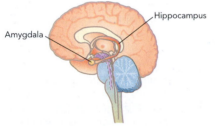

Hippocampus

Amygdala

**FIGURE 2.14** Key structures commonly associated with the limbic system

for a common parental warning—lying actually does seem to lead to more lies (see the following **Research Challenge**).

The **thalamus** is located at the top of the brainstem. It integrates input from the senses, and it may also function in learning and memory (Chiou et al., 2016; Wang et al., 2017; Zhou et al., 2016). The thalamus receives input from nearly all sensory systems, except smell, and then directs the information to the appropriate cortical areas. The thalamus also transmits some higher brain information to the cerebellum and medulla. Think

## Research Challenge

### Does Lying Lead to More Lies?

The short answer is yes! We now have scientific evidence that telling small lies desensitizes our brains to the associated negative emotions and may encourage us to tell bigger lies in the future (Garrett et al., 2016). In this particular study, the brains of 80 volunteer participants were scanned in an fMRI machine (see the photo) while they were shown pennies in a glass jar. Participants were then randomly assigned to different groups and given different incentives to lie about how much money they estimated that the jar contained. Their estimates were then sent via computer to an unseen partner.

In the baseline scenario, participants were told that aiming for the most accurate estimate would benefit both the participant and his or her partner. In various other conditions, overestimating or underestimating the amount would either benefit them at their

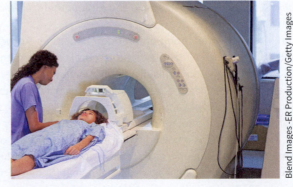

Blend Images -ER Production/Getty Images

partner's expense, would benefit both of them, would benefit their partner at their own expense, or would only benefit one of them with no effect on the other.

What do you think happened? When overestimating the amount would benefit the volunteer at the partner's expense, the volunteer started by slightly exaggerating his or her estimates, which in turn, elicited strong amygdala activation in the participant's brain. More importantly, as the experiment went on, participants' exaggerations escalated, but activation within the amygdala (shown by the fMRI scans) declined. How can this be explained? Just as our brains and nervous systems generally adapt to higher and higher levels of drugs (Chapter 5), the amygdala (which is responsible for emotional processing and arousal) apparently adapts and becomes desensitized to increasing levels of lying. In sum, we now have biological evidence (changes in the amygdala) for a so-called "slippery slope"—small lies often escalate to ever-larger ones.

**Test Yourself**

1. Based on the information provided, did the researchers in this study (Garrett et al., 2016) use descriptive, correlational, and/or experimental research?

2. If you chose:

    o *descriptive research*, is this a naturalistic observation, survey/interview, case study, and/or archival research?

    o *correlational research*, is this a positive, negative, and/or zero correlation?

    o *experimental research*, label the IV, DV, experimental group(s), and control group. (Note: If participants were not randomly assigned to groups, list it as a *quasi-experimental design*.)

    o both *descriptive* and *correlational*, answer the corresponding questions for both.

**Check your answers by clicking on the answer button or by looking in Appendix B.**

**Note:** The information provided in this study is admittedly limited, but the level of detail is similar to what is presented in most textbooks and public reports of research findings. Answering these questions, and then comparing your answers to those provided, will help you become a better critical thinker and consumer of scientific research.

---

of the thalamus as the switchboard in an air traffic control center that receives information from all aircraft and directs them to appropriate landing or takeoff areas.

Because the thalamus is the brain's major sensory relay center to the cerebral cortex, damage or abnormalities in the thalamus might cause the cortex to misinterpret or not receive vital sensory information. As you'll discover in Chapter 14, brain-imaging research links thalamus abnormalities to schizophrenia, a serious psychological disorder characterized by problems with sensory filtering and perception (Cho et al., 2016; Woodward & Heckers, 2016).

Beneath the thalamus lies the kidney bean–sized **hypothalamus**. (*Hypo-* means "under.") This organ has been called the "master control center" that helps govern drives, such as hunger, thirst, sex, and aggression, and hormones (e.g., Loveland & Fernald, 2017; Presti, 2016; Wright et al., 2016). See the following **Try This Yourself**, which explains how the hypothalamus affects weight and dieting.

Another well-known function of the hypothalamus is its role as part of the so-called "pleasure center," a set of brain structures whose stimulation leads to highly enjoyable feelings (Loonen & Ivanova, 2016; Naneix et al., 2016; Olds & Milner, 1954). Even though the hypothalamus and other structures and neurotransmitters are instrumental in emotions, the frontal lobes of the cerebral cortex also play an important role.

Hanging down from the hypothalamus, the *pituitary gland* is usually considered the "master endocrine gland" because it releases hormones that activate the other endocrine glands. The hypothalamus influences the pituitary through direct neural connections and through release of its own hormones into the blood supply of the pituitary.

**Hypothalamus** The small brain structure beneath the thalamus that helps govern drives (hunger, thirst, sex, and aggression) and hormones.

---

# Try This Yourself

### Diet and the Hypothalamus

Have you ever gone on a diet to try to lose weight or lost weight but then struggled to maintain your new weight? One of the reasons long-term weight loss is so hard for many people is that eating a high-fat diet can lead to long-term changes in the hypothalamus (Cordeira et al., 2014; Stamatakis et al., 2016; Zhang et al., 2015). These changes make it harder for the body to regulate its weight, meaning that you will continue to feel hungry even when you have just eaten plenty of food.

© donmedia/iStockphoto

© Billy R. Ray/Wiley

## Retrieval Practice 2.3 | A Tour Through the Brain

Completing this self-test and connections section, and then checking your answers by clicking on the answer button or by looking in Appendix B, will provide immediate feedback and helpful practice for exams.

**Self-Test**

1. Label the following structures/areas of the brain:

   a. corpus callosum
   b. amygdala
   c. cerebellum
   d. thalamus
   e. hippocampus
   f. cerebral cortex

2. Damage to the medulla can lead to loss of _____.

   a. vision                b. respiration
   c. hearing               d. smell

3. The pons, cerebellum, and the medulla are all _____.

   a. higher-level brain structures    b. cortical areas
   c. association areas                d. hindbrain structures

4. The brainstem is primarily involved with your _____.

   a. sense of smell and taste
   b. sense of touch and pain

   c. automatic survival functions
   d. emotional behavior

5. An interconnected group of forebrain structures particularly responsible for emotions is known as the _____.

   a. subcortical center
   b. homeostatic controller
   c. limbic system
   d. master endocrine gland

**Connections—Chapter to Chapter**

Answering the following question will help you "look back and look ahead" to see the important connections among the various subfields of psychology and chapters within this text.

In this chapter, you learned that the *limbic system* is a group of forebrain structures involved with memory and emotions (such as fear or pleasure). In Chapter 13 (Personality), you'll learn that activity in certain areas of the brain may contribute to some personality traits, such as shyness or extraversion. Explain how the limbic systems of shy or outgoing individuals might respond differently to unfamiliar people or situations.

## 2.4   The Cerebral Cortex

### LEARNING OBJECTIVES

**Retrieval Practice**   While reading the upcoming sections, respond to each Learning Objective in your own words.

**Summarize the key features and major divisions of the cerebral cortex.**

- **Discuss** the location and functions of the eight lobes of the cerebral cortex.
- **Describe** the brain's two specialized hemispheres and split-brain research.

*We sit on the threshold of important new advances in neuroscience that will yield increased understanding of how the brain functions and of more effective treatments to heal brain disorders and diseases. How the brain behaves in health and disease may well be the most important question in our lifetime.*

—Richard D. Broadwell (Neuroscientist, Author, Educator)

**Cerebral cortex**   The thin surface layer on the cerebral hemispheres that regulates most complex behavior, including sensations, motor control, and higher mental processes.

The gray, wrinkled **cerebral cortex**, the surface layer of the cerebral hemispheres, is responsible for most complex behaviors and higher mental processes (**Figure 2.15**). It plays such a vital role in human life that many consider it the essence of life. Without a functioning cortex, we would be almost completely unaware of ourselves and our surroundings.

Although the cerebral cortex is only about one-eighth of an inch thick, it's made up of approximately 30 billion neurons and nine times as many glial cells. Its numerous wrinkles, called *convolutions*, significantly increase its surface area. Interestingly, the amount of "wrinkling" or convolutions reflects the brain's functional complexity and information-processing capacity. This means that having fewer convolutions (a "smooth" brain) is correlated with lower levels of cognitive functioning (Tallinen et al., 2014).

**FIGURE 2.15** The cerebral cortex

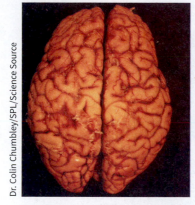

Dr. Colin Chumbley/SPL/Science Source

**a. A top-down view of the cerebral cortex** Looking at this photo of the top side of a human brain, all you can see is its outer, wrinkled surface, known as the cerebral cortex.

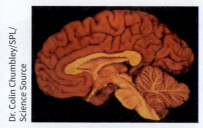

Dr. Colin Chumbley/SPL/Science Source

**b. A view inside the cerebral cortex** If you made a vertical cut along the center crevice of the brain, you would have this inside view of the right hemisphere. Note the wrinkled convolutions (folds) of the cerebral cortex around the top and the midbrain and hindbrain in the center and at the bottom.

NICHOLAS KAMM/AFP/Getty Images

**FIGURE 2.16** **Damage to the brain** A growing number of professional soccer organizations have enacted a new rule requiring doctors (instead of coaches) to determine whether a player can safely return to the game after experiencing a head injury. This rule was enacted following several high-profile cases in which players appeared to suffer concussions during World Cup games, yet quickly returned to the matches. In this photo, you see Morgan Brian of the U.S. Women's National Team colliding with another player in the semifinals of the 2015 Women's World Cup.

Damage to the cerebral cortex is linked to numerous problems, including suicide, substance abuse, and dementia (Flores et al., 2016; Presti, 2016; Sharma et al., 2015). Evidence suggests that such trauma is particularly common in athletes who experience head injuries in sports like football, ice hockey, boxing, and soccer (**Figure 2.16**).

Have you watched brain surgeries in movies or on television? After the skull is opened, you'll first see a gray, wrinkled, cerebral cortex that closely resembles an oversized walnut. Also like a walnut, the cortex has a division, or *fissure*, down the center marking the separation between the left and right *hemispheres* of the brain, which make up about 80% of the brain's weight. The hemispheres are mostly filled with axon connections between the cortex and the other brain structures. Each hemisphere controls the opposite side of the body (**Figure 2.17**).

## Lobes of the Brain

Each cerebral hemisphere is divided into four distinct areas, or lobes (**Figure 2.18**). To help you remember these areas, picture their relative locations—frontal lobes (behind your forehead), temporal lobes (above your ears), occipital lobes (back of your head) and parietal lobes (at the top and back of your head). Like the lower-level brain structures, the lobes specialize in somewhat different tasks, another example of localization of function. However, some functions overlap two or more lobes.

**Frontal Lobes** By far the largest of the cortical lobes, the two **frontal lobes** are generally what we think of as "the mind" because they're responsible for at least three major functions:

1. *Higher cognitive processes* Our frontal lobes control most complex cognitive processes, including **executive functions (EFs)**, intelligence, and personality. Research conducted by our famous introductory figure, Adele Diamond, suggests that EFs are composed of three major abilities—*cognitive flexibility* ("thinking outside the box"), *working memory*, and *impulse control*. She also believes that EFs are crucial for success in all parts of life, and her work with children has shown that they can be developed and improved with practice (Diamond, 2013, 2016).

2. *Speech production* Broca's area, located in the *left* frontal lobe near the bottom of the motor control area, plays a crucial role in speech production. In 1865, French physician

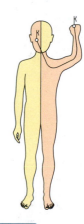

**FIGURE 2.17** **Information crossover** Our brains' right hemisphere controls the left side of our bodies, whereas the left hemisphere controls the right side.

**Frontal lobes** The two lobes at the front of the brain involved in higher cognitive processes, speech production, and voluntary motor control.

**Executive functions (EFs)** A set of higher-order cognitive processes controlled by the frontal lobes.

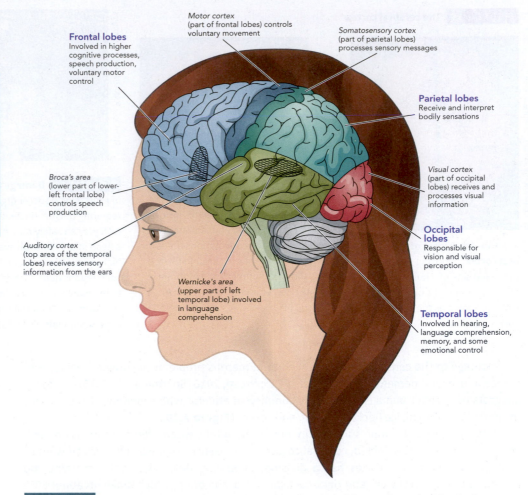

Motor cortex
(part of frontal lobes) controls
voluntary movement

Somatosensory cortex
(part of parietal lobes)
processes sensory messages

**Frontal lobes**
Involved in higher
cognitive processes,
speech production,
voluntary motor
control

**Parietal lobes**
Receive and interpret
bodily sensations

Broca's area
(lower part of lower-
left frontal lobe)
controls speech
production

Visual cortex
(part of occipital
lobes) receives and
processes visual
information

Auditory cortex
(top area of the temporal
lobes) receives sensory
information from the ears

**Occipital
lobes**
Responsible for
vision and visual
perception

Wernicke's area
(upper part of left
temporal lobe) involved
in language
comprehension

**Temporal lobes**
Involved in hearing,
language comprehension,
memory, and some
emotional control

**FIGURE 2.18** **Lobes of the brain** This is a view of the brain's left hemisphere showing its four lobes—*frontal, parietal, temporal*, and *occipital*. The right hemisphere has the same four lobes. Divisions between the lobes are marked by visibly prominent folds. Keep in mind that Broca's and Wernicke's areas occur only in the left hemisphere.

**Motor cortex** A region at the back of the frontal lobes responsible for voluntary movement.

Moxie Production/Getty Images

**FIGURE 2.19** **Can high-fat foods decrease cognitive efficiency?** We've all heard numerous warnings about the dangers of high-fat foods. Now we have scientific evidence that they even increase the chances of cognitive and psychiatric problems in later life—especially if these foods are consumed during the teen years (Labouesse et al., 2017). Why? Apparently, these foods deplete levels of a key protein that helps synapses in the frontal lobes function properly.

Paul Broca discovered that damage to this area causes difficulty in speech, but not language comprehension (see the **Study Tip**). This type of impaired language ability is known as Broca's aphasia.

3. *Voluntary motor control* At the very back of the frontal lobes lies the **motor cortex**, which sends messages to the various muscles that instigate voluntary movement. When you want to call your friend on your cell phone, the motor control area of your frontal lobes guides your fingers to press the desired sequence of numbers.

As you might imagine, damage to the frontal lobes seriously affects motivation, drives, creativity, self-awareness, initiative, and reasoning. In addition, individuals suffering from schizophrenia (Chapter 14) often show loss of tissue and abnormal brain activity in the frontal lobes (DeRosse et al., 2015; Lake et al., 2016; Watsky et al., 2016). Surprisingly, researchers have even found that a high-fat diet (particularly during adolescence) can negatively affect synapses in the frontal lobes (see **Figure 2.19**).

On a more encouraging note, updated information on the famous case of Phineas Gage, which is discussed in the following **Research Challenge**, indicates that damage to the frontal lobes may not be as permanent as we once thought, thanks to the two processes we discussed earlier— *neuroplasticity* and *neurogenesis*. Further good news regarding the power of your frontal lobes can be found in the **Psychology and Your Personal Success** following the Research Challenge.

## Research Challenge

### Phineas Gage—Myths Versus Facts

In 1848, a 25-year-old railroad foreman named Phineas Gage had a metal rod (13½ pounds, 3 feet 7 inches long, and 1¼ inches in diameter) accidentally blown through the front of his face, destroying much of his brain's left frontal lobe. Amazingly, Gage was immediately able to sit up, speak, and move around, and he did not receive medical treatment until about 1½ hours later. After his wound healed, he tried to return to work, but was soon fired. The previously friendly, efficient, and capable foreman was now "fitful, impatient, and lacking in deference to his fellows" (Macmillan, 2000). In the words of his friends: "Gage was no longer Gage" (Harlow, 1868).

This so-called "American Crowbar Case" is often cited in current texts and academic papers as one of the earliest in-depth studies of an individual's survival after massive damage to the brain's frontal lobes. The evidence is clear that Gage did experience several dramatic changes in his behavior and personality after the accident, but the extent and permanence of these changes are in dispute. Most accounts of post-accident Gage report him as impulsive and unreliable until his death. However, more reliable evidence later showed that Gage spent many years driving stagecoaches—a job that required high motor, cognitive, and interpersonal skills (Griggs, 2015; Macmillan & Lena, 2010).

So why bother reporting this controversy? As you'll note throughout this text, we discuss several popular misconceptions in psychology in order to clarify and correct them. Phineas Gage's story is particularly significant because it highlights how a small set of reliable facts can be distorted and shaped to fit existing beliefs and scientific theories. For example, at the time of Gage's accident, little was known about how the brain functions, and damage to it was believed to be largely irreversible. Do you see how our current research techniques, along with our new understanding of *neurogenesis* and *neuroplasticity*, might explain the previously ignored evidence of Gage's significant recovery in later life?

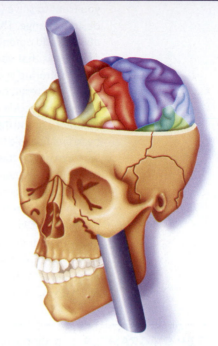

#### Test Yourself

1. Based on the information provided, did the various studies focusing on Phineas Gage use descriptive, correlational, and/or experimental research?

2. If you chose:

   - *descriptive research*, is this a naturalistic observation, survey/interview, case study, and/or archival research?

   - *correlational research*, is this a positive, negative, and or zero correlation?

   - *experimental research*, label the IV, DV, experimental group(s), and control group. (Note: If participants were not randomly assigned to groups, list it as a *quasi-experimental design*.)

   - both *descriptive* and *correlational*, answer the corresponding questions for both.

Check your answers by clicking on the answer button or by looking in Appendix B.

**Note:** The information provided in this study is admittedly limited, but the level of detail is similar to what is presented in most textbooks and public reports of research findings. Answering these questions, and then comparing your answers to those provided, will help you become a better critical thinker and consumer of scientific research.

## ❖ Psychology and Your Personal Success | How to Train Your Brain

Did you know that "enjoying life to the fullest" and "living a healthier lifestyle" were the top two New Year's resolutions in January 2016, yet by the second week of February about 80% of these resolutions had failed (Luciani, 2015; Quinn, 2016)? Being a college student, you'd probably add something about studying more, partying less, and so on—goals you're also unlikely to meet. Why? The general answer is faulty brain training! The good news is that by understanding your frontal lobes, you now have the power to create positive brain training that leads to lasting, healthy changes in your life.

As you can see in **Step-by-Step Diagram 2.4,** making a change in your life begins within your brain's frontal lobes (Step 1). Using your *executive functions*, first identify the problem you want to solve (a behavior you want to change). Next, develop a plan for implementing the desired change. Then activate your "I can do it" *growth mindset* (by reminding yourself of your abilities and potential for change and improvement—Chapter 1). For example, if your identified problem is that you need to study more to achieve your long-term goals, you might start by self-monitoring and keeping careful notes of what you do throughout a typical day.

If, as a result of the self-monitoring, you notice that you watch television every night instead of studying, decide what you need to do to increase your impulse control, delay your gratification (Chapter 12), and then implement the new behavior (Step 2). One way to accomplish all of this might be to create a rule that you cannot turn on your television until you've studied for an hour. You can later expand on this rule by thinking flexibly and maybe adding another alternative rule that you can only check your e-mail or social media after studying for 10 minutes. Keep in mind that these rewards should be small, immediate, and presented AFTER the appropriate behavior (Chapter 6).

In Step 3, remind yourself that in addition to a growth mindset the other major key to achievement is *grit*—perseverance and passion in pursuing long-term goals (Chapter 1). To increase your grit, frequently remind yourself that you deeply want to achieve your long-term goals and that your current behavior change (e.g., studying more) will help you attain them. Also, join a "gritty group." Being with other people who share your passion and perseverance will help motivate and guide you.

---

**STEP-BY-STEP DIAGRAM 2.4** | **Brain Training—A "Virtuous" Cycle**

**STOP!** This Step-by-Step Diagram contains essential information NOT found elsewhere in the text, which is likely to appear on quizzes and exams. Be sure to study it CAREFULLY!

Note the arrows joining the three steps. They signal that with repeated practice the new behavior change becomes self-reinforcing. Research has shown that healthy behaviors, exercise in particular, actually improve your brain's executive functions, including cognitive flexibility, impulse control, and other higher cognitive processes (Allan et al., 2016; Diamond, 2013, 2016). By pushing through the first few weeks of a new behavior change, you'll be ultimately rewarded with stronger frontal lobes and enhanced executive functions, which will transfer to all areas of your life.

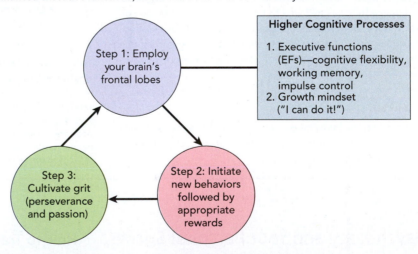

---

**Temporal lobes** The two lobes on the sides of the brain above the ears that are involved in hearing, language comprehension, memory, and some emotional control.

**Temporal Lobes**   The **temporal lobes** are responsible for hearing, language comprehension, memory, and some emotional control. The *auditory* (hearing) *cortex*, which processes sound, is located at the top front of each temporal lobe. This area is responsible for receiving incoming sensory information and sending it on to the parietal lobes, where it is combined with other sensory information.

A part of the left temporal lobe called *Wernicke's area* aids in language comprehension. About a decade after Broca's discovery, German neurologist Carl Wernicke noted that patients with damage in this area could not understand what they read or heard, but they could speak quickly and easily.

However, their speech was often unintelligible because it contained made-up words, sound substitutions, and word substitutions. This syndrome is now referred to as *Wernicke's aphasia.*

## Occipital Lobes

The **occipital lobes** are responsible for, among other things, vision and visual perception. Damage to the occipital lobes can produce blindness, even if the eyes and their neural connection to the brain are perfectly healthy.

## Parietal Lobes

The **parietal lobes** receive and interpret bodily sensations, including pressure, pain, touch, temperature, and location of body parts. A band of tissue on the front of the parietal lobes, called the **somatosensory cortex**, processes sensory information for touch, temperature, pain, and other bodily sensations. Areas of the body with more somatosensory and motor cortex devoted to them (such as the hands and face) are most sensitive to touch and have the most precise motor control (see **Concept Organizer 2.1** and the **Try This Yourself**).

## Association Areas

One of the most popular myths in psychology is that we use only 10% of our brains. This myth might have begun with early research which showed that approximately three-fourths of the cortex is "quiet" (with no precise, specific function responsive to electrical brain stimulation). These areas are not dormant, however. They are clearly engaged in interpreting, integrating, and acting on information processed by other parts of the brain. They are called **association areas** because they associate, or connect, various areas and functions of the brain. The association areas in the frontal lobes, for example, help in decision making and planning. Similarly, the association area right in front of the motor cortex aids in the planning of voluntary movement.

**Occipital lobes**   The two lobes at the back of the brain that are primarily responsible for vision and visual perception.

**Parietal lobes**   The two lobes at the top of the brain in which bodily sensations are received and interpreted.

**Somatosensory cortex**   A region in the parietal lobes responsible for processing information from bodily sensations, such as touch and temperature.

**Association areas**   The "quiet" areas in the cerebral cortex involved in interpreting, integrating, and acting on information processed by other parts of the brain.

---

**CONCEPT ORGANIZER 2.1**   **Body Representation of the Motor Cortex and Somatosensory Cortex**

**STOP!** This Concept Organizer contains essential information NOT found elsewhere in the text, which is likely to appear on quizzes and exams. Be sure to study it CAREFULLY!

This drawing shows a vertical cross-section taken from the left hemisphere's motor cortex and the right hemisphere's somatosensory cortex. If body areas were truly proportional to the amount of tissue on the motor and somatosensory cortices that affect them, our bodies would look like the oddly shaped human figures draped around the outside edge of the cortex.

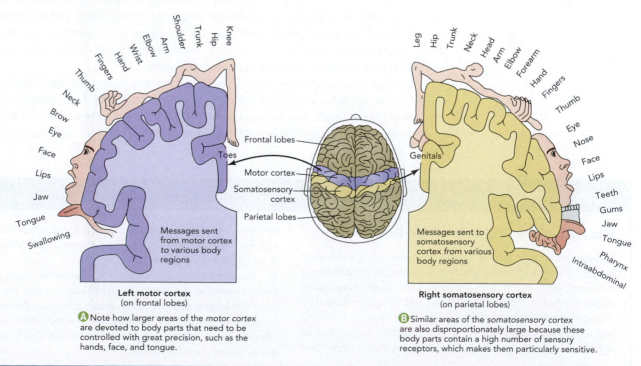

**Left motor cortex**
(on frontal lobes)

**A** Note how larger areas of the *motor cortex* are devoted to body parts that need to be controlled with great precision, such as the hands, face, and tongue.

**Right somatosensory cortex**
(on parietal lobes)

**B** Similar areas of the *somatosensory cortex* are also disproportionately large because these body parts contain a high number of sensory receptors, which makes them particularly sensitive.

## Try This Yourself

### Testing Your Motor Cortex and Somatosensory Cortex

1. ***Motor cortex*** Try wiggling each of your fingers one at a time. Now try wiggling each of your toes. Note in Concept Organizer 2.1 how the area of your motor cortex is much larger for your fingers than for your toes, thus explaining the greater control in your fingers.

2. ***Somatosensory cortex*** Ask a friend to close his or her eyes. Using a random number of fingers (one to four), press down on the skin of your friend's back for 1 to 2 seconds. Then ask, "How many fingers am I using?" Repeat the same procedure on the palm or back of the hand. Note the increased accuracy of reporting after pressing on the hand, which explains why the area of the somatosensory cortex is much larger for the hands than for the back, as well why our hands are much more sensitive than our backs.

## Two Brains in One?

We mentioned earlier that the brain's left and right cerebral hemispheres control opposite sides of the body. Each hemisphere also has separate areas of specialization. For example, the left hemisphere is generally considered our main language center, whereas the right hemisphere specializes in nonverbal information and spatial perception. This is another example of localization of function, technically referred to as *lateralization*. Recognizing that certain differences between our two hemispheres do exist, some people have jumped to unwarranted conclusions about the extent of these differences (see the following **Myth Busters**).

Interestingly, early researchers believed the right hemisphere was subordinate or nondominant to the left, with few special functions or abilities. In the 1960s, landmark **split-brain surgeries** began to change this view.

The primary connection between the two cerebral hemispheres is a thick, ribbon-like band of neural fibers under the cortex called the **corpus callosum** (**Figure 2.20**). In some rare cases of severe epilepsy, when other forms of treatment have failed, surgeons cut the corpus callosum to stop the spread of epileptic seizures from one hemisphere to the other. Because this operation cuts the only direct communication link between the two hemispheres, it reveals what each half of the brain can do in isolation from the other. The resulting research has profoundly improved our understanding of how the two halves of the brain function.

For example, when someone has a stroke and loses his or her language comprehension or ability to speak, we know this generally points to damage in the left hemisphere, because this is where *Wernicke's area*, which is responsible for language comprehension, and *Broca's area*, which controls speech production, are located (refer back to Figure 2.18). However, we now know that when specific regions of the brain are injured or destroyed their functions can sometimes be picked up by a neighboring region—even the opposite hemisphere.

Although most split-brain surgery patients generally show very few outward changes in their behavior, other than fewer epileptic seizures, the surgery does create a few unusual responses. For example, one split-brain patient reported that when he dressed himself, he sometimes pulled his pants down with his left hand and up with his right (Gazzaniga, 2009).

**Split-brain surgery** The cutting of the corpus callosum to separate the brain's two hemispheres; used medically to treat severe epilepsy; also provides information on the functions of the two hemispheres.

**Corpus callosum** A bundle of neural fibers that connects the brain's two hemispheres.

## Myth Busters

### The Myth of the "Neglected Right Brain"

Popular accounts of split-brain research have led to some exaggerated claims and unwarranted conclusions about differences between the left and right hemispheres. For example, courses and books directed at "right-brain thinking" and "drawing on the right side of the brain" often promise to increase our intuition, creativity, and artistic abilities by "waking up" our neglected and underused right brain. Contrary to this myth, research has clearly shown that the two hemispheres work together in a coordinated, integrated way, each making vital contributions (Garrett, 2015; Lilienfeld et al., 2015; Nitschke et al., 2017).

If you are a member of a soccer or basketball team, you can easily understand this principle. Just as you and your teammates often specialize in different jobs, such as offense and defense, the hemispheres also divide their workload to some extent. However, like good team players, each of the two hemispheres is generally aware of what the other is doing.

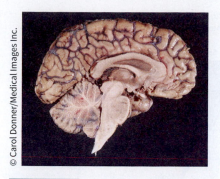

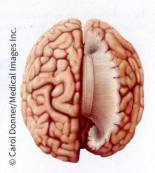

© Carol Donner/Medical Images Inc.

© Carol Donner/Medical Images Inc.

**FIGURE 2.20** **Views of the corpus callosum** In the side-view photo on the left, a human brain was sliced vertically from the top to the bottom to expose the corpus callosum, which conveys information between the two hemispheres of the cerebral cortex. The top-down illustration on the right has been cut open to show how fibers, or *axons*, of the corpus callosum link to both the right and left hemispheres. Note: The deep, extensive cuts shown in these images are to reveal the corpus callosum. In split-brain surgeries on live patients, only fibers within the corpus callosum itself are cut.

The subtle changes in split-brain patients normally appear only with specialized testing. See **Concept Organizer 2.2** for an illustration and description of this type of specialized test. Keep in mind that in actual split-brain surgery on live patients, only some fibers within the corpus callosum are cut (*not* the lower brain structures), and this surgery is performed only in rare cases of uncontrollable epilepsy.

In our tour of the nervous system, the principles of localization of function, lateralization, and specialization recur: dendrites receive information, the occipital lobes specialize in vision, and so on. Keep in mind, however, that all parts of the brain and nervous system also play overlapping and synchronized roles.

---

**CONCEPT ORGANIZER 2.2** | **Split-Brain Research**

**STOP!** This Concept Organizer contains essential information NOT found elsewhere in the text, which is likely to appear on quizzes and exams. Be sure to study it CAREFULLY!

Experiments on split-brain patients often present visual information to only the patient's left or right hemisphere, which leads to some intriguing results.

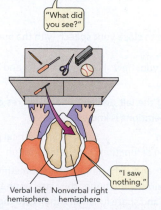

"What did you see?"

"I saw nothing."

Verbal left hemisphere    Nonverbal right hemisphere

"With your left hand, pick up what you saw"

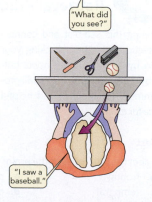

"What did you see?"

"I saw a baseball."

**A** When a split-brain patient is asked to stare straight ahead while a photo of a screwdriver is flashed only to the right hemisphere, he will report that he "saw nothing."

**B** However, when asked to pick up with his left hand what he saw, he can reach through and touch the items hidden behind the screen and easily pick up the screwdriver.

**C** When the left hemisphere receives an image of a baseball, the split-brain patient can easily name it.

Assuming you have an intact, nonsevered corpus callosum, if the same photos were presented to you in the same way, you could easily name both the screwdriver and the baseball. Can you explain why? The answers lie in our somewhat confusing visual wiring system (as shown in Figures D and E below).

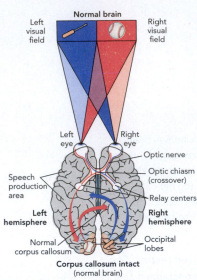

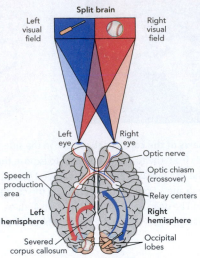

**D** As you can see, our eyes normally connect to our brains in such a way that, when we look straight ahead, information from the left visual field travels to our right hemisphere (the blue line). In contrast, information from the right visual field travels to our left hemisphere (the red line). The messages received by either hemisphere are then quickly sent to the other across the corpus callosum (the red and blue arrows).

**E** When the corpus callosum is severed (note the white line down the middle of the two hemispheres), the split-brain patient cannot state out loud the name of what he sees in the left visual field (in this case "screwdriver"). Why? It's because the image from the left visual field is sent to both eyes, but only to the right side of the brain. For most people, the speech-control center is in the left hemisphere, and information from either hemisphere is normally passed quickly to the other hemisphere across the corpus callosum. However, in the split-brain patient, the corpus callosum is severed and communication between the two hemispheres is blocked. (Compare how the red and blue arrows cross over to the opposite hemisphere in Figure D versus how the same arrows are limited to only one hemisphere here in Figure E.)

© Billy R. Ray/Wiley

## Retrieval Practice 2.4 | The Cerebral Cortex

Completing this self-test and connections section, and then checking your answers by clicking on the answer button or by looking in Appendix B, will provide immediate feedback and helpful practice for exams.

### Self-Test

1. Label the four lobes of the brain:
   a. frontal
   b. parietal
   c. temporal
   d. occipital

2. Imagine that you are giving a speech. Identify the cortical lobes involved when you are:

   a. seeing faces in the audience _____.
   b. hearing questions from the audience _____.

   c. remembering to close your speech with the quote you memorized _____.
   d. noticing that your new shoes are too tight and hurting your feet _____.

3. Specialization of the left and right hemispheres of the brain for particular operations is known as _____.

   a. centralization
   b. asymmetrical processing
   c. normalization of function
   d. lateralization

4. Although the left and right hemispheres sometimes perform different, specialized functions, they are normally in close communication and share functions, thanks to the _____.

   a. thalamus system
   b. sympathetic nervous
   c. corpus callosum
   d. cerebellum

5. Describe the major functions of the two hemispheres.

**Connections—Chapter to Chapter**

Answering the following question will help you "look back and look ahead" to see the important connections among the various subfields of psychology and chapters within this text.

In Chapter 7 (Memory), you will learn more about Alzheimer's, a progressive mental deterioration that occurs most often later in life. Individuals with this disease may have trouble remembering facts and personal life events, or they might become lost when traveling a familiar route. Using what you have learned in this chapter about the functions of the *frontal, parietal, temporal,* and *occipital lobes* of the brain, explain how damage to each lobe may be related to the symptoms of Alzheimer's.

**Study Tip**

*The WileyPlus program that accompanies this text provides for each chapter a* Media Challenge, Critical Thinking Exercise, *and* Application Quiz. *This set of study materials provides additional, invaluable study opportunities. Be sure to check it out!*

# Chapter Summary

## 2.1 Neural and Hormonal Processes 46

- **Neurons**, supported by **glial cells**, receive and send electrochemical signals to other neurons and to the rest of the body. Their major components are **dendrites**, a **cell body**, and an **axon**.

- Within a neuron, a neural impulse, or **action potential**, moves along the axon.

- Neurons communicate with each other using **neurotransmitters**, which are released at the **synapse** and attach to the receiving neuron. Neurons receive input from many synapses. Hundreds of different neurotransmitters regulate a wide variety of physiological processes. Many **agonist** and **antagonist** drugs and poisons act by mimicking or interfering with neurotransmitters.

- The **endocrine system** uses **hormones** to broadcast messages throughout the body. The system regulates long-term bodily processes, maintains ongoing bodily processes, and controls the body's response to emergencies.

**Test Your Critical Thinking**

1. Why is it valuable for scientists to understand how neurotransmitters work at a molecular level?

2. What are some examples of how hormones affect your daily life?

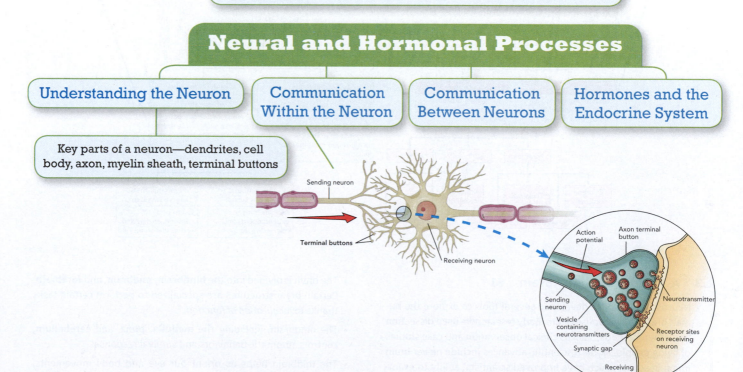

Psychology and a Contemporary Success: Adele Diamond

**Neural and Hormonal Processes**

| Understanding the Neuron | Communication Within the Neuron | Communication Between Neurons | Hormones and the Endocrine System |

Key parts of a neuron—dendrites, cell body, axon, myelin sheath, terminal buttons

Sending neuron

Terminal buttons

Receiving neuron

Action potential

Axon terminal button

Sending neuron

Neurotransmitter

Vesicle containing neurotransmitters

Receptor sites on receiving neuron

Synaptic gap

Receiving neuron

## 2.2   Nervous System Organization   54

- The **central nervous system (CNS)** includes the brain and spinal cord. The CNS allows us to process information and adapt to our environment in ways that no other animal can. The spinal cord transmits information between the brain and the rest of the body, and it initiates involuntary **reflexes**. Although the CNS is very fragile, research shows that the brain is capable of lifelong **neuroplasticity** and **neurogenesis**. Neurogenesis is made possible by **stem cells**.

- The **peripheral nervous system (PNS)** includes all the nerves outside the brain and spinal cord. It links the brain and spinal cord to the body's sense receptors, muscles, and glands. The PNS is subdivided into the **somatic nervous system (SNS)**, which controls voluntary movement, and the **autonomic**

**nervous system (ANS)**, which is responsible for automatic behavior.

- The ANS includes the **sympathetic nervous system** and the **parasympathetic nervous system**. The sympathetic nervous system mobilizes the body's fight-flight-freeze response. The parasympathetic nervous system returns the body to its normal functioning.

### Test Your Critical Thinking

**1.** Some stem cells used in research come from tissue taken from aborted fetuses, which has led to great controversy and severe restrictions in some states. Do you believe this specific form of research should be limited? If so, how and why?

**2.** What are some everyday examples of neuroplasticity—that is, of the way the brain is changed and shaped by experience?

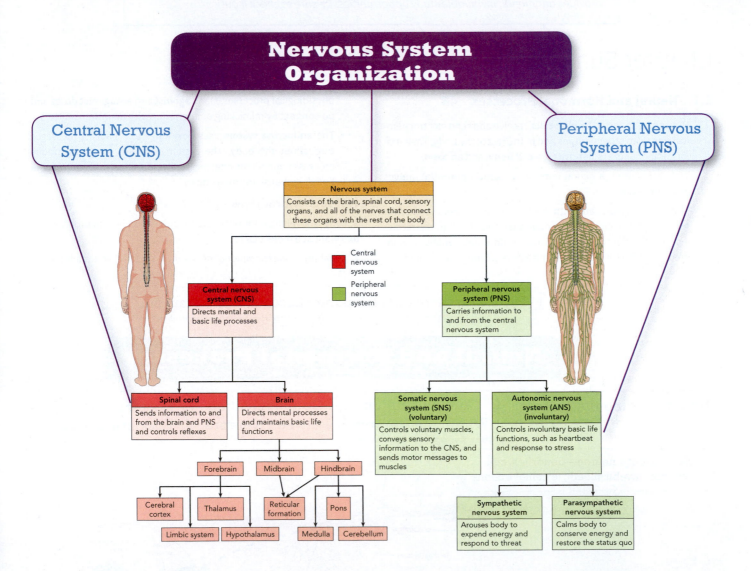

## 2.3   A Tour Through the Brain   61

- Neuroscientists have developed several tools to explore the human brain and nervous system. Early researchers used dissection and other methods, such as clinical observation and case studies of living people. Modern scientific advances include newer brain imaging scans, which have improved scientists' ability to examine these processes and do so noninvasively.

- The brain is divided into the **hindbrain**, **midbrain**, and **forebrain**. Certain brain structures are specialized to perform certain tasks thanks to *localization of function*.

- The hindbrain, including the **medulla, pons**, and **cerebellum**, controls automatic behaviors and survival responses.

- The midbrain helps us orient our eye and body movements, helps control sleep and arousal, and is involved with the neurotransmitter dopamine. The **reticular formation (RF)** runs through the core of the hindbrain, midbrain, and brainstem, and is responsible for screening information and managing our levels of alertness.

- Forebrain structures, including the **cerebral cortex, limbic system, thalamus**, and **hypothalamus**, integrate input from the senses, control basic motives, regulate the body's internal environment, and regulate emotions, learning, and memory.

**Test Your Critical Thinking**

**1.** Which tool for biological research do you consider the least invasive and damaging? Which would be the most dangerous?

**2.** Given that the limbic system is largely responsible for our emotional arousal and expression, do you think people with significant damage to this section should be held less responsible for violent crimes? Why or why not?

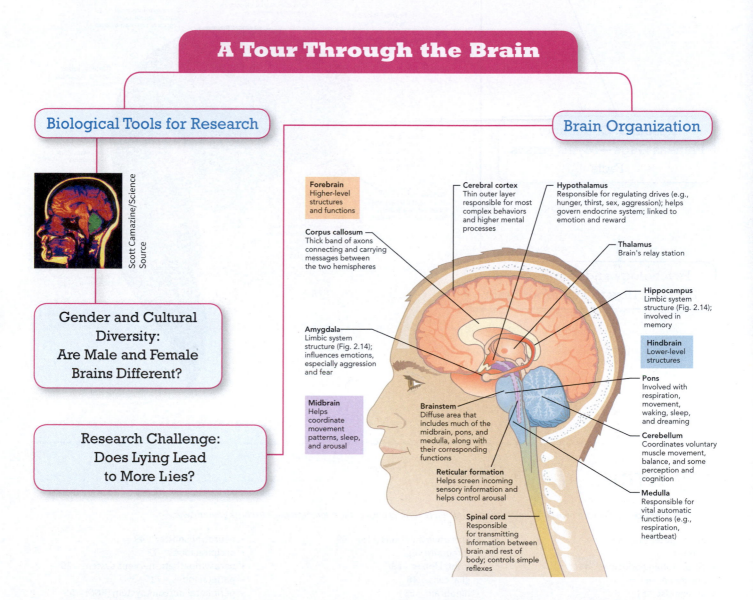

**A Tour Through the Brain**

**Biological Tools for Research**

Scott Camazine/Science Source

**Gender and Cultural Diversity: Are Male and Female Brains Different?**

**Research Challenge: Does Lying Lead to More Lies?**

**Brain Organization**

**Forebrain** Higher-level structures and functions

**Corpus callosum** Thick band of axons connecting and carrying messages between the two hemispheres

**Amygdala** Limbic system structure (Fig. 2.14); influences emotions, especially aggression and fear

**Midbrain** Helps coordinate movement patterns, sleep, and arousal

**Cerebral cortex** Thin outer layer responsible for most complex behaviors and higher mental processes

**Brainstem** Diffuse area that includes much of the midbrain, pons, and medulla, along with their corresponding functions

**Reticular formation** Helps screen incoming sensory information and helps control arousal

**Spinal cord** Responsible for transmitting information between brain and rest of body; controls simple reflexes

**Hypothalamus** Responsible for regulating drives (e.g., hunger, thirst, sex, aggression); helps govern endocrine system; linked to emotion and reward

**Thalamus** Brain's relay station

**Hippocampus** Limbic system structure (Fig. 2.14); involved in memory

**Hindbrain** Lower-level structures

**Pons** Involved with respiration, movement, waking, sleep, and dreaming

**Cerebellum** Coordinates voluntary muscle movement, balance, and some perception and cognition

**Medulla** Responsible for vital automatic functions (e.g., respiration, heartbeat)

## 2.4   The Cerebral Cortex   68

- The **cerebral cortex**, part of the forebrain, governs most higher processing and complex behaviors. It is divided into two hemispheres, each controlling the opposite side of the body. The **corpus callosum** links the hemispheres.

- Each hemisphere is divided into **frontal, parietal, temporal**, and **occipital lobes**. Each lobe specializes in somewhat different tasks, but a large part of the cortex is devoted to integrating actions performed by different brain regions.

- **Split-brain** research shows that the two hemispheres perform somewhat different functions, although they work in close communication.

**Test Your Critical Thinking**

**1.** Recognizing that high-impact sports may cause permanent and serious brain damage, would you allow your child to play these sports? Why or why not?

**2.** How would you explain to a friend the myth that people are "right-brained" or "left-brained"?

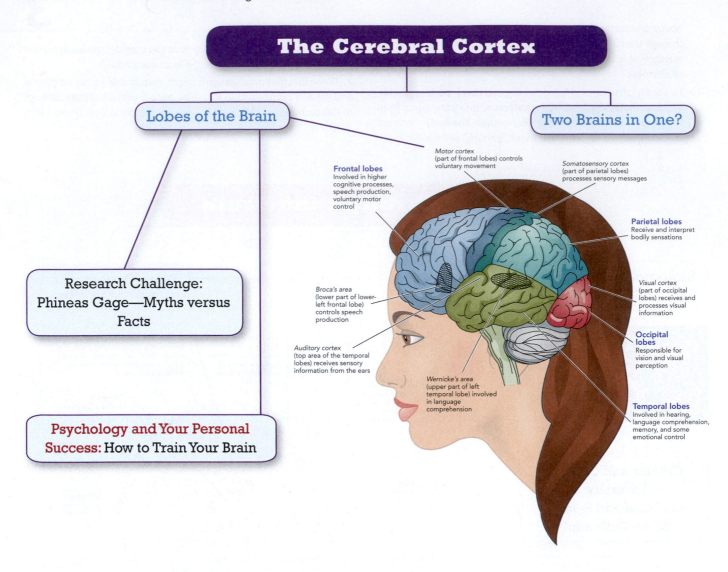

## The Cerebral Cortex

**Lobes of the Brain**

**Two Brains in One?**

Frontal lobes
Involved in higher cognitive processes, speech production, voluntary motor control

Motor cortex (part of frontal lobes) controls voluntary movement

Somatosensory cortex (part of parietal lobes) processes sensory messages

Parietal lobes
Receive and interpret bodily sensations

Broca's area (lower part of lower-left frontal lobe) controls speech production

Visual cortex (part of occipital lobes) receives and processes visual information

Occipital lobes
Responsible for vision and visual perception

Auditory cortex (top area of the temporal lobes) receives sensory information from the ears

Wernicke's area (upper part of left temporal lobe) involved in language comprehension

Temporal lobes
Involved in hearing, language comprehension, memory, and some emotional control

**Research Challenge: Phineas Gage—Myths versus Facts**

**Psychology and Your Personal Success: How to Train Your Brain**

# Key Terms

**Retrieval Practice**  *Write your own definition for each term before turning back to the referenced page to check your answer.*

- action potential   48
- agonist   51
- all-or-nothing principle   48
- amygdala   65
- antagonist   51
- association areas   73
- autonomic nervous system (ANS)   59
- axon   46
- brainstem   65
- cell body   46
- central nervous system (CNS)   55
- cerebellum   65
- cerebral cortex   68
- corpus callosum   74
- dendrites   46
- endocrine system   52
- endorphin   51

- executive functions (EFs)   69
- forebrain   65
- frontal lobes   69
- glial cells   46
- hindbrain   65
- hippocampus   65
- hormone   52
- hypothalamus   67
- limbic system   65
- medulla   65
- midbrain   65
- motor cortex   70
- myelin sheath   47
- nervous system   54
- neurogenesis   56
- neuron   46
- neuroplasticity   56

- neurotransmitter   49
- occipital lobes   73
- parasympathetic nervous system   60
- parietal lobes   73
- peripheral nervous system (PNS)   55
- pons   65
- reflex   57
- reticular formation (RF)   65
- somatic nervous system (SNS)   59
- somatosensory cortex   73
- split-brain surgery   74
- stem cells   56
- sympathetic nervous system   60
- synapse   49
- temporal lobes   72
- thalamus   66

© alexxl66/iStockphoto

# Stress and Health Psychology

| **CHAPTER OUTLINE** | **LEARNING OBJECTIVES** |
|---|---|

❖ **Psychology and a Contemporary Success**
Marcus Luttrell

---

**3.1 Understanding Stress**
• Sources of Stress
**GCD** **Gender and Cultural Diversity**
**What Are the Problems with Acculturative Stress?**
• Reactions to Stress
• Benefits of Stress
**RC** **Research Challenge**
**What Are the Hidden Benefits of Practice Testing?**

**Summarize the major issues and discoveries concerning stress.**
• **Define** stress and stressors.
• **Identify** the major sources of stress.
• **Describe** our physical and cognitive reactions to stress.
• **Review** the benefits of stress.

---

**3.2 Stress and Illness**
• Ulcers
• Chronic Pain
• Cancer
• Cardiovascular Disorders
• Posttraumatic Stress Disorder (PTSD)

**Review how stress contributes to major illnesses.**
• **Explain** how stress affects ulcers.
• **Discuss** how chronic pain is affected by stress.
• **Describe** the role of stress in cancer.
• **Discuss** how the development of cardiovascular disorders is affected by stress.
• **Explain** the role of stress in PTSD and the methods used to cope with this disorder.

---

**3.3 Stress Management**
• Cognitive Appraisal
• Personality and Individual Differences
• Resources for Healthy Living
❖ **Psychology and Your Personal Success**
Can Mindfulness Improve Your GPA?

**Review the major factors involved in managing and coping with stress.**
• **Discuss** the role of cognitive appraisal in coping with stress.
• **Describe** how personality and individual differences affect stress responses.
• **Summarize** the major resources for healthy living.

---

**3.4 Health Psychology**
• What Is Health Psychology?
• Health Psychology at Work
**GCD** **Gender and Cultural Diversity**
**Culture and Job Stress**
**RC** **Research Challenge**
**When Do Losers Actually Win?**

❖ **Psychology and Your Professional Success**
How Well Do You Cope with Job Stress?

**Summarize the field of health psychology and the role of stress in health psychology.**
• **Identify** health psychology.
• **Describe** the work of health psychologists.
• **Discuss** how health psychology can be used in the workplace.

---

## ❖ Psychology and a Contemporary Success | Marcus Luttrell

David Livingston/Getty Images

On June 28, 2005, an elite four-person Navy SEAL team was dropped by helicopter in the middle of the night into the remote mountains of Afghanistan, near the border with Pakistan. Their assignment was to find and capture Ahmad Shah, a leader of the Taliban. Unfortunately, the SEAL team soldiers were spotted early the next morning by three local goat herders—two men and a teenage boy. The team then made a fateful decision: they let the goat herders go even though they recognized they might alert Taliban forces to their presence. And as they feared, within the hour, dozens of Taliban forces arrived, firing machine guns and grenades at the four Americans. Three men died in the fight. The fourth, Marcus Luttrell (1975–) (see photo), was badly wounded from the attack and also suffered from a fall that shattered three of his vertebrae.

Despite his serious injuries, Luttrell managed to elude the Taliban. He crawled seven miles through the mountains and was eventually found by friendly Afghani men, who took him to their village and provided food, water, and shelter. The Taliban eventually discovered that this village was hiding the missing American soldier and demanded that Luttrell be turned over. The villagers refused. They secretly moved him from house to house for protection. Finally, Marine forces arrived and carried Luttrell to safety. Following his rescue, Luttrell received the Navy Cross for his heroism, and his story has been made into a best-selling book and popular movie, both with the same name —*Lone Survivor.*

## Chapter Overview

As you might expect, stress exists on a continuum, and it's often in the eye of the beholder. We would all agree that what Navy SEAL Marcus Luttrell endured was extreme, unimaginable stress. In comparison, if you've done poorly on previous exams and are only just now reading this chapter at the last minute before an exam, you may be experiencing personally high levels of stress. But if you're a student who's generally well prepared and performs well on exams, you're probably experiencing little or no stress getting ready for the exam. In short, stress depends largely on our interpretations of events and our perceived resources for coping with them.

In this chapter, we begin with a general description of stress, along with its sources, effects, and surprising benefits. Next, we discuss the various illnesses associated with stress. Then we explore the numerous ways we typically cope with stress, personality effects on coping, and tips for healthy living. We close with a discussion of the field of health psychology, its role in the workplace and its contribution to our understanding of stress.

## 3.1 | Understanding Stress

### LEARNING OBJECTIVES

**Retrieval Practice**    While reading the upcoming sections, respond to each Learning Objective in your own words.

**Summarize the major issues and discoveries concerning stress.**

- **Define** stress and stressors.
- **Identify** the major sources of stress.
- **Describe** our physical and cognitive reactions to stress.
- **Review** the benefits of stress.

**Stress**    The interpretation of specific events, called *stressors*, as threatening or challenging; the physical and psychological reactions to stress, known as the *stress response*.

**Stressor**    A trigger or stimulus that induces stress.

Everyone experiences **stress**, and we generally know what a person means when he or she speaks of being "stressed." But scientists typically define stress as the interpretation of specific events, called **stressors**, as threatening or challenging. The resulting physical and psychological reactions to stressors are known as the *stress response* (Anisman, 2016; Sanderson, 2013; Selye, 1936, 1983). Using these definitions, can you see how an upcoming exam on this material could be called a stressor, whereas your physical and psychological reactions are your stress response? In

## Myth Busters

### True or False?

_____ 1. Even positive events, like graduating from college and getting married, are major sources of stress.

_____ 2. As your number of friends on social media increases, so does your level of stress.

_____ 3. Small, everyday hassles can impair your immune system functioning.

_____ 4. Police officers, nurses, doctors, social workers, and teachers are particularly prone to "burnout."

_____ 5. Stress causes cancer.

_____ 6. Having a positive attitude can prevent cancer.

_____ 7. Optimistic personality types may cope better with stress.

_____ 8. Ulcers are caused primarily or entirely by stress.

_____ 9. Watching televised coverage of natural disasters can increase symptoms of PTSD.

Courtesy Lee Decker

_____ 10. Friendship is one of your best health resources.

_____ 11. Prolonged stress can lead to death.

_____ 12. You can control or minimize most of the negative effects of stress.

**Answers:** Three out of the 12 questions are false. Looking for the correct answers, while reading the chapter, will improve your mastery of the material.

this section, we'll discuss the key sources of stress, how it affects us, and its occasional benefits. Before going on, test your general knowledge of stress and health in the accompanying **Myth Busters**.

## Sources of Stress

As you might imagine, literally hundreds of things can cause stress in all our lives. We will discuss job stress in the health psychology section at the end of this chapter. For now, we focus on what psychological science has discovered regarding several major sources of stress (**Figure 3.1**).

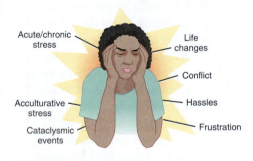

Acute/chronic stress
Life changes
Conflict
Acculturative stress
Hassles
Cataclysmic events
Frustration

**FIGURE 3.1** **Major sources of stress**

### Acute/Chronic Stress

When considering specific sources of stress, it's important to note that many stressors can fit into multiple categories. For example, life changes generally also include conflicts and frustrations. Furthermore, stressors can be either acute or chronic—and sometimes both. **Acute stress** is generally severe, but short term, with a definite endpoint, such as the stress that results from narrowly avoiding a bike or car accident or missing a critical deadline. In modern times, this type of immediate, short-term arousal is almost a daily occurrence, and it often leads to unhealthy emotions (anxiety, tension, irritability) and physical reactions (transient increases in blood pressure and heart rate, dizziness, chest pains). Thankfully, because acute stress is short term, it generally doesn't lead to the type of extensive damage associated with long-term stress.

In contrast to acute, short-term stress, **chronic stress** is continuous. Ongoing wars, a bad marriage, domestic violence, poor working conditions, poverty, prejudice, and discrimination (discussed in **Figure 3.2**) can all be significant sources of chronic stress (Chaby et al., 2015; Simons et al., 2016; Vliegenthart et al., 2016). Surprisingly, chronic stress can suppress sexual functioning in both men and women (Hamilton & Julian, 2014). And confirming what many have long suspected, chronic stress can even reduce the probability of conception (Akhter et al., 2016). It can also contribute to low birth weight in infants, negatively affect the structure and maturation of the adolescent brain, and lead to depression across the life span (Colman et al., 2014; Romeo, 2017; Witt et al., 2016).

While social support can help buffer the negative effects of stress, our social lives can be chronically stressful as well. Making and maintaining friendships require considerable thought and energy (Ehrlich et al., 2016; Flannery et al., 2017; Sriwilai & Charoensukmongkol, 2016). For example, although people often use social media to maintain friendships, research suggests that your stress level increases with the number of social media "friends" you have and the

**Acute stress** A short-term state of arousal in response to a perceived threat or challenge that has a definite endpoint.

**Chronic stress** A continuous state of arousal in which demands are perceived as greater than the inner and outer resources available for dealing with them.

© Valentin Casarsa/iStockphoto

**FIGURE 3.2** **Prejudice and discrimination as chronic stressors** Research has found that the chronic stress resulting from prejudice and discrimination is linked to serious physical and mental problems, including being at a higher risk of heart disease, inflammation, substance abuse, and suicide (Kershaw et al., 2016; Lea et al., 2014; Tebbe & Moradi, 2016).

amount of time you spend on social networking sites (APA Press Release, 2017; Bevan et al., 2014; Wegman & Brand, 2016). In fact, higher cortisol levels were found in teens who had more than 300 friends on Facebook. However, teens who acted in support of their Facebook friends—for example, by liking what they posted—had less stress, as measured by decreased cortisol levels (Morin-Major et al., 2016). (See the **Study Tip** for more information on cortisol.) And needless to say, the effects of some of the negative aspects of social media, such as social exclusion and cyberbullying, can be intense and long lasting (Underwood & Ehrenreich, 2017).

Research also shows that people who spend more time on social media experience lower levels of day-to-day happiness, lower overall feelings of life satisfaction, and higher levels of depression due to social comparison (Brooks, 2015; Rosenthal et al., 2016; Steers et al., 2014). Why is social comparison stressful? People may feel excluded from social events that are described and photographed on social media, experience pressure to be entertaining when they post, and fear that they are missing vital information if they don't check in repeatedly (e.g., Beyens et al., 2016). (As you may know, this fear of missing out is so common that it has its own acronym—FOMO.) The good news is that limiting how often you check your social media accounts and e-mail has been shown to decrease stress and increase overall well-being (Kushlev & Dunn, 2015; Shaw et al., 2015).

## Study Tip

What is cortisol? *As mentioned in Chapter 2 and discussed throughout this chapter, cortisol is the so-called "stress hormone" released from our adrenal glands when we're under physical or emotional stress. Cortisol releases glucose and fatty acids that provide energy for fast action, but as you'll see, it also suppresses our immune system. Cortisol levels are commonly measured in stress research.*

## Life Changes

Early stress researchers Thomas Holmes and Richard Rahe (1967) believed that any *life change* that required some adjustment in behavior or lifestyle could cause some degree of stress. They also believed that exposure to numerous stressful events in a short period could have a direct, detrimental effect on health.

To investigate the relationship between change and stress, Holmes and Rahe created the Social Readjustment Rating Scale (SRRS), which asks people to check off all the life events they have experienced in the previous year (see the **Try This Yourself**). The SRRS is an easy and popular tool for measuring stress, and cross-cultural studies have shown that most people rank the magnitude of their stressful events similarly (Bagheri et al., 2016; Loving & Sbarra, 2015; Smith et al., 2014). But the SRRS is not foolproof. For example, it only shows a correlation between stress and illness; it does not prove that stress actually causes illnesses.

## Try This Yourself

### Measuring Life Changes

To score yourself on the Social Readjustment Rating Scale (SRRS), add up the "life change units" for all life events you have experienced during the last year and compare your score with the following standards: 0–150 = No significant problems; 150–199 = Mild life crisis (33% chance of illness); 200–299 = Moderate life crisis (50% chance of illness); 300 and above = Major life crisis (80% chance of illness).

| Life Events | Life Change Units | Life Events | Life Change Units |
|---|---|---|---|
| Death of spouse | 100 | Gain of a new family member | 39 |
| Divorce | 73 | Business readjustment | 39 |
| Marital separation | 65 | Change in financial state | 38 |
| Jail term | 63 | Death of a close friend | 37 |
| Death of a close family member | 63 | Change to different line of work | 36 |
| Personal injury or illness | 53 | Change in number of arguments with spouse | 35 |
| Marriage | 50 | | |
| Fired at work | 47 | Mortgage or loan for major purchase | 31 |
| Marital reconciliation | 45 | Foreclosure on mortgage or loan | 30 |
| Retirement | 45 | Change in responsibilities at work | 29 |
| Change in health of family member | 44 | Son or daughter leaving home | 29 |
| Pregnancy | 40 | Trouble with in-laws | 29 |
| Sex difficulties | 39 | Outstanding personal achievement | 28 |

| Life Events | Life Change Units | Life Events | Life Change Units |
|---|---|---|---|
| Spouse begins or stops work | 26 | Mortgage or loan for lesser purchase (car, major appliance) | 17 |
| Begin or end school | 26 | Change in sleeping habits | 16 |
| Change in living conditions | 25 | Change in number of family get-togethers | 15 |
| Revision of personal habits | 24 | | |
| Trouble with boss | 23 | Change in eating habits | 15 |
| Change in work hours or conditions | 20 | Vacation | 13 |
| Change in residence | 20 | Christmas | 12 |
| Change in schools | 20 | Minor violations of the law | 11 |
| Change in recreation | 19 | | |
| Change in church activities | 19 | *Source:* Reprinted from the *Journal of Psychosomatic Research*, Vol. III; Holmes and Rahe: "The Social Readjustment Rating Scale," 213–218, 1967, with permission from Elsevier. | |
| Change in social activities | 18 | | |

## Conflict

**Conflict** Stress can also arise when we experience **conflict**—that is, when we are forced to make a choice between at least two incompatible alternatives. There are three basic types of conflict: **approach–approach**, **approach–avoidance**, and **avoidance–avoidance** (**Concept Organizer 3.1**).

Generally, approach–approach conflicts, in which two alternatives are equally desirable, are the easiest to resolve and produce the least stress. Avoidance–avoidance conflicts, on the other hand, are usually the most difficult and take the longest to resolve because either choice leads to unpleasant results. Furthermore, the longer any conflict exists, or the more important the decision, the more stress a person will experience.

Common sources of conflict at work come from *role conflict,* being forced to take on separate and incompatible roles, and *role ambiguity,* being uncertain about the expectations and demands of your role (Lu et al., 2016; Memili et al., 2015). Mid-level managers who report to several supervisors, while also working among the people they are expected to supervise, often experience both role conflict and role ambiguity.

**Conflict** A forced choice between two or more incompatible goals or impulses.

**Approach–approach conflict** A forced choice between two options, both of which have equally desirable characteristics.

**Approach–avoidance conflict** A forced choice involving one option with equally desirable and undesirable characteristics.

**Avoidance–avoidance conflict** A forced choice between two options, both of which have equally undesirable characteristics.

## Hassles

**Hassles** The minor **hassles** of daily living also can pile up and become a major source of stress. We all share many hassles, such as time pressures and financial concerns. But our reactions to them vary. Persistent hassles, among other factors, can lead to a form of physical, mental, and emotional exhaustion known as **burnout** (Cranley et al., 2016; Guveli et al., 2015; Zysberg et al., 2017). This is particularly true for some people in chronically stressful professions, such as firefighters, police officers, doctors, and nurses. Their exhaustion and "burnout" then lead to more work absences, reduced productivity, and increased risk of illness.

Some researchers believe hassles can be more significant than major life events in creating stress (Keles et al., 2016; Stefanek et al., 2012). Divorce is extremely stressful, but it may be so because of the increased number of hassles it brings—changes in finances, child-care arrangements, longer working hours, and so on.

**Hassles** The small problems of daily living that may accumulate and become a major source of stress.

**Burnout** A state of physical, mental, and emotional exhaustion resulting from chronic exposure to high levels of stress, with little personal control.

## Frustration

**Frustration** Like hassles, **frustration**, a negative emotional state resulting from a blocked goal, can cause stress. And the more motivated we are, the more frustrated we become when our goals are blocked. After getting stuck in traffic and being five minutes late to an important job interview, we may become very frustrated. However, if the same traffic jam causes us to be five minutes late showing up to a casual party, we may experience little or no frustration.

**Frustration** The unpleasant tension, anxiety, and heightened sympathetic activity resulting from a blocked goal.

## Cataclysmic Events

**Cataclysmic Events** Terrorist attacks, natural disasters, and other events that cause major damage and loss of life are what stress researchers call **cataclysmic events**. They occur suddenly and generally affect many people simultaneously. Politicians and the public often imagine that such catastrophes inevitably create huge numbers of seriously depressed and permanently scarred survivors. Relief agencies typically send large numbers of counselors to help with the psychological aftermath. However, researchers have found that because the catastrophe is shared by so many others, there is already a great deal of mutual social support from those touched by the same disaster, which may help people cope (Aldrich & Meyer, 2015; Ginzburg & Bateman, 2008).

**Cataclysmic event** A stressful occurrence that happens suddenly and generally affects many people simultaneously.

| CONCEPT ORGANIZER 3.1 | Types of Conflict |
|---|---|

**STOP!** This Concept Organizer contains essential information NOT found elsewhere in the text, which is likely to appear on quizzes and exams. Be sure to study it CAREFULLY!

| Process | Description/Resolution | Example/Resolution |
|---|---|---|
| Approach–approach [ + ] [ + ] | Forced choice between two options, both of which have equally desirable characteristics<br><br>Generally easiest and least stressful conflict to resolve | Two equally desirable job offers, but you must choose one of them<br><br>You make a pro/con list and/or "flip a coin"<br><br>(a) Approach–approach conflict |
| Approach–avoidance [ + ] [ − ] | Forced choice involving one option with equally desirable and undesirable characteristics<br><br>Moderately difficult choice, often resolved with a partial approach | One high-salary job offer that requires you to relocate to an undesirable location away from all your friends and family<br><br>You make a pro/con list and/or "flip a coin"; if you take the job you decide to only live in the new location for a limited time (a partial approach)<br><br>(b) Approach–avoidance conflict |
| Avoidance–avoidance [ − ] [ − ] | Forced choice between two options, both of which have equally undesirable characteristics<br><br>Difficult, stressful conflict, generally resolved with a long delay and considerable denial | Two equally undesirable options—bad job or no job—and you must choose one of them<br><br>You make a pro/con list and/or "flip a coin" and then delay the decision as long as possible, hoping for additional job offers<br><br>(c) Avoidance–avoidance conflict |

**Q Test Your Critical Thinking**

The expression on this man's face indicates that he's experiencing some form of conflict.

1. Can you explain how this could be both an avoidance–avoidance and an approach–avoidance conflict?

2. What might be the best way resolve this conflict?

Lisa Peardon/Taxi/Getty

Nevertheless, cataclysmic events are clearly devastating to all parts of the victims' lives. In fact, people who experience extreme stress, such as a natural disaster like the 9.0 magnitude earthquake that hit Japan and caused devastating tsunami waves, show changes in the brain as long as a year later (Sekiguchi et al., 2014). Specifically, the hippocampus and orbitofrontal cortex are smaller following stress. Some survivors may even develop a prolonged and severe stress reaction known as *posttraumatic stress disorder (PTSD)*, which we discuss later in this chapter.

In addition to the sources of stress just discussed, we also encounter significant stress when we must adapt to a new culture or even travel to another country. This is known as **acculturative stress**—see the following **Gender and Cultural Diversity**.

**Acculturative stress**   The stress resulting from the many changes and pressures of adapting to a new culture; also known as "culture shock."

## Gender and Cultural Diversity

### What Are the Problems with Acculturative Stress?

Have you ever dreamed of living in another country? If so, you probably imagine yourself fully enjoying all the excitement and adventure. But have you considered the stress and stressors that come with adapting to and surviving in the new culture? International travelers, military personnel, immigrants, refugees, individuals who move from one social class to another, and even Native Americans (like the young woman in these two photos) all fall victim to the unspoken and unforeseen stressors of adjusting their personal and family values, their cultural norms, and maybe even their style of dress to the new or dominant culture—see the photos. These required adjustments are referred to as *acculturation*, whereas the associated stress is called *acculturative stress*.

Naturally, this type of stress places great demands on almost every individual's psychological, social, and physical well-being (Berry et al., 1987; Corona et al., 2016; Zvolensky et al., 2016). However, many factors determine the degree of stress. For instance, acculturative stress is much higher for people who are forced to emigrate and if the new country is reluctant to accept newcomers and distrustful of ethnic and cultural diversity.

The degree of acculturative stress also depends in large part on the method of coping an individual chooses when entering a new society. Researchers have identified four major approaches to acculturation (Berry & Ataca, 2010; Urzúa et al., 2017):

Courtesy of Linda Locklear

Courtesy of Linda Locklear

- *Integration*—maintaining the original cultural identity while also attempting to form a relationship with members of the new culture.
- *Assimilation*—giving up the original cultural identity and completely adopting the new culture.
- *Separation*—maintaining the original cultural identity and rejecting the new culture.
- *Marginalization*—rejecting the old cultural identity while also being rejected by members of the new culture.

To check your understanding of these four patterns, see the following **Try This Yourself**.

## Try This Yourself

### Stress and "Culture Shock"

Imagine yourself as a college graduate offered a high-paying job that will allow you to move from a lower socioeconomic class to the middle or upper class. This change in your socioeconomic status will lead to considerable acculturative stress. In anticipation of this change, will you:

1. Adopt the majority culture and seek positive relations with the dominant culture?
2. Maintain your original cultural identity and avoid relations with the dominant culture?

As you can see in the following table, if you answered "yes" to the first question, you have chosen the path to integration. If you have chosen you answered "no" to the second question, you will likely become marginalized.

|     | Yes | No |
| --- | --- | --- |
| Yes | Integration | Separation |
| No | Assimilation | Marginalization |

As you might expect, *integration* typically leads to the lowest levels of acculturative stress. And, *marginalization* generally leads to the highest levels—presumably due to the fact that these people live on the "margins" and lack the connections and support of either the new or old cultures.

*Assimilation* has the second lowest level of stress, but there are still many problems, presumably due to the loss of cultural support from other members of the original culture who do not assimilate. Individuals in the *separation* group tend to have next to the highest level of acculturative stress, with even higher levels for those who are forcibly separated by prejudice and discrimination versus those who separate voluntarily.

Tinseltown/Shutterstock

Natalie Portman is a famous actress (see the photo) who's appeared in several films, including *Star Wars, V for Vendetta, Black Swan*, and *Thor*. She also graduated from Harvard University with a degree in psychology. Did you know that she was born in Jerusalem and maintains a dual citizenship in the United States and Israel? She has stated that although she really loves the States, she feels most at home in Jerusalem. Which of the four approaches to acculturation do you think she has followed? More importantly, can you see how you as an individual, or all of us as part of our general society, can celebrate diversity and thereby help to reduce the anxiety, depression, alienation, and physical illnesses associated with acculturative stress?

# Reactions to Stress

*It's not stress that kills us—it's our reaction to it.*
—Hans Selye (Austrian Endocrinologist, "Father" of Stress Research)

As we've just seen, there are numerous factors that contribute to stress, and while it may strike without warning, it also can be a chronic, lifelong situation. In this section, we'll take a close look at three ways our human bodies typically respond to both short- and long-term stress—the GAS, SAM, and HPA systems, changes in the immune system, and alterations in our cognitive functioning.

**Stress and the General Adaptation Syndrome (GAS)**   When mentally or physically stressed, our bodies undergo several biological changes that can be detrimental to our health. In 1936, Canadian physician Hans Selye (SELL-yay) described a generalized physiological reaction to stress that he called the **general adaptation syndrome (GAS)**. The GAS occurs in three phases—*alarm*, *resistance*, and *exhaustion*—activated by efforts to adapt to any stressor, whether physical or psychological (**Step-by-Step Diagram 3.1**).

**General adaptation syndrome (GAS)**   Selye's three-stage (alarm, resistance, exhaustion) reaction to chronic stress; a pattern of nonspecific, adaptational responses to a continuing stressor.

---

**STEP-BY-STEP DIAGRAM 3.1**    **General Adaptation Syndrome (GAS)**

**STOP!**  This Step-by-Step Diagram contains essential information NOT found elsewhere in the text, which is likely to appear on quizzes and exams. Be sure to study it CAREFULLY!

The three phases of Selye's syndrome (*alarm, resistance,* and *exhaustion*) focus on the biological response to stress—particularly the "wear and tear" on the body that results from prolonged stress.

**1  Alarm phase**   When surprised or threatened, your body enters an alarm phase during which your sympathetic nervous system (SNS) is activated (e.g., increased heart rate and blood pressure) and blood is diverted to your skeletal muscles to prepare you for the "fight-flight-freeze" response (Chapter 2).

**2  Resistance phase**   As the stress continues, your body attempts to resist or adapt to the stressor by summoning all your resources. Physiological arousal remains higher than normal, and there is an outpouring of stress hormones. During this resistance stage, people use a variety of coping methods. For example, if your job is threatened, you may work longer hours and give up your vacation days.

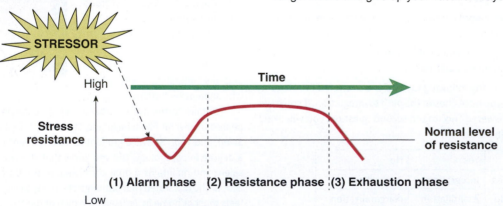

**3  Exhaustion phase**   Unfortunately, your body's resistance to stress can only last so long before exhaustion sets in. During this final phase, your reserves are depleted and you become more susceptible to serious illnesses, as well as potentially irreversible damage to your body. Selye maintained that one outcome of this exhaustion phase for some people is the development of *diseases of adaptation*, including asthma and high blood pressure. Unless a way of relieving stress is found, the eventual result may be complete collapse and death.

Most of Selye's ideas about the GAS pattern have proven to be correct. For example, studies have found that the primary behavioral response to stress by both men and women is to fight or flee—the classic "fight or flight" response. However, this two-option response does not include situations in which we become immobile and "freeze" in the face of stress. Therefore, many researchers have now replaced the previous label of "fight or flight" with a new three-option response, called *fight-flight-freeze* (Corr & Cooper, 2016; Friedman, 2015; Maack et al., 2015).

Keep in mind that different stressors evoke different responses and that people vary widely in their reactions to stressors. For example, women are more likely to "tend and befriend" (Israel-Cohen & Kaplan, 2016; Taylor, 2006, 2012; von Dawans et al., 2012). This means that when under stress women more often take care of themselves and their children (tending) while also forming strong social bonds with others (befriending). Interestingly, other research has found that after being administered oxytocin, the so-called "love hormone," which increases bonding, attachment, and empathy, both male and female participants showed enhanced compassion toward women but not toward men (Palgi et al., 2015). These researchers explain their results by suggesting that the females' "tend and befriend" behaviors may have evolved from a need to help vulnerable individuals of both sexes, rather than being a result of true gender differences.

What is Selye's take-home message? *Our bodies are relatively well designed for temporary stress but poorly equipped for prolonged stress.* As noted in **Figure 3.3**, the same biological processes that are adaptive in the short run, such as the fight-flight-freeze response, can be hazardous in the long run (Papathanasiou et al., 2015; Russell et al., 2014).

### Stress, the SAM System, and the HPA Axis

To understand these dangers, we need to first describe how our bodies (ideally) respond to stress. As you can see in **Step-by-Step Diagram 3.2**, once our brains identify a stressor, our **SAM** (sympatho–adreno–medullary) **system** and **HPA** (hypothalamic–pituitary–adrenocortical) **axis** then work together to increase our arousal and energy levels to deal with the stress (Anisman, 2016; Dieleman et al., 2016; Garrett, 2015). Once the stress is resolved, these systems turn off, and our bodies return to normal, baseline functioning, known as **homeostasis**.

Unfortunately, given our increasingly stressful modern lifestyle, our bodies are far too often in a state of elevated, chronic arousal, which can wreak havoc on our health. Some of the most damaging effects of stress are on our immune system and cognitive functioning.

### Stress and the Immune System

The discovery of the relationship between stress and our immune system has been very important. When people are under stress, the immune system is less able to regulate the normal inflammation system, which makes us more susceptible to diseases, such as bursitis, colitis, Alzheimer's disease, rheumatoid arthritis, periodontal disease, the common cold, and even neurodegenerative and psychiatric disorders (e.g., Campbell et al., 2015; Cohen et al., 2003, 2012; O'Farrell & Harkin, 2017).

Knowledge that psychological factors have considerable control over infectious diseases has upset the long-held assumption in biology and medicine that these diseases are strictly physical. The clinical and theoretical implications have been so influential that a new interdisciplinary field, called **psychoneuroimmunology**, has emerged. It studies the effects of psychological and other factors on the immune system.

Prolonged, excessive, and/or chronic stress also contributes to hypertension, depression, posttraumatic stress disorder (PTSD), drug and alcohol abuse, and low birth weight (Guardino et al., 2016; Kim et al., 2016; Nicolaides et al., 2015). It can also lead to premature aging and even death (Lohr et al., 2015; Prenderville et al., 2015; Simm & Klotz, 2015).

How does this happen? Cortisol, a key element of the HPA axis, plays a critical role in the long-term negative effects of stress. Although increased cortisol levels initially help us fight stressors, if these levels stay high, which occurs when stress continues over time, the body's

**FIGURE 3.3** **Stress in ancient times** As shown in these ancient cave drawings, the automatic "fight-or-flight" response was adaptive and necessary for early human survival. However, in modern society, it occurs as a response to ongoing situations where we often cannot fight or flee, and this repeated arousal can be detrimental to our health. (Note that this classic term of "fight or flight" has been expanded and is now called the fight-flight-freeze response.)

**SAM system** Our body's initial, rapid-acting stress response, involving the sympathetic nervous system and the adrenal medulla; called the sympatho–adreno–medullary (SAM) system.

**HPA axis** Our body's delayed stress response, involving the hypothalamus, pituitary, and adrenal cortex; called the hypothalamic–pituitary–adrenocortical (HPA) axis.

**Homeostasis** Our body's tendency to maintain equilibrium, or a steady state of internal balance, such as a constant internal temperature.

**Psychoneuroimmunology** The interdisciplinary field that studies the effects of psychological and other factors on the immune system.

**STEP-BY-STEP DIAGRAM 3.2**    **The SAM System and HPA Axis—Two Co-Actors in Our Stress Response**

**STOP!** This Step-by-Step Diagram contains essential information NOT found else-where in the text, which is likely to appear on quizzes and exams. Be sure to study it CAREFULLY!

Faced with stress, our sympathetic nervous system prepares us for immediate action—fight-flight-freeze. Our slower-acting HPA axis maintains our arousal. Here's how it happens:

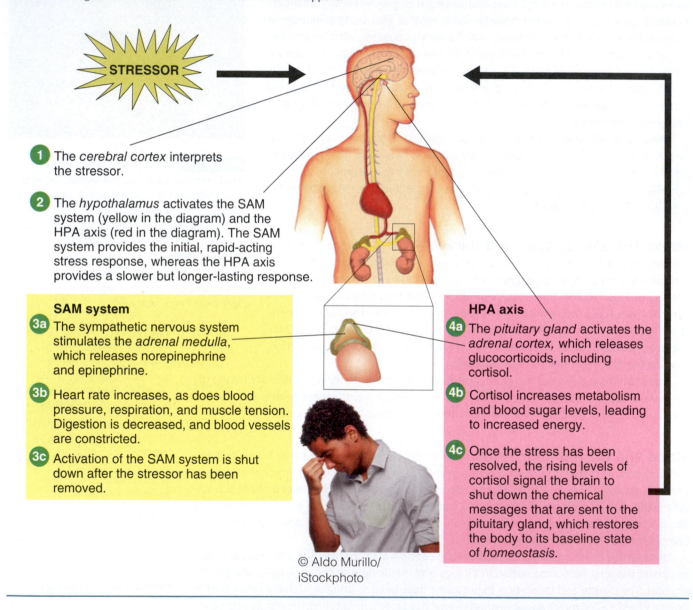

**STRESSOR**

1. The *cerebral cortex* interprets the stressor.

2. The *hypothalamus* activates the SAM system (yellow in the diagram) and the HPA axis (red in the diagram). The SAM system provides the initial, rapid-acting stress response, whereas the HPA axis provides a slower but longer-lasting response.

**SAM system**

3a. The sympathetic nervous system stimulates the *adrenal medulla,* which releases norepinephrine and epinephrine.

3b. Heart rate increases, as does blood pressure, respiration, and muscle tension. Digestion is decreased, and blood vessels are constricted.

3c. Activation of the SAM system is shut down after the stressor has been removed.

**HPA axis**

4a. The *pituitary gland* activates the *adrenal cortex,* which releases glucocorticoids, including cortisol.

4b. Cortisol increases metabolism and blood sugar levels, leading to increased energy.

4c. Once the stress has been resolved, the rising levels of cortisol signal the brain to shut down the chemical messages that are sent to the pituitary gland, which restores the body to its baseline state of *homeostasis.*

© Aldo Murillo/ iStockphoto

disease-fighting immune system is suppressed. For example, studies have found that both children and adults who are lonely—which is another type of chronic stressor—have an impaired HPA axis and immune response, leaving their bodies vulnerable to infections, allergies, and many of the other illnesses cited above (Drake et al., 2016; Jaremka et al., 2013; Zilioli et al., 2017).

**Stress and Cognitive Functioning**    What happens to our brains and thought processes when we're under immediate stress? As we've just seen, cortisol helps us deal with immediate dangers by mobilizing our energy resources. It also helps us create memories. For example, you'll discover in Chapter 7 that short-term stress can solidify our memories for highly emotional, "flashbulb" events.

Unfortunately, short-term stress can interfere with the retrieval of existing memories, the laying down of new memories, and general information processing (Banks et al., 2015; Rubin et al., 2016). For instance, when research participants are engaged in a stress-inducing task (keeping their hand in ice water for up to three minutes), they are less able to discriminate complex visual scenes than nonstressed participants (Paul et al., 2016). On a personal level, this may help explain why you forget important information during a big exam and why people too often become dangerously confused during a fire and are unable to find the exit. The good news is that once the cortisol washes out, memory performance generally returns to normal levels. Can you see why scientists believe our increased memories for emotional events may have evolved to help us remember what to avoid or protect in the future?

What happens to cognitive functioning during prolonged stress? Long-term exposure to cortisol can permanently damage cells in the hippocampus, a key part of the brain involved in memory (Chapter 7). Furthermore, once the hippocampus has been damaged, it cannot provide proper feedback to the hypothalamus, so cortisol continues to be secreted, and a vicious cycle can develop (**Figure 3.4**). Perhaps even more alarming is the finding that long-term stress in mice not only disturbs their short-term memory, but also causes changes in the brain, leading to lasting symptoms of depression and social avoidance (McKim et al., 2016).

**FIGURE 3.4**  **Our brains under chronic stress**

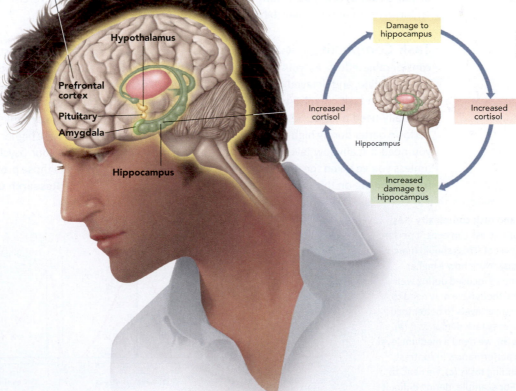

**a.  Stress and our prefrontal cortex**  Chronic stress results in a reduction in the size of neurons in the prefrontal cortex and a diminished performance during cognitive tasks.

**b.  Stress and our hippocampus**  Cortisol released in response to immediate stress can be beneficial. However, under chronic stress it can produce a vicious cycle leading to permanent damage to the hippocampu

Hypothalamus

Prefrontal cortex

Pituitary

Amygdala

Hippocampus

Damage to hippocampus

Increased cortisol

Increased cortisol

Hippocampus

Increased damage to hippocampus

To make matters worse, living below the poverty line (a chronic type of stressor) can literally make it harder to learn. For example, researchers have found poverty to be associated with particular differences in certain surface areas of the brain essential for academic success (Noble et al., 2015). In addition, brain scans of people currently living or growing up in poverty and experiencing maltreatment, compared to those from middle- and higher-income families, show several important differences in brain structures, including the frontal and temporal lobes, hippocampus, and gray matter (Hair et al., 2015; Harden et al., 2016; Wang et al., 2016). These areas of the brain are known to be among the most crucial for academic achievement.

## Benefits of Stress

So far in our discussion, we've focused primarily on the harmful, negative side of stress, but there are also some positive aspects. Our bodies are nearly always in some state of stress, whether pleasant or unpleasant, mild or severe. *Anything* placing a demand on the body can cause stress.

### Eustress versus Distress
We often think of stress as unpleasant and threatening. This sort of stress is called **distress** (Selye, 1974). When stress is pleasant or perceived as a manageable challenge, it can be beneficial. As seen in athletes, business tycoons, entertainers, or great leaders, this type of desirable stress, called **eustress**, helps arouse and motivate us to persevere and accomplish challenging goals. Consider large life events like graduating from college, securing a highly desirable job, and getting married. Each of these occasions involves enormous changes in our lives and inevitable conflicts, frustration, and other sources of stress, yet for most of us they are incredibly positive events.

Rather than being the source of discomfort and distress, *eustress* is pleasant and motivating. It encourages us to overcome obstacles and even enjoy the effort and work we expend toward achieving our goals. Physical exercise is a clear example of the benefits of eustress. When we're working out at a gym, or even just walking in a park, we're placing some level of stress on our bodies. However, this stress encourages the development and strengthening of all parts of our body, particularly our muscles, heart, lungs, and bones. Exercise also releases endorphins (Chapter 2), which help lift depression and overall mood.

### Task Complexity
Keep in mind that all the achievements related to eustress require considerable effort. As you well know, going through college requires long hours of study, self-discipline, and delayed gratification. Research also shows that your optimal level of stress depends on task complexity (**Figure 3.5**). For example, during well-learned, easy tasks, you generally need a higher level of stress to perform at your best. This is why athletes typically perform better during high-stakes competition—when their stress levels are higher. In contrast, you need a really low level of stress during a hard, complex exam in your psychology class (unless you've taken the time to work through a lot of practice tests, like those provided in this text). For more on the advantages of practice testing, see the following **Research Challenge**.

**Distress**   The unpleasant, undesirable stress caused by aversive conditions.

**Eustress**   The pleasant, desirable stress that arouses us to persevere and accomplish challenging goals.

**FIGURE 3.5**  **Stress and task complexity**   As you can see in this figure, stress can benefit performance. However, the level of stress should match the complexity of the task. Note how a higher level of stress helps keep us focused during well-learned, very easy tasks, though we may need to intentionally raise our stress levels to better focus our attention when the easy task demands it (**a**). During moderate tasks (**b**), we need a medium level of stress for maximum performance. In contrast, during complex, demanding tasks (**c**), we need to lower our stress level. For example, during difficult exams your performance will benefit from deep breathing and other methods of relaxation.

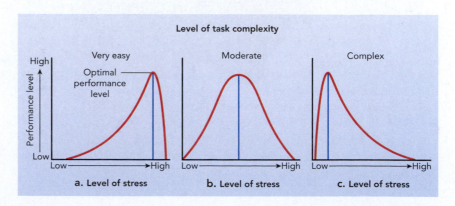

## Research Challenge

### What Are the Hidden Benefits of Practice Testing?

Are you planning a career as a teacher? Would you like to improve your own performance on exams? Interesting research has found that *practice testing* (repeated self-testing as described in Chapter 1) can improve your test grades while also protecting your memory from the negative effects of stress (Smith et al., 2016).

In this study, 120 volunteers were asked to learn a set of 30 words and 30 images displayed on a computer screen one item at a time for a few seconds each. After seeing each item, participants were given 10 seconds to type a sentence on a computer to simulate note taking. Next, participants were randomly assigned to one of two study groups. Group 1 was asked to use *study practice*, the traditional method of rereading material to memorize it. Group 2 studied using *retrieval practice* involving timed practice tests in which they freely recalled as many items as they could.

Following a one-day break, half of each group was placed in a stress-inducing situation that required them to give an unexpected, impromptu speech and to solve math problems in front of two judges, three peers, and a video camera. These participants then took two memory tests requiring them to recall the words and images they had studied the previous day. The other half of the participants took the same memory tests after performing a time-matched, nonstressful task.

Can you predict what happened? Among the participants who engaged in *retrieval practice*, the stressed participants remembered approximately 11 of 30 items, whereas the nonstressed participants recalled 10 items. In contrast, among participants who learned through *study practice*, the stressed participants remembered 7 items, and the nonstressed participants remembered 9 items.

In short, the traditional study practice of rereading material to memorize it was found to be less effective than retrieval practice in both stressful and nonstressful conditions. More importantly, numerous studies have shown that stress impairs memory (Chapter 7). However, this study shows that retrieval practice, discussed and promoted throughout this text, can protect memory against the adverse effects of stress.

kristian sekulic/iStockphoto

**Test Yourself**

1. Based on the information provided, did the researchers in this study (Smith et al., 2016) use descriptive, correlational, and/or experimental research?

2. If you chose:
   - *descriptive research*, is this a naturalistic observation, survey/interview, case study, and/or archival research?
   - *correlational research*, is this a positive, negative, or zero correlation?
   - *experimental research*, label the IV, DV, experimental group(s), and control group. (Note: If participants were not randomly assigned to groups, list it as a *quasi-experimental design*.)
   - both *descriptive* and *correlational*, answer the corresponding questions for both.

**Check your answers by clicking on the answer button or by looking in Appendix B.**

**Note:** The information provided in this study is admittedly limited, but the level of detail is similar to what is presented in most textbooks and public reports of research findings. Answering these questions, and then comparing your answers to those provided, will help you become a better critical thinker and consumer of scientific research.

## Stress and Social Support

Even highly stressful events can, in some cases, be surprisingly beneficial. Researchers compared data for psychological adjustment, including anxiety and depression, in female students before the 2007 shooting at Virginia Tech (as part of an already on-going study) and then again after the event (Mancini et al., 2016). They found that some students suffered continued distress after the shooting, while others showed relatively long-lasting psychological improvement and resilience. On the face of it, this sounds absurd. However, numerous studies have shown that the outpouring of social support after mass traumas can promote greater cooperation, sharing, solidarity, and bonding among the survivors. One researcher described it as "a paradise built in hell" (Solnit, 2009).

What's the takeaway message? The key "advantage" of mass trauma is that it often mobilizes broad-scale public support and cooperative behaviors—as seen in the media and public outpouring of support following the horrific Orlando, Florida, massacre in 2016. Sadly, the opposite is generally true after individual-level traumas, like rape or assault. Do you see then why group therapy is often so helpful for rape and assault survivors (Chapter 15)? Or why we all need to remember to offer strong social support to survivors of both mass and individual traumas—and to actively seek it for ourselves during stressful times?

© Billy R. Ray/Wiley

## Retrieval Practice 3.1 | Understanding Stress

Completing this self-test and the connections section, and then checking your answers by clicking on the answer button or by looking in Appendix B, will provide immediate feedback and helpful practice for exams.

### Self-Test

1. When John saw his girlfriend kissing another man at a party, he became very upset. In this situation, watching someone you love kiss someone else is _____, and becoming upset is _____.
   a. a stressor; a biological imperative
   b. distressing; a life change event
   c. a cataclysmic event; evidence of a burnout
   d. a stressor; a stress response

2. Briefly explain the three basic forms of conflict (approach–approach, approach–avoidance, and avoidance–avoidance).

3. A state of physical, emotional, and mental exhaustion resulting from chronic exposure to high levels of stress with little personal control is called _____.
   a. primary conflict
   b. technostress
   c. burnout
   d. secondary conflict

4. As Michael watches his instructor pass out papers, he suddenly realizes that this is the first major exam and he is unprepared. Which phase of the GAS is he most likely experiencing?
   a. resistance
   b. alarm
   c. exhaustion
   d. phase out

5. Stress that is pleasant and motivates us to accomplish challenging goals _____.
   a. can be beneficial
   b. is called eustress
   c. is described by both a and b
   d. is described by none of these options

### Connections—Chapter to Chapter

Answering the following question will help you "look back and look ahead" to see the important connections among the various subfields of psychology and chapters within this text.

In Chapter 2 (Neuroscience and Biological Foundations), you discovered that the *sympathetic* and *parasympathetic nervous systems* work together in a way that helps us to adapt to the demands of the environment, especially emergencies. How have the stressors in our modern world (sources of stress) challenged the adaptability and effectiveness of these two systems?

## 3.2 Stress and Illness

### LEARNING OBJECTIVES

**Retrieval Practice** While reading the upcoming sections, respond to each Learning Objective in your own words.

**Review how stress contributes to major illnesses.**

- **Explain** how stress affects ulcers.
- **Discuss** how chronic pain is affected by stress.
- **Describe** the role of stress in cancer.
- **Discuss** how the development of cardiovascular disorders is affected by stress.
- **Explain** the role of stress in PTSD and the methods used to cope with this disorder.

*A healthy body is a guest-chamber for the soul; a sick body is a prison.*
—Francis Bacon (Philosopher, Statesman, Scientist)

As we've just seen, stress has dramatic effects on our bodies. This section explores how stress is related to five serious conditions—ulcers, chronic pain, cancer, cardiovascular disorders, and posttraumatic stress disorder (PTSD).

### Ulcers

*Ulcers* are lesions in the lining of the stomach, esophagus, or upper small intestine that can be quite painful. In extreme cases, they may even be life-threatening. Beginning in the 1950s, psychologists reported strong evidence that stress can lead to ulcers. Studies found that people who live in stressful situations have a higher incidence of ulcers than people who don't.

And numerous experiments with laboratory animals have shown that stressors, such as shock, water-immersion, or confinement to a very small space, can produce ulcers in a few hours in some laboratory animals (e.g., Landeira-Fernandez, 2015; Shakya et al., 2015; Sun et al., 2016).

The relationship between stress and ulcers seemed well established until researchers identified a bacterium (*Helicobacter pylori*, or *H. pylori*) that appeared to be associated with ulcers. Later studies confirmed that this bacterium clearly damages the stomach wall and that antibiotic treatment helps many patients. However, approximately 75% of normal, healthy people's stomachs also have the bacterium. This suggests that the bacterium may cause the ulcer, but only in people who are compromised by stress. Furthermore, behavior modification and other psychological treatments, used alongside antibiotics, can help ease ulcers. In other words, although stress *by itself* does not cause ulcers, it is a contributing factor, along with other psychological and biological factors (Jaul et al., 2016; Southwick & Watson, 2015; Wang et al., 2017).

> ### Study Tip
>
> *Many believe that ulcers are "psychosomatic" and that this means they're imaginary. However, psychosomatic (*psyche *means "mind" and* soma *means "body") refers to symptoms or illnesses that are caused or aggravated by psychological factors, especially stress (Lipowski, 1986). Most researchers and health practitioners believe that almost all illnesses are partly psychosomatic in this sense.*

## Chronic Pain

Imagine having all your pain receptors removed so that you could race cars, downhill ski, skateboard, and go to the dentist without ever worrying about pain. Does this sound too good to be true? Think again. Pain is essential to the survival and well-being of humans and all other animals. It alerts us to dangerous or harmful situations and forces us to rest and recover from injury. In contrast, **chronic pain**, the type that comes with a chronic disease or continues long past the healing of a wound, generally does not serve a useful function. Sadly, an estimated 100 million Americans suffer from chronic pain (Lewis Rickert et al., 2016). Although psychological factors may not be the source of the chronic pain, they frequently intensify the related anxiety, depression, fatigue, and disability (Kerns et al., 2011; Miller-Matero et al., 2017; Vlaeyen et al., 2016).

**Chronic pain**   Continuous or recurrent pain over a period of six months or longer.

To treat chronic pain, medical professionals often prescribe opioids. Too often, though, these medications create serious side effects, and their misuse has led to epidemic forms of addiction (e.g., Jones & Comer, 2016). (See Chapter 5.) In comparison, health psychologists emphasize psychologically oriented treatments, such as behavior modification, biofeedback, and relaxation.

- *Behavioral interventions* Chronic pain is a serious problem with no simple solution. For example, behavior modification programs (Chapters 6 and 15) often emphasize "well behaviors" such as exercise, which is known to produce an increase in endorphins and a resulting decrease in pain (Chapter 2). Unfortunately, chronic pain patients tend to decrease their activity and exercise, but behavior modification programs have helped to address this problem (Nicassio & Azizoddin, 2016; Noel et al., 2016).

- *Biofeedback* In *biofeedback*, information about physiological functions, such as heart rate and blood pressure, is monitored, and the feedback helps the individual learn to control these functions (see **Figure 3.6**). Such feedback helps reduce some types of chronic pain.

- *Mindfulness-based meditation and relaxation techniques* Because the pain always seems to be there, chronic pain sufferers tend to talk and think about their pain whenever they are not thoroughly engrossed in an activity. Watching TV shows or films, attending parties, or performing any activity that diverts attention from the pain seems to reduce discomfort. Attention might also be diverted with mindfulness-based stress reduction (MBSR) meditation programs and special relaxation techniques like those discussed later in this chapter (Day, 2016). Relaxation techniques are taught in some childbirth classes. These techniques

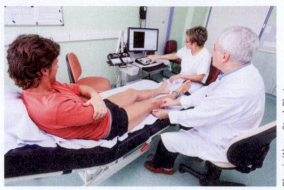

**FIGURE 3.6** **Biofeedback and pain control** Most biofeedback with chronic pain patients is done with the *electromyograph (EMG)*, which measures muscle tension by recording electrical activity in the skin. The EMG is most helpful when the pain involves extreme muscle tension, such as tension headache and lower back pain. Electrodes are attached to the site of the pain, and the patient is instructed to relax. When sufficient relaxation is achieved, the machine signals with a tone or a light. The signal serves as feedback, enabling the patient to learn how to relax. Research shows that biofeedback is helpful and sometimes as effective as more expensive and lengthier forms of treatment (Jensen et al., 2009; Urban, 2016). Apparently, it is successful because it teaches patients to recognize patterns of emotional arousal and conflict that affect their physiological responses. This self-awareness, in turn, enables them to learn self-regulation skills that help control their pain.

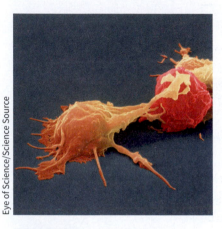

**FIGURE 3.7** **The immune system** The actions of a healthy immune system are shown here. The round red structures are leukemia cells. Note how the yellow killer cells are attacking and destroying the cancer cells.

focus the birthing mother's attention on breathing and relaxing the muscles, which helps distract her attention from the fear and pain of the birthing process. Similar techniques also can be helpful to chronic pain sufferers. Remember, however, that these techniques do not eliminate the pain. They merely allow the person to ignore it for a time.

## Cancer

*Cancer* is among the leading causes of death for adults in the United States. It occurs when a particular type of primitive body cell begins rapidly dividing and then forms a tumor that invades healthy tissue. Unless destroyed or removed, the tumor eventually damages organs and causes death. In a healthy person, whenever cancer cells start to multiply, the immune system checks the uncontrolled growth by attacking the abnormal cells (**Figure 3.7**).

More than 100 types of cancer have been identified. They appear to be caused by an interaction between environmental factors (such as diet, smoking, and pollutants) and inherited predispositions. Note that research does *not* support the popular myths that stress directly *causes* cancer or that positive attitudes can prevent it (Chang et al., 2015; Coyne & Tennen, 2010; Lilienfeld et al., 2010, 2015).

Of course, this is not to say that developing a positive attitude and reducing our stress levels aren't worthy health goals. As you read earlier, prolonged stress causes the adrenal glands to release hormones that negatively affect the immune system, and a compromised immune system is less able to resist infection or to fight off cancer cells (Antoni et al., 2016; Bick et al., 2015). In addition, it seems that stress can increase the spread of cancer cells to other organs, including the bones, which decreases the likelihood of survival (Chang et al., 2016; Levi et al., 2016).

## Cardiovascular Disorders

Cardiovascular disorders contribute to over half of all deaths in the United States (American Heart Association, 2013). Understandably, health psychologists are concerned because stress is a major contributor to these deaths (Marchant, 2016; Orth-Gomér et al., 2015; Taylor-Clift et al., 2016).

*Heart disease* is a general term for all disorders that eventually affect the heart muscle and lead to heart failure. *Coronary heart disease* occurs when the walls of the coronary arteries thicken, reducing or blocking the blood supply to the heart. Symptoms of such disease include *angina* (chest pain due to insufficient blood supply to the heart) and *heart attack* (death of heart muscle tissue).

How does stress contribute to heart disease? Recall that one of the major brain and nervous system autonomic reactions to stress is the release of epinephrine (adrenaline) and cortisol into the bloodstream. These hormones increase heart rate and release fat and glucose from the body's stores to give muscles a readily available source of energy. If no physical action is taken (and this is most likely the case in our modern lives), the fat that was released into the bloodstream is not burned as fuel. Instead, it may adhere to the walls of blood vessels. These fatty deposits are a major cause of blood-supply blockage, which, in turn, causes heart attacks. Of course, the stress-related buildup of fat in our arteries is not the only risk factor associated with heart disease. Other factors include smoking, obesity, a high-fat diet, and lack of exercise (Christian et al., 2015; Diaz et al., 2016; Steptoe et al., 2016).

To end on a more positive note, one group of researchers found that no matter how many, or how few, stressful events a person faces, those who perceive the events as more stressful or who experience a greater spike in negative emotions may be at the greatest risk for heart disease (Sin et al., 2016). This means that the resources for stress management discussed later in the chapter can be very helpful in changing your cognitive appraisal and stress reactions.

## Posttraumatic Stress Disorder (PTSD)

One of the most powerful examples of the effects of severe stress is **posttraumatic stress disorder (PTSD)** (American Psychiatric Association, 2013; Anisman, 2016; Levine, 2015). PTSD is a long-lasting, trauma- and stressor-related disorder that overwhelms an individual's ability to cope. It can occur in both adults and children.

Have you ever been in a serious car accident or been the victim of a violent crime? According to the National Institute of Mental Health (NIMH) (2014), it's natural to feel afraid in dangerous situations like these. But it's important to note that most people who experience traumatic events do not later suffer from PTSD. For example, our introductory famous figure, Marcus Luttrell, and his twin brother, Morgan, both served as Navy SEALs, and both experienced similar war-time traumas, yet neither developed PTSD. Interestingly, Morgan Luttrell, driven by his long-term goal to find the best treatment for veterans suffering from PTSD, went back to school and is now an accomplished neuroscientist (Tarrant, 2016).

For people who do suffer from PTSD, the normal fight-flight-freeze response is modified or damaged. This change helps explain why people with PTSD continue to experience extreme stress and fear, even when they're no longer in danger.

PTSD's essential feature is the development of characteristic symptoms (**Table 3.1**) following exposure to one or more traumatic events (American Psychiatric Association, 2013). These symptoms may continue for months or even years after the event. Unfortunately, some victims of PTSD turn to alcohol and other drugs to cope, which generally compounds the problem (Goldstein et al., 2016; McLean et al., 2015; Smith et al., 2016).

Sadly, one of the most dangerous problems associated with PTSD is the increased risk for suicide. Did you know that more U.S. troops have died from suicide over the last 15 years than have been killed in Afghanistan (National Veterans Foundation, 2016)? The precise cause

**Posttraumatic stress disorder (PTSD)**  A long-lasting, trauma- and stressor-related disorder that overwhelms an individual's ability to cope.

---

**TABLE 3.1**

### Key Characteristics of PTSD

1. *Direct exposure to trauma* through experiencing it personally, witnessing it, or discovering that it happened to others. Also, direct, ongoing exposure to traumatic events (e.g., first responders).
2. *Recurrent, intrusive symptoms*, including thoughts, feelings, memories, and bad dreams. Also, re-experiencing the trauma over and over through *flashbacks*.
3. *Avoidance symptoms*, such as feeling emotionally numb, losing interest in previously enjoyable activities, avoiding memories of the trauma and/or stimuli associated with the traumatic event.
4. *Chronic heightened arousal and reactivity*, including irritability, being easily startled, sleep disturbances, angry outbursts, and reckless/self-destructive behaviors.

Orlando Sentinel/Getty Images

**FIGURE 3.8    Stress and PTSD**    People who experience traumatic events, such as the survivors of the 2016 nightclub shooting massacre in Orlando, Florida, may develop symptoms of PTSD.

for this astronomically high number of suicides is unknown, but experts point to PTSD, along with combat injuries and the difficulties of readjusting to civilian life (Ashrafioun et al., 2016; Finley et al., 2015; Legarreta et al., 2015).

Lest you think PTSD only develops from military experiences, keep in mind that victims of natural disasters, physical or sexual assault, and terrorist attacks also may develop PTSD. In addition, research shows that simply watching televised coverage of major natural disasters, such as hurricanes, earthquakes, and tornados, can increase the number of PTSD symptoms, especially in children who are already experiencing other symptoms (Holman et al., 2014; Weems et al., 2012).

PTSD is not a new problem. During the Industrial Revolution, workers who survived horrific railroad accidents sometimes developed a condition very similar to PTSD. It was called "railway spine" because experts thought the problem resulted from a twisting or concussion of the spine. Later, doctors working with combat veterans referred to the disorder as "shell shock" because they believed it was a response to the physical concussion caused by exploding artillery. Today, we know that PTSD is caused by exposure to extraordinary stress (**Figure 3.8**).

What can we do to help? Professionals have had success with various forms of therapy and medication for PTSD (e.g., Castillo et al., 2016; Keller & Tuerk, 2016; Watts et al., 2016). They've also offered several constructive tips for the general public (see **Table 3.2** and the **Try This Yourself** feature).

**TABLE 3.2**

| Seven Important Tips for Coping with Crisis |
| --- |
| 1. If you have experienced a traumatic event, recognize your feelings about the situation, and talk to others about your fears. Know that these feelings are a normal response to an abnormal situation. |
| 2. If you know someone who has been traumatized, be willing to patiently listen to that person's account of the event, pay attention to his or her feelings, and encourage him or her to seek counseling, if necessary. |
| 3. Be patient and kind to yourself and others. It's natural to feel anxious, helpless, and/or frustrated, but give yourself a break. Also, tempers are short in times of crisis, and others may be feeling as much stress as you. |
| 4. Recognize normal crisis reactions, such as sleep disturbances and nightmares, withdrawal, reversion to childhood behaviors, and trouble focusing on work or school. |
| 5. Be mindful of your time. Feel free to say "NO" to others. Limit your news watching. Take time with your children, spouse, life partner, friends, and coworkers to do something you enjoy. |
| 6. Get plenty of sleep and avoid alcohol and other drugs. We all need a good night's sleep, especially during times of crisis. Alcohol and other drugs interfere with sleep and good decision making. |
| 7. Study and adopt stress management skills, such as the ones discussed in this chapter. |

**Source:** Based on information from Pomponio, 2002; Thorn, 2013; Tips for Coping with Crisis, 2015.

## Try This Yourself

### Helping Someone with PTSD

If you have a friend or loved one with PTSD, it may feel like you're walking through a minefield when you're attempting to provide comfort and help. What do the experts suggest that you say (or NOT say)? Here are a few general tips:

### What NOT to Do

**Don't trivialize the disease.** Like cancer or heart disease, PTSD, and its associated anxiety and depression, is a critical, life-threatening illness. Asking someone, "What do you have to be depressed about?" is akin to asking cancer patients why they have cancer or why they don't just smile and exercise more.

**Don't be a cheerleader or a Mr. or Ms. Fix-It.** You can't pep-talk someone out of PTSD, and offering cheap advice or solutions is the best way to ensure that you'll be the last person he or she will turn to for help.

## What Can You Do?

**Educate yourself.** Your psychology instructor, your college library, almost any book store, and the Internet all provide a wealth of information.

**Be Rogerian.** Carl Rogers's four key qualities of communication (*empathy, unconditional positive regard, genuineness*, and *active listening*, discussed in Chapter 13) are probably the best, and safest, approaches in any situation—including talking with someone who's suffering from PTSD.

**Get help!** The most dangerous problem associated with PTSD, and its commonly associated serious depression, is the high risk

of suicide. If a friend or loved one mentions suicide, or if you believe he or she is considering it, get help fast! Consider calling the police for emergency intervention, contacting a trusted friend or family member of the person, or calling the toll-free 7/24 hotline 1-800-SUICIDE.

John Gomez/Getty Images

© Billy R. Ray/Wiley

## Retrieval Practice 3.2 | Stress and Illness

Completing this self-test and the connections section, and then checking your answers by clicking on the answer button or by looking in Appendix B, will provide immediate feedback and helpful practice for exams.

### Self-Test

1. Briefly explain why psychosomatic illnesses are not imaginary.
2. Which of the following is true?
   a. Stress is a leading cause of cancer.
   b. Positive attitudes alone can prevent cancer.
   c. Both of these options.
   d. None of these options.
3. Stress may contribute to heart disease by releasing _____ and _____, which increase the level of fat in the blood.
   a. angina; cortisol
   b. hormones; GABA
   c. cynical hostility; hormones
   d. epinephrine (adrenaline); cortisol
4. Someone who experiences flashbacks, nightmares, and other forms of recurring intrusive symptoms following a life-threatening or other horrifying event may be _____.
   a. suffering from a substance abuse disorder
   b. experiencing symptoms of PTSD

   c. having a psychotic breakdown
   d. weaker than people who take such events in stride
5. _____ is not one of the key characteristics of PTSD identified in the text.
   a. Exposure to serious trauma
   b. Persistent avoidance of stimuli related to traumatic event
   c. Marked changes in arousal and reactivity
   d. Animistic behaviors

### Connections—Chapter to Chapter

Answering the following question will help you "look back and look ahead" to see the important connections among the various subfields of psychology and chapters within this text.

In this chapter, you discovered that the effects of prolonged stress may result in permanent damage to the *hippocampus*. Describe what you learned about the hippocampus in Chapter 2 (Neuroscience and Biological Foundations), and discuss what cognitive changes we might see in someone experiencing PTSD.

## 3.3 Stress Management

### LEARNING OBJECTIVES

**Retrieval Practice** While reading the upcoming sections, respond to each Learning Objective in your own words.

**Review the major factors involved in managing and coping with stress.**

- **Discuss** the role of cognitive appraisal in coping with stress.
- **Describe** how personality and individual differences affect stress responses.
- **Summarize** the major resources for healthy living

As noted at the beginning of this chapter, stress is a normal, and necessary, part of our lives. Therefore, *stress management* is the goal—not stress elimination (see the **Try This Yourself**). Although our initial bodily responses to stress are largely controlled by nonconscious, autonomic processes, our higher brain functions can help us avoid the serious damage caused by chronic overarousal. The key is to consciously recognize when we are overstressed and then to choose resources that activate our parasympathetic relaxation response. In this section, we'll first discuss the role of cognitive appraisal in coping with stress. Then, we'll explore how personality and individual differences affect our coping responses. Finally, we'll present several major resources for healthy living and stress management.

---

## Try This Yourself

### Stress and Illness

Think about a time when you were experiencing stress, such as studying for a difficult exam, having a fight with a loved one, or struggling to pay your bills. Both minor and major stressors can decrease the effectiveness of your immune system and thereby lead to both short- and long-term health problems. Given the previous discussion of all the ill effects of stress, can you see why it's so important not only to reduce your stress levels but also to improve your personal coping skills?

© Keeweeboy/iStockphoto

---

## Cognitive Appraisal

Because we can't escape stress, we need to learn how to effectively cope with it. Our first approach to stress management generally begins with a cognitive appraisal of the stressor (**Step-by-Step Diagram 3.3**).

One of the biggest challenges during the process of stress management is deciding whether to try to change the stressor itself or our emotional reactions to it. **Problem-focused coping** strategies work to deal directly with a stressor in order to eventually decrease or eliminate it (Delahaij & van Dam, 2016; Dixon et al., 2016; Mayordomo-Rodriquez et al., 2015). We tend to choose this approach, and find it most effective, when we have some control over a stressful situation. Although you may feel like you have little or no control over exams and other common academic stressors, our students have found that by using the various study tools provided throughout this text and on our text's website, they increased their personal control and success, while also decreasing their stress levels. Do you see how this approach of studying and adopting new study skills would be a good example of *problem-focused coping*?

Many times, however, it seems that little or nothing can be done to alter the stressful situation, so we turn to **emotion-focused coping**, in which we attempt to relieve or regulate our emotional reactions. If you're dealing with the death of a loved one, the pain and stress are out of your control. To cope with your painful emotions, you might try distraction, meditation, journaling, or talking to a friend and/or therapist, which are all healthy forms of *emotion-focused coping*.

Keep in mind that emotion-focused forms of coping can't change the problem, but they do make us feel better about the stressful situation. For example, teenagers who are asked to think about the "silver lining" benefits of a recent stressful event—such as having a traffic accident or losing a valued relationship—show increases in positive mood and decreases in negative mood (Rood et al., 2012). Instant messaging (IM) also helps distressed teenagers share their emotions and receive immediate social support and advice (Dolev-Cohen & Barak, 2013).

**Problem-focused coping**    The strategies we use to deal directly with a stressor to eventually decrease or eliminate it.

**Emotion-focused coping**    The strategies we use to relieve or regulate our emotional reactions to a stressful situation.

**STOP!**  This Step-by-Step Diagram contains essential information NOT found else-where in the text, which is likely to appear on quizzes and exams. Be sure to study it CAREFULLY!

Research suggests that when facing a serious stressor, we begin with a *primary appraisal* process to eval-uate the threat and decide whether it's harmless or potentially harmful. Next, during *secondary apprais-al*, we assess our available and potential resources for coping with the stress. Then, we generally choose either *emotion-* or *problem-focused* methods of coping. When attempting to resolve complex stressors, or a stressful situation that is in flux, we often combine both emotion- and problem-focused approaches.

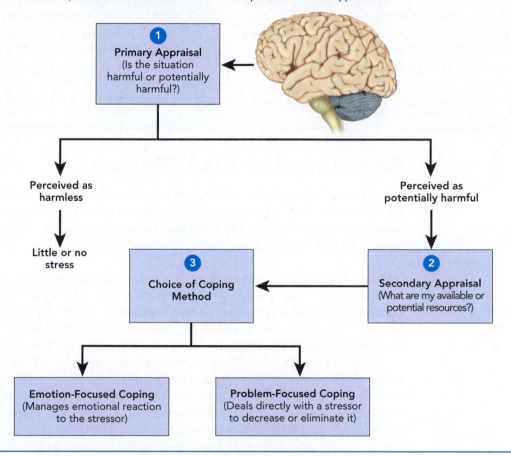

As you'll discover in Chapter 13, Sigmund Freud believed we commonly turn to another cognitive approach when facing uncomfortable or painful stressors. We use **defense mechanisms**, in which we unconsciously distort reality to protect our egos and to avoid anxiety (see **Table 3.3** and Chapter 13). These defense mechanisms can sometimes act as a beneficial type of emotion-focused coping. For example, when you're really angry at your boss and realize that you can't safely express that anger, you may take out your frustration by aggressively hitting a punching bag at the gym. This would be a healthy use of defense mechanisms. But if taken too far, defense mecha-nisms can be destructive. If we fail to get a promotion, and then resort to elaborate excuses (rationalizations) for our failure, it may block us from see-ing a situation more clearly and realistically, which in turn can prevent us from developing valuable skills (see the cartoon). In short, occasional use of defense mechanisms can be beneficial, as long as it's not excessive and does not distort reality (Hertel et al., 2015; Levine, 2015).

**Defense mechanisms**  Freud's term for the strategies the ego uses to reduce anxiety by uncon-sciously distorting reality.

*"Before we begin, I'd like to say a few words about the concept of 'defence mechanisms'."*

BART/CartoonStock

**TABLE 3.3** Sample Psychological Defense Mechanisms

| Defense Mechanism | Description | Example |
|---|---|---|
| Repression | Preventing painful or unacceptable thoughts from entering consciousness | Forgetting the details of a tragic accident |
| Sublimation | Redirecting socially unacceptable impulses into acceptable activities | Redirecting aggressive impulses by becoming a professional fighter |
| Denial | Refusing to accept an unpleasant reality | Alcoholics refusing to admit their addiction |
| Rationalization | Creating a socially acceptable excuse to justify unacceptable behavior | Justifying cheating on an exam by saying "everyone else does it" |
| Intellectualization | Ignoring the emotional aspects of a painful experience by focusing on abstract thoughts, words, or ideas | Discussing your divorce without emotion while ignoring the hidden, underlying pain |
| Projection | Transferring unacceptable thoughts, motives, or impulses to others | Becoming unreasonably jealous of your mate while denying your own attraction to others |
| Reaction formation | Not acknowledging unacceptable impulses and overemphasizing their opposite | Promoting a petition against adult bookstores even though you are secretly fascinated by pornography |
| Regression | Reverting to immature ways of responding | Throwing a temper tantrum when a friend doesn't want to do what you'd like |
| Displacement | Redirecting impulses from the original source toward a less threatening person or object | Yelling at a coworker after being criticized by your boss |

# Personality and Individual Differences

We've just seen how problem- and emotion-focused coping, as well as defense mechanisms, are used in stress management. Research has also found that various personality types and individual differences directly affect how we cope with stress. In this section, we discuss the various effects of locus of control, positive affect, and optimism.

**Locus of Control**  Perhaps one of the most important personal resources for stress management is a sense of personal control. People who believe they are the "masters of their own destiny" have what is known as an **internal locus of control**. Believing they control their own fate, they tend to make more effective decisions and healthier lifestyle choices, are more likely to follow treatment programs, and more often find ways to positively cope with a situation.

**Internal locus of control**  The belief that we control our own fate.

Do you see how an internal locus of control is closely related to a *growth mindset* and *grit*, and how our introductory famous figure, Marcus Luttrell, demonstrates all three of these traits? He obviously believes in his personal control, and his growth mindset and grit are shown when he talks about the Navy SEALS (including himself): "The real battle is won in the mind. It's won by guys who understand their areas of weakness, who sit and think about it, plotting and planning to improve. Attending to the detail. Work on their weaknesses and overcome them. Because they can" (Marcus Luttrell, n.d.).

Conversely, people with an **external locus of control** believe that chance or outside forces beyond their control determine their fate. Therefore, they tend to feel powerless to change their circumstances, are less likely to make effective and positive changes, and are more likely to experience high levels of stress (e.g., Au, 2015; Rotter, 1966; Zhang et al., 2014).

**External locus of control**  The belief that chance or outside forces beyond our control determine our fate.

**Positive Affect**  Have you ever wondered why some people survive in the face of great stress (personal tragedies, demanding jobs, or an abusive home life) while others do not? One answer may be that these "survivors" have a unique trait called **positive affect**, meaning they experience and express positive emotions, including feelings of happiness, joy, enthusiasm, and contentment. Interestingly, people who are high in positive affect also experience fewer colds and car accidents, as well as better sleep and an enhanced quality of life (Anisman, 2016; Pollock et al., 2016; Tavernier et al., 2016).

**Positive affect**  The experience or expression of positive feelings (affect), including happiness, joy, enthusiasm, and contentment.

Positive states are also sometimes associated with fewer physical symptoms, more biological indicators of good health, and less vision impairment (Cameron et al., 2015; Liu et al., 2016; Zhang & Han, 2016). In addition, one study that followed 3,777 participants for over 22 years found a significant association between positive affect and a longer life, even after adjustment for factors such as prior medical conditions (Gana et al., 2016). These studies provide intriguing evidence for the mind-body link.

Can you see how having positive affect is closely associated with a good sense of humor? Humor is one of the best methods you can use to reduce stress. The ability to laugh at oneself and at life's inevitable ups and downs allows us to relax and gain a broader perspective (**Figure 3.9**).

**Optimism**   Positive affect is also closely associated with **optimism**, the expectation that good things will happen in the future and bad things will not. If you agree with statements such as, "I tend to expect the best of others," or "I generally think of several ways to get out of a difficult situation," you're probably an optimist. The opposite is true if you tend to be a pessimist.

As you might expect, optimists are generally much better at stress management. Rather than seeing bad times as a constant threat and assuming personal responsibility for them, they generally assume that bad times are temporary and external to themselves. Optimists also tend to have better overall physical and psychological health, and they typically have longer and overall happier lives (Denovan & Macaskill, 2017; Hernandez et al., 2015; Kim et al., 2017).

Why are optimists healthier? To test this question, researchers in one study tracked 135 older adults (aged 60+) over six years (Jobin et al., 2014). Participants were asked about the level of stress they perceived in their day-to-day lives and whether they would rate themselves as optimists or pessimists. Saliva samples were then collected from each individual to measure his or her current level of cortisol. The results revealed that compared to self-described optimists, people who described themselves as pessimists had higher cortisol levels, a higher baseline level of stress, and more difficulty coping with stress. The researchers suggested that the optimists enjoyed better health because their lower cortisol levels and better coping strategies reduced the "wear-and-tear" of the biological effects of stress on their bodies.

The best news is that according to Martin Seligman, a leader in the field of positive psychology, optimism can be learned (Seligman, 2012). In short, he believes optimism requires careful monitoring and challenging of our thoughts, feelings, and self-talk. For example, if you don't get a promotion at work or you receive a low grade on an exam, don't focus on all the negative possible outcomes and unreasonably blame yourself. Instead, force yourself to think of alternate ways to meet your goals, and develop specific plans to improve your performance. Chapter 15 offers additional help and details for overcoming faulty thought processes.

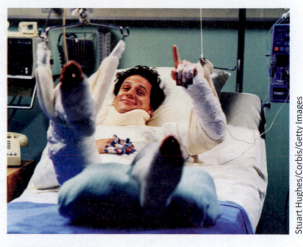

**FIGURE 3.9**   **Positive affect in action**   Based on his smile and cheery wave, it looks like this patient may be one of those lucky people with a naturally positive outlook on life. Can you see how this approach might help him cope and recuperate from his serious injuries?

Stuart Hughes/Corbis/Getty Images

**Optimism**   A tendency to expect the best and to see the best in all things.

## Resources for Healthy Living

As we've just seen, various cognitive appraisal techniques and personality and individual differences have significant effects on our stress management. In this section, we'll provide specific, evidence-based resources for stress management. Perhaps the most researched approach comes from the recent **mindfulness-based stress reduction (MBSR)** programs, which are based on developing a state of consciousness that attends to ongoing events in a receptive, nonjudgmental way. The practice of MBSR has proven to be particularly effective in managing stress and treating mood disturbances, and it's even been linked to positive, and perhaps permanent, cell and brain changes (Creswell et al., 2016; Felleman et al., 2016; Mallya & Fiocco, 2016). For more good news about mindfulness, see the following **Psychology and Your Personal Success**.

**Mindfulness-based stress reduction (MBSR)**   A stress reduction strategy based on developing a state of consciousness that attends to ongoing events in a receptive and nonjudgmental way.

## ❖ Psychology and Your Personal Success | Can Mindfulness Improve Your GPA?

Researchers interested in the potential usefulness of mindfulness training in academic settings assigned students either to a seven-week mental training program designed to tame mind wandering and increase focus or to a control group that received no training (Morrison et al., 2013). Students in the two groups did not differ at the start of the semester on levels of attention and mind wandering (two factors that lead to lower academic performance). However, by the end of the semester, students in the control group showed diminished attention and increased mind wandering. In contrast, those who participated in the mindfulness program showed significant improvements in attention and no increases in reported mind wandering.

Related studies with college students who engage in mindfulness-based stress reduction (MBSR) programs show improvements in reading comprehension and working memory capacity, as well as better overall adjustment to the college environment (Mrazek et al., 2013; Ramler et al., 2016). For younger children, a school-based mindfulness program, which includes breathing and movement exercises, helps many elementary school children manage their stress better and become more optimistic, more helpful, more caring, better liked by peers, and even better at math (Schonert-Reichl et al., 2015).

Another effective and frequently overlooked resource for stress management is *social support*. When we are faced with stressful circumstances, our friends and family often help us take care of our health, listen, hold our hands, make us feel important, and provide stability to offset the changes in our lives.

This support can help offset the stressful effects of chronic illness, pregnancy, physical abuse, job loss, and work overload. People who have greater social support also experience better health outcomes, including greater psychological well-being, greater physical well-being, faster recovery from illness, and a longer life expectancy (Diener & Tay, 2015; Flannery et al., 2017; Martínez-Hernáez et al., 2016). Even a single close childhood friendship seems to protect children in lower socioeconomic circumstances (which is an ongoing stressor) from several negative psychological risk factors (Graber et al., 2015).

These findings may help explain why married people live longer than unmarried people (Liu, 2009) and why a married person with cancer is 20% less likely to die from the disease than an unmarried person (Aizer et al., 2013). So what is the take-home message from this emphasis on social support? Don't be afraid to offer help and support to others—or to ask for the same for yourself!

Six additional resources for healthy living and stress management are exercise, social skills, behavior change, stressor control, material resources, and relaxation. These resources are summarized in **Concept Organizer 3.2**.

---

**CONCEPT ORGANIZER 3.2** | **Six Additional Stress Resources**

---

**STOP!** This Concept Organizer contains essential information NOT found elsewhere in the text, which is likely to appear on quizzes and exams. Be sure to study it CAREFULLY!

---

| **Exercise** | Exercising and keeping fit help minimize anxiety and depression, which are associated with stress. Exercise also helps relieve muscle tension; improves cardiovascular efficiency; and increases strength, flexibility, and stamina.<br><br>*Those who do not find time for exercise will have to find time for illness.*<br>—Edward Smith-Stanley | <br>© Rich Vintage/iStockphoto |
| --- | --- | --- |
| **Social skills** | People who acquire social skills (such as knowing appropriate behaviors for certain situations, having conversation starters up their sleeves, and expressing themselves well) suffer less anxiety than people who do not. Social skills not only help us interact with others but also communicate our needs and desires, enlist help when we need it, and decrease hostility in tense situations. | <br>© Henk Badenhorst/iStockphoto |

*(Continued)*

| | | |
|---|---|---|
| **Behavior change** | When under stress, do you smoke, drink, overeat, zone out in front of the TV or computer, sleep too much, procrastinate, or take your stress out on others? If so, substitute healthier choices. | *Louis A. Arana-Barradas/U.S. Air Force* |
| **Stressor control** | While not all stress can be eliminated, it helps to recognize and avoid unnecessary stress by analyzing your schedule and removing nonessential tasks and controlling your environment by avoiding people and topics that stress you. It also helps to find a less stressful job and to give yourself permission to say "no" to extra tasks and responsibilities. | *© PK-Photos/ iStockphoto* |
| **Material resources** | Money increases the number of options available for eliminating sources of stress or reducing the effects of stress. When faced with the minor hassles of everyday living, acute or chronic stressors, or major catastrophes, people with more money and the skills to use it effectively generally fare better. They experience less overall stress and can "buy" more resources to help them cope with what stressors they do have. | *© Juanmonino/ iStockphoto* |
| **Relaxation** | There are a variety of relaxation techniques. *Biofeedback* is often used in the treatment of chronic pain, but it is also useful in teaching people to relax and manage their stress. *Progressive relaxation* helps reduce or relieve the muscular tension commonly associated with stress (see the following **Try This Yourself**). | *Dynamic GraphicsValue/ SUPERSTOCK* |

## Test Your Critical Thinking

1. Health psychologists often advise personal and lifestyle changes like the ones in this feature. Do you think this is important? If so, what changes do you plan to make that would improve your own health and longevity?

2. Why do you think most people are so reluctant to make these lifestyle changes?

## Try This Yourself

### Practicing Progressive Relaxation

You can use progressive relaxation techniques whenever and wherever you feel stressed, such as before or during an exam. Here's how:

1. Sit in a comfortable position, with your head supported.

2. Start breathing slowly and deeply.

3. Let your entire body relax. Release all tension. Try to visualize your body getting progressively more relaxed with each breath.

4. Systematically tense and release each part of your body, beginning with your toes. Curl them tightly while counting to 10. Now, release them. Note the difference between the tense and relaxed states. Next, tense your feet to the count of 10. Then relax them and feel the difference. Continue upward with your calves, thighs, buttocks, abdomen, back muscles, shoulders, upper arms, forearms, hands and fingers, neck, jaw, facial muscles, and forehead. Try practicing progressive relaxation twice a day for about 15 minutes each time. You will be surprised at how quickly you can learn to relax—even in the most stressful situations.

© Billy R. Ray/Wiley

## Retrieval Practice 3.3 | Stress Management

Completing this self-test and the connections section, and then checking your answers by clicking on the answer button or by looking in Appendix B, will provide immediate feedback and helpful practice for exams.

### Self-Test

1. What is the major difference between emotion-focused coping and problem-focused coping?

2. Freud's term for the strategies the ego uses to reduce anxiety by unconsciously distorting reality is known as _____.
   a. "rose-colored glasses" syndrome
   b. defense mannerisms
   c. ego-denial apparatus
   d. defense mechanisms

3. Research suggests that people with _____ have less psychological stress than those with _____.

   a. an external locus of control; an internal locus of control
   b. an internal locus of control; an external locus of control
   c. an attributional coping style; a person-centered coping style
   d. an emotion-focused coping style; a problem-focused coping style

4. Demonstrating positive emotions, including feelings of happiness, joy, enthusiasm, and contentment, is known as _____.

   a. positive defect
   b. the positivity principle
   c. the Rogerian technique
   d. positive affect

5. Which of the following is *not* one of the ways to cope with stress outlined in the chapter?

   a. exercise
   b. sense of humor
   c. social support
   d. stimulant drugs

### Connections—Chapter to Chapter

Answering the following questions will help you "look back and look ahead" to see the important connections among the various subfields of psychology and chapters within this text.

1. In the Prologue, you learned about Critical Thinking Components (CTCs) such as empathizing (affective), accepting change (affective), and resisting overgeneralization (cognitive). Describe how practicing these CTCs may help you to cope with stressors in your life.

2. In Chapter 16 (Social Psychology), you'll explore the ways in which other people influence our thoughts, feelings, and actions in both positive and negative ways. Consider how your social relationships and interactions with the people in your life (friends, family, co-workers, classmates, and professors) influence you. How do some of these relationships help you to cope better with your life stressors? Or perhaps contribute to them?

# 3.4 Health Psychology

## LEARNING OBJECTIVES

**Retrieval Practice** While reading the upcoming sections, respond to each Learning Objective in your own words.

**Summarize the field of health psychology and the role of stress in health psychology.**

- **Identify** health psychology.
- **Describe** the work of health psychologists.
- **Discuss** how health psychology can be used in the workplace.

Did you know that according to the latest report, Americans' life expectancy recently dropped for the first time since 1993 (Centers for Disease Control, 2016)? And do you recall that, as mentioned earlier, ulcers, cancer, cardiovascular disorders, and PTSD significantly affect our physical well-being, as well as our cognitive, emotional, and behavioral responses? Such trends and effects are the concerns of health psychologists. In this final section, we'll discuss the work of health psychologists, followed by an exploration of stress in the workplace.

## What Is Health Psychology?

**Health psychology** A branch of psychology that studies how biological, psychological, and social (biopsychosocial) factors influence health, illness, and health-related behaviors.

**Health psychology** is the branch of psychology that studies how biological, psychological, and social factors influence health, illness, and health-related behaviors. It emphasizes wellness and the prevention of illness, as well as the interplay between our physical health and our psychological well-being.

As researchers, health psychologists are particularly interested in how changes in behavior can improve health outcomes (Anisman, 2016; Straub, 2014). They also emphasize the relationship between stress and the immune system. As we discovered earlier, a normally functioning immune system helps defend against disease. On the other hand, a suppressed immune system leaves the body susceptible to a number of illnesses.

As practitioners, health psychologists can work as independent clinicians or as consultants alongside physicians, physical and occupational therapists, and other health care workers. The goal of health psychologists is to reduce unhealthy behaviors and psychological distress among suffering individuals and affected family members (see **Figure 3.10**). They also help patients and families make critical decisions and prepare psychologically for surgery or other treatment. In fact, health psychologists have become so involved with health and illness that medical centers are one of their major employers (Considering a Career, 2011).

Health psychologists also educate the public about illness *prevention* and health *maintenance*. For example, they provide public information about the effects of stress, smoking, alcohol, lack of exercise, and other health issues. Let's look at smoking as an example. Tobacco use endangers both smokers and those who breathe secondhand smoke, so it's not surprising that health psychologists are concerned with preventing smoking and getting those who already smoke to stop.

Did you know that according to the U.S. Department of Health and Human Services, smoking has killed 10 times the number of Americans who died in all our nation's wars combined (Sebelius, 2014)? Thanks in large part to comprehensive mass media campaigns, smoke-free policies, restrictions on underage access to tobacco, and large price increases, adult smoking rates have fallen from about 43% in 1965 to about 15% in 2015. Unfortunately, cigarette smoking remains the leading cause of preventable death worldwide (Centers for Disease Control, 2016). Given that almost everyone recognizes the serious consequences of smoking, and the fact that the first puff is rarely pleasant, why do people start smoking? The answer can be found in the biopsychosocial model and the biology of addiction (**Figure 3.11**).

In addition to encouraging smokers to stop—and urging nonsmokers never to start—health psychologists help people cope with conditions such as chronic pain, diabetes, and high blood pressure, as well as unhealthful behaviors such as inappropriate anger and/or lack of assertiveness. If you're interested in a career in this field, check with your college's counseling or career center.

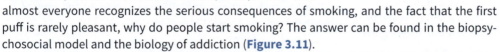

Dennis MacDonald/PhotoEdit

**FIGURE 3.10    Test your critical thinking**

1. How might both the mother and child in this photo be affected biologically, psychologically, and socially (the biopsychosocial model) by alcohol abuse?

2. What could a health psychologist do to improve the well-being of the mother and child?

**FIGURE 3.11    Understanding nicotine addiction**

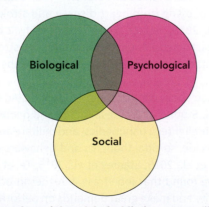

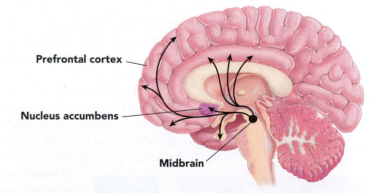

**a. The biopsychosocial model of addiction**    As you'll see throughout this text, the biopsychosocial model helps explain almost all human behavior, including nicotine addiction. From a psychological and social perspective, smokers learn to associate smoking with pleasant things, such as good food, friends, and sex. People also form such associations from seeing smoking in the movies, which is one reason researchers believe that requiring all movies with characters who smoke to be rated R would reduce smoking in teenagers by 20% (Sargent et al., 2012). From a biological perspective, nicotine is highly addictive. Once a person begins to smoke, there is a biological need to continue—as explained next.

**b. The biology of addiction**    Nicotine addiction appears to be very similar to heroin, cocaine, and alcohol addiction, and all four drugs are commonly associated with depression (Müller & Homberg, 2015; Torrens & Rossi, 2015; Wu et al., 2014). To make matters worse, nicotine quickly increases the release of acetylcholine and norepinephrine in our brains, increasing alertness, concentration, memory, and feelings of pleasure. Nicotine also stimulates the release of dopamine, the neurotransmitter most closely related to our brains' reward centers (shown in the figure above). This so-called "pleasure pathway" extends from an area in the midbrain, to the nucleus accumbens, and on to other subcortical structures and the prefrontal cortex.

## Health Psychology at Work

Have you ever dragged yourself home from work so tired you feared you couldn't make it to your bed? Do you think your job may be killing you? You may be right! The Japanese even have a specific word for this type of extreme job stress, "karoshi" [KAH-roe-she], which is translated literally as "death from overwork." See the following **Gender and Cultural Diversity**.

---

### Gender and Cultural Diversity

#### Culture and Job Stress

The term *karoshi* was first brought to public awareness in 1969 when a 29-year-old Japanese worker died of a stroke following long hours working under stressful conditions (Sullivan, 2014). During Japan's "Boom Years" of the 1980s and the "Lost Decade" of the 1990s, work-related deaths and illnesses increased, and Japanese health personnel officially recognized karoshi as a valid and potentially lethal condition.

Working under stressful conditions 10 or 12 hours a day, 6 and 7 days a week, year after year increases the risk of death or serious disabilities from strokes and diabetes. And researchers have also reported that more than 10,000 Japanese workers die each year from work-related cardiovascular diseases. But few victims of karoshi are compensated under the Japanese workers' compensation system (Eguchi et al., 2016; Steger, 2016; Tayama, 2014). In addition, job stressors leave many workers disoriented and suffering from serious stress even when they're not working. Sadly, working and living conditions in Japan are much worse today, after the country's catastrophic earthquake, tsunami, and nuclear accidents.

Similar deaths, disabilities, and psychological problems from overwork have spread to other Eastern countries, and things are not much better in the United States and Western Europe. Economic globalization appears to increase stressful job characteristics for the workers, such as additional and changing demands, low job control, effort-reward imbalances, job insecurity, and long work hours. Larger employer and economic factors, including precarious employment, downsizing/restructuring, privatization, and lean production, further exacerbate these problems (Nishiyama & Johnson, 2014; Schnall et al., 2016). Unfortunately, in our global economy, pressures to reduce costs and to increase productivity will undoubtedly continue, and job stress is a serious and growing health risk—as you'll see in the next section.

---

**Job Stress** As mentioned at the start of this chapter, among the top sources of stress for most people is *job stress*, which can result from unemployment, job change, and/or worries about job performance (see the photo). And, as we've just seen, job strain is increasing around the world. As in other countries, research in the United States finds that job stress and overwork can greatly increase the risk of dying from heart disease and stroke (Biering et al., 2015; Charles et al., 2014; Huang et al., 2015). In fact, a large meta-analysis of the correlation between job strain and coronary heart disease found that people with stressful jobs are 23% more likely to experience a heart attack than those without stressful jobs (Kivimäki et al., 2012).

Perhaps more troubling is the fact that job stress can contribute to suicide (Adams, 2015; Cartwright & Cooper, 2014; Rees et al., 2015). Studies of first responders and people in other high-risk professions, such as police officers, firefighters, paramedics, and military and medical personnel, have found an elevated risk of suicide, suicidal thoughts and behaviors, and post-traumatic stress disorder (PTSD) (Carpenter et al., 2015; Stanley et al., 2016; Tei et al., 2015). In addition, studies have found that job stress is higher in occupations that have little job security and make great demands on performance and concentration, with little or no allowance for creativity or opportunity for advancement (Bauer & Hämmig, 2014; Dawson et al., 2016; Sarafino & Smith, 2016).

Intense job stressors reportedly not only increase the risk for potentially lethal physical and psychological problems, but they also leave some workers disoriented and suffering from serious stress even when they're not working (Calderwood & Ackerman, 2016; Tayama et al., 2016; Tetrick & Peiró, 2016). Stress at work can also cause serious stress at home, not only for the worker but for other family members as well. These risks even apply to our world's top leaders (see the following **Research Challenge**).

PathDoc/Shutterstock

## Research Challenge

### When Do Losers Actually Win?

Can a high-pressure job actually take years off your life? To test this question, researchers in one study examined life expectancy of candidates for head-of-country elections—meaning president or prime minister—in a number of different countries (Olenski et al., 2015). Specifically, the researchers gathered data on the number of years candidates lived after their final campaign for office. They then compared whether candidates who won the election—and thus served as head of country—had fewer years of life than those who lost the election—and thus didn't serve in this capacity. The researchers gathered data from 17 countries (including the United States, Australia, the United Kingdom, and Canada) over nearly 300 years (from 1722 to 2015).

As they predicted, winning an election was actually bad for candidates' health. Candidates who lost the election lived an average of an additional 17.8 years, whereas those who won lived only an average of an additional 13.4 years. In this case, it actually hurts to win—the winning candidate lost an additional 4.4 years of life! Although these numbers don't explain exactly how winning an election led to a shorter life expectancy, researchers believe that the greater stress experienced by heads of country likely helps explain this difference.

JStone/Shutterstock

#### Test Yourself

1. Based on the information provided, did this study (Olenski et al., 2015) use descriptive, correlational, and/or experimental research?

2. If you chose:
   - *descriptive research,* is this a naturalistic observation, survey/interview, case study, and/or archival research?
   - *correlational research,* is this a positive, negative, or zero correlation?
   - *experimental research,* label the IV, DV, experimental group(s), and control group. (Note: If participants were not randomly assigned to groups, list it as a *quasi-experimental design.*)
   - *both descriptive and correlational,* answer the corresponding questions for both.

**Check your answers by clicking on the answer button or by looking in Appendix B.**

**Note:** The information provided in this study is admittedly limited, but the level of detail is similar to what is presented in most textbooks and public reports of research findings. Answering these questions, and then comparing your answers to those provided, will help you become a better critical thinker and consumer of scientific research.

**Technostress**    If you're not suffering from overwork, are you hassled and stressed by the ever-changing technology at your workplace? Do the expensive machines your employers install to "aid productivity" create stress-related problems instead? Does technology in your home allow you to accomplish several things simultaneously—talking on your cell phone, checking and responding to e-mails, warming your dinner in the microwave, doing a load of laundry—yet leave you feeling irritable and exhausted? If so, you may be suffering from the well-documented ill effects of **technostress**, a feeling of anxiety or mental pressure from overexposure or involvement with technology (Joo et al., 2016; Maier et al., 2015; Tarafdar et al., 2010).

Technology is often described as a way of bringing people together. Yet how often have you noticed busy executives frantically checking their e-mail while on vacation? It's even common to see families eating at restaurants while the children play video games or send text messages and the parents loudly talk on separate cell phones. In fact, simply placing a cell phone on the table between two people—even if no one ever picks it up—leads to lower levels of closeness, connection, and meaning in their conversation (Przybylski & Weinstein, 2013).

**Technostress**    A feeling of anxiety or mental pressure from overexposure or involvement with technology; stress caused by an inability to cope with modern technology.

### ❖ Psychology and Your Professional Success | How Well Do You Cope with Job Stress?

Experts suggest that we can (and must) control technology and its impact on our lives. Admittedly, we all find the new technologies convenient and useful. But how can we control technostress? First, evaluate each new technology on its usefulness for you and your lifestyle. It isn't a yes or no, "technophobe" or "technophile," choice. If something works for you, invest the energy to adopt it. Second, establish clear boundaries. Technology came into the world with an implied promise of a better and more productive life. But, for many, the servant has become the master. Like any healthy relationship, our technology interactions should be based on moderation and balance (Ashton, 2013).

Of course, technostress is not the only source of job-related stress. You can score your past, current, and potential future careers on several additional factors in the following **Try This Yourself**.

## Try This Yourself

### Workplace Stress

Start by identifying what you like and don't like about your current (and past) jobs. With this information in hand, you'll be prepared to find jobs that will better suit your interests, needs, and abilities, which will likely reduce your stress. To start your analysis, answer *Yes* or *No* to these questions:

1. Is there a sufficient amount of laughter and sociability in my workplace?
2. Does my boss notice and appreciate my work?
3. Is my boss understanding and friendly?
4. Am I embarrassed by the physical conditions of my workplace?
5. Do I feel safe and comfortable in my place of work?
6. Do I like the location of my job?
7. If I won the lottery and were guaranteed a lifetime income, would I feel truly sad if I also had to quit my job?
8. Do I watch the clock, daydream, take long lunches, and leave work as soon as possible?
9. Do I frequently feel stressed and overwhelmed by the demands of my job?
10. Compared to others with my qualifications, am I being paid what I am worth?
11. Are promotions made in a fair and just manner where I work?
12. Given the demands of my job, am I fairly compensated for my work?

Now score your answers. Give yourself one point for each answer that matches the following: 1. No; 2. No; 3. No; 4. Yes; 5. No; 6. No; 7. No; 8. Yes; 9. Yes; 10. No; 11. No; 12. No.

The questions you just answered are based on four factors that research shows are conducive to increased job satisfaction and reduced stress: supportive colleagues, supportive working conditions, mentally challenging work, and equitable rewards (Robbins, 1996). Your total score reveals your overall level of dissatisfaction. A look at specific questions can help identify which of these four factors is most important to your job satisfaction—and most lacking in your current job.

1. **Supportive colleagues (items 1, 2, 3):** For most people, work fills valuable social needs. Therefore, having friendly and supportive colleagues and superiors leads to increased satisfaction.
2. **Supportive working conditions (items 4, 5, 6):** Not surprisingly, most employees prefer working in safe, clean, and relatively modern facilities. They also prefer jobs close to home.
3. **Mentally challenging work (items 7, 8, 9):** Jobs with too little challenge create boredom and apathy, whereas too much challenge creates frustration and feelings of failure.
4. **Equitable rewards (items 10, 11, 12):** Employees want pay and promotions based on job demands, individual skill levels, and community pay standards.

© Billy R. Ray/Wiley

## Retrieval Practice 3.4 | Health Psychology

Completing this self-test and the connections section, and then checking your answers by clicking on the answer button or by looking in Appendix B, provides immediate feedback and helpful practice for exams.

### Self-Test

1. Briefly define health psychology and its major areas of emphasis.
2. According to the U.S. Department of Health and Human Services, _____ has killed 10 times as many Americans as all our nation's wars combined.

   a. cigarette smoking
   b. lack of exercise
   c. overeating
   d. heart disease

3. An increase in acetylcholine and norepinephrine is associated with _____.

   a. nicotine use          b. any alcohol consumption
   c. binge drinking        d. stress

4. Once you begin smoking, you continue _____.
   a. because nicotine is addictive
   b. because nicotine increases alertness
   c. because nicotine stimulates the release of dopamine
   d. because of all of these options

5. Technostress can be defined as _____.
   a. a feeling of euphoria from exposure or involvement with technology
   b. anxiety or mental pressure from overexposure to loud "techno" style music
   c. stress caused by an inability to cope with modern technology
   d. none of these options

**Connections—Chapter to Chapter**

Answering the following question will help you "look back and look ahead" to see the important connections among the various subfields of psychology and chapters within this text.

In Chapter 12 (Motivation and Emotion), you'll discover some of the factors that influence us to set goals and maintain the necessary behaviors to achieve those goals. Health psychologists are particularly interested in how changes in behavior can improve health outcomes. Although most of us know what we should do to be healthy, we sometimes lack the motivation to stick to that diet or exercise routine. Choose one aspect of improving your health (such as decreasing tobacco use or increasing exercise), and describe a way to motivate yourself to follow through with it.

---

**Study Tip**

*The WileyPLUS program that accompanies this text provides for each chapter a* Media Challenge, Critical Thinking Exercise, *and* Application Quiz. *This set of study materials provides additional, invaluable study opportunities. Be sure to check it out!*

# Chapter Summary

## 3.1 Understanding Stress    82

- **Stress** is the interpretation of specific events, called **stressors**, as threatening or challenging.

- Stress can be acute or chronic. **Acute stress** is a short-term state of arousal in response to a perceived threat or challenge. **Chronic stress** is a state of continuous physiological arousal, in which demands are perceived as greater than available coping resources. **Conflicts** are forced choices between two or more competing goals or impulses. They are often classified as **approach–approach, avoidance–avoidance,** or **approach–avoidance. Hassles** are little everyday life problems that pile up to cause major stress and possible **burnout. Frustration** refers to blocked goals. **Cataclysmic events** are disasters that occur suddenly and generally affect many people simultaneously.

- Hans Selye's **general adaptation syndrome (GAS)** describes our body's three-stage reaction to stress: the initial alarm reaction, the resistance phase, and the exhaustion phase (if resistance to stress is not successful). If stress is resolved, our bodies return to normal, baseline functioning, called **homeostasis**.

- The **SAM system** and the **HPA axis** control significant physiological responses to stress. The SAM system prepares us for immediate action; the HPA axis responds more slowly but lasts longer.

- Prolonged stress suppresses the immune system, which increases the risk for many diseases (e.g., colds, colitis, cancer). The new field of **psychoneuroimmunology** studies the effects of psychological and other factors on the immune system.

- During acute stress, cortisol can prevent the retrieval of existing memories, as well as the laying down of new memories and general information processing. Under prolonged stress, cortisol can permanently damage the hippocampus, a key part of the brain involved in memory.

- Our bodies are nearly always under stress, some of which has beneficial effects. **Eustress** is pleasant, desirable stress, whereas **distress** is unpleasant, undesirable stress.

**Test Your Critical Thinking**

1. What are the major sources of stress in your life?

2. Is chronic stress threatening your immune system? If so, how?

**Psychology and a Contemporary Success:** Marcus Luttrell

# Understanding Stress

**Sources of Stress**

**Gender and Cultural Diversity: What Are the Problems with Acculturative Stress?**

**Reactions to Stress**
- General adaptation syndrome (GAS)
- SAM system and HPA axis
- Immune system
- Cognitive functioning

**Benefits of Stress**
- Eustress versus distress
- Task complexity

**Research Challenge: What Are the Hidden Benefits of Practice Testing?**

Acute/chronic stress

Life changes

Conflict

Acculturative stress

Hassles

Cataclysmic events

Frustration

**1** **Alarm phase** When surprised or threatened, your body enters an alarm phase during which your sympathetic nervous system (SNS) is activated (e.g., increased heart rate and blood pressure) and blood is diverted to your skeletal muscles to prepare you for the "fight-flight-freeze" response (Chapter 2).

**2.** **Resistance phase** As the stress continues, your body attempts to resist or adapt to the stressor by summoning all your resources. Physiological arousal remains higher than normal, and there is an outpouring of stress hormones. During this resistance stage, people use a variety of coping methods. For example, if your job is threatened, you may work longer hours and give up your vacation days.

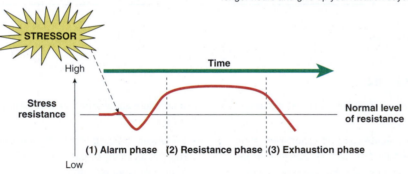

STRESSOR

High

Time

Stress resistance

Normal level of resistance

Low

(1) Alarm phase    (2) Resistance phase    (3) Exhaustion phase

**3** **Exhaustion phase** Unfortunately, your body's resistance to stress can only last so long before exhaustion sets in. During this final phase, your reserves are depleted and you become more susceptible to serious illnesses, as well as potentially irreversible damage to your body. Selye maintained that one outcome of this exhaustion phase for some people is the development of *diseases of adaptation*, including asthma and high blood pressure. Unless a way of relieving stress is found, the eventual result may be complete collapse and death.

## 3.2  Stress and Illness  94

- Scientists once believed that stress or the H. pylori bacterium, acting alone, could cause ulcers. Current research shows that biopsychosocial factors, including stress, interact to increase our vulnerability to the bacterium, which may then lead to ulcers.

- **Chronic pain** is a type of continuous or recurrent pain over a period of six months or longer. To treat chronic pain, health psychologists emphasize psychologically oriented treatments, such as behavior modification, biofeedback, and relaxation.

- Cancer appears to result from an interaction of heredity, environmental insults (such as smoking), and immune system deficiencies. Although stress is linked to a decreased immunity, research does *not* show that it *causes* cancer or that a positive attitude alone will prevent it.

- Increased stress hormones can cause fat to adhere to blood vessel walls, increasing the risk of cardiovascular disorders, including heart attacks.

- Exposure to extraordinary stress can cause **posttraumatic stress disorder (PTSD)**, a type of trauma- and stressor-related disorder characterized by the persistent re-experiencing of traumatic events. The condition results from directly or indirectly experiencing actual or threatened death, serious injury, or violence.

### Test Your Critical Thinking

**1.** How is stress a contributing factor to ulcers?

**2.** Has stress contributed to your own illnesses? If so, what can you do to avoid or decrease future illnesses?

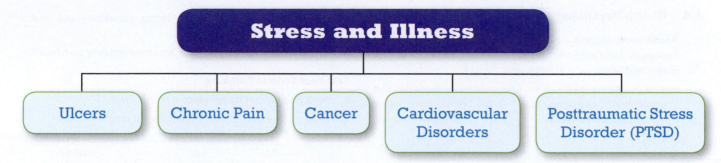

# Stress and Illness

| Ulcers | Chronic Pain | Cancer | Cardiovascular Disorders | Posttraumatic Stress Disorder (PTSD) |

## 3.3  Stress Management  99

- When facing a stressor, we generally engage in a three-step cognitive appraisal: We start with (Step 1) **primary appraisal** (deciding if a situation is harmless or potentially harmful) and (Step 2) **secondary appraisal** (assessing our resources and choosing a coping method). (Step 3) We then tend to choose either **emotion-focused coping** (managing emotional reactions to a stressor) or **problem-focused coping** (dealing directly with the stressor to decrease or eliminate it). People often combine problem-focused and emotion-focused coping strategies to resolve complex stressors or to respond to a stressful situation that is in flux.

- Freud proposed that we commonly cope with stress with **defense mechanisms,** which are strategies the ego uses to protect itself from anxiety, but they often distort reality and may increase self-deception.

- Personality and individual differences also affect stress management. Having an **internal locus of control** (believing that we control our own fate), as opposed to an **external locus of control** (believing that chance or outside forces beyond our control determine our fate), is an effective personal strategy for stress management. People with a **positive affect** and **optimism** tend to deal better with stress.

- **Mindfulness-based stress reduction (MBSR)** and social support are two important keys to stress management. Six additional resources include exercise, social skills, behavior change, stressor control, material resources, and relaxation.

### Test Your Critical Thinking

**1.** Do you generally prefer an emotion-focused style of coping or a problem-focused style of coping when faced with a stressful situation? Why?

**2.** Which of the various personality styles discussed in this section (e.g., internal versus external locus of control) best describes you? How could you use this information to improve your stress management?

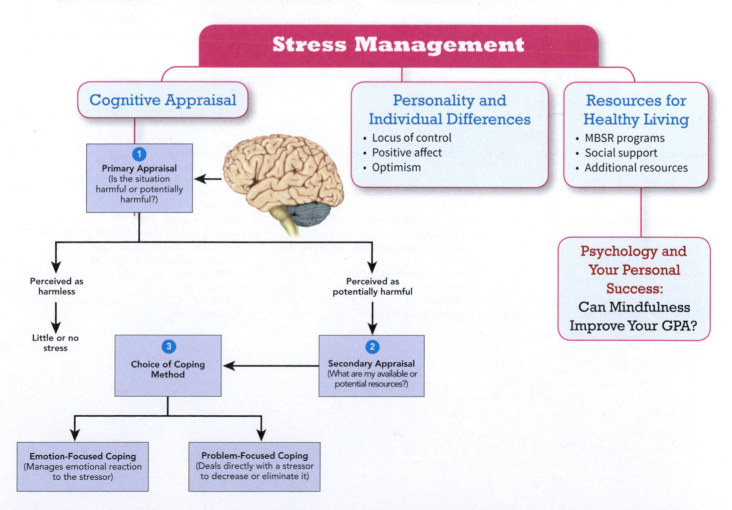

# Stress Management

### Cognitive Appraisal

**1** Primary Appraisal (Is the situation harmful or potentially harmful?)

Perceived as harmless → Little or no stress

Perceived as potentially harmful

**2** Secondary Appraisal (What are my available or potential resources?)

**3** Choice of Coping Method

Emotion-Focused Coping (Manages emotional reaction to the stressor)

Problem-Focused Coping (Deals directly with a stressor to decrease or eliminate it)

### Personality and Individual Differences
- Locus of control
- Positive affect
- Optimism

### Resources for Healthy Living
- MBSR programs
- Social support
- Additional resources

**Psychology and Your Personal Success:** Can Mindfulness Improve Your GPA?

## 3.4 Health Psychology 106

- **Health psychology** is a branch of psychology that studies how biological, psychological, and social factors influence health, illness, and health-related behaviors.

- Health psychologists focus on how changes in behavior can improve health outcomes. They often work as independent clinicians, or as consultants to other health practitioners, to educate the public about illness prevention and health maintenance.

- Health psychologists also study job stress and how to reduce it.

### Test Your Critical Thinking

1. Why is it so difficult for people to quit smoking?

2. Would you like to be a health psychologist? Why or why not?

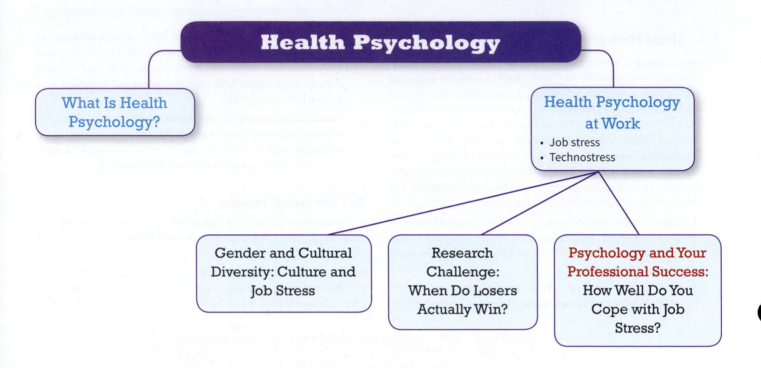

Health Psychology

What Is Health Psychology?

Health Psychology at Work
- Job stress
- Technostress

Gender and Cultural Diversity: Culture and Job Stress

Research Challenge: When Do Losers Actually Win?

Psychology and Your Professional Success: How Well Do You Cope with Job Stress?

## Key Terms

**Retrieval Practice** *Write your own definition for each term before turning back to the referenced page to check your answer.*

- acculturative stress 86
- acute stress 83
- approach–approach conflict 85
- approach–avoidance conflict 85
- avoidance–avoidance conflict 85
- burnout 85
- cataclysmic event 85
- chronic pain 95
- chronic stress 83
- conflict 85
- defense mechanisms 101

- distress 92
- emotion-focused coping 100
- eustress 92
- external locus of control 102
- frustration 85
- general adaptation syndrome (GAS) 88
- hassle 85
- health psychology 106
- homeostasis 89
- HPA axis 89
- internal locus of control 102

- mindfulness-based stress reduction (MBSR) 103
- optimism 103
- positive affect 102
- posttraumatic stress disorder (PTSD) 97
- problem-focused coping 100
- psychoneuroimmunology 89
- SAM system 89
- stress 82
- stressor 82
- technostress 109

© alexxl66/iStockphoto

CHAPTER **4**

# Sensation and Perception

**LEARNING OBJECTIVES**

**Review the key features and processes of sensation.**
- **Differentiate** sensation from perception.
- **Describe** how raw sensory stimuli are processed and converted to signals sent to our brains.
- **Discuss** how and why we reduce the amount of sensory information we receive and process.
- **Explain** psychophysics and subliminal stimuli.
- **Summarize** the factors involved in sensory adaptation and pain perception.

**Summarize the key components and processes of vision and audition.**
- **Identify** the key characteristics of light and sound waves.
- **Explain** the visual process, the key parts and functions of the human eye, and color vision.
- **Identify** vision's major problems and peculiarities.
- **Describe** audition, the key parts and functions of the human ear, and pitch perception.
- **Summarize** the two major types of hearing problems and what we can do to protect our hearing.

**Review the processes involved in smell, taste, and the body senses.**
- **Explain** the key factors in olfaction and gustation, and how the two senses interact.
- **Describe** how the body senses (skin, vestibular, and kinesthesis) work.

**Summarize the three processes involved in perception.**
- **Explain** illusions and why they're important.
- **Discuss** the process of selection and its three major factors.
- **Describe** the three ways we organize sensory data.
- **Review** the main factors in perceptual interpretation.
- **Discuss** the research findings on ESP and why so many people believe in it.

Helen Keller, No. 8

Alamy Stock Photo

❖ Psychology and a Classic
  Success | Helen Keller

Helen Keller (1880–1968) lost both her vision and hearing at the age of 19 months. But at the age of nine, she learned to speak by feeling her teacher Anne Sullivan's mouth when she talked. She also learned to use hand signals to communicate and to read and write in Braille—eventually becoming fluent in English, French, German, Greek, and Latin. As an adult (see the photo), Helen Keller graduated cum laude from Radcliffe College, becoming the first deaf-blind person to earn a Bachelor of Arts degree. She then went on to become a famous educator, author, and lecturer, as well as one of the 20th century's leading humanitarians (Thompson & Harrison, 2003). Keller received the Presidential Medal of Freedom in 1964 and was elected to the Women's Hall of Fame in 1965.

The story of Helen Keller has been told and retold as an inspiring example of how people can overcome incredible personal odds and go on to great heights of achievement. Her remarkable life also illustrates how the overarching themes of this text—having a *growth mindset* and *grit* (a combination of passion and perseverance)—can allow someone to triumph over adversity.

# Chapter Overview

Helen Keller's life and writings provide a fascinating glimpse into an entirely different way of sensing and perceiving the world. Imagine being able to recognize your friends by a touch of their face, or a house by the smell of its previous occupants. Most of us take our senses for granted, but this chapter might help change that. At this very moment, our bodies are being bombarded with stimuli from the outside world—light, sound, heat, pressure, texture, and so on—while our brains are floating in complete silence and utter darkness within our skulls. But Helen's story shows us that sensing the world is not enough. Our brains must receive, convert, and constantly adapt the information from our sense organs into useful mental representations of the world.

How we get the outside world inside to our brains, and what our brains do with this information, are the key topics of this chapter. We begin with an exploration of how sensation differs from perception and three key topics involved in sensation—processing, psychophysics, and sensory adaptation. Next, we examine vision, hearing, and our other important senses—smell, taste, and body senses. We conclude with a survey of the basic processes in perception—selection, organization, and interpretation.

## Myth Busters

### True or False?

1. Athletes have a higher pain tolerance than non-athletes.
2. Humans have one blind spot in each eye.
3. Using a higher-pitched voice can increase your perceived influence and power.
4. Loud music can lead to permanent hearing loss.
5. There are discrete spots on our tongues for specific tastes.
6. Humans have only five senses.
7. Illusions are not the same as hallucinations.
8. People tend to see what they expect to see.
9. There is strong scientific evidence for ESP.
10. Black football players are more likely to be penalized for touchdown celebrations than White football players.

(**Answers:** 1. True, 2. True, 3. False, 4. True, 5. False, 6. False, 7. True, 8. True, 9. False, 10. True. Detailed answers appear in this chapter)

# 4.1 | Understanding Sensation

## LEARNING OBJECTIVES

**Retrieval Practice**   While reading the upcoming sections, respond to each Learning Objective in your own words.

**Review the key features and processes of sensation.**

- **Differentiate** sensation from perception.
- **Describe** how raw sensory stimuli are processed and converted to signals sent to our brains.

- **Discuss** how and why we reduce the amount of sensory information we receive and process.
- **Explain** psychophysics and subliminal stimuli.
- **Summarize** the factors involved in sensory adaptation and pain perception.

*The world is full of magic things, patiently waiting for our senses to grow sharper.*

—W.B. Yeats (Irish Poet, Nobel Prize in Literature)

Psychologists are keenly interested in our senses because they are our mind's window to the outside world. We're equally interested in how our mind perceives and interprets the information it receives from the senses. In this chapter, we separate the discussion of sensation and perception, but in our everyday life the two normally blend into one apparently seamless process. We'll start with an explanation of how they differ.

## Sensation versus Perception

**Sensation** begins with specialized receptor cells located in our sense organs (eyes, ears, nose, tongue, skin, and internal body tissues). When sense organs detect an appropriate stimulus (light, mechanical pressure, chemical molecules), they convert it into neural impulses (action potentials) that are transmitted to our brains. Through the process of **perception**, the brain then assigns meaning to this sensory information (**Table 4.1**). Another clever way to differentiate sensation and perception is shown in **Figure 4.1**.

How do we unknowingly and automatically combine sensation and perception? It involves at least two processes (Johns & Jones, 2015; Sussman et al., 2016; van Ommen et al., 2016):

- In **bottom-up processing**, information processing starts at the "bottom" with an analysis of smaller features, and then builds on them to create complete perceptions. In other words, processing begins at the sensory level and works "up."

- During **top-down processing**, our brains create useable perceptions from the sensory messages based on prior knowledge and expectations. In this case, processing begins at the "top," our brain's higher-level cognitive processes, and works "down."

One additional way to understand the difference between bottom-up and top-down processing is to think about what happens when we "see" a helicopter flying overhead in the sky. According to the *bottom-up processing* perspective, receptors in our eyes and ears record the sight and sound of this large, loud object, and send these sensory messages on to our brains for interpretation. The other, top-down processing, approach suggests that our brains quickly make a "best guess," and interpret the large, loud object as a "helicopter," based on our previous knowledge and expectations.

**Sensation**   The process of detecting, converting, and transmitting raw sensory information from the external and internal environments to the brain.

**Perception**   The process of selecting, organizing, and interpreting sensory information into meaningful objects and events.

**Bottom-up processing**   A type of information processing that starts at the "bottom" with an analysis of smaller features, and then builds on them to create complete perceptions; data-driven processing that moves from the parts to the whole.

**Top-down processing**   A type of information processing that starts at the "top" with higher-level analysis (prior knowledge and expectations), and then works "down" to recognize individual features as a unified whole; conceptually driven processing that moves from the whole to the parts.

**FIGURE 4.1   Sensation and perception**   When you look at this drawing, do you see a young woman looking back over her shoulder or an older woman with her chin buried in a fur collar? Younger students tend to first see a young woman, and older students first see an older woman. Although the basic sensory input (sensation) stays the same, your brain's attempt to select, organize, and interpret the sensory information (perception) turns the black and white lines and shapes into meaningful objects—either a young or old face.

**TABLE 4.1**   **Sensation and Perception**

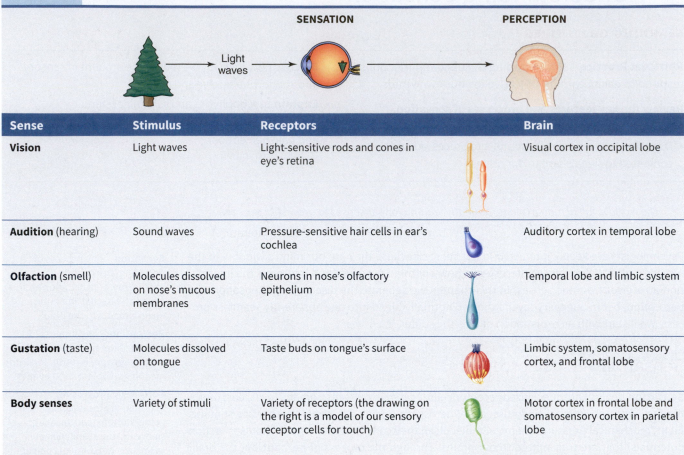

| | | SENSATION | | PERCEPTION |
|---|---|---|---|---|
| **Sense** | **Stimulus** | **Receptors** | | **Brain** |
| **Vision** | Light waves | Light-sensitive rods and cones in eye's retina | | Visual cortex in occipital lobe |
| **Audition** (hearing) | Sound waves | Pressure-sensitive hair cells in ear's cochlea | | Auditory cortex in temporal lobe |
| **Olfaction** (smell) | Molecules dissolved on nose's mucous membranes | Neurons in nose's olfactory epithelium | | Temporal lobe and limbic system |
| **Gustation** (taste) | Molecules dissolved on tongue | Taste buds on tongue's surface | | Limbic system, somatosensory cortex, and frontal lobe |
| **Body senses** | Variety of stimuli | Variety of receptors (the drawing on the right is a model of our sensory receptor cells for touch) | | Motor cortex in frontal lobe and somatosensory cortex in parietal lobe |

**Transduction**   The process of converting sensory stimuli into neural impulses that are sent along to the brain (for example, transforming light waves into neural impulses).

As you can see, the processes of sensation and perception are complex, but also very interesting. Now that you understand and appreciate the overall purpose of these two processes, let's dig deeper, starting with the first step of sensation—*processing*.

## Processing

Looking again at Table 4.1, note that our eyes, ears, skin, and other sense organs all contain special cells called receptors, which receive and process sensory information from the environment. For each sense, these specialized cells respond to a distinct stimulus, such as sound waves or odor molecules. Next, during the process of **transduction**, the receptors convert the energy from the specific sensory stimulus into neural impulses, which are then sent on to the brain. For example, in hearing, tiny receptor cells in the inner ear convert mechanical vibrations from sound waves into electrochemical signals. Neurons then carry these signals to the brain, where specific sensory receptors detect and interpret the information.

How does your brain differentiate between sensations, such as sounds and smells? Through a process known as **coding**, the brain interprets different physical stimuli as distinct sensations because their neural impulses travel by different routes and arrive at different parts of the brain (**Figure 4.2**).

We also have structures that purposefully reduce the amount of sensory information we receive. In this process of *sensory reduction,*

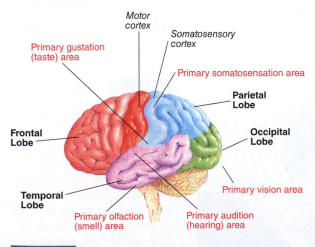

**FIGURE 4.2**   **Sensory processing within the brain**   Neural messages from the various sense organs must travel to specific areas of the brain in order for us to see, hear, smell, and so on. Shown here in the red-colored labels are the primary locations in the cerebral cortex for vision, hearing, taste, smell, and somatosensation (which includes touch, pain, and temperature sensitivity).

we analyze and then filter incoming sensations before sending neural impulses on for further processing in other parts of our brains. Without this natural filtering of stimuli, we would constantly hear blood rushing through our veins and feel our clothes brushing against our skin. Some level of filtering is needed to prevent our brains from being overwhelmed with unnecessary information.

All species have evolved selective receptors that suppress or amplify information for survival. Humans, for example, cannot sense ultraviolet light, electric or magnetic fields, the ultrasonic sound of a dog whistle, or infrared heat patterns from warm-blooded animals, as some other animals can.

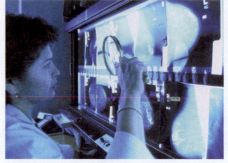

ER Productions/©Corbis

**FIGURE 4.3** **Why is our difference threshold important?** This radiologist is responsible for detecting the slightest indication of a tumor in this mammogram of a female breast. The ability to detect differences between stimuli (like the visual difference between normal and abnormal breast tissue) can be improved by special training, practice, and instruments. However, it's still limited by our basic sensory difference thresholds.

## Psychophysics

How can scientists measure the exact amount of stimulus energy it takes to trigger a conscious experience? The answer comes from the field of **psychophysics**, which studies and measures the link between the physical characteristics of stimuli and the psychological experience of them.

One of the most intriguing insights from psychophysics is that what is out there is not directly reproduced inside our bodies. At this moment, there are light waves, sound waves, odors, tastes, and microscopic particles touching us that we cannot see, hear, smell, taste, or feel. We are consciously aware of only a narrow range of stimuli in our environment.

German scientist Ernst Weber (1795–1878) was one of the first to study the smallest difference between two weights that could be detected (Goldstein, 2014; Schwartz & Krantz, 2016). This **difference threshold**, also known as *Weber's law of just noticeable differences* (*JND*), is the minimum difference that is consciously detectable 50% of the time (**Figure 4.3**).

Another scientist, Gustav Fechner (1801–1887), expanded on Weber's law to determine what is called the **absolute threshold**, the minimum stimulation necessary to consciously detect a stimulus 50% of the time. See **Table 4.2** for a list of absolute thresholds for our various senses.

To measure your senses, an examiner presents a series of signals that vary in intensity and asks you to report which signals you can detect. In a hearing test, the softest level at which you can consistently hear a tone is your absolute threshold. The examiner then compares your threshold with those of people with normal hearing to determine whether or not you have hearing loss (**Figure 4.4**).

Many nonhuman animals have higher or lower thresholds than humans. For example, a dog's absolute and difference thresholds for smell are far more sensitive than those of a human. This exceptional sensitivity allows specially trained dogs to provide invaluable help in sniffing

**Coding** The process in which neural impulses travel by different routes to different parts of the brain; it allows us to detect various physical stimuli as distinct sensations.

**Psychophysics** The study of the link between the physical characteristics of stimuli and the psychological experience of them.

**Difference threshold** The smallest physical difference between two stimuli that is consciously detectable 50% of the time; also called the *just noticeable difference* (*JND*).

**Absolute threshold** The minimum amount of stimulation necessary to consciously detect a stimulus 50% of the time.

**TABLE 4.2**   **Examples of Human Absolute Thresholds**

| Sense | Absolute Threshold |
|---|---|
| **Vision** | A candle flame seen from 30 miles away on a clear, dark night |
| **Audition** (hearing) | The tick of an old-fashioned watch at 20 feet |
| **Olfaction** (smell) | One drop of perfume spread throughout a six-room apartment |
| **Gustation** (taste) | One teaspoon of sugar in 2 gallons of water |
| **Body senses** | A bee's wing falling on your cheek from a height of about half an inch |

**Test Your Critical Thinking**

1. If scientists could improve your sensory thresholds (like vision and hearing) far beyond the normal range, would you volunteer for this treatment? What might be the advantages and disadvantages?

2. Why is it important to test all children's vision and hearing capabilities at a young age?

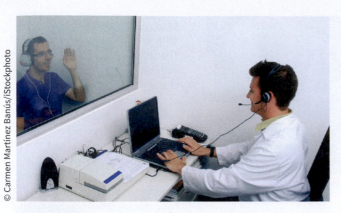

© Carmen Martinez Banús/iStockphoto

**FIGURE 4.4** **Measuring the absolute and difference thresholds for hearing**

out dangerous plants, animals, drugs, and explosives; tracking criminals; and assisting in search-and-rescue operations (Byrne et al., 2017; Porritt et al., 2015). Some researchers believe dogs can detect hidden corrosion, fecal contamination, and chemical signs of certain illnesses (such as diabetes or cancer) and may even be able to predict seizures in humans (Parker & Graham, 2016; Urbanová et al., 2015).

Interestingly, other research found that when dogs were presented with five different scents from humans and dogs, sensory receptors in the dogs' noses easily picked up all five scents (Berns et al., 2015). However, only the human scents activated a part of the dog's brain (the caudate nucleus) that has a well-known association with positive expectations. The researchers concluded that this brain activation, and the dog's positive association with human scents, point to the importance of humans in dogs' lives. A related study has shown that dogs can discriminate among many emotional expressions on human faces (Muller et al., 2015).

### Subliminal Stimuli

**Subliminal Stimuli** Have you heard some of the wild rumors about subliminal messages? During the 1970s, it was said that rock songs contained demonic messages, which could only be heard when the songs were played backwards! Similarly, in the 1990s, many suggested that some Disney films contained obscene subliminal messages. For example, in the film *Aladdin*, the lead character supposedly whispers, "all good teenagers take off your clothes," and *The Lion King* reportedly showed close-up shots of the dust with a secret spelling out of the word "sex." In addition, at one time movie theaters were reportedly flashing messages like "Eat popcorn" and "Drink Cola-Cola" on the screen. Even though the messages were so brief that viewers weren't aware of seeing them, it was believed they increased consumption of these products (Bargh, 2014; Blecha, 2004; Vokey & Read, 1985).

**Subliminal perception** The detection of stimuli below the absolute threshold for conscious awareness.

Can unconscious stimuli really affect our behavior? Experimental studies on **subliminal perception** have clearly shown that we *can* detect stimuli and information below our level of conscious awareness (Chiau et al., 2017; Rabellino et al., 2016; Urriza et al., 2016). These studies commonly use an instrument, called a *tachistoscope*, to flash images too quickly for conscious recognition, but slowly enough to be registered by the brain. How does this happen? As we've just seen, our "absolute threshold" is the point at which we can detect a stimulus half the time. *Subliminal stimuli* are just stimuli that fall below our 50% absolute threshold, and they can be detected without our awareness.

**Priming** An exposure (often unconscious) to previously stored information that predisposes (or *primes*) our response to related stimuli.

Furthermore, research on **priming** finds that certain unconscious or unnoticed stimuli can reach our brains and predispose (*prime*) us to make it easier or more difficult to recall related information already in storage (Ohtomo, 2017; Sassenberg et al., 2017; Xiao & Yamauchi, 2016). If a researcher shows you the words "red" and "fire engine," you'll be slightly faster to recognize the word "apple" because all of these words have been previously stored and closely associated in your memory.

Despite the fact that *subliminal perception* and *priming* do occur, it doesn't mean that such processes lead to significant behavioral changes. Subliminal stimuli are basically weak stimuli. In one recent experiment that used priming, for example, researchers offered participants implicit primes as well as direct, overt warnings about the danger of cyberattacks. Surprisingly, almost 80% of the participants nevertheless were willing to provide personal information, such as their e-mail addresses, and over 40% willingly provided 9 digits from their 18-digit bank account numbers (Junger et al., 2017). Apparently, our tendency to trust one another overrides priming, direct warnings, and even our common sense.

Nevertheless, subliminal stimuli sometimes have an effect on indirect, more subtle reactions, such as our more casual attitudes. Researchers in a clever study placed volunteers in different rooms with music playing in the background from one of three regions—the United States, China, or India (North et al., 2016). While listening to different types of music, each participant looked at a menu for 5 minutes with 30 dinner options. The scientists then asked them to recall as many dishes from the menu as they could, and then to choose one dish to order as a meal. Presumably due to subliminal stimuli from the music, participants better remembered and more often chose dishes that reflected the music they had listened to before looking at the menu. For example, those who listened to American music ("California Girls," "Surfin' U.S.A.," and "Good Vibrations" by the Beach Boys) chose foods like hamburgers and hot dogs.

## Sensory Adaptation

Imagine that friends have invited you to come visit their beautiful new baby kitten. As they greet you at the door, you are overwhelmed by the odor of the kitten's overflowing litter box. Why don't your friends do something about that smell? The answer lies in the previously mentioned sensory reduction, as well as **sensory adaptation**. When a constant stimulus is presented for a length of time, sensation often fades or disappears. Receptors in our sensory system become less sensitive. They get "tired" and actually fire less frequently.

Sensory adaptation can be understood from an evolutionary perspective. We can't afford to waste attention and time on unchanging, normally unimportant stimuli. "Turning down the volume" on repetitive information helps the brain cope with an overwhelming amount of sensory stimuli and enables us to pay attention to change. Sometimes, however, adaptation can be dangerous, as when people stop paying attention to a small gas leak in the kitchen.

Although some senses, like smell and touch, adapt quickly, we never completely adapt to visual stimuli or to extremely intense stimuli, such as the odor of ammonia or the pain of a bad burn. From an evolutionary perspective, these limitations on sensory adaptation aid survival by reminding us, for example, to keep a watch out for dangerous predators, avoid strong odors and heat, and take care of that burn.

**Sensory adaptation** The sensory receptors' innate tendency to fatigue and stop responding to unchanging stimuli; an example of bottom-up processing.

### Pain and Sensory Adaptation
Our differing reactions to pain offer an intriguing example of sensory adaptation. In certain situations, including times of physical exertion, the body releases natural, pain-killing neurotransmitters called *endorphins* (Chapter 2), which inhibit pain perception. This is the so-called "runner's high," which may help explain why athletes have been found to have a higher pain tolerance than nonathletes (Tesarz et al., 2012). (As a critical thinker, is it possible that individuals with a naturally high pain tolerance are just more attracted to athletics? Or might the experience of playing sports change your pain tolerance?)

Interestingly, the pain of athletes, soldiers, firefighters, and others is also greatly diminished when they're distracted by factors such as duty, competition, or fear (**Figure 4.5**). Similarly, surgical patients who listen to music—even while under anesthesia—have less anxiety, report a 20% reduction in post surgery pain, and need less pain medication during recovery (Hole et al., 2015). And, as you may recall from Chapter 2, dancing or singing in synchrony with others is linked to higher pain thresholds and increased social bonding (Tarr et al., 2016; Weinstein et al., 2016).

In addition to endorphin release and distraction, one of the most widely accepted explanations of pain perception is the **gate-control theory of pain**, first proposed by Ronald Melzack and Patrick Wall (1965). According to this theory, the experience of pain depends partly on whether the neural message gets past a "gatekeeper" in the spinal cord. Normally, the gate is kept shut, either by impulses

**Gate-control theory of pain** The theory that pain sensations are processed and altered by certain cells in the spinal cord, which act as gates to interrupt and block some pain signals while sending others on to the brain.

**FIGURE 4.5 Competition—a powerful pain distractor!** Manteo Mitchell broke his left leg in the qualifying heats of the 4 × 400-meter relay race in the 2012 Olympics. Recalling the moment of the accident, Manteo said, "I felt it break . . . it hurt so bad . . . it felt like somebody literally just snapped my leg in half" (Moore, 2013). However, he continued running so that the American team could get into the finals.

Ian MacNicol/Getty Images

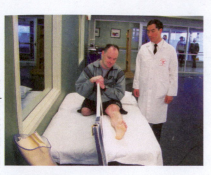

Navy Mass Communication Specialist
2nd Class Jeff Hopkins

**FIGURE 4.6** **Treating phantom limb pain** Using mirror therapy, an amputee patient places his or her intact limb on one side of the mirror, and the amputated limb on the other. He or she then concentrates on looking into the mirror on the side that reflects the intact limb, creating the visual impression of two complete undamaged limbs. The patient then attempts to move both limbs. Thanks to the artificial feedback provided by the mirror, the patient sees the complete limb, and the reflected image of the complete limb, moving. He or she then interprets this as the phantom limb moving.

coming down from the brain or by messages being sent from large-diameter nerve fibers that conduct most sensory signals, such as touch and pressure. However, when body tissue is damaged, impulses from smaller pain fibers open the gate (Price & Prescott, 2015; Rhudy, 2016; Zhao & Wood, 2015). Can you see how this gate-control theory helps explain why massaging an injury or scratching an itch can temporarily relieve discomfort? It's because pressure on large-diameter neurons interferes with pain signals. In addition, studies suggest that the pain gate may be chemically controlled. A neurotransmitter called *substance P* opens the pain gate, and endorphins close it (Fan et al., 2016; Krug et al., 2015; Wu et al., 2015).

In sum, endorphins, distraction, listening to music, singing and dancing in synchrony with others, pain gates, and substance P may all provide soothing comfort and pain reduction, especially for those who are very anxious (Bradshaw et al., 2012; Fan et al., 2016; Gardstrom & Sorel, 2015).

### Phantom Limb Pain (PLP)

Did you know that when normal sensory input is disrupted, the brain can also generate pain and other sensations entirely on its own, as is the case with *phantom limb pain (PLP)* (Bonnan-White et al., 2016; Melzack, 1999; Raffin et al., 2016)? After an amputation, people commonly report detecting their missing limb as if it were still there. And up to 80% of people who have had amputations sometimes "feel" pain (and itching, burning, or tickling sensations) in the missing limb, long after the amputation. Numerous theories attempt to explain this type of PLP, but one of the best suggests that there is a mismatch between the sensory messages sent and received in the brain.

Can you understand how this may be an example of our earlier description of how *bottom-up processes* (such as the sensory messages sent from our limbs to our brains) combine with our *top-down processes* (our brain's interpretation of these messages)? Messages are no longer being transmitted from the missing limb to the brain (bottom up), but areas of the brain responsible for receiving messages are still intact (top down). The brain's attempt to interpret the confusing messages may result in pain and other sensations.

In line with this idea of mismatched signals, when amputees wear prosthetic limbs, or when *mirror visual therapy* is used, phantom pain often disappears. In mirror therapy (**Figure 4.6**), pain relief apparently occurs because the brain is somehow tricked into believing there is no longer a missing limb (Deconinck et al., 2015; Foell et al., 2014; Thieme et al., 2016). Others believe that mirror therapy works because it helps the brain reorganize and incorporate this phantom limb into a new nervous system configuration (Guo et al., 2016).

Now that we've studied how we perceive pain, how we might ignore or "play through" it, and how we might misperceive it with phantom limb pain, you'll be interested to know that when we get anxious or dwell on our pain, we can intensify it (Lin et al., 2013; Miller-Matero et al., 2017; Ray et al., 2015). This is important because social and cultural factors, such as well-meaning friends or anxious parents who ask pain sufferers about their pain, may unintentionally reinforce and increase it. The following **Try This Yourself** offers an assessment and strategies for your personal pain management.

---

## Try This Yourself

### How Well Do You Manage Your Pain?

Score yourself on how often you use one or more of these strategies, using the following scale:
0 = never, 1 = seldom, 2 = occasionally, 3 = often, 4 = almost always, 5 = always.

____ **1.** I do something I enjoy, such as watching TV or listening to music.

____ **2.** I try to be around other people.

____ **3.** I do something active, like household chores or projects.

____ **4.** I try to feel distant from the pain, almost as if I'm floating above my body.

____ **5.** I try to think about something pleasant.

____ **6.** I replay in my mind pleasant experiences from the past.

____ **7.** I tell myself that I can overcome the pain.

____ **8.** I don't think about the pain.

These questions are based on effective pain management techniques, such as distraction, ignoring pain, and reinterpreting it. Review those items that you checked as "never" or "seldom" and consider adding them to your pain management skills.

© Billy R. Ray/Wiley

## Retrieval Practice 4.1 | Understanding Sensation

Completing this self-test and the connections section, and then checking your answers by clicking on the answer button or by looking in Appendix B, will provide immediate feedback and helpful practice for exams.

### Self-Test

1. Briefly describe how bottom-up processing differs from top-down processing.

2. Transduction is the process of converting _____ .

   a. sensory stimuli into neural impulses that are sent along to the brain
   b. receptors into transmitters
   c. a particular sensory stimulus into a specific perception
   d. receptors into neural impulses

3. The _____ is the minimum stimulation necessary to consciously detect a stimulus.

   a. threshold of excitation       b. difference threshold
   c. absolute threshold            d. low point

4. Experiments on subliminal perception have _____ .

   a. supported its existence, but shown that it has little or no effect on behavior
   b. shown that subliminal perception occurs only among children and some adolescents
   c. shown that subliminal messages affect only people who are highly suggestible
   d. failed to support the phenomenon

5. The _____ theory of pain helps explain why it sometimes helps to rub or massage an injured area.

   a. sensory adaptation            b. gate-control
   c. just noticeable difference    d. Lamaze

### Connections—Chapter to Chapter

Answering the following question will help you "look back and look ahead" to see the important connections among the various subfields of psychology and chapters within this text.

In Chapter 10 (Lifespan Development II), you'll learn about autism spectrum disorder (ASD). This neurodevelopmental disorder is characterized by impairments in social interaction and communication, as well as a need for routine and an avoidance of touch. One of the theories about autism is that the person experiences a "sensory overload." Discuss the process of *sensory reduction* and how it might relate to the symptoms of autism.

---

## 4.2 | How We See and Hear

### LEARNING OBJECTIVES

**Retrieval Practice**   While reading the upcoming sections, respond to each Learning Objective in your own words.

**Summarize the key components and processes of vision and audition.**

- **Identify** the key characteristics of light and sound waves.
- **Explain** the visual process, the key parts and functions of the human eye, and color vision.

- **Identify** vision's major problems and peculiarities.
- **Describe** audition, the key parts and functions of the human ear, and pitch perception.
- **Summarize** the two major types of hearing problems and what we can do to protect our hearing.

---

Many people mistakenly believe that what they see and hear is a copy of the outside world. In fact, vision and hearing are the result of what our brains create in response to light and sound waves. What we see and hear is based on wave phenomena, similar to ocean waves. Waves vary in wavelength and frequency, as explained in **Figure 4.7**. They also vary in height (technically called *amplitude*). This wave height/amplitude determines the intensity of sights and sounds. Finally, waves vary in range, or complexity, which mixes together waves of various wavelength/frequency and height/amplitude (**Figure 4.8**).

S. Greg Panosian/iStockphoto

**FIGURE 4.7   Waves of light and sound**   Ocean waves have a certain distance between them (the *wavelength*), and they pass by you at intervals. If you counted the number of passing waves in a set amount of time (for example, 5 waves in 60 seconds), you could calculate the *frequency* (the number of complete wavelengths that pass a point in a given time). Longer wavelength means lower frequency and vice versa.

**Wavelength**
The distance between successive peaks.

Time →

*Long wavelength/ low frequency = Reddish colors/ low-pitched sounds*

Time →

*Short wavelength/ high frequency = Bluish colors/ high-pitched sound*

**Wave amplitude**
The height from peak to trough.

Time →

*Low amplitude/ low intensity = Dull colors/ soft sounds*

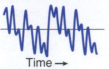

Time →

*High amplitude/ high intensity = Bright colors/ loud sounds*

**Range of wavelengths**
The mixture of waves.

Time →

*Small range/ low complexity = Less complex colors/ less complex sounds*

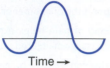

Time →

*Large range/ high complexity = Complex colors/ complex sounds*

**FIGURE 4.8** **Properties of light and sound**

# Vision

As you recall from our introductory story, Helen Keller lost her sight at a very young age, yet she was aware of something missing in her life (Keller, 1962). While on a long train trip, Helen's aunt improvised a doll for six-year-old Helen out of a few towels. It had no nose, no mouth, no ears, and no eyes—nothing to indicate a face. Helen found this disturbing. Most disturbing, though, was the lack of eyes. In fact, it agitated her so much that she was not content until she found some beads and her aunt attached them for eyes. Uncomprehending as she was of the myriad sensations our eyes bring us, Helen still seemed to know the importance of having eyes.

For example, our human eyes receive and process information amazingly fast. Did you know that professional baseball players can hit a 90-mile-per-hour fastball four-tenths of a second after it leaves the pitcher's hand? How is that possible? To understand the marvels of vision, we need to start with the basics—that light waves are a form of electromagnetic energy and only a small part of the full *electromagnetic spectrum* (**Figure 4.9**).

To fully appreciate how our eyes turn these light waves into the experience we call *vision*, we need to first examine the various structures in our eyes that capture and focus the light waves. Then, we need to understand how these waves are transformed (transduced) into neural messages (action potentials) that our brains can process into images we consciously see. (Be sure to carefully study this process in **Step-by-Step Diagram 4.1**.)

## Vision Problems and Peculiarities

Thoroughly understanding the processes detailed in Step-by-Step Diagram 4.1 offers clues that help us understand several visual peculiarities. For example, small abnormalities in the eye sometimes cause images to be focused in front of the **retina**, resulting in *nearsightedness (myopia)*. In contrast, the image is focused behind the retina in the case of *farsightedness (hyperopia)*. In addition, during middle age, most people's lenses lose elasticity and the ability to accommodate for near vision, a condition known as *presbyopia*. Corrective lenses or laser surgery can often correct all three of these visual acuity problems.

A visual peculiarity occurs where the optic nerve exits the eye. Because there are no receptor cells for visual stimuli in that area, we have a tiny hole, or **blind spot**, in our field of vision. (See Step-by-Step Diagram 4.1 for a demonstration.)

**Retina** The light-sensitive inner surface of the back of the eye, which contains the receptor cells for vision (rods and cones).

**Blind spot** The point at which the optic nerve leaves the eye, which contains no receptor cells for vision—thus creating a "blind spot."

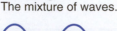
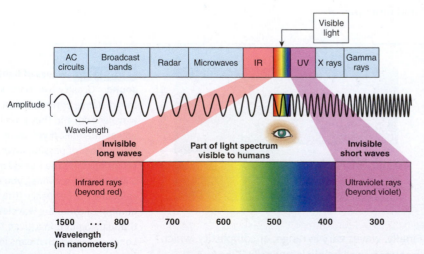

**a. Waves of the electromagnectic spectrum** Note that each type of wave has a different name and wavelength. Unlike sound waves, which need air to travel, these waves are vibrations of magnetic and electric fields, and they can move in a vacuum. The fact that light waves travel nearly 900,000 times faster than sound waves explains why we see a flash of lightning before we hear the thunder.

**b. What we see** Only the light waves in the middle of the electromagnetic spectrum can be seen by the human eye. Note that we perceive the longer visible wavelengths as red, whereas the shortest are seen as blue, with the rest of the colors in between.

**FIGURE 4.9** **The electromagnetic spectrum for vision**

| STEP-BY-STEP DIAGRAM 4.1 | **How Our Eyes See** |

**STOP!** This Step-by-Step Diagram contains essential information NOT found else-where in the text, which is likely to appear on quizzes and exams. Be sure to study it CAREFULLY!

Various structures of your eye work together to capture and focus the light waves from the outside world. Receptor cells in your retina (rods and cones) then convert these waves into messages that are sent along the optic nerve to be interpreted by your brain.

**3** The muscularly controlled lens then focuses incoming light into an image on the light-sensitive *retina*, located on the back surface of the fluid-filled eyeball.

**2** The light then passes through the *pupil*, a small adjustable opening. Muscles in the *iris* allow the *pupil* to dilate or constrict in response to light intensity or emotional factors.

**1** Light first enters through the *cornea*, which helps protect the eye and focus incoming light rays.

Labels: Lens, Vitreous humor, Retinal blood vessels, Retina, Lid, Iris, Sclera, Light, Light, Fovea, Pupil, Cornea, Blind spot, Optic nerve

**4** In the **retina**, light waves are detected and transduced into neural signals by vision receptor cells (rods and cones). Note how the image of the flower is inverted when it is projected onto the retina. Our brains later reverse the visual input into the final image that we perceive.

**5** The **fovea**, a tiny pit filled with cones, is responsible for our sharpest vision.

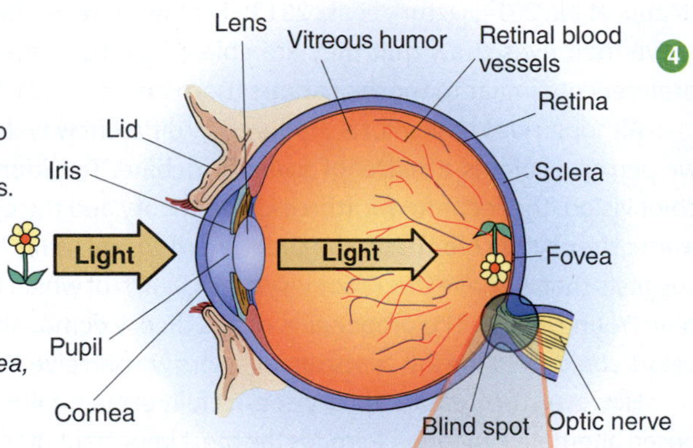

Labels: Rod, Bipolar cells, Ganglion cells, Light, Light, Light, Cone

**6** **Rods** are retinal receptor cells with high sensitivity in dim light, but low sensitivity to details and color.

**7** **Cones** are retinal receptor cells with sensitivity to color, but low sensitivity in dim light.

**8** The optic nerve, which consists of axons of the ganglion cells, then carries the message on to the brain.

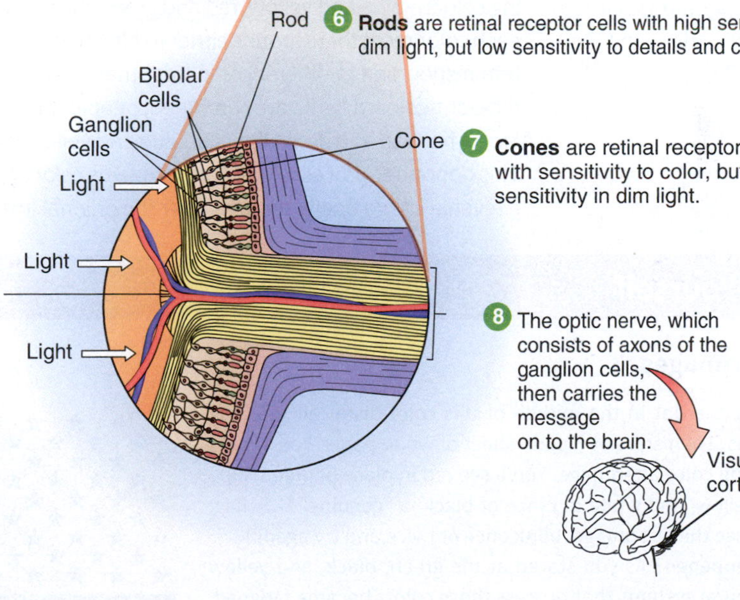

Labels: Visual cortex

**Do you have a blind spot?**
At the back of the retina lies an area that has no visual receptors at all and absolutely no vision. This **blind spot** is where blood vessels and nerves enter and exit the eyeball. To find yours, hold this book about one foot in front of you, close your right eye, and stare at the X with your left eye. Very slowly, move the book closer to you. You should see the worm disappear and the apple become whole.

Another peculiarity exists in the retina's vision receptor cells (the rods and cones). The **rods** are highly sensitive in dim light, but are less sensitive to detail and color. The reverse is true for the **cones**, which are highly sensitive to color and detail, and less sensitive in dim light. Do you recognize how this explains why you're cautioned to look away from bright headlights when driving or biking at night? Staring into the bright lights will activate your cones, which are less

**Rods** Retinal receptor cells with high sensitivity in dim light, but low sensitivity to details and color.

**Cones** Retinal receptor cells with high sensitivity to color and detail, but low sensitivity in dim light.

**FIGURE 4.10** **Primary colors**
Trichromatic theory found that the three primary colors (red, green, and blue) can be combined to form all colors. For example, a combination of green and red creates yellow.

**Fovea** A tiny pit in the center of the retina that is densely filled with cones; it is responsible for sharp vision.

**Trichromatic theory of color** The theory that color perception results from three types of cones in the retina, each most sensitive to either red, green, or blue; other colors result from a mixture of these three.

**Opponent-process theory of color** The theory that all color perception is based on three systems, each of which contains two color opposites (red versus green, blue versus yellow, and black versus white).

effective in dim light, whereas looking away activates the rods in your peripheral vision, which are more sensitive at night.

Two additional peculiarities happen when we go from a bright to dark setting and vice versa. Have you noticed that when you walk into a dark movie theater on a sunny afternoon, you're almost blind for a few seconds? The reason is that in bright light, the pigment inside the rods (refer to Step-by-Step Diagram 4.1) is bleached, making them temporarily nonfunctional. It takes a second or two for the rods to become functional enough again for you to see. This process of *dark adaptation* continues for 20 to 30 minutes.

In contrast, *light adaptation*, the adjustment that takes place when you go from darkness to a bright setting, takes about 7 to 10 minutes and is the work of the cones. Interestingly, a region in the center of the retina, called the **fovea**, has the greatest density of cones, which are most sensitive in brightly lit conditions. They're also responsible for color vision and fine detail.

## Color Vision
Our ability to perceive color is almost as remarkable and useful as vision itself. Humans may be able to discriminate among seven million different hues, and research conducted in many cultures suggests that we all seem to see essentially the same colored world (Maule et al., 2014; Ozturk et al., 2013). Furthermore, studies of infants old enough to focus and move their eyes show that they are able to see color nearly as well as adults and have color preferences similar to those of adults (Bornstein et al., 2014; Yang et al., 2015).

Although we know color is produced by different wavelengths of light, the actual way in which we perceive color is a matter of scientific debate. Traditionally, there have been two theories of color vision: the trichromatic (three-color) theory and the opponent-process theory. The **trichromatic theory of color** (from the Greek word *tri*, meaning "three," and *chroma*, meaning "color") suggests that we have three "color systems," each of which is maximally sensitive to red, green, or blue (Young, 1802). The proponents of this theory demonstrated that mixing lights of these three colors could yield the full spectrum of colors we perceive (**Figure 4.10**).

However, trichromatic theory doesn't fully explain color vision, and other researchers have proposed alternative theories. Perhaps the most important of these, the **opponent-process theory of color**, agrees that we have three color systems, but it says that each system is sensitive to two opposing colors—blue and yellow, red and green, black and white—in an "on/off" fashion. In other words, each color receptor responds either to blue or yellow, or to red or green, with the black-or-white system responding to differences in brightness levels. This theory makes a lot of sense because when different-colored lights are combined, people are unable to see reddish green and bluish yellow. In fact, when red and green lights or blue and yellow lights are mixed in equal amounts, we see white. This opponent-process theory also explains *color afterimages*, a fun type of optical illusion in which a reverse image briefly remains after the original image has faded (**Try This Yourself**).

## Try This Yourself

### Color Afterimages

Try staring at the dot in the middle of this color-distorted U.S. flag for 60 seconds. Then stare at a plain sheet of white paper. You should get a surprising color afterimage. You'll see red in place of green, blue in place of yellow, and white in place of black: a "genuine" U.S. flag. (If you don't see the afterimage, blink once or twice and try again.)

What happened? As you stared at the green, black, and yellow colors, the neural systems that process those colors became fatigued. Then when you looked at the plain white paper, which reflects all wavelengths, a reverse opponent process occurred: Each fatigued receptor responded with its opposing red, white, and blue colors! This is a good example of color afterimages—and further support for the opponent-process theory.

### Test Your Critical Thinking
1. In what situations do you think color afterimages are more likely to occur?

2. Other than learning that our eyes can play tricks on our brain, why might understanding illusions like this afterimage be useful?

Today we know that both trichromatic and opponent-process theories are correct—they just operate at different levels in visual processing. Color vision is processed in a trichromatic fashion in the retina. In contrast, color vision during opponent processing involves the retina, optic nerve, and brain.

### Color-Deficient Vision
Most people perceive three different colors—red, green, and blue—and are called *trichromats*. However, a small percentage of the population has a genetic deficiency in the red–green system, the blue–yellow system, or both. Those who perceive only two colors are called *dichromats*. People who are sensitive to only the black–white system are called *monochromats*, and they are totally color blind. If you'd like to test yourself for red–green color blindness, see the following **Try This Yourself**.

---

### Try This Yourself

#### Are You Color Blind?

People who suffer red–green color deficiency have trouble perceiving the number in this design. Although we commonly use the term *color blindness*, most problems are color confusion rather than color blindness. Furthermore, most people who have some color blindness are not even aware of it.

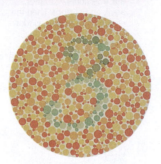

---

## Hearing

In this section, we examine **audition**, the sense of hearing, which we use nearly as much as our sense of vision. In fact, Helen Keller said she, "found deafness to be a much greater handicap than blindness. . . . Blindness cuts people off from things. Deafness cuts people off from people."

What is it about hearing that makes it so valuable? Audition has a number of important functions, ranging from alerting us to dangers to helping us communicate with others. In this section, we talk first about sound waves, then about the ear's anatomy and function, and finally about problems with hearing.

Like the visual process, which transforms light waves into vision, the auditory system is designed to convert sound waves into hearing. Sound waves are produced by air molecules moving in a particular wave pattern. For example, vibrating objects like vocal cords or guitar strings create waves of compressed and expanded air resembling ripples on a lake that circle out from a tossed stone. Our ears detect and respond to these waves of small air pressure changes, our brains then interpret the neural messages resulting from these waves, and we hear!

To fully understand this process, pay close attention to the information in **Step-by-Step Diagram 4.2**.

### Pitch Perception
How do we determine that certain sounds are from a child's voice, and not from an adult's? We distinguish between high- and low-pitched sounds by the *frequency* of the sound waves. The higher the frequency, the higher the *pitch*. There are three main explanations for how we perceive pitch:

- According to the **place theory for hearing**, we hear different pitches because different sound waves stimulate different sections (or *places*) on our cochlea's basilar membrane (see again Step-by-Step Diagram 4.2). Our brains figure out the pitch of a sound by detecting the position of the hair cells that sent the neural message. High frequencies produce large vibrations near the start of the basilar membrane—next to the oval window. However, this theory does not predict well for low frequencies, which tend to excite the entire basilar membrane.

**Audition** The sense or act of hearing.

**Place theory for hearing** The theory that pitch perception is linked to the particular spot on the cochlea's basilar membrane that is most stimulated.

## STEP-BY-STEP DIAGRAM 4.2 | How Our Ears Hear

**Outer ear**   The pinna, auditory canal, and eardrum structures, which funnel sound waves to the middle ear.

**Middle ear**   The hammer, anvil, and stirrup structures of the ear, which concentrate eardrum vibrations onto the cochlea's oval window.

**STOP!**   This Step-by-Step Diagram contains essential information NOT found elsewhere in the text, which is likely to appear on quizzes and exams. Be sure to study it CAREFULLY!

The **outer ear** captures and funnels sound waves into the eardrum. Next, three tiny bones in the **middle ear** pick up the eardrum's vibrations and transmit them to the **inner ear**. Finally, the snail-shaped **cochlea** in the inner ear transforms (transduces) the sound waves into neural messages (action potentials) that our brains process into what we consciously hear.

**1** The **outer ear** captures and funnels sound waves onto the tympanic membrane (ear drum).

**2** Vibrations of the tympanic membrane strike the **middle ear's** ossicles (hammer, anvil, and stirrup). Then the stirrup hits the oval window.

**3** Vibrations of the oval window create waves in the **inner ear's** cochlear fluid, which deflect the basilar membrane. This movement bends the hair cells.

**4** The hair cells communicate with the auditory nerve, which sends neural impulses to the brain.

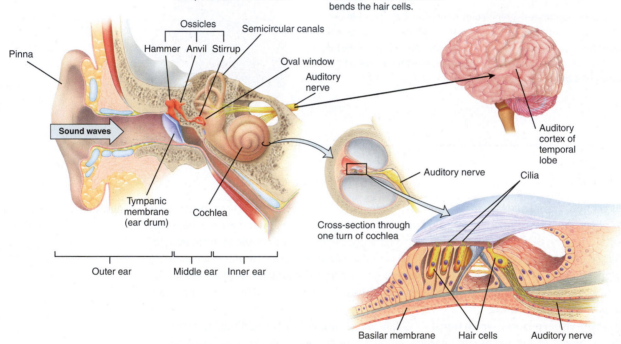

**Inner ear**   The semicircular canals, vestibular sacs, and cochlea, which generate neural signals that are sent to the brain.

**Cochlea [KOK-lee-uh]**   The fluid-filled, coiled tube in the inner ear that contains the receptors for hearing.

**Frequency theory for hearing**   The theory that pitch perception depends on how often the auditory nerve fires.

**Volley principle for hearing**   An explanation for pitch perception suggesting that clusters of neurons take turns firing in a sequence of rhythmic volleys, and that pitch depends on the frequency of these volleys.

- The **frequency theory for hearing** differs from place theory because it states that we hear pitch by the *frequency* of the sound waves traveling up the auditory nerve. High-frequency sounds trigger the auditory nerve to fire more often than do low-frequency sounds. The problem with this theory is that an individual neuron cannot fire faster than 1,000 times per second, which means that we could not hear many of the notes of a soprano singer.

- The **volley principle for hearing** solves the problem of frequency theory, which can't account for the highest-pitched sounds. It states that clusters of neurons take turns firing in a sequence of rhythmic *volleys*. Pitch perception depends upon the frequency of volleys, rather than the frequency carried by individual neurons.

Now that we've explored the mechanics of pitch and pitch perception, would you like a real-world example that you can apply to your everyday life? A recent experiment revealed that research participants who lowered the pitch of their voices were seen as being more influential, powerful, and intimidating (Cheng et al., 2016). This finding also held true in a second experiment in which the people listened to audio recordings of various voices. Can you see why the famous deep-voiced actor James Earl Jones was chosen as the voice of Darth Vader in the Star Wars films? Given that women generally tend to have higher-pitched voices, can you also see how this research might help explain why women often find it harder to gain leadership positions?

Interestingly, as we age, we tend to lose our ability to hear high-pitched sounds but are still able to hear low-pitched sounds. Given that young students can hear a cell phone ringtone that sounds at 17 kilohertz—too high for most adult ears to detect—they can take advantage of this age-related hearing difference and call or text one another during class (**Figure 4.11**). Ironically, the cell phone's ringtone that most adults can't hear is an offshoot of another device, called the Mosquito, which was originally designed to help shopkeepers annoy and drive away loitering teens!

### Softness versus Loudness

How we detect a sound as being soft or loud depends on its amplitude (or wave height). Waves with high peaks and low valleys produce loud sounds; waves with relatively low peaks and shallow valleys produce soft sounds. The relative loudness or softness of sounds is measured on a scale of *decibels* (dBs) (**Figure 4.12**).

### Hearing Problems

What are the types, causes, and treatments of hearing loss? **Conduction hearing loss**, also called conduction deafness, results from problems with the mechanical system that conducts sound waves to the cochlea. Hearing aids that amplify the incoming sound waves, and some forms of surgery, can help with this type of hearing loss.

In contrast, **sensorineural hearing loss**, also known as nerve deafness, results from damage to the cochlea's receptor (hair) cells or to the auditory nerve. Disease and biological changes associated with aging can result in sensorineural hearing loss. But it's most common (and preventable) cause is continuous exposure to loud noise, which can damage hair cells and lead to permanent hearing loss. Even brief exposure to really loud sounds, like a stereo or headphones at full blast, a jackhammer, or a jet airplane engine, can cause permanent nerve deafness (see again Figure 4.12). In fact, a high volume on earphones can reach the same noise level as a jet engine! All forms of high-volume noise can damage the coating on nerve cells, making it harder for the nerve cells to send information from the ears to the brain (Eggermont, 2015; Fagelson & Baguley, 2016; Jiang et al., 2016).

Keep in mind that damage to the auditory nerve or receptor cells is generally considered irreversible. Currently the best-known treatment is a small electronic device called a *cochlear implant*. If the auditory nerve is intact, the implant bypasses hair cells to stimulate the nerve. Unfortunately, cochlear implants produce only a crude approximation of hearing, but the technology is improving.

Given the limited benefits of medicine or technology to help improve hearing following damage, it's even more important to protect our sense of hearing. We can do this by avoiding exceptionally loud noises and wearing hearing protectors, such as earmuffs or earplugs, when we cannot avoid such stimuli (see photo). In fact, a recent study found that 42% of people not wearing earplugs experienced some hearing loss after being exposed to a loud sound, compared to only 8% who wore earplugs (Ramakers et al., 2016). It's also critical to pay attention to bodily warnings of possible hearing loss, including a change in our normal hearing threshold and *tinnitus*, a whistling or ringing sensation in the ears. These relatively small changes can have lifelong benefits.

**FIGURE 4.11** **Exploiting the teacher's age-related hearing loss**

**Conduction hearing loss** A type of hearing loss that results from damage to the mechanical system that conducts sound waves to the cochlea; also called conduction deafness.

**Sensorineural hearing loss** A type of hearing loss resulting from damage to the cochlea's receptor (hair) hearing cells or to the auditory nerve; also called nerve deafness.

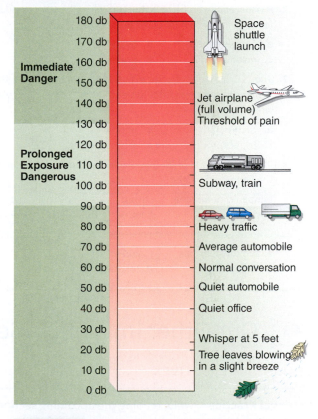

**FIGURE 4.12** **Beware of loud sounds** The higher a sound's decibel (dB) reading, the more damaging it is to the ear.

© Billy R. Ray/Wiley

## Retrieval Practice 4.2 | How We See and Hear

Completing this self-test and the connections section, and then checking your answers by clicking on the answer button or by looking in Appendix B, will provide immediate feedback and helpful practice for exams.

**Self-Test**

1. Identify the parts of the eye, placing the appropriate label on the figure to the right.

   | | | | |
   |---|---|---|---|
   | cornea | lens | cone | blind spot |
   | iris | retina | fovea | optic nerve |
   | pupil | rod | | |

2. A visual acuity problem that occurs when the cornea and lens focus an image in front of the retina is called _____ .

   **a.** farsightedness    **b.** hyperopia
   **c.** myopia    **d.** presbyopia

3. The _____ theory of color vision states that there are three systems of color opposites (blue-yellow, red-green, and black-white).

   **a.** trichromatic    **b.** opponent-process
   **c.** tri-receptor    **d.** lock-and-key

4. Identify the parts of the ear, placing the appropriate label on the figure to the right.

   | | | |
   |---|---|---|
   | tympanic membrane | stirrup | oval window |
   | anvil | hammer | cochlea |

5. Chronic exposure to loud noise can cause permanent _____ .

   **a.** auditory illusions    **b.** auditory hallucinations
   **c.** nerve deafness    **d.** conduction deafness

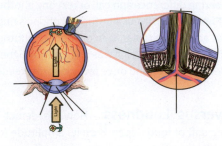

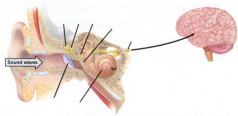

**Connections—Chapter to Chapter**

Answering the following question will help you "look back and look ahead" to see the important connections among the various subfields of psychology and chapters within this text.

In this chapter, you discovered that some people experience color-deficient vision. However, you may not realize that this condition usually affects men more than women and is genetic. Based on the discussion in Chapter 9 (Lifespan Development 1) about chromosomes and inherited characteristics, how might you explain the higher number of men versus women with color-deficient vision?

---

## 4.3 | Our Other Important Senses

### LEARNING OBJECTIVES

**Retrieval Practice**    while reading the upcoming sections, respond to each learning objective in your own words.

**Review the processes involved in smell, taste, and the body senses.**

- **Explain** the key factors in olfaction and gustation, and how the two senses interact.
- **Describe** how the body senses (skin, vestibular, and kinesthesis) work.

---

*I know by smell the kind of house we enter. I have recognized an old-fashioned country house because it has several layers of odors, left by a succession of families, of plants, perfumes, and draperies. Through the sense of touch I know the faces of friends, the illimitable variety of straight and curved lines, all surfaces, the exuberance of the soil, the delicate shapes of flowers, the noble forms of trees, and the range of mighty winds. . . . Footsteps, I discover, vary tactually according to the age, the sex, and the manners of the walker.*

(—Keller (1902, pp. 43–44, 46, 68–69)

These are the words of Helen Keller, the blind and deaf educator, author, and activist we introduced at the start of this chapter. Imagine being able to recognize a house by the smell of its previous occupants or your friends by a touch of their face. Vision and audition may be the most prominent of our senses, but the others—smell, taste, and the body senses—also help us navigate and gather vital information about our environment.

## Smell and Taste

Smell and taste are sometimes called the *chemical senses* because they both rely on chemoreceptors that are sensitive to certain chemical molecules. Have you wondered why we have trouble separating the two sensations? Smell and taste receptors are located near each other and closely interact (**Figure 4.13** and the following **Try This Yourself**).

**FIGURE 4.13** **Why we enjoy eating pizza: olfaction plus gustation** When we eat pizza, the crust, cheese, sauce, and other food molecules activate taste receptor cells on our tongue, while the pizza's odors activate smell receptor cells in our nose. This combined sensory information is then sent on to our brain where it is processed in various association regions of the cortex. Taste and smell also combine with sensory cells that respond to touch and temperature, which explains why cold, hard pizza "tastes" and "smells" different than hot, soft pizza.

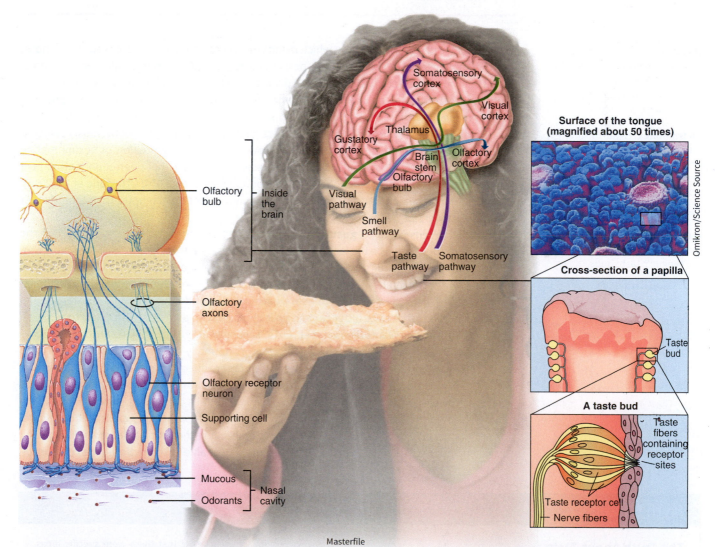

Omikron/Science Source

Masterfile

**a. The smell pathway** Olfactory receptor neurons (shown here in blue) transduce information from odorant molecules that enter the nose. The olfactory nerve carries this information into the olfactory bulb, where most information related to smell is processed before being sent on to other parts of the brain. (Note that olfaction is the only sensory system that is NOT routed through the thalamus.)

**b. The taste pathway** While eating and drinking, liquids and dissolved foods flow over the tongue's papillae (the lavender circular areas in the top photo) and into their pores. This activates the taste receptor cells, which then send messages on to the nerve fibers, which carry information on to the brain stem, thalamus, gustatory cortex, and somatosensory cortex.

## Try This Yourself

### The Art of Wine Tasting

Why do professional wine judges sniff the wine instead of just tasting it?

Don Tremain/Alamy

**Answer:** Most of what we perceive as taste or flavor is a combination of both smell and taste, which explains why wine-tasting judges use both their noses and mouths. More specifically, sniffing draws more smell molecules into the nose and helps speed their circulation, and the mouth is equally important because smells reach the nasal cavity by wafting up the throat like smoke in a chimney.

**Olfaction** The sense or act of smelling; receptors are located in the nose's nasal cavity.

**Pheromones [FARE-oh-mones]** Chemical signals released by organisms that trigger certain responses, such as aggression or sexual mating, in other members of the same species.

**Gustation** The sense or act of tasting; receptors are located in the tongue's taste buds.

Our sense of smell, **olfaction**, which results from stimulation of receptor cells in the nose, is remarkably useful and sensitive. We possess more than 1,000 types of olfactory receptors, which allow us to detect more than 10,000 distinct smells. The nose is more sensitive to smoke than any electronic detector. And people who are blind (like Helen Keller) can, with practice, learn to recognize others by their unique odors.

Chemicals called **pheromones**, which are released by animals and unconsciously detected through the sense of smell, trigger certain responses, such as aggression or sexual mating (Beny & Kimchi, 2016; Plush et al., 2016). Some research indicates that pheromones also affect human sexual response (Baum & Cherry, 2015; Jouhanneau et al., 2014; Ottaviano et al., 2015). However, other research suggests that human sexuality is far more complex than that of other animals (Chapters 11, 12, and 16).

Today, the sense of taste, **gustation**, which results from stimulation of receptor cells in the tongue's taste buds, may be the least critical of our senses. In the past, however, it probably contributed significantly to our survival. For example, humans and other animals have a preference for sweet foods, which are generally nonpoisonous and are good sources of energy. The major function of taste, aided by smell, is to help us avoid eating or drinking harmful substances. Because many plants that taste bitter contain toxic chemicals, an animal is more likely to survive if it avoids bitter-tasting plants (French et al., 2015; Sagong et al., 2014; Schwartz & Krantz, 2016).

Did you know that our taste and smell receptors normally die and are replaced every few days? This probably reflects the fact that these receptors are directly exposed to the environment, whereas vision receptors are protected by the eyeball and hearing receptors are protected by the eardrum. However, as we grow older, the number of taste cells diminishes, which helps explain why adults enjoy spicier foods than do infants. Scientists are particularly excited about the regenerative capabilities of the taste and olfactory cells because they hope to learn how to transfer this regeneration to other types of cells that are currently unable to self-replace when damaged.

## Myth Busters

### The Truth About Taste

Scientists once believed that we detected only four distinct tastes: *sweet, sour, salty,* and *bitter*. However, we now know that we have a fifth taste sense, *umami*, a word that means "delicious" or "savory" and refers to sensitivity to an amino acid called *glutamate* (Bredie et al., 2014; Lease et al., 2016). Glutamate is found in meats, meat broths, and monosodium glutamate (MSG).

It was also previously believed that there were specific areas on our tongues dedicated to detecting bitter, sweet, salty, and other tastes. Today we know that taste receptors, like smell receptors, respond differentially to the varying shapes of food and liquid molecules. The major taste receptors—taste buds—are distributed all over our tongues within little bumps called papillae. But a small number of taste receptors are also found in the palate and the back of our mouths. Thus, even people without a tongue experience some taste sensations.

**Learning and Culture**    Many food and taste preferences are learned from an early age and from personal experiences (Fildes et al., 2014; Nicklaus, 2016; Tan et al., 2015). For example, many Japanese children eat raw fish, and some Chinese children eat chicken feet as part of their normal diet. Although most U.S. children might consider these foods "yucky," they tend to love cheese, which children in many other cultures find repulsive.

In addition, our expectations and experiences can affect our taste preferences. For example, adults who are told a bottle of wine costs $90 (rather than its real price of $10) report that it tastes better than a supposedly cheaper brand. Ironically, these false expectations actually trigger areas of the brain that respond to pleasant experiences (Plassmann et al., 2008). This means that in a neurochemical sense, the wine we believe is better does, in fact, taste better! Regarding our experiences, other research has found that multiple-drug users and recreational cannabis users have a higher preference for salty and sour tastes, whereas daily tobacco and cannabis users have a higher preference for sweet and spicy tastes (Dovey et al., 2016).

Keep in mind that smell and taste are not the only two senses that overlap. We obviously enjoy a meal in a fine restaurant with beautiful music playing in the background far more than the same meal eaten alone while watching television. But did you know that music alone can even affect the taste of beer? See the following **Research Challenge**.

## The Body Senses

As you recall from our introductory story, Helen Keller's young teacher, Anne Sullivan, was able to break through Helen's barrier of isolation by taking advantage of her sense of touch. One day, Anne took Helen to the pump house and, as Anne recalled:

> I made Helen hold her mug under the spout while I pumped. As the cold water gushed forth, filling the mug, I spelled "w-a-t-e-r" in Helen's free hand. The word coming so close upon the sensation of cold water rushing over her hand seemed to startle her. She dropped the mug and stood as one transfixed. A new light came into her face (Keller, 1902, p. 23).

---

## Research Challenge

### Can Music Improve the Taste of Beer?

Research shows that what we see and hear can significantly affect our perception and enjoyment of different flavors (e.g., Seo & Hummel, 2015; Spence, 2016). Surprisingly, even the curvature of a product's design can influence its expected taste. For example, rounder designs lead to greater expectations of sweetness, whereas people more often expect more sour tastes with angular designs (Lunardo & Livat, 2016).

To investigate how taste and background music may interact, the Brussels Beer Project collaborated with a UK band, The Editors, to produce a porter-style beer with a custom-designed label that broadly corresponded to the band's latest album, "In Dreams" (Carvalho et al., 2016). The researchers then invited 231 drinkers to test the beer in three different conditions:

- Group 1 drank the beer from unlabeled bottles without listening to any specific song.

- Group 2 drank the beer from bottles with the special labels, again without listening to a song.

- Group 3 drank the beer from bottles with the special labels while listening to "Oceans of Light," one of the songs on the band's latest album.

Before being assigned to groups, participants rated how tasty they expected the beer to be. After tasting, they rated how much they liked the beer's taste. Can you explain why participants in Group

3 reported both greater enjoyment and better taste than those in Groups 1 and 2?

**Test Yourself**

1. Based on the information provided, did this research (Carvalho et al., 2016) use descriptive, correlational, and/or experimental research?

2. If you chose:
   - *descriptive research*, is this a naturalistic observation, survey/ interview, case study, and/or archival research?
   - *correlational research*, is this a positive, negative, or zero correlation?
   - *experimental research*, label the IV, DV, experimental groups(s), and control group. (Note: If participants were not randomly assigned to groups, list it as a *quasi-experimental design*.)
   - both *descriptive* and *correlational*, answer the corresponding questions for both.

**Check your answers by clicking on the answer button or by looking in Appendix B.**

**Note:** The information provided in this study is admittedly limited, but the level of detail is similar to what is presented in most textbooks and public reports of research findings. Answering these questions, and then comparing your answers to those provided, will help you become a better critical thinker and consumer of scientific research.

**FIGURE 4.14** **Our body senses**

**a. Skin senses** The sense of touch relies on a variety of receptors located in different parts of the skin. Both human and nonhuman animals are highly responsive to touch.

© Philip Dyer/iStockphoto

**Pain and temperature**

Free nerve endings for pain (sharp pain and dull pain)

Free nerve endings for temperature (heat or cold)

**Fine touch and pressure**

Meissner's corpuscle (touch)

Merkel's disc (light to moderate pressure against skin)

Ruffini's end organ (heavy pressure and joint movements)

Hair receptors (flutter or steady skin indentation)

Pacinian corpuscle (vibrating and heavy pressure)

© John Wiley and Sons, Inc.

**b. Vestibular sense** Part of the "thrill" of amusement park rides comes from our vestibular sense of balance becoming confused. The vestibular sense is used by the eye muscles to maintain visual fixation and sometimes by the body to change body orientation. We can become dizzy or nauseated if the vestibular sense becomes "confused" by boat, airplane, or automobile motion. Children between ages 2 and 12 years have the greatest susceptibility to motion sickness.

PomInOz/Shutterstock

Courtesy Kathy Young

**c. Kinesthesis** This athlete's finely-tuned behaviors are the result of information provided by receptors in her muscles, joints, and tendons that detect the location, orientation, and movement of her individual body parts relative to each other.

That one moment, brought on by the sensation of cold water on her hand, was the impetus for a lifetime of learning about, understanding, and appreciating the world through her remaining senses. In using her sense of touch, Helen was using one of the so-called body senses. In addition to smell and taste, we have three major body senses that help us navigate our world—skin senses, vestibular sense, and kinesthetic sense (**Figure 4.14**).

**Skin Senses** Our skin is uniquely designed for the detection of touch (or pressure), temperature, and pain (**Figure 4.14a**). The concentration and depth of the receptors for each of these stimuli vary. For example, touch receptors are most concentrated on the face and fingers and least concentrated in the back and legs. Getting a paper cut can feel so painful because we have many receptors on our fingertips. Some receptors respond to more than one type of stimulation. For example, itching, tickling, and vibrating sensations seem to be produced by light stimulation of both pressure and pain receptors.

The benefits of touch are so significant for human growth and development that the American Academy of Pediatrics recommends that all mothers and babies have skin-to-skin contact in the first hours after birth. This type of contact, which is called *kangaroo care*, is especially beneficial for preterm and low-birth-weight infants. Babies who receive this care experience greater weight gain, fewer infections, and improved cognitive and motor development. How does kangaroo care lead to these improvements in infant health? See **Figure 4.15**.

**Vestibular Sense** Our sense of balance, the **vestibular sense**, informs our brains of how our body (particularly our head) is oriented with respect to gravity and three-dimensional space

**Vestibular sense** The sense that provides information about balance and movement; receptors are located in the inner ear.

(**Figure 4.14b**). When our head tilts, liquid in the *semicircular canals*, located in our inner ear, moves and bends hair cell receptors. In addition, at the end of the semicircular canals are *vestibular sacs*, which contain hair cells sensitive to our bodily movement relative to gravity (as shown in Figure 4.14b). Information from the semicircular canals and the vestibular sacs is converted to neural impulses that are then carried to our brains.

### Kinesthesis

The sense that provides the brain with information about the location, orientation, and movement of individual body parts is called **kinesthesis** (**Figure 4.14c**). Kinesthetic receptors are found throughout the muscles, joints, and tendons of our body. They tell our brains which muscles are being contracted or relaxed, how our body weight is distributed, where our arms and legs are in relation to the rest of our body, and so on.

Mike Kemp/Getty Images

**FIGURE 4.15** **Infant benefits from kangaroo care** This type of skin-to-skin touch helps babies in several ways, including providing warmth, reducing pain (lower levels of arousal and stress increases pain tolerance and immune functioning), and improving sleep quality. Other research, including a meta-analysis (which combines results from multiple studies), also found that babies who receive kangaroo care have a 36% lower likelihood of death—as well as a lower risk of blood infection and similar positive long-term effects beyond infancy (Boundy et al., 2016; Burke-Aaronson, 2015; Nobre et al., 2016). As we'll discuss throughout this text, skin-to-skin contact, including holding hands and hugging, provides numerous physical and mental benefits for people of all ages.

**Kinesthesis** The sense that provides information about the location, orientation, and movement of individual body parts relative to each other; receptors are located in muscles, joints, and tendons.

© Billy R. Ray/Wiley

## Retrieval Practice 4.3 | Our Other Important Senses

Completing this self-test and the connections section, and then checking your answers by clicking on the answer button or by looking in Appendix B, will provide immediate feedback and helpful practice for exams.

### Self-Test

1. _____ results from stimulation of receptor cells in the nose.
   - **a.** Audition
   - **b.** Gustation
   - **c.** Olfaction
   - **d.** None of these options

2. Describe how olfaction and gustation interact.

3. Most of our taste receptors are found on the _____.
   - **a.** olfactory bulb
   - **b.** gustatory cells
   - **c.** frenulum
   - **d.** taste buds

4. The skin senses include _____.
   - **a.** pressure
   - **b.** pain
   - **c.** warmth and cold
   - **d.** all of these options

5. The _____ sense is located in the inner ear and is responsible for our sense of balance.
   - **a.** auditory
   - **b.** vestibular
   - **c.** kinesthetic
   - **d.** olfactory

### Connections—Chapter to Chapter

Answering the following question will help you "look back and look ahead" to see the important connections among the various subfields of psychology and chapters within this text.

In Chapter 2 (Neuroscience and Biological Foundations), you explored the functions of various structures in the brain. Imagine that you are giving a presentation in your U.S. history class. Name the areas involved in the following behaviors: (a) smelling the perfume of one of your classmates, (b) tasting the cough drop you just swallowed to prevent your coughs, (c) noticing that the tag of your new shirt is scratching the back of your neck.

## 4.4 Understanding Perception

### LEARNING OBJECTIVES

**Retrieval Practice** While reading the upcoming sections, respond to each Learning Objective in your own words.

**Summarize the three processes involved in perception.**

- **Explain** illusions and why they're important.
- **Discuss** the process of selection and its three major factors.

- **Describe** the three ways we organize sensory data.
- **Review** the main factors in perceptual interpretation.
- **Discuss** the research findings on ESP and why so many people believe in it.

*There are things known and unknown, and in between are the doors of perception.*
—Aldous Huxley (English Satiristt, Author of *Brave New World*)

We are ready to move from *sensation* and the major senses to *perception*, the process of selecting, organizing, and interpreting incoming sensations into useful mental representations of the world.

Normally, our perceptions agree with our sensations. When they do not, the result is called an **illusion**, a false or misleading impression produced by errors in the perceptual process or by actual physical distortions, as in the so-called *moon illusion*, in which the moon looks larger at the horizon than when it's overhead. Illusions are important to psychologists because they provide a unique tool for studying the normal process of perception (**Concept Organizer 4.1**).

**Illusion**    A false or misleading perception shared by others in the same perceptual environment.

## Selection

In almost every situation, we confront more sensory information than we can reasonably pay attention to. Three major factors help us focus on some stimuli and ignore others: *selective attention*, *feature detectors*, and *habituation*.

Certain basic mechanisms for perceptual selection are built into the brain. For example, we're able to focus our conscious awareness on a specific stimulus while filtering out other stimuli thanks to the process of **selective attention** (**Figure 4.16**). This type of focused attention

**Selective attention**    The process of focusing conscious awareness onto a specific stimulus, while filtering out a range of other stimuli occurring simultaneously.

---

### CONCEPT ORGANIZER 4.1    Understanding Perceptual Illusions

**STOP!**  This Concept Organizer contains essential information NOT found elsewhere in the text, which is likely to appear on quizzes and exams. Be sure to study it CAREFULLY!

As you may have noticed, this text highlights numerous popular *myths* about psychology because it's important to understand and correct our misperceptions. For similar reasons, you need to know how illusions mislead our normal information processing and recognize that "seeing is believing, but seeing isn't always believing correctly" (Lilienfeld et al., 2010, p. 7).

**Study Tip**

*Note that illusions are NOT the same as hallucinations or delusions.* Hallucinations *are false, imaginary sensory perceptions that occur without external, objective stimuli, such as hearing voices during a psychotic episode or seeing particular images after using some type of hallucinogenic drug, such as LSD or hallucinogenic mushrooms.* Delusions *refer to false, imaginary beliefs, often of persecution or grandeur, that may accompany psychotic episodes or drug experiences.*

**a. Müller-Lyer illusion**    Which vertical line is longer? In fact, the two vertical lines are the same length, but psychologists have learned that people who live in urban environments normally see the one on the right as longer. This is because they have learned to make size and distance judgments from perspective cues created by right angles and horizontal and vertical lines of buildings and streets.

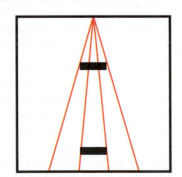

**b. Ponzo illusion**    Which of the two horizontal lines is longer? In fact, both lines are the exact same size, but the converging vertical lines provide depth cues telling you that the top dark, horizontal line is farther away than the bottom line and therefore much longer.

**Test Your Critical Thinking**

**1.** Can you see how illusions like these might create real-world dangers for our everyday lives?

**2.** When you watch films of moving cars, the wheels appear to go backward. Can you explain this common visual illusion?

**c. The horizontal-vertical illusion**    Which is longer, the horizontal (flat) or the vertical (standing) line? People living in areas where they regularly see long straight lines, such as roads and train tracks, perceive the horizontal line as shorter because of their environmental experiences.

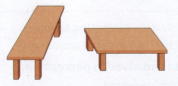

**d. Shepard's tables**    Do these two table tops have the same dimensions? Get a ruler and check it for yourself.

**FIGURE 4.16** **Selective attention** Have you noticed that when you're at a noisy party, you can still select and attend to the voices of people you find interesting, or that you can suddenly pick up on another group's conversation if someone in that group mentions your name? These are prime examples of *selective attention*, also called the "cocktail party phenomenon."

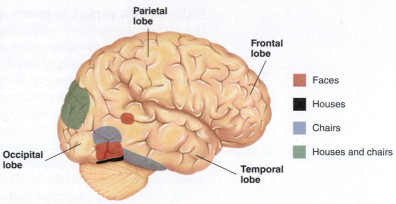

**FIGURE 4.17** **Feature detectors in our brains** Recall from Chapter 2 that during fMRI scans, specific areas of the brain are activated (they "light up"). In this case, researchers identified areas that are activated when people look at specific objects, such as faces, houses, chairs, and even combinations like houses and chairs. Given that our brains are not designed to waste time or processing power, can you see why humans have developed specific cells designed to recognize these particular shapes?

and concentration allows us to select only information that is essential to us and discard the rest (Chen et al., 2016; Howell et al., 2016; Rosner et al., 2015).

In addition to selective attention, the brains of humans and other animals contain specialized cells, called **feature detectors**, which respond only to specific characteristics of visual stimuli, such as shape, angle, or movement (**Figure 4.17**). For example, frogs are known to have specific "bug detector" cells that respond to small, dark, moving objects. Humans also have specific cells for detecting general motion in our peripheral vision, as well as feature detectors in the temporal and occipital lobes, some of which respond maximally to faces (see again Figure 4.17). Problems in these areas can produce a condition called *prosopagnosia* (*prosopon* means "face," and *agnosia* means "failure to know"). People with prosopagnosia can recognize that they are looking at a face. But, surprisingly, they cannot say whose face is reflected in a mirror, even if it is their own or that of a friend or relative (Lohse et al., 2016; Tanzer et al., 2014; Van Belle et al., 2015).

Other examples of the brain's ability to filter experience occurs with **habituation**, the brain's learned tendency to ignore or stop responding to unchanging information. Apparently the brain is "prewired" to pay more attention to changes in the environment than to stimuli that remain constant. As you'll discover in Chapter 9, developmental psychologists often use measurements of habituation to tell when a stimulus can be detected and discriminated by infants who are too young to speak. When presented with a new stimulus, infants initially pay attention, but with repetition they learn that the stimulus is unchanging, and their responses weaken. Habituation can also lead to serious relationship problems—see the following **Try This Yourself**.

**Feature detectors** Neurons in the brain's visual system that respond to specific characteristics of stimuli, such as shape, angle, or movement.

**Habituation** The brain's learned tendency to ignore or stop responding to unchanging information; an example of top-down processing.

## Try This Yourself

### Romance versus Habituation

Have you ever wondered why attention and compliments from a complete stranger seem more exciting and valuable to you than similar actions and words from your long-term romantic partner? Does this make you wonder if you're with the right person? Think again. Remember that we all habituate to unchanging stimuli. If we move on to other relationships, they too will soon fall victim to habituation.

What can we do to keep romance alive? If we're the person being complimented, we can be grateful that we've learned about habituation, and then remind ourselves to not be overly influenced by a stranger's attention. As the long-term romantic partner hoping to offset the dangers of habituation, we can take a note from advertisers by using more *intensity, novelty*, and *contrast* in our compliments and interactions with our loved ones.

### Habituation versus Sensory Adaptation

Before going on, let's look more closely at the distinction between habituation and sensory adaptation, which we discussed earlier. Recall that sensory adaptation refers to the *sensory receptors' innate* tendency to fatigue and stop responding to unchanging stimuli. In contrast, habituation is our *brain's learned* tendency to stop responding to unchanging stimuli. The first is innate and occurs at the sensory receptor level. The second is learned and occurs within the brain. Here's a simple example: If someone pulled the fire alarm at your college, you'd initially jump up and try to evacuate. However, if your instructor told you that this was a false alarm, which couldn't be immediately turned off, the loud noise of the alarm would slowly start to fade because your sensory receptors would automatically adapt to the unchanging noise. In contrast, if students keep pulling the fire alarm as a dangerous prank, you and others will soon learn to ignore the sound and stop trying to evacuate.

In sum, sensory adaptation happens to us and we respond automatically. Habituation is voluntary—we actively use our brains to deliberately redirect our attention away from the stimulus. Do you understand how both sensory adaptation and habituation may have serious consequences? If you ignore the smell of leaking gas in your apartment, you'll eventually adapt—and may die from the fumes! Similarly, repeated "prank" fire alarms, lock-down drills at schools, and national "red alert" terrorist warnings may lead all of us to become complacent (and less careful). Hopefully, your increased understanding of sensory adaptation and habituation will better prepare you for a proper response when a true need arises.

Given that sensory adaptation and habituation occur with unchanging stimuli, are you wondering why ads are so often repeated? Advertisers know that repetition builds brand familiarity, which generally increases sales. However, they're also well aware of the *wear-in/wear-out theory*, which suggests that repetition has an initial positive effect but that too much repetition generally diminishes an ad's effectiveness (Berlyne, 1970; Kapexhiu, 2015). You can be sure that advertisers take steps to avoid problems resulting from exposure. The good news is that your awareness of the psychological factors behind persuasive techniques may help you become a more informed consumer.

## Organization

In the previous section, we discussed how we select certain stimuli in our environment to pay attention to while disregarding other stimuli. The next step in perception is to organize this selected information into useful mental representations of the world around us. Raw sensory data are like the parts of a watch—the parts must be assembled in a meaningful way before they are useful. We organize visual sensory data in terms of *form, depth,* and *constancy*.

### Form Perception

Look at the two figures in **Figure 4.18a**. What do you see? Can you draw similar objects on a piece of paper? Most people without artistic training cannot reconstruct these drawings. Why? It's because pictures and drawings are naturally two-dimensional. However, these drawings were created using standard pictorial rules to create the illusion of three dimensions, while also breaking some of these same rules. For example, looking at each drawing in Figure a, you assume they're representing a normal structure and items. But as you try to sort out and organize the different lines into a stable, well-organized whole, you realize the lines and planes don't add up—they're

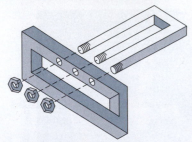

a. **Impossible figures**

Courtesy Linda Locklear

b. **An infant's early facial recognition**

**FIGURE 4.18** Understanding form perception

illogical or impossible. Why do psychologists study these aptly named "impossible figures"? It's because they offer intriguing insights into our visual processing and form perception.

Now look at **Figure 4.18b**. Even before they're two months of age, infants have learned how to piece together the components of the human face and easily recognize familiar faces, just as this infant recognizes her grandfather's face. Like the illusions studied earlier, impossible figures and infant perception help us understand perceptual principles—in this case, the principle of *form perception.*

**Gestalt psychologists** were among the first to study form perception and how the brain organizes sensory impressions into a *gestalt*—a German word meaning "form" or "whole." They emphasized the importance of organization and patterning in enabling us to perceive the whole stimulus rather than perceive its discrete parts as separate entities. The Gestaltists proposed several laws of organization that specify how people perceive form (**Figure 4.19**).

The most fundamental Gestalt principle of organization is our tendency to distinguish between the *figure* (our main focus of attention) and the *ground* (the background or surroundings). Your sense of figure and ground is at work in what you are doing right now—reading. Your brain is receiving sensations of black lines and white paper, but your brain is organizing these sensations into black letters and words on a white background. You perceive the letters as the figure and the white as the ground. If you make a great effort, you might be able to force yourself to see the page reversed, as though a black background were showing through letter-shaped holes in a white foreground.

There are times, however, when it is very hard to distinguish the figure from the ground, as you can see in **Figure 4.20**. This type of figure is known as a *reversible figure*. Your brain

**Gestalt psychology**   An early school of thought that emphasized the tendency to organize our perceptions into meaningful patterns and whole figures.

## Figure 4.19

**Figure–ground:**
The tendency to perceive one aspect as the figure and the other as the ground. (Here the red objects are the figure and the yellow background is the ground).

**Proximity:**
Objects that are physically close together are grouped together. (In this figure, we see 3 groups of 6 hearts, not 18 separate hearts.)

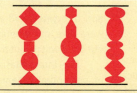

**Continuity:**
Objects that continue a pattern are grouped together. (When we see line **a,** we normally see a combination of lines **b** and **c** — not **d.**)

When we see this,

a.

we normally see this

b.

plus this.

c.

Not this.

d.

**Closure:**
The tendency to see a finished unit (triangle, square, or circle) from an incomplete stimulus.

**Similarity:**
Similar objects are grouped together (the green colored dots are grouped together and perceived as the number 5).

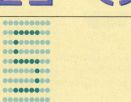

**FIGURE 4.19** **Understanding Gestalt principles of organization**   Gestalt principles are based on the notion that we all share a natural tendency to force patterns onto whatever we see. Although the examples of the Gestalt principles in this figure are all visual, each principle applies to other modes of perception as well. For example, the Gestalt principle of *contiguity* cannot be shown because it involves nearness in time, not visual nearness. Similarly, the aural (hearing) effects of figure and ground aren't shown in this figure, but you've undoubtedly experienced them in a movie theater. Despite nearby conversations in the audience, you can still listen to the voices on the film because you make them your focus (the figure) versus the ground.

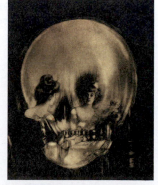

Rykoff Collection/Corbis/Getty Images

**FIGURE 4.20** **Understanding reversible figures**   This so-called *reversible figure* demonstrates alternating figure–ground relations. It can be seen as a woman looking in a mirror or as a skull, depending on what you see as figure or ground.

**Depth perception** The ability to perceive three-dimensional space and to accurately judge distance.

Kieran Meehan/CartoonStock

alternates between seeing the light areas as the figure and seeing them as the ground. Are you wondering how the Gestalt laws might vary among different cultures? See the following **Gender and Cultural Diversity**.

## Depth Perception

In our three-dimensional world, the ability to perceive the depth and distance of objects—as well as their height and width—is essential (see the cartoon). **Depth perception** is learned primarily through experience. However, research using an apparatus called the *visual cliff* (**Figure 4.22**) suggests that very young infants can perceive depth and will actively avoid it.

Some have suggested that this visual cliff research proves that depth perception, and avoidance of heights, is inborn. The modern consensus is that infants are, indeed, able to perceive depth. But the idea that infants' fear of heights causes their avoidance is not supported by research (Adolph et al., 2014). Instead, researchers found that infants display a flexible and adaptive response at the edge of a drop-off. They pat the surface, attempt to reach through the glass, and even rock back and forth at the edge. They decide whether or not to cross or avoid a drop-off based on previous locomotor experiences, along with gained knowledge of their own muscle strength, balance, and other criteria.

## Gender and Cultural Diversity

### Are the Gestalt Laws Universally True?

Gestalt psychologists conducted most of their work with formally educated people from urban European cultures. A. R. Luria (1976) was one of the first to question whether their laws held true for all participants, regardless of education and cultural setting. Luria recruited a wide range of participants living in what was then the U.S.S.R. He included Ichkeri women from remote villages (with no formal education), collective farm activists (who were semiliterate), and female students in a teachers' school (with years of formal education).

Luria found that when presented with the stimuli shown in **Figure 4.21,** the formally trained female students were the only ones who identified the first three shapes by their categorical name of "circle." Whether circles were made of solid lines, incomplete lines, or solid colors, they called them all circles. However, participants with no formal education named the shapes according to the objects they resembled. They called a circle a watch, a plate, or a moon, and referred to a square as a mirror, a house, or an

apricot-drying board. When asked if items 12 and 13 from Figure 4.21 were alike, one woman answered, "No, they're not alike. This one's not like a watch, but that one's a watch because there are dots."

One interpretation of Luria's findings is that the Gestalt laws of perceptual organization are valid only for people who have been schooled in geometric concepts. But an alternative explanation has also been suggested. Luria's study, as well as most research on visual perception and optical illusions, relied on two-dimensional presentations—either on a piece of paper or projected on a screen. It may be that experience with pictures and photographs (not formal education in geometric concepts) is necessary for learning to interpret two-dimensional figures as portraying three-dimensional forms. Westerners who have had years of practice learning to interpret two-dimensional drawings of three-dimensional objects may not remember how much practice it took to learn the cultural conventions for judging the size and shape of objects drawn on paper (Berry et al., 2011; Keith, 2010).

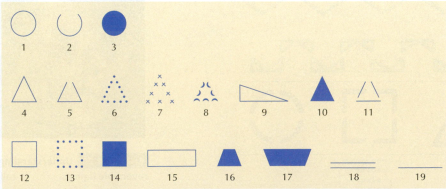

**FIGURE 4.21** **Luria's stimuli** When you see these shapes, you readily identify them as circles, triangles, and other geometric forms. According to cross-cultural research, this is due to your formal educational training. If you were from a culture without formal education, you might identify them instead as familiar objects in your environment—"the circle is like the moon."

*Source:* Reprinted by permission of the publisher from, *Cognitive Development: Its Cultural and Social Foundations* by A.R. Luria, translated by Martin Lopez-Morillas and Lynn Solotaroff, edited by Michael Cole, p. 33, Cambridge, Mass.: Harvard University Press Copyright © 1976 by the President and Fellows of Harvard College.

The notion that fear of heights is NOT innate is further supported by other research showing that infants and young children willingly approach photos and videos of snakes and spiders, and even live snakes and spiders, rather than withdrawing from them (LoBue, 2013). Although infants do show a heightened sensitivity to snakes, spiders, and heights—which may facilitate fear learning later in development—they do not innately fear them. In short, infants perceive depth, but their fear of heights apparently develops over time, like walking or language acquisition.

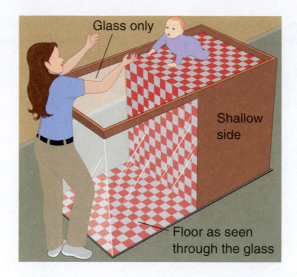

Glass only

Shallow side

Floor as seen through the glass

**FIGURE 4.22**  **Visual cliff** Given the desire to investigate depth perception, while also protecting infants and other experimental participants from actual falls, psychologists E. J. Gibson and R. D. Walk (1960) created a clever miniature cliff with a simulated drop-off. Infants were placed on the glass surface that covered the entire table and then encouraged (usually by their mothers) to crawl over either the shallow or the deep side. The research showed that most crawling infants hesitate or refuse to move to the "deep end" of the visual cliff, indicating that they perceive the difference in depth.

How, exactly, do we perceive depth? Although we do get some sense of distance based on hearing and even smell, most depth perception comes from several visual cues, which are summarized in **Figure 4.23**. The first mechanism we use is the interaction of both of our eyes, which produces **binocular cues** (**Figure 4.24**). However, the binocular cues of **retinal disparity** and **convergence** are inadequate in judging distances longer than the length of a football field. Luckily, we have several **monocular cues**, which need only one eye to work. Imagine yourself as an artist, and see whether you can identify each of the following monocular cues in this beautiful photo of the Taj Mahal, a famous mausoleum in India (**Figure 4.25**):

- **Linear perspective**  Parallel lines converge, or angle toward one another, as they recede into the distance.

- **Interposition**  Objects that obscure or overlap other objects are perceived as closer.

- **Relative size**  Close objects cast a larger retinal image than distant objects.

- **Texture gradient**  Nearby objects have a coarser and more distinct texture than distant ones.

- **Aerial perspective**  Distant objects appear hazy and blurred compared to close objects because of intervening atmospheric dust or haze.

- **Light and shadow**  Brighter objects are perceived as being closer than darker objects.

- **Relative height**  Objects positioned higher in our field of vision are perceived as farther away.

Two additional monocular cues for depth perception, **accommodation** of the lens of the eye and *motion parallax*, cannot be used by artists and are not shown in Figure 4.25. In *accommodation*, muscles that adjust the shape of the lens as it focuses on an object send neural messages to the brain, which interprets the signal to perceive distance. For near objects, the lens bulges; for far objects, it flattens. *Motion parallax* (also known as *relative motion*) refers to the fact that close objects appear to whiz by, whereas farther objects seem to move more slowly or remain stationary.

**Binocular cues**  Visual input from two eyes, which allows perception of depth or distance.

**Retinal disparity**  The binocular cue of distance in which the separation of the eyes causes different images to fall on the two retinas.

**Convergence**  A binocular depth cue in which the eyes turn inward (or converge) to fixate on an object.

**Monocular cues**  Visual input from a single eye alone that contributes to perception of depth or distance.

**Accommodation**  The process by which the eye's ciliary muscles change the shape (thickness) of the lens so that light is focused on the retina; adjustment of the eye's lens permitting focusing on near and distant objects.

**Perceptual constancy**  The tendency to perceive the environment as stable, despite changes in the sensory input.

**Constancies Perception**  To organize our sensations into meaningful patterns, we develop **perceptual constancies**, the learned tendency to perceive the environment as stable, despite changes in an object's *size*, *color*, *brightness*, and *shape*. Without perceptual constancy, things would seem to grow as we get closer to them, change shape

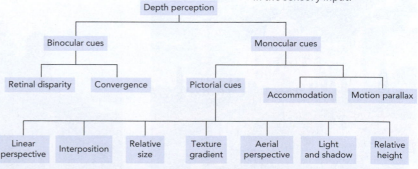

Depth perception

Binocular cues

Monocular cues

Retinal disparity

Convergence

Pictorial cues

Accommodation

Motion parallax

Linear perspective

Interposition

Relative size

Texture gradient

Aerial perspective

Light and shadow

Relative height

**FIGURE 4.23**  **Visual cues for depth perception**

**FIGURE 4.24**  **Binocular depth cues**    How do we perceive a three-dimensional world with a two-dimensional receptor system? One mechanism is the interaction of both eyes to produce binocular cues.

**a. Retinal disparity**    Stare at your two index fingers a few inches in front of your eyes with their tips half an inch apart. Do you see the "floating finger"? Move them farther away and the "finger" will shrink. Move them closer and it will enlarge. Because our eyes are about 2½ inches apart, objects at different distances (such as the "floating finger") project their images on different parts of the retina, an effect called *retinal disparity*. Far objects project on the retinal area near the nose, whereas near objects project farther out, closer to the ears.

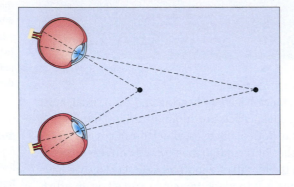

**b. Convergence**    Hold your index finger at arm's length in front of you and watch it as you bring it closer until it is right in front of your nose. The amount of strain in your eye muscles created by the *convergence* (turning inward) of your eyes is used as a cue by your brain to interpret distance.

as our viewing angle changes, and change color as light levels change (Albright, 2015; Schmidt & Fleming, 2016; Stiles et al., 2015).

- **Size constancy**    Regardless of an object's distance from us (or the size of the image it casts on our retina), *size constancy* allows us to interpret the object as always being the same size. For example, the image of the couple in the foreground of **Figure 4.26** is much larger on our retina than the trees behind them. However, thanks to size constancy, we perceive them to be of normal size. Without this constancy, we would perceive people as "shrinking" when they move away from us and "growing" when they move toward us. Although researchers have found evidence of size constancy in newborns, it also develops from learning and the environment. Case studies of people who have been blind since birth, and then have their sight restored, find that they initially have little or no size constancy (Sacks, 2015).

- **Color and brightness constancies**    Our perception of color and brightness remain the same even when the light conditions change. Look at the two children's red hair in **Figure 4.27**. We perceive the color and brightness as constant despite the fact that the wavelength of light reaching our retina may vary as the light changes.

- **Shape constancy**    One additional perceptual constancy is the tendency to perceive an object's shape as staying constant even when the angle of our view changes (**Figure 4.28**).

**FIGURE 4.25**  **Monocular depth cues and the Taj Mahal**

iStockphoto.com/adamkaz

courtesy Karen Huffman

**FIGURE 4.26**  **Size constancy**    Note how the couple in the foreground look larger than the trees and mountains in the background. Thanks to *size constancy*, we automatically adjust our perception and see them not as giants but as simply far closer to the photographer than the trees and mountains.

# Interpretation

In the previous two sections, we discussed how we select and organize all the available and incoming sensory information. Now we'll explore how our brains work to interpret this large data base. This final stage of perception—*interpretation*—is influenced by several factors, including sensory adaptation, perceptual set, and frame of reference.

Imagine that your visual field has been suddenly inverted and reversed. Things you normally expect to be on your right are now on your left, and those above your head are now below. How would you ride a bike, read a book, or even walk through your home? Do you think you could ever adapt to this upside-down world?

To answer that question, psychologist George Stratton (1896) invented, and for eight days wore, special prism goggles that flipped his view of the world from up to down and right to left. For the first few days, Stratton had a great deal of difficulty navigating in this environment and coping with everyday tasks. But by the third day, he noted:

> Walking through the narrow spaces between pieces of furniture required much less care than hitherto. I could watch my hands as they wrote, without hesitating or becoming embarrassed thereby.

By the fifth day, Stratton had almost completely adjusted to his strange perceptual environment, but when he later removed the headgear, he quickly readapted.

**Sensory Adaptation** What does this experiment have to do with our everyday life? Stratton's study illustrates the critical role that *sensory adaptation* plays in the way we interpret the information that our brains gather. Without his ability to adapt his perceptions to a skewed

**FIGURE 4.27** **Color and brightness constancies** Thanks to *color* and *brightness constancies*, we don't assume the children's red hair is dark brown or black in the shaded areas.

Courtesy of Sandy Harvey

**FIGURE 4.28** **Shape constancy**

    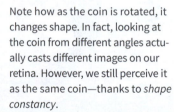

Note how as the coin is rotated, it changes shape. In fact, looking at the coin from different angles actually casts different images on our retina. However, we still perceive it as the same coin—thanks to *shape constancy*.

 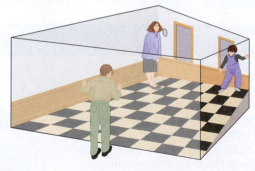

The Ames room illusion (shown in the two figures above) is found in many amusement parks. It's also been used in films to change the relative sizes of characters. In *The Lord of the Rings* trilogy, for instance, it was used to make Gandalf appear much larger than the hobbits. In the first diagram, the child on the right appears to be almost the same size as his adult mother on the left. How does this illusion work? To a viewer peering through the peephole (diagram on the right), the room appears to have a normal cubic shape. In fact, it's an artificially constructed, trapezoid-shaped room. The walls are slanted to the right, and the floor and ceiling are placed at an angle facing forward. Note

also how the right corner of the room is much closer to the observer. If you're the person looking through the peephole, can you now understand why the mother and child appear to be almost the same size? If so, you'll also understand, but still be amazed, that when the two individuals walk across to exchange places, they will appear to be growing and/or shrinking! While mind-challenging and fun, this illusion illustrates what happens when our normal perceptual processes of size constancy, shape constancy, and depth perception are disrupted. We have no perceptual experience with trapezoid-shaped rooms, so we compensate by distorting the relative size of the human figures.

## I2
## A I3 C
## I4

**FIGURE 4.29** **What is the middle figure?** If you look at the letters from left to right, you see the middle figure as a B. However, if you look at it from top to bottom, you see the number 13. Can you see how the "environment" created a perceptual set that affected how you interpreted the visual stimulus in the middle of the figure?

**Perceptual set** The readiness to perceive in a particular manner based on expectations.

Christian Petersen/Getty Images

environment, Stratton would not have been able to function. His brain's ability to retrain itself to interpret his new surroundings allowed him to create coherence from what would otherwise have been chaos.

**Perceptual Set**    As you can see in **Figure 4.29**, our previous experiences, assumptions, and expectations also affect how we interpret and perceive the world by creating a **perceptual set**, or a readiness to perceive in a particular manner based on expectations (Buckingham & MacDonald, 2016; Dye & Foley, 2017; Sella et al., 2017). In other words, we largely see what we expect to see.

In some cases, our perceptual sets, or expectations, can have hazardous effects. Studies find that perceptual sets concerning the wearing of protective devices, like helmets, actually lead many people to *increase* their risky behaviors (Fyhri & Phillips, 2013; Gamble & Walker, 2016; Phillips et al., 2011). Why? Apparently, wearing or using safety devices unconsciously primes us to expect greater levels of protection, so we then feel freer to ski, bike, or drive motorcycles faster than we otherwise would!

In a second example of the dangers of perceptual set, researchers asked both White and Black participants to play a video game in which they were told to shoot targets who were carrying a gun but not targets who were unarmed (Correll et al., 2002). Participants of both races made the decision to shoot an armed target more quickly if the target was Black, rather than White. They also chose NOT to shoot an unarmed target more quickly if the target was White, rather than Black. This study points to the influence of our expectations on real-life situations in which police officers must decide almost instantly whether to shoot a potential suspect—and may partially explain why Blacks are at greater risk than Whites of being accidentally shot by police officers.

Researchers have also examined how perceptual sets regarding race may influence judgments of football players (Hall & Livingston, 2012). In this study, participants read a scenario in which a Black or White NFL player scored a touchdown and then either showed no reaction to scoring or celebrated by spiking the ball and then doing his signature dance (see the photo). They were then asked to rate the player's level of arrogance and to determine if the player deserved a salary bonus for this touchdown. Perhaps not surprisingly, all players who celebrated after touchdowns were perceived as more arrogant than those who did not celebrate (regardless of race). Sadly, White players were seen as equally deserving of a bonus whether or not they had celebrated their touchdown, whereas Black players were judged as deserving a bonus only if they had NOT celebrated. These findings, termed the "hubris penalty," show that the same celebratory behavior is seen in different—and biased—ways as a function of the athlete's race. On a lighter note, perceptual sets may even influence our sex appeal, as described in the following **Research Challenge**.

**Frame of Reference**    Along with problems with perceptual sets, the way we perceive people, objects, or situations is also affected by the *frame of reference*, or

## Research Challenge

### Does Wearing Red Increase Your Sex Appeal?

Do women wearing red have more sex appeal? To examine this question, researchers recruited women who had on-line dating profiles expressing interest in meeting a man and had posted color photographs (Guéguen & Jacob, 2014). Through the magic of Photoshop, the researchers changed the color of the woman's shirt in the photograph every 12 weeks: the color rotated at random through red, black, white, yellow, blue, and green. The women were asked to notify the researchers of how many e-mails they received from men during the eight- to nine-month period of the study. As hypothesized, women received more contacts from men when they wore red as opposed to any of the other five colors. In fact, they received about a 5% increase in e-mails.

Does the color red also impact a man's sex appeal? In a related study, researchers showed female college students photographs of a man who was wearing a red, white, blue, or green shirt (Elliot

Reggie Casagrande/Getty Images

et al., 2010). They then asked the women to rate his attractiveness, as well as their interest in dating, kissing, and engaging in other types of sexual activity with him. As predicted, men who were wearing a red shirt seemed more powerful, attractive, and sexually desirable. This effect was also seen across a variety of cultures, including the United States, England, Germany, and China, suggesting that these links between the color red and perceptions of attractiveness are partially rooted in our biology, not merely social learning.

**Test Yourself**

1. Based on the information provided, did this research (Guéguen & Jacob, 2014; Elliot et al., 2010) use descriptive, correlational, and/or experimental research? (Tip: Be sure to look for two separate answers for the two different studies.)

2. If you chose:

   o *descriptive research*, is this a naturalistic observation, survey/interview, case study, and/or archival research?

   o *correlational research*, is this a positive, negative, or zero correlation?

   o *experimental research*, label the IV, DV, experimental groups(s), and control group. (Note: If participants were not randomly assigned to groups, list it as a *quasi-experimental design*.)

   o both *descriptive* and *correlational*, answer the corresponding questions for both.

**Check your answers by clicking on the answer button or by looking in Appendix B.**

**Note:** The information provided in this study is admittedly limited, but the level of detail is similar to what is presented in most textbooks and public reports of research findings. Answering these questions, and then comparing your answers to those provided, will help you become a better critical thinker and consumer of scientific research.

context. An elephant is perceived as much larger when it is next to a mouse than when it stands next to a giraffe. This is the reason professional athletes who make huge amounts of money sometimes feel underpaid: they're comparing what they make to the pay of those around them, who also make huge sums, and not to the average person in the United States!

**Science and ESP**    So far in this chapter, we've only discussed sensations provided by our eyes, ears, nose, mouth, and body senses. What about a so-called sixth sense? Can some people detect things that cannot be perceived through the usual sensory channels by using **extrasensory perception (ESP)**? Those who claim to have ESP profess to be able to read other people's minds (*telepathy*), perceive objects or events that are inaccessible to their normal senses (*clairvoyance*), or see and predict the future (*precognition*). (*Psychokinesis,* the ability to move or change objects with mind power alone, such as the ability to levitate a table, is generally not considered a type of ESP because, unlike the other three alleged abilities, it does not involve the senses, in the way that, for example, "seeing" the future does.)

In 1927, a professor at Duke University, J. B. Rhine, was apparently the first person to use the term ESP, and he is credited with developing the field of **parapsychology**, which studies paranormal phenomena, including ESP, ghosts, and other topics normally outside the realm of scientific psychology. As we discussed in Chapter 1, claims involving ESP generally fall under the name *pseudopsychology,* and almost all studies of ESP have been successfully debunked or have produced weak or controversial results (Baptista et al., 2015; Lilienfeld et al., 2015; Schick & Vaughn, 2014). Findings in ESP are notoriously "fragile" in that they do not hold up to scientific scrutiny.

Perhaps the most serious weakness of ESP is its failure of replication by rivals in independent laboratories, which is a core requirement for scientific acceptance (Francis, 2012; Hyman, 1996; Rouder et al., 2013). (Recall also from Chapter 1 that magician James Randi and the MacArthur Foundation offered $1 million to "anyone who proves a genuine psychic power under proper observing conditions." But even after many years, the money was never collected!)

Despite the lack of credible scientific evidence, a large percentage of adults in the United States believe in ESP (Gray & Gallo, 2016; Lamont, 2013; Moore, 2005). Why? One reason is that, as mentioned earlier in the chapter, our motivations and interests often influence our perceptions, driving us to selectively attend to things we want to see or hear. For example, a recent study found that the need to find meaning in life increases the belief in extraterrestrial intelligence (ETI) and that religious people are less likely to believe in ETI (Routledge et al., 2017).

In addition, the subject of extrasensory perception often generates strong emotional responses. When individuals feel strongly about an issue, they sometimes fail to recognize the faulty reasoning underlying their beliefs. Belief in ESP is particularly associated with nonreflective, illogical, or noncritical thinking (Bouvet & Bonnefon, 2015; Gray & Gallo, 2016; Lindeman & Svedholm-Häkkinen, 2016). For example, people often fall victim to the *confirmation bias*, noting and remembering events that confirm personal expectations and beliefs (the "hits") and ignoring nonsupportive evidence (the "misses") (e.g., Rogers et al., 2016). Other times, people fail to recognize chance occurrences for what they are. Finally, human information processing often biases us to notice and remember

**Extrasensory perception (ESP)** Perceptual, so-called "psychic," abilities that supposedly go beyond the known senses (for example, telepathy, clairvoyance, and precognition).

**Parapsychology** The study of paranormal phenomena, such as ESP, ghosts, and psychokinesis, that are inexplicable by science.

the most vivid information. Rather than relying on scientific research based on analyzing numerous data points, we prefer colorful anecdotes and heartfelt personal testimonials.

## ❖ Psychology and Your Personal Success | Helen Keller's Inspiring Advice

In this chapter, we've seen how a number of internal and external factors can affect sensation as well as all three stages of perception—selection, organization, and interpretation. Thanks to the story of Helen Keller, we've also seen how crucial sensation and perception are to all parts of our lives. She learned to "see" and "hear" with her sense of touch and often recognized visitors by their smell or by vibrations from their walk. Despite the heightened sensitivity of her functioning senses, however, Helen professed a lifelong yearning to experience a normal sensory world. She gave this advice to those whose senses are "normal"—advice that can help you and your goal for achieving maximum personal success:

*I who am blind can give one hint to those who see: use your eyes as if tomorrow you would be stricken blind. And the same method can be applied to the other senses. Hear the music of voices, the song of a bird, the mighty strains of an orchestra as if you would be stricken deaf tomorrow. Touch each object as if tomorrow your tactile sense would fail. Smell the perfume of flowers, taste with relish each morsel as if tomorrow you could never smell and taste again. Make the most of every sense; glory in all the facets of pleasure and beauty that the world reveals to you through the several means of contact which nature provides.*

—Helen Keller (cited in Harrity & Martin, 1962, p. 23)

© Billy R. Ray/Wiley

## Retrieval Practice 4.4 | Understanding Perception

Completing this self-test and the connections section, and then checking your answers by clicking on the answer button or by looking in Appendix B, will provide immediate feedback and helpful practice for exams.

### Self-Test

1. _____ Briefly explain how illusions differ from hallucinations and delusions.

2. In the _____ shown here, the discrepancy between figure and ground is too vague, and we may have difficulty perceiving which is figure and which is ground.
   a. illusion
   b. reversible figure
   c. optical illusion
   d. hallucination

   *Rykoff Collection/Corbis*

3. The tendency for the environment to be perceived as remaining the same even with changes in sensory input is called _____.
   a. perceptual constancy
   b. the constancy of expectation
   c. an illusory correlation
   d. Gestalt's primary principle

4. A readiness to perceive in a particular manner is known as _____.
   a. sensory adaptation        b. perceptual set
   c. habituation               d. frame of reference

5. Scientists sometimes find that one person will supposedly demonstrate ESP in one laboratory but not in another. This suggests that _____.
   a. replication of studies is useless
   b. one or both of the studies were probably flawed
   c. the researcher or the participant was biased against ESP
   d. ESP abilities have been scientifically proven to exist

### Connections—Chapter to Chapter

Answering the following questions will help you "look back and look ahead" to see the important connections among the various subfields of psychology and chapters within this text.

1. In Chapter 16 (Social Psychology), you'll discover more about prejudice and discrimination. Using the term *perceptual set*, explain how prejudice and discrimination are different and how they both might be created.

2. In the Prologue to this textbook, you learned about Critical Thinking Components (CTCs), including employing a variety of thinking processes (behavioral), analyzing data for value and content (cognitive), and employing metacognition (cognitive). Discuss how each of these CTCs is relevant to the issue of extrasensory perception, or ESP.

# Chapter Summary

## 4.1   Understanding Sensation   117

- **Sensation** is the process by which we detect, convert, and transmit raw sensory data from the environment to our brain. Through the process of **perception**, our brain then selects, organizes, and interprets this sensory information.

- Although sensation and perception are an interrelated, continuous process, our use of **bottom-up processing** versus **top-down processing** affects our interpretation of what we sense and perceive.

- **Transduction** is the process by which we convert sensory stimuli into neural signals that are sent to the brain. During **coding**, the neural impulses generated by different physical stimuli travel by separate routes and arrive at different parts of the brain. In *sensory reduction,* we filter and analyze incoming sensations.

- **Psychophysics** studies the link between physical characteristics of stimuli and our psychological experience. The **difference threshold**, or just noticeable difference (JND), is the smallest physical difference between two stimuli that is consciously detectable 50% of the time. The **absolute threshold** is the minimum stimulation necessary to consciously detect a stimulus 50% of the time.

- **Subliminal perception**, the detection of stimuli below conscious awareness, is a fact, and unconscious stimuli can **prime** certain responses. However, these processes don't lead to significant behavioral change.

- In **sensory adaptation**, sensory receptors fatigue and stop responding to unchanging stimuli. We never completely adapt to visual stimuli, however, or to extremely intense stimuli, such as the odor of ammonia or the pain of a bad burn.

- Because our body releases natural painkillers, called endorphins, we can persist in spite of pain. In addition, according to the **gate-control theory**, our experience of pain depends partly on whether the neural message gets past a "gatekeeper" in the spinal cord, which researchers believe is chemically controlled.

### Test Your Critical Thinking

**1.** Sensation and perception are closely linked. What is the central distinction between the two?

**2.** If we sensed and attended equally to each stimulus in the world, the amount of information would be overwhelming. What sensory and perceptual processes help us lessen the din?

---

**Psychology and a Classic Success:** Helen Keller

## Understanding Sensation

**Sensation versus Perception**

**Processing**
- Transduction
- Coding
- Sensory reduction

**Psychophysics**
- Difference threshold
- Absolute threshold
- Subliminal stimuli

**Sensory Adaptation**
- Pain and sensory adaptation
- Phantom limb pain (PLP)

---

## 4.2   How We See and Hear   123

- Light waves are a form of electromagnetic energy, and sound waves are produced when air molecules move in a particular wave pattern.

- Light enters the eye at the front of the eyeball. The cornea protects the eye and helps focus light rays. The lens further focuses light, adjusting to allow focusing on objects at different distances. At the back of the eye, incoming light waves reach the **retina**, which contains light-sensitive **rods** and **cones.** A network of neurons in the retina transmits neural information to the brain. There are two theories of color vision—**trichromatic** and **opponent process**.

- The sense of hearing is known as **audition**. The ear has three parts. The **outer ear** gathers sound waves, the **middle ear** amplifies and concentrates the sounds, and the **inner ear** changes the mechanical energy of sounds into neural impulses. The frequency of sounds determines how we distinguish among sounds of different pitches, and there are three explanations for pitch perception—**place theory, frequency theory**, and the **volley principle**. The amplitude of sound waves determines the softness or loudness of sounds.

**Test Your Critical Thinking**

1. Which sensation, vision or hearing, would you least like to lose? Why?

2. Many people believe that blind people have supernatural hearing. How would brain plasticity explain how enhanced hearing might result from greater reliance on hearing or from just using auditory information more effectively?

3. Using what you've learned about pitch, how would you explain why an older person often has an easier time hearing a man's voice than a woman's voice?

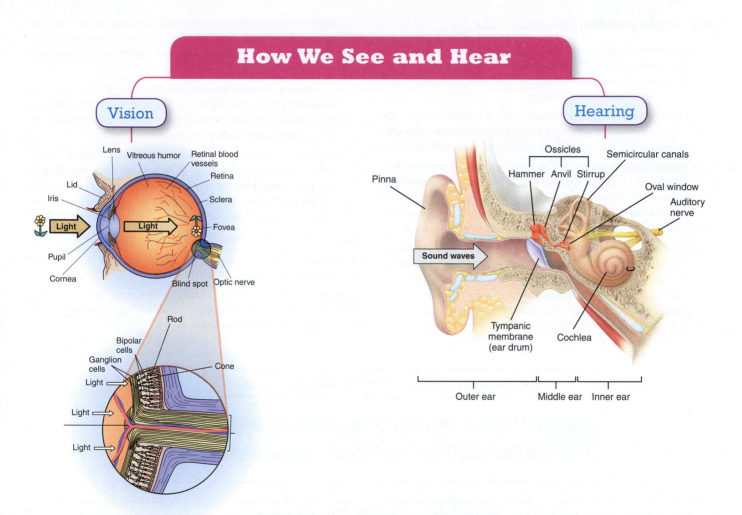

**How We See and Hear**

Vision

Hearing

### 4.3 Our Other Important Senses 130

- Smell and taste, sometimes called the chemical senses, involve chemoreceptors that are sensitive to certain chemical molecules. In **olfaction**, odor molecules stimulate receptors in the olfactory epithelium of the nose. The resulting neural impulse travels to the olfactory bulb, where the information is processed before being sent elsewhere in the brain. Our sense of taste (**gustation**) involves five tastes: sweet, sour, salty, bitter, and umami (umami means "savory" or "delicious"). The taste buds are distributed on our tongues within the papillae.

- The body senses—the skin senses, the **vestibular sense**, and **kinesthesis**—tell the brain what it's touching or being touched by, how the body is oriented, and where and how it is moving.

**Test Your Critical Thinking**

1. From an evolutionary perspective, which is more essential—smell or taste?

2. From a personal perspective, which sense is most important to you—smell, taste, skin senses, vestibular sense, or kinesthetic sense?

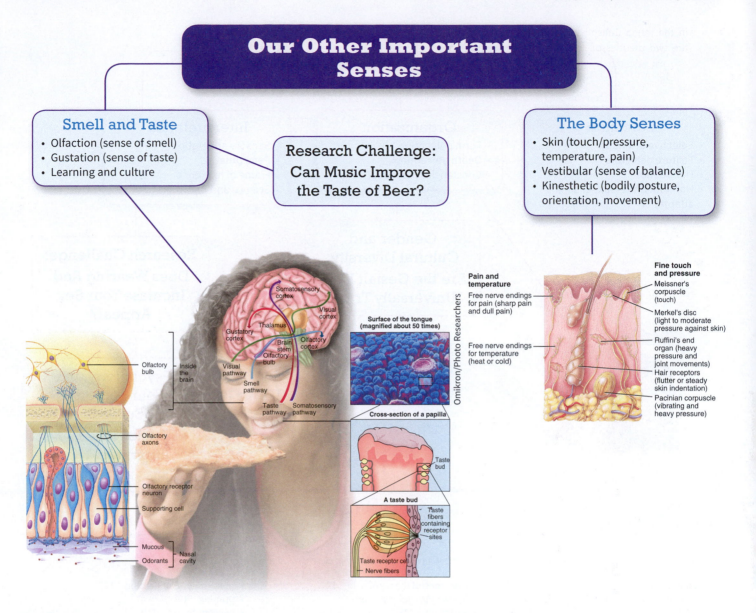

## Our Other Important Senses

**Smell and Taste**
- Olfaction (sense of smell)
- Gustation (sense of taste)
- Learning and culture

**Research Challenge: Can Music Improve the Taste of Beer?**

**The Body Senses**
- Skin (touch/pressure, temperature, pain)
- Vestibular (sense of balance)
- Kinesthetic (bodily posture, orientation, movement)

Omikron/Photo Researchers

*Labels in figure:*

Somatosensory cortex
Visual cortex
Thalamus
Gustatory cortex
Brain stem
Olfactory cortex
Olfactory bulb
Visual pathway
Smell pathway
Olfactory bulb
Inside the brain
Taste pathway
Somatosensory pathway

Olfactory axons
Olfactory receptor neuron
Supporting cell
Mucous
Odorants
Nasal cavity

Surface of the tongue (magnified about 50 times)
Cross-section of a papilla
Taste bud
A taste bud
Taste fibers containing receptor sites
Taste receptor cell
Nerve fibers

**Pain and temperature**
Free nerve endings for pain (sharp pain and dull pain)
Free nerve endings for temperature (heat or cold)

**Fine touch and pressure**
Meissner's corpuscle (touch)
Merkel's disc (light to moderate pressure against skin)
Ruffini's end organ (heavy pressure and joint movements)
Hair receptors (flutter or steady skin indentation)
Pacinian corpuscle (vibrating and heavy pressure)

## 4.4  Understanding Perception   135

- **Illusions** are false or misleading perceptions that can be produced by actual physical distortions, as in the full moon illusion, or by errors in perception. These errors give psychologists insight into normal perceptual processes.

- **Selective attention** allows us to filter out unimportant sensory messages. **Feature detectors** are specialized cells that respond only to certain sensory information. **Habituation** refers to our brain's learned tendency to stop responding to unchanging information.

- To be useful, sensory data must be organized in a meaningful way—in terms of form, depth, and constancy. **Gestalt psychologists** emphasize that we all share a natural tendency to force patterns onto whatever we see.

- Interpretation, the final stage of perception, can be influenced by *sensory adaptation*, **perceptual set**, and *frame of reference*.

- Research on **extrasensory perception (ESP)**, the supposed ability to perceive things that go beyond the normal senses, has produced "fragile" results, and critics condemn its lack of experimental control and replicability.

### Test Your Critical Thinking

**1.** Can you explain how your own perceptual sets might create prejudice or discrimination?

**2.** How has reading this chapter's information about ESP influenced your beliefs about this topic?

**3.** Why do you think no one ever collected the $1 million dollars?

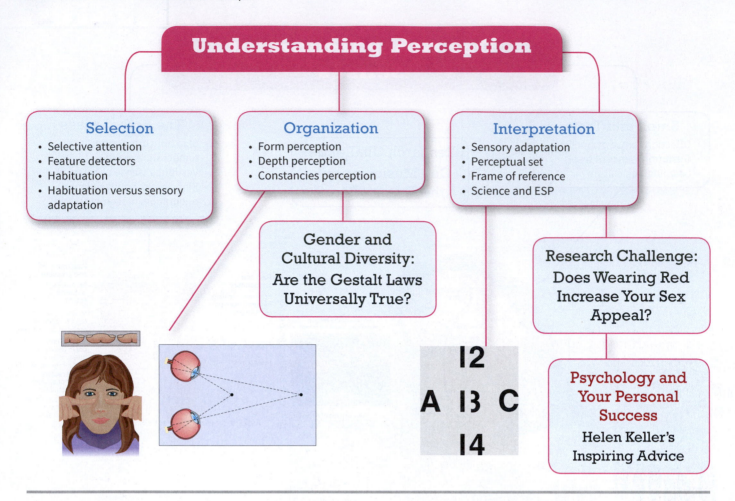

# Understanding Perception

### Selection
- Selective attention
- Feature detectors
- Habituation
- Habituation versus sensory adaptation

### Organization
- Form perception
- Depth perception
- Constancies perception

### Interpretation
- Sensory adaptation
- Perceptual set
- Frame of reference
- Science and ESP

**Gender and Cultural Diversity: Are the Gestalt Laws Universally True?**

**Research Challenge: Does Wearing Red Increase Your Sex Appeal?**

**Psychology and Your Personal Success**
Helen Keller's Inspiring Advice

# Key Terms

**Retrieval Practice**  *Write your own definition for each term before turning back to the referenced page to check your answer.*

- absolute threshold   119
- accommodation   141
- audition   127
- binocular cues   141
- blind spot   124
- bottom-up processing   117
- cochlea   128
- coding   119
- conduction hearing loss   129
- cones   125
- convergence   141
- depth perception   140
- difference threshold   119
- extrasensory perception (ESP)   145
- feature detectors   137
- fovea   126
- frequency theory for hearing   128

- gate-control theory of pain   121
- Gestalt psychology   139
- gustation   132
- habituation   137
- illusion   136
- inner ear   128
- kinesthesis   135
- middle ear   128
- monocular cues   141
- olfaction   132
- opponent-process theory of color   126
- outer ear   128
- parapsychology   145
- perception   117
- perceptual constancy   141
- perceptual set   144
- pheromones   132

- place theory for hearing   127
- priming   120
- psychophysics   119
- retina   124
- retinal disparity   141
- rods   125
- selective attention   136
- sensation   117
- sensorineural hearing loss   129
- sensory adaptation   121
- subliminal perception   120
- top-down processing   117
- transduction   118
- trichromatic theory of color   126
- vestibular sense   134
- volley principle for hearing   128

© alexxl66/iStockphoto

# States of Consciousness

AFP/Getty Images

## ❖ Psychology and a Classic Success | Albert Einstein

Albert Einstein (1879–1955) is widely considered the most influential physicist of the 20th century—and his name is synonymous with genius (see photo). His passion for inquiry eventually led him to develop the special and general theories of relativity, and his mass–energy equivalence formula ($E = mc^2$) is often called the world's most famous equation. In 1921, Einstein won the Nobel Prize for physics for his explanation of the photoelectric effect. His work had a major impact on the development of atomic energy, and his other achievements and honors are too numerous to mention. In short, Einstein changed the world.

It's important to note that Einstein achieved his incredible level of success despite serious personal struggles and anti-Semitism. For example, during his early years in Germany, he dropped out of formal schooling due to his frustration with the rigid educational style and emphasis on rote learning. He also faced challenges caused by his oft-reported spelling and speech problems. Einstein eventually earned a diploma from the Swiss Federal Polytechnic School. But, after graduation, he spent two frustrating years searching for a teaching position before finally accepting a job as an assistant in the Swiss Patent Office. Sadly, his greatest struggles lay ahead. During the 1930s, Jewish citizens were barred from many jobs. And Einstein, who at this point had returned to Germany, was himself targeted to be killed by the Nazis. As a result, in 1933, Einstein accepted a position at Princeton University in the United States and remained there until his death in 1955 (Albert Einstein—Questions and Answers, n. d.; Biography, 2017; Nobel Lectures, 1967).

## Chapter Overview

Are you surprised that we chose Albert Einstein as the famous figure for this chapter? First, he's known for saying that, "Failure is success in progress" and "It's not that I'm so smart. It's just that I stay with problems longer." These quotes highlight the two key themes of this text—having a *growth mindset* and *grit*. Second, there are several interesting (and quirky) facts about Einstein that relate to the content of this chapter. For example, did you know that his deep understanding of the nature of consciousness led to many of his greatest theories? Einstein also reportedly liked to sleep 10 to 11 hours a night—claiming that his dreams improved his creativity.

In this chapter, we begin with an exploration of the nature of consciousness. Next, we'll discuss several altered states of consciousness (ASCs)—sleep and dreaming—and follow that with a discussion of psychoactive drugs. And we'll finish with a description of the ASCs brought about by meditation and hypnosis. Before we begin, check your understanding of the topics in this chapter in the following **Myth Busters**.

## Myth Busters

**True or False?**

1. Our brains "turn off" when we sleep.
2. Some people never dream.
3. Judges dole out harsher punishments when they're sleep deprived than when they're not sleep deprived.
4. Using a computer or iPad late at night can make it harder to fall asleep.
5. People who suffer from narcolepsy may fall instantly asleep while walking, talking, or driving a car.
6. Facebook usage can lead to addiction.
7. Binge drinking may reduce condom use.
8. Even small initial doses of cocaine can be fatal because they can interfere with the electrical signals of the heart.
9. People can be hypnotized against their will.
10. Hypnotized people can perform acts of superhuman strength.

Paul Kuroda/SUPERSTOCK

**Answers:** 1. F, 2. F, 3. T, 4. T, 5. T, 6. T, 7. T, 8. T, 9. F, 10. F. Detailed answers can be found in this chapter.

## 5.1 | Understanding Consciousness

**LEARNING OBJECTIVES**

**Retrieval Practice**    While reading the upcoming sections, respond to each Learning Objective in your own words.

**Summarize how selective attention and levels of awareness affect consciousness.**

- **Define** consciousness and altered states of consciousness (ASCs).

- **Describe** the key factors in selective attention.
- **Review** how consciousness exists on various levels of awareness.

---

*Our normal waking consciousness is but one special type of consciousness, whilst all about it, parted from it by the filmiest of screens, there lie potential forms of consciousness entirely different.* —William James (American Philosopher, Psychologist)

This quote is from William James (1842–1910), one of the most famous early psychologists. What did he mean by "normal waking consciousness" and "entirely different" forms of consciousness? We all commonly use the term, but what exactly is **consciousness**? Most psychologists define it as a two-part awareness of both ourselves and our environment (Li, 2016; Thompson, 2015). This dual-natured awareness explains how we can be deeply engrossed in studying or a conversation with others and still hear the ping of an incoming message on our cell phones. However, if we're deeply asleep, we probably won't hear this same message ping because sleep is an **altered state of consciousness (ASC)**, which is defined as a temporary mental state other than ordinary waking consciousness. Later in this chapter we will discuss the ASCs of sleep, dreaming, meditation, and hypnosis. But we first need to explore the general nature of consciousness.

Before going on, we need to address the apparently never-ending philosophical debates over the *mind–body problem*. Is the "mind" (consciousness and other mental functions) fundamentally different from matter (the body)? How can a supposedly nonmaterial mind influence a physical body and vice versa? Most psychologists today believe the mind *is* the brain and *consciousness* involves an activation and integration of several parts of the brain (**Figure 5.1**). However, awareness is generally limited to the *cerebral cortex*, particularly the frontal lobes, and arousal generally results from *brain-stem activation*.

**Consciousness**   Our awareness of ourselves and our environment.

**Altered state of consciousness (ASC)**   A temporary mental state, other than ordinary waking consciousness, that occurs during sleep, dreaming, psychoactive drug use, and hypnosis.

**Selective attention**   The process of focusing conscious awareness onto a specific stimulus, while filtering out a range of other stimuli occurring simultaneously.

## Selective Attention

William James, quoted above, likened consciousness to a stream that's constantly changing yet always the same. It meanders and flows, sometimes where the person wills and sometimes not. The process of **selective attention** (Chapter 4) allows us to control this *stream of consciousness* through deliberate concentration and full attention. For example, when listening to a classroom lecture, your attention may drift away to thoughts of a laptop computer you want to buy or an attractive classmate. But you can catch and control this wandering stream of consciousness and willingly go back to selectively attending to the lecture.

There's another aspect of selective attention that you may find fascinating. Sometimes when we're fully focused and selectively attending, we can fail to notice clearly visible stimuli, particularly if they're unexpected and we're otherwise distracted. A case in point, a Boston police officer chasing a shooting suspect

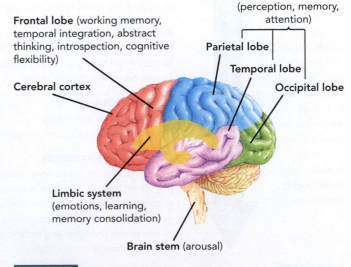

**Frontal lobe** (working memory, temporal integration, abstract thinking, introspection, cognitive flexibility)

(perception, memory, attention)

**Parietal lobe**

**Temporal lobe**

**Occipital lobe**

**Cerebral cortex**

**Limbic system** (emotions, learning, memory consolidation)

**Brain stem** (arousal)

**FIGURE 5.1**   **Consciousness and our brain**

on foot ran right past a brutal assault, but later claimed no memory of seeing the assault. Nevertheless, a jury convicted him of perjury and obstruction of justice (Lehr, 2009). Can you see how you might also fail to see such an assault if you were otherwise distracted?

Another example of this surprising phenomenon, known as **inattentional blindness**, can be found in popular YouTube videos in which observers fail to notice a grown man dressed in a gorilla costume as he repeatedly passes through a group of people. These videos are based on a clever experiment that asked participants to count the number of passes in a videotaped basketball game. Researchers then sent an assistant, dressed in a full gorilla suit, to walk through the middle of the ongoing game. Can you predict what happened? The research participants were so focused on their pass-counting task that they failed to notice the person in the gorilla suit (Simons & Chabris, 1999).

**Inattentional blindness** The failure to notice a fully visible, but unexpected, stimulus when our attention is directed elsewhere; also known as perceptual blindness.

Surprisingly, when the participants later watched the video without having to count the basketball passes, most could not believe they had missed seeing the gorilla. Can you now see why magicians ask us to focus on a distracting element, such as a deck of cards or beautiful assistant, while they manipulate the real object of their magic—removing an unsuspecting volunteer's wallet or watch? More significantly, this type of inattentional blindness can lead to serious problems for police officers focused on chasing suspects who might miss seeing an unexpected brutal assault, pilots concentrated on landing their plane who might fail to see a flock of birds, or a driver texting on a cell phone who fails to see the red light. In case you're wondering, this type of "blindness" also occurs in some of our other senses, such as *inattentional deafness*—failing to notice unexpected auditory stimuli when focusing on another task (Kreitz et al., 2016).

## Levels of Awareness

As this example of inattentional blindness indicates, our *stream of consciousness* also varies in its level of awareness. Consciousness is not an all-or-nothing phenomenon—conscious or unconscious. Instead, it exists along a continuum, ranging from high awareness and sharp, focused alertness at one extreme, to middle levels of awareness, to low awareness or even nonconsciousness and coma at the other extreme (**Figure 5.2**).

**Controlled processes** Mental activities that require focused attention and generally interfere with other ongoing activities.

**Automatic processes** Mental activities that require minimal attention and generally have little impact on other activities.

As you can see from the figure, our level of awareness depends in part on whether we are engaged in *controlled* or *automatic* processes. When you're working at a demanding task or learning something new, such as how to drive a car, your consciousness is at the high end of the continuum. These **controlled processes** demand focused attention and generally interfere with other ongoing activities (Cohen & Israel, 2015; Maher & Conroy, 2016; Peleg & Eviatar, 2017).

In sharp contrast to the high awareness and focused attention required for controlled processes, **automatic processes** require minimal attention and generally do not interfere with other ongoing activities. Think back to your teen years when you were first learning how to drive a car and it took all of your attention (controlled processing). The fact that you can now effortlessly steer a car and work the brakes at the same time (with little or no focused attention) is thanks to automatic processing. In short, learning a new task requires complete concentration and *controlled processing*. Once that task is well-learned, you can switch to *automatic processing*.

The following **Research Challenge** offers further insights and practical applications on the importance of selective attention and levels of awareness.

*ALTERED STATES OF CONSCIOUSNESS (ASCS)* can exist on many levels of awareness, from high awareness to no awareness (e.g., drugs, sensory deprivation, sleep, dreaming)

**CONTROLLED PROCESSES**

Require focused, maximum attention (e.g., studying for an exam, learning to drive a car)

**AUTOMATIC PROCESSES**

Require minimal attention (e.g., walking to class while talking on a cell phone, listening to your boss while daydreaming)

**SUBCONSCIOUS**

Below conscious awareness (e.g., subliminal perception, sleeping, dreaming)

**LITTLE OR NO AWARENESS**

Biologically based lowest level of awareness (e.g., head injuries, anesthesia, coma; also the *unconscious mind*—a Freudian concept discussed in Chapter 13—reportedly consisting of unacceptable thoughts and feelings too painful to be admitted to consciousness)

**FIGURE 5.2** Levels of awareness

## Research Challenge

Pamela Moore/iStock/Getty Images Inc.

### What's Wrong with Distracted Driving?

Thanks to repeated public service announcements and widespread media coverage, you've undoubtedly heard that using a cell phone while driving, including dialing, talking, texting, reaching for the phone, etc., greatly increases your risk of accidents and near collisions. In fact, research on all such forms of "distracted driving" firmly supports the dangers of cell phone use while driving (Dingus et al., 2016; Pope et al., 2017; Tucker et al., 2015). Even hands-free cell phones are essentially as risky to use as hand-held phones (Li et al., 2016a).

Given that motor vehicle crashes remain a leading cause of death and injury (LaVoie et al., 2016), and that we've all been repeatedly warned against cell phone use while driving, why is it still so common? Many drivers believe that talking on a cell phone while driving is no more dangerous than talking to another passenger. Is that true?

Using the latest in driving simulators, researchers set up four distinct driving scenarios: (1) driving alone without talking on a cell phone, (2) driving while talking with a passenger but not talking on a cell phone, (3) driving alone while speaking on a hands-free cell phone to someone in a remote location, and (4) driving under the same conditions as in scenario 3, but the person in the remote condition can see the driver's face and the driving scene through a videophone (Gaspar et al., 2014).

Note that in all conditions the drivers confronted fairly challenging highway situations, such as merging and navigating around unpredictable drivers in other cars. While the drivers were confronting these challenges, researchers measured the drivers' performance, including distance from other cars, speed, and collisions.

What do you think happened? As you probably predicted, driving alone without talking on a cell phone (Condition 1) was the safest option. The next safest option was when drivers talked with a passenger but not on a cell phone (Condition 2). In contrast, the likelihood of a collision tripled when drivers were talking on a cell phone to a person in a remote location who had no awareness of what was going on during the drive (Condition 3). Interestingly, when the driver was talking to someone who was not in the car but was on a specially designed videophone, and hence could see both the driver's face and the view out the front windshield (Condition 4), the risks of collision were about the same as when the driver was just talking to a passenger (Condition 2). Can you see why? Like a passenger in the car, the remote viewer using the videophone could help the driver by stopping speaking and pointing out potentially dangerous situations while they were talking.

What's the take-home message? Most of us are unaware of the limits of our attention and may mistakenly assume that we can safely drive while texting or talking on a cell phone. This study shows that traditional cell phone use is detrimental to driving precisely because it distracts the driver, while providing none of the assistance that a passenger in the car can typically provide.

#### Test Yourself

1. Based on the information provided, did this study (Gaspar et al., 2014) use descriptive, correlational, and/or experimental research?

2. If you chose:

   ○ *descriptive research*, is this a naturalistic observation, survey/interview, case study, and/or archival research?

   ○ *correlational research*, is this a positive, negative, or zero correlation?

   ○ *experimental research*, label the IV, DV, experimental group(s), and control group. (Note: If participants were not randomly assigned to groups, list it as a *quasi-experimental design*.)

   ○ both *descriptive* and *correlational*, answer the corresponding questions for both.

**Check your answers by clicking on the answer button or by looking in Appendix B.**

**Note:** The information provided in this study is admittedly limited, but the level of detail is similar to what is presented in most textbooks and public reports of research findings. Answering these questions, and then comparing your answers to those provided, will help you become a better critical thinker and consumer of scientific research.

## ❖ Psychology and Your Personal Success | Can Maximizing Your Consciousness Save Lives?

Before moving on, it's important to understand how several key concepts in this section have direct, real-world applications—especially to distracted driving. First, talking with a passenger and talking or texting while driving are all risky behaviors because they require shifting your *selective attention* back and forth between what's on the road and your conversations. Second, given that people missed seeing someone dressed in a gorilla suit when they were distracted, can you see how any form of distracted driving also increases the possibility of *inattentional blindness* to serious traffic hazards? Third, inexperienced drivers should decrease all forms of distraction and use fully focused *controlled processes* while learning to drive, whereas experienced drivers are generally better equipped to handle a few distractions, such as talking to a passenger, because driving is largely an *automatic process* for them (Klauer et al., 2014). However, it's still true that distracted driving remains a serious health threat to all drivers and passengers.

As you've just seen, distractions often lead to potentially serious problems—especially when it comes to complex tasks, like driving and avoiding accidents. But distractions and *multitasking* also negatively affect our ability to learn. For example, in a Stanford University study that involved 100 college students, researchers ran a series of three tests with the participants divided into two groups—those who regularly multitasked and those who didn't. The outcomes for all three tests were consistent: The self-described multitaskers paid less attention to detail, displayed poorer memory, and had more trouble switching from one task to another compared to participants who preferred doing only one task at a time (Ophir et al., 2009). A more recent study found that heavy media multitasking among adolescents, such as watching TV while texting, was associated with lower scores on statewide standardized achievement tests of math and English, poorer performance on behavioral measures of executive function (working memory capacity), and greater impulsivity and a lesser *growth mindset*—a key component to success (Cain et al., 2016).

Can you see how this explains why trying to listen to a lecture or drive a car, while simultaneously texting or playing games on a smartphone, may threaten both your physical life and your academic GPA? What's the good news? Being distracted and multitasking aren't always necessarily bad. In fact, listening to music while exercising or relaxing while watching TV and simultaneously texting can be very beneficial. Just remember that when you're in a dangerous situation or trying to learn something that you will need to later recall, you need to focus and use your controlled processes (see the **Study Tip**).

> *Control of consciousness determines the quality of life.*
> —Mihaly Csikszentmihaly (Hungarian Author, Professor)

## Study Tip

*Be sure to use highly focused, controlled processing while reading and studying this and other essential material. Also be aware that because reading is a well-learned, automatic process for most college students, you can't casually (automatically) read complex new material (like this text) if you want to do well on upcoming quizzes and exams.*

© Billy R. Ray/Wiley

## Retrieval Practice 5.1 | Understanding Consciousness

Completing this self-test and connections section, and then checking your answers by clicking on the answer button or by looking in Appendix B, will provide immediate feedback and helpful practice for exams.

### Self-Test

1. Define *consciousness*.

2. Mental states other than ordinary waking consciousness, such as sleep, dreaming, and hypnosis, are known as _____.

   a. altered states of consciousness
   b. intentional blindness
   c. automatic processes
   d. none of these options

3. Mental activities that require minimal attention without affecting other activities are called _____ processes.

   a. controlled          b. peripheral
   c. conscious           d. automatic

4. As you read this text, you should _____.

   a. be in an altered state of consciousness (ASC)
   b. employ controlled processing
   c. let your stream of consciousness take charge
   d. employ automatic processing

5. Which of the following is TRUE?

   a. Consciousness exists on a continuum.
   b. Selective attention allows us to control our stream of consciousness.
   c. Our consciousness varies in its level of awareness.
   d. All of these options are true.

### Connections—Chapter to Chapter

Answering the following questions will help you "look back and look ahead" to see the important connections among the various subfields of psychology and chapters within this text.

In Chapter 13 (Personality), you'll discover a lot about Freud and the psychoanalytic perspective—especially the unconscious mind. Describe how this chapter's levels of awareness differ from Freud's three levels of consciousness (the conscious, preconscious, and unconscious).

## 5.2 Understanding Sleep and Dreams

### LEARNING OBJECTIVES

**Retrieval Practice** While reading the upcoming sections, respond to each Learning Objective in your own words.

**Review the major processes that occur while we sleep and dream.**

- **Describe** circadian rhythms and how they affect our lives.

- **Review** what happens during the various stages of sleep.
- **Compare and contrast** the key factors and theories concerning sleep and dreams.
- **Describe** the major sleep–wake disorders and their possible treatment.

Having explored the definition and description of everyday, waking consciousness and its properties of selective attention and levels of awareness, we now can explore two of our most common *altered states of consciousness* (ASCs)—sleep and dreaming. These ASCs are fascinating to both scientists and the general public. Why are we born with a mechanism that forces us to sleep and dream for approximately a third of our lives? How can an ASC that requires reduced awareness and responsiveness to our environment be beneficial in an evolutionary sense? What are the functions and causes of sleep and dreams? To answer these questions and fully understand sleep and dreaming, we need to first discuss circadian rhythms.

### Circadian Rhythms and Sleep

Most animals have adapted to our planet's cycle of days and nights by developing a pattern of bodily functions that wax and wane over each 24-hour period. For humans, these **circadian rhythms** govern our sleep cycles, alertness, core body temperature, moods, learning efficiency, blood pressure, metabolism, immune responses, and pulse rate (Goh et al., 2016; Gumz, 2016; Hori et al., 2016). See **Concept Organizer 5.1**.

**Circadian rhythm** The internal biological clock governing bodily activities, such as the sleep/wake cycle, that occur on a 24- to 25-hour cycle. (*Circa* means "about," and *dies* means "day.")

**Suprachiasmatic nucleus (SCN)** A set of cells within the hypothalamus that respond to light and control the circadian rhythm.

---

**CONCEPT ORGANIZER 5.1** **Explaining Circadian Rhythms**

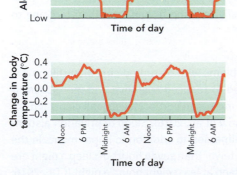

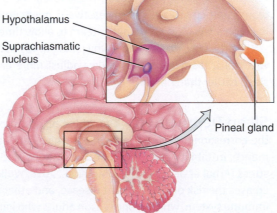

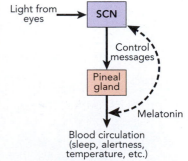

**a. Variations in circadian rhythms** Note how the 24-hour daily circadian rhythm affects our degree of alertness and core body temperature and how they rise and fall in similar ways.

**b. What controls our circadian rhythms?** A part of the hypothalamus, the **suprachiasmatic nucleus (SCN)**, receives information about light and darkness from our eyes and then sends control messages to our *pineal gland,* which releases the hormone *melatonin.*

**c. What regulates melatonin?** The level of melatonin in the blood is sensed by the SCN, which then adjusts the output of the pineal gland to maintain the "desired" level. This process is similar to other feedback loops in the body, which are essential in maintaining our body's internal balance or *homeostasis* (Chapters 3 and 12).

Do you remember having trouble going to bed at a "reasonable hour" when you were a teenager and then having a really difficult time getting up each morning? This common pattern of staying up late at night and then sleeping longer in the morning appears to be a result of the natural shift in the timing of circadian rhythms that occurs during puberty (Carskadon et al., 1998; Miano, 2017; Paiva et al., 2015). This shift is caused by a delay in the release of the hormone melatonin. In adults, this hormone is typically released around 10 p.m., signaling the body that it is time to go to sleep. But in teenagers, melatonin isn't released until around 1 a.m.—thus explaining why it's more difficult for teenagers to fall asleep as early as adults or younger children do.

Recognition of this unique biological shift in circadian rhythms among teenagers has led some school districts to delay the start of school in the morning. Research shows that even a 25- to 30-minute delay allows teenagers to be more alert and focused during class, and contributes to improvements in their moods and overall health (Boergers et al., 2014; Bryant & Gómez, 2015; Weintraub, 2016). More importantly, delaying the start of school in one large county in Kentucky was associated with a 16.5% decrease in car crashes among teenage drivers over the next two years (Danner & Philips, 2008).

As you've just seen, disruptions in circadian rhythms are particularly problematic for teenagers. However, such disruptions can put any of us at risk for serious health issues and personal concerns, including increased risk of cancer, heart disease, autoimmune disorders, obesity, sleep disorders, and accidents, as well as advanced aging and decreased cognitive abilities and productivity (e. g., Fang et al., 2017; Fleet et al., 2016; Lucassen et al., 2016).

Those who suffer the most immediate and obvious ill effects from sleep and circadian disturbances tend to be physicians, nurses, police, and others—about 20% of employees in the United States—whose occupations require rotating "shift work" schedules. Typically divided into a first shift (8 a.m. to 4 p.m.), second shift (4 p.m. to midnight), and third shift (midnight to 8 a.m.), these work shifts often change from week to week and clearly disrupt the workers' circadian rhythms. Some research suggests that productivity and safety increase when shifts are rotated every three weeks instead of every week and napping is allowed.

### Jet Lag and Circadian Rhythms
Like shift work, flying across several time zones can disrupt our circadian rhythms, cause fatigue and irritability, decrease alertness and mental agility, and worsen psychiatric disorders (Chiesa et al., 2015; Sharma et al., 2016; Wieczorek et al., 2016). Such effects are often referred to as *jet lag*.

Researchers have found that jet lag can have a significant effect on baseball teams. Specifically, it affects pitching location and velocity, which in turn impacts the number of home runs allowed (Song et al., 2016). These researchers suggest that starting pitchers for jet-lagged teams, particularly when flying eastward, might improve their pitching by traveling to the game location a few days ahead of the team to allow time to adjust to the new time zone.

By the way, do you know why jet lag tends to be worse when we fly eastward rather than westward? It's because our bodies adjust more easily to going to bed later than to going to sleep earlier than normal.

### Sleep Deprivation
One of the biggest problems with disrupted circadian rhythms is the corresponding *sleep deprivation*, which can lead to reduced cognitive and motor performance, irritability and other mood alterations, and increased cortisol levels—all clear signs of stress (Arnal et al., 2016; Collomp et al., 2016; Wolkow et al., 2016). Sleep deprivation also increases the risk of cancer, heart disease, and other illnesses, in addition to impairments in the immune system, which is one reason adults who get fewer than seven hours of sleep a night are four times as likely to develop a cold as those who sleep at least eight hours a night (CDC, 2016; Chaput & Dutil, 2016; Prather et al., 2015). Furthermore, sleep-deprived adolescents and adults are more likely to react emotionally, as shown in **Figure 5.3** (Demos et al., 2016). Surprisingly, when we're sleep deprived, we're also more likely to "remember" things that did not actually happen, a phenomenon you'll learn more about in Chapter 7 (Frenda et al., 2014).

Perhaps the most frightening and immediate danger is that lapses in attention among sleep-deprived pilots, truck drivers, physicians, and other workers too often cause serious accidents and cost thousands of lives each year (Bougard et al., 2016; Gonçalves et al., 2015; Lee et al., 2016a). Another serious concern is a recent plan to *increase* the existing 16-hour work limit for medical interns to 28 hours—without a break! Although one study found that interns could safely work these longer shifts (Bilimoria, 2016), the findings are controversial (Rau, 2016).

The good news is that more restrictive safety regulations and stronger enforcement of the limited hours of service for medical interns, truck drivers, and other public personnel could offset many of these public dangers. If you're concerned about your own levels of sleep deprivation, take the two-part test in the following **Try This Yourself**.

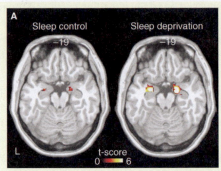

Yoo, Seung-Schik et al. Current Biology , Volume 17 , Issue 20, R877 - R878

**FIGURE 5.3** **Sleep deprivation, emotionality, and Impulse control** Note how our brain's emotional centers, particularly the amygdala (circled in red), are activated more under conditions of sleep deprivation. Research has clearly shown that sleep-deprived individuals are likely to respond with more emotionality (particularly to negative, fearful stimuli) and less impulse control (Demos et al., 2016). Other studies find that sleep-deprived individuals are more aggressive and violent, as well as being more likely to perceive transgressions by others as negative and menacing (Barber & Budnick, 2015; Krizan & Herlache, 2016). These findings are further supported by archival research showing that sleep-deprived judges dole out longer sentences to criminals than when they are not sleep deprived (Cho et al., 2017).

## Try This Yourself

### Are You Sleep Deprived?

Take the following test to determine whether you are sleep deprived.

**Part 1** Set up a small mirror next to this text and trace the black star pictured here, using your nondominant hand, while watching your hand in the mirror. The task is difficult, and sleep-deprived people typically make many errors. If you are not sleep deprived, it still may be difficult to trace the star, but you'll probably do it more accurately.

**Part 2** Give yourself one point each time you answer yes to the following:

_____ **1.** I generally need an alarm clock or my cell phone alarm to wake up in the morning.

_____ **2.** I sometimes fall asleep unintentionally in public places.

_____ **3.** I try to take only late morning or early afternoon college classes because it's so hard to wake up early.

_____ **4.** People often tell me that I look tired and sleepy.

_____ **5.** I often struggle to stay awake during class, especially in warm rooms.

_____ **6.** I find it hard to concentrate and often nod off while I'm studying.

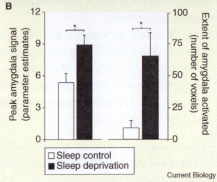
Leontura/Getty Images, Inc.

**Effects of sleep deprivation** Insufficient sleep can seriously affect your college grades, as well as your physical health, motor skills, and overall mood.

_____ **7.** I often feel sluggish and sleepy in the afternoon.

_____ **8.** I need several cups of coffee or other energy drinks to make it through the day.

_____ **9.** My friends often tell me I'm less moody and irritable when I've had enough sleep.

_____ **10.** I tend to get lots of colds and infections, especially around final exams.

_____ **11.** When I get in bed at night, I generally fall asleep within four minutes.

_____ **12.** I try to catch up on my sleep debt by sleeping as long as possible on the weekends.

The average student score is between 4 and 6. The higher your number, the greater your level of sleep deprivation.

*Sources:* Bianchi, 2014; Howard et al., 2014; National Sleep Foundation, 2012; Smith et al., 2012.

## Stages of Sleep

*The woods are lovely, dark and deep. But I have promises to keep, and miles to go before I sleep.*
—Robert Frost (American Poet, Educator)

Having discussed our daily circadian cycle and the problems associated with its disruption, we now turn our attention to our cyclical patterns and stages of sleep. We begin with an exploration of how scientists study sleep. Surveys and interviews can provide general information, but for more detailed and precise data researchers in sleep laboratories use a number of sophisticated instruments (**Concept Organizer 5.2**).

Imagine that you are a participant in a sleep experiment. When you arrive at the sleep lab, you are assigned one of several bedrooms. The researcher hooks you up to various physiological recording devices, which will require a night or two of adaptation before the researchers can begin to monitor your typical night's sleep (Concept Organizer 5.2a). After this adaptation, if you're like most sleepers, you'll begin the sleep cycle with a drowsy, presleep state followed by several distinct stages of sleep, each progressively deeper (Concept Organizer 5.2b). Then the sequence begins to reverse.

Note that we don't necessarily go through all sleep stages in this exact sequence (Concept Organizer 5.2c). But during the course of a night, people usually complete four to five cycles of light to deep sleep and then back up to light sleep. Each of these down and up cycles lasts about 90 minutes. Also note the two important divisions of sleep shown in Concept Organizer 5.2b and 5.3c: **rapid-eye-movement (REM) sleep** and **non-rapid-eye-movement (NREM) sleep** (Stages 1, 2, and 3).

**Rapid-eye-movement (REM) sleep** The fourth stage of sleep, marked by rapid eye movements, irregular breathing, high-frequency brain waves, paralysis of large muscles, and often dreaming.

**Non-rapid-eye-movement (NREM) sleep** The sleep stages (1 through 3) during which a sleeper does not show rapid eye movements.

---

**CONCEPT ORGANIZER 5.2**     **Scientific Study of Sleep and Dreaming**     Data collected in sleep labs has helped scientists understand the stages of sleep.

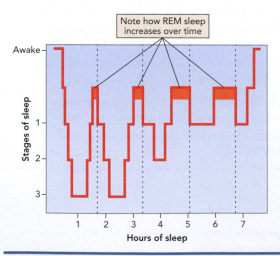

**a. Sleep lab recordings**     Participants in sleep research labs wear electrodes on their heads and bodies to measure brain and bodily responses during the sleep cycle. An electroencephalogram (EEG) detects and records brain-wave changes by means of small electrodes on the scalp. Other electrodes measure muscle activity and eye movements.

Philippe Garo/Science Source

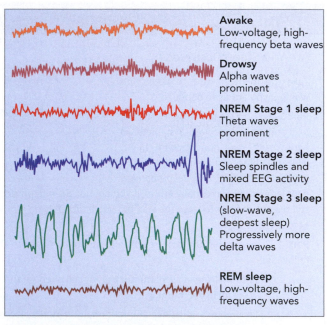

**c. Sleep related brain-wave changes**     The stages of sleep, defined by telltale changes in brain waves, are indicated by the jagged lines. The compact brain waves of alertness gradually lengthen as you descend downward through NREM Stages 1–3. The final stage in the 90-minute sleep cycle is called REM sleep, which as you can see involves compact, faster brain waves.

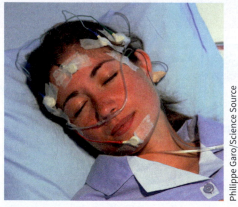

**b. Stages of sleep**     Your first sleep cycle generally lasts about 90 minutes from awake and alert, downward through NREM Stages 1–3, and then back up through NREM Stages 3–1, followed by a period of REM sleep. If you sleep 8 hours, you'll typically go through approximately four or five sleep cycles (as shown by the vertical dotted lines). Note how the overall amount of REM sleep increases as the night progresses, while the amount of deep sleep (Stage 3) decreases.

**REM and NREM Sleep**   During REM sleep, your brain's wave patterns are similar to those of a relaxed wakefulness stage, as shown in Concept Organizer 5.2c. Interestingly, your eyeballs also move up and down and from left to right. This rapid eye movement is a signal that dreaming is occurring. In addition, during REM sleep your breathing and pulse rates become fast and irregular, and your genitals may show signs of arousal. Yet your musculature is deeply relaxed and unresponsive, which may prevent you from acting out your dreams. Many people mistakenly interpret this type of sleep paralysis as a sign of being in the deepest versus the lightest stage of sleep. Because of these contradictory qualities, REM sleep is sometimes referred to as *paradoxical sleep.*

Although dreams occur most frequently during REM sleep, they also sometimes occur during NREM sleep (Askenasy, 2016; Jones & Benca, 2013). Note how *Stage 1* of NREM sleep is characterized by theta waves and drowsy sleep—see again Concept Organizer 5.2c. During this stage, you may experience *hypnagogic hallucinations*, during which you might hear your name called or a loud noise, or feel as if you're falling or floating weightlessly. The sensation of falling is often accompanied by sudden muscle movements called *myoclonic jerks.* In *Stage 2 sleep*, muscle activity further decreases, and sleep spindles occur, which involve a sudden surge in brain wave frequency. Stages 1 and 2 are relatively light stages of sleep, whereas *Stage 3 sleep* involves the deepest stage of sleep, often referred to as *slow wave sleep (SWS)* or simply *deep sleep*. Sleepers during this deep sleep are very hard to awaken, and if something does wake them, they're generally confused and disoriented at first. This is also a time that sleepwalking, sleep talking, and bedwetting occur. (Note that Stage 3 sleep was previously divided into Stages 3 and 4, but the American Academy of Sleep Medicine [AASM] removed the Stage 4 designation.)

---

## Try This Yourself

### The Sleep Cycle in Cats

During NREM (non–rapid-eye-movement) sleep, cats often sleep in an upright position. With the onset of REM sleep, cats normally lie down. Can you explain why?

**Answer:** During REM sleep, large muscles are temporarily paralyzed, which causes the cat to lose motor control and lie down.

Anna Hoychuk/Shutterstock.com

Anna Hoychuk/Shutterstock.com

---

## Why Do We Sleep and Dream?

There are many misconceptions about why we sleep and dream (see the **Myth Busters**). Fortunately, scientists have carefully studied what sleep and dreaming do for us and why we spend approximately 25 years of our life in these ASCs.

---

## Myth Busters

**True or False?**

Before reading the facts about each myth, place a check by any statement that you currently believe to be true.

1. _____ Everyone needs 8 hours of sleep a night to maintain sound mental and physical health.

2. _____ Dreams have special or symbolic meaning.

3. _____ Some people never dream.

4. _____ Dreams last only a few seconds and occur only in REM sleep.

5. _____ When genital arousal occurs during sleep, it means the sleeper is having a sexual dream.

6. _____ Most people dream only in black and white, and blind people don't dream.

7. _____ Dreaming of dying can be fatal.

8. _____ It's easy to learn new, complicated things, like a foreign language, while asleep.

## Facts:

1. *Fact:* Although sleep needs vary across ages, lifestyle, and health, the recommended average is 7.6 hours of sleep a night for adults. But some get by on much less. For example, the legendary artist Leonardo Da Vinci reportedly slept less than two hours a night! And some may need as much as 11 hours (Blunden & Galland, 2014; Bootzin et al., 2015; National Sleep Foundation, 2017). As mentioned earlier, Albert Einstein reportedly liked to sleep 10 to 11 hours a night.

2. *Fact:* Many people mistakenly believe that dreams can foretell the future, reflect unconscious desires, have secret meaning, reveal the truth, or contain special messages. But scientific research finds little or no support for these beliefs (Domhoff, 2010, 2017; Hobson et al., 2011; Lilienfeld et al., 2010, 2015).

3. *Fact:* In rare cases, adults with certain brain injuries or disorders do not dream (Solms, 1997). But otherwise, virtually all adults regularly dream, though many don't remember doing so. Even people who firmly believe they never dream report dreams if they are repeatedly awakened during an overnight study in a sleep laboratory. Children also dream regularly ages 3 and 8, they dream during approximately 25% of their sleep time (Foulkes, 1993, 1999; Mindell & Owens, 2015).

4. *Fact:* Research shows that most dreams occur in real time. Dream that seemed to last 20 minutes probably did last approximately 20 minutes (Dement & Wolpert, 1958). Dreams also sometimes occur in NREM sleep (Askenasy, 2016; Jones & Benca, 2013; Montangero & Cavallero, 2015).

5. *Fact:* When sleepers are awakened during this time, they are no more likely to report sexual dreams than at other times.

6. *Fact:* People frequently report seeing color in their dreams. Those who are blind do dream, but they report visual images only if they lost their sight after approximately age 7 (Bakou et al., 2014; Meaidi et al., 2014).

7. *Fact:* This is a good opportunity to exercise your critical thinking skills. Where did this myth come from? Although many people have personally experienced and recounted a fatal dream, how would we scientifically prove or disprove this belief?

8. *Fact:* Sleep is clearly essential for learning and memory consolidation, and some new learning can occur during the lighter stages (1 and 2) of sleep, but processing and retention of this material is minimal (Chambers & Payne, 2015; Lilienfeld et al., 2015; Takashima & Bakker, 2017). Wakeful learning is much more effective and efficient.

## Four Sleep Theories

How do scientists explain our shared need for sleep? There are four key theories:

**Adaptation/protection theory of sleep** The theory that sleep evolved to conserve energy and provide protection from predators.

**Repair/restoration theory of sleep** The theory that sleep allows organisms to repair their bodies or recuperate from depleting daily waking activities.

1. **Adaptation/protection theory** The most common explanation for sleep is that it evolved to conserve energy and provide protection from predators (Drew, 2013; Tsoukalas, 2012). From an evolutionary perspective, it's adaptive to sleep because it conserves calories, especially when food is scarce. Furthermore, sleeping at night helps us avoid becoming prey to animals that are more active at night. Indeed, as you can see in **Figure 5.4**, animals vary greatly in how much sleep they need each day. Those with the highest likelihood of being eaten by others, a higher need for food, and the lowest ability to hide tend to sleep the least.

2. **Repair/restoration theory** According to this theory, sleep helps us recuperate from the depleting effects of daily waking activities. Essential chemicals and bodily tissues are repaired or replenished while we sleep, and the brain repairs itself and clears potentially toxic waste products that accumulate (Iliff et al., 2012; Konnikova, 2014; Underwood, 2013; Xie et al., 2013). We recover not only from physical fatigue but also from emotional and intellectual demands (Blumberg, 2015). When deprived of REM sleep, most people "catch up" later by spending more time than usual in this state (the so-called REM rebound), which further supports this theory.

3. **Growth/development theory** In line with this theory, the percentage of deepest sleep (Stage 3) changes over the life span and coincides with changes in the structure and

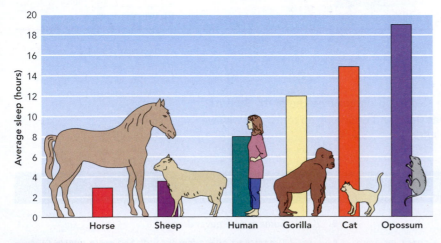

**FIGURE 5.4** **Average daily hours of sleep for different mammals** According to the adaptation/protection theory, differences in diet and number of predators affect different species' sleep habits. For example, opossums sleep many hours each day because they are relatively safe in their environment and are able to easily find food and shelter. In comparison, sheep and horses sleep very little because their diets require almost constant foraging for food in more dangerous open grasslands.

organization of the brain, as well as the release of growth hormones from the pituitary gland—particularly in children. As we age, our brains change less, and we release fewer of these hormones, grow less, and sleep less.

4. **Learning/memory theory** The fourth explanation for sleep centers on its role in learning and the consolidation, storage, and maintenance of memories (Bennion et al., 2015; Chambers & Payne, 2015; Vorster & Born, 2015). This is particularly true for REM sleep, which increases after periods of stress or intense learning. For example, infants and young children, who generally are learning more than adults, spend far more of their sleep time in REM sleep (**Figure 5.5**). Further support of the learning/memory theory comes from recent research that suggests sleep is necessary because we need to forget some of the unnecessary things we learn during the day (Diering et al., 2017). As you've discovered in other chapters, when we learn our brains grow new connections between neurons, thus enabling their signals between one another to become faster and more efficient. However, these connections often become so excessive and "noisy" that they interfere with learning and memory. Therefore, our brains automatically pare back some unnecessary connections while we sleep (Zimmer, 2017).

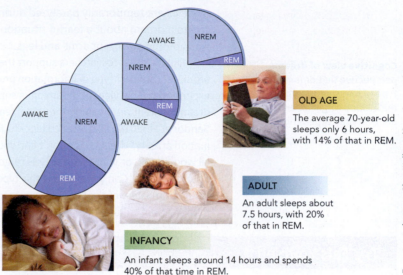

**OLD AGE**
The average 70-year-old sleeps only 6 hours, with 14% of that in REM.

**ADULT**
An adult sleeps about 7.5 hours, with 20% of that in REM.

**INFANCY**
An infant sleeps around 14 hours and spends 40% of that time in REM.

**FIGURE 5.5** **Aging and the sleep cycle** Our biological need for sleep changes throughout our life span. The pie charts in this figure show the relative amounts of REM sleep, NREM sleep, and awake time the average person experiences as an infant, an adult, and an elderly person.

## Three Dream Theories

As you can see, researchers have clearly shown that sleep serves a wide variety of vital functions. Although no one theory fully explains why we sleep, keep in mind that studying any topic from a variety of approaches yields a deeper understanding. Now let's look at three theories of why we dream—and whether dreams carry special meaning or information.

One of the oldest and most scientifically controversial explanations for why we dream is Freud's **wish-fulfillment view**. Freud proposed that unacceptable desires, which are reportedly normally repressed, rise to the surface of consciousness during dreaming. We avoid anxiety, Freud believed, by disguising our forbidden unconscious needs (what Freud called the dream's **latent content**) as symbols (**manifest content**) (Maggiolini & Codecà, 2016). For example, a journey supposedly symbolizes death; horseback riding and dancing could symbolize sexual intercourse; and a gun might represent a penis.

Most modern scientific research does not support Freud's view (Domhoff & Fox, 2015; Hobson, 2015; Siegel, 2010). Critics also say that Freud's theory is highly subjective and that the symbols can be interpreted according to the particular analyst's view or training.

In contrast to Freud's view, a biological view called the **activation–synthesis theory of dreams** suggests that dreams are a by-product of random, spontaneous stimulation of brain cells during sleep, which the brain combines (synthesizes) into coherent patterns, known as dreams (Hobson, 1999, 2005; Wamsley & Stickgold, 2010). Alan Hobson and Robert McCarley (1977) proposed that specific neurons in the brain stem fire spontaneously during REM sleep and that the cortex struggles to "synthesize," or make sense of, this random stimulation by manufacturing dreams. This is *not* to say that dreams are totally meaningless. Hobson suggests that even if our dreams begin with essentially random brain activity, our individual personalities, motivations, memories, and life experiences guide how our brains construct the dream.

Have you ever dreamed that you were trying to run away from a frightening situation but found that you could not move? The activation–synthesis hypothesis might explain this dream as random stimulation of the amygdala. As you recall from Chapter 2, the amygdala is a specific brain area linked to strong emotions, especially fear. If your amygdala is randomly

**Growth/development theory of sleep** The theory that deep sleep (Stage 3) is correlated with physical development, including changes in the structure and organization of the brain; infants spend far more time in Stage 3 sleep than adults.

**Learning/memory theory of sleep** The theory that sleep is important for learning and for the consolidation, storage, and maintenance of memories.

**Wish-fulfillment view of dreams** The Freudian belief that dreams provide an outlet for unacceptable desires.

**Latent content of dreams** According to Freud, a dream's unconscious, hidden meaning, which is transformed into symbols within the dream's manifest content (story line).

**Manifest content of dreams** In Freudian dream analysis, the "surface," or remembered, story line, which contains symbols that mask the dream's latent content (the true meaning).

**Activation–synthesis theory of dreams** The theory that dreams are a by-product of random, spontaneous stimulation of brain cells during sleep, which the brain combines (synthesizes) into coherent patterns, known as dreams.

stimulated and you feel afraid, you may try to run. But you can't move because your major muscles are temporarily paralyzed during REM sleep. To make sense of this conflict, you might create a dream about a fearful situation in which you were trapped in heavy sand or someone was holding onto your arms and legs.

**Cognitive view of dreams** The perspective that dreaming is a type of information processing that helps us organize and interpret our everyday experiences.

Finally, other researchers support the **cognitive view of dreams**, which suggests that dreams are simply another type of information processing that helps us organize and interpret our everyday experiences. This view of dreaming is supported by research showing strong similarities between dream content and waking thoughts, fears, and concerns (Domhoff, 2010; Domhoff & Fox, 2015; Sándor et al., 2014). Like most college students, you've probably experienced what are called "examination anxiety" dreams. You can't find your classroom, you're running out of time, your pen or pencil won't work, or you've completely forgotten a scheduled exam and show up totally unprepared. Sound familiar? Can you see how this type of dream fits best with the cognitive view of dreams? To test your mastery of the major dream theories, see the following **Try This Yourself**. For more information about cultural differences in dreams, check out the **Gender and Cultural Diversity** feature.

## Try This Yourself

### Practice Your Critical Thinking

The wish-fulfilment, activation-synthesis, and cognitive views of dreaming offer three widely divergent perspectives, and numerous questions remain. For example, how would the wish-fulfillment view of dreams explain why human fetuses show REM patterns? On the other hand, how would the activation–synthesis hypothesis explain complicated, story-like dreams or recurrent dreams? Finally, according to the cognitive view, how can we explain dreams that lie outside our everyday experiences? And how can we explain Albert Einstein's belief that his first insight into relativity theory occurred during a dream where he saw a beam of light and imagined himself chasing after it at its own speed? Similar questions arise about Elias Howe's dream and his later famous invention of the sewing machine—as depicted in the following.

Which of the three major theories of dreaming best explains Elias Howe's dream?

**a.** In the early 1800s, clothing was all made by hand using the standard hand-held needle with the threading hole at the top and the sharp end at the bottom.

**b.** In 1846, American inventor Elias Howe allegedly had a dream of being chased by men carrying spears with a hole in the tip.

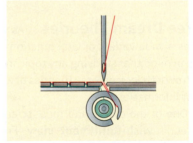

**c.** When Howe awoke, he realized his dream offered a key solution to problems with existing machine-operated sewing machines. Like the spear tips, the threading hole needed to be at the sharp end of the needle!

## Gender and Cultural Diversity

### Are There Differences in Dreams?

Men and women tend to share many of the common dream themes shown in **Table 5.1.** But women are more likely to report dreams of children, family members and other familiar people, household objects, and indoor events. In contrast, men tend to report dreams about strangers, violence, weapons, sexual activity, achievement, and outdoor events (Dale et al., 2016; Mathes et al., 2014; Mazandarani et al., 2013).

As a critical thinker, can you see how attitudes toward "proper" male and female gender roles might have affected what the participants were willing to report? For instance, might a male hesitate to report dreaming about caring for children? Might a female think it was inappropriate for her to report dreaming about guns and violence? Interestingly, a study of WWII prisoners of war found that their dreams contained less sexuality and even less aggression than the male norms (Barrett et al., 2014).

Dreams about basic human needs and fears (like sex, aggression, and death) seem to be found in all cultures. Children around the world often dream about large, threatening monsters or wild animals. Furthermore, dreams in most cultures typically include more misfortune than good fortune, and the dreamer is more often the victim of aggression than the cause of it (Dale et al., 2016; Domhoff, 2003, 2010; Krippner, 2015).

| TABLE 5.1 | Top Ten Common Dream Themes |
|---|---|

1. Being attacked or pursued
2. Falling
3. Sexual experiences
4. Being lost
5. Being paralyzed
6. Flying
7. Being naked in public
8. School, teachers, studying
9. Arriving too late
10. Death of a loved one or dead people as alive

Best View Stock/Getty Images, Inc.

**Test Your Critical Thinking**

1. Given that these 10 dream themes are found worldwide, what might be the evolutionary advantage of such dreams?

2. Imagine that someone marketed a drug that provided complete rest and recuperation with only one hour of sleep. However, it did stop you from dreaming. Would you take the drug? Why or why not?

*Sources*: Mathes et al., 2014; Mazandarani et al., 2013; Yu, 2012.

# Sleep–Wake Disorders

In any given year, an estimated 40 million Americans suffer from chronic sleep disorders, and another 30 million experience occasional sleep disorders serious enough to disrupt their daily activities (Larzelere & Campbell, 2016; National Sleep Foundation, 2017; Ng et al., 2015).

Judging by these statistics, and perhaps by your own experiences, it's not surprising to learn that almost everyone has difficulty sleeping at some point in his or her lifetime. The most common and serious of these disorders are summarized in **Table 5.2**.

Although it's normal to have trouble sleeping before an exciting event, as many as 1 person in 10 may suffer from **insomnia**. Those who suffer from this disorder may have persistent difficulty falling or staying asleep, or may wake up too early. Nearly everybody has insomnia at some time; a telltale sign is feeling poorly rested the next day. Most people with serious insomnia have other medical or psychological disorders as well (American Psychiatric Association, 2013; Bonnet & Arand, 2017; Primeau & O'Hara, 2015).

**Insomnia**   A sleep disorder characterized by persistent problems in falling or staying asleep, or awakening too early.

As a college student, you'll be particularly interested to know that students who send a high number of text messages are more likely to experience symptoms of insomnia (Murdock, 2013). Why? Researchers believe that most students feel pressured to immediately respond to texts and may be awakened by alerts from incoming texts, which can reduce both the quality and quantity of their sleep. On a related note, another study found that 10 to 30% of Americans experience long-term, *chronic* insomnia, compared to only 2% of hunter gatherers living in Africa and South America (Yetish et al., 2015). Could it be that our American culture, with its smartphones, television, and hectic pace, is interfering with our need for good-quality sleep?

To cope with insomnia, many people turn to nonprescription, over-the-counter sleeping pills, which generally don't work. In contrast, prescription tranquilizers and barbiturates do help people sleep, but they decrease Stage 3 and REM sleep, seriously affecting sleep quality. In the short term, limited use of drugs such as Ambien, Dalmane, Xanax, Halcion, and Lunesta may be helpful in treating sleep problems related to anxiety and acutely stressful situations. However, chronic users run the risk of psychological and physical drug dependence (Maisto et al., 2015; Mehra & Strohl, 2014; Taylor et al., 2016). The

| TABLE 5.2 | Sleep–Wake Disorders |
|---|---|
| **Label** | **Characteristics** |
| **Insomnia** | Persistent difficulty falling or staying asleep, or waking up too early |
| **Narcolepsy** | Sudden, irresistible onset of sleep during waking hours, such as sudden sleep attacks while standing, talking, or even driving |
| **Breathing-Related Sleep Disorder (Sleep Apnea)** | Repeated interruption of breathing during sleep, causing loud snoring or poor-quality sleep and excessive daytime sleepiness |
| **Nightmare** | Bad dream that significantly disrupts REM sleep |
| **NREM Sleep Arousal Disorder (Sleep Terror)** | Abrupt awakening with feelings of panic that significantly disrupts NREM sleep |

**Narcolepsy** A sleep order characterized by uncontrollable sleep attacks. (*Narco* means "numbness," and *lepsy* means "seizure.")

**Sleep apnea** A disorder of the upper respiratory system that causes a repeated interruption of breathing during sleep; it also leads to loud snoring, poor-quality sleep, and excessive daytime sleepiness.

hormone melatonin may provide a safer alternative. Some research suggests that taking even a relatively small dose (just .3 to .4 milligrams) can help people fall asleep and stay asleep (Hajak et al., 2015; Paul et al., 2015).

Thankfully, there are many effective strategies for alleviating sleep problems without medication. For example, research shows that not watching television or using electronic devices, like your computer, iPad, eReader, or cell phone, around bedtime makes it much easier to fall asleep (Chang et al., 2015; van der Lely et al., 2015; Weir, 2017). Why? Exposure to the light from the screens on these devices disrupts the circadian rhythm and reduces the level of melatonin in the body by about 22%, which makes it more difficult to fall asleep (especially for children and teenagers). See the following **Try This Yourself** for other recommendations about getting and staying asleep.

---

## Try This Yourself

### Natural Sleep Aids

Are you wondering what sleep experts recommend for sleep problems? Simple sleep hygiene tips and professional therapies provide consistent benefits that you can apply in your own life (Dolezal et al., 2017; Peterman et al., 2016; Taylor et al., 2014). When you're having a hard time going to sleep, don't keep checking the clock and worrying about your loss of sleep. In addition, remove all TVs, stereos, and books from your bedroom, and limit it to sleep rather than reading, watching movies, checking e-mail, and the like. If you need additional help, try some of the following suggestions.

### During the Day

- *Exercise.* Daily physical activity works away tension. But don't exercise vigorously late in the day, or you'll get fired up instead.
- *Keep regular hours.* An erratic schedule can disrupt biological rhythms. Get up at the same time each day.
- *Avoid stimulants.* Coffee, tea, soft drinks, chocolate, and some medications contain caffeine. Nicotine may be an even more potent sleep disrupter.

- *Avoid late meals and heavy drinking.* Overindulgence can interfere with your normal sleep pattern.
- *Stop worrying.* Focus on your problems at a set time earlier in the day.
- *Use presleep rituals.* Follow the same routine every evening: listen to music, write in a diary, meditate.
- *Practice yoga.* These gentle exercises help you relax.

### In Bed

- *Use progressive muscle relaxation.* Alternately tense and relax various muscle groups.
- *Use fantasies.* Imagine yourself in a tranquil setting. Feel yourself relax.
- *Use deep breathing.* Take deep breaths, telling yourself you're falling asleep.
- *Try a warm bath.* This can induce drowsiness because it sends blood away from the brain to the skin surface.

---

© Juniors/SuperStock

**FIGURE 5.6** **Narcolepsy** Research on specially bred narcoleptic dogs has found degenerated neurons in certain areas of the brain (Siegel, 2000). Whether human narcolepsy results from similar degeneration is a question for future research. Note how this hungry puppy has lapsed suddenly from alert wakefulness to deep sleep even when offered his preferred food.

**Narcolepsy**, a sleep disorder characterized by uncontrollable sleep attacks, afflicts about 1 person in 2,000 and generally runs in families (Ivanenko & Johnson, 2016; Lee & Radin, 2016; Williamson & Williamson, 2015). During an attack, REM-like sleep suddenly intrudes into the waking state of consciousness. Victims may experience sudden, incapacitating attacks of muscle weakness or paralysis (known as *cataplexy*). They may even fall asleep while walking, talking, or driving a car. The causes of narcolepsy are not fully understood, but researchers have discovered several genes believed to cause it in dogs and humans (**Figure 5.6**). Sadly, although long naps each day and stimulant or antidepressant drugs can help reduce the frequency of attacks, there is currently no known cure.

Perhaps the most serious sleep disorder is **sleep apnea**. People with sleep apnea may fail to breathe for a minute or longer and then wake up gasping for breath. When they do breathe during their sleep, they often snore. Sleep apnea seems to result from blocked upper airway passages and/or the brain's failure to send signals to the diaphragm, thus causing breathing to stop.

Unfortunately, people with sleep apnea are often unaware they have this disorder and fail to understand how their repeated awakening during the night leaves them feeling tired and sleepy during the day. More importantly, they should know that sleep apnea is linked with high blood pressure, strokes, cancer, depression, and heart attacks (Larzelere & Campbell, 2016; Lavie, 2015; Tekgol Uzuner & Uzuner, 2017).

Treatment for sleep apnea depends partly on its severity. If the problem occurs only when you're sleeping on your back, sewing tennis balls to the back of your pajama top may help remind you to sleep on your side. Because obstruction of the breathing passages is related to obesity and heavy alcohol use (Tan et al., 2015a; Yamaguchi et al., 2014), dieting and alcohol restriction are often recommended. For other sleepers, surgery, dental appliances that reposition the tongue, or CPAP (continuous positive airway pressure) machines that provide a stream of air to keep the airway open may provide help.

Research suggests that even "simple" snoring (without the breathing stoppage characteristic of sleep apnea) is associated with heart disease, hypertension, and other serious illnesses (Deeb et al., 2014; Schwartz et al., 2015). Although occasional mild snoring is fairly normal, chronic snoring is a possible warning sign that should prompt people to seek medical attention.

*Sleepwalking*, more formally known as *somnambulism*, usually occurs during the deepest stage of NREM sleep. (Recall that large muscles are paralyzed during REM sleep, which explains why sleepwalking normally occurs during NREM sleep.) Sleepwalking is normally harmless, and despite common beliefs, it's safe and advisable to awaken sleepwalkers, given that they may harm themselves while wandering around in the dark. An estimated 4% of U.S. adults—meaning over 8 million people—have at least one episode of sleepwalking each year. *Sleep talking* (also known as *somniloquy*) can occur during any stage of sleep, but it appears to arise most commonly during NREM sleep. It can consist of single, indistinct words or long, articulate sentences. It is even possible to engage some sleep talkers in a limited conversation.

Two additional sleep disturbances are **nightmares** and **sleep terrors** (**Figure 5.7**). Nightmares, sleep terrors, sleepwalking, and sleep talking are all more common among young children, but they can also occur in adults, usually during times of stress or major life events (Carter et al., 2014; Ivanenko & Johnson, 2016). Patience and soothing reassurance at the time of the sleep disruption are usually the only treatment recommended for both children and adults. However, some people, such as those with posttraumatic stress disorder (PTSD), suffer from such disabling and frightening nightmares that they may be at risk for suicide, which generally requires professional intervention (Littlewood et al., 2016). See Chapters 3 and 15.

© RyanJLane/iStockphoto

**FIGURE 5.7  Nightmare or sleep terror?**  Nightmares, or bad dreams, occur toward the end of the sleep cycle, during REM sleep. Less common but more frightening are sleep terrors, which occur late in the cycle, during Stage 3 of NREM sleep. Like the person in this photo, sleepers may sit bolt upright, screaming and sweating. They also may walk around, talk incoherently, and be almost impossible to awaken.

**Nightmares**  Anxiety-arousing dreams that generally occur near the end of the sleep cycle, during REM sleep.

**Sleep terrors**  Abrupt awakenings from NREM (non-rapid-eye-movement) sleep accompanied by intense physiological arousal and feelings of panic.

© Billy R. Ray/Wiley

## Retrieval Practice 5.2 | Understanding Sleep and Dreams

Completing this self-test and connections section, and then checking your answers by clicking on the answer button or by looking in Appendix B, will provide immediate feedback and helpful practice for exams.

### Self-Test

1. Briefly describe circadian rhythms.

2. The sleep stage marked by irregular breathing, eye movements, high-frequency brain waves, and dreaming is called _____ sleep.

   **a.** beta                    **b.** hypnologic
   **c.** REM                     **d.** transitional

3. The _____ theory says that sleep allows us to replenish what was depleted during daytime activities.

   **a.** repair/restoration      **b.** evolutionary/circadian
   **c.** supply-demand           **d.** conservation of energy

4. The _____ theory suggests dreams are by-products of random stimulation of brain cells.

   **a.** activation–synthesis    **b.** manifest-content
   **c.** wish fulfillment        **d.** information processing

5. A sleep disorder characterized by uncontrollable sleep attacks is known as _____ .

   **a.** dyssomnia               **b.** parasomnia
   **c.** narcolepsy              **d.** sleep apnea

### Connections—Chapter to Chapter

Answering the following questions will help you "look back and look ahead" to see the important connections among the various subfields of psychology and chapters within this text.

1. While dreaming, your brain is almost as active as it is when fully awake. Recalling what you learned in Chapter 2 (Neuroscience and Biological Foundations), identify which parts of your brain would be active when dreaming that you are (a) playing the piano, (b) late for your final exam, (c) listening to a concert, (d) walking a tightrope.

2. In Chapter 1 (Introduction and Research Methods), you learned about Freud and the psychoanalytic perspective. In this chapter, the psychoanalytic perspective was applied to dreaming. Briefly describe a dream you have had, and then try to identify and explain its manifest and latent content.

# 5.3 Psychoactive Drugs

## LEARNING OBJECTIVES

**Retrieval Practice** While reading the upcoming sections, respond to each Learning Objective in your own words.

**Summarize the major issues and concepts associated with psychoactive drugs.**

- **Identify** psychoactive drugs and the key terms associated with them.

- **Explain** how agonist and antagonist drugs produce their psychoactive effects.

- **Discuss** the four major categories of psychoactive drugs.

---

Virtually everyone routinely experiences the altered states of consciousness found in sleep and dreams. The vast majority of us also use *psychoactive drugs* (legal and/or illegal) to alter our moods, memory, concentration, and perception on a regular daily basis. As a busy college student, do you start your day with a routine cup of coffee? How about that glass of wine or a beer with your dinner that you use to help you relax after a hard day? If you're having trouble sleeping, do you reach for a couple of Tylenol PMs before going to bed? If you're like most people, you also manage to use these substances in moderation and without creating problems in your life. Therefore, you may be wondering why we're including these common drinks, pills, and behaviors as "drug use." If so, you'll be particularly interested in the next section.

## Understanding Psychoactive Drugs

**Psychoactive drug** A chemical that changes mental processes, such as conscious awareness, mood, and perception.

In our society, where the most popular **psychoactive drugs** are caffeine, tobacco, and ethyl alcohol, people often become defensive when these drugs are grouped with illicit drugs such as marijuana and cocaine. Similarly, marijuana users are disturbed that their drug of choice is grouped with "hard" drugs like heroin. Most scientists believe that there are good and bad uses of almost all drugs. The way drug use differs from drug abuse and how chemical alterations in consciousness affect a person, psychologically and physically, are important topics in psychology.

**Agonist** A substance that binds to a receptor and triggers a response that mimics or enhances a neurotransmitter's effect.

**Antagonist** A substance that binds to a receptor and triggers a response that blocks a neurotransmitter's effect.

Alcohol, for example, has a diffuse effect on neural membranes throughout the nervous system. Most psychoactive drugs, however, act in a more specific way: by either enhancing a particular neurotransmitter's effect, as does an **agonist** drug, or inhibiting it, as does an **antagonist** drug (**Step-by-Step Diagram 5.1**). Examples of agonist drugs are heroin and oxycodone. Naloxone is an example of an antagonist drug that is sometimes used to reverse a heroin overdose.

**Drug abuse** A type of drug taking that causes emotional or physical harm to the drug user or others.

**Addiction** A broad term that describes a compulsive craving for a substance, thing, or activity despite harmful consequences.

Is drug abuse the same as drug addiction? The term **drug abuse** generally refers to drug taking that causes emotional or physical harm to oneself or others. Drug consumption among abusers is also typically compulsive, frequent, and intense. **Addiction** is a broad term that refers to a compulsive craving for a substance, thing, or activity despite harmful consequences. Although we're talking primarily about addiction in this section, the term is applied to almost any type of compulsive activity, from video gaming to surfing the Internet (Sdrulla et al., 2015; Young, 2017). In fact, the latest version of the *Diagnostic and Statistical Manual (DSM-5)*, which officially classifies mental disorders, now includes *gambling disorders* in the substance-related and addictive disorders category (American Psychiatric Association, 2013). (Certain other disorders, including "sex addiction" and "exercise addiction" were not included because there was not enough evidence to support their inclusion.)

**Psychological dependence** The psychological desire or craving to achieve a drug's effect.

**Physical dependence** The changes in bodily processes that make a drug necessary for minimal functioning.

**Withdrawal** The discomfort and distress, including physical pain and intense cravings, experienced after stopping the use of an addictive drug.

In addition to distinguishing between drug abuse and addiction, many researchers distinguish between types of dependence. The term **psychological dependence** refers to the mental desire or craving to achieve a drug's effects. In contrast, **physical dependence** describes changes in bodily processes that make a drug necessary for minimum daily functioning. Physical dependence appears most clearly when the drug is withheld and the user undergoes **withdrawal** reactions, including physical pain and intense cravings.

## STEP-BY-STEP DIAGRAM 5.1   Agonist and Antagonist Drugs and Their Psychoactive Effects

**STOP!** This Step-by-Step Diagram contains essential information NOT found elsewhere in the text, which is likely to appear on quizzes and exams. Be sure to study it CAREFULLY!

Most psychoactive drugs produce their mood, energy, and perception-altering effects by changing the body's supply of neurotransmitters.

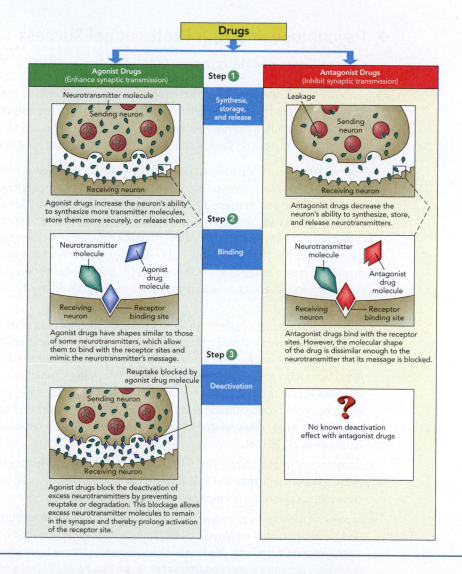

Keep in mind that psychological dependence is no less damaging than physical dependence. The craving in psychological dependence can be strong enough to keep the user in a constant drug-induced state—and to lure an addict back to a drug habit long after he or she has overcome physical dependence.

After repeated use of a drug, many of the body's physiological processes adjust to higher and higher levels of the drug, producing a decreased sensitivity called **tolerance**. Tolerance leads many users to escalate their drug use and experiment with other drugs in an attempt to re-create the original pleasurable altered state. Sometimes using one drug increases tolerance for another, a result known as *cross-tolerance*. Developing tolerance or cross-tolerance does not prevent drugs from seriously damaging the brain, heart, liver, and other organs.

Finally, note that some psychoactive drugs may induce symptoms of *psychosis,* which involves varying degrees of loss of contact with reality (see Chapter 15). For example,  individuals

**Tolerance**   The bodily adjustment to continued use of a drug in which the drug user requires greater dosages to achieve the same effect.

who abuse high doses of amphetamines for an extended period of time may develop *amphetamine psychosis* and compulsively pick at their skin, believing bugs are burrowing beneath the outer layer. In addition to this type of *hallucination* (a false, imaginary sensory perception), some individuals may become paranoid and extremely afraid of others, even those they've known for a long time. You can clearly see that someone who is experiencing these types of *delusions* (false, imaginary beliefs) or hallucinations is out of touch with reality and possibly extremely dangerous. Therefore, be very careful not to upset or antagonize such a person. The best way to help is to call 911. For more on how psychoactive drugs, and in particular, addiction, could affect your career, see the following.

## ❖ Psychology and Your Professional Success | Potential Career Costs of Addiction

As previously noted, addiction is a broad term referring to a compulsive craving for a substance, thing, or activity despite harmful consequences. Sadly, for both the addict and those who love him or her, it's most often heartbreaking. In this section, we will examine the serious negative effects addiction can have on your academic and job success in at least five major areas:

- *Time management* Virtually all compulsive behaviors are "time gobblers"! If you notice that your GPA is lower than you expect or that you're not advancing in your career, check out how much time you're spending on your various hobbies/addictions. For example, many college students and employees feel unreasonably compelled to check and use Facebook throughout the day and even late at night. What explains this type of addiction? Along with the self-reported "fear of missing out" (FOMO), researchers have found that using social media can create a high that's indistinguishable from that experienced during risky trading in the financial markets or with drug addiction (Buglass et al., 2017; Hong & Chiu, 2016; Suissa, 2015).

- *Quality and quantity of sleep* Heavy TV viewing, alcohol and other drug use, gambling, or any addiction can slowly disrupt or destroy your career and academic life by leading to sleep deprivation. As described earlier, lack of sleep is associated with numerous problems, including reduced cognitive and motor performance, which in turn affects your quality of work, productivity, and overall safety (Arnal et al., 2016; Barling et al., 2016). The lack of attention and concentration and slower reaction time associated with sleep deprivation also lead to many work-related injuries, accidents, and economic losses (Bougard et al., 2016; Lee et al., 2016a).

- *Interpersonal relationships* Due to the time-gobbling effect and the sleep losses associated with addictions, you may find it difficult to maintain successful social relationships with your classmates, coworkers, or employers.

- *Impression management* Having a legal record of drug abuse or DUIs will obviously negatively affect potential employers' perceptions of you. What you may not know is that many employers now commonly use Facebook and other social media sites to recruit, evaluate, and potentially fire employees (Goodmon et al., 2014; Head et al., 2016; Landers & Schmidt, 2016). The safest rule is to never post anything you don't want your current or future bosses to see!

- *Overall performance* Addictions are associated with inconsistent work quality, increased absenteeism, poorer concentration, and lack of focus, all of which lead to poorer overall academic and professional achievement. For example, marijuana is the drug most commonly used by college students, and research shows that it's linked with lower senior year enrollment, plans to graduate on time, GPA, and job performance (Firmin et al., 2016; Suerken et al., 2016).

In short, successful students, employees, and employers all know that they need to prioritize their studies and work in order to achieve. Each of us is allotted only 24-hours each day, and how we choose to spend this time is critical to our long-term success. What is more important to you—your addictions or your academic and professional life? If you need help, talk with your psychology instructor, college counselor, or other professionals.

# Four Drug Categories

Psychologists divide psychoactive drugs into four broad categories: *depressants, stimulants, opiates/opioids,* and *hallucinogens* (**Table 5.3**).

**Depressants**   The group of drugs called **depressants**, sometimes called "downers," act on the central nervous system to suppress or slow bodily processes and reduce overall responsiveness. Because tolerance and both physical and psychological dependence are rapidly acquired with these drugs, there is strong potential for abuse.

Although alcohol is primarily a depressant, at low doses it has stimulating effects, thus explaining its reputation as a "party drug." As consumption increases, symptoms of drunkenness appear. Alcohol's effects are determined primarily by the amount that reaches the brain (**Table 5.4**). Because the liver breaks down alcohol at the rate of about one ounce per hour, the number of drinks and the speed of consumption are both very important. People can die after drinking large amounts of alcohol in a short period of time. Moreover, men's bodies are more efficient than women's at breaking down alcohol. Even after accounting for differences in size and muscle-to-fat ratio, women have a higher blood-alcohol level than men following equal doses of alcohol.

**Depressant**   A drug that decreases bodily processes and overall responsiveness.

**TABLE 5.3   Effects of the Major Psychoactive Drugs**

| | Category | Desired Effects | Undesirable Effects |
|---|---|---|---|
| Giselleflissak/Getty Images | **Depressants (sedatives)** Alcohol, barbiturates, anxiolytics (antianxiety or tranquilizing drugs), alprazolam (xanax), flunitrazepam (rohypnol, "date-rape drug," "roofies"), ketamine (special K), gamma-hydroxybutyrate (GHB) | Tension reduction, euphoria, disinhibition, drowsiness, muscle relaxation | Anxiety, nausea, disorientation, impaired reflexes and motor functioning, amnesia, loss of consciousness, shallow respiration, convulsions, coma, death |
| Valentyn Volkov/Shutterstock | **Stimulants** Cocaine, amphetamine ("crystal meth," "speed"), 3,4-methylene-dioxy-methamphetamine (MDMA, "ecstasy," "molly") | Exhilaration, euphoria, high physical and mental energy, reduced appetite, perceptions of power, sociability | Irritability, anxiety, sleeplessness, paranoia, hallucinations, psychosis, elevated blood pressure and body temperature, convulsions, death |
| joe1719/Shutterstock.com | Caffeine | Increased alertness | Insomnia, restlessness, increased pulse rate, mild delirium, ringing in the ears, rapid heartbeat |
| | Nicotine | Relaxation, increased alertness, sociability | Irritability, increased blood pressure, stomach pains, vomiting, dizziness, cancer, heart disease, emphysema |
| JordiDelgado/Shutterstock.com | **Opiates/opioids (narcotics)** Morphine, heroin ("H," "smack," "horse"), codeine, oxycodone | Euphoria, "rush" of pleasure, pain relief, prevention of withdrawal, sleep | Nausea, vomiting, constipation, painful withdrawal, shallow respiration, convulsions, coma, death |
| Hysteria/Shutterstock | **Hallucinogens (psychedelics)** Lysergic acid diethylamide (LSD), mescaline (extract from the peyote cactus), psilocybin (extract from mushrooms) | Heightened aesthetic responses, euphoria, mild delusions, hallucinations, distorted perceptions and sensation | Panic, nausea, longer and more extreme delusions, hallucinations, perceptual distortions ("bad trips"), psychosis |
| | Marijuana | Relaxation, mild euphoria, nausea relief | Perceptual and sensory distortions, hallucinations, fatigue, increased appetite, lack of motivation, paranoia, possible psychosis |

### TABLE 5.4 Alcohol's Effect on Your Body and Behavior

| Number of Drinks[a] in Two Hours | Blood Alcohol Content (%)[b] | Effect |
| --- | --- | --- |
| (2) 🍺🍺 | 0.02. to 0.05 | Relaxed state but reduced inhibitions, impaired judgment, and lowered willpower |
| (3) 🍺🍺🍺 | 0.05 to 0.10 | Increased confidence and feelings of euphoria, but balance, coordination, speech, vision, and hearing somewhat impaired |
| (4) 🍺🍺🍺🍺 | 0.10 to 0.15 | Distinct impairment of mental faculties (judgment, concentration, reasoning, memory), slurred speech, poor coordination, and delayed reaction time |
| (7) 🍺🍺🍺🍺🍺🍺🍺 | 0.15 to 0.20 | Obvious intoxication, bloodshot eyes, and major loss of balance and coordination, along with major impairment of mental faculties |
| (12) 🍺🍺🍺🍺🍺🍺🍺🍺🍺🍺🍺🍺 | 0.20 to 0.40 | Severe intoxication, minimal control of mind and body, unconsciousness; high possibility of coma and death at the upper limit of 0.40 |

Nomadsoul1/Getty Images

**Fun partying or...?** Despite the personal risks associated with alcohol shown in this table, binge drinking and drunkenness remain common among college students. As you undoubtedly know, alcohol use also poses serious dangers to others, including drunk driving, sexual aggression, and intimate partner violence (Crane et al., 2016; Gilmore & Bountress, 2016; Li et al., 2016b).

[a]A drink refers to one 12-ounce beer, a 4-ounce glass of wine, or a 1.25-ounce shot of hard liquor.
[b]In the United States, the legal blood alcohol level for "drunk driving" varies from 0.05 to 0.12.

**FIGURE 5.8** **Alcohol and rape** In January 2016, 20-year-old Brock Turner was caught in the act and later convicted of sexually assaulting an unconscious woman he met earlier at a fraternity party. At the time of the rape, Turner's blood alcohol concentration was .17, twice the legal limit for driving. Turner was sentenced to six months in jail, was expelled from Stanford University, and must register as a sexual offender for the rest of his life.

HANDOUT/REUTERS/Newscom

#### Test Your Critical Thinking

1. Numerous protests erupted following the judge's sentencing of Brock Turner to six months. Many believed that such a short jail term was inappropriate in light of his crime. What do you think?

2. Given alcohol's widely accepted social role in many college functions, what could we do to decrease its link with sexual assault?

One of the most common, but seldom mentioned, risks with alcohol is that college students are more likely to have unprotected sex on days they binge drink, which may lead to serious problems such as STDs and unplanned pregnancies (Kerr et al., 2015). Sadly, overuse of alcohol and binge drinking has also been linked with major sexual crimes (**Figure 5.8**).

Before going on, you should also know that alcohol can be very dangerous when combined with certain other drugs. For example, combining alcohol and barbiturates—both depressants—can relax the diaphragm muscles to such a degree that the person suffocates (Marczinski, 2014). Does this information surprise you? Take the quiz in the following **Myth Busters** to discover if some of your other ideas about alcohol are really misconceptions.

## Myth Busters

**True or False?**

_____ 1. Alcohol increases sexual desire.

_____ 2. Alcohol helps you sleep.

_____ 3. Alcohol kills brain cells.

_____ 4. It's easier to get drunk at high altitudes.

_____ 5. Switching among different types of alcohol is more likely to lead to drunkenness.

_____ 6. Drinking coffee and taking a cold shower are great ways to sober up after heavy drinking.

_____ 7. Alcohol warms the body.

_____ 8. You can't become an alcoholic if you drink only beer.

_____ 9. Alcohol's primary effect is as a stimulant.

_____ 10. People experience impaired judgment after drinking only if they show obvious signs of intoxication.

**Answers:** All these statements are false. Detailed answers are provided in this chapter and in Lilienfeld et al., 2010.

**FIGURE 5.9** **Cocaine: An agonist drug in action**

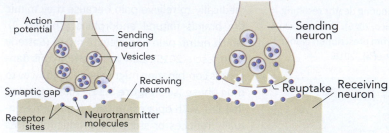

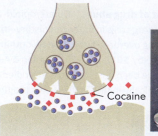

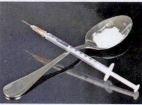

Douglas Sacha/Getty Images

**a. Normal neurotransmitter reuptake**  The two figures above depict how after releasing neurotransmitter into the synapse, the sending neuron normally reabsorbs (or reuptakes) excess neurotransmitter back into the vesicles, called terminal buttons.

**b. Cocaine blocks neurotransmitter reuptake**  This figure shows that when cocaine is present in the synapse, it will block the reuptake of dopamine, serotonin, and norepinephrine, and levels of these substances will increase. The result is overstimulation and a brief euphoric high. When the drug wears off, the depletion of the normally reabsorbed neurotransmitters may cause the drug user to "crash."

## Stimulants

Whereas depressants suppress central nervous system activity, **stimulants**, or "uppers," increase the overall activity and responsiveness of the central nervous system. Like depressants, stimulants also involve the potential for abuse.

Cocaine is a powerful central nervous system stimulant extracted from the leaves of the coca plant. It produces feelings of alertness, euphoria, well-being, power, energy, and pleasure. But it also acts as an *agonist drug* to block the reuptake of our body's natural neurotransmitters that produce these same effects. As you can see in **Figure 5.9**, cocaine's ability to block reuptake allows neurotransmitters to stay in the synapse longer than normal—thereby artificially prolonging the effects and depleting the user's neurotransmitters.

Surprisingly, cocaine was once widely used by doctors and dentists for numbing purposes, and many medicines as well as early Coca-Cola sodas contained traces of cocaine (**Figure 5.10**). Some people today still consider it to be a relatively harmless "recreational drug." However, even small initial doses can be fatal because cocaine interferes with the electrical system of the heart, causing irregular heartbeats and, in some cases, heart failure. It also can produce heart attacks, hypertension, and strokes by temporarily constricting blood vessels, as well as cognitive declines and brain atrophy (Levinthal, 2016; Siniscalchi et al., 2015; Vonmoos et al., 2014). In fact, the combined use of cocaine and alcohol may be the major cause of drug-related deaths (Burnett et al., 2016). Note too that the most dangerous form of cocaine is the smokable, concentrated version known as "crack," or "rock." Its lower price makes it affordable and attractive to a large audience. And its greater potency makes it more highly addictive.

Even legal stimulants can lead to serious problems. For example, cigarette smoking is among the most preventable causes of death and disease in the United States, and tobacco-related illnesses are among the leading economic concerns and causes of death worldwide (Goodchild et al., 2017; Herbst et al., 2014; World Facts, 2016). Like smoking, chewing tobacco is also extremely dangerous. Sadly, in 2014 fans mourned the loss of Hall of Fame baseball player Tony Gwynn, who died of mouth cancer, which he attributed to his lifelong use of chewing tobacco. Gwynn's family later filed a wrongful-death lawsuit against the tobacco industry on the grounds of negligence, fraud, and product liability (Kepner, 2016).

Given these well-known health hazards and the growing stigma against tobacco users, why do people ever start using tobacco? Two of the most compelling reasons are that nicotine is highly addictive and it offers significant cognitive rewards (Castaldelli-Maia et al., 2016; Herman et al., 2014; Li et al., 2014). In fact, nicotine's effects—relaxation, increased alertness, and diminished pain and appetite—are so powerfully reinforcing that some people continue to smoke even after having a cancerous lung removed.

## Opiates/Opioids

The drugs known as **opiates/opioids**, or narcotics, are derived from the opium poppy. They're sometimes classified as depressants because they do depress the central nervous system (CNS).

**Stimulant**  A drug that increases overall activity and general responsiveness.

**Opiate/opioid**  A drug derived from opium that numbs the senses and relieves pain.

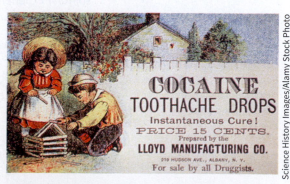

Science History Images/Alamy Stock Photo

**FIGURE 5.10**  **History of psychoactive drugs**  Before the Food and Drug Administration (FDA) regulated the sale of such drugs as heroin, opium, and cocaine, they were commonly found in over-the-counter, nonprescription drugs.

**FIGURE 5.11** **The high cost of drug abuse** Opiate/opioid abuse and addiction have recently been called the worst drug crisis in American history—rivaling the number of deaths from AIDS in the 1990s, with drug overdose fatalities now outnumbering deaths resulting from car accidents or guns (Grigsby, 2017; Katz, 2017; Nolan & Amico, 2016). The number of children and teenagers who have been hospitalized and/or died from prescription opioid poisoning also has risen dramatically in the last few years (Gaither et al., 2016).

*Ebet Roberts/Getty Images*

**a. Death of a Prince** In May 2016, world-famous musician Prince died at the age of 57 due to an opioid overdose and possible addiction to painkillers (Eldred & Eligon, 2016; Eligon et al., 2016).

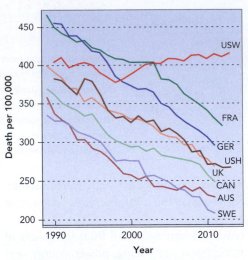

**b. Midlife mortality** The chart shows mortality from all causes, ages 45–54, for U.S. White non-Hispanics (USW), U.S. Hispanics (USH), and people in six comparison countries. As you can see, mortality rates have risen only for U.S. White non-Hispanics (Case & Deaton, 2015). This is particularly true for those with only a high school education or less. Increased rates of suicide and drug use along with economic inequality, have been cited as causes of the increase (Grigsby, 2017; Stiglitz, 2016). Some suggest that declining health among middle-aged White Americans helps explain the current political reaction on the right (e.g., Starr, 2015). What do you think?

However, they also excite areas of the CNS. Opiates like morphine and oxycodone are used medically to relieve pain because they mimic the brain's natural endorphins (Chapter 2), which numb pain and elevate mood (Satterly & Anitescu, 2015). Can you see how this dangerous combination might create a pathway to drug abuse (see **Figure 5.11**)? After repeated flooding with opiates/opioids, the brain eventually reduces or stops the production of its own natural, pain-reducing endorphins. If the user later attempts to stop, the brain lacks both artificial and natural pain-killing chemicals, and withdrawal becomes excruciatingly painful (**Figure 5.12**).

## Hallucinogens

Our fourth category of drugs, **hallucinogens**, produce sensory or perceptual distortions, including visual, auditory, and kinesthetic hallucinations. Some cultures have used hallucinogens for religious purposes, as a way to experience "other realities" or to communicate with the supernatural. However, in Western societies, most people use hallucinogens for their reported "mind-expanding" potential.

Hallucinogens are commonly referred to as *psychedelics* (from the Greek for "mind manifesting"). They include mescaline (derived from the peyote cactus), psilocybin (derived from mushrooms), PCP (phencyclidine, chemically derived), and LSD (lysergic acid diethylamide, derived from ergot, a rye mold). For many years, people who have used psychedelic drugs have claimed that the drugs allowed them to reach a "higher state of consciousness," and recent studies do back them up (e.g., Pultarova, 2017; Schartner et al., 2017). Brain scans have shown that neural activity in users' brains was, in fact, higher than during normal waking consciousness.

What are these experiences like? LSD, or "acid," produces dramatic alterations in sensation and perception, including an altered sense of time, synesthesia (blending of the senses), and spiritual experiences. Perhaps because the LSD experience is so powerful, few people "drop acid" on a regular basis. Nevertheless, LSD can be an extremely dangerous drug. Bad LSD "trips"

**Hallucinogen** A drug that produces sensory or perceptual distortions.

**FIGURE 5.12** **How opiates/ opioids may create physical dependence** Psychoactive drugs such as opiates/opioids affect the brain and body in a variety of ways.

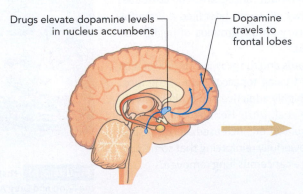

Drugs elevate dopamine levels in nucleus accumbens — Dopamine travels to frontal lobes

*igorstevanovic/Shutterstock.com*

**a. Reward pathway** Most researchers believe that increased dopamine activity in this so-called *reward pathway* of the brain accounts for the reinforcing effects of most addictive drugs.

**b. Withdrawal symptoms** Absence of the drug triggers withdrawal symptoms (e.g., intense pain and cravings).

can be terrifying and may lead to accidents, deaths, or suicide. One 32-year-old man, with no known psychiatric disorder, intentionally removed his own testes after his first and only use of LSD combined with alcohol (Blacha et al., 2013)!

Marijuana, or cannabis, is generally classified as a hallucinogen even though it has some properties of a depressant—it induces drowsiness and lethargy—and some of a narcotic—it acts as a weak painkiller. In low doses, marijuana produces mild euphoria; moderate doses may lead to an intensification of sensory experiences and the illusion that time is passing slowly. High doses may produce hallucinations, delusions, and distortions of body image (Bechtold et al., 2016; Maisto et al., 2015). The active ingredient in marijuana is THC, or tetrahydrocannabinol, which attaches to receptors that are abundant throughout the brain.

Some research has found marijuana to be therapeutic in treating glaucoma (an eye disease), and alleviating the nausea and vomiting associated with chemotherapy, as well as in dealing with chronic pain and other health problems (Loflin & Earleywine, 2015; Piomelli, 2015; Wilkie et al., 2016). In response to its potential medical benefits, and to free up police resources for fighting serious crime, many states have passed laws legalizing marijuana for medical and/ or recreational use. However, it remains relatively controversial for a variety of reasons (Alpár et al., 2016; Pacek et al., 2015).

One controversy involves possible health effects. Some researchers have reported several negative effects, such as chronic respiratory problems, reduced sperm count, psychosis, and disruption of the menstrual cycle and ovulation (e.g., Gage et al., 2016; Harley et al., 2016; National Academies of Sciences (2017). On the other hand, a longitudinal study that followed over a thousand cannabis versus tobacco users from the ages of 18 to 38 found no increase in physical health problems for the cannabis users, other than poorer periodontal health (Meier et al., 2016).

Along with the conflicting research on possible health problems, some research supports the popular belief that marijuana serves as a "gateway" to other illegal drugs. However, other studies find little or no connection (Firmin et al., 2016; Levinthal, 2016; Mosher & Akins, 2014).

A third area with contradictory research has to do with cognitive functioning. Some studies report that marijuana use leads to decreases in IQ, educational achievement, and overall cognitive functioning (Suerken et al., 2016; Thames et al., 2014). However, these findings have been questioned by a study on over two thousand teenagers (Mokrysz et al., 2016). As discussed in Chapter 1, correlational studies are always subject to the *third-variable problem*. A case in point, some earlier correlational studies that identified a connection between marijuana use and lowered IQ may have failed to control for the influence of cigarette smoking—the third variable. When the researchers in this last study isolated cigarette smoking, they found it to be the best predicting factor for lowered IQ.

As you can see, marijuana remains a controversial drug, and more research is needed. While waiting for more conclusive research, keep in mind that marijuana, like virtually all drugs, can cause pregnancy complications, and its regular use before age 18 is particularly hazardous because the brain is still developing. In addition, some researchers still believe that over time persistent use and dependence may be linked to psychotic illnesses and cognitive and motor declines (Alpár et al., 2016; Ganzer et al., 2016; Lu & Mackie, 2016). Furthermore, marijuana can be habit forming, though few users experience the intense cravings associated with cocaine or opiates/opioids. Withdrawal symptoms are mild because the drug dissolves in the body's fat and leaves the body very slowly, which explains why a marijuana user can test positive for days or weeks after the last use.

## Club Drugs

As you may know from television or newspapers, psychoactive drugs like Rohypnol (the "date rape drug," also called "roofies"), MDMA (3,4-methylenedioxymethylamphetamine, or Ecstasy), GHB (gamma-hydroxybutyrate), ketamine ("special K"), methamphetamine ("ice" or "crystal meth"), "bath salts," and LSD are all sometimes called "club drugs." This name reflects the fact that they're often used by teenagers and young adults at parties, bars, and nightclubs (NIDA, 2016). Unfortunately, these drugs can have very serious consequences (Dunne et al., 2015; NIDA, 2016; Weaver et al., 2015). For example, recreational use of Ecstasy is associated with potentially fatal damage to hippocampal cells in the brain, as well as a reduction in the neurotransmitter serotonin, which can lead to memory, sleep, mood, and appetite problems (Asl et al., 2015; Levinthal, 2016).

On the other hand, the club drug ketamine, "special K," shows promise as a treatment for major depression, suicidal behaviors, and bipolar disorders. Research has found that it appears to have an immediate and positive effect on parts of the brain responsible for executive functioning and emotion regulation (Kishimoto et al., 2016; Lee et al., 2016b; Li et al., 2016c).

Despite this one encouraging research finding and the favorable reports of some users, bear in mind that club drugs, like all illicit drugs, are particularly dangerous because there are no truth-in-packaging laws to protect buyers from unscrupulous practices. Sellers often substitute cheaper, and possibly even more dangerous, substances for the ones they claim to be selling. Also, club drugs (like most psychoactive drugs) affect the motor coordination, perceptual skills, and reaction time necessary for safe driving, bicycle riding, or even walking.

Impaired decision making is a serious problem as well. Just as "drinking and driving don't mix," club drug use may lead to risky sexual behaviors with increased risk of sexually transmitted infections. Add in the fact that some drugs, like Rohypnol, are odorless, colorless, and tasteless and can easily be added to beverages by individuals who want to intoxicate or sedate others, and you can see that the dangers of club drug use go far beyond the drugs themselves.

*I don't do drugs, my dreams are frightening enough.*

—M. C. Escher (Dutch Graphic Artist)

© Billy R. Ray/Wiley

## Retrieval Practice 5.3 | Psychoactive Drugs

Completing this self-test and connections section, and then checking your answers by clicking on the answer button or by looking in Appendix B, will provide immediate feedback and helpful practice for exams.

### Self-Test

1. Psychoactive drugs _____.

   a. change conscious awareness, mood, or perception
   b. are addictive, mind altering, and dangerous to your health
   c. are illegal unless prescribed by a medical doctor
   d. have all these effects

2. Drug taking that causes emotional or physical harm to the drug user or others is known as _____.

   a. addiction
   b. physical dependence
   c. psychological dependence
   d. drug abuse

3. Briefly explain how agonist drugs differ from antagonist drugs.

4. _____ act on the brain and nervous system to increase overall activity and responsiveness.

   a. Stimulants
   b. Opiates/opioids
   c. Depressants
   d. Hallucinogens

5. Depressants include all the following *except* _____.

   a. antianxiety drugs
   b. alcohol
   c. tobacco
   d. Rohypnol

### Connections—Chapter to Chapter

Answering the following question will help you "look back and look ahead" to see the important connections among the various subfields of psychology and chapters within this text.

In Chapter 3 (Stress and Health Psychology), you learned that some people with posttraumatic stress disorder (PTSD) turn to alcohol and other drugs to help reduce or cope with the stress. Based on what you discovered about the effects of alcohol in this chapter, how might this behavior make the symptoms of PTSD worse?

## 5.4 | Meditation and Hypnosis

### LEARNING OBJECTIVES

**Retrieval Practice**   While reading the upcoming sections, respond to each Learning Objective in your own words.

**Review the major features of meditation and hypnosis.**

• **Describe** meditation and its major effects.
• **Identify** hypnosis, its key features, and its major myths.

As we have seen, factors such as sleep, dreaming, and psychoactive drug use can create altered states of consciousness (ASCs). Changes in consciousness also can be achieved by means of meditation and hypnosis.

# Meditation

*Suddenly, with a roar like that of a waterfall, I felt a stream of liquid light entering my brain through the spinal cord . . . I experienced a rocking sensation and then felt myself slipping out of my body, entirely enveloped in a halo of light. I felt the point of consciousness that was myself growing wider, surrounded by waves of light.*

—Jiddu Krishnamurti (Indian Philosopher, Speaker, Writer)

This is how spiritual leader Krishnamurti described his experience with **meditation**, a group of techniques generally designed to focus attention, block out distractions, and produce an ASC (**Figure 5.13**). Most people in the beginning stages of meditation report a simpler, mellow type of relaxation, followed by a mild euphoria and a sense of timelessness. Some advanced meditators report experiences of profound rapture, joy, and/or strong hallucinations.

How can we explain these effects? Brain imaging studies suggest that meditation's requirement to focus attention, block out distractions, and concentrate on a single object, emotion, or word reduces the number of brain cells that must be devoted to the multiple, competing tasks normally going on within the brain's frontal lobes. This narrowed focus explains the feelings of timelessness and mild euphoria. This increased concentration also may explain Albert Einstein's famous saying that, "No problem can be solved from the same level of consciousness that created it." Can you see that this quote might be referring to the mind's normal, constant chattering of thoughts? Meditation is believed to disrupt this chatter, raise consciousness, and increase cognitive processing.

Research has also verified that meditation can produce dramatic changes in basic physiological processes, including heart rate, oxygen consumption, sweat gland responses, and brain activity. In addition, it's been somewhat successful in reducing pain, anxiety, and stress; lowering blood pressure; and improving overall cognitive functioning and mental health (Crescentini et al., 2016; Heffner et al., 2016; Taylor & Abba, 2015). Surprisingly, a meta-analysis (which combines results from multiple studies) revealed that 30 minutes of meditation may provide as much relief from anxiety and depression as antidepressants (Goyal et al., 2014).

As you can see in **Figures 5.13b** and **c**, studies have also found that meditation can change the body's sympathetic and parasympathetic responses and increase our responsiveness to sensory stimuli, as well as improving our decision making, emotion regulation, and attention processing (Esch, 2014; Tang et al., 2014; Xue et al., 2014).

A number of elite athletes use meditation to help prepare for competition. To help control arousal and pregame "jitters," NBA coach Phil Jackson led his LA Lakers team in meditation before games, former MLB star Derek Jeter meditated for an hour each day on non-game days, and marathon runner Deena Kastor meditates to reduce anxiety before a big race.

**Meditation** A group of techniques generally designed to focus attention, block out distractions, and produce an altered state of consciousness (ASC); it's believed to enhance self-knowledge and well-being through reduced self-awareness.

**FIGURE 5.13** **Benefits of meditation**

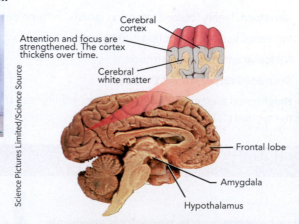

**a. Varieties of meditation** Some meditation techniques, such as tai chi and hatha yoga, include body movements and postures. In other techniques, the meditator remains motionless, chanting or focusing on a single point, like a candle flame.

**b. Sympathetic and parasympathetic changes** During meditation, the hypothalamus diminishes the sympathetic response and increases the parasympathetic response. Shutting down the fight-flight-freeze response in this way allows for deep rest, slower respiration, and overall relaxation.

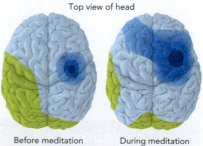

**c. Sensory responses** Researchers have found that an increased area of the brain responds to sensory stimuli during meditation, which also suggests that meditation enhances the coordination between the brain hemispheres (Kilpatrick et al., 2011; Kurth et al., 2014). Note how much the blue-colored areas enlarged and spread from the right to the left hemisphere during meditation.

| TABLE 5.5 | Hypnosis Myths and Facts |
|---|---|
| **Myth** | **Fact** |
| **Faking** <br> Hypnosis participants are "faking it" and playing along with the hypnotist. | There are conflicting research positions about hypnosis. Although most participants are not consciously faking hypnosis, some researchers believe the effects result from a blend of conformity, relaxation, obedience, suggestion, and role playing. Other theorists believe that hypnotic effects result from a special ASC. A group of "unified" theorists suggest that hypnosis is a combination of both relaxation/role playing and a unique ASC. |
| **Forced hypnosis** <br> People can be hypnotized against their will, or hypnotically "brainwashed." | Hypnosis requires a willing, conscious choice to relinquish control of one's consciousness to someone else. The best potential subjects are those who are able to focus attention, are open to new experiences, and are capable of imaginative involvement or fantasy. |
| **Unethical behavior** <br> Hypnosis can make people behave immorally or take dangerous risks against their will. | Hypnotized people retain awareness and control of their behavior, and they can refuse to comply with the hypnotist's suggestions. |
| **Superhuman strength** <br> Under hypnosis, people can perform acts of special superhuman strength. | When nonhypnotized people are simply asked to try their hardest on tests of physical strength, they generally can do anything that a hypnotized person can do. |
| **Exceptional memory** <br> Under hypnosis, people can recall things they otherwise could not. | Although the heightened relaxation and focus that hypnosis engenders improves recall for some information, it adds little (if anything) to regular memory. Hypnotized people are just more willing to guess. Because memory is normally filled with fabrication and distortion (Chapter 7), hypnosis generally increases the potential for error. |

*Sources:* Hilgard, 1978, 1992; Huber et al., 2014; Lilienfeld et al., 2010, 2015; Polito et al., 2014.

## Hypnosis

*Relax . . . your eyelids are so very heavy . . . your muscles are becoming more and more relaxed . . . your breathing is becoming deeper and deeper . . . relax . . . your eyes are closing . . . let go . . . relax.*

**Hypnosis** An altered state of consciousness (ASC) characterized by deep relaxation and a trance-like state of heightened suggestibility and intense focus.

Hypnotists use suggestions like these to begin **hypnosis**, a trance-like state of heightened suggestibility, deep relaxation, and intense focus. Once hypnotized, some people can be convinced that they are standing at the edge of the ocean, listening to the sound of the waves and feeling the ocean mist on their faces. Invited to eat a "delicious apple" that is actually an onion, the hypnotized person may relish the flavor. Told they are watching a very funny or sad movie, hypnotized people may begin to laugh or cry at their self-created visions.

For centuries, entertainers and quacks have used (and abused) hypnosis, leading to many myths and misconceptions (**Table 5.5**), but it has also long been employed as a clinical tool. Modern scientific research has removed much of the mystery surrounding hypnosis. A number of features characterize the hypnotic state (Huber et al., 2014; Spiegel, 2015; Yapko, 2015):

- Narrowed, highly focused attention (ability to "tune out" competing sensory stimuli)
- Increased use of imagination and hallucinations
- A passive and receptive attitude
- Decreased responsiveness to pain
- Heightened suggestibility, or a greater willingness to respond to proposed changes in perception ("This onion is an apple.")

## Try This Yourself

### Hypnosis or Simple Trick?

You can re-create a favorite trick that stage hypnotists promote as evidence of superhuman strength under hypnosis. Simply arrange two chairs as shown in the picture. You will see that hypnosis is not necessary—all that is needed is a highly motivated volunteer willing to stiffen his or her body.

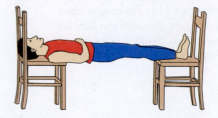

Today, even with available anesthetics, hypnosis is occasionally used in surgery and for the treatment of cancer, chronic pain, and severe burns (Adachi et al., 2014; Spiegel, 2015; Tan et al., 2015b). Hypnosis has found its best use in medical areas such as dentistry and childbirth, where patients have a high degree of anxiety, fear, and misinformation. For instance, some studies have found that women who use hypnosis in labor and childbirth experience lower levels of pain and a shorter duration of labor (Beebe, 2014; Madden et al., 2012). Because tension and anxiety strongly affect pain, any technique that helps the patient relax is medically useful. In psychotherapy, hypnosis can help patients relax and reduce anxiety (Alladin, 2016; Hope & Sugarman, 2015; Iglesias & Iglesias, 2014).

## One Final Note
Before closing this chapter, we'd like to take an unusual step for authors by offering you, our reader, a piece of caring, personal, and professional advice. A core problem while you're in any ASC is that you're less aware of external reality, which places you at high risk. This applies to both men and women. We generally recognize these dangers while sleeping and dreaming, and we've developed standard ways to protect ourselves. For example, when we're driving on a long trip and start to feel sleepy, we stop for coffee, walk around, and/or rent a hotel room before allowing ourselves to fall asleep. Unfortunately, we often fail to acknowledge that similar dangers exist with other ASCs.

Our simple advice is to follow this same "sleepy driver" logic and standards. If you decide to use drugs, meditate, undergo hypnosis, or engage in any other form of altered consciousness, research the effects and risks of your ASC and plan ahead for the best options for dealing with it—just like you set up a designated driver before drinking. Take care and best wishes,

*Karen R. Huffman*    *Katherine Dowdell*    *Cathrine A. Sanderson*

© Billy R. Ray/Wiley

## Retrieval Practice 5.4 | Meditation and Hypnosis

Completing this self-test and connections section, and then checking your answers by clicking on the answer button or by looking in Appendix B, will provide immediate feedback and helpful practice for exams.

### Self-Test

1. Altered states of consciousness (ASCs) can be achieved in which of the following ways?
   a. During sleep and dreaming
   b. Via chemical channels
   c. Through hypnosis and meditation
   d. In all these ways

2. Briefly explain how meditation differs from hypnosis.

3. Research on the effects of meditation has found _____.
   a. an increase in blood pressure
   b. a reduction in stress
   c. a lack of evidence for changes in any physiological functions
   d. all of these options

4. _____ is an ASC characterized by deep relaxation and a trance-like state of heightened suggestibility and intense focus.
   a. Meditation          b. Amphetamine psychosis
   c. Hypnosis            d. Daydreaming

5. Which of the following is NOT associated with hypnosis?
   a. the use of imagination
   b. exceptional memory
   c. a passive, receptive attitude
   d. decreased pain

### Connections—Chapter to Chapter
Answering the following question will help you "look back and look ahead" to see the important connections among the various subfields of psychology and chapters within this text.

In Chapter 7 (Memory), you'll discover that our memories can be distorted and filled with inaccuracies. What factors involved in hypnosis could jeopardize the accuracy of events recalled under its influence?

# Chapter Summary

## 5.1  Understanding Consciousness   153

- **Consciousness**, an organism's awareness of internal events and the external environment, includes ordinary waking consciousness as well as various **altered states of consciousness (ASCs)**, such as sleep and dreaming.

- **Selective attention** allows us to focus our conscious awareness onto specific stimuli, whereas **inattentional blindness** blocks us from seeing unexpected stimuli.

- Consciousness varies in its depth and exists along a continuum of awareness. **Controlled processes**, which require focused attention, are at the highest level of the continuum of awareness. **Automatic processes**, which require minimal attention, are found in the middle. Unconsciousness and coma are at the lowest level.

### Test Your Critical Thinking

**1.** Can you see how selective attention and inattentional blindness might explain why some arguments with friends and love partners are impossible to resolve?

**2.** How would automatic processing explain how you can walk all the way from one end of your college campus to the other and not remember anything you did or saw along the way?

**CONTROLLED PROCESSES**
Require focused, maximum attention (e.g., studying for an exam, learning to drive a car)

**AUTOMATIC PROCESSES**
Require minimal attention (e.g., walking to class while talking on a cell phone, listening to your boss while daydreaming)

**SUBCONSCIOUS**
Below conscious awareness (e.g., subliminal perception, sleeping, dreaming)

**LITTLE OR NO AWARENESS**
Biologically based lowest level of awareness (e.g., head injuries, anesthesia, coma; also the *unconscious mind*—a Freudian concept discussed in Chapter 13— reportedly consisting of unacceptable thoughts and feelings too painful to be admitted to consciousness)

High Awareness

Middle Awareness

Low Awareness

*ALTERED STATES OF CONSCIOUSNESS (ASCS)* can exist on many levels of awareness, from high awareness to no awareness (e.g., drugs, sensory deprivation, sleep, dreaming)

**Psychology and a Classic Success:** Albert Einstein

## Understanding Consciousness

**Selective Attention**
- Stream of consciousness
- Inattentional blindness

**Levels of Awareness**
Controlled versus automatic processes

**Research Challenge:** What's Wrong with Distracted Driving?

**Psychology and Your Personal Success:** Can Maximizing Your Consciousness Save Lives?

## 5.2   Understanding Sleep and Dreams   157

- Many physiological functions follow 24-hour **circadian rhythms**. Disruptions in these rhythms, as well as long-term sleep deprivation, lead to increased fatigue, cognitive and mood disruptions, and other health problems.

- During a normal night's sleep, we progress through several distinct stages of **non-rapid-eye-movement (NREM) sleep**, with periods of **rapid-eye-movement (REM) sleep** generally occurring at the end of each sleep cycle. Both REM and NREM sleep are important for our biological functioning.

- There are four major theories about why we sleep. **Adaptation/protection theory** proposes that sleep evolved to conserve energy and to provide protection from predators. The **repair/restoration theory** suggests that sleep helps us recuperate from the day's events. The **growth/development theory** argues that we use sleep for growth. The **learning/memory theory** says that we use sleep for consolidation, storage, and maintenance of memories.

- Three major theories about why we dream are Freud's **wish-fulfillment view**, the **activation–synthesis hypothesis**, and the **cognitive view**. Researchers have found many similarities and differences in dream content between men and women and across cultures.

- Sleep–wake disorders include **insomnia**, **narcolepsy**, **sleep apnea**, **nightmares**, and **sleep terrors**.

### Test Your Critical Thinking

**1.** How are you affected by sleep deprivation and disruption of your circadian rhythms?

**2.** Which of the major theories of dreaming best explains your own dreams?

# Understanding Sleep and Dreams

## Circadian Rhythms and Sleep

Light from eyes → SCN

SCN → Control messages → Pineal gland

Pineal gland → Melatonin

→ Blood circulation (sleep, alertness, temperature, etc.)

## Stages of Sleep
REM and NREM sleep

Philippe Garo/Science Source

Note how REM sleep increases over time

Awake

Stages of sleep
1
2
3

Hours of sleep
1  2  3  4  5  6  7

## Why Do We Sleep and Dream?

### Four Sleep Theories
- Adaptation/protection
- Repair/restoration
- Growth/development
- Learning/memory

### Three Dream Theories
- Wish-fulfillment
- Activation–synthesis
- Cognitive view

### Gender and Cultural Diversity:
Are There Differences in Dreams?

## Sleep–Wake Disorders
- Insomnia
- Narcolepsy
- Sleep apnea
- Nightmares
- Sleep terrors

© RyanJLane/iStockphoto

## 5.3   Psychoactive Drugs   168

- **Psychoactive drugs** influence the nervous system in a variety of ways. Alcohol affects neural membranes throughout the entire nervous system. Most psychoactive drugs act in a more specific

way, by either increasing a particular neurotransmitter's effect—an **agonist** drug—or inhibiting it—an **antagonist** drug.

- The term **drug abuse** refers to drug-taking behavior that causes emotional or physical harm to oneself or others. **Addiction** refers to a condition in which a person feels compelled to use a specific drug. **Psychological dependence** refers to the mental desire or craving to achieve a drug's effects. **Physical dependence** refers to biological changes that make a drug necessary for minimum daily functioning, so as to avoid **withdrawal** symptoms (pain and intense cravings experienced after stopping the use of an addictive drug). Repeated use of a drug can produce decreased sensitivity, or **tolerance**. Sometimes, using one drug increases tolerance for another (*cross-tolerance*).

- Psychologists divide psychoactive drugs into four categories: **depressants** (such as alcohol, barbiturates, Rohypnol, and Ketamine), **stimulants** (such as caffeine, nicotine, cocaine, and amphetamines), **opiates/opioids** (such as morphine, heroin, and codeine), and **hallucinogens** (such as marijuana and LSD). Almost all psychoactive drugs can cause serious health problems and, in some cases, even death.

- Club drugs are popular due to their desirable effects, but they can also cause serious health problems and impair good decision making.

**Test Your Critical Thinking**

**1.** Which is more important in creating addiction—physical dependence or psychological dependence?

**2.** Do you think marijuana use should be legal in all states? Why or why not?

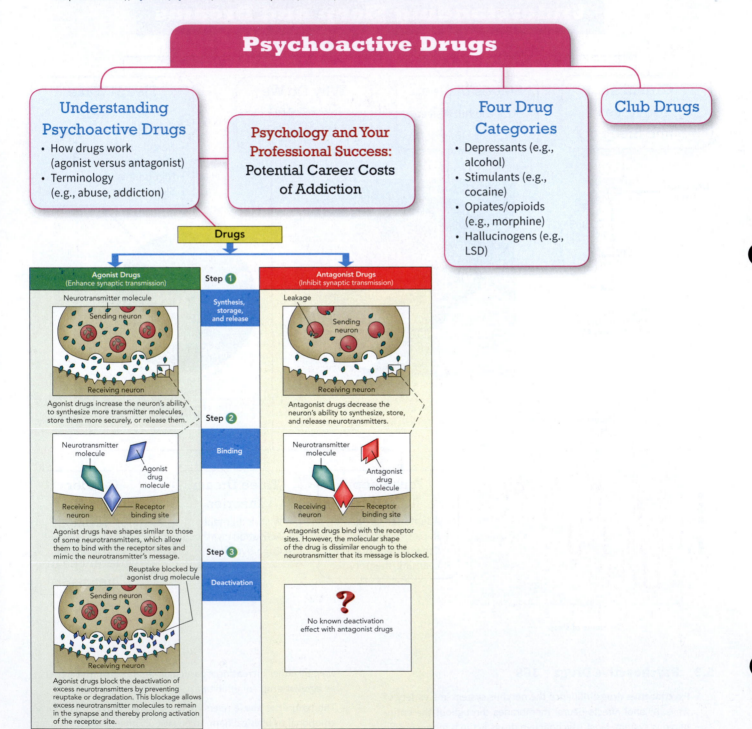

### 5.4  Meditation and Hypnosis  176

- **Meditation** refers to techniques designed to focus attention, block out distractions, and produce an altered state of consciousness (ASC).

- Modern research has removed the mystery surrounding **hypnosis**, a trance-like state of heightened suggestibility, deep relaxation, and intense focus.

**Test Your Critical Thinking**

1. Why is it almost impossible to hypnotize an unwilling participant?

2. Describe the possible health benefits of hypnosis and meditation.

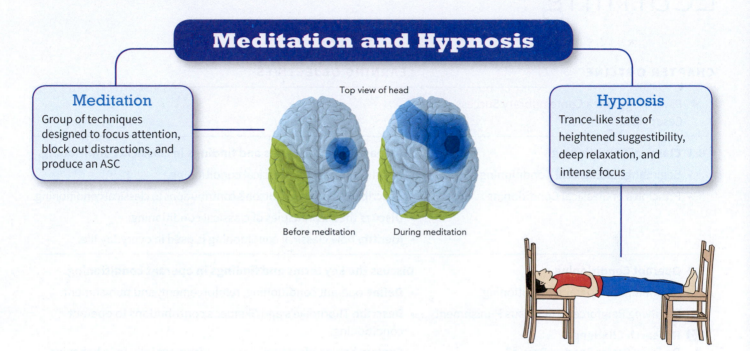

**Meditation and Hypnosis**

**Meditation**
Group of techniques designed to focus attention, block out distractions, and produce an ASC

Top view of head

Before meditation    During meditation

**Hypnosis**
Trance-like state of heightened suggestibility, deep relaxation, and intense focus

# Key Terms

**Retrieval Practice**  *Write a definition for each term before turning back to the referenced page to check your answer.*

- activation–synthesis theory of dreams  163
- adaptation/protection theory of sleep  162
- addiction  168
- agonist  168
- altered state of consciousness (ASC)  153
- antagonist  168
- automatic processes  154
- circadian rhythm  157
- cognitive view of dreams  164
- consciousness  153
- controlled processes  154
- depressant  171
- drug abuse  168

- growth/development theory of sleep  163
- hallucinogen  174
- hypnosis  178
- inattentional blindness  154
- insomnia  165
- latent content of dreams  163
- learning/memory theory of sleep  163
- manifest content of dreams  163
- meditation  177
- narcolepsy  166
- nightmares  167
- non-rapid-eye-movement (NREM) sleep  160

- opiate/opioid  173
- physical dependence  168
- psychoactive drug  168
- psychological dependence  168
- rapid-eye-movement (REM) sleep  160
- repair/restoration theory of sleep  162
- selective attention  153
- sleep apnea  164
- sleep terrors  167
- stimulant  173
- suprachiasmatic nucleus (SCN)  157
- tolerance  169
- wish-fulfillment view of dreams  163
- withdrawal  168

# Learning

| CHAPTER OUTLINE | LEARNING OBJECTIVES |
|---|---|
| ❖ **Psychology and a Contemporary Success**<br>Cesar Millan | |
| **6.1 Classical Conditioning**<br>• Beginnings of Classical Conditioning<br>• Principles of Classical Conditioning | **Summarize the key terms and findings in classical conditioning.**<br>• **Define** learning and classical conditioning.<br>• **Describe** Pavlov's and Watson's contributions to classical conditioning.<br>• **Discuss** the six principles of classical conditioning.<br>• **Identify** how classical conditioning is used in everyday life. |
| **6.2 Operant Conditioning**<br>• Beginnings of Operant Conditioning<br>• Clarifying Reinforcement versus Punishment<br>**RC Research Challenge**<br>**Do Dogs Prefer Food or Praise?**<br>• Principles of Operant Conditioning<br>❖ **Psychology and Your Professional Success**<br>Why Can't We Get Anything Done Around Here? | **Discuss the key terms and findings in operant conditioning.**<br>• **Define** operant conditioning, reinforcement, and punishment.<br>• **Describe** Thorndike's and Skinner's contributions to operant conditioning.<br>• **Explain** how reinforcement and punishment influence behavior.<br>• **Review** the five key principles in operant conditioning.<br>• **Identify** how operant conditioning is used in everyday life.<br>• **Summarize** the major similarities and differences between classical and operant conditioning. |
| **6.3 Cognitive–Social Learning**<br>• Insight Learning and Latent Learning<br>• Observational Learning<br>**RC Research Challenge**<br>**Does the Media Impact Our Body Size Preferences?**<br>❖ **Psychology and Your Personal Success**<br>Can Learning Principles Help You Succeed in College? | **Summarize the key terms and findings in the cognitive–social theory of learning.**<br>• **Describe** insight learning, cognitive maps, and latent learning.<br>• **Discuss** observational learning and Bandura's four key factors. |
| **6.4 Biology of Learning**<br>• Neuroscience and Learning<br>• Biological Primes and Constraints on Learning | **Review the biological factors in learning.**<br>• **Explain** how learning changes our brains.<br>• **Describe** how experiences and enriched environments affect our brains.<br>• **Discuss** the importance of mirror neurons.<br>• **Summarize** the role of evolution in learning. |

184

### ❖ Psychology and a Contemporary Success | Cesar Millan

Dogs live in about 45% of U.S. households. Any guess as to how many of those dogs are perfectly behaved and come every time they're called? Probably a fairly low number! Cesar Millan (1969–) is a world-renowned dog trainer and star of such television series as *Dog Whisperer*, *Cesar 911*, and *Leader of the Pack* (see photo). Millan was born in Mexico and grew up on a farm, where he began his lifelong connection to dogs and earned the nickname "El Perrero," or "dog boy." At the age of 21, he came to the United States illegally, knowing little or no English, and lived on the streets supporting himself with odd jobs, including car washer and dog groomer. Thanks to Millan's growing reputation as a successful handler of difficult animals, television producers eventually offered to create his first show, *Dog Whisperer*, which earned an Emmy Award nomination for outstanding reality program.

Despite achieving this initial public fame and success, being granted U.S. citizenship and marrying his first love, Millan also endured significant personal hardships—his wife asked him for a divorce, his two sons stopped talking to him, and his beloved dog died. Around the same time, he also discovered that he had virtually no money after all his years of hard work. He then attempted to take his own life with an overdose of pills, but was rescued and taken to a hospital. Today, he believes he's fully recovered and is enjoying his extraordinary work rehabilitating aggressive and misbehaving dogs and training their owners to be more effective "pack leaders." His TV series *Dog Whisperer* is broadcast in more than 80 countries and his first three books became *New York Times* best sellers (Mead, 2015; Peltier, 2007). What's his secret?

Mark J. Terrill/AP Photos

*No dog is too much for me to handle. I rehabilitate dogs, I train people. I am the dog whisperer.*

—Cesar Millan

# Chapter Overview

Why did we choose Cesar Millan as our opening famous figure? His life and work capture the essence of this text's two themes—a *growth mindset* and *grit*. Regarding the mindset, Millan has said, "I'm open for possibilities and always eager to learn." And his obvious love for his work and his struggles to overcome several serious life challenges exemplify the power of grit—passion and perseverance in pursuing long-term goals.

Millan's personal story and his work with out-of-control dogs also clearly demonstrate the basic terms, principles, and concepts in this chapter. Like Cesar Millan's dogs and other animals, we human animals need learning in order to survive on this planet. We learn that certain objects or events, such as food or pain, are critical to our well-being (classical conditioning). In addition, we learn to avoid punishing situations and to repeat acts that bring rewards (operant conditioning). Finally, we learn through our thought processes and from watching others (cognitive–social learning). In this chapter, we will study these three forms of learning, followed by an exploration of how our brain and nervous system change as we learn. Along the way, we'll also explore how learning theories and concepts impact our everyday lives (see **Why Study Psychology**).

## Why Study Psychology?

### Did you know that this chapter can . . .

- **Enhance your enjoyment of life?** Unfortunately, many people (who haven't read this text or taken an introductory psychology course) too often choose marital partners hoping to change or "rescue" them. Or they pursue jobs they hate because they want to "make a lot of money." If you carefully study and actively apply the information in this chapter, you can avoid these mistakes and thereby greatly enrich your life.

Tim Robbins/Mint Images/Getty Images

- **Expand your understanding and control of behavior?**    A core research finding from learning theory is that humans and nonhuman animals *do not persist in behaviors that are not reinforced*. Using this information, we can remove reinforcers of destructive or undesirable behaviors and recognize that bad habits will continue until we change the reinforcers. Keep in mind that behavior is not random! Although the reinforcers are sometimes hidden, there's a reason for everything we do.

- **Improve the predictability of your life?**    Another key finding from research in learning is that the *best predictor of future behavior is past behavior*. People can (and do) change, and learned behavior can be unlearned. However, the statistical odds are still high that old patterns of behavior will persist in the future. If you want to predict whether the person you're dating is good marriage or long-term relationship material, look to his or her past.

- **Help you change the world?**    Reinforcement also motivates greedy business practices, unethical political and environmental decisions, prejudice, and war. Knowing this, if we all work together to remove the inappropriate reinforcers, we can truly change the world. Admittedly, this sounds grandiose and simplistic. But we sincerely believe in the power of education and the usefulness of the material in this chapter. Your life and the world around you can be significantly improved with a "simple" application of learning principles.

## 6.1 | Classical Conditioning

### LEARNING OBJECTIVES

**Retrieval Practice**    While reading the upcoming sections, respond to each Learning Objective in your own words.

**Summarize the key terms and findings in classical conditioning.**

- **Define** learning and classical conditioning.

- **Describe** Pavlov's and Watson's contributions to classical conditioning.
- **Discuss** the six principles of classical conditioning.
- **Identify** how classical conditioning is used in everyday life.

*Being ignorant is not so much a shame, as being unwilling to learn.*
—Benjamin Franklin (American Statesman, Scientist, Author)

How did Millan's dogs learn to be less aggressive and out of control? How do dog owners learn to be more effective "pack leaders"? Much of what Millan does with these dogs and their owners is pulled right from the pages of this chapter on learning.

We normally think of learning in terms of classroom activities, such as math and reading, or motor skills, like riding a bike or playing the piano. But for psychologists, learning is an all-encompassing process allowing us to adapt to our ever-changing environment. For example, without the ability to learn, you would not be going to college. In fact, if people couldn't learn, there would be no colleges, no rocket ships to outer space, no computers, and virtually no human civilization. We simply could not exist.

**Learning**    A relatively permanent change in behavior or mental processes caused by experience.

Psychologists define **learning** as a *relatively permanent change in behavior or mental processes caused by experience*. This relative permanence applies to bad habits, like texting while driving or procrastinating instead of studying, as well as to useful behaviors and emotions, such as Millan's rehabilitation of aggressive and misbehaving dogs, your training as a college student to pursue your chosen profession, and even your experience of falling in love.

How do we change our bad habits? From previous experiences, we may have learned that bad habits can be very rewarding, which makes them difficult to change. The good news is that since learning is only "relatively" permanent, it can be changed. With new experiences, previous bad habits and problem behaviors can be replaced with new, more adaptive ones (Bull et al., 2017; Cheng et al., 2017; Gardner et al., 2016). Thus, to break the bad habit of texting while driving, you can force yourself to turn off your phone before starting the car (as we're reminded to do before a movie begins). Instead of procrastinating when it's time to study, you can practice the study skills sprinkled throughout this text.

We begin this chapter with a study of one of the earliest forms of learning, *classical conditioning*, made famous by Pavlov's salivating dogs.

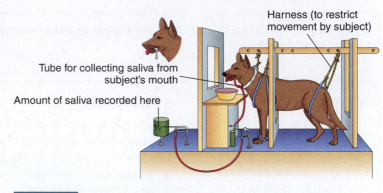

**FIGURE 6.1**  **Pavlov's experimental setup**

# Beginnings of Classical Conditioning

Why does your mouth water when you stare at a large slice of delicious cake or a juicy steak? The answer to this question was accidentally discovered in the laboratory of Russian physiologist Ivan Pavlov (1849–1936). Pavlov's initial plan was to study the role of saliva in digestion by using a tube attached to dogs' salivary glands (**Figure 6.1**).

During these experiments, one of Pavlov's students noticed that even before receiving the actual food, many dogs began salivating at the mere sight of the food, the food dish, the smell of the food, or even just the sight of the person who normally delivered the food! Pavlov's genius was in recognizing the importance of this "unscheduled" salivation. He realized that the dogs were not only responding on the basis of hunger (a biological need), but also as a result of experience or learning.

Excited by this accidental discovery, Pavlov and his students conducted several experiments, including sounding a tone on a tuning fork just before food was placed in the dogs' mouths. After several pairings of the tone and food, dogs in the laboratory began to salivate on hearing the tone alone.

Pavlov and later researchers found that many things can become conditioned stimuli for salivation if they are paired with food—a bell, a buzzer, a light, and even the sight of a circle or triangle drawn on a card. This type of learning, called **classical conditioning**, develops through involuntary, passive, paired associations (McSweeney & Murphy, 2017). More specifically, a neutral stimulus (such as the tone on a tuning fork) comes to elicit a response after repeated pairings with a naturally occurring stimulus (like food).

To fully understand classical conditioning and how it applies to our everyday life, the first step is to recognize that *conditioning* is simply another word for learning. Next, we need to explain that classical conditioning is a three-step process—*before*, *during*, and *after conditioning*. This process is explained in detail below and visually summarized in **Step-by-Step Diagram 6.1**.

**Step 1**  Before conditioning, the sound of the tone does NOT lead to salivation, which makes the tone a **neutral stimulus (NS)**. Conversely, food naturally brings about salivation, which makes food an *unlearned*, **unconditioned stimulus (US)**. The initial reflex of salivation also is *unlearned*, so it is called an **unconditioned response (UR)**.

**Step 2**  During conditioning, the tuning fork is repeatedly sounded right before the presentation of the food (US).

**Step 3**  After conditioning, the tone alone will bring about salivation. At this point, we can say that the dog is *classically conditioned*. The previously neutral stimulus (NS) (the tone) has now become a *learned*, **conditioned stimulus (CS)** that produces a *learned*, **conditioned response (CR)** (the dog's salivation). (Note that the "R" in UR in Step 1 and the CR in this Step 3 refers to both "reflex" and "response.")

**Classical conditioning**
Learning that develops through involuntarily paired associations; a previously neutral stimulus (NS) is paired (associated) with an unconditioned stimulus (US) to elicit a conditioned response (CR).

**Neutral stimulus (NS)**  A stimulus that, before conditioning, does not naturally bring about the response of interest.

**Unconditioned stimulus (US)**  A stimulus that elicits an unconditioned response (UR) without previous conditioning.

**Unconditioned response (UR)**  An unlearned reaction to an unconditioned stimulus (US) that occurs without previous conditioning.

**Conditioned stimulus (CS)**  A previously neutral stimulus (NS) that, after repeated pairings with an unconditioned stimulus (US), comes to elicit a conditioned response (CR).

**Conditioned response (CR)**  A learned reaction to a conditioned stimulus (CS) that occurs after previous repeated pairings with an unconditioned stimulus (US).

**STEP-BY-STEP DIAGRAM 6.1** | **The Beginnings and a Modern Application of Classical Conditioning**

**STOP!** This Step-by-Step Diagram contains essential information NOT found elsewhere in the text, which is likely to appear on quizzes and exams. Be sure to study it CAREFULLY!

**Study Tip**

*Use this figure to help you visualize and organize the three major stages of classical conditioning and their associated key terms. Also, remember conditioning is essentially the same as learning. In addition, when thinking of a US or UR, picture how a newborn baby, with little or no previous learning, would respond. The baby's innate, unlearned response to the US would be the UR.*

Pavlov's initial experiment used a metronome, a ticking instrument designed to mark exact time, and he later used a bell. However, his most scientifically researched and best-known method (depicted here) involved a tone from a tuning fork. As you can see, the basic process of classical conditioning is simple. Just as you've been classically conditioned to respond to your cell phone's tones, or possibly to just the sight of a pizza box, Pavlov's dogs learned to respond to a tuning fork's tone. Unfortunately, many students get confused by these technical terms. So here's a tip that might help: The actual stimuli (tone and food) remain the same—only their names change from neutral to conditioned or from unconditioned to conditioned. A similar name change happens for the response (salivation)—from unconditioned to conditioned.

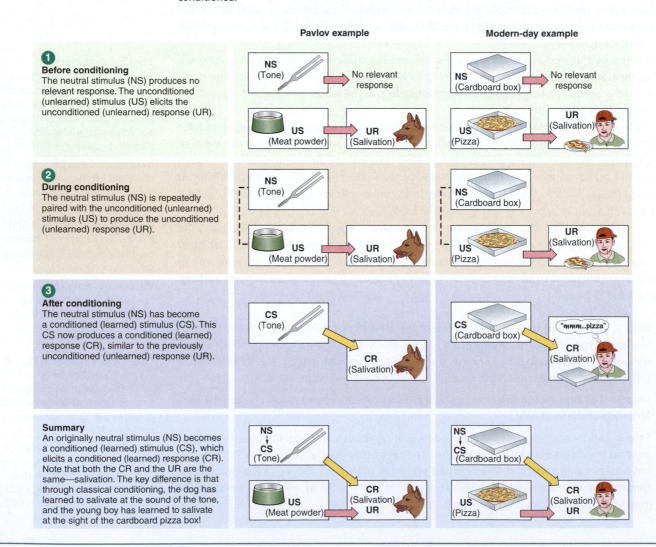

**Pavlov example**          **Modern-day example**

**1 Before conditioning**
The neutral stimulus (NS) produces no relevant response. The unconditioned (unlearned) stimulus (US) elicits the unconditioned (unlearned) response (UR).

**2 During conditioning**
The neutral stimulus (NS) is repeatedly paired with the unconditioned (unlearned) stimulus (US) to produce the unconditioned (unlearned) response (UR).

**3 After conditioning**
The neutral stimulus (NS) has become a conditioned (learned) stimulus (CS). This CS now produces a conditioned (learned) response (CR), similar to the previously unconditioned (unlearned) response (UR).

**Summary**
An originally neutral stimulus (NS) becomes a conditioned (learned) stimulus (CS), which elicits a conditioned (learned) response (CR). Note that both the CR and the UR are the same—salivation. The key difference is that through classical conditioning, the dog has learned to salivate at the sound of the tone, and the young boy has learned to salivate at the sight of the cardboard pizza box!

In sum, the overall goal of Pavlov's classical conditioning was for the dog to learn to associate the tone with the unconditioned stimulus (food) and then to show the same response (salivation) to the tone as to the food. Using similar classical conditioning techniques, Millan's dogs learn to associate a specific sound ("tsch") with an unwanted behavior. After training, the dog stops the behavior at the sound alone, without the need for additional correction.

So what do Pavlov's and Millan's dogs have to do with your everyday life? Classical conditioning is a fundamental way that all animals, including humans, learn. Just as you may have learned to salivate at the sight of a pizza box (see again Step-by-Step Diagram 6.1), alcoholics often report cravings for a drink after a quick glance at a TV commercial showing alcoholic beverages. Also, laboratory experiments show that cigarette smokers can be trained to develop cravings for a cigarette after seeing a simple geometric design if it was previously paired with cigarette-related cues (Deweese et al., 2016). Classical conditioning also explains why so many of us turn to food when we're upset (see **Figure 6.2**).

Like the cravings for cigarettes or comfort foods, most of our human emotions, including the excitement of gambling, love for our family and significant others, and the almost universal fear of public speaking, are learned through the process of classical conditioning. How do we learn to be afraid of public speaking or of typically harmless things like mice and elevators? In a now-famous experiment, John Watson and Rosalie Rayner (1920) demonstrated how a fear of rats could be classically conditioned.

In this study, a healthy 11-month-old child, later known as "Little Albert," was first allowed to play with a white laboratory rat. Like most other infants, Albert was curious and reached for the rat, showing no fear. Knowing that infants are naturally frightened by loud noises, Watson stood behind Albert and when he reached for the rat, Watson banged a steel bar with a hammer. The loud noise obviously frightened the child and made him cry. The rat was paired with the loud noise only seven times before Albert became classically conditioned and demonstrated fear of the rat even without the noise (**Figure 6.3**). The rat had become a CS that brought about the CR (fear).

Although this deliberate experimental creation of what's now called a **conditioned emotional response (CER)** remains a classic in psychology, it has been heavily criticized and would never be allowed today (Antes, 2016; Avieli et al., 2016; Ethical Principles of Psychologists, 2016). The research procedures used by Watson and Rayner violated several current ethical guidelines for scientific research (Chapter 1). They not only deliberately created a serious fear in a child, but they also ended their experiment without *extinguishing* (removing) it. In addition, the researchers have been criticized because they did not measure Albert's fear objectively. Their subjective evaluation raises doubt about the degree of fear conditioned.

**"I think we need to have a chat about your 'support team'..."**

**FIGURE 6.2** **Classical conditioning and emotional eating (EE)** As shown in this cartoon, and documented in a recent experiment (Bongers & Jansen, 2017), negative emotions can act as conditioned stimuli (CS) that lead to the conditioned response (CR) of hunger—particularly for so-called "comfort foods"—in this case, wine, cake, and cupcakes.

Tim Cordell/CartoonStock

**Conditioned emotional response (CER)** An emotion, such as fear, that becomes a learned, conditioned response to a previously neutral stimulus (NS), such as a loud noise.

**FIGURE 6.3** **Conditioning Little Albert's fears** Watson and Rayner's famous Little Albert study demonstrated how some fears can originate through conditioning. Using classical conditioning terms, we would say that the white rat (a neutral stimulus/NS) was initially paired with the loud noise (an unconditioned stimulus/US) to produce a conditioned stimulus (CS)—the white rat. Then, just the appearance of the white rat would elicit Little Albert's conditioned emotional response (CER)—his fear of the rat. Note again that just as the CR and UR (salivation) were the same for Pavlov's dogs, the CER and UR (fear) are the same for Little Albert. The key difference is that through classical conditioning the infant learned to fear just the sight of the white rat.

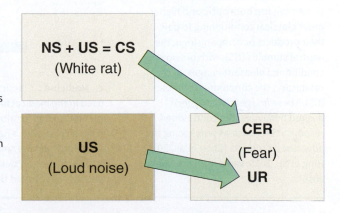

Despite such criticisms, this study of Little Albert and follow-up research led to our current understanding that many of our likes, dislikes, prejudices, and fears are examples of *conditioned emotional responses (CERs)*. For example, if your romantic partner always uses the same shampoo, simply the smell of that shampoo may soon elicit a positive response. In Chapter 15, you'll discover how Watson's research later led to powerful clinical tools for eliminating exaggerated and irrational fears of a specific object or situation, known as *phobias* (Cheng et al., 2017; Pear, 2016). For more examples of how classical conditioning impacts everyday life, see **Concept Organizer 6.1**.

---

## CONCEPT ORGANIZER 6.1

### Classical Conditioning in Everyday Life

**STOP!** This Concept Organizer contains essential information NOT found elsewhere in the text, which is likely to appear on quizzes and exams. Be sure to study it CAREFULLY!

**a. Prejudice** How do children, like the one holding the KKK sign in this photo, develop prejudice at such an early age? Research shows that prejudice may be a combination of psychological, biological, and cultural factors (Conger et al., 2012; Hughes et al., 2016; Mallan et al., 2013). As shown in the diagram, children are naturally upset and fearful (UR) when they see that their parents are upset and afraid (US). Over time, they may learn to associate their parents' reaction with all members of a disliked group (CS), thus becoming prejudiced like their parents.

**NS + US = CS**
(Member of disliked group)

**US**
(Parent's negative reaction)

**CR**
(Child is upset and fearful)
**UR**

Randy Olsen/NG Image Collection

Jim Holden/Alamy Stock Photo

**b. Advertising** Magazine ads, TV commercials, and business promotions often use both basic and higher-order classical conditioning to pair their products or company logo, the neutral stimulus (NS), with previously conditioned pleasant images, like celebrities, the conditioned stimulus (CS). These images then trigger desired behaviors, the conditioned response (CR), such as purchasing the advertised products (Chen et al., 2014; Hing et al., 2015; van der Pligt & Vliek, 2016).

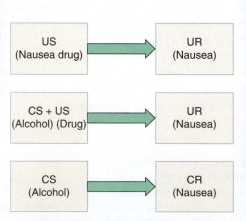

**US**
(Nausea drug) → **UR**
(Nausea)

**CS + US**
(Alcohol) (Drug) → **UR**
(Nausea)

**CS**
(Alcohol) → **CR**
(Nausea)

**c. Medicine** Classical conditioning also is used in the medical field. For example, a treatment designed for alcohol-addicted patients pairs alcohol with a nausea-producing drug. Afterward, just the smell or taste of alcohol makes the person sick. Some, but not all, patients have found this treatment helpful.

Rex/Shutterstock

**d. Politics** Politicians often use classical conditioning to create a positive conditioned emotional response (CER) toward themselves and/or a negative CER against their opponents. Can you see how this type of conditioning explains why politicians so often surround themselves with American flags or kiss babies? What other stimuli and symbols do politicians use that are based on classical conditioning?

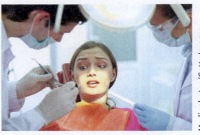

**FIGURE 6.4** **Why are so many people afraid of dentists?** Imagine being seated in a dental chair and hearing the sound of the dentist's drill. Even though the drill is nowhere near you, its sound immediately makes you feel anxious. Your anxiety is obviously not innate. Little babies don't cringe at the sound of a dental drill, unless it's very loud. Your fear is learned primarily through classical conditioning. The good news is that your dental fears and even serious dental phobias can be successfully treated (see Chapters 14 and 15).

*Mediaphotos/Getty Images*

## Principles of Classical Conditioning

We've just seen how a loud noise was used to condition Little Albert's fear of rats. But how would we explain common fears, such as being afraid of dentists or just the sound of a dentist's drill? As shown in **Figure 6.4**, your fear of the drill, and maybe of dentistry in general, is not innate. Instead, it involves one or more of the six classical conditioning principles summarized in **Concept Organizer 6.2** and discussed in detail below.

**CONCEPT ORGANIZER 6.2** **Six Principles and Applications of Classical Conditioning**

| Process | Description | Example |
|---|---|---|
| **Acquisition** | Learning occurs (is acquired) when an organism involuntarily links a neutral stimulus (NS) with an unconditioned stimulus (US), which in turn elicits the conditioned response (CR) and/or conditioned emotional response (CER) | You learn to fear (CER) a dentist's drill (CS) because you associate it with the pain of your dental work (US). |
| **Generalization** | Conditioned response (CR) and/or a conditioned emotional response (CER) come to be involuntarily elicited not only by the conditioned stimulus (CS), but also by stimuli similar to the CS; the opposite of discrimination | You generalize your fear of the dentist's drill to your dentist's office and other dentists' offices. |
| **Discrimination** | Learned ability to distinguish (discriminate) between similar stimuli so as NOT to involuntarily respond to a new stimulus as if it were the previously conditioned stimulus (CS); the opposite of generalization | You are not afraid of your physician's office because you've learned to differentiate it from your dentist's office. |
| **Extinction** | Gradual diminishing of a conditioned response (CR) and/or a conditioned emotional response (CER) when the unconditioned stimulus (US) is no longer paired with the conditioned stimulus (CS) | You return several times to your dentist's office for routine checkups, with no dental drill; your fear of the dentist's office (CER) gradually diminishes. |
| **Spontaneous recovery** | Reappearance of a previously extinguished conditioned response (CR) and/or conditioned emotional response (CER) | While watching a movie depicting dental drilling, your previous fear (CER) suddenly returns. |
| **Higher-order conditioning** | A new conditioned stimulus (CS) is created by pairing it with a previously conditioned stimulus (CS) | You fear the sign outside your dentist's office, an originally neutral stimulus (NS). Why? It has become a conditioned stimulus (CS) associated with the previously conditioned stimulus (CS) of the dental drill. |

### Try This Yourself

#### Identifying Principles of Classical Conditioning

____ **1.** The mere smell of coffee helps wake me up in the morning.

____ **2.** The sound of ocean waves makes me cringe but hearing raindrops falling makes me smile.

____ **3.** I used to enjoy eating hamburgers, but after months on a vegetarian diet, I no longer want to eat meat.

____ **4.** Pictures of my ex-girlfriend on Facebook made me suddenly sad even though we broke up months ago.

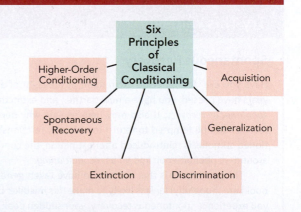

**Answers:** (1) acquisition, (2) discrimination, (3) extinction, (4) spontaneous recovery. Note that adding additional examples from your personal life will further help you understand, appreciate, and master the principles of classical conditioning.

**Acquisition (in classical conditioning)**  The process by which learning occurs (is acquired) when an organism involuntarily links a neutral stimulus (NS) with an unconditioned stimulus (US), which in turn elicits the conditioned response (CR).

**Generalization (in classical conditioning)**  The process by which a conditioned response (CR) spreads (generalizes) and comes to be involuntarily elicited not only by the conditioned stimulus (CS), but also by stimuli similar to the CS; the opposite of discrimination.

**Discrimination (in classical conditioning)**  A learned ability to distinguish (discriminate) between similar stimuli so as NOT to involuntarily respond to a new stimulus as if it were the previously conditioned stimulus (CS); the opposite of generalization.

**Extinction (in classical conditioning)**  The gradual diminishing of a conditioned response (CR) when the unconditioned stimulus (US) is no longer paired with the conditioned stimulus (CS).

**Spontaneous recovery**  The reappearance of a previously extinguished conditioned response (CR).

**Higher-order conditioning**  The process by which a new conditioned stimulus (CS) is created by pairing it with a previously conditioned stimulus (CS); also known as second-order conditioning.

1. **Acquisition**  In the basic **acquisition** phase, learning occurs (is acquired) when an organism involuntarily links a neutral stimulus (NS) with an unconditioned stimulus (US). This acquisition in turn elicits the conditioned response (CR). Pavlov's original (accidental) discovery of classical conditioning involved this mechanism, but he later went on to conduct numerous experiments beyond the acquisition phase.

2. **Generalization**  One of Pavlov's most interesting findings was that stimuli similar to the original conditioned stimulus (CS) also can elicit the conditioned response (CR). For example, after first conditioning dogs to salivate to the sound of low-pitched tones, Pavlov later demonstrated that the dogs would also salivate in response to higher-pitched tones. Similarly, after Watson and Rayner's conditioning experiment, Little Albert learned to fear not only rats, but also a rabbit, a dog, and a bearded Santa Claus mask. This process, by which a conditioned response (CR) spreads (generalizes) and comes to be involuntarily elicited not only by the conditioned stimulus (CS) but also by stimuli similar to the CS, is called stimulus **generalization** (Davidson et al., 2016; El-Bar et al., 2017; Pear, 2016).

3. **Discrimination**  Just as Pavlov's dogs learned to generalize and respond to similar stimuli in a similar way, they also learned to *discriminate* between similar stimuli. For example, when he gave the dogs food following a high-pitched tone, but not when he used a low-pitched tone, he found that they learned the difference between the two tones and only salivated to the high-pitched one. Likewise, Little Albert learned to recognize differences between rats and other stimuli and presumably overcame his fear of these other stimuli. This learned ability to distinguish (discriminate) between similar stimuli so as NOT to involuntarily respond to a new stimulus as if it were the previously conditioned stimulus (CS) is known as stimulus **discrimination**.

4. **Extinction**  What do you think happened when Pavlov repeatedly sounded the tone without presenting food? The answer is that the dogs' salivation gradually declined, a process Pavlov called **extinction**. This term is defined as the gradual diminishing of a conditioned response (CR) when the unconditioned stimulus (US) is no longer paired with the conditioned stimulus (CS). Without continued association with the US, the CS loses its power to elicit the CR.

5. **Spontaneous recovery**  It's important to note that extinction is not complete unlearning. It does not fully "erase" the learned connection between the stimulus and the response (González et al., 2016; John & Pineño, 2015). Pavlov found that sometimes, after a CR had apparently been extinguished, if he sounded the tone once again, the dogs would occasionally still salivate. This reappearance of a previously extinguished conditioned response (CR) is called **spontaneous recovery** (see the **Try This Yourself**).

6. **Higher-order conditioning**  The phenomenon of **higher-order conditioning** takes basic classical conditioning one step higher. Also known as "second-order conditioning," this process refers to a situation in which a previously neutral stimulus (NS) (like a tone) is first made into a conditioned stimulus (CS) by pairing it with an unconditioned stimulus (US) (such as food). Next, the previously conditioned stimulus (CS) is used as a basis for creating a NEW CS (like a flashing light) that produces its own conditioned response (CR). In short, a new CS is created by pairing it with a previously created CS (**Step-by-Step Diagram 6.2**).

## Try This Yourself

### Spontaneous Recovery

Have you ever felt renewed excitement at the sight of a former girlfriend or boyfriend, even though years have passed, you have a new partner, and extinction has occurred? This may be an example of *spontaneous recovery*. It also may help explain why people might misinterpret a sudden flare-up of feelings and be tempted to return to unhappy relationships. To make matters worse, when a conditioned stimulus is reintroduced after extinction, the conditioning occurs much faster the second time around—a phenomenon known as *reconditioning*.

The good news is that those who have taken general psychology (or are currently reading this book) are (hopefully) far less likely to make this mistake. Looking at **Figure 6.5**, you can see that even if you experience spontaneous recovery, your sudden peak of feelings for the old love partner will gradually return to their previously extinguished state. So don't overreact.

GoodMood Photo/Shutterstock

**FIGURE 6.5** **Three key principles of classical conditioning** During acquisition, the strength of the conditioned response (CR) rapidly increases and then levels off near its maximum. During extinction, the CR declines erratically until it is extinguished. After a "rest" period in which the organism is not exposed to the conditioned stimulus (CS), spontaneous recovery may occur, and the CS will once again elicit a (weakened) CR. Note that the CR once again gradually diminishes after the spontaneous recovery because the CS is alone and not paired with the US.

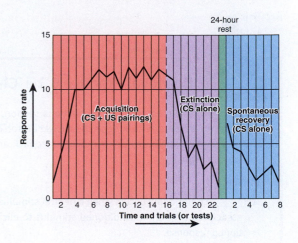

**STEP-BY-STEP DIAGRAM 6.2** | **The Power of Higher-Order Conditioning**

**STOP!** This Step-by-Step Diagram contains essential information NOT found elsewhere in the text, which is likely to appear on quizzes and exams. Be sure to study it CAREFULLY!

Children are not born salivating at the sight of McDonald's golden arches. So why do they beg adults to take them to "Mickey D's" after simply seeing an ad showing the golden arches? It's because of higher-order conditioning, which occurs when a new conditioned stimulus (CS) is created by pairing it with a previously conditioned stimulus (CS).

**Pavlov's dogs**    **Children and McDonald's**

**1 First-order conditioning**
If you wanted to demonstrate higher-order conditioning in Pavlov's dogs, you would first condition the dogs to pair up the sound of the tone with the food. Similarly, children first learn to pair McDonald's restaurants with the food.

**2 Pairing NS with previously conditioned CS**
Then, with Pavlov's dogs, you might pair a flash of light with the previously conditioned stimulus (CS)—the tone. Similarly, children learn to pair the two golden arches with the McDonald's restaurant.

**3 Higher-order conditioning**
Eventually, the dogs would salivate in response to the flash of light alone. Similarly, children salivate and beg to eat at Mickey D's when they see the golden arches.

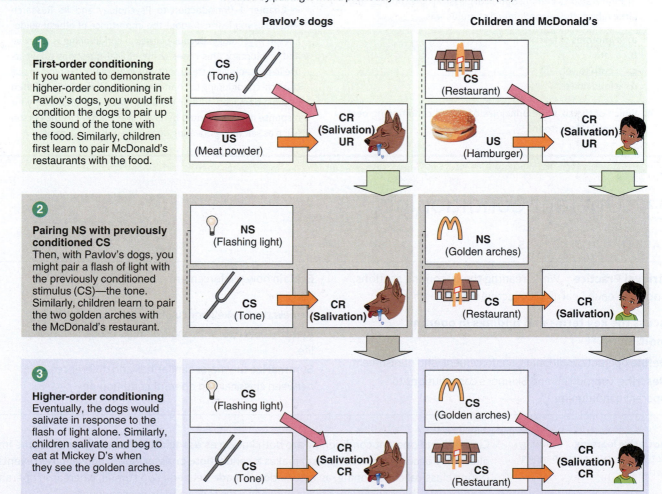

## Retrieval Practice 6.1 | Classical Conditioning

Completing this self-test and the connections section, and then checking your answers by clicking on the answer button or by looking in Appendix B, will provide immediate feedback and helpful practice for exams.

### Self-Test

1. _____ conditioning occurs when a neutral stimulus becomes associated with an unconditioned stimulus to elicit a conditioned response.

   a. Reflex
   b. Instinctive
   c. Classical
   d. Basic

2. A young child learns to fear dogs after being bitten. In this situation, the conditioned emotional response (CER) is _____.

   a. the dog
   b. the bite
   c. fear
   d. none of these options

3. In John Watson's demonstration of classical conditioning with Little Albert, the unconditioned stimulus was _____.

   a. symptoms of fear
   b. a rat
   c. a bath towel
   d. a loud noise

4. Which of the six basic principles of classic conditioning best explain(s) this cartoon? _____.

"I don't care if she is a tape dispenser.  I love her."

5. Extinction in classical conditioning occurs when the_____.

   a. conditioned stimulus is no longer paired with the unconditioned response
   b. unconditioned stimulus is withheld or removed
   c. conditioned response is no longer paired with the unconditioned stimulus
   d. unconditioned stimulus is ambiguous

### Connections—Chapter to Chapter

Answering the following question will help you "look back and look ahead" to see the important connections among the various subfields of psychology and chapters within this text.

In Chapter 1 (Introduction to Psychology and Its Research Methods), you learned about the importance of ethical guidelines in psychology. Because classical conditioning is reflexive and involuntary, this raises some ethical questions about its use in psychological treatment. For example, is it ethical to use classical conditioning to change unwanted behavior in children or brain-damaged adults? Would it make a difference to your response if the unwanted behavior was harmful to the person (such as self-biting or eating nonedible household items)?

---

## 6.2 | Operant Conditioning

### LEARNING OBJECTIVES

**Retrieval Practice**   While reading the upcoming sections, respond to each Learning Objective in your own words.

**Discuss the key terms and findings in operant conditioning.**

- **Define** operant conditioning, reinforcement, and punishment.
- **Describe** Thorndike's and Skinner's contributions to operant conditioning.

- **Explain** how reinforcement and punishment influence behavior.
- **Review** the five key principles in operant conditioning.
- **Identify** how operant conditioning is used in everyday life.
- **Summarize** the major similarities and differences between classical and operant conditioning.

---

**Associative learning**   Learning that two events occur or happen together.

Classical and operant conditioning are both known as **associative learning**. As the name implies, they occur when an organism makes a connection, or association, between two events. During classical conditioning, an association is made between two stimuli, whereas in operant conditioning the association is made between a response and its consequences.

**FIGURE 6.6** **Classical versus operant conditioning** Classical conditioning is based on involuntary behavior, whereas operant conditioning is based on voluntary behavior.

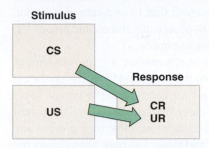

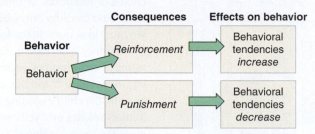

**a. Classical conditioning** The subject is passive while the previously neutral stimulus (NS) is paired with an unconditioned stimulus (US). After repeated pairings, the NS becomes a conditioned stimulus (CS) that leads to a conditioned response (CR).

**b. Operant conditioning** The subject is active and voluntarily "operates" on the environment. The consequences (reinforcement or punishment) that follow the behavior determine whether the behavioral tendencies will increase or decrease.

As we've just seen, classical conditioning is based on what happens *before* we *involuntarily* respond: Something happens to us, and we learn a new response. In contrast, **operant conditioning** is based on what happens *after* we *voluntarily* perform a behavior (McSweeney & Murphy, 2017; Pear, 2016). We do something and learn from the consequences. If a behavior is followed by reinforcement, it increases. If it's followed by punishment, it decreases (**Figure 6.6**).

The key point to remember is that *consequences* are the heart of operant conditioning. In classical conditioning, consequences are irrelevant—Pavlov's dogs still got to eat whether they salivated or not. But in operant conditioning, the organism voluntarily performs a behavior (an operant) that produces a consequence—either reinforcement or punishment—and the behavior then either increases or decreases. For example, Millan teaches pet owners to use operant conditioning to make their dogs earn all rewards by working for them.

It's also very important to note that **reinforcement** is the process by which adding or taking away a stimulus following a response increases the likelihood that the response will be repeated. **Punishment**, in contrast, involves adding or taking away a stimulus following a response and thereby decreasing the likelihood that the response will be repeated. Before going on, check your understanding of operant conditioning with the following **Myth Busters**.

## Beginnings of Operant Conditioning

In the early 1900s, Edward Thorndike, a pioneer of operant conditioning, was the first to identify that the frequency of a behavior is controlled by its consequences (Thorndike, 1911). Today this is known as Thorndike's **law of effect**, which further clarifies that any behavior followed by pleasant consequences is likely to be repeated, whereas any behavior followed by unpleasant consequences is likely to be stopped. Thorndike's findings were based on his study of cats in puzzle boxes (**Figure 6.7**).

B. F. Skinner later extended Thorndike's law of effect to more complex behaviors. However, he carefully avoided Thorndike's use of terms like *pleasant* and *unpleasant* because they are

**Operant conditioning** A form of associative learning in which behavior increases if followed by reinforcement and decreases if followed by punishment; also known as instrumental conditioning.

**Reinforcement** A process by which adding or removing a stimulus following a response increases the likelihood that the response will be repeated.

**Punishment** A process by which adding or removing a stimulus following a response decreases the likelihood that the response will be repeated.

**Law of effect** Thorndike's rule that any behavior followed by pleasant consequences is likely to be repeated, whereas any behavior followed by unpleasant consequences is likely to be stopped.

## Myth Busters

### True or False?

1. The most logical and efficient way to maintain a desired behavior is to reward every response.

2. Punishment is a very effective way to change long-term behavior.

3. Negative reinforcement is another type of punishment.

4. Prejudiced and superstitious people are born that way.

5. Gamblers persist because they're on a partial schedule of reinforcement.

**Answer:** All but one of these are false. Detailed answers can be found in the following pages.

**FIGURE 6.7** **Thorndike's law of effect** In his most famous experiment, Thorndike put a cat inside a specially built puzzle box. When the cat stepped on a pedal inside the box (at first by chance), the door opened, and the cat could get out and eat. Then, through trial and error, the cat learned what specific actions led to opening the door. With each additional success, the cat's actions became more purposeful, and it soon learned to open the door immediately (Thorndike, 1898).

subjective and not directly observable. Furthermore, Skinner argued that such words make unfounded assumptions about what an organism feels or wants and imply that behavior is due to conscious choice or intention. Skinner believed that to understand behavior, we should consider only external, observable stimuli and responses. We must look outside the learner, not inside.

Skinner also talked about reinforcement and punishment in terms of *increasing* or *decreasing* the likelihood of the response being repeated. If a toddler whines for candy, and the parent easily gives in, the child's whining will likely increase. But what if the parent initially refuses and yells at the child for whining, then gives in and gives the child a lollipop? The child might feel both happy to get the candy and sad because the parent is upset. Because we can't know the full extent of the child's internal, mixed feelings, it's cleaner (and more scientific) to limit our focus to observable behaviors and consequences. If the child's whining for lollipops increases, we can say that whining was reinforced. If it decreases, then it was punished.

In keeping with his focus on external, observable stimuli and responses, Skinner emphasized that reinforcement and punishment should always be presented *after* the targeted behavior has occurred. This was because Skinner believed that the only way to know how we have influenced an organism's behavior is to check whether it increases or decreases. As he pointed out, we too often think we're reinforcing or punishing behavior when we're actually doing the opposite (see the following **Try This Yourself**).

---

## Try This Yourself

### The Challenge of Reinforcement

A professor may think she is encouraging shy students to talk by repeatedly praising them each time they speak up in class. But what if you are one of those shy students and are embarrassed by this extra attention? If so, you may actually decrease the number of times you talk in class. Can you see why it's important to always remember that what is reinforcing or punishing for one person may not be so for another?

---

**Primary reinforcer** Any unlearned, innate stimulus (like food, water, or sex) that reinforces a response and thus increases the probability that it will recur.

**Secondary reinforcer** Any learned stimulus (like money, praise, or attention) that reinforces a response and thus increases the probability that it will recur.

**Positive reinforcement** A process by which adding (or presenting) a stimulus following a response increases the likelihood that the response will be repeated.

**Negative reinforcement** A process by which taking away (or removing) a stimulus following a response increases the likelihood that the response will be repeated.

## Clarifying Reinforcement versus Punishment

Until now, we've only discussed reinforcement and punishment in general terms. But we also need to clarify exactly how they either increase or decrease behavior. To begin, you need to understand that psychologists group reinforcers into two types, primary and secondary. A **primary reinforcer** is any unlearned, innate stimulus (like food, water, or sex) that reinforces a response and thus increases the probability that it will recur. A **secondary reinforcer** is any learned stimulus (like money, praise, or attention) that reinforces a response and thus increases the probability that it will recur. The key point is that "primary" is another word for unlearned, whereas "secondary" means learned. Note that the term *primary* may seem to imply that primary reinforcers are the most critical or powerful kind. But as you'll see in the following **Research Challenge**, that's not always the case.

It's also important to note that both primary and secondary reinforcers can produce **positive reinforcement** or **negative reinforcement**, depending on whether certain stimuli are added or taken away. *Positive reinforcement* is a process by which adding (or presenting) a stimulus following a response increases the likelihood that the response will be repeated.

## Research Challenge

### Do Dogs Prefer Food or Praise?

Did you know that dogs were the first domesticated species, or that they're currently the most loved household pets around the world, with the United States having the largest population of dogs, followed by Brazil and China (A Guide to Worldwide Pet Ownership, 2016)?

Both humans and dogs have clearly benefited from their shared social bonding. But how do we explain why dogs have become so uniquely gifted at attending to and interpreting social cues from humans (e.g., Müller et al., 2015)? Is it because humans generally provide dogs with food, a *primary reinforcer*? Or are dogs more interested in *secondary reinforcers*, like praise and human social interactions?

Previous studies attempting to answer this question have found it difficult to separate food and social rewards during training or to measure their relative contributions to learning. However, recent advances in canine fMRI brain scans (Andics et al., 2016; Cook et al., 2015) have allowed scientists to examine the precise neural mechanisms involved in the bond between humans and dogs.

For example, a recent examination of food versus social rewards (Cook et al., 2016) used scans of the brains of 15 dogs of various breeds. The researchers scanned the dogs' brains while their owners praised them and when they received food. The scans revealed that 13 of the 15 dogs showed equal or higher levels of activity in brain areas responsible for decision making and for signaling rewards when they were praised versus when they received food. To confirm that the differences were solely driven by the value of social praise, the researchers then conducted a follow-up brain-scan study in which the praise was withheld on some trials, and the findings strongly correlated with those of the first study.

To see how the dogs responded outside the brain-imaging equipment, the researchers then used a Y-shaped maze and placed the dogs' owners on one side of the Y, with a bowl of treats on the other. As predicted, most of the canines preferred to go the direction of their owner versus the food. Interestingly, the dogs that showed a greater reaction to food in the scanner also chose food in the maze.

Can you see why this research is so important? Millions of dogs are now providing invaluable services in a variety of occupations, including as guide dogs for the blind, as companions or therapy animals, and as herders, hunters, and trackers. They also serve in wars, in search-and-rescue operations, and in the detection of drugs and dangerous explosives. Given these multiple roles, the scientists in this study suggest that brain scans could better match certain dogs with specific service assignments. For example, therapy jobs requiring close human contact might be better for dogs with a higher preference for praise. In contrast, dogs with a

Winnie Au/fStop/Getty Images

lower need for praise might do better in more independent settings like herding and hunting, where the dogs traditionally receive a treat after successfully completing a task.

What's the take-home message for most of us who only ask our dogs to serve as our loyal friends and playmates? The authors of this study concluded that "social reinforcement is at least as effective as food—and probably healthier too" (Cook et al., 2016, p. 17).

#### Test Yourself

1. Based on the information provided, did the second follow-up study using the Y-shaped maze (Cook et al., 2016) use descriptive, correlational, and/or experimental research?

2. If you chose:

   ○ *descriptive research*, is this a naturalistic observation, survey/interview, case study, and/or archival research?

   ○ *correlational research*, is this a positive, negative, or zero correlation?

   ○ *experimental research*, label the IV, DV, experimental group(s), and control group. (Note: If participants were not randomly assigned to groups, list it as a *quasi-experimental design*.)

   ○ both *descriptive* and *correlational*, answer the corresponding questions for both.

**Check your answers by clicking on the answer button or by looking in Appendix B.**

**Note:** The information provided in this study is admittedly limited, but the level of detail is similar to what is presented in most textbooks and public reports of research findings. Answering these questions, and then comparing your answers to those provided, will help you become a better critical thinker and consumer of scientific research.

---

*Negative reinforcement* is a process by which taking away (or removing) a stimulus following a response increases the likelihood that the response will be repeated (**Table 6.1**).

We readily admit that this terminology is very confusing because positive normally means something "good" and negative generally means something "bad." But recall that Skinner cautioned us to avoid subjective terms like good and bad or pleasant and unpleasant because

**TABLE 6.1    How Reinforcement Increases (or Strengthens) Behavior**

| | Positive Reinforcement | Negative Reinforcement |
| --- | --- | --- |
| | Stimulus added (+) and behavior increases | Stimulus taken away (−) and behavior increases |
| **Primary Reinforcers** Unlearned, innate stimuli that reinforce and increase the probability of a response | You put money in the vending machine, and a snack comes out. The addition of the snack makes it more likely you will put money in the vending machine in the future.<br><br>You hug your baby and he smiles at you. The addition of his smile increases the likelihood that you will hug him again. | You switch from formal dress shoes to sneakers, and your foot pain goes away. The removal of your pain makes it more likely you will wear sneakers or other casual shoes in the future.<br><br>Your baby is crying, so you hug him, and he stops crying. The removal of crying increases the likelihood that you will hug him again when he cries. |
| **Secondary Reinforcers** Learned stimuli that reinforce and increase the probability of a response | Completing a quest in your video game increases your score and unlocks desirable game items. The addition of these items increases your video game playing behavior.<br><br>You study hard and receive a good grade on your psychology exam. The addition of the good grade makes it more likely that you'll study hard for future exams. | You mention all the homework you have to do, and your partner offers to do the dinner dishes. The removal of this chore increases the likelihood that you will again mention your homework the next time it's your turn to do the dishes.<br><br>You're allowed to skip the final exam because you did so well on your unit exams. The removal of the final exam makes it more likely that you'll work hard to do well on unit exams in the future. |

*© bryanregan/iStockphoto*

*© ferrantraite/iStockphoto*

**Primary punisher** Any unlearned, innate stimulus, such as hunger or thirst, that punishes a response and thus decreases the probability that it will recur.

**Secondary punisher** Any learned stimulus, such as poor grades or a parking ticket, that punishes a response and thus decreases the probability that it will recur.

**Positive punishment** A process by which adding (or presenting) a stimulus following a response decreases the likelihood that the response will be repeated.

**Negative punishment** A process by which taking away (or removing) a stimulus following a response decreases the likelihood that the response will be repeated.

they are not external and directly observable. Instead, he used *positive* and *negative*, as they're commonly used in mathematics and science. You'll find this section much easier if you always remember that "positive" is simply adding something (+), and "negative" is taking something away (−).

As with reinforcers, there are two kinds of punishers—primary and secondary. A **primary punisher** is any unlearned, innate stimulus, such as hunger or thirst, that punishes a response and thus decreases the probability that it will recur. In contrast, a **secondary punisher** is any learned stimulus, such as poor grades or a parking ticket, that punishes a response and thus decreases the probability that it will recur.

Also, as with reinforcement, there are two kinds of punishment—positive and negative. **Positive punishment** is a process by which adding (or presenting) a stimulus following a response decreases the likelihood that the response will be repeated. **Negative punishment** is a process by which taking away (or removing) a stimulus following a response decreases the likelihood that the response will be repeated (**Table 6.2**).

Remember, negative reinforcement is NOT punishment. In fact, the two concepts are actually complete opposites. Reinforcement (both positive and negative) *increases* a behavior, whereas punishment (both positive and negative) *decreases* a behavior. To check your understanding of the principles of both reinforcement and punishment, see **Figure 6.8**.

### Problems with Punishment

As you've seen, punishment is a tricky concept that's difficult to use appropriately and effectively. We often think we're punishing, yet the behaviors continue. Similarly, we too often mistakenly think we're reinforcing when we're actually punishing. The key thing to remember is that punishment, by definition, is a process that adds or takes away something, which causes a behavior to decrease. If the behavior does not decrease, it's NOT punishment!

In addition to these problems, to be effective punishment should always be *clear*, *direct*, *immediate*, and *consistent*. However, this is extremely hard to do. Police officers cannot stop all drivers each and every time they speed. And parents can't scold a child each time he or she curses.

**TABLE 6.2**   **How Punishment Decreases (or Weakens) Behavior**

| | Positive Punishment<br>Stimulus added (+) and behavior decreases (or weakens) | Negative Punishment<br>Stimulus taken away (−) and behavior decreases (or weakens) | |
|---|---|---|---|
| **Primary Punishers**<br>Unlearned, innate stimuli that punish and decrease the probability of a response | You must run four extra laps at soccer practice because you were late. Adding the four extra laps makes it less likely that you'll be late for soccer practice in the future.<br><br>You forget to apply sunscreen, and as a consequence you later suffer a painful sunburn. The addition of the sunburn makes it less likely that you'll forget to apply sunscreen in the future. | Your instructor takes away a significant number of points from your paper because you turned it in late. The loss of points makes it less likely that you'll be late turning in your papers in the future.<br><br>A hungry child is denied dessert because she refused to eat her dinner. The removal of the dessert option decreases the likelihood of the child refusing to eat her dinner in the future. |  <br>Fertnig/iStockphoto |
| **Secondary Punishers**<br>Learned stimuli that punish and decrease the probability of a response | You text on your cell phone while driving and receive a ticket. The addition of the ticket for texting makes it less likely you will text while driving in the future.<br><br>You study hard for your psychology exam and still receive a low grade. The addition of the low grade after studying hard decreases the likelihood that you will study hard for future exams. | A parent takes away a teen's cell phone following a poor report card. The removal of the phone makes it less likely that the teen will earn poor grades in the future.<br><br>You argue aggressively with your friend, and he or she goes home. The removal of your friend's presence decreases the likelihood that you'll argue aggressively in the future. |  <br>Arcady/Shutterstock |

**FIGURE 6.8**   **Using the "Skinner box" for both reinforcement and punishment**   To test his behavioral theories, Skinner created an operant conditioning chamber, popularly known as a "Skinner box." Using this device, experimenters can teach subjects (like rats or pigeons) to perform specific behaviors, such as pressing a lever or pecking at a disk, in response to specific signals, such as a light or sound. In many experiments, the subject's responses also are mechanically recorded. Do you see how this highly controlled environment helps reduce potential experimental errors?

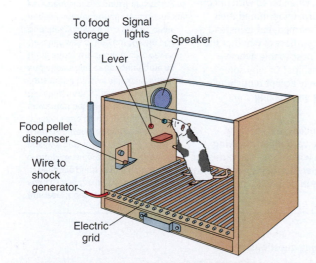

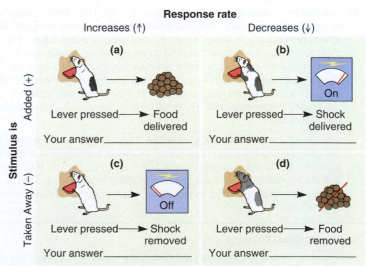

**a. The classic Skinner Box**   In Skinner's basic experimental design, an animal (such as a rat) could press a lever and food pellets or shocks (administered through an electric grid on the cage floor) could be used to administer reinforcement or punishment.

**b. Test Yourself**   Use the blank lines in the four boxes below to fill in the label of the correct learning principle—*positive reinforcement, negative reinforcement, positive punishment,* or *negative punishment.*

Answers: (a) positive reinforcement, (b) positive punishment, (c) negative reinforcement, (d) negative punishment

Don't worry. Psychologists recognize that there are situations when punishment is necessary, such as when a child takes something that doesn't belong to him or her. However, even in limited circumstances like this, it can still have at least seven key drawbacks (**Table 6.3**). After considering all these potential problems with punishment, you may be feeling a bit overwhelmed and wondering what to do instead. The most important reminder is that punishment teaches us *what not to do*, whereas reinforcement teaches us *what to do*.

---

**TABLE 6.3** **Potential Side Effects of Punishment**

1. **Undesirable emotional responses** For the recipient, punishment often leads to fear, anxiety, frustration, anger, and hostility—obviously, not the responses most punishers intend. For example, modern parents generally disapprove of physical punishment. But how often have you seen a parent threaten to leave a child in the store if he or she doesn't hurry and catch up? The parent may see this as a simple way to obtain compliance, whereas the child may interpret it as a threat of abandonment and experience one or more of these unintended, undesirable emotional responses.

2. **Passive aggressiveness** Most of us have learned from experience that retaliatory aggression toward a punisher (especially one who is bigger and/or more powerful) is often followed by more punishment. So instead, we may resort to subtle techniques, called *passive aggressiveness*, in which we deliberately show up late, "forget" to do an assigned chore, or complete the chore in a half-hearted way.

3. **Lying and avoidance behavior** No one likes to be punished, so we naturally try to avoid the punishment by lying or by avoiding the punisher. Do you see how this is an example of negative reinforcement, which will actually increase the behavior? If lying gets you out of trouble, you'll be more likely to do it again in the future. Similarly, if every time you come home, your parent or spouse starts yelling at you, you'll learn to delay coming home—or you'll find another place to go.

Is placing a child in "time out" a form of positive or negative punishment?

4. **Inappropriate modeling** Have you ever seen a parent spank or hit his or her child for hitting another child? Ironically, the punishing parent may unintentionally serve as a "model" for the same behavior he or she is attempting to stop.

5. **Temporary suppression versus elimination** Punishment generally suppresses the behavior only temporarily, while the punisher is nearby, and the effects of the punishment tend to fade with time. For example, a recent study found that after experiencing a severe collision, automobile drivers initially decreased their risky driving, but only temporarily (O'Brien et al., 2017). In addition, the recipient only learns what NOT to do, but not necessarily what he or she SHOULD do.

6. **Learned helplessness** Early researchers theorized that nonhuman animals, when faced with uncontrollable aversive events, learned that nothing they did mattered, which, in turn, undermined their attempts to escape. However, recent studies suggest that this passivity is not learned, but is instead a biologically based response that inhibits escape (Maier & Seligman, 2016). Regardless of whether the helplessness response was learned or unlearned, can you see how repeated, inescapable aversive punishments might explain, in part, why some people stay in abusive relationships? Or why some students who've experienced many failures in academic settings might passively accept punishingly low grades and/or engage in self-defeating behaviors, such as procrastinating and making minimal effort?

7. **Inappropriate rewards and escalation** Because punishment often produces a decrease in the undesired behavior, at least for the moment, the punisher is in effect rewarded for applying punishment. To make matters worse, a vicious cycle may be established in which both the punisher and the recipient are reinforced—the punisher for punishing, and the recipient for being fearful and submissive. This side effect may partially explain the escalation of violence in domestic abuse and bullying.

**Answer:** It depends on the circumstances and the individual. This type of negative punishment ("time out") is often considered more ethical than positive punishment. And it's often en used by parents and preschool teachers as a consequence for unwanted behavior. It does remove the child from what the punisher considers a pleasurable environment and allows him or her quiet time to think about the situation. However, if the child was acting out to gain attention, being placed in a special chair may be unintentionally reinforcing the very behavior the punisher is trying to decrease.

---

**Test Your Critical Thinking**

Using one or more of these seven side effects of punishment, answer the following questions:

1. Why do you think roommates, children, and spouses refuse to load the dishwasher despite repeated nagging?

2. Why do drivers quickly slow down when they see a police car following behind and then quickly resume speeding once the police officer is out of sight?

---

**Sources:** Besemer et al., 2016; Lapré & Marsee, 2016; Maier & Seligman, 2016; McSweeney & Murphy, 2017; Miller et al., 2012; Seligman & Maier, 1967; Walker & Gresham, 2016.

# Principles of Operant Conditioning

Earlier, we discussed the six principles of classical conditioning. In this section, we explore five principles of operant conditioning: *acquisition, generalization, discrimination, extinction,* and *shaping* (**Figure 6.9**). Note that the first four of these principles are very similar to those in classical conditioning, except that in classical conditioning the response is involuntary, whereas it is voluntary in operant conditioning.

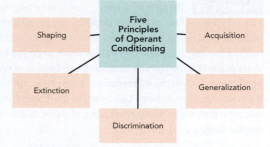

1. **Acquisition**  Recall that acquisition in classical conditioning refers to learning that occurs (is acquired) when an organism involuntarily links a neutral stimulus (NS) with an unconditioned stimulus (US). This acquisition then elicits the conditioned response (CR) and/or conditioned emotional response (CER). However, during **acquisition** in operant conditioning, learning occurs (is acquired) when an organism voluntarily links a response with a consequence, such as a reward.

2. **Generalization**  Generalization in classical conditioning occurs when the CR is involuntarily elicited not only by the CS, but also by stimuli similar to the CS. In comparison, **generalization** in operant conditioning refers to voluntarily responding to a new stimulus as if it is the original, previously conditioned stimulus (CS). A pigeon that's been trained to peck at a green light might also peck at a red light. And a young child who is rewarded for calling her father "Daddy" might generalize and call all men "Daddy." [Study tip: Remember that in classical conditioning the CR is *involuntarily elicited*, whereas in operant conditioning the CR is a *voluntary response*.]

3. **Discrimination**  Discrimination in classical conditioning refers to the learned ability to distinguish (discriminate) between stimuli that differ from the CS. In operant conditioning, **discrimination** refers to the learned ability to distinguish (discriminate) between similar stimuli based on whether responses to the stimuli are reinforced or punished and then to voluntarily respond accordingly. A pigeon might be punished after pecking at a green light, and not after pecking at a red light. As a result, it would quickly learn to peck only at red and to stop pecking at green. Similarly, a child who is only reinforced for calling her father "Daddy" will quickly learn to stop calling all men "Daddy."

4. **Extinction**  Recall that extinction in classical conditioning involves a gradual diminishing of the conditioned response (CR) when the unconditioned stimulus (US) is withheld or removed. Similarly, **extinction** in operant conditioning refers to a gradual diminishing of a response when it is no longer reinforced. Skinner quickly taught pigeons to peck at a certain stimulus using food as a reward (Bouton & Todd, 2014; van den Akker et al., 2015). However, once the reinforcement stopped, the pigeons quickly stopped pecking. How does this apply to human behavior? If a local restaurant stops serving our favorite dishes, we'll soon stop going to that restaurant. Similarly, if we routinely ignore compliments or kisses from a long-term partner, he or she may soon stop giving them.

5. **Shaping**  How do seals in zoos and amusement parks learn how to balance beach balls on their noses or how to clap their flippers together on command from the trainers? For new and complex behaviors such as these, which aren't likely to occur naturally, **shaping** is the key. Skinner believed that shaping, or *rewarding successive approximations*, explains a variety of abilities that each of us possesses, from eating with a fork to playing a musical instrument. Parents, athletic coaches, teachers, therapists, and animal trainers all use shaping techniques (Diefenbach et al., 2017; Pear, 2016). See **Figure 6.10**.

Now that we've discussed how we learn complex behaviors through shaping, you may want to know how to maintain them. This issue involves **schedules of reinforcement**—specific patterns of reinforcement that determine when a behavior will be reinforced.

**Acquisition (in operant conditioning)**  The process by which learning occurs (is acquired) when an organism voluntarily links a response with a consequence, such as a reward.

**Generalization (in operant conditioning)**  Voluntarily responding to a new stimulus as if it were the original, previously conditioned stimulus (CS); the opposite of discrimination.

**Discrimination (in operant conditioning)**  A learned ability to distinguish (discriminate) between similar stimuli based on whether responses to the stimuli are reinforced or punished and then to voluntarily respond accordingly; the opposite of generalization.

**Extinction (in operant conditioning)**  The gradual diminishing of a conditioned response when it is no longer reinforced.

**Shaping**  Delivering reinforcement following successive approximations of the desired response.

**Schedules of reinforcement**  Specific patterns of reinforcement (either fixed or variable) that determine when a behavior will be reinforced.

**FIGURE 6.10** **Shaping in action** How does a dog learn to ride on a paddle board? This pet owner undoubtedly used common shaping techniques. He probably began by standing on the paddle board holding the dog in his arms in shallow water or on dry land. Then he likely placed the dog on the board and used praise or rewards (small doggy treats) when the dog remained there. Next, the owner probably gradually moved the paddle board in small steps into increasingly deeper water, while calmly reassuring, praising, and/or rewarding the dog for staying on the board.

**Continuous reinforcement** Reinforcement in which every correct response is reinforced.

**Partial (intermittent) reinforcement** Reinforcement in which some, but not all, correct responses are reinforced.

**Fixed ratio (FR) schedule** Schedule in which a reinforcer is delivered for the first response made after a fixed number of responses.

**Variable ratio (VR) schedule** Schedule in which a reinforcer is delivered for the first response made after a variable number of responses.

**Fixed interval (FI) schedule** Schedule in which a reinforcer is delivered for the first response made after a fixed period of time has elapsed.

**Variable interval (VI) schedule** Schedule in which a reinforcer is delivered for the first response made after a variable period of time has elapsed.

**Schedules of Reinforcement** When Skinner was training his animals, he found that learning was most rapid if the correct response was reinforced every time it occurred—a pattern called **continuous reinforcement**. Although most effective during the initial training/learning phase, continuous reinforcement unfortunately also leads to rapid *extinction*—the gradual diminishing of a response when it is no longer reinforced. Furthermore, in the real world, continuous reinforcement is generally not practical or economical. When teaching our children, we can't say, "Good job! You brushed your teeth!" every morning for the rest of their lives. As an employer, we can't give a bonus for every task our employees accomplish. For pigeons in the wild, and people in the real world, behaviors are almost always reinforced only occasionally and unpredictably—a pattern called **partial (or intermittent) reinforcement**.

Given the impracticality, and near impossibility, of continuous reinforcement, let's focus on the good news regarding partially reinforced behaviors—they're highly resistant to extinction. Skinner found that pigeons that were reinforced on a continuous schedule would continue pecking approximately a hundred times after food was removed completely—indicating extinction. In contrast, pigeons reinforced on a partial schedule continued to peck thousands of times (Skinner, 1956). Moving from pigeons to people, consider the human behavior of persistent gambling, as described in **Figure 6.11**.

When using partial reinforcement, it's also critical to note that some partial schedules of reinforcement are better suited for maintaining or changing behavior than others (Craig et al., 2014; Kono, 2016; Thrailkill & Bouton, 2015). There are four schedules—**fixed ratio (FR), variable ratio (VR), fixed interval (FI)**, and **variable interval (VI)**. **Table 6.4** defines these terms, compares their respective response rates, and provides examples. Note that in general, ratio schedules consistently elicit higher response rates than interval schedules because the intervals are more predictable. In addition, variable schedules generally produce higher response rates than fixed schedules because schedules are more predictable. Therefore, do you see why variable ratios (VRs) elicit the highest response rate, whereas fixed intervals (FIs) produce the lowest?

**FIGURE 6.11** **Gambling—a partial schedule of reinforcement** Gambling should be a punishing situation, and easily extinguished, because gamblers generally lose far more than they win. However, the fact that they occasionally, and unpredictably, win keeps them "hanging in there." In addition to this dangerous *partial schedule* of *reinforcement*, which is highly resistant to extinction, some research demonstrates that pathological gamblers are less able to make an association between negative events, such as losing lots of money, and the stimuli that cause those events, such as gambling (Stange et al., 2016; Templeton et al., 2015). As a critical thinker, do you recognize how this inability to see connections between losses and gambling might also be an example of the *confirmation* bias (discussed in Chapters 1 and 8)? Most gamblers are far more likely to note and remember their wins—and ignore their losses.

**TABLE 6.4**    **Four Schedules of Partial (Intermittent) Reinforcement**

| | Definitions | Response Rates | Examples |
|---|---|---|---|
| **Ratio Schedules (Response Based)** | | | |
| **Fixed ratio (FR)** | Reinforcement occurs after a fixed, predetermined number of responses | Relatively high rate of response, but a brief drop-off just after reinforcement | You receive a free flight from your frequent flyer program after accumulating a given number of flight miles. |
| **Variable ratio (VR)** | Reinforcement occurs after a varying number of responses | Highest response rate, no pause after reinforcement; variability also makes it resistant to extinction | Slot machines are designed to pay out after an average number of responses (maybe every 10 times), but any one machine may pay out on the first response, then the seventh, then the twentieth. |
| **Interval Schedules (Time Based)** | | | |
| **Fixed Interval (FI)** | Reinforcement occurs after the first response, following a fixed period (interval) of time | Lowest response rate; responses increase near the time for the next reinforcement but drop off after reinforcement and during intervals | You receive a monthly paycheck. Health inspectors visit a restaurant every 6 months. |
| **Variable interval (VI)** | Reinforcement occurs after the first response, following varying periods (intervals) of time | Relatively low, but steady, response rates because respondents cannot predict when reward will come; variability also makes it resistant to extinction | Your professor gives pop quizzes at random times throughout the course. A dog receives a treat if he stays in a sit position for a variable, unpredictable length of time. |

> **Study Tip**
>
> *Remember that intervals are* time *based, whereas ratios are* response *based.*

How do we know which schedule to choose? The type of partial schedule selected depends on the type of behavior being studied and on the speed of learning desired (Lubar, 2015; Pear, 2016; Snider et al., 2016). For example, suppose you want to teach your dog to sit. First, you could reinforce your dog with a cookie every time he sits (continuous reinforcement). To make his training more resistant to extinction, you then could switch to a partial reinforcement schedule. Using the fixed ratio schedule, you would offer a cookie only after your dog sits a certain number of times. As you can see in **Figure 6.12**, a fixed ratio leads to the highest overall response rate. But each of the four types of partial schedules has different advantages and disadvantages (see again Table 6.4).

Before going on, it's important to recognize that operant conditioning principles are commonly used by teachers, animal trainers (like our famous figure Cesar Millan), and therapists to bring about desired changes in behavior (Chapter 15). **Figure 6.13** offers even more examples of how operant conditioning applies to your everyday life. In addition, the following **Psychology and**

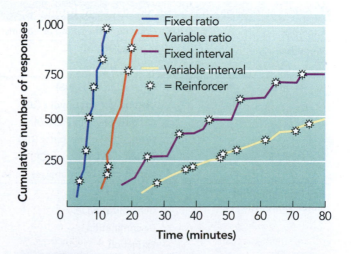

**FIGURE 6.12**    **Which schedule is best?**    Each of the different schedules of reinforcement produces its own unique pattern of response. The best schedule depends on the specific task—see Table 6.4. (The "stars" on the lines represent the delivery of a reinforcer.) (Based on Skinner, 1958.)

**FIGURE 6.13** **Operant conditioning in everyday life** Reinforcement and punishment shape behavior in many aspects of our lives.

**a. Prejudice and discrimination** Although prejudice and discrimination show up early in life, children are not born believing others are inferior. How might posters like this one discourage children from developing (and adults from perpetuating) prejudice and discrimination?

**b. Superstition** Like prejudice and discrimination, superstition is not something we're born with. These attitudes are learned—partly through operant conditioning. For example, the baseball player sticking gum on his helmet in the photo might have once placed his gum on his helmet and then hit a home run. He associated the gum with winning and continued the practice in later games.

**c. Biofeedback** To treat ailments such as anxiety or chronic pain, patients may be connected to electrodes and watch a monitor with a series of flashing lights that display changes in their internal bodily functions. The patients then use this "feedback" (flashing lights) to gauge their progress as they try various relaxation strategies to receive relief from the pain of muscle tension.

**Your Professional Success** demonstrates how these same principles can be used to improve your success in the business world. And, finally, if you're feeling a bit overwhelmed with all the terms and concepts for both classical and operant conditioning, carefully study the summary provided in **Table 6.5**.

**TABLE 6.5** **Comparing Classical and Operant Conditioning**

| | **Classical Conditioning** | **Operant Conditioning** |
|---|---|---|
| **Example** | Cringing at the sound of a dentist's drill | A baby cries and you pick her up |
| **Pioneers** | Ivan Pavlov | Edward Thorndike |
| | John B. Watson | B. F. Skinner |
| **Key Terms** | Neutral stimulus (NS) | Reinforcers and punishers (primary/secondary) |
| | Unconditioned stimulus (US) | Reinforcement (positive/negative) |
| | Conditioned stimulus (CS) | Punishment (positive/negative) |
| | Unconditioned response (UR) | Superstition |
| | Conditioned response (CR) | Shaping |
| | Conditioned emotional response (CER) | Schedules of reinforcement (continuous/partial) |
| **Key Principles and Major Similarities** | Acquisition | Acquisition |
| | Generalization | Generalization |
| | Discrimination | Discrimination |
| | Extinction | Extinction |
| | Spontaneous recovery | Shaping |
| | Higher-order conditioning | |
| **Major Differences** | Passive/involuntary response | Active/voluntary response |
| | NS presented *before* the US | Consequences presented *after* the behavior |

### ❖ Psychology and Your Professional Success | Why Can't We Get Anything Done Around Here?

Imagine yourself as an employee who's just been promoted to manager for a big company (see photo). Unfortunately, this company is in serious trouble and is currently losing business primarily due to low productivity and employee-related problems. Your bonuses (and job) depend on your ability to motivate these employees and increase their production. How could you use reinforcement and punishment to meet your goals?

Hero Images/Getty Images

1. **Provide clear directions and feedback.**   Have you noticed how frustrating it is when a boss asks you to do something but doesn't give you clear directions or helpful feedback on your work? When using either reinforcement or punishment, be sure to provide specific, frequent, and clear directions and feedback to the employee whose behavior you want to encourage or change. When using punishment, it is particularly important to clearly explain and perhaps demonstrate the desired response. Remember that punishment is merely an indication that the current response is undesirable, and employees, like all of us, need to know precisely what to do, as well as what NOT to do.

2. **Be consistent.**   To be effective, both reinforcement and punishment must be consistent. As a student, have you noticed how some of your classmates get out of difficult assignments or gain extra time or make-up arrangements because they're constantly complaining or begging? This same pattern is often seen in business situations. Recalling what you've learned in this chapter, can you see how some business managers (and college instructors) may begin with refusals but then eventually give in when the complaining persists?

   Do you see how this creates a vicious cycle? First, the employee is being *positively reinforced* for complaining and begging, which almost guarantees that these inappropriate behaviors are likely to increase. To make matters worse, the manager's inconsistency (saying "no" and then giving in) places the employee's bad behavior on a *partial schedule of reinforcement*—and thus makes it highly resistant to extinction. Like a toddler screaming for a lollipop or a gambler continuing to play despite the odds, the employee will continue his or her inappropriate behavior in hopes of the occasional payoff. Because effective punishment requires constant surveillance and consistent responses, it's almost impossible to be a "perfect punisher." It's best (and easiest) to use consistent reinforcement for good behavior and extinction for bad behavior.

3. **Use appropriate timing.**   Reinforcers and punishers should be presented as close in time to the response as possible. If you're trying to increase production, don't tell your staff that you'll have a large party at the end of the year if they reach a significant goal. Instead, reward them with immediate compliments and small bonuses. The same is true for punishment. When you notice inappropriate behaviors, such as employees surfing the Internet rather than working, you should immediately confront them and remind them to get back to work. Do you see how waiting until a performance review or even the end of the day to confront workers is obviously inappropriate and less effective? The delayed punishment is no longer associated with the inappropriate response.

4. **Follow correct order of presentation.**   As a teenager, did you ever ask for a few extra dollars as an advance on your allowance or promise to mow the grass before the end of the week? Did you later conveniently "forget" the advance or your promise? As a manager, you can understand why providing reinforcement before the desired response occurs generally leads to increased requests for advances and broken promises. At the same time, imagine how an employee might feel if he or she asked to telecommute (or work from home) but you immediately denied the request because you believe all employees "slough off if they're not being watched." Here, refusing the request before the negligent behavior occurs typically

leads to frustration, resentment, and lowered productivity. Both reinforcement and punishment should come *after* the behavior, never *before*.

5. **Combine key learning principles.**    In sum, the overall best management strategy in business (as in most areas of your life) is to combine the major principles: reinforce appropriate behavior, extinguish inappropriate behavior, and save punishment for the most extreme cases (such as harassment, bullying, or stealing). Interestingly, Cesar Millan suggests that to be a good "pack leader," dog owners must use these very same principles—providing clear and immediate direction, consistency, and so on. But he also insists that the owners maintain a calm, assertive demeanor, which is also good advice for managers, parents, and others who want to become more effective leaders.

© Billy R. Ray/ Wiley

## Retrieval Practice 6.2 | Operant Conditioning

Completing this self-test and the connections section, and then checking your answers by clicking on the answer button or by looking in Appendix B, will provide immediate feedback and helpful practice for exams.

### Self-Test

1. Learning in which voluntary responses are controlled by their consequences is called _____.

2. An employer who gives employees a cash bonus after they've done a good job is an example of _____.
   a. positive reinforcement    b. incremental conditioning
   c. classical conditioning    d. bribery

3. _____ reinforcers normally satisfy an unlearned biological need.
   a. Positive            b. Negative
   c. Primary             d. None of these

4. The overall best method for changing behavior is to _____.
   a. reinforce appropriate behavior
   b. extinguish inappropriate behavior

   c. save punishment for extreme cases
   d. use all of these options

5. Gamblers become addicted partially because of _____.
   a. previously generalized response discrimination
   b. previously extinguished response recovery
   c. partial (intermittent) reinforcement
   d. behavior being learned and not conditioned

### Connections—Chapter to Chapter

Answering the following question will help you "look back and look ahead" to see the important connections among the various subfields of psychology and chapters within this text.

The connection between operant conditioning and motivation (Chapter 12, Motivation and Emotion) seems an easy one to make: you can motivate someone to change behavior by rewards or punishments. But is it really that easy? Describe a time when reinforcement or punishment did not work for you. How was your motivation to do (or not do) something a factor in the ineffectiveness of operant conditioning?

## 6.3    Cognitive–Social Learning

### LEARNING OBJECTIVES

**Retrieval Practice**    While reading the upcoming sections, respond to each Learning Objective in your own words.

**Summarize the key terms and findings in the cognitive—social theory of learning.**

- **Describe** insight learning, cognitive maps, and latent learning.
- **Discuss** observational learning and Bandura's four key factors.

*He who learns but does not think is lost! He who thinks but does not learn is in great danger.*
—Confucius (Chinese Philosopher, Teacher, Politician)

So far, we have examined learning processes that involve associations between a stimulus and an observable behavior—the key to both classical and operant conditioning. Although some behaviorists believe that almost all learning can be explained in such stimulus–response terms, cognitive psychologists disagree. **Cognitive–social learning theory** (also called cognitive–behavioral theory) incorporates the general concepts of conditioning. But rather than relying on a simple S–R (stimulus and response) model, this theory emphasizes the interpretation or thinking that occurs within the organism: S–O–R (stimulus–organism–response).

According to this view, humans have attitudes, beliefs, expectations, motivations, and emotions that affect learning. Furthermore, humans and many nonhuman animals also are social creatures that are capable of learning new behaviors through the observation and imitation of others. For example, Cesar Millan suggests that dogs naturally imitate their owner's emotions and behaviors. He reminds them, "if you feel anxious, the dog becomes anxious with you." And if your dog is misbehaving, ask yourself, "What am I doing wrong?" In this section, we first look at insight and latent learning, followed by observational learning.

**Cognitive–social learning theory** A theory that emphasizes the roles of thinking and social learning.

## Insight Learning and Latent Learning

Early behaviorists likened the mind to a "black box" whose workings could not be observed directly. German psychologist Wolfgang Köhler (1887–1967) wanted to look inside the box. He believed that there was more to learning—especially learning to solve a complex problem—than responding to stimuli in a trial-and-error fashion.

In one of a series of experiments, Köhler placed a piece of fruit and a long stick just outside the reach of one of his brightest chimpanzees, named Sultan. Köhler also placed a short stick inside Sultan's cage. Sultan quickly picked up the stick and tried to rake the fruit into his reach outside the cage, but the stick was too short. Köhler noticed that the chimp did not solve the problem in a random trial-and-error fashion. Instead, he seemed to sit and think about the situation for a while. Then, in a flash of *insight*, Sultan picked up the shorter stick and used it to drag the longer stick within his reach. He then used the longer stick to rake in the fruit (Köhler, 1925). Köhler called this **insight learning** because some internal mental event, which he could only describe as *insight*, or an "aha" experience, went on between the presentation of the fruit and the use of the two sticks to retrieve it. See **Figure 6.14** for another example of how Sultan solved a similar "out-of-reach banana" problem.

Like Köhler, Edward C. Tolman (1898–1956) believed that previous researchers underestimated human and nonhuman animals' cognitive processes and cognitive learning. He noted that, when allowed to roam aimlessly in an experimental maze with no food reward at the end, rats seemed to develop a **cognitive map**, or mental representation of the maze.

To further test the idea of cognitive learning, Tolman allowed one group of rats to aimlessly explore a maze, with no reinforcement. A second group was reinforced with food whenever they reached the end of the maze. The third group was not rewarded during the first 10 days of the trial, but starting on day 11, they found food at the end of the maze.

As expected from simple operant conditioning, the first and third groups were slow to learn the maze, whereas the second group, which had reinforcement, showed fast, steady improvement. However, when the third group started receiving reinforcement (on the 11th day), their learning quickly caught up to the group that had been reinforced every time (Tolman & Honzik, 1930). This showed that the nonreinforced rats had been thinking and building cognitive maps of the area during their aimless wandering and that their **latent learning**, or implicit learning, only showed up when there was a reason to display it (the food reward).

Cognitive maps and latent learning are not limited to rats. For example, a chipmunk will pay little attention to a new log in its territory (after initially checking it for food). When a predator comes along, however, the chipmunk heads directly for and hides beneath the log. Recent experiments provide additional clear evidence of latent learning and the existence

**Insight learning** A sudden understanding or realization of how a problem can be solved.

**Cognitive map** A mental image of a three-dimensional space that an organism has navigated.

**Latent learning** Hidden learning that exists without behavioral signs; also known as implicit learning.

**FIGURE 6.14 Cognitive–social learning** In a second Köhler experiment, chimpanzees were placed in a room with several scattered boxes, none of which was high enough to enable them to reach the banana. They initially ran around and unproductively jumped for the banana. Then, all of a sudden, Sultan saw the solution—he stacked the boxes and used them to climb up and grab the banana! (Also, note how the chimp in the background is engaged in observational learning, our next topic.)

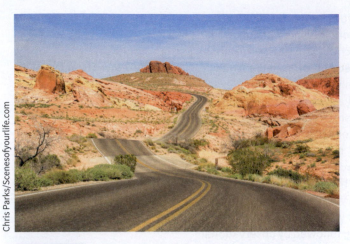

**FIGURE 6.15** **Cognitive maps in humans** People who live or work near these beautiful red rocks in Nevada undoubtedly know what lies beyond the last turn in this highway. That's because they have developed a detailed cognitive map of the area. Can you think of examples of similar cognitive maps from your own life?

**Observational learning** The learning of new behaviors or information by watching and imitating others (also known as social learning or modeling).

**FIGURE 6.16** **Bandura's Bobo doll study**

of internal cognitive maps in both human and nonhuman animals (Brunyé et al., 2015; Geronazzo et al., 2016; Leising et al., 2015). See **Figure 6.15**. Do you remember your first visit to your college campus? You probably just wandered around checking out the various buildings, without realizing you were engaging in "latent learning" and building your own "cognitive maps." This exploration undoubtedly came in handy when you later needed to find your classes and the cafeteria!

## Observational Learning

In addition to classical and operant conditioning and cognitive processes (such as insight learning and latent learning), we learn many things through **observational learning**, which is also called *imitation* or *modeling*. From birth to death, observational learning is essential to our biological, psychological, and social survival (the *biopsychosocial model*). Watching others helps us avoid dangerous stimuli in our environment, teaches us how to think and feel, and shows us how to act and interact socially (Askew et al., 2016; Pauen & Hoehl, 2015; Pear, 2016).

For example, toddlers typically go through a picky eating phase, but research shows that toddlers who watched their parents eating a novel food were far more likely to try that food than toddlers who were only repeatedly prompted by parents (Edelson et al., 2016). Unfortunately, observational learning also may lead to negative outcomes. One study found that even some very young toddlers showed a clear preference for looking at average-sized versus obese figures (Ruffman et al., 2016). The toddlers' responses were correlated with their mothers' anti-fat attitudes and were not related to the parents' body mass index (BMI, a measure of obesity) or education or to the children's television viewing time. The researchers concluded that the toddlers' prejudices most likely resulted from modeling and observational learning. A similar example of bad modeling may come from research on math-anxious parents who help with their children's math homework. This study found that the children of these parents actually learn less math over a school year and are more likely to develop math anxiety themselves (Maloney et al., 2015).

Interestingly, the work of our introductory famous figure, Cesar Millan, provides a contrary, positive example for modeling. When faced with extremely out-of-control dogs that do not respond to his initial training, Millan takes them to his *Dog Psychology Center*. There, they seem to quickly learn the desired behaviors by watching and imitating the behaviors of other, well-trained dogs.

Much of our knowledge about the power of observational learning initially came from the work of Albert Bandura and his colleagues (Bandura, 2011; Bandura et al., 1961; Bandura & Walters, 1963). Wanting to know whether children learn to be aggressive by watching others be aggressive, Bandura and his colleagues set up several experiments in which children watched a live or televised adult model punch, throw, and hit a large inflated Bobo doll (**Figure 6.16** top).

Later, the children were allowed to play in the same room with the same Bobo doll. As Bandura hypothesized, children who had watched the live or televised aggressive model were much more aggressive with the Bobo doll than children who had not seen the modeled aggression (**Figure 6.16** bottom). In other words, "Monkey see, monkey do" (see cartoon).

Thanks to the Bobo doll studies and his other experiments, Bandura established that observational learning requires at least four separate processes: *attention, retention, reproduction*, and *motivation* (**Figure 6.17**).

**Cognitive–Social Learning and Everyday Life** We use cognitive–social learning in many ways in our everyday lives (as humorously depicted in the cartoon on

**FIGURE 6.17** **Bandura's four key factors in observational learning** A child who wants to become a premier ballerina—or you, if you want to learn to paint, ski, or play a musical instrument—will need to incorporate these four factors to maximize learning.

**a. Attention** Observational learning requires attention. This is why teachers insist on having students watch their demonstrations.

**b. Retention** To learn new behaviors, we need to carefully note and remember the model's directions and demonstrations.

**c. Reproduction** Observational learning requires that we imitate the model.

Erik Isakson/Getty Images, Inc.

**d. Motivation** We are more likely to repeat a modeled behavior if the model is reinforced for the behavior (for example, with applause or other recognition).

the left). However, one of the most powerful examples is frequently overlooked—*media influences*. Experimental and correlational research clearly show that when we watch television or movies, read books or magazines, or visit websites that portray people of color, women, or others in demeaning and stereotypical roles, we often learn to expect these behaviors and to accept them as "natural." Exposure of this kind initiates and reinforces the learning of prejudice (Dill & Thill, 2007; Scharrer & Ramasubramanian, 2015; van der Pligt & Vliek, 2016).

In addition to prejudice and stereotypes, watching popular media also teaches us what to eat, what toys to buy, what homes and clothes are most fashionable, and what constitutes "the good life." When a TV commercial shows children enjoying a particular cereal and beaming at their mom in gratitude (and mom is smiling back), both children and parents in the audience are participating in a form of observational learning. They learn that they, too, will be rewarded for buying the advertised brand (with happy children). Sadly, as shown in the following **Research Challenge**, the media may strongly influence our ideal body image.

At risk of leaving you with the impression that observational learning is primarily negative, we'd like to end on a more positive note. A cross-cultural study tested levels of empathy and helpfulness in thousands of adolescents and young adults in seven different countries (Australia, China, Croatia, Germany, Japan, Romania, and the United States). And, happily,

"THEY PICK IT UP FROM THE TOURISTS"

Jackson Graham/CartoonStock

## Research Challenge

### Does the Media Impact Our Body Size Preferences?

How do media images of women's bodies influence preferences for particular body shapes and sizes? To examine this question, researchers compared preferences for different body sizes in men and women living in three distinct parts of Nicaragua (Boothroyd et al., 2016). One group was living in an urban area, with regular access to most forms of media. The second group resided in a village with only television access. The third group was living in a remote area with little access to electricity and hence low rates of any media viewing. Participants in each of the three areas were shown images of women's bodies, like those on the right, that varied on degree of thinness and were then asked to rate their attractiveness on a scale of 1 to 5.

Can you predict their findings? As the researchers hypothesized, people living in the village with little access to media rated the thinner female bodies as the least attractive, whereas those living in the urban area with more media exposure rated the thinner female bodies as most attractive. Moreover, rates of dieting by women were in line with the participants' degree of exposure to media. Those living in urban areas with regular media access reported the strongest desire to lose weight, whereas women living in the area without regular exposure to television showed the least. These findings suggest that the thin ideal so commonly shown in the media may change both men's and women's beliefs about what is considered attractive in a given culture.

Why do you think the researchers limited their study to Nicaragua? Can you see how it would be difficult to find areas in more developed nations that are relatively free of media influences? How might this type of maladaptive observational learning contribute to body dissatisfaction, excessive dieting, and eating disorders, such as bulimia and anorexia (Chapter 12)?

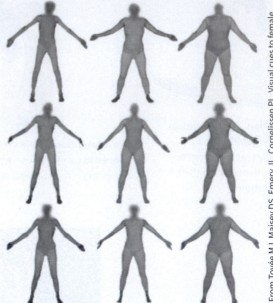

From Tovée MJ, Maisey DS, Emery JL, Cornelissen PL. Visual cues to female physical attractiveness. Proceedings of the Royal Society B: Biological Sciences. 1999;266(1415):211-218. by permission of the Royal Society

**Test Yourself**

1. Based on the information provided, did this study (Boothroyd et al., 2016) use descriptive, correlational, and/or experimental research?

2. If you chose:
   - *descriptive research*, is this a naturalistic observation, survey/interview, case study, and/or archival research?
   - *correlational research*, is this a positive, negative, or zero correlation?
   - *experimental research*, label the IV, DV, experimental group(s), and control group. (Note: If participants were not randomly assigned to groups, list it as a *quasi-experimental design*.)
   - both *descriptive* and *correlational*, answer the corresponding questions for both.

**Check your answers by clicking on the answer button or by looking in Appendix B.**

**Note:** The information provided in this study is admittedly limited, but the level of detail is similar to what is presented in most textbooks and public reports of research findings. Answering these questions, and then comparing your answers to those provided, will help you become a better critical thinker and consumer of scientific research.

---

the researchers found that greater exposure to *prosocial media*—meaning video games, movies, or TV programs showing helpful, caring, and cooperative behaviors—led to higher levels of helping behavior among the viewers (Prot et al., 2014). In conclusion, the following **Psychology and Your Personal Success** provides a quick, helpful way to review the three major forms of learning while also improving your student success skills.

## ❖ Psychology and Your Personal Success | Can Learning Principles Help You Succeed in College?

Having studied the principles of classical, operant, and cognitive–social learning, see if you can apply this new information to your overall educational goals.

1. **Classical conditioning** If you're overly anxious when taking exams, and you can see that this might be a personal CER, describe how you could use the principle of extinction to weaken this response.

2. **Operant conditioning** List three ways you can positively reinforce yourself for studying, completing assignments, and attending class.

3. **Cognitive–social learning** Discuss with friends what they do to succeed in college classes and how participating in club and campus activities can reinforce your commitment to education.

© Billy R. Ray/Wiley

## Retrieval Practice 6.3 | Cognitive-Social Learning

Completing this self-test and the connections section, and then checking your answers by clicking on the answer button or by looking in Appendix B, will provide immediate feedback and helpful practice for exams.

### Self-Test

1. Briefly describe how cognitive–social learning differs from classical conditioning and operant conditioning.

2. Insight learning is _____.
   a. based on unconscious classical conditioning
   b. an innate human reflex
   c. a sudden flash of understanding
   d. an artifact of operant conditioning

3. When walking to your psychology class, you note that the path you normally take is blocked for construction, so you quickly choose an alternate route. This demonstrates that you've developed _____ of your campus.
   a. a neural map
   b. insight learning into the layout
   c. a cognitive map
   d. none of these representations

4. Latent learning occurs without being rewarded and _____.
   a. remains hidden until a future time when it is needed
   b. is easily extinguished

c. serves as a discriminative stimuli
d. has been found only in nonhuman species

5. Bandura's observational learning studies focused on how _____.
   a. rats learn cognitive maps through exploration
   b. children learn aggressive behaviors by observing aggressive models
   c. cats learn problem solving through trial and error
   d. chimpanzees learn problem solving through reasoning

### Connections—Chapter to Chapter

Answering the following question will help you "look back and look ahead" to see the important connections among the various subfields of psychology and chapters within this text.

In Chapter 14 (Psychological Disorders), you'll learn that anxiety disorders affect more people than any other group of disorders. Why are so many people anxious and afraid? Has the dangerousness of our world changed so much? Or is it that our perception and awareness of its dangers have increased? What relationship might this have to the prevalence of anxiety disorders? Consider these questions from the perspective of *cognitive–social theory* of learning.

## 6.4 Biology of Learning

### LEARNING OBJECTIVES

**Retrieval Practice**    While reading the upcoming sections, respond to each Learning Objective in your own words.

**Review the biological factors in learning.**

- **Explain** how learning changes our brains.

- **Describe** how experiences and enriched environments affect our brains.
- **Discuss** the importance of mirror neurons.
- **Summarize** the role of evolution in learning.

Now that we've discussed how we learn through classical conditioning, operant conditioning, and cognitive–social learning, we need to explore the key biological factors in all forms of learning. In this section, we will examine both neurological and evolutionary influences on learning.

**FIGURE 6.18** **How our brains respond to reinforcement versus punishment**

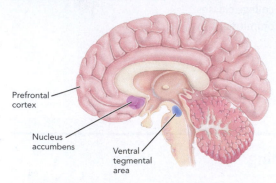

**a. Brain areas responsive to reinforcement** Learning from reinforcement primarily involves sections of the ventral tegmental area, nucleus accumbens, and prefrontal cortex.

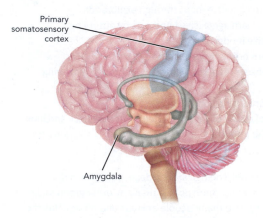

**b. Brain areas responsive to punishment** Learning from punishment involves some of the same brain regions as in reinforcement, but the amygdala and primary somatosensory cortex are particularly responsive, due to their role in fear and pain.

# Neuroscience and Learning

Each time we learn something, either consciously or unconsciously, that experience creates new synaptic connections and alterations in a wide network of our brain's structures, including the cortex, cerebellum, hippocampus, hypothalamus, thalamus, and amygdala. Interestingly, it appears that somewhat different areas of our brains respond to reinforcement and punishment (Correia & Goosens, 2016; Jean-Richard-Dit-Bressel & McNally, 2015; Ollmann et al., 2015). See **Figure 6.18**.

Evidence that learning changes brain structure first emerged in the 1960s, from studies of animals raised in *enriched* versus *deprived* environments. Compared with rats raised in a stimulus-poor environment, those raised in a colorful, stimulating "rat Disneyland" had a thicker cortex, increased nerve growth factor (NGF), more fully developed synapses, more dendritic branching, and improved performance on many tests of learning and memory (Ahlbeck et al., 2016; Hong et al., 2016; Lima et al., 2014).

Admittedly, it is a big leap from rats to humans, but research suggests that the human brain also responds to environmental conditions (**Figure 6.19**). For example, older adults who are exposed to stimulating environments generally perform better on intellectual and perceptual tasks than those in restricted environments (Petrosini et al., 2013; Rohlfs Domínguez, 2014; Schaeffer et al., 2014). Similarly, babies who spend their early weeks and months of life in an orphanage, and receive little or no one-on-one care or attention, show deficits in the cortex of the brain, indicating that early environmental conditions may have a lasting impact on cognitive development (Behen & Chugani, 2016; Moutsiana et al., 2015; Perego et al., 2016). The good news, however, is that children who are initially placed in an orphanage but later move on to foster care—where they receive more individual attention—show some improvements in brain development.

**Mirror Neurons** Researchers have identified another neurological influence on learning processes, particularly imitation and observational learning. When an adult models a facial expression, even

**FIGURE 6.19** **Environmental enrichment and the brain** Given that environmental conditions play such an essential role in enabling learning, can you see why it's so important to a child's brain development that he or she has the opportunity to attend classrooms like the one on the left, which is filled with stimulating toys, games, and books? Similarly, how might an "enriched" cage environment like the one on the right encourage brain growth in rats and mice?

very young infants will immediately respond with a similar expression (**Figure 6.20**). At nine months, infants will imitate facial actions a full day after first seeing them (Heimann & Meltzoff, 1996).

How can newborn infants so quickly imitate the facial expressions of others? Using fMRIs and other brain-imaging techniques, researchers have identified specific **mirror neurons** believed to be responsible for human empathy and imitation (Ahlsén, 2008; Fox et al., 2016; Praszkier, 2016). When we see other people in pain, one reason we empathize and "share their pain," while seemingly unconsciously imitating their facial expressions, may be that our mirror neurons are firing.

Mirror neurons were first discovered by neuroscientists who implanted wires in the brains of monkeys to monitor areas involved in planning and carrying out movement (Ferrari et al., 2005; Rizzolatti, 2014; Rizzolatti et al., 1996, 2008). When these monkeys moved and grasped an object, specific neurons fired, but they also fired when the monkeys simply observed another monkey performing the same or similar tasks.

Scientists are excited about the promising links between mirror neurons and the thoughts, feelings, and actions of both human and nonhuman animals (**Figure 6.21**). We do not yet know the full extent of the influence of mirror neurons, nor do we know how they develop. However, we do appreciate that, thanks to our mirror neurons, we're born prepared to imitate, and imitation is essential to survival in our complex, highly developed social world.

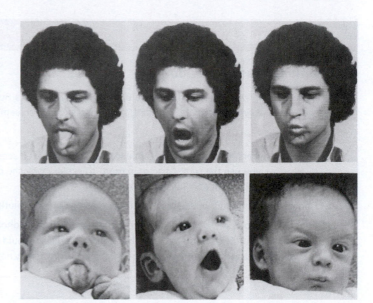

A.N. Meltzoff & M.K. Moore,"Imitation of facial and manual gestures by human neonates." Science, 1977, 198, 75–78

**FIGURE 6.20**  **Infant imitation—evidence of mirror neurons?** In a series of well-known studies, Andrew Meltzoff and M. Keith Moore (1977, 1985, 1994) found that newborns could easily imitate such facial movements as tongue protrusion, mouth opening, and lip pursing.

## Biological Primes and Constraints on Learning

In addition to being born with brains that adapt and change with learning, humans and other animals are also born with various innate reflexes and instincts that help ensure their survival. However, these evolutionary responses are inherently inflexible, whereas learning allows us to more flexibly respond to complex environmental cues, such as spoken words and written symbols, which in turn enables us to survive and prosper in a constantly changing world. As we've seen, learning even enables nonhuman animals to be classically conditioned to salivate to tones and operantly conditioned to perform a variety of novel behaviors, such as a seal balancing a ball on its nose.

**Mirror neurons**  Neurons that fire (or are activated) when an action is performed, as well as when the actions or emotions of another are observed; believed to be responsible for empathy, imitation, language, and the deficits of some mental disorders.

### Classical Conditioning
Evolutionary and learning theorists initially believed that the fundamental laws of conditioning would apply to almost all species and all behaviors. However, researchers have discovered that some associations are much more readily learned than others. As you recall, Pavlov's experiments required several pairings of the NS with the US before it elicited a response. However, it normally only requires a single pairing of a specific taste with nausea to produce a learned dislike for, and avoidance of, that taste. Like other classically conditioned responses, this reaction, known as a **conditioned taste aversion**, develops involuntarily (see the **Try This Yourself**).

**Conditioned taste aversion**  A classically conditioned dislike for, and avoidance of, a specific taste when followed by nausea; normally occurs after only one association.

**FIGURE 6.21**  **Mirror neurons**   Have you noticed how spectators at an athletic event sometimes slightly move their arms or legs in synchrony with the athletes? Mirror neurons may be the underlying biological mechanism for this imitation. Deficiencies in these neurons also might help explain the emotional deficits of children and adults with autism or schizophrenia, who often misunderstand the verbal and nonverbal cues of others (Alaerts et al., 2015; Brown et al., 2016; van der Weiden et al., 2015).

Carlos E. Santa Maria/Shutterstock

## Try This Yourself

### Conditioned Taste Aversion

Years ago, a young woman named Rebecca unsuspectingly bit into a Butterfinger candy bar filled with small, wiggling maggots. Horrified, she ran gagging and screaming to the bathroom.

#### Test Your Critical Thinking

1. After many years, Rebecca still feels nauseated when she even sees a Butterfinger candy bar. Can you use the term "discrimination" to explain why she doesn't feel similarly nauseated by the sight of a Snickers candy bar?

2. Under what conditions would a conditioned taste aversion be evolutionarily maladaptive?

3. Imagine someone developed a secret pill that could make alcohol, tobacco, and fatty foods an immediate conditioned taste aversion for everyone. Would that be good or bad? Assuming it was totally safe, would you take the pill? Why or why not?

© robtek/iStockphoto

The initial discovery of conditioned taste aversions is credited to psychologists John Garcia and his colleague Robert Koelling (1966). They produced a taste aversion in lab rats by pairing sweetened water (NS) and a nausea-producing drug (US). After being conditioned and then recovering from the illness, the rats refused to drink the sweetened water (CS) because of the conditioned taste aversion. As discussed earlier, when alcohol is paired with a nausea-producing drug (US), alcoholics may similarly learn to avoid drinking alcohol.

Conditioned taste aversions illustrate a critical evolutionary process. Being biologically prepared to quickly associate nausea with food or drink is obviously adaptive because it helps us avoid that specific food or drink, and similar ones, in the future (Buss, 2015; Goldfinch, 2015; Shepherd, 2017).

Similarly, perhaps because of the more "primitive" evolutionary threat posed by snakes, darkness, spiders, and heights, people tend to more easily develop phobias of these stimuli, compared to guns, knives, and electrical outlets. Research also shows that both adults and very young children have an innate ability to very quickly identify the presence of a snake, whereas they are less able to quickly identify other (non-life-threatening) objects, including a caterpillar, flower, or toad (LoBue & DeLoache, 2008; Mallan et al., 2013; Young et al., 2012). We apparently inherit a built-in (innate) readiness to form associations between certain stimuli and responses—but not others. This is known as **biological preparedness**.

**Biological preparedness** The built-in (innate) readiness to form associations between certain stimuli and responses.

### Operant Conditioning

As we've just seen, there are both biological primes and limits on classical conditioning. The same is true in operant conditioning. It's relatively easy to train pigeons to peck at a light because this is among their natural food-searching behaviors. However, other researchers have found that an animal's natural behavior pattern can interfere with the learning of certain operant responses. For example, early researchers tried to teach a chicken to play a modified form of baseball (Breland & Breland, 1961). Through shaping and reinforcement, the chicken first learned to pull a loop that activated a swinging bat and then learned to time its response to actually hit the ball. Surprisingly, the researchers had more difficulty training the chicken to run to first base. Instead, it would often chase the moving ball as if it were food. Regardless of the lack of reinforcement for chasing the ball, the chicken's natural predatory behavior for chasing moving objects took precedence. This tendency for a conditioned behavior to revert (drift back) to innate response patterns is known as **instinctive drift**.

**Instinctive drift** The tendency for conditioned responses to revert (drift back) to innate response patterns.

### Final Note

In this chapter, we've discussed three general types of learning: classical, operant, and cognitive–social. We've also examined several biological effects on learning. What is the most important "take-home message"? As humans, we have the ability to learn and change! Using what you've discovered in this chapter, we hope you'll remember to avoid using punishment whenever possible and "simply" reinforce desired behaviors. This basic principle can also be successfully applied on a national and global scale.

© Billy R. Ray/Wiley

## Retrieval Practice 6.4 | Biology of Learning

Completing this self-test and the connections section, and then checking your answers by clicking on the answer button or by looking in Appendix B, will provide immediate feedback and helpful practice for exams.

### Self-Test

1. Rats _____ developed a thicker cortex, more fully developed synapses, and improved test performances.
   a. given a restricted diet
   b. injected with nerve growth factor (NGF)
   c. raised in an enriched environment
   d. in none of these conditions

2. _____ neurons may be responsible for human empathy and imitation.

3. Rebecca's story of becoming nauseated and vomiting after eating a spoiled candy bar is a good example of _____.
   a. a biological imperative     b. a conditioned taste aversion
   c. learned empathy              d. negative reinforcement

4. Being innately predisposed to form associations between certain stimuli and responses is called _____.
   a. biological readiness
   b. vicarious learning
   c. superstitious priming
   d. biological preparedness

5. The fact that chickens trained to play baseball tend to chase the ball, rather than running to first base, is an example of _____.
   a. latent learning
   b. biological unpreparedness
   c. instinctive drift
   d. none of these options

### Connections—Chapter to Chapter

Answering the following question will help you "look back and look ahead" to see the important connections among the various subfields of psychology and chapters within this text.

In Chapter 2 (Neuroscience and Biological Foundations), you learned about the role of neurotransmitters in the brain, including those involved in learning. If you had the option to take a drug that would enhance learning by changing your brain's levels of neurotransmitters, would you consider it? What are the potential advantages and disadvantages?

---

### Study Tip

*The WileyPLUS program that accompanies this text provides for each chapter a* Media Challenge, Critical Thinking Exercise, *and* Application Quiz. *This set of study materials provides additional, invaluable study opportunities. Be sure to check it out!*

# Chapter Summary

## 6.1 Classical Conditioning   186

- **Learning** is a relatively permanent change in behavior or mental processes caused by experience. Pavlov discovered a fundamental form of **conditioning** (learning) called **classical conditioning**, which develops through involuntarily paired associations. A previously **neutral stimulus (NS)** becomes associated with an **unconditioned stimulus (US)** to elicit a **conditioned response (CR)**.

- In the Little Albert study, Watson and Rayner demonstrated how many of our likes, dislikes, prejudices, and fears are examples of a **conditioned emotional response (CER)**.

- **Acquisition**, the first of six key principles of classical conditioning, is the initial learning (acquisition) that occurs when an organism involuntarily links an NS with a US, which then elicits the CR. **Generalization** occurs when a CR is involuntarily elicited not only by the CS, but also by stimuli similar to the CS. In contrast, **discrimination** is the learned ability to involuntarily distinguish (discriminate) so as NOT to respond to a new stimulus as if it were the previous CS. **Extinction** is a gradual diminishing of a CR when the US is withheld or removed. However, if a CS is reintroduced after extinction, an extinguished response may **spontaneously recover**. **Higher-order conditioning** occurs when a new CS is created by pairing it with a previous CS.

**Test Your Critical Thinking**

**1.** How might Watson and Rayner, who conducted the famous Little Albert study, have designed a more ethical study of conditioned emotional responses (CERs)?

**2.** Most classical conditioning is involuntary. Considering this, is it ethical for politicians and advertisers to use classical conditioning to influence our thoughts and behavior? Why or why not?

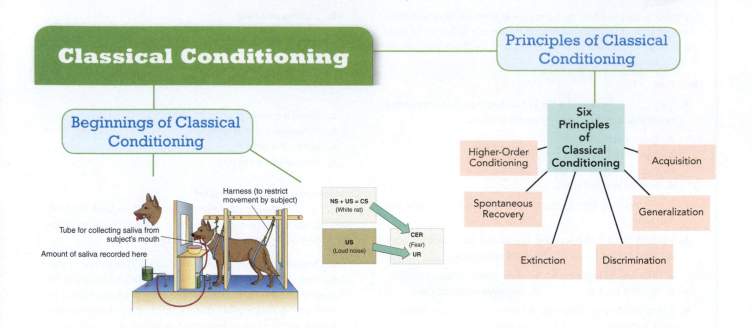

## 6.2 Operant Conditioning   194

- Both classical and operant conditioning are forms of **associative learning**. In **operant conditioning**, an organism learns as a result of voluntary behavior and its subsequent consequences. **Reinforcement** increases the response, while **punishment** decreases the response.

- Thorndike developed the **law of effect**, in which any behavior followed by pleasant consequences is likely to be repeated, whereas any behavior followed by unpleasant consequences is likely to be stopped. Skinner extended Thorndike's law of effect to more complex behaviors, with a special emphasis on external, observable behaviors.

- **Primary reinforcers** and **primary punishers** are innate, whereas **secondary reinforcers** and **secondary punishers** are learned. Each type of reinforcer can produce **positive reinforcement** or **negative reinforcement**, and both of these forms of reinforcement increase the response they follow. Negative reinforcement is NOT punishment. Both **positive punishment** and **negative punishment** decrease a response.

- Punishment can have serious side effects: undesirable emotional responses, passive aggressiveness, lying and avoidance behavior, inappropriate modeling, temporary suppression versus elimination, learned helplessness, and inappropriate rewards and escalation.

- In the context of operant conditioning, **acquisition** occurs when an organism voluntarily links a response with a consequence,

such as a reward. **Generalization** refers to voluntarily responding to a new stimulus as if it is the original, previously conditioned stimulus (CS). In contrast, **discrimination** is the learned ability to distinguish (discriminate) between similar stimuli based on whether the responses to the stimuli are reinforced or punished and then to voluntarily respond accordingly. **Extinction** refers to a gradual diminishing of a response when it is no longer reinforced. **Shaping** involves delivering reinforcement for successive approximations of the desired response. **Schedules of reinforcement** refer to patterns of reinforcement (fixed or variable) that determine when a behavior is reinforced. Most behavior is rewarded and maintained through one of four partial schedules of reinforcement: fixed ratio (FR), variable ratio (VR), fixed interval (FI), or variable interval (VI).

- Both classical and operant conditioning share terms, including acquisition, generalization, discrimination, and extinction. The key difference is that classical conditioning is learning through passive, involuntary paired associations, whereas operant conditioning is learning through active, voluntary behavior and its subsequent consequences.

**Test Your Critical Thinking**

**1.** You observe a parent yelling "No!" to a child who is screaming for candy in a supermarket. Given what you've learned about operant conditioning, can you predict how both the parent and the child will respond in similar future situations?

**2.** Can you think of a better alternative to yelling "No!"?

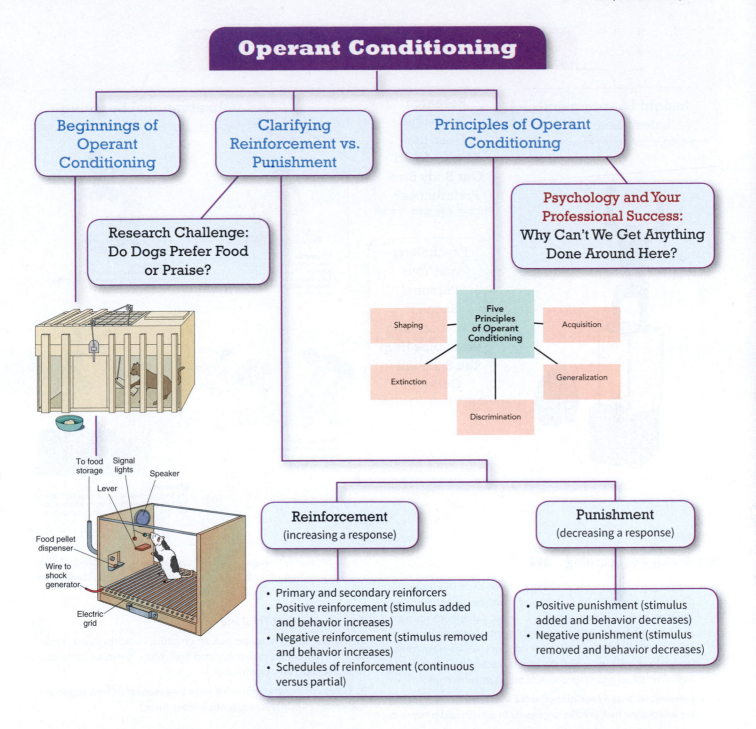

# Operant Conditioning

**Beginnings of Operant Conditioning**

**Clarifying Reinforcement vs. Punishment**

Research Challenge: Do Dogs Prefer Food or Praise?

**Principles of Operant Conditioning**

Psychology and Your Professional Success: Why Can't We Get Anything Done Around Here?

Five Principles of Operant Conditioning

Shaping · Acquisition · Extinction · Generalization · Discrimination

To food storage · Signal lights · Speaker · Lever · Food pellet dispenser · Wire to shock generator · Electric grid

**Reinforcement** (increasing a response)

- Primary and secondary reinforcers
- Positive reinforcement (stimulus added and behavior increases)
- Negative reinforcement (stimulus removed and behavior increases)
- Schedules of reinforcement (continuous versus partial)

**Punishment** (decreasing a response)

- Positive punishment (stimulus added and behavior decreases)
- Negative punishment (stimulus removed and behavior decreases)

## 6.3 Cognitive–Social Learning   206

- **Cognitive–social learning theory** emphasizes the roles of thinking and social learning. Köhler discovered that animals sometimes learn through sudden **insight learning**, rather than through trial and error. Tolman provided evidence of hidden, **latent learning** and internal **cognitive maps**.

- Bandura's research found that children who watched an adult behave aggressively toward an inflated Bobo doll became more aggressive themselves. **Observational learning** requires attention, retention, reproduction, and motivation.

### Test Your Critical Thinking

**1.** What are some examples of how insight learning has benefited you in your life?

**2.** Are there instances in which observational learning has worked to your advantage?

# Cognitive–Social Learning

**Insight Learning and Latent Learning**

**Research Challenge: Does the Media Affect Our Body Size Preferences?**

**Psychology and Your Personal Success: Can Learning Principles Help You Succeed in College?**

## Observational Learning

**A** **Attention**
Observational learning requires attention. This is why teachers insist on having students watch their demonstrations.

**B** **Retention**
To learn new behaviors, we need to carefully note and remember the model's directions and demonstrations.

**C** **Reproduction**
Observational learning requires that we imitate the model.

**D** **Motivation**
We are more likely to repeat a modeled behavior if the model is reinforced for the behavior (for example, with applause or other recognition).

## 6.4 Biology of Learning   211

- Learning creates structural changes in the brain. For example, different areas of our brains respond to reinforcement and punishment. Early evidence for such changes came from research on animals raised in enriched environments versus deprived environments. Another neurological influence on learning comes from **mirror neurons**, which fire when an action is performed, as well as when actions or emotions of others are observed.

- Learning, such as a **conditioned taste aversion**, is an evolutionary adaptation that enables organisms to survive and prosper in a constantly changing world. However, there are biological constraints that may alter or limit conditioning, such as **biological preparedness** and **instinctive drift**.

### Test Your Critical Thinking

**1.** If mirror neurons explain human empathy, could they also explain why first responders (like police and firefighters) are more vulnerable to job burnout? Why or why not?

**2.** Do you have any conditioned taste aversions? If so, how would you use information in this chapter to remove them?

## Biology of Learning

**Neuroscience and Learning**

**Biological Primes and Constraints on Learning**

Mirror Neurons

Top-Pet-Pics/Alamy

From A.N. Meltzoff & M.K. Moore, "Imitation of Facial and Manual Gestures by Human Neonates," Science, 1977, 198, 75–78 Reprinted with permission from AAAS

- Classical conditioning (conditioned taste aversion, biological preparedness)
- Operant conditioning (instinctive drift)

# Key Terms

**Retrieval Practice**    *Write your own definition for each term before turning back to the referenced page to check your answer.*

- acquisition (in classical conditioning)   192
- acquisition (in operant conditioning)   201
- associative learning   194
- biological preparedness   214
- classical conditioning   187
- cognitive map   207
- cognitive-social learning theory   207
- conditioned emotional response (CER)   189
- conditioned response (CR)   187
- conditioned stimulus (CS)   187
- continuous reinforcement   202
- conditioned taste aversion   213
- discrimination (in classical conditioning)   192
- discrimination (in operant conditioning)   201
- extinction (in classical conditioning)   192
- extinction (in operant conditioning)   201

- fixed interval (FI) schedule   202
- fixed ratio (FR) schedule   202
- generalization (in classical conditioning)   192
- generalization (in operant conditioning)   201
- higher-order conditioning   192
- insight learning   207
- instinctive drift   214
- latent learning   207
- law of effect   195
- learning   186
- mirror neurons   213
- negative punishment   198
- negative reinforcement   196
- neutral stimulus (NS)   187
- observational learning   208

- operant conditioning   195
- partial (intermittent) reinforcement   202
- positive punishment   198
- positive reinforcement   196
- primary punisher   198
- primary reinforcer   196
- punishment   195
- reinforcement   195
- schedules of reinforcement   201
- secondary punisher   198
- secondary reinforcer   196
- shaping   201
- spontaneous recovery   192
- unconditioned response (UR)   187
- unconditioned stimulus (US)   187
- variable interval (VI) schedule   202
- variable ratio (VR) schedule   202

© alexxl66/iStockphoto

# CHAPTER 7

# Memory

| CHAPTER OUTLINE | LEARNING OBJECTIVES |
|---|---|

### ❖ Psychology and a Contemporary Success | Elizabeth Loftus

©AP/Wide World Photos

When Elizabeth Loftus (1944–) was 14 years old, her mother drowned in their pool. As she grew older, the details surrounding her mother's death became increasingly vague (see photo). Decades later, a relative told Elizabeth that she, Elizabeth, had been the one to find her mother's body. Despite her initial shock, memories slowly started coming back.

> *I could see myself, a thin, dark-haired girl, looking into the flickering blue-and-white pool. My mother, dressed in her nightgown, is floating face down. I start screaming. I remember the police cars, their lights flashing, and the stretcher with the clean, white blanket tucked in around the edges of the body. The memory had been there all along, but I just couldn't reach it (Loftus & Ketcham, 1994, p. 45).*

Loftus went on to study mathematics and psychology and was admitted to Stanford University as a graduate student in mathematical psychology in 1966. Due to her talkative, outgoing nature, her colleagues at Stanford voted her the "least likely to succeed as a psychologist" (Zagorski, 2005). Ironically, Loftus is now a distinguished professor of psychology who has earned numerous awards and is recognized around the world for her groundbreaking research on the nature of memory. In 2002, she was the highest-ranked woman in a list of the 100 most influential psychological researchers of the 20th century, and in 2016 she was awarded the John Maddox Prize for promoting sound science on a matter of public interest (Sample, 2016).

## Chapter Overview

How could a psychologist famous for her research on memory forget finding her mother's body? In this chapter, you'll discover more details about Loftus's "recovered memory" regarding her mother's body, along with the story's shocking ending. You'll also learn many other fascinating facts about memory. We begin the chapter with a look at the nature of memory. Next, we explore the basic theories and factors in forgetting and the biological bases of memory. Then we examine when, how, and why we sometimes distort our memories. The chapter closes with a summary of the best memory-improvement tools for your academic success.

## 7.1   The Nature of Memory

**LEARNING OBJECTIVES**

**Retrieval Practice**   While reading the upcoming sections, respond to each Learning Objective in your own words.

**Summarize the key factors, research findings, and major models of memory.**
- **Define** memory and its constructive process.

- **Discuss** the four major memory models.
- **Explain** the function and process of sensory memory.
- **Review** the core principles of short-term memory (STM) and how it compares to working memory.
- **Describe** the core features, functions, and various types of long-term memory (LTM), and how to improve it.

*One lives in the hope of becoming a memory.* —Antonio Porchia (Argentinian Poet, Author, Philosopher)

In Chapter 6, we discussed how the ability to learn is essential to our very survival because it allows us to learn and adapt to our ever-changing environment. But we cannot learn unless we can remember our past, weave it into our present, and then use our vast storehouse of

**Memory** The persistence of learning over time; process by which information is encoded, stored, and retrieved.

memories in the future. Can you see why psychologists are so fascinated by **memory** and why it's generally defined as *learning that persists over time*?

Why should you be interested in this chapter? You may have noticed that people often create journals and collect souvenirs on their trips, along with taking literally thousands of photos of themselves and their everyday lives. Given such common and obvious efforts to collect concrete evidence of experiences to preserve memories, it's ironic that the public tends to think of memory as a gigantic library or an automatic video recorder. As you'll discover later in this chapter, our memories are, in fact, highly fallible and very selective, and the public's unwarranted faith in eyewitness testimony has led to serious problems in legal settings and other situations (Baddeley et al., 2015; Matlin & Farmer, 2016; Wan et al., 2017).

**Constructive process** The process of organizing and shaping information during encoding, storage, and retrieval of memories.

In reality, studies find that memory is a **constructive process** through which we actively organize and shape information as it is being encoded, stored, and retrieved (Herriot, 2014; Karanian & Slotnick, 2015; Robins, 2016). This construction often leads to serious errors and biases, which we'll discuss throughout the chapter. If you'd like proof of the constructive nature of your own memory, see the following **Try This Yourself.**

## Try This Yourself

### A Personal Memory Test

Carefully read through all the words in the following list.

| Sour | Chocolate | Pie | Bitter |
| Nice | Heart | Honey | Good |
| Honey | Cake | Candy | Taste |
| Artichoke | Tart | Sugar | Tooth |

Now cover the list and write down all the words you remember. *Scoring:*

15 to 16 words = excellent
10 to 14 words = average
5 to 9 words = below average
4 or fewer words = you might need a nap

How did you do? Did you recall seeing the words "sour" and "tooth"? Most students do, and it's a good example of the *serial-position effect*—the first and last words in the list are more easily remembered than those in the middle. Did you remember the words "artichoke" and "honey"? If you recalled "artichoke," it illustrates the power of *distinctiveness*, whereas if you remembered seeing "honey" it's because it was repeated two times. Both of these examples demonstrate how distinctive and/or repeated material are more easily encoded, stored, and recalled.

Finally, did you recall the word "sweet"? If so, look back over the list. That word is not there, yet students commonly report seeing it. Why? Many of the items on the list are sweets, so they wrongly assume that word is also on the list. As mentioned above, memory is not a faithful duplicate of an event; it is a *constructive process*. We actively shape and build on information as it is encoded and retrieved.

#### Test Your Critical Thinking

1. Other than this example of seeing the word "sweet," can you think of another example in which you may have created a false memory?

2. How might constructive memories create misunderstandings at work and in our everyday relationships?

## Memory Models

**Encoding, storage, and retrieval (ESR) model** A memory model that involves three processes: *encoding* (getting information in), *storage* (retaining information for future use), and *retrieval* (recovering information).

**Encoding** The first step of the ESR memory model; process of moving sensory information into memory storage.

**Storage** The second step of the ESR memory model; retention of encoded information over time.

**Retrieval** The third step of the ESR memory model; recovery of information from memory storage.

To understand memory (and its constructive nature), you need a model of how it operates. In **Figure 7.1**, we provide a visual comparison of the four major models of memory, followed by a brief discussion of each model. Then we'll explore the fourth model in greater depth.

### Encoding, Storage, and Retrieval (ESR) Model
According to the **encoding, storage, and retrieval (ESR) model**, the barrage of information that we encounter every day goes through three basic operations: *encoding, storage*, and *retrieval*. Each of these processes represents a different function that is closely analogous to the parts and functions of a computer (**Step-by-Step Diagram 7.1**).

To input data into a computer, you begin by typing letters and numbers on the keyboard. The computer then translates these keystrokes into its own electronic language. In a roughly similar fashion, our brains **encode** sensory information (sound, visual images, and other senses) into a neural code (language) it can understand and use. Once information is encoded, it must be **stored**. Computer information is normally stored on a flash drive or hard drive, whereas human information is stored in our brains. Finally, information must be **retrieved**, or taken out of storage. We retrieve stored information by going to files on our computer or to "files" in our brains.

## FIGURE 7.1 Comparing memory models

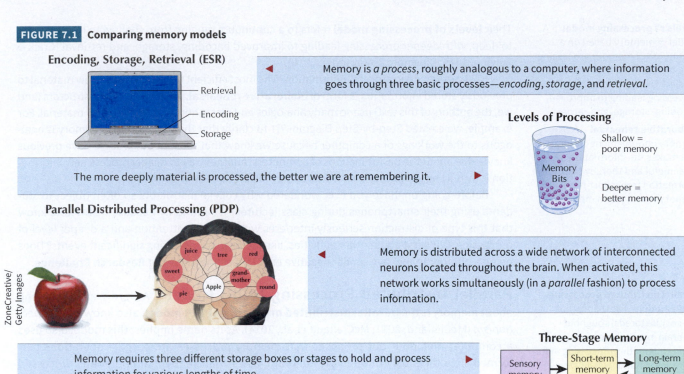

**Encoding, Storage, Retrieval (ESR)**

Retrieval
Encoding
Storage

◄ Memory is *a process*, roughly analogous to a computer, where information goes through three basic processes—*encoding*, *storage*, and *retrieval*.

The more deeply material is processed, the better we are at remembering it. ►

**Levels of Processing**

Shallow = poor memory

Memory Bits

Deeper = better memory

**Parallel Distributed Processing (PDP)**

juice   tree   red
sweet          grand-
pie    Apple   mother
               round

ZoneCreative/ Getty Images

◄ Memory is distributed across a wide network of interconnected neurons located throughout the brain. When activated, this network works simultaneously (in a *parallel* fashion) to process information.

Memory requires three different storage boxes or stages to hold and process information for various lengths of time. ►

**Three-Stage Memory**

Sensory memory → Short-term memory (STM) → Long-term memory (LTM)

---

## STEP-BY-STEP DIAGRAM 7.1   Encoding, Storage, and Retrieval (ESR) Model Compared with a Computer

**STOP!** This Step-by-Step Diagram contains essential information NOT found elsewhere in the text, which is likely to appear on quizzes and exams. Be sure to study it CAREFULLY!

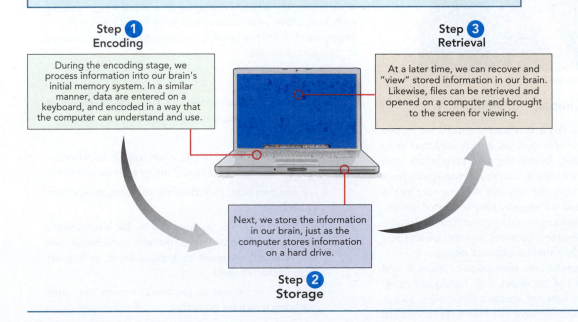

**Step 1 Encoding**

During the encoding stage, we process information into our brain's initial memory system. In a similar manner, data are entered on a keyboard, and encoded in a way that the computer can understand and use.

**Step 3 Retrieval**

At a later time, we can recover and "view" stored information in our brain. Likewise, files can be retrieved and opened on a computer and brought to the screen for viewing.

**Step 2 Storage**

Next, we store the information in our brain, just as the computer stores information on a hard drive.

---

Keep this model in mind. To do well in college, or almost any other pursuit, you must successfully encode, store, and retrieve a large amount of facts and concepts. Throughout this chapter, we'll discuss ways to improve your memory during each of these steps.

## Levels of Processing Model
Fergus Craik and Robert Lockhart (1972) were the first to suggest that encoding can be influenced by how *deeply* we process and store information.

**Levels of processing model** A model of memory based on a continuum of memory processing ranging from shallow to intermediate to deep, with deeper processing leading to improved encoding, storage, and retrieval.

**Elaborative rehearsal** A memory improvement method that makes the information more meaningful and thereby transfers information from short-term memory to long-term memory.

Their **levels of processing model** refers to a continuum ranging from shallow to intermediate to deep, with deeper processing leading to improved encoding, storage, and retrieval (Craik & Tulving, 1975; Dinsmore & Alexander, 2016).

How can we "deep process" information? The most efficient way is to link the new material to previously stored information, a form of **elaborative rehearsal**. This is why your instructors (and we, the authors of this text) use so many analogies and metaphors to introduce new material. For example, we created Step-by-Step Diagram 7.1 to clarify that the ESR model of memory is analogous to the workings of a computer because we know that most of our readers have previous knowledge about the basic functions of computers. Another way to deeply process new information is by putting it into your own words and/or talking about it with others.

Before going on, have you ever wondered why college instructors so often object to students using their smartphones during class lectures? It's primarily because instructors know that this type of distraction seriously interferes with selective attention and a deeper level of processing. But what about other activities, like taking pictures during significant events? Does being a photographer have similar negative effects? See the following **Research Challenge**.

**Parallel distributed processing (PDP) model** The theory that memory is stored throughout the brain in web-like connections among interacting processing units operating simultaneously, rather than sequentially; also known as connectionism.

**Parallel Distributed Processing (PDP) Model** A third way of thinking about memory is the **parallel distributed processing (PDP) model**, also known as *connectionism* (McClelland, 2011; McClelland et al., 2014). As its name implies, this model also uses a computer metaphor but proposes that memory processes are *parallel* operations performed simultaneously throughout the brain rather than sequential operations processed one at a time. In addition, memory is spread out, or *distributed*, throughout the brain in a web-like network of processing units.

## Research Challenge

Gemma Ferrando/Getty Images

### Can Taking Photos Impair Our Memories?

Researchers interested in this and related questions set up two studies using participants who were led on a guided tour of an art museum (Henkel, 2014). During the tour, participants were asked to take note of certain objects, either by photographing them or by simply observing them. The next day, their memory for the specific objects was tested. As you may have suspected, participants were less accurate in recognizing the objects they had photographed than those they had only observed, and they weren't able to answer as many questions about the objects' details.

In contrast, when participants were asked to zoom in and photograph a specific part of the object, their subsequent recognition and detail memory were not impaired. Surprisingly, participants' memories for features that were NOT zoomed in on were just as strong as those for features that were zoomed in on. Can you see how the selective attention and deeper levels of processing engaged by this focused activity improve overall encoding and may eliminate the photo-taking-impairment effect?

This research has valuable practical applications. Given that it's difficult to always pay full focused attention, we need to keep in mind

that while we're mindlessly taking numerous "selfies" and other photos we may encode fewer details. Furthermore, taking photos the whole time we're on vacation or during a child's dance recital may interfere with not only our full enjoyment of the event, but our actual memories of those special occasions as well! (Study Tip: While reading this and other college texts and listening to lectures, you can improve your learning and memory by consciously directing your brain to pay focused, selective attention and "zooming in" on essential details.)

**Test Yourself**

1. Based on the information provided, did this study (Henkel, 2014) use descriptive, correlational, and/or experimental research?

2. If you chose:
   - *descriptive research*, is this a naturalistic observation, survey/interview, case study, and/or archival research?
   - *correlational research*, is this a positive, negative, or zero correlation?
   - *experimental research*, label the IV, DV, experimental group(s), and control group. (Note: If participants were not randomly assigned to groups, list it as a *quasi-experimental design*.)
   - *both descriptive and correlational*, answer the corresponding questions for both.

**Check your answers by clicking on the answer button or by looking in Appendix B.**

**Note:** The information provided in this study is admittedly limited, but the level of detail is similar to what is presented in most textbooks and public reports of research findings. Answering these questions, and then comparing your answers to those provided, will help you become a better critical thinker and consumer of scientific research.

For example, if you're swimming in the ocean and see a large fin nearby, your brain does not conduct a one-by-one search of all fish with fins before urging you to begin a rush to shore. Instead, you conduct a mental *parallel* search. You note the color of the fish, the shape of the fin, and the potential danger all at the same time. Because the processes are parallel, you can quickly process the information—and possibly avoid being eaten by the shark!

The PDP model seems consistent with neurological information about brain activity (Chapter 2). Thanks to our richly interconnected synapses, activation of one neuron can influence many other neurons. This model also has been useful in explaining perception (Chapter 4), language (Chapter 8), and decision making (Chapter 8). Perhaps most importantly, it allows a faster response time to sharks and other threats to our survival.

### Three-Stage Memory Model

Since the late 1960s, the most highly researched and widely used memory model has been the **three-stage memory model** (Atkinson & Shiffrin, 1968; Eichenbaum, 2013; Li, 2016). Today, this model remains the leading paradigm in memory research because it offers a convenient way to organize the major research findings. Like the ESR model, the three-stage memory model has been compared to a computer, with input, processing, and output. However, in the three-stage model, the three different storage "boxes," or memory stages, all perform both encoding and storage functions (**Step-by-Step Diagram 7.2**). Let's consider each stage in more detail.

**Three-stage memory model**
A memory model based on the passage of information through three stages: sensory, short-term, and long-term memory; also known as the Atkinson-Shiffrin theory.

---

**STEP-BY-STEP DIAGRAM 7.2** | **An Update to the Traditional Three-Stage Memory Model**

**STOP!** This Step-by-Step Diagram contains essential information NOT found elsewhere in the text, which is likely to appear on quizzes and exams. Be sure to study it CAREFULLY!

Each "box" in this model represents a separate memory storage system that differs in purpose, duration, and capacity from the others. When information is not transferred from sensory memory or short-term memory (STM), it is assumed to be lost. Information stored in long-term memory (LTM) can be retrieved and send back to short-term memory for use. In addition to the three traditional stages, modern research has discovered other routes to memory formation, such as through *automatic encoding*. As shown by the dotted line, and as you may know from personal experience, some information from the environment bypasses Steps 1 and 2 and gets into our long-term memory without our conscious awareness.

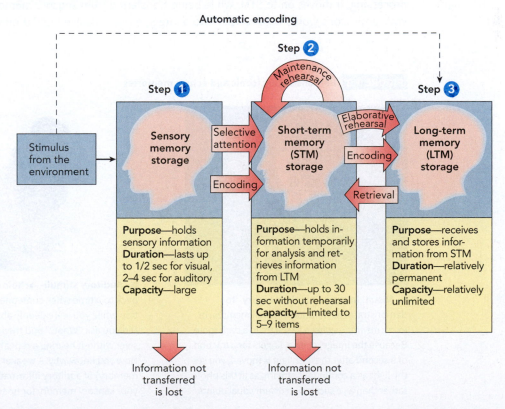

## Stage 1: Sensory Memory

**Sensory memory** The initial memory stage, which holds sensory information; it has relatively large capacity, but the duration is only a few seconds.

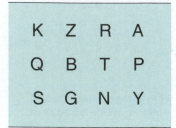

**FIGURE 7.2** **Sperling's test for iconic sensory memory**

Everything we see, hear, touch, taste, and smell must first enter our **sensory memory**. Once it's entered, the information remains in sensory memory just long enough for our brains to locate relevant bits of data and transfer it on to the next stage of memory. For visual information, known as *iconic memory*, the visual image (icon) stays in sensory memory only about one-half a second before it rapidly fades away.

In an early study of iconic sensory memory, George Sperling (1960) flashed an arrangement of 12 letters like the ones in **Figure 7.2** for 1/20 of a second. Most people, he found, could recall only 4 or 5 of the letters. But when instructed to report just the top, middle, or bottom row, depending on whether they heard a high, medium, or low tone, they reported almost all the letters correctly. Apparently, all 12 letters are held in sensory memory right after they're viewed, but only those that are immediately attended to are noted and processed.

Like the fleeting visual images in iconic memory, auditory stimuli (what we hear) is temporary. Yet a weaker "echo," or *echoic memory*, of this auditory input lingers for up to four seconds (Erviti et al., 2015; Kojima et al., 2014; Neisser, 1967). Why are visual and auditory memories so fleeting? We cannot process all incoming stimuli, so lower brain centers need only a few seconds to "decide" if the information is significant enough to promote to conscious awareness (**Figure 7.3**).

Early researchers believed that sensory memory had an unlimited capacity. However, later research suggests that sensory memory does have limits and that stored images are fuzzier than once thought (Cohen, 2014; Franconeri et al., 2013; Howes & O'Shea, 2014).

## Stage 2: Short-Term Memory (STM)

**Short-term memory (STM)** The second memory stage, which temporarily stores sensory information and transmits information to and from long-term memory (LTM); its capacity is limited to five to nine items, and it has a duration of about 30 seconds.

The second stage of memory processing, **short-term memory (STM)**, temporarily stores and processes sensory stimuli. Unlike sensory memory, STM does not store exact *duplicates* of information but rather stores a mixture of perceptual analyses.

For example, when your sensory memory registers the sound of your professor's voice, it holds the actual auditory information for only a few seconds. If the information requires further processing, it moves on to STM. While being transferred from sensory memory, the sound of your professor's words is converted into a larger, more inclusive type of message capable of

**FIGURE 7.3** **Demonstrating iconic and echoic memories**

Francesco Balbusso/EyeEm/Getty Images

**a. Visual images—iconic memory** To demonstrate the duration of visual memory, or *iconic memory*, swing a flashlight in a dark room. Because the image, or icon, lingers for a fraction of a second after the flashlight is moved, you see the light as a continuous stream, as in this photo, rather than as a succession of individual points.

Blue Jean Images/Getty Images

**b. Auditory stimuli—echoic memory** Think back to a time when someone asked you a question while you were deeply absorbed in a task. Did you ask "What?" and then immediately answer without hearing a repeat of the question? Now you know why. A weaker "echo" (echoic memory) of auditory information is available in your sensory memory for up to four seconds.

being analyzed and interpreted in STM. If you decide the information is important (or may be on a test), your STM organizes and sends it along to relatively permanent storage, called long-term memory (LTM).

Both the *duration* and *capacity* of STM are relatively limited. Although some researchers extend the time to a few minutes, most research shows that STM holds information for approximately 30 seconds (Bankó & Vidnyánsky, 2010; Nairne & Neath, 2013). STM also holds a restricted *amount* of new information, from five to nine items. As with sensory memory, information in STM either is transferred quickly into the next stage (LTM), or it decays and is theoretically lost.

### Improving Your STM
As just mentioned, the capacity and duration of STM are limited. To extend the *capacity* of STM, you can use a technique called **chunking**, which involves grouping separate pieces of information into larger, more manageable units (Gilbert et al., 2015; Miller, 1956; Portrat et al., 2016). Have you noticed that your credit card, social security card, and telephone numbers are almost always grouped into three or four distinct units (sometimes separated by hyphens)? The reason is that it's easier to remember numbers in chunks rather than as a string of single digits.

Chunking even helps in football. What do you see when you observe the arrangement of players from a page of a sports playbook shown in **Figure 7.4**? To the inexpert eye, it looks like a random assembly of lines and arrows. But experienced players and seasoned fans generally recognize many or all of the standard plays. To them, the scattered lines form meaningful patterns—classic arrangements that recur often. Just as you group the letters of this sentence into meaningful words and remember them long enough to understand the meaning of the sentence, expert football players group the different football plays into easily recalled patterns (or chunks).

You can also extend the *duration* of your STM almost indefinitely by consciously "juggling" the information—a process called **maintenance rehearsal**. You are using maintenance rehearsal when you look up a phone number and repeat it over and over until you key in the number.

As you may know, people who are good at remembering names often take advantage of maintenance rehearsal. They repeat the name of each person they meet, aloud or silently, to keep it active in STM. They also make sure that other thoughts (such as their plans for what to say next) don't intrude.

### Working Memory
According to the traditional three-stage memory model, STM is a storehouse for information until it is either lost or moves along to LTM. However, we now know that STM is not just a "box" that passively stores information. Instead, it is a working, active system that allows us to hold information temporarily while also performing cognitive tasks. To reflect this combination of STM and active processing, modern researchers use the term **working memory** (Baddeley, 1992, 2007; Radvansky & Ashcraft. 2016).

As you can see in **Figure 7.5**, working memory is composed of a *visuospatial sketchpad*, a *phonological loop*, and a *central executive*. To understand this three-part system, consider what's happening when we "channel surf." As we all know, this "simply" involves pushing the channel selector on our television's remote control to quickly switch from channel to channel until we find something interesting to watch. But did you know that this process actually requires a complex interaction between all parts of our working memory system? During this "surfing," the visuospatial sketchpad allows us to keep a brief mental image of each channel in mind, while the phonological loop enables us to continually mentally rehearse the auditory information. Even more amazing is the fact that we're simultaneously actively retrieving previously stored information from our LTM. We then use all of this information to decide whether or not we like the particular programs we're briefly seeing on each channel.

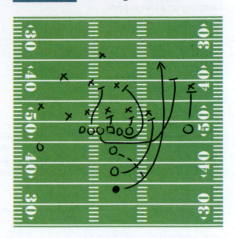

**FIGURE 7.4  Chunking in football**

**Chunking**  A memory technique involving grouping separate pieces of information into larger, more manageable units (or chunks).

**Maintenance rehearsal**  The act of repeating information over and over to maintain it in short-term memory (STM).

**Working memory**  A newer understanding of short-term memory (STM) that emphasizes the active processing of information.

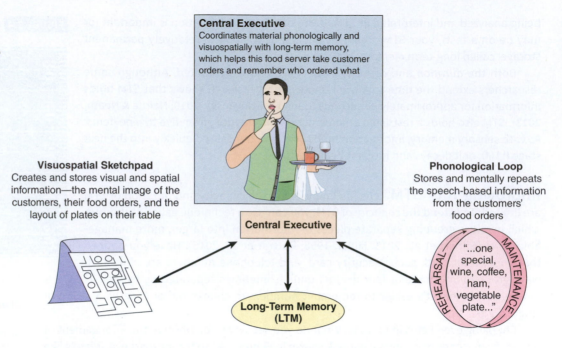

**Working memory as a three-part system** The *central executive* supervises and coordinates two subsystems, the *phonological loop* and the *visuospatial sketchpad*, while also sending and retrieving information to and from LTM. Picture yourself as a food server in a busy restaurant. A couple has just given you a complicated food order. When you mentally rehearse the food order (the phonological loop) and combine it with a mental picture of your customers, their food orders, and the layout of plates on their table (the visuospatial sketchpad), you're using your central executive.

**Central Executive**
Coordinates material phonologically and visuospatially with long-term memory, which helps this food server take customer orders and remember who ordered what

**Visuospatial Sketchpad**
Creates and stores visual and spatial information—the mental image of the customers, their food orders, and the layout of plates on their table

**Phonological Loop**
Stores and mentally repeats the speech-based information from the customers' food orders

**Central Executive**

**Long-Term Memory (LTM)**

REHEARSAL · MAINTENANCE · "...one special, wine, coffee, ham, vegetable plate..."

**Long-term memory (LTM)**
The third stage of memory, which stores information for long periods of time; the capacity is virtually limitless, and the duration is relatively permanent.

**Explicit/declarative memory**
A subsystem of long-term memory (LTM) that involves conscious, easily described (declared) memories; consists of semantic memories (facts) and episodic memories (personal experiences).

## Stage 3: Long-Term Memory (LTM)

Once information has been transferred from STM, it is organized and integrated with other information in **long-term memory (LTM)**. LTM serves as a storehouse for information that must be kept for long periods. When we need the information, it is sent back to STM for our conscious use. Compared with sensory memory and short-term memory, long-term memory has relatively unlimited *capacity* and *duration* (Eichenbaum, 2013). But, just as with any other possession, the better we label and arrange our memories, the more readily we'll be able to retrieve them.

How do we store the vast amount of information we collect over a lifetime? Several types of LTM exist (**Figure 7.6**). **Explicit/declarative memory** refers to intentional learning or conscious knowledge. If asked to remember your phone number or your mother's name, you can easily state (*declare*) the answers directly (*explicitly*). Explicit/declarative memory is further

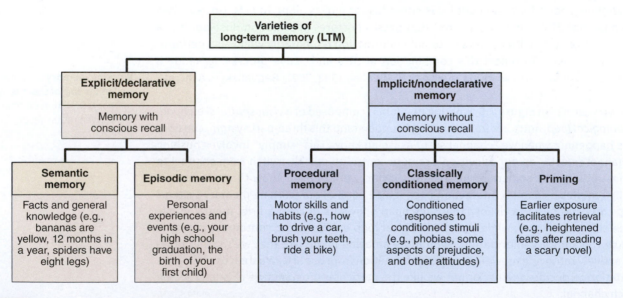

**Varieties of long-term memory (LTM)**

| Explicit/declarative memory | | Implicit/nondeclarative memory | | |
|---|---|---|---|---|
| Memory with conscious recall | | Memory without conscious recall | | |
| **Semantic memory** | **Episodic memory** | **Procedural memory** | **Classically conditioned memory** | **Priming** |
| Facts and general knowledge (e.g., bananas are yellow, 12 months in a year, spiders have eight legs) | Personal experiences and events (e.g., your high school graduation, the birth of your first child) | Motor skills and habits (e.g., how to drive a car, brush your teeth, ride a bike) | Conditioned responses to conditioned stimuli (e.g., phobias, some aspects of prejudice, and other attitudes) | Earlier exposure facilitates retrieval (e.g., heightened fears after reading a scary novel) |

**LTM is divided and subdivided into various types**

subdivided into two parts. **Semantic memory** is memory for general knowledge, rules, events, facts, and specific information. It is our mental encyclopedia. In contrast, **episodic memory** is like a mental diary. It records the major events (*episodes*) in our lives. Some of our episodic memories are short-lived, whereas others can last a lifetime.

**Implicit/nondeclarative memory** refers to unintentional learning or unconscious knowledge. As you recall from Step-by-Step Diagram 7.2, certain memories get stored in LTM without going through the normal steps. This type of *automatic encoding* occurs without our conscious awareness and is a form of implicit/nondeclarative memory. Try telling someone how you tie your shoelaces without demonstrating the actual behavior. Because your memory of this skill is unconscious and hard to describe (*declare*) in words, this type of memory is sometimes referred to as *nondeclarative*.

Implicit/nondeclarative memory consists not only of *procedural motor skills*, like tying your shoes or riding a bike, but also of *classically conditioned emotional responses* (CERs), such as fears and prejudices (Chapter 6). In addition, implicit/nondeclarative memory includes **priming**, in which exposure (often unconscious) to previously stored information predisposes (or primes) our responses to related stimuli (Cesario, 2014; Clark et al., 2014). As you may recall from Chapter 4, research on *subliminal perception* finds that certain unconscious (unnoticed) stimuli can reach our brains and predispose (*prime*) us to make it easier or more difficult to recall related information already in storage (Loebnitz & Aschemann-Witzel, 2016; Xiao & Yamauchi, 2016). For example, if a researcher shows you the words "red" and "fire engine," you're more likely to quickly recognize the word "apple" because those words are already stored and closely associated in your memory. Additional examples are provided in the following **Try This Yourself**.

**Semantic memory**  A subsystem of long-term memory (LTM) that stores general knowledge; a mental encyclopedia or dictionary.

**Episodic memory**  A subsystem of long-term memory (LTM) that stores autobiographical events and the contexts in which they occurred; a mental diary of a person's life.

**Implicit/nondeclarative memory**  A subsystem within long-term memory (LTM) that contains memories independent of conscious recall; consists of procedural motor skills, priming, and simple classically conditioned responses.

**Priming**  An exposure (often unconscious) to previously stored information that predisposes (or primes) one's response to related stimuli.

## Try This Yourself

### Can Our Emotions Be Primed?

Have you ever felt nervous being home alone while reading a Stephen King novel, experienced sadness after hearing about a tragic event in the news, or developed amorous feelings while watching a romantic movie? These are all examples of how the situation we are in may influence our mood, in conscious or unconscious ways. Given this new insight into how priming can "set you up" for certain emotions, do you understand how those who haven't studied psychology might be more likely to mislabel or overreact to their feelings?

© CBW/Alamy Inc.

Before going on, have you ever wondered why most adults can recall almost nothing of the years before they reached age 3? This so-called *infantile amnesia* reflects the fact that memory in the first few years of life is primarily implicit/nondeclarative. Research suggests that the development of a concept of self and sufficient language, as well as growth of multiple brain regions, may be necessary for us to recall early events many years later (Lambert & Lavenex, 2017; Madsen & Kim, 2016; Uehara, 2015). In other words, we start with implicit/nondeclarative memory and only later develop explicit/declarative memory, which is necessary for us to encode, store, retrieve, and later discuss early memories. But even with this later development, some memories are more lasting than others. A case in point, many older adults describe their most lasting memories as occurring between the ages of 17 and 24, in part because our most notable life transitions—such as getting married, attending college, starting a first job, and having children— often happen during this period of time (Steiner et al., 2014).

### Improving Your LTM
There are three major ways we can improve LTM—*organization*, *rehearsal*, and *retrieval tips*.

### Organization
To successfully encode information, we need to *organize* material into hierarchies. This means arranging a number of related items into broad categories that we further divide and subdivide. (This organizational strategy for LTM is similar to the strategy of grouping and chunking material in STM.) For instance, we arrange content throughout this text in subheadings under larger, main headings and within diagrams, tables, and so on in order to make the material in the book more understandable and *memorable*.

Admittedly, organization takes time and work, so you'll be happy to know that some memory organization and filing is done automatically while you sleep or nap (Adi-Japha & Karni, 2016; Cona et al., 2014; Nielsen et al., 2015). In fact, people who rest and close their eyes for as little as 10 minutes show greater memory for details of a story they've just heard (Dewar et al., 2012). Unfortunately, despite claims to the contrary, research shows that we can't recruit our sleeping hours to memorize new material, such as a foreign language.

**Rehearsal**   As mentioned in Chapter 1 and discussed later in this chapter, the rehearsal that comes from *practice testing* and *distributed practice* (versus "cramming") is the most effective method for improving your LTM—and exam scores (Carpenter & Yeung, 2017; Putnam et al., 2016; Trumbo et al., 2016). Why? Like organization, *rehearsal* improves encoding. If you need to hold information in STM for longer than 30 seconds, you can simply keep repeating it (maintenance rehearsal). But storage in LTM requires *deeper levels of processing* through methods such as *elaborative rehearsal*. As described earlier, this simply involves making new information more meaningful in some way. For example, to remember the exact order of the colors of the rainbow, teachers often use the acronym "Roy G. Biv."

How does deeper processing and elaborative rehearsal apply to your academic life? An intriguing study found that students who took notes on laptops performed worse on conceptual questions than students who took notes on paper (Mueller & Oppenheimer, 2014). The researchers suggested that students who take notes using a laptop tend to just transcribe lectures verbatim (*shallow processing*), rather than reframing lecture material in their own words (*deeper processing*). (Additional tips for improving elaborative rehearsal and deeper levels of processing are provided in the following **Try This Yourself**.)

## Try This Yourself

### Improving Elaborative Rehearsal

Think about the other students in your college classes. Have you noticed that older students often tend to get better grades? This is, in part, because they've lived longer and can tap into a greater wealth of previously stored material. If you're a younger student (or an older student just returning to college), you can learn to process information at a deeper level and build your elaborative rehearsal skills by:

- ***Expanding (or elaborating on) the information***   The more you elaborate, or try to understand something, the more likely you are to remember it. People who have a chance to reflect on a task show better learning and memory than those who don't (Schlichting & Preston, 2014). This study has clear implications for teachers. Asking students to reflect on what they've just learned helps prompt them to remember that information better. As a student, you can discuss the major points of a lecture with your study group or practice repeating or reading something aloud. It's another form of elaborative rehearsal (Lafleur & Boucher, 2015).

- ***Linking new information to yourself***   All humans think about themselves many times each day. Therefore, creating links between new information and our own experiences, beliefs, and memories will naturally lead to easier, and more lasting, memories. In addition to applying new information to your personal life, which is known as the *self-reference effect,* research shows that *visual imagery* (such as the numerous figures, photos and tables in this text and the personal images you create yourself) greatly improves LTM and decreases forgetting (Collins et al., 2014; Leblond et al., 2016; Paivio, 1995).

- ***Finding meaningfulness***   When studying new terms in this book and other college textbooks, try to find meaning. If you want to add the term *iconic memory* to your LTM, ask yourself, "What does the word *iconic* mean"? By looking it up on your smartphone, you'll discover that it comes from the Greek word for "image" or "likeness," which adds meaning to the word and thereby increases your retention. Similarly, when you meet new people and want to remember their names, ask about their favorite TV shows, career plans, political beliefs, or anything else that requires deeper analysis. You'll be much more likely to remember their names.

**Retrieval cues**   A prompt or stimulus that aids recall or retrieval of a stored piece of information from long-term memory (LTM).

**Retrieval Tips**   Finally, effective *retrieval* is critical to long-term memory. There are two types of **retrieval cues**. *Specific* cues require you only to *recognize* the correct response. *General* cues require you to *recall* previously learned material by searching through all possible matches in LTM—a much more difficult task. Can you see how this explains why multiple-choice exams are generally easier than essay exams? See **Figure 7.7**.

Whether cues require recall or only recognition is not all that matters. Imagine that while house hunting, you walk into a stranger's kitchen and are greeted with the unmistakable smell of freshly baked bread. Instantly, the aroma transports you back to your grandmother's kitchen,

**FIGURE 7.7** **Essay exams, retrieval cues, and planets** Are you wondering what these three things have in common? If so, stop and try to *recall* the names of all the planets in our solar system. Almost everyone finds this difficult because recall requires retrieval using only general, nonspecific cues—as in naming the planets or taking an essay exam. In contrast, a *recognition* task requires you only to identify the correct response, as in a multiple-choice exam. Note how much easier it is to recognize the names of the planets when you're provided a specific retrieval cue, in this case the first three letters of each planet's name: Mer-, Ven-, Ear-, Mar-, Jup-, Sat-, Ura-, Nep-, Plu-. (Note that in 2006, Pluto was officially declassified as a planet and is now considered a "dwarf planet.")

where you spent many childhood afternoons doing your homework. You find yourself suddenly thinking of the mental shortcuts your grandmother taught you to help you learn your multiplication tables. You hadn't thought about these little tricks for years, but somehow a whiff of baking bread brought them back to you. Why?

In this imagined bread-baking episode, you have stumbled upon the **encoding-specificity principle** (Tulving & Thompson, 1973). In most cases, we're able to remember better when we attempt to recall information in the *same* context in which we learned it (Gao et al., 2016; Grzybowski et al., 2014; Unsworth et al., 2012). Have you noticed that you tend to do better on exams when you take them in the same seat and classroom in which you originally studied the material? This happens because the matching location acts as a retrieval cue for the information.

We also remember information better when our moods during learning and retrieval match (Forgas & Eich, 2013; Rokke & Lystad, 2014). This phenomenon, called *mood congruence*, occurs because a given mood tends to evoke memories that are consistent with a similar mood. When you're sad (or happy or angry), you're more likely to remember events and circumstances from other times when you were sad (or happy or angry).

Retrieval is also improved when we are in the same state of consciousness as when the memory was formed. For example, people who are intoxicated will better remember events that happened in a previous drunken state, compared to when they were sober. This is called *state-dependent retrieval* or *state-dependent memory* (Hunt & Barnet, 2016; Jafari-Sabet et al., 2014; Zarrindast et al., 2014).

**Encoding-specificity principle**
The principle that retrieval of information is improved if cues received at the time of recall are consistent with those present at the time of encoding.

> **Study Tip**
>
> *If you're confused by these seemingly overlapping terms* (retrieval cues, *the* encoding-specificity principle, mood congruence, *and* state-dependent retrieval), *just remember that they're essentially different ways of improving retrieval by recreating the original learning environment. Just as the smell of bread might bring back specific memories of being in Grandma's house, you will do better on exams if your studying environment matches your testing environment.*

One final trick for giving your recall a boost is to use **mnemonic** devices to encode items in a special way (**Concept Organizer 7.1**). However, these devices take practice and time, and some students find that they get better results using the other well-researched principles discussed throughout this chapter.

**Mnemonic** A strategy device that uses familiar information during the encoding of new information to enhance later recall.

## CONCEPT ORGANIZER 7.1 | Improving Your Memory Using Mnemonic Devices

These three mnemonics improve memory by tagging information to physical locations (*method of loci*), organizing information into main and subsidiary topics (an *outline*), and using familiar information to remember the unfamiliar (*acronyms*).

**a. Method of loci** Greek and Roman orators developed the *method of loci* to keep track of the many parts of their long speeches. Orators would imagine the parts of their speeches attached to places in a courtyard. As shown below, if an opening point in a speech was the concept of *justice*, they might visualize a courthouse placed in the back corner of their garden. Continuing this imaginary garden walk, the second point the orator might make would be about the prison system, and the third would be a set of scales, symbolizing the need for balance in government.

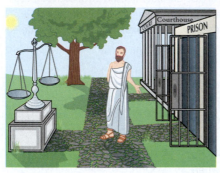

**b. Outlining organization** When listening to lectures and/or reading this text, draw a vertical line approximately 3 inches from the left margin of your notebook paper. Write main headings from the chapter outline to the left of the line and add specific details and examples from the lecture or text on the right, as in this example:

| Outline | Details and Examples from Lecture and Text |
|---|---|
| 1. Nature of Memory | _____ |
| a. Memory Models | _____ |
| b. Sensory Memory | _____ |
| c. Short-Term Memory (STM) | _____ |

**c. Acronyms** To use the *acronym method*, create a new code word from the first letters of the items you want to remember. For example, to recall the names of the Great Lakes, use the common acronym *HOMES* (Huron, Ontario, Michigan, Erie, Superior). Visualizing homes on each lake also helps you remember the acronym *homes*.

### Test Your Critical Thinking

1. How could you use the method of loci to remember several items on your grocery shopping list?

2. How would you use the acronym method to remember the names of the last seven presidents of the United States?

---

© Billy R. Ray/Wiley

## Retrieval Practice 7.1 | The Nature of Memory

Completing this self-test and the connections section, and then checking your answers by clicking on the answer button or by looking in Appendix B, will provide immediate feedback and helpful practice for exams.

### Self-Test

1. Describe how the ESR model of memory can be compared to the workings of a computer.

2. Information in _____ lasts only a few seconds or less and has a relatively large (but not unlimited) storage capacity.
   a. perceptual processes
   b. working memory
   c. short-term storage
   d. sensory memory

3. _____ is the process of grouping separate pieces of information into a single unit.
   a. Chunking
   b. Collecting
   c. Conflation
   d. Dual-coding

4. In answering this question, the correct multiple-choice option may serve as a _____ for recalling accurate information from your long-term memory.
   a. specificity code
   b. retrieval cue
   c. priming pump
   d. flashbulb stimulus

5. The encoding-specificity principle says that information retrieval is improved when _____.
   a. both maintenance and elaborative rehearsal are used
   b. reverberating circuits consolidate information
   c. conditions of retrieval are similar to encoding conditions
   d. long-term potentiation is accessed

**Connections—Chapter to Chapter**
Answering the following question will help you "look back and look ahead" to see the important connections among the subfields of psychology and chapters within this text.

In Chapter 4 (Sensation and Perception), you discovered the Gestalt principles of organization, which are based on our nat-ural tendency to force patterns onto whatever we see. Explain how *chunking* (discussed in this chapter) might be considered an extension of Gestalt principles. Which of the principles (*figure-ground, proximity, continuity, closure, similarity*) do we use in chunking?

## 7.2    Forgetting

**LEARNING OBJECTIVES**

**Retrieval Practice**    While reading the upcoming sections, respond to each Learning Objective in your own words.

**Review the research, major theories, and important factors in forgetting.**

- **Describe** Ebbinghaus's research on learning and forgetting.
- **Review** the five basic theories of forgetting.
- **Identify** three key factors involved in forgetting.

We've all had numerous experiences with *forgetting*—the inability to remember information that was previously available. We misplace our keys, forget the name of a familiar person, and even miss major exams! Although forgetting can be annoying and sometimes even catastrophic, it's generally adaptive. If we remembered everything we ever saw, heard, or read, our minds would be overwhelmed with useless information.

### Ebbinghaus's Forgetting Curve

Psychologists have long been interested in how and why we forget. Hermann Ebbinghaus first introduced the experimental study of learning and forgetting in 1885. Using himself as a research participant, Ebbinghaus calculated how long it took him to learn and then forget a list of three-letter *nonsense syllables*, such as *SIB* and *RAL*. As you can see in **Figure 7.8**, his research revealed that forgetting begins soon after we learn something and then gradually tapers off (Ebbinghaus, 1885).

If this dramatic "curve of forgetting" discourages you from studying, keep in mind that meaningful material is far more memorable than Ebbinghaus's nonsense syllables. Furthermore, after some time had passed and Ebbinghaus thought he had completely forgotten the material, he discovered that *relearning* it took less time than the initial learning. Similarly, if your college requires you to repeat some of the math or foreign language courses you took in high school, you'll be happily surprised by how much you recall and how much easier it is to relearn the information the second time around.

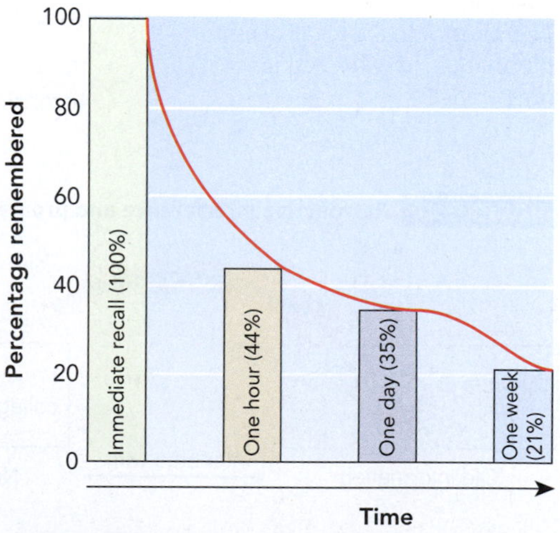

### Theories of Forgetting

As mentioned earlier, the ability to forget is essential to the proper functioning of memory, and psychologists have developed several theories to explain why forgetting occurs: *decay, interference, motivated forgetting, encoding failure,* and *retrieval failure*. As shown in **Figure 7.9**, each theory focuses on a different stage of the memory process or a particular problem with encoding or retrieval.

**FIGURE 7.8    How quickly we forget**    Ebbinghaus's research involved learning lists of three-letter nonsense syllables. He found that one hour after he knew a list perfectly, he remembered only 44% of the syllables. A day later, he recalled 35%, and a week later only 21%.

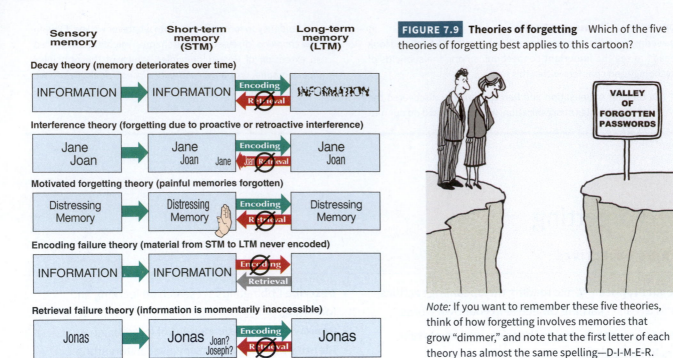

**Sensory memory** | **Short-term memory (STM)** | **Long-term memory (LTM)**

**Decay theory (memory deteriorates over time)**

INFORMATION → INFORMATION → Encoding / Retrieval → INFORMATION

**Interference theory (forgetting due to proactive or retroactive interference)**

Jane Joan → Jane Joan Jane → Encoding / Joan Retrieval → Jane Joan

**Motivated forgetting theory (painful memories forgotten)**

Distressing Memory → Distressing Memory → Encoding / Retrieval → Distressing Memory

**Encoding failure theory (material from STM to LTM never encoded)**

INFORMATION → INFORMATION → Encoding / Retrieval →

**Retrieval failure theory (information is momentarily inaccessible)**

Jonas → Jonas Joan? Joseph? → Encoding / Retrieval → Jonas

**FIGURE 7.9** **Theories of forgetting** Which of the five theories of forgetting best applies to this cartoon?

VALLEY OF FORGOTTEN PASSWORDS

Cartoon Resource/Shutterstock

*Note:* If you want to remember these five theories, think of how forgetting involves memories that grow "dimmer," and note that the first letter of each theory has almost the same spelling—D-I-M-E-R.

- In *decay theory*, memory is processed and stored in a physical form—for example, in a network of neurons. Connections between neurons probably deteriorate over time, leading to forgetting. This theory explains why skills and memory often degrade if they go unused ("use it or lose it").

- According to *interference theory*, forgetting is caused by two competing memories, particularly memories with similar qualities. At least two types of interference exist: *retroactive* and *proactive* (**Figure 7.10**). When new information disrupts (*interferes* with) the recall of OLD, "retro" information, it is called **retroactive interference** (acting backward in time). Learning your new home address may cause you to forget your old home address. Conversely, when old information disrupts (*interferes* with) the recall of NEW information, it is called **proactive interference** (acting forward in time). Old information (like the Spanish you learned in high school) may interfere with your ability to learn and remember material from your new college course in French.

- *Motivated forgetting theory* is based on the idea that we forget some information for a reason. According to Freudian theory (Chapter 13), people forget unpleasant or anxiety-producing

**Retroactive interference**
A memory problem that occurs when new information disrupts (*interferes* with) the recall of old, "retro" information; backward-acting interference.

**Proactive interference**
A memory problem that occurs when old information disrupts (*interferes* with) the recall of new information; forward-acting interference.

**FIGURE 7.10** **Retroactive interference and proactive interference**

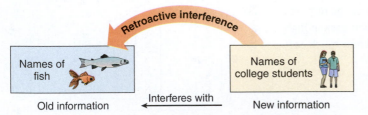

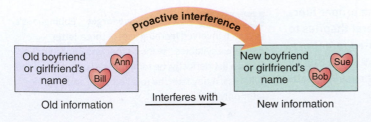

**a. Retroactive interference** This so-called *backward-acting* interference occurs when new information interferes with old information. This example comes from a story about an absent-minded ichthyology professor (fish specialist) who refused to learn the name of his college students. Asked why, he said, "Every time I learn a student's name, I forget the name of a fish!"

**b. Proactive interference** Referred to as *forward-acting*, this type of interference occurs when old information interferes with new information. Have you ever been in trouble because you used an old partner's name to refer to your new partner? You now have a guilt-free explanation—proactive interference.

information, either consciously or unconsciously, such as the box of cookies you ate last night. Interestingly, in the first few moments after finishing a marathon race, athletes often rate the intensity and unpleasantness of their pain about a 5.5 on a scale of 1 to 10. However, when these same people are asked 3 to 6 months later to report how they felt after the race, they've forgotten their initial level of pain, and guess that it was about a 3 (Babel, 2016). Do you see how the runners probably enjoyed the overall experience of the event and are motivated to forget the pain? For similar reasons, this motivated forgetting theory may even help explain why all children aren't only children—mothers tend to forget the actual pain of childbirth!

- In *encoding failure theory*, our sensory memory receives information and passes it to STM. But during the short time the information is in STM, we may overlook precise details and may not fully encode it, which results in a failure to pass along a complete memory to LTM (see the following **Try This Yourself**).

- According to *retrieval failure theory*, memories stored in LTM aren't forgotten. They're just momentarily inaccessible. The **tip-of-the-tongue (TOT) phenomenon**—the feeling that a word or an event you are trying to remember will pop out at any second—is an example of retrieval failure that results from interference, faulty cues, and high emotional arousal.

**Tip-of-the-tongue (TOT) phenomenon**  A strong, confident feeling of knowing something, while not being able to retrieve it at the moment.

## Factors Involved in Forgetting

In addition to the five basic theories of forgetting, there are five specific explanations for why we forget: the *misinformation effect*, the *serial-position effect*, *source amnesia*, *spacing of practice,* and *culture*.

1. **Misinformation effect**  As mentioned earlier, our memories are highly fallible and filled with personal constructions that we create during encoding, storage, and retrieval. Research on the **misinformation effect** shows that misleading information that occurs *after an event* may further alter and revise those constructions. Can you see how this is another example of *retroactive interference*? Our original memories are forgotten or altered because of misleading post-event information. For example, as you will see, our introductory famous figure, Elizabeth Loftus, experienced the misinformation effect when her aunt told her that she, Elizabeth, had been the one to discover her own mother's body. Elizabeth actually altered her previous memories to fit with this new information.

**Misinformation effect**  A memory error resulting from misleading information presented after an event, which alters memories of the event itself.

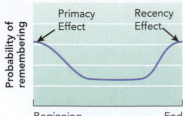

**FIGURE 7.11** **The serial-position effect** When we try to recall a list of similar items, we tend to remember the first and last items best. Do you see how you can use this information to improve your chances for employment success? If a potential employer calls you to set up an interview, you can increase the likelihood that the interviewer will remember you (and your application) by asking to be either the first (*primacy effect*) or last (*recency effect*) candidate.

**Serial-position effect** A characteristic of memory retrieval in which information at the beginning and end of a series is remembered better than material in the middle.

**Source amnesia** A memory error caused by forgetting the origin of a previously stored memory; also called source confusion or source misattribution.

**Distributed practice** A learning strategy in which studying or practice is broken up into a number of short sessions over a period of time; also known as spaced repetition.

**Massed practice** A study technique in which time spent learning is grouped (or massed) into long, unbroken intervals; also called cramming.

Another example comes from a study in which participants completed an interview in one room and then answered questions about it in another room (Morgan et al., 2013). Participants who received neutral questions like, "Was there a telephone in the room?" answered accurately for the most part, making errors on only 10% of the interview questions. However, other participants were asked questions such as, "What color was the telephone?" which falsely implied that there had been a telephone in the room. Of these respondents, 98% "remembered" a telephone. Other experiments have documented the misinformation effect by showing participants doctored photos of themselves taking a completely fictitious hot-air balloon ride or by asking participants to simply imagine an event, such as having a nurse remove a skin sample from their finger. In these and similar cases, a large number of participants later believed that the misleading information was correct and that the fictitious or imagined events actually occurred (Kaplan et al., 2016; Kirk et al., 2015; Takarangi et al., 2016).

2. **Serial-position effect** Stop for a moment, and write down the names of all the U.S. presidents that you can immediately recall. How did you do? Research shows that most people recall presidents from the beginning of history (e.g., Washington, Adams, Jefferson) and the more recent past (e.g., Clinton, Bush, Obama, Trump). This is known as the **serial-position effect** (**Figure 7.11**). We tend to recall items at the beginning (*primacy effect*) and the end (*recency effect*) better than those in the middle of the list. And when we do remember presidents in the middle, like Abraham Lincoln, it's normally because they are associated with significant events, such as Lincoln and the Civil War.

3. **Source amnesia** Each day we read, hear, and process an enormous amount of information, and it's easy to get confused about how we learned who said what to whom, and in what context. Forgetting the origin of a previously stored memory is known as **source amnesia** (Ferrie, 2015; Leichtman, 2006; Paterson et al., 2011). (See **Figure 7.12**.)

4. **Spacing of practice** You've probably heard of *Lumosity,* a website heavily promoted on the Internet and in television ads. This website, along with similar websites and software programs, is fairly recent in origin. They promise to dramatically decrease forgetting and improve our memory, while revolutionizing the way we learn (Schroers, 2014; Weir, 2014). Interestingly, most of these "new" programs are based on the older, well-established principle of **distributed practice**, in which studying or practice is broken up into a number of short sessions spaced out over time to allow numerous opportunities for "drill and practice." As you first discovered in the *Tools for Student Success* at the end of Chapter 1, this type of spaced learning is widely recognized as one of the very best tools for learning and grade improvement (Dunlosky et al., 2013; Küpper-Tetzel, 2014; Mettler et al., 2016). In response to these research findings on the superiority of distributed practice, we've built in numerous opportunities for distributed practice and self-tests throughout this text. Unfortunately, many students do the exact opposite! They put off studying and believe they're better off using **massed practice** or "cramming" right before an exam, which is proven to be far less effective than distributed practice.

5. **Culture** Finally, as discussed in the following **Gender and Cultural Diversity**, cultural factors can play a role in memory and how well people remember what they have learned (Gutchess & Huff, 2016; Wang, 2011).

**FIGURE 7.12** **Source amnesia and negative political ads** Think back to a recent political election. What type of television advertisements most readily come to mind? Research shows that we're more likely to recall ads that rely on creating negative feelings about one of the candidates. They stick in our memory even if we initially have negative feelings about them (Lariscy & Tinkham, 1999). In addition, over time the negative "facts" stay in our memory, and we forget the source—*source amnesia!* The good news for politicians, and in your personal life, is that direct rebuttals of negative ads are generally effective and unlikely to backfire (Weeks & Garrett, 2014).

© Maciej Dakowicz/Alamy Stock Photo

## Gender and Cultural Diversity

### Does Culture Affect Memory?

As discussed in Chapter 1, we're often unaware of how cultural forces affect us, and this is particularly true of how they affect what we value and remember. People raised in *individualistic cultures*, such as North American and Western European, tend to value the needs and goals of the individual, whereas those who grow up in collectivistic cultures, such as Asian and West African, generally emphasize the needs and goals of the group. Research has revealed several cross-cultural differences between these two groups, including variations in cognitive biases, memory for objects versus background, episodic memory, and even emotional memories evoked by music (Guchess & Huff, 2016; Juslin et al., 2016; Schwartz et al., 2014).

These studies clearly show that culture shapes our memories. However, maybe it's more valuable to understand how and why these differences develop. For that, let's look at everyday experiences and some classic historical research. For example, how do you remember the dates for all your college quizzes, exams, and assignments or the items you need to buy at the supermarket? Most people from industrialized societies rely on written shopping lists, calendars, or computers to store information and prevent forgetting. What would it be like if you had to rely solely on your memory to store and retrieve all your learned information? Do people raised in preliterate societies with rich oral traditions develop better memory skills than do people raised in literate societies?

Ross and Millson (1970) designed a cross-cultural study to explore these questions. They compared American and Ghanaian college students' abilities to remember stories that were read aloud. Students listened to the stories without taking notes and without being told they would be tested. Two weeks later, all students were asked to write down as much as they could remember. The Ghanaian students had better recall than the Americans. Their superior performance was attributed to their culture's long oral tradition, which requires developing greater skill in encoding oral information.

Does this mean that people from cultures with an oral tradition simply have better memories? Recall from Chapter 1 that a core requirement for scientific research is *replication* and the generation of related hypotheses and studies. In this case, when other researchers orally presented nonliterate African participants with lists of words instead of stories, they did *not* perform better (Cole et al., 1971). However, when both educated Africans and uneducated Africans were compared for memory of lists of words, the educated Africans performed better (Scribner, 1977). This suggests that formal schooling helps people develop memory strategies for things like lists of words. Preliterate participants may see such lists as unrelated and meaningless (Berry et al., 2011).

Wagner (1982) conducted a study with Moroccan and Mexican children that helps explain the effect of formal schooling.

Participants were first presented with seven cards that were placed face down in front of them, one at a time. They were then shown a card and asked to point out which of the seven cards was its duplicate. Everyone, regardless of culture or amount of schooling, was able to recall the latest cards presented (the *recency effect*). However, the amount of schooling significantly affected overall recall and the ability to recall the earliest cards presented (*primacy effect*).

Wagner suggests that the primacy effect depends on *rehearsal*—the silent repetition of things you're trying to remember—and that this strategy is strongly related to schooling. As a child in a typical classroom, you were expected to memorize letters, numbers, multiplication tables, and a host of other basic facts. This type of formal schooling provides years of practice in memorization and in applying these skills in test situations. According to Wagner, memory has a "hardware" section that does not change across culture. But it also contains a "software" part that develops particular strategies for remembering, which are learned.

In summary, research indicates that the "software" part of memory is affected by culture. In cultures in which communication relies on oral tradition, people develop good strategies for remembering orally presented stories (**Figure 7.13**). In cultures in which formal schooling is the rule, people learn memory strategies that help them remember lists of items. From these studies, we can conclude that, across cultures, people tend to remember information that matters to them. They develop memory skills to match the demands of their environment.

**FIGURE 7.13**  **Culture and memory**   In many societies, tribal leaders pass down vital information through stories related orally. Because of this rich oral tradition, children living in these cultures have better memories for information related through stories than do other children.

(c) Ferdinando Scianna/Magnum Photos, Inc.

© Billy R. Ray/Wiley

## Retrieval Practice 7.2 | Forgetting

Completing this self-test and the connections section, and then checking your answers by clicking on the answer button or by looking in Appendix B, will provide immediate feedback and helpful practice for exams.

**Self-Test**

1. Briefly explain the decay theory of forgetting.

2. The _____ theory suggests that forgetting is caused by two competing memories, particularly memories with similar qualities.
   a. decay
   b. interference
   c. motivated forgetting
   d. encoding failure

3. The _____ effect suggests that people will recall information presented at the beginning and end of a list better than information from the middle of a list.
   a. recency
   b. latency
   c. serial position
   d. primacy

4. Distributed practice is a learning technique in which _____.
   a. students are distributed (spaced) equally throughout the room
   b. learning periods are broken up into a number of short sessions over a period of time
   c. learning decays faster than it can be distributed
   d. several students study together, distributing various subjects according to their individual strengths

5. Which of the following is *not* one of the key factors that contribute to forgetting outlined in the text?
   a. misinformation effect
   b. serial-position effect
   c. consolidation
   d. source amnesia

**Connections—Chapter to Chapter**

Answering the following question will help you "look back and look ahead" to see the important connections among the subfields of psychology and chapters within this text.

Remember the picture of different versions of the penny in Chapter 1? Now that you've read about memory, explain why it is so difficult to pick out the correct version of the penny from among the imposters.

## 7.3 Biological Bases of Memory

### LEARNING OBJECTIVES

**Retrieval Practice**    While reading the upcoming sections, respond to each Learning Objective in your own words.

**Summarize the biological factors involved in memory.**

- **Describe** the synaptic and neurotransmitter changes that occur when we learn and remember.

- **Identify** the major areas of the brain involved in memory storage.
- **Explain** how emotional arousal affects memory.
- **Discuss** the biological factors in memory loss.

So far we have explored the nature of memory and various models of how it is organized. We've also examined various theories and factors involved in forgetting. In this section, we'll explore the biological bases of memory—synaptic and neurotransmitter changes, where memories are stored, the effects of emotional arousal, and the biological factors in memory loss.

### Synaptic and Neurotransmitter Changes

In Chapters 2 and 6, we discussed how learning and memory modify our brains' neural networks. For instance, for people learning to play tennis, repeated practice builds specific neural pathways that make it progressively easier to get the ball over the net. These same pathways later enable players to remember how to play the game the next time they go out onto the tennis court.

**Long-term potentiation (LTP)**
A long-lasting increase in neural sensitivity; a biological mechanism for learning and memory.

How do these biological changes, called **long-term potentiation (LTP)**, occur? They happen in at least two ways. First, early research with rats raised in enriched environments found that repeated stimulation of a synapse strengthens it by causing the dendrites to grow more spines (Rosenzweig et al., 1972). This repeated stimulation further results in more synapses and additional receptor sites, along with increased sensitivity. Research on long-term potentiation (LTP) in humans also supports the idea that LTP is one of the major biological mechanisms underlying learning and memory (Baddeley et al., 2015; Camera et al., 2016; Panja & Bramham, 2014).

Second, when learning and memory occur, there is a measurable increase in the amount of neurotransmitter released, which in turn increases the neuron's efficiency in message transmission. Research with *Aplysia* (a type of sea slug) clearly demonstrates this effect (**Figure 7.14**). Further evidence of the importance of neurotransmitters in memory comes from research with genetically engineered "smart mice," which have extra receptors for a neurotransmitter named NMDA (N-methyl-d-aspartate). These mice perform significantly better on memory tasks than do normal mice (Lin et al., 2014; Plattner et al., 2014; Tsien, 2000).

Although it is difficult to generalize from rats, mice, and sea slugs to humans, such research does show that synaptic and neurotransmitter changes within neurons are the biological bases of *encoding*—the essential first step to creating a new memory. Normal, everyday encoding begins with somewhat "unconscious" attention to a particular sensory message, such as a visual image, a sound, a taste, or some other sensation. This attention causes our neurons to fire more frequently and release more neurotransmitters, which makes the experience more intense. This, in turn, increases the likelihood that the event will be encoded and sent along to be stored in LTM.

© Wolfgang Pölzer/Alamy Inc.

**FIGURE 7.14**   **How does a sea slug learn and remember?**   After repeated squirting with water, followed by a mild shock, the sea slug Aplysia releases more neurotransmitters at certain synapses. These synapses then become more efficient at transmitting signals that cause the slug to withdraw its gills when squirted. As a critical thinker, can you explain why this ability might provide an evolutionary advantage?

## The Brain's Role in Memory

We've just seen how synaptic and neurotransmitter changes lead to encoding and to storage in LTM. We turn now to exactly where and how those memories are processed and stored in our brains (**Figure 7.15**).

Encoding begins with a focusing of our attention, which is controlled by our *thalamus* and *frontal lobes*. The encoded neural messages are then decoded (interpreted) in various areas in our cerebral cortex. Next, they're sent along to the *hippocampus*, which "decides" which of these messages will be stored in LTM. As you will see, emotional arousal tends to increase attention, and those messages and resulting memories are primarily processed and stored in the *amygdala*, a brain structure involved in emotion.

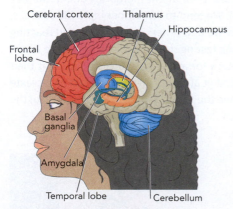

Cerebral cortex    Thalamus
Hippocampus
Frontal lobe
Basal ganglia
Amygdala
Temporal lobe    Cerebellum

**Test Your Critical Thinking**

1. What effect might damage to the amygdala have on a person's relationships with others?

2. How might damage to your thalamus affect your day-to-day functioning?

**FIGURE 7.15**   **Major areas of the brain involved in memory**

| Area of the Brain | Effects on Memory |
|---|---|
| Amygdala | Emotional memories |
| Basal ganglia and cerebellum | Creation and storage of basic memory and implicit/nondeclarative LTM (such as skills, habits, and simple classically conditioned responses) |
| Hippocampal formation (hippocampus and surrounding area) | Explicit/declarative and implicit/nondeclarative LTM, as well as sequences of events |
| Thalamus | Formation of new memories and spatial and working memory; implicit/nondeclarative and explicit/declarative LTM |
| Cerebral cortex | Encoding, storage, and retrieval of explicit/declarative and implicit/nondeclarative LTM |

*Sources:* Baddeley et al., 2015; Emilien & Durlach, 2015; Furuya et al., 2014; Garrett, 2015; Hara et al., 2014; McCormick et al., 2015; Radvansky & Ashcraft, 2016; Yamazaki et al., 2015.

Keep in mind that memory is not a single process. Different types of memory involve different neural systems (Foerde & Shohamy, 2011). For example, the *basal ganglia* are important in implicit/nondeclarative memory (motor skills and habits, conditioned responses, and priming). In contrast, the *temporal lobes* are key to explicit/declarative memory (facts and general knowledge, as well as personal experiences).

Early memory researchers believed that memory was *localized,* or stored in a particular brain area. Today, research techniques are so advanced that we can identify specific brain areas that are activated or changed during memory processes by using functional magnetic resonance imaging (fMRI) brain scans. From these scans and other research methods, we now know that, in fact, memory tends to be distributed in many areas throughout the brain (see again Figure 7.15).

## Emotional Arousal and Memory

As we've just seen, memory formation begins when we pay attention to certain stimuli. This attention then triggers synaptic and neurotransmitter changes that result in encoding, which, in turn, produces neural messages that are processed and stored in various areas of our brains. Interestingly, high levels of emotional arousal appear to lead to a type of *attention narrowing*. This results in details directly connected with the source of the arousal being more strongly encoded than the peripheral details, which are often fuzzy or lost. Does this help explain why if you're attacked by a mugger with a knife you might remember a lot about the knife but little about the attacker or the surroundings?

What are the biological processes behind this type of attention narrowing? When stressed or excited, we naturally produce neurotransmitters and hormones that arouse the body, such as *epinephrine* and *cortisol* (Chapter 3). These chemicals also affect parts of the brain, including the amygdala, the hippocampus, and the cerebral cortex. Research has shown that these chemicals can interfere with, as well as enhance, how we encode, store, and retrieve our memories (Conway, 2015; Emilien & Durlach, 2015; Quas et al., 2016).

Surprisingly, some studies suggest that sexual arousal due to exposure to pornography can also disrupt memory. Researchers in one study asked men to view a series of both pornographic and nonpornographic images and judge whether they had previously seen each image (Laier et al., 2013). Men who saw the nonsexual images gave 80% correct answers, whereas men who saw the pornographic images gave only 67% correct answers.

Rather than disrupting memory, emotional arousal can sometimes lead to memory enhancement. During significant historical, public, or autobiographical events, like the 9/11 attack or the 2016 presidential election, it appears that our minds automatically create **flashbulb memories (FBMs)**—vivid, detailed, and near-permanent memories of emotionally significant moments or events (Brown & Kulik, 1977). We tend to remember incredible details, such as where we were, what was going on, and how we and others were feeling and reacting at that moment in time. And these memories are long lasting. In fact, researchers have found that people have retained their FBMs of the 9/11 attack for as long as 10 years and that their confidence in these memories has remained high (Hirst et al., 2015). We also sometimes create uniquely personal (and happy) FBMs (**Figure 7.16**) (See the **Study Tip** for an explanation of the term "flashbulb.").

**Flashbulb memory (FBM)**
A vivid, detailed, and near-permanent memory of an emotionally significant moment or event; memory resulting from a form of automatic encoding, storage, and later retrieval.

### Study Tip

*Note that the term "flashbulb" refers to older times, when a photographer would snap a photo and at that moment a noticeably strong flashbulb would go off to increase the light exposure and improve the photo's quality. Today, we use the term FBM to capture the idea that during moments of exceptionally high emotional arousal, our minds take an automatic "picture" and create a lasting memory of that event.*

**FIGURE 7.16** **Common FBMs** Why do most people clearly remember their college graduations and wedding ceremonies? Most of us experience higher levels of emotionality during these happy occasions, as shown in this photo of one of your authors, Catherine Sanderson, and her husband on their wedding day. Therefore, we tend to automatically create detailed, long-lasting flashbulb memories (FBMs) of our thoughts, feelings, and actions during such momentous events.

**Thinking Critically**

1. Do your personal memories of highly emotional events fit with what FBM research suggests? Why or why not?

2. Despite documented errors with FBMs, most people are very confident in the accuracy of their personal FBMs. What problems might result from this overconfidence?

Catherine Sanderson

How does this happen? It's as if our brains command us to take "flash pictures" of these highly emotional events in order for us to "pay attention, learn, and remember." As we've seen, a flood of neurotransmitters and hormones helps create strong, immediate memories. Furthermore, as discussed in Chapter 3, the flood of the hormone cortisol that happens during traumatic events has been studied as a contributor to long-lasting memories and, sadly, to PTSD (Drexler et al., 2015). Along with these chemical changes, we actively replay these memories in our minds again and again, which further encourages stronger and more lasting memories (**Figure 7.17**).

Angela Hampton Picture Library/Alamy Stock Photo

**FIGURE 7.17**  **A negative (and thankfully uncommon) FBM**  In 2001, Air Transit (AT) Flight 236 ran out of fuel over the Atlantic Ocean and everyone on board prepared for a water landing. Thankfully, the plane was able to glide safely to an island military base (McKinnon et al., 2015). Although no one was seriously hurt, virtually everyone experienced severe anxiety for the 25 minutes spent preparing to ditch at sea. This near accident occurred in 2001, and research on the passengers' memory of the event was conducted in 2014. Despite the passage of time, the passengers showed enhanced episodic recall of the event, including details like the oxygen masks coming down, jumping down the slide, and putting on life jackets.

Keep in mind that research shows that our FBMs for specific details, particularly the time and place the emotional event occurred, are fairly accurate (Rimmele et al., 2012). However, these FBMs also suffer the same alterations and decay as all other forms of memory. They're NOT perfect recordings of events (Hirst et al., 2015; Lanciano et al., 2010; Schmidt, 2012). For instance, President George W. Bush's memory for how he heard the news of the September 11, 2001, attacks contained several errors (Greenberg, 2004). Similarly, shortly after the death of Michael Jackson, researchers asked participants to report on their FBMs and other reactions to the news of his death. When these same people were interviewed again 18 months later, researchers found that despite several discrepancies in their memories, confidence in their personal accuracy remained high (Day & Ross, 2014).

In sum, FBMs, like other forms of memory, are subject to alterations. What separates them from ordinary, everyday memories is their vividness and our subjective confidence in their accuracy. But confidence is not the same as accuracy—an important point we'll return to in the last part of this chapter. Perhaps the most important take-home message is that our memory processes are sometimes impaired during high emotional arousal (**Figure 7.18**).

## The Biology of Memory Loss

So far in this section, we've discussed the neuronal and synaptic changes that occur when we learn and remember, the major brain areas involved in memory activation and storage, and how emotional arousal affects memory. Now we will explore the biological processes linked to memory loss.

Chris Clor/Getty Images

**Traumatic Brain Injury (TBI)**  One of the leading causes of neurological disorders—including memory loss—among young U.S. men and women between the ages of 15 and 25 is *traumatic brain injury (TBI)*. These injuries most commonly result from car accidents, falls, blows, and gunshot wounds. TBI happens when the skull suddenly collides with another object. Compression, twisting, and distortion of the brain inside the skull all cause serious and sometimes permanent damage to the brain. The frontal and temporal lobes often take the heaviest hit because they directly collide with the bony ridges inside the skull.

One of the most troubling, and controversial, causes of TBIs is severe or repeated blows to the head during sports participation (CDC, 2016; Pearce et al., 2015; Solomon & Zuckerman, 2015). Both professional and nonprofessional athletes frequently experience *concussions*, a form of TBI, and multiple concussions can lead to *chronic traumatic encephalopathy (CTE)*. Sadly, the frequency of sports-related brain injuries may have been grossly underestimated (Baugh et al., 2015), and a growing body of research connects these multiple brain injuries to diseases and

**FIGURE 7.18**  **How emotional arousal may threaten our survival!**  News reports are filled with stories of people becoming dangerously confused during fires or other emergencies because they panic and forget vital survival tips, such as the closest exit routes. Does this help explain why airlines and fire departments routinely provide safety and evacuation drills? And why it's dangerous to drive when we're arguing with a loved one or to discipline our children when we're very angry? Recognizing that we're sometimes "not in our right minds" during times of high emotional arousal may save our lives—and our relationships!

**FIGURE 7.19** **Professional sports and brain damage** Junior Seau (photo on the left), a 10-time all-pro linebacker in the National Football League (NFL), died as a result of suicide in 2012 at the age of 43. Experts later concluded that Seau suffered from chronic traumatic encephalopathy (CTE), a serious neurological disease linked to concussions—and to similar deaths of other sports players (CDC, 2016; Park, 2016; Pearce et al., 2015). Due to his personal concerns over concussions, NFL linebacker Chris Borland, one of the league's top rookies (photo on the right), quit playing in 2015 despite being in the prime of his athletic career.

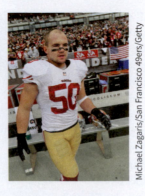

**Retrograde amnesia** The inability to retrieve information from the past; backward-acting amnesia.

**Consolidation** The process by which LTM memories become stable in the brain; neural changes that take place when a memory is formed.

**Anterograde amnesia** The inability to form new memories; forward-acting amnesia.

disorders like Alzheimer's, depression, and even suicide (**Figure 7.19**).

**Amnesia** Now that we know a little more about brain injuries, let's examine the general topic of *amnesia*, or memory loss, which may be caused by brain injuries. Although being completely amnesic about your past and not knowing who you are is a common plot in movies and on television, real-life amnesia generally doesn't cause a complete loss of self-identity. Instead, the individual typically has trouble retrieving more widespread and general old memories or forming new ones. These two forms of amnesia are called *retrograde* and *anterograde* (**Figure 7.20**).

Like retrograde interference (discussed earlier), **retrograde amnesia** acts backward in time. The person has no memory (is amnesic) for events that occurred *before* the brain injury because those memories were never stored in LTM. However, the same person has no trouble remembering things that happened after the injury. As the name implies, only the old, "retro," memories are lost.

What causes retrograde amnesia? We learned earlier that during long-term potentiation (LTP), our neurons change to accommodate new learning. In addition, we know that it takes a certain amount of time for these neural changes to become fixed and stable in long-term memory, a process known as **consolidation**. Like heavy rain on wet cement, the brain injury "wipes away" unstable memories because the cement has not yet had time to harden. In cases where the individual is only amnesic for the events right before the brain injury, the cause may be a failure of consolidation.

In contrast to retrograde amnesia, in which people lose memories for events *before* a brain injury, some people lose memory for events that occur *after* a brain injury, which is called **anterograde amnesia**. Like anterograde interference (discussed earlier), this type of amnesia acts forward in time. The victim has no memory (is amnesic) for events after the brain injury. This type of amnesia generally results from a surgical injury or from diseases, such as chronic alcoholism or senile dementia—a form of severe mental deterioration in old age. Continuing our analogy with cement, anterograde amnesia would be like having permanently hardened cement, which prevents the laying down of new memories.

Keep in mind that retrograde amnesia is normally temporary and somewhat common, such as what happens to football players after a head injury. In contrast, anterograde amnesia is relatively rare and most often permanent. However, patients often show surprising abilities to learn and remember procedural motor skills, such as mowing a lawn.

Also note that some individuals have both forms of amnesia. For example, a famous patient (officially referred to as H.M.) was 27 when he underwent brain surgery to correct his severe epileptic seizures. Although the surgery improved his medical problem, something was clearly wrong with H.M.'s LTM. When his uncle died, he grieved in a normal way. But soon after, he began to ask why his uncle never visited him. H.M. had to be repeatedly reminded of his uncle's death, and each reminder would begin a new mourning process.

**FIGURE 7.20** **Two types of amnesia**

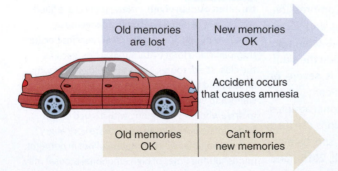

Old memories are lost | New memories OK

Accident occurs that causes amnesia

Old memories OK | Can't form new memories

**a. Retrograde amnesia** After an accident or other brain injury, individuals with *retrograde amnesia* have no trouble forming new memories, but they do experience *amnesia* (loss of memories) for segments of the past. Old, "retro" memories are lost.

**b. Anterograde amnesia** In contrast, people with *anterograde amnesia* have no trouble recovering old memories, but they do experience *amnesia* (cannot form new memories) after an accident or other brain injury. New, "antero" memories are lost.

Can you see how H.M.'s loss of memory for his uncle's death is an example of extreme anterograde amnesia? H.M. lost the ability to form new memories. But he also suffered mild memory loss for events and people before the operation—retrograde amnesia. Sadly, H.M. lived another 55 years after the operation not recognizing the people who cared for him daily. Each time he met his caregivers, read a book, or ate a meal, it was as if for the first time (Augustinack et al., 2014; Corkin, 2013; Mauguière & Corkin, 2015). H.M. died in 2008—never having regained his long-term memory.

### Alzheimer's Disease (AD)
Like TBIs, which can cause amnesia, various diseases can alter the physiology of the brain and nervous system and thereby disrupt memory processes. For example, *Alzheimer's disease (AD)* is a progressive mental deterioration that occurs most commonly in old age (**Figure 7.21**). The most noticeable early symptoms are disturbances in memory, which become progressively worse until, in the final stages, the person fails to recognize loved ones, needs total nursing care, and ultimately dies.

**FIGURE 7.21** **The effect of Alzheimer's disease (AD) on the brain**

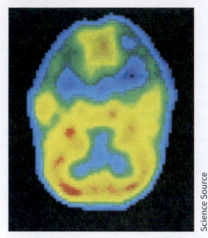
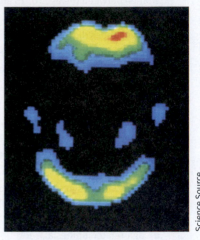

Science Source

**a. Normal brain** In this PET scan of a normal brain, note the high amount of red and yellow (signs of brain activity).

**b. Brain of a person with AD** In this PET scan of a person with AD, note how the reduced activity in the brain is most significant in the temporal and parietal lobes (the mostly black areas in the center and on the sides of this AD patient's brain). These are the major areas for storing memories.

Alzheimer's does not attack all types of memory equally. A hallmark of the disease is an extreme decrease in *explicit/declarative memory*—failing to recall facts, information, and personal life experiences (Howes & O'Shea, 2014; Müller et al., 2014; Redondo et al., 2015). However, those who suffer from AD generally retain some *implicit/nondeclarative* memories, such as simple classically conditioned responses and procedural tasks like brushing their teeth.

What causes AD? Brain autopsies of people with Alzheimer's show unusual *tangles* (structures formed from degenerating cell bodies) and *plaques* (structures formed from degenerating axons and dendrites). Early-onset Alzheimer's typically strikes its victims between the ages of 45 and 55, and a genetic mutation is generally the cause. In contrast, late-onset Alzheimer's normally develops from brain changes that occur over decades and from a mixture of multiple factors (Guekht, 2016; Kumar et al., 2016; Tousseyn et al., 2015).

Unfortunately, at this time, there is no effective means for early diagnosis of Alzheimer's. However, there is promising research based on tell-tale changes in the retina of the human eye (Tsai et al., 2014). In addition, individuals with AD may benefit from a healthy diet and exercise program. One encouraging study found that 9 out of 10 patients with AD who adopted such a program showed substantial improvement in memory and cognitive function, yet they are still expected to continue to deteriorate over time (Bredesen, 2014).

© Billy R. Ray/Wiley

## Retrieval Practice 7.3 | Biological Bases of Memory

Completing this self-test and the connections section, and then checking your answers by clicking on the answer button or by looking in Appendix B, will provide immediate feedback and helpful practice for exams.

**Self-Test**

1. Define long-term potentiation (LTP).

2. Your vivid memory of what you were doing when you were first informed about your parents' impending divorce might be an example of _____.

   a. encoding specificity
   b. long-term potentiation (LTP)
   c. latent learning
   d. a flashbulb memory (FBM)

3. The leading cause of memory loss among young U.S. men and women between the ages of 15 and 25 is _____.

  **a.** age-related amnesia (A-RA)   **b.** long-term potentiation (LTP)
  **c.** Alzheimer's disease (AD)   **d.** traumatic brain injury (TBI)

4. Ralph can't remember anything that happened to him before he fell through the floor of his tree house. His lack of memory of events before his fall is called _____ amnesia.

  **a.** retroactive         **b.** proactive
  **c.** retrograde         **d.** anterograde

5. A progressive mental deterioration characterized by severe memory loss that occurs most commonly in elderly people is called _____.

  **a.** retrieval loss syndrome deterioration
  **b.** prefrontal cortex disease (PCD)
  **c.** Alzheimer's disease (AD)
  **d.** age-related amnesia (A-RA)

**Connections—Chapter to Chapter**

Answering the following questions will help you "look back and look ahead" to see the important connections among the subfields of psychology and chapters within this text.

1. In Chapter 2 (Neuroscience and Biological Foundations), you learned about biological research methods and tools, including functional magnetic resonance imaging (fMRI). Describe how you could use fMRI to discover where memories of music reside in the brain.

2. In Chapter 12 (Motivation and Emotion), you'll discover the *optimal arousal theory*, which states that we're motivated to maintain a level of arousal that maximizes our performance. Too little or too much arousal can hurt our performance. Explain how this theory is similar to how arousal affects memory.

## 7.4   Memory Distortions and Improvement

**LEARNING OBJECTIVES**

**Retrieval Practice**   While reading the upcoming sections, respond to each Learning Objective in your own words.

**Summarize how our memories get distorted and the resulting problems.**

• **Discuss** how our need for logic, consistency, and efficiency contributes to some memory distortions.

• **Describe** the memory problems associated with eyewitness testimony.
• **Discuss** false versus repressed memories.
• **Review** the ten tips for memory improvement.

---

*Remembrance of things past is not necessarily the remembrance of things as they were.*
—Marcel Proust (French Author, Critic)

At this point in your life, you've undoubtedly experienced a painful breakup of a serious love relationship and/or witnessed such breakups among your close friends. During these breakups, did you wonder how the reported experiences of two people in the same partnership could be so different? Why would each partner reconstruct his or her own personal memory of the relationship? How can we explain such common memory distortions?

### Understanding Memory Distortions

There are several reasons why we shape, rearrange, and distort our memories. One of the most common is our need for *logic* and *consistency*. When we're initially forming new memories or sorting through old ones, we fill in missing pieces, make corrections, and rearrange information to make it logical and consistent with our previous experiences or personal desires. For example, if you left a relationship because you found a new partner, you might rearrange your memories to suit your belief that you two were mismatched from the beginning and that the new partner is your true, forever "soul mate." However, if you were the one left behind, you might reconstruct your memories and now believe that you're lucky that the relationship ended because your partner was a manipulative "player" from the beginning.

We also edit, summarize, and augment new information and tie it to previously stored memories for the sake of *efficiency*. Unfortunately, this "efficient" shaping and constructing sometimes results in a loss of specific details that we may need later on. For instance, when taking notes during lectures, you can't (and shouldn't) record every word. Instead, you edit, summarize, and (hopefully) augment what you hear and tie it to other related material. However, your note taking may occasionally miss essential details that later trip you up during exams!

Despite all their problems and biases, our memories are normally fairly accurate and serve us well in most situations. Human memory has evolved to encode, store, and retrieve general and/or vital information, such as the location of various buildings on our college campus or the importance of looking both ways when we cross the street. However, when faced with tasks that require encoding, storing, and retrieving precise details like those in a scholarly text, remembering names and faces of potential clients, or recalling where we left our house keys, our brains are not as well-equipped.

## Eyewitness Testimony

Unfortunately, when our natural, everyday memory errors come into play in the criminal justice system, they may lead to wrongful judgments of guilt or innocence with possible life or death consequences. In the past, one of the best forms of trial evidence a lawyer could have was an *eyewitness*—"I was there; I saw it with my own eyes." However, research has identified several problems with eyewitness testimony (Loftus, 1993, 2013; Michael & Garry, 2016; Wan et al., 2017). For example, if multiple eyewitnesses talk to one another after a crime, they may "remember" and corroborate erroneous details that someone else reported, which explains why police officers try to separate eyewitnesses while taking their reports.

As a critical thinker, do you recognize how the details and problems we discussed earlier about flashbulb memories (FBMs) might also apply to eyewitness testimony? Traumatic events, like watching a crime, often create FBMs for eyewitnesses. Despite high confidence in their personally vivid memories, they can make serious errors, such as identifying an innocent person as the perpetrator (**Figure 7.22**).

Problems with eyewitness recollections are so well established that most judges now allow expert testimony on the unreliability of eyewitness testimony and routinely instruct jurors on its limits (Loftus, 2013; Pozzulo, 2017; Safer et al., 2016). If you serve as a member of a jury or listen to accounts of crimes in the news, remind yourself of these problems. Also, keep in mind that research participants in eyewitness studies generally report their inaccurate memories with great self-assurance and strong conviction (DeSoto & Roediger, 2014; Kaplan et al., 2016; Morgan & Southwick, 2014).

Interestingly, research now suggests that eyewitness statements taken at the time of the initial identification of a suspect are quite reliable (Wixted et al., 2015). And the overall accuracy of eyewitness testimony can be improved if people are asked to make very fast judgments (Brewer et al., 2012). In fact, giving people only a few seconds to identify the culprit in a lineup increases the accuracy of such identifications by 20 to 30%, compared to allowing people to take as long as they want to make a decision. Surprisingly, even simply asking people to close their eyes when they're trying to remember leads to greater accuracy in both audio and visual details (Nash et al., 2016). **Figure 7.23** offers further insights on eyewitness testimony.

## False Versus Repressed Memories

> *We invent memories. Without thinking. If we tell ourselves something happened often enough, we start to believe it, and then we can actually remember it.*
>
> —S. J. Watson (British Writer)

Like eyewitness testimony, false memories can have serious legal, personal, and social implications. Do you recall our introductory story about memory researcher Elizabeth Loftus's

ZUMA Press, Inc./Alamy Stock Photo

**FIGURE 7.22** | **Dangerous eyewitness testimony**  With minimal physical evidence and a single eyewitness with something to gain by his testimony, Andre Hatchett was convicted of the murder of Neda Mae Carter in 1991. Tragically, Mr. Hatchett spent 25 years in prison before finally being exonerated, and eyewitness misidentification reportedly plays a role in more than 70% of the wrongful convictions that are later overturned through DNA testing (Augenstein, 2016; Innocence Project, 2016).

**FIGURE 7.23** **Understanding and improving eyewitness testimony**

© The New Yorker Collection 2006
Tom Cheney from Cartoonbank.com

*"Thank you, gentlemen—you may all leave except for No. 3."*

**Eyewitnesses and police lineups** As humorously depicted in this cartoon, officials now recommend that suspects should never "stand out" from the others in a lineup. Witnesses also are cautioned to not assume that the real criminal is in the lineup, and they should never "guess" when asked to make an identification.

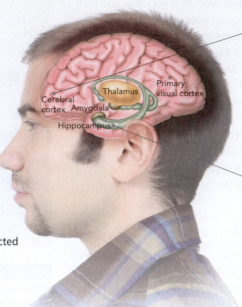

**Recalling information** During eyewitness recall and courtroom testimony, memories are retrieved from neurons in the cerebral cortex.

Primary visual cortex
Thalamus
Cerebral cortex
Amygdala
Hippocampus

**Storing the memory** The hippocampus plays a major role in the formation and consolidation of new memories, and it is also activated when we recall old memories of facts and events.

Masterfile

amazing recovered memory of finding her drowned mother's body? If so, you might be even more shocked to discover that the relative who told Elizabeth that she had been the one to discover her mother's body later remembered—and other relatives confirmed—that it had actually been Aunt Pearl, not Elizabeth. Loftus, a world-renowned expert on memory distortions, had unknowingly created her own *false memory*.

## Understanding False Memories
As demonstrated by Loftus's personal experience, extensive research has shown that it's relatively easy to create false memories (Kaplan et al., 2016; Lindner & Henkel, 2015; Lynn et al., 2015). In fact, even innocent adult participants can be convinced, over the course of a few hours, that as teenagers they committed serious crimes (Shaw & Porter, 2015). This finding comes from a study in which researchers brought college students to the lab for three 40-minute interviews that took place about a week apart. In the first interview, the researchers told each student about two events he or she experienced as a teen, only one of which actually happened. These false events were serious, such as an assault, a theft, or a personal injury. (Each false-event story included some true details about that time in the student's life, which the researchers obtained from the student's parent or guardian.) Participants were then asked to explain what happened in both the true and false events. When they had difficulty explaining the false event, the interviewer encouraged them to try anyway, explaining that if they used specific memory strategies they might be able to recall more details. In the second and third interviews, the researchers again asked the students to recall as much as they could about both events. Surprisingly, over half the students had developed a false memory of the event, and many included elaborate details of their false experience.

Similarly, a recent meta-analysis found that when presented with totally fabricated (but plausible) events that had supposedly happened to them when they were children, 46% of participants believed they had actually experienced the fake event, such as trouble with a teacher or taking a hot-air balloon ride (Scoboria et al., 2017). Even more worrisome is the fact that 30% of these believers went on to invent further details that supposedly happened to them during the fictitious event.

Do you recall our earlier discussion of the *misinformation effect* and how experimenters created a false memory of seeing a telephone in a room? Participants who were asked neutral questions, such as, "Was there a telephone in the room?" made errors on only 10% of the queries (Morgan et al., 2013). In contrast, when participants were asked, "What color was the telephone?" falsely implying that a telephone had been in the room, 98% "remembered" it being there.

To make matters worse, once false memories have been formed, they can multiply over time—and last for years. Researchers in one study showed participants pictures of an event, such as a girl's wallet being stolen (Zhu et al., 2012). Participants then read a series of statements about the event, which included both accurate information (for instance, the person who took the girl's wallet was a man) and false information (the person who took the girl's wallet put it in his pants pocket). (In reality, the picture showed him hiding the wallet in his jacket.) Initially, after reading these statements, participants identified only 31% of the false events as having occurred. However, when participants were asked 1½ years later which events had occurred, they identified 39% of the false statements as true.

As you can see, research like this has serious implications for the legal system. The good news is that research using brain scans has shown that different areas of the brain are activated during true versus false memories, which may lead to more reliable tests of memory (**Figure 7.24**).

Are you wondering how all this research applies to our everyday life? In addition to serious legal problems with eyewitness testimony, false memories can influence our attitudes and behaviors, as well as our interpersonal relationships. Furthermore, even trained professionals may find it difficult to determine when someone is recalling a true or false memory (Scoboria et al., 2017). In short, remember that we're all vulnerable to creating and believing false memories. Just because something feels true, doesn't mean that it is (see the following **Try This Yourself**).

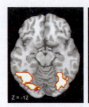

Image provided courtesy of Roberto Cabeza, Duke University. From Cabeza, cerebral cortex, 2007, Figure 4. Reproduced with permission of Oxford University Press.

**FIGURE 7.24** **Brain scans detecting true versus false memories**   Note how different areas of the primary visual cortex are activated (the orange/white areas) when both true and false memories are recalled (the scan on the left) versus when only true memories are recalled (the scan on the right).

---

## Try This Yourself

### "False Daughter" Memories

The following is a personal memory experience from a fellow psychologist. Do you think it qualifies as a true "false memory"? Why or why not?

*One of the co-authors of this book, Karen Huffman, is a dear friend of mine and we've co-taught intro psych for many years. During our times together in the classroom, we've often told stories about our own children to provide real-life examples of various psychological principles. Ironically, in the chapter on memory, we suddenly realized that some of the stories we were currently telling our students about our respective daughters were becoming blended in our own minds. I couldn't remember whether certain events happened to one of my three daughters or to Karen's only daughter! For us, this became a perfect, personal example of the constructive nature of memory, as well as source amnesia!*
—Katie Townsend-Merino (Professor, Meditation Educator, Writer)

Courtesy of Katie Townsend-Merino

---

## Understanding Repressed Memories

Creating false memories may be somewhat common, but can we recover true memories that are buried in childhood? There is a great deal of debate regarding so-called *repressed memories* (Boag, 2012; Brodsky & Gutheil, 2016; Kaplan et al., 2016). **Repression** is Sigmund Freud's term for a basic coping or defense mechanism that prevents anxiety-provoking thoughts, feelings, and memories from reaching consciousness (Chapter 13).

According to some research, repressed memories are *actively* and *consciously* "forgotten" in an effort to avoid the pain of their retrieval (Anderson et al., 2004; Boag, 2012). Do you recognize how in this case repression might be a form of motivated forgetting, which we discussed earlier? Others suggest that some memories are so painful that they exist only in an *unconscious* corner of the mind, making them inaccessible to the individual (Haaken, 2010; Mancia & Baggott, 2008). In these cases, therapy supposedly would be necessary to unlock the hidden memories.

**Repression**   According to Freud's psychoanalytic theory, a basic coping or defense mechanism that prevents anxiety-provoking thoughts, feelings, and memories from reaching consciousness.

On the other hand, critics of repressed memories contend that most people who have witnessed or experienced a violent crime or have survived childhood sexual abuse have intense, persistent memories. They have trouble *forgetting*, not remembering. Other skeptics wonder whether therapists may sometimes inadvertently create false memories in their clients during therapy. They propose that if a clinician suggests the possibility of abuse, the client's own *constructive processes* may lead him or her to create a false memory. The client also might start to incorporate portrayals of abuse from movies and books into his or her own memory, forgetting their original sources (a form of *source amnesia*) and eventually coming to see them as reliable.

As you can see, the notion of repressed memory is hotly contested. What's the final answer? Repression is a complex and controversial topic in psychology. No one doubts that some memories are forgotten and later recovered. What some question is the idea that *repressed memories* of painful experiences (especially childhood sexual abuse) are stored in the unconscious mind, especially since these memories may play a deciding role in certain judicial processes (Howe & Knott, 2015; Lampinen & Beike, 2015; Loftus & Cahill, 2007). The stakes are high because lawsuits and criminal prosecutions of sexual abuse are sometimes based on recovered memories of childhood sexual abuse. However, the so-called, "memory wars" may be getting less heated. Comparing attitudes in the 1990s to today, researchers found less belief in repressed memories among mainstream psychologists, as well as among undergraduates with greater critical-thinking abilities (Patihis et al., 2014).

**Summing Up**   While the debate over repressed memories continues, we must be careful not to ridicule or condemn people who remember or recover true memories of abuse. In the same spirit, we must protect innocent people from wrongful accusations that come from false memories. Hopefully, with continued research (and perhaps new technology) we may someday better protect the interests of both the victim and the accused.

To close on another encouraging note, we're providing a final, brief section that summarizes the most effective strategies for memory improvement. One of the many beauties of our human brain is that we can recognize the limits and problems of memory and then develop appropriate coping mechanisms. Just as our ancestors domesticated wild horses and cattle to overcome the physical limits of the human body, we can develop similar approaches to improve our mental limits—especially those responsible for fine detail.

## ❖ Psychology and Your Personal Success | Can Memory Improvement Increase Success?

The following TEN TIPS for memory improvement are based on material discussed throughout this chapter, and they're particularly helpful for increasing college success and reducing wasted time. Given that the three basic steps in memory are *encoding, storage,* and *retrieval* (the ESR model), we've arranged these tips accordingly. To get the maximum benefits, first read through the list placing a check mark ✓ in the blank space next to items you're currently using, a + mark by the tips you want to add, and a − mark by those strategies you don't plan to try. After adding the new skills to your daily study habits, look back and reconsider those items with a − mark. We'd like to hear how these strategies work out for you (khuffman@palomar.edu, kdowdell@dmacc.edu, casanderson@amherst.edu).

**Encoding**   As discussed earlier, the first step in memory is successful *encoding*. To improve your study skills and exam performance, try these encoding tips:

- _____ *Pay attention and reduce interference.* When you really want to remember something, you must *selectively attend* to that information and ignore distractions. During class, focus on the instructor, and sit away from distracting people or views outside. When studying, choose a place with minimal interferences. Also, recall from earlier chapters that *multitasking* while studying or listening to lectures greatly increases interference and reduces your ability to pay attention.

- _____ *Strive for a deeper level of processing.* Some students try to study important terms or concepts by highlighting, rereading, or simply repeating the information over and over to themselves. As you recall from Chapter 1, highlighting and rereading are the LEAST effective study techniques. While repeating information (maintenance rehearsal) does extend the duration of STM beyond the normal limits of about 30 seconds, this type of rehearsal, as well as highlighting and rereading, are all forms of *shallow processing*. They're not efficient for LTM or for preparing for exams. If you want to effectively encode (and later successfully retrieve) information, you need a deeper level of processing, which involves active reading and taking notes. Another way to deeply process is *elaborative* rehearsal, which involves thinking about the material and relating it to previously stored information. Hopefully, you've noticed that we formally define each key term immediately in the text and generally give a brief explanation with one or two examples for each term. While studying this text, use these tools to help your elaborative rehearsal—and thereby ensure a deeper level of processing. Also try making up your own examples. The more elaborate the encoding of information, the more memorable it will become.

- _____ *Counteract the serial-position effect.* Because we tend to remember information that occurs at the beginning or end of a sequence, spend extra time with information in the middle. When reading or reviewing the text, start at different places—sometimes at the second section, sometimes near the end.

**Storage**    The second step in successful memory is *storage*. The best way to create an effective storage system, in either your brain or your computer, is through logical filing and good organization. Try these two helpful tips:

- _____ *Use chunking.* Although the storage capacity of STM is only around five to nine items, you can expand it by chunking information into groups. For example, if you need to remember a 12-digit number, try grouping it into four groups of three numbers.

- _____ *Create hierarchies.* An efficient way to organize and store a large body of information is to create hierarchies, which involves grouping concepts from most general to most specific. Chapter outlines and the tables and figures in this text are examples of hierarchies. Be sure to study them carefully—and make up your own versions whenever possible.

**Retrieval**    The third and final stage of successful memory is *retrieval*. As you know, your grades in most courses are primarily determined by some form of quizzing or exams, both of which rely exclusively on retrieval. Here are five tips for improving retrieval:

- _____ *Engage in practice testing.* Recall from Chapter 1 that research clearly shows that practice testing is one of the very best ways to improve your retrieval—and course grades (Carpenter & Yeung, 2017; Putnam et al., 2016; Trumbo et al., 2016). Taking tests is not a favorite pastime for most people. However, if you think of it as "practice," then it becomes more attractive and logical. Just as we all need to practice our skateboarding tricks, golf swing, or dance routine, we need to practice testing ourselves—BEFORE any exam. This is why we provide so many self-testing options within this text (e.g., the learning objectives questions that start each section, the self-tests at the end of each major heading, and the key term review at the end of each chapter). We also offer numerous additional free tests within *WileyPlus* (e.g., ORION adaptive practice, application quizzes, and practice tests). Be sure to take advantage of these options.

- _____ *Distribute your practice.* In addition to practice testing, the next best way to improve your memory is through distributed practice. Researchers have found that we encode, store, and retrieve information better when our study sessions are distributed (or spaced out) over time (Carpenter & Yeung, 2017; Dunlosky et al., 2013; Kornmeier et al., 2014). Although *massed practice* (cramming) can produce speedy short-term learning, it's far less effective than distributed practice. There are at least two other major problems with staying up late or "pulling an all-nighter" to cram for exams: (1) being drowsy while studying or taking an exam negatively affects overall performance, and (2) during sleep we process and store most of the new information we acquired when awake (Chapter 5).

**FIGURE 7.25** **What's wrong with this picture?** Many students claim they study best while listening to music or while in a noisy environment. However, as you recall from Chapter 1, this type of multitasking almost always decreases overall performance, and that's particularly true when you're attempting to learn something new. Just as people are trained to give public speeches in front of an audience and deep-sea divers practice their diving underwater, you should, when you study, try to recreate the academic environment under which you initially learn and will later perform. For example, when taking a test, most instructors will not allow you to wear headphones and will attempt to keep the room as quiet as possible. Therefore, this is the environment you need to recreate while studying.

Ulrich Baumgarten/Getty Images

• _____ *Employ self-monitoring.* When studying a text, you should periodically stop and test your understanding of the material using the built-in self-testing throughout each chapter. This type of self-monitoring is a common strategy of successful students. Even when you are studying a single sentence, you need to monitor your understanding. Furthermore, poor readers tend to read at the same speed for both easy and difficult material. Good readers (and more successful students) tend to monitor themselves, and they slow down or repeat difficult material. Keep in mind that if you evaluate your learning only while you're reading the material, you may overestimate your understanding (because the information is still in STM). However, if you delay for at least a few minutes, and then test your understanding, your evaluation will be more accurate.

• _____ *Overlearn essential material.* Successful students know that the best way to ensure their full understanding of material (and success on an exam) is through *overlearning*—studying information even after you think you already know it. Don't just study until you *think* you know it. Work hard until you *know* you know it!

• _____ *Recreate the original learning environment.* As mentioned earlier, the terms *retrieval cues, encoding-specificity principle, mood congruence,* and *state-dependent retrieval* all emphasize a central point—characteristics of the internal and external environment are key to the formation and retrieval of your memories (**Figure 7.25**). Therefore, since you naturally encode a lot of material during class lectures, avoid "early takes" or makeup exams, because they're generally scheduled in a setting different from your original classroom. The *context* will be different, and your retrieval will suffer. Similarly, when you take a test, try to recreate the psychological and physiological states you were in when you originally learned the material. According to the mood-congruence effect, you will recall more if the mood of your test taking matches the mood of the original learning. Given that you'll naturally be somewhat anxious when taking a test, try to "hype yourself up" during class and while you're studying by reminding yourself of how important it is to do well on your upcoming exams. Similarly, in line with the *state-dependent memory* research, if you normally drink coffee while studying, drink it again before or during your exams.

## A Final Word
As we've seen throughout this chapter, our memories are remarkable—yet highly fickle. Recognizing our commonly shared frailties of memory will make us better jurors in the courtroom, more informed consumers, and more thoughtful, open-minded parents, teachers, students, and friends. Unfortunately, sometimes our memories are better than we would like. Traumatic, and extremely emotional, memories can persist even when we would very much like to forget. Though painful, these memories can sometimes provide valuable personal insights. As Elizabeth Loftus suggests in a letter to her deceased mother:

> *I thought then [as a 14-year-old] that eventually I would get over your death. I know today that I won't. But I've decided to accept that truth. What does it matter if I don't get over you? Who says I have to? David and Robert still tease me: "Don't say the M word or Beth will cry." So what if the word mother affects me this way? Who says I have to fix this? Besides, I'm too busy* (Loftus, 2002, p. 70).

© Billy R. Ray/Wiley

## Retrieval Practice 7.4 | Memory Distortions and Improvement

Completing this self-test and the connections section, and then checking your answers by clicking on the answer button or by looking in Appendix B, will provide immediate feedback and helpful practice for exams.

**Self-Test**

1. Briefly describe why we sometimes shape, rearrange, or distort our memories.

2. Researchers have demonstrated that it is _____ to create false memories.

   a. relatively easy     b. rarely possible
   c. moderately difficult     d. never possible

3. Dave was told the same childhood story of his father saving his neighbor from a fire so many times that he is now sure it is true, but all the evidence proves it never happened. This is an example of _____.

   a. a repressed memory   b. deluded childhood fantasies
   c. a false memory     d. early-onset juvenile dementia

4. _____ memories are related to anxiety-provoking thoughts or events that are supposedly prevented from reaching consciousness.

   a. Suppressed     b. Flashbulb
   c. Flashback     d. Repressed

5. To improve your encoding, you should _____.

   a. pay attention and reduce interference
   b. strive for a deeper level of processing
   c. counteract the serial-position effect
   d. use all of these options

**Connections—Chapter to Chapter**

Answering the following question will help you "look back and look ahead" to see the important connections among the subfields of psychology and chapters within this text.

In Chapter 11 (Gender and Human Sexuality), you'll learn about *child sexual abuse* and *rape*. In this chapter, you discovered why we shape, rearrange, and distort our memories out of our need for logic and consistency, as well as for the sake of efficiency. Using this information on how and why we distort our memories, explain why victims might unintentionally distort their memories of childhood sexual abuse.

---

**Study Tip**

*The WileyPLUS program that accompanies this text provides for each chapter a* Media Challenge, Critical Thinking Exercise, *and* Application Quiz. *This set of study materials provides additional, invaluable study opportunities. Be sure to check it out!*

# Chapter Summary

## 7.1 The Nature of Memory   221

- **Memory** is an internal representation of some prior event or experience. It's also a **constructive process** that organizes and shapes information as it's being processed, stored, and retrieved.

- Major perspectives on memory include the **encoding, storage, and retrieval (ESR) model**, the **levels of processing model**, the **parallel distributed processing (PDP) model**, and the **three-stage memory model**. This last approach, which is the dominant model, proposes that information is stored and processed in **sensory memory**, **short-term memory (STM)**, and **long-term memory (LTM)**. Each stage differs in its purpose, duration, and capacity.

- Sensory memory has a relatively large capacity, but the duration is only a few seconds. Visual sensory memory (**iconic memory**) only holds for about one-half of a second, whereas auditory sensory memory (**echoic memory**) lasts for up to 4 seconds.

- Short-term memory (STM) has a limited capacity and duration. Material is retained for as long as 30 seconds, but it's limited to 5 to 9 bits of information. **Chunking** and **maintenance rehearsal** improve STM's duration and capacity.

- Given that STM is passive and that conscious, active processing of information also occurs in STM, researchers now often refer to **working memory**, which is composed of a three-part system—a *phonological loop, visuospatial sketchpad,* and a *central executive.*

- LTM is an almost unlimited storehouse for information that must be kept for long periods. The two major types of LTM are **explicit/ declarative memory** and **implicit/nondeclarative memory**. Organization and **elaborative rehearsal** improve encoding. **Retrieval cues** help stimulate retrieval of information from LTM. According to the **encoding-specificity principle**, retrieval is improved when conditions of recovery are similar to encoding conditions.

**Test Your Critical Thinking**

**1.** What are some of the possible advantages and disadvantages of memory being a constructive process?

**2.** If you were forced to lose one type of memory—sensory, short-term, or long-term—which would you select? Why?

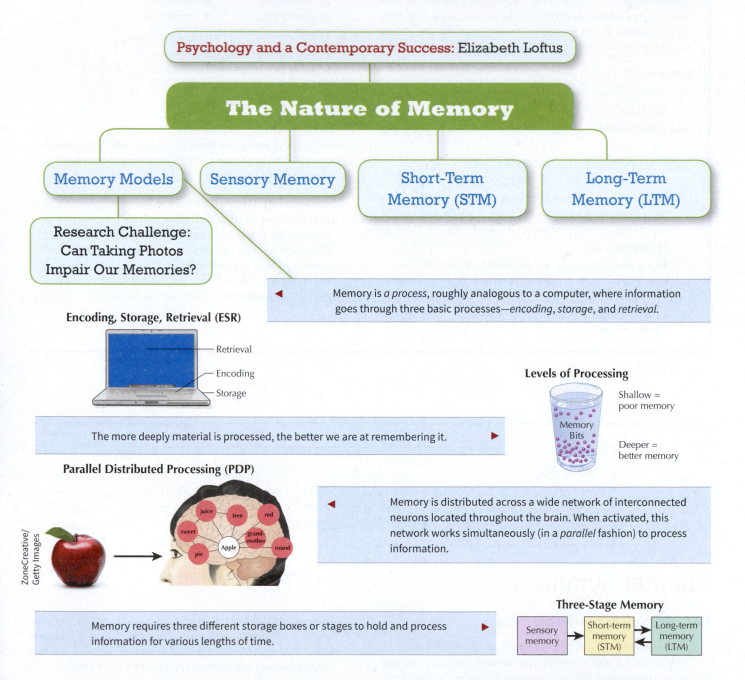

Psychology and a Contemporary Success: Elizabeth Loftus

## The Nature of Memory

- Memory Models
- Sensory Memory
- Short-Term Memory (STM)
- Long-Term Memory (LTM)

Research Challenge: Can Taking Photos Impair Our Memories?

Memory is *a process*, roughly analogous to a computer, where information goes through three basic processes—*encoding*, *storage*, and *retrieval*.

**Encoding, Storage, Retrieval (ESR)**

— Retrieval
— Encoding
— Storage

The more deeply material is processed, the better we are at remembering it.

**Levels of Processing**

Shallow = poor memory

Memory Bits

Deeper = better memory

**Parallel Distributed Processing (PDP)**

ZoneCreative/ Getty Images

juice    tree    red
sweet    grand-mother
pie    Apple    round

Memory is distributed across a wide network of interconnected neurons located throughout the brain. When activated, this network works simultaneously (in a *parallel* fashion) to process information.

Memory requires three different storage boxes or stages to hold and process information for various lengths of time.

**Three-Stage Memory**

Sensory memory → Short-term memory (STM) ⇄ Long-term memory (LTM)

## 7.2    Forgetting    233

- Early research by Ebbinghaus showed that we tend to forget newly learned information quickly, but we relearn the information more readily the second time.

- Researchers have proposed five major theories to explain forgetting— decay, **retroactive** and **proactive interference**, motivated forgetting, encoding failure, and retrieval failure. The **tip-of-the-tongue phenomenon** is an example of the retrieval failure theory.

- There are several major factors that help explain why we forget: the **misinformation effect**, the **serial-position effect**, **source amnesia**, spacing of practice, and culture.

**Test Your Critical Thinking**

**1.** Briefly describe an example from your own life of source amnesia.

**2.** Why might advertisers of shoddy services or products benefit from channel surfing, especially if the television viewer is skipping from news programs to cable talk shows to infomercials?

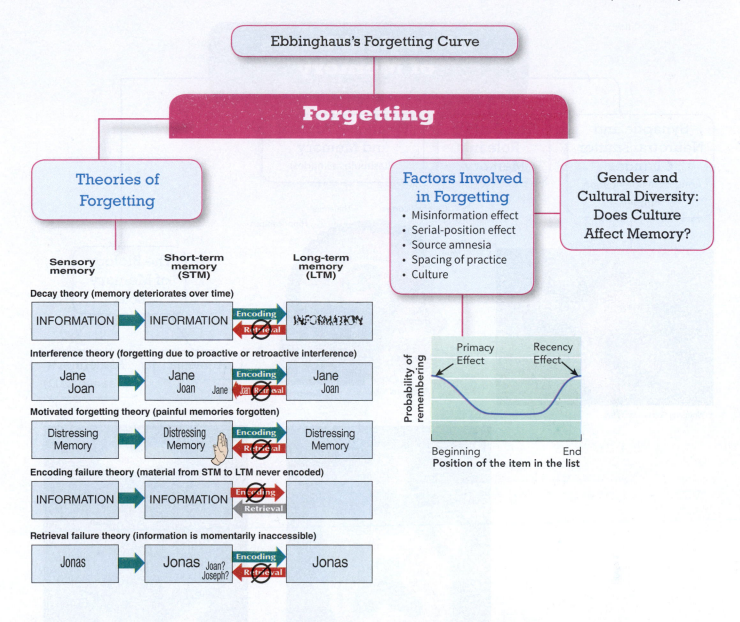

Ebbinghaus's Forgetting Curve

**Forgetting**

**Theories of Forgetting**

**Factors Involved in Forgetting**
- Misinformation effect
- Serial-position effect
- Source amnesia
- Spacing of practice
- Culture

**Gender and Cultural Diversity: Does Culture Affect Memory?**

Sensory memory | Short-term memory (STM) | Long-term memory (LTM)

**Decay theory (memory deteriorates over time)**
INFORMATION → INFORMATION → Encoding / Retrieval ⊘ → INFORMATION

**Interference theory (forgetting due to proactive or retroactive interference)**
Jane Joan → Jane Joan Jane → Encoding / Jean Retrieval ⊘ → Jane Joan

**Motivated forgetting theory (painful memories forgotten)**
Distressing Memory → Distressing Memory → Encoding / Retrieval ⊘ → Distressing Memory

**Encoding failure theory (material from STM to LTM never encoded)**
INFORMATION → INFORMATION → Encoding / Retrieval

**Retrieval failure theory (information is momentarily inaccessible)**
Jonas → Jonas Joan? Joseph? → Encoding / Retrieval ⊘ → Jonas

Probability of remembering

Primacy Effect    Recency Effect

Beginning    End
**Position of the item in the list**

## 7.3   Biological Bases of Memory   238

- Learning modifies the brain's neural networks through **long-term potentiation (LTP)**, strengthening particular synapses and affecting the ability of neurons to release their neurotransmitters.

- Memory formation begins with attention to certain stimuli. This attention then triggers synaptic and neurotransmitter changes that result in encoding, which, in turn, produces neural messages that are processed and stored in various areas of the brain.

- Emotional arousal increases neurotransmitters and hormones that affect several parts of the brain. Heightened arousal also can

increase the encoding and storage of new information and the formation of **flashbulb memories (FBMs)**.

- Traumatic brain injuries and disease, such as Alzheimer's disease (AD), can cause memory loss. Two major types of amnesia are **retrograde** and **anterograde amnesia**. The lack of **consolidation** may help explain retrograde amnesia.

### Test Your Critical Thinking

**1.** What might be the evolutionary benefit of flashbulb memories?

**2.** How might anterograde amnesia affect a person's relationships with others?

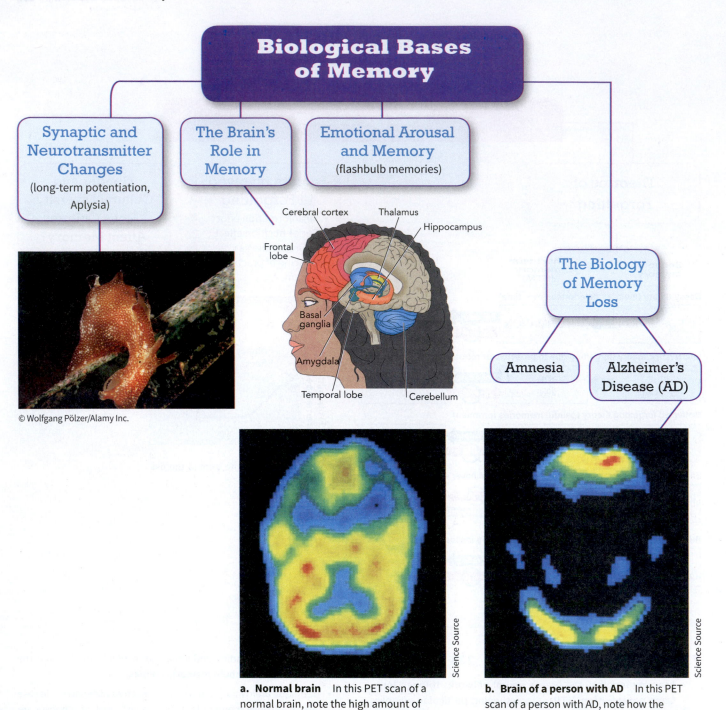

## Biological Bases of Memory

**Synaptic and Neurotransmitter Changes** (long-term potentiation, Aplysia)

**The Brain's Role in Memory**

**Emotional Arousal and Memory** (flashbulb memories)

**The Biology of Memory Loss**

**Amnesia**

**Alzheimer's Disease (AD)**

© Wolfgang Pölzer/Alamy Inc.

Cerebral cortex

Thalamus

Hippocampus

Frontal lobe

Basal ganglia

Amygdala

Temporal lobe

Cerebellum

Science Source

Science Source

**a. Normal brain** In this PET scan of a normal brain, note the high amount of the red and yellow color (signs of brain activity).

**b. Brain of a person with AD** In this PET scan of a person with AD, note how the reduced activity in the brain is most significant in the temporal and parietal lobes (the mostly black areas in the center and on the sides of this AD patient's brain). These are the key areas for storing memories.

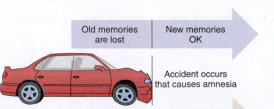

Old memories are lost | New memories OK

Accident occurs that causes amnesia

Old memories OK | Can't form new memories

**a. Retrograde amnesia** After an accident or other brain injury, individuals with *retrograde amnesia* have no trouble forming new memories, but they do experience *amnesia* (loss of memories) for segments of the past. Old, "retro" memories are lost.

**b. Anterograde amnesia** In contrast, people with *anterograde amnesia* have no trouble recovering old memories, but they do experience *amnesia* (cannot form new memories) after an accident or other brain injury. New, "antero" memories are lost.

### 7.4   Memory Distortions and Improvement   244

- People shape, rearrange, and distort their memories in order to create logic, consistency, and efficiency. Despite all their problems and biases, our memories are normally fairly accurate and usually serve us well.

- When memory errors occur in the context of the criminal justice system, they can have serious legal and social consequences. Problems with eyewitness testimony are so well established that judges often allow expert testimony on the unreliability of eyewitnesses.

- False memories are well-established phenomena that are relatively common and easy to create. However, memory **repression** (especially of childhood sexual abuse) is a complex and controversial topic.

- How can we improve our memory? When *encoding*, pay attention and reduce interference, strive for a deeper level of processing, and counteract the serial-position effect. During *storage*, use chunking and hierarchies. During *retrieval*, practice test taking (in-text quizzes, website quizzes, etc.), use distributed rather than massed practice, employ self-monitoring and overlearning, and, finally, recreate the original learning environment.

**Test Your Critical Thinking**

**1.** As an eyewitness to a crime, how could you use information in this chapter to improve your memory for specific details?

**2.** If you were a juror, what would you say to the other jurors about the reliability of eyewitness testimony?

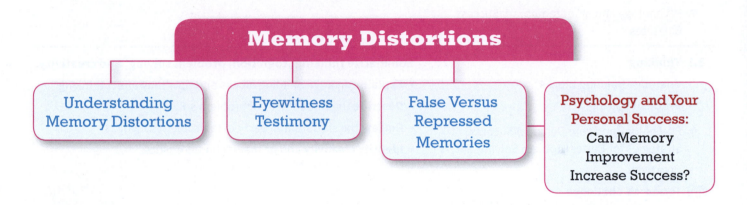

## Key Terms

**Retrieval Practice**   *Write a definition for each term before turning back to the referenced page to check your answer.*

- anterograde amnesia   242
- chunking   227
- consolidation   242
- constructive process   222
- distributed practice   236
- elaborative rehearsal   224
- encoding   222
- encoding-specificity principle   231
- encoding, storage, and retrieval (ESR) model   222
- episodic memory   229
- explicit/declarative memory   228
- flashbulb memory (FBM)   240
- implicit/nondeclarative memory   229

- levels of processing model   224
- long-term memory (LTM)   228
- long-term potentiation (LTP)   238
- maintenance rehearsal   227
- massed practice   236
- memory   222
- misinformation effect   235
- mnemonic   231
- parallel distributed processing (PDP) model   224
- priming   229
- proactive interference   234
- repression   247
- retrieval   222

- retrieval cue   230
- retroactive interference   234
- retrograde amnesia   242
- semantic memory   229
- sensory memory   226
- serial-position effect   236
- short-term memory (STM)   226
- source amnesia   236
- storage   222
- three-stage memory model   225
- tip-of-the-tongue (TOT) phenomenon   235
- working memory   227

© alexxl66/iStockphoto

# Thinking, Language, and Intelligence

**LEARNING OBJECTIVES**

**Summarize thinking, cognition, problem solving, and creativity.**
• **Explain** cognitive building blocks and how they affect thinking.
• **Describe** the three stages of problem solving.
• **Review** the six potential barriers to problem solving.
• **Identify** creativity and its major characteristics.

**Summarize the key characteristics and theories of language.**
• **Identify** language and its major building blocks.
• **Describe** the prominent theories of language and thinking and how they interact.
• **Discuss** the major stages of language development, including the language acquisition device (LAD).
• **Review** the evidence and controversy surrounding nonhuman animals' acquisition and use of language.

**Summarize the nature and measurement of intelligence.**
• **Define** intelligence.
• **Compare** the different forms and theories of intelligence.
• **Describe** how intelligence is measured and the groups that fall at the extremes.

**Review the major controversies surrounding intelligence.**
• **Identify** the various theories and controversies concerning multiple intelligences.
• **Discuss** the relative contributions of nature and nurture to IQ.
• **Describe** how and why groups differ in mental ability tests.

### ❖ Psychology and a Contemporary Success | Bill Gates

You've undoubtedly heard of Bill Gates (1955–), the American entrepreneur, philanthropist, investor, and author, who cofounded Microsoft and subsequently became one of the richest people in the world. But did you know that as a child he was a voracious reader of reference books, such as encyclopedias, and seemed so bored and withdrawn that his parents worried that he might become a loner? Or that at the age of 15 he started his first business venture with his friend Paul Allen and sold his first computer program for $20,000? Although he wanted to start his own company at this age, his parents pushed him to go on to college to become a lawyer. Gates agreed and attended Harvard University for a short time before he dropped out to focus full time on his ultimate career in computers.

Today, Bill Gates is extremely rich and famous, and he's also incredibly generous. Gates and his wife, Melinda, have earned many awards for their philanthropic work in the areas of health and education. As a result of his outstanding achievements and untiring efforts, Gates has been awarded numerous accolades, including several honorary doctorates from around the world. *Time* magazine has named him one of the most influential people of the 20th century, and in 2016 President Barack Obama presented Bill and Melinda Gates with the Presidential Medal of Freedom (see the photo). Perhaps most impressive is his incredible optimism. Gates believes all errors and huge problems, such as global poverty and climate change, can be fixed. They just need to be debugged (Bennet, 2015; Bill Gates Biography, n.d.; Goodell, 2014). Let's hope he's right!

Alex Wong/Getty Images

# Chapter Overview

*Life is not fair — get used to it!* —Bill Gates

As suggested by this quote, Bill Gates's path to extraordinary fame and success was not easy. In fact, it was filled with long hours of tedious work and numerous business and personal setbacks. But Gates persevered. His display of passion and perseverance (grit), along with his obvious "can do" attitude (growth mindset), explain why we chose him as our famous figure. In this chapter, we focus on thinking, language, and intelligence—each of which was central to Gates's achievements.

We begin with an exploration of the mental processes involved in thinking, problem solving, and creativity. Then we look at the world of language—its components, its interrelationship with thinking, how it develops, and whether nonhuman animals use true language. We close with the definition and measurement of intelligence and the controversies that surround it.

## Why Study Psychology?

### Did you know that

- . . . engaging in outdoor activities or simply taking a walk may improve your creativity?
- . . . personal traits and character strengths may be better predictors of achievement than IQ?
- . . . Bill Gates is judged as sexy based on his creative genius?
- . . . chimps and dolphins can use nonvocal language to make simple sentences and communicate with human trainers?
- . . . children all over the world go through similar stages in language development at about the same age, and their babbling is the same in all languages?
- . . . speaking multiple languages can make you smarter?
- . . . many cultures have no language equivalent for our notion of intelligence?
- . . . watching TV dramas can increase your emotional intelligence?

Mariday/Shutterstock

# 8.1    Thinking

**Retrieval Practice**    While reading the upcoming sections, respond to each Learning Objective in your own words.

**Summarize thinking, cognition, problem solving, and creativity.**

- **Explain** cognitive building blocks and how they affect thinking.
- **Describe** the three stages of problem solving.
- **Review** the six potential barriers to problem solving.
- **Identify** creativity and its major characteristics.

**Cognition**    The mental activities involved in acquiring, storing, retrieving, and using knowledge.

If you go on to major in psychology, you'll discover that researchers often group thinking, language, and intelligence under the larger umbrella of **cognition**, the mental activities of acquiring, storing, retrieving, and using knowledge (Groome et al., 2014; Matlin, 2016). Technically, we discuss cognition throughout this text (for example, in chapters on sensation and perception, consciousness, learning, and memory). However, in this section we limit our discussion to *thinking*—what it is and where it's located.

Every time we take in information and mentally act on it, we're thinking. These thought processes are both localized and distributed throughout our brains in networks of neurons. For example, during decision making, our brains are most active in the *prefrontal cortex*. This region associates complex ideas; makes plans; forms, initiates, and allocates attention; and supports multitasking. The prefrontal cortex also links to other areas of the brain, such as the limbic system (Chapter 2), to synthesize information from several senses (Haas et al., 2015; Schmitgen et al., 2016; Viviani et al., 2015).

**Artificial intelligence (AI)**    The scientific field concerned with creating machines that can simulate human thought processes and performance.

As you may know, scientists have struggled for decades to create machines that can simulate human thought processes and performance. So far, this field, known as **artificial intelligence (AI)**, has successfully developed computers that can outperform humans on several complex information-processing tasks and games—particularly those that require speed, perseverance, and a huge memory—since they never get tired, distracted, or take a break (Jee, 2017; Koch, 2015; Lemley et al., 2017)! Thanks to AI research, we now enjoy incredible advances, such as Google's Deep Learning and IBM's Watson, as well as personal assistants like Apple's Siri, Google Now, and Microsoft's Cortana. Will AI someday match human thinking in flexibility, emotional capacity, and consciousness? Some have estimated that computers will surpass human brains around the year 2040 (van Paaschen, 2017). Time alone will tell!

Before concluding that our brains (or AI machines) are the center of all cognition, it's important to note that our bodies also affect our thoughts, perceptions, attitudes, and judgments. Research shows that just holding a hot cup of coffee or being in a comfortably heated room warms our feelings toward strangers (Carpenter, 2011; Williams & Bargh, 2008; Zhong & Leonardelli, 2008). In this chapter, we'll discuss how just taking a walk increases our creativity, and in Chapter 12 you'll discover how cosmetic injections of Botox in the facial muscles tend to lift depression but also decrease empathy (Baumeister et al., 2016; Maasumi et al., 2015; Sifferlin, 2017). These examples of **embodied cognition** show us that our thought processes are not just centered in our brains, but are also shaped ("grounded") by our bodily sensations and interactions with our environment.

**Embodied cognition**    The theory that cognitive processes are influenced by bodily sensations and interactions with the environment.

## Cognitive Building Blocks

Now that we know where thinking occurs, let's look at its basic components. Imagine yourself lying, relaxed, in the warm, gritty sand on an ocean beach. Do you see palms swaying in the wind? Can you smell the salty sea and taste the dried salt on your lips? Can you hear children playing in the surf? What you've just created is a *mental image*, a mental representation of a previously stored sensory experience, which includes visual, auditory, olfactory, tactile, motor, and gustatory imagery (McKellar, 1972). We all have a mental space where we visualize and manipulate our sensory images. Interestingly, research shows that when we create mental images and thoughts about "healthy foods," we tend to consider them less filling and actually order larger portions and eat more (Suher et al., 2016)! See the following **Try This Yourself** to test your skills in manipulating mental images.

In addition to mental images, our thinking includes forming *concepts*, or mental representations of a group or category. Concepts can be concrete (like car and concert) or abstract (like intelligence and beauty). They are essential to thinking and communication because they simplify and organize information. Normally, when you see a new object or encounter a new situation, you relate it to your existing conceptual structure and categorize it according to where it fits. If you see a metal box with four wheels driving on the highway, you know it is a car, even if you've never seen that particular model before.

### Try This Yourself

#### Manipulating Mental Images

How are the two yellow figures the same, and how are the two blue figures different? Solving this problem requires mental imagery and manipulation. Those of you who are familiar with the computer game Tetris might find this puzzle rather simple. Others might want to turn to Appendix B for an explanation.

How do we learn concepts? They develop through the environmental interactions of three major building blocks—prototypes, artificial concepts, and hierarchies (Ferguson & Casasola, 2015; McDaniel et al., 2014). See **Figure 8.1**.

**Prototype**  A mental image or best example that embodies the most typical features of a concept or category.

- **Prototypes** When initially learning about birds, a young child develops a general concept based on a typical representative, or **prototype** (**Figure 8.1a**), of *bird* after a parent points out a number of examples. Once the child develops the prototype of a bird, he or she then is able to quickly classify all flying animals, such as this robin, correctly.

- **Artificial concepts** We create *artificial* (or formal) *concepts* (**Figure 8.1b**) from logical rules or definitions. When an example doesn't quite fit the prototype, like a penguin, we must review our artificial concept of a bird: warm-blooded animals that fly, have wings and beaks, and lay eggs. Although this penguin doesn't fly, it has wings and a beak and lays eggs. So it must be a bird.

- **Hierarchies** Creating *hierarchies*, or subcategories within broader concepts, helps us master new material more quickly and easily (**Figure 8.1c**). Note, however, that we tend to begin with basic-level concepts (the middle row on the diagram) when we first learn something (Rosch, 1978). For example, a child develops the basic-level concept for *bird* before learning the higher-order concept *animal* or the lower-order concept *robin*.

## Problem Solving

Many years ago in Los Angeles, a 12-foot-high tractor-trailer reportedly got stuck under a bridge that was 6 inches too low. After hours of towing, tugging, and pushing, the police and transportation workers were stumped. Then a young boy happened by and asked, "Why don't you let some air out of the tires?" It was a simple, creative suggestion—and it worked.

Like this young boy—and like Köhler's chimps that stacked boxes to reach bananas (Chapter 6)—we all sometimes solve problems with a sudden flash of *insight*. These "aha" moments and sudden bursts of understanding often lead to more accurate solutions than those found through logical reasoning and analysis (Salvi et al., 2016). However, insight is somewhat unconscious and automatic, so it can't be rushed. When we're stumped on a problem, it sometimes helps to mentally set our problem aside for a while, in an *incubation period*, and the solution may then come to mind without further conscious thought.

**a. Prototypes**

Tom Biegalski/Shutterstock.com

**b. Artificial concepts**

FLPA/Alamy Stock Photo

**c. Hierarchies**

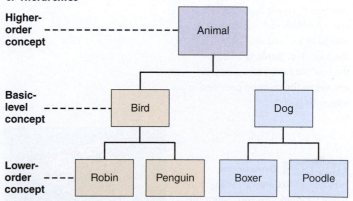

**FIGURE 8.1**  **Concepts**  When learning concepts, we most often use prototypes, artificial concepts, and hierarchies to simplify and categorize information. When we encounter a new type of bird, we fit it into our existing concept of a bird.

**Algorithm** A logical, step-by-step procedure that, if followed correctly, will always eventually solve the problem.

**Heuristic** An educated guess, or "rule of thumb," often used as a shortcut for problem solving; does not guarantee a solution to a problem but does narrow the alternatives.

**Mental set** A fixed-thinking approach to problem solving that only sees solutions that have worked in the past.

**Functional fixedness** A barrier to problem solving that comes from thinking about objects as functioning only in their usual or customary way.

**Availability heuristic** A cognitive strategy (or shortcut) that estimates the frequency or likelihood of an event based on information that is readily available in our memory.

What can we do if we've struggled with a problem, waited, and still have no insightful solution? Some problems are solved through *trial and error*. If you're stuck in a traffic jam, having trouble sleeping, or trying to lose weight, you may just try different solutions until you're successful—or give up.

In contrast to such "hit or miss" approaches, a more generally effective problem-solving method involves a logical progression from a given state (the problem) to a goal state (the solution). This process usually has three steps: *preparation*, *production*, and *evaluation* (Bourne et al., 1979).

Note in **Step-by-Step Diagram 8.1** that during the preparation stage, we identify and separate relevant from irrelevant facts and define the ultimate goal. Then, during the production stage, we generate possible solutions, called hypotheses, by using *algorithms* and *heuristics*. **Algorithms** are logical, step-by-step procedures that if followed correctly will always lead to an eventual solution. But they are not practical in many situations. **Heuristics**, or simplified rules based on experience, are much faster but do not guarantee a solution. Finally, during the evaluation stage we judge the hypotheses generated during the production stage against the criteria established in the preparation stage.

## Six Potential Barriers to Problem Solving

As we've just seen, insight, trial and error, algorithms, and heuristics all help us solve problems in our daily life. In this section, we'll discuss six potential barriers to effective problem solving. Why do we say "potential"? It's because most of these factors have both positive and negative influences.

1. *Mental sets* Why are some problems so difficult to solve? The reason may be that we often stick to problem-solving strategies that have worked in the past, called **mental sets**, rather than trying new, possibly more effective ones (**Figure 8.2**).

2. *Functional fixedness* We also sometimes fail to see solutions to our problems because we tend to view objects as functioning only in the usual or customary way—a phenomenon known as **functional fixedness** (Chrysikou et al., 2016; Ness, 2015; Wright et al., 2015). When a child uses sofa cushions to build a fort, or you use a table knife instead of a screwdriver to tighten a screw, you both have successfully avoided functional fixedness. Similarly, the individual who discovered a way to retrofit diesel engines to allow them to use discarded restaurant oil as fuel also overcame functional fixedness—and may become very wealthy! For practice with functional fixedness, see **Figure 8.3**.

3. *Availability heuristic* Every summer, we see repeated programs and "BREAKING NEWS" reports about shark attacks on unsuspecting swimmers, which lead viewers to a mistaken perception that such attacks are highly likely. In reality, ocean-goers are 1,817 times more likely to drown than to die from a shark attack! How might this type of media coverage also increase prejudice against certain groups, such as viewing all Muslims as terrorists, or create unrealistic dreams and expectations of personal success (see **Figure 8.4**)? These are just some of the many examples of the **availability heuristic**, in which we take a

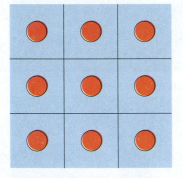

**FIGURE 8.2** **The nine-dot problem** Can you connect all nine dots without lifting your pencil or using more than four lines? If not, the reason may be that you're trying to use *mental sets*—problem-solving strategies that have worked well for you in the past. Try "thinking outside the box" and then compare your answer to the solution provided in Appendix B.

**FIGURE 8.3** **Overcoming functional fixedness** Using only these supplies, can you mount the candle on a wall so that it can be lit in the normal way and without toppling over? The solution is provided in Appendix B.

**FIGURE 8.4** **The availability heuristic in action** Thanks to repeated ads about lottery winners, yoy may overestimate your personal chances of winning the jackpot (the availability heuristic). Before you start buying lottery tickets, however, consider the fact that any one individual's odds of winning either the MegaMillions or Powerball jackpot are about 175 million to one, whereas your chances of dying in a plane crash are 25 million to one and a car crash 5,000 to one (Amadeo, 2016).

Siphotography/Getty Images

## STEP-BY-STEP DIAGRAM 8.1 | Three Steps to the Goal

**STOP!** This **Step-by-Step** Diagram contains essential information NOT found elsewhere in the text, which is likely to appear on quizzes and exams. Be sure to study it CAREFULLY!

There are three stages of problem solving that help you attain a goal, such as moving to a new home.

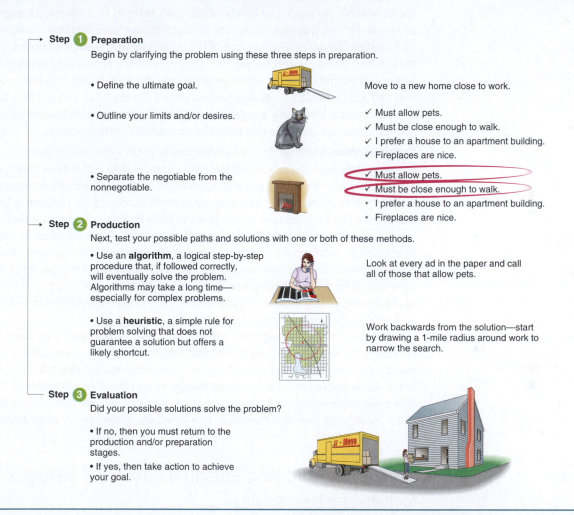

Step **1** **Preparation**

Begin by clarifying the problem using these three steps in preparation.

• Define the ultimate goal.

Move to a new home close to work.

• Outline your limits and/or desires.

✓ Must allow pets.
✓ Must be close enough to walk.
✓ I prefer a house to an apartment building.
✓ Fireplaces are nice.

• Separate the negotiable from the nonnegotiable.

✓ Must allow pets.
✓ Must be close enough to walk.
\* I prefer a house to an apartment building.
\* Fireplaces are nice.

Step **2** **Production**

Next, test your possible paths and solutions with one or both of these methods.

• Use an **algorithm**, a logical step-by-step procedure that, if followed correctly, will eventually solve the problem. Algorithms may take a long time—especially for complex problems.

Look at every ad in the paper and call all of those that allow pets.

• Use a **heuristic**, a simple rule for problem solving that does not guarantee a solution but offers a likely shortcut.

Work backwards from the solution—start by drawing a 1-mile radius around work to narrow the search.

Step **3** **Evaluation**

Did your possible solutions solve the problem?

• If no, then you must return to the production and/or preparation stages.

• If yes, then take action to achieve your goal.

---

mental shortcut by estimating the frequency or likelihood of an event based on information that is most readily *available* in our memories. In other words, we give greater credence to information and examples that readily spring to mind (Bruine de Bruin et al., 2016; Mase et al., 2015; Tversky & Kahneman, 1974, 1993).

4. ***Representativeness heuristic*** When walking in the woods, have you ever immediately frozen or jumped away because you thought you saw a dangerous snake, when in fact it was just a curved stick on the ground? If so, this would be an example of the **representativeness heuristic**, in which we estimate the probability of an event based on how well something matches (or *represents*) an existing prototype or stereotype in our minds (Bernard et al., 2016; Lien & Yuan, 2015; Peteros & Maleyeff, 2015). We all have a prototype of a snake in our minds, and the curved stick matches this prototype, which explains why this is also an example of the *availability heuristic*. While walking in the woods, you're primed to look out for snakes, and the sight of the curved stick brings immediate images of a snake to your mind.

**Representativeness heuristic**
A cognitive strategy (or shortcut) that involves making judgments based on how well something matches (represents) an existing prototype or stereotype.

**Confirmation bias** The tendency to prefer information that confirms our preexisting positions or beliefs and to ignore or discount contradictory evidence; also known as remembering the "hits" and ignoring the "misses."

**Cognitive offloading** The use of external resources to reduce the information processing requirements of a task in order to reduce the cognitive demand.

5. **Confirmation bias** Are you wondering why the U.S. Congress can't seem to solve serious national problems, like our deteriorating bridges and highways? Or why we can't resolve ongoing disputes with our roommates or spouses? It may be that we too often seek confirmation for our preexisting positions or beliefs and tend to ignore or discount contradictory evidence. As discussed in Chapters 1 and 4, this type of faulty thinking and barrier to problem solving is known as the **confirmation bias** (Dibbets & Meesters, 2017; Nickerson, 1998; Webb et al., 2016). Like gamblers who keep putting coins into slot machines, we all have preexisting beliefs and biases that may lead us to focus only on our "hits" and ignore our "misses." To make matters worse, the confirmation bias is closely related to what's called *belief perseverance*—our tendency to stick to our positions and beliefs even when we hear contrary information.

Real-world examples of the confirmation bias (coupled with belief perseverance) are all around us—people who believe (or don't believe) that climate change is caused by human factors, that gun control can (or cannot) save lives, and that immigration helps (or hurts) our economy. Perhaps one of the most dramatic examples occurred during the 2016 United States presidential election. Do you recall the widespread shock in the United States and around the world when Donald Trump, the Republican nominee, won the election and not the widely presumed winner, Hillary Clinton? Can you see how both voters and observers undoubtedly sought out polls that supported their favored candidate and ignored or discounted those that provided contradictory information?

6. **Cognitive offloading** What do you do when you're lost in a new area of town, or you want to know the definition of a new word? Most of us immediately pull out our smartphones and ask for help. So it's disturbing to learn that our increasing reliance on the Internet and online resources may be negatively affecting our thought processes for problem solving, recall, and general learning (Storm et al., 2017). In the study that gave rise to these findings, participants were asked to answer challenging trivia questions. Some participants were allowed to use Google, whereas the others used only their memory. Next they were allowed to use either method to answer easier questions. The researchers found that participants who had used Google for the challenging questions were significantly more likely to use it again, and to use it more quickly. More surprising, 30% of these Google users failed to even attempt to answer a single simple question from memory.

The general idea of **cognitive offloading** is that rather than cognitively processing entirely in our head, we're likely to "offload" information and problem solving out into the world via online resources or just writing down the information (Gilbert, 2015; Risko & Dunn, 2015). Given that our use of and reliance on cognitively offloading will undoubtedly increase over time, some researchers conclude that our memory and problem-solving abilities will suffer accordingly. Does this mean that if we "don't use it, we lose it"? What do you think?

## ❖ Psychology and Your Personal Success | Strategies for Better Problem Solving

Are you feeling overwhelmed by all the potential barriers to problem solving? If so, keep in mind that some of these cognitive strategies, such as the availability and representativeness heuristics, provide mental shortcuts that are generally far more likely to help than to hurt us (Pohl et al., 2013). They allow immediate "inferences that are fast, frugal, and accurate" (Todd & Gigerenzer, 2000, p. 736). If you note that several houses on your street have safety bars on their windows, you might be motivated to add your own safety bars and thereby decrease your chances of being burglarized. Likewise, if you're hiking in an area with dangerous snakes, and you see a curved stick on the ground, it's smart to initially freeze or jump away. When faced with an immediate decision, we often don't have time to investigate all the options. We need to make quick decisions based on the currently available information.

What about other, long-term decisions, such as choosing your college major and your future career? How can you use the material we've been discussing to improve your personal success? You obviously can't try all possible options using algorithms to solve your career-planning problems. Instead, the three heuristics presented in **Table 8.1** may help focus your search and desired outcomes.

**TABLE 8.1    Three Problem-Solving Heuristics and Your Career**

| Problem-Solving Heuristics | Description | Example |
|---|---|---|
| **Working backward** | Starts with the solution, a known condition, and works backward through the problem. Once the search has revealed the steps to be taken, the problem is solved. | Deciding you want to be an experimental psychologist, you ask your psychology professor to recommend graduate programs at various colleges and universities. Then you contact these institutions for information on their academic requirements and admission policies. Next, you adapt your current college courses to fit those institutional requirements and policies. |
| **Means–end analysis** | Problem solver determines what measures would reduce the difference between the existing, given state and the end goal. Once the means to reach the goal are determined, the problem is solved. | You know you need a high GPA to get into a good graduate school for experimental psychology. Therefore, you ask your professors for study suggestions and interview several "A" students to compare their study habits to your own. You then determine the specific means (the number of hours and study techniques) required to meet your end goal of a high GPA. |
| **Creating subgoals** | Large, complex problems are broken down into a series of small subgoals. These subgoals then serve as a series of stepping stones, which can be taken one at a time to reach the end goal. | Getting a good grade in many college courses requires subgoals, like writing a successful term paper. To do this, you first choose a topic, and then go to the library and Internet to locate information related to that topic. Once you have the information, you organize it, create an outline, write the paper, review the paper, rewrite, rewrite again, and then submit the final paper, on or before the due date. |

# Creativity

*Effective philanthropy requires a lot of time and creativity—the same kind of focus and skills that building a business requires.* —Bill Gates

Everyone exhibits a certain amount of creativity in some aspects of life. Even when doing ordinary tasks, like planning an afternoon of errands, you are being somewhat creative. Similarly, if you've ever used a plastic garbage bag as a temporary rain jacket, or placed a thick college textbook on a chair as a booster seat for a child, you've found creative solutions to problems.

How would psychologists operationally define creativity? Conceptions of creativity are obviously personal and influenced by culture, but most agree that a creative solution or performance generally produces original, appropriate, and valued outcomes in a novel way. Three characteristics are generally associated with **creativity**: *originality*, *fluency*, and *flexibility*. Nikola Tesla and his numerous technological developments offer a prime example of each of these characteristics (**Table 8.2**).

**Creativity** The ability to produce original, appropriate, and valued outcomes in a novel way; consists of three characteristics— originality, fluency, and flexibility.

**TABLE 8.2    Three Elements of Creative Thinking**

| | Explanations | Nikola Tesla Examples |
|---|---|---|
| **Originality** | Seeing unique or different solutions to a problem | After noting the limitations of Thomas Edison's direct current (DC) transmission system, Tesla devised a means of transmitting power via an alternating current (AC), which greatly reduced power loss over long distances. |
| **Fluency** | Generating a large number of possible solutions | Tesla developed numerous alternating current (AC) systems, including generators, motors, and transformers. |
| **Flexibility** | Shifting with ease from one type of problem-solving strategy to another | Tesla was a prolific inventor who held over 300 patents worldwide. He played a key role in developing fluorescent bulbs, neon signs, X-rays, the radio, lasers, remote controls, robotics, and even the technology used in modern cell phones. |

### Test Your Critical Thinking

1. Can you identify which of the three characteristics of creativity (originality, fluency, or flexibility) best explains your personal experiences with being creative?

2. Creativity is usually associated with art, poetry, and the like. What are other areas in which creativity should be highly valued?

**Divergent thinking** A type of thinking that produces many solutions to the same problem.

**Convergent thinking** A type of thinking that seeks the single best solution to a problem.

Interestingly, research shows that creative people are judged to be more sexually attractive than less creative individuals (Geher & Kaufman, 2013; Lange & Euler, 2014). As a case in point, a survey of 815 undergraduates found that Bill Gates would be considered sexy based on his applied/technological creativity, whereas others might be considered sexy based on their ornamental/aesthetic or everyday/domestic creativity (Kaufman et al., 2016).

How do we measure creativity? Most tests focus on **divergent thinking**, a type of thinking in which we develop many possibilities from a single starting point (Palmiero et al., 2016; van de Kamp et al., 2015). Divergent thinking is open-ended and focused on generating multiple, novel solutions. You're using divergent thinking when you're brainstorming or thinking of multiple ways to remodel your home. **Convergent thinking** is the opposite of divergent thinking. Instead of looking for multiple solutions, it looks for the one, single best answer. You're using convergent thinking when you're searching for the answer to a math problem or a multiple-choice question.

Although divergent thinking and convergent thinking are very different, we generally use both to successfully problem solve. "Thinking outside the box" and generating many ideas (divergent thinking) increase the odds of finding a solution. But you also need convergent thinking to bring all the differing ideas together to identify (or *converge* on) the single best solution.

As you can see, creative, divergent thinking is highly desirable, and it helps us avoid some of the barriers to problem solving, such as functional fixedness. Unfortunately, this type of thinking is seldom emphasized in formal education. Furthermore, most people have a narrow, limited idea of creativity—thinking it applies only to artists and creative writers. However, as mentioned before, creativity consists of three major characteristics—originality, fluency, and flexibility—that can apply to any of us.

Psychologists have developed several tests for creativity. For example, the Unusual Uses Test requires you to think of as many uses as possible for an object, such as a brick. In the Anagrams Test, you're asked to reorder the letters in a word to make as many new words as possible. To test your overall creativity, see the following **Try This Yourself** feature.

## Try This Yourself

### Are You Creative?

- Find 10 coins and arrange them in the configuration shown here. By moving only 2 coins, form two rows, each containing 6 coins. The solution is provided in Appendix B.
- In five minutes, see how many words you can make using the letters in the word *hippopotamus*.
- In five minutes, list all the things you can do with a paper clip.

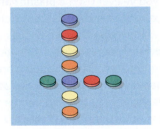

How can we increase general creativity? For children, outdoor activities—such as climbing, jumping, and exploring—have a positive effect (Brussoni et al., 2015). See **Figure 8.5**. For adults, even a simple walk will increase creativity. This was documented by an experiment that asked participants to think about alternative ways of using a common object (Oppezzo & Schwartz, 2014). For the word "button," a person might say, "as a doorknob on a dollhouse." Half the participants did this task while sitting at

**FIGURE 8.5** **Children and creativity** How do outdoor activities increase creativity? Unstructured free playtime (both indoors and outdoors) allows safe practice for skills necessary for adult activities, which serves as an evolutionary advantage to both human and nonhuman animals (Holmes et al., 2015; Kuczaj, 2017; Tsai, 2015). It also appears to build the skills essential to success in the arts, entrepreneurship, and even fields like science and engineering.

Courtesy of Sandy Harvey

| TABLE 8.3 | Resources of Creative People |
|-----------|------------------------------|
| **Affective processes** | Emotional intelligence and joy in creative expression |
| **Intellectual ability** | Enough intelligence to see problems in a new light |
| **Knowledge** | Sufficient basic knowledge of the problem to effectively evaluate possible solutions |
| **Thinking style** | Novel ideas, divergent thinking, and ability to distinguish between the worthy and worthless |
| **Personality** | Conscientiousness, openness, and willingness to grow and change, take risks, and work to overcome obstacles |
| **Motivation** | Sufficient motivation to accomplish the task and more internal than external motivation |
| **Environment** | An environment that supports creativity |

Which of these seven resources do you think best explains artist Vincent Van Gogh's great creativity? Although he reportedly only sold one painting in his lifetime, Van Gogh's portrait of *Dr. Gachet* is one of the 10 most expensive paintings in history, selling for $82.5 million dollars in 1990.

M. Flynn/Alamy Stock Photo

*Sources:* Chrysikou et al., 2016; Crilly, 2015; How Many Paintings, 2017; Li et al., 2015; Sternberg, 2014, 2015; van de kamp et al., 2015.

a desk facing a blank wall. The other half did it while walking on a treadmill facing a blank wall. Next, researchers repeated the study with participants walking outside and participants sitting at a desk outdoors, and in both conditions the walkers outperformed the sitters in creativity.

What are the obvious take-home messages? If you're a parent, teacher, or child's caregiver, this research on the value of outdoor activities and unstructured free playtime is particularly important given the increasing pressure on parents and schools to emphasize science, math, and other structured activities. In your own life, carve out time for play the next time you need to be creative—or simply take a walk!

If you'd like further suggestions for increasing your own creativity, researchers have found that it requires the coming together of at least seven interrelated resources, as shown in **Table 8.3**. Can you think of ways to apply some or all of this information to your own life?

So far we've only presented the positive side of creativity. But what about the famous stories of creative geniuses who suffer from psychological disorders? Are these based on myths or on reality? For more information on this controversial topic, see the following **Research Challenge**.

## Research Challenge

### Is Creativity Linked with Psychological Disorders?

What do you picture when you think of a creative genius? Thanks to movies, television, and novels, many people share the stereotypical image of an eccentric inventor or deranged artist, like the lead ballerina in the film *Black Swan*, portrayed by Natalie Portman (see the photo).

Thinking back to Chapter 1 and the mistaken belief that a full moon leads to more crime, can you see how this might be a simple illusory correlation—a mistaken perception that a relationship exists between two variables when no such relationship actually exists?

Or could there be small kernel of truth to the stereotyped link between creativity and psychological disorders? Researchers interested in this question analyzed years of stored data from more than a million people, including their professions, whether they had ever been diagnosed and treated for a psychological disorder, and, if so, what type of disorder (Kyaga et al., 2012). The researchers found that individuals in generally creative professions (scientific or artistic) were no more likely to suffer from most psychiatric disorders than those in other professions. However, one illness, *bipolar disorder*—which is characterized by extreme high and low mood swings (Chapter 14)—*was* found to be significantly more common in artists and scientists, and particularly in authors.

But could an individual's choice of occupation have confounded these results (Patra & Balhara, 2012; Rothenberg, 2014)? As you'll discover in Chapter 14, there is a strong genetic component in bipolar disorders. Furthermore, we're all much more likely to enter a profession similar to that of our parents because of familiarity, access, and modeling. So children of artists, scientists, and authors are more likely to choose the same professions as their parents. Might it be that the modest link between creativity and bipolar disorder is actually due to kinship, and the profession is incidental?

What do you think? How would you explain this intriguing association between certain types of creativity and bipolar disorder? If there is a true link, does the manic phase increase the energy levels of artists, scientists, and authors, giving them greater access to creative ideas than they would otherwise have? Or does it interfere with their overall output?

© Fox Searchlight Pictures/Photofest

If you find these questions fascinating and the lack of answers frustrating, you may be the perfect candidate for a career as a research psychologist. Recall from Chapter 1 that the scientific method is circular and never-ending—but guaranteed to excite!

### Test Yourself

1. Based on the information provided, did this study (Kyaga et al., 2012) use descriptive, correlational, and/or experimental research?

2. If you chose:

    ○ *descriptive research*, is this a naturalistic observation, survey/interview, case study, and/or archival research?

    ○ *correlational research*, is this a positive, negative, or zero correlation?

○ *experimental research*, label the IV, DV, experimental group(s), and control group. (Note: If participants were not randomly assigned to groups, list it as a *quasi-experimental design*.)

○ both *descriptive* and *correlational* research, answer the corresponding questions for both

**Check your answers by clicking on the answer button or by looking in Appendix B.**

**Note:** The information provided in this study is admittedly limited, but the level of detail is similar to what is presented in most textbooks and public reports of research findings. Answering these questions, and then comparing your answers to those provided, will help you become a better critical thinker and consumer of scientific research.

© Billy R. Ray/Wiley

## Retrieval Practice 8.1 | Thinking

Completing this self-test and the connections section, and then checking your answers by clicking on the answer button or by looking in Appendix B, will provide immediate feedback and helpful practice for exams.

### Self-Test

1. Briefly define *cognition*.

2. _____ is a logical step-by-step procedure that, if followed, will always eventually solve the problem.

    a. An algorithm
    b. A problem-solving set
    c. A heuristic
    d. Brainstorming

3. Rosa is shopping in a new supermarket and wants to find a standard type of mustard. Which problem-solving strategy would be most efficient?

    a. algorithm       b. heuristic
    c. instinct         d. mental set

4. _____ is a fixed-thinking approach to problem solving that only sees solutions that have worked in the past.

    a. Problem-solving set    b. Functional fixedness
    c. Mental set              d. Incubation

5. _____ is the ability to produce original, appropriate, and valued outcomes in a novel way.

    a. Problem solving        b. Functional flexibility
    c. Incubation             d. Creativity

### Connections Chapter to Chapter

Answering the following question will help you "look back and look ahead" to see the important connections among the subfields of psychology and chapters within this text.

In Chapter 14 (Psychological Disorders), you'll learn more about how attitudes toward mental illness develop. Explain how the availability heuristic might influence your thoughts and feelings about whether people with mental illness are violent or dangerous.

## 8.2    Language

### LEARNING OBJECTIVES

**Retrieval Practice**    While reading the upcoming sections, respond to each Learning Objective in your own words.

**Summarize the key characteristics and theories of language.**

• **Identify** language and its major building blocks.

• **Describe** the prominent theories of language and thinking and how they interact.

• **Discuss** the major stages of language development, including the language acquisition device (LAD).

• **Review** the evidence and controversy surrounding nonhuman animals' acquisition and use of language.

**FIGURE 8.6**   **The three major building blocks of language**

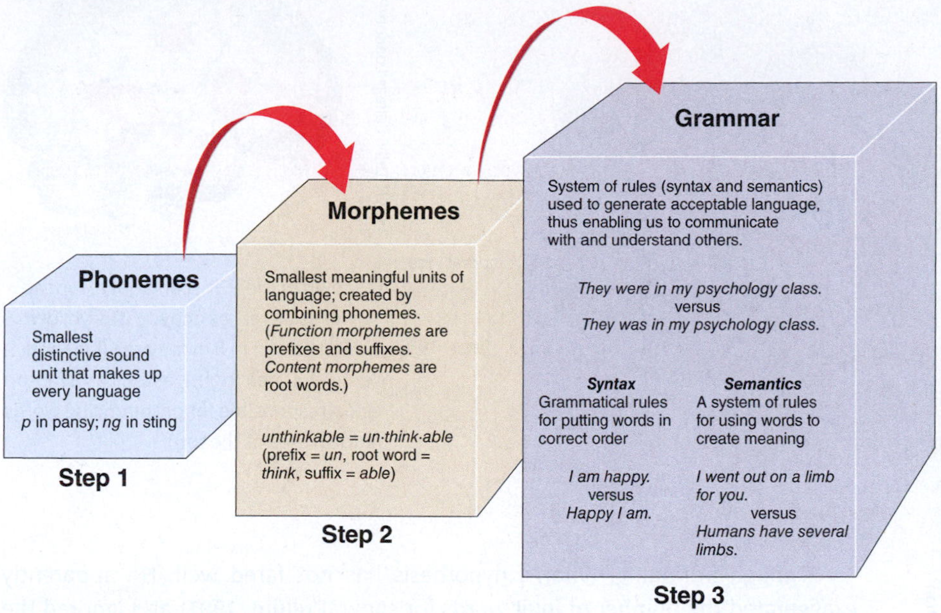

**Phonemes**

**Smallest distinctive sound unit that makes up every language**

*p* in pansy; *ng* in sting

**Step 1**

**Morphemes**

Smallest meaningful units of language; created by combining phonemes. (*Function morphemes* are prefixes and suffixes. *Content morphemes* are root words.)

*unthinkable* = *un·think·able* (prefix = *un*, root word = *think*, suffix = *able*)

**Step 2**

**Grammar**

System of rules (syntax and semantics) used to generate acceptable language, thus enabling us to communicate with and understand others.

*They were in my psychology class.*
versus
*They was in my psychology class.*

**Syntax**
Grammatical rules for putting words in correct order

*I am happy.*
versus
*Happy I am.*

**Semantics**
A system of rules for using words to create meaning

*I went out on a limb for you.*
versus
*Humans have several limbs.*

**Step 3**

"That wasn't me barking, that was me giving a motivational speech."

Cartoon Resource/Shutterstock

**Language** is critical to thinking because it enables us to mentally manipulate symbols, thereby expanding our thinking. Whether it's spoken, written, or signed, language also allows us to communicate our thoughts, ideas, and feelings (Harley, 2014; Jandt, 2016).

## Language Characteristics

To produce language, we first build words using **phonemes** [FO-neems] and **morphemes** [MOR-feems]. Then we string words into sentences using rules of **grammar**, including *syntax* and *semantics* (**Figure 8.6**).

What happens in our brains when we produce and comprehend language? Language, like our thought processes, is both localized and distributed throughout our brains (**Figure 8.7**). For example, the amygdala is active when we engage in a special type of language—cursing or swearing. Why? Recall from Chapter 2 that the amygdala is linked to emotions, especially fear and rage. So it's logical that the brain regions activated by swearing or hearing swear words would be the same as those for fear and aggression.

As shown in Figure 8.7, additional parts of the brain are involved in language, including *Broca's area* (which is responsible for speech generation) and *Wernicke's area* (which controls language comprehension). Keep in mind that several additional areas of the brain, not shown on this figure, are activated during different types of language generation and listening.

How do we know which parts of the brain are involved with language? Scientists can track brain activity through a *positron emission tomography (PET) scan*. Injection of the radioactive isotope oxygen-15 into the bloodstream of the participant makes areas of the brain with high metabolic activity "light up" in red and orange on the scan (see again Figure 8.7).

## Language Theories

Does the fact that you speak English instead of German—or Chinese instead of Swahili—determine how you reason, think, and perceive the world? Linguist Benjamin Whorf (1956) believed so. As evidence for his *linguistic relativity hypothesis*, Whorf offered a now classic example: Because Inuits (previously known as Eskimos) supposedly have many words for snow (*apikak* for "first snow falling," *pukak* for "snow for drinking water," and so on), they can reportedly perceive and think about snow differently from English speakers, who have only one word—*snow*.

**Language**   A form of communication using sounds or symbols combined according to specified rules.

**Phoneme**   The smallest basic unit of speech or sound in any given language.

**Morpheme**   The smallest meaningful unit of language; formed from a combination of phonemes.

**Grammar**   The set of rules (syntax and semantics) governing the use and structure of language.

**FIGURE 8.7** **Language and the brain**

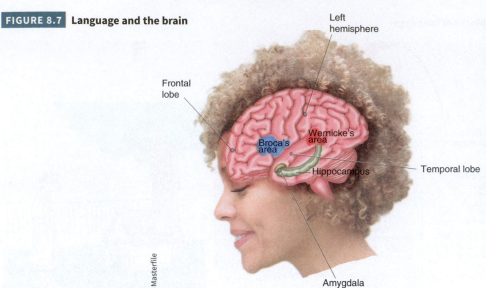

Left hemisphere

Frontal lobe

Broca's area

Wernicke's area

Hippocampus

Temporal lobe

Amygdala

Masterfile

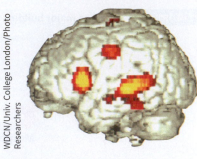

WDCN/Univ. College London/Photo Researchers

As shown in the PET scan above, repeating words increases activity (the yellow and red colors) in Broca's area (left) and Wernicke's area (right), as well as a motor region responsible for pronouncing words (reddish area at the top).

(c) Gallo Images-Dave Hamman/Getty Images

**FIGURE 8.8** **Language distortions** Our words clearly influence the thinking of those who hear them. That's why companies avoid *firing* employees. Instead, they're *outplaced* or *nonrenewed*. And the military uses terms like *preemptive strike* to cover the fact that they attacked first and *tactical redeployment* to refer to a retreat. Similarly, the dentist who shot the African lion known as Cecil apologized for this act by saying, "I had no idea the lion I took was a known, local favorite." But he didn't "take" the lion. He killed it!

Though intriguing, Whorf's hypothesis has not fared well. He apparently exaggerated the number of Inuit words for snow (Pullum, 1991) and ignored the fact that English speakers have a number of terms to describe various forms of snow, such as *slush*, *sleet*, *hard pack*, and *powder*. Other research has directly contradicted Whorf's theory. Eleanor Rosch (1973) found that although people of the Dani tribe in New Guinea possess only two color names—one indicating cool, dark colors, and the other describing warm, bright colors—they discriminate among multiple hues as well as English speakers do.

Whorf apparently was mistaken in his belief that language *determines* thought. But there is no doubt that language *influences* thought (Bylund & Athanasopoulos, 2015; Yang, 2016; Zhong et al., 2015). For example, a university cafeteria increased vegetable consumption by 25% just by adding flavorful, exciting, and indulgent descriptors, like "rich, buttery, roasted sweet corn" (Turnwald et al., 2017). In addition, people who speak multiple languages report that the language they're currently using affects their sense of self and how they think about events (Berry et al., 2011; Lai & Narasimhan, 2015). In support of this view, people who speak both Chinese and English report that they tend to conform to Chinese cultural norms when speaking Chinese and to Western norms when speaking English. Interestingly, research shows that speaking multiple languages, or even just learning one new language, offers a wide range of benefits that might make you smarter, including increased attention, better communication skills, and more gray matter in key brain regions (Bak et al., 2016; Fan et al., 2015; Olulade et al., 2016). For additional insights on language effects, see **Figure 8.8.**

## Language Development

Although children's language development varies in timing, virtually all children follow a similar sequence (see **Table 8.4**). The various stages within this table are believed to be universal, meaning that all children progress through similar stages regardless of the culture they're born into or what language(s) they ultimately learn to speak.

Corbis/VCG/Getty Images

**FIGURE 8.9** **Can you identify this emotion?** Infants as young as 2.5 months can nonverbally express emotions, such as joy, surprise, or anger.

### Prelinguistic Stage
From birth, a child communicates through facial expressions, eye contact, and body gestures (**Figure 8.9**). Babies only hours old begin to "teach" their caregivers when and how they want to be held, fed, and played with. Babies even start to learn language before they are born. Researchers in one study played sounds from two different languages—English and Swedish—for babies at hospitals in both the United States and Sweden shortly after birth (Moon et al., 2013). These babies were given special pacifiers that were hooked up to a computer, and the more times they sucked on the pacifier, the more times

**TABLE 8.4    Language Acquisition**

| Birth to 12 Months | |
|---|---|
| **Features** | **Examples** |
| Crying (reflexive in newborns) becomes more purposeful | hunger cry, anger cry, and pain cry |
| Cooing (vowel-like sounds) at 2–3 months | "ooooh," "aaaah" |
| Babbling (consonants added) at 4–6 months | "bahbahbah," "dahdahdah" |

| 12 Months to 2 Years | |
|---|---|
| **Features** | **Examples** |
| Babbling resembles language of the environment, and child understands that sounds relate to meaning | "mama," "da da" |
| Speech consists of one-word utterances | "juice," "up" |
| Expressive ability more than doubles once words are joined into short phrases | "daddy milk," "no night-night!" |
| Overextension (using words to include objects that do not fit the word's meaning) | all men = "daddy," all furry animals = "doggy" |

| 2 Years to 5 Years | |
|---|---|
| **Features** | **Examples** |
| Telegraphic speech (like telegrams, omits nonessential connecting words) | "Me want cookie" "Grandma go bye-bye?" |
| Vocabulary increases at a phenomenal rate | |
| Child acquires a wide variety of grammar rules | adding *-ed* for past tense, adding s to form plurals |
| Overgeneralization (applying basic rules of grammar even to cases that are exceptions to the rule) —see the **Study Tip** | "I goed to the zoo," "two mans" |

Photo credits (left margin): Jaimie Duplass/iStockphoto; iStockphoto; © kate_sept2004/iStockphoto

they heard the sounds. Half the babies heard sounds from the language they'd been exposed to in utero, whereas the others heard sounds from a different language. In both countries, the babies who heard the foreign sounds sucked more frequently than those who heard sounds from their native language, suggesting that babies have already become familiar—through listening to their mother's voice—with the sounds in their native language and are now more interested in hearing novel sounds.

Regarding infant cries, have you ever wondered why a crying baby on a plane is so stressful for all passengers? Thanks to evolution, it appears that crying is a primitive behavior shared by most mammals that plays a crucial role in infant survival (Darwin, 1872; Raine, 2016). In fact, the sounds of infant mammals are highly similar, which may explain why both children and adults respond to the cries of kittens and puppies and why deer will respond to the cries of infant humans, seals, and cats (Lingle & Riede, 2014).

Why is it so particularly hard to ignore these cries? Research has shown that infant cries modulate our hormone levels and activate specific areas of our brains responsible for attention and empathy (Quintana et al., 2016; Reim et al., 2011; Swain & Ho, 2012). Furthermore, all mammals tend to cry primarily when they're upset, in pain, or alone, with a pitch and sound specifically designed to attract attention and responses from their caregivers (Lingle et al., 2015). Although some parents seem to be able to distinguish between their baby's different cries, the overall function of crying is to signal infant distress. This distress signal, in turn, creates distress and discomfort in others, leading to a helping response (Esposito et al., 2017; Lin et al., 2016). In short, everyone on the plane wants someone to comfort and quiet the crying baby!

**Study Tip**

*Are you having difficulty differentiating between overextension and overgeneralization? Remember the "g" in overgeneralize as a cue that this term applies to problems with grammar.*

### Linguistic Stage

After the prelinguistic stage, infants quickly move toward full language acquisition (see again Table 8.4). By age 5, most children have mastered basic grammar and typically use about 2,000 words (a level of mastery considered adequate for getting by in any given culture). Past this point, vocabulary and grammar gradually improve throughout life (Levey, 2014; Oller et al., 2014).

### Theories of Language Development

Some theorists believe that language capability is innate, primarily a matter of maturation. Noam Chomsky (1968, 1980) suggests that children are "prewired" with a neurological ability within the brain, known as a **language acquisition device (LAD)**, that enables them to analyze language and to extract the basic rules of grammar. This mechanism needs only minimal exposure to adult speech to unlock its potential. As evidence for this *nativist position*, Chomsky observes that children everywhere progress through the same stages of language development at about the same ages. He also notes that babbling is the same in all languages and that deaf babies babble just like hearing babies.

*Nurturists* argue that the nativist position doesn't fully explain individual differences in language development. They hold that children learn language through a complex system of rewards, punishments, and imitation. For example, parents smile and encourage any vocalizations from a very young infant. Later, they respond even more enthusiastically when the infant babbles "mama" or "dada." In this way, parents unknowingly use *shaping* (Chapter 6) to help babies learn language. Unfortunately, researchers have found a wide variability in how much parents talk or read to their children, and low levels of these activities can lead to serious gaps in their language development (Hirsh-Pasek et al., 2015; Hutton et al., 2015; Ockerman, 2016).

**Language acquisition device (LAD)** According to Chomsky, an innate mechanism within the brain that enables a child to analyze language and extract the basic rules of grammar.

---

## Gender and Cultural Diversity

### Can Your Nonverbal Language Reveal Your Roots?

Now that we've reviewed the characteristics and theories of language and how it develops, let's give some thought to *nonverbal language*—communication through gestures, facial expressions, and other nonverbal means. Specifically, we're going to explore some of the cultural factors behind nonverbal language—particularly the power of accents. Just as an Irish brogue or a Minnesota lilt betrays one's background, facial expressions and body language can reveal our cultural origins. These "nonverbal accents" also convey information about mental, social, and physical states (Rosenberg et al., 2016).

Nonverbal language and behavior are sometimes considered to be universal—wherever you go, a groan sounds like a groan and a smile looks like a smile. However, a growing body of research suggests that where we live shapes both how we display emotion and how we perceive it in others. In one study, researchers found that American volunteers could distinguish American from Australian faces when the faces were photographed smiling, but not when they were photographed with neutral expressions (Marsh et al., 2007). In addition, the way Americans and Australians walk or wave in greeting not only telegraphs their nationality but also apparently triggers stereotypes about the two groups. In this particular study, Americans were judged more dominant (think, "Carry a big stick") and Australians more likable (think, "G'day, mate!").

What explains cultural variations in nonverbal communication? A recent study suggests that some differences may be the result of *historical heterogeneity*—meaning the degree to which a

Blend Images/Getty Images

country's present-day population descended from migrants who came from many countries over a period of 500 years (Rychlowska et al., 2015). To test this hypothesis, the researchers carefully analyzed existing data on cultural rules for displaying emotions from 32 countries (Matsumoto et al., 2008). As predicted, countries with less migration tended to be less expressive. Why? The researchers suggest that over time homogeneous countries—those with less diversity—develop stronger display rules for how emotions should be openly expressed. In relatively homogeneous Japan, for instance, when subordinates are upset around their bosses, they're likely to conceal these feelings with smiles. In countries with a more diverse past, though, people needed to beef up their facial expressions, perhaps to overcome cultural and language barriers.

In their follow-up research, the team zeroed in on a particular kind of facial expression: the smile (Rychlowska et al., 2015). They conducted a new study of 726 people in nine countries, including the United States, Japan, and France. Participants were asked to complete a questionnaire regarding cultural rules for emotional expression. But in this case, they were asked to consider what constituted a good reason for someone else to smile, such as that he or she "is a happy person," "wants to sell you something," and "feels inferior to you." The participants rated each reason to smile on a scale from Strongly Disagree to Strongly Agree. The researchers then compared the results for each country with their migration numbers. In further support of their initial hypothesis, countries with less migration and less diversity thought smiles were related to the social hierarchy—people smile because they "feel inferior to you." In contrast, countries with greater and more diverse immigration over the past 500 years were more likely to interpret smiles as friendly gestures.

Other research suggests that people from different cultures are attuned to different nonverbal cues. Americans, who tend to express emotion overtly, look to the mouth to interpret others' true feelings (Yuki et al., 2007). However, Japanese, who tend to be more emotionally guarded, give greater weight to the eyes, which are less easily controlled. "These studies show both that people can be sensitive to cultural cues that they are barely aware of, and also that their own cultural norms can lead them astray," comments Judith Hall, who studies nonverbal communication at Northeastern University. "Americans who think the Japanese are unexpressive mistake subtlety for lack of expression. These Americans would misjudge facial cues that Japanese might be very successful at interpreting." Do you recognize how such misjudgments can lead to cross-cultural misunderstandings? And why improving our awareness of these differences might go a long way toward improving cross-cultural interactions.

*Source*: Parts of this feature were originally published in *Scientific American Mind*, August/September 2007, p. 13. Reprinted with permission of author, Siri Carpenter.

## Language and Other Species

Can human animals talk with nonhuman animals? Without question, nonhuman animals communicate. They regularly send warnings, signal sexual interest, share locations of food sources, and so on. But can nonhuman animals master the complexity of human language? Since the 1930s, many language studies have attempted to answer this question by probing the language abilities of chimpanzees, gorillas, and other animals (Hoeschele & Fitch, 2016; Scott-Phillips, 2015; Zuberbühler, 2015).

One of the most successful early studies was conducted by Beatrice and Allen Gardner (1969), who recognized chimpanzees' manual dexterity and ability to imitate gestures. The Gardners used American Sign Language (ASL) with a chimp named Washoe. By the time Washoe was 4 years old, she had learned 132 signs and was able to combine them into simple sentences such as "Hurry, gimme toothbrush" and "Please tickle more." The famous gorilla Koko also uses ASL to communicate; she reportedly uses more than 1,000 signs (**Figure 8.10**).

In another well-known study, a chimp named Lana learned to use symbols on a computer to get things she wanted, such as food, a drink, and a tickle from her trainers, and to have her curtains opened (Rumbaugh et al., 1974). See **Figure 8.11**.

Dolphins also are often the subject of interesting language research (see cartoon) (Kuczaj et al., 2015; Pack, 2015). Communication with dolphins is typically conducted with hand signals or audible commands transmitted through an underwater speaker system. In one typical study, trainers gave dolphins commands made up of two- to five-word sentences, such as "Big ball—square—return," which meant that they should go get the big ball, put it in the floating square, and return to the trainer (Herman et al., 1984). By varying the syntax (the order of the words) and specific content of the commands, the researchers showed that dolphins are sensitive to these aspects of language.

Scientists disagree about how to interpret the findings on chimps, apes, and dolphins. Most believe nonhuman animals

"ALTHOUGH HUMANS MAKE SOUNDS WITH THEIR MOUTHS AND OCCASIONALLY LOOK AT EACH OTHER, THERE IS NO SOLID EVIDENCE THAT THEY ACTUALLY COMMUNICATE WITH EACH OTHER."

Sidney Harris/ScienceCartoonPlus.com

Bettmann/Contributor/Getty Images

**FIGURE 8.10**  **Koko learning sign language**  In this photo, Koko is signaling to her mentor, 28-year-old graduate student Penny Patterson, that she wants to listen to the phone. She hasn't yet learned the ASL sign for phone, but she clearly understands the relationship between gestures and communication.

**FIGURE 8.11** **Computer-aided communication** Apes lack the necessary anatomical structures to vocalize the way humans do. For this reason, language research with chimps and gorillas has focused on teaching the animals to use sign language or to "speak" by pointing to symbols on a keyboard. Do you think this amounts to using language the same way humans do?

Michael Nichols/NG Image Collection

definitely communicate, but that they're not using true language because they don't convey subtle meanings, use language creatively, or communicate at an abstract level. Other critics propose that these animals do not truly understand language but are simply operantly conditioned (Chapter 6) to imitate symbols to receive rewards. Finally, many language scientists contend that data regarding animal language has not always been well documented (Beran et al., 2014; Savage-Rumbaugh, 1990; Terrace, 1979).

Proponents of animal language respond that apes can use language creatively and have even coined some words of their own. Koko supposedly signed "finger bracelet" to describe a ring and "eye hat" to describe a mask (Patterson & Linden, 1981). Proponents also argue that, as demonstrated by the dolphin studies, animals can be taught to understand basic rules of sentence structure. As you can see, the jury is still out on whether nonhuman animals use "true" language or not. Stay tuned!

© Billy R. Ray/Wiley

## Retrieval Practice 8.2 | Language

Completing this self-test and the connections section, and then checking your answers by clicking on the answer button or by looking in Appendix B, will provide immediate feedback and helpful practice for exams.

### Self-Test

1. Briefly explain how we first produce language.

2. Which rule of English is violated by this sentence? *Going to college I really enjoy.*

   **a.** deep structure  **b.** phonemic structure
   **c.** semantics  **d.** syntax

3. "I goed to the zoo" and "I hurt my foots" are examples of _____.

   **a.** prelinguistic verbalizations
   **b.** overexposure to adult "baby talk"
   **c.** overgeneralization
   **d.** Noam Chomsky's theory of language acquisition

4. According to Chomsky, the innate mechanism that enables a child to analyze language is known as a(n) _____.

   **a.** telegraphic understanding device (TUD)

   **b.** language acquisition device (LAD)
   **c.** language and grammar translator (LGT)
   **d.** overgeneralized neural net (ONN)

5. Some researchers believe nonhuman animals are not using true language because they don't _____.

   **a.** convey subtle meanings
   **b.** use language creatively
   **c.** communicate at an abstract level
   **d.** do any of these things

### Connections—Chapter to Chapter

Answering the following question will help you "look back and look ahead" to see the important connections among the subfields of psychology and chapters within this text.

In Chapter 6 (Learning), you studied several forms of learning: classical conditioning, operant conditioning, and observational learning. Explain how each type of learning might be used in learning a language.

## 8.3 | Intelligence

### LEARNING OBJECTIVES

**Retrieval Practice** While reading the upcoming sections, respond to each Learning Objective in your own words.

**Summarize the nature and measurement of intelligence.**

- **Define** intelligence.
- **Compare** the different forms and theories of intelligence.
- **Describe** how intelligence is measured and the groups that fall at the extremes.

*I don't think there's anything unique about human intelligence. All the neurons in the brain that make up perceptions and emotions operate in a binary fashion. —Bill Gates*

Many people equate intelligence with "book smarts." For others, the definition of intelligence depends on the characteristics and skills that are valued in a particular social group or culture (Goldstein et al., 2015; Plucker & Esping, 2014; Suzuki et al., 2014). As a case in point, the Mandarin word that corresponds most closely to the word *intelligence* is a character meaning "good brain and talented" (Matsumoto, 2000). In other cultures, intelligence is associated with traits like imitation, effort, and social responsibility (Keats, 1982). An experiment carried out in seven countries even found that smiling versus non-smiling affected judgments of intelligence (Krys et al., 2014). Interestingly, German respondents perceived smiling individuals as being more intelligent, whereas Chinese participants judged smilers as less intelligent.

Even among Western psychologists there is considerable debate over the definition of intelligence. In this discussion, we rely on a formal definition of **intelligence**—*the global capacity to think rationally, act purposefully, profit from experience, and deal effectively with the environment* (Wechsler, 1944, 1977). See the **Study Tip**.

## The Nature of Intelligence

In the 1920s, British psychologist Charles Spearman first observed that high scores on separate tests of mental abilities tend to correlate with each other. Spearman (1923) thus proposed that intelligence is a single factor, which he termed **general intelligence (g)**. He believed that *g* underlies all intellectual behavior, including reasoning, solving problems, and performing well in all areas of cognition. Spearman's work laid the foundations for today's standardized intelligence tests (Bouchard, 2016; Cooper, 2015; Woodley of Menie & Madison, 2015).

About a decade later, L. L. Thurstone (1938) proposed seven primary mental abilities: verbal comprehension, word fluency, numerical fluency, spatial visualization, associative memory, perceptual speed, and reasoning. J. P. Guilford (1967) later expanded this number, proposing that as many as 120 factors are involved in the structure of intelligence.

Around the same time, Raymond Cattell (1963, 1971) reanalyzed Thurstone's data and argued against the idea of multiple intelligences. He believed that two subtypes of *g* exist:

- **Fluid intelligence (gf)** refers to the ability to think speedily and abstractly and to solve novel problems. Fluid intelligence is relatively independent of education and experience, and like most biological capacities, it declines with age (Gazes et al., 2016; Gerstorf et al., 2015; Klein et al., 2015).

- **Crystallized intelligence (gc)** refers to the store of knowledge and skills gained through experience and education (Santos, 2016; Sternberg, 2014, 2015). Crystallized intelligence tends to increase over the life span.

## Measuring Intelligence

Different IQ tests approach the measurement of intelligence from different perspectives. However, most are designed to predict grades in school. Let's look at the most commonly used IQ tests.

The *Stanford-Binet Intelligence Scale* is loosely based on the first IQ tests developed in France around the turn of the twentieth century by Alfred Binet. In the United States, Lewis Terman (1916) developed the Stanford-Binet (at Stanford University) to test the intellectual ability of U.S.-born children ages 3 to 16. The test is revised periodically—most recently in 2003. The test is administered individually and consists of such tasks as copying geometric designs, identifying similarities, and repeating number sequences.

After administering the individual test to a large number of people, researchers discovered that their scores typically are distributed in a **normal distribution** that forms a symmetrical, bell-shaped curve (**Figure 8.12**). This means that a majority of the scores fall in the middle of the curve and a few scores fall on the extremes. In addition to intelligence, measurements on many physical traits, like height and weight, also create a "bell curve" normal distribution.

**Intelligence** The global capacity to think rationally, act purposefully, profit from experience, and deal effectively with the environment.

**General intelligence (g)** Spearman's term for a common skill set that underlies all intellectual behavior.

**Study Tip**

*Intelligence is not a thing. It has no mass. It occupies no space. There are no specific sites within the brain where intelligence resides. When people talk about intelligence as though it were a concrete, tangible object, they commit an error in reasoning (known as reification). Like consciousness and memory, intelligence is a hypothetical, abstract construct.*

**Fluid intelligence (gf)** The ability to think speedily and abstractly and to solve novel problems; *gf* tends to decrease over the life span.

**Crystallized intelligence (gc)** The store of knowledge and skills gained through experience and education; *gc* tends to increase over the life span.

**Normal distribution** A statistical term used to describe how traits are distributed within a population; IQ scores usually form a symmetrical, bell-shaped curve, with most scores falling near the average and fewer scores near the extremes.

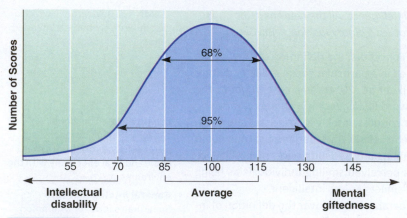

**FIGURE 8.12** **The normal distribution (bell curve) of scores on intelligence tests** The term "bell curve" refers to the fact that the graph used to depict the normal distribution of scores (shown here) is shaped like a bell. The highest point at the top of the bell represents the most likely, probable score (100 points), whereas all the other scores are equally distributed around this center point. Note that 68% of people score 15 points above or below the national average, which is 100 points.

**Mental age (MA)** An individual's level of mental development relative to that of others; mental age was initially used in comparison to chronological age (CA) to calculate IQ.

**Intelligence quotient (IQ)** An index of intelligence derived from standardized tests; originally computed by dividing mental age (MA) by chronological age (CA) and then multiplying by 100 but now derived by comparing individual scores with the scores of others of the same age.

**Standardization** A set of uniform procedures for administering and scoring a test; also, establishing norms by comparison with scores of a pretested group.

**Reliability** The degree to which a test produces similar scores each time it is used; stability or consistency of the scores produced by an instrument.

In the original version of the Stanford-Binet test, results were expressed in terms of a **mental age (MA)**, which refers to an individual's level of mental development relative to that of others. If a 7-year-old's score equaled that of an average 8-year-old, the child was considered to have a mental age of 8. To determine the child's **intelligence quotient (IQ)**, mental age was divided by the child's chronological age (actual age in years) and multiplied by 100.

The most widely used intelligence test today, the *Wechsler Adult Intelligence Scale (WAIS),* was developed by David Wechsler in the early 1900s. He later created a similar test for school-aged children. Like the Stanford-Binet, Wechsler's tests yield an overall intelligence score, along with separate index scores related to four specific areas: verbal comprehension, perceptual reasoning, working memory, and processing speed. See **Figure 8.13** for samples of Wechsler's perceptual reasoning test items.

Today, most intelligence test scores are expressed as a comparison of a single person's score to a national sample of similar-aged people. Even though the actual IQ is no longer calculated using the original formula comparing mental and chronological ages, the term *IQ* remains as a shorthand expression for intelligence test scores.

## Principles of Test Construction

What makes a good test? How are the tests developed by Binet and Wechsler any better than those published in popular magazines and presented on television programs? To be scientifically acceptable, all psychological tests must fulfill three basic requirements (Dombrowski, 2015; Jackson, 2016; Suzuki et al., 2014):

- **Standardization** in intelligence tests (as well as personality, aptitude, and most other tests) involves following a certain set of uniform procedures when administering a test. First, every test must have *norms*, or average scores, developed by giving the test to a representative sample of people (a diverse group of people who resemble those for whom the test is intended). Second, testing procedures must be standardized. All test takers must be given the same instructions, questions, and time limits, and all test administrators must follow the same objective score standards.

- **Reliability** is usually determined by retesting participants to see whether their test scores change significantly. Retesting can be done via the *test–retest method*, in which participants' scores on two separate administrations of the same test are compared, or via the *split-half method*, which splits a test into two equivalent parts (such as odd and even questions) and determines the degree of similarity between the two halves.

**FIGURE 8.13** **Items similar to those on the Wechsler adult intelligence scale (WAIS)** These simulated items resemble those found in the Wechsler Adult Intelligence Scale, Fourth Edition (WAIS-IV). Previous editions of the WAIS included sections, such as Picture Arrangement, Block Design, and Object Assembly, which were dropped to increase reliability and user friendliness. WAIS-IV also takes less time to administer, and the results show smaller differences based on level of education or racial/ethnic group membership. Answers to the two puzzles here are provided in Appendix B.

*Source*: Based on simulated items from the Wechsler Adult Intelligence Scale, Fourth Edition (WAIS-IV).

**a. Visual puzzles** The test administrator asks: "Which three pieces go together to make this puzzle?"

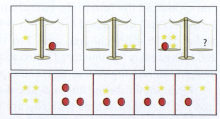

**b. Figure weights** The test administrator asks: "Which one of these works to balance the scale?"

- **Validity** is the ability of a test to measure what it is designed to measure. The most important type of validity is *criterion-related validity*, or the accuracy with which test scores can be used to predict another variable of interest (known as the criterion). Criterion-related validity is expressed as the *correlation* (Chapter 1) between the test score and the criterion. If two variables are highly correlated, then one can be used to predict the other. Thus, if a test is valid, its scores will be useful in predicting an individual's behavior in some other specified situation. One example is using intelligence test scores to predict grades in college.

> **Validity** The degree to which a test measures what it is intended to measure.

Do you see why a test that is standardized and reliable but not valid is worthless? For example, a test for skin sensitivity may be easy to standardize (the instructions specify exactly how to apply the test agent), and it may be reliable (similar results are obtained on each retest). But it certainly would not be valid for predicting college grades.

## Extremes in Intelligence

One of the best methods for judging the validity of a test is to compare people who score at the extremes. And intelligence tests provide one of the major criteria for assessing mental ability at the extremes—specifically, for diagnosing *intellectual disability* and *mental giftedness*.

### Intellectual Disability
The clinical label *intellectually disabled* (previously referred to as *mentally retarded*) is applied when someone has considerable deficits in general mental abilities, such as reasoning, problem solving, and academic learning. These deficits may also result in impairments of adaptive functioning, including communication, social participation, and personal independence (American Psychiatric Association, 2013; Kumin, 2015).

Fewer than 3% of people are classified as having an intellectual disability (see **Table 8.5**). Of this group, 85% have only mild intellectual disability, and many become self-supporting, integrated members of society. Furthermore, people can score low on some measures of intelligence and still be average or even gifted in others (Miller et al., 2016; Treffert, 2014; Werner & Roth, 2014). The most dramatic examples are people with *savant syndrome*. People with savant syndrome generally score very low on IQ tests (usually between 40 and 70), yet they demonstrate exceptional skills or brilliance in specific areas, such as rapid calculation, art, memory, or musical ability (**Figure 8.14**).

Some forms of intellectual disability stem from genetic abnormalities, such as Down syndrome, fragile-X syndrome, and phenylketonuria (PKU). Other causes are environmental, including prenatal exposure to alcohol and other drugs, extreme deprivation or neglect in early

**FIGURE 8.14** **Savant syndrome—an unusual form of intelligence** Derek Paravicini, a musical savant, pictured here, was born premature, blind, and with a severe learning disability. In spite of these challenges, he plays the concert piano entirely by ear and has a repertoire of thousands of pieces.

Charley Gallay/Getty Images

**TABLE 8.5** **Degrees of Intellectual Disability**

| | Level of Disability | IQ Scores | Characteristics |
|---|---|---|---|
| General population; Intellectually disabled 1–3%; 85% Mild; 1–2% Profound; 3–4% Severe; 10% Moderate | Mild (85%) | 50–70 | Usually able to become self-sufficient; may marry, have families, and secure full-time jobs in low-skilled occupations |
| | Moderate (10%) | 35–49 | Generally able to perform simple, low-skilled tasks; may contribute to a certain extent to their livelihood |
| | Severe (3–4%) | 20–34 | Generally able to follow daily routines, but need supervision; with training, may learn basic communication skills |
| | Profound (1–2%) | below 20 | Generally able to perform only the most rudimentary behaviors, such as walking, feeding themselves, and saying a few phrases |

life, and brain damage from physical trauma, such as car accidents or sports injuries. However, in many cases, there is no known cause of the intellectual disability.

**Mental Giftedness**   At the other end of the intelligence spectrum are people with especially high IQs (typically defined as an IQ of 130 or higher). In the early 1900s, Lewis Terman identified 1,500 gifted children—affectionately nicknamed the "Termites"—with IQs of 140 or higher (Terman, 1925). He and his colleagues then tracked their progress through adulthood. The number who became highly successful professionals was many times the number a random group would have produced (Kreger Silverman, 2013; Plucker & Esping, 2014; Terman, 1954). Researchers noted, however, that those who were most successful tended to have extraordinary motivation, and they typically had someone at home or school who was especially encouraging (Goleman, 1980). Unfortunately, similar to the general population, some of the "Termites" became alcoholics, got divorced, and died as a result of suicide (Campbell & Feng, 2011; Leslie, 2000; Terman, 1954).

In sum, a high IQ is no guarantee of success in every endeavor. As shown by the "Termites" study, and as emphasized at the end of this chapter and often in this text, personal traits and character strengths, like self-control, motivation, and perseverance, may be the strongest predictors of overall achievement and well-being. Having a growth mindset is particularly valuable for intellectual achievement (Dweck, 2012; Mischel, 2014; Rattan et al., 2015).

© Billy R. Ray/Wiley

## Retrieval Practice 8.3 | Intelligence

Completing this self-test and the connections section, and then checking your answers by clicking on the answer button or by looking in Appendix B, will provide immediate feedback and helpful practice for exams.

### Self-Test

1. What is the formal definition of *intelligence*?

2. The store of knowledge and skills gained through experience and education is known as _____ intelligence.

   **a.** crystallized      **b.** fluid
   **c.** general           **d.** specific

3. Which is the most widely used intelligence test?

   **a.** Wechsler Intelligence Scale for Children
   **b.** Wechsler Adult Intelligence Scale
   **c.** Stanford-Binet Intelligence Scale
   **d.** Binet-Terman Intelligence Scale

4. If a test gives you the same score each time you take it, that test would be _____.

   **a.** reliable          **b.** valid
   **c.** standardized      **d.** none of these options

5. Validity refers to the ability of a test to _____.

   **a.** return the same score on separate administrations of the test
   **b.** measure what it is designed to measure
   **c.** avoid discrimination between different cultural groups
   **d.** give a standard deviation of scores

### Connections—Chapter to Chapter

Answering the following questions will help you "look back and look ahead" to see the important connections among the subfields of psychology and chapters within this text.

*Employing precise terms*, one of the Critical Thinking Components (CTCs) identified in the Prologue, is especially relevant to the word "intelligence." The section on intelligence in this chapter examines the controversies surrounding the definition of this term. How do you define intelligence? How well would a standard IQ test measure your definition of intelligence?

## 8.4   Intelligence Controversies

### LEARNING OBJECTIVES

**Retrieval Practice**   While reading the upcoming sections, respond to each Learning Objective in your own words.

**Review the major controversies surrounding intelligence.**

- **Identify** the various theories and controversies concerning multiple intelligences.

- **Discuss** the relative contributions of nature and nurture to IQ.
- **Describe** how and why groups differ in mental ability tests.

*I'm grateful to intelligent people. That doesn't mean educated. That doesn't mean intellectual. I mean really intelligent.* —Maya Angelou (American Poet, Author, Dancer)

Psychologists have long debated several important questions related to intelligence: Is intelligence a general ability or a number of specific talents and aptitudes? Is IQ mostly inherited, or is it molded by our environment? Do men and women or racial and ethnic groups differ in mental abilities? If so, how and why?

## Multiple Intelligences

For some time, psychologists have debated whether intelligence is a general ability or a collection of separate abilities. Earlier we discussed the history of the concept of *g* as an overall, general measure of intelligence—at least in terms of "academic smarts." In this section, we'll explore why many contemporary cognitive theorists believe we all possess multiple intelligences.

### Gardner's and Sternberg's Theories
The fact that brain-damaged patients often lose some intellectual abilities, while retaining others, suggested to psychologist Howard Gardner that different intelligences are located in discrete areas throughout the brain. According to *Gardner's theory of multiple intelligences* (1983, 2008), people have different profiles of intelligence because they are stronger in some areas than others (**Table 8.6**). And they use their intelligences differently to learn new material, perform tasks, and solve problems. Moreover, Gardner's research suggests that most people possess one or more natural intelligences critical to success in various occupations. Carefully consider each of the multiple intelligences in Table 8.6 and how it might help guide you toward a satisfying career.

Robert Sternberg's **triarchic theory of intelligence** also assumes multiple abilities. As shown in **Table 8.7**, Sternberg believes there are three separate, learned aspects of intelligence: (1) *analytic*, (2) *creative*, and (3) *practical* (Sternberg, 1985, 2015).

**Triarchic theory of intelligence** Sternberg's theory that intelligence involves three forms: analytical, creative, and practical.

---

**TABLE 8.6    Gardner's Multiple Intelligences**

| Type of Intelligence | Possible Careers |
|---|---|
| **Linguistic** <br> Language, such as speaking, reading a book, writing a story | Novelist, journalist, teacher |
| **Spatial** <br> Mental maps, such as figuring out how to pack multiple presents in a box or how to draw a floor plan | Engineer, architect, pilot |
| **Bodily/kinesthetic** <br> Body movement, such as dancing, soccer, and football | Athlete, dancer, ski instructor |
| **Intrapersonal** <br> Understanding oneself, such as setting achievable goals or recognizing self-defeating behaviors | Increased success in almost all careers |
| **Logical/mathematical** <br> Problem solving or scientific analysis, such as following a logical proof or solving a mathematical problem | Mathematician, scientist, engineer |
| **Musical** <br> Musical skills, such as singing or playing a musical instrument | Singer, musician, composer |
| **Interpersonal** <br> Social skills, such as managing diverse groups or people | Salesperson, manager, therapist, teacher |
| **Naturalistic** <br> Being attuned to nature, such as noticing seasonal patterns or using environmentally safe products | Biologist, naturalist |
| **Spiritual/existential** <br> Attunement to meaning of life and death and other conditions of life | Philosopher, theologian |

Frederic Legrand - COMEO/Shutterstock

Eagle9/Shutterstock

Laszlo Szirtesi/Shutterstock

*Source:* Based on Gardner, 1983, 2008.

| TABLE 8.7 | Sternberg's Triarchic Theory of Successful Intelligence | | |
|---|---|---|---|
| | **Analytical intelligence** | **Creative intelligence** | **Practical intelligence** |
| **Sample skills** | Good at analysis, evaluation, judgment, and comparison skills | Good at invention, coping with novelty, and imagination skills | Good at application, implementation, execution, and utilization skills |
| **Methods of assessment** | Intelligence tests that measure traditional verbal and mathematical skills | Open-ended tasks, writing a short story, creating a piece of art, solving a scientific problem requiring insight | Tasks requiring solutions to practical, personal problems |

Sternberg emphasizes the process underlying thinking, rather than just the product. He also stresses the importance of applying mental abilities to real-world situations, rather than testing mental abilities in isolation. In short, Sternberg avoids the traditional idea of intelligence as an innate form of "book smarts." Instead, he emphasizes successful intelligence as the learned ability to adapt to, shape, and select environments in order to accomplish personal and societal goals.

### Goleman's Emotional Intelligence (EI)

Have you ever wondered why some people who are very intelligent, in terms of "book smarts," still experience frequent conflicts and repeated failures in their friendships and work situations? In addition to Gardner's and Sternberg's theories of multiple intelligences, Daniel Goleman's research (1995, 2000, 2008) and best-selling books have popularized the concept of **emotional intelligence (EI)**, based on original work by Peter Salovey and John Mayer (1990). Emotional intelligence (EI) is generally defined as *the ability to perceive, understand, manage, and utilize emotions accurately and appropriately*. If you'd like a brief self-test of your own emotional intelligence, see the following **Try This Yourself** feature.

**Emotional intelligence (EI)** The ability to perceive, understand, manage, and utilize emotions accurately and appropriately.

---

### Try This Yourself

#### Key Traits for Emotional Intelligence (EI)

**True or False?**

_____ **1.** Some of the major events of my life have led me to re-evaluate what is important and not important.

_____ **2.** I can tell how other people are feeling just by looking at them.

_____ **3.** I seek out activities that make me happy.

_____ **4.** I am aware of my emotions as I experience them.

_____ **5.** I am aware of the nonverbal messages I send to others.

_____ **6.** I compliment others when they have done something well.

*Scoring:* Each of these items represents one or more of the traits of an emotionally intelligent person. A higher number of "True" responses indicates a higher level of overall EI.

---

Proponents of EI have suggested that traditional measures of human intelligence ignore a crucial range of abilities that characterize people who are high in EI and tend to excel in real life: self-awareness, impulse control, persistence, zeal, self-motivation, empathy, and social deftness (Garg et al., 2016; Ruiz-Arranda et al., 2014; Stein & Deonarine, 2015). These proponents have also said that parents can play an instrumental role in the development of EI, as shown in **Figure 8.15**. Surprisingly, research has even shown that people who watch televised dramas—such as *Mad Men*—show increases in emotional intelligence, more so than those who watch documentaries (Black & Barnes, 2015). This suggests that just seeing dramas may help expose us to different emotions, which increases our awareness of emotions.

Although the idea of emotional intelligence is very appealing, critics fear that a handy term like EI invites misuse. Their strongest reaction is to Goleman's proposals for widespread teaching of EI. Paul McHugh, director of psychiatry at Johns Hopkins University, suggests that Goleman is "presuming that someone has the key to the right emotions to be taught to children. We don't even know the right emotions to be taught to adults" (cited in Gibbs, 1995, p. 68).

**FIGURE 8.15** **How do we develop emotional intelligence?** The mother in this photo appears to be empathizing with her young daughter and helping her to recognize and manage her own emotions. According to Goleman, this type of modeling and instruction is vital to the development of emotional intelligence.

**Test Your Critical Thinking**

1. Should preschools and elementary schools be required to teach children emotional intelligence? Why or why not?

2. What is the role of emotional intelligence in business? Should it be a factor in hiring and promotions? What might be the advantages and drawbacks if it were?

# Nature, Nurture, and IQ

How is brain functioning related to intelligence? What factors—environmental or hereditary—most influence an individual's intelligence? These specific questions, and the controversies surrounding them, are discussed in this section.

## The Brain's Influence on Intelligence
A basic tenet of neuroscience is that all mental activity (including intelligence) results from neural activity in the brain, which explains why most research on intelligence has focused on brain functioning. For example, neuroscientists have found that people who score highest on intelligence tests also respond more quickly on tasks requiring perceptual judgments (Hofman, 2015; Sternberg, 2014, 2015; Wagner et al., 2014).

In addition, research using positron emission tomography (PET) scans to measure brain activity (Chapter 2) suggests that intelligent brains work smarter, or more efficiently, than less-intelligent brains (Jung & Haier, 2007; Neubauer et al., 2004; Posthuma et al., 2001). See **Figure 8.16**.

Does size matter? It makes logical sense that bigger brains would be smarter. In fact, imaging studies have found a significant correlation between brain size (adjusted for body size) and intelligence (Bouchard, 2016; Moller & Erritzoe, 2014). However, Albert Einstein's brain was no larger than normal (Witelson et al., 1999). In fact, some of Einstein's brain areas were actually smaller than average, but the area responsible for processing mathematical and spatial information was 15% larger than average.

## Genetic and Environmental Influences on Intelligence
When we observe strong similarities in IQ among the members of a particular family, we might be tempted to attribute them to heredity. Such similarities, however, are due to a combination of hereditary (shared genetic material) and environmental factors (similar living arrangements and experiences).

Researchers who are interested in the role of heredity in intelligence often focus on identical (monozygotic) twins because they share 100% of their genetic material, as shown in **Figure 8.17**. One example is the long-running Minnesota Study of Twins, an investigation of identical twins raised in different homes and reunited only as adults, which found that genetic factors appear to play a surprisingly large role in the IQ scores of identical twins (Bouchard, 2016; Rushton & Jensen, 2010).

In contrast, those who emphasize environmental influences on intelligence would say that these twin study results are not conclusive. Adoption agencies tend to look for similar criteria in their choice of adoptive parents. Therefore, the homes of these "reared apart" twins were actually quite similar. Moreover, these twins shared the same 9-month prenatal environment, which might

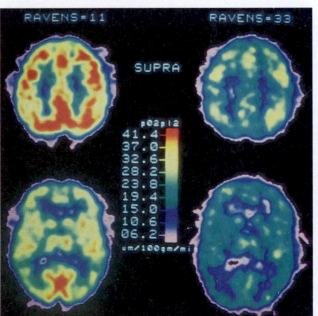

**FIGURE 8.16** **Do intelligent brains work more efficiently?** In PET scan images, red and yellow indicate more activity in relevant brain areas. Note how during problem-solving tasks, low-IQ brains (left) show more activity than high-IQ brains (right). This research suggests that lower-IQ brains actually work harder, although less efficiently, than higher-IQ brains.

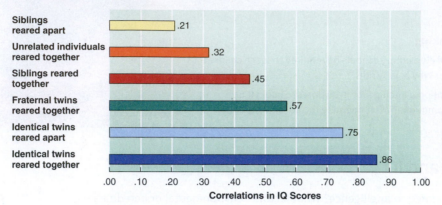

FIGURE 8.17 **Genetic and environmental influences on IQ** Note the higher correlations between identical twins' IQ test scores compared to correlations between all other pairs. Genes no doubt play a role in intelligence, but these effects are difficult to separate from environmental influences. (Based on Bouchard, 2016; Bouchard & McGue, 1981; Plomin & Deary, 2015.)

PhotoDisc, Inc./Getty Images

have influenced their brain development and hence their intelligence (Felson, 2014; White et al., 2002).

Additional evidence of environmental influences on intelligence comes from studies of the multiple effects of abuse and neglect in childhood, as well as from brain scans of children who are seriously neglected (**Figure 8.18**). Likewise, early malnutrition, which affects over 113 million children worldwide, can retard a child's intellectual development, curiosity, and motivation for learning (Peter et al., 2016; Schoenmaker et al., 2015; Venables & Raine, 2016).

Also supporting environmental effects is research indicating that only children have higher gray-matter volume than children with siblings (Yang et al., 2016). Other research has found that breast-fed babies have higher gray-matter volume and higher IQ scores than non-breast-fed babies (Horta et al., 2015; Luby et al., 2016). Gray-matter volume is associated with intelligence.

In short, genetics and environment play interacting and inseparable roles. Intelligence is like a rubber band. Heredity equips each of us with innate intellectual capabilities (our personal rubber band). But our environment helps shrink or stretch this band, which significantly influences whether or not we reach our full intellectual potential.

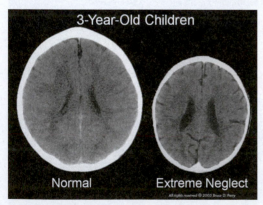

FIGURE 8.18 **Neglect and IQ** These images illustrate the negative impact of neglect on the developing brain. The brain on the left is from a normal developing child, whose brain size is in the 50th percentile. The brain on the right is from a child suffering from severe sensory deprivation neglect, whose brain size is in the lowest third percentile.

*Source:* Photo supplied with kind permission from Springer Science+Business Media: Perry, B.D. Childhood experience and the expression of genetic potential: what childhood neglect tells us about nature and nurture Brain and Mind 3: 79-100, 2002.

## Group Differences in IQ Scores

As we've just seen, intelligence in general does show a high degree of heritability. However, it's VERY important to recognize that heritability cannot explain *between*-group differences! Note the overall difference between the average height of plants on the left and those on the right in **Figure 8.19**. Just as we cannot say that the difference *between* these two groups of plants is due to heredity, we similarly cannot say that differences in IQ *between* any two groups of people are due to heredity.

Note also the considerable variation in height *within* the group of plants on the left and those *within* the group on the right. Just as some plants are taller than others, there are individuals who score high on IQ tests and others who score low. Always remember that when we compare individuals' IQ scores, we can only compare individuals *within* groups—not between groups.

### Controversial Racial and Ethnic Differences
One of the most long-standing controversies in this area revolves around reported differences in IQ scores between racial and ethnic groups. This focus on racial and ethnic differences explains why the debate is so heated. It also highlights why the distinction between within- and between-group differences is so essential. Consider that intelligence is often linked with financial success. If you were in a

group at the top of the economic ladder, and you believed that intelligence was primarily inherited, you might believe that your position and privilege were part of your intellectual birthright, without considering that you were also born with special advantages that maximized any inherited abilities. Can you see how this mindset ignores the "fertile soil" idea? See again Figure 8.19.

We've already seen that heredity does contribute to individual differences in IQ, but group differences in any heritable trait are highly dependent on environment. Setting aside the political implications, let's carefully consider five key research findings:

- *Environmental and cultural factors may override genetic potential and later affect IQ test scores.* Like plants that come from similar seeds, but are placed in poor soil, children of color are more likely to grow up in stressful, lower socioeconomic conditions, which may hamper their true intellectual potential. Furthermore, in some ethnic groups and economic classes, a child who excels in school may be ridiculed for trying to be different from his or her classmates. Moreover, if children's own language and dialect do not match their education system or the IQ tests they take, they are obviously at a disadvantage (Davies et al., 2014; Suzuki et al., 2014; von Stumm & Plomin, 2015).

- *Traditional IQ tests may be culturally biased.* If standardized IQ tests contain questions that reflect White middle-class culture, they will discriminate against test takers with differing language, knowledge, and experience (Chapman et al., 2014; Stanovich, 2015). Researchers have attempted to create a *culture-fair* or *culture-free* IQ test, but they have found it virtually impossible to do. Past experiences, motivation, test-taking abilities, and previous experiences with tests are powerful influences on IQ scores. The good news is that positive environmental messages can help offset some of these problems. For example, simply including aspects of Black culture—*The Color Purple*, BET, Black History Month—within a university setting has been linked to positive academic outcomes (Brannon et al., 2015).

- *Intelligence (as measured by IQ tests) is not a fixed trait.* Around the world, IQ scores have increased over the past half century. This well-established phenomenon, known as the *Flynn effect*, may be due to improved nutrition, better public education, more proficient test-taking skills, and rising levels of education for a greater percentage of the world's population (Flynn, 1987, 2010; Flynn et al., 2014; Woodley of Menie et al., 2016). Fortunately, research shows that simply believing that intelligence is *not* a fixed trait is correlated with higher academic grades and fewer feelings of helplessness (De Castella & Byrne, 2015; Romero et al., 2014).

- *Race and ethnicity, like intelligence itself, are almost impossible to define.* Depending on the definition we use, there are between 3 and 300 races, and no race is pure in a biological sense (Humes & Hogan, 2015; Kite, 2013). Furthermore, like former President Barack Obama, Tiger Woods, and Mariah Carey, many people today self-identify as multiracial.

- *Negative stereotypes about people of color can cause some group members to doubt their abilities.* This phenomenon, called **stereotype threat**, may, in turn, reduce their intelligence test scores (Boucher et al., 2015; Kaye & Pennington, 2016; Steele & Aronson, 1995). In the first study of stereotype threat, Claude Steele and Joshua Aronson (1995) recruited Black and White college students (with similar ability levels) to complete a difficult verbal exam. Students in one group were told that the exam was diagnostic of their intellectual abilities, and in this group, Blacks underperformed in relation to Whites. However, in the second group, where students were told the exam was not diagnostic, there were no differences between the two groups' scores.

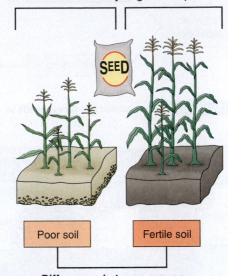

**Differences *within* groups are due almost entirely to genetics (the seed).**

Poor soil      Fertile soil

**Differences *between* groups are due almost entirely to environment (the soil).**

**FIGURE 8.19** **Genetics versus environment** Note that even when you begin with the same package of seeds (genetic inheritance), the average height of corn plants in fertile soil will be greater than the average height of corn plants in poor soil (environmental influences). Therefore, no valid or logical conclusions can be drawn about the overall genetic differences between the two groups of plants because the two environments (soil) are so different. Similar logic must be applied to intelligence scores between groups.

**Stereotype threat** The awareness of a negative stereotype directed toward a group, which leads members of that group to respond in a self-fulfilling way that impairs their performance.

### Stereotype Threat
Given the potential lasting impact of stereotype threat, let's explore it in more depth. First, why did the Blacks in the first group underperform and not in the

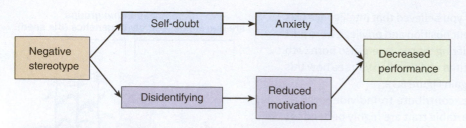

FIGURE 8.20    **How stereotype threat leads to decreased performance**

FIGURE 8.21    **"Obama effect" versus stereotype threat**    Some research has found a so-called "Obama effect," which reportedly offsets problems related to the stereotype threat (Dillon, 2009; Meirick & Schartel Dunn, 2015). However, other studies found either no relationship between test performance and positive thoughts about Obama or mixed results (Aronson et al., 2009; Stricker & Rock, 2015).

other? It appears that members of stereotyped groups are anxious that they will fulfill their group's negative stereotype, and their anxiety hinders their performance on tests. Some people cope with stereotype threat by *disidentifying*, telling themselves they don't care about the test scores (Major et al., 1998; Rothgerber & Wolsiefer, 2014). Understandably, this attitude reduces motivation and leads to decreased performance (**Figure 8.20**).

Stereotype threat affects people in many social groups, including those who are elderly or low-income, people of color, women, and White male athletes (Bouazzaoui et al., 2016; Hively & El-Alayhi, 2014; Kaye & Pennington, 2016). Researchers in one study examined high school women's interest in computer science after they were given descriptions and photographs of both a stereotypical and a nonstereotypical computer science classroom (Master et al., 2016). The stereotypical classroom contained objects such as *Star Wars* items, tech magazines, and science fiction books. The nonstereotypical classroom had objects such as nature pictures, general magazines, and plants. On average, women expressed heightened interest in taking a computer science class after seeing the nonstereotypical classroom. Men's interest, in comparison, did not differ by classroom. Studies like this suggest that when women are under-represented in particular fields, like computer science, the underrepresentation may be due not to women's ability but rather to subtle social and environmental factors.

Research on stereotype threat helps explain some group differences in intelligence and achievement tests. In doing so, it underscores why relying solely on such tests to make critical decisions affecting individual lives—in hiring, college admissions, or clinical application—is unwarranted and possibly even unethical.

What's the good news? First, some early research found that having Barack Obama as president improved academic performance in people of color—thus offsetting stereotype threat (Marx et al., 2009). See **Figure 8.21**. Second, people who have the opportunity to self-affirm, or validate, their identities in some meaningful way do not show the negative effects of stereotype threat. For example, Black first-year college students who receive information about how to feel more connected to their college or university show higher GPAs. They likewise experience better health three years later compared to those who do not receive the "how to connect" information (Walton & Cohen, 2011).

## ❖ Psychology and Your Professional Success | Is a High IQ Essential to High Achievement?

In our culture, high IQ and high financial status are generally idolized, and Bill Gates and Albert Einstein are revered icons (see the photos). Why? As you've just seen, modern research suggests that intelligence is not entirely the result of inherited traits. In fact, both IQ and great economic success are the result of numerous personality, social, and biological factors.

**Personality Factors**    How do we explain Bill Gates's and Albert Einstein's genius-level achievements? Several studies have found that personal attributes such as a *growth mindset* and *grit*, along with *self-discipline, impulse control,*

and *motivation*, are the best predictors of achievement (e.g., Claro et al., 2016; Duckworth, 2016; Dweck, 2012).

Let's examine the importance of *perseverance* and *passion*—the two key components of grit. Research has shown that internationally recognized experts in a variety of fields (e.g., athletics, music, science, writing, mathematics) required approximately 10 years of intensive training before reaching their level of success (Ericsson, 1993, 2006; Mooradian et al., 2016). Clearly, that takes perseverance.

Others suggest that it's not just the willingness to practice for extended periods of time that matters. Instead, they believe the one factor most predictive of expertise is the number of hours spent in what they call *deliberate practice*. Highly competent professionals not only practice more—they practice *better*. When they train, experts constantly evaluate their own performance and then concentrate more time and energy in areas where they are weak (Eskreis-Winkler et al., 2016; Keith et al., 2016).

What if you're not an expert? Research shows that deliberate practice can even improve undergraduates' end-of-semester grades (Eskreis-Winkler et al., 2016). Can you see how this type of self-monitoring followed by focused practice can be invaluable to both your academic and career success? While reading a text or listening to lectures, and training for a new job or promotion, be sure to carefully monitor your understanding of the material and note the areas where you need to apply extra time and effort. If you've been using the WileyPLUS adaptive practice testing—an accompaniment to this text—you've undoubtedly noticed the benefits of this type of deliberate practice.

**Social Factors**    What Gates and Einstein had were not just a growth mindset, grit, and the ability to focus and practice for long periods of time. They also came from cultures that placed high value on literacy and education and from high-income families—though family income matters somewhat less. Such families tend to have children who are more likely to develop their intellectual abilities to their highest potential (Claro et al., 2016; Liu & Xie, 2016). Also, when a culture, community, and family assume that hard work is more important than innate abilities, that education and learning should be a joy, and that a child's accomplishments reflect on the family and the community, the child is likely to internalize the same values and attempt to achieve maximum success (Chua & Rubenfeld, 2014; Ricci & Lee, 2016; Shin et al., 2016).

One study followed Chinese American students from elementary school until high school. At first, IQ tests did not show an advantage of Asian Americans over other Americans. However, over time, their academic abilities flourished in comparison to their peers. By high school, their grades were significantly higher than their peers with similar IQ scores (Flynn, 1991). Researchers concluded that cultural beliefs about education and hard work played a dominant role in their accomplishments.

**Biological Factors**    Are you wondering if high-achieving athletes, like Olympic-medal-winning gymnast Simone Biles or swimmer Michael Phelps, have biological advantages that we don't? Years ago, researchers presumed star athletes were born with faster reflexes, larger hearts, superior lung capacity, more muscle tissue, and so on. This is not necessarily the case. Most athletes develop these characteristics thanks to years of intensive training.

**Take-Home Message**    Whether it's great financial, intellectual, or athletic achievement, the media and public appear most interested in the innate genetics and "hard wiring" supposedly underlying great success. However, as you've discovered throughout this text, our brains are remarkably "plastic," and the latest research combining personality, social, and biological factors reinforces once again the importance of the biopsychosocial model.

If you're questioning your ability to be a physician or a member of any other profession because of supposed intellectual barriers, be sure to critically reevaluate your concerns and consider all your options. Also, talk to successful people in your desired career field. You'll undoubtedly discover that personal behaviors and character strengths, like self-control, motivation, deliberate practice, grit, and a growth mindset, are generally the best predictors of lifetime achievement (e.g., Duckworth, 2016; Dweck, 2012; Eskreis-Winkler et al., 2016).

## Retrieval Practice 8.4 | Intelligence Controversies

Completing this self-test and the connections section, and then checking your answers by clicking on the answer button or by looking in Appendix B, will provide immediate feedback and helpful practice for exams.

### Self-Test

1. Briefly explain how brain size might affect intelligence.

2. Which of the following persons would be most likely to have similar IQ test scores?

   **a.** identical twins raised apart
   **b.** identical twins raised together
   **c.** fraternal twins raised apart
   **d.** brothers and sisters from the same parents

3. By examining identical twins raised in different homes and reunited only as adults, _____ found that genetic factors appear to play a surprisingly large role in the IQ scores of identical twins.

   **a.** the Minnesota Study of Twins
   **b.** Lewis Terman's "Termites" research
   **c.** the Stanford-Binet Intelligence Studies
   **d.** David Wechsler's research

4. Howard Gardner proposed a theory of _____.

   **a.** language development
   **b.** fluid and crystallized intelligence
   **c.** culture specificity intelligence
   **d.** multiple intelligences

5. Awareness of a negative stereotype that affects oneself and may lead to impairment in performance is known as _____.

   **a.** the Flynn effect        **b.** the "Obama effect"
   **c.** a bell curve            **d.** stereotype threat

### Connections—Chapter to Chapter

Answering the following question will help you "look back and look ahead" to see the important connections among the subfields of psychology and chapters within this text.

In Chapter 13 (Personality), you'll discover several criticisms about how psychologists typically measure personality, whereas in this chapter, we discussed the criticisms of IQ assessment. How do the two sets of criticism overlap and how are they different?

---

### Study Tip

*The WileyPLUS program that accompanies this text provides for each chapter a Media Challenge, Critical Thinking Exercise, and Application Quiz. This set of study materials provides additional, invaluable study opportunities. Be sure to check it out!*

# Chapter Summary

## 8.1 Thinking 258

- Thinking is a central aspect of **cognition**. Thought processes are distributed throughout the brain in neural networks and grounded within the body. Mental images and concepts aid our thought processes. There are three major building blocks for concepts—**prototypes**, artificial concepts, and hierarchies.

- Problem solving often involves *insight* and/or *trial and error*. However, a more deliberative approach usually has three steps: *preparation*, *production*, and *evaluation*. **Algorithms** are logical step-by-step procedures that eventually solve the problem. **Heuristics** are a cognitive strategy, or "rule of thumb," for problem solving.

- Barriers to problem solving include **mental sets, functional fixedness, availability heuristic, representativeness heuristic, confirmation bias**, and **cognitive offloading**.

- **Creativity** is the ability to produce original, appropriate, and valued outcomes in a novel way. Creative thinking involves *originality, fluency,* and *flexibility*. Tests of creativity usually focus on **divergent thinking**, which involves generating as many alternatives or ideas as possible. In contrast, **convergent thinking**—or conventional thinking—works toward a single correct answer.

### Test Your Critical Thinking

1. During problem solving, do you use primarily algorithms or heuristics? What are the advantages of each?

2. Would you prefer to be highly creative or highly intelligent? Why?

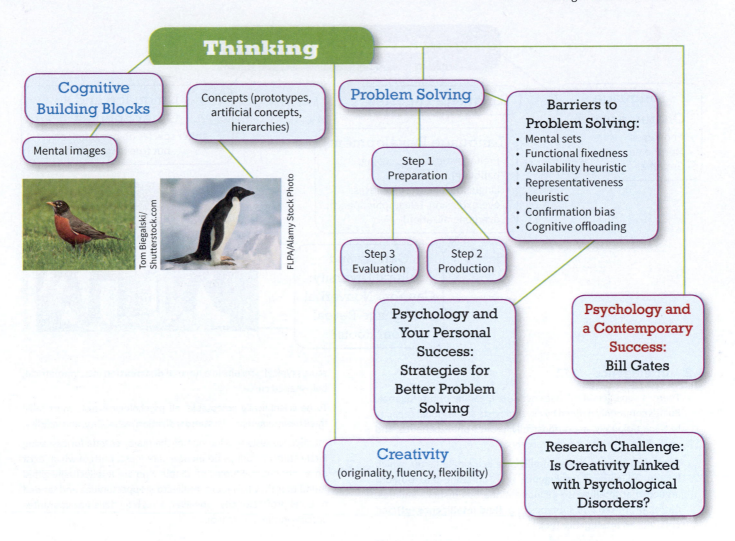

## Thinking

**Cognitive Building Blocks**

Mental images

Concepts (prototypes, artificial concepts, hierarchies)

Tom Biegalski/ Shutterstock.com

FLPA/Alamy Stock Photo

**Problem Solving**

Step 1 Preparation

Step 3 Evaluation

Step 2 Production

**Barriers to Problem Solving:**
- Mental sets
- Functional fixedness
- Availability heuristic
- Representativeness heuristic
- Confirmation bias
- Cognitive offloading

**Psychology and Your Personal Success:** Strategies for Better Problem Solving

**Psychology and a Contemporary Success:** Bill Gates

**Creativity** (originality, fluency, flexibility)

**Research Challenge:** Is Creativity Linked with Psychological Disorders?

### 8.2  Language  266

- **Language** supports thinking and enables us to communicate. To produce language, we use **phonemes, morphemes**, and **grammar** (syntax and semantics). Several different parts of our brains are involved in producing and listening to language.

- According to Whorf's *linguistic relativity hypothesis*, language determines thought. Generally, this hypothesis is not supported, but it's clear that language does strongly influence thought.

- Children communicate nonverbally from birth. Their language development proceeds in stages: *prelinguistic*, which includes crying, cooing, and babbling, and *linguistic*, which includes single utterances, telegraphic speech, and acquisition of the basic rules of grammar.

- According to nativists, like Chomsky, humans are "prewired" with a **language acquisition device (LAD)** that enables children to develop language with minimal environmental input. Nurturists hold that children learn language through rewards, punishments, and imitation. Most psychologists hold an intermediate, interactionist view.

- Research with chimpanzees, gorillas, and dolphins suggests that these animals can learn and use basic rules of language. However, critics suggest nonhuman animal language is less complex, less creative, and not as rule laden as human language.

#### Test Your Critical Thinking

**1.** Describe a personal example of language influencing your thinking.

**2.** Review the evidence that nonhuman animals are able to learn and use language. Do you think apes and dolphins have true language? Why or why not?

## Language

### Language Characteristics
- Phonemes
- Morphemes
- Grammar

### Language Theories

### Language Development
- Prelinguistic (crying, cooing, babbling)
- Linguistic (one word, phrases, overextension, telegraphic speech, overgeneralization)

### Gender and Cultural Diversity: Can Your Nonverbal Language Reveal Your Roots?

### Language and Other Species
Other species do communicate, but true language?

Blend Images/Getty Images

## 8.3    Intelligence    272

- There is considerable debate over the meaning of **intelligence**. But it's commonly defined by psychologists as the global capacity to think rationally, act purposefully, profit from experience, and deal effectively with the environment.

- Spearman proposed that intelligence is a single factor, which he termed **general intelligence (g)**. Thurstone and Guilford argued that intelligence included numerous distinct abilities. Cattell proposed two subtypes of *g*: **fluid intelligence (gf)** and **crystallized intelligence (gc)**.

- Early intelligence tests computed a person's **mental age (MA)** to arrive at an **intelligence quotient (IQ)**. Today, two of the most widely used intelligence tests are the *Stanford-Binet Intelligence Scale* and the *Wechsler Adult Intelligence Scale (WAIS)*. Intelligence tests commonly compare the performance of an individual with other individuals of the same age. The distribution of these test scores typically results in a **normal distribution** in a symmetrical, bell-shaped curve.

- To be scientifically acceptable, all psychological tests must fulfill three basic requirements: **standardization, reliability**, and **validity**.

- Intelligence tests provide one of the major criteria for assessing *intellectual disability* and *mental giftedness*, both of which exist on a continuum. Studies of people who are intellectually gifted found that they had more intellectual opportunities and tended to excel professionally. However, a high IQ does not guarantee success in every endeavor.

### Test Your Critical Thinking

1. Is fluid intelligence (gf) more important than crystallized intelligence (gc)? Why or why not?

2. Do you believe IQ tests are more reliable than valid? Explain.

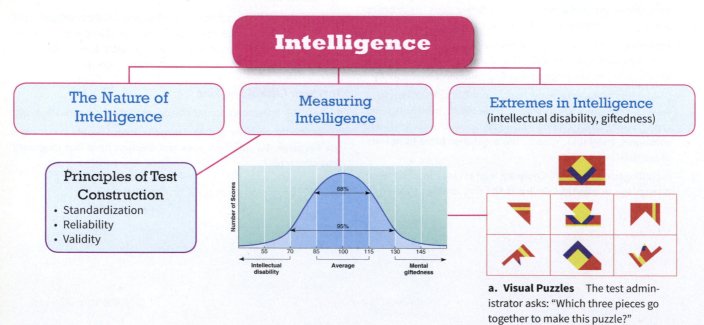

## Intelligence

### The Nature of Intelligence

#### Principles of Test Construction
- Standardization
- Reliability
- Validity

### Measuring Intelligence

### Extremes in Intelligence
(intellectual disability, giftedness)

**a. Visual Puzzles**    The test administrator asks: "Which three pieces go together to make this puzzle?"

### 8.4  Intelligence Controversies  276

- Rather than a single *g* factor of intelligence, many contemporary cognitive theorists, including Gardner and Sternberg, believe that intelligence is a collection of many separate specific abilities. Goleman believes that **emotional intelligence (EI)**, the ability to empathize and manage our emotions and relationships, is just as important as any other kind of intelligence.

- Most research suggests that both nature and nurture are interacting influences on intelligence. Research on the biology of intelligence has focused on brain functioning, not size, and it indicates that intelligent people's brains respond especially quickly and efficiently.

- In answer to the questions of group differences and how gender and/or ethnicity affect IQ, heredity and the environment are always interacting, inseparable factors.

**Test Your Critical Thinking**

**1.** How would someone with exceptionally low or high EI behave?

**2.** Do you believe IQ tests are biased against certain groups? Why or why not?

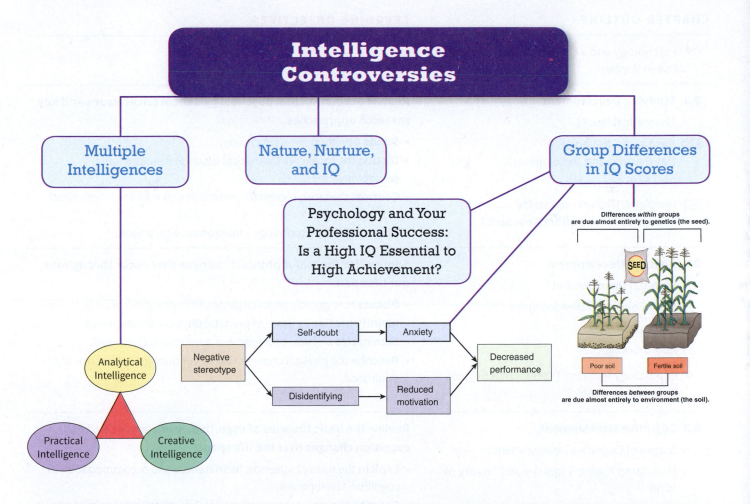

# Key Terms

**Retrieval Practice**    *Write your own definition for each term before turning back to the referenced page to check your answer.*

- algorithm   260
- artificial intelligence (AI)   258
- availability heuristic   260
- cognition   258
- cognitive offloading   262
- confirmation bias   262
- convergent thinking   264
- creativity   263
- crystallized intelligence (gc)   273
- divergent thinking   264
- embodied cognition   258

- emotional intelligence (EI)   278
- fluid intelligence (*gf*)   273
- functional fixedness   260
- general intelligence (*g*)   273
- grammar   267
- heuristic   260
- intelligence   273
- intelligence quotient (IQ)   274
- language   267
- language acquisition device (LAD)   270
- mental age (MA)   274

- mental set   260
- morpheme   267
- normal distribution   273
- phoneme   267
- prototype   259
- reliability   274
- representativeness heuristic   261
- standardization   274
- stereotype threat   281
- triarchic theory of intelligence   277
- validity   275

© alexxl66/iStockphoto

# Life Span Development I

### ❖ Psychology and a Contemporary Success |

## Oprah Winfrey

Born into poverty to a teenage single mother, Oprah Winfrey (1954–) grew up on her grandmother's farm, where her grandmother provided love and support (see photo). Oprah's life changed when, at the age of 6, she was sent to live with her mother in Milwaukee. While her mother worked as a housemaid, Oprah was left alone in their city apartment. Starting at the age of 9, she was severely beaten and sexually molested by two relatives and a family friend. At the age of 13, Oprah ran away from home. She became pregnant at 14 and gave birth to a baby boy who died in infancy.

At this point, Oprah's life finally took a positive turn. Her mother sent her to live with her father, who was a demanding and strict disciplinarian. However, he also provided the secure environment Oprah needed to become an honor student and earn several other awards, including a full scholarship to college and the Miss Black Tennessee beauty pageant. The pageant award led to a job in radio and then to success as a local news co-anchor at the age of 19. Oprah later moved on to take a position on a daytime talk show in Chicago, and the *Oprah Winfrey Show* became the number one talk show for 24 consecutive seasons.

In addition to her award-winning television programs, Oprah is also an actress, writer, publisher, and producer. Furthermore, she has been hailed as the "Queen of all Media," the greatest Black philanthropist in American history, and the most influential woman of her generation. In 2013, Oprah was awarded the Presidential Medal of Freedom by President Barack Obama (Jacques, 2013; Oprah Winfrey Net Worth, n. d.; Oswald, 2010).

Louis Myrie/WireImage/Getty Images

# Chapter Overview

*Whatever your goal, you can get there if you're willing to work.*—Oprah Winfrey

Based on this quote and her incredible life story, it's easy to see why we chose Oprah Winfrey as our famous figure for this chapter. She is the perfect exemplar for our text's themes—having a *growth mindset* and *grit*—and her "can do" attitude, passion, and perseverance remind all of us what we can achieve with dedication and hard work.

Unlike Oprah, with her harrowing childhood, are you one of the lucky ones who grew up with loving parents who documented every stage of your development with photos, videos, and/or journals—starting with your birth, first smile, first day of school, all the way to your high school graduation? If so, you have a head start on the material in this chapter. As you might expect, studying development across the entire life span is a monumental task, so we need two chapters to adequately cover the material. We've organized this first chapter into three major sections—*physical, cognitive,* and *social-emotional development.* Then, in Chapter 10, we'll explore *moral development, personality development,* and *special issues* related to development. Keep in mind that topics in both chapters are intricately interwoven.

## Why Study Psychology?

### Did you know that

- . . . at the moment of conception, you were smaller than the period at the end of a sentence?
- . . . during the last few months of pregnancy, you (as a fetus) could hear sounds outside your mother's womb?
- . . . prenatal exposure to smoke increases the risk of obesity in later life?
- . . . at birth, your head was approximately one-fourth of your total body size, but as an adult it's only one-eighth?

Cavid M Phillips/Science Source

- ... within the first few days of life, newborns breast-fed by their mothers recognize and show preference for the odor and taste of their own mother's milk?
- ... human brains aren't fully developed until the mid-20s?

- ... attachment patterns you form as an infant may have lasting effects on your adult romantic relationships?
- ... young people are more supportive of gay marriage than older people?

# 9.1   Studying Development

## LEARNING OBJECTIVES

**Retrieval Practice**   While reading the upcoming sections, respond to each Learning Objective in your own words.

**Review developmental psychology's theoretical issues and key research approaches.**

- **Define** developmental psychology.

- **Discuss** the three core theoretical issues in developmental psychology.
- **Contrast** the cross-sectional research design with the longitudinal research design.
- **Discuss** cultural psychology's four research guidelines.

**Developmental psychology**
The study of age-related behavior and mental processes from conception to death.

Just as some parents carefully document their child's progress throughout his or her life, the field of **developmental psychology** studies growth and change throughout the eight major stages of life—from conception to death, or "womb to tomb" (**Table 9.1**). These studies have led to three key theoretical issues.

## Theoretical Issues

Almost every area of research in human development frames questions around three major issues:

1. **Nature or nurture?**   How do genetics (nature) and life experiences (nurture) influence development? According to the *nature position*, development is largely governed by automatic, genetically predetermined signals in a process known as *maturation*. Just as a flower unfolds in accord with its genetic blueprint, humans crawl before we walk and walk before we run.

**Critical period**   A specific time during which an organism must experience certain stimuli in order to develop properly in the future.

In addition, naturists believe there are **critical periods**, or windows of opportunity, that occur early in life when exposure to certain stimuli or experiences is necessary for

**TABLE 9.1   Life Span Development**

| Stage | Approximate Age |
|-------|-----------------|
| Prenatal | Conception to birth |
| Infancy | Birth to 18 months |
| Early childhood | 18 months to 6 years |
| Middle childhood | 6 to 12 years |
| Adolescence | 12 to 20 years |
| Young adulthood | 20 to 45 years |
| Middle adulthood | 45 to 60 years |
| Late adulthood | 60 years to death |

THE FOUR AGES OF MAN

INFANCY   CHILDHOOD   YOUTH   MATURITY

proper development. For example, many newborn animals form rigid attachments to particular stimuli shortly after birth, a process called **imprinting** (**Figure 9.1**).

Human children may also have critical periods for normal development. For instance, infants who are born with *cataracts*, a condition in which the eye's lens is cloudy and distorts vision, are able to see much better if they're operated on as infants than if they're operated on after the age of eight. In addition, research has shown that appropriate social interaction with adults in the first few weeks of life is essential for creating normal cognitive and social development (Berger, 2015; Harker et al., 2016; Mermelshtine & Barnes, 2016). Sadly, a study of both Israeli and Palestinian children found that exposure to serious military/political violence at age 8 is associated with more aggressive behavior later on, whereas witnessing such violence at later ages doesn't lead to aggression (Boxer et al., 2013). These and similar studies provide further evidence for critical periods—at least in the early years (see the **Research Challenge**).

2. **Stages or continuity?** Some developmental psychologists suggest that development generally occurs in *stages* that are discrete and qualitatively different from one another, whereas others believe it follows a *continuous pattern*, with gradual but steady and quantitative (measurable) changes (**Figure 9.2**).

3. **Stability or change?** Which of our traits are stable and present throughout our life span, and what aspects will change? Psychologists who emphasize *stability* hold that measurements of personality taken during childhood are major predictors of adult personality; those who emphasize *change* disagree.

REUTERS/Roger Schneider/Newscom

**FIGURE 9.1** **Critical periods and imprinting** Some animals, like these baby cranes, simply attach to, or imprint on, the first large, moving object they see—in this case, French pilot Christian Moullec, who raised the cranes from birth.

**Imprinting** The process by which attachments are formed during critical periods in early life.

---

## Research Challenge

### Deprivation and Development

What happens if a child is deprived of appropriate stimulation during a critical period of development? Consider the story of Genie, the so-called "wild child." From the time she was 20 months old until authorities rescued her at age 13, Genie (see photo) was locked alone in a tiny, windowless room. By day, she sat naked and tied to a child's toilet with nothing to do and no one to talk to. At night, she was immobilized in a kind of straitjacket and "caged" in a covered crib. Genie's abusive father forbade anyone to speak to her for those 13 years. If Genie made noise, her father beat her while he barked and growled like a dog.

AP/Wide World Photos

Genie's tale is a heartbreaking account of the lasting scars from a disastrous childhood. In the years after her rescue, Genie spent thousands of hours receiving special training, and by age 19 she could use public transportation and was adapting well to special classes at school. Genie was far from normal, however. Her intelligence scores were still close to the cutoff for intellectual disability. And although linguists and psychologists worked with her for many years, she was never able to master grammatical structure, and was limited to sentences like "Genie go" (Rymer, 1993).

These findings suggest that because of her extreme childhood isolation and abuse, Genie, like other seriously neglected or environmentally isolated children, missed a necessary critical period for language development (Curtiss, 1977; Raaska et al., 2013; Sylvestre &

Mérette, 2010). To make matters worse, she was also placed in a series of foster homes, some of which were emotionally and physically abusive. According to the latest information, Genie now lives in a privately run facility for mentally underdeveloped adults (James, 2008).

**Test Yourself**

1. Based on the information provided, did this study (Rymer, 1993) use descriptive, correlational, and/or experimental research?

2. If you chose:
   - *descriptive research*, is this a naturalistic observation, survey/interview, case study, and/or archival research?
   - *correlational research*, is this a positive, negative, or zero correlation?
   - *experimental research*, label the IV, DV, experimental group(s), and control group. (Note: If participants were not randomly assigned to groups, list it as a *quasi-experimental design*.)
   - both *descriptive* and *correlational*, answer the corresponding questions for both.

**Check your answers by clicking on the answer button or by looking in Appendix B.**

**Note:** The information provided in this study is admittedly limited, but the level of detail is similar to what is presented in most textbooks and public reports of research findings. Answering these questions, and then comparing your answers to those provided, will help you become a better critical thinker and consumer of scientific research.

**FIGURE 9.2**    **Stages versus continuity in development**    There is an ongoing debate about whether development is better characterized by discrete stages or by gradual, continuous development.

**a.** Stage theorists think development results from discrete, qualitative changes.

**b.** Continuity theorists believe development results from gradual, quantitative (incremental) changes.

**Cross-sectional design**    In developmental psychology, a research technique that measures individuals of various ages at one point in time and provides information about age differences.

**Longitudinal design**    In developmental psychology, a research design that measures individuals over an extended period and gives information about age changes.

Which of these positions is most correct? Psychologists generally do not take a hard line either way. Rather, they prefer an interactionist perspective and/or the biopsychosocial model. For instance, in the nature-versus-nurture debate, psychologists agree that development emerges from unique genetic predispositions *and* environmental experiences (Auger, 2016; Cavanaugh & Blanchard-Fields, 2015; Gallagher & Jones, 2016).

## Research Approaches

To investigate these three controversies and other questions, developmental psychologists typically use all the research methods discussed in Chapter 1. To study the entire human life span, they also need two additional techniques—*cross-sectional* and *longitudinal* research **(Figure 9.3)**.

The **cross-sectional design** measures individuals of various ages at a single point in time to provide information about age differences. One cross-sectional study included women in three different age groups (ages 22–34, 35–49, and 50–65) to examine whether body weight dissatisfaction changes with age (Siegel, 2010). Unfortunately, female body dissatisfaction appears to be quite stable—and relatively high—across the life span.

In contrast, a **longitudinal design** takes repeated measures of one person or a group of same-aged people over a long period of time to see how the individual or the group changes over time. For example, a group of developmental researchers wondered if peer ratings of personality taken during childhood might be better predictors of later adult personality than self-ratings (Martin-Storey et al., 2012). They first asked grade school children in 1976–1978 to rate themselves and their peers on several personality factors, such as likeability, aggression, and social withdrawal. In 1999–2003, the researchers returned and asked the same participants, now in mid-adulthood, to complete a second series of personality tests. As hypothesized, the peer ratings were better than self-ratings in predicting adult personality. Does this finding surprise you? If so, try contacting some of your childhood peers and then compare notes on how you remember one another's personality as children and how this evaluation predicted your personalities as adults.

| CROSS-SECTIONAL RESEARCH | | | Advantages | Disadvantages |
|---|---|---|---|---|
| **Different** participants of various ages are compared at one point in time to determine age-related *differences* | **Group One** 20-year-old participants **Group Two** 40-year-old participants **Group Three** 60-year-old participants | Research done in 2018 | • Provides information about age differences • Quick and less expensive • Typically larger sample | • Cohort effects difficult to separate • Restricted generalizability (measures behaviors and mental processes at only one point in time) |

| LONGITUDINAL RESEARCH | | | Advantages | Disadvantages |
|---|---|---|---|---|
| The **same** participants are studied at various ages to determine age-related *changes* | **Study One** Participants are 20 years old | Research done in 2018 | • Provides information about age changes • Increased confidence in results • More in-depth information per participant | • More expensive and time consuming • Restricted generalizability (typically smaller sample due to participant dropouts over time) |
| | **Study Two** Same participants are now 40 years old | Research done in 2038 | | |
| | **Study Three** Same participants are now 60 years old | Research done in 2058 | | |

**FIGURE 9.3**    **Cross-sectional versus longitudinal research**    To study development, psychologists may use a cross-sectional research design, a longitudinal research design, or both.

Now that you have a better idea of these two types of research, if you were a developmental psychologist interested in studying intelligence in adults, which design would you choose—cross-sectional or longitudinal? Before you decide, note the different research results shown in **Figure 9.4**.

Why do the two methods show such different results? Cross-sectional studies sometimes confuse genuine age differences with *cohort effects*—differences that result from specific histories of the age group studied. As shown in the top line in Figure 9.4, the 81-year-olds measured by the cross-sectional design have dramatically lower scores than the 25-year-olds. But is this due to aging or instead to broad environmental differences, such as less formal education or poorer nutrition?

A prime example of possible environmental effects on cross-sectional studies is a recent survey of attitudes towards gay marriage that found young people are much more in favor of gay marriage than older people (Pew Research Center, 2016). So does this mean that people grow more opposed to gay marriage as they age? Probably not. These differences most likely reflect cohort and generational effects. Young people today are generally more liberal and more positive toward different sexual orientations, and therefore more likely to support gay marriage. They'll also probably maintain their current attitudes as they age.

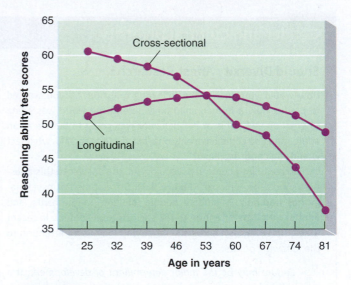

**FIGURE 9.4** **Which results are true?** Cross-sectional studies have shown that reasoning and intelligence reach their peak in early adulthood and then gradually decline. In contrast, longitudinal studies have found that a marked decline does not begin until about age 60.

Adapted from Schaie, 1994, with permission.

The essential thing to remember is that because the different age groups, called *cohorts*, grew up in different historical periods, research results that apply to them may not apply to people growing up at other times. With the cross-sectional design, age effects and cohort effects are sometimes inextricably tangled. (As a critical thinker, can you see how *cohort effects* are a unique research problem for cross-cultural studies, just as the *third-variable problem* poses a unique threat to correlational studies—discussed in Chapter 1?)

Longitudinal studies have their own share of limits and disadvantages. They are expensive in terms of time and money, and it is difficult for us to generalize their results. Because participants often drop out or move away during the extended test period, the experimenter may end up with a self-selected sample that differs from the general population in crucial ways. Each method of research has strengths and weaknesses (as you recall from the right-hand side of Figure 9.3). Keep these differences in mind when you read the findings of developmental research.

Also note that modern researchers sometimes combine both cross-sectional and longitudinal designs into one study. In Chapter 10, we will discuss a study that examined whether well-being decreases with age (Sutin et al., 2013). When these researchers examined combined cross-sectional and longitudinal data from two independent samples taken over 30 years, they initially found that well-being *declined* with age. However, when they then controlled for the fact that older cohorts started out with lower levels of well-being, they found that all the cohorts *increased* rather than decreased in well-being with age. The reversal in findings was explained by the fact that the older group of people had experienced instances of major turmoil in their younger years, including America's Great Depression during the 1930s. This means that this group started out with lower levels of well-being. Sadly, they apparently maintained these attitudes into their later years, compared to those who grew up during more prosperous times.

Why is this combination of two research designs valuable? It offers a more accurate and positive view of well-being in old age than what was indicated in either the cross-sectional design or the longitudinal design. It also suggests some troubling possibilities for today's young adults who are entering a stagnant workforce with high unemployment. As the study's authors say, this "economic turmoil may impede [their] psychological, as well as financial, growth even decades after times get better" (Sutin et al., 2013, p. 384). If you're one of these young adults, you'll be happy to hear that there's some very encouraging research showing that individuals who enter their teens and early 20s during a recession are less narcissistic than those who come of age in more prosperous times (Bianchi, 2014, 2015). In fact, CEOs who were in their teens and early 20s during bad economic times later paid themselves less compared to other top executives. The following **Gender and Cultural Diversity** offers more information regarding research across cultures.

## Gender and Cultural Diversity

### Should Diversity Affect Research?

How would you answer the following question: "If you wanted to predict how a human child anywhere in the world was going to grow up—what his or her behavior was going to be like as an adult—and you could have only one fact about that child, what fact would you choose to have?"

According to cultural psychologists, the answer to this question should be "culture" (**Figure 9.5**). Developmental psychology has traditionally studied people (children, adolescents, and adults) with little attention to the sociocultural context. In recent times, however, psychologists are paying increasing attention to the following points:

- *Culture may be the major determinant of development.* If a child grows up in an individualistic/independent culture (such as those of the United States, Canada, and most countries in Western Europe), we can predict that this child will probably be competitive and question authority as an adult. Were this same child reared in a collectivist/interdependent culture (common in Africa, Asia, and Latin America), she or he would most likely grow up to be cooperative and respectful of elders (Berry et al., 2011; Greenfield et al. 2012; Manago & Greenfield, 2011).

- *Human development cannot be studied outside its sociocultural context.* In parts of Korea, most teenagers see a strict, authoritarian style of parenting as a sign of love and concern (Kim & Choi, 1995). Korean American and Korean Canadian teenagers, however, see the same behavior as a sign of rejection. Thus, rather than studying any general response to "authoritarian parenting styles," discussed later in this chapter, researchers in child development prefer to study children only within their *developmental niche* (Hewlett & Roulette, 2014; Torney-Purta, 2013; Yamagishi, 2011). A developmental niche has three components: the physical and social contexts in which the child lives, the rearing and educational practices of the child's culture, and the psychological characteristics of the parents (Bugental & Johnston, 2000; Harkness et al., 2007).

- *Each culture's ethnotheories are key determinants of behavior.* Within every culture, people have a prevailing set of ideas and beliefs that attempt to explain the world around them (an *ethnotheory*) (Carra et al., 2014; Kartner et al., 2013; Lau, 2010). In the area of child development, for example, cultures have specific ethnotheories about how children should be trained. As a critical thinker, you can anticipate that differing ethnotheories can lead to problems between cultures. In fact, the very idea of "critical thinking" is part of our North American ethnotheory regarding education. And it, too, can produce culture clashes. Concha Delgado-Gaitan (1994) found that Mexican immigrants from a rural background have a difficult time adjusting to U.S. schools, which teach children to question authority and think for themselves. In their culture of origin, these children are trained to respect their elders, be good listeners, and participate in conversation only when their opinion is solicited. Children who argue with adults are reminded not to be *malcriados* (naughty or disrespectful).

- *Culture is largely invisible to its participants.* Culture consists of ideals, values, and assumptions that are widely shared among a given group and that guide specific behaviors (Angeloni, 2014; Matsumoto & Juang, 2013; Ratner, 2011). Precisely because these ideals and values are widely shared, they are seldom discussed or directly examined. Just as a "fish doesn't know it's in water," we take our culture for granted, operating within it, though being almost unaware of it. See the following **Try This Yourself**.

Bartosz Hadyniak/E+/Getty Images    Hero Images/Getty Images

**FIGURE 9.5** **Cultural influences on development** As you're reading these two chapters on development (Chapters 9 and 10), ask yourself how culture might affect the lifespan development of these two groups of adolescents.

### Try This Yourself

#### Culture Invisibility

If you'd like a personal demonstration of the invisibility of culture, try this simple experiment: The next time you walk into an elevator, don't turn around. Remain facing the rear wall. Watch how others respond when you don't turn around (or when you stand right next to them rather than going to the other side of the elevator). Our American culture has rules that prescribe the "proper" way to ride in an elevator, and people become very uncomfortable when those rules are violated.

© Billy R. Ray/Wiley

## Retrieval Practice 9.1 | Studying Development

Completing this self-test and the connections section, and then checking your answers by clicking on the answer button or by looking in Appendix B, will provide immediate feedback and helpful practice for exams.

**Self-Test**

1. What does the field of developmental psychology study?

2. _____ is governed by automatic, genetically predetermined signals.
   - **a.** The cohort effect
   - **b.** Secondary aging
   - **c.** Thanatology
   - **d.** Maturation

3. A specific time during which an organism must experience certain stimuli in order to develop properly in the future is known as _____.
   - **a.** the cohort years
   - **b.** a critical period
   - **c.** the thanatology phase
   - **d.** maturation

4. What three major questions are studied in developmental psychology?
   - **a.** nature versus nurture, stages versus continuity, and stability versus change
   - **b.** nature versus nurture, "chunking" versus continuity, and instability versus change
   - **c.** nature versus nurture, stages versus continuity, and stagnation versus instability
   - **d.** none of these options

5. _____ studies are the most time-efficient method, whereas _____ studies provide the most in-depth information per participant.
   - **a.** Latitudinal; longitudinal
   - **b.** Neo-gerontology; longitudinal
   - **c.** Cross-sectional; longitudinal
   - **d.** Class-racial; longitudinal

**Connections—Chapter to Chapter**

Answering the following question will help you "look back and look ahead" to see the important connections among the subfields of psychology and chapters within this text.

In Chapter 1 (Introduction to Psychology and Its Research Methods), you discovered how various scientists approach research questions. In this chapter, you learned about two additional research designs: cross-sectional and longitudinal. Using these two methods, explain how you could test for age-related changes in reaction times.

## 9.2    Physical Development

### LEARNING OBJECTIVES

**Retrieval Practice**   While reading the upcoming sections, respond to each Learning Objective in your own words.

**Summarize the major physical changes that occur throughout our life span.**

- **Discuss** how genetic material passes from one generation to the next.

- **Identify** the three phases of prenatal physical development.
- **Summarize** physical development during early childhood.
- **Describe** the physical changes that occur during adolescence and adulthood.

After studying the photos of your textbook authors as they've aged over the life span (**Figure 9.6**), or after reviewing your own similar photos, you may be amused and surprised by all the dramatic changes in physical appearance. But have you stopped to appreciate the incredible underlying process that transforms all of us from birth to death? In this section, we will explore the fascinating process of physical development from conception through childhood, adolescence, and adulthood.

### Prenatal Development

At the moment of your conception, your biological mother and father each contributed 23 **chromosomes**, which are threadlike, linear strands of **DNA** (deoxyribonucleic acid) encoded

**Chromosome**   A threadlike molecule of DNA (deoxyribonucleic acid) that carries genetic information.

**DNA**   The main constituent of chromosomes found in all living organisms, which transmits hereditary characteristics from parents to children; short for *deoxyribonucleic acid*.

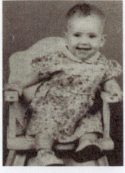

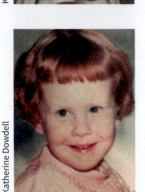

Karen Huffman

Katherine Dowdell

Catherine Sandersen

**FIGURE 9.6** **Changes in physical development over the life span** As this series of photos of your textbook authors shows, physical changes occur throughout our lives. Our cognitive, social, and emotional processes, as well as our personalities, also are continually changing, but the changes aren't as visible. (The top row is Karen Huffman at ages 1, 10, and 60. The second row is Katherine Dowdell at ages 2, 10, and 50; The third row is Catherine Sanderson at ages 1, 10, and 30.)

**Gene** A segment of DNA (deoxyribonucleic acid) that occupies a specific place on a particular chromosome and carries the code for hereditary transmission.

**Behavioral genetics** The study of the relative effects of heredity and the environment on behavior and mental processes.

**Epigenetics** The study of how nongenetic factors, such as age, environment, lifestyle, and disease, affect how (and if) genes are expressed; "epi" means "above" or "outside of."

with their **genes** (**Figure 9.7**). Interestingly, DNA of all humans (except identical twins) has unique, distinguishing features, much like the details on our fingerprints. This uniqueness is commonly used in forensics to exclude or identify criminal suspects. Furthermore, DNA analysis is often used for genetic testing during prenatal development to identify existing or potential future disorders.

Note that *genes* are the basic building blocks of our entire biological inheritance (Garrett, 2015; Scherman, 2014). Each of our human characteristics and behaviors is related to the presence or absence of particular genes that control the transmission of traits. For some traits, such as blood type, a single pair of genes (one from each parent) determines what characteristics we will possess. When two genes for a given trait conflict, the outcome depends on whether the gene is *dominant* or *recessive*. A dominant gene reveals its trait whenever the gene is present. In contrast, the gene for a recessive trait is normally expressed only if the other gene in the pair is also recessive.

Unfortunately, there are numerous myths and misconceptions about traits supposedly genetically *determined* by dominant genes. For example, we once assumed that characteristics such as eye color, hair color, and height were the result of either one dominant gene or two paired recessive genes. But modern geneticists now believe that these characteristics are *polygenic*, meaning they are controlled by multiple genes. One of the major goals of the new field of **behavioral genetics**, which studies the interplay of heredity and the environment, is to identify and study these polygenic traits.

Another new and related field of research, known as **epigenetics**, studies how nongenetic factors can dramatically affect how (and if) inherited genes are expressed throughout our lives

**FIGURE 9.7**    **Conception and your hereditary code**

**a. Before conception**    Millions of sperm are released when a man ejaculates into a woman's vagina, but only a few hundred sperm survive the arduous trip up to the egg.

**b. Conception**    Although a joint effort is required to break through the outer coating, only one sperm will actually fertilize the egg. At the moment of conception, a father's sperm and a mother's egg each contribute 23 chromosomes, for a total of 46.

**c. Cell nucleus**    Each cell in the human body (except red blood cells) contains a nucleus.

**d. Chromosomes**    Each cell nucleus contains 46 chromosomes, which are threadlike molecules of DNA (deoxyribonucleic acid).

**e. DNA and genes**    Each DNA molecule contains thousands of genes, which are the most basic units of heredity.

Francis Leroy/Biocosmos/Science Source

Thierry Berrod, Mona Lisa Production/ Science Source

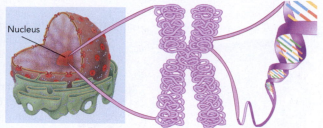

Nucleus

(Brody et al., 2016; Iakoubov et al., 2015; Wallack & Thornburg, 2016). Unlike simple genetic transmission, which is based on changes in the DNA sequence, changes in gene expression can have other causes, such as age, environment, lifestyle, or disease. (The term "epi" means "above" or "outside of"—see the **Study Tip**.) In other words, nurture can shape nature! Epigenetic factors can switch genes "ON" or "OFF." As a case in point, an epigenetic factor like malnutrition or childhood abuse can prevent a child from reaching his or her full potential genetic height or maximum genetic intelligence (Denholm et al., 2013; Venables & Raine, 2016). The good news is that with environmental changes even identical twins are not destined to develop the same diseases.

### Three Stages of Prenatal Development

Now that we've discussed the general principles of how our genes and our environment interact to form us as unique individuals, let's go back to the moment of your conception. At that point in time, you were a single cell barely 1/175 of an inch in diameter—smaller than the period at the end of this sentence. This new cell, called a *zygote*, then began a process of rapid cell division that resulted in a multimillion-celled infant (you) some nine months later.

The (see Study Tip) vast changes that occur during the nine months of a full-term pregnancy are usually divided into three stages: the **germinal period**, **embryonic period**, and **fetal period** (**Step-by-Step Diagram 9.1**). Prenatal growth and growth during the first few years after birth are *proximodistal* (near to far), which means that the innermost parts of the body develop before the outermost parts. Thus, a fetus's arms develop before its hands and fingers. Development at this stage also proceeds *cephalocaudally* (head to tail)—a fetus's head is disproportionately large compared with the lower part of its body. Can you see how these two terms—proximodistal and cephalocaudal—help explain why an infant can lift its head before it can lift its arms and lift its arms before lifting its legs?

### Hazards to Prenatal Development

As we've just seen, human development begins with the genes we inherit from our biological parents, and epigenetic factors, like age, lifestyle, and diseases, can dramatically affect how (and if) these inherited genes are expressed. During pregnancy, for example, the *placenta* connects the fetus to the mother's uterus and serves as the link for delivery of food and excretion of wastes. Moreover, it screens out some, but not all, harmful substances. As you can see in **Table 9.2**, environmental hazards such as X-rays and toxic waste, drugs, and diseases can still cross the placental barrier and have an *epigenetic effect*—meaning they leave a chemical mark on the DNA that abnormally switches the fetus's genes on or off. These influences generally have the most devastating effects during the first three months of pregnancy, making this a *critical period* in development.

Perhaps the most important—and generally avoidable—danger to a fetus comes from drugs, both legal and illegal. Nicotine and alcohol are major **teratogens**, environmental agents

**Germinal period**    The first stage of prenatal development, beginning with ovulation and followed by conception and implantation in the uterus; the first two weeks of pregnancy.

**Embryonic period**    The second stage of prenatal development, which begins after uterine implantation and lasts through the eighth week.

**Fetal period**    The third, and final, stage of prenatal development (eight weeks to birth).

**Teratogen**    Any factor that causes damage or fetal death during prenatal development.

| STEP-BY-STEP DIAGRAM 9.1 | **Prenatal Development** |

**STOP!** This Step-by-Step Diagram contains essential information NOT found elsewhere in the text, which is likely to appear on quizzes and exams. Be sure to study it CAREFULLY!

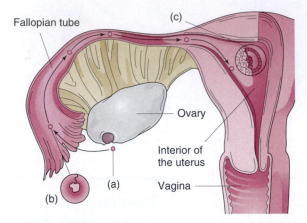

Fallopian tube
(c)
Ovary
Interior of the uterus
(a)
Vagina
(b)

**Step 1. Germinal period: From conception to implantation**
After discharge from either the left or right ovary (a), the ovum travels to the opening of the fallopian tube.

If fertilization occurs (b), it normally takes place in the first third of the fallopian tube. The fertilized ovum is referred to as a zygote.

When the zygote reaches the uterus, it implants itself in the wall of the uterus (c) and begins to grow tendril-like structures that intertwine with the rich supply of blood vessels located there. After implantation, the organism is known as an embryo.

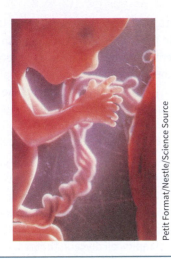

Petit Format/Nestle/Science Source

**Step 3. Fetal period: From eight weeks to birth** After the eighth week, and until the moment of birth, the embryo is called a fetus. At four months, all the actual body parts and organs are established. The fetal stage is primarily a time for increased growth and "fine detailing."

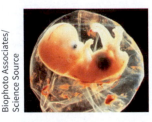

Biophoto Associates/ Science Source

**Step 2. Embryonic period: From implantation to eight weeks**
At eight weeks, the major organ systems have become well differentiated. Note that at this stage, the head grows at a faster rate than other parts of the body.

that cause damage during prenatal development. Mothers who smoke tobacco or drink alcohol during pregnancy have significantly higher rates of premature births, low-birth-weight infants, and fetal deaths. Their children also show increased behavior and cognitive problems (Doulatram et al., 2015; Roozen et al., 2016).

As you can see in **Figure 9.8**, heavy maternal drinking may lead to a cluster of serious abnormalities called *fetal alcohol spectrum disorders (FASD)*. The most severe form of this disorder is known as *fetal alcohol syndrome (FAS)*. Recent research suggests that alcohol may leave chemical marks on DNA that abnormally turn off or on specific genes (Mason & Zhou, 2015). In addition, children whose mothers smoked during pregnancy are more likely to be obese as adolescents, perhaps because in-utero exposure to nicotine changes a part of the brain that increases a preference for fatty foods (Haghighi et al., 2013, 2014).

The pregnant mother obviously plays a primary role in prenatal development because her nutrition, her health, and almost everything she ingests can cross the placental barrier (a better term might be placental sieve). However, the father also plays a role. A father's smoking can pollute the air the mother breathes—an epigenetic environmental factor.

**FIGURE 9.8** **Fetal alcohol syndrome** Prenatal exposure to alcohol can result in fetal alcohol spectrum disorders (FASD). The most severe form of FASD, called *fetal alcohol syndrome (FAS)*, causes facial abnormalities and stunted growth. But the most disabling features of FAS are brain damage and neurobehavioral problems, ranging from hyperactivity and learning disabilities to intellectual disability, depression, and psychoses (Centers for Disease Control, 2016; Doulatram et al., 2015; Roozen et al., 2016).

Andy Levin / Science Source

**TABLE 9.2**   **Sample Prenatal Environmental Conditions That Endanger a Child**

| Maternal Factors | Possible Effects on Embryo, Fetus, Newborn, or Young Child | |
| --- | --- | --- |
| **Malnutrition** | Low birth weight, malformations, less developed brain, greater vulnerability to disease | |
| **Exposure to:** Environmental toxins, X-rays, excessive stress | Low birth weight, malformations, cancer, hyperactivity, irritability, feeding difficulties | |
| **Legal and illegal drugs:** Certain prescription drugs, alcohol, nicotine, cocaine, methamphetamine | Inhibition of bone growth, hearing loss, low birth weight, fetal alcohol spectrum disorders (FASD), intellectual disability, attention deficits in childhood, death | |
| **Diseases:** Heart and thyroid disease, diabetes, asthma, infectious diseases | Blindness, deafness, intellectual disability, heart and other malformations, brain infection, spontaneous abortion, premature birth, low birth weight, death | |

Courtesy of Sandy Harvey

**Sources:** Centers for Disease Control (CDC), 2016; Doulatram et al., 2015; Maisto et al., 2015; Roozen et al., 2016.

Genetically, the father can transmit heritable diseases, and alcohol, opiates, cocaine, various gases, lead, pesticides, and industrial chemicals can all damage sperm (Finegersh et al., 2015; Ji et al., 2013; Vassoler et al., 2014). Likewise, children of older fathers may be at higher risk of a range of mental difficulties, including attention deficits, bipolar disorder, autism, and schizophrenia (D'Onofrio et al., 2014; McGrath et al., 2014).

## Early Childhood Development

*What is learned in the cradle, lasts to the grave.*—French proverb

Like the prenatal period, early childhood is a time of rapid physical development. Let's explore three major areas of change in early childhood: *brain*, *motor*, and *sensory/perceptual development*.

**Brain Development**   Our brains and other parts of the nervous system grow faster than any other part of the body during both prenatal development and the first two years of life, as illustrated in **Concept Organizer 9.1**. This brain development and learning occur primarily because neurons grow in size. Also, the number of dendrites, as well as the extent of their connections, increases (Bornstein et al., 2014; Garrett, 2015; Swaab, 2014).

**Motor Development**   Compared to the hidden, internal changes in brain development, the orderly emergence of active movement skills, known as *motor development*, is easily observed and measured. A newborn's first motor abilities are limited to *reflexes*, or involuntary responses to stimulation (Chapter 2). For example, the rooting reflex occurs when something touches a baby's cheek—the infant will automatically turn its head, open its mouth, and root for a nipple.

Along with these innate simple reflexes, the infant also soon begins to show voluntary control over the movement of various body parts (**Figure 9.9**). Thus, a helpless newborn, who cannot even lift her head, is soon transformed into an

Chin up — 2.2 mo.
Rolls over — 2.8 mo.
Sits with support — 2.9 mo.
Sits alone — 5.5 mo.
Stands holding furniture — 5.8 mo.
Walks holding on — 9.2 mo.
Stands alone — 11.5 mo.
Walks alone — 12.1 mo.
Walks up steps — 17.1 mo.

**FIGURE 9.9**   **Milestones in motor development**   The acquisition and progression of motor skills, from chin up to walking up steps, is generally the same for all children, but the environment and personal experiences also play a role. In short, each child will follow his or her own personal timetable (Adolph & Berger, 2012; Berger, 2015).

## CONCEPT ORGANIZER 9.1

**Brain Development**

The brain undergoes dramatic changes from conception through the first few years of life. Keep in mind, however, that our brains continue to change and develop throughout our life span.

**STOP!** This Concept Organizer contains essential information NOT found elsewhere in the text, which is likely to appear on quizzes and exams. Be sure to study it CAREFULLY!

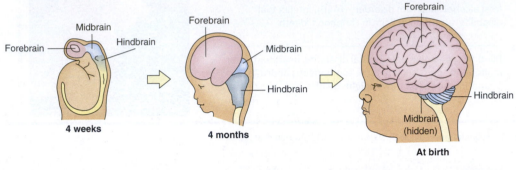

**4 weeks** · **4 months** · **At birth**

**a. Prenatal brain development** Recall from Chapter 2 that the human brain is divided into three major sections— the forebrain, midbrain, and hindbrain. Note how at three weeks after conception these three brain sections are one long neural tube, which later becomes the brain and spinal cord.

**At birth** · **3 months** · **15 months** · **6 years** · **14 years**

**b. Brain growth during the first 14 years** As infants learn and develop, synaptic connections between active neurons strengthen, and dendritic connections become more elaborate. Synaptic pruning (reduction of unused synapses) helps support this process. Myelination, the accumulation of fatty tissue coating the axons of nerve cells, continues until early adulthood.

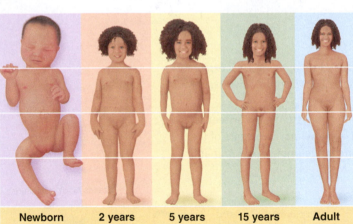

**Newborn** · **2 years** · **5 years** · **15 years** · **Adult**

**c. Brain and body changes over our life span** There are dramatic changes in our brains and body proportions as we grow older. At birth, our head was one-fourth our total body's size, whereas in adulthood, our head is one-eighth.

active toddler capable of crawling, walking, and climbing. In fact, babies are highly motivated to begin walking because they can move faster than when crawling, and they get better with practice (Adolph & Berger, 2012; Berger, 2015). Keep in mind that motor development is largely due to natural maturation, but, like brain development, it can be affected by environmental influences, such as disease and neglect.

Certain cultural differences in child-rearing also can explain some accelerated or delayed onset ages of major physical milestones, such as walking and crawling. In some regions of the world, for example, infants begin sitting, standing, and walking at earlier than expected ages due to special baby-swimming activities, or because their caregivers vigorously massage and exercise them as part of daily bathing routines, stretching their limbs, tossing them into the air, and propping them into sitting and walking positions (Karasik et al., 2010; Sigmundsson et al., 2017; Super & Harkness, 2015). Interestingly, the relatively recent practice in the United States of putting infants to sleep on their backs rather than their stomachs has resulted in delayed onset of crawling.

## Sensory and Perceptual Development

At birth, and during the final trimester of pregnancy, the developing child's senses are quite advanced (Bardi et al., 2014; Levine & Munsch, 2014; National Institutes of Health, 2016). Research shows that a newborn infant prefers his or her mother's voice, providing evidence that the developing fetus can hear sounds outside the mother's body (Lee & Kisilevsky, 2014; Von Hofsten, 2013). This raises the intriguing possibility of fetal learning, and some have advocated special stimulation for the fetus as a way of increasing intelligence, creativity, and general alertness (Jarvis, 2014; Van de Carr & Lehrer, 1997).

Interestingly, a newborn can smell most odors and distinguish between sweet, salty, and bitter tastes. Breast-fed newborns also recognize the odor of their mother's milk compared to other mothers' milk, formula, and other substances (Allam et al., 2010; Nishitani et al., 2009). Similarly, newborns' sense of touch and pain is highly developed, as evidenced by reactions to circumcision and to heel pricks for blood testing, and by the fact that their pain reactions are lessened by the smell of their own mother's milk (Nishitani et al., 2009; Rodkey & Riddell, 2013; Vinall & Grunau, 2014).

The newborn's sense of vision, however, is poorly developed. At birth, an infant is estimated to have vision between 20/200 and 20/600 (Haith & Benson, 1998). Imagine what the infant's visual life is like: The level of detail you see at 200 or 600 feet (if you have 20/20 vision) is what an infant sees at 20 feet. Within the first few months, vision quickly improves, and by 6 months it is 20/100 or better. At 2 years, visual acuity is nearly at the adult level of 20/20 (Courage & Adams, 1990).

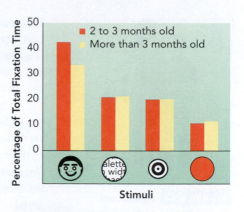

**FIGURE 9.10** **Infant visual preferences**

## Scientific Research with Infants

At this point, are you wondering how psychologists conduct research with infants—especially before they can even talk? One of the earliest experimenters, Robert Fantz (1956, 1963), designed a "looking chamber" to find out what infants can see and what holds their attention. Babies are placed on their backs inside the chamber facing a lighted "testing" area above them. Using this apparatus, Fantz and his colleagues measured how long infants stared at various stimuli. They found that infants prefer complex rather than simple patterns and pictures of faces rather than pictures of nonfaces (**Figure 9.10**).

Other researchers use newborns' heart rates and certain innate abilities, such as the sucking reflex, to study learning and perceptual development (Bendersky & Sullivan, 2007; Bornstein et al., 2014). For example, to study the sense of smell, researchers measure changes in newborns' heart rates when odors are presented. Presumably, if they can smell one odor but not another, their heart rates will change in the presence of the first but not the second. As you may recall from Chapter 4, what all of these researchers are measuring is *habituation*—decreased responsiveness after repeated stimulation. Brain scans, such as fMRI, MRI, and CTs, also help developmental scientists detect changes in infants' brains.

# Adolescence

> *Adolescents are not monsters. They are just people trying to learn how to make it among the adults in the world, who are probably not so sure themselves.*
>
> —Virginia Satir (American Author, Social Worker)

*Adolescence* is the loosely defined transition period of development between childhood and adulthood. In the United States, it roughly corresponds to the teenage years. However, the concept of adolescence and its meaning vary greatly across cultures (**Figure 9.11**).

Adolescence officially begins with **puberty**, the period of time when we mature sexually and become capable of reproduction. And one of the clearest and most dramatic physical signs of puberty is the *growth spurt*, which is characterized by rapid increases in height, weight, and skeletal growth (**Figure 9.12**), along with significant changes in reproductive structures and sexual characteristics. Maturation and hormone secretion cause rapid development of the ovaries, uterus, and vagina and the onset of menstruation (*menarche*) in the adolescent female. In the adolescent male, the testes, scrotum, and penis develop, and he experiences his first ejaculation (*spermarche*). The testes and ovaries produce hormones

**Puberty** The biological changes during adolescence that lead to sexual maturation and the ability to reproduce.

**FIGURE 9.11** **Ready for responsibility?** Adolescence is not a universal concept. Unlike the United States and other Western nations, some nonindustrialized countries have no need for a slow transition from childhood to adulthood; children simply assume adult responsibilities as soon as possible.

**FIGURE 9.12 Adolescent growth spurt** Note the gender differences in height gain during puberty. Most girls are about two years ahead of boys in their growth spurt and are therefore taller than most boys between the ages of 10 and 14.

that lead to the development of secondary sex characteristics, such as the growth of pubic hair, deepening of the voice and growth of facial hair in men, and growth of breasts in women (**Figure 9.13**). Do you recall how changes in height and weight, breast development and menstruation for girls, and a deepening voice and beard growth for boys were such important milestones for you and your adolescent peers?

Puberty has another physical effect that is far less dramatic than changes in secondary sex characteristics and the growth spurt but is still very interesting. Have you ever wondered why teenagers seem to sleep so much? Researchers have found that puberty is triggered by changes in the brain, including the release of certain hormones, which occurs only during periods of *deep sleep* (D'Ambrosio & Redline, 2014; Shaw et al., 2012). This finding suggests that getting adequate, deep (slow-wave) sleep (see Chapter 5) during adolescence is an essential part of activating the reproductive system. Can you see why the increasing number of sleep problems in adolescents is a cause for concern and why parents should actually be encouraging "over-sleeping" in their teenagers?

**The Teenage Brain** As you recall, the brain and other parts of the nervous system grow faster than any other part of the body during both prenatal development and the first two years of life. In contrast to the rapid synaptic growth experienced in the earlier years, the adolescent's brain actively destroys (prunes) unneeded connections. Although it may seem counterintuitive, this pruning actually improves brain functioning by making the remaining connections between neurons more efficient. Perhaps more surprising, full maturity of the frontal lobes is not accomplished until the mid-20s (**Figure 9.14**). Do you recall your teenage years as a time of exaggerated self-consciousness, feelings of special uniqueness, and risky behaviors? Psychologists now believe these effects may be largely due to your less-than-fully-developed frontal lobes (Casey et al., 2014; Fuhrmann et al., 2015; Pokhrel et al., 2013)!

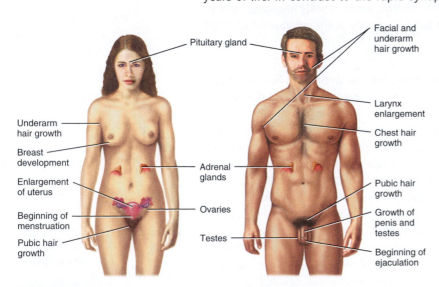

**FIGURE 9.13 Secondary sex characteristics** Complex physical changes in puberty primarily result from hormones secreted from the ovaries and testes, the pituitary gland in the brain, and the adrenal glands near the kidneys.

**FIGURE 9.14 Changes in the brain**

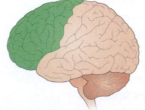

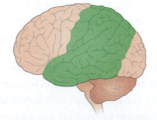

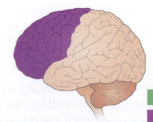

Growth

Pruning

**a. Risky behaviors** Recall from Chapter 2 that the frontal lobes are responsible for judgment, impulse control, and planning ahead, which may explain this type of risky teenage behavior.

**b. Frontal lobe changes** During early childhood (ages 3–6), the frontal lobes experience a significant increase in the connections between neurons, which helps explain a child's rapid cognitive growth.

**c. Temporal and parietal lobe changes** This rapid synaptic growth shifts to the temporal and parietal lobes during the ages of 7 to 15, which corresponds to notable increases in language and motor skills.

**d. Synaptic pruning** During ages 16–20, synaptic pruning of unused connections in the frontal lobes leads to increased brain efficiency, but full frontal lobe maturity only occurs in the mid-20s.

# Adulthood

When does adulthood begin? In most Western cultures, children are typically considered adults once they graduate from high school or college or get their first stable job and become self-sufficient. For greater precision and research purposes, scientists commonly divide adulthood into at least three periods: emerging/young adulthood (ages 20–45), middle adulthood (ages 45–60), and late adulthood (ages 60 to death).

**Emerging/Young Adulthood**  Although young adulthood is generally considered to begin at age 20, many developmental psychologists have added a new term, **emerging adulthood**, to refer to the time from the end of adolescence through the first few years of the young-adult stage, approximately ages 18–25. This stage, which is found primarily in modern cultures, is characterized by the search for a stable job, self-sufficiency, and/or marriage and parenthood, along with five distinguishing features (Arnett, 2000, 2015; Munsey, 2006; Newman & Newman, 2015):

1. *Identity exploration*—young people decide who they are and what they want out of life.
2. *Instability*—a time marked by multiple changes in residence and relationships.
3. *Self-focus*—freed from social obligations and commitments to others, young people at this stage are focused on what they want and need before constraints of marriage, children, and career.
4. *Feeling in-between*—although taking responsibility for themselves, they still feel in the middle between adolescence and adulthood.
5. *Age of possibilities*—a time of optimism and belief that their lives will be better than those of their parents.

During emerging adulthood, some individuals experience modest increases in height and muscular development, and most of us find this to be a time of maximum strength, sharp senses, and overall stamina. However, a decline in strength and speed becomes noticeable in the 30s, and our hearing starts to decline as early as our late teens.

> **Emerging adulthood**  The age period from approximately 18–25 in which individuals in modern cultures have left the dependency of childhood but not yet assumed adult responsibilities.

**Middle Adulthood**  Many physical changes during young adulthood happen so slowly that most people don't notice them until they enter their late 30s or early 40s. For example, around the age of 40, we first experience difficulty in seeing things close up and after dark, thinning and graying of our hair, wrinkling of our skin, and gradual loss in height coupled with weight gain (Landsberg et al., 2013; Saxon et al., 2014).

For women ages 45–55, *menopause*, the cessation of the menstrual cycle, is the second major life milestone in physical development. The decreased production of estrogen (the dominant female hormone) produces certain physical changes, including decreases in some types of cognitive and memory skills (Doty et al., 2015; Hussain et al., 2014; Pines, 2014). However, the popular belief that menopause (or "the change of life") causes serious psychological mood swings is not supported by current research. In fact, younger women are more likely to report irritability and mood swings, whereas women at midlife generally report positive reactions to aging and the end of the menstrual cycle. They're also less likely to have negative experiences such as headaches (Sievert et al., 2007; Sugar et al., 2014).

In contrast to women, men experience a more gradual decline in hormone levels, and most men can father children until their 70s or 80s. Physical changes such as unexpected weight gain, decline in sexual responsiveness, loss of muscle strength, and graying or loss of hair may lead some men to feel depressed and to question their life progress. They often see these alterations as a biological signal of aging and mortality. Such physical and psychological changes in men are generally referred to as the *male climacteric* (or *andropause*). However, the popular belief that almost all men go through a deeply disruptive midlife crisis, experiencing serious dissatisfaction with their work and personal relationships, is largely a myth.

**Late Adulthood**  After middle age, most physical changes in development are gradual and occur in the heart and arteries and in the sensory receptors. Cardiac output (the volume of blood pumped by the heart each minute) decreases, whereas blood pressure increases due to the thickening and stiffening of arterial walls. Visual acuity and depth perception decline, hearing acuity lessens (especially for high-frequency sounds), smell sensitivity decreases, and some decline in cognitive and memory skills occurs (Dupuis et al., 2015; Fletcher & Rapp, 2013; Newman & Newman, 2015).

Why do we go through so many physical changes? What causes us to age and die? Setting aside aging and deaths resulting from disease, abuse, or neglect, known as *secondary aging*, let's focus on *primary aging* (gradual, inevitable age-related changes in physical and mental processes).

According to *cellular-clock theory*, primary aging is genetically controlled. Once the ovum is fertilized, the program for aging and death is set and begins to run. Researcher Leonard Hayflick (1965, 1996) found that human cells seem to have a built-in life span. After about 100 doublings of laboratory-cultured cells, they cease to divide. Based on this limited number of cell divisions, Hayflick suggests that we humans have a maximum life span of about 120 years—we reach the *Hayflick limit*. Why? One answer may be that small structures on the tips of our chromosomes, called *telomeres*, shorten each time a cell divides. After about 100 replications, the telomeres are too short and the cells can no longer divide (Broer et al., 2013; Hayashi et al., 2015; Rode et al., 2015).

The second major explanation of primary aging is *wear-and-tear theory*. Like any machine, repeated use and abuse of our organs and cell tissues cause our human bodies to simply wear out over time.

**The Brain in Late Adulthood**   What about changes in the brain in later years? The public and most researchers long believed aging was inevitably accompanied by declining cognitive abilities and widespread death of neurons in the brain. Although this decline does happen with degenerative disorders like Alzheimer's disease (AD), it is no longer believed to be an inevitable part of normal aging (Hillier & Barrow, 2011; Whitbourne & Whitbourne, 2014). Furthermore, age-related cognitive problems are not on a continuum with AD. That is, normal forgetfulness does not mean that serious dementia is around the corner.

Aging does seem to take its toll on the *speed* of information processing (Chapter 7). Decreased speed of processing may reflect problems with *encoding* (putting information into long-term storage) and *retrieval* (getting information out of storage). If memory is like a filing system, older people may have more filing cabinets, and it may take them longer to initially file and later retrieve information.

Although mental speed declines with age, general mental abilities are largely unaffected (Carey, 2014; Ramscar et al., 2014; Whitbourne & Whitbourne, 2014). Have you noticed that older returning students often do as well as or better than their younger counterparts in college classes? Their superior performance is likely due to their generally greater academic motivation, but it also reflects the importance of prior knowledge. Cognitive psychologists have clearly demonstrated that the more people know, the easier it is for them to lay down new memories (Goldstein, 2014; Matlin, 2016). Older students, for instance, generally find this chapter on development easier to master than younger students. Their interactions with children and greater accumulated knowledge about life changes create a framework on which to hang new information.

In short, the more you know, the more you can learn. Furthermore, gaining more education and having an intellectually challenging life may help you stay mentally sharp in your later years—another reason for going to college and engaging in life-long learning (Branco et al., 2014; Huang & Zhou, 2013; Sobral et al., 2015).

**Ageism**   Unfortunately, television, magazines, movies, and advertisements generally portray aging as a time of balding and graying hair, sagging body parts, poor vision, hearing loss, and, of course, no sex life. Can you see how our personal fears of aging and death, combined with these negative media portrayals, contribute to our society's widespread **ageism**—prejudice and discrimination based on physical age?

**Ageism**   A form of prejudice or discrimination based on physical age; similar to racism and sexism in its negative stereotypes.

Ageism is also a big factor in job discrimination. According to the latest data from the U.S. Bureau of Labor Statistics, almost 20% of Americans over the age of 65 are now working and delaying retirement—some out of desire but most because they need the money (Steverman, 2016). Although age discrimination in employment is illegal in the United States, two-thirds of older job seekers report experiencing it, and those who face such discrimination have significantly lower physical and emotional health, as well as greater declines in health, than those who do not (Applewhite, 2016; Sutin et al., 2015). But the news about ageism and your professional career isn't all bad. Check out the following.

### ❖ Psychology and Your Professional Success  |  Does Ageism Matter?

First the bad news: Did you know that many potential employers assume that older applicants are more likely to be burned out, absent due to illness, and reluctant to travel, as well as less creative and productive? If you're a young millennial (aged 18–34), you may not realize that many people, including potential employers, also criticize your group for "needing to have your hands held," "acting entitled," and having no "work ethic" (Applewhite, 2016; Reade, 2015).

Now for some good news: These and other stereotypes about older workers and millennials are seldom based on facts. For example, a recent large-scale analysis of scientific careers revealed that age is truly just a number! In this study, the researchers found that scientific success comes from a combination of elements, including intelligence, luck, personality, and a new element they called "Q" (Sinatra et al., 2016). This Q factor includes personal skills and strengths, as well as high levels of drive, motivation, openness to new ideas, and ability to work well with others (Carey, 2016). (As you can see, many of these same traits reflect our text's two central themes, a *growth mindset* and *grit*—composed of passion and perseverance in pursuit of long-term goals.)

And some modestly good news comes from recent changes in those previously mentioned negative media and advertising portrayals of older people. Marketing experts have noted the large number of aging baby boomers and are now producing a few ads with a more positive and accurate portrayal of aging as a time of vigor, interest, and productivity. And, as noted in this chapter and in Chapter 2, our brains are constantly changing, and our cognitive abilities and overall achievements can grow and improve throughout our life span (see **Figure 9.15**).

Tim Sloan/Getty Images    Mark Wilson/Getty Images

**FIGURE 9.15**  **Grit in action!**  As you've seen throughout this text, thanks to grit (passion and perseverance) we can all grow and improve throughout our life span, as demonstrated by the achievements of people like Justices Ruth Bader Ginsburg and Antonin Scalia of the U.S. Supreme Court. Justice Scalia served from 1986 until his death in 2016, just shy of his 80th birthday. For decades Justice Scalia was the leading conservative voice on the Court. In her younger years, Justice Ginsburg worked tirelessly as a staunch courtroom advocate. Now in her 80s, she serves as a leading liberal voice on the Supreme Court.

Fun fact: Despite their diametrically opposed political and legal philosophies, Justice Scalia and Justice Ginsburg had a great deal of mutual respect for one another and were known to be very close friends.

© Billy R. Ray/Wiley

### Retrieval Practice 9.2  |  Physical Development

Completing this self-test and the connections section, and then checking your answers by clicking on the answer button or by looking in Appendix B, will provide immediate feedback and helpful practice for exams.

#### Self-Test

1. Define *behavioral genetics*.

2. Teratogens are _____.
   a. maternal defects that cause damage during neonatal development.
   b. factors that cause damage during prenatal development.
   c. popular children's toys that studies have shown cause damage during early childhood development.
   d. environmental diseases that cause damage during early childhood development.

3. _____ is the first stage of prenatal development, which begins with conception and ends with implantation in the uterus (the first two weeks).
   a. The embryonic period
   b. The germinal period
   c. The critical period
   d. None of these options

4. The clearest and most physical sign of puberty is the_____, characterized by rapid increases in height, weight, and skeletal growth.
   a. menses               b. spermarche
   c. growth spurt         d. age of fertility

5. Some employers are reluctant to hire older workers (50 years of age and older) because of a generalized belief that they are sickly and will take too much time off. This is an example of _____.
   a. discrimination       b. prejudice
   c. ageism               d. all of these options

#### Connections—Chapter to Chapter

Answering the following question will help you "look back and look ahead" to see the important connections among the subfields of psychology and chapters within this text.

In this chapter, you discovered that the prefrontal cortex of the adolescent's brain is one of the later areas to develop. Review what you learned in Chapter 2 (Neuroscience and Biological Foundations) about the higher-order functions of the frontal lobes. Provide an example of adolescent behavior that might be explained by the slower development of this area of the brain.

## 9.3 | Cognitive Development

### LEARNING OBJECTIVES

**Retrieval Practice** While reading the upcoming sections, respond to each Learning Objective in your own words.

**Review the basic theories of cognitive development and how cognition changes over the life span.**

• **Explain** the roles of schemas, assimilation, and accommodation in cognitive development.

• **Describe** the major characteristics of Piaget's four stages of cognitive development.

• **Compare** Piaget's theory of cognitive development to Vygotsky's.

Just as a child's body and physical abilities change, his or her way of knowing and perceiving the world also grows and changes. Jean Piaget [pee-ah-ZHAY] provided some of the first great demonstrations of how children develop thinking and reasoning abilities (Piaget, 1952). He showed that an infant begins at a cognitively "primitive" level and that intellectual growth progresses in distinct stages, motivated by an innate need to know.

To appreciate Piaget's contributions, we need to consider three major concepts: schemas, assimilation, and accommodation. **Schemas** are the most basic units of intellect. They act as patterns that organize our interactions with the environment, like an architect's drawings or a builder's blueprints. For most of us, a common, shared schema for a car would likely be "a moving object with wheels and seats for passengers." However, we also develop unique schemas based on differing life experiences (see the **Try This Yourself**).

In the first few weeks of life, the infant apparently has several *schemas* based on innate reflexes such as sucking and grasping. These schemas are primarily motor activities and may be little more than stimulus-and-response mechanisms—the nipple is presented, and the baby sucks. Soon, other schemas emerge. The infant develops a more detailed schema for eating solid food, a different schema for the concepts of "mother" and "father," and so on.

**Schema** A Piagetian term for a cognitive framework, or "blueprint," formed through interaction with an object or event.

### Try This Yourself

#### Do You Have an Artistic Schema?

Study the "impossible figure" to the right, and then try drawing this figure without tracing it. Students with artistic training generally find it relatively easy to reproduce, whereas the rest of us find it very hard or "impossible." This is because we lack the necessary artistic schema and cannot assimilate what we see. With practice and training, we could accommodate the new information and easily draw the figure.

**Assimilation** In Piaget's theory, the incorporation (assimilation) of new information into existing schemas.

**Accommodation** According to Piaget, the process of adjusting (accommodating) existing schemas to incorporate new information.

*Assimilation* and *accommodation* are the two major processes by which schemas grow and change over time. **Assimilation** is the process of absorbing new information into existing schemas. For instance, infants use their sucking schema not only in sucking nipples, but also in sucking blankets and fingers. In **accommodation**, existing ideas are modified to fit new information. Accommodation generally occurs when new information or stimuli cannot be assimilated. New schemas are developed or old schemas are changed to better fit with the new information. An infant's first attempt to eat solid food with a spoon is a good example of accommodation (**Figure 9.16**).

# Stages of Cognitive Development

According to Piaget, all children go through approximately the same four stages of cognitive development, regardless of the culture in which they live (**Step-by-Step Diagram 9.2**). Piaget also believed that none of these stages can be skipped because skills acquired at earlier stages are essential to mastery at later stages (Berger, 2015).

Courtesy of Terese Jacob

**FIGURE 9.16**  **Accommodation** When feeding from a spoon, infants initially try to suck on the spoon—an example of assimilation. However, when that doesn't work, they learn to shape their lips around the spoon and pull the food into their mouths—an example of accommodation.

| STEP-BY-STEP DIAGRAM 9.2 | Piaget's Four Stages of Cognitive Development |
| --- | --- |

> **STOP!**  This Step-by-Step Diagram contains essential information NOT found elsewhere in the text, which is likely to appear on quizzes and exams. Be sure to study it CAREFULLY!

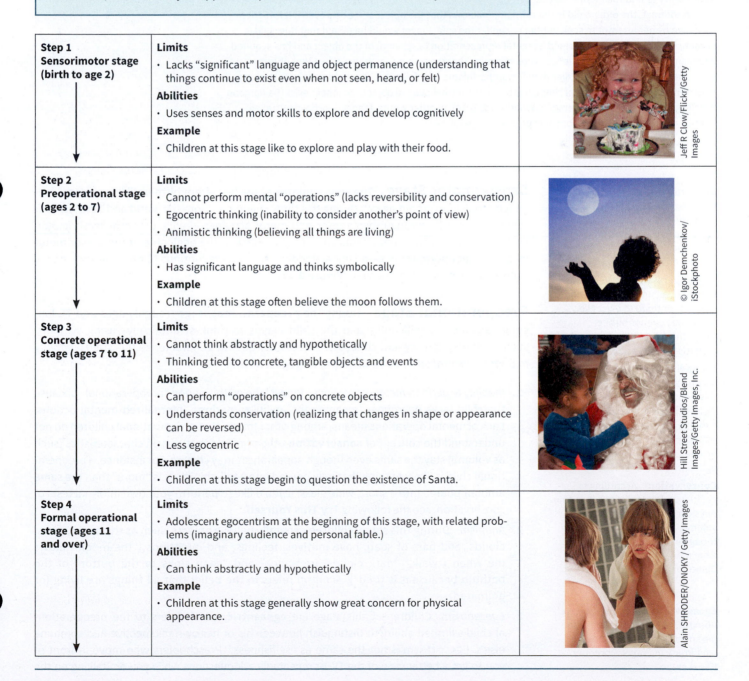

| | | |
| --- | --- | --- |
| **Step 1**<br>**Sensorimotor stage (birth to age 2)** | **Limits**<br>• Lacks "significant" language and object permanence (understanding that things continue to exist even when not seen, heard, or felt)<br>**Abilities**<br>• Uses senses and motor skills to explore and develop cognitively<br>**Example**<br>• Children at this stage like to explore and play with their food. | Jeff R Clow/Flickr/Getty Images |
| **Step 2**<br>**Preoperational stage (ages 2 to 7)** | **Limits**<br>• Cannot perform mental "operations" (lacks reversibility and conservation)<br>• Egocentric thinking (inability to consider another's point of view)<br>• Animistic thinking (believing all things are living)<br>**Abilities**<br>• Has significant language and thinks symbolically<br>**Example**<br>• Children at this stage often believe the moon follows them. | © Igor Demchenkov/iStockphoto |
| **Step 3**<br>**Concrete operational stage (ages 7 to 11)** | **Limits**<br>• Cannot think abstractly and hypothetically<br>• Thinking tied to concrete, tangible objects and events<br>**Abilities**<br>• Can perform "operations" on concrete objects<br>• Understands conservation (realizing that changes in shape or appearance can be reversed)<br>• Less egocentric<br>**Example**<br>• Children at this stage begin to question the existence of Santa. | Hill Street Studios/Blend Images/Getty Images, Inc. |
| **Step 4**<br>**Formal operational stage (ages 11 and over)** | **Limits**<br>• Adolescent egocentrism at the beginning of this stage, with related problems (imaginary audience and personal fable.)<br>**Abilities**<br>• Can think abstractly and hypothetically<br>**Example**<br>• Children at this stage generally show great concern for physical appearance. | Alain SHRODER/ONOKY / Getty Images |

Doug Goodman/Photo Researchers/Getty Images    Doug Goodman/Photo Researchers/Getty Images    Heleen Sitter/The Image Bank/Getty Images

**FIGURE 9.17** **Object permanence** Piaget believed that infants younger than about 8 months of age lack object permanence. For instance, in the Piagetian view, the child in the first two photos believes the toy no longer exists once it is blocked from sight. This is supposedly shown by the fact that the child does not try to find the hidden object.

In contrast, the older child in the third photo knows that the object still exists even if it is hidden—as shown by her attempt to seek out the toy under the sofa. Piaget would have said that this child is demonstrating that she has formed a mental representation (a schema) of the object and has acquired a recognition of object permanence. Note, however, that modern researchers believe that object permanence appears much earlier than 8 months. Infants may fail to look for hidden objects because they don't know how to look for them, not because they believe the objects no longer exist (Baillargeon & DeVos, 1991; Berger, 2015; Gerson & Woodward, 2014). In other words, Piaget may have mistaken infants' motor incompetence for conceptual incompetence.

**Sensorimotor stage** Piaget's first stage of cognitive development (birth to approximately age 2), in which schemas are developed through sensory and motor activities.

**Object permanence** According to Piaget, an understanding that objects continue to exist even when they cannot be seen, heard, or touched directly; a hallmark of Piaget's preoperational stage.

**Preoperational stage** Piaget's second stage of cognitive development (roughly ages 2 to 7); it is characterized by significant language, but the child lacks operations (reversible mental processes), and thinking is egocentric and animistic.

**Conservation** According to Piaget, the understanding that certain physical characteristics (such as volume) remain unchanged, even though appearances may change; a hallmark of Piaget's concrete operational stage.

**Egocentrism** In cognitive development, the inability to take the perspective of another person; a hallmark of Piaget's preoperational stage.

## Sensorimotor Stage

The **sensorimotor stage** lasts from birth until "significant" language acquisition (about age 2). During this time, children explore the world and develop their schemas primarily through their senses and motor activities—hence the term *sensorimotor*. One important concept that infants are thought to lack at the beginning of the sensorimotor stage is **object permanence**—an understanding that objects continue to exist even when they cannot be seen, heard, or touched (**Figure 9.17**).

## Preoperational Stage

During the **preoperational stage** (roughly ages 2 to 7), language advances significantly, and the child begins to think symbolically—using symbols, such as words, to represent concepts. Three other qualities characterize this stage: *inability to perform mental operations, animism,* and *egocentrism*.

1. *Inability to perform mental operations.* Piaget labeled this period "preoperational" because the child lacks *operations,* meaning the ability to perform internalized mental actions. Lack of mental operations means, among other things, that preoperational children do not understand the concept of **conservation**—the principle that certain characteristics (such as volume) stay the same even though appearances may change. For instance, a preoperational child is likely to think that milk poured into a tall, thin glass is "more" than the same amount poured into a short, wide glass. If you'd like to perform your own informal tests of conservation, see the following **Try This Yourself**.

2. *Animism.* During this stage, children generally believe objects, such as the moon, trees, clouds, and bars of soap, have motives, feelings, and intentions ("the moon follows me when I walk," "dark clouds are angry," and "soap sinks to the bottom of the bathtub because it is tired"). *Animism* refers to the belief that all things are living (or animated).

3. *Egocentrism.* Children at this stage are **egocentric**, which refers to the preoperational child's limited ability to distinguish between his or her own perspective and someone else's. Egocentrism is not the same as "selfishness." Preschoolers who move in front of you to get a better view of the TV, or repeatedly ask questions while you are talking on the

## Try This Yourself

### Putting Piaget to the Test

If you have access to children in the preoperational or concrete operational stages, try some of the following experiments, which researchers use to test Piaget's various forms of conservation. The equipment is easily obtained, and you will find their responses fascinating. Keep in mind that this should be done as a game. The child should not feel that he or she is failing a test or making a mistake.

| Type of conservation task (average age at which concept is fully grasped) | Your task as experimenter . . . | Child is asked . . . |
|---|---|---|
| **Length** (ages 6–7) | **Step 1** Center two sticks of equal length. Child agrees that they are of equal length. **Step 2** In full view of the child, move one stick sideways. | **Step 3** "Which stick is longer?" Preoperational child will say that one of the sticks is longer. Child in concrete stage will say that they are both the same length. |
| **Substance amount** (ages 6–7) | **Step 1** Center two identical clay balls. Child acknowledges that the two have equal amounts of clay. **Step 2** While the child is watching, flatten one ball. | **Step 3** "Do the two pieces have the same amount of clay?" Preoperational child will say that the flat piece has more clay. Child in concrete stage will say that the two pieces have the same amount of clay. |
| **Liquid volume** (ages 7–8) | **Step 1** Present two identical glasses with liquid at the same level. Child agrees that liquid is at the same height in both glasses. **Step 2** In full view of the child, pour the liquid from one of the short, wide glasses into the tall, thin one. | **Step 3** "Do the two glasses have the same amount of liquid?" Preoperational child will say that the tall, thin glass has more liquid. Child in concrete stage will say that the two glasses have the same amount of liquid. |
| **Area** (ages 8–10) | **Step 1** Center two identical pieces of cardboard with wooden blocks placed on them in identical positions. Child acknowledges that the same amount of space is left open on each piece of cardboard. **Step 2** While the child is watching, scatter the blocks on one piece of the cardboard. | **Step 3** "Do the two pieces of cardboard have the same amount of open space?" Preoperational child will say that the cardboard with scattered blocks has less open space. Child in concrete stage will say that both pieces have the same amount of open space. |

### Test Your Critical Thinking

1. Based on their responses, are the children you tested in the preoperational or concrete stage?
2. If you repeat the same tests with each child, do their answers change? Why or why not?

telephone, are not being selfish. They are demonstrating their natural limits and egocentric thought processes. Children in this stage naively assume that others see, hear, feel, and think exactly as they do. Consider the following telephone conversation between a 3-year-old, who is at home, and her mother, who is at work:

MOTHER: Emma, is that you?

EMMA: (Nods silently.)

MOTHER: Emma, is Daddy there? May I speak to him?

EMMA: (Twice nods silently.)

Egocentric preoperational children fail to understand that the phone caller cannot see their nodding heads. Charming as this is, preoperational children's egocentrism also sometimes leads them to believe their "bad thoughts" caused their sibling or parent to get sick or that their misbehavior caused their parents' marital problems. Because they think the world centers on them, they often cannot separate reality from what goes on inside their own heads.

**Concrete operational stage**
Piaget's third stage of cognitive development (roughly ages 7 to 11), in which the child can think logically about concrete, tangible objects and events.

### Concrete Operational Stage
At approximately age 7, children enter the **concrete operational stage**. During this time, many important thinking skills emerge. However, as the name implies, thinking tends to be limited to *concrete*, tangible objects and events. Youngsters in this stage are less egocentric in their thinking than preoperational children and become capable of true logical thought. As most parents know, children now stop believing in Santa Claus because they logically conclude that one man can't deliver presents to everyone in one night.

Because they are capable of thinking logically, concrete operational children recognize that certain physical attributes remain unchanged although the outward appearance is altered. This understanding of conservation is a hallmark of children in the concrete stage.

**Formal operational stage**
Piaget's fourth stage of cognitive development (around age 11 and beyond), characterized by abstract and hypothetical thinking.

### Formal Operational Stage
The final period in Piaget's theory, the **formal operational stage**, typically begins around age 11. In this stage, children begin to apply their operations to abstract concepts in addition to concrete objects. They become capable of hypothetical thinking ("What if?"), which allows systematic formulation and testing of concepts. Before filling out applications for part-time jobs, adolescents may think about possible conflicts with school and friends, the number of hours they want to work, and the kind of work for which they are qualified. Formal operational thinking also allows the adolescent to construct a well-reasoned argument based on hypothetical concepts and logical processes. Consider the following argument:

1. If you hit a glass with a feather, the glass will break.
2. You hit the glass with a feather.

What is the logical conclusion? The correct answer, "The glass will break," is contrary to fact and direct experience. Therefore, the child in the concrete operational stage would have difficulty with this task, whereas the formal operational thinker understands that this problem is about abstractions that need not correspond to the real world.

Along with the benefits of this cognitive style come several problems. Adolescents in the early stages of the formal operational period demonstrate a type of egocentrism different from that of the preoperational child (see **Figure 9.18** and the following **Try This Yourself**). Adolescents certainly recognize that others have unique thoughts and perspectives. However, they may fail to differentiate between what they are thinking and what others are thinking. If they change hairstyles or fail to make the sports team, they may be overly concerned about how others will react. Instead of considering that everyone is equally wrapped up in his or her own appearance, concerns, and plans, they tend to believe that they are the center of others' thoughts and attentions. David Elkind (1967, 2007) referred to this as the *imaginary audience*.

In addition to believing they are special and unique and that others are always watching and evaluating them (the imaginary audience), adolescents also tend to believe they are invulnerable and that life's normal problems, difficulties, and dangers do not apply to them. Sadly, these feelings of special uniqueness and invulnerability, known as the *personal fable,* are associated with several forms of risk taking, such as engaging in sexual intercourse without protection, driving dangerously, indoor tanning, and experimenting with drugs (Banerjee et al., 2015; Landicho et al., 2014). Adolescents apparently recognize the dangers of

antoniodiaz/Shutterstock

**FIGURE 9.18 Adolescent egocentrism or narcissism?** Piaget describes most children and adolescents as being egocentric, and egocentrism is a major characteristic of narcissism, which is defined as having an excessive interest in or admiration of oneself. Consider the growing popularity of taking and posting self-portraits ("selfies") on social media. Have you ever wondered if this practice might increase narcissism? Research on this topic has found that narcissistic individuals do in fact take and post more "selfies" and that these actions have a self-reinforcing effect that maintains the narcissist's positive self-views (Halpern et al., 2016).

## Try This Yourself

### Reliving Your Own Adolescent Egocentrism

Do these descriptions of the imaginary audience and personal fable ring true for you? If so, do you now understand how these beliefs might help explain some of the problems and challenges you faced in adolescence? As implied in this photo, many teens have difficulty accepting comfort and support from parents due to their belief that no one has ever felt or experienced what they have. One young woman remembered being very upset in middle school when her mother tried to comfort her over the loss of an important relationship. "I felt like she couldn't possibly know how it felt—no one could. I couldn't believe that anyone had ever suffered like this or that things would ever get better." Best advice for parents? Have patience and be comforting and reassuring. Teenagers whose parents use harsh verbal discipline (yelling or making serious threats) show more symptoms of depression and more behavior problems (lying, trouble in school, fighting with peers) (Wang & Kenny, 2014).

risky activities, but they believe the rules and statistics just don't apply to them. Recall from the discussion earlier that psychologists now believe these effects may be largely due to the teen's less-than-fully-developed frontal lobes (Casey et al., 2014; Pokhrel et al., 2013).

In sum, the imaginary audience apparently results from an inability to differentiate the self from others, whereas the personal fable may be a product of differentiating too much. Thankfully, these two forms of adolescent egocentrism tend to decrease during later stages of the formal operational period.

## Evaluating Piaget: Vygotsky and Theory of Mind

As influential as Piaget's account of cognitive development has been, there are two major criticisms. First, research shows that Piaget may have underestimated young children's cognitive development. As we discussed earlier, infants seem to develop concepts like object permanence much earlier than Piaget suggested. As you recall, Piaget also believed that infancy and early childhood were a time of extreme egocentrism, in which children have little or no understanding of the perspective of others. However, research finds that empathy develops at a relatively young age (**Figure 9.19**). Even newborn babies tend to cry in response to the cry of another baby (Diego & Jones, 2007; Geangu et al., 2010). And, preschoolers will adapt their speech by using shorter, simpler expressions when talking to 2-year-olds than when talking with adults.

Second, Piaget's model, like other stage theories, has been criticized for not sufficiently taking into account genetic and cultural differences (Newman & Newman, 2015; Shweder, 2011). During Piaget's time, the genetic influences on cognitive abilities were poorly understood, but as in the case of epigenetics, there has been a rapid explosion of information in this field in the last few years. In addition, formal education and specific cultural experiences can significantly affect cognitive development. Consider the following example from a researcher attempting to test the formal operational skills of a farmer in Liberia (Scribner, 1977):

> RESEARCHER: All Kpelle men are rice farmers. Mr. Smith is not a rice farmer. Is he a Kpelle man?
> KPELLE FARMER: I don't know the man. I have not laid eyes on the man myself.

Instead of reasoning in the "logical" way of Piaget's formal operational stage, the Kpelle farmer reasoned according to his specific cultural and educational training, which apparently emphasized personal knowledge. Not

**FIGURE 9.19**  **Are preoperational children always egocentric?**  Some toddlers and preschoolers clearly demonstrate empathy for other people. How does this ability to take another's perspective contradict Piaget's beliefs about egocentrism in very young children?

Upper limit
(tasks beyond
reach at present)

Zone of proximal
development (ZPD)
(tasks achievable
with guidance)

Lower limit
(tasks achieved
without help)

omgimages/iStockphoto

**FIGURE 9.20**  **Vygotsky's zone of proximal development (ZPD)**   Have you heard of "instructional scaffolding"? This term refers to providing support during the learning process that is tailored to the needs of the student. Vygotsky was one of the first to apply the general idea of scaffolding to early cognitive development. He proposed that the most effective teaching focuses on tasks between those a learner can do without help (the lower limit) and those he or she cannot do even with help (the upper limit). In this middle, *zone of proximal development (ZPD)*, tasks and skills can be "stretched" to higher levels with the guidance and encouragement of a more knowledgeable person.

**Zone of proximal development (ZPD)**   Vygotsky's concept of the difference between what children can accomplish on their own and what they can accomplish with the help of others who are more competent.

**Theory of mind (ToM)**   The understanding that other people don't have the same thoughts and feelings that we do, which generally develops during early childhood.

knowing Mr. Smith, the Kpelle farmer did not feel qualified to comment on him. Thus, Piaget's theory may have underestimated the effect of culture on a person's cognitive functioning.

Before going on, let's consider two prominent alternative views on cognitive development. In contrast to Piaget's focus on internal schemas, Russian psychologist Lev Vygotsky emphasized the sociocultural influences on a child's cognitive development (Vygotsky, 1962). According to Vygotsky, children construct knowledge through their culture, language, and collaborative social interactions with more experienced thinkers (Mahn & John-Steiner, 2013; Scott, 2015; Yasnitsky, 2015). Unlike Piaget, Vygotsky also believed that adults play an essential instructor role in development and that this instruction is particularly helpful when it falls within a child's **zone of proximal development (ZPD)**, described in **Figure 9.20**.

In addition to Vgotsky's emphasis on the sociocultural influences in cognitive development, researchers have questioned why children in the preoperational stage cannot take another's point of view and how they eventually learn to do so. In response to these inquiries, an entire area of research has emerged regarding how young children think about their own minds and the minds of others. According to this research, children become less egocentric when they begin to understand that other people don't have the same thoughts and feelings that they do—an achievement called **theory of mind (ToM)** (Kuhnert et al., 2017; Mar et al., 2010; Weimer et al., 2017).

One of the first experiments on ToM was conducted with children between the ages of 3 and 9 (Wimmer & Perner, 1983). The children first listen to a story about Maxi and how his mother moves some chocolate from a blue cupboard to a green one (see **Figure 9.21**). When asked where Maxi will look for the chocolate, the children not only have to remember that the chocolate was moved but also, more importantly, must recognize that Maxi has no way of knowing that his mom moved the chocolate, since he was playing outside during the move. Therefore, Maxi will assume the chocolate is still in the blue cupboard. Interestingly, 3- and 4-year-olds often fail such tests, pointing to the actual position of the chocolate versus where Maxi will think it is. They apparently are unable to understand that although they know where the chocolate is, Maxi doesn't. On the other hand, most 6-year-olds succeed.

This type of experimentation supports Piaget's notion that young preoperational children are highly egocentric. But it goes on to explain that most children eventually do develop the understanding that their thoughts and feelings differ from those of others through a combination of maturation and social experiences. Can you see how the apparently simple task in Figure 9.21 actually requires a high level of thought? And why children who have difficulty in developing their ToM will find it difficult to engage in pretend play or understand why people do and say the things they do? Some researchers believe the lack of ToM also helps explain the problems with communication and social interactions typical of children with autism spectrum disorder (ASD) and attention-deficit/hyperactivity disorder (ADHD)—two developmental disorders discussed in Chapter 10 (Cantio et al., 2016; Kuijper et al., 2017; Peterson et al., 2012).

Despite these alternative views and the direct criticisms of Piaget's theory, his contributions to psychology are enormous. As one scholar put it, "assessing the impact of Piaget on developmental psychology is like assessing the impact of Shakespeare on English literature or Aristotle on philosophy—impossible" (Beilin, 1992, p. 191).

**FIGURE 9.21** **Theory of mind**    Each child research participant is told a story about a boy named Maxi who watches while his mother places some chocolate she plans to use to make a cake in a blue cupboard (a). Maxi then goes out to play (b), and while he is outside his mother makes the cake and puts the leftover chocolate in a green cupboard (c). Then Maxi comes back in, wanting some chocolate (d). At this point, the researcher asks the child listening to the story not where the chocolate is, but which cupboard Maxi will look in.

a.

b.

c.

d.

## Retrieval Practice 9.3 | Cognitive Development

Completing this self-test and the connections section, and then checking your answers by clicking on the answer button or by looking in Appendix B, will provide immediate feedback and helpful practice for exams.

### Self-Test

1. _____ was one of the first scientists to demonstrate that a child's intellect is fundamentally different from that of an adult.

   **a.** Baumrind      **b.** Beck
   **c.** Piaget        **d.** Elkind

2. Briefly explain how assimilation and accommodation differ.

3. A child who believes that trees have feelings is probably in the _____ stage of development.

   **a.** sensorimotor    **b.** preoperational
   **c.** egocentric      **d.** concrete operational

4. The ability to think abstractly and hypothetically occurs in Piaget's _____ stage.

   **a.** egocentric         **b.** postoperational
   **c.** formal operational  **d.** concrete operational

5. In Vygotsky's theory of cognitive development, the area between what children can accomplish on their own and what they can accomplish with the help of others who are more competent is called the _____.

   **a.** concrete operational area    **b.** postoperational zone
   **c.** formal operational limits     **d.** zone of proximal development

### Connections—Chapter to Chapter

Answering the following question will help you "look back and look ahead" to see the important connections among the subfields of psychology and chapters within this text.

In Chapter 2 (Neuroscience and Biological Foundations), we discussed the functions of the lobes and structures of the brain. Name the brain lobes and/or structures most involved in Piaget's four stages of cognitive development—sensorimotor, preoperational, concrete operational, and formal operational.

# Social-Emotional Development

**LEARNING OBJECTIVES**

**Retrieval Practice**   While reading the upcoming sections, respond to each Learning Objective in your own words.

**Summarize how social-emotional factors affect development across the life span.**

- **Review** attachment and its contributions across the life span.
- **Describe** the four main parenting styles.

Along with physical and cognitive development, developmental psychologists also study the way social and emotional factors affect development over the life span. In this section, we focus on *attachment* and *parenting styles*.

## Attachment

**Attachment**   A strong emotional bond with special others that endures over time.

An infant arrives in the world with a multitude of behaviors that encourage a strong bond of **attachment** with primary caregivers. Returning to our earlier discussion of the nature–nurture controversy, researchers who advocate the "nature" position suggest that newborn infants are biologically equipped with verbal and nonverbal behaviors (such as crying, clinging, and smiling) and imprinting ("following") behaviors (such as crawling and walking after the caregiver) that elicit instinctive nurturing responses from the caregiver (Bowlby, 1969, 1989, 2000).

Studies have found numerous benefits to a child's good attachment, including lower levels of aggressive behavior, fewer sleep problems, and less social withdrawal (Ding et al., 2014). But as was the sad case with Genie, discussed at the start of this chapter, some children never form appropriate, loving attachments. What happens to these children? Researchers have investigated this question by looking at children and adults who spent their early years in institutions without the stimulation and love of a regular caregiver, as well as those who lived at home but were physically isolated under abusive conditions.

Tragically, infants raised in impersonal or abusive surroundings suffer from a number of problems. They seldom cry, coo, or babble; they become rigid when picked up; and they have few language skills. As for their social-emotional development, they tend to form shallow or anxious relationships. Some appear forlorn, withdrawn, and uninterested in their caretakers, whereas others seem insatiable in their need for affection. They also tend to show intellectual, physical, and perceptual deficiencies, along with increased susceptibility to infection and neurotic "rocking" and isolation behaviors. There are even cases where healthy babies who were well-fed and kept in clean diapers—but seldom held or stimulated—died from lack of attachment (Bowlby, 2000; Duniec & Raz, 2011; Spitz & Wolf, 1946). Some research suggests that childhood emotional abuse and neglect is as harmful, in terms of long-term mental problems, as physical and sexual abuse (Spinazzola et al., 2014).

Nina Leen/Life Picture Service/Getty Images

**FIGURE 9.22 Harlow's study and contact comfort**   Although Harlow's studies of attachment in infant monkeys would be considered unethical today, they did clearly demonstrate that *contact comfort*, and not *feeding*, is crucial to attachment.

**Touch**   Harry Harlow and his colleagues (1950, 1971) also investigated the variables that might affect attachment. They created two types of wire-framed surrogate (substitute) "mother" monkeys: one covered by soft terry cloth and one left uncovered (**Figure 9.22**). The infant monkeys were fed by either the cloth or the wire mother, but they otherwise had access to both mothers. The researchers found that the infant monkeys overwhelmingly preferred the soft, cloth surrogate—even when the wire surrogate was the one providing the food. In addition, monkeys "reared" by a cloth mother clung frequently to the soft material of their surrogate mother and developed greater emotional security and curiosity than did monkeys assigned to a wire mother.

Thanks in part to Harlow's research, psychologists discovered that *contact comfort*, the pleasurable tactile sensations provided by a soft and cuddly "parent," is one of the most important variables in attachment (**Figure 9.23**). Further support comes from the fact that, as discussed in Chapter 4, hospitals now encourage "kangaroo care" for premature babies, which provides them with skin-to-skin contact with caregivers (Head, 2014; Metgud & Honap, 2015). For more information on how touch affects us—even as adults—see the following.

### ❖ Psychology and Your Personal Success | The Power of Touch

As we've just seen, contact comfort is critical for the physical and mental well-being of both monkeys and human infants. But did you know that the touch of others is an invaluable asset throughout our life span? Human touch has been repeatedly shown to be an effective way to solicit and provide social support (e.g., Robinson et al., 2015). It also can reduce the perception of pain, lower heart rate and blood pressure, and increase levels of oxytocin.

Unfortunately, some individuals, such as elderly nursing home residents, often feel lonely and ostracized, and their unsatisfied desire for social touch can lead to "touch hunger" (Ben-Zeév, 2014; Rydé & Hjelm, 2016; Uvnäs-Moberg et al., 2015). Even something as simple as a hand massage can reduce disruptive behaviors in patients with dementia (Fu et al., 2013).

Hugs appear to be a particularly effective way of touching (see the photo). In fact, one study found that people who get more frequent hugs are less susceptible to infection and experience less severe illness symptoms (Cohen et al., 2015). However, keep in mind that while hugs and other forms of loving touch can reduce stress and promote emotional well-being, uninvited touch from a stranger generally makes us uncomfortable or even (see photo) angry (Harjunen et al., 2017). Even a friendly pat on the back or "high five" may be too personal among strangers. When contemplating hugging or touching other people, it's wise to carefully monitor their physical reactions. Ask yourself questions such as "Do they relax and lean in when I try to hug them, or do they stiffen and move backward?" and "Do they initiate similar touching, or is it only one-sided?" It's always safer to ask, "Would you like (or mind) a hug?"

Moreover, touch of any kind is a particularly "touchy" situation in the workplace and with young children. The most loving and best-intentioned touch can be seen as as a power play, as intimidating or aggressive, or as sexual harassment. The general rule is "Hands off!" And parents and caregivers are advised to teach children about "good touch" versus "bad touch" (Chapter 11).

### Ainsworth's Levels of Attachment

Although physical contact between caregiver and child appears to be an innate, biological part of attachment, Mary Ainsworth and her colleagues (1967, 1978) discovered several differences in the type and level of human attachment (**Figure 9.24**). Infants with a secure attachment style generally had caregivers who were sensitive and responsive to their signals of distress, happiness, and fatigue. In contrast, anxious/avoidant infants had caregivers who were aloof and distant, and anxious/ambivalent infants had inconsistent caregivers, who alternated between strong affection and indifference. Caregivers of disorganized/disoriented infants tended to be abusive or neglectful (Ainsworth, 1967; Ainsworth et al., 1978; Zeanah & Gleason, 2015).

As a critical thinker, can you offer additional explanations for attachment, other than differences in caregivers? What about the infants themselves? Researchers have found that the temperament of the child also affects levels of attachment. An infant who is highly anxious and avoidant might not accept or respond to a caregiver's attempts to comfort and soothe. Furthermore, children and their parents share genetic tendencies, and attachment patterns may reflect these shared genes. Finally, critics have suggested that Ainsworth's research does not account for cultural variations, such as cultures that encourage infants to develop attachments to multiple caregivers (Rothbaum et al., 2007; van IJzendoorn & Bakermans-Kranenburg, 2010).

Marili Forastieri/Digital Vision/Getty Images

**FIGURE 9.23** **The power of touch** Parents around the world tend to kiss, nuzzle, comfort, and respond to their children with lots of physical contact, which points out its vital role in infant development. It also provides support for the biological, nature argument for attachment.

Darren Kemper/Corbis/Getty Images

**FIGURE 9.24** **Research on infant attachment** For most children, parents are the earliest and most important factor in social development, and the attachment between parent and child is of particular interest to developmental psychologists.

1. After mother and baby spend some time in the experimental room, a stranger enters.

2. The mother then leaves the baby alone with the stranger.

3. The mother returns, and the stranger leaves.

4. The mother leaves, and the baby is alone until the stranger returns.

5. Once again, the mother returns, and the stranger leaves.

**a. Strange situation procedure** To measure attachment between infants and their mothers, Mary Ainsworth and her colleagues (1967, 2010) observed how infants responded to the presence or absence of their mother and a stranger.

Banana Stock/AgeFotostock

Secure attachment 60%

Disorganized/disoriented attachment 15%

15%

10%

Anxious/avoidant attachment

Anxious/ambivalent attachment

| | |
|---|---|
| **Secure** | Infant seeks closeness with mother when stranger enters. Uses her as a safe base from which to explore, shows moderate distress on separation from her, and is happy when she returns. |
| **Anxious/ambivalent** | Infant becomes very upset when mother leaves the room and shows mixed emotions when she returns. |
| **Anxious/avoidant** | Infant does not seek closeness or contact with the mother and shows little emotion when the mother departs or returns. |
| **Disorganized/disoriented** | Infant exhibits avoidant or ambivalent attachment, often seeming either confused or apprehensive in the presence of the mother. |

**b. Degrees of attachment** Using the strange situation procedure, Ainsworth found that children could be divided into three groups: *secure, anxious/avoidant,* and *anxious/ambivalent.* Later, psychologist Mary Main added a fourth category, *disorganized/disoriented* (Main & Solomon, 1986, 1990).

## Attachment Styles in Adulthood

In addition to finding varying levels of infant attachment to parents, researchers have examined adult attachment patterns independent of their earlier infant patterns, with several interesting—and sometimes troublesome—results. For example, a secure attachment pattern is associated with higher subjective well-being (SWB), whereas adolescents and young adults with avoidant and anxious attachment patterns show more depressive symptoms (Desrosiers et al., 2014; Galinha et al., 2014). Another study found an association between pathological jealousy and the anxious/ambivalent style of attachment (Costa et al., 2015).

Researchers also looked at how varying types of attachment as infants might shape our later adult styles of romantic love (Fraley & Roisman, 2015; Salzman et al., 2014; Sprecher & Fehr, 2011). If we developed a secure, anxious/ambivalent, anxious/avoidant, or disorganized/disoriented style as infants, we tend to follow these same patterns in our adult approach to intimacy and affection. Young adults who experienced either unresponsive or overintrusive parenting during childhood are more likely to avoid committed romantic relationships as

## Try This Yourself

### What's Your Romantic Attachment Style?

Thinking of your current and past romantic relationships, place a check next to the statement that best describes your feelings about relationships.

___**1.** *I find it relatively easy to get close to others and am comfortable depending on them and having them depend on me. I don't often worry about being abandoned or about someone getting too close.*

___**2.** *I am somewhat uncomfortable being close. I find it difficult to trust partners completely or to allow myself to depend on them. I am nervous when anyone gets close, and love partners often want me to be more intimate than is comfortable for me.*

___**3.** *I find that others are reluctant to get as close as I would like. I often worry that my partner doesn't really love me or won't stay with me. I want to merge completely with another person, and this desire sometimes scares people away.*

© GlobalStock/iStockphoto

According to research, 55% of adults agree with item 1 (secure attachment), 25% choose number 2 (anxious/avoidant attachment), and 20% choose item 3 (anxious/ambivalent attachment) (adapted from Fraley & Shaver, 1997; Hazan & Shaver, 1987). Note that the percentages for these adult attachment styles do not perfectly match those in Figure 9.24b, partly because the disorganized/disoriented attachment pattern was not included in this measurement of adult romantic attachments.

### Test Your Critical Thinking

**1.** Do your responses as an adult match your childhood attachment experiences?

**2.** Does your romantic attachment style negatively affect your present relationship? If so, how might you use this new information to make positive changes?

---

adults (Dekel & Farber, 2012). You can check your own romantic attachment style in the **Try This Yourself**. However, keep in mind that it's always risky to infer causation from correlation (see Chapter 1). Even if early attachment experiences are correlated with our later relationships, they do not determine them. Throughout life, we can learn new social skills and different approaches to all our relationships.

## Parenting Styles

*For your children, you may house their bodies but not their souls. For their souls dwell in the house of tomorrow, which you cannot visit, not even in your dreams. You may strive to be like them, but seek not to make them like you.* —Anonymous

How much of our personality comes from the way our parents treat us as we're growing up? Researchers since the 1920s have studied the effects of parental behaviors and different methods of child-rearing on children's physical and mental development (Lee, 2017; Whitbourne & Whitbourne, 2014) and mental health. One study found that teenagers whose parents used a controlling style—such as withholding love or creating feelings of guilt—later have more difficulty working out conflicts with friends and romantic partners (Oudekerk et al., 2015).

Studies by (see Study Tip) Diana Baumrind (1980, 2013) found that parenting styles could be reliably divided into four broad patterns—*permissive-neglectful, permissive-indulgent, authoritarian*, and *authoritative*—which can be differentiated by their degree of *control/demandingness (C)* and *warmth/responsiveness (W)* (**Table 9.3**). See the **Study Tip**.

As you might expect, authoritative parenting, which encourages independence but still places controls and limits on behavior, is generally the most beneficial for both parents and children (Gherasim et al., 2016; Gouveia et al., 2016; Rodriguez et al., 2015). Unfortunately, research has found a link between permissive parenting and college students' sense of "academic entitlement," which in turn is associated with more perceived stress and poorer

### Study Tip

*The names of the last two parenting styles (authoritarian and authoritative) are very similar. An easy way to remember and differentiate them is to notice the two Rs in authoRitaRian, and imagine a Rigid Ruler. Then note the last two Ts in authoriTaTive, and picture a Tender Teacher.*

**TABLE 9.3**   **Parenting Styles**

| Parenting Style | Description | Example | Effect on Children |
|---|---|---|---|
| **Permissive-neglectful** (low C, low W) | Parents make few demands, with little structure or monitoring (low C). They also show little interest or emotional support; may be actively rejecting (low W). | "I don't care about you—or what you do." | Children tend to have poor social skills and little self-control (being overly demanding and disobedient). |
| **Permissive-indulgent** (low C, high W) | Parents set few limits or demands (low C), but are highly involved and emotionally connected (high W). | "I care about you—and you're free to do what you like!" | Children often fail to learn respect for others and tend to be impulsive, immature, and out of control. |
| **Authoritarian** (high C, low W) | Parents are rigid and punitive (high C), but low on warmth and responsiveness (low W). | "I don't care what you want. Just do it my way, or else!" | Children tend to be easily upset, moody, and aggressive and often fail to learn good communication skills. |
| **Authoritative** (high C, high W) | Parents generally set and enforce firm limits (high C), while being highly involved, tender, and emotionally supportive high W). | "I really care about you, but there are rules, and you need to be responsible." | Children become self-reliant, self-controlled, high achieving, and emotionally well adjusted; also seem more content, goal oriented, friendly, and socially competent. |

**Sources:** Baumrind, 2013; Berger, 2015; Bornstein et al., 2014; Topham et al., 2011.

mental health among college students (Barton & Hirsh, 2016). Authoritarian parenting also is linked with increased behavior problems (Tavassolie et al., 2016).

Cross-cultural and longitudinal studies also suggest that lack of parental warmth and/ or parental rejection may have long-lasting negative effects (Friesen et al., 2017; Suizzo et al., 2016; Wu & Chao, 2011). The neglect and indifference shown by rejecting parents tend to be correlated with hostile, aggressive children who have a difficult time establishing and maintaining close relationships. As might be expected, these children are more likely to develop psychological problems that require professional intervention.

### Evaluating Baumrind's Research
Before you conclude that the authoritative pattern is the only way to raise successful children, you should know that many children raised in the other styles also become caring, cooperative adults. Criticism of Baumrind's findings generally falls into three areas:

1. *Child temperament.* Research shows that a child's unique temperament may affect the parents' chosen parenting style, just as the parenting style may shape a child's temperament (Bradley & Corwyn, 2008; Miller et al., 2011; Pitzer et al., 2017). In other words, the parents of mature and competent children may have developed the authoritative style because of the children's behavior, rather than vice versa.

2. *Parent and child expectations.* Cultural research suggests that a parent's expectations of a child's temperament and a child's expectations of how parents should behave also play important roles in parenting (Laungani, 2007; Manczak et al., 2016; Zhang et al., 2011). As you read earlier in this chapter, adolescents in Korea expect strong parental control and interpret it as a sign of love and deep concern. Adolescents in North America, however, might interpret the same behavior as a sign of parental hostility and rejection.

3. *Limited attention to father's role in parenting.* Until recently, the father's role in discipline and child care was largely ignored by most developmental researchers. But fathers in Western countries have begun to take a more active role in child-rearing, and there has been a corresponding increase in research. From these studies, we now know that children do best with authoritative dads, who are absorbed with, excited about, and responsive to their children. Children also do best when parents share the same, consistent parenting style. However, mothers and fathers often differ in their approaches, and research shows that such differences may increase marital conflict and child behavior problems (Tavassolie et al., 2016).

© Billy R. Ray/ Wiley

## Retrieval Practice 9.4 | Social-Emotional Development

Completing this self-test and the connections section, and then checking your answers by clicking on the answer button or by looking in Appendix B, will provide immediate feedback and helpful practice for exams.

### Self-Test

1. According to Harlow's research with cloth and wire surrogate mother monkeys, _____ is one of the most important variable in attachment.

   a. contact comfort
   b. "comfort food"
   c. neonatal breast feeding
   d. age group peer contact ("free play" periods)

2. Which of the following terms are correctly matched?

   a. Lorenz, ageism
   b. Piaget, permissive parenting
   c. Harlow, contact comfort
   d. Baumrind, accommodation

3. Ainsworth's research suggests that a(n) _____ infant is more likely to become very upset when mother leaves the room and to show mixed emotions when she returns.

   a. securely attached
   b. anxious/avoidant
   c. anxious/ambivalent
   d. demanding

4. Using Hazan and Shaver's research on adult attachment styles, identify the following adults with their probable type of infant attachment:

   _____ Mary is nervous around attractive partners and complains that lovers often want her to be more intimate than she finds comfortable.

   _____ Bob complains that lovers are often reluctant to get as close as he would like.

   _____ Rashelle finds it relatively easy to get close to others and seldom worries about being abandoned.

5. Briefly explain Baumrind's four parenting styles.

### Connections—Chapter to Chapter

Answering the following question will help you "look back and look ahead" to see the important connections among the subfields of psychology and chapters within this text.

In this chapter, you learned about Baumrind's parenting styles. Using operant conditioning (Chapter 6, Learning), explain how a permissive parent and an authoritative parent might respond differently to a child's misbehavior. Use the terms *positive punishment, negative punishment, positive reinforcement,* and/or *negative reinforcement,* as applicable, in your response.

---

### Study Tip

*The WileyPLUS program that accompanies this text provides for each chapter a* Media Challenge, Critical Thinking Exercise, *and* Application Quiz. *This set of study materials provides additional, invaluable study opportunities. Be sure to check it out!*

---

# Chapter Summary

## 9.1 Studying Development  290

- **Developmental psychology** is the study of age-related changes in behavior and mental processes, including stages of growth, from conception to death. Development is an ongoing, lifelong process.

- The three most important debates or questions in human development concern *nature versus nurture* (including studies of

maturation and **critical periods**), *stages versus continuity*, and *stability versus change*.

- Developmental psychologists use two special techniques in their research: **cross-sectional design** and **longitudinal design**. Although both have valuable attributes, each has disadvantages. Cross-sectional studies can confuse genuine age differences with *cohort effects*. On the other hand, longitudinal studies are expensive and time consuming. Both research techniques also suffer from restricted generalizability.

- Cultural psychologists suggest that (1) culture may be the major determinant of development, (2) human development cannot be studied outside its sociocultural context, (3) each culture's ethnotheories are key determinants of behavior, and (4) culture is largely invisible to its participants.

**1.** Which of the three debates or questions in developmental psychology do you find most valuable? Why?

**2.** Based on what you have learned about critical periods, can you think of a time in your own development, or that of a friend, when a critical period might have been disrupted or lost?

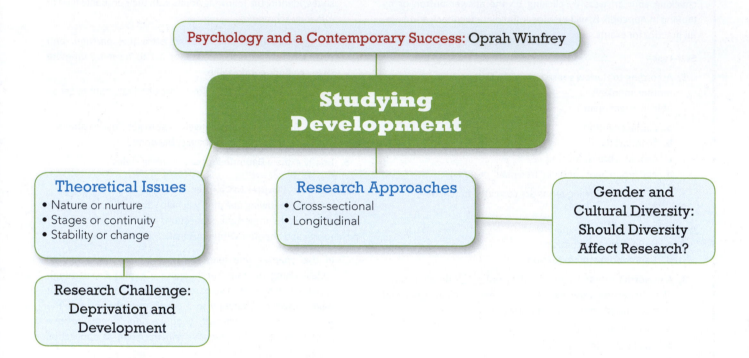

## 9.2   Physical Development   295

- Prenatal development begins at conception and is divided into three stages: the **germinal period** (ovulation to implantation), the **embryonic period** (implantation to 8 weeks), and the **fetal period** (8 weeks to birth).

- Throughout our life span, environmental, **epigenetic** factors affect how our inherited genes are expressed. During pregnancy, the placenta serves as the link for food and the excretion of wastes, and it screens out some harmful substances—but not **teratogens**, such as alcohol and nicotine.

- Early childhood is a time of rapid physical development, including brain, motor, and sensory/perceptual development.

- During *adolescence*, both boys and girls undergo dramatic changes in appearance and physical capacity. Adolescence begins with **puberty**, when a person becomes capable of reproduction.

- During the period of **emerging adulthood**, approximately ages 18–25, individuals in Western nations have left the dependency of childhood but have not yet assumed adult responsibilities.

- During adulthood, most individuals experience only minor physical changes until middle age. Around age 45–55, women

experience *menopause*, the cessation of the menstrual cycle. At the same time, men experience a gradual decline in the production of sperm and testosterone, as well as other physical changes, known as the *male climacteric*.

- After middle age, most physical changes in development are gradual and occur in the heart and arteries and in the sensory receptors.

- Aging was once believed to involve widespread death of neurons in the brain, but that is no longer believed to be a part of normal aging. Although mental speed declines with age, general mental abilities are largely unaffected by the aging process. One of the greatest problems for the elderly is the various negative stereotypes that contribute to our society's widespread **ageism**.

**Test Your Critical Thinking**

**1.** If a pregnant woman knowingly ingests a quantity of alcohol, which causes her child to develop fetal alcohol syndrome (FAS), is she guilty of child abuse? Why or why not?

**2.** Based on what you have learned about development during late adulthood, do you think this period is inevitably a time of physical and mental decline? Why or why not?

# Physical Development

## Prenatal and Early Childhood
- Germinal, embryonic, and fetal periods
- Epigenetic factors affect expression of inherited genes
- Early childhood is a time of rapid physical growth

## Adolescence and Adulthood
- Adolescence: Transitional period between childhood and adulthood
- Puberty: Period of sexual maturation
- Teen brain: Pruning taking place, frontal lobes not fully developed
- Emerging/young adulthood: Characterized by modest physical changes
- Middle adulthood: Women experience menopause, while men undergo the male climacteric
- Late adulthood: Characterized by gradual physical changes
- Explanations of primary aging: Cellular-clock theory (Hayflick limit) and wear-and-tear theory
- Brain in late adulthood: Information processing slower but general abilities largely unaffected

### Psychology and Your Professional Success:
**Does Ageism Matter?**

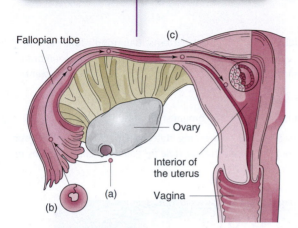

Fallopian tube
(c)
Ovary
Interior of the uterus
(a)
(b)
Vagina

## 9.3 Cognitive Development   306

- Piaget believed an infant's intellectual growth progresses in distinct stages, motivated by an innate need to know. He also proposed three major concepts: **schemas**, patterns that organize our interactions with the environment; **assimilation**, absorbing new information "as is" into existing schemas; and **accommodation**, adjusting old schemas or developing new ones to fit with new information.

- According to Piaget, all children progress through four stages of cognitive development: the **sensorimotor stage**, the **preoperational stage**, the **concrete operational stage**, and the **formal operational stage**.

- In the sensorimotor stage, children acquire **object permanence**. During the preoperational stage, children are better equipped to use symbols. But their language and thinking are limited by their lack of operations, by animism, and by **egocentrism**. In the concrete operational stage, children learn to perform concrete operations (to think about concrete things while not actually doing them) and to understand the principle of **conservation**. During the formal operational stage, the adolescent is able to think abstractly and deal with hypothetical situations, but is prone to a type of adolescent egocentrism.

- Piaget's account of cognitive development has been enormously influential, but it has received significant criticisms. Piaget has been criticized for underestimating children's abilities and for paying insufficient attention to the genetic and cultural influences on cognitive development. Vygotsky emphasized the sociocultural influences on cognitive development, such as the child's **zone of proximal development (ZPD)**. The **theory of mind (ToM)** presents another alternative to Piaget. It proposes that children become less egocentric when they recognize that other people don't have the same thoughts and feelings that they do.

### Test Your Critical Thinking

**1.** Piaget's theory states that all children progress through all the stages of cognitive development in order and without skipping any. Do you agree with this theory? Do you know any children who seem to contradict this theory?

**2.** Based on what you've learned about schemas, what are some new schemas you've developed as part of your transition from high school to college?

## Cognitive Development

### Piaget's Theory
- Schema
- Assimilation
- Accommodation

### Stages of Cognitive Development

#### Piaget's Four Stages
- Sensorimotor
- Preoperational
- Concrete operational
- Formal operational

### Evaluating Piaget: Vygotsky and Theory of Mind
- Piaget underestimated abilities, as well as genetic and cultural influences.
- Vygotsky emphasized sociocultural influences, such as the ZPD.
- Developing a theory of mind (ToM) leads to less egocentrism.

### 9.4  Social-Emotional Development   314

- Harlow and his colleagues' research with monkeys raised by cloth or wire "mothers" found that *contact comfort* might be the most important factor in **attachment**.

- Using the strange situation procedure, Ainsworth found that children could be divided into three groups: secure, anxious/avoidant, and anxious/ambivalent. Mary Main later added a fourth category, disorganized/disoriented.

- In addition to attachment patterns, Baumrind's four parenting styles—*permissive-neglectful, permissive-indulgent, authoritarian*, and *authoritative*—also affect a child's social development.

### Test Your Critical Thinking

1. Which of Ainsworth's attachment styles best describes you?

2. Which of Baumrind's parenting styles was most like that of your parents? Would you use a similar style for your own children? Why or why not?

Nina Leen/Life Picture Service/Getty Images

## Social-Emotional Development

### Attachment
- Imprinting
- Harlow's contact comfort
- Ainsworth's four types: secure, anxious/ambivalent, anxious/avoidant, disorganized/disoriented

### Parenting Styles
Baumrind's four styles: permissive-neglectful, permissive-indulgent, authoritarian, authoritative

### Psychology and Your Personal Success:
The Power of Touch

# Key Terms

**Retrieval Practice**   *Write a definition for each term before turning back to the referenced page to check your answer.*

- accommodation  306
- ageism  304
- assimilation  306
- attachment  314
- behavioral genetics  296
- chromosome  295
- concrete operational stage  310
- conservation  308
- critical period  290
- cross-sectional design  292
- developmental psychology  290

- DNA  295
- egocentrism  308
- emerging adulthood  303
- embryonic period  297
- epigenetics  296
- fetal period  297
- formal operational stage  310
- gene  296
- germinal period  297
- imprinting  290
- longitudinal design  292

- object permanence  308
- preoperational stage  308
- puberty  301
- schema  306
- sensorimotor stage  308
- temperament  000
- teratogen  297
- theory of mind (ToM)  312
- zone of proximal development (ZPD)  312

© alexxl66/iStockphoto

# Life Span Development II

## ❖ Psychology and a Classic Success | Nelson Mandela

Louise Gubb/Contributor/Getty Images

Nelson Mandela (1918–2013) was born in Mvezo, South Africa (see photo). His father was a polygamist with four wives and nine daughters, and Nelson grew up with his mother and two sisters tending herds as a cattle boy. Both of his parents were illiterate, and, according to Mandela, "no one in my family had ever attended school" (Mandela, 1994, p. 19). However, his mother was a devout Christian and sent him to a local Methodist school, where his first teacher gave him the name "Nelson." It was the custom among Africans in those days to give all schoolchildren English Christian names.

Unfortunately, Nelson's father died while he was very young. He was made a ward of the tribe and adopted by a high-ranking tribesman who helped groom him for a leadership role. Said "grooming" was obviously very successful. Beginning in the 1940s, Mandela was part of the African National Congress (ANC), where he spent many years as a "freedom fighter." His actions as a leader of both peaceful protests and armed resistance resulted in his imprisonment for almost three decades. After being released from prison, Mandela became a central figure in the eradication of apartheid, and he was elected in 1994 in a fully representative democratic election as the first Black president of South Africa. He was later awarded the Nobel Peace Prize, along with former South African president F. W. de Klerk, for fostering racial reconciliation and for overseeing his country's transition from a system of racial segregation.

After leaving the presidency, Mandela remained an activist, philanthropist, and champion for peace and social justice, earning over 250 honors before his death in 2013 at the age of 95. Today, he is remembered as perhaps the greatest African leader of our time and as a global symbol for human rights (Biography of Nelson Mandela, n.d.; Nelson Mandela, n. d).

# Chapter Overview

> *Everyone can rise above their circumstances and achieve success if they are dedicated to and passionate about what they do.*   —Nelson Mandela

Mandela's personal *growth mindset* and *grit* (passion plus perseverance) are on clear display in this quote and in the brief description of his life and achievements. This explains, in part, why we chose him as our famous figure for this chapter. In addition, the challenges of his unusual childhood and his long imprisonment, along with his growth and development throughout his life span, provide examples of the topics we'll cover in this chapter.

Recall that Chapter 9 explored life span changes in physical development, cognitive development, and social-emotional development. In this chapter, we start with a look at moral development, followed by the major theories and factors in personality development. Then we cover two of the most common neurodevelopmental disorders—ADHD and ASD. We close with an exploration of the many challenges of adulthood.

## Why Study Psychology?

### Did you know that

- ... traveling abroad may lead to an increase in immoral behaviors?
- ... juvenile chimpanzees will soothe a frightened or injured peer?
- ... letting your partner influence you is key to maintaining successful relationships?
- ... older adults are better at remembering and paying attention to positive information than are younger people?
- ... parents typically experience their highest levels of marital satisfaction before children are born and after they leave home?
- ... Kübler-Ross believed that most people go through five predictable psychological stages when facing death?

franckreporter/Getty Images

# 10.1 | Moral Development

## LEARNING OBJECTIVES

**Retrieval Practice**   While reading the upcoming sections, respond to each Learning Objective in your own words.

**Summarize the key concepts and theories of how morality develops and changes across our life span.**

- **Describe** the research and central characteristics of Kohlberg's theory of moral development.
- **Review** the three major criticisms of Kohlberg's theory.

> *Morality is the basis of things and truth is the substance of all morality.*
> —Mahatma Gandhi (Leader Of Indian Independence, Philosopher)

In Chapter 9, we noted that newborns cry when they hear another baby cry. But did you know that by age two, most children use words like *good* or *bad* to evaluate actions that are aggressive or that might endanger their own or another's welfare? Or that juvenile chimpanzees will soothe a frightened or injured peer, and adult social birds and mammals show reciprocity and helping behaviors within their groups (Freidin et al., 2017; Goodall, 1990; Smith & Warneken, 2014)? How can we explain such early emergence and cross-species evidence of **morality**—the ability to take the perspective of, or empathize with, others and to distinguish between right and wrong?

From a biological perspective, some researchers suggest that morality may be prewired and evolutionarily based (Decety & Yoder, 2017; Keltner et al., 2014; Workman & Reader, 2014). Behaviors like infants' empathic crying and animals' helping behaviors promote the survival of the species. Therefore, evolution may have provided us with a biological basis for moral acts. But biology is only one part of the *biopsychosocial model*. In this section, we will focus our attention on the psychological and social factors that explain how moral thoughts, feelings, and actions change over the life span.

**Morality**   The ability to take the perspective of, or empathize with, others and to distinguish right from wrong.

## Kohlberg's Research

Consider the following situation.

> *In Europe, a cancer-ridden woman was near death, but an expensive drug existed that might save her. The woman's husband, Heinz, begged the druggist to sell the drug at a lower price, or to let him pay later, but the druggist refused. Heinz became desperate and broke into the druggist's store and stole it* (Kohlberg, 1964, pp. 18–19).

Was Heinz right to steal the drug? What do you consider moral behavior? Is morality "in the eye of the beholder," or are there universal truths and principles? Whatever your answer, your ability to think, reason, and respond to Heinz's dilemma demonstrates another type of development that is very important to psychology—*moral development*.

One of the most influential researchers in moral development was Lawrence Kohlberg (1927–1987). He presented what he called "moral stories" like the Heinz dilemma to people of all ages, not to see whether they judged Heinz right or wrong but to examine the reasons they gave for their decisions. On the basis of his findings, Kohlberg (1964, 1984) developed a model of moral development with three broad levels, each composed of two distinct stages (**Step-by-Step Diagram 10.1**). Individuals at various levels may or may not support Heinz's stealing of the drug, but their reasoning changes from level to level.

**Preconventional morality** is self-centered and based on rewards, punishments, and exchange of favors. In contrast, **conventional morality** is based on compliance with the rules and values of society. Finally, at the highest level—**postconventional morality**—individuals develop personal standards for right and wrong. They define morality in terms of abstract principles and values that apply to all situations and societies.

**Preconventional morality**   Kohlberg's first level of moral development, in which morality is based on rewards, punishment, and exchange of favors.

**Conventional morality**   Kohlberg's second level of moral development, in which moral judgments are based on compliance with the rules and values of society.

**Postconventional morality**   Kohlberg's third and highest level of moral development, in which individuals develop personal standards for right and wrong, and define morality in terms of abstract principles and values that apply to all situations and societies.

## STEP-BY-STEP DIAGRAM 10.1    Kohlberg's Three Levels of Moral Development

**STOP!** This Step-by-Step Diagram contains essential information NOT found elsewhere in the text, which is likely to appear on quizzes and exams. Be sure to study it CAREFULLY!

**Preconventional morality**   The first level of Kohlberg's theory of moral development, in which morality is based on rewards, punishment, and exchange of favors.

**Conventional morality**
The second level of Kohlberg's theory of moral development, in which moral judgments are based on compliance with the rules and values of society.

**Postconventional morality**
The highest level of Kohlberg's theory of moral development, in which individuals develop personal standards for right and wrong, and define morality in terms of abstract principles and values that apply to all situations and societies.

### STEP 1: PRECONVENTIONAL MORALITY

**(Stages 1 and 2—young children to adolescence)** Moral judgment is *self-centered*. What is right is what one can get away with or what is personally satisfying.

**1 Punishment-obedience orientation**

Focus is on self-interest—obedience to authority and avoidance of punishment. Because children at this stage have difficulty considering another's point of view, they ignore people's intentions.

**2 Instrumental-exchange orientation**

Children become aware of others' perspectives, but their morality is based on reciprocity—an equal exchange of favors.

### STEP 2: CONVENTIONAL MORALITY

**(Stages 3 and 4—adolescence to adulthood)**
Moral reasoning is *other-centered*. Conventional societal rules are accepted because they help ensure the social order.

**3 Good-child orientation**

Primary moral concern is being nice and gaining approval; judges others by their intentions—"His heart was in the right place."

**4 Law-and-order orientation**

Morality based on a larger perspective—societal laws. Understanding that if everyone violated laws, even with good intentions, there would be chaos.

### STEP 3: POSTCONVENTIONAL MORALITY

**(Stages 5 and 6—adulthood)**
Moral judgments based on *personal standards for right and wrong*. Morality is defined in terms of abstract principles and values that apply to all situations and societies.

**5 Social-contract orientation**

Appreciation for the underlying purposes served by laws. Societal laws are obeyed because of the "social contract," but they can be morally disobeyed if they fail to express the will of the majority or fail to maximize social welfare.

**6 Universal-ethics orientation**

"Right" is determined by universal ethical principles (e.g., nonviolence, human dignity, freedom) that moral authorities might view as compelling or fair. These principles apply whether or not they conform to existing laws.

**Sources:** Based on Kohlberg, L. "Stage and Sequence: The Cognitive Developmental Approach to Socialization," in D. A. Goslin, *The handbook of socialization theory and research.* Chicago: Rand McNally, 1969, p. 376 (Table 6.2).

## Assessing Kohlberg's Theory

*When morality comes up against profit, it is seldom that profit loses.*
    —Shirley Chisholm (Politician, Author, Educator)

Kohlberg's ideas have led to considerable research on how we think about moral issues. One area of research concerns the relationship of moral reasoning to moral behavior. That is, are people who achieve higher stages on Kohlberg's scale really more moral than others? Or do they just "talk a good game"?

Some researchers have shown that people's sense of moral identity, meaning their use of moral principles to define themselves, is often a good predictor of their behavior in real-world situations (Johnston et al., 2013). Others have found that situational factors are better predictors of moral behavior (Antonaccio et al., 2017; Bandura, 1986, 2008). For example, employees are more likely to voluntarily participate in environmentally "green" behaviors at work if their supervisors model such behaviors themselves (Kim et al., 2017a). And both men and women will tell more sexual lies during casual relationships than during close relationships (Williams, 2001).

Other areas of research into Kohlberg's theory involve possible gender bias and the influence of cultural differences. See the following **Gender and Cultural Diversity** for more about this research.

## Gender and Cultural Diversity

### Effects on Moral Development

Are there gender differences in moral development? In Kohlberg's studies, women tended to be classified at a lower level of moral reasoning than men. As noted in **Figure 10.1**, researcher Carol Gilligan suggested that this was true because Kohlberg's theory emphasizes values more often held by men, such as rationality and independence, while deemphasizing common female values, such as concern for others and belonging (Gilligan, 1977, 1990, 1993). Gilligan later expanded on this "care versus justice" difference between women and men by saying that these two positions are not mutually exclusive (Gilligan, 2011). And most follow-up studies in this area have not found consistent support for gender differences in moral reasoning (Giammarco, 2016; Gibbs, 2014; Mercadillo et al., 2011).

Interestingly, a study of over 6,000 participants (Friesdorf et al., 2015) did clarify that women are more likely than men to have a stronger emotional aversion to causing harm to others, but they are no less rational. In line with other studies, women were found to be more empathic, but contrary to stereotypes, being more emotional or empathic does not mean being less rational.

A focus on emotion is also central to recent research on the importance of *moral intuition*, or "gut instincts" in moral judgments. One of the leaders in the field, Johnathan Haidt (2001, 2012), developed the *social intuitionist model* (SIM), which suggests that we typically make quick, automatic, emotion-laden moral judgments—rather than employing logical, deliberative reasoning. What do you think? What might be the advantages of the SIM as a scientific model, or of the practice of making quick emotional judgments rather than using reasoning?

Does culture also affect moral development? Several cross-cultural studies do support Kohlberg's model, whereas other studies find significant differences (Csordas, 2014; Endicott & Endicott, 2014; Rest et al., 1999). For instance, cross-cultural comparisons of responses to Heinz's moral dilemma show that Europeans and Americans tend to consider whether they like or identify with the victim in questions of morality. In contrast, Hindu Indians consider social responsibility and personal concerns two separate issues (Miller & Bersoff, 1998). Researchers suggest that the difference reflects the Indians' broader sense of social responsibility. Furthermore, in India, Papua New Guinea, and China, as well as in Israeli kibbutzim, people don't choose between the rights of the individual and the rights of society (as the top levels of Kohlberg's model require). Instead, most people seek a compromise solution that accommodates both

Jonathan Nourok/Stone/Getty Images

**FIGURE 10.1  Gilligan versus Kohlberg** According to Carol Gilligan, women score "lower" on Lawrence Kohlberg's stages of moral development because they are socialized to assume more responsibility for the care of others. What do you think?

interests (Killen & Hart, 1999; Miller & Bersoff, 1998). Thus, Kohlberg's standard for judging the highest level of morality (the postconventional level) may be more applicable to cultures that value individualism over community and interpersonal relationships.

Looking beyond cultural differences in Kohlberg's specific stages of moral development, modern researchers (e.g., Graham et al., 2016) emphasize the need to examine a broader range of factors *within* a given culture, such as religion, social ecology (weather, crop conditions, residential mobility), and social institutions (kinship structures and economic markets), rather than the differences *between* cultures mentioned above.

Before going on, we'd like to share a particularly intriguing study related to cultural differences and morality. Given the common belief that foreign travel experiences enhance one's education and reduce intergroup bias, many will be disturbed by a recent study that reveals a darker side to travel (Lu et al., 2017). These researchers found that experiences abroad encouraged not only cognitive flexibility but also a type of moral flexibility or relativism that may lead to immoral behaviors! However, this effect seemed to apply only to broad, brief travel to many countries, which exposes the traveler to a wide variety of differing moral codes over a short time.

Recognizing that travel time is limited for most people and that tourists often want to visit several countries in one trip, the authors of this study suggest that travelers review their own moral values and standards before leaving home. Can you see how the popular "Study Abroad" programs offered at many universities and colleges, in which students typically spend several weeks or a semester in one country, might be ideal? They provide more time and experiences that should lead to a deeper understanding of the differing moral codes and values of the host country (see the photo).

Courtesy of Lee Decker

© Billy R. Ray/Wiley

## Retrieval Practice 10.1 | Moral Development

Completing this self-test and connections section, and then checking your answers by clicking on the answer button or by looking in Appendix B, will provide immediate feedback and helpful practice for exams.

### Self-Test

1. Briefly define morality.

2. According to Kohlberg, at what level of moral development is moral judgment self-centered and based on obtaining rewards and avoiding punishment?

3. Calvin would like to wear baggy, torn jeans and a nose ring, but he is concerned that others will disapprove. Calvin is at Kohlberg's _____ level of morality.

   a. conformity          b. approval seeking
   c. conventional        d. preconventional

4. Five-year-old Tyler believes "bad things are what you get punished for." Tyler is at Kohlberg's _____ stage of morality.

   a. law-and-order orientation
   b. punishment-obedience orientation

   c. good-child orientation
   d. social-contract orientation

5. Which of the following is NOT one of the major areas of research into Kohlberg's theory?

   a. possible gender bias
   b. cultural differences
   c. experimenter bias
   d. moral reasoning versus moral behavior

### Connections—Chapter to Chapter

Answering the following question will help you "look back and look ahead" to see the important connections among the subfields of psychology and chapters within this text.

In Chapter 16 (Social Psychology), you will discover three factors that contribute to conformity—normative social influence, informational social influence, and reference groups. How might each of these factors apply to Kohlberg's various stages and/or levels of moral development?

## 10.2 Personality Development

### LEARNING OBJECTIVES

**Retrieval Practice**    While reading the upcoming sections, respond to each Learning Objective in your own words.

**Review the key concepts and theories of how personality develops and changes across our life span.**

- **Describe** Thomas and Chess's temperament theory.
- **Summarize** Erikson's eight psychosocial stages of development.
- **Review** the major criticisms of Erikson's theory.

## Thomas and Chess's Temperament Theory

As an infant, did you lie quietly and seem oblivious to loud noises? Or did you tend to kick and scream and respond immediately to every sound? Did you respond warmly to people, or did you fuss, fret, and withdraw? Your answers to these questions help determine what developmental psychologists call your **temperament**, an individual's disposition or innate, biological behavioral style and characteristic emotional response.

One of the earliest and most influential theories regarding temperament came from the work of psychiatrists Alexander Thomas and Stella Chess (Thomas & Chess, 1977, 1987, 1991). Thomas and Chess found that approximately 65 percent of the babies they observed could be reliably separated into three categories:

1. *Easy children* These infants were happy most of the time, relaxed and agreeable, and adjusted easily to new situations (approximately 40 percent).

2. *Difficult children* Infants in this group were moody, easily frustrated, tense, and overreactive to most situations (approximately 10 percent).

3. *Slow-to-warm-up children* These infants showed mild responses, were somewhat shy and withdrawn, and needed time to adjust to new experiences or people (approximately 15 percent).

Follow-up studies have found that certain aspects of these temperament styles tend to be consistent and enduring throughout childhood and even adulthood (Bates et al., 2014; Coplan & Bullock, 2012; Sayal et al., 2014). That is not to say every shy, cautious infant ends up a shy adult. Many events take place between infancy and adulthood that shape an individual's development.

One of the most influential factors in early personality development is *goodness of fit* between a child's nature, parental behaviors, and the social and environmental setting (Granader et al., 2014; Seifer et al., 2014; Smiley et al., 2016). A slow-to-warm-up child does best if allowed time to adjust to new situations. Similarly, a difficult child thrives in a structured, understanding environment but not in an inconsistent, intolerant home. Alexander Thomas, the pioneer of temperament research, thinks parents should work with their child's temperament rather than trying to change it. Can you see how this idea of goodness of fit is yet another example of how nature and nurture interact?

**Temperament** An individual's innate disposition or behavioral style and characteristic emotional response.

## Erikson's Psychosocial Theory

Like Piaget and Kohlberg, Erik Erikson proposed a stage theory of development. He identified eight **psychosocial stages** of development from infancy to old age. Each stage is marked by a "psychosocial" task that a person must successfully resolve in order to develop healthy interpersonal relationships and emotional well-being (**Step-by-Step Diagram 10.2**).

The name for each psychosocial stage reflects the specific crisis encountered at that stage and identifies two possible outcomes. For example, the crisis or task of most young adults is *intimacy versus isolation*. This age group's developmental task is establishing deep, meaningful relations with others. Those who don't meet this developmental challenge risk social isolation. Erikson believed that the more successfully we overcome each psychosocial crisis, the better chance we have to develop in a healthy manner (Erikson, 1950).

**Psychosocial stages** Erikson's stages of development, each involving a psychosocial task that must be successfully resolved at a particular place in the life span.

## Evaluating Erikson's Theory

Many psychologists agree with Erikson's general idea that psychosocial crises, which are based on interpersonal and environmental interactions, do contribute to social development (Gonzales-Backen et al., 2015; Kuiper et al., 2016; Major et al., 2016). As an example, researchers have found that adolescence is a critical time for consolidating one's identity and developing sexual and nonsexual intimacy—thus supporting Erikson's Stage 6 (Brandell and Brown, 2015). These researchers also found that successful resolution of this stage may be harder in modern times due to adolescents' increased exposure to social media websites, Internet pornography, casual "hook-ups," and recreational drugs and alcohol.

| STEP-BY-STEP DIAGRAM 10.2 | Erikson's Eight Stages of Psychosocial Development |

**STOP!** This Step-by-Step Diagram contains essential information NOT found elsewhere in the text, which is likely to appear on quizzes and exams. Be sure to study it CAREFULLY!

Courtesy of Sandy Harvey

**Stage 1**
**Trust versus mistrust (birth–age 1)**

Infants learn to *trust* or *mistrust* their caregivers and the world based on whether or not their needs—such as food, affection, and safety—are met.

Courtesy of Karen Huffman

**Stage 2**
**Autonomy versus shame and doubt (ages 1–3)**

Toddlers start to assert their sense of independence (*autonomy*). If caregivers encourage this self-sufficiency, the toddler will learn to be independent versus feeling *shame* and *doubt*.

Courtesy of Sandy Harvey

**Stage 3**
**Initiative versus guilt (ages 3–6)**

Preschoolers need to learn to *initiate* activities and develop self confidence and a sense of social responsibility. If they do not, they feel irresponsible, anxious, and *guilty*.

Courtesy of Linda Locklear

**Stage 4**
**Industry versus inferiority (ages 6–12)**

Elementary-school-aged children who succeed in learning new, productive life skills develop a sense of pride and competence (*industry*). Those who fail to develop these skills feel inadequate and unproductive (*inferior*).

Courtesy of Richard Hosey

**Stage 5**
**Identity versus role confusion (ages 12–20)**

Adolescents develop a coherent and stable self-definition (*identity*) by exploring many roles and deciding who or what they want to be in terms of career, attitudes, etc. Failure to resolve this **identity crisis** may lead to apathy, withdrawal, and/or *role confusion*.

wavebreakmedia/Shutterstock

**Stage 6**
**Intimacy versus isolation (early adulthood)**

Young adults need to form lasting, meaningful relationships, which help them develop a sense of connectedness and *intimacy* with others. If they are not able to form such relationships, they become psychologically *isolated*.

Courtesy of Lee Decker

**Stage 7**
**Generativity versus stagnation (middle adulthood)**

The challenge for middle-aged adults is in nurturing the young and making contributions to society through their work, family, or community activities (*generativity*). Failing to meet this challenge leads to self-indulgence and a sense of *stagnation*.

Courtesy of Lee Decker

**Stage 8**
**Ego integrity versus despair (late adulthood)**

During this stage, older adults reflect on their past. If this reflection reveals a life well spent, the person experiences self-acceptance and satisfaction (*ego integrity*). If not, he or she experiences regret and deep dissatisfaction (*despair*).

Erikson's conclusions have been criticized in three major areas (Kroger, 2015; Robinson, 2016; Schwartz et al., 2016). First, his narrow focus on only one challenge for each developmental stage ignores other critical tasks in the same period. Second, Erikson's psychosocial stages are difficult to test scientifically. Third, the labels Erikson used to describe the eight stages may not be entirely appropriate cross-culturally. In individualistic cultures, *autonomy* is highly preferable to *shame and doubt*. But in collectivist cultures, the preferred resolution might be *dependence* or *merging relations* (Berry et al., 2011).

Despite their limits, Erikson's stages have greatly contributed to the study of North American and European psychosocial development. By suggesting that development continues past adolescence, Erikson's theory has encouraged ongoing research and theory development.

© Billy R. Ray/Wiley

## Retrieval Practice 10.2 | Personality Development

Completing this self-test and connections section, and then checking your answers by clicking on the answer button or by looking in Appendix B, will provide immediate feedback and helpful practice for exams.

**Self-Test**

1. Briefly define temperament.

2. According to Thomas and Chess's temperament theory, _____ children are somewhat shy and withdrawn and need time to adjust to new experiences or people.

   a. difficult
   b. emotionally delayed
   c. slow-to-warm-up
   d. none of these

3. According to Erikson, the key crisis or task of most young adults is _____.

   a. identity versus role confusion
   b. trust versus mistrust
   c. intimacy versus isolation
   d. industry versus inferiority

4. Erikson suggested that problems in adulthood are sometimes related to unsuccessful resolution of one of his eight stages. For each of the following individuals, identify the most likely "problem" stage:

   a. _____ Marcos has trouble keeping friends and jobs because he feels unsafe, and he continually asks for guarantees and reassurance of his worth.

   b. _____ Ann has attended several colleges without picking a major, has taken several vocational training programs, and has had numerous jobs over the last 10 years.

   c. _____ Teresa is reluctant to apply for a promotion even though her coworkers have encouraged her to do so. She lacks self-confidence and feels guilty that she will be taking a job from someone else.

   d. _____ George continually obsesses over the value of his life. He regrets that he left his wife and children for a job in another country and failed to maintain contact.

**Connections—Chapter to Chapter**

Answering the following questions will help you "look back and look ahead" to see the important connections among the subfields of psychology and chapters within this text.

1. In Chapter 9 (Life Span Development I), you discovered some of the ongoing theoretical debates in developmental psychology: nature or nurture, stages or continuity, and stability or change. Apply each of these issues to the development of personality across childhood into adulthood.

2. In what ways are attachment theory (Chapter 9) and Erikson's psychosocial theory similar?

## 10.3 Neurodevelopmental Disorders

### LEARNING OBJECTIVES

**Retrieval Practice**   While reading the upcoming sections, respond to each Learning Objective in your own words.

**Review the major concepts and theories that help explain neurodevelopmental disorders.**

- **Discuss** attention-deficit/hyperactivity disorder (ADHD), including its symptoms, causal factors, and treatment options.
- **Describe** autism spectrum disorder (ASD), including its symptoms, causal factors, and treatment options.

Our study of life span development so far has focused on normal or typical development. But as we all know, everything doesn't always happen according to the book (even a textbook). Some children and their families are challenged by physical, cognitive, or socioemotional symptoms that may make learning or social relationships more difficult. These **neurodevelopmental disorders** usually begin during childhood and arise from abnormal brain development. They can result in a wide range of disorders, including intellectual disability (discussed in Chapter 8), as well as difficulties in communication and learning. We will focus on two of the more common neurodevelopmental disorders: *attention-deficit/hyperactivity disorder* and *autism spectrum disorder*.

**Neurodevelopmental disorders** A group of disorders that usually begin in early life, causing problems with communication, cognitive abilities, social relationships, and/or behavior.

## Attention-Deficit/Hyperactivity Disorder (ADHD)

Do you find it difficult to sit through a typical college class lecture or to focus on studying? Do you often fail to meet deadlines or forget to pay your bills? Although most of us find these tasks challenging at times, we can generally force ourselves to power through and do what needs to be done. Someone with ADHD, though, often finds such tasks nearly impossible.

**Attention-deficit/hyperactivity disorder (ADHD)** A common developmental disorder characterized by a pattern of inattention and/or hyperactivity-impulsivity.

**Attention-deficit/hyperactivity disorder (ADHD)** is a developmental disorder characterized by a pattern of inattention and/or hyperactivity-impulsivity that is present in multiple settings and interferes with social, educational, or work functioning (American Psychiatric Association, 2013). According to the American Psychiatric Association's *Diagnostic and Statistical Manual of Mental Disorders (DSM-5)*, about 5% of children have ADHD, with about twice as many boys as girls meeting the official diagnostic criteria. Symptoms typically begin prior to the age of 12 and, in many cases, last into adulthood.

What causes ADHD? Like most psychological processes, it's likely to result from an interaction of both biological and psychosocial causes, but the greatest contributors appear to be neurological and genetic factors (Barkley, 2017; Kim et al., 2017b; Thapar & Cooper, 2016). Interestingly, research finds that children with ADHD fail to get enough high-quality sleep, but it's unclear whether this is a possible cause or just a side effect and symptom of the disorder (Virring et al., 2016).

The symptoms of ADHD cause various problems. For example, a child with *hyperactivity* and *impulsivity* may have significant difficulty in school due to his inability to remain seated during class or to carefully read through instructions or test questions. He may run into difficulty with peers when he doesn't follow the rules or wait patiently for his turn at games. An *inattentive* child may not call as much attention to herself as a hyperactive child, but she will often forget to turn in assignments, daydream in class instead of listening to the teacher, and lose track of her books, pencils, and other items.

Experts once believed most children would "grow out" of ADHD. Today, evidence suggests that some aspects of the disorder tend to persist into adolescence and adulthood (Guelzow et al., 2017). Specifically, symptoms of hyperactivity generally decline with age, whereas inattention and impulsivity persist. Women with ADHD are more likely than men to experience the *inattentive* symptoms of ADHD, such as being easily sidetracked at work, missing appointments or important details in a meeting, and misplacing significant items like car keys or a wallet. Men with ADHD more often exhibit *impulsivity* symptoms, such as having difficulty waiting their turn while standing in line, butting into others' conversations, or blurting out the answer to a question before it has been completed.

Do you see how these symptoms of ADHD would naturally impede success at school or work (Weyandt et al., 2017)? They also can have a deep impact on self-esteem and interpersonal relationships. In addition, people with ADHD are more likely to suffer from serious anxiety, depression, and substance abuse disorders and to self-injure or even commit suicide (Barkley, 2017; Chen et al., 2014; Rucklidge et al., 2016).

These findings have prompted researchers and clinicians to closely examine and evaluate the various causes and treatments of ADHD. One of the most puzzling and controversial aspects of this disorder is determining how many children actually have ADHD. The Center for Disease Control (CDC) reports that that the percentage of children who have received a diagnosis of ADHD by a health care provider varies by state, from a low of 5.6% in Nevada to a high of 18.7% in Kentucky (Visser et al., 2014). Moreover, it seems that the number of children being diagnosed with ADHD is increasing.

So what's going on? It's certainly possible that ADHD is being overdiagnosed. Children today are more likely to be in institutional settings, such as day care and preschool, at very young ages. These environments may require more attention and behavioral control than some children can handle, prompting caregivers or parents to seek a medical solution. Yet another contributing factor could be that almost all children today spend more time indoors with less opportunity for exercise than in the past, which tends to exacerbate the symptoms of ADHD. For older kids, teens, and young adults, the increased pressure for high standardized test scores and academic or career success becomes particularly troublesome for those suffering from ADHD. Others suggest that the rise in ADHD is due to misdiagnosis and confusion with other disorders. The increase has also been attributed to parents, teachers, and medical practitioners who label normal behavior as pathological, as well as aggressive campaigning by pharmaceutical companies (Molina & Pelham, 2014; Monastra, 2014).

The most common treatment for ADHD is stimulant medication (such as Ritalin or Adderall). And the use of ADHD medication has markedly increased in the last 20 years (Bachmann et al., 2017). Contrary to what you might expect, the areas of the brain that help us to focus, pay attention, and control behavior are actually underaroused in someone with ADHD. For many people with ADHD, stimulant medications help to reduce hyperactivity and improve their ability to pay attention. For others, though, the medication's side effects may be unacceptable, and finding the correct medication and dosage can be challenging.

An additional concern is the increased recreational use of ADHD drugs. They're also being abused to increase academic and job performance and as weight-loss aids (Bagot & Kaminer, 2014; Schwarz, 2013.) One large-scale survey of 8th, 9th, and 11th graders found that Ritalin and other ADHD medications were the prescription drugs most frequently used for nonmedical purposes—even outranking opiate-based painkillers (Forster et al., 2017). Although the effectiveness of ADHD medications is well-documented, there is little information regarding how it affects non-ADHD users. And one worrisome study noted changes in the brain chemistry resulting in increased risk-taking behaviors and disruptions in the sleep-wake cycle (Robison et al., 2017).

Fortunately, many who suffer from ADHD may benefit from behavioral interventions at home and at school. These behavioral strategies include giving clear, step-by-step instructions, immediate feedback on tasks, and ample warning before transitioning between activities (e.g., Monastra, 2014). An example of behavioral interventions comes from renowned Olympic athlete Michael Phelps, who was diagnosed with ADHD in childhood (**Figure 10.2**). At 10 years of age, Michael became so upset at coming in second at a swim meet that he angrily threw his goggles onto the pool deck. His mother quickly reminded him that sportsmanship counted as much as winning, and together they designed a C-shaped hand signal that she could give him from the stands that stood for "compose yourself" (Dutton, 2014). Like many others with ADHD, Michael found that competitive sports helped him focus and successfully deal with his disorder.

Bloomberg/Getty Images

**FIGURE 10.2** **Attention-deficit hyperactivity disorder (ADHD)** Olympic swimming legend Michael Phelps was diagnosed with ADHD when he was in 6th grade.

**Test Your Critical Thinking**

1. Given the core symptoms of ADHD—inattention and/or hyperactivity-impulsivity—how could Michael Phelps endure the long and grueling years of practice and training required to become a star Olympic athlete?

2. If you or a loved one has been diagnosed with ADHD, how has it affected your college and personal life?

## Autism Spectrum Disorder (ASD)

**Autism spectrum disorder (ASD)** is a developmental disorder that begins in early childhood and involves problems with social communication and social interaction, as well as restricted, repetitive patterns of behavior, interests, or activities.

Interestingly, autism may be one of the most familiar yet least understood of the developmental disorders. As with ADHD, the reported cases of ASD have risen sharply in recent years and experts disagree about the explanations for this increase (e.g., Graf et al., 2017). Sadly, film and television portrayals of the disorder far too often create a distorted view of a person with extraordinary talents (such as a mathematical or musical prodigy) and a complete lack of emotional or social skills. Actually, the truth is somewhere in between (see **Figure 10.3**).

The most recent *Diagnostic and Statistical Manual of Mental Disorders* (DSM-5) made a significant change in the way autism-related disorders are categorized. The previously separate diagnoses (autistic, Asperger's, childhood disintegrative, and pervasive developmental

**Autism spectrum disorder (ASD)**   A developmental disorder that begins in early childhood and involves problems with social communication and social interaction, as well as restricted, repetitive patterns of behavior, interests, or activities.

Jim Steele/Popperfoto/Getty Images

**FIGURE 10.3** **Susan Boyle and autism spectrum disorder (ASD)** The world was shocked when Susan Boyle first appeared on the *Britain's Got Talent* show in 2009, but she quickly impressed the judges and later rose to great fame and fortune. Her iconic version of the song "I Dreamed a Dream," along with her trouble-filled life story, due in large part to her ASD, are great examples of the power of a growth mindset and grit.

disorders) are now combined into a single category, *autism spectrum disorder (ASD)*. The use of the term "spectrum" refers to a *range* of symptoms and disabilities, with no single identified cause. In order to be diagnosed, a child must show symptoms from an early age. However, those symptoms may not be problematic until the child is in an environment (such as school) that would highlight the deficits.

ASD symptoms fall into two main types: social/communicative and behavioral. People with ASD have difficulty with both verbal and nonverbal communication. They may respond inappropriately in conversations, misinterpret abstract or emotional content, or fail to interpret nonverbal cues (such as looking pointedly at one's watch or rolling one's eyes). In conversations, people with ASD may seem to be talking *at* rather than *with* you, because they focus entirely on their own interests and ideas. Some individuals with ASD may lack the ability to speak at all or may have cognitive impairments (such as low IQ). In such cases, communication may be made easier through the use of handheld, touchscreen technologies that allow for messaging or e-mailing. Those who are non-verbal and cannot read or write may be able to communicate by choosing pictures on a touchscreen—a picture of a food item they might want to eat, or a picture that indicates they need to use the bathroom.

The behavioral symptoms vary quite a bit, but most people with ASD show a strong preference for routine and are upset by and resistant to any efforts to change things. People with ASD also tend to have intense, restricted interests, often focused on inappropriate objects (such as train schedules or light switches). In more severe cases, the behavioral symptoms may take the form of self-injury, such as head-banging or self-biting.

ASD is a complex neurodevelopmental condition that is associated with many different causes. However, most research suggests that biological factors are the greatest contributors (Butler, 2017; Geschwind & State, 2015; Kim et al., 2017b). For instance, the heritability of ASD is high, and brain development in infants with autism is abnormal. Researchers have found that infants later diagnosed with autism had smaller-than-average head size at birth but had heads and brains much larger than normal by 6 to 14 months (Libero et al., 2016; Martinez-Murcia et al., 2016; Sacco et al., 2015). Brain imaging studies suggest that the areas of the cortex most affected by these abnormal growth patterns, the frontal lobes, are those areas essential to complex functions such as attention, social behavior, and language.

Interestingly, research suggests that ASD's established link with a lack of theory of mind (ToM) is also probably biologically based (e.g., Cheng et al., 2015; Frith, 2016; Hutchins & Prelock, 2015). As discussed in Chapter 9, ToM is the ability to understand that others don't share the same thoughts and feelings that we do. And experts believe that this impediment helps explain the communication and social interaction problems typical of people with ASD, as well as those with ADHD.

ASD is especially disruptive to development because of its very early onset. Although symptoms and severity may vary widely, ASD treatment should begin as early as possible. Treatment options usually focus on increasing effective communication, learning social skills, and decreasing problematic behaviors. Many treatment programs use *operant conditioning*, a form of therapy that you learned about in Chapter 6. This approach attempts to shape and reward desired behaviors (such as making eye contact) through the use of reinforcement. Children with ASD may also need speech and/or occupational therapy to directly address language or motor difficulties. Although there is no medication that specifically targets autism, children who also have other symptoms, such as hyperactivity or anxiety, may benefit from medication.

Before going on, it's important to dispel the persistent myth that ASD is caused by vaccines or by the preservatives used in vaccines. Numerous studies have failed to find a causal link between vaccinations and autism, and it appears that one well-known study reporting such a link was fraudulent (Jain et al., 2015; Lilienfeld et al., 2010; McGuinness, 2015). There is a similar lack of strong evidence for other dietary or environmental factors. It is easy to understand, though, how well-meaning parents would grasp at any potential solution to prevent or treat this devastating disorder. Unfortunately, experts strongly believe that parents who refuse to vaccinate their children risk even more dangerous consequences.

© Billy R. Ray/ Wiley

## Retrieval Practice 10.3 | Neurodevelopmental Disorders

Completing this self-test and connections section, and then checking your answers by clicking on the answer button or by looking in Appendix B, will provide immediate feedback and helpful practice for exams.

**Self-Test**

1. Which of the following is TRUE of ADHD?
   a. More girls than boys are diagnosed with this disorder.
   b. Symptoms typically begin after the age of 12.
   c. Symptoms often last into adulthood.
   d. All of these are true.

2. Describe the major symptoms of ADHD.

3. Women with ADHD are more likely than men to experience the _____ symptoms of ADHD, whereas men more often exhibit _____ symptoms.
   a. inattentive; impulsivity
   b. behavioral; cognitive
   c. depressive; anxiety
   d. hyperactivity; inattentive

4. ASD symptoms fall into two main types: _____ and _____.

   a. verbal communication; nonverbal
   b. social/communicative; behavioral
   c. cognitive impairments; behavioral difficulties
   d. genetic; environmental

5. Which of the following is FALSE about ASD?
   a. Treatment should begin as early as possible.
   b. In ASD, the term "spectrum" refers to a *range* of symptoms and disabilities, with no single identified cause.
   c. Most experts believe it is caused by preservatives in vaccines.
   d. There is no medication that specifically targets autism.

**Connections—Chapter to Chapter**

Answering the following question will help you "look back and look ahead" to see the important connections among the subfields of psychology and chapters within this text.

In Chapter 14 (Psychological Disorders), we discuss the four major criteria for identifying abnormal behavior—deviance, dysfunction, distress, and danger. How do these four criteria apply to ADHD?

## 10.4 | Challenges of Adulthood

**LEARNING OBJECTIVES**

**Retrieval Practice** While reading the upcoming sections, respond to each Learning Objective in your own words.

**Summarize the key challenges of adulthood and how we can best cope with them.**

- **Discuss** the key factors in relationships.
- **Review** the personal challenges of aging.
- **Discuss** the major issues surrounding grief, death, and dying.

Now that we've completed our whirlwind trip through the major theories and concepts explaining morality, personality development, and neurodevelopmental disorders, you may be wondering how this applies to your current adult life. In this section, we will explore several critical developmental tasks we all face as adults: developing a long-term, committed relationship with another person, coping with the challenges of family life, finding rewarding work and retirement, and the major issues of grief, death, and dying.

## Relationships

One of the most essential tasks faced during adulthood is that of establishing some form of continuing, loving, sexual relationship with another person. Research shows that marriage is associated with improved overall health outcomes, greater life satisfaction, lower stress, less depression, and lower waking blood pressure (e.g., Blekesaune, 2017; Effects of Marriage, 2016;

Lim & Raymo, 2016). As expected, same-sex partnerships and opposite-sex unions offer similar health benefits (Frech et al., 2016).

**Divorce**   Despite the obvious advantages to committed relationships, they also pose significant challenges. For example, many marriages end in divorce, which has serious implications for both adults and children (Braithwaite et al., 2016; Chun et al., 2016; Shafer et al., 2016). For the adults, both spouses generally experience emotional as well as practical difficulties and are at high risk for depression and physical health problems. However, many problems assumed to be due to divorce are actually present before marital disruption, and, for some, divorce can be life enhancing. In a "healthy" divorce, ex-spouses must accomplish three tasks: *let go, develop new social ties*, and, when children are involved, *redefine parental roles* (Everett & Everett, 1994).

In addition to stresses on the divorcing couple, some research shows that children also suffer both short-term and long-lasting effects. Compared with children in continuously intact two-parent families, children of divorce exhibit more behavioral problems, poorer self-concepts, more psychological problems, lower academic achievement, and more substance abuse and social difficulties, according to some researchers (Friesen et al., 2017; Hosokawa & Katsura, 2017; Shafer et al., 2016). Other researchers, however, find little or no effect on children's social and behavioral problems. Still other researchers have suggested that both parents and children may do better without the constant tension and fighting of an intact, but unhappy, home (Bernet & Ash, 2007; Hakvoort et al., 2011).

Whether children become "winners" or "losers" in a divorce depends on the (1) individual attributes of the child, (2) qualities of the custodial family, (3) continued involvement with noncustodial parents, and (4) resources and support systems available to the child and parents (Ferraro et al., 2016; Modecki et al., 2015; Vélez et al., 2011). If you or your parents are currently considering or going through a divorce, you may want to keep these four factors in mind when making legal and other decisions about children. Before going on, it's important to dispel the popular myth that over half of all marriages in the United States end in divorce. In actuality, the rate of divorce has been declining since the 1970s. Today, only about a third of marriages end in divorce (Swanson, 2016).

## ❖ Psychology and Your Personal Success:  |  What Are the Secrets to Enduring Love?

*By Thomas Frangicetto, Northampton Community College, Bethlehem, PA*

Have you ever wished you knew the secrets of happy marriages and committed romantic relationships—as shown in the photo? Renowned psychologist and marriage researcher John Gottman believes he knows, and there's nothing secret about them (see photo). Based on over four decades of rigorous scientific observation, Gottman and his colleagues have identified seven basic principles they believe explain why some relationships grow and flourish, whereas others deteriorate and die (Gottman, 2011; Gottman & Gottman, 2015; Navarra et al., 2016).

To evaluate your own relationship, take the following quiz based on these same seven principles. (Note: Although written primarily for marital spouses, the principles apply to all long-term relationships—friends, lovers, and even parents and children.)

### Principle 1: Enhance your "love maps."

*Does your partner know about the major events in your life and your goals, worries, and dreams for the future? Do you know the same about him or her? Yes ___ No ___*

Emotionally intelligent couples are "intimately familiar" with each other's lives because both partners pay attention to one another and are willing to share their innermost thoughts and feelings. Gottman says this type of attention and sharing leads to the creation of richly detailed "*love maps*." Our partner should be the one person in the world who knows us almost as well as we know ourselves—and vice versa.

### Principle 2: Nurture your fondness and admiration.

*Do you basically like and respect your partner? Yes ___ No ___*

Although happily married couples may, at times, feel annoyed by their partner's personality quirks, they still consider their spouse worthy of honor and respect. Nurturing fondness and expressing admiration are essential factors in a mutually rewarding and durable romance. How important is this principle? Gottman answers: "When this sense is completely missing from a marriage, the relationship cannot be revived."

### Principle 3: Turn toward each other instead of away.

*Do you and your partner believe it's okay to tune each other out when your conversations become boring or mundane? Yes ___ No ___*

Think again. According to Gottman: "When couples stay tuned to one another, even when their talking seems trivial, and when they engage in lots of chitchat, I can be pretty sure that they will stay happily married." While these exchanges may seem inconsequential, they represent moments of bonding—the couple is *turning toward each other*. Couples headed for divorce rarely have these small, but crucial, moments of connection. Turning toward one another is the basis of emotional connection, romance, passion, and a good sex life.

### Principle 4: Let your partner influence you.

*Do you believe that "welcoming divergent views" doesn't necessarily include your partner's views? Yes ___ No ___*

It may take two to "make or break a marriage," but on this principle, women tend to have the positive edge. Gottman's research reveals that women more often "let their husbands influence their decision making by taking their opinions and feelings into account." And men? "They often do not return the favor." Gottman advises men to adopt the female approach because the most successful and stable marriages are those in which power and influence are shared.

### Principle 5: Solve your solvable problems.

*Do you believe that "love conquers all" or that good communication can solve all your problems? Yes ___ No ___*

Gottman suggests that what makes a good marriage is not communication, but how partners perceive one another and how they handle inevitable conflicts. He puts it simply: "When a husband and wife respect each other and are open to each other's point of view, they have a good basis for resolving any differences that arise." In addition to focusing on our partner's positive traits and accepting that he or she has our best interests at heart, Gottman suggests five steps for successful problem solving: (1) Soften your startup. (It's not what you say as much as how you say it.) (2) Learn to make and receive "repair attempts." (3) Soothe yourself and each other. ("Turn toward" one another with words or behaviors that help soften the conflict.) (4) Compromise. (5) Be tolerant of one another's faults.

Unfortunately, when we're really angry with our partner and emotionally threatened, we may not be able to remember these five steps. We become overwhelmed by "emotional flooding," and our physiological "fight-flight-freeze" response kicks in—we want to attack, tune out (freeze), or run away! To make matters worse, during this time of high arousal, our higher, logical cognitive processes are limited (Chapter 3). In this heightened state, we may fail to recognize and/or accept repair attempts, as well as the need to soothe ourselves and our partner. Can you see why this lethal combination so often leads to an inevitable increase in tension and anger? The good news is that you can successfully cope with experiences of "flooding" by saying things like, "Let's stop for now. I need to calm down." Then agree when and where you'll resume your discussion.

### Principle 6: Overcome gridlock.

*Do you believe that major differences of opinion will destroy a marriage? Yes ___ No ___*

Gottman finds that about 70% of marital conflicts are unsolvable! Do you find this surprising? It actually should be reassuring. Knowing that we all have "irreconcilable differences" with those we love means that we don't need to assume that they will automatically lead to divorce or the loss of valuable relationships. Instead of wasting huge amounts of time and energy arguing our case in the hopes of changing our partner's opinions, we need to recognize that serious and perpetual problems are generally about core values and personal views of the world—which seldom change! The goal in ending "gridlock"—those situations that seemingly won't yield to agreement—is *not* to solve the problem as much as it is to progress from gridlock to engage in dialogue. Gottman's unhappy couples are often stuck in "loss-loss loops," whereas his successful couples learn to engage in dialogue and then "live with the problem."

Keep in mind that gridlock is often rooted in oppositional hopes or dreams. Gottman's happy couples recognize this and understand that helping each other realize their competing desires is one of the goals of marriage. They try to establish some level of "initial compromise," and then continue working on bridging or ending the gridlock with mutual respect and compromise.

**Principle 7: Create shared meaning.**

*Do you and your partner work to create an intentional, shared purpose for your relationship? Yes ___ No ___*

While similar to establishing "love maps," this principle encourages partners to work at developing a *deeper sense of shared meaning*. Successful couples go out of their way to create traditions and rituals that help them stay connected. For example, they routinely schedule and honor holiday and birthday get-togethers, they have a designated date night or family home evening, or they always hug or kiss before bed or leaving one another in the morning. This results in the sort of shared history that becomes an almost "spiritual dimension that has to do with creating an inner life together—a culture rich with symbols and rituals."

Bottom line: If we want our love and relationships to not only last, but also flourish, we need to be willing to work at nurturing, repairing, and protecting them. For additional information on John Gottman's extensive research and available book titles, go to: www.gottman.com.

### Domestic Violence
Families can be warm and loving. They also can be cruel and abusive. Maltreatment and abuse are more widely recognized than in the past. However, it is difficult to measure domestic violence because it usually occurs in private and victims are reluctant to report it out of shame, feelings of powerlessness, or fear of reprisal. Nevertheless, every year millions of cases of domestic violence, child abuse, intimate partner violence (IPV), and elder abuse are known to occur, and many more are not reported to police or social service agencies (e.g., Edwards et al., 2017; Reuter et al., 2017; Stover & Lent, 2014).

What causes domestic violence? Research shows that it occurs more often in families experiencing marital conflict, pregnancy, substance abuse, mental disorders, and economic stress (Labrum & Solomon, 2016; Low et al., 2017; Miller-Graff & Cheng, 2017). Keep in mind that abuse and violence occur at all socioeconomic levels. However, abuse and violence do occur more frequently in families disrupted by unemployment or other financial distress.

In addition, many abusive family members are socially isolated and lack good communication and parenting skills. Their anxiety and frustration may explode into spouse, child, or elder abuse. In fact, one of the clearest identifiers of abuse potential is *impulsivity*. People who abuse their children, their dating partners or spouses, or their elderly parents seem to lack impulse control, especially when stressed. They also respond to stress with more intense emotions and greater arousal (Chamorro et al., 2012; Finkenauer et al., 2015; Leone et al., 2016). This impulsivity is related not only to psychosocial factors like economic stress and social isolation (with no one to turn to for help or feedback) but also to possible biological influences.

Biologically, three regions of the brain are closely related to the expression and control of aggression: the amygdala, the prefrontal cortex, and the hypothalamus (see Chapter 2 to review these regions). Interestingly, head injuries, strokes, dementia, schizophrenia, alcoholism, abuse of stimulant drugs, and nonmedical use of prescription drugs have all been linked to these three areas and to aggressive outbursts (e.g., Low et al., 2017; Parks et al., 2017; Smith et al., 2016).

When people hear about domestic violence, they often wonder why the victim doesn't immediately report the abuse to authorities and/or simply leave. As with most social problems, the causes of domestic violence are complex, and the solutions are far from simple (Low et al., 2017; Murray et al., 2016; Pill et al., 2017):

- First, abuse is almost never a single, isolated explosion. Instead, it generally involves numerous events that follow a cyclical and escalating pattern. In the beginning, perpetrators can be devoted and caring partners or parents, but when disagreements happen the abusers respond with increasing levels of intimidation, bullying, and violence, while the victims learn that the only way to calm the situation is to respond with increasing levels of compliance and subservience.
- Second, abuse occurs in many forms (physical, verbal, and emotional), which makes it harder to identify and report. And domestic violence is much more difficult to report and prosecute than attacks by strangers. Child abuse may be dismissed as a parent's right to discipline, and spousal assault is often ignored or treated as insignificant.
- Third, the victims' own mixed feelings may stop them from leaving. Given that abuse is about power and control, victims are typically afraid of what will happen if they leave. It's also difficult to admit that they've been abused, and some even believe that abuse is normal. Many also stay for cultural and religious reasons, and others because they still have feelings of love for the abuser and want to keep the relationship or family together.
- Fourth, and possibly most importantly, many victims are financially or physically dependent on the abuser and simply see no alternative.

Despite these obstacles, there is help if you or someone you know is involved in domestic violence. You can reach trained counselors 24 hours a day anywhere in North America by calling 1-800-799-SAFE, and on the Internet at www.thehotline.org.

*If your friends and family are telling you to run, not walk away from a relationship, take their advice!*
                                                                                              —Anonymous

# Challenges of Aging

Having discussed the difficulties of finding and keeping committed relationships, we now turn to other important challenges of adulthood.

### Work and Retirement
Throughout most of our adult lives, work defines us in fundamental ways. It affects our health, our friendships, where we live, and even our leisure activities. How can we find personally satisfying and long-lasting careers? Choosing an occupation is one of the most influential decisions in our lives, and the task is becoming ever more difficult and complex as career options rapidly change due to increasing specialization, job fluctuations, and the global economy. The *Dictionary of Occupational Titles*, a government publication, currently lists more than 200,000 job categories. One way to learn more about these job categories and potential careers is to visit your college career center. These centers typically offer an abundance of resources, as well as interesting and helpful vocational interest tests.

Work is a big part of adult life and self-identity. But the large majority of men and women in the United States choose to retire sometime in their sixties. Fortunately, the loss of self-esteem and depression that are commonly assumed to accompany retirement may be largely a myth. Life satisfaction after retirement appears to be most strongly related to good health, control over one's life, social support, adequate income, and participation in community services and social activities (e.g., Henning et al., 2016; Li & Loo, 2016; Tovel & Carmel, 2014).

### Theories of Aging
Active involvement in community and social activities is the key ingredient to a fulfilling old age, according to the **activity theory of aging**. In contrast, **disengagement theory** holds that successful aging is a natural and graceful withdrawal from life (Achenbaum & Bengtson, 1994; Cavanaugh & Blanchard-Fields, 2014; Cummings & Henry, 1961) (**Figure 10.4**). Today, disengagement theory has been largely abandoned. Successful aging does *not* require withdrawal from society. We mention this theory because of its historical relevance and also because of its connection to an influential modern perspective, **socioemotional selectivity theory**.

**Activity theory of aging** A theory holding that successful aging is fostered by a full and active commitment to life.

**Disengagement theory of aging** A theory holding that successful aging is characterized by mutual withdrawal between older people and society.

**Socioemotional selectivity theory of aging** A theory holding that a natural decline in social contact occurs as older adults become more selective with their time.

Steve Cole/Getty Images

**FIGURE 10.4**   **Disengagement versus activity**   The disengagement theory of aging suggests that older people naturally disengage and withdraw from life. However, judging by the apparently happy people in this photo, activity theory may be a better model to follow because it suggests that everyone should remain active and involved throughout the entire life span.

This latest model helps explain the predictable decline in social contact that almost everyone experiences as they move into their older years (Carstensen et al., 2011; English & Carstensen, 2014; Williams et al., 2017). According to socioemotional selectivity theory, we don't naturally withdraw from society in our later years—we just become more *selective* with our time. We deliberately choose to decrease our total number of social contacts in favor of familiar people who provide emotionally meaningful interactions (see the **Try This Yourself**).

Although older people do tend to reduce their number of social contacts, they're surprisingly happier! Contrary to stereotypes about "grumpy old people," psychological research consistently finds an increase in happiness and well-being as we grow older (Kern et al., 2014; Riediger & Luong, 2016; Sutin et al., 2013). Why? Research finds that older people tend to have stronger relationships, to value their time more than money, and to become more selective with their time and friendships (offering further support for socioemotional selectivity theory) (Birditt & Newton, 2016; Vaillant, 2012; Whillans et al., 2016).

## Try This Yourself

### Socioemotional selectivity

Note how our emotional needs appear to change over our life span (see photo). Can you explain why?

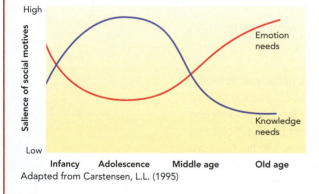

Adapted from Carstensen, L.L. (1995)

Courtesy Sandy Harvey

**Answer:** During infancy, emotional connection is essential to our survival. During childhood, adolescence, and early adulthood, information gathering is critical, and the need for emotional connection declines. During late adulthood, emotional satisfaction is again more important—we tend to invest our time in those who can be counted on in times of need.

**Age-related positivity effect**   The preference in older adults for positive over negative information and events in attention and memory.

In addition, according to the **age-related positivity effect**, older adults generally prefer and pay more sustained attention to positive versus negative information and events (Carstensen, 1993, 2006; Livingstone & Isaacowitz, 2016; Mikels & Shuster, 2016). Further research finds that this age-related positivity effect may even increase immune functioning and overall well-being after charitable giving (Bjälkebring et al., 2016; Kalokerinos et al., 2014).

Younger people, in contrast, tend to show an opposite approach—preferring and paying more attention to negative versus positive information and events. Do you see how this might help explain why the college years can feel so painful and troublesome in your 20s, while in later years they might be remembered as "the best years of your life"? It appears that older adults have developed greater emotional regulation, and that they deliberately focus their attention and memory in a positive direction. How can we use this information to improve our lives regardless of age? See the following **Try This Yourself**.

## Try This Yourself

### Increasing Your Positivity

At first glance, the answer to becoming more positive is "simple"—just focus on positive information and events. Obviously, this is harder than it appears. For more help, recall from Chapter 3 that this type of optimistic thinking is a personality trait that can be learned and developed. In addition, Chapter 15 offers tips for overcoming faulty thought processes.

Interestingly, recent research shows that practicing *gratitude exercises* may be the fastest way to become a more optimistic and positive person while also enhancing well-being, happiness, life satisfaction, interpersonal relationships, and even physical health (Alkozei et al., 2017; Layous et al., 2017; Yoshimura & Berzins, 2017). Try these simple exercises:

Louise Gubb/Contributor/Getty Images

1. Create a daily gratitude list of the things that you're grateful for, and review the list each morning.

2. Put things in perspective. Gratitude isn't just for the good things in life. When things go wrong, ask yourself, "What's good about this?" and "What can I learn from this?"

3. Send thank you e-mails or letters to the special people who have had a favorable impact on your life. Even better—visit them in person.

For more information on the age-related positivity effect, see the following **Research Challenge**.

## Research Challenge

### Are Brain Differences Associated with Age-Related Happiness?

To test possible neural changes underlying the positive attention and memory bias exhibited by older people, researchers asked both younger adults (ages 19–31) and older adults (ages 61–80) to look at a series of photographs with positive and negative themes, such as a skier winning a race or a wounded soldier, and to remember as much as they could about the photographs (Addis et al., 2010). While participants viewed these images, researchers measured their brain activity through the use of functional magnetic resonance imaging (fMRI) scans (Chapter 2).

Surprisingly, they found no difference between brain activity in the encoding of information among younger and older adults as they looked at negative images. However, when viewing the positive images, areas of older adults' brains that process emotions (the amygdala and the ventromedial prefrontal cortex) directly affected the hippocampus. (As you recall, the hippocampus is responsible for encoding and storage of memories.) In contrast, in the younger adults' brains, the thalamus (a "simple" relay station) had a bigger influence on the hippocampus. This suggests that older adults may be better at sustaining attention on positive information and remembering more good times because brain regions that process positive emotions are instructing the hippocampus to "remember this."

ViewStock/Getty Images

2. If you chose:
   - *descriptive research*, is this a naturalistic observation, survey/interview, case study, and/or archival research?
   - *correlational research*, is this a positive, negative, or zero correlation?
   - *experimental research*, label the IV, DV, experimental group(s), and control group. (Note: If participants were not randomly assigned to groups, list it as a *quasi-experimental design*.)
   - both *descriptive* and *correlational,* answer the corresponding questions for both.

Check your answers by clicking on the answer button or by looking in Appendix B.

**Note:** The information provided in this study is admittedly limited, but the level of detail is similar to what is presented in most textbooks and public reports of research findings. Answering these questions, and then comparing your answers to those provided, will help you become a better critical thinker and consumer of scientific research.

#### Test Yourself

1. Based on the information provided, did the researchers in this study (Addis et al., 2010) use descriptive, correlational, and/or experimental research?

## Myth Busters

### Myths of Development

A number of popular beliefs about age-related crises are not firmly supported by research. The popular idea of a *midlife crisis* began largely as a result of Gail Sheehy's national best-seller *Passages* (1976). Sheehy drew on the theories of Daniel Levinson (1959, 1977, 1996) and psychiatrist Roger Gould (1975), as well as her own interviews. She popularized the idea that almost everyone experiences a "predictable crisis" at about age 35 for women and 40 for men. Middle age often is a time of reexamining one's values and lifetime goals. However, Sheehy's book led many people to automatically expect a midlife crisis with drastic changes in personality and behavior. Research suggests that a severe reaction or crisis may be quite rare and unlike what most people experience during middle age (Freund & Ritter, 2009; Lilienfeld et al., 2010; Whitbourne & Mathews, 2009).

Many people also believe that when the last child leaves home, most parents experience *empty-nest syndrome*—a painful separation and time of depression for the mother, the father, or both parents. Again, research suggests that the empty-nest syndrome may be an exaggeration of the pain experienced by a few individuals. Societal and cultural norms, as well as the quality of the family relationships, also play a role in empty-nest perceptions (Mitchell & Wister, 2015; Proulx & Helms, 2008). For example,

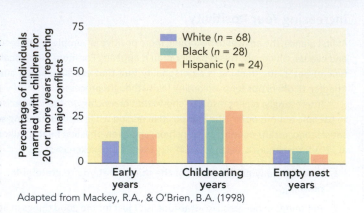

Adapted from Mackey, R.A., & O'Brien, B.A. (1998)

**FIGURE 10.5**  **Myth of the empty nest**

one major benefit of the empty nest is a decrease in conflicts and an increase in marital satisfaction (**Figure 10.5**). Moreover, parent–child relationships do continue once the child leaves home. As one mother said, "The empty nest is surrounded by telephone wires" (Troll et al., 1979, p. 34). Fortunately, this is even more true today with cell phones, e-mail, and video chat services.

# Grief, Death, and Dying

One unavoidable part of life is its end. How can we understand and prepare ourselves for the loss of our own life and those of loved others? In this section, we look at the four stages of grief. We then consider cultural and age-related differences in attitudes toward death. We conclude with death itself as a final developmental crisis.

> *Quien teme la muerte no goza la vida. (He who fears death cannot enjoy life)*
>
> —Spanish Proverb

## Grief—A Lesson in Survival

> *What do I do now that you're gone? Well, when there's nothing else going on, which is quite often, I sit in a corner and I cry until I am too numbed to feel. Paralyzed motionless for a while, nothing moving inside or out. Then I think how much I miss you. Then I feel fear, pain, loneliness, desolation. Then I cry until I am too numbed to feel. Interesting pastime* (Colgrove et al., 1991, p. 18).

Have you ever felt like this? If so, you are not alone. Loss and grief are an inevitable part of all our lives. Feelings of desolation, loneliness, and heartache, accompanied by painful memories, are common reactions to loss, disaster, and misfortune. Ironically, such painful emotions may serve a useful function. Evolutionary psychologists suggest that bereavement and grief may be adaptive mechanisms for both human and nonhuman animals. The pain may motivate parents and children or mates to search for one another. Obvious signs of distress also may be adaptive because they bring the group to the aid of the bereaved individual. Furthermore, grief makes us aware of the fragile nature of life, and reminds us to protect, cherish, and feel grateful for the many gifts that remain.

What does it mean if someone seems emotionless after a significant loss? Grieving is a complicated and personal process. Just as there is no right way to die, there is no right way to grieve (**Figure 10.6**). People who restrain their grief may be following the rules for emotional display that prevail in their cultural group. Moreover, although outward signs of strong emotion may be the most obvious expression of grief, they are not the only way grief is expressed.

Some theorists have proposed that there are four stages in the "normal" grieving process (Bowlby, 1994; Morrow, 2016; Parkes, 1972, 2015). In the initial phase, *shock and numbness*, bereaved individuals may seem dazed and may feel little emotion other than numbness or emptiness. They also may deny the death, insisting that a mistake has been made.

In the second stage, individuals enter a period of *yearning and searching*, experiencing intense longing for the loved one and pangs of guilt, anger, and resentment. They may also experience illusions. They "see" the deceased person in his or her favorite chair or in the face of a stranger. They also report having vivid dreams in which the deceased is still alive, or they feel the "presence" of the dead person. In addition, they may experience strong guilt feelings ("If only I had gotten her to a doctor sooner" "I should have been more loving") and anger or resentment ("Why wasn't he more careful?" "It isn't fair that I'm the one left behind").

Sharon Gekoski-Kimmel/KRT/Newscom

**FIGURE 10.6    Grieving**   Individuals vary in their emotional reactions to loss.

Once the powerful feelings of yearning subside, bereaved individuals reportedly enter the third stage, *disorganization and despair*. Life seems to lose its meaning. The mourners feel listless, apathetic, and submissive. As time goes by, however, they gradually begin to accept the loss both intellectually (the loss makes sense) and emotionally (memories are pleasurable as well as painful). This acceptance, combined with building a new self-identity ("I am a single mother" "We are no longer a couple"), characterizes the fourth and final stage of grief—*reorganization and recovery*.

This is just one model for how some people may grieve, and once again, grief is obviously not the same for everyone. We all vary in the way we grieve, the supposed stages of grief we experience, and the length of time needed for "recovery" (Hooghe, 2017; Neimeyer, 2014; Tseng et al., 2014).

Before going on, it's important to note a seldom mentioned fact—death sometimes also brings strong feelings of guilt and anger or even relief and happiness! When death ends the suffering of a loved one, a tormented or abusive relationship, or the burden of caring for a terminally ill person, it's normal to experience such emotions. Unfortunately, most people are ashamed of these feelings and suffer alone with their mixed emotions, never knowing that such feelings are common and healthy responses. One of the many benefits of studying psychology is discovering that our "shameful" emotions are almost always a natural part of the human experience. For more information on this topic, a riveting book called *Liberating Losses*, by Jennifer Elison and Chris McGonigle (2004), provides a personal and pragmatic look at what they call "relieved grievers." The following **Try This Yourself** offers general tips for dealing with your own and others' grief.

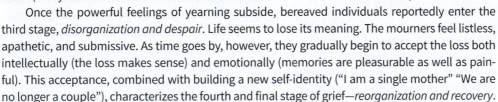

## Try This Yourself

### Dealing with Grief

What can you say or do to help another who has recently lost a loved one? Recognizing the large variation in how people grieve, your quiet presence and caring are generally the best type of response. Take your cues from the bereaved persons. If they're busily working around the house, or mention wanting to get out of the house, or go to a movie, join them. If they want to talk, listen.

When it comes to dealing with your own losses and grief, you may find the following tips helpful (Cacciatore & Rubin, 2016; Goldman, 2014; Neimeyer & Kosminsky, 2014).

1. *Expect the unexpected.* Although grief is an inevitable part of all our lives, we're generally unprepared for the magnitude and range of mixed emotions that it often entails. Heartache, sadness, and loneliness are expected. But as we've just seen, we also may feel relieved, angry, or happy. Recognizing that you have a right to your emotions, whatever they are, and that the intensity of feelings will soften over time, are valuable aids to successful coping. Mindfulness practices may also be helpful (Chapters 3 and 5).

2. *Take care of yourself.* Accept the company and comfort of others. Most people genuinely want to help, and assigning them tasks and chores is a gift for all concerned. Comfort yourself by avoiding unnecessary stress, getting plenty of rest, and giving yourself permission to enjoy life whenever possible.

3. *Set up a daily activity schedule.* One of the best ways to offset the lethargy and depression of grief is to force yourself to fill your time with useful activities (studying, washing your car, doing the laundry, and so on). Outings with friends will help you focus on something other than your loss. If you want to relax and avoid talking about your loss, plan activities like going to a movie or an athletic event.

4. *Seek help.* Having the support of loving friends and family helps offset the loneliness and stress of grief. Recognize, however, that professional counseling may be necessary in cases of extreme or prolonged numbness, anger, guilt, or depression. (You'll learn more about depression and its treatment in Chapters 14 and 15.)

Mel Evans/AP Photos

**FIGURE 10.7   Culture influences our response to death**   In October 2006, a dairy truck driver took over a one-room Amish schoolhouse in Pennsylvania, killed and gravely injured several young girls, then shot himself. Instead of responding in rage, his Amish neighbors attended his funeral. Amish leaders urged forgiveness for the killer and called for a fund to aid his wife and three children. Rather than creating an on-site memorial, the schoolhouse was razed, to be replaced by pasture. What do you think of this response? The fact that many Americans were offended, shocked, or simply surprised by the Amish reaction illustrates how strongly culture affects our emotion, beliefs, and values.

## Attitudes toward Death and Dying

Cultures around the world interpret and respond to death in widely different ways: "Funerals are the occasion for avoiding people or holding parties, for fighting or having sexual orgies, for weeping or laughing, in a thousand combinations" (Metcalf & Huntington, 1991, p. 62).

Similarly, subcultures within the United States also have different responses to death (**Figure 10.7**). Irish Americans are likely to believe the dead deserve a good send-off—a wake with food, drink, and jokes. Blacks in America traditionally regard funerals as a time for serious grief, demonstrated in some congregations by wailing and singing spirituals. And most Japanese Americans try to restrain their grief and smile so as not to burden others with their pain. They also want to avoid the shame associated with losing emotional control (Corr et al., 2009; Kastenbaum, 2012; Schim et al., 2007).

Attitudes toward death and dying vary not only among cultures and subcultures but also with age. As adults, we understand death in terms of three basic concepts: (1) *permanence*—once a living thing dies, it cannot be brought back to life; (2) *universality*—all living things eventually die; and (3) *nonfunctionality*—all living functions, including thought, movement, and vital signs, end at death.

Research shows that permanence, the notion that death cannot be reversed, is the first and most easily understood concept (**Figure 10.8**). Understanding of universality comes slightly later. By about the age of seven, most children have mastered nonfunctionality and have an adultlike understanding of death. Adults may fear that discussing death with children and adolescents will make them unduly anxious. But those who are offered open, honest discussions of death have an easier time accepting it (Kastenbaum, 2012; Neimeyer & Kosminsky, 2014; Sori & Biank, 2016).

Susan Van Etten/PhotoEdit

**FIGURE 10.8   How do children understand death?**   Preschoolers seem to accept the fact that the dead person cannot get up again, perhaps because of their experiences with dead butterflies and beetles found while playing outside (Furman, 1990). Later, they begin to understand all that death entails and that they, too, will someday die.

**Death—Our Final Developmental Task**   Have you thought about your own death? Would you like to die suddenly and alone? Or would you prefer to know ahead of time so you could plan your funeral and spend time saying good-bye to your family and friends? If you find thinking about these questions uncomfortable, it may be because most people in Western societies try to avoid thinking about death. However, the better we understand death, and the more wisely we approach it, the more fully we can live until it comes.

During the Middle Ages (from about the fifth until the sixteenth century), people were expected to recognize when death was approaching so they could say their farewells and die with dignity, surrounded by loved ones. In recent times, Western societies have moved death out of the home and put it into the hospital and funeral parlor. Rather than personally caring for our dying family and friends, we have shifted responsibility to "experts"—physicians and morticians. We have made death a medical failure rather than a natural part of the life cycle.

This avoidance of death and dying may be changing, however. Since the late 1990s, right-to-die and death-with-dignity advocates have been working to bring death out in the open. And mental health professionals have suggested that understanding the psychological processes of death and dying may play a significant role in good adjustment (Leaming & Dickinson, 2011).

Confronting our own death is the last major crisis we face in life. What is it like? Is there a "best" way to prepare to die? Is there such a thing as a "good death"? After spending hundreds of hours at the bedsides of the terminally ill, Elisabeth Kübler-Ross developed a controversial stage theory of the psychological processes surrounding death (1983, 1997, 1999).

Based on interviews with individuals facing imminent death, Kübler-Ross proposed that most people go through five sequential stages when facing death:

- *Denial* of the terminal condition ("This can't be true; it's a mistake!")
- *Anger* ("Why me? It isn't fair!")
- *Bargaining* ("God, if you let me live, I'll dedicate my life to you!")
- *Depression* ("I'm losing everyone and everything I hold dear.")
- *Acceptance* ("I know that death is inevitable and my time is near.")

For more information on Kübler-Ross's theory and dealing with your own and others' death anxiety, see the following **Myth Busters** and the **Try this Yourself**.

*Let us endeavor so to live that when we come to die even the undertaker will be sorry.*
—Samuel Clemens (Mark Twain) (Author, Humorist)

**thanatology [than-uh-TAHL-uh-gee]** The study of death and dying; the term comes from *thanatus*, the Greek name for a mythical personification of death, and was borrowed by Freud to represent the death instinct.

## Myth Busters

### Kübler-Ross's Theory—A National Myth?

Like the proposed four stages of grief, the five-stage sequence for dying has not been scientifically validated. Some critics point out that each person's bereavement or death is a unique experience and that some people don't have time to go through all five stages. Furthermore, the dying person's emotions and reactions depend on personality, life situation, age, and so on. Others worry that popularizing such a stage theory will cause further avoidance and stereotyping of those who are grieving or dying ("He's just in the anger stage right now") and that grieving or dying people may feel pressured to conform to the stages Kübler-Ross described (Corr, 2015; Flamez et al., 2016; Lilienfeld et al., 2010).

In spite of these drawbacks, Kübler-Ross's theory has encouraged research into a long-neglected topic. **Thanatology**, the study of death and dying, has become a major topic in human development. Thanks in part to thanatology research, the dying are being helped to die with dignity by the *hospice* movement. These organizations have trained staff and volunteers to provide loving support for the terminally ill and their families in special facilities, hospitals, or the persons' own homes (Franz & LaForge, 2016; Goel et al., 2014; Kasl-Godley et al., 2014).

One influential contribution by Kübler-Ross (1975) may have been her suggestion that:

> It is the denial of death that is partially responsible for [people] living empty, purposeless lives; for when you live as if you'll live forever, it becomes too easy to postpone the things you know you must do. In contrast, when you fully understand that each day you awaken could be the last you have, you take the time that day to grow, to become more of who you really are, to reach out to other human beings (p. 164).

## Try This Yourself

### Coping with Your Own Death Anxiety

Woody Allen once said, "It's not that I'm afraid to die. I just don't want to be there when it happens." Although some people who are very old and in poor health may welcome death, most of us have difficulty facing it.

One of the most important elements of critical thinking is *self-knowledge*, which includes the ability to critically evaluate our deepest and most private fears.

*Death Anxiety Questionnaire*
To test your own level of death anxiety, indicate your response according to the following scale:

| 0 | 1 | 2 |
|---|---|---|
| not at all | somewhat | very much |

____ **1.** Do you worry about dying?

____ **2.** Does it bother you that you may die before you have done everything you wanted to do?

____ **3.** Do you worry that you may be very ill for a long time before you die?

____ **4.** Does it upset you to think that others may see you suffering before you die?

____ **5.** Do you worry that dying may be very painful?

____ **6.** Do you worry that the persons closest to you won't be with you when you are dying?

____ **7.** Do you worry that you may be alone when you are dying?

____ **8.** Are you bothered by the thought that you might lose control of your mind before death?

____ **9.** Do you worry that expenses connected with your death will be a burden to other people?

____ **10.** Does it worry you that your will or instructions about your belongings may not be carried out after you die?

____ **11.** Are you afraid that you may be buried before you are really dead?

_____ **12.** Does the thought of leaving loved ones behind when you die disturb you?

_____ **13.** Do you worry that those you care about may not remember you after your death?

_____ **14.** Are you worried by the thought that with death you will be gone forever?

_____ **15.** Are you worried about not knowing what to expect after death?

How does your total score compare to the national average of 8.5? When this same test was given to nursing-home residents, senior citizens, and college students, researchers found no significant differences, despite the fact that those tested ranged in age from 18 to 80.

**Source:** H. R. Conte, M. B. Weiner, & R. Plutchik (1982). Measuring death anxiety: Conceptual, psychometric, and factor-analytic aspects. *Journal of Personality and Social Psychology, 43*, 775–785. Reprinted with permission.

© Billy R. Ray/ Wiley

## Retrieval Practice 10.4 | Challenges of Adulthood

Completing this self-test and connections section, and then checking your answers by clicking on the answer button or by looking in Appendix B, will provide immediate feedback and helpful practice for exams.

### Self-Test

1. Researchers suggest that during a _____ divorce, ex-spouses learn how to let go, develop new social ties, and redefine parental roles (when children are involved).

   **a.** midlife
   **b.** patrimonial
   **c.** healthy
   **d.** Gottman-style

2. Which of the following is NOT one of the seven principles recommended for enduring love?

   **a.** Solve your solvable problems.
   **b.** Maintain a separate identity.
   **c.** Nurture your fondness and admiration.
   **d.** Let your partner influence you.

3. Briefly describe why someone might not report or leave an abusive relationship.

4. The _____ theory of aging says that one should remain active and involved in fulfilling activities as long as possible.

   **a.** social facilitation
   **b.** activity
   **c.** involvement
   **d.** life-enhancement

5. Match the following statements with Elisabeth Kübler-Ross's five-stage theory of death and dying:

   **a.** "I understand that I'm dying, but if I could just have a little more time . . ."
   **b.** "I refuse to believe the doctors. I want a fourth opinion."
   **c.** "I know my time is near. I'd better make plans for my spouse and children."
   **d.** "Why me? I've been a good person. I don't deserve this."
   **e.** "I'm losing everything. I'll never see my children again. This is so hard."

### Connections—Chapter to Chapter

Answering the following question will help you "look back and look ahead" to see the important connections among the subfields of psychology and chapters within this text.

In Chapter 16 (Social Psychology), we will explore some of the many factors that explain groupthink, which is a type of faulty decision making that occurs when maintaining group harmony becomes more desirable than making a good decision. In this chapter, we discussed some of the reasons people may stay in abusive relationships. How might groupthink also explain why someone decides to stay?

---

**Study Tip**

*The WileyPLUS program that accompanies this text provides for each chapter a* Media Challenge, Critical Thinking Exercise, *and* Application Quiz. *This set of study materials provides additional, invaluable study opportunities. Be sure to check it out!*

# Chapter Summary

## 10.1 **Moral Development** 325

- From a biological perspective, **morality** may be prewired and evolutionarily based.

- According to Kohlberg, morality progresses through three levels. Each level consists of two stages. **Preconventional morality** is based on rewards, punishment, and exchange of favors. **Conventional morality** reflects compliance with societal rules and values. **Postconventional morality** develops from personal standards for right and wrong.

- Kohlberg's theory has been criticized as measuring moral reasoning more than moral behavior, as well as for possible culture and gender bias.

**Test Your Critical Thinking**

**1.** Which do you believe is the better predictor of morality—the person or the situation?

**2.** Which Kohlbergian stage of moral development do you think you would qualify for, and do you agree or disagree with this categorization?

**3.** Do you believe men and women reason differently about morality? If so, what might be the pros and cons of these differences?

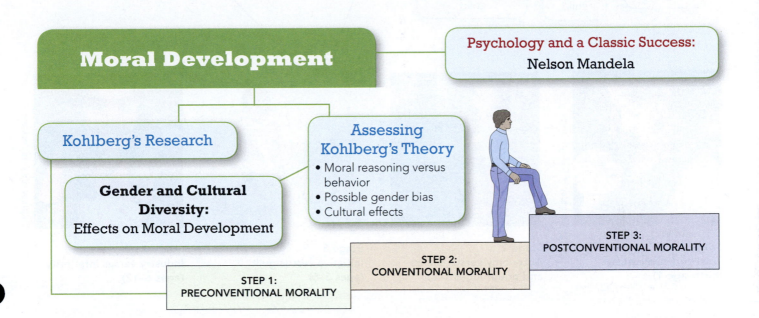

10.2 **Personality Development**  328

- Thomas and Chess emphasized the innate biological components of traits such as sociability. They observed that babies often exhibit three categories of **temperament** shortly after birth—*easy*, *difficult*, and *slow-to-warm-up*—and that these patterns appear to be consistent throughout childhood and adulthood.

- Erikson's eight **psychosocial stages** of development cover the entire life span, with each stage involving a psychosocial crisis or conflict related to a specific developmental task. The four stages that occur during childhood are *trust versus mistrust*, *autonomy versus shame and doubt*, *initiative versus guilt*, and *industry versus inferiority*. The major psychosocial crisis of adolescence is the search for *identity versus role*

*confusion*. During young adulthood, the individual's task is to establish *intimacy versus isolation*. During middle adulthood, the person must deal with *generativity versus stagnation*. At the end of life, the older adult faces *ego integrity versus despair*.

- Erikson's eight stages are difficult to test scientifically, and they may not apply across cultures.

**Test Your Critical Thinking**

**1.** If your parents are available, ask them if you were an "easy," "difficult," or "slow-to-warm-up" child. Do you agree with their answer? Does this label match your adult personality?

**2.** Which Eriksonian stage do you think best explains your current personality and life choices?

## Personality Development

**Thomas and Chess's Temperament Theory**

- Easy child
- Difficult child
- Slow-to-warm-up child

**Evaluating Erikson's Theory**

**Erikson's Psychosocial Theory**

**Stage 1**
Trust versus mistrust (birth–age 1)

*Courtesy of Sandy Harvey*

**Stage 2**
Autonomy versus shame and doubt (ages 1–3)

*Courtesy of Karen Huffman*

**Stage 3**
Initiative versus guilt (ages 3–6)

*Courtesy of Sandy Harvey*

**Stage 4**
Industry versus inferiority (ages 6–12)

*Courtesy of Linda Locklear*

**Stage 5**
Identity versus role confusion (ages 12–20)

*Courtesy of Richard Hosey*

**Stage 6**
Intimacy versus isolation (early adulthood)

*wavebreakmedia/Shutterstock*

**Stage 7**
Generativity versus stagnation (middle adulthood)

*Courtesy of Lee Decker*

**Stage 8**
Ego integrity versus despair (late adulthood)

*Courtesy of Lee Decker*

## 10.3 Neurodevelopmental Disorders 331

- **Attention-deficit/hyperactivity disorder (ADHD)** is one of the most common **neurodevelopmental disorders**, and it is characterized by a pattern of inattention and/or hyperactivity-impulsivity. It's most likely to result from an interaction of biological and psychosocial causes, but the greatest contributors appear to be neurological and genetic factors.

- **Autism spectrum disorder (ASD)** is a developmental disorder that begins in early childhood and involves problems with social communication and social interaction, as well as restricted, repetitive patterns of behavior, interests, or activities. The term

"spectrum" refers to a *range* of symptoms and disabilities, with no single identified cause.

### Test Your Critical Thinking

**1.** What might be the problem with taking ADHD medications if you don't actually have the disorder?

**2.** Given the scientific evidence that vaccinations are not related to autism spectrum disorder (ASD), how would you talk to a parent who is refusing to vaccinate his or her child? Should children who are not vaccinated be allowed to attend public schools? Why or why not?

# Neurodevelopmental Disorders

## Attention-Deficit/Hyperactivity Disorder (ADHD)
Pattern of inattention and/or hyperactivity-impulsivity

## Autism Spectrum Disorder (ASD)
Problems with social communication and social interaction, as well as restricted, repetitive patterns of behavior, interests, or activities

Bloomberg/Getty Images

Jim Steele/Popperfoto/Getty Images

## 10.4 Challenges of Adulthood   335

- Establishing and maintaining a committed relationship is one of the most difficult and essential tasks of adulthood. Such relationships provide great benefits but also pose significant challenges. About a third of marriages in the United States end in divorce, for instance, with serious implications for both adults and children.

- Domestic violence has a significant effect on development. It is more widely recognized than in the past. However, it is difficult to measure because it usually occurs in private and victims are reluctant to report it out of shame, powerlessness, or fear of reprisal.

- The kind of work we do can affect our health, friendships, where we live, and even our leisure activities. Life satisfaction after retirement appears to be most strongly related to good health, control over one's life, social support, and participation in community services and social activities. Contrary to stereotypes, psychological research consistently finds an increase in happiness and well-being as we grow older—thanks to the **age-related positivity effect**.

- One theory of successful aging, **activity theory**, says people should remain active and involved throughout the life span. Another theory, **disengagement theory**, says the elderly naturally and gracefully withdraw from life. Although the disengagement theory is no longer in favor, the **socioemotional selectivity theory** does find that the elderly tend to decrease their total

number of social contacts as they become more selective with their time.

- Grief is a natural and painful reaction to a loss. For many people, grief consists of four major stages—*shock and numbness, yearning and searching, disorganization and despair*, and *reorganization and recovery*.

- Attitudes toward death and dying vary greatly across cultures and among age groups. Some cultures regard death as a time for celebration, whereas others see it as a time for serious grief. Although adults understand the *permanence, universality*, and *nonfunctionality* of death, children often don't master these concepts until around age 7.

- Kübler-Ross's theory of the five-stage psychological process of facing death—*denial, anger, bargaining, depression*, and *acceptance*—has been widely criticized. However, the study of death and dying, **thanatology**, has become a significant topic in human development.

### Test Your Critical Thinking

**1.** Which of the factors discussed in this section on committed relationships did you find most helpful? Why?

**2.** If you or someone you know is experiencing domestic violence or grief, what advice would you give on how to deal with the situation?

**3.** Did the description of Kübler-Ross's five-stages of death seem true from your experience with dying friends or relatives? Why or why not?

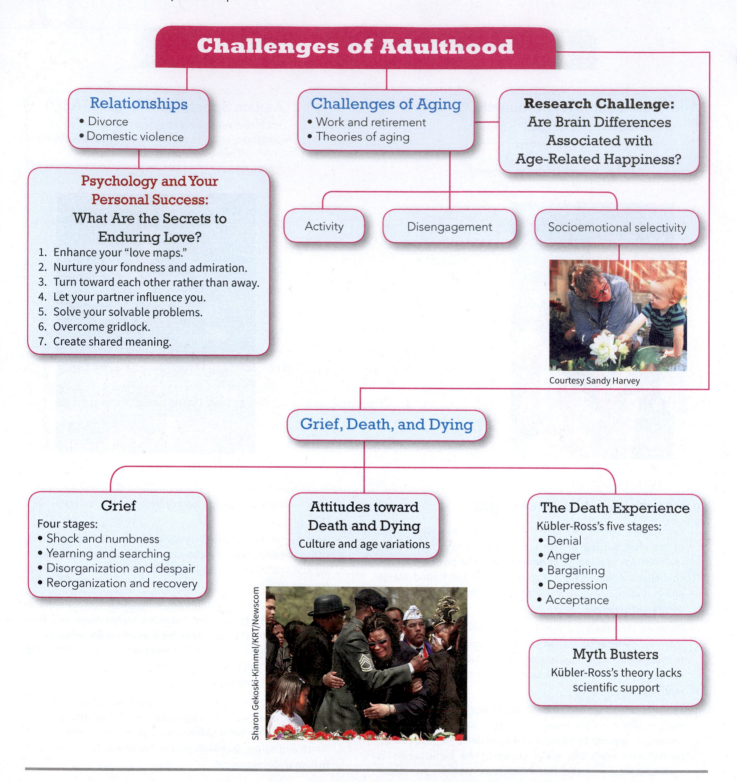

# Challenges of Adulthood

## Relationships
- Divorce
- Domestic violence

### Psychology and Your Personal Success:
**What Are the Secrets to Enduring Love?**
1. Enhance your "love maps."
2. Nurture your fondness and admiration.
3. Turn toward each other rather than away.
4. Let your partner influence you.
5. Solve your solvable problems.
6. Overcome gridlock.
7. Create shared meaning.

## Challenges of Aging
- Work and retirement
- Theories of aging

## Research Challenge:
**Are Brain Differences Associated with Age-Related Happiness?**

- Activity
- Disengagement
- Socioemotional selectivity

Courtesy Sandy Harvey

## Grief, Death, and Dying

### Grief
Four stages:
- Shock and numbness
- Yearning and searching
- Disorganization and despair
- Reorganization and recovery

### Attitudes toward Death and Dying
Culture and age variations

Sharon Gekoski-Kimmel/KRT/Newscom

### The Death Experience
Kübler-Ross's five stages:
- Denial
- Anger
- Bargaining
- Depression
- Acceptance

### Myth Busters
Kübler-Ross's theory lacks scientific support

# Key Terms

**Retrieval Practice**  *Write your own definition for each term before turning back to the referenced page to check your answer.*

- activity theory of aging  339
- age-related positivity effect  340
- attention-deficit/hyperactivity disorder (ADHD)  332
- autism spectrum disorder (ASD)  333
- conventional morality  325

- disengagement theory of aging  339
- morality  325
- neurodevelopmental disorders  332
- postconventional morality  325
- preconventional morality  325
- psychosocial stages  329

- socioemotional selectivity theory of aging  339
- temperament  229
- thanatology [than-uh-tahl-uh-gee]  345

© alexxl66/iStockphoto

# Gender and Human Sexuality

## LEARNING OBJECTIVES

**Summarize the early studies and modern research in human sexuality.**
• **Describe** the limits and contributions of the early studies of sexuality.
• **Discuss** the advances in modern sexuality research and the major findings and value of cross-cultural studies of sexuality.

**Review the key terms and concepts underlying sex versus gender.**
• **Contrast** sex, gender, and gender role.
• **Differentiate** among being transgender, cross-dressing, and sexual orientation.
• **Discuss** the major physical and psychological sex and gender differences.
• **Describe** the two major theories of gender-role development.

**Summarize the research findings about the sexual response cycle and sexual orientation.**
• **Review** Masters and Johnson's sexual response cycle and the key gender differences and similarities.
• **Discuss** the myths and latest research on sexual orientation.

**Summarize the major problems in sexuality.**
• **Describe** the paraphilic disorders, including fetishism and exhibitionism, and their treatment.
• **Explain** how biological, psychological, and social factors influence sexual dysfunction.
• **Discuss** the major treatments for sexual dysfunctions.
• **Identify** the major issues related to sexually transmitted infections (STIs) and the special problem of AIDS.

**Summarize the major issues of sex and modern life.**
• **Discuss** the risks and methods of prevention for sexual victimization, including child sexual abuse and rape.
• **Describe** why and how gender differences, conflict, and assertiveness are key elements of sexual communication.

Axelle/Bauer-Griffin/FilmMagic/Getty Images

## ❖ Psychology and a Contemporary Success | Ellen DeGeneres

Ellen DeGeneres (1958–) is an American comedian, humanitarian, animal rights activist, television host, actress, writer, and producer (see photo). She is also a prominent gay/lesbian role model. Over the years, Ellen has won many honors and accolades, including *People's Choice* and *Daytime Emmy* awards for favorite actress and comedian and a GLADD Media award from the Gay and Lesbian Alliance against Defamation. She was named Woman of the Year by People for the Ethical Treatment of Animals (PETA) and was ranked by *Forbes* magazine as one of the "Most Powerful Women in the World." *Forbes* estimated her net worth as $250 million as of 2015. Perhaps her most prestigious award came in 2016 when she received the Presidential Medal of Freedom, one of the nation's two highest civilian awards.

DeGeneres was born and raised in Metairie, Louisiana, but in her teens moved with her mother to Texas following her parents' painful divorce. Interestingly, Ellen's comedic talents and motivation apparently began with repeated efforts to make her mother laugh during rough times before and after the divorce. When growing up, she dreamed of becoming a veterinarian but eventually gave up, fearing she was not "book smart." After graduating from high school, Ellen attended Tulane University for a short time and then dropped out to support herself with jobs as a clerical worker in a law firm, a waitress, a house painter, and a bartender. She eventually discovered her true calling when she earned praise for her stand-up comedy, and she received her first important breakthrough with her appearance on *The Tonight Show Starring Johnny Carson*.

Although DeGeneres is celebrated today as one of America's greatest talents, when she first publicly came out as a lesbian in 1997 and became a staunch advocate of lesbian, gay, bisexual, and transgender (LGBT) rights, she generated a violent media storm and serious backlash. While many fans wrote supportive letters, others were outraged. Her popular TV show, *Ellen*, began to lose viewers, several major advertisers pulled out, and the show was canceled after the 1997–1998 season. After that, she went through a difficult period of personal depression and professional losses (Biography.com, n.d.; Famous People, n.d.; Stack, 2016).

Thankfully, DeGeneres eventually recovered her bubbly, positive personality. Her public support began to grow again when, in 2001, she hosted the *Primetime Emmy Awards* program, which had been delayed twice after the terrorist attacks of September 11. That night, despite the somber state of the nation, Ellen received several standing ovations for her wit and grace under pressure, including this comment: "Think about it—what would bug the Taliban more than seeing a gay woman in a suit surrounded by Jews?" (Ford, 2013).

# Chapter Overview

As shown by the quote that closes our opening feature, Ellen DeGeneres has a wonderful sense of humor and irony. Why did we choose her as our famous figure? First, her life story and many accomplishments clearly demonstrate the values of a *growth mindset* and *grit*. Second, the discrimination and hardships DeGeneres and others endure due to their sexual orientation are key topics of this chapter. Finally, Ellen's exceptional wit and self-acceptance once again shine through with the following satirical advice:

*Accept who you are. Unless you're a serial killer.* —Ellen DeGeneres

This chapter begins with a brief look at how we study sexuality. Next, we discuss core issues in sexual identity, followed by a discussion of sexual arousal, sexual response, and sexual orientation. Then, we explore sex problems and their causes and treatments. We close with a look at sex in modern life, including sexual victimization and sexual communication.

## Myth Busters

**True or False?**

1. The breakfast cereal Kellogg's Corn Flakes was originally developed to discourage masturbation.

2. Nocturnal emissions and masturbation are signs of abnormal sexual adjustment.

3. Sex and gender are essentially the same.

4. Androgyny is a type of homosexuality.

5. Transsexual is just another word for a transvestite.

6. Men and women are more alike than different in their sexual responses.

7. Sexual skill and satisfaction are learned behaviors that can be increased through education and training.

8. The American Psychiatric Association and the American Psychological Association (APA) consider homosexuality a type of mental illness.

George Shelley Productions/Getty Images, Inc.

9. Sex education should begin as early as possible.

10. Rape is a crime of passion.

11. Men can't be raped.

12. Assertiveness is just another word for aggressiveness.

**Answers:** 1. T 2. F 3. F 4. F 5. F 6. T 7. T 8. F 9. T 10. F 11. F 12. F

---

## 11.1 Studying Human Sexuality

### LEARNING OBJECTIVES

**Retrieval Practice** While reading the upcoming sections, respond to each learning objective in your own words.

**Summarize the early studies and modern research in human sexuality.**

- **Describe** the limits and contributions of the early studies of sexuality.

- **Discuss** the advances in modern sexuality research and the major findings and value of cross-cultural studies of sexuality.

**Sexuality** is generally described as the ways in which we experience and express ourselves as sexual beings. Throughout time, it has been a major component of human happiness and well-being, and people have probably always been interested in learning more about their own and others' sexuality. But cultural and religious forces have often attempted to suppress this interest.

**Sexuality** The ways in which we experience and express ourselves as sexual beings; includes sexual arousal, orientation, and behaviors.

### Early Studies

During the nineteenth century, people in polite society avoided mentioning any part of the body covered by clothing, so the breast of chickens became known as "white meat." Male doctors examined female patients in totally dark rooms, and some people even covered piano legs for the sake of propriety (Carroll, 2016; Orrells, 2015; Pettit & Hegarty, 2014).

Throughout this Victorian period, medical experts warned that masturbation led to blindness, impotence, acne, and insanity. Believing a bland diet helped suppress sexual desire, Dr. John Harvey Kellogg and Sylvester Graham developed the original Kellogg's Corn Flakes and graham crackers and marketed them as foods that would discourage masturbation (Maunder, 2016; Money et al., 1991; Perelman, 2014). One of the most serious concerns of many doctors was nocturnal emissions (during so-called "wet dreams"), which were believed to cause brain damage and death. Special devices were even marketed for men to wear at night to prevent sexual arousal (**Figure 11.1**).

In light of modern knowledge, it is hard to understand these practices and myths. One of the first physicians to question them was Havelock Ellis (1858–1939). When he first heard of the dangers of nocturnal emissions, Ellis was frightened; he had had personal experience with the problem. His fear led him to frantically search the medical literature, where instead of a cure he found only predictions of gruesome illness and eventual death. He was so upset he contemplated suicide.

Ellis eventually decided he could give meaning to his life by keeping a detailed diary of his deterioration. He planned to dedicate the book to science when he died. However, after several months of careful observation, Ellis realized that the experts were wrong. He wasn't dying. He wasn't even sick. Angry that he had been so misinformed, he spent the rest of his life developing reliable and accurate sex information. Today, thanks in part to his informal case study of his own sexuality, Havelock Ellis is acknowledged as one of the most influential pioneers in the field of sex research.

## Modern Research

One of the earliest efforts in modern sex research came from Alfred Kinsey and his colleagues (1948, 1953), who personally surveyed and interviewed more than 18,000 participants, asking detailed questions about their sexual activities and preferences. The results shocked the nation. Kinsey reported, for instance, that 37% of men and 13% of women had engaged in adult same-sex behavior to the point of orgasm. Although Kinsey's interviewing techniques were excellent, his data has been heavily criticized for violating certain ethical and research standards.

Since Kinsey's time, literally thousands of similar surveys and interviews have been conducted on such topics as contraception, abortion, premarital sex, sexual orientation, and sexual behavior (Flores et al., 2016; Laumann et al., 1994; Sandberg, 2016). By comparing Kinsey's data to the responses found in later surveys, we can see how sexual practices have changed over the years. Given the value of empirical, scientifically based surveys and interviews, particularly for the lesbian, gay, bisexual, and transgender (LGBT) community, the American Psychological Association recently adopted an official resolution recommending that research studies include sexual orientation and gender identity in their data collection (American Psychological Association, 2016).

In addition to surveys, interviews, and case studies, some researchers have employed biological research methods, as well as direct laboratory experimentation and observational methods. For example, modern biological researchers have found that tasks that trigger sexual arousal, such as looking at erotic photographs, activate different parts of the brain than tasks that trigger feelings of love, such as looking at a photograph of a beloved sibling or parent (Cacioppo et al., 2012).

Direct laboratory experimentation and observation were first conducted by William Masters and Virginia Johnson (1961, 1966, 1970) and their research colleagues. To experimentally document the physiological changes that occur in sexual arousal and response, they first enlisted several hundred male and female volunteers. Then, using intricate physiological measuring devices, the researchers carefully monitored participants' bodily responses as they masturbated or engaged in sexual intercourse. Masters and Johnson's research findings have been hailed as a major contribution to our knowledge of sexual physiology. A brief summary of their results is presented later in this chapter.

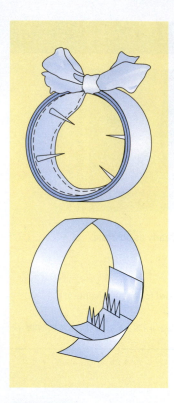

**FIGURE 11.1 Victorian sexual practice** During the nineteenth century, men were encouraged to wear spiked rings around their penises at night. Can you explain why?

**Answer:** The Victorians believed nighttime erections and emissions ("wet dreams") were dangerous. If the man had an erection, the spikes would cause pain and awaken him.

## Gender and Cultural Diversity

### Sexuality Across Cultures

Sex researchers interested in both similarities and variations in human sexual behavior often conduct cross-cultural studies of sexual practices, techniques, and attitudes (e.g., Beach, 1977; Buss, 2011; Espinosa-Hernández et al., 2016). Their studies of different societies put sex in a broader perspective. To illustrate, a cross-cultural study asked both U.S. and Dutch parents whether they would allow their teenage child to spend the night with a dating partner in their own home. Interestingly, only 9% of U.S parents said they would allow such a sleepover, compared to a whopping 93% of the Dutch parents (Schalet, 2011). This difference in perspectives illustrates cultural differences in attitudes about sexuality, and in particular about adolescent sexuality. In the Netherlands, and many Scandinavian countries, comprehensive sex education, including information about birth control and sexual pleasuring, is required. In contrast, such programs continue to be controversial in the United States.

Cross-cultural studies of sex also help counteract *ethnocentrism*, the tendency to judge our own cultural practices as "normal" and preferable to those of other groups. For example, did you know that less than half of the 168 cultures studied around the world engage in romantic/sexual kissing (Jankowiak et al., 2015)? In fact, couples in Sub-Saharan Africa, New Guinea, the Amazon, and many native cultures in Central America find this type of kissing uncomfortable or even repulsive!

Members of Tiwi society, who inhabit islands off the northern coast of Australia, believe young girls will not develop breasts or menstruate unless they first experience intercourse. In some cultures, adolescent boys routinely undergo harsh ceremonies, such as *superincision*, to initiate them into adulthood. During superincision, the foreskin of the penis is slit horizontally along the upper length of the foreskin, without removing any tissue (Gregersen, 1996; Marshall, 1971; Schlegel & Barry, 2017). **Figure 11.2** gives other examples of cultural variations in sexuality.

Although other cultures' practices may seem unnatural and strange to us, we often forget that our own sexual rituals may appear equally curious to others. If the description of the practice of superincision bothered you, how do you feel about our own culture's routine circumcision of infant boys? At one point, the American Academy of Pediatrics (AAP) decided that the reported medical benefits of circumcision were so statistically small that the procedure should *not* be routinely performed (American Academy of Pediatrics, 1999, 2005). This position was later revised. In 2012, the AAP concluded that the health benefits of newborn male circumcision outweighed the risks, though the choice should still be left to parents (American Academy of Pediatrics, 2012). However, physicians and health experts in other parts of the

Israel images/Alamy

Western world, including Europe, Canada, and Australia, contend that there is no compelling medical benefit to newborn circumcision, and that the AAP reversal may reflect a cultural or religious rationale (Earp, 2015; Frisch et al., 2013; Myers, 2015). Others have argued that, at a minimum, we should wait until the boys are old enough to decide for themselves (Erlings, 2016).

| Mangaia (Polynesian Island) | Yolngu (Island near Australia) | Inis Beag (Irish Island) |
|---|---|---|
| **Childhood sexuality:** <br> • Children readily exposed to sex. <br> • Adolescents are given direct instruction in techniques for pleasuring their sexual partners. <br> • Both boys and girls are encouraged to have many partners. | **Childhood sexuality:** <br> • Permissive attitude toward childhood sexuality. <br> • Parents soothe infants by stroking their genitals. <br> • Nudity accepted from infancy through old age. | **Childhood sexuality:** <br> • Sexual expression is strongly discouraged. <br> • Children learn to abhor nudity and are given no information about sex. <br> • Young girls are often shocked by their first menstruation. |
| **Adult sexuality:** <br> • After marriage, three orgasms per night are not uncommon for men. <br> • Men are encouraged to "give" three orgasms to their female partner for every one of their own. <br> • Adults practice a wide range of sexual behaviors. | **Adult sexuality:** <br> • Men can have many wives and are generally happy with their sex life. <br> • Women are given no choice in marital partner and little power in the home. <br> • Women are apathetic about sex, seldom orgasmic, and generally unhappy. | **Adult sexuality:** <br> • Little sex play before intercourse. <br> • Female orgasm is unknown or considered deviant. <br> • Numerous misconceptions about sex (e.g., intercourse can be debilitating, menopause causes insanity). |

**FIGURE 11.2    Cross-cultural differences in sexual behavior**    Note: "Inis Beag" is a pseudonym used to protect the privacy of residents of this Irish island, which is another interesting cultural difference. The other communities cited apparently don't require pseudonyms.

*Sources:* Crooks & Baur, 2016; Marshall, 1971; Money et al., 1991.

© Billy R. Ray/Wiley

# Retrieval Practice 11.1 | Studying Human Sexuality

Completing this self-test and connections section, and then checking your answers by clicking on the answer button or by looking in Appendix B, will provide immediate feedback and helpful practice for exams.

## Self-Test

1. Describe how masturbation and nocturnal emissions were viewed during the Victorian period.

2. _____ was a major pioneer in sex research who used an informal case study method to record his own sexuality.

    **a.** B. F. Skinner      **b.** Sigmund Freud

    **c.** Alfred Kinsey      **d.** Havelock Ellis

3. Some of the earliest and most extensive surveys and interviews of human sexual behavior in the United States were conducted by _____.

    **a.** Havelock Ellis

    **b.** William Masters and Virginia Johnson

    **c.** Emily and John Roper

    **d.** Alfred Kinsey and his colleagues

4. Direct laboratory experimentation and observation of human sexuality were first conducted by _____.

   a. Alfred Kinsey
   b. William Masters and Virginia Johnson
   c. Havelock Ellis
   d. all of these individuals

5. Cross-cultural studies of human sexuality help counteract _____, the tendency to view our culture's sexual practices as normal and preferable to those of other groups.

   a. sexual prejudice      b. ethnic typing
   c. ethnocentrism         d. sexual predation

**Connections—Chapter to Chapter**

Answering the following questions will help you "look back and look ahead" to see the important connections among the subfields of psychology and chapters within this text.

In Chapter 1 (Introduction and Research Methods), you discovered the limitations of survey data and the problems of sampling bias. Given that much of what we know about sexual behavior is gathered by surveys, what potential concerns do you have about some of the sexuality data reported in this chapter? What kinds of sexual behaviors may be overreported or underreported?

## 11.2 | Sexual Identity

### LEARNING OBJECTIVES

**Retrieval Practice**   While reading the upcoming sections, respond to each Learning Objective in your own words.

**Review the key terms and concepts underlying sex versus gender.**

- **Contrast** sex, gender, and gender role.

- **Differentiate** among being transgender, cross-dressing, and sexual orientation.

- **Discuss** the major physical and psychological sex and gender differences.

- **Describe** the two major theories of gender-role development.

Why is it that the first question most people ask after a baby is born is "Is it a girl or a boy?" What would life be like if there were no divisions according to maleness or femaleness? Would your career plans or friendship patterns change? These questions reflect the role of *sex* and *gender* in our lives.

### Describing Sex and Gender

*We allow our ignorance to prevail upon us and make us think we can survive alone, alone in patches, alone in groups, alone in races, even alone in genders.*

—Maya Angelou (American Poet, Author, Dancer)

**Sex**   The state of being biologically male or female; also, sexual activities.

**Gender**   The psychological and sociocultural traits typically associated with one sex.

**Gender identity**   One's sense of self-identification as belonging to the male or female sex.

**Gender roles**   The culturally and socially defined prescriptions and expectations about the thoughts, feelings, and actions of men and women.

**Gender stereotypes**   Gender role prescriptions and beliefs that are overly generalized and applied to all men and women.

The term **sex** generally refers to the biological differences between men and women (such as having a penis or vagina) or to sexual activities (such as masturbation and intercourse). **Gender**, on the other hand, encompasses the psychological and sociocultural traits typically associated with one sex (such as "masculinity" and "femininity"). There are at least seven dimensions or elements of sex and two of gender (**Table 11.1**). In short, *sex* is physical and *gender* is mental.

It's also important to point out that **gender identity**—our multifaceted sense of self-identification as belonging to the male or female sex— is formed in our first few years of life. Similarly, we develop an understanding of **gender roles**, meaning the culturally and socially defined prescriptions and expectations about the thoughts, feelings, and actions of men and women, largely before we are consciously aware of them (Brannon, 2016; Keatley et al., 2017; Tosh, 2016). Yet they are very influential in our adult lives.

When gender role prescriptions and beliefs are overly general, and applied to all men and women, they're known as **gender stereotypes**. In our culture, these stereotypes include various beliefs and expectations. For instance, men are expected to be more independent, aggressive, dominant, and achieving than women. In contrast, women are expected to be more dependent, passive, emotional, and "naturally" interested in children than men (Leaper & Farkas, 2015; O'Neil, 2015; Wood & Fixmer-Oraiz, 2016).

### TABLE 11.1    Dimensions of Sex and Gender

| | Male | Female |
|---|---|---|
| ***Sex Dimensions*** | | |
| **1.** Chromosomes | XY | XX |
| **2.** Gonads | Testes | Ovaries |
| **3.** Hormones | Mainly androgens | Mainly estrogens |
| **4.** External genitals | Penis, scrotum | Labia minor, clitoris, vaginal opening |
| **5.** Internal accessory organs | Prostate gland, seminal vesicles, vas deferens, ejaculatory duct, Cowper's gland | Vagina, uterus, fallopian tubes, cervix |
| **6.** Secondary sex characteristics | Beard, lower voice, wider shoulders, sperm emission | Breasts, wider hips, menstruation |
| **7.** Sexual orientation | Heterosexual, gay, bisexual | Heterosexual, lesbian, bisexual |
| ***Gender Dimensions*** | | |
| **8.** Gender identity (self-definition) | Perceives self as male | Perceives self as female |
| **9.** Gender-role (societal expectations) | Masculine ("Boys like trucks and sports") | Feminine ("Girls like dolls and clothes") |

*People give me such a hard time because I don't wear dresses. What's that got to do with anything?*
—Ellen DeGeneres

This quote by Ellen DeGeneres and the public pressure for her to wear dresses is a good example of which dimension of gender?

Axelle/Bauer-Griffin/FilmMagic/Getty Images

Can you predict some of the inherent dangers with these stereotypes? One study found, for instance, that identifying a job searcher as either male or female on a Google ad search for jobs made a big difference. Ads for highly paid executive positions were successfully responded to 1,816 times by male applicants, but only 311 times by female applicants (Datta et al., 2015). And, as you've probably heard, women in the United States still tend to earn lower salaries than men, even when they hold the same job (Gibbs, 2014; Hegewisch & DuMonthier, 2016; Wright, 2016). See the following **Research Challenge**.

## Research Challenge

### Is Gender Income Inequality Real?

Do you recall the heavy focus on income inequalities between the rich and all other groups during the presidential election in 2016? Although most Americans were unhappy with the wealth and income distribution, very little was said about the persistent gender, race, and ethnicity income disparities.

A study from the U.S. Bureau of Labor Statistics clearly addressed this issue (Hegewisch & DuMonthier, 2016). Researchers found that the gender wage gap for weekly full-time workers in the United States widened from 2014 to 2015 (the latest available data). Between 2014 and 2015, women's earnings increased by 0.09%, whereas men's earnings increased by 2.6%.

As you can see in **Table 11.2**, women of all major racial and ethnic groups earn less than men of the same groups. Note also that Hispanic workers have the lowest overall median weekly earnings, whereas Asian workers have the highest overall median weekly earnings.

How can we explain these findings? The lower earnings for women may result from several factors. One is occupational segregation—the fact that many women work in occupations dominated mainly by women. Women also face discrimination in compensation, recruitment, and hiring, as well as in bonuses and promotions. Can you see how these same factors might also explain the income disparities between racial and ethnic groups? Or how these disparities might be causally linked with poorer educational opportunities,

"You ever get the feeling that this economy benefits some people

Cartoon Resource/Shutterstock

**TABLE 11.2** Median Weekly Earnings and Gender Earnings Ratio for Full-Time Workers, 16 Years and Older by Race/Ethnic Background, 2014 and 2015

| Racial/Ethnic Background | 2015 | | | | 2014 (in 2015 dollars) | | | |
| --- | --- | --- | --- | --- | --- | --- | --- | --- |
| | Women | Men | Female Earnings as % of Male Earnings of Same Group | Female Earnings as % of White Male Earnings | Women | Men | Female Earnings as % of Male Earnings of Same Group | Female Earnings as % of White Male Earnings |
| All Races/Ethnicities | $726 | $895 | 81.1% | N/A | $720 | $872 | 82.5% | N/A |
| White | $743 | $920 | 80.8% | 80.8% | $735 | $898 | 81.8% | 81.8% |
| Black | $615 | $680 | 90.4% | 66.8% | $612 | $681 | 89.9% | 68.1% |
| Hispanic | $566 | $631 | 89.7% | 61.5% | $549 | $617 | 89.0% | 61.1% |
| Asians | $877 | $1,129 | 77.7% | 95.3% | $842 | $1,081 | 77.9% | 93.8% |

**Sources:** The Gender Wage Gap (2016); U.S. Bureau of Labor Statistics (2016).

housing, and mental and physical health outcomes for members of these groups (Alvarez et al., 2016; Smith & Trimble, 2016; Williams et al., 2016)?

**Test Yourself**

1. Based on the information provided, did this study (Hegewisch & DuMonthier, 2016) use descriptive, correlational, and/or experimental research?

2. If you chose:

   o *descriptive research*, is this a naturalistic observation, survey/interview, case study, or/and archival research?

   o *correlational research*, is this a positive, negative, or zero correlation?

   o *experimental research*, label the IV, DV, experimental group(s), and control group. (Note: If participants were not randomly assigned to groups, list it as a *quasi-experimental design*.)

   o both *descriptive* and *correlational*, answer the corresponding questions for both.

**Check your answers by clicking on the answer button or by looking in Appendix B.**

**Note:** The information provided in this study is admittedly limited, but the level of detail is similar to what is presented in most textbooks and public reports of research findings. Answering these questions, and then comparing your answers to those provided, will help you become a better critical thinker and consumer of scientific research.

Along with earning less, women are underrepresented in certain types of stereotypically male occupations in science, engineering, and technology. Why? Researchers in one study asked science faculty from a research-intensive university to evaluate the application materials of a student who was applying for a laboratory manager position (Moss-Racusin et al., 2012). Identical applications were assigned either a male name or a female name. Sadly, but in line with predictions, faculty members rated the applicant who was given a male name as significantly more competent and hirable than the (identical) applicant with a female name. The faculty also suggested a higher starting salary for the male applicant. Both male and female professors were equally likely to make these gender-biased decisions. If even highly educated college professors of both sexes show such bias, does this explain why there are still relatively few women in certain careers? More importantly, can you think of ways to change these and other examples of gender bias?

Before going on, keep in mind that men also suffer from traditional gender roles. And a recent meta-analysis of almost 20,000 participants found that conforming to masculine norms is linked with poorer social functioning and mental health, as well as with being less willing to seek psychological help (Wong et al., 2017).

**Androgyny** One way to diminish gender bias and/or gender-role stereotypes is to encourage the expression of both the "masculine" and "feminine" characteristics and traits found in virtually every individual. For instance, both men and women could learn to be assertive and aggressive when necessary, but also gentle and nurturing. Combining characteristics in this way is known as **androgyny [an-DRAH-juh-nee]** (see the following **Try This Yourself**). Interestingly, research finds that this blending of traits leads to higher self-esteem and more success and adjustment in today's complex society because it allows us to display whatever behaviors and traits are most appropriate in a given situation (Bem, 1981, 1993; Brannon, 2016; Wood & Fixmer-Oraiz, 2016).

**Androgyny [an-DRAH-juh-nee]**
A combination of masculine and feminine characteristics and traits; from the Greek andro for "male" and gyn for "female."

---

## Try This Yourself

### Are You Androgynous?

Social psychologist Sandra Bem (1974, 1993) developed a personality measure for androgyny that has been widely used in research. You can take this version of Bem's test by rating yourself on the following items. Give yourself a number between I (never or almost never true) and 7 (always or almost always true):

1. _____ Analytical
2. _____ Affectionate
3. _____ Competitive
4. _____ Compassionate
5. _____ Aggressive
6. _____ Cheerful
7. _____ Independent
8. _____ Gentle
9. _____ Athletic
10. _____ Sensitive

Now add up your points for all the odd-numbered items; then add up your points for the even-numbered items. If you have a higher total on the odd-numbered items, you are more "masculine." If you scored higher on the even-numbered items, you are more "feminine" in your adherence to traditional gender roles. If your score is fairly even, you are more androgynous.

---

Studies also show that gender roles are becoming less rigidly defined (Brannon, 2016; Levant & Wong, 2017; Signorielli, 2014). However, a survey of college students at a comparatively liberal university in California found that more than two-thirds of both women and men strongly prefer traditional gender roles when it comes to marriage proposals. In fact, the title of the research article is: "Girls don't propose! Ew." (Robnett & Leaper, 2013). Furthermore, over 60% of the women surveyed were either "very willing" or "somewhat willing" to take their husband's surname.

In a later, related study on traditional heterosexual dating and courtship patterns, researchers found that both women and men generally agreed that men should initiate and pay for a date, hold the door open for the woman, and propose marriage, whereas women should take the man's surname after marriage (Paynter & Leaper, 2017). Rachael Robnett, the lead author on the first study, suggested that this type of "benevolent sexism" looks positive on the surface, but it contributes to power differentials between men and women and does a disservice to women (Lasnier, 2013). What do you think? Would relationships be better if both men and women were free to initiate and pay for dates, open their own doors, and propose marriage, as well as if they both kept their own names when they married?

> It is fatal to be a man or woman pure and simple; one must be woman-manly or man-womanly. . . . Some marriage of opposites has to be consummated.
> —Virginia Woolf (Author, Journalist)

## Explaining Sex and Gender

In the previous section, we *described* sex and gender. Now we need to *explain* some of their core issues. How do we develop our gender identity? Are there clear gender and sex differences between men and women? If so, what causes these differences, and are they important? These are some of the most controversial questions in the ongoing nature versus nurture debate. Scientists on the nature side suggest that inborn genetic and biological factors not only determine our physical sex, but also help program our gender identity. In contrast, those on the nurture side believe that most aspects of gender and human sexuality are determined largely by social influences. As you've seen throughout this text, the answer to the debate is almost always provided by the *biopsychosocial model*, which proposes an interaction among biology, psychology, and social forces.

**Gender Identity**   One of the best ways to illustrate the significance of gender identity, and the fine nuances of gender and sex differences, is through the famous case study of "John/Joan." In 1963, identical twin boys were taken to their family doctor to be

**FIGURE 11.3**  **David, previously known as "John/Joan"**

**Transgender**  The state of having a gender identity that does not match one's biological sex; being born with the biological characteristics of one sex but feeling psychologically as if belonging to the other gender.

**FIGURE 11.4**  **The struggle for gender identity**  In 2015, the public was fascinated by the story of Bruce Jenner's famous journey from being a male Olympic decathlon icon, referred to as the "world's greatest athlete," to a woman, Caitlyn Jenner (pictured here). Caitlyn gave extensive interviews about this journey and her painful gender identity struggles, which were best summarized with her simple statement that "nature made a mistake" (Bissinger, 2015).

circumcised. Tragically, the first twin's penis was damaged beyond repair. Following the medical experts' advice, the child's testes were removed, his genitalia modified, and estrogen administered so he could be raised as a girl.

During their childhood, the twins were brought to Johns Hopkins Hospital each year for physical and psychological evaluations, and the story of "John/Joan" (the name used by Johns Hopkins) was heralded as proof that gender is made—not born. Unfortunately, follow-up studies indicate that, despite being raised from infancy as a girl, "Joan" did not feel like a girl and avoided most female activities and interests. As she entered adolescence, her appearance and masculine way of walking led classmates to tease her and call her "cave woman." By age 14, she was so unhappy that she contemplated suicide. Her father tearfully explained what had happened earlier, and for Joan, "All of a sudden everything clicked. For the first time, things made sense, and I understood who and what I was" (Thompson, 1997, p. 83).

After the truth came out, "John/Joan" reclaimed his male gender identity and renamed himself David (**Figure 11.3**). Following a double mastectomy (removal of both breasts) and construction of an artificial penis, he married a woman and adopted her children. David, his parents, and his twin brother all suffered enormously from the original accident and its long aftermath. In 2004, David died by suicide. No one knows what went through David's mind when he decided to end his life. However, he had just separated from his wife, lost his job, and experienced the failure of a big investment. His twin brother had also ended his own life shortly before. Most suicides, experts say, "have multiple motives, which come together in a perfect storm of misery" (Colapinto, 2004).

If you apply the dimensions of sex and gender, which we discussed earlier and displayed in Table 11.1, to the case of "John/Joan," you can see why this is such an influential case study. Although he was born a chromosomal male, the child's genital sex was altered first by the doctor who accidentally destroyed his penis, and later by surgeons who removed his testes and created a "preliminary" vagina. Experts at the time believed this surgery, along with female hormones and "appropriate" gender-role expectations of the parents, would be enough to create a stable female gender identity. But David ultimately rejected this female gender assignment.

In contrast to the rare, tragic accident that created serious problems with gender identity for David, a much larger group of people who also struggle with gender identity were born with the biological characteristics of one sex, but identify with the other. This is known as being **transgender** (having a gender identity that does not match one's biological sex).

What causes this type of gender identity confusion? Is gender identity a choice? People who are transgender often report feeling as if they are victims of a "birth defect," and they tend to have a deep and lasting discomfort with their sexual anatomy. In fact, there is ample evidence (e.g., Saraswat et al., 2015) that gender identity is biologically driven, so it does not appear to be a personal choice or something that can be changed through therapy. Further evidence comes from a study with 32 transgender children, ages 5 to 12, indicating that their gender identity is deeply held and is not the result of confusion about gender identity or pretense (Olson et al., 2015). The study used implicit measures that operate outside conscious awareness and are, therefore, less susceptible to modification than self-report measures. These and other studies of transgender children suggest that gender identity is really deeply held and not just a phase that could be "outgrown."

Sadly, transgender children and adults are more likely to experience ostracism, harassment, bullying, and psychological problems, including self-mutilation, suicide attempts, and drug abuse (Ghabrial, 2017; Rinehart & Espelage, 2016; Tosh, 2016). In some cases, they undergo medical procedures and/or drug therapies to change their bodies physically to be more like the other sex (**Figure 11.4**). The good news is that transgender kids (ages 3 to 12) who have transitioned, and are treated like the gender they identify with, do not differ from other kids on rates of depression and are only slightly higher on anxiety (Olson et al., 2016). So, this study suggests that living as the "wrong gender" leads to depression, not being transgender.

People sometimes confuse being transgender with *transvestism*, *gender-bending*, or *cross-dressing*, in which individuals adopt the dress and often the gender-role behaviors typical of the other sex. Some individuals occasionally or routinely dress up as the other sex for personal or erotic pleasure, and some entertainers cross-dress as part of their job. People who are transgender often dress in clothing opposite to their biological sex, but they're not considered to be "cross-dressing." Their motivation is to look like the "right" sex, the one that matches their gender identity (Buehler, 2014; Colizzi et al., 2014; Tosh, 2016).

In addition, many people confuse cross-dressing and/or being transgender with **sexual orientation**, our emotional and erotic attraction toward the other sex (heterosexual), our own sex (gay or lesbian), or both sexes (bisexual). Sexual orientation will be further discussed later in this chapter, but at this point note that cross-dressers are usually heterosexual, whereas people who are transgender can be heterosexual, gay, lesbian, or bisexual.

**Sexual orientation**   Emotional and erotic attraction, which can be directed primarily toward members of the same sex (gay, lesbian), both sexes (bisexual), or the other sex (heterosexual).

## Sex and Gender Differences
As we've just seen, gender identity is confusing to many. Also potentially confusing is the relationship of sex to gender and to the gender roles prescribed by societal expectations. Let's take some time to clarify how the two sexes differ.

Physical anatomy is the most obvious biological sex difference between men and women (**Concept Organizer 11.1**). Recall from Chapter 9 that puberty is a time during early

---

| CONCEPT ORGANIZER 11.1 | Major Physical Differences Between the Sexes |
|---|---|

**STOP!** This Concept Organizer contains essential information NOT found elsewhere in the text, which is likely to appear on quizzes and exams. Be sure to study it CAREFULLY!

### Body Size and Shape
The average man is 35 pounds heavier, has less body fat, and is 5 inches taller than the average woman. Men typically have broader shoulders, slimmer hips and slightly longer legs in proportion to their height.

### Brain
The corpus callosum, the bridge joining the two halves of the brain, is larger in women. This size difference is interpreted by some to mean that women can more easily integrate information from the two halves of the brain and more easily perform more than one task simultaneously.

An area of the hypothalamus that causes men to have a relatively constant level of sex hormones, whereas women have cyclic sex hormone production and menstrual cycles.

Differences in cerebral hemispheres may help explain reported sex differences in verbal and spatial skills.

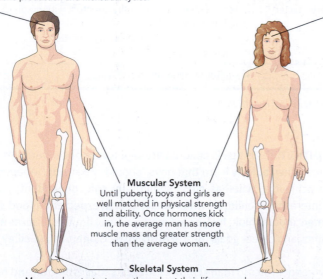

### Muscular System
Until puberty, boys and girls are well matched in physical strength and ability. Once hormones kick in, the average man has more muscle mass and greater strength than the average woman.

### Skeletal System
Men produce testosterone throughout their life span, whereas estrogen production virtually stops when a women goes through menopause. Because estrogen helps rejuvenate bones, women are more likely to have brittle bones. Women also are more prone to knee damage because a woman's wider hips may place a greater strain on the ligaments joining the thigh to the knee.

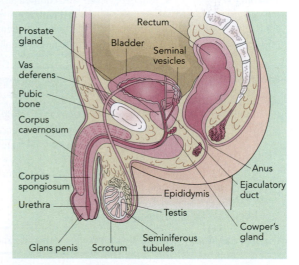

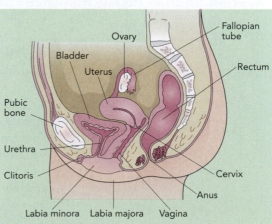

© John Wiley and Sons, Inc.

adolescence in which maturation and hormone secretions lead to rapid development and changes in the female's ovaries, uterus, clitoris, and vagina, as well as in the male's testes, scrotum, and penis. Maturation and hormones also drive the development of *secondary sex characteristics*, such as enlarged breasts in women and facial hair in men, along with pubic hair in both sexes. In addition to biological sex differences, scientists have noted numerous psychological differences that affect our cognitive and personality development (**Table 11.3**). A recent study found an interesting combination of biological and psychological factors in how men and women absorb visual information. Specifically, although the general visual process is the same for both groups, women pay more attention to faces than men and are more comfortable with increased eye contact (Coutrot et al., 2016).

| TABLE 11.3 | **Research-Supported Sex and Gender Differences** (Note that these variations are statistically small and represent few meaningful differences.) | |
| --- | --- | --- |
| **Behavior** | **More Often Shown by Men** | **More Often Shown by Women** |
| **Sexual** | • Begin masturbating sooner in life cycle and higher overall occurrence rates<br>• Start sexual life earlier and have first orgasm through masturbation<br>• More likely to recognize their own sexual arousal<br>• More orgasm consistency with sexual partner | • Begin masturbating later in life cycle and lower overall occurrence rates<br>• Start sexual life later and have first orgasm from partner stimulation<br>• Less likely to recognize their own sexual arousal<br>• Less orgasm consistency with sexual partner |
| **Touching** | • Touched, kissed, and cuddled less by parents<br>• Less physical contact with other men and respond more negatively to being touched<br>• More likely to initiate both casual and intimate touch with sexual partner | • Touched, kissed, and cuddled more by parents<br>• More physical contact with other women and respond more positively to being touched<br>• Less likely to initiate either casual or intimate touch with sexual partner |
| **Friendship** | • Larger number of friends and express friendship by shared activities | • Smaller number of friends and express friendship by shared communication about self |
| **Personality** | • More aggressive from a very early age<br>• More self-confident of future success<br>• Attribute success to internal factors and failures to external factors<br>• Achievement more task oriented; motives are mastery and competition<br>• More self-validating<br>• Higher self-esteem | • Less aggressive from a very early age<br>• Less self-confident of future success<br>• Attribute success to external factors and failures to internal factors<br>• Achievement more socially directed, with emphasis on self-improvement<br>• More dependent on others for validation<br>• Lower self-esteem |
| **Cognitive abilities** | • Slightly superior in math and visuospatial skills | • Slightly superior in verbal skills |

*Sources*: Carroll, 2016; Chaplin, 2015; Eagly, 2015; Forgasz et al., 2015; Hofstede et al., 2015; Schmitt, 2015.

**Gender-Role Development**    By age 2, children are well aware of gender roles. From parents and other social forces, they quickly learn that boys "should" be strong, independent, aggressive, dominant, and achieving, whereas girls "should" be soft, dependent, passive, emotional, and "naturally" interested in children. Unfortunately, such expectations and stereotypes for how women and men should think, feel, or act may seriously limit both sexes in their choice of friendships, activities, and career goals (Best & Bush, 2016; Gianettoni & Guilley, 2016; Latu & Schmid Mast, 2016).

The existence of similar gender roles in many cultures suggests that evolution and biology may play a role in their formation. However, most research emphasizes two major psychosocial theories of gender-role development: social-learning theory and cognitive-developmental theory (**Figure 11.5**). *Social-learning theory* emphasizes the power of the immediate situation and observable behaviors on gender-role development. Girls learn how to be "feminine," and boys learn how to be "masculine" in two major ways: (1) They receive rewards or punishments for specific gender-role behaviors, and (2) they watch and imitate the behavior of others,

**FIGURE 11.5** **Gender-role development**   Social-learning theory focuses on a child's passive process of learning about gender through observation, rewards, and punishments, whereas cognitive-developmental theory emphasizes a child's active role in building a gender schema. Which theory do you think best explains how the children in this photo learn what type of clothes are "appropriate" for their respective genders?

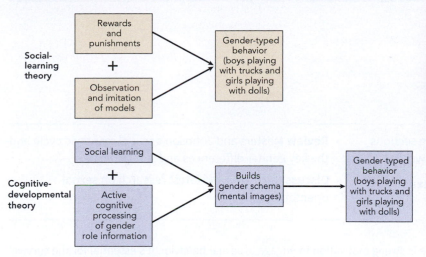

Courtesy of Sandy Harvey

particularly their same-sex parent (Bandura, 1989, 2008; Risman & Davis, 2013). A boy who puts on his father's tie or baseball cap wins big, indulgent smiles from his parents. But what would happen if he put on his mother's nightgown or lipstick? Parents, teachers, and friends generally reward or punish behaviors according to traditional gender-role expectations. Thus, a child "socially learns" what it means to be male or female.

According to *cognitive-developmental theory*, social learning is part of gender-role development, but it's much more than a passive process of receiving rewards or punishments and modeling others. Instead, cognitive developmentalists argue that children actively observe, interpret, and judge the world around them (Bem, 1981, 1993; Leaper, 2013; Starr & Zurbriggen, 2017). As children process information about the world, they also create internal rules governing correct behaviors for boys and for girls. On the basis of these rules, they form *gender schemas* (mental images) of how they should act.

© Billy R. Ray/Wiley

## Retrieval Practice 11.2 | Sexual Identity

Completing this self-test and connections section, and then checking your answers by clicking on the answer button or by looking in Appendix B, will provide immediate feedback and helpful practice for exams.

### Self-Test

1. Briefly describe how the term "gender" differs from "sex."

2. _____ refers to one's self-identification as either a man or a woman.

   a. Sex role          b. Assigned sex
   c. Gender dysphoria  d. Gender identity

3. Androgynous is another word for _____.

   a. transgender, gay, or lesbian
   b. having both male and female traits

c. having an oversupply of androgens during prenatal development
d. transvestite

4. A transgender person has a _____.

   a. mismatch between his or her gender identity and biological sex
   b. mismatch between his or her gender role and biological sex
   c. heterosexual preference for sexual gratification
   d. need to wear clothing of the other sex for sexual gratification

5. John has a male lover but also enjoys sexual relationships with women. His probable sexual orientation is _____.

   a. gay          b. transgender
   c. bisexual     d. heterosexual

▼ **Connections—Chapter to Chapter**
Answering the following question will help you "look back and look ahead" to see the important connections among the subfields of psychology and chapters within this text.

In Chapter 9 (Lifespan Development I), you learned about schemas, the foundation of Piaget's theory of cognitive development. Explain how schemas are involved in the way that children learn and understand gender roles.

## 11.3 | Sexual Behavior

### LEARNING OBJECTIVES

**Retrieval Practice** While reading the upcoming sections, respond to each Learning Objective in your own words.

**Summarize the research findings about the sexual response cycle and sexual orientation.**

- **Review** Masters and Johnson's sexual response cycle and the key gender differences and similarities.

- **Discuss** the myths and latest research on sexual orientation.

**Pair bonding** The formation of enduring relationships between adult mates.

Obviously, there is strong motivation to engage in sexual behavior. It's essential for the survival of our species, and it's also pleasurable. But *sexuality* includes much more than reproduction. For most humans (and some other animals), a sexual relationship fulfills many needs, including the need for connection, intimacy, pleasure, and the release of sexual tension. Interestingly, sex may also play a critical role in **pair bonding**—the formation of enduring relationships between adult mates. A recent longitudinal study found that sexual satisfaction remained elevated approximately 48 hours after sex and that spouses who experienced stronger, lingering "afterglows" reported significantly higher marital satisfaction over time (Meltzer et al., 2017). However, another study revealed that engaging in more frequent sex is associated with greater overall well-being—but only up to a point (Muise et al., 2015). Past the frequency of once a week, satisfaction and well-being level off. It isn't that having sex more than once a week lessens satisfaction, it's just that you don't get more satisfaction past the "break-even point" of once a week.

### Sexual Arousal and Response

Men and women, like waffles and pancakes, have the same basic ingredients when it comes to sexual arousal and response—and, overall, we are much more alike than different. But we also have obvious differences. How do we know this? How do researchers scientifically test what happens to the human body when an individual or a couple engages in sexual activities?

As mentioned earlier, William Masters and Virginia Johnson (1966) were the first to conduct laboratory studies on what happens to the human body during sexual activity. They attached recording devices to male and female volunteers and monitored or filmed their physical responses as they moved from nonarousal, to orgasm, and back to nonarousal. They labeled the bodily changes during this series of events a **sexual response cycle** (**Step-By-Step Diagram 11.1**). Later researchers expanded on their work, documenting differences between the male and female sexual response pattern (**Figure 11.6**).

**Sexual response cycle** Masters and Johnson's model of the typical human sexual response, consisting of four stages—excitement, plateau, orgasm, and resolution.

### Sexual Orientation

Of course, an essential part of our sexuality concerns whom we are sexually attracted to. What leads people to be sexually interested in members of their own sex, the opposite sex, or both sexes? The roots of human sexual orientation are poorly understood. However, most studies suggest that genetics and biology play a major role (Breedlove, 2017; DeBord et al., 2017; LeVay, 2003, 2012). A comprehensive review of the scientific literature suggests that, along with biological factors, certain environmental forces (particularly in the prenatal environment) may play some role in influencing sexual orientation (Bailey et al., 2016). However, these environmental forces do not

**STEP-BY-STEP DIAGRAM 11.1**    Masters and Johnson's View of the Sexual Response Cycle

**STOP!**  This Step-by-Step Diagram contains essential information NOT found elsewhere in the text, which is likely to appear on quizzes and exams. Be sure to study it CAREFULLY!

Masters and Johnson identified a typical, four-stage pattern of sexual response. Note that this simplified description does not account for individual variation, and should not be used to judge what's "normal."

**2** During the **plateau phase**, physiological and sexual arousal continue at heightened levels. Heart, circulation, and respiration rates, as well as muscle tension, all continue at elevated levels in both sexes. Sexual pleasure intensifies with increased stimulation. As arousal reaches its peak, both sexes may experience a feeling that orgasm is imminent and inevitable.

**3** The **orgasm phase** involves a highly intense and pleasurable release of tension. In women, muscles around the vagina squeeze the vaginal walls in and out, and the uterus pulsates. Muscles at the base of the penis contract in men, causing ejaculation—the discharge of seminal fluid.

Plateau

Orgasm

Resolution

Excitement

**1** The **excitement phase** can last for minutes or hours. Arousal is initiated through touching, fantasy, or erotic stimuli. Heart rate and respiration increase. Elevated blood flow to the genital region causes penile or clitoral erection, as well as vaginal lubrication in women.

After one orgasm, most men enter a **refractory period**, during which further excitement to orgasm is quite rare. Many women (and some men), however, are capable of multiple orgasms in fairly rapid succession.

**4** Physiological responses gradually return to normal during the **resolution phase**.

**Excitement Phase**   The first stage of the sexual response cycle, characterized by increasing levels of arousal and engorgement of the genitals.

**Plateau Phase**   The second stage of the sexual response cycle; period of sexual excitement prior to orgasm.

**Orgasm Phase**   The third stage of the sexual response cycle, when pleasurable sensations peak and orgasm occurs.

**Refractory Period**   A period of time following orgasm, during which further orgasm is considered physiologically rare for men.

**Resolution Phase**   The fourth, and final, stage of the sexual response cycle, when the body returns to its unaroused state.

**FIGURE 11.6**  **Comparing male and female sexual response patterns**   Although the overall pattern of sexual response is similar in the two sexes, there is more variation in specific patterns among women.

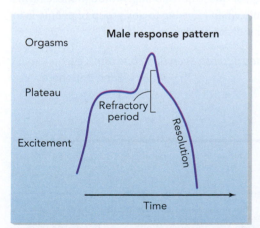

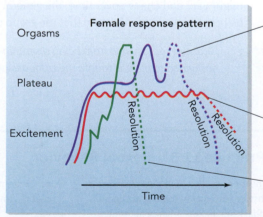

Resembles the male pattern, but with the possibility of multiple orgasms without falling below the plateau level

Represents nonorgasmic arousal

Portrays a rapid rise to orgasm, no definitive plateau, and a quick resolution

**a.  Typical Male sexual response pattern**
Immediately after orgasm, men generally enter a refractory period, which lasts from several minutes to up to a day.

**b.  Typical Female sexual response pattern**
Note the greater variety in sexual response among women versus men.

## TABLE 11.4 Sexual Orientation Myths

Patsy Lynch/Polaris/Newscom

*Myth #1: Seduction theory:* Gays and lesbians were seduced as children by adults of their own sex.

*Myth #2: "By default" theory:* Gays and lesbians were unable to attract partners of the other sex or have had unhappy heterosexual experiences.

*Myth #3: Poor parenting theory:* Sons become gay because of domineering mothers and weak fathers. Daughters become lesbians because their mothers were weak or absent or their fathers were their primary role model.

*Myth #4: Modeling theory:* Children raised by gay and lesbian parents usually end up adopting their parents' sexual orientation.

**Marriage equality** In 2013, the U.S. Supreme Court ruled the federal Defense of Marriage Act (DOMA), which defined marriage as a union between one man and one woman, unconstitutional. In 2015, in the case of *Obergefell* v. *Hodges*, the court went further and held that all states are required to issue marriage licenses to same-sex couples, and to recognize same-sex marriages validly performed in other jurisdictions. These decisions, along with other judicial and legislative action and changing societal views surrounding gay marriage, have lessened the misunderstandings and myths surrounding sexual orientation.

involve the social environment, and this study does not support the notion that sexual orientation can be taught or learned. Most importantly, the causes of homosexuality, biological or otherwise, should have no bearing on any individual's right to equality (Soh, 2017).

Can you see how a biological foundation for sexual orientation challenges some of the most enduring myths and misconceptions about sexual orientation (see **Table 11.4**)? Unfortunately, these false beliefs often contribute to **sexual prejudice**, which is a negative attitude directed toward an individual because of his or her sexual orientation. Many gay, lesbian, bisexual, and transgender people experience discrimination, as well as serious verbal and physical attacks, disrupted family and peer relationships, and high rates of anxiety, depression, and suicide (Elder, 2016; Ghabrial, 2017; Semlyen et al., 2016). Sadly, the risk of suicide may be particularly high among youths in the earliest stages of "coming out"—publicly revealing their gay sexual orientation (Dirkes et al., 2016).

Note that the term *sexual prejudice* is now preferred over the older, outdated term *homophobia*. In part, that's because *homophobia* implies an individual pathology, whereas *sexual prejudice* reflects the fact that, like all forms of prejudice, this type is socially constructed. Also note that a new acronym, LGBTQ, is sometimes used today to refer to people who identify themselves as lesbian, gay, bisexual, transgender, or queer/questioning. Although these terms might vary and change over time, the general rule when referring to any group of people is to be respectful and use the term that the group or individual prefers.

**Sexual prejudice** A negative attitude toward an individual because of her or his sexual orientation.

> *I learned compassion from being discriminated against. Everything bad that's ever happened to me has taught me compassion.*
> —Ellen DeGeneres

© Billy R. Ray/Wiley

## Retrieval Practice 11.3 | Sexual Behavior

Completing this self-test and connections section, and then checking your answers by clicking on the answer button or by looking in Appendix B, will provide immediate feedback and helpful practice for exams.

**Self-Test**

1. In this text's diving-board analogy for the sexual response cycle, climbing up the ladder is analogous to the _____ phase.

**a.** excitement      **b.** plateau
**c.** orgasm      **d.** resolution

2. The _____ occurs after the orgasm phase and before the resolution phase of the sexual response cycle.

**a.** spermarche      **b.** woman's refractory period
**c.** man's refractory period      **d.** sex flush

3. Orgasm refers to _____.
   a. the final phase of the sexual response cycle
   b. the male refractory period
   c. a highly intense and pleasurable release of tension
   d. the peak of the excitement phase
4. Which is true of research on the causes of sexual orientation?
   a. It has helped overcome many misconceptions and myths.
   b. It provides evidence of a biological foundation.
   c. It is inconclusive.
   d. All of these options are true.
5. Briefly explain how sexual prejudice differs from homophobia.

**Connections—Chapter to Chapter**
Answering the following question will help you "look back and look ahead" to see the important connections among the subfields of psychology and chapters within this text.

In Chapter 16 (Social Psychology), you'll discover the four most common sources of prejudice—learning, limited resources, displaced aggression, and mental shortcuts. Briefly discuss how each of these sources might explain sexual prejudice.

## 11.4  Sex Problems

### LEARNING OBJECTIVES

**Retrieval Practice**   While reading the upcoming sections, respond to each Learning Objective in your own words.

**Summarize the major problems in sexuality.**

- **Describe** the paraphilic disorders, including fetishism and exhibitionism, and their treatment.

- **Explain** how biological, psychological, and social factors influence sexual dysfunction.
- **Discuss** the major treatments for sexual dysfunctions.
- **Identify** the major issues related to sexually transmitted infections (STIs) and the special problem of AIDS.

When we are functioning well sexually, we generally take this part of our lives for granted. But what happens when things don't go smoothly? Why are some people sexually aroused by exposure to objects or situations that are potentially self-destructive or that victimize others? Why does normal sexual functioning stop for some people and never begin for others? What are the major diseases that can be spread through sexual behavior? We will explore these questions in the following section.

## Paraphilic Disorders

People obviously have differing preferences for particular types of sexual activities. Some may engage in "kinky" or unusual sexual behavior, such as sex in socially unacceptable situations or with unusual stimuli, whereas others may participate in sexual violence or pedophilia (Balon, 2016; Merrick, 2016). Unusual sexual practices between two consenting adults are generally not a problem, unless the practices are potentially harmful or cause personal distress. In such cases, they may be classified as a **paraphilic disorder**—a group of psychosexual disorders involving disturbing and repetitive sexual fantasies, urges, or behaviors that cause distress or impairment to the person and/or harm or risk of harm to others (American Psychiatric Association, 2013). Let's examine two of the most common paraphilias—*fetishistic disorder* and *exhibitionistic disorder*.

**Paraphilic disorder**   Any of a group of psychosexual disorders involving disturbing and repetitive sexual fantasies, urges, or behaviors that cause distress or impairment to the person and/or harm or risk of harm to others.

**Fetishistic Disorder**   In *fetishistic disorder*, the individual uses inanimate objects or unusual parts of the human body to achieve sexual arousal and satisfaction (American Psychiatric Association, 2013; Trail, 2015). Someone with a fetish might become aroused by seeing and touching silky material or by touching or smelling someone's shoe or foot. Or the person may simply find a particular object or body part appealing and arousing. In contrast to this type of *fetishism*, individuals with a clinical fetishistic disorder experience significant distress and/or impairment of their sexual, social, and other key areas of functioning. For example, they may find it impossible to become aroused or achieve orgasm when the preferred fetish object or body part is unavailable.

**Exhibitionistic Disorder**    *Exhibitionistic disorder*, often called "indecent exposure," involves recurrent and intense sexual arousal from fantasies, urges, or behaviors associated with exposing the genitals to unsuspecting and nonconsenting observers (American Psychiatric Association, 2013). This exhibitionistic ("flashing") behavior sometimes includes masturbating or performing sexual acts in a public location. A key aspect of the arousal is the surprise experienced by the victim. The exhibitionist generally does not desire any sexual contact with that person. People who have this paraphilia may actually engage in exhibitionism or may have recurring, obsessive sexual fantasies about doing so.

**Explaining and Treating Paraphilic Disorders**    As you'll discover in Chapter 14, the precise cause of psychological disorders is often difficult to determine, in part because numerous biological, psychological, and sociocultural factors may interact and contribute to such disorders (Balon, 2016; Kingston, 2016; Saadat, 2015). When looking for the causes of paraphilias, some researchers emphasize the importance of biological factors, such as traumatic brain injury (TBI), hormones, and alcohol abuse. Those who take the psychoanalytic perspective, in contrast, believe that paraphilias represent a return to a sexual habit or behavior from childhood.

The learning, or behaviorist, perspective describes paraphilias as a result of conditioning. In this view, particular sexual habits and paraphilias are learned from observing other people or from receiving reinforcement or reward for engaging in them. A person who engages in exhibitionistic behavior, for example, may experience increased arousal from anxiety about being caught engaging in such behavior, which can be quite rewarding.

Regardless of the cause, treatments are clearly needed to help people with such disorders find healthier and more positive outlets for their sexual pleasures. For example, some individuals have difficulty forming relationships with others, and group therapy can help build their social skills. Therapy also encourages them to empathize with their victims and take responsibility for their actions.

Paraphilias also can be treated using aversion therapy, which focuses on replacing the positive associations between sexual pleasure and a particular object or behavior with negative ones (see Chapters 6 and 15). During this form of therapy, the person might be told to imagine a particularly arousing scene (such as the fetish object and/or exhibitionism). Then the person would be asked to immediately visualize a negative outcome, such as getting arrested or seriously injured. After creating new negative associations with the fetish object or behavior to replace the previously positive ones, the therapist can work on creating healthier associations.

## Common Sexual Difficulties

In contrast to paraphilic disorders, many sexual problems involve common, everyday difficulties. These problems come under the official label **sexual dysfunction**, or difficulty in sexual functioning (**Table 11.5**). In this section, we discuss how biology, psychology, and social forces, as represented in the *biopsychosocial model*, all contribute to sexual difficulties.

**Sexual dysfunction**    A difficulty in sexual functioning; a significant disturbance in a person's ability to respond sexually or to experience sexual pleasure.

**Biological Factors**    Although many people may consider it unromantic, a large part of sexual arousal and behavior is clearly the result of biological processes (Crooks & Baur, 2016; Segarra-Echebarría et al., 2015; Shackelford & Hansen, 2015). *Erectile dysfunction*, the inability to get or maintain an erection firm enough for intercourse, and *orgasmic dysfunction*, the inability to respond to sexual stimulation to the point of orgasm, often reflect lifestyle factors like cigarette smoking. They are also related to medical conditions such as diabetes, alcoholism, circulatory problems, and reactions to certain prescription and nonprescription drugs. Furthermore, many people fail to recognize that drinking alcohol, even in moderate doses, can interfere with sexual functioning. Sexual responsiveness is also affected by stress, illness, and simple fatigue. In addition, hormones (especially testosterone) have a clear effect on sexual desire in both men and women, though their precise role is not well understood.

**TABLE 11.5**  **Common Male and Female Sexual Dysfunctions**

| Male | | Female | | Both Male and Female | |
|---|---|---|---|---|---|
| **Disorder** | **Causes** | **Disorder** | **Causes** | **Disorder** | **Causes** |
| **Erectile disorder***  *Marked difficulty in obtaining or maintaining an erection during sexual activity or until its completion; marked decrease in erectile rigidity*  • Lifelong (present since beginning of sexual activity) or acquired (began after a period of relatively normal sexual functioning)  *Must be experienced on almost all or all occasions of sexual activity (approximately 75% to 100%) | **Physical:** Chronic illness, diabetes, circulatory conditions, heart disease, drugs, fatigue, alcohol, hormones, inappropriate or inadequate stimulation  **Psychological:** Performance anxiety, difficulty expressing desires, not wanting to have sex, peer pressure, antisexual education or upbringing | **Female orgasmic disorder** *Marked delay, infrequency, or absence of orgasm; markedly reduced intensity of orgasmic sensations*  • Generalized (not limited to certain types of stimulation, situations, or partners), or situational (only occurs with certain types of stimulation, situations or partners) | **Physical:** Chronic illness, diabetes, drugs, fatigue, alcohol, hormones, pelvic disorders, inappropriate or inadequate stimulation  **Psychological:** Guilt, fear of discovery, hurried experiences, difficulty expressing desires, severe relationship distress, antisexual education or upbringing | **Female sexual interest/arousal disorder, male hypoactive sexual desire disorder** *Avoids sexual relations due to disinterest* | **Physical:** Hormones, drugs, alcohol, chronic illness  **Psychological:** Antisexual education or upbringing, depression, anxiety, sexual trauma, relationship problems  **Primarily psychological:** Antisexual education or upbringing, sex trauma, partner pressure, gender identity confusion |
| **Premature (early) ejaculation** *Persistent or recurrent pattern of ejaculation during partnered sexual activity within approximately one minute following vaginal penetration and before the individual wishes it*  • Generalized (not limited to certain types of stimulations, or partners) or situational (only occurs with certain types of stimulation, situations, or partners) | **Primarily psychological:** Guilt, fear of discovery, hurried experiences, learning to ejaculate as quickly as possible | **Vaginismus** *Involuntary vaginal spasms making penile insertion impossible or difficult and painful* | **Primarily psychological:** Inadequate lubrication, learned association of pain or fear with intercourse, antisexual education or upbringing | **Substance/ medication-induced sexual dysfunction** | **Physical:** Substance intoxication or withdrawal from drugs (e.g., alcohol, cocaine) or after exposure to medication |

Although sex therapists typically divide sexual dysfunction into "male, "female," or "both," problems should never be considered "his" or "hers." Couples are almost always encouraged to work together to find solutions.

For more information, check www.goaskalice.columbia.edu/Cat6.html.

**Sources:** Based on American Psychiatric Association, 2013; Balon, 2015; Carroll, 2016; Crooks & Baur, 2016; Strassberg et al., 2015.

Sexual arousal for both men and women is partially reflexive and somewhat analogous to simple reflexes (see Chapter 2). Just as a puff of air produces an automatic closing of the eye, certain stimuli, such as stroking of the genitals, can lead to automatic arousal in both men and women. In response to such stimuli, nerve impulses from the receptor site travel to the spinal cord. The spinal cord then responds by sending messages to target organs or glands. Normally, the blood flow into organs and tissues through the arteries is balanced by an equal outflow through the veins. During sexual arousal, however, the arteries dilate beyond the capacity of the veins to carry the blood away. This results in erection of the penis in men and an engorged clitoris and surrounding tissue in women.

As we've just seen, the human body is biologically prepared to become aroused and respond to erotic stimulation. Generally, if a man or woman stays in arousal long enough, an orgasm will occur. If this is so automatic, why do some people have difficulty getting aroused? Unlike the case in simple reflexes such as the eye blink, psychological factors, such as negative thoughts or high emotional states, may block sexual arousal. Recall from Chapter 2 that the *autonomic nervous system (ANS)* is intricately linked to emotional and sexual responses. It is composed of two subsystems: the sympathetic, which prepares the body for "fight-flight-freeze," and the parasympathetic, which maintains bodily processes at a steady, even balance. The *parasympathetic* branch is dominant during initial sexual excitement and throughout the plateau phase. The *sympathetic* branch dominates during ejaculation and orgasm.

### Psychological Influences

Do you see why the parasympathetic branch must be in control during arousal? The person needs to be relaxed enough to allow blood to flow to the genital area. Anxieties associated with certain sexual experiences, such as fear of pregnancy or sexually transmitted infections, may cause sympathetic dominance, which in turn blocks sexual arousal. Many individuals discover that they need locked doors, committed relationships, and reliable birth control to fully enjoy sexual relations.

**Performance anxiety** The fear of being judged in connection with sexual activities.

**Sexual scripts** The learned, socially constructed guidelines for our sexual interactions.

Another psychological block to sexual arousal is **performance anxiety**, the fear of being judged in connection with sexual activity (see the cartoon). Men commonly experience problems with erections or sufficient arousal (especially after drinking alcohol), and both men and women wonder whether their "performance" will satisfy their partner. Both partners also frequently worry about their attractiveness and their ability to reach orgasm. Do you see how these performance fears can lead to sexual problems? Once again, increased anxiety causes the sympathetic nervous system to dominate, which blocks blood flow to the genitals.

Many psychological factors affect our sexual functioning (Clarke et al., 2015; Gosselin, 2016; Rajkumar & Kumaran, 2015). Consider one more example. People who are having difficulty becoming pregnant and are using fertility treatments such as in vitro fertilization may experience lower levels of sexual desire and pleasure (Daniluk et al., 2014; Smith et al., 2015). And on a related note, research has recently confirmed what was long suspected—women who are highly stressed are less likely to conceive (Akhter et al., 2016). In other words, psychological factors, such as anxiety about not becoming pregnant or high levels of stress, may interfere not only with the enjoyment of sex but also with the ability to become pregnant.

### Snapshots

Another form of performance anxiety.

### Social and Cultural Factors

There are numerous social and cultural factors that provide explicit **sexual scripts** about what to do and when, where, how, and with whom we should do it (Gagnon, 1990; Leiting & Yeater, 2017; Wright & Bae, 2016). During the 1950s, societal messages said the "best" sex was at night, in a darkened room, only between a man and a woman, with the man on top and the woman on bottom. Today, the messages are bolder and more varied, partly because of media portrayals. Compare the sexual scripts portrayed in **Figure 11.7**.

**FIGURE 11.7** **Changing sexual scripts** Television and movies in the 1950s and 1960s allowed only married couples to be shown in a bedroom setting (and only in long pajamas and separate twin-size beds). Contrast this with modern times, where very young, unmarried couples are commonly portrayed in one bed, scantily dressed or nude, and sometimes even engaging in various stages of intercourse.

Sexual scripts may be less rigid today than they once were, but a major difficulty remains. Many sexual behaviors do not fit society's scripts and expectations, and we all unconsciously internalize societal messages without recognizing that they affect our values and behaviors. A recent study of 7th grade students found that those who believed that their peers were having sex were 2.5 times more likely themselves to have sex by 9th grade. Can you see how this increase in sexual behavior demonstrates the power of perceived peer norms and sexual scripts in influencing behavior (Johnson-Baker et al., 2016)?

Another change is the increasing prevalence of "hooking up" among high school and college students. Not so recently, dating was the major route to sexual interactions. Following predictable scripts, the man was expected to initiate the first date, organize it, and initiate sexual activity, whereas the woman waited to be asked out and accepted or rejected the man's sexual overtures.

Today, more casual, no-strings-attached, hooking-up relationships have at least partially replaced the more traditional romantic dating relationships (Allison, 2016; Olmstead et al., 2015; Prestage et al., 2015). Some research, however, suggests the "hookup" culture on college campuses has been overstated. For example, one study of first-year college women found that 56% of the women reported having sex with a romantic partner, whereas only 40% reported having sex in the context of a hookup (Fielder et al., 2012).

Sexual behaviors are also related to the **double standard**, which tends to encourage male sexuality and discourage female sexuality. Despite many changes in recent years, men are still generally encouraged to explore their sexuality and bring a certain level of sexual knowledge into relationships. In contrast, women are generally expected to permit or stop male advances and to refrain from sexual activity until married—or at least "in love." For example, researchers found that when male adolescents reported "having sex," they gained in peer acceptance, whereas female adolescents reporting the same behavior experienced decreases in peer acceptance (Kreager et al., 2016). However, these gender differences reversed when it came to "making out." In this case, male adolescents' peer acceptance declined, while the female adolescents' acceptance increased.

You can see how traditional sexual scripts and the double standard might affect our sexual behaviors and attitudes, but what about political beliefs? See the following **Research Challenge** to explore this question.

**Double standard** The beliefs, values, and norms that subtly encourage male sexuality and discourage female sexuality.

## Sex Therapy

People experiencing sex problems often benefit from therapy. How do therapists work with sex problems? Clinicians usually begin with interviews and examinations to determine whether the problem is biological, psychological, or, more likely, a combination of both (Atwood, 2015; McAnulty & Milling, 2015; Tolman et al., 2014).

## Research Challenge

### Does Political Affiliation Reflect Sexual Behavior?

Historically, the general American view has been that liberals typically believe the government's major function is to ensure equal opportunity and equality for all, whereas conservatives believe that government should focus on national defense and the freedom to pursue individual goals. But little was known about how each group's political values aligned with their sexual behaviors and attitudes—until now.

Using a web-based sampling technique, researchers directly asked American participants about their individual sexual practices and their political preferences (Hatemi et al., 2017). As might be expected, those with more conservative attitudes, ideologies, and partisan leanings tended to report engaging in more traditional sexual behaviors, such as kissing and missionary position (man on top) sex. In contrast, those who are more liberal politically reported more masturbation and more adventurous sex, such as using sex toys. They also engage in "liberal sex," such as having sex with someone they met on the same day, and have more sexual partners in their lifetime. Interestingly, those with more conservative orientations tend to report being more satisfied with their sex life.

What do you think? Does this fit with what you know about liberals and conservatives? Why do you think conservatives are more satisfied with their sex life? Can you predict the problems that might arise in a sexual union between two people who held strong and opposite political views?

Jon Feingersh/Getty Images

#### Test Yourself

1. Based on the information provided, did this study (Hatemi et al., 2017) use descriptive, correlational, and/or experimental research?

2. If you chose:
   - *descriptive research,* is this a naturalistic observation, survey/interview, case study, or/and archival research?
   - *correlational research,* is this a positive, negative, or zero correlation?
   - *experimental research,* label the IV, DV, experimental group(s), and control group. (Note: If participants were not randomly assigned to groups, list it as a *quasi-experimental design.*)
   - both *descriptive* and *correlational,* answer the corresponding questions for both.

**Check your answers by clicking on the answer button or by looking in Appendix B.**

**Note:** The information provided in this study is admittedly limited, but the level of detail is similar to what is presented in most textbooks and public reports of research findings. Answering these questions, and then comparing your answers to those provided, will help you become a better critical thinker and consumer of scientific research.

---

As mentioned earlier, biological causes of sexual dysfunction include medical conditions such as diabetes and heart disease, medications such as antidepressants, and drugs such as alcohol and tobacco—see **Table 11.6**. In fact, many who are addicted to drugs or alcohol experience sexual problems even after they stop using these substances (Del Río et al., 2015; Vallejo-Medina & Sierra, 2013). Erectile disorders are the problems most likely to have an organic component, and numerous drugs and other medical procedures have been developed to treat them.

Sex therapists also emphasize psychological and social factors. Years ago, the major psychological treatment for sexual dysfunction was long-term psychoanalysis. This treatment was based on the assumption that sexual problems resulted from deep-seated conflicts that originated in childhood. During the 1950s and 1960s, behavior therapists proposed that sexual dysfunction was learned. (See Chapter 15 for a more complete description of both psychoanalysis and behavior therapy.) It wasn't until the early 1970s and the publication of Masters and Johnson's *Human Sexual Inadequacy* that sex therapy gained national recognition. Because the model that Masters and Johnson developed is still a popular choice of many sex therapists, we will use it as our example of how psychological sex therapy is conducted.

| TABLE 11.6 | Sexual Effects of Legal and Illegal Drugs |
|---|---|
| **Drug** | **Effects** |
| Alcohol | Moderate to high doses inhibit arousal; chronic abuse causes damage to testes, ovaries, and the circulatory and nervous systems |
| Tobacco | Decreases blood flow to the genitals, thereby reducing the frequency and duration of erections and vaginal lubrication |
| Cocaine and amphetamines | Moderate to high doses and chronic use result in inhibition of orgasm and decrease in erection and lubrication |
| Barbiturates | Moderate to high doses lead to decreased desire, erectile disorders, and delayed orgasm |

**Sources:** Crooks & Baur, 2013; Hyde et al., 2014; King, 2012.

**Masters and Johnson's Sex Therapy Program**   The approach developed by William Masters and Virginia Johnson (see photo) is founded on four major principles:

1. **Relationship focus**   Unlike forms of therapy that focus on the individual, Masters and Johnson's sex therapy focuses on the relationship between two people. To counteract any blaming tendencies, each partner is considered fully involved in and affected by sexual problems. Both partners are taught positive communication and conflict resolution skills.

2. **Investigation of both biological and psychosocial factors**   Medication and many physical disorders can cause or aggravate sexual dysfunctions. Therefore, Masters and Johnson emphasize the importance of medical histories and exams. They also explore psychosocial factors, such as how the couple first learned about sex and their current attitudes, gender-role training, and sexual scripts.

3. **Emphasis on cognitive factors**   Recognizing that many problems result from performance anxiety and *spectatoring*—mentally watching and evaluating responses during sexual activities—therapists discourage couples from setting goals and judging sex in terms of success or failure.

4. **Specific behavioral techniques**   Couples are seen in an intensive two-week counseling program. They explore their sexual values and misconceptions and practice specific behavioral exercises. "Homework assignments" usually begin with a *sensate focus* exercise in which the partners take turns gently caressing each other and communicating what is pleasurable. There are no goals or performance demands. Later exercises and assignments are tailored to the couple's particular sex problem. For more suggestions for healthy sexuality, see the following **Try This Yourself**.

**Experiments in Sex**
William Masters and Virginia Johnson were the first researchers to use direct laboratory experimentation and observation to study human sexuality.

*Diana Walker/Time & Life Pictures/Getty Images, Inc.*

---

## Try This Yourself

### Tips for Healthy Sexuality

Sex therapists generally recommend:

- Beginning sex education as early as possible. Children should be given positive feelings about their bodies and an opportunity to discuss sexuality in an open, honest fashion.

- Avoiding goal- or performance-oriented approaches. Therapists often remind clients that there really is no "right" way to have sex. When couples or individuals attempt to judge or evaluate their sexual lives or to live up to others' expectations, they risk making sex a job rather than a pleasure.

- Communicating openly with your partner. Mind reading belongs onstage, not in the bedroom. Partners need to tell each other what feels good and what doesn't. Sexual problems should be openly discussed without blame, anger, or defensiveness. If the problem does not improve within a reasonable time, consider getting professional help.

---

# Sexually Transmitted Infections (STIs)

As we've just seen, early sex education and open communication between partners are essential for full sexual functioning. They're also key to avoiding and controlling **sexually transmitted infections (STIs)**, formerly called sexually transmitted diseases (STDs), venereal disease (VD), or social diseases. STIs are infections that are generally passed from one person to another through vaginal, oral, or anal sex. There are more than 25 infectious organisms that can be transmitted through sexual activity.

As you've undoubtedly heard, it's extremely important for sexually active people to get medical diagnosis and treatment for any suspicious symptoms and to inform their partners. If left untreated, many STIs can cause severe problems, including infertility, ectopic pregnancy, cancer, and even death. Each year, of the millions of North Americans who contract one or more STIs, a substantial majority are under age 35. Also, as **Figure 11.8** shows, women are at much greater risk than men of contracting major STIs.

**Sexually transmitted infection (STI)**   An infection generally transmitted by vaginal, oral, or anal sex.

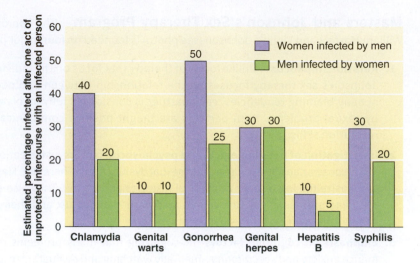

**FIGURE 11.8**  **Male–female differences in suscepti-bility to STIs**  These percentages represent the relative chances of infection for men and women after a single act of intercourse with an infected partner.

**AIDS (acquired immunodefi-ciency syndrome)**  A disease in which the human immuno-deficiency virus (HIV) destroys the immune system's ability to fight other diseases, thus leaving the body vulnerable to a variety of opportunistic infections and cancers.

**HIV positive**  The state of being infected by the human immuno-deficiency virus (HIV).

STIs such as genital warts and chlamydial infections have reached epidemic proportions. Yet **AIDS (acquired immunodeficiency syndrome)** has received the largest share of public attention. AIDS results from infection with the *human immunodeficiency virus* (*HIV*). A standard blood test can determine whether someone is **HIV positive**, which means he or she has been infected by HIV. Keep in mind that being infected is not the same as having AIDS. AIDS is the final stage of the HIV infection process.

Note also that with the right medications, people can have a normal, or near-normal, life span with HIV or AIDS (Helleberg et al., 2015; May et al., 2014; Naghavi et al., 2015). The key is early treatment with antiretroviral drugs. Nonetheless, there is no known cure for HIV in most cases, and AIDS remains a serious, potentially fatal health risk.

Sadly, myths about AIDS are still widespread. Many people still believe AIDS can be transmitted through casual contact, such as sneezing, shaking hands, sharing drinking glasses or towels, kissing, or contact with sweat or tears. Some even mistakenly believe that you can contract HIV while donating blood. Others are mistrustful of gay people, be-cause gay men were the first highly visible victims. All of these are *false* beliefs.

HIV spreads only by direct contact with bodily fluids—primarily blood, semen, and vag-inal secretions, but also occasionally through breast milk and nonsterile needles. Note that

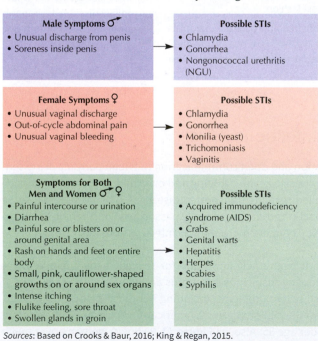

**FIGURE 11.9**  **Common sex-ually transmitted infections (STIs)**  Keep in mind that you may have an STI without having any of the danger signs listed here. If you have symptoms or concerns, see your doctor and follow all medical recommendations. This generally includes returning for a checkup to make sure you are no longer infected. If you would like more information, check www.niaid.nih.gov/factsheets/stdinfo.htm. For further, detailed information about STIs, visit www.safesex.org.

contrary to popular stereo-types, anyone can get HIV and AIDS, including men, women, children, and people who are gay or straight (Hall et al., 2015; Heeren et al., 2014; Malavé et al., 2014).

At this point, we need to offset these depressing facts about STIs with some good news. Most STIs are readily cured in their early stages. See **Figure 11.9** for an overview of the signs and symptoms of the most common STIs. As you study this figure, remember that many infected people are *asymptomatic*, meaning they lack obvious symptoms. You can have one or more of the

*Sources*: Based on Crooks & Baur, 2016; King & Regan, 2015.

diseases without knowing it. And it is often impossible to tell whether a sexual partner is infectious. That's why the best strategy is prevention and regular testing (see the following **Try This Yourself**).

---

## Try This Yourself

### Protecting Yourself and Others from STIs

The following "safer sex" suggestions are intended not to be moralistic but to help reduce your chances of contracting HIV/AIDS and other STIs:

1. **Remain abstinent or have sex with one mutually faithful, uninfected partner**. Be selective about sexual partners and postpone physical intimacy until laboratory tests verify that you are both free of STIs.

2. **Don't share needles, syringes, or other drug equipment— and don't have sex with someone who does**. If you must share, use bleach to clean and sterilize your needles and syringes. Also, if you're engaging in tattooing and/or body piercing, be sure the needles are sterilized.

3. **Don't have sex if you or your partner is impaired by alcohol or other drugs**. The same is true for your friends: "Friends don't let friends drive (or have sex) when drunk (or

drug impaired)." Sadly, one study found that almost 20% of college men have committed some kind of sexual assault, and 4% have committed rape (Mouilso & Calhoun, 2016). And other research shows that an estimated 7% of women are raped while incapacitated due to the influence of alcohol or drugs during their first year at college (Carey et al., 2015).

4. **Use condoms**. Although condoms do not provide 100% protection, when used consistently and correctly, using them is still one of the very best ways to decrease your chances of contracting STIs, while simultaneously helping to prevent unwanted pregnancies.

5. **Educate yourself**. Learn the signs and symptoms of STIs. If you have more than one sexual partner, experts recommend having regular medical exams (every three to six months), and if you think you might be infected, get help right away.

---

© Billy R. Ray/ Wiley

## Retrieval Practice 11.4 | Sex Problems

Completing this self-test and connections section, and then checking your answers by clicking on the answer button or by looking in Appendix B, will provide immediate feedback and helpful practice for exams.

### Self-Test

1. Define *paraphilic disorder*.

2. _____ teach us "what to do, when, where, how, and with whom."

   a. Sex surrogates     b. Sexual scripts
   c. Sex manuals     d. Sex therapists

3. The fear of being judged in connection with sexual activity is known as _____.

   a. decreased sexual desire    b. sexual dysfunctions
   c. inhibited orgasm     d. performance anxiety

4. All of the following are principles of Masters and Johnson's approach to sex therapy except _____.

   a. setting goals to improve sexual performance
   b. examining the relationship between the two people

   c. using medical histories and physical examinations
   d. exploring individual attitudes and sex education

5. Having AIDS generally refers to being infected with a virus that attacks the _____.

   a. central nervous system
   b. peripheral nervous system
   c. immune system
   d. mucous membranes

### Connections—Chapter to Chapter

Answering the following question will help you "look back and look ahead" to see the important connections among the subfields of psychology and chapters within this text.

In Chapter 6 (Learning), we discussed how operant conditioning and observational learning can shape behavior. How do these two processes contribute to our understanding of sexual scripts and the double standard for men and women?

# 11.5 | Sex and Modern Life

## LEARNING OBJECTIVES

**Retrieval Practice**   While reading the upcoming sections, respond to each Learning Objective in your own words.

**Summarize the major issues of sex and modern life.**

- **Discuss** the risks and methods of prevention for sexual victimization, including child sexual abuse and rape.
- **Describe** why and how gender differences, conflict, and assertiveness are key elements of sexual communication.

Sexuality can be a source of vitality and tender bonding. But when sexual activity becomes a forcible act against the wishes of another person, it can be very traumatizing. In this section, we look at the dark side of human sexuality—*sexual victimization*. Then, we address perhaps the most valuable topic of all—*sexual communication*.

## Sexual Victimization

Any sexual activity that includes lack of consent, or the coercion, exploitation, or assault of another, is a serious problem. Although we often think about sexual violence as caused by a stranger, in most cases it is committed by someone known to the victim, such as a friend, neighbor, or family member. Both men and women can experience sexual victimization. In this section we examine two types of sexual violence: *child sexual abuse* and *rape*.

### Child Sexual Abuse (CSA)

**Child sexual abuse (CSA)**   A sexual act with a child that is intended to provide sexual gratification for the perpetrator; it includes both physical acts and noncontact exploitation.

A substantial number of children and adolescents are *sexually abused* by adults or other adolescents. **Child sexual abuse (CSA)**, also known as *child molestation* or *pedophilia*, refers to a sexual act with a child that is intended to provide sexual gratification for the perpetrator. It can refer to a number of different behaviors, including touching a child's genitals, masturbating in front of a child, or engaging in digital penetration, oral-genital stimulation, or vaginal or anal intercourse. It can also occur in the absence of any physical contact, such as when an abuser watches a child undress or exposes their genitals to a child. Soliciting a child to engage in acts for the sexual gratification of others or viewing or disseminating child pornography are also considered child sex abuse (American Psychiatric Association, 2013; Crosson-Tower, 2015; Delmonico & Griffin, 2014). See **Figure 11.10**.

Not surprisingly, children who are sexually abused may experience long-term psychological, physical, and behavioral problems. Common reactions include depression, anxiety, guilt, fear, sexual dysfunction, withdrawal, acting out, and problems with sleeping, eating, or school performance. In addition, sexually abused children may show inappropriate knowledge of, or interest in, sexual activity. As adults, they're also at increased risk of sexual revictimization, as well as depression, anxiety, insomnia, posttraumatic stress disorder (PTSD), problems with alcohol and drugs, aggressive and criminal behaviors, and difficulty in adult sexual relationships (Nguyen et al., 2017; Teicher & Samson, 2016; Waldron et al., 2015).

The effects of CSA vary according to a number of factors, but in general, the longer the abuse occurred, the closer the relationship between the perpetrator and the victim, and the more violent the assault, the greater the negative effects (Carroll, 2016; Karakurt & Silver, 2014; Many et al., 2014). The consequences also vary in part depending on

**FIGURE 11.10** **"Stranger danger"? The reality of child sex abusers**   Did you know that up to 30% of CSA is committed by family members and that up to 60% is committed by acquaintances and people the family trusts (Deblinger et al., 2015; Finkelhor, 2012; Whealin & Barnett, 2014)? Ironically, most people believe strangers are the major perpetrators of sexual abuse, which leaves parents and the public less alert to the real dangers from relatives, coaches, and even trusted religious leaders! As shown in this photo, the systemic child abuse practiced by numerous Roman Catholic priests was highlighted in the Academy Award-winning 2015 film *Spotlight*.

Photos 12/Alamy Stock Photo

whether and how quickly a child reports the abuse. Children who confide shortly after the abuse in an adult who believes them generally experience less trauma than children who do not disclose the offense. Sadly, many children wait years to tell someone about what occurred. In fact, one study found that half of all victims wait as long as five years before telling someone, and 25% never disclose the abuse (Hébert et al., 2009).

Why would a child not reveal this type of abuse immediately? Adult sexual predators typically lie and distort their abusive sexual behaviors as a way of manipulating and confusing the intended child victim. Even before the abuse begins, most abusers engage in a "seduction stage" in which they typically "groom" their victims by gradually and methodically building trust with the child and the adults who surround him or her. During the abuse, the predator then uses power, fear, isolation, and verbal threats ("no one will believe you") and/or physical threats ("I'll kill you and/or your family") to discourage the child from revealing the abuse. Thus, the child may stay silent, deny the abuse, misremember, or even forcibly forget in order to protect himself or herself or a loved one (Belli, 2013; Bennett & O'Donohue, 2016; McNally & Robinaugh, 2015).

The good news is that a cross-cultural meta-analysis (which combined results from 24 studies) found that school-based programs teaching children about sexual abuse leads to more disclosure (Walsh et al., 2015). Furthermore, many victims of this type of abuse can and do recover to have fulfilling romantic and sexual relationships. This is not to say that CSA isn't a very serious crime, and our top priority must be to prevent it. The following general tips are drawn from the work of numerous specialists. For more information, contact the National Children's Alliance (www.nca-online.org) or the National Child Abuse hotline (1-800-4-A-Child).

1. **Education** Adults should learn the risks and facts about child sexual abuse. Starting in early childhood, present this information to both male and female children in concrete terms, using age-appropriate language. During these prevention discussions, be sure to include the positive aspects of loving touch and sexuality, which the child will discover as an adult.

2. **Reduce the risk** Recognizing that abusers are most often family members, friends, or trusted people in positions of authority, create and lobby for open-door policies and the reduction or elimination of private, one-adult/one-child situations.

3. **Child empowerment** Teach children to know the difference between "good touch" and "bad touch" and to trust their own feelings when they think something is wrong. Remind them that they have rights. They can say "no" to any adult who asks them to participate in any activity or bodily contact that makes them feel uncomfortable. Also, instruct children that no matter what anyone tells them, "body secrets" are not okay, and reassure them that they will not get in trouble by reporting the secret. If you suspect abuse, or if a child reports it, stay calm, protect the child from further contact with the abuser, and report it to the police.

**Rape**    The legal definition of **rape** varies from state to state, but it is generally defined as unlawfully engaging in oral, anal, or vaginal penetration with a person through force or threat of force and without consent or with a person incapable of giving consent (due to age or physical or mental incapacity). As clear-cut as this definition seems, many people misunderstand what constitutes rape. To test your own knowledge, see the following **Try This Yourself**.

As with CSA, only around 10% of rapes are committed by strangers. In the United States alone, more than 2 million women are raped each year (Centers for Disease Control and Prevention, 2015). Nationwide surveys reveal that 8% of high school students (11.8% of female students and 4.5% of male students) report having been forced to have sex, as do 20% to 25% of college women. Considering that most rapes are never reported to the police, you can see why the official numbers most likely underestimate the true prevalence of such violence.

**Rape**    The unlawful act of engaging in oral, anal, or vaginal penetration with a person through force or threat of force and without consent or with a person incapable of giving consent (due to age or physical or mental incapacity).

## Try This Yourself

### True or False?

____ **1.** Rape usually occurs between strangers.

____ **2.** A man cannot be raped by a woman.

____ **3.** Rape is a crime of passion.

____ **4.** Women secretly want to be raped.

____ **5.** Male sexuality is biologically overpowering and beyond control.

____ **6.** Rape is usually violent.

____ **7.** There are many false reports of rape.

____ **8.** Most people report rape or sexual assault to the police.

____ **9.** If a person didn't fight back, he or she wasn't really raped.

____ **10.** Women and girls sometimes play hard to get and say "no" when they really mean "yes."

All these statements are false. But popular culture and media often support these myths, and a large number of men and women believe them (Carroll, 2016; Garland et al., 2016; Schwartz & Kempner, 2015). Using your critical thinking skills, can you explain how gender role conditioning, media portrayals, and lack of general information help perpetuate these myths?

Keith Srakocic/AP Photos

**Without consent, it's rape!**
In March 2013, Trent Mays, age 17, and Ma'lik Richmond, age 16, were found guilty of sexually assaulting a 16-year-old female classmate who was intoxicated and thus unable to give legal consent. Sadly, this type of sexual assault occurs far too often in both high schools and colleges.

Sadly, the impact of rape is often long lasting and can include physical, psychological, and social consequences. Victims may experience chronic pain, headaches and migraines, back pain, and gynecological and gastrointestinal problems. Equally serious psychological and social consequences include lasting fear, anxiety, depression, guilt, distrust of others, and strained relationships with family members, friends, and romantic partners. Some victims develop PTSD and experience painful flashbacks in which they mentally reexperience the trauma of the attack. Some respond by engaging in unhealthy behaviors, including taking drugs, smoking cigarettes, vomiting, overeating, and even attempting suicide (Çelikel et al., 2015; Crooks & Baur, 2016; Zinik & Padilla, 2016).

Recovering from sexual violence takes time. Victims of rape may go through an initial period of coping with the immediate physical and emotional trauma, followed by a lengthy "reorganization" phase in which they try to get back to their normal life. They often benefit from group therapy with other survivors. When PTSD has developed, cognitive therapy or treatment with antidepressants may be useful. The victim's family, friends, and sexual partners also need support, education, and counseling to deal with their own feelings, as well as guidance in dealing appropriately with the victim.

Preventing rape is obviously a crucial goal, and the best general strategies are to:

- Provide education about healthy sexuality and safe dating relationships.

- Help parents identify violent attitudes and behaviors in their children.

- Create and enforce policies in school and work environments that address sexual violence and harassment.

- Develop mass media messages—on television, on the Internet, and in newspapers and magazines—that promote violence-free relationships and norms.

- Increase public awareness of sexual violence and the importance of bystanders stepping in to prevent an assault.

For more information, contact the Rape, Abuse & Incest National Network (www.rainn.org) or the National Sexual Violence Against Women Prevention Research Center (www.musc.edu/vawprevention).

# Sexual Communication

*Men and women, women and men. It will never work.*

—Erica Jong (American Author, Poet, Teacher)

As we've just seen, communication can help to reduce sexual victimization. It's also the foundation for finding and maintaining a healthy sexual relationship. We need to learn how to clearly communicate with words, as well as through facial expressions, eye contact, and body language (e.g., Adams & Nelson, 2016; Hwang & Matsumoto, 2016). In this section, we focus on three key topics and potential problems with communication: male/female differences, managing conflict, and saying "no."

### Male/Female Differences in Communication

Have you heard that men and women communicate so differently that they seem to be from two separate cultures or planets—as in the title of the popular book *Men Are from Mars, Women Are from Venus?* This idea is appealing because of popular stereotypes and our own occasional difficulties communicating "across genders." However, research shows that these differences are small and not characteristic of all men and women or of all mixed-gender conversations (Carothers & Reis, 2013; Hyde, 2014; Martey et al., 2014). Still, they may help explain and prevent some communication misunderstandings.

Take, for example, the finding that in general men use speech to convey information, exert control, preserve independence, and enhance their status. In contrast, women more often use speech to achieve and share intimacy, promote closeness, and maintain relationships (**Table 11.7**). If men more often see conversations as a contest they must "win" and women use

---

**TABLE 11.7** **Communication Differences Between the Genders**

| In General, Men Tend to | In General, Women Tend to | |
|---|---|---|
| Use speech to convey information, exert control, preserve independence, and enhance their status. | Use speech to achieve and share intimacy, promote closeness, and maintain relationships. | **What's wrong with this communication?** Can you use information from this table to identify possible gender-related explanations? |
| Talk more than women, interrupt women more than women interrupt men, and interrupt women more often than they interrupt other men. | Talk more than men when they have more power in a relationship. | |
| Be more directive and assertive ("I want to get there by noon"). | Be more indirect and tentative, using hedges ("kind of") and disclaimers ("I'm not sure what time we should get there"). | |
| Talk more about politics, sports, and careers when they're in same-gender pairs. | Talk more about feelings and relationships when they're in same-gender pairs. | |
| Remain calm and problem oriented during conflict and seek compromise solutions to problems. | Become more sensitive to the feelings of others during conflict, more easily express both positive and negative emotions, and send double messages (such as smiling while making a critical comment). | |
| Prefer spoken communication. | Prefer written communication. | |
| Prefer to work out their problems by themselves. | Prefer to talk out solutions with another person. | |
| Make critical comments on the work of a colleague. | Compliment the work of a colleague. | |
| Be less sensitive to reading and sending nonverbal messages. | Be better at reading and sending nonverbal messages. | |

Jakubzak/iStock/Getty Images, Inc.

**Sources:** Brannon, 2016; Crooks & Baur, 2016; Levant & Wong, 2017; Matlin, 2016; Tannen, 1990, 2007, 2011; Wood & Fixmer-Oralz, 2016.

Joseph Farris / CartoonStock

language as a way to "bond with others," it's easy to see why the two sexes might have certain communication problems. Do you see how a woman who sees language as a way to maintain relationships might call her partner at work to ask how his day is going or when he will be home? And how, in turn, the man might interpret her call as a challenge to his freedom and resist what he perceives as controlling behavior? To make matters worse, at home that night, the same man may feel like relaxing. If he doesn't have information to convey or anyone to defend against, he sees little reason to talk. In comparison, the woman may have spent her day having few opportunities to build closeness through language, and she looks forward to a quiet dinner and "relationship talk" with her mate.

Obviously, this scenario exaggerates gender differences and overlooks individual situations. But we use this extreme example to demonstrate why the two sexes are sometimes at cross-purposes when they talk (see cartoon). Researcher Deborah Tannen (1990, 2007, 2011) believes that boys and girls learn different styles of communication from early childhood and that these styles sometimes carry over into most of their adult social interactions. In her book *You Just Don't Understand*, Tannen (1990) says that the first steps in improving communication between men and women are accepting that there are some differences in gender communication styles, realizing it is not a matter of one style being right or wrong, and then working to understand the other gender's occasionally differing styles.

Since the publication of Tannen's research, a large number of investigations have looked at gender differences in communication. These studies have verified that some differences do exist, but they are relatively small. Moreover, they may reflect differences in status and power more than gender (Brannon, 2016; Leaper, 2015; McGlone & Pfiester, 2015). This is good news. Given that communication is essential for healthy sexuality, as well as in our professional and personal lives, men and women can use this information to better understand one another and work around their small, but sometimes meaningful, gender differences.

## ❖ Psychology and Your Personal Success | Are Your Conflicts Constructive or Destructive?

One of the most essential, and most difficult, areas of communication is conflict management, and the way we handle it is a major predictor of relationship satisfaction and longevity. It's also an inevitable part of life. By understanding it and identifying your own conflict patterns, you can use it as an opportunity to improve and solidify your relationships.

Carol Rusbult and her colleagues describe four of the most common types of responses that people typically use in handling conflict—*voice, loyalty, neglect,* and *exit* (Drigotas et al., 1995; Rusbult & Zembrodt, 1983; Rusbult et al., 1982).

The first, and generally seen as the most constructive, strategy is *voice*, which means talking things over to try to resolve the conflict. When done properly, it helps maintain and affirm the relationship because it involves direct problem solving and creative "win-win" solutions. Thus, if your partner seems to be avoiding your sexual advances, you could discuss how his or her resistance makes you feel and how the problem could be solved. (Perhaps he or she is exhausted from work, and you could renegotiate the work load at home.)

*Loyalty* is defined as remaining committed to the relationship and simply waiting patiently for things to get better. It is characterized by quiet forgiveness, acceptance, and accommodation. Loyalty sounds as if it could be a good strategy, but it's less often associated with favorable consequences for conflict management, possibly because it is a less visible and more indirect strategy (Cahn, 2013; Kammrath & Dweck, 2006).

The other two conflict strategies are clearly destructive. *Neglect*, giving up on the relationship and withdrawing from it emotionally, and *exit*, leaving or threatening to leave the relationship, are far too common and should be avoided if you want to build or maintain a healthy relationship. Not surprisingly, people who have high relationship investment and satisfaction are more likely to use a constructive strategy for resolving conflicts (see the following **Try This Yourself**).

---

### Try This Yourself

#### How Do You Handle Conflict?

Rate how likely you would be to use each strategy for handling conflict in a romantic relationship on a scale of 1 to 5 (1 meaning "I would definitely not do this" and 5 meaning "I would definitely do this").

1. I would end the relationship.
2. I would tell my partner to leave.
3. I would talk to my partner about what was bothering me.
4. I would suggest things that I thought would help us.
5. I would hope that if I just hung in there, things would get better.
6. I would wait patiently.
7. I guess I would just sort of let things fall apart.
8. I would get angry and wouldn't talk at all.

What were your highest and lowest scores? Items 1 and 2 measure exit, items 3 and 4 measure voice, items 5 and 6 measure loyalty, and items 7 and 8 measure neglect (Rusbult et al., 1982).

---

Another researcher, John Gottman, has conducted extensive research on relationship conflict (Gottman, 2015; Gottman & Silver, 2012). Using a variety of measures (physiological, nonverbal, verbal, and questionnaire) to assess and follow large samples of couples over long periods of time, his research has revealed four styles of conflict that are particularly destructive:

- *Criticism*—complaining about some features of the relationship.
- *Contempt*—acting as if sickened or repulsed by the partner.
- *Defensiveness*—protecting the self.
- *Stonewalling*—emotionally withdrawing and refusing to participate in conversation.

All these strategies can lead to increased isolation and withdrawal. In fact, Gottman calls these styles of conflict the "Four Horsemen of the Apocalypse," meaning that the end of a relationship, the *apocalypse*, will be brought on by four horsemen—the four negative styles of conflict.

The *stonewalling* approach is part of another conflict style, called the *demand/withdraw interaction pattern*, in which one partner attempts to start a discussion by criticizing, complaining, or suggesting change (Baucom et al., 2015; King & DeLongis, 2013; Knobloch-Fedders et al., 2014). The other partner then attempts to end this discussion—or avoid the issue—by maintaining silence or withdrawing from the situation. In a heterosexual relationship, the man is more likely to withdraw from conflict and the woman is more likely to take a leading role in initiating and discussing it.

In contrast to the demand/withdraw pattern of interaction, some couples just avoid and deny the presence of any conflict in a relationship. Unfortunately, denial prevents couples from solving their problems at early stages, which can lead to even greater problems later on. On the other hand, expressing anger and disagreement also leads to lower marital satisfaction (Bloch et al., 2014; Gottman, 2015; MacKenzie et al., 2014). In fact, couples who show high levels of negative communication in their first few years of marriage are more likely than others to get divorced (Lavner & Bradbury, 2012; Worthington et al., 2015).

As we've just seen, demanding, withdrawing, avoiding, denying, and expressing anger and disagreement all seem to lead to relationship problems. So what's the answer? Given that conflict is an inevitable and even healthy part of all our relationships, we need to learn better strategies for working through conflicts in a positive and productive way (Buehler, 2014; Flora & Segrin, 2015; Marigold & Anderson, 2016). See the following **Try This Yourself**.

## Try This Yourself

### Conflict Resolution Skills

What can we do to successfully manage conflict in our own relationships? Understanding the other person's point of view and putting ourselves in their place is a good first step. People who can adopt their partner's perspective show more constructive responses to conflict.

Second, because conflict and disagreements are an inevitable part of close relationships, people need to be able to forgive personal wrongdoings and apologize (Enright & Fitzgibbons, 2015; Flora & Segrin, 2015). Those who remember relationship transgressions their partner committed in a more positive and less severe light are more likely to have lasting and satisfying relationships (Gottman, 2015). Similarly, apologies minimize conflict, lead to forgiveness, and help you maintain relationship closeness.

What makes for an effective apology? Research has identified six components (Lewicki et al., 2016):

- Acknowledgment of responsibility
- Offer of repair
- Declaration of repentance
- Expression of regret
- Explanation of what went wrong
- Request for forgiveness

JGI/Jamie Grill/Getty Images

Research also shows that the first two items on this list, acknowledgment of responsibility and an offer of repair, are the most important. Keep these tips in mind after your next conflict. A good apology will save or strengthen all your relationships—romantic and otherwise.

---

**Saying "No"** When faced with sexual or other types of conflict, how do you respond? Are you *passive*, *aggressive*, or *assertive*? In this section, we'll clarify the differences among these terms, help you identify and increase your own level of assertiveness, and improve your conflict resolution skills.

Let's begin with *passive behavior*, which means failing to stand up for your rights even when you are fully justified in doing so. Although passive individuals often "get along" with everyone, they are less respected and less likely to achieve their personal goals. They also are self-denying and self-inhibiting, experience low self-esteem, and feel hurt and anxious (Alberti & Emmons, 2008; Brassard et al., 2015; Hays, 2014). Furthermore, passive sex partners may be seen as lackluster and as contributing little to the relationship.

As will be discussed in Chapter 16, *aggression* is any behavior intended to harm another. During conflict, an aggressive person will stand up for his or her rights, disregarding potential harm to others and possibly using insults, threats, and even physical intimidation and attacks. Aggressive behavior is more likely than passive behavior to get you what you want in the short term. But like passiveness, it too has negative long-term consequences. Others may initially give in to aggressive people and feel intimidated by them, yet they rarely like or respect them. Think about how much you liked or respected classroom or playground bullies when you were growing up. Furthermore, aggressive behavior far too often provokes aggressive responses that can easily escalate into violence.

**Assertiveness** The behavior of confidently and directly standing up for your rights, or putting forward your views, without infringing on the rights or views of others; striking a balance between passivity and aggression.

**Assertiveness**, which is defined as confidently and directly standing up for your rights without infringing on those of others, strikes a balance between passive and aggressive behavior. It means you directly and honestly request things you want and say "no" to things you don't want. As you might expect, assertive people tend to have higher levels of self-esteem, self-worth, and self-satisfaction because they have more control over their life choices and direction (Brassard et al., 2015; Hays, 2014; Sarkova et al., 2013). They're also more likely to avoid serious conflicts and to resolve them more effectively. Perhaps most importantly, assertiveness generally leads to higher goal attainment and to greater respect from others.

How assertive are you in your everyday life? Do you stick up for your rights, or do you allow others to walk all over you? Do you say what you feel, or do you say what you think other people want you to say? Beginning in childhood, most of us were socialized to be "nice," to say "yes," and to please others. Regrettably, being overly nice often means sacrificing our own needs, which in turn allows hostility and frustration to accumulate and weaken our relationships. For tips on assertiveness, see the following **Try This Yourself**.

### How to Say "No"

A key step in becoming assertive is learning how to say "no." When faced with a sexual or other situation in which you want to refuse the requests of another or to protect your own rights, try the following:

- **Be assertive nonverbally.** Look the person in the eye, keep your head up, and keep your body firm but relaxed. Stand at an appropriate distance—not too close or too far away. Don't be a "shrinking violet."

- **Use strong verbal signals.** Speak clearly, firmly, and at a volume that can be easily heard.

- **Be strong.** People are often persistent in their requests. Be prepared to repeat your refusal. Stick to your guns!

- **Just say "no."** You don't have to explain why you're refusing. If you feel that you must explain why you're declining, try saying: "Thanks, but no. I really can't. . . ." "I really appreciate the offer, but no. I'm not interested/too busy/don't want any. . . ." "Please don't take this personally. I like you, but no, I don't . . ." or "I enjoy your company, and I'd like to do something together, but no. . . ."

Can you see how accepting our right to be assertive may strengthen our resolve to speak up and defend ourselves in sexual situations and in all other parts of life? Keep in mind that assertive behavior doesn't guarantee that we'll achieve our goals or force others to respect our rights. But it can definitely increase our chances of doing so.

© Billy R. Ray/ Wiley

## Retrieval Practice 11.5 | Sex and Modern Life

Completing this self-test and connections section, and then checking your answers by clicking on the answer button or by looking in Appendix B, will provide immediate feedback and helpful practice for exams.

### Self-Test

1. List some suggestions for counseling parents and other caregivers about avoiding child sexual abuse.

2. Which of the following is a myth about rape?
   a. A man cannot be raped by a woman.
   b. All women secretly want to be raped.
   c. Women cannot be raped against their will.
   d. All these options are myths about rape.

3. Research has shown that _____ are more likely to use speech to convey information, exert control, preserve independence, and enhance their status, whereas _____ tend to use speech to achieve and share intimacy, promote closeness, and maintain relationships.
   a. older men; younger men
   b. older women; younger women
   c. men; women
   d. heterosexuals; women and men

4. According to John Gottman's research, _____ means emotionally withdrawing and refusing to participate in conversation.
   a. defensiveness      b. contempt
   c. stonewalling       d. neglect

5. _____ is defined as confidently and directly standing up for your rights without infringing on those of others.
   a. Androgyny
   b. Assertiveness
   c. Ambitiousness
   d. Each of these options

### Connections—Chapter to Chapter

Answering the following question will help you "look back and look ahead" to see the important connections among the subfields of psychology and chapters within this text.

In Chapter 14 (Psychological Disorders), you'll discover that women are much more likely than men to suffer from depression. How might some of the biological, psychological, and social factors related to sex and gender explained in this chapter contribute to sexual victimization and depression in women?

### Study Tip

*The WileyPLUS program that accompanies this text provides for each chapter a* Media Challenge, Critical Thinking Exercise, *and* Application Quiz. *This set of study materials provides additional, invaluable study opportunities. Be sure to check it out!*

# Chapter Summary

## 11.1 Studying Human Sexuality 353

- Although sex has always been a vital part of human interest, motivation, and behavior, it received little scientific attention before the twentieth century. Havelock Ellis was among the first to study human sexuality despite the repression and secrecy of Victorian times.

- Alfred Kinsey and his colleagues conducted large-scale, systematic surveys and interviews of the sexual practices and preferences of U.S. adults during the 1940s and 1950s. In the 1960s, the research team William Masters and Virginia Johnson pioneered the use of laboratory measurement and observation of human physiological response during sexual activity.

- Cross-cultural studies provide important information about the similarities and variations in human sexuality. They also help counteract *ethnocentrism*—the tendency to judge our culture as "normal" and preferable to others.

### Test Your Critical Thinking

**1.** Which of the major sex researchers (Ellis, Kinsey, or Masters and Johnson) do you think contributed the most valuable information to the field of human sexuality? Why?

**2.** Which of the cross-cultural sexual practices do you find most interesting? Why?

## Studying Human Sexuality

**Psychology and a Contemporary Success:** Ellen DeGeneres

### Early Studies
- Sexuality suppressed during Victorian times
- Havelock Ellis conducted early sex research

**Gender and Cultural Diversity:** Sexuality Across Cultures

### Modern Research
- Alfred Kinsey used surveys in sex research
- Masters and Johnson introduced laboratory and observational sex research

## 11.2 Sexual Identity 356

- **Sex** refers to biological differences between men and women, such as having a penis or vagina, as well as to sexual activities, such as masturbation and intercourse. **Gender** encompasses the socially constructed differences between men and women, such as "masculinity" and "femininity."

- Our **gender identity** (self-identification as a man or woman) and our understanding of **gender roles** (culturally and socially defined prescriptions and beliefs about the thoughts, feelings, and actions of men and women) are largely formed in the first few years of life. When gender role prescriptions and beliefs are overly general, and applied to all men and women, they're known as **gender stereotypes**.

- People who are **transgender** experience a mismatch between their biological sex and their gender identity. **Sexual orientation** (being heterosexual, gay, lesbian, or bisexual) refers to our primary emotional and erotic attraction.

- There are several obvious physical sex differences, such as height, body build, and reproductive organs, as well as some gender differences (such as in aggression and verbal skills). But the cause of these differences (either nature or nurture) is controversial.

- *Social-learning theory* of gender-role development emphasizes rewards, punishments, observation, and imitation, whereas *gender-schema theory* combines social-learning theory with active cognitive processing.

### Test Your Critical Thinking

**1.** Do you believe gender roles are primarily determined by innate biological factors or learned from society?

**2.** Why do you think attitudes in Western society have become more accepting of gay marriage and the LGBT community in recent years?

## Sexual Identity

### Describing Sex and Gender
- Sex = biological
- Gender = psychological and sociocultural
- Gender identiy = self-identification as belonging to the male or female sex

**Research Challenge:** Is Gender Income Inequality Real?

### Explaining Sex and Gender
- Transgender
- Sexual orientation

## 11.3  Sexual Behavior     364

- The human motivation for sex is extremely strong. Masters and Johnson first studied and described the **sexual response cycle**, the series of physiological and sexual responses that occur during sexual activity.

- Most studies suggest that genetics and biology play the dominant role in determining a person's sexual orientation but this remains a divisive issue. People who are gay, lesbian, bisexual, and transgender often confront **sexual prejudice**.

### Test Your Critical Thinking

**1.** What did you find most interesting or helpful about Masters and Johnson's sexual response cycle? Why?

**2.** Why is sexual prejudice still so pervasive in our society? How is it socially reinforced?

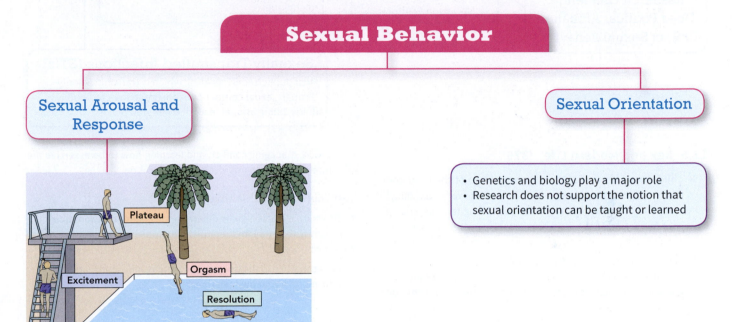

## 11.4  Sex Problems     367

- People who experience personal distress over their sexual interests or whose sexual arousal or response depends entirely on these interests may be classified as having a **paraphilic disorder**, such as *fetishistic disorder* or *exhibitionistic disorder*.

- Biology plays a key role in both sexual arousal and sexual response. Ejaculation and orgasm are partly reflexive, and the parasympathetic nervous system must be dominant for sexual arousal to occur. The sympathetic nervous system must be dominant for orgasm to occur. Psychological factors like negative early sexual experiences, fears of negative consequences from sex, and **performance anxiety** contribute to **sexual dysfunction**. Sexual arousal and response are also related to social forces, such as early gender-role training and **sexual scripts**, which teach us what to consider as the "best" sex.

- During sex therapy, tests and interviews are often used to determine the cause(s) of the sexual dysfunction. William Masters and Virginia Johnson emphasize the couple's relationship, biological and psychosocial factors, cognitions, and specific behavioral techniques.

- The dangers and rates of **sexually transmitted infections (STIs)** are high, and they are higher for women than for men. However, most STIs can be cured in their early stages. **AIDS (acquired immunodeficiency syndrome)** is transmitted only through sexual contact or exposure to infected bodily fluids, though many people have irrational fears of contagion.

### Test Your Critical Thinking

**1.** Do you believe biological, psychological, or social factors best explain sexual problems?

**2.** If you had a sexual problem, would you go to a sex therapist? Why or why not?

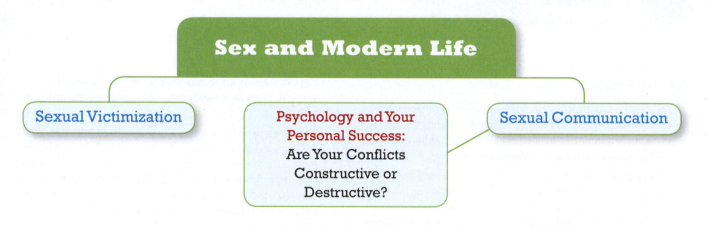

## Sex Problems

**Paraphilic Disorders**

**Research Challenge: Does Political Affiliation Reflect Sexual Behavior?**

**Common Sexual Difficulties**
*Possible causes:* biological, psychological, social, and cultural

**Sex Therapy**
Masters and Johnson emhasize couple's relationship, biological and psychological factors, cognitions, and behavioral techniques

**Sexually Transmitted Infections (STIs)**
Most publicized STI is AIDS, which is transmitted only through sexual contact or exposure to infected bodily fluids, but irrational fears of contagion persist

### 11.5 Sex and Modern Life 376

- **Child sexual abuse (CSA)** and **rape** are two of the most common forms of sexual victimization. The effects vary according to a number of factors, but they often cause long-term psychological, physical, and behavioral problems. There are several ways to prevent or reduce the risks of sexual victimization.

- Effective sexual communication not only reduces the risks of sexual victimization but is also essential in healthy sexual relationships. Understanding male/female differences in communi-cation, managing conflict, and learning how to be **assertive** are three key steps to improved communication.

#### Test Your Critical Thinking

**1.** Do you think male/female differences in communication contribute significantly to sexual and relationship problems between the sexes? Why or why not?

**2.** How can you use the tips on managing conflict and learning to say "no" to improve your own relationships?

## Sex and Modern Life

**Sexual Victimization**

**Psychology and Your Personal Success: Are Your Conflicts Constructive or Destructive?**

**Sexual Communication**

---

# Key Terms

**Retrieval Practice**  *Write a definition for each term before turning back to the referenced page to check your answer.*

- AIDS (acquired immunodeficiency syndrome)  374
- androgyny  359
- assertiveness  382
- child sexual abuse (CSA)  376
- double standard  371
- excitement phase  365
- gender  356
- gender identity  356
- gender roles  356

- gender stereotypes  356
- HIV positive  374
- orgasm phase  365
- pair bonding  364
- paraphilic disorder  367
- performance anxiety  370
- plateau phase  365
- rape  377
- refractory period  365
- resolution phase  365

- sex  356
- sexuality  353
- sexual dysfunction  368
- sexual orientation  361
- sexual prejudice  366
- sexual response cycle  364
- sexual scripts  370
- sexually transmitted infection (STI)  373
- transgender  360

© alexxl66/iStockphoto

# Motivation and Emotion

**LEARNING OBJECTIVES**

**Summarize the major theories of motivation.**
- **Define** motivation.
- **Discuss** the three key biological theories of motivation.
- **Describe** two psychological theories of motivation.
- **Explain** how biopsychosocial theories apply to motivation.

**Review how the key factors of motivation affect behavior.**
- **Discuss** the major factors that influence hunger and eating.
- **Describe** the major eating problems and disorders.
- **Define** achievement motivation and list the characteristics of high achievers.
- **Compare** extrinsic and intrinsic motivation.

**Summarize the major components and theories of emotion.**
- **Define** emotion.
- **Discuss** emotion's biological, cognitive, and behavioral components.
- **Compare** the three major theories of emotion and the facial-feedback hypothesis.

**Review how emotions affect behavior.**
- **Describe** the role of culture and evolution in emotion.
- **Discuss** the psychosocial factors that influence emotions.
- **Summarize** the problems with using polygraph testing as a lie detector.
- **Discuss** the major components of happiness.

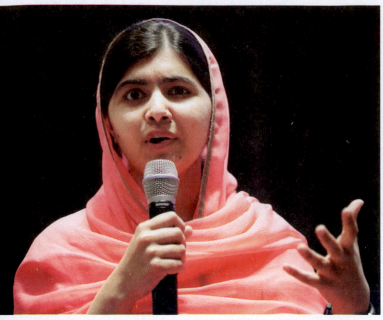

Xinhua/Alamy Stock Photo

### ❖ Psychology and a Contemporary Success | Malala Yousafzai

Malala Yousafzai (1997–) (see photo) was born in the Swat Valley of Pakistan, which was once called "the Switzerland of Pakistan" (Husain, 2013). Growing up, her father stressed the need to speak out against injustice and the critical importance of education for all children. However, when Malala was very young, most of the Swat Valley was taken over by a group affiliated with the Taliban that banned education for girls and destroyed more than a hundred girls' schools.

In defiance of the ban, brave, precocious Malala wrote a blog for the BBC describing her life under the Taliban and her desire for all girls to have the chance to be educated. Although this blog was initially written under a pseudonym, her identity was later revealed when she volunteered for interviews and a televised documentary. Once her identity was known, she began to receive worldwide recognition for her courageous activism (Blumberg, 2017).

Sadly, this early activism also brought Malala to the dangerous attention of the Taliban. In 2012, at the age of 15, her life was changed forever when two Taliban gunmen shot her in the head. Malala was rushed to a nearby hospital and endured several surgeries. Despite her near-fatal injury, she made an outstanding recovery. Nine months after the shooting, on her 16th birthday, Malala gave a powerful speech at the United Nations that was broadcast around the world. Parts of her speech were later set to music as a part of International Women's Day on March 8, 2017 (Wilkinson, 2017).

Malala's ongoing bravery and passionate activism have garnered international awareness and support for her struggle for a girl's right to be educated and to protest the ongoing the tragedies in her homeland. In addition to several other honors, she is the youngest person ever to win the Nobel Peace Prize. Today, Malala Yousafzai is best known as "the girl who stood up for education and changed the world!"

# Chapter Overview

*I don't want to be remembered as the girl who was shot. I want to be remembered as the girl who stood up.*
—Malala Yousafzai

What motivates Malala? Why is she not afraid of further retaliation? How can such a young woman achieve so much in such a short time? Research in *motivation* and *emotion* attempts to answer such "what," "why," and "how" questions. *Motivation* refers to a set of factors that activate, direct, and maintain behavior, usually toward some goal. *Emotion*, on the other hand, refers to subjective responses, including arousal, cognitions, and expressive behaviors. In other words, motivation energizes and directs behavior, whereas emotion is the "feeling" response. (Both *motivation* and *emotion* come from the Latin *movere*, meaning "to move.")

In this chapter, we begin with the major theories and concepts of motivation, followed by two key sources of motivation—hunger and achievement. Then we turn to the basic components and theories related to emotion, as well as how culture and evolution affect it. We conclude with discussions of the polygraph and the psychology of happiness.

## Myth Busters

**True or False?**

1. Being either too excited or too relaxed can interfere with performance.

2. Cognitive expectancies may lead to problem drinking.

3. Just looking at pictures of high-fat foods can make you feel hungry.

4. Heavy use of social media may increase the risk of eating disorders.

5. Having a growth mindset and grit are two of the best predictors of success.

6. Getting paid for your hobbies may reduce your overall creativity and enjoyment.

7. Smiling can make you feel happy and frowning can create negative feelings.

8. Emotions are contagious.

9. Polygraph tests are reliable lie detectors.

10. America is not one of the top 10 happiest nations in the world.

**Answers:** All but one are true. Check the text for details.

## 12.1   Theories of Motivation

### LEARNING OBJECTIVES

**Retrieval Practice**   While reading the upcoming sections, respond to each Learning Objective in your own words.

**Summarize the major theories of motivation.**

• **Define** motivation.

• **Discuss** the three key biological theories of motivation.

• **Describe** two psychological theories of motivation.

• **Explain** how biopsychosocial theories apply to motivation.

Years of research on motivation has created six major theories, which fall into three general categories—*biological*, *psychological*, and *biopsychosocial* (**Table 12.1**). While studying these theories, try to identify which theory best explains your personal behaviors, such as going to college or choosing a lifetime partner. This type of personal focus will not only improve your exam performance but also may lead to increased self-knowledge and personal motivation!

### Biological Theories

There are three key biological theories of **motivation**—*instinct*, *drive reduction*, and *optimal arousal*.

**Motivation**   A set of factors that activate, direct, and maintain behavior, usually toward some goal.

1. **Instinct**   One of the earliest researchers, William McDougall (1908), proposed that humans have numerous instincts, such as repulsion, curiosity, and self-assertiveness.

**TABLE 12.1**   **Six Major Theories of Motivation**

Tetra Images/SuperStock, Inc.

**Name That Theory**   Curiosity is a key aspect of both human and nonhuman experience. Which of the six theories of motivation best explains this behavior?

| Theory | Description |
|---|---|
| **Biological** | |
| 1. Instinct | Motivation results from innate biological instincts, which are unlearned responses found in almost all members of a species. |
| 2. Drive reduction | Motivation begins with a biological need (a lack or deficiency) that elicits a *drive* toward behavior that will satisfy the original need and restore homeostasis. |
| 3. Optimal arousal | Organisms are motivated to achieve and maintain an optimal level of arousal. |
| **Psychological** | |
| 4. Incentive | Motivation results from external stimuli that "pull" the organism in certain directions. |
| 5. Cognitive | Motivation is affected by expectations and attributions, or how we interpret or think about our own or others' actions. |
| **Biopsychosocial** | |
| 6. Maslow's hierarchy of needs | Lower needs like hunger and safety must be satisfied before advancing to higher needs (such as belonging and self-actualization). |

**FIGURE 12.1** Instincts

**a. Instincts and nonhuman animals** Instinctual behaviors are obvious in many animals. Birds build nests, bears hibernate, and salmon swim upstream to spawn.

**b. Do humans have instincts?** Sociobiologists such as Edward O. Wilson (1975, 1978) believe that humans also have instincts, like competition and aggression, which are genetically transmitted from one generation to another.

© imaginary_nl/iStockphoto
a.

Cultura RF/Getty Images
b.

**Instinct** The fixed, unlearned response patterns found in almost all members of a species.

**Drive-reduction theory** The theory that motivation begins with a physiological need (a lack or deficiency) that elicits a drive toward behavior that will satisfy the original need; once the need is met, a state of balance (homeostasis) is restored, and motivation decreases.

**Homeostasis** The body's tendency to maintain equilibrium, or a steady state of internal balance.

Other researchers later added their favorite instincts, and by the 1920s, the list of recognized instincts had become impossibly long. One researcher found listings for more than 10,000 human instincts (Bernard, 1924).

In addition, the label *instinct* led to unscientific, circular explanations—"men are aggressive because they are instinctively aggressive" or "women are maternal because they have a natural maternal instinct." However, in recent years, a branch of biology called sociobiology (Apicella et al., 2017; Shenkman, 2016; Wilson, 2013) has revived the case for **instincts** when strictly defined as *fixed, unlearned response patterns found in almost all members of a species* (**Figure 12.1**).

2. **Drive reduction** In the 1930s, the concept of drive reduction began to replace the theory of instincts. According to **drive-reduction theory** (Hull, 1952), when biological needs such as the needs for food, water, and oxygen are unmet, a state of tension known as a *drive* is created. The organism is then motivated to reduce that drive. The overall goal of drive reduction is to restore **homeostasis**—the body's tendency to maintain equilibrium, or a steady state of internal balance (**Step-by-Step Diagram 12.1**). To keep our bodies

**STEP-BY-STEP DIAGRAM 12.1**    Drive-Reduction Theory

**STOP!** This Step-by-Step Diagram contains essential information NOT found elsewhere in the text, which is likely to appear on quizzes and exams. Be sure to study it CAREFULLY!

When we are hungry or thirsty, the disruption of our normal state of equilibrium creates a drive that motivates us to search for food or water. Once action is taken and the need is satisfied, homeostasis is restored, and our motivation decreases.

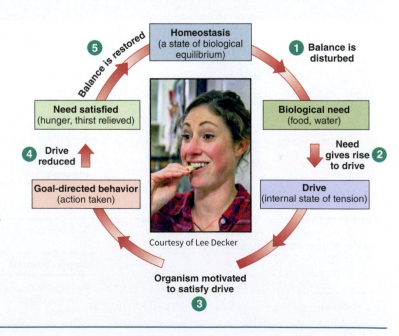

Balance is restored ⑤

**Homeostasis** (a state of biological equilibrium)

① **Balance is disturbed**

**Need satisfied** (hunger, thirst relieved)

**Biological need** (food, water)

④ **Drive reduced**

**Need gives rise to drive** ②

**Goal-directed behavior** (action taken)

**Drive** (internal state of tension)

Courtesy of Lee Decker

**Organism motivated to satisfy drive** ③

functioning at an appropriate level, numerous biological states must be balanced within a certain range, including hunger, blood glucose, temperature, and oxygenation.

3. **Optimal arousal** In addition to having obvious biological needs, humans and other animals are innately curious and require a certain amount of novelty and complexity from the environment. According to **optimal-arousal theory**, organisms are motivated to achieve and maintain an optimal level of arousal that maximizes their performance. Both too much and too little arousal diminish performance (**Figure 12.2**). The desired amount of arousal also may vary from person to person (see the following **Try This Yourself**).

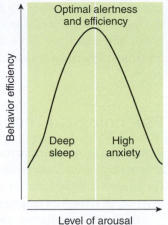

**FIGURE 12.2** **Optimal level of arousal** Our need for stimulation (the arousal motive) suggests that behavior efficiency increases as we move from deep sleep to increased alertness. However, once we pass the optimal level of arousal, our performance declines.

**Optimal-arousal theory** The theory that organisms are motivated to achieve and maintain an optimal level of arousal, which maximizes their performance.

---

## Try This Yourself

### Sensation Seeking

What motivates people to bungee jump over deep canyons or white-water raft down dangerous rivers? According to research, these "high-sensation seekers" may be biologically "prewired" to need a higher-than-usual level of stimulation (Zuckerman, 1979, 2014; Zuckerman & Aluja, 2015). Researchers have also identified several characteristics of sensation seeking (Drane et al., 2017; Maples-Keller et al., 2016; Zuckerman & Aluja, 2015):

- Thrill and adventure seeking (skydiving, driving fast, or traveling to an unusual, "off the beaten path" location).
- Experience seeking (unusual friends, exotic foods or restaurants, drug experimentation).
- Disinhibition ("letting loose").
- Susceptibility to boredom (lower tolerance for repetition and sameness).

To sample the questions asked on tests for sensation seeking, circle the choice (a or b) that best describes you:

1. **a.** I would like a job that requires a lot of traveling.
   **b.** I would prefer a job in one location.

2. **a.** I get bored seeing the same old faces.
   **b.** I like the comfortable familiarity of everyday friends.

3. **a.** The most important goal of life is to live it to the fullest and experience as much as possible.
   **b.** The most important goal of life is to find peace and happiness.

4. **a.** I would like to try parachute jumping.
   **b.** I would never want to try jumping out of a plane, with or without a parachute.

5. **a.** I prefer people who are emotionally expressive even if they are a bit unstable.
   **b.** I prefer people who are calm and even-tempered.

*Source:* Zuckerman, M. (1978, February). The search for high sensation, *Psychology Today*, pp. 38–46.

MAGEMORE Co, Ltd./Getty Images

### Think Critically

1. If you answered mostly "a" to these five questions, you're probably a high-sensation seeker. If so, what do you do to satisfy that urge, and what can you do to make sure it doesn't get out of control?

2. If you are low in sensation seeking, has this trait interfered with some aspect of your life? If so, what could you do to improve your functioning in this area?

3. How might having either a very high or very low score on these questions cause trouble in relationships or in your choice of a career?

---

In addition to the need for an optimal overall level of arousal and stimulation, keep in mind that the degree of maximal arousal changes with the difficulty of a task. According to the **Yerkes-Dodson law**, maximum performance on complex, unfamiliar tasks requires a moderately low level of arousal, whereas simple, well-learned tasks require a moderately high arousal level (**Figure 12.3**). How can this information be helpful in your everyday life? Have you ever "blanked out" during a stressful exam and been unable to answer questions that you thought you knew? This was probably due to overarousal. And it helps explain why *overlearning* is so critical—especially if you're someone who

**Yerkes-Dodson law** The law stating that maximum performance is related to levels of arousal; complex tasks require a relatively low level of arousal, whereas simple tasks require a relatively high arousal level.

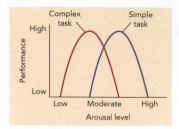

**FIGURE 12.3** **The Yerkes-Dodson law** Note how we generally perform complex, unfamiliar tasks (red line) best when our arousal level is moderately low. In contrast, we're best at simple, well-learned tasks (blue line) when our arousal level is moderately high.

**Incentive theory** The theory that motivation results from external stimuli that "pull" an organism in certain directions.

suffers from test anxiety. As discussed in Chapter 1, you need to study and practice until the information is firmly locked in place. On the other hand, if you find yourself getting bored and distracted while studying, do something to raise your arousal level, such as drinking coffee, taking a walk, and/or reminding yourself how critical it is to do well on the exam.

## Psychological Theories

Instinct and drive-reduction theories explain some motivations, but why do we continue to eat after our biological need has been completely satisfied? Why do some of us work overtime when our salary is sufficient to meet all basic biological needs? These questions are best answered by psychological theories that emphasize incentives and cognition.

Unlike drive-reduction theory, which states that internal factors *push* people in certain directions, **incentive theory** maintains that external stimuli *pull* people toward desirable goals or away from undesirable ones. Most of us initially eat because our hunger "pushes" us (drive-reduction theory). But the sight of apple pie or ice cream too often "pulls" us toward continued eating (incentive theory). As you may know, highly processed foods with added salt, fats, and/or refined carbohydrates also increase the motivation to eat and may even create cravings and like eating (Ma et al., 2017; Polk et al., 2016; Soto-Escageda et al., 2016).

According to *cognitive theories*, motivation is directly affected by *attributions*, or the ways in which we interpret or think about our own and others' actions (see the **Try This Yourself**).

---

### Try This Yourself

#### Using Attributions to Explain Grades

Imagine that you receive a high grade on a test in your psychology course. You can interpret that grade in several ways: You earned it because you really studied, you "lucked out" because the test was easy, or the textbook was exceptionally interesting and helpful (our preference!). As you might expect, people who attribute their successes to personal control and effort tend to work harder toward their goals than people who attribute their successes to luck (Aruguete & Hardy, 2016; Gorges & Göke, 2015; Weiner, 1972, 2015).

---

**FIGURE 12.4** **Expectancies as psychological motivators** What expectations might these people have about the champagne that will motivate them to drink it? Think about all the advertisements for alcohol and the pressure from others to "join in." Can you see how these expectancies and pressures might contribute to problem drinking?

*Expectancies*, or what we believe or assume will happen, are also important to motivation (Best et al., 2016; Dietrich et al., 2017). If you anticipate that you will receive a promotion at work, you're more likely to work overtime for no pay than if you do not expect a promotion. Similarly, expectancies that alcohol will increase sociability and decrease anxiety and negative emotions lead many people to increase their alcohol consumption, particularly in unfamiliar social settings (Anthenien et al., 2017; Baines et al., 2016; Fairbain & Bresin, 2017). See **Figure 12.4**.

## Biopsychosocial Theories

Research in psychology generally emphasizes either biological or psychosocial factors (nature or nurture). But biopsychosocial factors almost always provide the best explanation, and the theories of motivation are no exception. One researcher who believed in biopsychosocial factors as predictors of motivation was Abraham Maslow (1954, 1999). He believed we all have numerous needs that compete for fulfillment but that some needs are more vital than others. For example, food and shelter are typically more critical than good grades.

As you can see in **Figure 12.5**, Maslow proposed a **hierarchy of needs**, starting with survival needs at the bottom level (which must be met before others) and self-actualization needs at the top. **Self-actualization** is the inborn drive to develop all our talents and capabilities. This seems intuitively correct: A starving person would first look for food, then security, then love and friendship, and so forth.

The hierarchy of needs and related humanistic concepts have played major roles in psychology, economics, and other related fields (D'Souza & Gurin, 2016; Hsu, 2016; Winston et al., 2017). One example comes from standard marketing texts, which often use the hierarchy of needs to imply that brand consumption is a natural, driving force in shopping behaviors. Ironically, Maslow's work and humanistic ideals would emphasize less, not more, consumption (Hackley, 2007).

Maslow's critics argue that parts of his theory are poorly researched and biased toward Western preferences for individualism. Furthermore, his theory presupposes that the lower needs must be satisfied before someone can achieve self-actualization, but people sometimes seek to satisfy higher-level needs even when their lower-level needs have not been met (Cullen & Gotell, 2002; Kress et al., 2011; Neher, 1991). For example, people all over the world have used starvation as a way to protest unfair laws and political situations.

Which of Maslow's five levels of need are most likely on display in this photo? How might the needs of the infant differ from those of his mother?

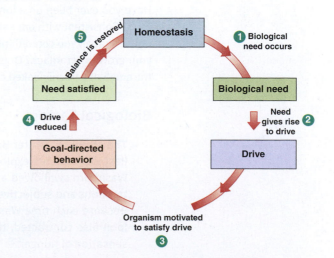
Courtesy of Lee Decker

**FIGURE 12.5** **Maslow's hierarchy of needs** Maslow's theory of motivation suggests that we all share a compelling need to "move up"—to grow, improve ourselves, and ultimately become "self-actualized."

**Hierarchy of needs** Maslow's view that basic human motives form a hierarchy; the lower motives (such as physiological and safety needs) must be met before advancing to higher needs (such as belonging and self-actualization).

**Self-actualization** The humanistic term for the inborn drive to develop all one's talents and capabilities.

---

© Billy R. Ray/Wiley

## Retrieval Practice 12.1 | Theories of Motivation

Completing this self-test and the connections section, and then checking your answers by clicking on the answer button or by looking in Appendix B, will provide immediate feedback and helpful practice for exams.

### Self-Test

1. Define *motivation*.
2. This diagram illustrates the _____ theory, in which motivation decreases once homeostasis occurs.
   a. cognitive
   b. hierarchy of needs
   c. incentive
   d. drive-reduction

3. _____ says people are "pulled" by external stimuli to act a certain way.
   a. Cognitive theory
   b. Incentive theory
   c. Maslow's hierarchy of needs
   d. Drive-reduction theory

4. According to Maslow's _____, lower-level motives have to be satisfied before a person can advance to fulfilling higher motives.
   a. psychosexual stages of development
   b. moral stages of development
   c. psychosocial stages of development
   d. hierarchy of needs

5. The humanistic term for the inborn drive to develop all one's talents and capabilities is known as _____.
   a. a cognitive "peak"
   b. self-actualization
   c. a hierarchy of needs
   d. drive-perfection theory

**Connections—Chapter to Chapter**

Answering the following question will help you "look back and look ahead" to see the important connections among the subfields of psychology and chapters within this text.

In Chapter 11 (Gender and Human Sexuality), you discovered how social-learning theory and cognitive-developmental theory explain how we form our attitudes, beliefs, and expectations about gender roles. In this chapter, you read about how incentives and cognitions affect motivation. How might social-learning theory and cognitive-developmental theory help to explain why some people are more motivated than others?

# 12.2   Motivation and Behavior

## LEARNING OBJECTIVES

**Retrieval Practice**   While reading the upcoming sections, respond to each Learning Objective in your own words.

**Review how the key factors of motivation affect behavior.**
• **Discuss** the major factors that influence hunger and eating.

• **Describe** the major eating problems and disorders.
• **Define** achievement motivation and list the characteristics of high achievers.
• **Compare** extrinsic and intrinsic motivation.

Why do people put themselves in dangerous situations? Why do salmon swim upstream to spawn? Behavior results from many motives. For example, we discuss the need for sleep in Chapter 5, and we look at aggression, altruism, and interpersonal attraction in Chapter 16. Here, we focus on the basic motivational processes underlying hunger and eating, eating problems and disorders, and achievement. Then we turn to a discussion of how extrinsic versus intrinsic motivation affects our performance.

## Hunger and Eating

Have you ever been on a long hike, camping trip, or similar situation in which you ran out of food? Consistent with our earlier discussion of Maslow's first and lowest level of needs, did you notice that all you could think or talk about was food? What specifically motivates hunger? Is it your growling stomach? Or is it your daydreams or the actual the sight of a juicy hamburger or the smell of a freshly baked cinnamon roll?

### Biological Factors

• **The stomach** Walter B. Cannon and A. L. Washburn (1912) conducted one of the earliest experiments exploring the internal factors in hunger (**Figure 12.6**). In this study, Washburn swallowed a balloon and then inflated it in his stomach. His stomach contractions and subjective reports of hunger feelings were then simultaneously recorded. Because each time Washburn reported having stomach pangs (or "growling") the balloon also contracted, the researchers concluded that stomach movement *caused* the sensation of hunger.

Can you identify what's wrong with this study? As you discovered in Chapter 1, correlation does not mean causation. Furthermore, researchers must always control for the possibility of *confounding variables*, factors that contribute irrelevant data and confuse the results. In this case, it was later found that an empty stomach is relatively inactive. The stomach contractions experienced by Washburn were an experimental artifact—something resulting from the presence of the balloon. Washburn's stomach had been tricked into thinking it was full and was responding by trying to digest the balloon!

In sum—as dieters who drink lots of water to keep their stomachs feeling full have been disappointed to discover—sensory input from an empty stomach is not essential for feeling hungry. In fact, humans and nonhuman animals without stomachs continue to experience hunger.

However, there is a connection between the stomach and feeling hungry. Receptors in the stomach and intestines detect levels of nutrients, and specialized pressure receptors in the stomach walls signal feelings of either emptiness or *satiety* (fullness). The stomach and other parts of the gastrointestinal tract also release chemical signals that play a role in hunger (Feinle-Bissett, 2016; François et al., 2015; Washington et al., 2016).

- **Biochemistry** The brain and other parts of the body produce numerous neurotransmitters, hormones, enzymes, and other chemicals that affect hunger and satiety (Herisson et al., 2016; Hsu et al., 2016; van Avesaat et al., 2015). Research in this area is complex because of the large number of known (and unknown) bodily chemicals and the interactions among them. It's unlikely that any one chemical controls our hunger and eating. Other internal factors, such as *thermogenesis*—the heat generated in response to food ingestion—also play a role (Hudson et al., 2015; Williams, 2014).

- **The brain** Specific brain structures also influence hunger and eating. Let's look at the *hypothalamus*, which helps regulate eating, drinking, and body temperature. Early research suggested that one area of the hypothalamus, the lateral hypothalamus (LH), stimulates eating, while another area, the ventromedial hypothalamus (VMH), creates feelings of satiety, signaling the animal to stop eating. When the VMH area was destroyed in rats, researchers found that the rats overate to the point of extreme obesity (**Figure 12.7**). In contrast, when the LH area was destroyed, the animals starved to death if they were not force-fed.

Later research, however, showed that the LH and VMH areas are not simple on–off switches for eating. Damage to the VMH not only leads ultimately to severe weight gain, but also makes animals picky eaters that reject a wide variety of foods. Can you see how this picky eating doesn't match the idea that rats with a damaged VMH overeat because they aren't satiated and just can't stop eating? Furthermore, normal rats force-fed to become overweight also become picky eaters. Today, researchers know that the hypothalamus plays a key role in hunger and eating, but it is not the brain's "eating center." In fact, hunger and eating, like virtually all other behaviors, are influenced by numerous factors interacting throughout various areas of our brains (Herisson et al., 2016; Hofmann et al., 2017a; Seeley & Berridge, 2015).

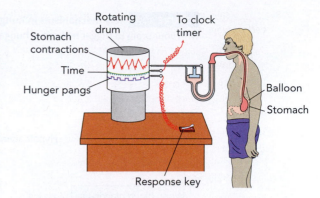

**FIGURE 12.6** **Cannon and Washburn's classic experiment on hunger** As a participant in his own study, Washburn swallowed a special balloon designed to detect stomach movement. His stomach movements were automatically recorded on graph paper attached to a rotating drum. Whenever Washburn experienced "hunger pangs," he would press a key that made a recording on the same graph paper. The two recordings (stomach movements and hunger sensations) were then compared. Finding that Washburn's stomach contractions occurred at the same time as his feelings of hunger led these early researchers to conclude that stomach movements caused hunger. Later research altered this conclusion.

**FIGURE 12.7** **How the brain affects eating** Several areas of the brain are active in the regulation of hunger, but the hypothalamus is a key player.

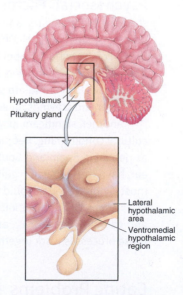

Olivier Voisin/Science Source

**a. Hunger and the hypothalamus** This diagram shows a section of the human brain, including the ventromedial hypothalamus (VMH) and the lateral hypothalamus (LH), which are involved in the regulation of hunger.

**b. Damage to the hypothalamus** After the ventromedial area of the hypothalamus of the rat on the left was destroyed, it overate to the point that its body weight tripled compared to the normal weight rat on the right.

**FIGURE 12.8**  **Key mechanisms in hunger regulation**  Different parts of your body communicate with your brain to trigger feelings of hunger.

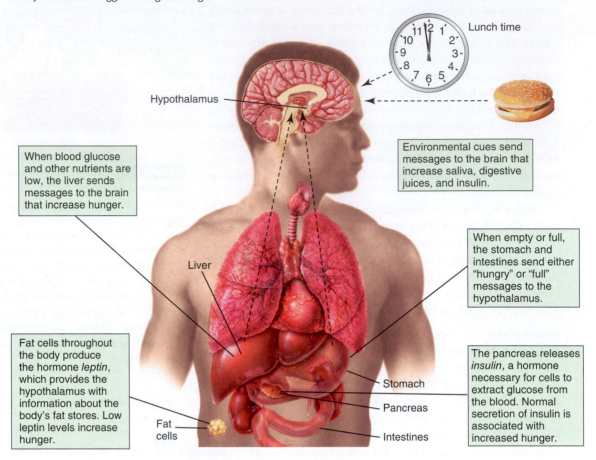

When blood glucose and other nutrients are low, the liver sends messages to the brain that increase hunger.

Environmental cues send messages to the brain that increase saliva, digestive juices, and insulin.

When empty or full, the stomach and intestines send either "hungry" or "full" messages to the hypothalamus.

Fat cells throughout the body produce the hormone *leptin*, which provides the hypothalamus with information about the body's fat stores. Low leptin levels increase hunger.

The pancreas releases *insulin*, a hormone necessary for cells to extract glucose from the blood. Normal secretion of insulin is associated with increased hunger.

Hypothalamus

Lunch time

Liver

Stomach

Pancreas

Fat cells

Intestines

**Psychosocial Factors**  The internal motivations for hunger we've discussed (the stomach, biochemistry, and the brain) are powerful. But *psychosocial factors*—spying a luscious dessert or smelling a McDonald's hamburger, or even simply noticing that it's almost lunchtime—can be equally important stimulus cues for hunger and eating. In fact, researchers have found that simply looking at pictures of high-fat foods, such as hamburgers, cookies, and cheesecake, can stimulate parts of the brain in charge of appetite, thereby increasing feelings of hunger and cravings for sweet or salty foods (Luo et al., 2015; Schüz et al., 2015).

Another significant psychosocial influence on when, what, where, and why we eat is cultural conditioning. People in the United States typically eat dinner at around 6 p.m., whereas people in Spain and South America tend to eat around 10 p.m. When it comes to *what* we eat, have you ever eaten guinea pig, dog, or horse meat? This might sound repulsive to you, yet most Hindus in India would feel a similar revulsion at the thought of eating meat from cows.

In sum, numerous biological and psychosocial factors operate in the regulation of hunger and eating (**Figure 12.8**), and researchers are still struggling to discover and explain how all these processes work together.

## Eating Problems and Disorders

The same biopsychosocial forces that explain hunger and eating also play a role in four serious eating problems and disorders: *obesity, anorexia nervosa, bulimia nervosa,* and *binge-eating disorder (BED).*

**Obesity**  Imagine that you were born and lived your life on another planet, but you could receive all the Earth's normal television channels. Given that almost all the television stars, newscasters, and commercial spokespeople you've ever seen are very thin, would you wonder why there are so many ads promoting weight loss? How would you explain the recent news that obesity has reached epidemic proportions in the United States and other developed nations?

Obviously, there is a large gap between the select few appearing on television and those of us in the real world. In fact, more than one-third of adults in the United States are considered to be overweight, and another third are considered to be medically obese (Flegal et al., 2016; Reed, 2015). In 2013, obesity was officially classified as a disease in the latest version of the *Diagnostic and Statistical Manual of Mental Disorders* (*DSM*) (American Psychiatric Association, 2013). (See Chapter 14 for a discussion of the *DSM*.)

What is **obesity**? The most widely used measure of weight status is *body mass index (BMI)*, which is a single numerical value that calculates height in relation to weight. Having a BMI of 30.0 and above is considered obese (see the **Try This Yourself**). Sadly, obesity is one of our greatest health threats because of its significant contribution to serious illnesses like heart disease, diabetes, ischemic stroke, and certain cancers (Guo & Garvey, 2016; Kroll et al., 2016; Miller & Brooks-Gunn, 2015). In addition, each year billions of dollars are spent treating serious and life-threatening medical problems related to obesity, with consumers spending billions more on largely ineffective weight-loss products and services.

**Obesity**  An eating problem involving a body mass index of 30 or above, based on height and weight.

## Try This Yourself

### Calculating Your Own BMI

To determine your BMI, use the *Adult BMI Calculator* at the Centers for Disease Control and Prevention site: http://www.cdc.gov/healthyweight/assessing/bmi/adult_bmi/

You also can compute your BMI by following these three steps:

1. Multiply your weight in pounds by 703.
2. Multiply your height in inches by itself (e.g., if your height is 63 inches, you would multiply 63 × 63).
3. Divide step 1 by step 2.

| If your BMI is: | You are: |
| --- | --- |
| 18.5 and below | Underweight |
| 18.5 to 24.9 | Healthy weight |
| 25.0 to 29.9 | Overweight |
| 30.0 and above | Obese |

**Note:** If your BMI is due to muscle or bone, rather than fat, it's possible to have a high BMI and still be healthy.

*Source:* Centers for Disease Control and Prevention, 2017.

Controlling weight is a particularly difficult task for people in the United States. For one thing, calorie-dense snack foods, like candy and chips, are heavily advertised, and many retail stores deliberately "corral" customers through their checkout lines so that it's necessary to pass by (and actively resist) these tempting treats (Basch et al., 2016). Indeed, Americans are constantly bombarded with advertisements for fattening foods, and we've become accustomed to "supersized" cheeseburgers, "Big Gulp" drinks, and huge servings of dessert (Almiron-Roig et al., 2015; Fast et al., 2015; Folkvord et al., 2016).

Moreover, we've been taught that we should eat three meals a day, whether we're hungry or not; that "tasty" food requires lots of salt, sugar, and fat; and that food is an essential part of the workplace and almost all social gatherings (**Figure 12.9**). To make matters worse, research clearly shows that both children and adults eat more calories when they're sleep-deprived (Al Khatib et al., 2017; Mullins et al., 2016). And Americans are among the most sleep-deprived (Chapter 5), and most sedentary— that is, least physically active—people in the world.

Dave Kotinsky/Getty Images

Christian Thomas/Getty Images

**FIGURE 12.9**  **A fattening environment**  A popular television program, *The Biggest Loser*, shows how difficult it is for contestants to lose weight. Even more difficult, and seldom shown, is how hard it is to maintain weight loss. To make it permanent, we need to make lasting lifestyle changes regarding exercise, as well as the amount and types of foods we eat. Can you see how our everyday environments, such as the workplace shown here, might make it harder for a person who wants to make healthier lifestyle changes?

What about those people who can seemingly eat anything they want and still not add pounds? This may be a result of their ability to burn more calories in the process of thermogenesis, a higher metabolic rate, and other possible individual and environmental factors (Pérusse et al., 2014; van Dongen et al., 2015; Zhou et al., 2015). Ironically, research consistently finds that low-calorie sweeteners, such as saccharin and sucralose, negatively affect thermogenesis and metabolism and are linked to weight gain and increased obesity (e.g., Fowler, 2016).

In addition, researchers have isolated a large number of genes that contribute to normal and abnormal weight (Albuquerque et al., 2015; Dubois et al., 2016; van Dijk et al., 2015). The good news is that one of these identified genes may provide a potential genetic explanation for why some people overeat and run a greater risk for obesity (e.g., Levitan et al., 2017; Nascimento et al., 2016; Pedram et al., 2017). Research finds that people who carry variants of the FTO gene don't feel full after eating and overeat because they have higher blood levels of ghrelin—a known hunger-producing hormone (Hess & Brüning, 2014; Tunçel et al., 2016; van Name et al., 2015). Fortunately, ghrelin can be reduced by engaging in exercise and eating a high-protein diet (Bailey et al., 2015; Hofmann et al., 2017b; Williams, 2013). But scientists caution that more research is needed and that human appetite and obesity are undoubtedly more complex than a single hormone.

### Eating Disorders

The three major eating disorders—*anorexia nervosa, bulimia nervosa,* and *binge-eating disorder* (*BED*)—are found in all ethnicities, all socioeconomic classes, and both sexes. However, they are more common in women (American Psychiatric Association, 2013; Bohon, 2015; Eddy et al., 2016). **Anorexia nervosa** is characterized by an overwhelming fear of becoming obese, a need for control, the use of dangerous weight-loss measures, and a body image that is so distorted that even a skeletal, emaciated body is perceived as fat. The resulting extreme malnutrition often leads to osteoporosis, bone fractures, interruption of menstruation in women, and loss of brain tissue. One study suggests that anorexia is linked with particular brain activation patterns—such as the part of the brain linked with automatic responding (Foerde et al., 2015). This means that anorexic people may make food decisions based on habit (e.g., I only eat low-fat foods), and not on reward centers, as do healthy people.

Occasionally, a person suffering from anorexia nervosa succumbs to the desire to eat and gorges on food, then vomits or takes laxatives. However, this type of sporadic bingeing and purging is more characteristic of **bulimia nervosa**. Individuals with bulimia go on recurrent eating binges and then purge by self-induced vomiting or the use of laxatives. They generally feel out of control during the binge episodes and alternate between overeating and fasting. In addition, people with bulimia are often impulsive—sometimes engaging in excessive shopping, alcohol abuse, or petty shoplifting (Mustelin et al., 2016; Pearson et al., 2015; Slane et al., 2014). The vomiting associated with bulimia nervosa causes severe damage to the teeth, throat, and stomach. It also leads to cardiac arrhythmia, metabolic deficiencies, and serious digestive disorders.

Note that bulimia is similar to but not the same as **binge-eating disorder (BED)**. Like bulimia, this disorder involves recurrent episodes of consuming large amounts of food in a short period of time while feeling a lack of control over eating. However, the individual does not try to purge (American Psychiatric Association, 2013; Amianto et al., 2015). Individuals with BED also generally eat more rapidly than normal, eat until they are uncomfortably full, and eat when not feeling physically hungry. In addition, they frequently eat alone because of embarrassment at the large quantities they are consuming, and they feel disgusted, depressed, and/or very guilty after bingeing.

There are many suspected causes of anorexia nervosa, bulimia nervosa, and binge-eating disorder (BED). Some theories focus on physical causes, such as hypothalamic disorders, low levels of various neurotransmitters, and genetic or hormonal disorders. Other theories emphasize psychosocial factors, such as a need for perfection, a perceived loss of control, a drive for thinness, destructive thought patterns, depression, dysfunctional families, distorted body image, and emotional or sexual abuse (e.g., American Psychiatric Association, 2013; Bodell et al., 2017; Evans et al., 2017). In addition, heavy use of social media appears to be associated with an increased risk of eating disorders. Apparently, browsing sites like Facebook leads to

**Anorexia nervosa** An eating disorder characterized by an obsessive fear of obesity, a need for control, self-imposed starvation, and a severe loss of weight.

**Bulimia nervosa** An eating disorder characterized by recurrent episodes of consuming large quantities of food (bingeing), followed by self-induced vomiting or laxative use (purging).

**Binge-eating disorder (BED)** An eating disorder characterized by recurrent episodes of consuming large amounts of food (bingeing), not followed by purge behaviors.

| TABLE 12.2 | Symptoms of Anorexia Nervosa, Bulimia Nervosa, and Binge-Eating Disorder (BED) | | |
| --- | --- | --- | --- |
| **Anorexia Nervosa** | **Bulimia Nervosa** | **Binge-Eating Disorder (BED)** | |
| • Weight less than 85% of normal for age and height<br>• Intense fear of gaining weight, even when underweight<br>• Persistent behavior to avoid weight gain<br>• Distorted body image, denial of seriousness of weight loss | • Repeated episodes of binge eating, consuming unusually large amounts of food in a short period of time<br>• Feeling out of control over eating during the binge episode<br>• Purging behaviors after eating, including vomiting, use of laxatives or other medications, and/or excessive exercise<br>• Alternating between overeating and fasting | • Repeated episodes of binge eating, consuming unusually large amounts of food in a short period of time<br>• Feeling out of control over eating during the binge episode<br>• Eating much more rapidly than normal, eating large amounts when not feeling physically hungry<br>• Feeling ashamed and guilty after bingeing<br>• No compensatory purging behaviors, such as vomiting, laxatives, and/or excessive exercise | Many celebrities, like Lady Gaga, have publicly shared their battles with eating disorders. But does this type of publicity increase or decrease the chance that their fans will suffer similar problems?<br><br><br>Chris Wolf/Getty Images |

more body dissatisfaction. Women who compare their own photos with those of their friends, and women who overvalue receiving comments and "likes" on their status updates, are at particular risk of eating disorders (Mabe et al., 2014).

Culture and ethnicity also play significant roles in eating disorders (Brewerton & Dennis, 2016; Reyes-Rodríguez et al., 2016; Smart & Tsong, 2014). For instance, U.S. Blacks report fewer overall eating disorders and greater satisfaction with their bodies than other U.S. groups.

Regardless of the causes of these eating disorders, it's important to recognize the symptoms of anorexia, bulimia, and binge-eating disorder (**Table 12.2**) and to seek therapy if the symptoms apply to you. The key point to remember is that all eating disorders are serious and chronic conditions that require treatment. In fact, some studies find that they have the highest mortality rates of all mental illnesses (Goldberg et al., 2015; Zerwas et al., 2015).

# Achievement Motivation

Although hunger is a primary motivator in all animals, we humans experience complex psychological and social needs that drive us throughout our lifespan. Consider what motivates you to go to college. Your first answer might be "to get a good job." But what motivates you to compete with your classmates for a better grade? According to psychologist David McClelland's concept of **achievement motivation**, most people have a desire to excel, especially in competition with others. We also want to succeed at attaining our goals, mastering skills or ideas, and gaining control of our lives.

One of the earliest tests for achievement motivation was devised by Christiana Morgan and Henry Murray (1935). Using a series of ambiguous pictures called the *Thematic Apperception Test* (TAT), these researchers asked participants to make up a story about each picture (see the following **Try This Yourself**). The participants' responses were then scored for different motivational themes, including achievement.

In addition to the TAT, researchers have developed several other questionnaires and interview methods designed to measure the *need for achievement (nAch)*. And thanks to their research findings, we now know that some individuals are significantly more achievement oriented than others.

Think back to our opening story of Malala Yousafzai, the Nobel Prize–winning teenager. What motivates her to continue her dangerous crusade for education for young girls despite being shot and under continual threats? Or what drives someone like Oprah Winfrey, the

**Achievement motivation**
The desire to excel, especially in competition with others.

## Try This Yourself

### Measuring Achievement

This card is a sample from the *Thematic Apperception Test* (TAT). The strength of an individual's need for achievement is reportedly measured by stories he or she tells about the TAT drawings. If you want an informal test using this method, look closely at the two people in the photo, and then write a short story answering the following questions:

1. What is happening in this picture, and what led up to it?
2. Who are the people is this picture, and how do they feel?
3. What is going to happen in the next few moments, and in a few weeks?

**Scoring**  Give yourself 1 point each time any of the following is mentioned: (1) defining a problem, (2) solving a problem, (3) obstructions to solving a problem, (4) techniques that can help overcome the problem, (5) anticipation of success or resolution of the problem. The higher your score on this test, the higher your supposed overall need for achievment.

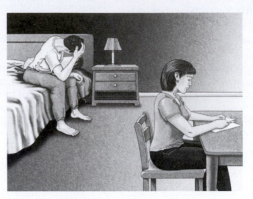

famous television star, thriving businesswoman, and generous philanthropist? What motivates Olympic athletes to work so hard for a gold medal?

Researchers have found that high achievers tend to have had parents, teachers, or other close adults who encouraged independence and frequently rewarded success (Ganimian & Murnane, 2016; Gaudreau et al., 2016; Pomerantz & Kempner, 2013). Other aspects of the environment, cultural values, and genetics also affect achievement needs (Al-Sharfi et al., 2016; Greenfield & Quiroz, 2013; Luginbuhl et al., 2016). Interestingly, a study of 13,000 identical and fraternal twins from six different countries found that academic motivation (enjoyment of reading, math, science, etc.) is determined about half by cultural values and differing environmental experiences, with the other half governed by genetics (Kovas et al., 2015).

Given that we have little or no control over our parents, early childhood environment, or cultural values, achievement is largely up to us as individuals. As you've seen repeatedly throughout this text, having a *growth mindset* and *grit* (passion and perseverance) are the keys to success and achievement in both work and academic settings (Claro et al, 2016; Datu et al., 2015; Dweck, 2007, 2012). Although some people may have been taught, or may have developed on their own, a *fixed mindset*, and believe that their abilities are set in stone, we all have a great capacity to change, adapt, and grow.

For a personal test of your own type of achievement needs and more information on the specific traits that distinguish high achievers, see the following **Try This Yourself**.

## Try This Yourself

### Need for Achievement (nAch)

Researchers have identified at least six traits that distinguish people with a high nAch (Harwood et al., 2015; McClelland, 1958, 1993; Schunk & Zimmerman, 2013; Stadler et al., 2017). Place a check mark next to each trait that applies to you or to traits that you may want to work to develop:

- _____ *Preference for moderately difficult tasks* People high in nAch avoid tasks that are too easy because they offer little challenge or satisfaction. They also avoid extremely difficult tasks because the probability of success is too low.

- _____ *Competitiveness* High-achievement-oriented people are more attracted to careers and tasks that involve competition and an opportunity to excel.

- _____ *Preference for clear goals with competent feedback* High-achievement-oriented people typically prefer tasks with clear outcomes and situations in which they can receive feedback on their performance. Likewise, they prefer criticism from a harsh but competent evaluator to criticism from one who is friendlier but less competent.

- _____ *Self-regulation and personal responsibility* High-achievement-oriented people purposefully control their thoughts and behaviors to attain their goals. In addition, they prefer being personally responsible for a project so that they can feel satisfied when the task is well done.

- _____ *Mental toughness and persistence* High-achievement-oriented people have a mindset that allows them to persevere through difficult circumstances. It includes attributes like sacri-

fice and self-denial, which help them maintain concentration and motivation when things aren't going well.

- _____ *More accomplished* People who have high nAch scores do better than others on exams, earn better grades in school, and excel in their chosen professions.

## Extrinsic Versus Intrinsic Motivation

Have you ever noticed that for all the money and glory they receive, professional athletes often don't look like they're enjoying themselves very much? What's the problem? Why don't they appreciate how lucky they are to be able to make a living by playing games?

One way psychologists attempt to answer questions about motivation is by distinguishing between **extrinsic motivation**, based on external rewards or avoidance of punishments, and **intrinsic motivation**, based on internal, personal satisfaction from a task or activity (Deci & Moller, 2005; Ryan & Deci, 2013). As you can see in the photo of the child jumping into the pool, when people do something for no ulterior purpose, they have internal, personal reasons ("I like it"; "It's fun") (see the photo). But when extrinsic rewards are added, the explanation shifts to external, impersonal reasons ("I did it for the money"; "I did it to please my parents"). This shift often decreases enjoyment and hampers performance. This is as true for professional athletes as it is for anyone else.

A classic experiment demonstrating this effect was conducted with preschool children who liked to draw (Lepper et al., 1973). These researchers found that children who were given paper and markers, and promised a reward for their drawings, were subsequently less interested in drawing than children who were not given a reward or who were given an unexpected reward for their pictures when they were done. Likewise, a decade-long study of over 10,000 West Point cadets found that those who were motivated to pursue a military career for internal reasons, such as personal ambition, were more likely to receive early career promotions than those who attended a military academy for external reasons, such as family expectations (Wrzesniewski et al., 2014).

As it turns out, however, there is considerable controversy over individual differences in what motivates someone, as well as under what conditions giving extrinsic rewards increases or decreases motivation (Bareket-Bojmel et al., 2017; Deci & Ryan, 1985, 2012; Zhang et al., 2017). Furthermore, research shows that not all extrinsic motivation is bad. In one study, elementary school students were simply mailed books weekly during the summer, were mailed books along with a reading incentive, or were assigned to a control group with no books or incentives. The researchers found that students who were initially more motivated to read were also more responsive to incentives (Guryan et al., 2015). As you can see in **Figure 12.10**, extrinsic rewards with "no strings attached" can actually increase motivation.

How does this apply to you and your everyday life? As a college student facing many high-stakes exams, have you noticed how often professors try to motivate their students with "scare tactics," such as frequently reminding you of how your overall GPA and/or scores on certain exams may be critical for entry into desirable jobs or for admittance to graduate programs? Does this type of extrinsic motivation help or hurt your motivation? One study found that when instructors use extrinsic consequences, such as fear tactics, as motivational tools, their students' intrinsic motivation and exam scores decrease (Putwain & Remedios, 2014; von der Embse et al., 2015). In fact, fear of failure may be one of the greatest detriments to intrinsic motivation (Covington & Müeller, 2001; Ma et al., 2014; Martin & Marsh, 2006).

What should teachers and students do instead? Rather than emphasizing high exam scores or overall GPA, researchers recommend focusing on specific behaviors required to avoid failure and attain success. In other words, as a student you can focus on improving your overall study techniques and test-taking skills. See again the *Tools for Student Success* at the end of Chapter 1. For additional help, check with your professor and/or your college counseling center. For help with increasing your overall motivation, see the following **Psychology and Your Professional Success** discussion.

**Extrinsic motivation** A type of motivation for a task or activity based on external incentives, such as rewards and punishments.

**Intrinsic motivation** A type of motivation for a task or activity based on internal incentives, such as enjoyment and personal satisfaction.

Courtesy of Sandy Harvey

**Intrinsic motivation** Judging by the expression on this child's face, he is jumping in the pool for the sheer joy and pleasure of swimming—intrinsic motivation.

**FIGURE 12.10** **How extrinsic rewards can sometimes be motivating**

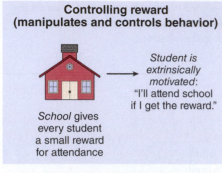

**Controlling reward
(manipulates and controls behavior)**

*School* gives every student a small reward for attendance

*Student is extrinsically motivated*: "I'll attend school if I get the reward."

**Approval reward
(praise and approval for desired behavior)**

*Parents*: "We'll be very happy if you get A's like our neighbor's boy."

*Student is extrinsically motivated*: "I'll get good grades to get their approval."

**Informing reward
(feedback or information on level of performance)**

*School* gives small reward for students with outstanding attendance

*Student is intrinsically motivated*: "I enjoy going to school every day."

**"No strings" treat
(unexpected reward with no contingencies attached)**

*Parents*: "You've been studying pretty hard tonight. Let's take a break and go out for ice cream."

*Student is intrinsically motivated*: "It's nice that Dad noticed me studying and an ice cream sounds great."

**a. Controlling or approval rewards**
If extrinsic rewards are used to control or to gain approval, they generally decrease motivation. For example, when schools pay all students for simple attendance, or when parents give children approval or privileges for achieving good grades, they may unintentionally decrease the children's motivation to attend school or to get good grades.

**b. Informing or "no strings" rewards**
Extrinsic rewards can be motivating if they are used to inform and if there are "no strings" attached. For instance, when a small reward is provided for outstanding attendance, or a surprise treat is offered for good grades, it may increase both motivation and enjoyment.

❖ **Psychology and Your Professional Success** | What Are the Best Ways to Increase Motivation?

Both intrinsic and extrinsic motivation are essential for advancing your career, running a business, or even studying this text. If you want to improve your effectiveness in any of these areas, consider the following guidelines:

1. **Emphasize intrinsic reasons for behaviors.** Rather than thinking about all the people you'll impress with good grades or all the great jobs you'll get when you finish college, focus instead on personally satisfying, intrinsic reasons. Think about how exciting it is to learn new things, or the value of becoming an educated person and a critical thinker.

2. **Limit extrinsic rewards.** In general, it is almost always better to use the least possible extrinsic reward and for the shortest possible time period. When children are first learning to play a musical instrument, it may help to provide small rewards until they gain a certain level of mastery. But once a child is working happily or practicing for the sheer joy of it, it is best to leave him or her alone. Similarly, if you're trying to increase your study time, begin by rewarding yourself for every significant improvement. But don't reward yourself when you're handling a difficult assignment easily. Save rewards for when you need them. Keep in mind that we're speaking primarily of concrete extrinsic rewards. Praise and positive feedback are generally safe to use and often increase intrinsic motivation.

3. **Provide appropriate rewards.** Use extrinsic rewards to provide feedback for competency or outstanding performance—not for simply engaging in the behavior. Schools can enhance intrinsic motivation by giving medals or privileges to students with no absences, rather than giving money for simple attendance. As a manager, you can provide informing, "no strings attached" rewards by giving or sharing credit with your employees for worthy accomplishments. On a personal level, treat yourself to a movie or a call to a friend *after* you've studied exceptionally hard for your scheduled time period or done particularly well on an exam. Don't reward yourself for half-hearted attempts.

4. **Just do it!** We've mentioned many times the value of distributed practice. You really can't "cram" when it comes to workouts, brushing your teeth, losing and maintaining weight,

or keeping up with employer demands. You "simply" have to get up and get started. Don't think! Just do! The first few minutes of exercise are always the hardest, and the same is true for almost every aspect of life. Get up, get started, power through! You'll thank yourself later.

*You have brains in your head. You have feet in your shoes. You can steer yourself in any direction you choose. You're on your own, and you know what you know. And you are the guy who'll decide where to go.*

*—Theodor Seuss Geisel, "Dr. Seuss" (American Writer, Poet, Cartoonist)*

© Billy R. Ray/Wiley

## Retrieval Practice 12.2  |  Motivation and Behavior

Completing this self-test and the connections section, and then checking your answers by clicking on the answer button or by looking in Appendix B, will provide immediate feedback and helpful practice for exams.

### Self-Test

1. Briefly describe the biological and psychosocial factors in hunger.

2. Motivation for eating is found _____ .
   a. in the stomach
   b. in the ventromedial section of the hypothalamus
   c. throughout the brain
   d. throughout the body

3. Maria appears to be starving herself and has obviously lost a lot of weight in just a few months. You suspect she might be suffering from _____ .
   a. anorexia nervosa
   b. bulimia nervosa
   c. obesity phobia
   d. none of these options

4. The desire to excel, especially in competition with others, is known as _____ .
   a. drive-reduction theory
   b. intrinsic motivation

   c. achievement motivation
   d. all these options

5. A high school began paying students $5 for each day they attended school. Overall rates of attendance increased in the first few weeks and then fell below the original starting point. The most likely reason is that _____ .
   a. the students felt going to school wasn't worth $5
   b. money is a secondary reinforcer, not a primary one
   c. extrinsic rewards decreased the intrinsic value of attending school
   d. the students' expectancies changed to fit the situation

### Connections—Chapter to Chapter

Answering the following question will help you "look back and look ahead" to see the important connections among the subfields of psychology and chapters within this text.

In this chapter, you discovered several factors that influence hunger, such as responding to stimulus cues and eating according to the clock, rather than when we are hungry. In Chapter 6 (Learning), you learned about *classical conditioning*, a form of learning that pairs learned environmental cues (stimuli) with reflexive responses (such as hunger or eating). How can we use classical conditioning to explain why we start to feel hungry around our usual lunch time each day?

## 12.3 | Components and Theories of Emotion

### LEARNING OBJECTIVES

**Retrieval Practice**    While reading the upcoming sections, respond to each learning objective in your own words.

**Summarize the major components and theories of emotion.**

• **Define** emotion.

• **Discuss** emotion's biological, cognitive, and behavioral components.

• **Compare** the three major theories of emotion and the facial-feedback hypothesis.

**FIGURE 12.11** **The three components of emotion—in action!** This politician shows his anger in various ways, including his red face (biological component), his clear appraisal that the reporter's question is unfair (cognitive component), and his yelling at the reporter and gesturing with his hands and arms (behavioral components).

**Emotion** A complex pattern of feelings that includes three components: biological (arousal), cognitive (thinking), and behavioral (expressions).

Emotions play an essential role in our lives. They color our dreams, memories, and perceptions. And emotion-related psychological problems, such as anxiety disorders and mood disorders, are among the most common of all psychological disorders and are major contributors to public health problems (de Jonge et al., 2016; National Institute of Mental Health, 2017; Risal et al., 2016). High levels of anger and anxiety have even been associated with an increased risk of a heart attack (Buckley et al., 2015). But what do we really mean by the term **emotion**? In everyday usage, we use it to describe feeling states; we feel "thrilled" when our political candidate wins an election, "dejected" when our candidate loses, and "miserable" when our loved ones reject us. Obviously, what we mean by these terms, and what we personally experience with different emotions, can vary greatly among individuals.

*All I want is an education, and I am afraid of no one.* —Malala Yousafzai

## Three Components of Emotion

Psychologists define and study emotion according to three basic components—*biological*, *cognitive*, and *behavioral* (see **Figure 12.11**).

**Biological (Arousal) Component** Internal physical changes occur in our bodies whenever we experience an emotion. Imagine walking alone on a dark street and having someone jump from behind a stack of boxes and start running toward you. How would you respond? Like most people, you would probably interpret the situation as threatening and would run. Your predominant emotion, fear, would inspire several physiological reactions, such as increased heart rate and blood pressure, perspiration, and goose bumps (piloerection). Such biological reactions are controlled by certain brain structures and by the autonomic branch of the nervous system (ANS).

Our emotional experiences appear to result from interactions between several areas of the brain, particularly the *cerebral cortex* and *limbic system* (Klapwijk et al., 2016; Meau & Vuilleumier, 2016; Panksepp, 2017). As we discussed in Chapter 2, the cerebral cortex, the outermost layer of the brain, serves as our body's ultimate control and information processing center, enabling us to recognize and regulate our emotions.

**Amygdala** A brain structure near the hippocampus that controls emotions, especially aggression and fear, and the formation of emotional memory; part of the limbic system.

Studies of the limbic system, located in the innermost part of the brain, have shown that one area, the **amygdala**, plays a key role in emotion—especially fear (**Figure 12.12**). It sends signals to the other areas of the brain, causing increased heart rate and other physiological reactions related to fear. Interestingly, children with high levels of anxiety tend to have larger amygdalae, as well as stronger connections between the amygdala and other parts of the brain (Qin et al., 2014).

Emotional arousal sometimes occurs without our conscious awareness. According to psychologist Joseph LeDoux (1996, 2014), when the *thalamus* (the brain's sensory switchboard) receives sensory inputs, it sends separate messages up to the cortex, which "thinks" about the stimulus, and to the amygdala, which immediately activates the body's alarm system (**Figure 12.13**). Although this dual pathway occasionally leads to "false alarms," such as when we mistake a stick for a snake, LeDoux believes it is a highly adaptive warning system essential to our survival. He states that "the time saved by the amygdala in acting on the thalamic interpretation, rather than waiting for the cortical input, may be the difference between life and death" (LeDoux, 1996, p. 166).

As vital as the brain is to emotion, it is the *autonomic nervous system* (Chapter 2) that produces the obvious signs of arousal. These largely automatic responses result from interconnections between the ANS and various glands and muscles (**Figure 12.14**).

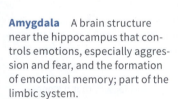

Hippocampus

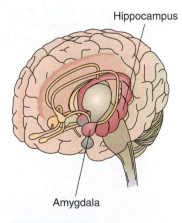

Amygdala

**FIGURE 12.12** **The limbic system's role in emotion** In addition to being involved in drive regulation, memory, and other functions, the limbic system plays a key role in the experience and expression of our emotions. It consists of several subcortical structures that form a border (or limbus) around the brain stem.

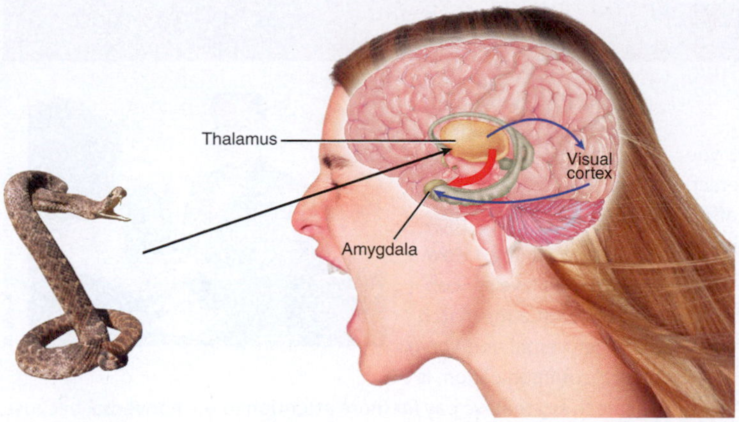

*Jack Goldfarb/Design Pics/Corbis Images*

| Sympathetic | | Parasympathetic |
|---|---|---|
| Pupils dilated | **Eyes** | Pupils constricted |
| Decreased saliva | **Mouth** | Increased saliva |
| Vessels constricted (skin cold and clammy) | **Skin** | Vessels dilated (normal blood flow) |
| Respiration increased | **Lungs** | Respiration normal |
| Increased heart rate | **Heart** | Decreased heart rate |
| Increased epinephrine and norepinephrine | **Adrenal glands** | Decreased epinephrine and norepinephrine |
| Decreased motility | **Digestion** | Increased motility |

Masterfile

**FIGURE 12.13** **Fast and slow pathways for fear** When visual sensory input arrives at the thalamus, the thalamus sends it along a fast route directly to the amygdala (the red arrow), as well as along a slower, more indirect route to the visual cortex (the blue arrow). The speedy, direct route allows us to quickly respond to a feared stimulus (like the snake) even before we're consciously aware of our emotions or behaviors. In contrast, the indirect route, engaging the visual cortex, provides more detailed information that allows us to consciously evaluate the danger of this particular snake and our most appropriate response.

**FIGURE 12.14** **Emotion and the autonomic nervous system (ANS)** During emotional arousal, the sympathetic branch of the autonomic nervous system (ANS) prepares the body for fight-flight-freeze. (The hormones epinephrine and norepinephrine keep the system under sympathetic control until the emergency is over.) The parasympathetic branch returns the body to a more relaxed state (homeostasis).

**Cognitive (Thinking) Component** Emotional reactions are very individual: What you experience as intensely pleasurable may be boring or aversive to another. To study the cognitive (thought) component of emotions, psychologists typically use self-report techniques, such as surveys and interviews. However, people are sometimes unable or unwilling to accurately remember or describe their emotional states. For these reasons, our cognitions about our own and others' emotions are difficult to measure scientifically. This is why many researchers supplement participants' reports on their emotional experiences with methods that assess emotional experience indirectly (e.g., measuring physiological responses such as heart rate, pupil dilation, blood flow).

People who undergo trauma often find it difficult to identify and manage their overwhelming emotions. Fortunately, a new imaging method that measures activity within the amygdala may provide help (Keynan et al., 2016). Can you see how providing someone with specific cognitive feedback on his or her particular level of arousal could help that person manage not only the arousal itself (the emotional component) but also the behavioral expression component (next section)?

**Behavioral (Expressive) Component** In addition to the biological and cognitive components, emotions also have a behavioral component, which can be verbal and/or nonverbal. We can verbally tell people that we love them and/or show them nonverbally through actions, such as gentle touches. However, facial expressions may be our most common form of emotional communication. As you'll discover later in this chapter, even newborn infants show distinct expressions of emotion that closely match adult facial expressions. Researchers have also developed sensitive techniques to measure subtleties of feeling and to differentiate honest expressions from fake ones. Perhaps most intriguing is the difference between the *social smile* and the *Duchenne smile* (named after French anatomist Duchenne de Boulogne, who first described it in 1862). See **Figure 12.15**. A recent meta-analysis, which combines data from numerous studies, found that people with Duchenne smiles are rated as more authentic, genuine, real, attractive, and trustworthy than those displaying non-Duchenne smiles (Gunnery & Ruben, 2016).

The Duchenne smile illustrates the importance of nonverbal means of communicating emotion. We all know that people communicate in ways other than speaking or writing. However, few people recognize the full importance of nonverbal signals (see the **Try This Yourself**).

*Courtesy of Karen Huffman*

**a. False, social smile**

*Courtesy of Karen Huffman*

**b. True Duchenne smile**

**FIGURE 12.15** **Duchenne smile** In a false, social smile (**a**), our voluntary cheek muscles are pulled back, but our eyes are unsmiling. Smiles of real pleasure use the muscles not only around the cheeks but also around the eyes (**b**).

## Try This Yourself

### The Power of Nonverbal Cues

Imagine yourself as a job interviewer. Your first applicant greets you with a big smile, full eye contact, a firm handshake, and an erect, open posture. The second applicant doesn't smile, looks down, offers a weak handshake, and slouches. Whom do you think you will hire?

Psychologist Albert Mehrabian would say that you're much less likely to hire the second applicant due to his or her "mixed messages." Mehrabian's research suggests that when we're communicating feelings or attitudes and our verbal and nonverbal dimensions don't match, the receiver trusts the predominant form of communication, which is about 93% nonverbal and consists of the way the words are said and the facial expression rather than the literal meaning of the words (Mehrabian, 1968, 1971, 2007).

Unfortunately, Mehrabian's research is often overgeneralized, and many people misquote him as saying that "over 90% of communication is nonverbal." Clearly, if a police officer says, "Put your hands up," his or her verbal words might carry 100% of the meaning. However, when we're confronted with a mismatch between verbal and nonverbal communication, it is safe to say that we pay far more attention to the nonverbal because we believe it more often tells us what someone is really thinking or feeling. The importance of nonverbal communication, particularly facial expressions, is further illustrated by the popularity of smileys and other emoticons in our everyday e-mail and text messages.

wavebreakmedia/Shutterstock

Keep in mind, however, that there are obvious limits to the power of nonverbal cues. For instance, a study of airport security found that agents who were trained not only to observe nonverbal cues but also to talk with passengers were more accurate at detecting dishonesty than those who only examined body language, such as lack of eye contact, nervousness, and fidgeting (Ormerod & Dando, 2015). Given that most of us will never serve as airport security personnel, the following **Research Challenge** offers an even more important warning about an overreliance on nonverbal cues.

## Research Challenge

### Does Wearing "Sexy" Clothing Signal Sexual Interest?

What do you think of the women in this photo? Do you think those who are wearing "sexier" clothes are more interested in sex than those who are dressed more modestly? This is the core question researchers attempted to answer when they sampled 276 female and 220 male college students (Treat et al., 2017).

Participants in this study were first presented with photographs of different women and were then asked to express their first thoughts on whether the women showed sexual interest or not. To improve their judgments, half of the participants were given instructions regarding specific nonverbal emotional cues (e.g., body language or facial expressions) before seeing the photos.

Interestingly, the researchers found that when judging the sexual interest of the women in the photographs, both male and female college students relied not only on the women's facial expressions and body language but also on the provocativeness of their clothing and their attractiveness. Although male and female participants showed similar ratings, the women relied more than the men on women's facial expressions, whereas the men relied more on the women's attractiveness.

Why is this important? Given that appearance-related cues such as clothing and physical beauty are less accurate signals of a woman's current (or momentary) sexual interest than her nonverbal emotional cues (facial expression and body language), these results suggest "sexy" clothing may be misinterpreted as sexual

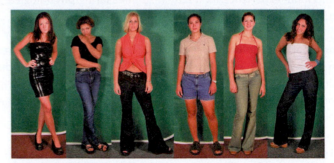

*Source:* Teresa A. Treat, Erin K. Church, Richard J. Viken. Effects of gender, rape-supportive attitudes, and explicit instruction on perceptions of women's momentary sexual interest. *Psychonomic Bulletin & Review*, 2017.

interest. Even more troubling is that all participants were also asked to complete an assessment about their attitudes toward rape, such as: "Rape happens when a man's sex drive gets out of control" or "Being raped isn't as bad as being mugged and beaten." And both male and female students who endorsed more rape-supportive attitudes relative to their peers focused more on women's clothing style and attractiveness to judge sexual interest and less on nonverbal cues.

As you know and as discussed in Chapter 11, rape is a horrific crime with long-lasting physical and psychological effects on the victim. The one encouraging note in this study was that participants who received instruction on nonverbal cues before assessing the photographs later paid more attention to these cues than to the women's clothing and physical beauty.

**▼ Test Yourself**

1. Based on the information provided, did this study (Treat et al., 2017) use descriptive, correlational, and/or experimental research?

2. If you chose:

   ○ *descriptive research*, is this a naturalistic observation, survey/interview, case study, and/or archival research?

   ○ *correlational research*, is this a positive, negative, or zero correlation?

   ○ *experimental research*, label the IV, DV, experimental group(s), and control group. (Note: If participants were not randomly assigned to groups, list it as a *quasi-experimental design.*)

   ○ both *descriptive* and *correlational* research, answer the corresponding questions for both.

**Check your answers by clicking on the answer button or by looking in Appendix B.**

**Note:** The information provided in this study is admittedly limited, but the level of detail is similar to what is presented in most textbooks and public reports of research findings. Answering these questions, and then comparing your answers to those provided, will help you become a better critical thinker and consumer of scientific research.

# Three Major Theories of Emotion

Researchers generally agree that emotion has biological, cognitive, and behavioral components, but there is less agreement about *how* we become emotional. The major competing theories are the *James-Lange theory*, the *Cannon-Bard theory*, and *Schachter and Singer's two-factor theory* (**Step-by-Step Diagram 12.2**).

Imagine that you're walking in the forest and suddenly see a coiled snake on the path next to you. What emotion would you experience? Most people would say they would be very afraid. But why? Common sense tells us that our hearts pound and we tremble when we're afraid and that we cry when we're sad. But according to the **James-Lange theory**, felt emotions begin with physiological arousal of the ANS (discussed in the preceding section). This arousal (a pounding heart, breathlessness, trembling all over) then causes us to experience the emotion

**James-Lange theory** A theory of emotion suggesting that the subjective experience of emotion results from physiological arousal, rather than being its cause ("I feel sad because I'm crying"); in this view, each emotion is physiologically distinct.

---

**STEP-BY-STEP DIAGRAM 12.2**    **Comparing Three Major Theories of Emotion**

**STOP!**  This Step-by-Step Diagram contains essential information NOT found elsewhere in the text, which is likely to appear on quizzes and exams. Be sure to study it CAREFULLY!

**Stimulus**

Maria Dryfhout/Shutterstock.com

**James-Lange theory**
Perception of an environmental stimulus (snake) triggers physiological arousal, which we experience as a felt emotion (fear).

→ Physiological arousal → Emotion: **FEAR**

**Cannon-Bard theory**
Perception of an environmental stimulus (snake) triggers the thalamus to send a simultaneous message that activates physiological arousal at the same time as the felt emotion (fear).

→ Thalamus relays information → Physiological arousal / Emotion: **FEAR**

**Schachter and Singer's two-factor theory**
Perception of an environmental stimulus (snake) triggers physiological arousal, which we cognitively appraise and label ("I'm afraid"). Then, the appraisal (label) is felt as the emotion (fear).

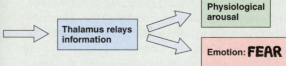
→ Physiological arousal → Label ("I'm scared") → Emotion: **FEAR**

we call "fear." Contrary to popular opinion, James wrote: "We feel sorry because we cry, angry because we strike, afraid because we tremble" (James, 1890, pp. 449–450).

In contrast, the **Cannon-Bard theory** proposes that arousal and emotion occur separately but simultaneously. Following perception of an emotion-provoking stimulus, the thalamus sends two simultaneous messages: one to the ANS, which causes physiological arousal, and one to the brain's cortex, which causes awareness of the felt emotion.

Finally, Schachter and Singer's **two-factor theory** suggests that our emotions start with physiological arousal followed by a conscious, cognitive appraisal. We then look to external cues from the environment and from others around us to find a label and explanation for the arousal. Therefore, if we cry at a wedding, we label our emotion as joy or happiness. If we cry at a funeral, we label the emotion as sadness.

In their classic study demonstrating this effect, Schachter and Singer (1962) gave research participants injections of epinephrine (adrenaline), a hormone/neurotransmitter that produces feelings of arousal, or saline shots (a placebo) and then exposed the participants to either a happy or an angry confederate (**Concept Organizer 12.1**). The way participants responded

**Cannon-Bard theory**  A theory proposing that emotions and physiological changes occur simultaneously ("I'm crying and feeling sad at the same time"); in this view, all emotions are physiologically similar.

**Two-factor theory**  Schachter and Singer's theory that emotion depends upon two factors—physiological arousal and cognitive labeling of that arousal.

---

| **CONCEPT ORGANIZER 12.1** | **Schachter and Singer's Classic Study** |
|---|---|

**STOP!**  This Concept Organizer contains essential information NOT found elsewhere in the text, which is likely to appear on quizzes and exams. Be sure to study it CAREFULLY!

| Experimenter | Informed group | Ignorant group | Misinformed group | Placebo group |
|---|---|---|---|---|
| | Got epinephrine; told about effects | Got epinephrine; told nothing about effects | Got epinephrine; deceived about effects | Got saline instead of epinephrine; told nothing about effects |

**a. Part 1 of the experiment**  Participants in this study were first told that it was a study of how certain vitamins affect visual skills, and then they were asked for permission to be injected with a small shot of the vitamin "Suproxin." (This injection actually was a shot of the hormone/neurotransmitter epinephrine, or adrenaline, which triggers feelings of arousal such as racing heart, flushed skin, and trembling hands.) Those participants who gave permission were then divided into four groups and given injections. Participants in three of the groups received epinephrine. One of these groups was correctly informed about the drug's effects, one was told nothing, and the third was misinformed about the effects. Those in the fourth placebo group received a neutral saline solution.

**Happy confederate**

| | | | |
|---|---|---|---|
| I feel strange, it must be the injection | I feel strange, sort of "happy" like that fella | I feel strange. I guess I feel very happy like that guy over there | I feel strange, sort of happy like that fella |

**b. Part 2 of the experiment**  Each participant was then placed in a room with either a "happy" or an "angry" trained confederate (who was actually an accomplice of the experimenter). Both the participants and the confederate were told that before they could take the supposed vision test, they needed to complete a questionnaire and allow time for the drug to take effect. The confederate was instructed in each condition to behave in line with his supposed emotion: He acted joyously in the happy condition—flying paper airplanes, bouncing a ball, etc.—and acted irate in the angry condition—complaining about the experiment, refusing to answer some items on the questionnaire, etc. As predicted, when participants were placed in a room with the happy confederate, they rated themselves as happy. They also engaged in more "happy" acts, just like the confederate had modeled. When placed with the angry, irritated confederate, they reported feeling angry and behaved more irately. Although the participants were feeling similar effects of the epinephrine, they labeled those effects differently (happy or angry), depending on the external cues in their environment, and acted accordingly.

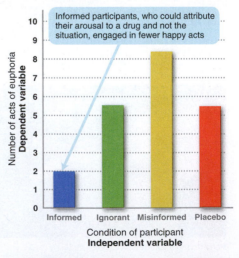

Informed participants, who could attribute their arousal to a drug and not the situation, engaged in fewer happy acts

Number of acts of euphoria
**Dependent variable**

Condition of participant
**Independent variable**

**c. Results of the experiment**  This effect on emotions was most apparent in the groups that were misinformed about the true effects of the injections. Why? Those in the informed group correctly attributed their arousal to the drug rather than to the environment.

suggested that arousal could be labeled happiness or anger, depending on the context. Thus, Schachter and Singer's research demonstrated that emotion is determined by two factors: physiological arousal and cognitive appraisal (labeling).

Schachter and Singer's two-factor theory may have several practical implications. Depending on the cues present in our environment, we apparently can interpret exactly the same feelings of arousal in very different ways. Research on this type of *misattribution of arousal* has had intriguing results (e.g., Greenaway et al., 2015; Shaked & Clore, 2016). For instance, one study found that female participants rated photos of male models as being more attractive when they were told—falsely—that their heart rates increased when they looked at the photos (Jouffre, 2015). The women apparently wrongly attributed their supposedly increased heart rates to feelings of increased attraction to the male model. This type of misattribution also explains why, when you're frustrated by something that happened at work or school, you might yell at your family or friends. On a more positive note, if you're shy or afraid of public speaking, try interpreting your feelings of nervousness as the result of too much coffee or the heating in the room.

Before going on, we need to add one more approach that helps expand our understanding of our emotional reactions. According to the **facial-feedback hypothesis**, movements of our facial muscles produce or intensify our subjective experience of emotion (see the following **Try This Yourself**). More specifically, sensory input (such as seeing a snake) is first routed to subcortical areas of the brain that activate facial movements. These facial changes then initiate and intensify emotions (Adelmann & Zajonc, 1989; Kulczynski et al., 2016; Lamer et al., 2015). For instance, researchers in one study asked participants to maintain a smile while they were engaging in a stress-inducing task, such as keeping their hand in a bucket of very cold ice water (Kraft & Pressman, 2012). Compared to participants who held their face in a neutral position, those who smiled had lower heart rates, showing that smiling can help reduce the experience of stress—thus supporting the facial-feedback hypothesis. Further evidence supporting this hypothesis comes from the cosmetic treatment Botox (see **Figure 12.16**).

**Facial-feedback hypothesis**
The hypothesis that movements of the facial muscles produce and/or intensify our subjective experience of emotion.

## Try This Yourself

### Testing the Facial-Feedback Hypothesis

Hold a pen or pencil between your teeth with your mouth open. Spend about 30 seconds in this position. How do you feel? According to research, pleasant feelings are more likely when teeth are showing than when they are not.

**Source:** Based on Strack et al., 1988.

Mark Owens/John Wiley & Sons, Inc.

Digital Vision/Getty Images

**FIGURE 12.16    Botox and the facial-feedback hypothesis**    Injections of the botulinum toxin (Botox) into the forehead muscles work well to relax frown lines for cosmetic purposes, but they also appear to reduce depression (Finzi & Rosenthal, 2014; Maasumi et al., 2015; Sifferlin, 2017). One study found that depression scores dropped 42% in Botox patients versus 15% for patients who received placebo injections (Magid et al., 2014). Unfortunately, given that Botox injections also inhibit our unconscious imitation of other's facial expressions, they may similarly inhibit our sensitive understanding and empathy for others. Research shows that this is particularly true when the expressions of others are subtle (Baumeister et al., 2015, 2016; Sifferlin, 2017).

Surprisingly, research suggests that even watching another's facial expressions causes an automatic, *reciprocal* change in our own facial muscles (Dimberg & Thunberg, 1998; Pawling et al., 2017; Wood et al., 2016). When people are exposed to pictures of angry faces, for example, the eyebrow muscles involved in frowning are activated. In contrast, the smile muscles show a significant increase in activity when participants are shown photos of a happy face. In follow-up research using the *subliminal perception* techniques discussed in Chapter 4, scientists have shown that this automatic, matching response occurs even *without* the participant's attention or conscious awareness (e.g., Dimberg et al., 2000).

This automatic, innate, and generally unconscious imitation of others' facial expressions has several practical applications. Given that the facial-feedback hypothesis suggests that facial expressions can influence moods, you can see how a treatment that prevents frowning might logically make someone feel less depressed. It also explains why you might feel depressed after just listening to a friend's problems. In addition, the theory may provide personal insights for therapists who constantly work with depressed clients and for actors who simulate emotions for their livelihood. Finally, if you're considering having Botox injections, consider the fact that these treatments may affect your ability to pick up on others' subtle facial cues and to properly empathize with their emotions. In everyday social interactions, failing to detect sudden changes in mood or small facial expressions can make the difference between successful communication and communication breakdown (Sissa Medialab, 2016).

### Evaluating Theories of Emotion

Which theory of emotion is correct? As you may imagine, each theory has its limits. The *James-Lange theory* fails to acknowledge that physiological arousal can occur without emotional experience (e.g., when we exercise). Furthermore, this theory requires a distinctly different pattern of arousal for each emotion. Otherwise, how do we know whether we are sad, happy, or mad? Positron emission tomography (PET) scans of the brain do show subtle differences in the overall physical arousal with basic emotions, such as happiness, fear, and anger (Levenson, 1992, 2007; Werner et al., 2007). But most people are not aware of these slight variations. Thus, there must be other explanations for how we experience emotion.

The *Cannon-Bard theory* (that arousal and emotions occur simultaneously and that all emotions are physiologically similar) has received some experimental support. Instead of the thalamus, however, other research shows that it is the limbic system, hypothalamus, and prefrontal cortex that are activated in emotional experience (Junque, 2015; LeDoux, 2007; Schulze et al., 2016).

As mentioned earlier, research on the *facial-feedback hypothesis* has found a distinctive physiological response for emotions such as fear, sadness, and anger—thus partially confirming James-Lange's initial position. Facial feedback does seem to contribute to the intensity of our subjective emotional experience and our overall moods. So, if you want to change a bad mood or intensify a particularly good emotion, adopt the appropriate facial expression. Try smiling when you're sad and expanding your smiles when you're happy.

Finally, Schachter and Singer's *two-factor theory* emphasizes the importance of cognitive labels in emotions. But research shows that some neural pathways involved in emotion bypass the cortex and go directly to the limbic system. Recall our earlier example of jumping at the sight of a supposed snake and then a second later using the cortex to interpret what it was. This and other evidence suggest that emotions can take place without conscious cognitive processes. Thus, emotion is not simply the labeling of arousal.

In sum, certain basic emotions are associated with subtle differences in arousal. These differences can be produced by changes in facial expressions or by organs controlling the autonomic nervous system. In addition, "simple" emotions (fear and anger) do not initially require conscious cognitive processes. This allows a quick, automatic emotional response that can later be modified by cortical processes. On the other hand, "complex" emotions (jealousy, grief, depression, embarrassment, love) seem to require more extensive cognitive processes.

© Billy R. Ray/Wiley

## Retrieval Practice 12.3 | Components and Theories of Emotion

Completing this self-test and the connections section, and then checking your answers by clicking on the answer button or by looking in Appendix B, will provide immediate feedback and helpful practice for exams.

### Self-Test

1. Briefly describe the three components of emotion.

2. You feel anxious because you are sweating and your heart is beating rapidly. This statement illustrates the _____ theory of emotion.

   a. two-factor
   b. James-Lange
   c. Cannon-Bard
   d. physiological feedback

3. According to the _____, arousal and emotions occur separately but simultaneously.

   a. Cannon-Bard theory
   b. James-Lange theory
   c. facial-feedback hypothesis
   d. two-factor theory

4. Schacter and Singer's two factor theory emphasizes the _____ component of emotion.

   a. stimulus-response
   b. physiological
   c. behavioral-imitation
   d. cognitive

5. You grin broadly while your best friend tells you she was just accepted to medical school. The facial-feedback hypothesis predicts that you will feel _____.

   a. happy
   b. envious
   c. angry
   d. all of these emotions

### Connections—Chapter to Chapter

Answering the following question will help you "look back and look ahead" to see the important connections among the subfields of psychology and chapters within this text.

In Chapter 15 (Therapy), you will discover that *empathy*, a sensitive understanding and sharing of another's inner experience, is a major therapeutic technique among humanistic therapists. In this chapter, you learned about the facial-feedback hypothesis and read about research that suggests even watching another's facial expressions causes an automatic, reciprocal change in our own facial muscles. Explain how Botox injections might affect a therapist's empathy toward his or her clients.

---

## 12.4 | Experiencing Emotions

### LEARNING OBJECTIVES

**Retrieval Practice**   While reading the upcoming sections, respond to each Learning Objective in your own words.

**Review how emotions affect behavior.**

- **Describe** the role of culture and evolution in emotion.

- **Discuss** the psychosocial factors that influence emotions.

- **Summarize** the problems with using polygraph testing as a lie detector.

- **Discuss** the major components of happiness.

How do culture and evolution affect our emotions? Is the polygraph an effective way to detect lies? Why are some people happier than others? Can romantic love survive long-distance relationships? These are just a few of the questions, topics, and emotional experiences we'll explore in this section.

## Gender and Cultural Diversity

### Are Emotions Affected by Culture and Evolution?

Are emotions the same across all cultures? Given the seemingly vast array of emotions within our own culture, it may surprise you to learn that some researchers believe that all our feelings can be condensed into a few primary, culturally universal emotions (**Table 12.3**).

These researchers hold that more complex emotions, such as love, are simply combinations of primary emotions with variations in intensity. As you can see in Table 12.3, there is considerable agreement among the theorists, and the most recent cross-cultural research (Jack et al., 2016) suggests that basic emotions can be combined and reduced to just four: happiness, sadness, surprise/fear, and disgust/

**TABLE 12.3** **Sample Basic Emotions**

*(Note the strong similarities among the various theories and how the last column collapses all emotions into four general categories)*

| Carroll Izard | Paul Ekman and Wallace Friesen | Silvan Tomkins | Robert Plutchik | Rachael Jack et al. |
|---|---|---|---|---|
| Fear | Fear | Fear | Fear | Surprise/fear |
| Anger | Anger | Anger | Anger | Disgust/anger |
| Disgust | Disgust | Disgust | Disgust | Disgust/anger |
| Surprise | Surprise | Surprise | Surprise | Surprise/fear |
| Sadness | Sadness | — | Sadness | Sadness |
| Joy | Happiness | Enjoyment | Joy | Happiness |
| Shame | — | Shame | — | |
| Contempt | Contempt | Contempt | — | |
| Interest | — | Interest | Anticipation | |
| Guilt | — | — | — | |
| — | — | — | Acceptance | |
| — | — | Distress | — | |

**Test Yourself**

Using this list of emotions, try to identify the specific emotion reflected in each of the infant faces.
Do you agree that disgust and anger look the same and that surprise and fear look the same?

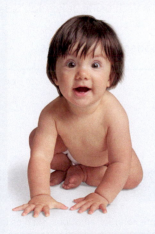

Vladimir Godnik/beyond fotomedia/Getty Images
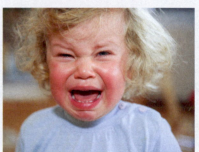
ICHIRO/Getty Images

arnoaltix/Getty Images

John Lund/Annabelle Breakey/Getty Images

© Flashon Studio/Shutterstock
Rubberball/Nicole Hill/Getty Images

**Answers:** From left to right (top row) = fear, sadness, anger, (bottom row) = surprise, joy/happiness, disgust.

anger. Regardless of the exact number, researchers generally agree that across cultures, the facial expression of certain emotions is interpreted similarly. Thus, a smile is recognized by all as a sign of pleasure, whereas a frown is recognized as a sign of displeasure.

From an evolutionary perspective, the idea of universal facial expressions makes adaptive sense because such expressions signal others about our current emotional state (Awasthi & Mandal, 2015; Ekman & Keltner, 1997; Hwang & Matsumoto, 2015). Charles Darwin first advanced the evolutionary theory of emotion in 1872. He proposed that expression of emotions evolved in different species as a part of survival and natural selection. For example, expressions of fear help other human and nonhuman animals avoid danger, whereas expressions of anger and aggression are useful when fighting for mates or resources. Modern evolutionary theory suggests that emotions originate in the limbic system. Given that higher brain areas like the cortex developed later than the subcortical limbic system, evolutionary theory proposes that emotions evolved before thought.

Studies with infants provide further support for an evolutionary basis for emotions. Interestingly, infants only a few hours old show distinct expressions of emotion that closely match adult facial expressions, and by the age of 7 months they can reliably interpret and recognize emotional information across both face and voice (Cole & Moore, 2015; Jessen & Grossman, 2015; Meltzoff & Moore, 1977, 1994). And all infants, even those who are born deaf and blind, show similar facial expressions in similar situations (Denmark et al., 2014; Field et al., 1982; Gelder et al., 2006). In addition, a study showed that families may have characteristic facial expressions, shared even by family members who have been blind from birth (Peleg et al., 2006). This collective evidence points to a strong biological, evolutionary basis for emotional expression and decoding.

Even though we may all share similar facial expressions for some emotions, each culture has its own *display rules* (see the **Try This Yourself**) that govern how, when, and where to express these emotions (de Gelder & Huis, 2016; Ekman, 1993, 2004; Schug et al., 2017).

## Try This Yourself

### Understanding Cultural Display Rules

How do we learn when, where, and how our emotions should be appropriately expressed? Parents and other adults pass along their culture's specific emotional **display rules** to children by responding negatively or ignoring some emotions and being supportive and sympathetic to others.

Public physical contact is also governed by display rules. Did you know that Americans, Europeans, and Asians are less likely than people in other cultures to touch one another and that only the closest family members and friends might hug in greeting or farewell? In contrast, Latin Americans and Middle Easterners often kiss, embrace, and hold hands as a sign of casual friendship (Axtell, 2007). In fact, some Middle Eastern men commonly greet one another with a kiss (as shown in the photo). Can you imagine this same behavior among men in the United States, who generally just shake hands or pat one another's shoulders? Keep these cultural differences in mind when you're traveling. The "thumbs

Behrouz Mehri/AFP/Getty Images

up" gesture is widely used in America to mean everything is okay or to show the desire to hitch a ride. However, in many Middle Eastern countries, the same gesture is similar to an American's raised middle finger!

# Psychosocial Factors and Emotion

**Display rules**  A set of informal cultural norms that control when, where, and how emotions should be expressed.

In addition to culture and evolution, psychosocial factors also clearly affect our emotions and their expression. For example, research shows that college football victories in the two weeks before gubernatorial elections can add three to four percentage points to the incumbent party vote (Lee et al., 2017). These researchers concluded that the football victories increased voters' happiness and well-being, which apparently spread to their current governor and thereby affected their voting behaviors.

Other research has shown that our emotions are sometimes contagious! To test the hypothesis that certain emotions might spread through social media, researchers first evaluated both positive and negative emotions conveyed in Facebook posts (Coviello et al., 2014). Then, they compared the frequency of these emotional expressions with the amount of rainfall in each poster's city. As you might expect, people tend to post more negative emotions and fewer positive emotions on rainy days. The researchers then examined how one person's Facebook post could impact the mood expressions posted by his or her friends living in other cities. They found that having a friend post something negative on Facebook increases the probability of writing a negative post and decreases the likelihood of a positive post.

In short, emotions are much more complex than originally thought. Culture, evolution, the environment, other people, gender, family background, norms, and individual differences all influence our emotions and their expression (Gendron et al., 2014; Hsu, 2016; Hwang & Matsumoto, 2015).

## The Polygraph as a Lie Detector

**Polygraph** An instrument that measures physiological indicators (heart rate, respiration rate, blood pressure, and skin conductivity) to detect emotional arousal, which in turn supposedly reflects lying.

Let's now we turn our attention to one of the hottest, and most controversial, topics in emotion research—the **polygraph**. The polygraph is a machine that measures physiological indicators (such as heart rate and blood pressure) to detect emotional arousal, which supposedly reflects whether or not you are lying. Traditional polygraph tests are based on the assumption that when people lie, they feel stressed, and that this stress can be measured. As you can see in **Figure 12.17**, during a polygraph test multiple (poly) signals from special sensors assess four major indicators of stress and autonomic arousal: heart rate (pulse), blood pressure, respiration (breathing) rate, and perspiration (or skin conductivity). If the participant's bodily responses significantly increase when responding to key questions, the examiner will infer that the participant is lying (Ginton, 2017; Grubin, 2016; Meijer & Verschuere, 2015).

Can you imagine what problems might be associated with the polygraph? First, many people become stressed even when telling the truth, whereas others can conceal their stress and remain calm when deliberately lying. Second, emotions cause physiological arousal, and a polygraph cannot tell which emotion is being felt (anxiety, irritation, excitement, or any other emotion). For this reason, some have suggested the polygraph should be relabeled as an "arousal detector." In fact, people can be trained to beat a lie detector (Kaste, 2015; Wollan, 2015). When asked a general, control question ("Where do you live?"), participants wishing to mislead the examiner can artificially raise their arousal levels by imagining their worst fears (being burned to death or buried alive). Then when asked relevant/guilty knowledge questions ("Did you rob the bank?"), they can calm themselves by practicing meditation tricks (imagining themselves relaxing on a beach).

In response to these and other problems, countless research hours and millions of dollars have been spent on new and improved lie-detection techniques. Although most people

**FIGURE 12.17** **Lie detecting or simple arousal?** Polygraph testing is based on the assumption that when we lie, we feel guilty, fearful, or anxious.

© Mark Burnett/Alamy

**a. Polygraph testing** During a standard polygraph test, a band around the person's chest measures breathing rate, a cuff monitors blood pressure, and finger electrodes measure sweating, or galvanic skin response (GSR).

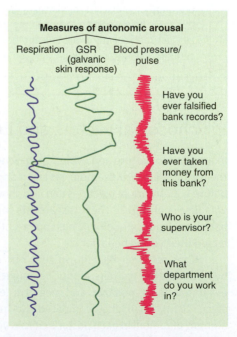

**b. Guilty knowledge questions** Note how the GSR rises sharply in response to the question, "Have you ever taken money from this bank?"

(including many police officers) believe that nonverbal cues—such as gaze aversion and increased movement—are indicative of deception, there is limited support for these beliefs (Bogaard et al., 2016). Perhaps the most promising method for lie detection is the use of brain scans, like *functional magnetic resonance imaging (fMRI)* (Farah et al., 2014; Jiang et al., 2015). Unfortunately, though, all lie-detection techniques have potential problems. Researchers have questioned their application, reliability, and validity, while civil libertarians and judicial scholars raise doubts about their ethics and legality (Lilienfeld et al., 2015; Vrij & Fisher, 2016; Zaitsu, 2016). While research on improved methods for lie detection continues, note that most courts do not accept polygraph test results, laws have been passed to restrict their use, and we should remain skeptical of their ability to detect guilt or innocence (Granhag et al., 2015; Handler et al., 2013; Tomash & Reed, 2013).

## The Psychology of Happiness

What emotion is most important for your overall life satisfaction? If you said "happiness," you're on the right track. Does money buy happiness? Although some people do report wanting to be wealthy, research around the world repeatedly finds that once we have enough money to meet our basic needs for comfort and security, additional funds fail to significantly increase our level of happiness (Diener & Biswas-Diener, 2002, 2008; Wang et al., 2017; Whillans et al., 2016). In short, more is not always better. As a case in point, America, the wealthiest nation in the world, ranked 13th out of 157 nations on happiness (Pullella, 2016). This report measures things like per capita gross domestic product (GDP), social support, and healthy years of life expectancy.

### ❖ Psychology and Your Personal Success | Are There Research-Based Secrets to Happiness?

If we're chasing the wrong things and money can't buy happiness, what can we do? Here are five research-based suggestions:

1. **Build and maintain close relationships.** One of the most consistent findings in positive psychology is that other people make us happy (see the photo). While building and maintaining long-term relationships typically improve our overall happiness and well-being, even just talking with strangers leads to higher levels of happiness (Diener & Tay, 2015; Galinha et al., 2016; Gander et al., 2017). Researchers who asked riders on trains and buses either to quietly sit alone or to talk to a stranger found that those who talked to a stranger reported more positive feelings than those who sat alone (Epley & Schroeder, 2014). Furthermore, positive social interactions with others increase our overall relationship satisfaction (O'Connell et al., 2016). Social acceptance and social connectedness are particularly vital to adolescents' well-being (Arslan, 2017; You et al., 2017).

   In short, powerful evidence suggests that forming and maintaining human connections are significant predictors of happiness. This even applies to nonhuman animals. As you might expect, the stress levels of dogs admitted to animal shelters is high. However, just 15 minutes of human interaction and petting can significantly reduce the dogs' cortisol levels, which as you recall from Chapter 3 is a common and reliable measure of stress (Willen et al., 2017).

2. **Express gratitude.** Consider the striking effects of this experiment. Participants were first randomly assigned to one of three groups, and then simply asked to write down:

   - "Five things you're grateful for in your life over the last week." The lists of participants in this first group included such things as God, kindness from friends, and the Rolling Stones. (Group 1: Gratitude condition.)

   - "Five daily hassles from the last week." Participants in this second group listed items like too many bills to pay, trouble finding parking, and a messy kitchen. (Group 2: Hassles condition.)

   - "Five events that occurred in the last week." This group's list included events such as attending a music festival, learning CPR, and cleaning out a closet. (Group 3: Events condition.)

Courtesy of Sandy Harvey

**Malala Yousafzai—a model of gratitude** Malala's father, Ziauddin Yousafzai, says she is very grateful for the chance to pursue her life goals. This gratitude and her incredible courage set an example for all of us of the importance of standing up for what is right.

Before the experiment started, all participants kept daily journals recording their moods, physical health, and general attitudes, which the researchers later used to compare how people in these three groups changed over time (Emmons & McCullough, 2003).

As you might have expected, participants in the gratitude condition reported feeling happier. In fact, they were 25% happier from this very simple assignment! Likewise, they were more optimistic about the future and felt better about their lives. What was unexpected was that this group did almost 1.5 hours more exercise a week than those in the hassles or events condition and had fewer symptoms of illness.

Further evidence of a positive link between gratitude and happiness comes from studies showing that developing and expressing gratitude are linked with reduced cardiac risk and fewer depression and anxiety symptoms, as well as with improved relationships with others and a less critical and more compassionate relationship with yourself (Mills et al., 2015; Petrocchi & Couyoumdjian, 2016). Keep in mind that your everyday expressions of gratitude can be very small. Simply thanking people who have helped us or given us good service at a restaurant, or writing down three things we are grateful for each night before going to bed, can have a substantial positive impact on our well-being, happiness, and life satisfaction (see photo of Malala and her father).

3. **Change your behavior.** As you discovered in Chapters 3 and 5, getting enough exercise and sleep and spending time in nature all help make us feel better (Panza et al., 2017; Song et al., 2016; Wassing et al., 2016). Surprisingly, research shows that simply reading a book you love increases happiness (Berns et al., 2013). Reading apparently helps us feel connected to characters in a book, which in turn helps us feel connected with other people. Reading also can increase positive feelings, especially if the book inspires you to think about your own life in a new way or to take action toward reaching your own goals. So grab a book you find personally enjoyable (not one you "should read"). Then make a point of reading every day—a few minutes before bed, on a lunch break, or during your daily commute on public transportation.

Another easy behavioral change that will increase your happiness is to act happy! Research shows that just changing your voice to a happier tone actually increases happiness (Aucouturier et al., 2016). In addition, as you discovered earlier in this chapter with the facial-feedback hypothesis, simply holding a pencil between your teeth (to force a simulated smile) increases pleasant feelings.

4. **Spend your money and time wisely.** People who spend money on life experiences—*doing things*—show greater enduring happiness than those who spend money buying material possessions—*having things*. Spending money on tickets to the "big game," a Broadway show, or a fabulous trip is a great way to increase happiness. In contrast, the pleasure we get from spending money on an expensive car, watch, or shoes is limited and momentary.

Why? One factor is anticipation. It's more enjoyable to anticipate experiences than to anticipate acquiring possessions. The pleasure we get from looking forward to a two-week trip is substantially greater than the pleasure we get from anticipating buying a new car. Another explanation is that we're far more likely to share experiences with others, whereas we generally acquire material possessions for solo use.

A second way to spend your money wisely is to share it with others! Research shows that giving to others and performing acts of kindness and service are powerful ways to increase happiness (Aknin et al., 2017; Nelson et al., 2016).

Just as it's critical to spend money wisely, the same is true about time. In fact, the two are often inseparable—money is simply something you trade your life energy for (Robin et al., 2009). If you're currently making $10 an hour and you're considering buying a new iPhone for $650, calculate the real time/money cost. Are you willing to work 65 hours for that new phone? Really?

5. **Choose and pursue worthy goals.** This final tip for increasing happiness involves making a list of your most personally valuable and worthy goals and the specific things you

want to accomplish—daily and long-term. As a college student you may be finding it hard to even choose your major, much less your most valuable and worthy goals. But just knowing that having a college degree is critical to most jobs today is enough as a beginning goal and as a motivator to study and stay in school. When thinking about your college major or lifetime goals, consider your most passionate and enjoyable personal interests. What television programs or podcasts do you naturally enjoy? What do you do in your spare time? This type of self-inquiry may give you insights into your personal passions and possible careers.

Remember that a growth mindset and grit (passion and perseverance) are key to long term success. Note, however, that pursuing happiness (or money) for its own sake can backfire! Have you heard about people who win the lottery and later become less happy and satisfied? This type of **adaptation-level phenomenon** reflects the fact that we tend to judge a new situation or stimuli relative to a neutral level defined by our previous experiences. We win the lottery or get a new job with a higher income and naturally experience an initial surge of pleasure. We then adjust our neutral level higher, which, in turn, requires ever-increasing improvements to gain a similar increase in happiness.

In other words, happiness, like all emotions, is fleeting, and it's incredibly difficult to go backwards. This so-called *hedonic treadmill* shows us that the pleasures we acquire in all parts of our lives—money, material possessions, status, and even our relationships—can quickly become part of our everyday baseline and taken for granted—until they're taken away. Can you see how the previous tips on this list—building and maintaining close relationships, expressing gratitude, changing your behavior, and spending your time and money wisely—can help offset the dangers of this adaptation?

*You can only become truly accomplished at something you love. Don't make money your goal. Instead, pursue the things you love doing, and then do them so well that people can't take their eyes off you.*

—Maya Angelou (American Poet, Author, Dancer)

**Adaptation-level phenomenon**
A tendency to judge a new situation or stimulus relative to a neutral, "normal" level based on our previous experiences; we then adapt to this new level, and it becomes the new "normal."

© Billy R. Ray/Wiley

## Retrieval Practice 12.4 | Experiencing Emotions

Completing this self-test and the connections section, and then checking your answers by clicking on the answer button or by looking in Appendix B, will provide immediate feedback and helpful practice for exams.

### Self-Test

1. According to evolutionary theory, basic emotions, like fear and anger, seem to originate in _____.
   a. higher cortical areas of the brain
   b. subtle changes in facial expressions
   c. the limbic system
   d. the interpretation of environmental stimuli

2. What are display rules?

3. Which of the following is(are) recommended for increasing happiness?
   a. Express gratitude.
   b. Spend your money and time wisely.
   c. Choose worthy goals.
   d. All of these options.

4. The polygraph, or lie detector, measures primarily the _____ component of emotions.
   a. physiological          b. articulatory
   c. cognitive              d. subjective

5. Which of the following is TRUE about the polygraph?
   a. It does in fact measure physiological arousal.
   b. It cannot tell which emotion is being felt.
   c. People can be trained to beat a polygraph.
   d. All of these options are true.

### Connections—Chapter to Chapter

Answering the following question will help you "look back and look ahead" to see the important connections among the subfields of psychology and chapters within this text.

In Chapter 8 (Thinking, Language, and Intelligence), we discussed decision making from a cognitive perspective, using algorithms and heuristics. In this chapter, you learned about the cognitive component of emotions, as well as the biological and behavioral components. Explain how emotions can function as a type of heuristic in making daily decisions.

# Chapter Summary

## 12.1 Theories of Motivation   389

- Biological theories of **motivation** emphasize **instincts**, drives (produced by the body's need for **homeostasis**), and arousal (the need for novelty, complexity, and stimulation).

- Psychological theories focus on the role of incentives and cognition, including attributions and expectancies.

- Maslow's **hierarchy of needs** theory takes a biopsychosocial approach. It prioritizes needs, with survival needs at the bottom and higher needs at the top.

### Test Your Critical Thinking

**1.** Why are modern biological theories of instincts more scientifically useful than older instinct theories?

**2.** At what level would you rank yourself on Maslow's hierarchy of needs? What can you do to advance to a higher level?

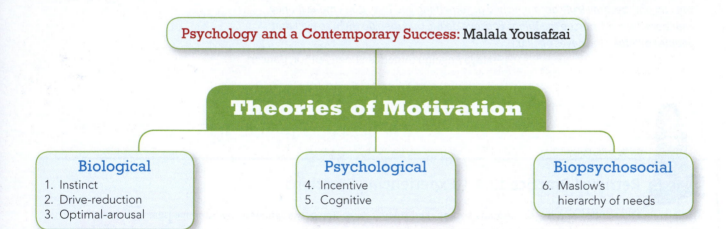

**Psychology and a Contemporary Success:** Malala Yousafzai

**Theories of Motivation**

**Biological**
1. Instinct
2. Drive-reduction
3. Optimal-arousal

**Psychological**
4. Incentive
5. Cognitive

**Biopsychosocial**
6. Maslow's hierarchy of needs

## 12.2 Motivation and Behavior   394

- Both biological factors (the stomach, biochemistry, the brain) and psychosocial factors (stimulus cues and cultural conditioning) affect hunger and eating.

- Biological and psychosocial factors also play a role in **obesity, anorexia nervosa, bulimia nervosa,** and **binge-eating disorder (BED)**.

- A high need for achievement (nAch), or **achievement motivation**, is generally learned in early childhood primarily through interactions with parents.

- Providing **extrinsic motivation** like money or praise for an intrinsically satisfying activity can undermine people's enjoyment and interest—their **intrinsic motivation**—for the activity. However, under the right conditions, extrinsic rewards can sometimes be motivational.

### Test Your Critical Thinking

**1.** Most adults (and many children) find it difficult to control their weight. Using information from this chapter, can you identify the factors or motives that best explain their experience?

**2.** How can you restructure elements of your personal, work, or school life to increase your intrinsic versus extrinsic motivation?

## Motivation and Behavior

### Hunger and Eating
- Biological factors (stomach, biochemistry, brain)
- Psychosocial factors (stimulus cues, cultural conditioning)

### Eating Problems and Disorders
- Obesity
- Anorexia nervosa
- Bulimia nervosa
- Binge-eating disorder

### Achievement Motivation
Desire to excel, especially in competition with others

### Extrinsic vs. Intrinsic Motivation
- Extrinsic = external rewards and/or punishments
- Intrinsic = internal, personal satisfaction

### Psychology and Your Professional Success:
What Are the Best Ways to Increase Motivation?

### 12.3 Components and Theories of Emotion 403

- All **emotions** have three basic components: *biological* (e.g., heart pounding), *cognitive* (thoughts, values, and expectations), and *behavioral* (e.g., smiles, frowns, running). Studies of the biological component find that emotions involve general, nonspecific arousal of the autonomic nervous system.

- According to the **James-Lange theory**, emotions follow from physiological changes. The **Cannon-Bard theory** holds that emotions and physiological changes occur simultaneously. The **two-factor theory** suggests that emotions depend on two factors—physiological arousal and cognitive labeling of that arousal. According to the **facial-feedback hypothesis**, facial movements produce and/or intensify emotions.

**Test Your Critical Thinking**

**1.** If you were going on a date with someone or applying for an important job, how might you use the three key theories of emotion to increase the chances that things will go well?

**2.** Why do you think people around the world experience and express the same basic emotions, and what evolutionary advantages might help explain these similarities?

## Components and Theories of Emotion

### Research Challenge: Does Wearing "Sexy" Clothing Signal Sexual Interest?

### Three Components of Emotion
- *Biological* (arousal—increased heart rate)
- *Cognitive* (thoughts—expectations)
- *Behavioral* (expressions—smiles, running)

### Three Major Theories of Emotion

### James-Lange
Subjective emotion follows physiological arousal

### Cannon-Bard
Emotions and physiological arousal occur simultaneously

### Schachter's Two-Factor
Emotions depend on two factors—physical arousal and cognitive labeling

## 12.4 Experiencing Emotions 411

- Some researchers believe that across all cultures people experience several basic, universal emotions and express and recognize these emotions in essentially the same way. Studies with infants support this evolutionary theory of emotion. However, other researchers note that **display rules** for emotional expression vary across cultures.

- Psychosocial factors, such as the environment and other people, also influence our emotions and their expression.

- **Polygraph** tests attempt to detect lying by measuring physiological signs of guilt, fear, and/or anxiety. Due to several problems with the polygraph's underlying assumptions and accuracy, most courts do not accept polygraph test results, laws have been passed to restrict its use, and we should remain skeptical.

- Happiness research finds that once basic needs for comfort and security are met, more money is not necessarily better. Tips for increasing happiness include building and maintaining close relationships, expressing gratitude, changing your behavior, spending your money and time wisely, and choosing worthy goals.

### Test Your Critical Thinking

**1.** How might differing cultural display rules explain why American tourists are often criticized by local residents for being "too loud and aggressive"?

**2.** After reading the section on polygraph tests, would you be willing to take a "lie detector" test if you were accused of a crime? Why or why not?

## Experiencing Emotions

**Psychosocial Factors and Emotions**
Numerous factors, such as the environment and other people, influence our emotions and their expression

**Gender and Cultural Diversity:**
Are Emotions Affected by Culture and Evolution?

**The Polygraph as a Lie Detector**
Polygraph machine measures sympathetic arousal to detect emotional arousal, which in turn supposedly reflects lying

**The Psychology of Happiness**
Once basic needs for comfort and security are met, more money is not necessarily better

**Psychology and Your Personal Success:**
Are There Research-Based Secrets to Happiness?

---

# Key Terms

**Retrieval Practice**   *Write a definition for each term before turning back to the referenced page to check your answer.*

- achievement motivation   399
- adaptation-level phenomenon   417
- amygdala   404
- anorexia nervosa   398
- binge-eating disorder (BED)   398
- bulimia nervosa   398
- Cannon-Bard theory   408
- display rules   413
- drive-reduction theory   390

- emotion   404
- extrinsic motivation   401
- facial-feedback hypothesis   409
- hierarchy of needs   393
- homeostasis   390
- incentive theory   392
- instinct   390
- intrinsic motivation   401
- James-Lange theory   407

- motivation   389
- obesity   397
- optimal-arousal theory   391
- polygraph   414
- self-actualization   393
- two-factor theory   408
- Yerkes-Dodson law   391

© alexxl66/iStockphoto

# CHAPTER 13

# Personality

| CHAPTER OUTLINE | LEARNING OBJECTIVES |
|---|---|

❖ **Psychology and a Classic Success:**
Abraham Lincoln

---

**13.1 Psychoanalytic/Psychodynamic Theories**

- Freud's Psychoanalytic Theory
- Neo-Freudians and the Psychodynamic Perspective
- Evaluating Psychoanalytic Theories

**Summarize the major concepts of psychoanalytic/ psychodynamic theories of personality.**

- **Define** personality.
- **Review** the major concepts of Freud's psychoanalytic theory.
- **Compare** psychoanalytic and psychodynamic theories of personality.
- **Discuss** the major criticisms of psychoanalytic theories.

---

**13.2 Trait Theories**

- Early Trait Theorists
- Modern Trait Theory
- **RC Research Challenge**
  Do Nonhuman Animals Have Unique Personalities?
- Evaluating Trait Theories

❖ **Psychology and Your Personal Success**
Can (and Should) We Improve Our Personalities?

**Review the major concepts of the various trait theories.**

- **Explain** how early trait theorists approached the study of personality.
- **Describe** the Big Five personality traits.
- **Summarize** the major contributions and criticisms of trait theory.

---

**13.3 Humanistic Theories**

- Rogers's Theory
- Maslow's Theory
- Evaluating Humanistic Theories

**Summarize the major concepts of humanistic theories of personality.**

- **Discuss** the importance of self-actualization in humanistic theories.
- **Explain** why self-concept and unconditional positive regard are key aspects of Rogers's theory of personality.
- **Describe** how Maslow's hierarchy of needs affects personality.
- **Evaluate** the strengths and weaknesses of humanistic theories of personality.

---

**13.4 Social-Cognitive Theories**

- Bandura's and Rotter's Approaches
- Evaluating Social-Cognitive Theories

❖ **Psychology and Your Personal Success**
Could You Pass the Stanford Marshmallow Test?

**Review the major concepts of social-cognitive theories of personality.**

- **Explain** Bandura's and Rotter's approaches to personality.
- **Summarize** the strengths and weaknesses of the social-cognitive perspective on personality.

SSPL/Getty Images

## ❖ Psychology and a Classic Success | Abraham Lincoln

Abraham Lincoln (1809–1865) was the 16th president of the United States (see photo). Although he served only four years, from 1861 until his assassination in 1865, Lincoln is the one American president whom historians and academicians most consistently rank as the best of all time (e.g., Rottinghaus & Vaughn, 2015; Von Drehle, 2017).

Lincoln did not have an easy life. Born in a one-room log cabin in Kentucky, he was forced to move with his family in 1811 and again in 1816 due to land disputes. When Lincoln was 9 years old, his mother died of milk sickness, a kind of poisoning. In addition, his younger brother died in infancy, his first serious romantic interest died at the age of 22, and three of his own four children died at early ages. Lincoln apparently suffered from intense bouts of *melancholia*, which is now known as *depression,* throughout his life. Even as a young man, he reportedly talked more than once of suicide. And the deaths of their three sons had serious depressive effects on both Lincoln and his wife, Mary Todd Lincoln (Abraham Lincoln Biography, n.d.).

Today, Abraham Lincoln is remembered as the quintessential self-made man, rising from humble beginnings to the highest positions of power and prestige. Among his long list of accomplishments, he is credited with freeing the slaves, launching the Transcontinental Railroad, and holding together a divided nation during the Civil War. Lincoln is also remembered for his exceptional oratory skills and his ability to communicate clearly and concisely. Although it was only a few minutes long, his Gettysburg Address, delivered in 1863, is considered one of the greatest speeches in all of American history. And his talent for capturing complex ideas in few words is shown in the following quote:

*Whenever I hear anyone arguing for slavery I feel a strong impulse to see it tried on him personally.*

—Abraham Lincoln

# Chapter Overview

As you can easily see from this brief biography, Abraham Lincoln clearly demonstrates the central themes of our text—having a *growth mindset* and *grit* (passion and perseverance). Despite his humble beginnings and considerable adversities, including serious depression, he went on to the highest levels of achievement. In fact, unlike other great figures who overcame their adversities, Lincoln appears to have used his lifelong melancholia to find personal lessons and as "fuel for the fire of his great work" (Shenk, 2005).

We also chose him as this chapter's famous figure because Abraham Lincoln is noted for his embodiment of distinctive personality traits, such as introversion and conscientiousness. Given his incredible success as an orator and a public figure, it's hard to recognize Lincoln as an introvert. But as you'll discover later in the chapter, there are many myths about introversion. In contrast, his trait of conscientiousness is easy to see. As you may remember from the history books, Lincoln is well known for having walked six miles to return a three-cent overcharge to a customer when he was working as a store clerk (Nichols, 2013).

This chapter focuses on what makes Lincoln (and each of us) unique—our individual personalities—as well as on what personality is and how we study and assess it. We begin with an examination of the five leading theories of personality (psychoanalytic/psychodynamic, trait, humanistic, social-cognitive, and biological). We then discuss the tools and techniques psychologists have developed to measure, compare, and evaluate our individual personalities.

---

## Why Study Psychology?

### Did you know that

- . . . Sigmund Freud believed that between the ages of 3 and 6, little boys develop a sexual longing for their mothers and jealousy and hatred of their fathers?

- . . . early personality theorists identified more than 4,500 traits to describe personality?

- . . . some research finds that nonhuman animals have unique personalities?

- . . . Carl Rogers believed that children raised with conditional positive regard might later have poorer mental health as adults?

- . . . spending time in a foreign country may change your personality?

- . . . in the 1800s phrenologists believed personality could be measured by reading the bumps on your skull?

- . . . some measures of personality require respondents to interpret inkblots?

- . . . your social media postings can be used to assess your personality?

Chris Stein/Getty Images

---

## 13.1 | Psychoanalytic/Psychodynamic Theories

### LEARNING OBJECTIVES

**Retrieval Practice**   While reading the upcoming sections, respond to each Learning Objective in your own words.

**Summarize the major concepts of psychoanalytic/ psychodynamic theories of personality.**

- **Define** personality.

- **Review** the major concepts of Freud's psychoanalytic theory.

- **Compare** psychoanalytic and psychodynamic theories of personality.

- **Discuss** the major criticisms of psychoanalytic theories.

**Temperament** An individual's innate disposition or behavioral style and typical emotional response.

**Character** Value judgments about an individual's morals, values, and ethical behaviors.

**Personality** Our unique and relatively stable pattern of thoughts, feelings, and actions.

Before we begin our journey through the various theories of personality, note that not all psychologists agree about exactly what personality includes. Many psychologists consider temperament and character to be vital aspects of personality. However, others believe personality is not equivalent to **temperament**, which refers to our innate disposition or behavioral style and typical emotional response. (Recall from Chapter 10 that there are three main categories of temperament—easy, difficult, or slow-to-warm-up.) Nor is it the same as **character**, which refers to value judgments about an individual's morals, values, and ethical behaviors, such as honesty, integrity, and kindness.

Throughout this chapter and this text, then, we will separate our discussion of personality from temperament and character, and rely on this widely accepted definition of **personality**: our unique and relatively stable pattern of thoughts, feelings, and actions. In other words, personality describes how we are different from other people and what patterns of behavior are typical of us. Just as the words *introversion* and *conscientiousness* can be used to characterize Abraham Lincoln's personality, each of us has terms that can be used to describe our unique personalities.

## Freud's Psychoanalytic Theory

One of the earliest theories of personality was Sigmund Freud's psychoanalytic perspective, which emphasized unconscious processes and unresolved past conflicts. Working from about 1890 until he died in 1939, Freud developed a theory of personality that has been one of the most influential—and controversial—theories in all of science (Bornstein & Huprich, 2015; Carducci, 2015; Elliott & Prager, 2016). Let's examine some of Freud's most basic and debatable concepts.

**Conscious** In Freudian terms, thoughts or motives that a person is currently aware of.

**Preconscious** Freud's term for thoughts, motives, or memories that exist just beneath the surface of awareness and can be called to consciousness when necessary.

**Unconscious** Freud's term for the reservoir of largely unacceptable thoughts, feelings, memories, and other information that lies beneath conscious awareness; in modern terms, subliminal processing that lies beneath the absolute threshold (Chapter 4).

### Levels of Consciousness
Freud called the mind the "psyche" and asserted that it contains three *levels of consciousness*, or awareness: the **conscious**, the **preconscious**, and the **unconscious** (**Figure 13.1**). For Freud, the unconscious is all-important because it serves as a reservoir that stores our largely unacceptable thoughts, feelings, memories, and other information. It lies beneath our conscious awareness. However, its contents supposedly have an enormous impact on personality development—like the hidden part of the iceberg that sunk the ocean liner *Titanic*.

Interestingly, because many of our unconscious thoughts and motives are unacceptable and threatening, Freud believed that they are normally *repressed* (held out of awareness)—unless they are unintentionally revealed by dreams or slips of the tongue, later called *Freudian slips* (**Figure 13.2**).

**FIGURE 13.1** **Freud's three levels of consciousness**

Although Freud never used this analogy, his levels of awareness are often compared to an iceberg:

- The tip of the iceberg would be analogous to the *conscious* mind—above the water and easily inspected.

- The *preconscious* mind (shallowly submerged) contains information available with a little extra effort.

- The large base of the iceberg is somewhat like the *unconscious*, completely hidden from personal inspection.

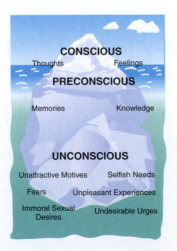

CONSCIOUS
Thoughts        Feelings
PRECONSCIOUS
Memories        Knowledge
UNCONSCIOUS
Unattractive Motives    Selfish Needs
Fears        Unpleasant Experiences
Immoral Sexual    Undesirable Urges
Desires

"So how's everything down in the dog pound ... I mean, the bullpen?"

Cartoon Resource/Shutterstock

**FIGURE 13.2** **Freudian slips** Freud believed that a small slip of the tongue (now known as a *Freudian slip*) can reflect unconscious feelings that we normally keep hidden.

## Personality Structure

In addition to the mind's three levels of consciousness, Freud also believed our personalities are composed of three mental structures: the *id*, *ego*, and *superego* (**Figure 13.3**).

According to Freud, the **id** is present at birth, completely unconscious, and focused on meeting basic drives, such as hunger, sex, and aggression. It is immature, impulsive, and irrational. When its primitive drives build up, the id seeks immediate gratification—a concept known as the *pleasure principle*. The id is like a newborn baby: It wants what it wants when it wants it!

As children develop, they discover they cannot act on their every impulse—grabbing others' candy or shoving them off the swing set. In response, the second personality structure, the **ego**, develops to deal with the real world. The ego is somewhat conscious and serves as the "executive" responsible for planning, problem solving, and controlling the potentially destructive energy of the id in ways that are compatible with the external world. Thus, the ego is responsible for delaying gratification when necessary. (Be careful not to confuse this Freudian personality structure with the more common usage of the term "ego"—meaning a person's sense of self-esteem or self-importance.)

The final part of the psyche to develop is the **superego**, which serves as the center of morality. It provides internalized ideals and standards for judgment, and is often referred to as the "conscience." When thinking about having sex, the superego might warn, "only when you're married," whereas the id would demand it "right now." Trying to meet the demands of both the id and superego, the ego might say, "let's practice safe sex in a committed relationship."

## Defense Mechanisms

As you can see, the "morality" demands of the superego often conflict with the "infantile" needs and drives of the id. When the ego fails to satisfy both the id and the superego, anxiety slips into conscious awareness. Because anxiety is uncomfortable, Freud believed we avoid it through **defense mechanisms**, strategies the ego uses to reduce anxiety. Although defense mechanisms do help relieve the conflict-created anxiety, they distort reality and may increase self-deception. **Figure 13.4** explains how this can happen with the defense mechanisms of intellectualization and rationalization. Freud also identified several other defense mechanisms, which are defined and illustrated in Table 3.3 in Chapter 3.

**FIGURE 13.3** **Freud's personality structure** According to Freud, personality is composed of three structures—the id, ego, and superego. Note how the ego is primarily conscious and preconscious, whereas the id is entirely unconscious.

**Id** In Freud's view, the personality structure that is present at birth, is completely unconscious, and strives to satisfy basic drives, such as hunger, sex, and aggression; it operates on the pleasure principle.

**Ego** In Freud's view, the somewhat conscious personality structure that develops out of the need to deal with the demands of the real world; it operates on the reality principle.

**Superego** In Freud's view, the personality structure that develops last and serves as the center of morality, providing internalized ideals and standards for judgment; often referred to as the "conscience."

**Defense mechanisms** Freud's term for the strategies the ego uses to reduce anxiety by unconsciously distorting reality.

**FIGURE 13.4** **Defense mechanisms in action**

**a. Advantages** Freud believed defense mechanisms help us deal with unconscious conflicts, which explains why these physicians may *intellectualize* and distance themselves from the gruesome aspects of their work to avoid personal anxieties. Defense mechanisms can be healthy and helpful if we use them in moderation or on a temporary basis.

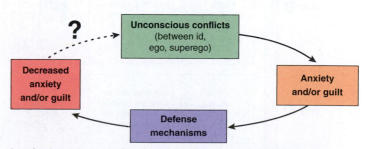

**b. Disadvantages** Unfortunately, defense mechanisms generally distort reality, and they create some of our most dangerous habits through a vicious self-reinforcing cycle. An alcoholic who uses his paycheck to buy drinks may feel very guilty, but he can easily reduce this conflict by *rationalizing* that he deserves to relax and unwind with alcohol because he works so hard.

## Psychosexual Stages

Although defense mechanisms are now an accepted part of modern psychology, other Freudian ideas are more controversial (Boag, 2015; Breger, 2014). For example, according to Freud, strong biological urges residing within the id push all children through five universal **psychosexual stages** (**Step-by-Step Diagram 13.1**). The term *psychosexual* reflects Freud's belief that children experience sexual feelings from birth (in different forms from those experienced by adolescents and adults). Each of the five psychosexual stages is named for the type of sexual pleasure that supposedly characterizes the stage—for instance, the oral phase is named for the mouth, the key erogenous zone during infancy.

According to Freud, at each psychosexual stage the id's impulses come into conflict with social demands. Furthermore, if a child's needs are not met, or are overindulged, at one particular stage, the child supposedly may *fixate,* and a part of his or her personality will remain stuck at that stage. Freud believed most individuals successfully pass through each of the five stages. But during stressful times, they may return (or *regress*) to an earlier stage in which prior needs were badly frustrated or overgratified.

**Psychosexual stages** In Freudian theory, five developmental periods (oral, anal, phallic, latency, and genital) during which particular kinds of pleasures must be gratified if personality development is to proceed normally.

---

**STEP-BY-STEP DIAGRAM 13.1**    **Freud's Five Psychosexual Stages of Development**

> **STOP!** This Step-by-Step Diagram contains essential information NOT found elsewhere in the text, which is likely to appear on quizzes and exams. Be sure to study it CAREFULLY!

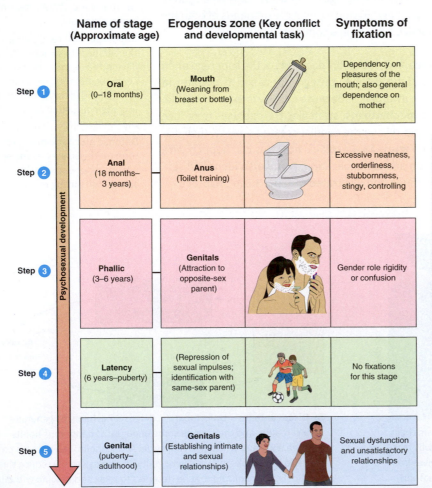

| | Name of stage (Approximate age) | Erogenous zone (Key conflict and developmental task) | Symptoms of fixation |
|---|---|---|---|
| Step 1 | **Oral** (0–18 months) | **Mouth** (Weaning from breast or bottle) | Dependency on pleasures of the mouth; also general dependence on mother |
| Step 2 | **Anal** (18 months–3 years) | **Anus** (Toilet training) | Excessive neatness, orderliness, stubbornness, stingy, controlling |
| Step 3 | **Phallic** (3–6 years) | **Genitals** (Attraction to opposite-sex parent) | Gender role rigidity or confusion |
| Step 4 | **Latency** (6 years–puberty) | (Repression of sexual impulses; identification with same-sex parent) | No fixations for this stage |
| Step 5 | **Genital** (puberty–adulthood) | **Genitals** (Establishing intimate and sexual relationships) | Sexual dysfunction and unsatisfactory relationships |

(Psychosexual development)

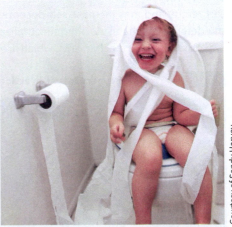

**Toilet training or great fun?** What do you think Freud would say about this child's stage of development?

Courtesy of Sandy Harvey

1. **Oral stage** (birth to 18 months)  During this period, an infant receives satisfaction through sucking, eating, biting, and so on. Because the infant is highly dependent on parents and other caregivers to provide opportunities for oral gratification, fixation at this stage can easily occur. If caregivers overindulge an infant's oral needs, the child may fixate and as an adult become gullible ("swallowing" anything), dependent, and passive. The under-indulged child, however, will develop into an aggressive, sadistic person who exploits others. According to Freud, orally fixated adults often orient their life around their mouth—chewing their nails, smoking cigarettes, overeating, becoming alcoholics, or talking a great deal.

2. **Anal stage** (18 to 36 months)  Once the child becomes a toddler, his or her erogenous zone shifts to the anus. The child supposedly receives satisfaction by having and retaining bowel movements. Because this is the time when most parents begin toilet training, the child's desire to control his or her own bowel movements often leads to strong conflict. Adults who are fixated at this stage, in Freud's view, may develop an *anal-retentive* personality and be highly controlled and compulsively neat. Or they may be very messy, disorderly, rebellious, and destructive—the so-called *anal-expulsive* personality.

3. **Phallic stage** (3 to 6 years)  During the *phallic stage*, the major center of pleasure is the genitals. Masturbation and "playing doctor" with other children are common during this time. According to Freud, a 3- to 6-year-old boy also develops an unconscious sexual longing for his mother and jealousy and hatred for the rival father. This attraction creates a conflict Freud called the **Oedipus complex**, named after *Oedipus*, the legendary Greek king who unwittingly killed his father and married his mother. The young boy reportedly experiences guilt and fear that his father will punish him for his feelings, perhaps by cutting off his penis—so-called *castration anxiety*. If this stage is not resolved completely or positively, or the child fixates at this stage, the boy grows up resenting his father and generalizes this feeling to all authority figures.

    What happens with little girls? Because a girl does not have a penis, she does not fear castration and fails to fully complete this stage and move on to successful identification with her mother. According to Freud, she develops *penis envy* and fails to develop an adequate superego, which Freud believed resulted in women being morally inferior to men. (You are undoubtedly surprised or outraged by this statement, but remember that Freud was a product of his time. Sexism was common at this point in history. And most modern psychodynamic theorists reject Freud's notion of penis envy, as we will see in the next section.)

> **Oedipus complex**  According to Freud, a young boy's development, during the phallic stage (ages 3 to 6 years), of sexual attraction to his mother and rivalry with his father.

4. **Latency period** (6 years to puberty)  Following the phallic stage, children supposedly repress sexual thoughts and engage in nonsexual activities, such as developing social and intellectual skills. The task of this stage is to develop successful interactions with same-sex peers and refine appropriate gender roles.

5. **Genital stage** (puberty to adulthood)  With the beginning of adolescence, the genitals are again erogenous zones. Freud automatically assumed heterosexuality and believed adolescents seek to fulfill their sexual desires through emotional attachment to members of the opposite sex. Unsuccessful outcomes at this stage lead to participation in sexual relationships based only on lustful desires, not on respect and commitment.

### Freud and Modern Western Culture
Before going on, keep in mind that many of Freud's terms and concepts have been heavily criticized and are not widely accepted in modern, scientific psychology—particularly his psychosexual stages of development. However, we discuss them here because words like *id, ego, superego, anal-retentive,* and *Oedipus complex* remain in common, everyday usage as part of our culture. In fact, Freud's impact on Western intellectual history cannot be overstated. His wide-ranging and revolutionary ideas attempted to explain dreams, religion, social groupings, family dynamics, neurosis, psychosis, humor, the arts, and literature. You need to be aware of Freud's major ideas, as well as of the criticisms that will be further discussed later.

## Neo-Freudians and the Psychodynamic Perspective

Some initial followers of Freud later extended his theories, often in social and cultural directions. They became known as neo-Freudians, or "new" Freudians. These theorists accepted

**FIGURE 13.5** **An upside to feelings of inferiority?** Adler suggested that the will-to-power could be positively expressed through social interest—by identifying with others and cooperating with them for the social good. Can you explain how these volunteers might be fulfilling their will-to-power interest?

**Inferiority complex** Adler's idea that feelings of inferiority develop from early childhood experiences of helplessness and incompetence.

**Collective unconscious** Jung's name for the deepest layer of the unconscious, which contains universal memories and archetypes shared by all people due to our common ancestral past.

**Archetypes** Jung's term for the collective, universal images and patterns, residing in the unconscious, that have symbolic meaning for all people.

most of Freud's basic ideas, such as the id, ego, superego, and defense mechanisms, but broke away for various reasons.

**Alfred Adler** As one of the first to leave Freud's inner circle, Alfred Adler (1870–1937) believed behavior is purposeful and goal directed, instead of being motivated by unconscious forces. According to his *individual psychology*, we are motivated by our goals in life—especially our goals of obtaining security and overcoming feelings of inferiority (Carlson & Englar-Carlson, 2013).

Adler believed that almost all of us suffer from an **inferiority complex**, or deep feelings of inadequacy and incompetence that arise from our feelings of helplessness as infants (Adler, 1927/1954). According to Adler, these early feelings result in a "will-to-power" that can take one of two paths. It can lead children to strive to develop superiority over others through dominance, aggression, or expressions of envy. Or, on a more positive note, it can encourage them to develop their full potential and creativity and to gain mastery and control of their lives (**Figure 13.5**).

**Carl Jung** Another early Freud follower turned dissenter, Carl Jung (1875–1961), developed *analytical psychology*. Like Freud, Jung (pronounced "Yoong") emphasized unconscious processes, but he believed that the unconscious contains positive and spiritual motives as well as sexual and aggressive forces.

Jung also thought that we have two forms of the unconscious mind: the personal unconscious and the collective unconscious. The *personal unconscious* is created from our individual experiences, whereas the **collective unconscious** is identical in all of us and is inherited (Jung, 1933, 1936/1969). The collective unconscious consists of primitive images and patterns of thought, feeling, and behavior that Jung called **archetypes** (**Figure 13.6**).

Because of archetypal patterns in the collective unconscious, we supposedly perceive and react in certain predictable ways. One set of archetypes refers to gender roles (Chapter 9). Jung claimed that both males and females have patterns for feminine aspects of personality—*anima*—and masculine aspects of personality—*animus*—which allow us to express both masculine and feminine personality traits and to understand the opposite sex.

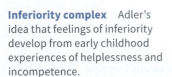

Micah Hanson/Alamy Stock Photo

**FIGURE 13.6** **Archetypes in the collective unconscious?** According to Jung, the collective unconscious is the ancestral memory of the human race. This may explain common similarities in religion, art, and dream imagery across cultures, such as the repeated symbol of the snake in this ancient Egyptian tomb painting. Can you think of other explanations, such as the fact that snakes pose an evolutionary danger across time and cultures?

**Karen Horney** Like Adler and Jung, psychoanalyst Karen Horney [HORN-eye] (1885–1952) was an influential follower of Freud who later came to reject major aspects of Freudian theory. She is credited with having developed a creative blend of Freudian, Adlerian, and Jungian theory, along with the first feminist critique of Freud's theory (Horney, 1939, 1945). She also emphasized women's positive traits and suggested that most of Freud's ideas about female personality reflected male bias and misunderstanding. As an example, Horney proposed that women's everyday experience with social inferiority led to power envy, not to Freud's idea of biological *penis envy*.

Horney also believed personality development depends largely on social relationships—particularly the one between parent and child. She believed that when a child's needs are not met by nurturing parents, the child may develop lasting feelings of helplessness and insecurity. The way people respond to this **basic anxiety**, in Horney's view, sets the stage for later adult psychological health. She believed that everyone copes with this basic anxiety in one of three ways—we move toward, away from, or against other people—and that psychological health requires a balance among these three styles.

In sum, Horney proposed that our adult personalities are shaped by our childhood relationships with our parents—not by fixation or regression at some stage of psychosexual development, as Freud argued.

Keep in mind that most of the major ideas of Adler, Jung, and Horney, along with concepts from other key figures such as Erik Erikson (Chapter 10), have evolved into the modern *psychodynamic perspective* described in Chapter 15. In contrast to the traditional Freudian focus on the id, ego, superego, and psychosexual stages, psychodynamic theorists emphasize the *dynamic* relations between conscious and unconscious processes and current problems (Barber & Solomonov, 2016; Beail, 2016).

**FIGURE 13.7** **Oral fixation or simple self-soothing?** Is this an example of Freud's earliest stage of psychosexual development or just a part of all infants' normal sucking behaviors?

© PonyWang/iStockphoto

**Basic anxiety** According to Horney, feelings of helplessness and insecurity that adults experience because as children they felt alone and isolated in a hostile environment.

## Evaluating Psychoanalytic Theories

Let's consider the major criticisms of Freud's psychoanalytic theories (Carducci, 2015; Gagnepain et al., 2014; Tummala-Narra, 2016):

- **Inadequate empirical support** Many psychoanalytic concepts—such as the psychosexual stages—cannot be empirically tested.
- **Overemphasis on sexuality, biology, and unconscious forces** Modern psychologists believe Freud underestimated the role of learning and evolution in shaping personality (**Figure 13.7**).
- **Sexism** Beginning with Karen Horney, many psychologists have rejected Freud's theories as derogatory toward women.

Despite claims of inadequate empirical support, there is reliable evidence for certain psychoanalytic concepts, such as defense mechanisms and the belief that a lot of our information processing occurs outside our conscious awareness (*automatic processing*, Chapter 5, and *implicit memories*, Chapter 7).

In addition, people who identify as having a heterosexual orientation, but show a strong sexual attraction to same-sex people in psychological tests, tend to show more sexual prejudice and higher levels of hostility toward gay people (Weinstein et al., 2012). Can you see how Freud's theory might suggest that these negative attitudes and beliefs spring from unconscious repression of same-sex desires?

Finally, many contemporary clinicians still value Freud's insights about childhood experiences and unconscious influences on personality development (de Tychey et al., 2016; Sand, 2014; Schimmel, 2014).

To sum up, Freud was clearly wrong on many counts. However, he still ranks as one of the giants of psychology. Furthermore, it's easy to criticize Freud if you don't remember that he began his work at the start of the twentieth century and lacked the benefit of modern research findings and technology. We can only imagine how our current theories will look 100 years from now. Right or wrong, Freud has earned a lasting place among the pioneers in psychology.

© Billy R. Ray/Wiley

## Retrieval Practice 13.1 | Psychoanalytic/Psychodynamic Theories

Completing this self-test and the connections section, and then checking your answers by clicking on the answer button or by looking in Appendix B, will provide immediate feedback and helpful practice for exams.

### Self-Test

1. Define *personality*.

2. In Freudian terms, the _____ seeks immediate gratification. The _____ is the "executive" that deals with the demands of reality, and the _____ is the center of morality that provides standards for judgment.

   a. psyche, ego, id
   b. id, ego, superego
   c. conscious, preconscious, unconscious
   d. oral stage, anal stage, phallic stage

3. According to Freud, when anxiety slips into our conscious awareness, we often avoid it through the use of _____.

   a. latency overcompensation
   b. the Oedipus complex
   c. regression to the oral stage
   d. defense mechanisms

4. During the _____ phase, the Oedipus complex is reportedly the major conflict in psychosexual development.

   a. oral            b. latent
   c. phallic         d. genital

5. Three of the most influential neo-Freudians were _____.

   a. Plato, Aristotle, and Descartes
   b. Dr. Laura, Dr. Phil, and Dr. Ruth
   c. Adler, Jung, and Horney
   d. None of these options

### Connections—Chapter to Chapter

Answering the following question will help you "look back and look ahead" to see the important connections among the subfields of psychology and chapters within this text.

In Chapter 14 (Psychological Disorders), you will learn about *personality disorders* (such as *borderline* and *antisocial personality disorders*). Using what you have learned about *personality* (general definition), explain how personality could become disordered or cause problems.

---

## 13.2   Trait Theories

### LEARNING OBJECTIVES

**Retrieval Practice**   While reading the upcoming sections, respond to each Learning Objective in your own words.

**Review the major concepts of the various trait theories.**

- **Explain** how early trait theorists approached the study of personality.

- **Describe** the Big Five personality traits.
- **Summarize** the major contributions and criticisms of trait theory.

When describing another's personality, we generally use terms that refer to that person's most typical and distinctive characteristics. As we mentioned earlier, Abraham Lincoln is remembered today in part for his distinctive characteristics of introversion and conscientiousness. But he also is known for his wonderful, self-effacing sense of humor. When accused of being two-faced, for instance, Lincoln quickly replied, "If I had two faces, do you think I'd be wearing *this* face?"

These examples of distinctive and defining characteristics are the foundation for the *trait approach*, which seeks to discover what characteristics form the core of human personality.

### Early Trait Theorists

**Trait**   A relatively stable personality characteristic that describes a pattern of thinking, feeling, and acting.

When early researchers began to investigate personality **traits**, they had to decide just what to include. An early study of dictionary terms found almost 4,500 words that fit the researchers' definition of personality traits (Allport & Odbert, 1936). Faced with this enormous list, Gordon Allport

(1937) believed that the best way to understand personality was to arrange a person's unique personality traits into a hierarchy, with the most pervasive or important traits at the top.

Later psychologists reduced the list of possible personality traits using a statistical technique called *factor analysis*, in which large arrays of data are grouped into more basic units (factors). Raymond Cattell (1950, 1990) condensed the list of traits to 16 source traits (see the **Try This Yourself**). Hans Eysenck (1967, 1990) reduced the list even further. He described personality as a relationship among three basic types of traits: *extraversion–introversion*, *neuroticism* (the tendency toward insecurity, anxiety, guilt, and moodiness), and *psychoticism* (being out of touch with reality).

**Five-factor model (FFM)** A model of personality traits that includes five basic dimensions: openness, conscientiousness, extraversion, agreeableness, and neuroticism; informally called the Big Five.

## Try This Yourself

### Constructing Your Own Personality Profile

Note how Cattell's 16 source traits exist on a continuum, from low to high. There are extremes at either end, such as reserved and less intelligent at the far left and outgoing and more intelligent at the far right. Average falls somewhere in the middle. To construct your own profile, add a dot on each line that represents your own degree of each personality trait, and then connect the dots with a line.

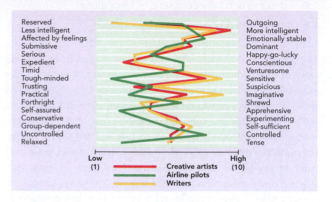

## Modern Trait Theory

Factor analysis was also used to develop the **five-factor model (FFM)**, which is the most promising modern trait theory (Costa & McCrae, 2011; McCrae, 2015; McCrae & Costa, 2013). A handy way to remember this model is to note that the first letters of the five words spell *ocean* (**Figure 13.8**).

Combining previous research findings and the long list of possible personality traits, researchers discovered that these five traits came up repeatedly, even when different tests were used:

**Openness** refers to people who are generally open to new ideas and experiences and willing to try new things. For instance, if you score high on this dimension, you probably enjoy talking with people with sharply different opinions because you realize that what the other person is saying may have value. People low on this trait generally like routine and prefer to maintain the status quo.

**Conscientiousness** applies to people who are typically highly organized, dependable, and careful about their belongings. If you are often late to class or social events, and commonly misplace things, you may be low on conscientiousness.

**Extraversion** refers to people who are generally outgoing, talkative, and assertive. In contrast, introversion describes individuals who tend to be retiring, quiet, and mild mannered. If you dislike being the center of attention and enjoy your time alone, you're probably more

**FIGURE 13.8** **The five-factor model (FFM)** Different adjectives may describe your personality, depending on whether you score high or low in each of the "Big Five" traits. Note that each factor exists on a continuum. If you'd like more details, take the five-factor online self-test at www.personalitytest.org.uk

| Big Five traits | High scorers | Low scorers |
|---|---|---|
| 1 **O**penness | Imaginative<br>Independent<br>Curious<br>Prefer variety | Practical<br>Conforming<br>Cautious<br>Prefer routine |
| 2 **C**onscientiousness | Organized<br>Dependable<br>Careful<br>Disciplined | Disorganized<br>Unreliable<br>Careless<br>Impulsive |
| 3 **E**xtraversion | Sociable<br>Talkative<br>Assertive<br>Prefer company | Retiring<br>Quiet<br>Mild-mannered<br>Prefer to be alone |
| 4 **A**greeableness | Soft-hearted<br>Trusting<br>Cooperative<br>Good natured | Ruthless<br>Suspicious<br>Competitive<br>Irritable |
| 5 **N**euroticism | Emotionally unstable<br>Anxious<br>Insecure<br>Self-pitying | Emotionally stable<br>Calm<br>Secure<br>Self-satisfied |

### Think Critically

1. Do you think these five factors accurately reflect your key personality traits? Why or why not?

2. Some have said that the first four factors are the "nice" traits. Under what conditions could scoring low on extraversion (being *introverted*) be advantageous?

## Myth Buster

### Misconceptions about Introversion and Extraversion

**True or False?**

1. Introverts don't like people and always want to be alone.

2. Introverts don't like to talk.

3. Introverts are shy.

4. Extraverts are bad listeners.

5. Extraverts are shallow.

6. Extraverts don't like quiet time or being alone.

7. You're either an introvert or an extravert.

Each of these statements is false (Cain, 2016; Laney, 2013; Tartakovsky, 2013). Introverts and extraverts just have differing ways of interacting with others and processing information. For example, introverts value people—particularly close friends—and while they're very comfortable being alone, introverts also crave authentic and sincere connections with a few others. Similarly, many believe introverts don't like to talk and are shy. In reality, they just avoid "small talk" and prefer to think about what they want to say before speaking. Furthermore, keep in mind that shyness and introversion are not the same. Unlike shy people, introverts are not necessarily afraid of others or of being judged by them. They just prefer less stimulating environments with fewer people.

Gary Morrow/EyeEm/Getty Images, Inc.

There are also several myths about extraversion. For instance, extraverts are sometimes mistakenly considered to be bad listeners or shallow because of their talkativeness and high sociability. While extraverts do like a certain amount of quiet time and being alone, they also enjoy socializing in large groups because they tend to process thoughts and information as they're speaking and interacting with others. In contrast, introverts process their thoughts and information through self-reflection.

Regarding the myth that you're either an introvert or an extravert, you've discovered throughout this text that most aspects of human nature fall on a continuum and that most people fall somewhere in the middle. Personality is like creativity, intelligence, and psychological disorders. We all have relative amounts of different traits. No one is either totally introverted or totally extraverted.

*I am rather inclined to silence, and whether that be wise or not, it is at least more unusual nowadays to find a man who can hold his tongue than to find one who cannot.*
—Abraham Lincoln

introverted. The reverse is true for someone who is extraverted. (As mentioned in the chapter opener, there are many myths about introversion and extraversion. To clarify these misunderstandings, check out the **Myth Busters**.)

**Agreeableness** describes a person's basic emotional style. Individuals who score high in this factor are typically easy going and pleasant to be around, whereas low scorers are often irritable and difficult to be around.

**Neuroticism (or *emotional stability*)** refers to an individual's emotional stability or instability. People who score high in neuroticism are generally anxious and moody, whereas low scorers tend to be calm and even-tempered.

The five-factor model (FFM) has led to numerous research follow-ups and intriguing insights about personality (Barceló, 2017; Choi & Shin, 2017; Suso-Ribera & Gallardo-Pujol, 2016). A recent large-scale study of profile photos on social media found several interesting correlations with the FFM (Liu et al., 2016). For instance, users high in agreeableness or extraversion tended to post colorful pictures of people that convey emotion, whereas people high in openness or neuroticism posted fewer photos of people.

Other studies indicate that these five personality traits are linked with real-world outcomes. Extraversion and neuroticism, for instance, are linked with greater procrastination (Kim et al., 2017). Researchers have also found that conscientiousness, agreeableness, and openness are reliable predictors for success, with conscientiousness being strongly linked with academic grade point average (GPA) (Rahafar et al., 2016; Steinmayr & Kessels, 2017; Vecchione et al., 2016). Based on your own college experience, can you see why this makes intuitive sense? How would you explain why extraversion does not positively correlate with GPA?

What about nonhuman animals? Do you think they have distinct personalities? If so, what implications might specific personality traits have? To find out, read the following **Research Challenge**.

## Research Challenge

### Do Nonhuman Animals Have Unique Personalities?

Pet owners have long believed that their dogs and cats have unique personalities, and a growing body of research tends to support these beliefs (Cote et al., 2014; Cussen & Mench, 2014; Gosling & John, 1999). The same is true of various animals, including macaques, bonobos, marmosets, orangutans, and chimpanzees (Adams et al., 2015; Iwanicki & Lehmann, 2015; Weiss et al., 2015; Wergård et al., 2016). Furthermore, chimpanzee personality traits have been found to be quite similar to those described by the FFM of human personality (Latzman et al., 2015). Research has even found evidence of personality traits in cockroaches (Planas-Sitjà et al., 2015)!

Dog lovers might be interested in knowing that when 78 dogs of all shapes and sizes were rated by both owners and strangers, a strong correlation was found in ratings on traits such as affection, aggression, anxiety, calmness, and intelligence. In addition, these researchers found that personalities vary widely within a breed, which means that not all pit bulls are aggressive and not all Labrador retrievers are affectionate (Gosling et al., 2004).

In one interesting study, researchers wanted to find out whether particular personality traits were associated with a longer life expectancy in nonhuman animals. These researchers studied 298 gorillas in zoos and sanctuaries across North America. Using standardized measures similar to the FFM, they asked zookeepers, volunteers, researchers, and caretakers who knew the gorillas well to score each gorilla's personality. With these scorings, they reliably identified four distinct personality traits: *dominance*, *extraversion*, *neuroticism*, and *agreeableness* (Weiss et al., 2013).

Next, the researchers examined the association between levels of each of these personality traits and life expectancy. They found that gorillas scoring high on extraversion, which included behaviors such as sociability, activity, play, and curiosity, lived longer. This link was found in both male and female gorillas and across all the different types of environments in which this research was conducted.

What might explain this link? One possibility is that extraverted apes—just like extraverted people—develop stronger social

Martin Harvey/Digital Vision/ Getty Images

networks, which helps increase survival and reduce stress. Can you think of other possible explanations?

**Test Yourself**

1. Based on the information provided, did this study (Weiss et al., 2013) use descriptive, correlational, and/or experimental research?

2. If you chose:
   - *descriptive research*, is this a naturalistic observation, survey/interview, case study, and/or archival research?
   - *correlational research*, is this a positive, negative, or zero correlation?
   - *experimental research*, label the IV, DV, experimental group(s), and control group. (Note: If participants were not randomly assigned to groups, list it as a *quasi-experimental design*.)
   - both *descriptive* and *correlational*, answer the corresponding questions for both.

**Check your answers by clicking on the answer button or by looking in Appendix B.**

**Note:** The information provided in this study is admittedly limited, but the level of detail is similar to what is presented in most textbooks and public reports of research findings. Answering these questions, and then comparing your answers to those provided, will help you become a better critical thinker and consumer of scientific research.

## Evaluating Trait Theories

The FFM is the first model to achieve the major goal of trait theory—to describe and organize personality characteristics using the smallest number of traits. There is also research support for the FFM. Psychologist David Buss and his colleagues (1989, 2008) surveyed more than 10,000 men and women from 37 countries and found a surprising level of agreement in the characteristics that men and women value in a mate (**Table 13.1**). Note that both sexes generally prefer mates with traits that closely match the FFM—dependability (conscientiousness), emotional stability (low neuroticism), pleasing disposition (agreeableness), and sociability (extraversion).

Why is there such a high degree of shared preferences for certain personality traits? Scientists suggest that these traits may provide an evolutionary advantage to people who are more conscientious, extraverted, and agreeable—and less neurotic. For instance, people who are conscientious have better health, which is clearly advantageous (Israel et al., 2014). The evolutionary advantage is also confirmed by cross-cultural studies and comparative studies with dogs, chimpanzees, and other highly social species (e.g., Carlo et al., 2014; Gosling, 2008; Valchev et al., 2014).

| TABLE 13.1 | Mate Preferences and the Five-Factor Model (FFM) | |
|---|---|---|
| **What Men Most Want in a Mate** | **What Women Most Want in a Mate** | |
| 1. Mutual attraction—love | 1. Mutual attraction—love | |
| 2. Dependable character | 2. Dependable character | |
| 3. Emotional stability and maturity | 3. Emotional stability and maturity | |
| 4. Pleasing disposition | 4. Pleasing disposition | |
| 5. Good health | 5. Education and intelligence | |
| 6. Education and intelligence | 6. Sociability | |
| 7. Sociability | 7. Good health | |
| 8. Desire for home and children | 8. Desire for home and children | |
| 9. Refinement, neatness | 9. Ambition and industriousness | |
| 10. Good looks | 10. Refinement, neatness | |

© Michelle Marsan/Shutterstock

**Source:** Based on Buss et al., 1990.

Along with having strong cross-cultural support, trait theories like the FFM allow us to predict real-life preferences and behaviors, such as our political attitudes, beliefs, and voting preferences, and even how much time we spend on Facebook (Bakker et al., 2016; Barceló, 2017; Hart et al., 2015). Furthermore, people who are extraverted have been found to prefer upbeat, energetic, and rhythmic types of music, such as rap and hip-hop. In contrast, people who are open to experience prefer complex, intense, and rebellious music, such as classical and rock (Langemeyer et al., 2012).

Despite their relative successes, critics argue that trait theories merely describe personality rather than explaining it. Moreover, they generally fail to consider situational determinants of personality or to offer sufficient explanations for why people develop specific traits (Chamorro-Premuzic, 2011; Cheung et al., 2011; Furguson et al., 2011). And although trait theories have shown personality to be fairly stable, they have failed to identify which characteristics last a lifetime and which are most likely to change (Carlo et al., 2014; Hosie et al., 2014; McCrae, 2011). Interestingly, research does show that certain stressful life events, such as being unemployed or experiencing natural disasters, can change our personalities (Boyce et al., 2015; Kandler et al., 2015; Milojev et al., 2014). Moreover, we can sometimes deliberately change our personalities if we have specific goals in mind (Hudson & Fraley, 2015). Would you like to be a more positive person and maybe change some parts of your own personality? See the following discussion.

## ❖ Psychology and Your Personal Success | Can (and Should) We Improve Our Personalities?

Have you ever admired the personalities of others and wished you could be more like them? The good news is that many personality traits can increase through training. In one study, researchers randomly divided 178 adults into three groups for a period of ten weeks (Proyer et al., 2013). One group focused on increasing the traits of "curiosity," "gratitude," "hope," "humor," and "zest." The second group trained on the strengths of "appreciation of beauty," "creativity," "kindness," "love of learning," and "perspective." The third group served as a control and did not complete any type of training.

People in the two treatment groups completed brief exercises at some point each day, such as writing a thank you letter (to practice gratitude) or paying attention to things they found beautiful in the world (to train their appreciation of beauty). As predicted, findings revealed that participants who focused on increasing traits such as curiosity, gratitude, and hope (Group 1) experienced greater life satisfaction at the end of the training sessions than those in the other two groups. In addition, both training groups reported greater well-being after the interventions concluded than did those in the control group.

Although this study suggests that we can change certain personality traits, keep in mind that psychologists only *describe* personality traits. We don't advise on what traits *should be changed*. That's for you as an individual to decide. Moreover, like beauty, personality traits are largely in the eye of the beholder. What traits people decide are preferable over others depends on the group, culture, and history.

For example, given our fast-paced, highly competitive society, you may think that to be successful you need to be an apparent extravert, like Stephen Colbert (see the photo). However, Colbert, Albert Einstein, Bill Gates, Meryl Streep, Lady Gaga, Selena Gomez, and Abraham Lincoln are all either self-described introverts or have been classified as introverts.

In short, before deciding to change your personality, note that almost all personality traits have both positive and negative characteristics. And, as mentioned earlier, all our traits exist on a continuum. No one is entirely extraverted nor always introverted.

Frederick M. Brown/Getty Images

**TV talk show host Stephen Colbert**   How would you describe his personality?

© Billy R. Ray/Wiley

## Retrieval Practice 13.2 | Trait Theories

Completing this self-test and the connections section, and then checking your answers by clicking on the answer button or by looking in Appendix B, will provide immediate feedback and helpful practice for exams.

### Self-Test

1. Briefly explain factor analysis.

2. What are the "Big Five" personality traits in the five-factor model?
   a. conscientiousness, openness, extraversion, agreeableness, and neuroticism
   b. shyness, conscientiousness, extraversion, agreeableness, and neuroticism
   c. shyness, conscientiousness, introversion, agreeableness, and neuroticism
   d. none of these options

3. People who score high in _____ are emotionally unstable and prone to insecurity, anxiety, guilt, worry, and moodiness.
   a. openness
   b. conscientiousness
   c. extraversion
   d. neuroticism

4. Trait theories of personality have been criticized for _____.
   a. failing to explain why people develop specific traits
   b. not including a large number of central traits
   c. failing to identify which traits last and which are transient
   d. not considering situational determinants of personality
   e. all but one of these options

5. Which of the following is NOT associated with the trait theories of personality?
   a. Cattell        b. Allport
   c. Rorschach      d. Eysenck

### Connections—Chapter to Chapter

Answering the following question will help you "look back and look ahead" to see the important connections among the subfields of psychology and chapters within this text.

In Chapter 3 (Stress and Health Psychology), you discovered that certain personality and individual differences directly affect how we cope with stress. Which characteristics of the five-factor model of personality are similar to the traits that may interact in a positive or negative way with stress, as identified in Chapter 3?

---

## 13.3 | Humanistic Theories

### LEARNING OBJECTIVES

**Retrieval Practice**   While reading the upcoming sections, respond to each Learning Objective in your own words.

**Summarize the major concepts of humanistic theories of personality.**

- **Discuss** the importance of self-actualization in humanistic theories.

- **Explain** why self-concept and unconditional positive regard are key aspects of Rogers's theory of personality.

- **Describe** how Maslow's hierarchy of needs affects personality.

- **Evaluate** the strengths and weaknesses of humanistic theories of personality.

Humanistic theories of personality emphasize each person's internal feelings, thoughts, and sense of basic worth. In contrast to Freud's generally negative view of human nature, humanists believe that people are naturally good (or, at worst, neutral) and that they possess a natural tendency toward **self-actualization**, the inborn drive to develop all their talents and capabilities.

According to this view, our personality and behavior depend on how we perceive and interpret the world, not on traits, unconscious impulses, or rewards and punishments. Humanistic psychology was developed largely by Carl Rogers and Abraham Maslow.

**Self-actualization** The humanistic term for the inborn drive to realize our full potential and to develop all our talents and capabilities.

## Rogers's Theory

**Self-concept** The image of oneself that develops from interactions with significant others and life experiences.

To psychologist Carl Rogers (1902–1987), the most important component of personality is our **self-concept**, the way we see and feel about ourselves. Rogers emphasized that mental health and adjustment reflect the degree of overlap (congruence) between our perceived real and ideal selves (see the following **Try This Yourself**). This self-perception is relatively stable over time and develops from our life experiences, particularly the feedback and perception of others.

© The New Yorker Collection 1996. Mike Twohy from cartoonbank.com. All Rights Reserved.

Why do some people develop negative self-concepts and poor mental health, such as the man in the cartoon? Rogers believed that such outcomes generally result from early childhood experiences with parents and other adults who make their love and acceptance *conditional* and contingent on the child's behaving in certain ways and expressing only certain feelings. Imagine being a child who is repeatedly told that your naturally occurring negative feelings and behaviors (which we all have) are totally unacceptable and unlovable. Can you see how your self-concept may become distorted? And why as an adult you might develop a closed, avoidant personality, always doubting the love and approval of others because they don't know "the real person hiding inside"?

To help children develop their fullest potential, Rogers cautioned that adults need to create an atmosphere of **unconditional positive regard**—love and acceptance with no "strings" (contingencies) attached (Ray & Jayne, 2016; Roth et al., 2016; Schneider et al., 2015). Interestingly, parents who engage in responsive caregiving, a form of unconditional positive regard, also tend to show this same pattern of behavior toward their spouses, which in turn leads to higher levels of relationship satisfaction (Millings et al., 2013). This suggests that unconditional positive regard is invaluable for all types of relationships.

**Unconditional positive regard** Rogers's term for love and acceptance with no "strings" (contingencies) attached.

---

## Try This Yourself

### Measuring Your Personal Self-concept

Stop for a moment and briefly describe yourself as you'd *ideally* like to be and as how you *actually* are. Now draw two circles, labeled "real self" and "ideal self," depicting how much your two perceived selves overlap.

**(a)** According to Carl Rogers, if your real self and ideal self are nearly the same, with considerable overlap in the two circles, you have *congruence* between your two "selves" and a positive self-concept.

**(b)** Unfortunately, many people have experienced negative life events and feedback from others that have led to negative self-concepts. In Rogers's view, poor mental health and personality maladjustment develop from a mismatch, or *incongruence*, between our ideal and real selves.

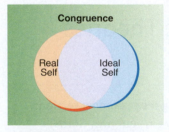

**a. Well-adjusted individual**
Considerable overlap between the ideal and real selves

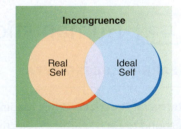

**b. Poorly adjusted individual**
Little overlap between the ideal and real selves

This is *not* to say that adults must approve of everything a child does. Rogers emphasizes that we must separate the value of the person from his or her behaviors—encouraging the person's innate positive nature, while discouraging destructive or hostile behaviors. Humanistic psychologists in general suggest that both children and adults must control their behavior so they can develop a healthy self-concept and satisfying relationships with others (**Figure 13.9**).

## Maslow's Theory

Like Rogers, Abraham Maslow believed there is a basic goodness to human nature and a natural tendency toward *self-actualization*—the inborn drive to develop all one's talents and capabilities (D'Souza & Gurin, 2016; Schneider et al., 2015; Winston et al., 2017). Maslow also saw personality development as a natural progression from lower to higher levels—a basic *hierarchy of needs* (Chapter 12). As newborns, we focus on physiological needs like hunger and thirst, and then as we grow and develop, we move on through four higher levels (**Figure 13.10**). Surveys from 123 countries found that people from around the world do share a focus on the same basic needs, and when those needs are met, they report higher levels of happiness (Tay & Diener, 2011).

According to Maslow, self-actualization requires understanding our own potential, accepting ourselves and others as unique individuals, and taking a problem-centered approach to life (Maslow, 1970). As an example, Abraham Lincoln accepted the fact that he didn't like hunting or farming very early in his life, and he understood that his way to get ahead would be through his mind, not through hard physical labor. So he became a largely self-educated man who constantly read throughout his entire lifetime.

Maslow believed that only a few rare individuals, such as Abraham Lincoln, Albert Einstein, Mohandas Gandhi, and Eleanor Roosevelt, become fully self-actualized. However, he saw self-actualization as part of every person's basic hierarchy of needs and as an ongoing process of growth rather than an end product or accomplishment.

David Laurens/PhotoAlto/Corbis

**FIGURE 13.9    Unconditional positive regard**
In response to a child who is angry and hits his or her younger sibling, the parent acknowledges that it is the behavior that is unacceptable, and not the child: "I know you're angry with your sister, but we don't hit. And you won't be able to play with her for a while unless you control your anger."

## Evaluating Humanistic Theories

Humanistic psychology was extremely popular during the 1960s and 1970s. It was seen as a refreshing new perspective on personality after the negative determinism of the psychoanalytic approach and the mechanical nature of learning theories (Chapter 6). Although this early popularity has declined, humanistic theories have provided valuable insights that are useful for personal growth and self-understanding. They likewise play a major role in contemporary counseling and psychotherapy, as well as in modern childrearing, education, and managerial practices (D'Souza & Gurin, 2016; Proctor et al., 2016; Schneider et al., 2015).

However, humanistic theories have been criticized (Berger, 2015; Henwood et al., 2014; Nolan, 2012) for the following:

1. **Naive assumptions** Some critics suggest that humanistic theories are unduly optimistic and overlook the negative aspects of human nature. They point out that Hitler was "self-actualized,"

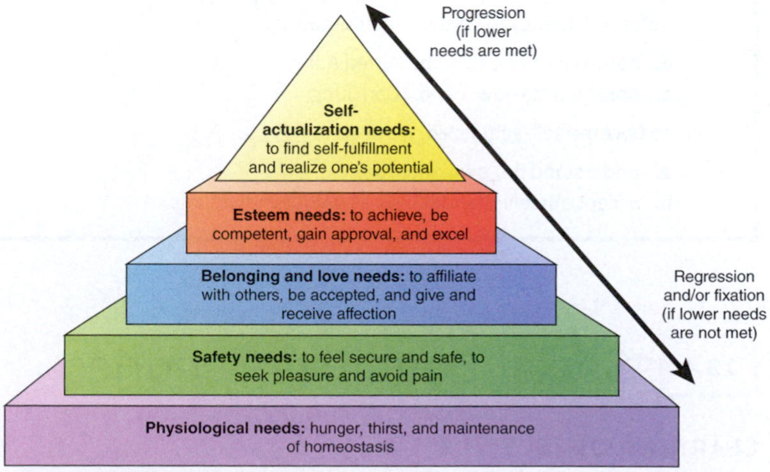

Progression
(if lower
needs are met)

**Self-actualization needs:** to find self-fulfillment and realize one's potential

**Esteem needs:** to achieve, be competent, gain approval, and excel

**Belonging and love needs:** to affiliate with others, be accepted, and give and receive affection

**Safety needs:** to feel secure and safe, to seek pleasure and avoid pain

**Physiological needs:** hunger, thirst, and maintenance of homeostasis

Regression
and/or fixation
(if lower needs
are not met)

**FIGURE 13.10    Maslow's hierarchy of needs**    Although our natural movement is upward from physical needs toward the highest level, *self-actualization*, Maslow believed we sometimes "regress" toward a lower level—especially under stressful conditions. For example, during national disasters, people first rush to stockpile food and water (physiological needs) and then often clamor for a strong leader to take over, enforce the rules, and make things right (safety needs).

was goal-driven, and believed he was fulfilling his potential. Furthermore, how would humanists explain deliberate mass genocide of large groups of people, horrific racist and terrorist attacks, and humankind's ongoing history of war and murder?

2. **Poor testability and inadequate evidence** Like many psychoanalytic terms and concepts, humanistic concepts such as unconditional positive regard and self-actualization are difficult to define operationally and to test scientifically. Furthermore, people sometimes overlook basic needs to pursue larger needs, such as by engaging in hunger strikes to protest political conditions. How does that fit into Maslow's hierarchy of needs?

3. **Narrowness** Like trait theories, humanistic theories have been criticized for merely describing personality rather than explaining it. To illustrate, where does the motivation for self-actualization come from? To say that it is an "inborn drive" doesn't satisfy those who favor using experimental research and scientific standards to study personality.

© Billy R. Ray/ Wiley

## Retrieval Practice 13.3 | Humanistic Theories

Completing this self-test and the connections section, and then checking your answers by clicking on the answer button or by looking in Appendix B, will provide immediate feedback and helpful practice for exams.

**Self-Test**

1. Describe the humanistic approach to personality theory.

2. Rogers suggested that _____ is necessary for a child to develop his or her fullest potential.

   a. authoritative parenting
   b. a challenging environment
   c. unconditional positive regard
   d. a friendly neighborhood

3. _____ believed in the basic goodness of individuals and their natural tendency toward self-actualization.

   a. Karen Horney       b. Alfred Adler
   c. Abraham Maslow     d. Carl Jung

4. To become self-actualized, we need to _____.

   a. understand our own potential
   b. accept ourselves and others as unique individuals

   c. take a problem-centered approach to life
   d. do all of these things

5. A major criticism of humanistic psychology is that most of its concepts and assumptions _____.

   a. are invalid
   b. are unreliable
   c. are naive
   d. lack a theoretical foundation

**Connections—Chapter to Chapter**

Answering the following question will help you "look back and look ahead" to see the important connections among the subfields of psychology and chapters within this text.

In Chapter 15 (Therapy), we will discuss client-centered therapy, which is based on Carl Rogers's humanistic theory of personality. According to Rogers, poor mental health and maladjustment develop from early childhood experiences with *conditional love* and *conditional acceptance*. How might a therapist create an experience of *unconditional positive regard* for such a client?

## 13.4 | Social-Cognitive Theories

### LEARNING OBJECTIVES

**Retrieval Practice**   While reading the upcoming sections, respond to each Learning Objective in your own words.

**Review the major concepts of social-cognitive theories of personality.**

• **Explain** Bandura's and Rotter's approaches to personality.

• **Summarize** the strengths and weaknesses of the social-cognitive perspective on personality.

As you've just seen, psychoanalytic/psychodynamic, trait, and humanistic theories all focus on internal, personal factors in personality development. In contrast, *social-cognitive* theories emphasize the influence of our *social* interpersonal interactions with the environment, along with our *cognitions*—our thoughts, feelings, expectations, and values.

## Bandura's and Rotter's Approaches

Albert Bandura (see Chapter 6) has played a major role in reintroducing thought processes into personality theory. Cognition, or thought, is central to his concept of **self-efficacy**, which is very similar to our everyday notion of self-confidence (Bandura, 1997, 2011; Herrero-Hahn et al., 2017). Abraham Lincoln's personality offers numerous examples of self-efficacy. He often self-confidently took the blame for others, shared credit for successes, and quickly conceded his errors. He also refused to bear grudges. Opponent Edwin Stanton called him a "long-armed ape" and deliberately shunned and humiliated him. However, when Lincoln needed a new War Secretary, he appointed Stanton because he considered Stanton the best man for this very important position (Goodwin, 2005).

According to Bandura, if you have a strong sense of self-efficacy, as Lincoln apparently did, you believe you can generally succeed and reach your goals, regardless of past failures and current obstacles. Your degree of self-efficacy will in turn affect which challenges you choose to accept and the effort you expend in reaching your goals (Bruning & Kauffman, 2016; Phan & Ngu, 2016). (See the **Try This Yourself**.) Interestingly, perceived self-efficacy in older adults is associated with better cognitive functions, and researchers suggest it might even help reduce stress and prevent cognitive decline (Korten et al., 2017).

How does self-efficacy affect personality? Bandura sees personality as being shaped by **reciprocal determinism**, which means that internal factors within the *person* (his or her personality, thoughts, expectations, etc.), the external *environment*, and the person's *behavior* all work as interacting (reciprocal) determinants of each other (**Figure 13.11**). Using Bandura's concept of self-efficacy, do you see how your own beliefs will affect how others respond to you and thereby influence your chance for success? Your belief ("I can succeed") will affect behaviors ("I'll work hard and ask for a promotion"), which in turn will affect the environment ("My employer recognized my efforts and promoted me").

**Self-efficacy**    Bandura's term for a person's learned expectation of success in a given situation; another term for self-confidence.

**Reciprocal determinism** Bandura's belief that internal personal factors, the environment, and the individual's behavior all work as interacting (reciprocal) determinants of each other.

---

## Try This Yourself

### Self-efficacy in Daily Life

The classic children's story *The Little Engine That Could* illustrates how we learn self-efficacy through our personal experiences with success. The little engine starts up a steep hill, saying, "I think I can, I think I can." After lots of hard work and perseverance, she ends up at the top of the hill and says, "I thought I could, I thought I could."

Bandura emphasized that self-efficacy is a *learned* expectation of success, but only in a given situation. It doesn't necessarily transfer to other circumstances. Bandura would suggest that the little engine's new-found self-efficacy will help her climb future hills. However, it wouldn't necessarily improve her overall speed or ability to turn sharp corners. Similarly, self-defense training significantly affects a woman's belief that she can improve her odds of escaping from or disabling a potential assailant or rapist. But it does not lead her to feel more capable in all areas of her life (Weitlauf et al., 2001).

How then can you transfer self-efficacy from one part of your academic or professional life to another? If you've experienced success as an athlete, a parent, or even a videogame player, consider how the skills you've demonstrated in these areas can be transferred to your academic life. Instead of saying, "I just can't find time to study" or "I never do well on tests," remind yourself of how your ongoing success in athletics, parenting, or videogames has resulted from good time management, hours of practice, patience, hard work, and perseverance. Applying skills that are the same as or similar to skills you've successfully used before will help move you from "I can't" to "I think I can." And then when you get your first high grade in a difficult course, you can move on to "I know I can, I know I can!"

*Courtesy of Lee Decker*

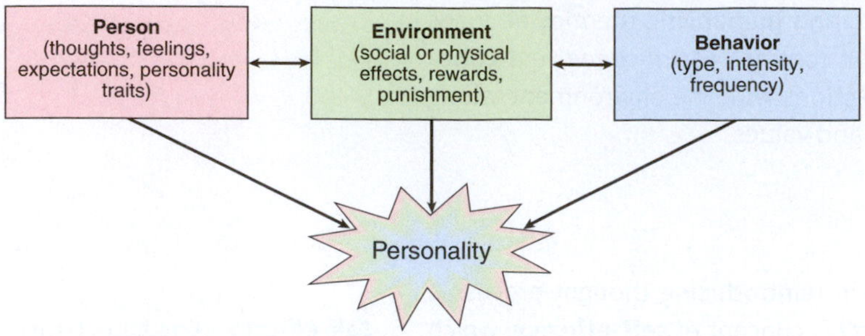

Person
(thoughts, feelings,
expectations, personality
traits)

Environment
(social or physical
effects, rewards,
punishment)

Behavior
(type, intensity,
frequency)

Personality

**FIGURE 13.11** **Bandura's theory of reciprocal determinism** According to Albert Bandura, personality is determined by a three-way, reciprocal interaction of the internal characteristics of the person, the external environment, and the person's behavior.

Julian Rotter's theory is similar to Bandura's in that it suggests that learning experiences create *cognitive expectancies* that guide behavior and influence the environment (Rotter, 1954, 1990). According to Rotter, your behavior or personality is determined by (1) what you expect to happen following a specific action and (2) the reinforcement value attached to specific outcomes.

To understand personality and behavior, Rotter used personality tests that measure internal versus external *locus of control* (Chapter 3). Rotter's tests ask participants to respond to statements such as, "People get ahead in this world primarily by luck and connections rather than by hard work and perseverance" and "When someone doesn't like you, there is little you can do about it." As you may suspect, people with an *external locus of control* think the environment and external forces have primary control over their lives, whereas people with an *internal locus of control* think they can personally control events in their lives through their own efforts (**Figure 13.12**).

## Evaluating Social-Cognitive Theories

The social-cognitive perspective holds several attractions. First, it offers testable, objective hypotheses and operationally defined terms, and it relies on empirical data. Second, social-cognitive theories emphasize the role of cognitive processes in personality and that both personality and situations predict behavior in real-world situations (Sherman et al., 2015). Relatedly, high school students who study abroad (thereby experiencing a change in environment) show greater changes in personality than those who do not (Hutteman et al., 2015). For instance, exchange students showed substantial increases in their self-esteem compared to those who stayed home (see the photo).

As we discussed earlier, there's a wealth of modern research connecting the Big Five personality traits to success in both work and academic settings, and these traits are closely related to the social-cognitive traits of self-efficacy and an internal locus of control. Furthermore, psychologist Carol Dweck has shown that our beliefs about our own abilities (*mindset*) influence how hard we try to achieve. For example, children who have a "fixed" mindset believe that intelligence is stable over time, so they aren't particularly motivated to try harder in school, since they believe such efforts won't really matter. In contrast, children who have a "growth" mindset believe that their efforts can make a difference, so they try harder in school, and, not surprisingly, perform better (Dweck, 2006, 2012; Yeager et al., 2016).

On the other hand, critics argue that social-cognitive theories focus too much on situational influences. They also suggest that this approach fails to adequately acknowledge the stability of personality, as well as sociocultural, emotional, unconscious, and biological influences (Ahmetoglu & Chamorro-Premuzic, 2013; Berger, 2015; Cea & Barnes, 2015). One of the most influential studies on the potential stability of personality traits is the now classic "marshmallow test"—the lead researcher, Walter Mischel, was even a guest on Stephen Colbert's *The Colbert Report*. For more information, see the following discussion.

Courtesy of Lee Decker

"The Self Esteem Seminar seems to have helped you."

Cartoon Resource/Shutterstock

**FIGURE 13.12** **Locus of control and achievement** Despite this cartoon's humorous message, research does link a perception of control with higher achievement, greater life satisfaction, and better overall mental health (e.g., Albert & Dahling, 2016; Nowicki, 2016).

## ❖ Psychology and Your Personal Success | Could You Pass the Stanford Marshmallow Test?

Beginning in the early 1960s and 1970s, psychologist Walter Mischel and his colleagues conducted numerous experiments on *delayed gratification*, which is defined as "putting off a pleasurable experience in exchange for a larger but later reward." In their most famous study, they recruited more than 600 children between the ages of 4 and 6 who attended a preschool at Stanford University (Mischel & Ebbesen, 1970). Each child was led into a room and seated alone at a table with a very tempting marshmallow within easy reach. They were then told they could eat the marshmallow at any time, but if they waited for 15 minutes, they would get two marshmallows. The child was then left alone, while the researchers watched and recorded how long each child would wait before giving into temptation. Can you imagine what happened? See **Figure 13.13**.

Courtesy of Lee Decker

**FIGURE 13.13**  **Psychology and marshmallows?**  Some children in this study quietly stared at the marshmallow while waiting for the experimenter to return. Others wiggled in their chairs, kicked at the table, smelled or petted the marshmallow, sang songs, or simply looked away—all in an attempt to resist temptation. And, as expected of preschoolers, a large number of children immediately ate the marshmallow as soon as the researcher left the room! Only a third of the preschoolers delayed gratification long enough to get the second marshmallow.

What makes this very simple research so compelling is that the researchers continued to study the children for more than 40 years—with dramatic results! The amount of time the children were able to delay eating the first marshmallow, and wait for the second one (delayed gratification), was a significant predictor of later success. Those who delayed gratification ended up with higher SAT scores, lower levels of substance abuse, lower likelihood of obesity, better responses to stress, greater academic performance and social skills as reported by their parents, and generally better scores in a range of other life measures (Caleza et al., 2016; Mischel, 1966, 2014; Mischel et al., 2011).

There are two important things to remember about this marshmallow study. First, it clearly illustrates the value of longitudinal research (**Figure 13.14**). Second, keep in mind that at every stage of our lives there will be numerous "marshmallows"—a fun party versus studying, an attractive new sexual partner versus our current one, a new car versus saving for retirement—that will potentially distract us from our long-term goals and personal best interests. The "simple" answer appears to be that when faced with critical decisions we need to continually make mindful choices. If you'd like more information on the importance of self-control and delay of gratification with numerous practical applications, see Mischel's book *The Marshmallow Test* (Mischel, 2014).

**FIGURE 13.14**  Interestingly, the spouse of one of the authors of this book (CAS) was one of the original participants in the marshmallow study, and the researchers have continued to follow up with him—and his wife and children. As evidence of psychology's strict ethical guidelines for research, even now, over 40 years later, the researchers will not disclose whether or not the author's husband ate the marshmallow!

© Billy R. Ray/ Wiley

## 13.5 | Biological Theories

**LEARNING OBJECTIVES**

**Retrieval Practice** While reading the upcoming sections, respond to each Learning Objective in your own words.

**Summarize the role that biology plays in personality.**

• **Discuss** how brain structures, neurochemistry, and genetics influence personality.

• **Explain** the contributions and limitations of biological theories.

• **Describe** how the biopsychosocial model blends various approaches to personality.

In this section, we explore how biological factors influence our personalities. We conclude with a discussion of how all theories of personality ultimately interact in the *biopsychosocial model*.

## Three Major Contributors to Personality

Hans Eysenck, the trait theorist mentioned earlier in the chapter, was one of the first to propose that personality traits are biologically based—at least in part. And modern research supports the theory that certain brain structures, neurochemistry, and genetics all may contribute to some personality characteristics (e.g., Boyle et al., 2016).

**Brain Structures** How do we decide in the real world which risks are worth taking and which are not (see the photo)? Modern research using functional magnetic resonance imaging (fMRI) and other brain-mapping techniques documents specific areas of the brain that correlate with trait impulsiveness and areas that differ between people with risk-averse versus risk-seeking personalities (Rass et al., 2016; Schilling et al., 2014). Research has also found that increased electroencephalographic (EEG) activity in the left frontal lobe of the brain is associated with sociability or extraversion, whereas greater EEG activity in the right frontal lobes is associated with shyness and introversion (Fishman & Ng, 2013; Tellegen, 1985).

**Neurochemistry** A major limitation of research on brain structures and personality is the difficulty of identifying which structures are uniquely connected with particular personality traits. Neurochemistry seems to offer more precise data on how biology influences personality. For example, sensation seeking (Chapter 12) has consistently been linked with high levels of monoamine oxidase (MAO), an enzyme that regulates levels of neurotransmitters such as dopamine (Trofimova & Robbins, 2016; Zuckerman, 1994, 2004, 2014). Likewise, dopamine seems to be correlated with addictive personality traits, novelty seeking, and extraversion (Blum et al., 2013; Harris et al., 2015; Norbury & Husain, 2015; Schilling et al., 2014).

How can neurochemistry have such effects? Studies suggest that high-sensation seekers and extraverts generally experience less physical arousal than introverts from the same stimulus (Fishman & Ng, 2013; Munoz & Anastassiou-Hadjicharalambous, 2011). Extraverts' low arousal apparently motivates them to seek out situations that will elevate their arousal. Moreover, it is believed that a higher arousal threshold is genetically transmitted. In other words, personality traits like sensation seeking and extraversion may be inherited. Our genes may also predict how we parent and even possible criminal behaviors, including arrest records (Armstrong et al., 2014; Klahr & Burt, 2014; van den Berg et al., 2016).

**Behavioral genetics** The study of the relative effects of heredity and the environment on behavior and mental processes.

**Genetics** This recognition that genetic factors have a significant influence on personality has contributed to the relatively new field called **behavioral genetics**, which attempts to determine the extent to which behavioral differences among people are due to genetics as opposed to the environment (Chapter 9). One interesting study found that individuals with a "niceness gene" were more likely to report engaging in various types of prosocial behaviors, such as giving blood, volunteering, and donating to charitable organizations (Poulin et al., 2012).

One way to measure genetic influences is to compare similarities in personality between identical twins and fraternal twins (see **Figure 13.15**). Twin studies of the FFM, for example, suggest

**FIGURE 13.15** **Identical versus fraternal twins**

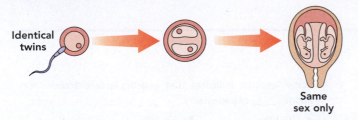

**a. Identical twins** Identical (*monozygotic*—one egg) twins share 100% of the same genes because they develop from a single egg fertilized by a single sperm. They also share the same placenta and are always the same sex.

**b. Fraternal twins** Fraternal (*dizygotic*—two eggs) twins share, on average, 50% of their genes because they are formed when two separate sperm fertilize two separate eggs. Although they share the same general environment within the womb, they are no more genetically similar than non-twin siblings. They're simply nine-month "womb mates."

that genetic factors account for about 40 to 50% of personality traits (Bouchard, 1997, 2013; McCrae et al., 2010; Plomin et al., 2016).

In addition to conducting twin studies, researchers compare the personalities of parents with those of their biological children and their adopted children (see **Figure 13.16**). Studies of extraversion and neuroticism have found that parents' traits correlate moderately with those of their biological children and hardly at all with those of their adopted children (Bouchard, 1997; McCrae et al., 2000).

## Evaluating Biological Theories

Modern research in biological theories has provided exciting insights and established clear links between some personality traits and various brain areas, neurotransmitters, and genes. However, researchers are careful to emphasize that personality traits are never the result of a single biological process (Cicchetti, 2016; Latzman et al., 2015; Turkheimer et al., 2014). Some believe the importance of the unshared environment—aspects of the environment that differ from one individual to another, even within a family—has been overlooked. Others fear that research on "genetic determinism" could be misused to "prove" that an ethnic or a racial group is inferior, that male dominance is natural, or that social progress is impossible.

In sum, there is no doubt that biological studies have produced valuable results. However, as is true for all the theories discussed in this chapter, no single theory explains everything we need to know about personality. Each theory offers different insights into how a person develops the distinctive set of characteristics we call "personality." That's why, instead of adhering to any one theory, many psychologists believe in the *biopsychosocial approach*, or the idea that several factors—biological, psychological, and social—overlap in their contributions to personality (**Figure 13.17**).

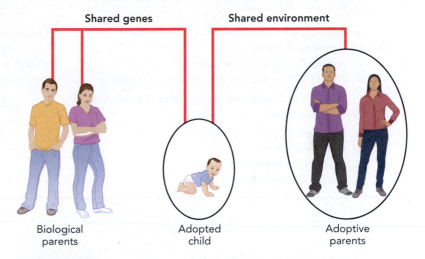

**FIGURE 13.16** **Adoption studies** If adopted children are more like their biological family in some trait, then genetic factors probably had the greater influence. Conversely, if adopted children resemble their adopted family, even though they do not share similar genes, then environmental factors may predominate.

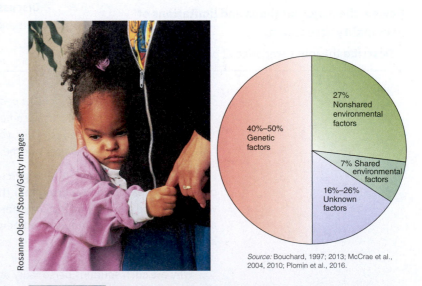

*Source:* Bouchard, 1997; 2013; McCrae et al., 2004, 2010; Plomin et al., 2016.

**FIGURE 13.17** **Multiple influences on personality** Research has identified three important influences on personality that might contribute to this child's apparent shyness. Still, some factors remain unknown.

© Billy R. Ray/ Wiley

## Retrieval Practice 13.5 | Biological Theories

Completing this self-test and the connections section, and then checking your answers by clicking on the answer button or by looking in Appendix B, will provide immediate feedback and helpful practice for exams.

### Self-Test

1. Discuss Hans Eysenck's contribution to theories of personality.

2. Dopamine is reportedly involved in the personality traits of _____.

   a. conscientiousness, extraversion, and altruism
   b. extraversion and neuroticism
   c. impulsivity, aggression, and altruism
   d. novelty seeking, extraversion, and sensation seeking

3. _____ theories emphasize the importance of genetics in the development of personality.

   a. Behavioral genetics
   b. Behavioral metrics
   c. Social/personal genetics
   d. Biometrical engineering

4. Some research indicates that genetic factors account for about _____ of personality.

   a. 10–12%        b. 12–25%
   c. 25–38%        d. 40–50%

5. Which approach represents a blending of several theories of personality?

   a. Inherited basis     b. Biopsychosocial
   c. Social/overlap      d. None of these options

### Connections—Chapter to Chapter

Answering the following question will help you "look back and look ahead" to see the important connections among the subfields of psychology and chapters within this text.

In Chapter 2 (Neuroscience and Biological Foundations), we discussed the role of different neurotransmitters in behavior and biological processes. In this chapter, you learned that personality has a biological component. Explain how neurochemistry may be involved in a personality characteristic such as sensation seeking or impulsivity.

## 13.6    Personality Assessment

### LEARNING OBJECTIVES

**Retrieval Practice**    While reading the upcoming sections, respond to each Learning Objective in your own words.

**Review the major methods and limitations of personality assessment.**

• **Describe** the four categories of personality assessment.

• **Explain** the key benefits and limitations of personality assessment.

• **Discuss** the logical fallacies associated with pseudo-personality assessment.

*You have a strong need for other people to like and admire you. You tend to be critical of yourself. Although you have some personality weaknesses, you are generally able to compensate for them. At times, you have serious doubts about whether you have made the right decision or done the right thing.*    —Adapted from Ulrich et al., 1963

Does this sound like you? A high percentage of research participants who read a similar personality description reported that the description was "very accurate"—even after they were informed that it was a *phony* horoscope (Hyman, 1981). Other research shows that about three-quarters of adults read newspaper horoscopes and that many of them believe astrological horoscopes were written especially for them (Sugarman et al., 2011; Wyman & Vyse, 2008).

Why are such spurious personality assessments so popular? One reason is that they seem to tap into our unique selves. Supporters of these horoscopes, however, ignore the fact that the traits they supposedly reveal are characteristics that almost everyone shares. Do you know anyone who doesn't "have a strong need for other people to like and admire" them?

Like this phony horoscope, a variety of other unscientific methods have been used over the years to assess personality (**Figure 13.18**). Even today, some people consult fortune-tellers, tarot cards, and fortune cookies in Chinese restaurants. But scientific research has provided much more reliable and valid methods for measuring personality (Berger, 2015; Dana, 2014). Clinical and counseling psychologists, psychiatrists, and other helping professionals use these modern methods to help with the diagnosis of patients and to assess their progress in therapy. Personality assessments can be grouped into a few broad categories: *interviews*, *observation*, *objective tests*, and *projective tests*.

## Interviews and Observation

We all use informal "interviews" to get to know other people. When first meeting someone, we usually ask about his or her job, academic interests, family, or hobbies. Psychologists also use interviews. In an unstructured format, interviewers get impressions and pursue hunches or let the interviewee expand on information that promises to disclose personality characteristics. In structured interviews, the interviewer asks specific questions in order to evaluate the interviewee's responses more objectively and compare them with others' responses.

Along with conducting interviews, psychologists also assess personality by directly and methodically observing behavior. They look for examples of specific behaviors and follow a careful set of evaluation guidelines. For instance, a psychologist might arrange to observe a troubled client's interactions with his or her family. Does the client become agitated by the presence of certain family members and not others? Does he or she become passive and withdrawn when asked a direct question? Through careful observation, the psychologist gains valuable insights into the client's personality as well as family dynamics (**Figure 13.19**).

As a further complement to face-to-face observations, psychologists have used social media outlets—such as Facebook—to observe personality. For instance, thanks to social media postings, selfies, "likes," and other responses, researchers can now study and sometimes predict a number of personality characteristics and attributes, including self-efficacy, FFM traits, sexual orientation, ethnicity, religious and political views, intelligence, happiness, use of addictive substances, parental separation, age, and gender (e.g., Choi & Shin, 2017; Hong et al., 2017; Kosinski et al., 2013). If you'd like to learn more about how Facebook posts can be used to predict your own personality, here's a link: https://applymagicsauce.com/demo.html.

## Objective Tests

*Objective personality tests*, or inventories, are the most widely used method of assessing personality, for two reasons: They can be administered to a large number of people relatively quickly, and they can be evaluated in a standardized fashion. Some objective tests measure one specific personality trait, such as sensation seeking (Chapter 12) or locus of control. However, psychologists in clinical, counseling, and industrial settings often wish to assess a range of personality traits. To do so, they generally use multi-trait, *multiphasic*, inventories.

The most widely researched and clinically used self-report method of personality assessment is the **Minnesota Multiphasic Personality Inventory (MMPI)**—or its revisions, the MMPI-2 and the MMPI-2-RF (Butcher, 2000, 2011; Chmielewski et al., 2017; Williams & Lally, 2016). The latest version, the MMPI-2-RF, consists of 338 statements. Participants respond with True, False, or Cannot Say. The following are examples of the kinds of statements found on the MMPI:

My stomach frequently bothers me.

I have enemies who really wish to harm me.

I sometimes hear things that other people can't hear.

I would like to be a mechanic.

I have never indulged in any unusual sex practices.

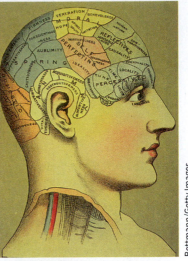

**FIGURE 13.18** **Personality and bumps on the head?**   In the 1800s, if you wanted to have your personality assessed, you would go to a phrenologist, who would determine your personality by measuring the bumps on your skull. The phrenologist would then compare those measurements with a chart that associated different areas of the skull with particular traits, such as *sublimity* (ability to squelch natural impulses, especially sexual) and *ideality* (ability to live by high ideals). What traits might be measured if we still believed in phrenology today?

**Minnesota Multiphasic Personality Inventory (MMPI)** The most widely researched and clinically used self-report method of personality assessment; originally designed to reveal abnormal personality traits and behaviors, it's also used for various screening purposes.

**FIGURE 13.19** **Behavioral observation**   How might careful observation help a psychologist better understand a troubled client's personality and family dynamics?

Did you notice that some of these questions are about very unusual, abnormal behavior? Although there are many "normal" questions on the full MMPI, the test was originally designed to reveal abnormal personality traits and behaviors, and it's currently used to help clinical and counseling psychologists diagnose psychological disorders. The MMPI is also sometimes employed for various screening purposes, such as in hiring decisions and forensic settings.

Other objective personality measures are less focused on abnormal personality traits. A good example is the NEO Personality Inventory–Revised, which assesses the dimensions of the five-factor model.

Note that personality tests like the MMPI are often confused with *career inventories*, or vocational interest tests. Career counselors use these latter tests (along with aptitude and achievement tests) to help people identify occupations and careers that match their unique traits, abilities, and interests.

## Projective Tests

**Projective test** A method of personality assessment that uses a standardized set of ambiguous stimuli, such as inkblots or abstract drawings, which allow test takers to "project" their underlying motives, conflicts, and personality traits onto the test materials.

**Rorschach Inkblot Test** The most widely used projective personality test, which is based on test takers' projections onto 10 inkblots.

**Thematic Apperception Test (TAT)** A projective personality test based on the stories test takers make up about ambiguous scenes.

Unlike objective tests, **projective tests** use ambiguous stimuli that people can perceive in many ways. When you listen to a piece of music or look at a picture, you might say that the music is sad or that the people in the picture look happy—but not everyone would have the same interpretation. Some psychologists believe that these different interpretations reveal important things about each individual's personality.

As the name implies, projective tests are meant to allow test takers to "project" their underlying motives, conflicts, and personality traits onto the test materials. Because respondents may be unable or unwilling to express their true feelings if asked directly, the ambiguous stimuli reportedly provide an indirect "psychological X-ray" of unconscious processes (Hogan, 2013). The **Rorschach Inkblot Test** and **Thematic Apperception Test (TAT)** are two of the most widely used projective tests (Cashel, 2016; Silverstein, 2013). See **Concept Organizer 13.1**.

---

**CONCEPT ORGANIZER 13.1**    **Sample Projective Tests**    The verbal or written responses participants make to projective tests reportedly reflect unconscious, hidden parts of their personalities that they unintentionally "project" onto the stimuli.

**STOP!** This Concept Organizer contains essential information NOT found elsewhere in the text, which is likely to appear on quizzes and exams. Be sure to study it CAREFULLY!

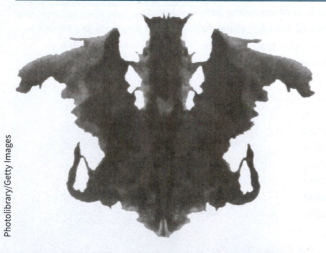

Photolibrary/Getty Images

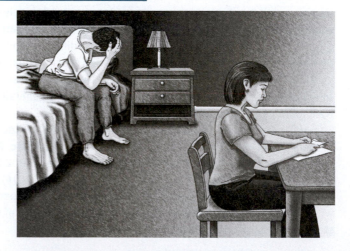

**a. Rorschach Inkblot Test**    This is one of many examples of the "inkblot" test first introduced in 1921 by Swiss psychiatrist Hermann Rorschach. Test takers are shown 10 inkblots like the one shown here, one at a time, and are asked to report what figures or objects they see in each of them.

**b. Thematic Apperception Test (TAT)**    Created by personality researcher Henry Murray in 1938, this test consists of a series of ambiguous black-and-white pictures, like this one, that are shown to the test taker, who is asked to create a story related to each one.

# Evaluating Personality Assessments

Let's evaluate the strengths and the challenges of each of the four methods of personality assessment: *interviews*, *observations*, *objective tests*, and *projective tests*.

**Interviews and Observations**   Both interviews and observations can provide valuable insights into personality, but they are time-consuming and expensive. Furthermore, raters of personality tests frequently disagree in their evaluations of the same individuals. Interviews and observations also take place in unnatural settings. In fact, the very presence of an observer can alter a person's behavior. For example, can you recall a time when you were nervous in a job interview and didn't act quite the same as you would have in a more relaxed setting?

**Objective Tests**   Tests like the MMPI-2 provide specific, objective information about a broad range of personality traits in a relatively short period. However, they are subject to at least three major criticisms:

1. **Problems with self-reports**  Some items on personality inventories are easy to see through, so respondents may fake particular personality traits. In addition, some respondents want to look good and will answer questions in ways that they perceive are socially desirable. For instance, people might try to come across as less hostile and more kind to others in their responses to some test items. Interestingly, self-report data among some groups can also be misleading because the respondents do not see themselves accurately. As an example, narcissists typically have an excessive form of self-love and overevaluate their performance (Guedes, 2017).

   To avoid these problems, the MMPI-2 has built-in validity scales. Furthermore, personality researchers and some businesses avoid self-reports. Instead, they rely on other people, such as friends or coworkers, to rate individuals' personalities, as well as how their personalities influence their work performance (Connelly & Hülsheger, 2012). In fact, three meta-analyses, involving over 44,000 participants, found that ratings from others were better predictors of actual behavior, academic achievement, and job performance than those based on self-reports (Connelly & Ones, 2010).

2. **Diagnostic difficulties**  When self-report inventories are used for diagnosis, overlapping items sometimes make it difficult to pinpoint a disorder (Ben-Porath, 2013; Hogan, 2013; Hunsley et al., 2015). Clients with severe disorders sometimes score within the normal range, and normal clients sometimes score within the elevated range (Borghans et al., 2011; Morey, 2013). Furthermore, one study found that computer-based tests were more accurate at determining someone's personality than those delivered by humans (Youyou et al., 2015).

3. **Cultural bias and inappropriate use**  Some critics think the standards for "normalcy" on objective tests fail to recognize the impact of culture (Dana, 2014; Geisinger & McCormick, 2013; Malgady et al., 2014). To illustrate, research examining personality traits in members of the Tsimané culture, a community of foragers and farmers in Bolivia with relatively little contact with the outside world, reveals two distinct dimensions of personality—prosociality and industriousness—instead of the more widely accepted five personality traits (Gurven et al., 2013).

   Differences in personality may also be seen in different parts of a single country (Rentfrow, 2014). For example, one study of over half a million people in the United States revealed regional differences in personality traits linked with entrepreneurial activity, defined as business-creation and self-employment rates (Obschonka et al., 2013). As you can see in **Figure 13.20**, certain regions are much more entrepreneurial than others. Why? The authors of the study suggest that the higher scores in the West, for example, might reflect America's historical migration patterns of people moving into the West from the East (or from outside of America). They cite other research (e.g., Rentfrow et al., 2008) that suggests this selective migration may have had a lasting effect on personality due to the heritability of personality traits and the passing on of norms and values within the regions.

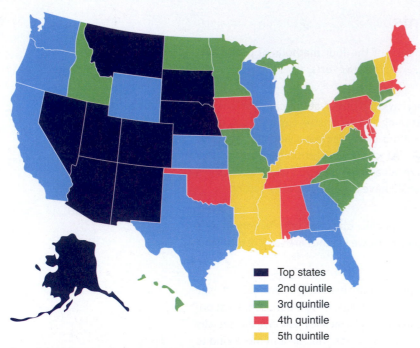

- ■ Top states
- ■ 2nd quintile
- ■ 3rd quintile
- ■ 4th quintile
- ■ 5th quintile

Copyright ©2013 by the American Psychological Association. Reproduced with permission. Obschonka, et al. The regional distribution and correlates of an entrepreneurship-prone personality profile in the United States, Germany, and the United Kingdom: A socioecological perspective. Journal of Personality and Social Psychology, Vol 105(1), Jul 2013, 104–122. The use of APA information does not imply endorsement by APA.

**FIGURE 13.20** **Entrepreneurship in the United States**

What do you think? How would you explain the differences? Can you see the overall value of expanding our study of personality from just looking at differences between individuals to examining regional differences? And can you see how this expansion might increase our understanding of how personality is formed and its potential applications? If you're interested in seeing how personality research can be applied to your career choice, see the following.

## ❖ Psychology and Your Professional Success | Should You Match Your Personality with Your Career?

As mentioned earlier, the FFM traits of conscientiousness, agreeableness, and openness are clearly linked with job success. But what about other factors, such as job satisfaction? Do some personality characteristics make you better suited for certain jobs than others? According to psychologist John Holland's *personality–job fit theory*, a match (or "good fit") between our individual personality and our career choice is a major factor in determining job satisfaction (Holland, 1985, 1994). Research shows that a good fit between personality and occupation helps increase subjective well-being, job success, and job satisfaction. In other words, people are generally happier and like their work when they're well matched to their jobs (Hagmann-von Arx et al., 2016; Joeng et al., 2013; Sundstrom et al., 2016). Check **Table 13.2** to see what job would be a good match for your personality.

**TABLE 13.2**

| Personality Characteristics | Holland Personality Type | Matching/Congruent Occupations |
|---|---|---|
| Shy, genuine, persistent, stable, conforming, practical | 1. *Realistic:* Prefers physical activities that require skill, strength, and coordination | Mechanic, drill press operator, assembly-line worker, farmer |
| Analytical, original, curious, independent | 2. *Investigative:* Prefers activities that involve thinking, organizing, and understanding | Biologist, economist, mathematician, news reporter |
| Sociable, friendly, cooperative, understanding | 3. *Social:* Prefers activities that involve helping and developing others | Social worker, counselor, teacher, clinical psychologist |
| Conforming, efficient, practical, unimaginative, inflexible | 4. *Conventional:* Prefers rule-regulated, orderly, and unambiguous activities | Accountant, bank teller, file clerk, manager |
| Imaginative, disorderly, idealistic, emotional, impractical | 5. *Artistic:* Prefers ambiguous and unsystematic activities that allow creative expression | Painter, musician, writer, interior decorator |
| Self-confident, ambitious, energetic, domineering | 6. *Enterprising:* Prefers verbal activities with opportunities to influence others and attain power | Lawyer, real estate agent, public relations specialist, small business manager |

**Source:** Adapted and reproduced with special permission of the publisher, Psychological Assessment Resources, Inc., 16204 North Florida Avenue, Lutz, Florida 33549, from the *Dictionary of Holland Occupational Codes*, 3rd edition, by Gary D. Gottfredson, Ph.D., and John L. Holland, Ph.D., Copyright 1982, 1989, 1996. Further reproduction is prohibited without permission from PAR, Inc.

## Projective Tests

Although projective tests are extremely time-consuming to administer and interpret, their proponents say that because the method is unstructured, respondents may be more willing to talk honestly about sensitive topics. Critics point out, however, that the *reliability* and *validity* of projective tests is among the lowest of all tests of personality (Hartmann & Hartmann, 2014; Hunsley et al., 2015; Koocher et al., 2014). (Recall from Chapter 8 that reliability—the consistency of test results—and validity—whether the test actually measures what it was designed to measure—are essential criteria for a good test.)

As you can see, each of these methods has limits, which is why psychologists typically combine the results from various scientific methods to create a fuller picture of any individual's personality. However, you're unlikely to have access to this type of professional analysis, so what's the most important take-home message? Beware of pop-psych books and pop-culture personality quizzes in magazines and on websites! They may be entertaining, but they're rarely based on standardized testing or scientific research of any kind, and you should never base decisions on their input.

Finally, throughout this text, we have emphasized the value of critical thinking, and it's particularly useful in evaluating personality tests (see the **Try This Yourself**).

---

## Try This Yourself

### What's Wrong with Pseudo-Personality Quizzes?

The phony personality horoscope presented earlier in this section contains several logical fallacies. Using your critical thinking skills, can you see how the following three factors help explain why so many people believe in fake personality descriptions and predictions?

### Barnum Effect

We often accept phony personality descriptions and horoscope predictions because we think they are accurate. We generally believe these tests have somehow tapped into our unique selves. In fact, they are ambiguous, broad statements that fit just about anyone (e.g., "You have a strong need for other people to like and admire you"). The existence of such generalities led to the term the *Barnum effect*, named for the legendary circus promoter P. T. Barnum, who said, "Always have a little something for everyone" (Wyman & Vyse, 2008).

### Confirmation Bias

Look again at the introductory personality profile and count the number of times you agree with the statements. According to the *confirmation bias* (Chapter 8), we tend to notice and remember events that confirm our expectations and ignore those that are nonconfirming (Dibbets & Meesters, 2017; Digdon, 2017; Kukucka & Kassin, 2014). If we see ourselves as independent thinkers, for example, we ignore the "needing to be liked by others" part.

### Self-Serving Biases

Now check the overall tone of the bogus personality profile. Do you see how the traits are generally positive and flattering—or at least neutral? According to several *self-serving biases*, we typically maximize the positivity of our self-view by preferring information that maintains our positive self-image (Sanjuán & Magallares, 2014; Sedkides & Alicke, 2012). In fact, research shows that the more favorable a personality description is, the more people believe it, and the more likely they are to believe it is personally unique (Guastello et al., 1989).

### Snapshots

Jason Love/CartoonStock

CartoonStock.com

Taken together, these three logical fallacies help explain the common support for pop-psych personality tests and newspaper horoscopes. They offer something for everyone (*Barnum effect*). We pay attention only to what confirms our expectations (*confirmation bias*). And we like flattering descriptions (*self-serving biases*).

### Think Critically

Using the information in this *Try This Yourself*, can you identify the two major fallacies in this cartoon?

**Answer:** self-serving biases and the Barnum effect.

© Billy R. Ray/Wiley

## Retrieval Practice 13.6 | Personality Assessment

Completing this self-test and the connections section, and then checking your answers by clicking on the answer button or by looking in Appendix B, will provide immediate feedback and helpful practice for exams.

### Self-Test

1. What is phrenology?

2. The most widely researched and clinically used self-report personality test is the _____.

   **a.** MMPI      **b.** Rorschach Inkblot Test
   **c.** TAT      **d.** SVII

3. During a(n) _____, individuals are asked to respond to a standardized set of ambiguous stimuli.

   **a.** projective test      **b.** objective test
   **c.** MMPI exam      **d.** phrenology exam

4. The Rorschach Inkblot Test is an example of which of the following?

   **a.** Projective
   **b.** Ambiguous stimuli

   **c.** Inkblot
   **d.** All these options

5. Two essential criteria for evaluating the usefulness of tests used to assess personality are _____.

   **a.** concurrence and prediction
   **b.** reliability and validity
   **c.** consistency and correlation
   **d.** diagnosis and prognosis

### Connections—Chapter to Chapter

Answering the following question will help you "look back and look ahead" to see the important connections among the subfields of psychology and chapters within this text.

> In Chapter 8 (Thinking, Language, and Intelligence), we explored how intelligence is measured. In this chapter, we examined how personality is assessed. How are the two methods of assessment most similar, and how are they primarily different?

---

### Study Tip

*The WileyPLUS program that accompanies this text provides for each chapter a* Media Challenge, Critical Thinking Exercise, *and* Application Quiz. *This set of study materials provides additional, invaluable study opportunities. Be sure to check it out!*

# Chapter Summary

## 13.1 Psychoanalytic/Psychodynamic Theories 423

- **Personality** is defined as our unique and relatively stable pattern of thoughts, feelings, and actions.

- Freud, the founder of psychodynamic theory, believed that the mind contained three *levels of consciousness*: conscious, preconscious, and **unconscious**. He proposed that most psychological disorders originate from unconscious memories and instincts.

- Freud also asserted that personality was composed of the **id**, **ego**, and **superego**. When the ego fails to satisfy both the id and the superego, anxiety slips into conscious awareness, which triggers **defense mechanisms**.

- Freud believed that all children go through five **psychosexual stages**: oral, anal, phallic, latency, and genital. How specific conflicts at each of these stages are resolved is supposedly important to personality development.

- *Neo-Freudians* such as Adler, Jung, and Horney were influential followers of Freud who later rejected major aspects of Freudian theory. Adler emphasized the inferiority complex and the compensating will-to-power. Jung introduced the **collective unconscious** and **archetypes**. Horney stressed the importance of basic anxiety and refuted Freud's idea of penis envy, replacing it with power envy.

- Critics of the psychoanalytic approach, especially Freud's theories, argue that the approach lacks adequate empirical support, overemphasizes sexuality, biology, and unconscious forces, and is sexist. Despite these criticisms, Freud remains a notable pioneer in psychology.

### Test Your Critical Thinking

**1.** If scientists have so many problems with Freud, why do you think his theories are still popular with the public? Should psychologists continue to discuss his theories (and include them in textbooks)?

**2.** What is a possible example of sexism in Freud's psychoanalytic theory?

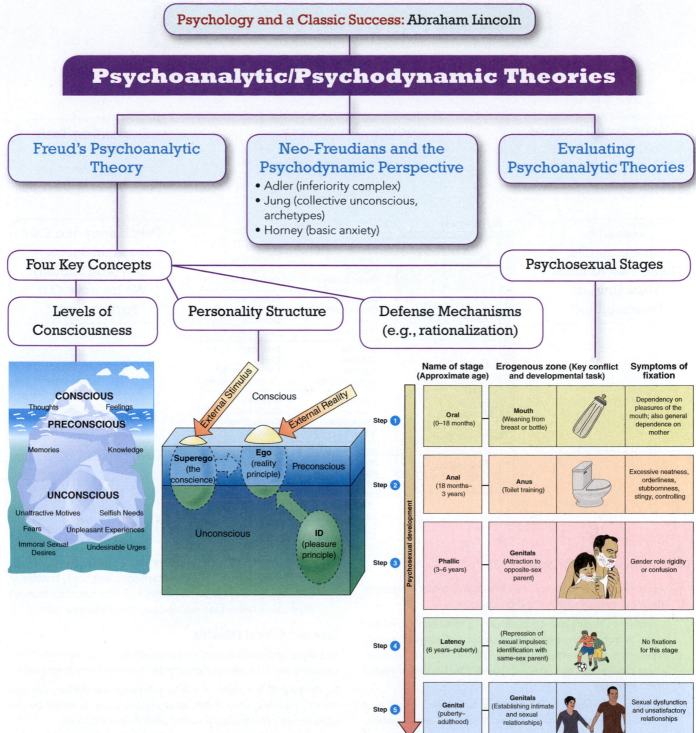

Psychology and a Classic Success: Abraham Lincoln

# Psychoanalytic/Psychodynamic Theories

**Freud's Psychoanalytic Theory**

**Neo-Freudians and the Psychodynamic Perspective**
- Adler (inferiority complex)
- Jung (collective unconscious, archetypes)
- Horney (basic anxiety)

**Evaluating Psychoanalytic Theories**

**Four Key Concepts**

**Psychosexual Stages**

**Levels of Consciousness**

**Personality Structure**

**Defense Mechanisms (e.g., rationalization)**

CONSCIOUS
Thoughts    Feelings
PRECONSCIOUS
Memories    Knowledge
UNCONSCIOUS
Unattractive Motives    Selfish Needs
Fears    Unpleasant Experiences
Immoral Sexual Desires    Undesirable Urges

External Stimulus    External Reality
Conscious
Superego (the conscience)    Ego (reality principle)    Preconscious
Unconscious    ID (pleasure principle)

| Name of stage (Approximate age) | Erogenous zone (Key conflict and developmental task) | | Symptoms of fixation |
|---|---|---|---|
| Step 1 — Oral (0–18 months) | Mouth (Weaning from breast or bottle) | | Dependency on pleasures of the mouth; also general dependence on mother |
| Step 2 — Anal (18 months–3 years) | Anus (Toilet training) | | Excessive neatness, orderliness, stubbornness, stingy, controlling |
| Step 3 — Phallic (3–6 years) | Genitals (Attraction to opposite-sex parent) | | Gender role rigidity or confusion |
| Step 4 — Latency (6 years–puberty) | (Repression of sexual impulses; identification with same-sex parent) | | No fixations for this stage |
| Step 5 — Genital (puberty–adulthood) | Genitals (Establishing intimate and sexual relationships) | | Sexual dysfunction and unsatisfactory relationships |

Psychosexual development

## 13.2 Trait Theories  430

- Allport believed that the best way to understand personality was to arrange a person's unique personality **traits** into a hierarchy. Cattell and Eysenck later reduced the list of possible personality traits using *factor analysis*.

- The **five-factor model (FFM)** identified the *Big Five* major dimensions of **personality:** *openness, conscientiousness, extraversion, agreeableness*, and *neuroticism*.

- Evolutionary research and cross-cultural studies support the five-factor model. But trait theories have been criticized for failing

to consider situational determinants of personality, to offer explanations for why people develop certain traits, or to identify which characteristics endure and which are transient.

### Test Your Critical Thinking

**1.** After reading the descriptions for each of the Big Five personality dimensions, how well do you think they describe someone you know very well? Can you predict how he or she might score on each of these traits?

**2.** Do you believe someone can change his or her core personality traits? Why or why not?

## Trait Theories

```
Trait Theories
├── Early Trait Theories (Allport, Cattell, and Eysenck)
├── Modern Trait Theory — Five-Factor Model (FFM)
└── Evaluating Trait Theories
```

**Early Trait Theories**
(Allport, Cattell, and Eysenck)

**Modern Trait Theory**
Five-Factor Model (FFM)

**Evaluating Trait Theories**

**Research Challenge: Do Nonhuman Animals Have Unique Personalities?**

**Psychology and Your Personal Success: Can (and Should) We Improve Our Personalities?**

**Big Five traits**

| # | Trait | High scorers | Low scorers |
|---|-------|--------------|-------------|
| 1 | **O**penness | Imaginative / Independent / Curious / Prefer variety | Practical / Conforming / Cautious / Prefer routine |
| 2 | **C**onscientiousness | Organized / Dependable / Careful / Disciplined | Disorganized / Unreliable / Careless / Impulsive |
| 3 | **E**xtraversion | Sociable / Talkative / Assertive / Prefer company | Retiring / Quiet / Mild-mannered / Prefer to be alone |
| 4 | **A**greeableness | Soft-hearted / Trusting / Cooperative / Good natured | Ruthless / Suspicious / Competitive / Irritable |
| 5 | **N**euroticism | Emotionally unstable / Anxious / Insecure / Self-pitying | Emotionally stable / Calm / Secure / Self-satisfied |

## 13.3 Humanistic Theories 435

- Humanistic theories focus on the individual's internal experiences (thoughts and feelings) and **self-concept**.

- According to Rogers, mental health and self-esteem are related to the degree of congruence between our **self-concept** and life experiences. Rogers argued that poor mental health results when young children do not receive **unconditional positive regard** from caregivers.

- Maslow saw personality as the quest to fulfill basic physiological needs and to move toward the highest level of **self-actualization**.

- Critics of the humanistic approach argue that these theories are based on naive assumptions and are not scientifically testable or well supported by empirical evidence. In addition, their focus on description, rather than explanation, makes them narrow.

### Test Your Critical Thinking

**1.** Do you agree with Rogers that unconditional positive regard from parents is key to healthy personality development? Why or why not?

**2.** Thinking of the traits of a fully self-actualized person, can you identify someone who exhibits all or most of these qualities? Do you consider self-actualization a worthy goal? Why or why not?

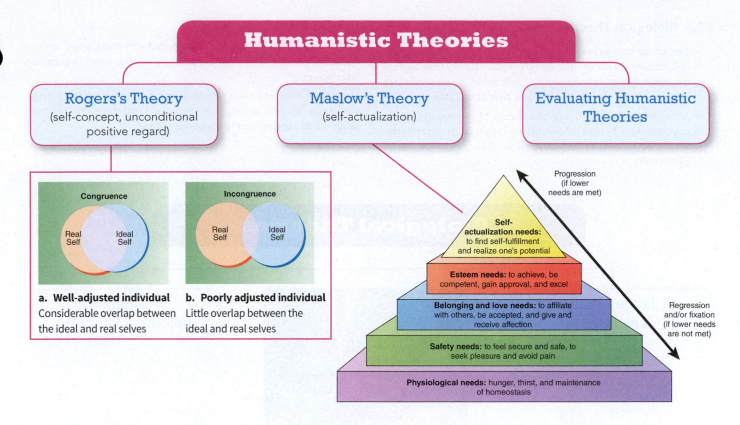

# Humanistic Theories

### Rogers's Theory
(self-concept, unconditional positive regard)

### Maslow's Theory
(self-actualization)

### Evaluating Humanistic Theories

**Congruence**

Real Self   Ideal Self

**a. Well-adjusted individual**
Considerable overlap between the ideal and real selves

**Incongruence**

Real Self   Ideal Self

**b. Poorly adjusted individual**
Little overlap between the ideal and real selves

Progression (if lower needs are met)

**Self-actualization needs:** to find self-fulfillment and realize one's potential

**Esteem needs:** to achieve, be competent, gain approval, and excel

**Belonging and love needs:** to affiliate with others, be accepted, and give and receive affection

**Safety needs:** to feel secure and safe, to seek pleasure and avoid pain

**Physiological needs:** hunger, thirst, and maintenance of homeostasis

Regression and/or fixation (if lower needs are not met)

## 13.4 Social-Cognitive Theories 438

- Social-cognitive theorists emphasize the importance of our interactions with the environment and how we interpret and respond to these external events.

- Cognition is central to Bandura's concept of **self-efficacy**. According to Bandura, self-efficacy affects which challenges we choose to accept and the effort we expend in reaching goals. His concept of **reciprocal determinism** states that internal personal factors, the environment, and the individual's behavior work as interacting reciprocal determinants.

- Rotter's theory says that learning experiences create *cognitive expectancies* that guide behavior and influence the environment. Rotter believed that having an internal versus external *locus of control* affects personality and achievement.

- Social-cognitive theories are credited for their attention to scientific standards, reliance on empirical data, and ability to predict behavior in real-world situations. However, they have been criticized for their narrow focus on situational factors, and for their lack of attention to the stability of personality, as well as to sociocultural, emotional, unconscious, and biological influences on personality.

### Test Your Critical Thinking

**1.** How would Bandura's social-cognitive concept of self-efficacy explain why bright students sometimes don't do well in college?

**2.** Do you have an internal or external locus of control? How might this affect your academic and lifetime achievement?

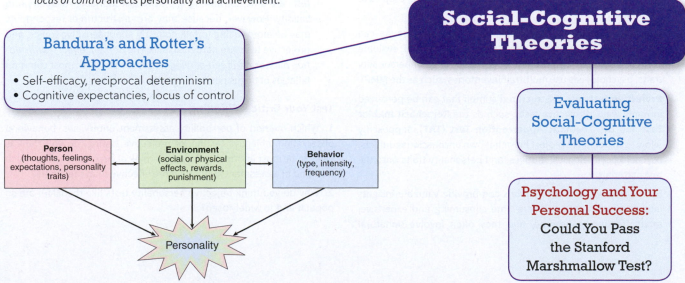

# Social-Cognitive Theories

### Bandura's and Rotter's Approaches
- Self-efficacy, reciprocal determinism
- Cognitive expectancies, locus of control

**Person**
(thoughts, feelings, expectations, personality traits)

**Environment**
(social or physical effects, rewards, punishment)

**Behavior**
(type, intensity, frequency)

Personality

### Evaluating Social-Cognitive Theories

### Psychology and Your Personal Success:
Could You Pass the Stanford Marshmallow Test?

## 13.5 Biological Theories 442

- Certain brain areas may contribute to personality. However, neurochemistry seems to offer more precise data on how biology influences personality. Research in *behavioral genetics* indicates that genetic factors also strongly influence personality.

- Instead of adhering to any one theory of personality, many psychologists believe in the biopsychosocial approach—the idea that several factors overlap in their contributions to personality.

**Test Your Critical Thinking**

**1.** If biological factors explain certain personality traits, what advice would you give to someone who is painfully shy and wants to become more outgoing?

**2.** Many of the same brain structures most closely associated with personality are also linked with emotions. What does this suggest about the role of emotions in our personalities?

## Biological Theories

**Three Major Contributors**
(brain, neurochemistry, genetics)

**Evaluating Biological Theories**

## 13.6 Personality Assessment 444

- Psychologists use four basic methods to measure or assess personality: interviews, observations, objective tests, and projective techniques.

- **Objective personality tests** are widely used because we can administer them broadly and relatively quickly and evaluate them in a standardized fashion. To assess a range of personality traits, psychologists use multitrait inventories, such as the **MMPI**.

- **Projective tests** use unstructured stimuli that can be perceived in many ways. Projective tests, such as the **Rorschach Inkblot Test** and the **Thematic Apperception Test (TAT)**, supposedly allow each person to project his or her own unconscious conflicts, psychological defenses, motives, and personality traits onto the test materials.

- Both *interviews* and *observations* can provide valuable insights into personality, but they are time consuming and expensive, raters frequently disagree, and they often involve unnatural

settings. *Objective tests* provide specific, objective information, but they are limited because of problems with self-reports, diagnostic difficulties, cultural bias, and inappropriate use. *Projective tests* are time consuming and have questionable reliability and validity. However, because they are unstructured, respondents may be more willing to talk honestly about sensitive topics, and projective tests are harder to fake. The *Barnum effect*, *confirmation bias*, and the *self-serving* biases are the three most common fallacies of bogus personality tests.

**Test Your Critical Thinking**

**1.** Which method of personality assessment (interviews, behavioral observation, objective testing, or projective testing) do you think is likely to be most informative? Can you think of circumstances in which one kind of assessment might be more effective than the others?

**2.** Why do you think objective personality tests like the MMPI are so popular and so widely used?

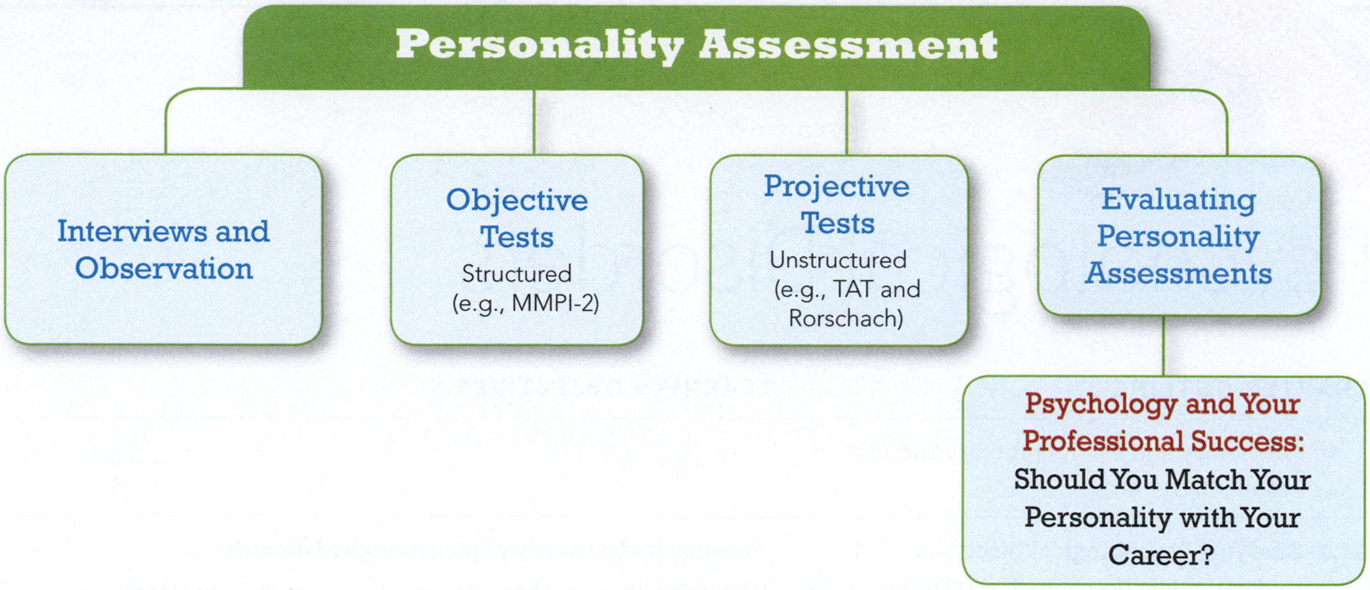

## Personality Assessment

- **Interviews and Observation**

- **Objective Tests**
  Structured
  (e.g., MMPI-2)

- **Projective Tests**
  Unstructured
  (e.g., TAT and Rorschach)

- **Evaluating Personality Assessments**

  - **Psychology and Your Professional Success:** Should You Match Your Personality with Your Career?

---

# Key Terms

**Retrieval Practice**   *Write a definition for each term before turning back to the referenced page to check your answer.*

- archetypes   428
- basic anxiety   429
- behavioral genetics   442
- character   424
- collective unconscious   428
- conscious   424
- defense mechanisms   425
- ego   425
- five-factor model (FFM)   431
- id   425

- inferiority complex   428
- Minnesota Multiphasic Personality Inventory (MMPI)   445
- Oedipus complex   427
- personality   424
- preconscious   424
- projective test   446
- psychosexual stages   426
- reciprocal determinism   439
- Rorschach Inkblot Test   446

- self-actualization   436
- self-concept   439
- self-efficacy   439
- superego   425
- temperament   424
- Thematic Apperception Test (TAT)   446
- trait   430
- unconditional positive regard   436
- unconscious   424

© alexxl66/iStockphoto

CHAPTER **14**

# Psychological Disorders

## CHAPTER OUTLINE

❖ Psychology and a Contemporary Success
  Jennifer Lawrence

**14.1 Studying Psychological Disorders**
  • Understanding Psychological Disorders
  ❖ Psychology and Your Personal Success
    Can Resilience Promote Mental Health in
    Children and Adults?
  • Classifying Psychological Disorders
  • Describing and Evaluating the *DSM*
  • Special Issues in Psychological Disorders

**14.2 Anxiety Disorders**
  • Describing Anxiety Disorders
  • Explaining Anxiety Disorders

**14.3 Depressive and Bipolar Disorders**
  • Describing Depressive and Bipolar Disorders
  • Explaining Depressive and Bipolar Disorders
  **RC Research Challenge**
    Are Head Injuries Related to Depressive
    and Other Psychological Disorders?

**14.4 Schizophrenia**
  • Symptoms of Schizophrenia
  • Classifying Schizophrenia
  • Explaining Schizophrenia

**14.5 Other Disorders**
  • Obsessive-Compulsive Disorder
  • Dissociative Disorders
  • Personality Disorders

## LEARNING OBJECTIVES

**Summarize the study of psychological disorders.**
  • **Describe** abnormal behavior and the four criteria for identifying
    psychological disorders.
  • **Explain** how perspectives on the causes of psychological disorders
    have changed throughout history.
  • **Discuss** the *Diagnostic and Statistical Manual of Mental Disorders
    (DSM)*, and its pros and cons.
  • **Review** the key factors in the stigma of mental illness and the
    increased risk of suicide.

**Summarize the major types of anxiety disorders.**
  • **Describe** the characteristics of generalized anxiety disorder (GAD),
    panic disorder, and phobias.
  • **Explain** how psychological, biological, and sociocultural factors
    contribute to anxiety disorders.

**Review the symptoms, causal factors, and dangers of depressive
and bipolar disorders.**
  • **Describe** depressive disorders and bipolar disorders, and how
    they differ.
  • **Summarize** research on the biological and psychosocial factors that
    contribute to depressive and bipolar disorders.

**Review how psychologists define, classify, and explain
schizophrenia.**
  • **Identify** schizophrenia and its common characteristics.
  • **Compare** the positive versus negative symptoms of schizophrenia.
  • **Summarize** the biological and psychosocial factors that contribute to
    schizophrenia.

**Review the main features of obsessive-compulsive, dissociative,
and personality disorders.**
  • **Identify** obsessive-compulsive disorder and its major symptoms.
  • **Describe** dissociative disorders.
  • **Discuss** personality disorders, including antisocial and borderline.

**Summarize gender and cultural differences in psychological disorders.**

- **Discuss** the possible gender differences in depression.
- **Explain** why it is difficult to directly compare psychological disorders, such as schizophrenia, across cultures.
- **Describe** how understanding culture-general symptoms and culture-bound disorders helps us overcome ethnocentrism in psychological disorders.
- **Discuss** how resilience promotes mental health.

## ❖ Psychology and a Contemporary Success | Jennifer Lawrence

VCG/Getty Images

Jennifer Lawrence (1990–) was born in Kentucky to loving parents who brought her up to be "tough" like her two older brothers (see photo). Her acting career began at the age of 14 when she traveled to Manhattan and was spotted by an agent who asked her to do a "cold read" (Jennifer Lawrence Biography, n.d.). And, as they say, the rest is history!

After graduating from high school two years early in order to begin acting, Lawrence played minor roles in several commercials and in a few small movies. Her big break came in 2012, when she was awarded a starring role in the movie *Winter's Bone*. An even bigger break came when she was cast as Katniss Everdeen in the unbelievably popular *Hunger Games* series of movies starting in 2012. Lawrence's leading role in *Silver Linings Playbook* in that same year earned her the Academy Award for Best Actress. Jennifer has also received other accolades, including the Golden Globe Award, the Screen Actors Guild Award, seven MTV Movie Awards, and six People's Choice Awards.

Today, Lawrence earns about $10 million per film, with estimated annual earnings of over $100 million, making her, according to *Forbes*, the world's highest-paid actress (Robehmed, 2015). In 2012 and 2015, she was named Entertainer of the Year, and in 2013 *Time* magazine called her "one of the 100 most influential people in the world." Perhaps most impressive is that she's used her incredible fame and fortune to fund numerous charities and to establish her own charitable organization (Jennifer Lawrence, n.d.).

At this point, you may be thinking that Jennifer Lawrence has had an ideal life—growing up in a loving, supportive family, achieving astonishing fame and success at a very early age in a field she loves, earning numerous acting awards, and being widely adored as "America's sweetheart." Moreover, with her extreme wealth, she's financially set for the rest of her life! But did you know that as a child Lawrence was so hyperactive that her nickname was "Nitro," as in nitroglycerin? Or that as an adult, she suffers from a serious psychological disorder known as *social anxiety*? Here's how she describes her high school days in Kentucky:

> I was a weirdo. I wasn't picked on or anything. And I wasn't smarter than the other kids; that's not why I didn't fit in. I've always had this weird anxiety.
>
> —Jennifer Lawrence, cited in *Vogue* (September 2013)

## Chapter Overview

Despite her youth, Jennifer Lawrence clearly demonstrates a *growth mindset* and *grit*, and you'll learn more about her social anxiety disorder throughout this chapter. Are you excited? Throughout history, psychological disorders have been the subject of intense fascination, and this chapter is the one our intro psych students are most eager to study. Hopefully, while reading this chapter you'll recognize how the earlier chapters have prepared you for a better understanding and appreciation of the complex issues surrounding abnormal behavior. We begin with a discussion of how psychological disorders are identified, explained, and classified. Next we explore the three major categories: anxiety disorders, depressive and bipolar disorders, and schizophrenia. Then we discuss other categories of abnormal behavior, including obsessive-compulsive disorder (OCD), dissociative disorders, and personality disorders. We close with a look at gender and cultural factors related to psychological disorders.

*My good fortune is not that I've recovered from mental illness. I have not, nor will I ever. My good fortune lies in having found my life.*

—Elyn Saks (Author, Professor of Law and Psychiatry)

## Why Study Psychology?

### Did you know that

- . . . the insanity defense is rarely used and seldom successful in criminal trials?
- . . . stigmatizing mental illness may discourage individuals from seeking help when they need it?
- . . . anxiety disorders are considered the most "contagious" of all psychological disorders?
- . . . high Internet and cell phone use may increase the risk of depression and anxiety disorders?

- . . . individuals with schizophrenia do not have multiple personalities?
- . . . certain mental disorders exist in some cultures, but not in others?
- . . . unequal pay for equal work may help explain gender disparities in anxiety and depression?
- . . . men may be underdiagnosed for serious depression due to stereotypes regarding the symptoms?

## 14.1 Studying Psychological Disorders

### LEARNING OBJECTIVES

**Retrieval Practice**  While reading the upcoming sections, respond to each Learning Objective in your own words.

**Summarize the study of psychological disorders.**

- **Describe** abnormal behavior and the four criteria for identifying psychological disorders.

- **Explain** how perspectives on the causes of psychological disorders have changed throughout history.
- **Discuss** the *Diagnostic and Statistical Manual of Mental Disorders* (DSM), and its pros and cons.
- **Review** the key factors in the stigma of mental illness and the increased risk of suicide.

**Psychological disorder**  A clinically significant collection of symptoms (a syndrome) characterized by serious disruptions in an individual's thoughts, feelings, and/or actions.

Did you know that over 40 million American adults, more than the population of New York and Florida combined, currently suffer from a mental health condition (The State of Mental Health, 2017)? That means that one in six American adults suffers from a **psychological disorder** (or multiple psychological disorders). This type of disorder is defined as a clinically significant collection of symptoms (a syndrome) characterized by serious disruptions in an individual's thoughts, feelings, and/or actions.

When do such disruptions rise to the level of a "disorder?" Most people agree that neither the artist who stays awake for 72 hours finishing a painting nor the shooter who kills 20 young school children is behaving normally. But what exactly is "normal"? How do we distinguish between eccentricity in the first case and abnormal behavior in the second?

### Understanding Psychological Disorders

As you can see, it can be difficult to distinguish normal from abnormal behavior, and psychologists have struggled to create a precise definition. However, mental health professionals generally agree that **abnormal behavior** (or psychopathology) can be identified as patterns of behaviors, thoughts, or emotions considered pathological (diseased or disordered) for one or more of these four reasons: *deviance, dysfunction, distress,* and/or *danger* (**Concept Organizer 14.1**). Keep in mind that abnormal behavior, like intelligence and creativity, is not composed of two discrete categories—"normal" and "abnormal." Instead, mental health lies along a continuum, with people being unusually healthy at one end and extremely disturbed at the other (Angermeyer et al., 2015; Schomerus et al., 2016; Sue et al., 2016).

When considering the four criteria for abnormal behavior, remember that no single criterion is adequate by itself. Furthermore, judgments of what is personally distressing, and what is deviant or dysfunctional, vary historically and cross-culturally. Perhaps the most damaging issue surrounding abnormal behavior is that the public generally overestimates the danger posed by those who suffer from psychological disorders. In fact, they are far more likely to be the *victims* of violence than the perpetrators. See **Table 14.1** for more about this and other myths of mental illness.

What causes abnormal behavior? Historically, evil spirits and witchcraft have been blamed (Campbell et al., 2017; Iheanacho et al., 2016; Stefanovics et al., 2016). Some Stone Age people, for instance, believed that abnormal behavior stemmed from demonic possession. The "therapy" was to bore a hole in the skull so the evil spirit could escape, a process we call *trephining*. During the European Middle Ages, abnormal behavior was sometimes treated with *exorcism*, which was a religious or spiritual practice designed to evict the demons by making the troubled person's body inhospitable through lengthy prayers, fasting, and beatings. During the later Renaissance period (14th to the 17th century), many believed that some individuals

**Abnormal behavior**    Patterns of behaviors, thoughts, or emotions considered pathological (diseased or disordered) for one or more of these four reasons: deviance, dysfunction, distress, and/or danger.

---

| **CONCEPT ORGANIZER 14.1** | **Four Criteria for Identifying Abnormal Behavior** |
| --- | --- |

**STOP!** This Concept Organizer contains essential information NOT found elsewhere in the text, which is likely to appear on quizzes and exams. Be sure to study it CAREFULLY!

Mandy Godbehear/Shutterstock

**a. Deviance**  Behaviors, thoughts, or emotions may be considered abnormal when they deviate from a society or culture's norms or values. For example, it's normal to be a bit concerned if friends are whispering, but abnormal if you're equally concerned when total strangers are whispering.

Axel Bueckert/Shutterstock.com

**b. Dysfunction**  When someone's behavior interferes with his or her daily functioning, it is considered abnormal behavior. A person who drinks to the point that it interferes with holding a job, staying in school, or maintaining a relationship is exhibiting dysfunction.

Peter Dazeley/Photographer's Choice/Getty Image, Inc.

**c. Distress**  Behaviors, thoughts, or emotions that cause significant personal distress may qualify as abnormal. Self-abuse, serious relationship problems, and suicidal thoughts all indicate significant personal distress and unhappiness.

**d. Danger**  If someone's thoughts, emotions, or behaviors present a danger to self or others, such as when a person engages in road rage to the point of physical confrontation, it is considered abnormal.

Digital Vision/Getty Images

**TABLE 14.1** **Common Myths About Mental Illness**

- **Myth: Mentally ill people are often dangerous and unpredictable.**
  **Fact:** Only a few disorders, such as some psychotic and antisocial personality disorders, are associated with violence. Only about 3% of the violent crimes in America are committed by people with serious mental illness. The stereotype that connects mental illness and violence persists because of prejudice, selective media attention, and negative portrayals in movies and on television.

- **Myth: People with psychological disorders act in bizarre ways and are very different from normal people.**
  **Fact:** This is true for only a small minority of individuals and during a relatively brief portion of their lives. In fact, sometimes even mental health professionals find it difficult to distinguish normal from abnormal behaviors without formal screening.

- **Myth: Psychological disorders are a sign of personal weakness.**
  **Fact:** Like all other illnesses, psychological disorders are a function of many factors, such as exposure to stress, genetic predispositions, a host of personal and sociocultural experiences, and family background. Mentally disturbed individuals can't be blamed for their illness any more than we blame people who develop cancer or other illnesses.

**Is this behavior abnormal?** Eccentric? Yes. Mentally disordered? Probably not.

*Corbis/VCG/Getty Images*

- **Myth: A mentally ill person is only suited for low-level jobs and never fully recovers.**
  **Fact:** Once again, like all other illnesses, psychological disorders are complex, and their symptoms, severity, and prognoses differ for each individual. With therapy, the vast majority of those who are diagnosed as mentally ill eventually improve and lead normal, productive lives. Moreover, the extreme symptoms of some psychological disorders are generally only temporary. Jennifer Lawrence, our famous figure for this chapter, as well as U.S. President Abraham Lincoln, British Prime Minister Winston Churchill, scientist Isaac Newton, and other high-achieving people all suffered from serious psychological disorders at various times throughout their careers.

**Sources:** Arkowitz & Lilienfeld, 2017; Bell, 2016; Knoll & Annas, 2016; National Alliance on Mental Health, 2015.

*Bettmann/Getty Images*

**FIGURE 14.1** **Witchcraft or mental illness?** During the European Renaissance, some people who may have been suffering from mental disorders were accused of witchcraft and tortured or hung.

**Psychiatry** The branch of medicine that deals with the diagnosis, treatment, and prevention of mental disorders.

chose to consort with the Devil. These supposed witches were often tortured, imprisoned for life, or executed (**Figure 14.1**).

As the Renaissance ended, special mental hospitals called *asylums* began to appear in Europe. Initially designed to provide quiet retreats from the world and to protect society, the asylums unfortunately became overcrowded, inhumane prisons (Radhika et al., 2015; Shiraev, 2015).

Improvement came in 1792, when Philippe Pinel, a French physician, was placed in charge of a Parisian asylum. Believing that inmates' behavior was caused by underlying physical illness, he insisted that they be unshackled and removed from their dark, unheated cells. Many inmates improved so dramatically that they could be released. Pinel's actions reflect the ideals of the modern *medical model*, which assumes that diseases (including mental illness) have physical causes that can be diagnosed, treated, and possibly cured and prevented. This medical model is the foundation of the branch of medicine, known as **psychiatry**, that deals with the diagnosis, treatment, and prevention of mental disorders.

In contrast, psychologists believe that focusing on "mental illness" overlooks critical social and cultural factors, as well as our own personal thoughts, feelings, and actions that contribute to psychological disorders. Therefore, we take a multifaceted approach to explaining abnormal behavior, as shown in **Figure 14.2**.

## Classifying Psychological Disorders

Along with identifying and explaining abnormal behavior, we need to classify it—that is, place it in specific categories. Why? Without a clear, reliable system for classifying the wide range of psychological disorders, scientific research on them would be almost impossible, and communication among mental health professionals would be seriously impaired. Fortunately, mental health specialists share a uniform classification system, the *Diagnostic and Statistical Manual of Mental Disorders (DSM)*. This manual has been updated and revised several times, and the fifth edition was published in 2013 (American Psychiatric Association, 2013).

Each revision of the *DSM* has expanded the list of disorders and changed the descriptions and categories to reflect the latest scientific research. Consider the terms *neurosis* and *psychosis*. In previous editions of the *DSM*, the term **neurosis** reflected Freud's belief that all neurotic conditions arise from unconscious conflicts (Chapter 13). Now, conditions that were previously grouped under the heading *neurosis* have been formally studied and redistributed as separate categories.

Unlike *neurosis*, the term *psychosis* is still listed in the current edition of the *DSM* because it remains useful for distinguishing the most severe psychological disorders, such as schizophrenia. **Psychosis** is generally defined as a serious psychological condition in which thoughts and perceptions are so impaired that the individual loses contact with external reality. This loss of contact with reality is most evident in the two key features of psychosis—delusions and hallucinations. **Delusions** are false, imaginary beliefs that persist despite clear evidence to the contrary, such as delusions of grandeur or persecution. In comparison, **hallucinations** are false, imaginary sensory perceptions that occur without an external objective source, such as hearing voices that others do not hear (**Figure 14.3**).

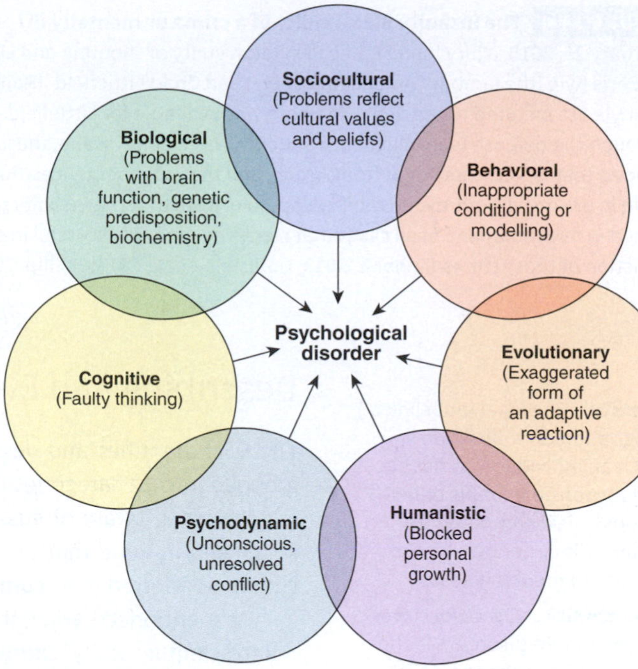

An example is the infamous case of Andrea Yates, who methodically drowned her five children in their bathtub. She may have been suffering from *postpartum depression*—a rare form of depression caused by hormonal changes after giving birth. Yates told police that Satan had ordered her to kill the children, and drowning them was all she could think about (Sher & Braswell, 2011). Yates was later judged to have been psychotic and in a delusional state at the time of the killings.

Note that psychosis, along with delusions and hallucinations, also may occur with substance abuse. In *amphetamine psychosis* (Chapter 5), for instance, users may experience a loss of contact with reality, hallucinate, and become delusional. In this chapter, however, we'll focus on psychological disorders, and be aware that psychosis, delusions, and hallucinations may occur to varying degrees with several different psychological disorders.

What about the term *insanity*? **Insanity** is a legal term indicating that a person cannot be held responsible for his or her actions or is incompetent to manage his or her own affairs because of mental illness. In the law, the definition of mental illness rests primarily on a person's inability to tell right from wrong (**Figure 14.4**). Andrea Yates was one of the rare cases in which someone was found not guilty by reason of insanity. The court found that, because of her psychotic condition at the time of the crime, she did not know her actions were wrong. Since her trial, Yates has been in continuous residence in a state hospital in Texas, where her lawyer reports she's doing remarkably well after 15 years of therapy (Wilkinson & Spargo, 2016). In conclusion, bear in mind that the term "insanity" often appears in public conversations, but it's seldom used by psychologists. People suffer from specific psychological disorders—they're not "insane."

**FIGURE 14.2** **Seven psychological perspectives** As you can see in this diagram, the seven major perspectives differ in their explanations for the general causes of psychological disorders, but there is still considerable overlap.

*Diagnostic and Statistical Manual of Mental Disorders (DSM)* A manual developed by the American Psychiatric Association that is used primarily to classify psychological disorders.

**Neurosis** A condition in which a person does not have signs of brain abnormalities and does not display grossly irrational thinking or violate basic norms but does experience subjective distress; no longer included in the *DSM*.

**Psychosis** A serious psychological condition in which thoughts and perceptions are so impaired that the individual loses contact with external reality.

**Delusion** A false, imaginary belief that persists despite clear evidence to the contrary, such as delusions of grandeur; a symptom associated with psychosis.

**Hallucination** A false, imaginary sensory perception that occurs without an external, objective source, such as hearing voices that others cannot hear; a symptom associated with psychosis.

Christopher Chan/Getty Images

**FIGURE 14.3** **Illusions, hallucinations, and delusions** As you may recall from Chapter 4, delusions and hallucinations are not the same as *illusions*. Delusions and hallucinations are false, imaginary, and experienced by someone who is out of touch with reality. In contrast, *illusions* are misleading perceptions of reality that are similarly experienced by others. The moon illusion, shown here, in which the moon appears larger near the horizon than it does higher up in the sky, is a classic example. In this case, virtually everyone shares the same visual experience.

**FIGURE 14.4** **The insanity plea—guilty of a crime or mentally ill?**   On February 25, 2015, a jury found Eddie Ray Routh guilty of shooting and killing Chris Kyle (the famous "American Sniper") and Chad Littlefield. (Routh and Kyle are pictured to the right. No photo was available for Littlefield.) Although the defense team claimed that Routh was legally insane, the jury decided that he did know right from wrong, and the judge sentenced Routh to life in prison without the possibility of parole. Note that the insanity plea is used in fewer than 1% of all cases that reach trial and is successful in only a fraction of those (Dirks-Linhorst, 2013; Goldstein et al., 2013; Phillip, 2015).

Eddie Ray Routh          Chris Kyle

Texas Department of Criminal Justice/AP Images

Chris Haston/NBC/NBCU Photo Bank/Getty Images, Inc.

**Insanity**   The legal (not clinical) designation for a situation in which an individual cannot be held responsible for his or her actions or is incompetent to manage his or her own affairs because of mental illness.

**Comorbidity**   The co-occurrence of two or more disorders in the same person at the same time, as when a person suffers from both depression and alcoholism.

## Describing and Evaluating the *DSM*

The *DSM* identifies and describes the symptoms of approximately 400 disorders, which are grouped into 22 categories (**Table 14.2**). Note that we focus on only the first 7 in this chapter (categories 8–14 are discussed in other chapters; 15–22 are beyond the scope of this book). Also, keep in mind that people may be diagnosed with more than one disorder at a time, a condition referred to as **comorbidity**.

As mentioned earlier, the *DSM's* type of classification of psychological disorders is essential to scientific study. Without a system such as the *DSM*, we could not effectively identify and diagnose the wide variety of disorders, predict their future courses, or suggest appropriate treatment. Moreover, the *DSM* facilitates communication among professionals and patients, and serves as a valuable educational tool.

Unfortunately, the *DSM* does have limitations and potential problems (Aragona, 2015; Bornstein, 2015; Gonçalves et al., 2016). Some critics have proposed that the latest revision lacks an official discussion of the ethical, political, economic, and related values underlying the classification and diagnostic processes involved. Others contend that the *DSM* may be casting too wide a net and *overdiagnosing*. Given that insurance companies compensate physicians and psychologists only if each client treated for a mental disorder is assigned a specific *DSM* code number, can you see how compilers of the *DSM* may be encouraged to add more diagnoses?

The *DSM* has also been criticized for a potential *cultural bias*. It does provide a culture-specific section and a glossary of culture-bound syndromes, such as ataque de nervios (attack of nerves), dhat syndrome (semen loss), khyâl cap (wind attack), kufingisisa (thinking too much), and taijin kyofusho (interpersonal fear disorder). However, the overall classification still reflects a Western European and U.S. perspective (Hsu, 2016; Jacob, 2014; Jani et al., 2016).

Perhaps the most troubling criticism of the *DSM* is its possible overreliance on the medical model and the way it may unfairly label people. Consider a classic (and controversial) study conducted by David Rosenhan (1973) in which he and seven colleagues presented themselves at several hospital admissions offices complaining of hearing voices (a classic symptom of schizophrenia). Aside from making this single false complaint and providing false names and occupations, the researchers answered all questions truthfully. Not surprisingly, given their reported symptom, they were all diagnosed with psychological disorders and admitted to the hospital. Once there, the "patients" stopped reporting any symptoms and behaved as they normally would, yet none were ever recognized by hospital staff as phony. All eight of these pseudo-patients were eventually released after an average stay of 19 days. However, all but one were assigned a label on their permanent medical records of "schizophrenia in remission."

## Special Issues in Psychological Disorders

What do you think about the Rosenhan study just described? Do you see how it demonstrates the inherent dangers and "stickiness" of all forms of labels? This particular study has been criticized, but few doubt that the stigma, prejudice, and discrimination surrounding mental illness often create lifetime career and social barriers for those who are already struggling with the psychological disorder itself. In the following section, we will explore two major issues related to psychological disorders—the stigma of mental illness and the increased risk of suicide.

## TABLE 14.2    Subcategories of Mental Disorders

© RapidEye/iStockphoto

© Aldo Murillo/iStockphoto

1. **Anxiety disorders** Problems associated with excessive fear and anxiety and related behavioral disturbances.

2. **Depressive disorders** Problems characterized by the presence of sad, empty, or irritable mood.

3. **Bipolar and related disorders** Problems associated with alternating episodes of depression and mania.

4. **Schizophrenia spectrum and other psychotic disorders** Group of disorders characterized by delusions, hallucinations, disorganized thinking or motor behavior, and negative symptoms, such as diminished emotional expression.

5. **Obsessive-compulsive and related disorders** Group of disorders characterized by the presence of obsessions, compulsions, preoccupations, and/or repetitive behaviors or mental acts.

6. **Dissociative disorders** Group of disorders characterized by a disruption and/or discontinuity in the normal integration of consciousness, memory, identity, emotion, perception, body representation, motor control, and behavior.

7. **Personality disorders** Problems related to an enduring pattern of experience and behavior that deviates markedly from the expectations of an individual's culture and leads to distress or impairment.

8. **Trauma- and stressor-related disorders** Problems associated with exposure to a traumatic or stressful event (see Chapter 3).

9. **Sleep–wake disorders** Dissatisfaction regarding the quality, timing, and amount of sleep (see Chapter 5).

10. **Substance-related and addictive disorders** A cluster of cognitive, behavioral, and physiological symptoms related to alcohol, tobacco, other drugs, and gambling (see Chapter 5).

11. **Feeding and eating disorders** Problems related to persistent disturbance of eating or eating-related behavior (see Chapter 12).

12. **Paraphilic disorders** Problems involving an intense and persistent sexual interest causing distress or impairment to the person or whose satisfaction has entailed personal harm, or risk of harm, to others (see Chapter 11).

13. **Sexual dysfunctions** A significant disturbance in a person's ability to respond sexually or to experience sexual pleasure (see Chapter 11).

14. **Gender dysphoria** Distress that may accompany the incongruence between a person's experienced or expressed gender and one's assigned gender (see Chapter 11).

15. **Neurodevelopmental disorders** Developmental deficits that typically manifest early in life, often before the child enters grade school, and produce impairments of personal, social, academic, or occupational functioning (see Chapter 10).

16. **Somatic symptom and related disorders** Problems related to unusual preoccupation with physical health or physical symptoms producing significant distress and impairment.

17. **Elimination disorders** Problems related to the inappropriate elimination of urine or feces, usually first diagnosed in childhood or adolescence.

18. **Disruptive, impulse-control, and conduct disorders** Problems related to kleptomania (impulsive stealing), pyromania (setting of fires), and other disorders characterized by inability to resist impulses, drives, or temptations to perform certain acts harmful to self or others.

19. **Neurocognitive disorders** A group of disorders involving cognitive function, including Alzheimer's disease, Huntington's disease, and physical trauma to the brain (see Chapters 2 and 7).

20. **Other mental disorders** Residual category of mental disorders that cause significant distress or impairment but do not meet the full criteria for any other disorder in DSM-5.

21. **Medication-induced movement disorders and other adverse effects of medication** These are not mental disorders but are included because of their importance in the management by medication and differential diagnosis of mental disorders.

22. **Other conditions that may be a focus of clinical attention** These are not mental disorders but are included to draw attention to and document issues that may be encountered in routine clinical practice.

SFM ITALY F//Alamy Stock Photo

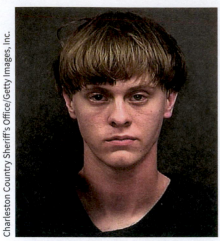

Charleston Country Sheriff's Office/Getty Images, Inc.

**Dylann Roof in 2015**

### The Stigma of Mental Illness

Today, public attitudes toward mental illness may be more negative than ever because of the media's intensive coverage of mass shootings by people with mental disorders. For example, many Americans were shocked and deeply saddened on June 17, 2015, when 21-year-old Dylann Roof (see the photo) shot and killed nine people who were attending a church prayer service in Charleston, South Carolina. Roof later confessed to the crime, saying that he murdered the Black church members because he wanted to ignite a race war. Following the shootings, the news media focused on issues of race and gun control. However, many also expressed the view that mental illness was a motivating factor and a common thread in mass shootings (Gonyea & Montanaro, 2015; Lysiak, 2015). Can you see how this type of intensive media coverage increases myths, misconceptions, and exaggerated fears of mental illness? To make matters worse, the media seldom, if ever, mention the fact that people with mental illness are less often perpetrators of violence than they are victims of violence or of their own self-destructive behaviors (Arkowitz & Lilienfeld, 2017; Metzl & MacLeish, 2015).

In 2010, the U.S. Surgeon General published a landmark mental health report identifying stigma as a public health concern. Unfortunately, the stigma still exists. Two serious consequences of stigmatizing mental illness are that it discourages individuals from seeking help when they need it, and it decreases public support for funding the treatment of mental illness. These reactions can lead to devastating, even life-threatening, consequences (Gilberti, 2016; Knoll & Annas, 2016). Given the approximately 450 million people worldwide who have a mental illness and the serious problems of labeling, you can see why we need to put an end to the stigma and discrimination that currently surround this condition (Baker, 2015). Along with providing counseling and services for the victims, we need to transform our public perception and media coverage of mental illness.

### The Increased Risk of Suicide

Did you know that close to 800,000 people die worldwide each year due to suicide (World Health Organization, 2017a)? Even people who enjoy enormous fame and financial success may be at risk, including well-known actors, comedians, and musicians, like Robin Williams and Kurt Cobain; professional athletes, like Olympic medalist Jeret Peterson and football player Junior Seau; and influential writers and artists, like Virginia Woolf, Ernest Hemingway, and Vincent van Gogh. Tragically, many of these deaths by suicide were permanent solutions to what might have been temporary problems.

What can we do? The first step might be to identify the many suicide myths and misunderstandings. We also need to recognize the danger signs and when to seek help for ourselves and others (see **Concept Organizer 14.2**).

| CONCEPT ORGANIZER 14.2 | Understanding and Preventing Suicide |
| --- | --- |

**STOP!** This Concept Organizer contains essential information NOT found elsewhere in the text, which is likely to appear on quizzes and exams. Be sure to study it CAREFULLY!

#### Common Myths about Suicide

Because of the shame and secrecy surrounding suicide, there are many misconceptions and stereotypes. Can you identify which of the following are true and which are false?

1. People who talk about suicide are less likely to actually complete it.
2. Suicide usually takes place with little or no warning.
3. Suicides can trigger "copycat" attempts.
4. Suicidal people are fully intent on dying.
5. Children of parents who attempt suicide are at greater risk of dying by suicide.
6. Suicidal people remain so forever.
7. Men are more likely than women to kill themselves by suicide.
8. When a suicidal person has been severely depressed, and seems to be "snapping out of it," the danger of suicide decreases substantially.
9. Only depressed people die by suicide.
10. Thinking about suicide is rare.
11. Asking a depressed person about suicide will push him or her over the edge and cause a suicidal act that might not otherwise have occurred.
12. Self-injury, such as cutting, burning, and/or hitting oneself, inevitably escalates to suicide.

© Bubbles Photolibrary/Alamy Stock Photo

Now, compare your responses to the experts' answers and explanations:

1. and 2. **False** Up to three-quarters of those who take their own lives talk about it and give warnings about their intentions beforehand. They may say, "If something happens to me, I want you to . . . " or, "Life just isn't worth living." They also provide behavioral clues, such as giving away valued possessions, withdrawing from family and friends, and losing interest in favorite activities.

3. **True** There is substantial evidence that media reports of deaths by suicide, particularly those of celebrities, increase the number of copycat suicides (e.g., Çelik et al., 2016; Schäfer & Quiring, 2015; Suh et al., 2015). Although the term "copycat" has been criticized for possibly trivializing the deep suffering that leads to suicide (Owens, 2016), keep in mind that intense media coverage does increase a type of mimicry among some individuals.

4. **False** Only about 3% to 5% of suicidal people truly intend to die. Most are just unsure about how to go on living. Unfortunately, they can't see their problems objectively enough to recognize alternative courses of action. They often gamble with death, arranging it so that fate or others will save them. However, once the suicidal crisis passes, they're generally grateful to be alive.

5. **True** Children of parents who attempt or die by suicide are at much greater risk of following in their footsteps. It has been said that: "The person who dies by suicide puts his psychological skeleton in the survivor's emotional closet" (cited in Schneidman, 1969, p. 225).

6. **False** People who want to kill themselves are usually suicidal only for a limited period.

7. **True** Although women are much more likely to attempt suicide, men are far more likely to actually complete it. This is true because men generally use more effective and lethal methods, such as guns instead of pills.

8. **False** When people are first coming out of a depression, they are at greater risk because they now have the energy to actually attempt suicide.

9. **False** Suicide rates are highest among people with major depressive disorders. However, suicide is also the leading cause of premature death in people who suffer from schizophrenia, as well as a major cause of death in people with anxiety disorders and alcohol and other substance-related disorders. Furthermore, poor physical health, serious illness, loneliness, unemployment, and even natural disasters may push some people over the edge. Interestingly, people who work in careers that have great pressure for perfectionism—doctors, lawyers, architects, those in leadership roles—are at elevated risk.

10. **False** Estimates from various studies are that 40% to 80% of the general public have thought about attempting suicide at least once in their lives.

11. **False** Because society often considers suicide a terrible, shameful act, asking directly about it can give the person permission to talk. In fact, not asking is more likely to lead to further isolation and depression.

12. **False** Although people who engage in self-injuring behaviors are at significantly greater risk of suicide (e.g., Chesin et al., 2017), their intention is not to kill themselves, and the behaviors don't inevitably lead to suicide. This problem is officially known as nonsuicidal self-injury (NSSI). Most common among adolescents and young adults, NSSI usually results from attempts to punish oneself for perceived faults, to provide distraction from painful emotions through physical pain, and to express internal feelings in an external way (Bresin et al., 2017; Mayo Clinic, 2017). This is particularly true for individuals who are unaware of and less able to cope with feelings of anger (Thomassin et al., 2017).

**Nonsuicidal self-injury (NSSI)**   A serious behavior problem in which people deliberately harm themselves without lethal intent.

### Danger Signs for Suicide

What are the key signals for impending suicide? Let's consider the major symptoms, risk factors, and emergency signs:

*General symptoms:*

- the three H's—feeling Helpless, Hopeless, and Hapless.
- alcohol and other drug abuse
- irritability
- loss of interest in daily activities
- persistent fatigue and lack of energy and strength
- insomnia or excessive sleeping
- difficulty concentrating or feeling very restless
- noticeably reduced or increased appetite

*Risk factors:*

- previous history of substance abuse or suicide attempt
- family history of substance abuse, suicide attempt, suicide, or mental illness
- firearms, medications, or other methods for suicide readily available
- recent emotional trauma, such as incarceration, loss of a loved one, or loss of an important job

*Emergency signs:*

- increasing use of alcohol and other drugs
- acting anxious or agitated or displaying extreme mood swings
- talking about unbearable pain, feeling trapped, or being a burden to others
- talking about wanting to die or of having no reason to live
- talking about wanting to kill oneself or seeking revenge
- social withdrawal and/or sleeping too little or too much
- seeking methods for suicide, such as buying a gun

If you or someone you know is currently feeling suicidal, remember that: **Suicide is a permanent response to what is generally a temporary problem! Get immediate help!** Also see the following **Try This Yourself**.

**Sources:** American Association of Suicidology, 2016; Arkowitz & Lilienfeld, 2017; Birmaher & Brent, 2016; Depression the Second Time Around, n.d.; Lilienfeld et al., 2015; National Institute of Mental Health, 2016; Suicide Basic Facts, 2015.

## Try This Yourself

### Getting Help When You Think Someone Is Suicidal

If you have a friend or loved one with serious depression, it may feel like you're walking through a minefield when you're attempting to comfort and help them. What do the experts suggest?

**What NOT to Do:**

- **Don't ignore the warning signs.** (See again the previous list of danger signs for suicide.) Depression, like cancer or heart disease, is a critical, life-threatening disease. Knowing the signs of suicide risk can increase your confidence in how and when to intervene (Ramchand et al., 2016).

- **Don't equate suicide with "selfishness."** Just as we wouldn't say that someone suffering from diabetes or cancer died because he or she lacked courage and was being selfish, we need to recognize the courage and strength of the chronically and deeply depressed who struggle each day NOT to die.

- **Don't be afraid to discuss suicide.** In a calm voice, ask the person a direct question, such as, "Are you thinking of hurting yourself?" Many people fear the topic of suicide because they think they might put that idea into the other person's head. As mentioned before, the reality is that virtually every adult knows what suicide is, and many have even considered it for themselves. Furthermore, people who are told "you can't be seriously considering suicide" often feel even more alone, become less likely to share their true feelings, and become more likely to actually attempt suicide.

- **Don't abandon the person after the suicidal crisis has seemingly passed.** Depression and suicidal thoughts don't magically disappear. For many, the fight against depression is a painful, lifelong struggle, and your friend or loved one needs your ongoing support.

**What to Do:**

- **Stay with the person.** Encourage him or her to talk to you rather than to withdraw. Show the person that you care, but do not give false reassurances that "everything will be okay." If you feel like you can't handle the crisis by yourself, share your suspicions with parents, friends, or others who can help in a suicidal crisis. To save a life, you may have to betray a secret when someone confides in you.

- **Be Rogerian.** As mentioned in Chapters 13 and 15, Carl Rogers's four essential qualities of communication (*empathy, unconditional positive regard, genuineness*, and *active listening*) are probably the best, and safest, approach for any situation—including talking with a depressed, suicidal person.

- **Find help fast!** If a friend or loved one mentions suicide, or if you believe he or she is considering it, remove any weapons, medications, or other means the person might use to harm himself or herself. Discourage the person from using alcohol or illegal drugs, and get professional help fast! Most cities have walk-in centers that provide emergency counseling. Also, consider talking to the person's family, a therapist, or the toll-free 7/24 hotline 1-800-SUICIDE or 1-800-273-TALK. If you think the situation calls for emergency intervention, call 911 or go to the emergency room without delay.

---

Before we close this section and begin our discussion of the various psychological disorders, we'd like to offer a somewhat uplifting note. Research shows that one of the best ways to reduce suicides is to pass laws that limit access to handguns. Compared with states without such laws, those with background checks have a 53% lower gun suicide rate, those with mandated gun locks have a 68% lower gun suicide rate, and those with restrictions on open carry have a 42% lower gun suicide rate. Similarly, the longer the waiting period to buy a gun, the lower the gun suicide rate (Anestis et al., 2015; Metzl & MacLeish, 2015, Stroebe, 2016).

> *The mentally ill frighten and embarrass us. And so we marginalize the people who most need our acceptance. What mental health needs is more sunlight, more candor, more unashamed conversation.*
>
> —Glenn Close (Actress, Mental Health Advocate)

© Billy R. Ray/Wiley

## Retrieval Practice 14.1 | Studying Psychological Disorders

Completing this self-test and the connections section, and then checking your answers by clicking on the answer button or by looking in Appendix B, will provide immediate feedback and helpful practice for exams.

**Self-Test**

1. What is the *DSM*, and how is it used?

2. In the early treatment of psychological disorders, _____ was used to allow evil spirits to escape, whereas _____

was designed to drive the Devil out through prayer, fasting, and so on.

 **a.** trephining; exorcism
 **b.** demonology; hydrotherapy
 **c.** the medical model; the dunking test
 **d.** exorcism; stoning

**3.** _____ is the branch of medicine that deals with the diagnosis, treatment, and prevention of psychological disorders.

 **a.** Psychology    **b.** Psychiatry
 **c.** Psychobiology    **d.** Psychodiagnostics

**4.** Label the seven psychological perspectives on psychological disorders.

**5.** The DSM provides _____ for mental disorders.

 **a.** categorical descriptions    **b.** a global perspective
 **c.** a classification system    **d.** all but one of these options

**Connections—Chapter to Chapter**

Answering the following question will help you "look back and look ahead" to see the important connections among the subfields of psychology and chapters within this text.

In this chapter, you learned that the seven major perspectives of psychology emphasize different factors in explaining psychological disorders. In Chapter 15 (Therapy), you will learn about several forms of therapy and the approach each takes to treating psychological disorders. If you were suffering from a psychological disorder, do you think you would you prefer a biological (medication) or psychological (talk or insight) type of treatment?

## 14.2  Anxiety Disorders

### LEARNING OBJECTIVES

**Retrieval Practice**  While reading the upcoming sections, respond to each Learning Objective in your own words.

**Summarize the major types of anxiety disorders.**

- **Describe** the characteristics of generalized anxiety disorder (GAD), panic disorder, and phobias.
- **Explain** how psychological, biological, and sociocultural factors contribute to anxiety disorders.

Have you ever faced a critical, "high stakes" exam, job interview, or first date and broken out in a cold sweat, felt your heart pounding, and had trouble breathing? If so, you have some understanding of anxiety. But when the experiences and symptoms of fear and anxiety become disabling (uncontrollable and disrupting), mental health professionals may diagnose an **anxiety disorder**. Although twice as many women as men are diagnosed with anxiety disorders, men also suffer from this widespread disease. In fact, these disorders are among the most frequently occurring psychological disorders in the general population (Anxiety and Depression Association of America, 2016; Essau & Petermann, 2013; National Institute of Mental Health, 2016). Fortunately, they are among the easiest disorders to treat and offer some of the best chances for recovery (see **Figure 14.5** and Chapter 15).

**Anxiety disorder**  One of a group of psychological disorders characterized by disabling (uncontrollable and disruptive) fear or anxiety, accompanied by physiological arousal and related behavioral disturbances.

### Describing Anxiety Disorders

In this section, we discuss three anxiety disorders: *generalized anxiety disorder* (GAD), *panic disorder*, and *phobias* (**Figure 14.6**). Although we cover these disorders separately, their symptoms overlap, and they often occur together (Allan et al., 2016; Dibbets et al., 2015; Zinbarg et al., 2015).

**Generalized Anxiety Disorder**  Sufferers of **generalized anxiety disorder (GAD)** experience persistent, uncontrollable, and free-floating, nonspecified anxiety. The fears and anxiety are referred to as "free-floating" because they're unrelated to any specific threat—thus the term "generalized" anxiety disorder. Sadly, the fears and anxieties of GAD are generally

**Generalized anxiety disorder (GAD)**  An anxiety disorder characterized by persistent, uncontrollable, and free-floating, nonspecified anxiety.

Alamy Stock Photo

**FIGURE 14.5** **Coping with anxiety disorders**  Did you know that Emma Stone, 2017 winner of the Best Actress Oscar for *La La Land*, experienced her first panic attack as a young child (Begley, 2017; Lang, 2016)? These attacks became so debilitating and frequent that she developed agoraphobia and could barely leave her home to go to school. Thanks to therapy and her acting career, she's since developed healthy coping styles and speaks openly about her illness and personal experiences, hoping to boost public awareness of psychological illness.

uncontrollable and chronic—lasting at least six months (Louie & Roberts, 2015; Szkodny & Newman, 2014). Because of persistent muscle tension and autonomic fear reactions, people with this disorder may develop headaches, heart palpitations, dizziness, and insomnia, making it even harder to cope with normal daily activities. The disorder affects twice as many women as men (American Psychiatric Association, 2013; Watson & Greenberg, 2017).

**Panic Disorder**  Most of us have experienced feelings of intense panic, such as after narrowly missing a potentially fatal traffic collision. However, people with **panic disorder** endure repeated, sudden onsets of extreme terror and inexplicable *panic attacks*. Symptoms include severe heart palpitations, trembling, dizziness, difficulty breathing, and feelings of impending doom. The reactions are so intense that many sufferers believe they are having a heart attack. Panic disorder is diagnosed when several apparently spontaneous panic attacks lead to a persistent concern about future attacks. A common complication of panic disorder is agoraphobia, discussed in the next section.

**Panic disorder**  An anxiety disorder characterized by repeated, sudden onsets of intense terror and inexplicable panic attacks.

**Phobia**  A persistent and intense, irrational fear and avoidance of a specific object, activity, or situation.

**Phobias**  Just as most of us have experienced feelings of panic, we may also share a common fear of spiders, sharks, or snakes. However, people who suffer from **phobias** experience a persistent, intense, irrational fear and avoidance of a *specific* object, activity, or situation. Their fears are so disabling that they significantly interfere with daily life. Although the person recognizes that the level of fear is irrational, the experience is still one of overwhelming anxiety, and a full-blown

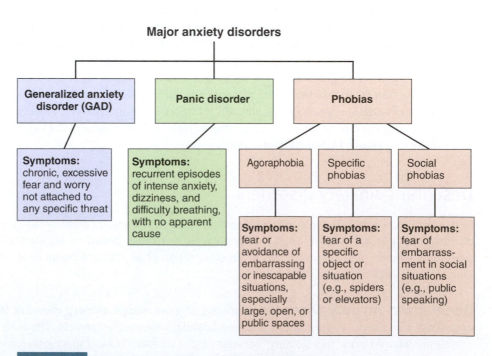

**FIGURE 14.6**  **The three major categories of anxiety disorders**

panic attack may follow. The fifth edition of the *DSM* divides phobias into separate categories: agoraphobia, specific phobias, and social anxiety disorder (social phobia).

People with *agoraphobia* restrict their normal activities because they fear having a panic attack in crowded, enclosed, or wide-open places where they would be unable to receive help in an emergency. In severe cases, people with agoraphobia may refuse to leave the perceived safety of their homes.

A *specific phobia* is a fear of a specific object or situation, such as needles, rats, spiders, or heights. Claustrophobia (fear of closed spaces) and acrophobia (fear of heights) are the specific phobias most often treated by therapists. People with specific phobias generally recognize that their fears are excessive and unreasonable, but they are unable to control their anxiety and will go to great lengths to avoid the feared stimulus.

People with *social anxiety disorder* (formerly called *social phobia*) are irrationally fearful of embarrassing themselves in social situations. Fear of public speaking and of eating in public are the two most common social phobias. The fear of public scrutiny and potential humiliation may become so pervasive that normal life is disrupted. People with this disorder are also four times more likely to abuse alcohol (Buckner & Terlecki, 2016).

As you may recall from our chapter opener, Jennifer Lawrence suffers from social anxiety disorder. Other famous people, including Britney Spears, Barbra Streisand, and Adele, also share this disorder, which can interfere with normal functioning. Ironically, for Jennifer Lawrence, being on stage actually relieves anxiety. Jennifer's mother remembers her as being curious about everything and having "a light within her." When she entered school, however, the light went out. Jennifer says: "We never knew what it was, a kind of social anxiety" (D'Aconti, 2013). Luckily, her struggles with anxiety subsided when she started acting. Jennifer recalls that moment in time: "On stage, my mother saw the change taking place in me. She saw my anxieties disappear. . . . I felt capable whereas before I felt good for nothing. This is why mom fought for me to become an actress" (cited in Harris, 2013).

## Explaining Anxiety Disorders

Why do people develop anxiety disorders? Research has focused on the roles of psychological, biological, and sociocultural processes (the *biopsychosocial model*) (**Figure 14.7**).

**Psychological Factors**    Researchers have identified two major psychological contributors to anxiety disorders:

1. *Faulty cognitive processes*    People with anxiety disorders may have habits of thinking, or cognitive processes, that make them prone to fear. These faulty cognitions, in turn, make them hypervigilant—meaning they constantly scan their environment for signs of danger and ignore signs of safety. Furthermore, they often magnify uncertain information and ordinary threats and failures and are hypersensitive to others' opinions of them (Helbig-Lang et al., 2015; Oglesby et al., 2016; Wild & Clark, 2015).

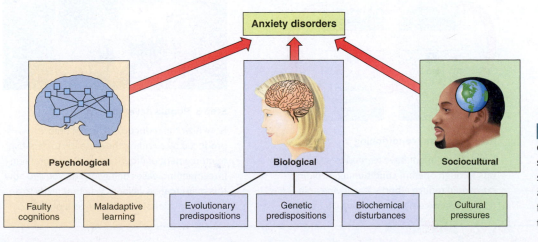

**FIGURE 14.7** **Anxiety disorders and the biopsychosocial model** The biopsychosocial model takes into account the wide variety of factors than can contribute to anxiety disorders.

© imageBROKER/Alamy Stock Photo

2. *Maladaptive learning* In contrast to this cognitive explanation, learning theorists suggest that anxiety disorders result from inadvertent and improper conditioning (Duits et al., 2015; Kunze et al., 2015; van Meurs et al., 2014). As we discovered in Chapter 6, during classical conditioning, if a neutral stimulus (NS), such as a harmless spider, becomes paired with an unconditioned stimulus (US), such as a sudden, frightening noise, it becomes a conditioned stimulus (CS) that elicits a conditioned emotional response (CER)—in this case, fear. To make matters worse, the person who experiences this conditioned fear often begins to actively avoid all spiders, which may eventually lead to a spider phobia. See **Step-by-Step Diagram 14.1**.

Along with maladaptive learning through classical and operant conditioning, anxiety disorders may develop from modeling and imitation (e.g., Schindler et al., 2016). In fact, research suggests that this type of social learning makes anxiety disorders the most "contagious" of all psychological disorders (Dean, 2015). By comparing 385 sets of identical twins and 486 sets of fraternal twins, researchers found direct environmental (versus genetic) transmission from parents to offspring (Eley et al., 2015). Note that in this case the word "contagious" does not mean that we can catch anxiety disorders from a sneeze or cough, but rather that children "catch it" primarily by watching and modeling their anxious caregivers' behavior (see the photo). The role of social learning in the transmission of anxiety is well-established. But the good news for parents with anxiety disorders is that certain behaviors, such as monitoring your own anxiety and encouraging your children to take small, age-appropriate risks, can minimize the chances of passing it on to your children (Dean, 2015).

**Biological Factors**   Some researchers believe phobias reflect an evolutionary, genetic predisposition to fear things that were dangerous to our ancestors (Bas-Hoogendam et al., 2016; Mineka & Oehlberg, 2008; New & German, 2015). In addition, some people with panic

---

**STEP-BY-STEP DIAGRAM 14.1**   **Conditioning and Phobias**   Classical conditioning combined with operant conditioning can lead to phobias. Consider the example of Little Albert's classically conditioned fear of rats, discussed in Chapter 6.

**STOP!** This Step-by-Step Diagram contains essential information NOT found elsewhere in the text, which is likely to appear on quizzes and exams. Be sure to study it CAREFULLY!

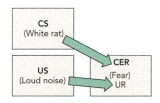

**Step 1   Classical conditioning**

John Watson and his assistant, Rosalie Rayner, paired a white rat with a loud noise (a hammer hitting a steel bar) to condition an infant (named "Little Albert") to fear rats.

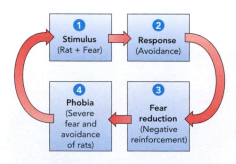

**Step 2   Operant conditioning**

Later, Albert might have learned to avoid rats through operant conditioning. Avoiding rats would reduce Albert's fear, giving unintended reinforcement to his fearful behavior.

© Jsteck/iStockphoto

**Step 3   Phobia development**

Note how the reduction in fear in Step 2 produced by avoiding the rat leads to negative reinforcement of Albert's fears. Given that reinforcement increases behavior, can you see how this may create a vicious cycle that leads to an intense, irrational fear, known as a phobia?

disorder seem genetically predisposed toward an overreaction of the autonomic nervous system, further supporting arguments for a biological explanation.

Given that women greatly outnumber men in diagnoses of anxiety disorders, biochemical research suggests that sex hormones, such as estrogen and progesterone, may be involved (Li & Graham, 2017). Further evidence for a biochemical disturbance comes from the fact that hyperventilation, as well as drugs such as caffeine and nicotine, can trigger a panic attack. Interestingly, recent research shows that disturbed sleep is linked to both anxiety disorders and chronic depression (Wassing et al., 2016).

**Sociocultural Factors**    As expected, many sociocultural factors contribute to anxiety. For instance, research shows children who are psychologically abused—including bullying, severe insults, overwhelming demands, and isolation—are at greater risk for developing GAD and social anxiety disorder (Flett et al., 2016; Spinazzola et al., 2014).

Research on cultural factors notes the sharp rise in anxiety disorders in the past 50 years, particularly in Western industrialized countries. Can you see how our fast-paced lives—along with our increased mobility, decreased job security, and decreased family support—might contribute to anxiety? Unlike the dangers early humans faced in our evolutionary history, today's threats are less identifiable and less immediate. This may in turn lead some people to become hypervigilant and predisposed to anxiety disorders.

Further support for sociocultural influences on anxiety disorders is our recognition that they can have dramatically different forms in other cultures. Some Japanese, for instance, experience a type of social phobia called *taijin kyofusho (TKS)*, a morbid dread of doing something to embarrass *others*. This disorder is quite different from the Western version of social phobia, which centers on a fear of criticism and self-embarrassment.

© Billy R. Ray/Wiley

## Retrieval Practice 14.2 | Anxiety Disorders

Completing this self-test and the connections section, and then checking your answers by clicking on the answer button or by looking in Appendix B, will provide immediate feedback and helpful practice for exams.

**Self-Test**

1. Label the three key anxiety disorders.

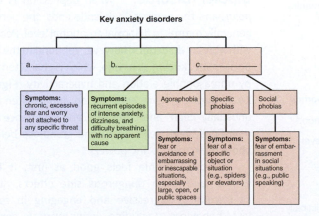

2. Persistent, uncontrollable, and free-floating, nonspecified anxiety might be diagnosed as _____.

   **a.** a generalized anxiety disorder   **b.** a panic disorder
   **c.** a phobia                          **d.** all these options

3. In _____ disorder, the individual suffers brief attacks of intense apprehension.

   **a.** phobic              **b.** posttraumatic stress
   **c.** panic               **d.** dissociative fugue

4. A persistent and intense, irrational fear and avoidance of a specific object or situation is known as _____.

   **a.** a panic disorder         **b.** a phobia
   **c.** the "scared-cat" syndrome   **d.** paranoia

5. In the Japanese social phobia called TKS, people fear that they will _____.

   **a.** evaluate others negatively   **b.** embarrass themselves
   **c.** embarrass others             **d.** be embarrassed by others

**Connections—Chapter to Chapter**

Answering the following question will help you "look back and look ahead" to see the important connections among the subfields of psychology and chapters within this text.

In Chapter 6 (Learning), we discussed cognitive-social theory and its emphasis on the roles of thinking and social learning in behavior. In this chapter, you learned that social learning theorists propose that some fears or anxieties may result from modeling and imitation. Explain how parents might develop fears concerning relatively uncommon events (such as child abductions by strangers) through social learning.

# 14.3 | Depressive and Bipolar Disorders

## LEARNING OBJECTIVES

**Retrieval Practice** While reading the upcoming sections, respond to each Learning Objective in your own words.

**Review the symptoms, causal factors, and dangers of depressive and bipolar disorders.**

- **Describe** depressive disorders and bipolar disorders, and how they differ.
- **Summarize** research on the biological and psychosocial factors that contribute to depressive and bipolar disorders.

**Depressive disorders** A group of psychological disorders characterized by profound and persistent sadness, despair, and/or decreased interest in things that were once pleasurable; moods severe enough to interfere with the ability to function.

**Major depressive disorder (MDD)** A psychological disorder characterized by significant symptoms of depression that occur nearly every day and last for two weeks or more.

**Bipolar disorder** A psychological disorder characterized by repeated episodes of mania (unreasonable elation, often with hyperactivity) alternating with depression.

**Mania** A state of abnormally elevated mood (either euphoric or irritable); also characterized by mental and physical hyperactivity, insomnia, and poor judgment.

Both depressive disorders and bipolar disorders are characterized by extreme disturbances in emotional states. Thus, both are sometimes referred to as *mood disorders.*

## Describing Depressive and Bipolar Disorders

We all experience shifts in our emotions on a somewhat regular basis—you may experience intense sadness when you fail a critical exam and high elation when you receive an A in a different course. Such emotional shifts are generally linked to life experiences, but when the shifts occur for no apparent reason and the extreme emotions are prolonged, they may qualify as **depressive disorders**.

### Major Depressive Disorder
Along with experiencing normal mood changes, almost everyone also feels depressed at some point in his or her lifetime—especially following the loss of a job, end of a relationship, or death of a loved one. But people suffering from **major depressive disorder (MDD)** may become so deeply sad and discouraged that they have trouble sleeping, lose (or gain) significant weight, and feel so fatigued that they cannot go to work or school or even comb their hair and brush their teeth.

Individuals with MDD also have trouble concentrating, making decisions, and being social. In addition, they often have difficulty recognizing common "thinking errors," such as *tunnel vision,* which involves focusing on only certain aspects of a situation (usually the negative parts) and ignoring other interpretations or alternatives. Do you see how this type of depressed thinking would deepen depression and possibly even lead to suicide (Connor et al., 2016; Polanco-Roman et al., 2016; Sue et al., 2016)?

**FIGURE 14.8** **Depressive versus bipolar disorders** If depressive disorders and bipolar disorders were depicted on a graph, they might look something like this. Remember that only in bipolar disorders do people experience manic episodes.

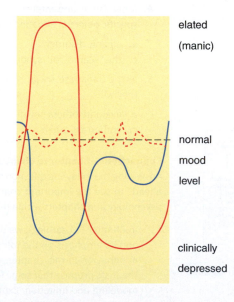

elated
(manic)

normal
mood
level

clinically
depressed

—— Bipolar Disorder

—— Major Depressive Disorder

### Bipolar Disorder
When depression is *unipolar*, and the depressive episode ends, the person generally returns to a normal emotional level. People with **bipolar disorders**, however, rebound to the opposite state, known as **mania**, which is characterized by unreasonable elation and hyperactivity (**Figure 14.8**). During a manic episode, individuals often feel unusually "high" and optimistic, and experience unrealistically high self-esteem and grandiose beliefs about their abilities and powers.

Although mania feels good at first, it has serious and often dangerous side effects, such as becoming aggressive and engaging in reckless behaviors, including inappropriate sexual activity, gambling away savings, giving away valuable possessions, or going on wild spending sprees. Also, during a manic episode, people are often hyperactive and may not sleep for days at a time without becoming apparently fatigued. Thinking is faster than normal and can change abruptly to new topics, showing "rapid flight of ideas." Speech is also rapid ("pressured speech"), making it difficult for others to get a word in edgewise. A manic episode may last a few days or a few months, and it generally ends abruptly. The ensuing depressive episode generally lasts three times as long as the mania (Leigh, 2015; Ray, 2015).

The lifetime risk for bipolar disorder is low—between 0.5 and 1.6%—but it can be one of the most debilitating and lethal disorders. Due in part to the impulsivity associated with this disorder, the suicide rate is between 10 and 20% among sufferers (Depp et al., 2016; Ketter & Miller, 2015).

To end on a more positive note, if you're suffering from a depressive or bipolar disorder, you are not alone. Many successful writers, scientists, and musicians suffer from depression. And television journalist Jane Pauley, award-winning actors Carrie Fisher and Catherine Zeta Jones, and action hero Jean-Claude Van Damme have all been diagnosed with bipolar disorder. Thanks to their courage and willingness to publicly discuss their lives, these famous figures have increased support, understanding, and funding for both depressive and bipolar disorders, as well as decreasing the associated stigma and stereotypes (**Figure 14.9**).

## Explaining Depressive and Bipolar Disorders

As we've seen, depressive and bipolar disorders are characterized by extreme disturbances in emotional states. What causes these extreme emotions? In this section, we will look at the biological, psychological, and sociocultural factors that contribute to depressive and bipolar disorders.

**Biological Factors**   Several biological factors are implicated in both depressive and bipolar disorder, including neurotransmitters, genes, and brain structure and function. For example, recent research points to imbalances of neurotransmitters, including GABA, serotonin, norepinephrine, and dopamine, as possible causes of mood disorders (Morgan, 2017; Peacock et al., 2017; Yin et al., 2016). And both depressive disorders and bipolar disorders are sometimes treated with antidepressants, which affect the amount or functioning of these same neurotransmitters. Another biochemical factor is suggested by a surprising link between depression and what we eat (**Figure 14.10**). Perhaps even more surprising is the recent finding that *psilocybin*, a hallucinogen from "magic" mushrooms, can help reduce the symptoms of depression (Mithoefer et al., 2016). Can you see how the chemicals in such foods and drugs might lead to physiological changes in the brain and body?

Along with neurotransmitter and other biochemical effects, genes appear to contribute to mood disorders (Boulos et al., 2017; Post et al., 2017; Strachan et al., 2017). Research shows that both depressive and bipolar disorder may be inherited (Antypa et al., 2016; Jacobs et al., 2015; Pandolfo et al., 2015). Other research, from an evolutionary perspective, suggests that moderate depression may be a normal and healthy adaptive response to a very real loss, such as the death of a loved one, because it helps us conserve energy and allows us to step back and reassess our goals (Beck & Bredemeier, 2016; Neumann & Walter, 2015). Clinical, severe depression may just be an extreme version of this generally adaptive response.

Finally, brain structures and functions also play a critical role. Many studies have found diminished brain activity in depression and increased activity during the manic phase of bipolar disorder (Brady et al., 2017; Cantisani et al., 2016; Carlson et al., 2017). Given the strong American (and international) love for high-impact professional sports, one of the most disturbing topics related to brain functioning is the mounting evidence that athletes who play these sports are at risk of developing depressive and bipolar disorders and other problems as they age. For more details, see the following **Research Challenge**.

United Archives GmbH/Alamy Stock Photo

**FIGURE 14.9   Carrie Frances Fisher (1956–2016)—a mental health hero**   The original Princess Leia of the famous *Star Wars* film series, Carrie Fisher, is remembered today as a famous and beloved Hollywood star. She's also celebrated as a mental health hero for her groundbreaking stance against the stigma of mental illness. Fisher told the Huffington Post, "At times, being bipolar can be an all-consuming challenge, requiring a lot of stamina and even more courage, so if you're living with this illness and functioning at all, it's something to be proud of, not ashamed of" (Holmes, 2016).

runzelkorn/Shutterstock.com

**FIGURE 14.10   Junk food and depression?**   Surprisingly, some studies have found that people who regularly eat junk food and commercially produced baked goods (such as croissants and doughnuts) are at increased risk of developing depression (Gangwisch et al., 2015; Sánchez-Villegas et al., 2011).

## Research Challenge

### Are Head Injuries Related to Depression and Other Psychological Disorders?

Concussions, or mild traumatic brain injuries (mTBIs), are common occurrences for athletes, military personnel, accident victims, and even ordinary people engaging in everyday sports and activities. The symptoms vary but typically include difficulty concentrating, sleep disturbances, fatigue, irritability, headaches, vertigo, depression, and/or anxiety (Broshek et al., 2015). Less common but more serious reactions occur after repeated concussions and brain trauma. Professional athletes often experience numerous concussions and may develop *chronic traumatic encephalopathy* (CTE), a progressive, degenerative brain disease. Sadly, individuals with CTE are more likely to develop depressive and bipolar disorders, as well as Parkinson's Disease, PTSD, schizophrenia, stroke, and other serious problems (Bajwa et al., 2016; Montenigro et al., 2017; Strain et al., 2017). CTE can even lead to suicide (**Figure 14.11**).

Despite this depressing opener, there is some good news. Researchers have identified for the first time how head injuries can alter genes, leading to serious brain diseases (Meng et al., 2017). This group of researchers first trained 20 rats to escape from a maze, a small tunnel-like structure commonly used to study spatial learning and memory in rodents. Next, they produced brain injuries by randomly choosing 10 of the 20 rats and injecting them with a special fluid. The other 10 rats did not receive the injections. When they later tested the rats in the same maze, it took the brain-injured rats about 25% longer to solve the maze than the noninjured rats. The researchers then examined the genes from five animals in each group and found major changes in the genes of the injured group (University of California—Los Angeles, 2017).

Why is this good news? Many of the rats' altered genes have counterparts in humans, and the study identified specific genes that are affected by traumatic brain injuries (TBIs). Knowing which genes are affected identifies them as the best targets for better diagnosis and possible future treatments for several neurological and psychological disorders.

#### Test Yourself

1. Based on the information provided, did this study (Meng et al., 2017) use descriptive, correlational, and/or experimental research?

**FIGURE 14.11** **Brain damage and professional sports** Junior Seau, who played in the NFL for 20 years, died by suicide from a gunshot wound to his chest in 2012 at the age of 43. Later studies confirmed that he suffered from CTE.

Kent C. Horner/Getty Images

2. If you chose:
   - *descriptive research*, is this a naturalistic observation, survey/interview, case study, and/or archival research?
   - *correlational research*, is this a positive, negative, or zero correlation?
   - *experimental research*, label the IV, DV, experimental group(s), and control group. (Note: If participants were not randomly assigned to groups, list it as a *quasi-experimental design*.)
   - both *descriptive* and *correlational* research, answer the corresponding questions for both.

**Check your answers by clicking on the answer button or by looking in Appendix B.**

**Note:** The information provided in this study is admittedly limited, but the level of detail is similar to what is presented in most textbooks and public reports of research findings. Answering these questions, and then comparing your answers to those provided, will help you become a better critical thinker and consumer of scientific research.

---

**Learned helplessness**
Seligman's term for a state of helplessness, or resignation, in which human or nonhuman animals fail to act to escape from a situation due to a history of repeated failures in the past.

## Psychological Factors
Psychological explanations of depression and bipolar disorder come from all the major perspectives. For instance, the psychoanalytic approach sees depression as the result of anger turned inward or as the aftermath of experiencing a real or imagined loss, which is internalized as guilt, shame, self-hatred, and ultimately self-blame. The cognitive perspective explains depression as caused, at least in part, by negative thinking patterns, including a tendency to ruminate, or obsess, about problems (Arora et al., 2015; Izadpanah et al., 2017; Topper et al., 2017). As you can see in **Figure 14.12**, this pattern of depressive thinking may, in turn, lead to a vicious, self-perpetuating cycle. The humanistic school says that depression results when a person demands perfection of himself or herself or when positive growth is blocked (McCormack & Joseph, 2014; Short & Thomas, 2015).

From the behavioral perspective, learning experiences also play a critical role. According to the **learned helplessness** theory (Seligman, 1975, 2007), depression occurs when people (and other animals) become resigned to the idea that they are helpless to escape from a painful situation because of a history of repeated failures. For humans, learned helplessness may be particularly likely to trigger depression if the person attributes failure to causes that are internal ("my own weakness"), stable ("this weakness is long-standing and unchanging"), and global ("this weakness is a problem in lots of settings") (Barnum et al., 2013; Smalheiser et al., 2014; Travers et al., 2015).

### Sociocultural Factors

In contrast to the biological and psychological theories, sociocultural explanations of depression and bipolar disorder focus on environmental stressors (such as poverty and unemployment), disturbances in interpersonal relationships, and histories of abuse or assault (Frodl et al., 2017; Holshausen et al., 2016; Massing-Schaffer et al., 2015). A surprising finding in the area of social factors is that high Internet and cell phone use are linked with mental health problems, including depression and anxiety (Panova & Lleras, 2016). This is particularly true when they're used to avoid negative experiences or feelings. However, no link was found if they're used merely to escape boredom.

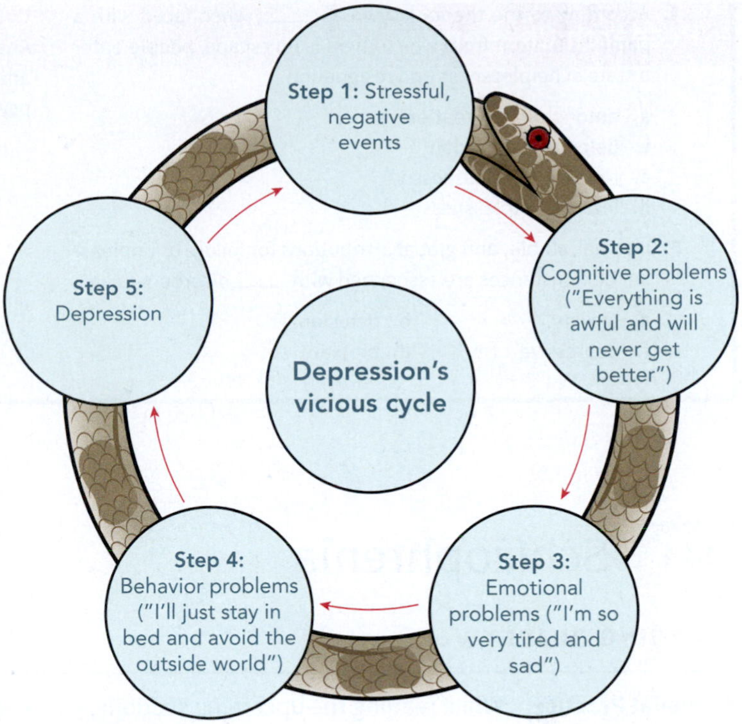

### Summing Up

Before going on, keep in mind that depression is more than a mental disorder. It also affects the entire body, which might help explain why people suffering from depression often feel so extremely tired and fatigued, as well as why they're at increased risk for cancer, cardiovascular disease, and dying younger (Batty et al., 2017; Jiménez-Fernández et al., 2015). One of the major culprits appears to be inflammation and/ or oxidative stress—a bodily imbalance that inhibits the ability to destroy toxic substances (Lindqvist et al., 2017; Liu et al., 2017; Peacock et al., 2017). The good news is that treatment with antidepressants can significantly reduce or remove these negative effects and greatly improve overall functioning (Black et al., 2017; Data-Franco et al., 2017).

However, note that suicide is a particular danger associated with both depressive disorder and bipolar disorder. If you or someone you know seem at risk, please review the myths, danger signs, and tips for what to do and what not to do discussed earlier in this chapter.

**FIGURE 14.12**  **Depression as a vicious cycle**  Have you heard that: *Depression is a snake that bites its own tail?* This somewhat common expression reflects cognitive theories that suggest depression results from a vicious cycle of destructive thoughts, emotions, and behaviors. Following one or more stressful, negative events (Step 1), people may ruminate and obsessively think about their personal failures and problems, while also worrying about events that are generally outside their control (Step 2). As a result of these persistent, negative thoughts, individuals tend to develop feelings of hopelessness, helplessness, sadness, and low self-esteem (Step 3). These emotional problems then generally lead to behavior problems, including decreased activities, social withdrawal, and decreased productivity (Step 4). Do you recognize how this cycle leads to depression (Step 5), and how other future stressors will inevitably add to and perpetuate this cycle? (See Chapter 15 for tips on how to break this cycle.)

© Billy R. Ray/Wiley

## Retrieval Practice 14.3 | Depressive and Bipolar Disorders

Completing this self-test and the connections section, and then checking your answers by clicking on the answer button or by looking in Appendix B, will provide immediate feedback and helpful practice for exams.

### Self-Test

1. How are depressive disorders different from bipolar disorder?

2. When experiencing _____, the individual is typically highly excited and impulsive and has unrealistically high self-esteem.

   **a.** hyperarousal        **b.** mania
   **c.** elation-excess syndrome (EES)   **d.** pituitary overload

3. Depressive and bipolar disorders are sometimes treated with _____, which affect the amount or functioning of norepinephrine, dopamine, and serotonin in the brain.

   **a.** antidepressants        **b.** antipsychotics
   **c.** mood congruence drugs    **d.** none of these options

4. According to the theory known as _____, when faced with a painful situation from which there is no escape, people enter a state of helplessness and resignation.

    a. autonomic resignation
    b. helpless resignation
    c. resigned helplessness
    d. learned helplessness

5. Internal, stable, and global attributions for failure or unpleasant circumstances are associated with _____ disorders.

    a. anxiety          b. delusional
    c. depressive      d. bipolar

**Connections—Chapter to Chapter**

Answering the following question will help you "look back and look ahead" to see the important connections among the subfields of psychology and chapters within this text.

In Chapter 3 (Stress and Health Psychology), you learned that some people have an *internal locus of control* (a belief that they can influence or control major factors in their lives), and some people have an *external locus of control* (believing that chance or outside forces beyond their control determine their fate). In this chapter, you read about the *learned helplessness* model of depression. Explain how locus of control and learned helplessness are related to each other and to depression.

# 14.4   Schizophrenia

## LEARNING OBJECTIVES

**Retrieval Practice**   While reading the upcoming sections, respond to each Learning Objective in your own words.

**Review how psychologists define, classify, and explain schizophrenia.**

- **Identify** schizophrenia and its common characteristics.
- **Compare** the positive versus negative symptoms of schizophrenia.
- **Summarize** the biological and psychosocial factors that contribute to schizophrenia.

Imagine that your 17-year-old son's behavior has changed dramatically over the past few months. He has gone from being actively involved in sports and clubs to suddenly quitting all activities and refusing to go to school. He now talks to himself—mumbling and yelling out at times—and no longer regularly showers or washes his hair. Recently he announced, "The voices are telling me to jump out the window" (Kotowski, 2012).

This description is taken from the true case history of a patient who suffers from **schizophrenia**. As shown in this example and discussed in this section, people with schizophrenia have major disturbances in *perception* (seeing or hearing things that others don't), *language* (bizarre words and meanings), *thought* (impaired logic), *emotion* (exaggerated or blunted), and/or *behavior* (peculiar movements and social withdrawal). Furthermore, some may have serious problems caring for themselves, relating to others, and holding a job. The *DSM* places schizophrenia within the category of "schizophrenic spectrum and other psychotic disorders." Recall that psychosis refers to a serious loss of contact with reality. In extreme cases, the illness is so severe that it's considered a psychosis, and treatment may require institutional or custodial care.

Schizophrenia is a widespread and devastating group of psychological disorders. Approximately 1% of people in any given adult population will develop it in their lifetime, and approximately half of all people who are admitted to mental hospitals are diagnosed with this disorder (Brown & Lau, 2016; Castle & Buckley, 2015; Gottesman, 1991). Schizophrenia usually emerges between the late teens and the mid-30s and only rarely prior to adolescence or after age 45. It seems to be equally prevalent in men and women, but it's generally more severe and strikes earlier in men (Brown & Lau, 2016; Castle & Buckley, 2015; Silber, 2014; Zorrilla et al., 2015).

Many people confuse schizophrenia with dissociative identity disorder, which is sometimes referred to as *split* or *multiple personality disorder*. *Schizophrenia* means "split mind," but when Eugen Bleuler coined the term in 1911, he was referring to the fragmenting of thought processes and emotions, not of personalities (Neale et al., 1983). As we discuss later in this chapter, dissociative identity disorder is popularly referred to as having a "split personality"—the rare and controversial condition of having more than one distinct personality (see the **Myth Busters**).

**Schizophrenia**   A group of severe psychological disorders involving major disturbances in perception, language, thought, emotion, and/or behavior.

## Myth Busters

### Do People with Schizophrenia Have Multiple Personalities?

As shown in this cartoon and as portrayed in many popular movies and television shows, schizophrenia is commonly confused with *multiple personality disorder* (now known as *dissociative identity disorder*). This widespread error persists in part because of confusing terminology. Literally translated, *schizophrenia* means "split mind," referring to a split from reality that shows itself in disturbed perceptions, language, thought, emotions, and/or behavior. In contrast, dissociative identity disorder refers to the condition in which two or more distinct personalities exist within the same person at different times. People with schizophrenia have only one personality.

Why does this matter? Confusing schizophrenia with multiple personalities is not only technically incorrect, it also trivializes the devastating effects of both disorders, which may include severe anxiety, social isolation, unemployment, homelessness, substance abuse, clinical depression, and even suicide (Arkowitz & Lilienfeld, 2017; Lasalvia et al., 2015; Lilienfeld et al., 2015).

"THANKS FOR CURING MY SCHIZOPHRENIA— WE'RE BOTH FINE NOW!"

## Symptoms of Schizophrenia

Schizophrenia, as mentioned, is characterized by a disturbance in one or more of the following areas: *perception, language, thought, affect* (emotions), and/or *behavior.*

**Perception**    The senses of people with schizophrenia may be either enhanced or blunted. The filtering and selection processes that allow most people to concentrate on whatever they choose are impaired, and sensory stimulation is jumbled and distorted. People with schizophrenia may experience *hallucinations*—false, imaginary sensory perceptions that occur without external stimuli. Auditory hallucinations (hearing voices and sounds) are among the most commonly noted and reported symptoms of schizophrenia. Individuals with schizophrenia may also experience visual hallucinations (seeing things that others cannot see) and olfactory hallucinations (smelling things others do not smell). In other words, people with schizophrenia may hear, see, and smell things that aren't real.

Are these voices and visions dangerous? On rare occasions, people with schizophrenia hurt others in response to their distorted perceptions. But a person with schizophrenia is more likely to be self-destructive and suicidal than violent toward others.

**Language and Thought**    For people with schizophrenia, words lose their usual meanings and associations, logic is impaired, and thoughts are disorganized and bizarre. When language and thought disturbances are mild, the individual jumps from topic to topic. With more severe disturbances, the person jumbles phrases and words together (into a "word salad") or creates artificial words. The most common—and frightening—thought disturbance experienced by people with schizophrenia is lack of contact with reality (psychosis).

*Delusions*—false, imaginary beliefs that are maintained despite clear evidence to the contrary—are also common in people with schizophrenia (see the cartoon). We all experience exaggerated thoughts from time to time, such as thinking a friend is trying to avoid us, but the delusions of schizophrenia are much more extreme. If someone falsely believes that the postman who routinely delivers mail to his house every afternoon is a co-conspirator in a plot to kill him, it will likely qualify as a *delusion of persecution,* or paranoia. In *delusions of grandeur*, people believe that they are someone very important, perhaps Jesus Christ or the Queen of England. In *delusions of control,* people believe that their thoughts or actions are being controlled by outside or alien forces—"the CIA is controlling my thoughts."

**Emotion**    Changes in emotion usually occur in people with schizophrenia. In some cases, emotions are exaggerated and fluctuate rapidly. At other times, they

"The company is happy to address your concerns about surveillance."

become blunted. Some people with schizophrenia have *flattened affect*—almost no emotional response of any kind.

**Behavior** Disturbances in behavior may take the form of unusual actions that have special meaning to the sufferer. For example, one patient massaged his head repeatedly to "clear it" of unwanted thoughts. People with schizophrenia also may become *cataleptic* and assume a nearly immobile stance for an extended period.

## Classifying Schizophrenia

For many years, researchers divided schizophrenia into five subtypes: *paranoid*, *catatonic*, *disorganized*, *undifferentiated*, and *residual*. Critics suggested that this system does not differentiate in terms of prognosis, cause, or response to treatment and that the undifferentiated type was merely a catchall for cases that are difficult to diagnose (Castle & Buckley, 2015; McNally, 2016). For these reasons, researchers have proposed an alternative classification system:

1. **Positive schizophrenia symptoms** are additions to or exaggerations of normal functions. Delusions and hallucinations are examples of positive symptoms. (In this case, and as discussed in Chapter 6, "positive" means that "something is added" above and beyond normal levels.)

2. **Negative schizophrenia symptoms** include the loss or absence of normal functions. Impaired attention, limited or toneless speech, flat or blunted affect, and social withdrawal are all classic negative symptoms of schizophrenia. (Recall again that "negative" is *not* the same as unpleasant or bad. It means that "something is taken away." In this case daily functioning is "taken away" because it's so far below normal levels.)

Positive symptoms are more common when schizophrenia develops rapidly, whereas negative symptoms are more often found in slow-developing schizophrenia. Positive symptoms are associated with better adjustment before the onset and a better prognosis for recovery.

## Explaining Schizophrenia

Because schizophrenia comes in many different forms, It's likely to be associated with multiple biological causes and prenatal and environmental influences. Let's look at biological contributions first.

**Biological Factors** Most biological explanations of schizophrenia focus on genetics, biochemistry, and brain abnormalities.

- **Genetics** Current research indicates that the risk for schizophrenia increases with genetic similarity (Arnedo et al., 2015; Gottesman, 1991; Reble et al., 2017). This means that people who share more genes with a person who has schizophrenia are more likely to develop the disorder (**Figure 14.13**).

- **Biochemistry** Recent research suggests that disruptions in gonadal and other hormones may play a role in schizophrenia (Riecher-Rössler, 2017). According to the *dopamine hypothesis*, overactivity of certain dopamine neurons in the brain causes some forms of schizophrenia (Gilani et al., 2014; Howes et al., 2017; Stopper & Floresco, 2015). This hypothesis is based on

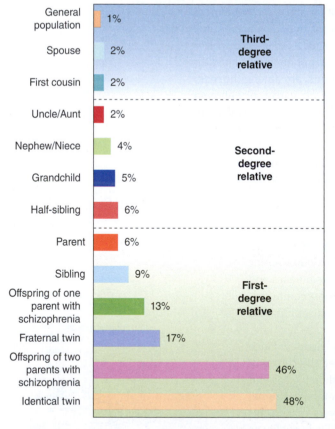

**Relationship to person with schizophrenia**

| Relationship | Risk | Category |
|---|---|---|
| General population | 1% | Third-degree relative |
| Spouse | 2% | |
| First cousin | 2% | |
| Uncle/Aunt | 2% | Second-degree relative |
| Nephew/Niece | 4% | |
| Grandchild | 5% | |
| Half-sibling | 6% | |
| Parent | 6% | First-degree relative |
| Sibling | 9% | |
| Offspring of one parent with schizophrenia | 13% | |
| Fraternal twin | 17% | |
| Offspring of two parents with schizophrenia | 46% | |
| Identical twin | 48% | |

**Percentage of risk**

**FIGURE 14.13** **Genetics and schizophrenia** As dramatically shown by this figure, the lifetime risk of developing schizophrenia is strongly linked with genetic inheritance. Is this a positive or negative correlation?

**Answer:** A positive correlation—the risk of developing schizophrenia increases as genetic relatedness to an individual with schizophrenia increases.

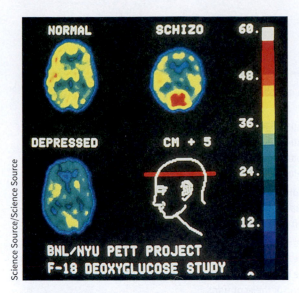

**FIGURE 14.14**   **Brain activity in schizophrenia**
Using these positron emission tomography (PET) scans, compare the normal levels of brain activity (upper left) with those of a person with schizophrenia (upper right), and then with those of a person with depression (lower left). Warmer colors (reds, yellows) indicate increased brain activity, whereas cooler colors (blues and greens) indicate decreased activity.

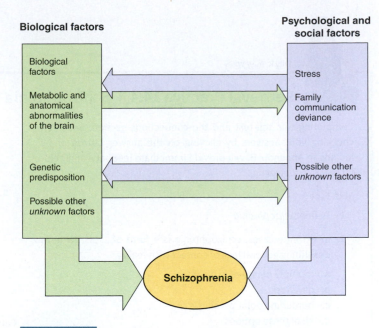

**FIGURE 14.15**   **The biopsychosocial model and schizophrenia**

two observations. First, administering amphetamines increases the amount of dopamine and can produce (or worsen) some symptoms of schizophrenia, especially in people with a genetic predisposition to the disorder. Second, drugs that reduce dopamine activity in the brain reduce or eliminate some symptoms of schizophrenia.

- **Brain abnormalities** A third area of research in schizophrenia explores links to abnormalities in brain function and structure. Researchers, for example, have found larger cerebral ventricles (fluid-filled spaces in the brain) and right hemisphere dysfunction in some people with schizophrenia (Guo et al., 2015; Woodward & Heckers, 2015; Young & Wimmer, 2017). Also, some people with chronic schizophrenia have lower levels of activity in specific areas of the brain (**Figure 14.14**).

### Prenatal and Other Environmental Influences

Clearly, biological factors play a key role in schizophrenia. However, consider that, in a pair of identical twins, if one twin has schizophrenia, the other has about a 50% chance of suffering from the disease at some point. This tells us that nongenetic factors must contribute the other 50%. Furthermore, as we've seen throughout this text, *epigenetic* (meaning "in addition to genetic") factors often influence whether or not specific genes will be expressed. Most psychologists believe there are several possible environmental and psychosocial contributors, including prenatal stress and viral infections, birth complications, low birth weight, immune responses, maternal malnutrition, and advanced paternal age (Kneeland & Fatemi, 2013; Meyer, 2016; Webb, 2016).

According to the **diathesis-stress model** of schizophrenia, stress plays an essential role in triggering schizophrenic episodes in people with an inherited predisposition (or diathesis) toward the disease (Brown & Lau, 2016; Frau et al., 2015; Howes et al., 2017). In line with this model, children who experience severe trauma before age 16 are three times more likely than other people to develop schizophrenia (Bentall et al., 2012; DeRosse et al., 2014). People who experience stressful living environments, including poverty, unemployment, and crowding, are also at increased risk (Brown & Lau, 2016; Kirkbride et al., 2014; Sweeney et al., 2015).

How should we evaluate the different theories about the causes of schizophrenia? Like virtually all psychological disorders, nature and nurture interact. Most scientists believe schizophrenia is probably the result of a combination of known and unknown interacting factors (**Figure 14.15**).

**Diathesis-stress model**   An explanation for the cause of certain disorders, such as schizophrenia, which suggests that people inherit a predisposition (or "diathesis") that increases their risk for psychological disorders when exposed to environmental or emotional stress; also known as the stress-vulnerability model.

© Billy R. Ray/ Wiley

## Retrieval Practice 14.4 | Schizophrenia

Completing this self-test and the connections section, and then checking your answers by clicking on the answer button or by looking in Appendix B, will provide immediate feedback and helpful practice for exams.

**Self-Test**

1. Define *schizophrenia.*

2. In extreme cases, schizophrenia is a form of _____, a term describing general lack of contact with reality.

   a. multiple personality disorder
   b. psychosis
   c. borderline polar psychosis
   d. all of these options

3. _____ refers to "split mind," whereas _____ refers to "split personality."

   a. Psychosis; neurosis
   b. Insanity; multiple personalities
   c. Schizophrenia; dissociative identity disorder (DID)
   d. Paranoia; borderline

4. Perceptions for which there are no appropriate external stimuli are called _____, and the most common type among people suffering from schizophrenia is _____ .

   a. hallucinations; auditory
   b. hallucinations; visual
   c. delusions; auditory
   d. delusions; visual

5. According to _____, people inherit a predisposition that increases their risk for mental disorders if they are exposed to certain extremely stressful life experiences.

   a. the stress-reactivity model
   b. the diathesis-stress model
   c. the envirogenetics hypothesis
   d. none of these options

**Connections—Chapter to Chapter**

Answering the following question will help you "look back and look ahead" to see the important connections among the subfields of psychology and chapters within this text.

In Chapter 4 (Sensation and Perception), you discovered that *sensation* and *perception* work together to help us understand the world around us. In this chapter, you learned that these two processes can become disordered in a person suffering with schizophrenia. Explain how some symptoms in schizophrenia may arise from problems with sensation and perception.

## 14.5 Other Disorders

### LEARNING OBJECTIVES

**Retrieval Practice**   While reading the upcoming sections, respond to each Learning Objective in your own words.

**Review the main features of obsessive-compulsive, dissociative, and personality disorders.**

- **Identify** obsessive-compulsive disorder and its major symptoms.
- **Describe** dissociative disorders.
- **Discuss** personality disorders, including antisocial (ASPD) and borderline (BPD).

Having discussed anxiety disorders, mood disorders, and schizophrenia, we now explore three additional disorders: obsessive-compulsive, dissociative, and personality disorders.

### Obsessive-Compulsive Disorder (OCD)

**Obsessive-compulsive disorder (OCD)**   A psychological disorder characterized by persistent, unwanted, fearful thoughts (obsessions) and/or irresistible urges to perform repetitive and/or ritualized behaviors (compulsions).

Do you occasionally worry about whether or not you locked your doors and sometimes feel compelled to run back and check? Most people do. However, people with **obsessive-compulsive disorder (OCD)** experience persistent, unwanted, fearful thoughts (obsessions) and/or irresistible urges to perform repetitive and/or ritualized behaviors (compulsions) to help relieve the anxiety created by the obsession. In adults, women are affected at a slightly higher rate than men, whereas men are more commonly affected in childhood (American Psychiatric Association, 2013).

Common examples of obsessions are fear of germs, fear of being hurt or of hurting others, and troubling religious or sexual thoughts. Examples of compulsions are repeatedly checking, counting, cleaning, washing all or specific body parts, putting things in a certain order, and hoarding (Berman et al., 2016; Bottesi et al., 2017; De Putter et al., 2017). As mentioned before, everyone worries and sometimes double-checks, but people with OCD have these thoughts and do these rituals for at least an hour or more each day, often longer.

Imagine what it would be like to worry so obsessively about germs that you compulsively wash your hands hundreds of times a day, until they are raw and bleeding. Most sufferers of OCD realize that their actions are senseless. But when they try to stop the behavior, they experience mounting anxiety, which is relieved only by giving in to the compulsions. Given that numerous biological and psychological factors contribute to OCD, it is most often treated with a combination of drugs, cognitive behavior therapy (CBT), and remediation therapy (Bennett, 2016; Emslie et al., 2016; van Passel, 2016). See Chapter 15 and **Figure 14.16**.

**FIGURE 14.16** **Managing OCD** Many celebrities suffer from OCD, including singer/actor Justin Timberlake (pictured here), soccer star David Beckham, and actors Megan Fox, Cameron Diaz, and Leonardo DiCaprio. Fortunately, people can learn to manage the symptoms of OCD, through therapy and/or medication, and lead highly productive and fulfilling lives.

JStone/Shutterstock

## Dissociative Disorders

If you've ever been daydreaming while driving home from your college campus, and then could not remember making one single turn, you may have experienced a normal form of *dissociation*, meaning a mild disconnection from your immediate surroundings.

The most dramatic extremes of this type of detachment are the **dissociative disorders**, characterized by a sudden break (*dissociation*) in conscious awareness, self-identity, and/or memory. Note that this is a disconnection or detachment from immediate surroundings or from physical or emotional experience. It is very different from the loss of contact with reality seen in psychosis (**Figure 14.17**). There are several forms of dissociative disorders, including dissociative amnesia and dissociative identity disorder (DID). However, all are characterized by a splitting apart (a *dis-association*) of critical aspects of experience from memory or consciousness.

The most controversial, and least common, dissociative disorder is **dissociative identity disorder (DID)**—previously known as multiple personality disorder (MPD). An individual with this disorder has at least two separate and distinct personalities, or *identities* (**Figure 14.18**). Each personality has unique memories, behaviors, and social relationships. Transition from one personality to another occurs suddenly, and is often triggered by psychological stress and trauma (Brand et al., 2016; Huntjens et al., 2016). Typically, there is a "core" personality, who has no knowledge or awareness of the alternate personalities but is often aware of lost memories and lost periods of time. The disorder is diagnosed about equally among men and women (American Psychiatric Association, 2013).

**Dissociative disorder** One of a group of psychological disorders characterized by a sudden break (*dissociation*) in conscious awareness, self-identity, and/or memory.

**Dissociative identity disorder (DID)** A psychological disorder characterized by the presence of two or more distinct personality systems (or identities) in the same individual; previously known as multiple personality disorder (MPD).

Image Source/Getty Images

**FIGURE 14.17** **Dissociation as an escape** A common factor in dissociative disorders is the need to escape and cope with extreme stress (Spiegel et al., 2013). Imagine witnessing a loved one's death in a horrible car accident. Can you see how your mind might cope by blocking out all memory of the event?

**FIGURE 14.18** **A personal account of DID** Herschel Walker, Pro Bowl NFL football player, Olympic bobsledder, and business and family man, now suggests that all of the people who played these roles were his "alters," or alternate personalities. He has been diagnosed with the controversial *dissociative identity disorder (DID)*. Although some have suggested that the disorder helped him succeed as a professional athlete, it played havoc with his personal life. He's now in treatment and has written a book, *Breaking Free*, hoping to change the public's image of DID.

Stephen Dunn/Allsport/Getty Images.

**Personality disorder** A psychological disorder characterized by chronic, inflexible, maladaptive personality traits, which cause significant impairment of social and occupational functioning.

**Antisocial personality disorder (ASPD)** A personality disorder characterized by egocentrism and a lack of conscience, remorse, or empathy for others.

DID is a controversial diagnosis. Some experts suggest that many cases are faked or can be attributed to fantasy-prone individuals, false memories, or an unconscious need to please a therapist (Arkowitz & Lilienfeld, 2017; Lynn et al., 2016; Merckelbach et al., 2016). In contrast, a recent study of women with genuine diagnoses of DID, female actors asked to simulate DID, women with PTSD, and healthy controls supported previous findings that DID is rooted in traumatic experiences, such as neglect or abuse in childhood (Vissia et al., 2016).

## Personality Disorders

What would happen if the characteristics of someone's personality were so inflexible and maladaptive that they significantly impaired that person's ability to function? This is what occurs with **personality disorders**. Several types of personality disorders are included in the fifth edition of the DSM, but here we will focus on antisocial personality disorder (ASPD) and borderline personality disorder (BPD) (American Psychiatric Association, 2013).

**Antisocial Personality Disorder (ASPD)** People with **antisocial personality disorder (ASPD)**—sometimes called *psychopaths* or *sociopaths*—are typically egocentric and exhibit a lack of conscience, remorse, or empathy for others. They're also manipulative, deceitful, and willing to use others for personal gain. These behaviors typically begin in childhood or early adolescence and continue through adulthood. They also lie so far outside the ethical and legal standards of society that many consider ASPD the most serious of all psychological disorders.

Unlike people with anxiety disorders, mood disorders, and schizophrenia, those with this diagnosis feel little personal distress (and may not be motivated to change). And, as shown in **Figure 14.19**, the maladaptive behaviors of those with ASPD often cause considerable harm to others (e.g., Baskin-Sommers et al., 2016; Brem et al., 2017; Newcorn et al., 2016). Individuals with ASPD typically act impulsively, without giving thought to the consequences. They are usually poised when confronted with their destructive behavior and feel contempt for anyone they are able to manipulate. Moreover, they typically change jobs and relationships suddenly, and often have a history of truancy from school or of being expelled for destructive behavior. Surprisingly, people with antisocial personalities can be charming and persuasive, and they often have remarkably good insight into the needs and weaknesses of other people.

**FIGURE 14.19** **Famous people with ASPD** Serial killers like Jeffrey Dahmer (pictured here) and Charles Manson are often seen as classic examples of people with ASPD. However, most people who have this disorder harm others in less dramatic ways—as crooked politicians or ruthless businessmen, such as the character portrayed by Michael Douglas in the movie *Wall Street,* for instance.

EUGENE GARCIA/AFP/Getty Images

Twin and adoption studies suggest a possible genetic predisposition to ASPD (Dhamija et al., 2016; Rosenström et al., 2017). Researchers also have found abnormally low autonomic activity during stress, right hemisphere abnormalities, reduced gray matter in the frontal lobes, and biochemical disturbances in people with ASPD (Jiang et al., 2015; Kumari et al., 2014; Smith et al., 2016). For example, MRI brain scans of criminals currently in prison for violent crimes, such as rape, murder, or attempted murder, and showing little empathy and remorse for their crimes, reveal reduced gray matter volume in the prefrontal cortex (Gregory et al., 2012).

Evidence also exists for environmental or psychological causes. People with antisocial personality disorder often come from homes characterized by severely abusive parenting styles, emotional deprivation, harsh and inconsistent disciplinary practices, residential mobility, and antisocial parental behavior (Crego & Widiger, 2016; Dargis et al., 2016; Mok et al., 2016). Still other studies show a strong interaction between both heredity and environment (Dhamija et al., 2016; Rosenström et al., 2017).

## Borderline Personality Disorder (BPD)

> *Mary's troubles first began in adolescence. She began to miss curfew, was frequently truant, and her grades declined sharply. Mary later became promiscuous and prostituted herself several times to get drug money. . . . She also quickly fell in love and overly idealized new friends. But when they quickly (and inevitably) disappointed her, she would angrily cast them aside. . . . Mary's problems, coupled with a preoccupation with inflicting pain on herself (by cutting and burning) and persistent thoughts of suicide, eventually led to her admittance to a psychiatric hospital at age 26 (Kring et al., 2010, pp. 354–355).*

**FIGURE 14.20  Girl Interrupted**  In this film, the Angelina Jolie character portrays several symptoms of BPD, as well as strong antisocial characteristics. The two personality disorders are often *comorbid*, meaning they occur together.

Mary's experiences are all classic symptoms of **borderline personality disorder (BPD)**. The core features of this disorder include a pervasive pattern of instability in emotions, relationships, and self-image, along with impulsive and self-destructive behaviors, such as truancy, promiscuity, drinking, gambling, and eating sprees (**Figure 14.20**). In addition, people with BPD may attempt suicide and sometimes engage in self-mutilating ("cutting") behaviors (Calati & Courtet, 2016; Khan et al., 2017; Sher et al., 2016).

**Borderline personality disorder (BPD)**  A psychological disorder characterized by severe instability in emotions, relationships, and self-image, along with impulsive and self-destructive behaviors.

Those with BPD also tend to see themselves and everyone else in absolute terms—as either perfect or worthless. Constantly seeking reassurance from others, they may quickly erupt in anger at the slightest sign of disapproval. As you might expect, this disorder is typically marked by a long history of broken friendships, divorces, and lost jobs.

In short, people with this disorder appear to have a deep well of intense loneliness and a chronic fear of abandonment. Unfortunately, given their troublesome personality traits, friends, lovers, and even family members and therapists often do "abandon" them—thus creating a tragic self-fulfilling prophecy. Sadly, this disorder is among the most commonly diagnosed and functionally disabling of all personality disorders (Arntz, 2015; Gunderson & Links, 2014; Rizvi & Salters-Pedneault, 2013). The good news is that BPD can be reliably diagnosed, and it does respond to professional intervention—particularly in young people (Bateman & Fonagy, 2016; Edel et al., 2017; Rizvi et al., 2017).

What causes BPD? Some research points to environmental factors, such as a childhood history of neglect, emotional deprivation, and/or physical, sexual, or emotional abuse, and trauma (Bichescu-Burian et al., 2017; Chesin et al., 2015; Hunt et al., 2015). From a biological perspective, BPD also tends to run in families, and some data suggest that it is a result of impaired functioning of the brain's frontal lobes and limbic system, areas that control impulsive behaviors (Denny et al., 2016; Soloff et al., 2017; Visintin et al., 2016). For instance, research using neuroimaging reveals that people with BPD show more activity in parts of the brain associated with the experience of negative emotions, coupled with less activity in parts of the brain that help suppress negative emotion (Ruocco et al., 2013). As in almost all other psychological disorders, most researchers agree that BPD results from an interaction of biopsychosocial factors (Crego & Widiger, 2016; McMurran & Crawford, 2016; Stone, 2014).

© Billy R. Ray/Wiley

## Retrieval Practice 14.5  |  Other Disorders

Completing this self-test and the connections section, and then checking your answers by clicking on the answer button or by looking in Appendix B, will provide immediate feedback and helpful practice for exams.

**Self-Test**

1. Compare obsessions and compulsions.

2. A disorder characterized by disturbances in conscious awareness, self-identity, and/or memory is known as a(n) _____.

   **a.** dissociative disorder
   **b.** disoriented disorder
   **c.** displacement disorder
   **d.** identity disorder

3. _____ is characterized by the presence of two or more separate and distinct personality systems in the same individual.

   **a.** Multiple-personality dysfunction (MPD)
   **b.** Disassociation disorder (DD)
   **c.** Fictional-actor delusion (FAD)
   **d.** Dissociative identity disorder (DID)

4. A serial killer would likely be diagnosed as a(n) _____ personality in the *Diagnostic and Statistical Manual (DSM)*.

   **a.** dissociative disorder
   **b.** antisocial personality disorder
   **c.** multiple personality disorder
   **d.** borderline psychosis

5. Instability in emotions, relationships, and self-image, along with impulsive and self-destructive behaviors, are characteristic of the _____ personality disorder.

   **a.** manic depressive
   **b.** bipolar
   **c.** borderline
   **d.** antisocial

### Connections—Chapter to Chapter

Answering the following question will help you "look back and look ahead" to see the important connections among the subfields of psychology and chapters within this text.

In Chapter 7 (Memory), we discussed the heated and ongoing controversy over false versus repressed memories. In this chapter, you discovered a similar controversy over dissociative identity disorder (DID). Explain the role of false memories in both controversies.

## 14.6 | Gender and Cultural Effects

### LEARNING OBJECTIVES

**Retrieval Practice** While reading the upcoming sections, respond to each Learning Objective in your own words.

**Summarize gender and cultural differences in psychological disorders.**

• **Discuss** the possible gender differences in depression.

• **Explain** why it is difficult to directly compare psychological disorders, such as schizophrenia, across cultures.

• **Describe** how understanding culture-general symptoms and culture-bound disorders helps us overcome ethnocentrism in psychological disorders.

• **Discuss** how resilience promotes mental health.

Among the Chippewa, Cree, and Montagnais-Naskapi Indians in Canada, there is a disorder called *wedigo* or *wiitiko—psychosis*, characterized by delusions and cannibalistic impulses. Believing they have been possessed by the spirit of a windigo, a cannibal giant with a heart and entrails of ice, victims become severely depressed (Faddiman, 1997). As the malady begins, the individual typically experiences loss of appetite, diarrhea, vomiting, and insomnia, and he or she may see people turning into beavers and other edible animals. In later stages, the victim becomes obsessed with cannibalistic thoughts and may even attack and kill loved ones in order to devour their flesh (Berreman, 1971; Thomason, 2014).

If you were a therapist, how would you treat this disorder? Does it fit neatly into any category of psychological disorders that we've just discussed? We began this chapter by discussing the complexities and problems with defining, identifying, and classifying abnormal behavior. Before we close, we need to add two additional confounding factors: gender and culture. In this section, we explore a few of the many ways in which men and women differ in their experience of abnormal behavior. We also look at cultural variations in abnormal behavior.

### Gender Differences

When you picture someone suffering from depression, anxiety, alcoholism, or antisocial personality disorder, what is the gender of each person? Most people tend to visualize a woman for the first two and a man for the last two. There is some truth to these stereotypes.

Research has found many gender differences in the prevalence rates of various psychological disorders. Let's start with the well-established fact that around the world, the rate of severe depression for women is about double that for men, and these differences tend to peak during adolescence. The gender gap narrows in early adulthood and then remains relatively stable in middle and late adulthood (Kuehner, 2017; Salk et al., 2017; World Health Organization, 2017b).

Why is there such a striking gender difference? Certain risk factors for depression (such as genetic predisposition, marital problems, pain, and illness) are common to both men and women. However, poverty is a well-known contributor to many psychological disorders, and women are far more likely than men to fall into the lowest socioeconomic groups. Women also experience more wage disparity and discrimination in the work force, sexual harassment and trauma, partner abuse, and chronic stress in their daily lives, which are all well-known contributing factors in depression and other disorders (Kelly et al., 2016; Oram et al., 2017; Salk et al., 2017). For more on income inequality, see the following **Research Challenge**.

## Research Challenge

### Does Unequal Pay for Equal Work Increase Female Anxiety and Depression?

Both anxiety and depression are more common among women than men, and a recent study provides an intriguing explanation (Platt et al., 2016). Given their initial hypothesis that the women's higher rate for both disorders may be due to discrimination in the workplace, researchers examined data from a national sample of over 20,000 adults (ages 30 to 65), who were interviewed in 2001–2002. Participants were asked questions about their education, work experience, and income, as well as questions to identify symptoms of depression and anxiety.

As predicted, women who made less than men (but had the same level of education and years in the workforce) were more likely to have both generalized anxiety disorder and major depressive disorder. More specifically, women whose income was equivalent to or greater than men's at the same level were somewhat more likely to show symptoms of anxiety, whereas those who made less money were more than four times as likely to show such symptoms. Similarly, women with equivalent levels of education and job experience but lower income had a rate of major depression nearly 2.5 times higher than men's. However, there was no gender difference in rates of depression among women whose income was the same as or better than men's.

Can you understand how these findings suggest that gender differences in rates of anxiety and depression may be at least in part a function of the consistently lower pay women receive in the workplace, and not merely a function of gender differences in biological predisposition to such disorders? Women may conclude that they are paid relatively less for equivalent work because of inferior merit and work quality, which, in turn, may cause feelings of depression and anxiety. Policies that mandate equal pay for equal work could therefore potentially help reduce the prevalence of these disorders in women.

**Test Yourself**

1. Based on the information provided, did this study (Platt et al., 2016) use descriptive, correlational, and/or experimental research?

2. If you chose:

   o *descriptive research*, is this a naturalistic observation, survey/interview, case study, and/or archival research?

   o *correlational research*, is this a positive, negative, or zero correlation?

   o *experimental research*, label the IV, DV, experimental group(s), and control group (Note: If participants were not randomly assigned to groups, list it as a *quasi-experimental design*.)

   o both *descriptive* and *correlational* research, answer the corresponding questions for both.

**Check your answers by clicking on the answer button or by looking in Appendix B.**

**Note:** The information provided in this study is admittedly limited, but the level of detail is similar to what is presented in most textbooks and public reports of research findings. Answering these questions, and then comparing your answers to those provided, will help you become a better critical thinker and consumer of scientific research.

© Yuri_Arcurs/iStockphoto

Research also suggests that some gender differences in depression may relate to the way women and men most often internalize or externalize their emotions. For instance, women tend to "vent" (express their emotions to others) more than men. They also generally ruminate more frequently than men, which means they are more likely to obsess and focus repetitively on their depressive thoughts and emotions, whereas men typically suppress their depressive thoughts and emotions (Malooly et al., 2017; Polanco-Romano et al., 2016; Rice et al., 2014).

Can you see how these gender differences might lead to differential diagnoses for depression? The most common symptoms of stereotypical depression, such as crying, low energy, dejected facial expressions, and withdrawal from social activities, are more socially acceptable for women than for men. In contrast, men in Western societies are typically socialized to believe that they should show their distress by acting out (being aggressive), acting impulsively (driving recklessly and committing petty crimes), and/or engaging in substance abuse. Given these differences in socialization and behaviors, combined with the fact that gender differences in depression are more pronounced in cultures with traditional gender roles, male depression may "simply" be expressed in less stereotypical ways, and therefore be underdiagnosed (Fields & Cochran, 2011; Pérez & Gaviña, 2015; Seedat et al., 2009). See the following **Try This Yourself.**

## Try This Yourself

### Gender Strategies for Managing Depression

In order to prevent or reduce depression, women may benefit from learning better stress reduction and thought control (Chapter 3). On the other hand, if it's true that men more often express their depression through impulsive, acting-out behaviors, then rewarding deliberate, planned behaviors over unintentional, spur-of-the moment ones may be helpful for treating some forms of male depression (Eaton et al., 2012). It's also important to stress that just because women are twice as likely to suffer from depression than men, it doesn't mean that the distress and impairment of depressed men should be overlooked or minimized.

© Piotr Marcinski/Shutterstock

**FIGURE 14.21** **What is stressful?**

David Alan Harvey/Magnum Photos, Inc.

**a.** Some stressors are culturally specific, such as feeling possessed by evil forces or being the victim of witchcraft.

Benelux/Corbis/VCG/Getty Images

**b.** Other stressors are shared by many cultures, such as the unexpected death of a loved one or loss of a job (Al-Issa, 2000; Cechnicki et al., 2011; Ramsay et al., 2012).

Understanding the importance of genetic predispositions, external environmental factors (like poverty), and cognitive factors (like internalizing versus externalizing emotions and problems) may help mental health professionals better understand individual and gender-related differences in depression.

## Culture and Psychological Disorders

Individuals from different cultures experience psychological disorders in a variety of ways. For example, the reported incidence of schizophrenia varies in different cultures around the world. It is unclear whether these differences result from actual differences in prevalence of the disorder or from differences in definition, diagnosis, or reporting (Hsu, 2016; Luhrmann et al., 2015; McLean et al., 2014). The symptoms and beliefs about the causes of schizophrenia also vary across cultures (Barnow & Balkir, 2013; Campbell et al., 2017; López & Guarnaccia, 2016), as do the particular stressors that may trigger its onset (**Figure 14.21**).

Finally, despite the advanced treatment facilities and methods in industrialized nations, the prognosis for people with schizophrenia is sometimes better in nonindustrialized societies. The reason may be that the core symptoms of schizophrenia (poor rapport with others, incoherent speech, and so on) make it more difficult to survive in highly industrialized countries. Furthermore, in most industrialized nations, families and other support groups are less likely to feel responsible for relatives and friends who have schizophrenia (Akyeampong et al., 2015; Burns et al., 2014; Eaton et al., 2012). On the other hand, some countries, such as Indonesia, still shackle and confine their mentally ill in filthy cells without basic human rights (Quiano, 2016).

**TABLE 14.3**    **Culture-General Symptoms of Mental Health Difficulties**

| Nervous | Trouble sleeping | Low spirits |
|---|---|---|
| Weak all over | Personal worries | Restless |
| Feel apart, alone | Can't get along | Hot all over |
| Worry all the time | Can't do anything worthwhile | Nothing turns out right |

**Source:** Brislin, 2000.

## Avoiding Ethnocentrism

Most research on psychological disorders originates and is conducted primarily in Western cultures. Do you see how such a restricted sampling can limit our understanding of these disorders? And how this limited view could lead to an ethnocentric view—a view that one's own culture is "correct?"

Fortunately, cross-cultural researchers have devised ways to overcome these difficulties. Robert Nishimoto (1988) has found several *culture-general symptoms* that are useful in diagnosing disorders across cultures (**Table 14.3**). Nishimoto also found several *culture-bound symptoms*, which are unique to different groups and generally appear only in one population. When talking about their psychological problems, for instance, Vietnamese and Chinese respondents more often report "fullness in head," Mexican respondents note "problems with [their] memory," and Anglo-American respondents report "shortness of breath" and "headaches." Apparently, people learn to express their problems in ways that are acceptable to others in the same culture (Brislin, 2000; Hsu, 2016; Shannon et al., 2015).

This division between culture-general and culture-bound symptoms also helps us better understand depression. Certain symptoms of depression (such as intense sadness, poor concentration, and low energy) seem to exist across all cultures (Walsh & Cross, 2013; World Health Organization, 2011). But there is evidence of some culture-bound symptoms. Feelings of guilt, for instance, are found more often in North America and Europe than in other parts of the world. And in China, *somatization* (the conversion of depression into bodily complaints) occurs more frequently than it does in other parts of the world (Grover & Ghosh, 2014; Lim et al., 2011).

Just as there are culture-bound symptoms, researchers also have found culture-bound disorders (**Figure 14.22**). The earlier example of windigo psychosis, a disorder limited to a few groups of Canadian Indians, illustrates just such a case. Interestingly, the distinctions between many culture-bound and cultural-general symptoms and disorders may be disappearing as a result of globalization (Kato & Kanba, 2016; Ventriglio et al., 2016).

As you can see, culture has a strong effect on psychological disorders (Campbell et al., 2017; López & Guarnaccia, 2016; Stefanovics et al., 2016). Studying the similarities and differences across cultures can lead to better diagnosis and understanding. It also helps all of us avoid, or at least minimize, our ethnocentrism.

Before closing this chapter, we need to offer a cautionary note. Students who first learn about these disorders often become overly concerned when they recognize some of the symptoms in themselves and others (Griffiths, 2016). This is so common that it actually has a name—**psychology student syndrome (PSS)**. Although it's tempting to use the information you've gained to diagnose yourself or others, only professionals are adequately trained to do so. If you're concerned about your own mental health or that of others, be sure to contact one of these professionals. Chapter 15 provides an overview of the various forms of therapy and tips for finding a good therapist. The following **Psychology and Your Personal Success** feature further explains how resilience offers an interesting, positive approach to mental health.

**Psychology student syndrome (PSSS)**   A condition often seen in psychology students concerned that they are experiencing the symptoms of a psychological disorder they're studying; also, using what is learned in a psychology class to "diagnose" someone of a psychological condition without full knowledge or proper certification.

| Puerto Rican and other Latin cultures | Southeast Asian, Malaysian, Indonesian, Thai | West African | Ethiopian | South Chinese and Vietnamese | Westerners |
|---|---|---|---|---|---|
| *Ataque de nervios* ("attack of nerves") | Running amok | Brain fag | Possession by the *Zar* | *Koro* | *Anorexia nervosa* (as other countries become Westernized they're showing an increase in cases of anorexia) |
| **Symptoms:** Trembling, heart palpitations, and seizure-like episodes often associated with the death of a loved one, accidents, or family conflict | **Symptoms:** Wild, out-of-control, aggressive behaviors and attempts to injure or kill others | **Symptoms:** "Brain tiredness," a mental and physical response to the challenges of schooling | **Symptoms:** Involuntary movements, mutism, or incomprehensible language | **Symptoms:** Belief that the penis is retracting into the abdomen and that when it is fully retracted, death will result; attempts to prevent the supposed retraction may lead to severe physical damage | **Symptoms:** Occurs primarily among young women; preoccupied with thinness, they exercise excessively and refuse to eat; death can result |

**FIGURE 14.22   Culture-bound disorders**   Some disorders are fading as remote areas become more Westernized, whereas other disorders (such as anorexia nervosa) are spreading as other countries adopt Western values.

## ❖ Psychology and Your Personal Success | Can Resilience Promote Mental Health in Children and Adults?

*The bamboo that bends is stronger than the oak that resists.* —Japanese proverb

Children fortunate enough to grow up with days filled with play and discovery, nights that provide rest and security, and dedicated, loving parents usually turn out fine. But what about those who are raised in violent, impoverished, or neglectful situations? Researchers have found that a troubled childhood is associated with higher risks of serious psychological disorders, along with physical, emotional, and behavioral problems. Yet some children living in harsh circumstances survive and prosper—as shown perhaps in this photo of a family in a refugee camp. What makes the difference?

**Resilience**   The ability to recover from or adapt effectively in the face of adversity.

The answer apparently is **resilience**—the ability to recover and adapt effectively in the face of adversity. Like bamboo that bends in strong winds, a resilient person flexes in response to hard times. Resilience has been studied throughout the world in a variety of situations, including ill health, homelessness, natural disasters, war, and family violence (e.g., Gibbons & Hickling, 2016; Gil-Rivas & Kilmer, 2016; Reynolds, 2017). And it is of particular interest to psychologists because it can teach us better ways to reduce risk, promote competence, and shift the course of development in more positive directions. Moreover, researchers using a meta-analysis, which compares data from multiple studies, found a solid link between resilience and mental health (Mortazavi & Yarolahi, 2015).

What characterizes a resilient child? Two pioneering researchers—Ann Masten and Douglas Coatsworth (1998)—identified several traits and environmental circumstances that might account for the resilient child's success: (1) good intellectual functioning; (2) relationships with caring adults; and, as they grow older, (3) the ability to regulate their attention, emotions, and behavior. These traits obviously overlap. Good intellectual functioning, for example, may help resilient children solve problems or protect themselves from adverse conditions, as well as attract the interest of teachers who serve as nurturing adults. Their greater intellectual skills also may help them learn from their experiences and from the caring adults, so in later life they have better self-regulation skills.

Resilience can develop in adulthood as well as in childhood. Surprisingly, in adults, adversity can actually promote healthy development (Konnikova, 2016). A recent study examined how some people benefit even after experiencing an extraordinarily stressful event, such as a mass school shooting (Mancini

et al., 2016). These researchers compared data in psychological adjustment, including anxiety and depression, in female students before the 2007 shooting at Virginia Tech (as part of an already ongoing study) and then again after the event. As you would expect, some students showed continued distress. But other students showed psychological improvement and resilience following these attacks, a phenomenon known as *posttraumatic growth*, which suggests that trauma can, at least at times, lead to positive outcomes (Tedeschi & Blevins, 2015; Zhou & Wu, 2016).

What can be done to promote adult resilience? One recent study found that practicing *self-* and *other compassion*, along with *meditation* (see Chapters 3 and 5), are valuable components of resilience (Newman, 2016). According to psychologist George Bonanno (2012), another component is *perception*. Do you perceive adversity as filled with meaning and an opportunity to grow and change? Or do you see it as devastating and uncontrollable? The good news is that we can develop a more resilient perception of adversity by cultivating the trait of *self-efficacy* and an *internal locus of control* (Chapter 13), as well as a more *optimistic, attributional style* (Chapter 16). In keeping with our text's focus on a growth mindset, recent research has found that individuals who have an anxiety growth mindset—that is, who believe that anxiety, like intelligence, is not a fixed trait—showed more resilience and positive coping than those without this mindset (Schroder et al., 2017).

Finally, bear in mind that a focus on resilience, when taken to extremes, may lead to a dangerous form of "blaming the victim." People who are homeless or mentally ill, for example, have been blamed for lacking resilience. While resilience is a useful concept, and while it is worth cultivating, we must consider all the factors leading to adversity and avoid placing all the responsibility for an individual's survival on that individual's resilience (Sehgal, 2015). Thinking back to the resilient child, Masten and Coatsworth remind us, "if we allow the prevalence of known risk factors for development to rise while resources for children fall, we can expect the competence of individual children and the human capital of the nation to suffer" (Masten & Coatsworth, 1998, p. 216).

© Billy R. Ray/ Wiley

## Retrieval Practice 14.6 | Gender and Cultural Effects

Completing this self-test and the connections section, and then checking your answers by clicking on the answer button or by looking in Appendix B, will provide immediate feedback and helpful practice for exams.

### Self-Test

1. How does depression differ in men and women?

2. Which of the following are examples of culture-general symptoms of mental health difficulties that are useful in diagnosing disorders across cultures?

    a. Trouble sleeping
    b. Worry all the time
    c. Can't get along
    d. All of these options

3. Symptoms of mental illness that generally only appear in one population group are known as _____.

    a. culture-bound symptoms
    b. group specific disorders
    c. group-think syndrome
    d. culture-specific maladies

4. What disorder has the following symptoms: wild, out-of-control, aggressive behaviors and attempts to injure or kill others?

    a. Brain fag
    b. Running amok
    c. Possession by the Zar
    d. Koro

5. Somatization (the conversion of depression into bodily complaints) occurs more frequently in _____.

    a. North and Central America
    b. China
    c. India
    d. Europe

### Connections—Chapter to Chapter

Answering the following question will help you "look back and look ahead" to see the important connections among the subfields of psychology and chapters within this text.

In Chapter 1 (Introduction and Research Methods), we discussed ethnocentrism and how it might affect general psychological research. In this chapter, we explored how it might play a role in research on psychological disorders. Identify the potential problems caused by ethnocentrism in both contexts.

# Chapter Summary

## 14.1  Studying Psychological Disorders  458

- **Abnormal behavior** is defined as patterns of behavior, thoughts, or emotions considered pathological for one or more of these four criteria: *deviance, dysfunction, distress,* and *danger.* Mental health exists on a continuum—not discrete categories of "normal" and "abnormal."

- Historically, abnormal behavior was blamed on evil spirits and witchcraft. These beliefs were eventually replaced by the *medical model,* which in turn gave rise to the modern specialty of **psychiatry**. In contrast to the medical model, psychology offers a multifaceted approach to explaining abnormal behavior.

- The *Diagnostic and Statistical Manual of Mental Disorders (DSM)* provides detailed descriptions and classifications of psychological disorders. It also allows standardized diagnosis and improved communication among professionals and between professionals

and patients. The *DSM* has been criticized for not discussing the ethical, political, economic, and related values, overdiagnosing, and potential cultural bias.

- The stigma surrounding mental illness is increased due to negative media coverage, and the stigma creates serious public health concerns. Death by suicide is an increased risk for people with psychological disorders.

### Test Your Critical Thinking

**1.** Can you imagine cases in which someone might have a psychological disorder not described by the four criteria deviance, dysfunction, distress, and danger?

**2.** Do you think the insanity plea, as it is currently structured, should be abolished? Why or why not?

---

**Psychology and a Contemporary Success:** Jennifer Lawrence

## Studying Psychological Disorders

**Understanding Psychological Disorders**

Four criteria:
1. Deviance
2. Dysfunction
3. Distress
4. Danger

**Classifying Psychological Disorders**
(Neurosis, psychosis, delusions, hallucinations, insanity)

**Describing and Evaluating the *DSM***
(*DSM* describes and classifies psychological disorders)

**Special Issues in Psychological Disorders**
- The stigma of mental illness
- Increased risk of suicide

## 14.2   Anxiety Disorders   467

- **Anxiety disorders** include **generalized anxiety disorder (GAD)**, **panic disorder**, and **phobias** (including agoraphobia, specific, and social anxiety disorder).

- Psychological factors (faulty cognitions and maladaptive learning), biological factors (evolutionary and genetic predispositions, biochemical disturbances), and sociocultural factors (cultural pressures in industrialized nations) likely all contribute to

anxiety. Classical and operant conditioning also can contribute to phobias.

**Test Your Critical Thinking**

**1.** Why do you suppose anxiety disorders are among the easiest disorders to both "catch" and treat?

**2.** How would you explain the high number of anxiety disorders in the United States?

### Anxiety Disorders

**Describing Anxiety Disorders**
- Generalized anxiety disorder (GAD)
- Panic disorder
- Phobias

**Explaining Anxiety Disorders**
- Psychological factors
- Biological factors
- Sociocultural factors

## 14.3   Depressive and Bipolar Disorders   472

- Both depressive disorder and bipolar disorder are characterized by extreme disturbances in emotional states. People suffering from **major depressive disorders (MDDs)** may experience a lasting depressed mood without a clear trigger. In contrast, people with **bipolar disorder** alternate between periods of depression and **mania** (characterized by elevated mood, hyperactivity, and poor judgment).

- Biological factors, including neurotransmitters, genes, and brain structures and functions, play a significant role in depressive

and bipolar disorders. Psychological theories focus on thought processes, self-concept, and learning history, including **learned helplessness**. Sociocultural factors include environmental stressors, disturbances in relationships, and abuse or assault.

**Test Your Critical Thinking**

**1.** Have you ever felt seriously depressed? How would you distinguish between "normal" depression and a serious depressive disorder?

**2.** Can you think of a personal example of how major depression might provide an evolutionary advantage?

### Depressive and Bipolar Disorders

**Describing Depressive and Bipolar Disorders**
Those with depressive disorders may experience a lasting depressed mood without a clear trigger, whereas those with bipolar disorder alternate between periods of depression and mania.

**Research Challenge: Are Head Injuries Related to Depressive and Other Psychological Disorders?**

**Explaining Depressive and Bipolar Disorders**
Biological, psychological, and sociocultural factors

## 14.4   Schizophrenia   476

- **Schizophrenia** is a group of disorders characterized by a disturbance in perception (including **hallucinations**), language, thought (including **delusions**), emotions, and/or behavior.

- In the past, researchers divided schizophrenia into multiple subtypes. More recently, researchers have proposed focusing instead on *positive schizophrenia symptoms* versus *negative schizophrenia symptoms*.

- Most biological theories of schizophrenia focus on genetics, biochemistry, and brain abnormalities. Psychologists have also identified several environmental and psychosocial contributors. According to the **diathesis-stress model**, stress can trigger schizophrenic episodes in people with an inherited predisposition (diathesis) toward the disease.

**1.** Most of the disorders discussed in this chapter have some evidence for a genetic predisposition. What would you tell a friend who has a family member with one of these disorders and fears that he or she might develop the same disorder?

**2.** What do you think are the key biological and psychosocial factors that contribute to schizophrenia?

## Schizophrenia

### Symptoms of Schizophrenia

Disturbances in:
- Perception
- Language and thought
- Emotion
- Behavior

### Classifying Schizophrenia

Positive and negative symptoms

### Explaining Schizophrenia

Biological factors and prenatal and environmental influences

## 14.5 Other Disorders  480

- **Obsessive-compulsive disorder (OCD)** involves persistent, unwanted, fearful thoughts (obsessions) and/or irresistible urges to perform an act or repeated rituals (compulsions), which help relieve the anxiety created by the obsession. Given that numerous biological and psychological factors contribute to OCD, it is most often treated with a combination of drugs, cognitive behavior therapy (CBT), and remediation therapy.

- **Dissociative disorders** are characterized by a sudden break (dissociation) in conscious awareness, self-identity, and/or memory A controversial subtype of these disorders, **dissociative identity disorder (DID)**, involves the presence of two or more distinct personality systems in the same individual. Environmental variables appear to be the primary cause of dissociative disorders. Dissociation can be a form of escape from a past trauma.

- **Personality disorders** occur when inflexible, maladaptive personality traits cause significant impairment of social and occupational functioning. **Antisocial personality disorder (ASPD)** is a pattern of disregard for, and violation of, the rights of others. The most common personality disorder is **borderline personality disorder (BPD)**. Its core features are impulsivity and instability in mood, relationships, and self-image.

**1.** How would you explain to others that schizophrenia is not the same as dissociative identity disorder (DID), formerly called multiple personality disorder?

**2.** Does the fact that research shows a genetic component to antisocial personality disorder change your opinion regarding the degree of guilt and responsibility of a mass-murdering terrorist after a vicious shooting spree?

## Other Disorders

### Obsessive-Compulsive Disorder (OCD)

Characterized by persistent, unwanted, fearful thoughts, or *obsessions*, and/or irresistible behaviors, or *compulsions*

### Dissociative Disorders

Characterized by a sudden break in conscious awareness, self-identity, and/or memory

### Personality Disorders

- Antisocial (ASPD)
- Borderline (BPD)

### 14.6    Gender and Cultural Effects    484

- Men and women differ in their rates and experiences of abnormal behavior. For instance, the rate of severe depression for women is almost double that for men. In the case of depression, research suggests that the gender differences may reflect an underlying predisposition toward internalizing or externalizing emotions and problems.

- People of different cultures experience psychological disorders in a variety of ways. For example, the reported incidence of schizophrenia varies in different cultures around the world, as do the disorder's symptoms, triggers, and prognosis.

- Some symptoms of psychological disorders, as well as some disorders themselves, are *culture general*, whereas others are *culture bound*.

- Our mental health can be improved and protected by developing **resilience**—the ability to recover or adapt effectively in the face of adversity.

#### Test Your Critical Thinking

**1.** Culture clearly has strong effects on psychological disorders. How does this influence what you think about what is normal or abnormal?

**2.** As you've seen, some research suggests that depression in men is often overlooked because men are socialized to suppress their emotions and encouraged to express their distress by acting out, being impulsive, or engaging in substance abuse. Does this ring true with your own experiences or observations of others? If so, how might we change this situation?

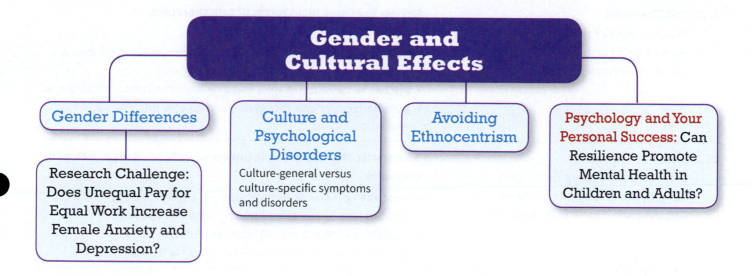

## Key Terms

**Retrieval Practice**    *Write a definition for each term before turning back to the referenced page to check your answer.*

- abnormal behavior   459
- antisocial personality disorder (ASPD)    482
- anxiety disorder   467
- bipolar disorder   472
- borderline personality disorder (BPD)    483
- comorbidity   462
- delusion   461
- depressive disorders   472
- *Diagnostic and Statistical Manual of Mental Disorders (DSM)*   461
- diathesis-stress model   479

- dissociative disorder   481
- dissociative identity disorder (DID)   481
- generalized anxiety disorder (GAD)   467
- hallucination   461
- insanity   462
- learned helplessness   474
- major depressive disorder (MDD)   472
- mania   472
- neurosis   461
- nonsuicidal self-injury (NSSI)   465
- obsessive-compulsive disorder (OCD)   480

- panic disorder   468
- personality disorder   482
- phobia   468
- psychiatry   460
- psychological disorder   458
- psychology student syndrome (PSS)   487
- psychosis   461
- resilience   488
- schizophrenia   476

© alexxl66/iStockphoto

# CHAPTER 15

# Therapy

| CHAPTER OUTLINE | LEARNING OBJECTIVES |
|---|---|

❖ **Psychology and a Contemporary Success**
J. K. Rowling

---

**15.1 Talk Therapies**
- Psychoanalysis/Psychodynamic Therapies
- Humanistic Therapies
- Cognitive Therapies

**Review the three main forms of talk therapies.**
- **Define** psychotherapy.
- **Describe** psychoanalysis and its core techniques and criticisms, along with modern psychodynamic therapies.
- **Discuss** humanistic therapies and their key techniques and evaluation.
- **Summarize** cognitive therapies and their core principles and evaluation.

---

**15.2 Behavior Therapies**
- Classical Conditioning Techniques
- Operant Conditioning Techniques
- Observational Learning Techniques

**Summarize the treatment techniques and criticisms of behavior therapies.**
- **Describe** how classical conditioning is used in therapy.
- **Explore** how operant conditioning is used in therapy.
- **Explain** how observational learning is used in therapy.
- **Discuss** the major criticisms of behavior therapies.

---

**15.3 Biomedical Therapies**
- Psychopharmacology
- Electroconvulsive Therapy and Psychosurgery

**Review the types of biomedical therapies and their risks and benefits.**
- **Describe** biomedical therapies.
- **Identify** the major types of drugs used to treat psychological disorders.
- **Explain** what happens in electroconvulsive therapy and psychosurgery.
- **Summarize** the risks and benefits associated with biomedical therapies.

---

**15.4 Psychotherapy in Perspective**
- Therapy Goals and Effectiveness

**RC Research Challenge**
Can Watching Movies Prevent Divorce?
- Therapy Formats
- Institutionalization

**GCD Gender and Cultural Diversity**
Therapy in Action

❖ **Psychology and Your Personal Success:**
What Are the Keys to Good Mental Health?

**Review the key issues in psychotherapy.**
- **Summarize** the goals and overall effectiveness of psychotherapy.
- **Describe** group, marital, family, and telehealth/electronic therapies.
- **Discuss** the issues involved in institutionalization.
- **Identify** the key cultural and gender issues important in therapy.
- **Summarize** the major career options for someone interested in becoming a mental health professional.

### ❖ Psychology and a Contemporary Success | J. K. Rowling

PA Images/Alamy Stock Photo

Joanne Rowling, best known as J. K. Rowling (1965–), is a British novelist, screenwriter, and film producer famous for her authorship of the *Harry Potter* series of fantasy novels (see photo). Rowling (pronounced *rolling*) was born in Yate, England, to parents who, as she says, "came from impoverished backgrounds and neither of whom had been to college." They did, however, love to read, and Rowling grew up surrounded by books to become the classic "bookworm." After graduating from Exeter University, Rowling moved to Portugal, where she met and married a Portuguese journalist. The marriage soon ended in divorce, and Rowling moved with her daughter to live near her sister in Edinburgh, Scotland. Struggling to support herself and her young daughter, she reluctantly signed up for welfare benefits, saying that she was "as poor as it is possible to be . . . without being homeless." Rowling sold her first novel in the Harry Potter series for only $4,000. Since then, though, this series of books has sold over 450 million copies (McClurg, 2017; Rowling, n.d.).

Despite her apparently wildly successful life, Rowling has endured numerous hardships. She reports that her teenage years were very unhappy due to her mother's protracted illness and a strained relationship with her father. The period after her divorce and her mother's painful death from multiple sclerosis was a particularly difficult time for Rowling. She saw herself as such a dismal failure that she even contemplated suicide. Fortunately, therapy helped her climb out of her diagnosed clinical depression, and she later reported that it was her experiences with such deep despair that led her to create the *Dementors*—the soul-sucking monsters found in the *Harry Potter* series (Bennett, 2012; Oppenheim, 2016; Rowling, n.d.).

Today, Rowling is ranked as Britain's 13th wealthiest woman—making her richer than even the Queen of England! Along with the famous *Harry Potter* series, she has authored several other books, including a collection of five fables from which Rowling generously donates all royalties to support institutionalized children in Eastern Europe. In addition to her impressive contributions to numerous causes and organizations, Rowling has received many honors and awards, including an Order of the British Empire (OBE) for services to children's literature and the PEN America Literary Service Award in 2016 (Biography.com, n.d.; Rowling, 2016).

> *I think you have a moral responsibility when you've been given far more than you need to do wise things with it and give intelligently.*
> —J. K. Rowling

## Chapter Overview

Based on her personal struggles and her ultimate achievements, Rowling clearly demonstrates a *growth mindset* and *grit*. Clinical depression was one of the serious issues Rowling had to deal with. Chapter 14 offered much on suicide and depression, and this chapter adds valuable information about its treatment.

In this chapter, we'll focus on the three major approaches to psychotherapy (**Figure 15.1**). We begin with what are known as the *talk therapies*, including psychoanalysis/psychodynamic, humanistic, and cognitive. Next we look at *behavior therapies* and the roles of classical conditioning, operant conditioning, and observational learning. Then we examine *biomedical* (or *biological*) *therapies*, including the topics of psychopharmacology, electroconvulsive therapy, and psychosurgery. Our final section looks at psychotherapy in perspective—its goals and effectiveness, its formats, and its cultural and gender issues. Along the way we'll work to demystify and destigmatize the practice of psychotherapy and dispel some unfortunate myths (see the **Myth Busters**).

**FIGURE 15.1** **An overview of the three major approaches to therapy**

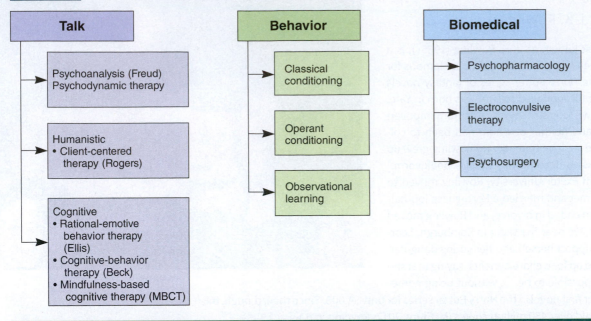

| Talk | Behavior | Biomedical |
|------|----------|------------|
| Psychoanalysis (Freud) Psychodynamic therapy | Classical conditioning | Psychopharmacology |
| Humanistic • Client-centered therapy (Rogers) | Operant conditioning | Electroconvulsive therapy |
| Cognitive • Rational-emotive behavior therapy (Ellis) • Cognitive-behavior therapy (Beck) • Mindfulness-based cognitive therapy (MBCT) | Observational learning | Psychosurgery |

## Myth Busters

### Myths About Therapy

- *Myth: There is one best therapy.*
  **Fact:** Many problems can be treated equally well with many different forms of therapy.

- *Myth: Therapists can read your mind.*
  **Fact:** Good therapists often seem to have an uncanny ability to understand how their clients are feeling and to know when someone is trying to avoid certain topics. This is not due to any special mind-reading ability; it simply reflects their specialized training and daily experience working with troubled people.

- *Myth: Therapy is only for deeply disturbed individuals.*
  **Fact:** Most people seek counseling because of stress in their lives or because they realize that therapy can improve their level of functioning (see the photo). It is difficult to be objective about our own problems. Seeking therapy is a sign of wisdom and personal strength.

- *Myth: Only the rich can afford therapy.*
  **Fact:** Therapy can be expensive. But many clinics and therapists charge on a sliding scale, based on the client's income. Some insurance plans also cover psychological services.

- *Myth: If I am taking meds, I don't need therapy.*
  **Fact:** Medications, such as antidepressants, are only one form of therapy. They can change brain chemistry, but they can't teach us to think, feel, or behave differently. Research suggests that a combination of drugs and psychotherapy may be best for some situations, whereas in other cases, psychotherapy or drug therapy alone may be most effective.

Georges De Keerle/Getty Images

**Prince Harry sought counseling over his mother's death** In an effort to help end the stigma around mental illness, Britain's Prince Harry publicly admitted that he had suffered for years over the death of his mother, Princess Diana, and that he recently sought therapy at the urging of his older brother, Prince William (Olivenness, 2017).

**Sources:** Arkowitz & Lilienfeld, 2017; Lilienfeld et al., 2010, 2015; Magnavita & Anchin, 2014; Seay & Sun, 2016.

## 15.1 Talk Therapies

### LEARNING OBJECTIVES

**Retrieval Practice** While reading the upcoming sections, respond to each Learning Objective in your own words.

**Review the three main forms of talk therapies.**
- **Define** psychotherapy.

- **Describe** psychoanalysis and its core techniques and criticisms, along with modern psychodynamic therapies.
- **Discuss** humanistic therapies and their key techniques and evaluation.
- **Summarize** cognitive therapies and their core principles and evaluation.

Throughout this text, we have emphasized the *science* of psychology, and this chapter is no exception. Now, we'll explore how therapists apply this science during **psychotherapy** to help us all improve our overall psychological functioning and adjustment to life and to assist people suffering from psychological disorders. Unfortunately, research finds that over 56% of American adults with a diagnosed psychological disorder are not receiving treatment (The State of Mental Health in America, 2017). This may be due in large part to the common stereotype and stigma that therapy is only for deeply disturbed individuals. Therefore, keep in mind that therapy provides an opportunity for *everyone* to have his or her specific problems addressed, as well as to learn better thinking, feeling, and behavioral skills useful in everyday life.

We begin our discussion of professional psychotherapy with traditional psychoanalysis and its modern counterpart, psychodynamic therapies. Then we explore humanistic and cognitive therapies. Although these therapies differ significantly, they're often grouped together as "talk therapies" because they emphasize communication between the therapist and client, as opposed to the behavioral and biomedical therapies we discuss later.

## Psychoanalysis/Psychodynamic Therapies

In **psychoanalysis**, a person's *psyche* (or mind) is *analyzed*. Traditional psychoanalysis is based on Sigmund Freud's central belief that abnormal behavior is caused by unconscious, unresolved conflicts (see photo). The therapist's major goal is to provide insight and to bring these conflicts into conscious awareness. During psychoanalysis, the individual comes to understand the reasons for his or her dysfunction and realizes that the childhood conditions under which the conflicts developed no longer exist. Once this realization or insight occurs, the conflicts can be resolved, and the client can develop more adaptive behavior patterns (Barber & Solomonov, 2016; Bonomi, 2015).

**Major Therapy Techniques**    As you recall from Chapter 13, in Freudian theory, unconscious conflicts occur among the three parts of the psyche—the id, the ego, and the superego. Unfortunately, according to Freud, the ego has strong *defense mechanisms* that block unconscious thoughts from coming to light. Thus, to gain insight into the unconscious, the ego must be "tricked" into relaxing its guard. To meet that goal, psychoanalysts employ five major methods: *free association*, *dream analysis*, *analyzing resistance*, *analyzing transference*, and *interpretation* (**Figure 15.2**).

**Free Association**    According to Freud, when you let your mind wander and remove conscious censorship over thoughts—a process called **free association**—interesting and even bizarre connections seem to spring into awareness. Freud believed that the first thing to come to a patient's mind is often an important clue to what the person's unconscious wants to conceal. Having the client recline on a couch, with only the ceiling to look at, is believed to encourage free association (**Figure 15.3**).

**Dream Analysis**    Recall from Chapter 5 that, according to Freud, our psychological defenses are lowered during sleep. Therefore, our forbidden desires and unconscious conflicts are supposedly more freely expressed during dreams. Even while dreaming, however, we recognize these feelings and conflicts as unacceptable and must disguise them as images that have deeper symbolic meaning. Thus, using Freudian **dream analysis**, a dream of riding a horse or driving a car might be analyzed as just the surface description, or *manifest content*. In contrast, the hidden, underlying meaning, or *latent content*, might be analyzed as a desire for, or concern about, sexual intercourse.

**Analysis of Resistance**    During free association or dream analysis, Freud found that clients often show an inability or unwillingness to confront unpleasant or fearful unconscious conflicts. For example, a client may suddenly "forget" what he or she was saying or completely change the subject. It is the therapist's job to identify

**Psychotherapy**    Any of a group of therapies used to treat psychological disorders and to improve psychological functioning and adjustment to life.

© Hulton-Deutsch Collection/CORBIS/Corbis/Getty Images

**Sigmund Freud (1856–1939)**
Freud believed that during psychoanalysis, the therapist's (or psychoanalyst's) major goal was to bring unconscious conflicts into consciousness.

**Psychoanalysis**    A type of talk therapy, originated by Sigmund Freud, that emphasizes bringing unconscious thoughts and conflicts into conscious awareness.

**Free association**    In psychoanalysis, reporting whatever comes to mind without monitoring its contents.

**Dream analysis**    In psychoanalysis, interpretation of the underlying true meaning of dreams to reveal unconscious processes.

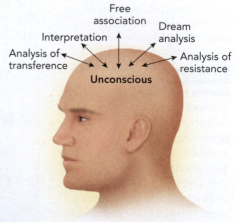

**FIGURE 15.2**    **The five key techniques for psychoanalysis**

"I'LL BARK, AND YOU BARK THE FIRST THING THAT COMES TO MIND."

S.Harris/www.CartoonStock.com

**FIGURE 15.3** **Freud's free association** As satirized in this popular cartoon, psychoanalysis is often stereotypically portrayed as a client lying on a couch engaging in free association. Freud believed that this arrangement—with the client relaxed and the therapist out of his or her view—helps the client let down his or her defenses, making the unconscious more accessible.

these possible cases of **resistance** and then help the client face his or her unconscious conflicts and learn to deal with them more realistically.

**Analysis of Transference** Freud believed that during psychoanalysis, clients disclose intimate feelings and memories, and the relationship between the therapist and client may become complex and emotionally charged. As a result, clients often apply, or *transfer*, some of their unresolved emotions and attitudes from past relationships onto the therapist. For instance, a client might interact with the therapist as if the therapist were a lover or parent. The therapist uses this process of **transference** to help the client "relive" painful past relationships in a safe, therapeutic setting so that he or she can move on to healthier relationships.

**Interpretation** The core of all psychoanalytic therapy is **interpretation**. During free association, dream analysis, resistance, and transference, the analyst listens closely and tries to find patterns and hidden conflicts. At the right time, the therapist explains or interprets the underlying meanings to the client.

**Resistance** A psychoanalytic therapy technique that examines a client's inability or unwillingness to confront unpleasant or fearful unconscious conflicts.

**Transference** A psychoanalytic therapy technique that explores situations in which a client attaches (transfers) to the therapist emotional reactions related to someone else in the client's life.

**Interpretation** A psychoanalyst's explanation of a client's free associations, dreams, resistance, and transference; more generally, any statement by a therapist that presents a problem in a new way.

**Psychodynamic therapies** A group of talk therapies that focus on conscious processes and current problems; briefer, more directive, and more modern forms of psychoanalysis.

**Psychodynamic Therapies** A modern derivative of Freudian psychoanalysis, **psychodynamic therapies**, includes both Freud's theories and those of his major followers—Carl Jung, Alfred Adler, Karen Horney, and Erik Erikson. In contrast to psychoanalysis, psychodynamic therapies are shorter and less intensive (once or twice a week versus several times a week and only for a few weeks or months versus years). Also, the client is treated face-to-face rather than reclining on a couch, and the therapist takes a more directive approach. Rather than waiting for unconscious memories and desires to slowly be uncovered, the psychodynamic therapist is more likely to offer advice or support.

Contemporary psychodynamic therapists also focus less on unconscious, early-childhood roots of problems and more on conscious processes and current problems (Barber & Solomonov, 2016; Göttken et al., 2014; Short & Thomas, 2015). Such refinements have helped make treatments shorter, more available, and more effective for an increasing number of people. See **Figure 15.4** for one of the most popular modern forms of psychodynamic therapies.

**Evaluating Psychoanalysis/Psychodynamic Therapies** Research shows that traditional psychoanalysis can be effective for those who have the time and money (Busch, 2014, 2015; Huber & Klug, 2016; Watkins, 2016). Psychodynamic therapies lead to similar benefits, and because they take place over a shorter time, they're also less expensive (Goldstone, 2017; Sell et al., 2017).

**FIGURE 15.4** **Interpersonal therapy (IPT)** IPT, a variation of psychodynamic therapy, focuses on current relationships, with the goal of relieving immediate symptoms and teaching better ways to solve interpersonal problems. Research shows that it's effective for a variety of disorders, including depression, marital conflict, eating and personality disorders, and drug addiction (Dimaggio et al., 2017; Driessen et al., 2015; Normandin et al., 2015).

© Wavebreak Media/Alamy Stock Photo

On the other hand, there are three major criticisms of these therapies (Grünbaum, 2015; Miltenberger, 2011; Ng et al., 2015):

- *Question of repressed memories and unconscious conflic*t As you've just seen, psychoanalysis is largely rooted in the assumption that repressed memories and unconscious conflicts actually exist. But, as we noted in Chapters 7 and 13, this assumption is the subject of heated, ongoing debate.

- *Limited applicability* Psychoanalysis is time-consuming (often lasting several years with four to five sessions a week) and expensive. Furthermore, critics suggest that it applies only to a select group of highly motivated, articulate clients with less severe disorders and not to such complex disorders as schizophrenia.

- *Lack of scientific credibility* According to critics, it is difficult, if not impossible, to scientifically document the major tenets of psychoanalysis. How do we prove or disprove the existence of an unconscious mind or the meaning of unconscious conflicts and symbolic dream images?

# Humanistic Therapies

**Humanistic therapies** are based on the belief that psychological disorders result from blocked personal growth. Therefore, the therapist's major goal is to maximize the individual's growth and potential, inherent capacity for self-actualization, free will, and self-awareness. Humanistic therapists assume that when obstacles are removed, the individual is free to become the self-accepting, self-actualized person everyone is capable of being (D'Souza & Gurin, 2016; Schneider et al., 2015; Winston et al., 2017).

Rather than emphasizing the unconscious, humanistic therapies focus on providing an accepting atmosphere and encouraging healthy emotional experiences. And humanistic therapists believe clients are responsible for discovering their own maladaptive patterns, whereas psychoanalysts and psychodynamic therapists rely on the therapist's analysis to provide insight.

*We do not need magic to transform our world. We carry all of the power we need inside ourselves already.*

—J. K. Rowling

**Carl Rogers (1902–1987)**

## Carl Rogers

One of the best-known humanistic therapists is Carl Rogers (see photo), who developed an approach that encourages people to actualize their potential and to relate to others in genuine ways (Rogers, 1961, 1980). His approach is referred to as **client-centered therapy** (**Figure 15.5**). (Rogers used the term *client* because he believed the label *patient* implied that someone was sick or mentally ill rather than responsible and competent.)

## Major Therapy Techniques

Rogerian therapists create a therapeutic relationship by focusing on four key elements of communication: *empathy*, *unconditional positive regard*, *genuineness*, and *active listening*.

**Empathy** Using the technique of **empathy**, a sensitive understanding and sharing of another person's inner experience, therapists pay attention to body language and listen for subtle cues to help them understand the emotional experiences of clients. To further help clients explore their feelings, the therapists use open-ended statements such as "You found that upsetting" or "You haven't been able to decide what to do about this" rather than asking questions or offering explanations.

**Unconditional Positive Regard** Regardless of the clients' problems or behaviors, humanistic therapists offer them **unconditional positive regard**, a genuine caring and nonjudgmental attitude toward people based on their innate value as individuals. They avoid evaluative statements such as

**Humanistic therapies** A group of talk therapies that emphasize maximizing a client's inherent capacity for self-actualization by providing a nonjudgmental, accepting atmosphere.

**Client-centered therapy** A form of talk therapy, developed by Carl Rogers, that provides a warm, supportive atmosphere that encourages self-actualization and improves the client's self-concept; techniques include empathy, unconditional positive regard, genuineness, and active listening.

**Empathy** In Rogerian terms, a sensitive understanding and sharing of another's inner experience.

**Unconditional positive regard** Rogers's term for love and acceptance with no "strings" (conditions) attached.

**FIGURE 15.5** **Nurturing growth** Recall how you've felt when you've been with someone who considers you to be a worthy and good person with unlimited potential, a person who believes that your "real self" is unique and valuable. These are the feelings that are nurtured in client-centered therapy.

**FIGURE 15.6  Unconditional versus conditional positive regard**  According to Rogers, clients need to feel unconditionally accepted by their therapists in order to recognize and value their own emotions, thoughts, and behaviors. As this cartoon sarcastically implies, some parents withhold their love and acceptance unless their children live up to their expectations.

**Genuineness**  In Rogerian terms, being personally authentic and sincere; the awareness of one's true inner thoughts and feelings and the ability to share them honestly with others.

**Active listening**  A communication technique that requires listening with total attention to what another is saying; techniques include reflecting, paraphrasing, and clarifying what the person says and means.

*"Just remember, son, it doesn't matter whether you win or lose—unless you want Daddy's love."*

"That's good" and "You did the right thing" because such comments imply that the therapist is judging the client. Rogers believed that most of us receive conditional acceptance from our parents, teachers, and others, which leads to poor self-concepts and psychological disorders (**Figure 15.6**).

*Genuineness*  Humanists believe that when therapists use **genuineness** and honestly share their thoughts and feelings with their clients, the clients will in turn develop self-trust and honest self-expression.

**Active Listening**  Using **active listening**, which includes reflecting, paraphrasing, and clarifying what clients are saying, therapists communicate that they are very interested and paying close attention (see the **Try This Yourself**).

*In my early professional years, I was asking the question: How can I treat, or cure, or change this person? Now I would phrase the question in this way: How can I provide a relationship which this person may use for his own personal growth?*
—Carl Rogers (Founder of Client-Centered Therapy)

## Try This Yourself

### Using Active Listening Personally and Professionally

If you want to try active listening in your personal life, keep in mind that to *reflect* is to hold a mirror in front of the person, enabling that person to see him- or herself. To *paraphrase* is to summarize in different words what the other person is saying. To *clarify* is to check that both the speaker and listener are on the same wavelength.

When a professional uses active listening, he or she might notice a client's furrowed brow and downcast eyes while he is discussing his military experiences and then might respond, "It sounds like you're angry with your situation and feeling pretty miserable right now." Can you see how this statement reflects the client's anger, paraphrases his complaint, and gives feedback to clarify the

communication? This type of attentive, active listening is a relatively simple and well-documented technique that you can use to improve your communication with virtually anyone—professors, employers, friends, family, and especially your romantic partner.

**Evaluating Humanistic Therapies**  Supporters say humanistic therapies emphasize the positives of human nature, and they point out that there is empirical evidence for the efficacy of client-centered therapy. However, critics argue that outcomes such as self-actualization and self-awareness are difficult to test scientifically. Furthermore, research on specific humanistic techniques has had mixed results (Cain et al., 2016; Erekson & Lambert, 2015; Xu & Tracey, 2016).

**Cognitive therapies**  A group of talk therapies that focus on changing faulty, distorted thoughts (cognitions); based on the assumption that thoughts intervene between events and reactions.

## Cognitive Therapies

**Cognitive therapies** assume that faulty, distorted thoughts (cognitions) are the primary source of problems and that the therapist's key goal is to help clients identify and correct this faulty thinking (Calkins et al., 2016; Clark, 2016; Craske, 2017).

**FIGURE 15.7**   **Using cognitive restructuring to improve sales**

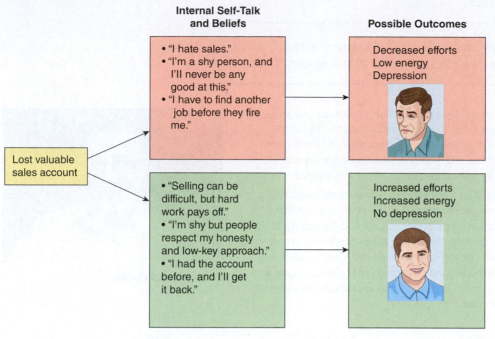

**a.  Negative self-talk**   Note how the negative interpretation and destructive self-talk leads to destructive and self-defeating outcomes.

**b.  Cognitive restructuring**   Cognitive therapy teaches clients to challenge and change their negative beliefs and negative self-talk. Developing positive beliefs and self-talk leads, in turn, to more positive outcomes. Can you think of other situations in which such reinterpretation could be helpful?

Like psychoanalysts and humanists, cognitive therapists believe that exploring unexamined beliefs can produce insight into the reasons for disturbed thoughts, feelings, and behaviors. However, instead of believing that a change occurs because of insight, cognitive therapists suggest that addressing *negative self-talk*, the unrealistic things a person tells himself or herself, is most important. For example, research with women suffering from eating disorders found that changing a client's irrational thoughts and self-talk, such as "If I eat that cake, I will become fat instantly" or "I'll never have a dating relationship if I don't lose 20 pounds," resulted in their having fewer negative thoughts about their bodies (Bhatnagar et al., 2013).

Through a process called **cognitive restructuring**, clients learn to identify, dispute, and replace their irrational or maladaptive thoughts with more realistic and positive beliefs. Do you see how if we first identify our irrational thoughts, then we can logically challenge them, which in turn enables us to become more effective (**Figure 15.7**)?

**Cognitive restructuring**   A therapeutic process of learning to identify, dispute, and replace irrational or maladaptive thoughts with more realistic and positive beliefs.

### Ellis's Rational-Emotive Behavior Therapy (REBT)   One of the best-known cognitive therapists, Albert Ellis, suggested that irrational beliefs are the primary culprit in problem emotions and behaviors. He proposed that most people mistakenly believe they are unhappy or upset because of external events, such as receiving a bad grade on an exam. In reality, according to Ellis, these negative emotions result from faulty interpretations and irrational beliefs (such as interpreting the bad grade as a sign of your incompetence and an indication that you'll never qualify for graduate school or a good job).

To deal with these irrational beliefs, Ellis developed **rational-emotive behavior therapy (REBT)** (Ellis & Ellis, 2011, 2014; Stephenson et al., 2017; Turner, 2016). (See **Step-by-Step Diagram 15.1** and the following **Try This Yourself**.)

**Rational-emotive behavior therapy (REBT)**   A form of talk therapy, developed by Albert Ellis, that focuses on eliminating negative emotional reactions through logic, confrontation, and examination of irrational beliefs.

*The best years of your life are the ones in which [you] decide your problems are your own. You do not blame them on your mother, the ecology, or the president. You realize that you control your own destiny.*

—Albert Ellis

## STEP-BY-STEP DIAGRAM 15.1 | Ellis's Rational-Emotive Behavior Therapy (REBT)

**STOP!** This Step-by-Step Diagram contains essential information NOT found elsewhere in the text, which is likely to appear on quizzes and exams. Be sure to study it CAREFULLY!

If you receive a poor performance evaluation at work, you might directly attribute your bad mood to the negative feedback. Psychologist Albert Ellis would argue that your self-talk ("I always mess up") between the event and the feeling is what actually upsets you. Furthermore, ruminating on all the other times you've "messed up" in your life maintains your negative emotional state and may even lead to anxiety disorders, depression, or other psychological disorders.

To treat these problems, Ellis developed an A–B–C–D approach: **A** stands for *activating event*, **B** the person's *belief system*, **C** the emotional *consequences*, and **D** the act of *disputing* erroneous beliefs. During therapy, Ellis helped his clients identify the A, B, C's underlying their irrational beliefs by actively arguing with, cajoling, and teasing them—sometimes in very blunt, confrontational language. Once clients recognized their self-defeating thoughts, he worked with them on how to *dispute* those beliefs and create and test out new, rational ones. These new beliefs then changed the maladaptive emotions—thus breaking the vicious cycle. (Note the arrow under D that goes backwards to B.)

**Albert Ellis (1913–2007)**

Bettman/Getty Images

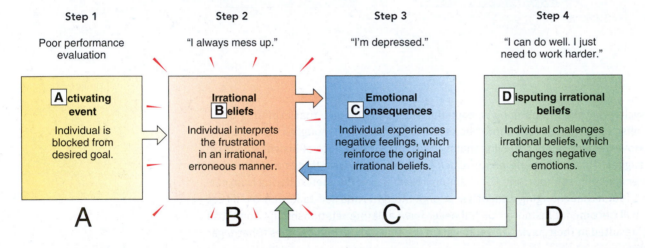

## Try This Yourself

### Overcoming Irrational Misconceptions

Albert Ellis believed that people often require the help of a therapist to see through their defenses and to challenge their self-defeating thoughts. For mild, everyday problems, our students have found that they can improve their own irrational beliefs and responses with the following suggestions:

1. **Identify and confront your belief system** Identify your irrational beliefs by asking yourself why you feel the particular emotions you do. Then, by confronting your thoughts and feelings, you can discover the irrational assumptions creating the problem consequences.

2. **Evaluate consequences** Rather than perpetuating negative emotions by assuming they must be experienced, focus on

whether your reactions make you more effective and enable you to solve your problems. It's gratifying when people you cherish love you in return. But if they don't, continuing to pursue them, or insisting that they must love you, will only be self-defeating.

3. **Practice effective ways of thinking and behaving** Imagine and rehearse thoughts and behaviors that are more effective and outcomes that are more successful.

*Why do I talk about the benefits of failure? . . . I was set free because my greatest fear had been realized, . . . and so rock bottom became a solid foundation on which I rebuilt my life.*
　　　　　　　　　　　　　　　　　　　—J. K. Rowling

### Beck's Cognitive-Behavior Therapy (CBT)

Another well-known cognitive therapist, Aaron Beck, also believes psychological problems result from illogical thinking and destructive self-talk (Beck, 1976, 2000; Calkins et al., 2016; Cristea et al., 2017). But Beck seeks to directly confront and change the behaviors associated with destructive cognitions. Beck's **cognitive-behavior therapy (CBT)** is designed to reduce *both* self-destructive thoughts *and* self-destructive behaviors.

In CBT, clients are first taught to recognize and keep track of their destructive thoughts (**Figure 15.8**). Next, CBT therapists help clients test these automatic thoughts against reality, thereby discovering that their faulty and illogical thoughts are feeding their depression (see the following **Try This Yourself**).

Once clients have recognized their destructive cognitions and tested them against reality, they are asked to confront and change their behaviors. Clients who suffer from depression, for instance, often lose motivation, even for experiences they used to find enjoyable. Taking an active rather than a passive role and reconnecting with enjoyable experiences can help lift their depression.

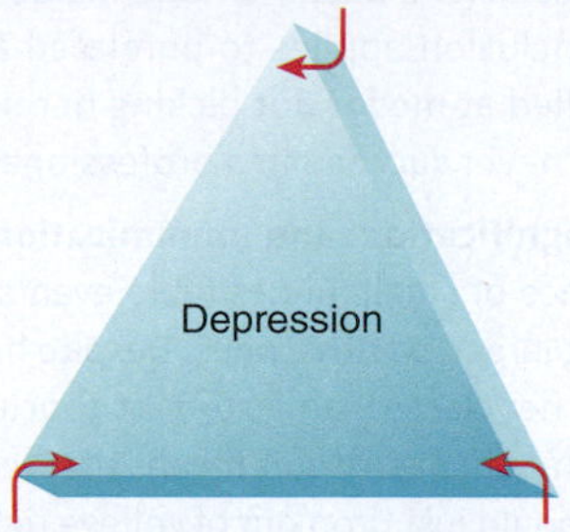

### Mindfulness-Based Cognitive Therapy (MBCT)

Building on CBT and the mindfulness meditation discussed in Chapter 3, **mindfulness-based cognitive therapy (MBCT)** helps clients to focus on their streams of thoughts, including their fears, anxieties, and worries. However, MBCT emphasizes that clients need to become mindful of their thinking processes at the very moment they're occurring (Forkmann et al., 2016; Helmes & Ward, 2017). Clients are taught how to pay attention to their ongoing thoughts, feelings, and events in a receptive and nonjudgmental way—as mere passing events of the mind. MBCT has been successfully applied in treatments for PTSD (**Figure 15.9**), as well as depression, personality disorders, and substance abuse (Dimidjian et al., 2016; Fortuna & Vallejo, 2015; Ottavi et al., 2016).

**Negative thoughts about oneself:**
"I'm a social failure."

Depression

**Negative thoughts about one's experiences:**
"Every encounter I have with people is a total disaster."

**Negative thoughts about the future:**
"Things will never improve. I'll never get along with people."

**FIGURE 15.8  The cognitive triad of depression**
According to Beck, some individuals typically think about themselves and their futures, along with their personal life experiences, in destructive, illogical ways. This so-called "cognitive triad" of negative thinking leads people to see themselves as inadequate, to view the future as bleak, and to exaggerate everyday negative experiences. Do you recognize how this triad of negativity feeds into and maintains depression?

**Cognitive-behavior therapy (CBT)**  A type of therapy, developed by Aaron Beck, that combines cognitive therapy (changing faulty thinking) with behavior therapy (changing maladaptive behaviors).

**Mindfulness-based cognitive therapy (MBCT)**  A therapy based on developing a state of consciousness that attends to ongoing thoughts, feelings, and events in a receptive and nonjudgmental way.

Howard Lipin/U-T San Diego/ZUMAWire/Alamy Stock Photo

**FIGURE 15.9  MBCT and the military**  To test the effectiveness of MBCT, 62 veterans suffering from PTSD were divided into two groups (Possemato et al., 2016). One group received the standard primary care, whereas the other received training in MBCT (see the photo). While both groups improved, those in the mindfulness group had significantly larger reductions in symptoms of PTSD and depression, and they maintained their gains in the 8-week follow up. Can you see how by accepting their fears and worries rather than trying to eliminate them, the veterans were less upset and affected by them?

---

## Try This Yourself

### A Cognitive Approach to Lifting Depression

One of the most successful applications of Beck's CBT is in the treatment of depression (Beck et al., 2012, 2015; Dobson, 2016; Hundt et al., 2016). Beck identified several thinking patterns believed to be common among depression-prone people, which are listed below. Recognizing these patterns in our own thought processes may help prevent or improve the occasional bad moods we all experience.

In CBT treatment, clients are first taught the three Cs—to *Catch* (identify), *Challenge*, and *Change* their irrational or maladaptive

thought patterns. Here, we provide an example of how to label the three C's for the first thinking pattern, *selective perception*. Then try to do the same for the other four maladaptive patterns.

- **Selective perception** Focusing selectively on negative events while ignoring positive events. (*Catch the thought* = "Why am I the only person alone at this party?" *Challenge it* = "I notice four other single people at this party." *Change it* = "Being single has several advantages. I'll bet some of the couples are actually envying my freedom.")

- **Overgeneralization** Drawing sweeping, global, negative conclusions based on one incident and then assuming that conclusion applies to unrelated areas of life. "My girlfriend yelled at me for not picking her up on time. I'm so forgetful. I'll never succeed in a professional career."

- **Magnification and minimization** Exaggerating the importance of small, undesirable events and grossly underestimating larger, positive ones. Despite having earned high grades in all her classes, an A student concludes: "This B on my last organic chemistry quiz means that I can't go on to med school, so I should just drop out of college right now."

- **Personalization** Taking responsibility and blame for events that are actually unrelated to the individual. "My adult child is unmarried and doesn't want to have children. I must have been a bad parent."

- **All-or-nothing thinking** Seeing things in terms of black-or-white categories—where everything is either totally good or bad, right or wrong, a success or a failure. ("If I don't get straight A's, I'll never get a good job.")

Clem Murray/MCT/NewsCom

**Aaron Beck (1921–)**

**Evaluating Cognitive Therapies**   Cognitive therapies are highly effective treatments for depression, as well as anxiety disorders, bulimia nervosa, anger management, addiction, and even some symptoms of schizophrenia and insomnia (Hundt et al., 2016; Palermo et al., 2016; Sankar et al., 2015).

There are, however, three major criticisms of cognitive therapies. First, critics suggest that a client's dysfunctional thinking may result from, not cause, abnormal functioning. For instance, the delusions and disturbed thinking characteristic of schizophrenia are generally believed to result from problems with brain functioning and biochemistry—not the thoughts themselves.

Second, cognitive therapies have been criticized for ignoring or denying the client's unconscious dynamics and minimizing the importance of the client's past.

Third, some critics suggest that cognitive therapies are successful because they employ behavior techniques, not because they change the underlying cognitive structure (Bandura, 1969, 2008; Granillo et al., 2013; Walker & Lampropoulos, 2014). Imagine that you sought treatment for depression and learned to curb your all-or-nothing thinking, along with identifying activities and behaviors that lessened your depression. You can see why it's difficult to identify whether changing your cognitions or changing your behavior was the most essential therapeutic factor. But to clients who have benefited, it doesn't matter. CBT combines both, and it has a proven track record for lifting depression!

© Billy R. Ray/Wiley

## Retrieval Practice 15.1  |  Talk Therapies

Completing this self-test and the connections section, and then checking your answers by clicking on the answer button or by looking in Appendix B, will provide immediate feedback and helpful practice for exams.

### Self-Test

1. Why are psychoanalysis/psychodynamic therapies, humanistic therapies, and cognitive therapies often grouped together?

2. The system of psychotherapy developed by Freud that seeks to bring unconscious conflicts into conscious awareness is known as _____.

   **a.** transference
   **b.** cognitive restructuring

   **c.** psychoanalysis
   **d.** the "hot seat" technique

3. A _____ therapist emphasizes the importance of empathy, unconditional positive regard, genuineness, and active listening.

   **a.** psychodynamic
   **b.** phenomenological behavior
   **c.** cognitive-behavior
   **d.** client-centered

4. According to rational-emotive behavior therapy (REBT), _____ often lead to depression and/or anxiety.

   **a.** unmet expectations     **b.** stimulus events
   **c.** conditioning experiences   **d.** irrational beliefs

5. Aaron Beck practices _____ therapy, which attempts to change not only destructive thoughts but the associated behaviors as well.

a. psycho-behavior   b. cognitive-behavior
c. thinking-acting   d. belief-behavior

**Connections—Chapter to Chapter**
Answering the following question will help you "look back and look ahead" to see the important connections among the subfields of psychology and chapters within this text.

In Chapter 12 (Motivation and Emotion), you discovered that emotion often depends on our cognitive appraisal or interpretation of events (*Schachter and Singer's two-factor theory*). In this chapter, you learned about *rational-emotive behavior therapy (REBT)*, a form of cognitive therapy that links irrational thoughts to problem emotions and behaviors. How are REBT and the two-factor theory alike?

# 15.2 Behavior Therapies

## LEARNING OBJECTIVES

**Retrieval Practice** While reading the upcoming sections, respond to each Learning Objective in your own words.

**Summarize the treatment techniques and criticisms of behavior therapies.**

- **Describe** how classical conditioning is used in therapy.
- **Explore** how operant conditioning is used in therapy.
- **Explain** how observational learning is used in therapy.
- **Discuss** the major criticisms of behavior therapies.

The previously discussed talk therapies are often called "insight therapies" because they focus on self-awareness, but sometimes having insight into a problem does not automatically solve it. As humorously depicted in the cartoon, the focus in **behavior therapies** is on the problem behavior itself rather than on any underlying causes (Spiegler, 2016; Stoll & Brooks, 2015). Although the person's feelings and interpretations are not disregarded, they're also not emphasized.

Given that behavior therapists believe that psychological disorders are primarily caused by inappropriate conditioning and learning, their major goals are to reduce or eliminate maladaptive behaviors and to increase adaptive ones. To do so, they generally rely on the learning principles of *classical conditioning, operant conditioning,* and *observational learning* (Chapter 6).

**Behavior therapies** A group of therapies that uses learning principles to reduce or eliminate maladaptive behaviors; techniques are based on classical and operant conditioning, along with observational learning.

**Systematic desensitization** A behavior therapy technique in which a client is first asked to create a hierarchy of ordered fears and then taught to relax while gradually confronting the feared stimulus.

## Classical Conditioning Techniques

Behavior therapists use the principles of classical conditioning to decrease maladaptive behaviors by creating new associations to replace the faulty ones. We will explore two techniques based on these principles: *systematic desensitization* and *aversion therapy*.

**Systematic Desensitization** Recall from Chapter 6 that classical conditioning occurs when a neutral stimulus (NS) becomes associated with an unconditioned stimulus (US) to elicit a conditioned response (CR). Sometimes a classically conditioned fear response becomes so extreme that we call it a "phobia." To treat phobias, behavior therapists often use **systematic desensitization**, which begins with relaxation training, followed by imagining or directly experiencing various versions of a feared object or situation while remaining deeply relaxed (Schare et al., 2015; Tyner et al., 2016; Wolpe & Plaud, 1997). See

SidneyHarris/ScienceCartoonsPlus.com

Most

Amount of anxiety

In a crowded elevator as doors close

Stepping onto elevator with a few other people

Doors open to empty elevator

Pressing the elevator call button

Approaching a bank of elevator doors

Least   Looking at a building with outside elevators

**FIGURE 15.10** **Systematic desensitization**   In systematic desensitization, the therapist and client together construct a *fear hierarchy*, a ranked listing of 10 or so related anxiety-arousing images—from the least fearful to the most. Then, while in a state of relaxation, the client mentally visualizes, or physically experiences, anxiety-producing items at the lowest level of the hierarchy. After becoming comfortable with the mild stimulus, the client then works his or her way up to the most anxiety-producing items at the top. In sum, each progressive step on the fear hierarchy is repeatedly paired with relaxation, until the fear response or phobia is extinguished.

**Figure 15.10** for a description of systematic desensitization useful for overcoming a fear of riding in an elevator.

How does relaxation training desensitize someone? Recall from Chapter 2 that the parasympathetic nerves control autonomic functions when we are relaxed. Because the opposing sympathetic nerves are dominant when we are anxious, it is physiologically impossible to be both relaxed and anxious at the same time. The key to success is teaching the client how to replace his or her fear response with relaxation when *exposed* to the fearful stimulus, which explains why these and related approaches are often referred to as *exposure therapies* (Hundt et al., 2017; Jordan et al., 2017).

For instance, if you or a friend suffers from a spider phobia, you may be amazed to know that after just two or three hours of therapy, starting with simply looking at photos of spiders (see the photo), and then moving next to a tarantula in a glass aquarium, clients are able to eventually pet and hold the spider with their bare hands (Hauner et al., 2012)! Modern virtual reality technology also uses systematic desensitization to expose clients to feared situations right in a therapist's office (**Figure 15.11**).

**Aversion Therapy**   As we've just seen, systematic desensitization substitutes a pleasant (relaxed) response to an unpleasant, fearful stimulus (like a spider) in order to reduce the fear. In contrast, **aversion therapy** uses classical conditioning techniques to substitute an unpleasant (aversive) response to a pleasant, desired stimulus (like alcohol) in order to reduce excessive drinking. Problem drinkers build up a number of pleasurable associations with alcohol. These pleasurable associations cannot always be

© Okea/iStockphoto

© Syracuse Newspapers/D.Lassman/ The Image Works

**FIGURE 15.11** **Virtual reality therapy**   Virtual reality therapy replaces mental images and actual physical experiences of fearful situations with headsets and data gloves. A client with a fear of heights, for example, can have experiences ranging from climbing a stepladder all the way to standing on the edge of a tall building.

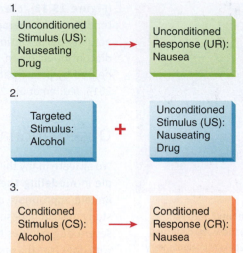

1.

| Unconditioned Stimulus (US): Nauseating Drug | → | Unconditioned Response (UR): Nausea |

2.

| Targeted Stimulus: Alcohol | + | Unconditioned Stimulus (US): Nauseating Drug |

3.

| Conditioned Stimulus (CS): Alcohol | → | Conditioned Response (CR): Nausea |

**FIGURE 15.12** **Aversion therapy** The goal of aversion therapy is to create an undesirable, or *aversive*, response to a stimulus a person would like to avoid, such as alcohol. Here, a man savors his drink just before the nauseating effects of the drug Antabuse begin. After repeated pairings of alcohol with nausea, the person learns a new, undesirable association—alcohol leads to vomiting!

prevented. Therefore, aversion therapy provides *unpleasant associations* to compete with the pleasurable ones (**Figure 15.12**).

**Aversion therapy** A type of behavior therapy that pairs an aversive (unpleasant) stimulus with a maladaptive behavior in order to elicit a negative reaction to the target stimulus.

## Operant Conditioning Techniques

As we discovered in Chapter 6, consequences are the heart of operant conditioning. Using a form of therapy called *behavior modification*, therapists provide reinforcement as a consequence for appropriate behaviors, and they withhold reinforcement for inappropriate behaviors. To develop complex behaviors, they often use *shaping*, which provides immediate rewards for successive approximations of the target behavior. Therapists have found this technique particularly successful in developing language skills in children with autism. First, the child is rewarded for connecting pictures or other devices with words; later, rewards are given only for using the pictures to communicate with others. This type of shaping can even be helpful if you suffer from the common problem of excessive shyness (see the following **Try This Yourself**).

### Try This Yourself

#### Overcoming Shyness

Shaping can help people acquire social skills and greater assertiveness. If you are painfully shy, for instance, a clinician might first ask you to role-play simply saying hello to someone you find attractive. Then you might practice behaviors that gradually lead you to suggest a get-together or date. During such role-playing, or behavior rehearsal, the clinician gives you feedback and reinforcement for each successive step you take toward the end goal.

For clients in an inpatient treatment facility, adaptive behaviors can be taught or increased with techniques that provide immediate reinforcement in the form of *tokens*, which are objects or symbols that can be later exchanged for primary rewards, such as food, TV time, a private room, or outings. In a program like this, which is called a **token economy**

**Token economy** A form of behavior therapy involving awarding "tokens" for desired behavior that can be exchanged later for rewards.

**FIGURE 15.13** **A familiar token economy?** Do you remember checking off items on a list to show you'd finished your chores? Or receiving stars or other stickers in elementary school for the number of books you read? A similar system is used in various mental health settings to reward clients for behaviors designed to improve their psychological functioning.

**Modeling therapy** A type of therapy characterized by watching and imitating models who demonstrate desirable behaviors.

**FIGURE 15.14** **Observational learning** During modeling therapy, a client might learn how to interview for a job by first watching the therapist role-play the part of the interviewee. The client then imitates the therapist's behavior and plays the same role. Over the course of several sessions, the client becomes gradually desensitized to the anxiety of interviews.

(**Figure 15.13**), clients might at first be given tokens for merely attending group therapy sessions. Later they will be rewarded only for actually participating in the sessions. Eventually, the tokens can be discontinued when the clients receive the reinforcement of being helped by participation in the therapy sessions (Jowett Hirst et al., 2016; Mullen et al., 2015).

## Observational Learning Techniques

We all learn many things by observing others. Therapists use this principle in **modeling therapy**, in which clients are asked to observe and imitate appropriate models as they perform desired behaviors. In one study, researchers successfully treated 4- and 5-year-old children with severe dog phobias by asking them first to watch other children play with dogs (see the photo), and then to gradually approach and get physically closer to the dogs themselves (May et al., 2013). When this type of therapy combines live modeling with direct and gradual practice, it is called *participant modeling*. This type of modeling is also effective in social skills training and assertiveness training (**Figure 15.14**).

**Evaluating Behavior Therapies** Criticisms of behavior therapy fall into three major categories:

- *Generalizability* Critics argue that in the real world, clients are not consistently reinforced or punished, and their newly acquired behaviors may disappear. Interestingly, a recent study found that drivers who were involved in a severe collision (punishment) initially reduced their risky driving, but only for the first month after the collision (O'Brien et al., 2017). To deal with this possibility, behavior therapists work to encourage clients to better recognize existing real-world rewards and to generate their own internal reinforcements, which they can then apply at their own discretion.

- *Neglect of other approaches* Some opponents contend that behavior therapies ignore or diminish the importance of unconscious, cognitive, and biological factors that also contribute to psychological disorders.

- *Ethics* Critics contend that it is unethical for one person to control another's behavior. Behaviorists, however, argue that rewards and punishments already control our behaviors. Behavior therapy actually increases our freedom by making these controls overt and by teaching people how to change their own behavior.

Despite these criticisms, behavior therapy is generally recognized as one of the most widely researched and scientifically documented forms of treatment. It's been shown to be highly effective for numerous problems, including phobias, obsessive-compulsive disorder, eating disorders, sexual dysfunctions, autism, intellectual disabilities, and delinquency (Cusack et al., 2016; Spiegler, 2016; Stoll & Brooks, 2015). For an immediate practical application of behavior therapy to your college life, see the following **Try This Yourself**.

## Try This Yourself

### Do You Have Test Anxiety?

Nearly everyone is somewhat anxious before a critical exam. If you find this anxiety helpful and invigorating, skip this activity. On the other hand, if the days and evenings before a major exam are ruined by your anxiety and you sometimes "freeze up" while taking a test, try these tips, based on the three major forms of behavior therapy.

**1. Classical Conditioning**

This informal type of systematic desensitization will help decrease your feelings of anxiety:

Step 1: Review and practice the relaxation technique taught in Chapter 3.

Step 2: Create a 10-step "test-taking" hierarchy—starting with the least anxiety-arousing image (perhaps the day your instructor first mentions an upcoming exam) and ending with actually taking the exam.

Step 3: Beginning with the least-arousing image—say, hearing about the exam—picture yourself at each stage. While maintaining a calm, relaxed state, mentally work your way through all 10 steps. If you become anxious at any stage, stay there, repeating your relaxation technique until the anxiety diminishes.

Step 4: If you start to feel anxious the night before the exam, or even during the exam itself, remind yourself to relax. Take a few moments to shut your eyes and review how you worked through your hierarchy.

**2. Operant Conditioning**

One of the best ways to avoid "freezing up" or "blanking out" on a test is to be fully prepared. To maximize your preparation, "shape" your behavior! Remember to start small. Try answering

Stockbyte/Getty Images

the multiple-choice and short answer questions at the end of each major section of the chapter, and then checking your answers by clicking on the answer button or by looking in Appendix B. Then move on to the longer self-grading quizzes that are available in the WileyPLUS program. Following each of these "successive approximations," be sure to reward yourself in some way—call a friend, play with your children or pets, watch a video, or maybe check your Facebook page.

**3. Observational Learning**

Talk with your classmates who are getting good grades. Ask them for tips on how they prepare for exams and how they handle their own test anxieties. This type of modeling and observational learning can be very helpful—and it's a nice way to make friends.

© Billy R. Ray/Wiley

## Retrieval Practice 15.2 | Behavior Therapies

Completing this self-test and the connections section, and then checking your answers by clicking on the answer button or by looking in Appendix B, will provide immediate feedback and helpful practice for exams.

### Self-Test

1. Describe the main goals of behavior therapy.

2. _____ pairs relaxation with a graduated hierarchy of anxiety-producing situations to extinguish the anxiety.

   a. Modeling
   b. Shaping
   c. Systematic desensitization
   d. Maslow's pyramid training

3. In behavior therapy, _____ techniques use shaping and tokens to increase adaptive behaviors.

   a. classical conditioning
   b. modeling
   c. social learning
   d. operant conditioning

4. In contrast to systematic desensitization, _____ uses classical conditioning techniques to create anxiety rather than prevent its arousal.

   a. anxiety-modeling therapy
   b. aversion therapy
   c. anxiety therapy
   d. subversion therapy

5. Asking clients with snake phobias to watch other (nonphobic) people handle snakes is an example of _____ therapy.

  **a.** time out  **b.** aversion
  **c.** participative  **d.** modeling

**Connections—Chapter to Chapter**
Answering the following question will help you "look back and look ahead" to see the important connections among the subfields of psychology and chapters within this text.

In Chapter 1 (Introduction to Psychology and Its Research Methods), you learned about psychology's ethical guidelines for research. In this chapter, you discovered several behavior therapies for treating psychological disorders. What might be the major ethical concerns with behavior therapies?

# 15.3 | Biomedical Therapies

## LEARNING OBJECTIVES

**Retrieval Practice**  While reading the upcoming sections, respond to each Learning Objective in your own words.

**Review the types of biomedical therapies and their risks and benefits.**

• **Describe** biomedical therapies.

• **Identify** the major types of drugs used to treat psychological disorders.

• **Explain** what happens in electroconvulsive therapy and psychosurgery.

• **Summarize** the risks and benefits associated with biomedical therapies.

**Biomedical therapies**  A group of therapies designed to alter brain functioning with biological or physical techniques, such as drugs, electroconvulsive therapy, and psychosurgery; also known as biological therapy.

Some problem behaviors seem to be caused, at least in part, by biological disruptions in brain structures, biochemistry, and/or genetics. And therapists attempt to improve this disturbed functioning and to relieve symptoms through **biomedical therapies**. Psychiatrists or other medical personnel are generally the only ones who use biomedical (biological) therapies. However, in some states, licensed psychologists can prescribe certain medications, and they often work with clients receiving biomedical therapies. In this section, we will discuss three aspects of biomedical therapies: *psychopharmacology*, *electroconvulsive therapy (ECT)*, and *psychosurgery*.

## Psychopharmacology

**Psychopharmacology**  The use of drugs to relieve or control the major symptoms of psychological disorders.

Since the 1950s, the field of **psychopharmacology** has effectively used drugs to relieve or control the major symptoms of psychological disorders. In some instances, using a psychotherapeutic drug is similar to administering insulin to people with diabetes, whose own bodies fail to manufacture enough. In other cases, drugs have been used to relieve or suppress the symptoms of psychological disturbances even when the underlying cause was not thought to be biological. As shown in **Table 15.1**, psychotherapeutic drugs are classified into four major categories: *antianxiety*, *antipsychotic*, *mood stabilizer*, and *antidepressant*.

How do the four categories differ? Antianxiety drugs generally create feelings of tranquility and relaxation, while also decreasing over-arousal in the brain. In contrast, antipsychotic drugs are designed to diminish or eliminate symptoms of psychosis, such as hallucinations and delusions. And mood-stabilizer drugs attempt to level off the emotional highs and lows of bipolar disorder. Interestingly, antidepressants are designed to lift depression—hence their name. However, they're now being successfully used to treat some anxiety disorders, obsessive-compulsive disorder (OCD), posttraumatic stress disorder (PTSD), and certain eating disorders.

**Explaining Drug Therapy**   How do drug treatments actually work? For most psychotherapeutic medications, including antidepressants, the best-understood action of the drugs
is to correct an imbalance in the levels of neurotransmitters in the brain (**Figure 15.15**). Surprisingly, research has found that the drug *ketamine* (sometimes called "Special K"), a dangerous date rape/party drug, also works to manage the symptoms of major depression, suicidal
behaviors, and bipolar disorders. Widely known in the medical field for its anesthetic properties, ketamine changes the levels of brain neurotransmitters and appears to decrease thoughts
of suicide because it targets parts of the brain responsible for executive and emotional

**TABLE 15.1**   **Psychotherapeutic Drug Treatments for Psychological Disorders**

| | Description | Examples (Trade Names) |
|---|---|---|
| **Antianxiety Drugs** Medications used to reduce anxiety and decrease over-arousal in the brain; also known as anxiolytics or minor tranquilizers. | **Antianxiety drugs** lower the sympathetic activity of the brain—the crisis mode of operation—so that anxiety is diminished and the person is calmer and less tense. Unfortunately, they're also potentially dangerous because they can reduce alertness, coordination, and reaction time. Moreover, they can have a synergistic (intensifying) effect with other drugs, which may lead to a severe drug reaction—and even death. | Ativan Halcion Klonopin Librium Restoril Tranxene Valium Xanax |
| **Antipsychotic Drugs** Medications used to diminish or eliminate symptoms of psychosis; also known as neuroleptics or major tranquilizers. | **Antipsychotic drugs** reduce the agitated behaviors, hallucinations, delusions, and other symptoms associated with psychotic disorders, such as schizophrenia. Traditional antipsychotics work by decreasing activity at the dopamine receptors in the brain. A large number of clients markedly improve when treated with antipsychotic drugs. | Clozaril Invega Latuda Haldol Risperdal Seroquel Thorazine Zyprexa |
| **Mood-Stabilizer Drugs** Medications used to treat the combination of manic episodes and depression characteristics of bipolar disorders. | **Mood-stabilizer drugs** help steady mood swings, particularly for those suffering from bipolar disorder, a condition marked by extremes of both mania and depression. Because these drugs generally require up to three or four weeks to take effect, their primary use is in preventing future episodes and helping to break the manic-depressive cycle. | Depakote Eskalith CR Lamictal Lithium Neurontin Tegretol Topamax Trileptal |
| **Antidepressant Drugs** Medications used to treat depression, some anxiety disorders, obsessive-compulsive disorder, posttraumatic stress disorder, and certain eating disorders (such as bulimia). | **Antidepressant drugs** are used primarily to reduce depression. There are several types of antidepressant drugs, including *selective serotonin reuptake inhibitors (SSRIs), serotonin and norepinephrine reuptake inhibitors (SNRIs), norepinephrine and dopamine reuptake inhibitors (NDRIs),* and *atypical antidepressants.* Each class of drugs affects neurochemical pathways in the brain in a slightly different way, increasing or decreasing the availability of certain chemicals. SSRIs (such as *Paxil* and *Prozac*) are by far the most commonly prescribed antidepressants. The atypical antidepressants are prescribed for those who fail to respond to, or experience undesirable side effects from, other antidepressants. Note that it can take weeks or months for antidepressants to achieve their full effect. | Anafranil Celexa Cymbalta Effexor Elavil Lexapro Nardil Norpramin Parnate Paxil Pristiq Prozac Sarafem Tofranil Wellbutrin Zoloft |

**FIGURE 15.15** **How antidepressants affect the brain** Antidepressants are believed to work by increasing the availability of serotonin or norepinephrine, neurotransmitters that normally elevate mood and arousal. Shown here is the action of some of the most popular antidepressants—Prozac, Paxil, and other selective serotonin reuptake inhibitors (SSRIs).

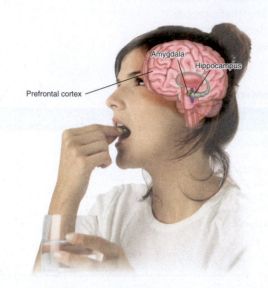

MedioImages/Photodisc/Getty Images, Inc.

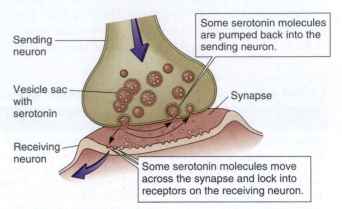

Some serotonin molecules are pumped back into the sending neuron.

Sending neuron

Vesicle sac with serotonin

Synapse

Receiving neuron

Some serotonin molecules move across the synapse and lock into receptors on the receiving neuron.

**b. Normal neural transmission** Sending neurons normally release an excess of neurotransmitters, including serotonin. Some of the serotonin locks into receptors on the receiving neuron, but excess serotonin is pumped back into the sending neuron (called *reuptake*) for storage and reuse. If serotonin is reabsorbed too quickly, there is less available to the brain, which may result in depression.

**a. Serotonin's effect on the brain** Some people with depression are believed to have lower levels of serotonin. Serotonin works in the prefrontal cortex, the hippocampus, and other parts of the brain to regulate mood, sleep, and appetite, among other things.

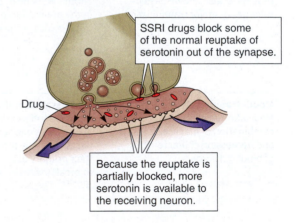

SSRI drugs block some of the normal reuptake of serotonin out of the synapse.

Drug

Because the reuptake is partially blocked, more serotonin is available to the receiving neuron.

**c. Partial blockage of reuptake by SSRIs** SSRIs, like Prozac, partially block the normal reuptake of excess serotonin, which leaves more serotonin molecules free to stimulate receptors on the receiving neuron. This increased neural transmission restores the normal balance of serotonin in the brain.

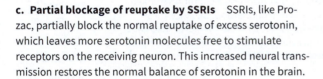

© Archive Image/Alamy Stock Photo

processing (Lee et al., 2016). Due to its anti-suicide effects, rapid onset, high efficacy, and good tolerability, ketamine shows promise as a potential treatment for depression and bipolar disorders (Kishimoto et al., 2016; Li et al., 2016; Reardon, 2015). However, it remains controversial due to the relative lack of empirical evidence on its effects, some serious side effects, and the potential for abuse (Zhang et al., 2016). For additional, intriguing (and controversial) psychotherapeutic drug research, see the following **Try This Yourself**.

In addition to correcting imbalances in the brain's neurotransmitters, other studies suggest that psychotherapeutic drugs, primarily antidepressants, may relieve depression and thoughts of suicide in three additional ways. They may increase *neurogenesis,* the production of new neurons, may increase *synaptogenesis,* the production of new synapses, and/or may stimulate activity in various areas of the brain (Miller & Hen, 2015; Samuels et al., 2016; Walker et al., 2015).

**Does "Acid" Cause Mental Illness?** What do you know about "psychedelic drugs"? Beginning in the 1960s (see the photo), there was considerable debate about these drugs, as well as widespread reports of "acid casualties" and increased mental health disorders among people who experimented with popular psychedelics, such as LSD, psilocybin (the active ingredient in "magic mushrooms"), and mescaline (found in the peyote cactus). As you may know, these drugs have been illegal in the United States since 1970 and are classified as schedule 1 drugs—"the most dangerous drugs," with no medicinal use.

Surprisingly, two studies contradict these earlier assumptions. In the first study, researchers analyzed data from more than 135,000 people who took part in the annual U.S. National Survey on Drug Use and Health (NSDUH) conducted from 2008 to 2011 (Johansen & Krebs, 2015). Of the 14% who reported use of psychedelics, the researchers found no increased risk of mental disorders, including schizophrenia, anxiety disorders, psychosis, depression, and suicide attempts. The second study, which analyzed 190,000 NSDUH respondents from 2008 to 2012, also found no link between psychedelic use and adverse mental health outcomes (Hendricks et al., 2015a). In fact, both studies suggested that psychedelic drug use may have produced lasting positive improvements in mental health. Other researchers have reviewed clinical trials, many that were double-blind and placebo-controlled, that showed positive relief of anxiety and depression in cancer patients and similar benefits with both alcohol and nicotine addiction, as well as in the prevention of suicide (dos Santos et al., 2016; Hendricks et al., 2015b; Nichols, 2016).

What do you think? Should psychedelics be used to treat physical and mental illnesses? Is this recent interest in psychedelics a flashback or a flash-in-the-pan? Only further research can fully answer these questions. (In the meantime, please remember that our inclusion of this research on psychedelics is not a recommendation for their use—either medically or recreationally.)

## Electroconvulsive Therapy and Psychosurgery

There is a long history of using electrical stimulation to treat psychological disorders. In **electroconvulsive therapy (ECT)**, also known as electroshock therapy (EST), a moderate electrical current is passed through the brain. This can be done by placing electrodes on the outside of both sides of the head (bilateral ECT) or on only one side of the head (unilateral ECT). The current triggers a widespread firing of neurons, or brief seizures. ECT can quickly reverse symptoms of certain mental illnesses and often works when other treatments have been unsuccessful. The electric current produces many changes in the central and peripheral nervous systems, including activation of the autonomic nervous system, increased secretion of various hormones and neurotransmitters, and changes in the blood–brain barrier (**Figure 15.16**).

Despite not knowing exactly how ECT works, and the possibility that it may cause some short-term and long-term memory problems, the risks of untreated, severe depression are generally considered greater than the risks of ECT (Andrade et al., 2016; Berman & Prudic, 2013). Today, ECT is used almost exclusively to treat serious depression when drugs and psychotherapy have failed or in cases where rapid response is needed— as is the case with suicidal clients (Fligelman et al., 2016; Kellner et al., 2015; Vallejo-Torres et al., 2015).

The most extreme, and least used, biomedical therapy is **psychosurgery**—brain surgery performed to reduce serious, debilitating psychological problems. Attempts to change disturbed thoughts, feelings, and behavior by altering the brain have a long history. In Roman times, for example, it was believed that a sword wound to the head could relieve insanity. In 1936, Portuguese neurologist Egaz Moniz first treated uncontrollable psychoses with a form of psychosurgery called a **lobotomy**, in which he cut the nerve fibers between the frontal lobes (where association areas for monitoring and planning behavior are found) and the thalamus and hypothalamus.

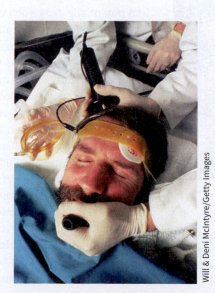

Will & Deni McIntyre/Getty Images

**Electroconvulsive therapy (ECT)** A biomedical therapy based on passing electrical current through the brain; it is used almost exclusively to treat serious depression when drugs and psychotherapy have failed.

**Psychosurgery** A form of biomedical therapy that involves alteration of the brain to bring about desirable behavioral, cognitive, or emotional changes; it is generally used when clients have not responded to other forms of treatment.

**Lobotomy** An outmoded neurosurgical procedure for mental disorders that involved cutting nerve pathways between the frontal lobes and the thalamus and hypothalamus.

**FIGURE 15.16** **Electroconvulsive therapy (ECT)** Modern ECT treatments are conducted with considerable safety precautions, including muscle-relaxant drugs that dramatically reduce muscle contractions and medication to help clients sleep through the procedure. Note, however, that ECT is used less often today, generally only when other treatments have failed, due to possibly serious side effects.

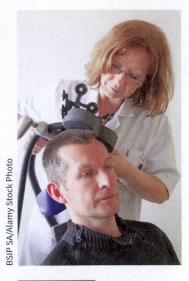

**FIGURE 15.17** **Repetitive transcranial magnetic stimulation (rTMS)** Powerful electromagnets generate pulsed magnetic fields that are targeted at specific areas of the brain to treat depression.

**Repetitive transcranial magnetic stimulation (rTMS)** A biomedical treatment that uses repeated magnetic field pulses targeted at specific areas of the brain.

Although these surgeries did reduce emotional outbursts and aggressiveness, some clients were left with debilitating brain damage. Two of the most notable examples of the damage from early lobotomies are Rosemary Kennedy, the sister of President John F. Kennedy, and Rose Williams, sister of American playwright Tennessee Williams. Both women were permanently incapacitated from lobotomies performed in the early 1940s. Thankfully, psychosurgery virtually stopped in the mid-1950s, when antipsychotic drugs came into use.

### Evaluating Biomedical Therapies

Like all other forms of therapy, biomedical therapies have both proponents and critics. In this section, we'll consider the pros and cons of each of the biomedical therapies—*psychopharmacology, ECT,* and *psychosurgery.*

**Psychopharmacology** In modern times, psychotherapeutic drugs have led to revolutionary changes in mental health. Before the use of drugs, some patients were destined to spend a lifetime in psychiatric institutions. Today, most improve enough to return to their homes and lead successful lives—if they continue to take their medications to prevent relapse.

However, drug therapy has been criticized on several grounds. First, although drugs may relieve symptoms for some people, they seldom provide cures, and some individuals become physically dependent. Furthermore, psychiatric medications can cause a variety of side effects, ranging from mild fatigue to severe impairments in memory and movement (Lawrence et al., 2017; Mentzel et al., 2017).

It's encouraging to note that drug therapy is more effective when combined with talk therapy. As an example, researchers have examined whether children and teenagers experiencing clinical depression would benefit from receiving cognitive behavioral therapy (CBT) along with medication to treat this disorder. In one study, 75 youths (ages 8 to 17) received either an antidepressant alone or an antidepressant along with CBT for 6 months (Kennard et al., 2014). Of those who received only the drug, 26.5% experienced continued depression, compared to only 9% of those who received the drug as well as CBT.

**ECT** As mentioned earlier, ECT is a controversial form of treatment, yet it still serves as a valuable last resort for severe depression. In recent years, many therapists have been using an alternative treatment, **repetitive transcranial magnetic stimulation (rTMS)**, in which an electromagnetic coil is placed on the scalp. Unlike ECT, which uses electricity to stimulate parts of the brain, rTMS uses magnetic pulses (**Figure 15.17**). To treat depression, the coil is usually placed over the prefrontal cortex, a region linked to deeper parts of the brain that regulate mood. Currently, rTMS's advantages over ECT are unclear, but studies have shown marked improvement in depression, and clients experience fewer side effects (Bakker et al., 2015; Yadollahpour et al., 2016; Zhang et al., 2015).

**Psychosurgery** Given that all forms of psychosurgery are generally irreversible and potentially dangerous with serious or even fatal side effects, some critics say that it should be banned altogether. For these reasons, psychosurgery is considered experimental and remains a highly controversial treatment.

Recently, psychiatrists have been experimenting with a much more limited and precise neurosurgical procedure called *deep brain stimulation (DBS)*. The surgeon drills two tiny holes into the skull and implants electrodes in the area of the brain believed to be associated with a specific disorder (**Figure 15.18**). These electrodes are then connected to a "pacemaker" implanted in the chest or stomach that sends low-voltage electricity to the problem areas in the brain. Over time, this repeated stimulation can bring about noticeable improvement in Parkinson's disease, epilepsy, major depression, and other disorders (Fields, 2015; Kim et al., 2016; Lipsman et al., 2015). Research has also shown that clients who receive DBS along with antidepressants show lower rates of depression than those who receive either treatment alone (Brunoni et al., 2013).

Before going on, **Table 15.2** provides a side-by-side comparison of all the major forms of therapy we've discussed so far. It will provide you with a handy way to review and master all the key terms and concepts.

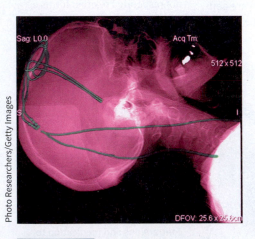

**FIGURE 15.18** **Deep brain stimulation (DBS)** Stimulation from the implanted electrodes in the client's brain may bring relief to those suffering from Parkinson's disease, epilepsy, major depression, and other disorders.

**TABLE 15.2** Side-by-Side Comparison of Treatments for Psychological Disorders

| Type of Treatment | Key Assumptions and Goals | Major Techniques | Strengths | Weaknesses |
|---|---|---|---|---|
| **Psychoanalysis/ Psychodynamic** | *Key assumption about cause of disorder* Unconscious, unresolved conflicts *Key goal of therapy* Provide insight by bringing unconscious thoughts and conflicts into conscious awareness | *Psychoanalysis* (Freud) • Free association • Dream analysis • Analysis of resistance • Analysis of transference • Interpretation *Psychodynamic therapies* • Face-to-face • Techniques similar to psychoanalysis but more likely to offer advice and support | *Psychoanalysis* • Can be effective for those who have the time and money *Psychodynamic therapies* • Benefits similar to those of psychoanalysis with shorter duration of treatment | • Question of repressed memories and unconscious conflicts • Limited applicability • Lacks scientific support |
| **Humanistic** | *Key assumption about cause of disorder* Blocked personal growth *Key goal of therapy* Maximize clients' inherent capacity for self-actualization, free will, and self-awareness | *Client-centered therapy* (Rogers) • Empathy • Unconditional positive regard • Genuineness • Active listening *General humanistic therapy* • Emphasis on providing an accepting atmosphere and encouraging healthy emotional experiences • Focus on conscious processes and present versus past experiences • Clients responsible for discovering their own maladaptive patterns | • Recognizes positives of human nature • Some empirical evidence of efficacy | • Self-actualization and self-awareness difficult to test scientifically • Mixed research results on specific humanistic techniques |
| **Cognitive** | *Key assumption about cause of disorder* Faulty, distorted thinking *Key goal of therapy* Help clients identify and correct faulty, distorted thinking | • Cognitive restructuring • Rational-emotive behavior therapy (REBT) (Ellis) • Cognitive-behavior therapy (CBT) (Beck) • Mindfulness-based cognitive therapy (MBCT) | Highly effective treatments for depression, as well as anxiety disorders, bulimia nervosa, anger management, addiction, and even some symptoms of schizophrenia and insomnia | • Dysfunctional thinking may result from, not cause, abnormal functioning • May neglect unconscious dynamics and importance of client's past • Success may be due to behavior techniques, not to changes in faulty thinking |
| **Behavior** | *Key assumption about cause of disorder* Inappropriate conditioning and learning *Key goal of therapy* Reduce or eliminate maladaptive behaviors and increase adaptive ones | • Classical conditioning (desensitization, aversion therapy) • Operant conditioning (behavior modification, shaping, token economies) • Observational learning (modeling, social-skills and assertiveness training) | Most widely researched and scientifically documented treatments; highly effective for phobias, obsessive-compulsive disorder, and other psychological disorders | • Effects of treatment may not generalize to the real world • May neglect unconscious, cognitive, and biological processes • May be unethical to control another's behavior |

| Type of Treatment | Key Assumptions and Goals | Major Techniques | Strengths | Weaknesses |
|---|---|---|---|---|
| Biomedical | *Key assumption about cause of disorder* Problems with brain structure or functioning, genetics, biochemistry  *Key goal of therapy* Improve structural or biochemical brain functioning and relieve symptoms | • Psychopharmacology • Electroconvulsive therapy • Psychosurgery | Often effective when problems don't respond to other treatments | • Psychopharmacology may relieve symptoms but seldom provides cures; also, problems with side effects and possible physical drug dependence • ECT and psychosurgery may have dangerous and permanent side effects |

© Billy R. Ray/ Wiley

## Retrieval Practice 15.3 | Biomedical Therapies

Completing this self-test and the connections section, and then checking your answers by clicking on the answer button or by looking in Appendix B, will provide immediate feedback and helpful practice for exams.

### Self-Test

1. Compare psychiatry and psychology in their use of biomedical therapies.

2. The effectiveness of antipsychotic drugs is thought to result primarily from decreasing activity at which receptors?

   **a.** Serotonin      **b.** Dopamine
   **c.** Epinephrine    **d.** All these options

3. In electroconvulsive therapy (ECT), _____.

   **a.** current is never applied to the left hemisphere
   **b.** seizures activate the central and peripheral nervous systems, stimulate hormone and neurotransmitter release, and change the blood–brain barrier
   **c.** convulsions are extremely painful and long lasting
   **d.** most clients receive hundreds of treatments because it is safer than in the past

4. ECT is used primarily to treat _____.

   **a.** phobias
   **b.** conduct disorders
   **c.** severe depression
   **d.** schizophrenia

5. The original form of psychosurgery developed by Egaz Moniz disconnected the _____ lobes from the thalamus and hypothalamus.

   **a.** occipital      **b.** parietal
   **c.** temporal       **d.** frontal

### Connections—Chapter to Chapter

Answering the following question will help you "look back and look ahead" to see the important connections among the subfields of psychology and chapters within this text.

In Chapter 16 (Social Psychology), you will learn about prejudice and discrimination. In this chapter, you discovered several myths about therapy. How do you think stereotypes about biomedical therapies, such as drug therapies, ECT, and psychosurgery, develop?

## 15.4 | Psychotherapy in Perspective

### LEARNING OBJECTIVES

**Retrieval Practice** While reading the upcoming sections, respond to each Learning Objective in your own words.

**Review the key issues in psychotherapy.**
• **Summarize** the goals and overall effectiveness of psychotherapy.
• **Describe** group, marital, family, and telehealth/ electronic therapies.

• **Discuss** the issues involved in institutionalization.
• **Identify** the key cultural and gender issues important in therapy.
• **Summarize** the major career options for someone interested in becoming a mental health professional.

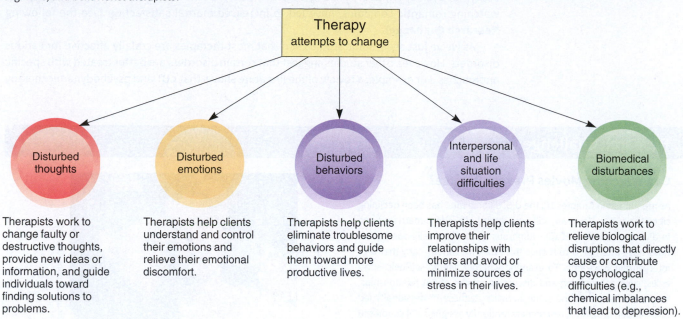

**FIGURE 15.19**    **The five most common goals of therapy**    Most therapies focus on one or more of these five goals. Can you identify which would be of most interest to psychodynamic, humanistic, cognitive, and behaviorist therapists?

**Therapy**
attempts to change

| Disturbed thoughts | Disturbed emotions | Disturbed behaviors | Interpersonal and life situation difficulties | Biomedical disturbances |

Therapists work to change faulty or destructive thoughts, provide new ideas or information, and guide individuals toward finding solutions to problems.

Therapists help clients understand and control their emotions and relieve their emotional discomfort.

Therapists help clients eliminate troublesome behaviors and guide them toward more productive lives.

Therapists help clients improve their relationships with others and avoid or minimize sources of stress in their lives.

Therapists work to relieve biological disruptions that directly cause or contribute to psychological difficulties (e.g., chemical imbalances that lead to depression).

It's currently estimated that there are more than a thousand approaches to psychotherapy, and the number is continuing to rise (Gaudiano et al., 2015; Magnavita & Anchin, 2014). Given this high number and wide variety of approaches, how would you choose one for yourself or someone you know? In the first part of this section, we discuss five goals common to all psychotherapies. Then we explore specific formats for therapy as well as considerations of culture and gender. Our aim is to help you synthesize the material in this chapter and put what you have learned about each of the major forms of therapy into a broader context.

## Therapy Goals and Effectiveness

All major forms of therapy are designed to help the client in five specific areas (**Figure 15.19**). Although most therapists work with clients in several of these areas, the emphasis varies according to the therapist's training and whether it is psychodynamic, cognitive, humanistic, behaviorist, or biomedical. Clinicians who regularly borrow freely from various theories are said to take an **eclectic approach**.

Does therapy work? After years of controlled studies and *meta-analysis*—a method of statistically combining and analyzing data from many studies—researchers have fairly clear evidence that it does. Furthermore, the major nonbiomedical therapies are as effective as biomedical therapies, and combined treatments are more effective than either of these alone (Cuijpers, 2017; Weisz et al., 2017). See **Figure 15.20**.

**Eclectic approach**    A treatment approach that draws from various therapies to best suit the client and the situation; also known as integrative therapy.

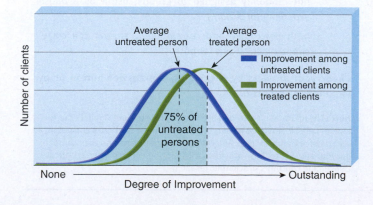

**FIGURE 15.20**    **Is therapy generally effective?**    An early meta-analytic review combined studies of almost 25,000 people and found that the average person who received treatment was better off than 75% of the untreated control clients (Smith et al., 1980; Smith & Glass, 1977).

Studies also show that short-term treatments can sometimes be as effective as long-term treatments and that several therapies are equally effective for various disorders (Goldstone, 2017; Goodyer et al., 2017; Lilliengren et al., 2016). Even informal therapy techniques, like watching romantic comedies, have led to increased marital satisfaction (see the following **Research Challenge**).

As we've just seen, some studies find that most therapies are equally effective for various disorders. However, other studies suggest that certain disorders are better treated with specific approaches. For example, a review of the literature shows that CBT and psychodynamic therapy

## Research Challenge

### Can Watching Movies Prevent Divorce?

As mentioned in Chapter 10, the U.S. divorce rate has been declining since the 1970s. However, still over a third of modern marriages end in divorce (Swanson, 2016). Numerous secular and religious institutions have attempted to reduce this rate with various early marriage intervention programs. To examine whether simple self-help strategies, such as watching and discussing movies about relationships, might offer some of the same benefits as these professionally led intervention programs, researchers randomly assigned 174 couples to one of four groups (Rogge et al., 2013):

MAD_Production/Shutterstock

- Group 1 (control) received no training or instructions.

- Group 2 (conflict management) learned active listening strategies to help discuss heated issues.

- Group 3 (compassion and acceptance training) learned strategies for finding common ground and showing empathy.

- Group 4 (minimal intervention—movie and talk) attended a 10-minute lecture on relationship awareness and how watching couples in movies could help increase awareness of their own behaviors.

Members of all the groups were similar in terms of age, education, ethnicity, relationship satisfaction, and other dimensions.

Following the initial assignment to groups, Group 1 received no training at all. Groups 2 and 3 attended weekly lectures, completed homework assignments, and met with a trained therapist periodically. In contrast, Group 4 attended a 10-minute lecture, watched a romantic comedy, and then discussed 12 questions about the screen couple's interactions (such as, "Did they try using humor to keep things from getting nasty?"). They were then sent home with a list of 47 relationship-oriented movies and allowed to choose their favorite one to watch and discuss once a week for the next month.

The researchers followed up with all couples 3 years later to see which of these approaches was most effective for preventing divorce. Much to their surprise, couples in all three of the intervention groups were much less likely to get divorced than those in the control group. Specifically, 24% of couples in the control group were divorced, compared to only 11% of those in any of the other three groups. Even more surprising, this study shows that a simple self-help strategy of watching and discussing five relationship movies over 1 month's time can be just as effective at reducing the divorce or separation rate as more intensive early marriage counseling programs led by trained psychologists.

Do you see how this study has exciting wide-scale, national applications? If "movie date night" can double as therapy, many

U.S. couples might be saved from the very high emotional and financial costs of divorce. What about your own current or future relationships? If simply sharing and discussing a relationship movie now and then with your romantic partner might strengthen that relationship, why not try it? You can learn more about this study (and see a list of recommended movies with guided discussion questions) at www.couples-research.com.

**Test Yourself**

1. Based on the information provided, did this study (Rogge et al., 2013) use descriptive, correlational, and/or experimental research?

2. If you chose:
   - *descriptive research*, is this a naturalistic observation, survey/interview, case study, and/or archival research?
   - *correlational research*, is this a positive, negative, or zero correlation?
   - *experimental research*, label the IV, DV, experimental group(s), and control group. (Note: If participants were not randomly assigned to groups, list it as a *quasi-experimental design*.)
   - both *descriptive* and *correlational*, answer the corresponding questions for both.

**Check your answers by clicking on the answer button or by looking in Appendix B.**

**Note:** The information provided in this study is admittedly limited, but the level of detail is similar to what is presented in most textbooks and public reports of research findings. Answering these questions, and then comparing your answers to those provided, will help you become a better critical thinker and consumer of scientific research.

are the most effective for depression (Goldstone, 2017). In contrast, symptoms of schizophrenia can be significantly relieved with medication (Bullis & Hofmann, 2016; Gillihan & Foa, 2016; Iglesias et al., 2016; Short & Thomas, 2015).

Finally, in recent years, **evidence-based practice in psychology (EBPP)** has been gaining momentum. As you have seen throughout this text, psychology is founded on empirically supported evidence backed by rigorous scientific standards. However, when it comes to therapy and treatment decisions for particular clients, relying solely on research can be difficult. Evidence for some disorders is conflicting or nonexistent. Furthermore, each client has his or her own specific characteristics, culture, and preferences, and those needs must be respected when designing the optimal treatment plan.

A special task force of the American Psychological Association recognized these competing positions, which led to their endorsement of EBPP (APA Presidential Task Force, 2006). As you can see in **Figure 15.21**, this approach provides flexibility for the clinician, while also incorporating the needs of the client and the best scientific evidence (Hamilton et al., 2016; Jordan et al., 2017; Kaminer & Eagle, 2017). Like all other movements, EBPP has been criticized. But this type of empirically based research promises to be helpful for therapists and clients alike in their treatment decisions.

Before going on, note that the most important factor in effective therapy is the relationship between the therapist and the client. This bond, known as the **therapeutic alliance**, should be one of mutual trust, respect, understanding, and cooperation (Constantino et al., 2017; Doran et al., 2017; Zilcha-Mano et al., 2016). Unfortunately, this is generally not the case with radio and television so-called therapists. Moreover, there is no assurance that these individuals have adequate training or licensing—*therapist* and *counselor* are generally not protected, licensed terms. For more tips on finding a qualified therapist for yourself or a loved one, see Table 15.3 in a later section and the following **Try This Yourself**.

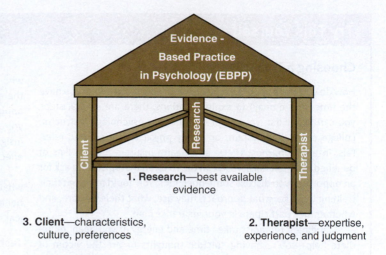

**FIGURE 15.21** **Evidence-based practice in psychology (EBPP)** The ideal treatment plan has been compared to a three-legged stool, supported by: (1) the best available research regarding whether and why a specific treatment works, (2) the therapist's expertise, experience, and judgment, and (3) the client's personal characteristics, culture, and preferences.

**Evidence-based practice in psychology (EBPP)** A newer approach to therapy that integrates the best available evidence with the clinician's expertise, along with the client's characteristics, culture, and preferences.

**Therapeutic alliance** A bond between the therapist and client based on mutual trust, respect, understanding, and cooperation; an essential factor in successful therapy.

## Therapy Formats

The therapies described earlier in this chapter are conducted primarily in a face-to-face, therapist-to-client format. In this section, we focus on several major alternatives: *group*, *family*, and *marital therapies*, which treat multiple individuals simultaneously, and *telehealth/electronic therapy*, which treats individuals via the Internet, e-mail, and/or smartphones.

### Group Therapies
In **group therapies**, multiple people meet together to work toward therapeutic goals. Typically, a group of 8 to 10 people meets with a therapist on a regular basis to talk about problems in their lives.

A variation on group therapy is the **self-help group**. Unlike other group approaches, self-help groups are not guided by a professional. They are simply circles of people who share a common problem, such as alcoholism, obesity, or breast cancer, and who meet to give and receive support. Programs such as Alcoholics Anonymous, Narcotics Anonymous, and Spenders Anonymous are examples of self-help groups.

Although group members don't get the same level of individual attention found in one-on-one therapies, group and self-help therapies provide their own unique advantages (Bateganya et al., 2015; Castillo et al., 2016; Friedman et al., 2017). They are far less expensive than one-on-one therapies and provide a broader base of social support. Group members also can learn from each other's experiences, share insights and coping strategies, and role-play social interactions together.

**Group therapies** A form of therapy in which a number of people with similar concerns meet together to work toward therapeutic goals.

**Self-help group** A leaderless or non–professionally guided group in which members assist each other with a specific problem, as in Alcoholics Anonymous.

## Try This Yourself

### Choosing a Therapist

How do you find a good therapist for your specific needs? If you have the time (and money) to explore options, there are several steps you can take. First, you might consult your psychology instructor, college counseling system, or family physician for specific referrals. In addition, most HMOs and health insurers provide lists of qualified professionals. Next, call the referred therapists and ask for an opportunity to discuss some questions. You could ask what their training was like, what approach they use, what their fees are, and whether they participate in your insurance plan.

Finding a therapist takes time and energy. If you need immediate help—you're having suicidal thoughts or are the victim of abuse—you should see if your community is one of the many that have medical hospital emergency services and telephone hotlines that provide counseling services on a 24-hour basis. Most colleges and universities also have counseling centers that provide immediate, short-term therapy to students free of charge.

Finally, if you're concerned about a friend or family member who might need therapy, you can follow these tips to help locate a therapist and then possibly offer to go with him or her on the first appointment. If the individual refuses help and the problem affects you, it is often a good idea to seek therapy yourself. You will gain insights and skills that will help you deal with the situation more effectively.

For general help in locating a skilled therapist, identifying what types of initial questions to ask, learning how to gain the most benefits during therapy, and so on, consult the American Psychological Association (APA) website.

#### Test Your Critical Thinking

1. If you were looking for a therapist, would you want the therapist's gender to be the same as yours? Why or why not?

2. Do you think all insurance companies should be required to offer mental health coverage? Why or why not?

---

Interestingly, researchers have studied group sessions in 12-step programs, like Alcoholics Anonymous, and they've found that group participants suffering from a combination of social anxiety disorders and substance abuse disorders, as well as recovering alcoholics, show lower rates of relapse than those who don't participate in these self-help groups. This is particularly true if they also provide help to others (Pagano et al., 2013, 2015). In sum, research on self-help groups for alcoholism, obesity, and other disorders suggests that they can be very effective, either alone or in combination with individual psychotherapy (Kendra et al., 2015; McGillicuddy et al., 2015; O'Farrell et al., 2016). Bear in mind that therapists often recommend these alternative formats to their clients as an additional resource while they continue in individual therapy.

**Marital and Family Therapies**  Given that a family or marriage is a system of interdependent parts, the problem of any one individual inevitably affects everyone. Therefore, all members are potential beneficiaries of therapy (Gunn et al., 2015; McGeorge et al., 2015; Smith, 2016). The line between family and marital or couples therapy is often blurred. Here, our discussion will focus on *family therapy*, in which the primary aim is to change maladaptive family interaction patterns (**Figure 15.22**). All members of the family attend therapy sessions, though at times the therapist may see family members individually or in twos or threes.

Family therapy is useful in treating a number of disorders and clinical problems. For instance, the therapist can help families improve their communication styles and reframe their problems as family issues rather than individual issues. Family therapy can also be the most favorable setting for the treatment of adolescent substance abuse and eating disorders (Dodge, 2016; Horigian & Szapocnik, 2015; Kanbur & Harrison, 2016).

**FIGURE 15.22  Family therapy**  Many families initially come into therapy believing that one member is the cause of all their problems. However, family therapists often find that this "identified client" is a scapegoat for deeper disturbances. How could changing ways of interacting within the family system promote the health of individual family members and the family as a whole?

Lisa F. Young /Shutterstock

**Telehealth/Electronic Therapy**    Today, millions of people are receiving advice and professional therapy in electronic formats, such as the Internet, e-mail, virtual reality (VR), and interactive web-based conference systems. This latest form of electronic therapy, often referred to as *telehealth*, allows clinicians to reach more clients and provide them with greater access to information regarding their specific problems.

Studies have long shown that therapy outcomes improve with increased client contact, and the electronic/telehealth format may be the easiest and most cost-effective way to increase this contact (Acierno et al., 2016; Ophuis et al., 2017; Schröder et al., 2017). A recent study of 132 veterans suffering from PTSD found that home-based telehealth treatment was as effective as standard in-person therapy, and it also greatly reduced the travel time, travel cost, lost work, and stigma that can be associated with in-person therapy (Acierno et al., 2017).

Using electronic options such as the Internet and smartphones does provide alternatives to traditional one-on-one therapies, but, as you might expect, these approaches also raise concerns. Professional therapists fear, among other things, that without interstate and international licensing or a governing body to regulate this type of therapy, there are no means to protect clients from unethical practices or incompetent therapists. What do you think? Would you be more likely to participate in therapy if it were offered via your smartphone, e-mail, or a website? Or is this too impersonal for you?

If you've enjoyed this section on the various forms and formats of psychotherapy, and are interested in seeking therapy for yourself or someone else, or are considering a career as a therapist, refer to **Table 15.3**. It provides a handy and quick overview of the major types of mental health professionals.

**TABLE 15.3**    **Careers in Mental Health**

Most colleges have counseling or career centers with numerous resources and trained staff to help you with your career choices. To give you an overview of the general field of psychotherapy, we've included a brief summary of the major types of mental health professionals, degrees, required education beyond the bachelor's degree, job description, and type of training.

| Major Types of Mental Health Professionals | | |
|---|---|---|
| **Occupational Title** | **Degree** | **Nature of Training** |
| **Clinical psychologists** | PhD (doctor of philosophy) PsyD (doctor of psychology) | Most clinical psychologists have a doctoral degree with training in research and clinical practice and a supervised one-year internship in a psychiatric hospital or mental health facility. As clinicians, they work with clients suffering from mental disorders, but many also work in colleges and universities as teachers and researchers. |
| **Counseling psychologists** | MA (master of arts) PhD (doctor of philosophy) PsyD (doctor of psychology) EdD (doctor of education) | Counseling psychologists typically have a doctoral degree with training that focuses on less severe mental disorders, such as emotional, social, vocational, educational, and health-related concerns. In addition to providing psychotherapy, other career paths are open, such as teaching, research, and vocational counseling. |
| **Pastoral counselors** | None MA (master of arts) PhD (doctor of philosophy) DD (doctor of divinity) | Pastoral counselors combine spiritual advice and psychotherapy. Generally, they must hold a license and at least a master's or doctoral degree in their field of study. They typically work for counseling centers, churches, community programs, and hospitals. |
| **Psychiatrists** | MD (doctor of medicine) | Psychiatrists must complete four years of medical school followed by an internship and residency in psychiatry, which include supervised practice in psychotherapy techniques and biomedical therapies. In most states in the United States, psychiatrists are the only mental health specialists who can regularly prescribe drugs. |
| **Psychiatric nurses** | RN (registered nurse) MA (master of arts) PhD (doctor of philosophy) | Psychiatric nurses usually have a bachelor's or master's degree in nursing, followed by advanced training in the care of patients in hospital settings and clients in mental health facilities. |

| | | |
|---|---|---|
| **Psychiatric social workers** | MSW (master of social work) DSW (doctor of social work) PhD (doctor of philosophy) | Psychiatric social workers usually have a master's degree in social work, followed by advanced training and experience in hospitals or outpatient settings working with people who have psychological problems. |
| **School psychologists** | MA (master of arts) PhD (doctor of philosophy) PsyD (doctor of psychology) EdD (doctor of education) | School psychologists generally begin with a bachelor's degree in psychology, followed by graduate training in psychological assessment and counseling for school-related issues and problems. |

*Sources:* Jaekel & Kortegast, 2016; Metz, 2016; Silvia et al., 2017; Sternberg, 2017; U.S. Bureau of Labor Statistics, 2017.

## Institutionalization

We all believe in the right to freedom. But what about people who threaten suicide or are potentially violent? Should some people be involuntarily committed to protect them from their own mental disorders? Despite Hollywood film portrayals, forced institutionalization of people with mental illness is generally reserved for only the most serious and life-threatening situations. And even so, it poses serious ethical problems.

**Involuntary Commitment**    The legal grounds for involuntary commitment vary from state to state and nation to nation (e.g., Holder et al., 2017; Ryan & Callagan, 2017). Generally, though, people can be sent to psychiatric hospitals against their will in the following circumstances.

- They are believed to pose a danger to themselves (usually suicidal) or to others (potentially violent).

- They are in serious need of treatment (indicated by bizarre behavior and loss of contact with reality).

- There is no reasonable, less restrictive alternative.

In emergencies, psychologists and other professionals can authorize temporary commitment for 24 to 72 hours. During this observation period, laboratory tests can be performed to rule out medical illnesses that could be causing the symptoms. Clients can also receive psychological testing, medication, and short-term therapy during this period.

**Deinstitutionalization**    Although the courts have established stringent requirements for involuntary commitment, abuses do occur. There are also problems with long-term, chronic institutionalization. And properly housing and caring for people with mental illness is very expensive. In response to these problems, many states have a policy of *deinstitutionalization*, which involves discharging clients from mental hospitals as soon as possible and discouraging admissions.

Deinstitutionalization has been a humane and positive step for many. But some clients are discharged without continuing provision for their protection. Many of these people end up living in rundown hotels or understaffed nursing homes, in jails, or on the street with no shelter or means of support (e.g., Roy et al., 2016; Ventriglio et al., 2015). Keep in mind that a sizable percentage of homeless people suffer from some form of serious mental illness (Allday, 2016; Diaz et al., 2016; National Alliance on Mental Illness, n.d.). (The rise in homelessness is also due to such economic factors as increased unemployment, underemployment, and a shortage of low-income housing.)

What else can be done? Rather than returning clients to state hospitals, most clinicians suggest expanding and improving community care (**Figure 15.23**). They also recommend that general

**FIGURE 15.23** **Outpatient support**  Community mental health (CMH) centers are a prime example of alternatives to institutionalization. CMH centers provide outpatient services, such as individual and group therapy and prevention programs. They also coordinate short-term inpatient care and programs for discharged clients, such as halfway houses and aftercare services. The major downside of CMH centers and their support programs is that they are expensive. Investing in primary prevention programs (such as more intervention programs for people at high risk for mental illness) could substantially reduce these costs.

James Shaffer/PhotoEdit

hospitals be equipped with special psychiatric units where those who are acutely ill receive inpatient care. For less disturbed individuals and chronically ill clients, they often recommend walk-in clinics, crisis intervention services, improved residential treatment facilities, and psychosocial and vocational rehabilitation. State hospitals can then be reserved for the most unmanageable cases.

## Gender and Cultural Diversity

### Therapy in Action

In this concluding section, we'll examine important cultural and gender issues in therapy. As you can probably imagine, we find both similarities and differences in therapies across cultures. We find, too, that gender poses several key issues for therapy.

### Cultural Issues in Therapy

The therapies described in this chapter are based on Western European and North American culture. Does this mean they are unique to this culture? Or do these psychotherapists accomplish some of the same things that, say, a native healer or shaman does? When we look at therapies in all cultures, we find that they have certain key features in common (Barnow & Balkir, 2013; Braakmann, 2015; Hall & Ibaraki, 2016):

- **Naming the problem** People often feel better just knowing that others experience the same problem and that the therapist has had experience with it.

- **Demonstrating the right qualities** Clients must feel that the therapist is caring, competent, approachable, and concerned with finding solutions to their problems.

- **Establishing credibility** Word-of-mouth testimonials and status symbols, such as diplomas on the wall, establish a therapist's credibility. A native healer may earn credibility by serving as an apprentice to a revered healer.

- **Placing the problem in a familiar framework** Some cultures believe evil spirits cause psychological disorders, so therapy is directed toward eliminating these spirits. Similarly, in cultures that emphasize the importance of early childhood experiences and the unconscious mind as the cause of mental disorders, therapy will be framed around these familiar issues.

- **Applying techniques to bring relief** In all cultures, therapy includes action. Either the client or the therapist must do something, and what the therapist does must fit the client's expectations—whether it is performing a ceremony to expel demons or talking with the client about his or her thoughts and feelings.

- **Meeting at a special time and place** The fact that therapy occurs outside the client's everyday experiences seems to be an essential and shared feature of all therapies.

Although there are basic similarities in therapies across cultures, there are also significant differences. In the traditional Western European and North American model, the emphasis is on the client's self and on his or her having independence and control over his or her life—qualities that are highly valued in individualistic cultures.

Sky Bonillo/PhotoEdit

**FIGURE 15.24** **Emphasizing Interdependence** In Japanese Naikan therapy, clients sit quietly from 5:30 a.m. to 9:00 p.m. for seven days and are visited by an interviewer every 90 minutes. During this time, they reflect on their relationships with others in order to discover personal guilt for having been ungrateful and troublesome and to develop gratitude toward those who have helped them (Itoh & Hikasa, 2014; Zhang et al., 2014).

In contrast, within collectivist cultures (**Figure 15.24**), the focus of therapy is on interpersonal sensitivity, interdependence, and the acceptance of life realities (Lee et al., 2015; Liao et al., 2016; Seay & Sun, 2016).

Not only does culture affect the types of therapy that are developed, but it also influences the perceptions of the therapist. What one culture considers abnormal behavior may be quite common—and even healthy—in others. For this reason, recognizing cultural differences is key to building trust between therapists and clients and for effecting behavioral change (La Roche et al., 2015; Strauss et al., 2015; Weiler et al., 2015).

### Gender and Therapy

In our individualistic Western culture, men and women present different needs and problems to therapists. Research has identified four unique concerns related to gender and psychotherapy (Moulding, 2016; Sáenz Herrero, 2015; Zerbe Enns et al., 2015):

1. **Rates of diagnosis and treatment of mental disorders** Women are diagnosed and treated for mental illness at a much higher rate than men. Are women "sicker" than men as a group, or are they just more willing to admit their problems? Or are the categories of illness biased against women? More research is needed to answer these questions.

2. **Stresses of poverty** Women are disproportionately likely to be poor. Poverty contributes to stress, which is directly related to many psychological disorders.

3. **Violence against women** Rape, incest, and sexual harassment—which are much more likely to happen to women than to men—may lead to depression, insomnia, posttraumatic stress disorder, eating disorders, and other problems.

4. **Stresses of multiple roles and gender-role conflict** Despite the many changes in gender roles in modern times, restrictive definitions of femininity and masculinity still limit

both genders' well-being and human potential. Furthermore, most men and women today serve in many roles, as family members, students, wage earners, and so forth. The conflicting demands of their multiple roles often create special stresses unique to each gender.

Therapists must be sensitive to possible connections between clients' problems and their gender, as well as to issues of gender diversity (De Bord et al., 2017; Levant & Powell, 2017). Rather than just emphasizing drugs to relieve depression, it may be more appropriate for therapists to explore ways to relieve the stresses of multiple roles or poverty for both women and men. Can you see how helping a single parent identify parenting resources, such as play groups, parent support groups, and high-quality child care, might be just as effective at relieving depression as prescribing drugs? In the case of men, can you see how relieving loneliness or depression might help decrease their greater problems with substance abuse and aggression?

We'd like to leave this chapter on a positive note. The psychotherapy techniques we've discussed are generally directed toward improving psychological disorders. However, psychologists are also committed to enhancing overall well-being and daily psychological functioning. In line with that, we offer the following.

## ❖ Psychology and Your Personal Success | What Are the Keys to Good Mental Health?

As you've seen throughout this text, psychology focuses on three major areas—*thoughts, feelings,* and *actions*. Therefore, to increase your everyday well-being and protect your mental health, consider the following research-based tips for each area:

1. **Recognize and control your thoughts.** Would you like to be happier and more often in a great mood? You might start by reviewing and implementing the suggestions in the *Psychology and Your Personal Success* section on happiness in Chapter 12. Also, as discussed earlier, the three Cs of Beck's cognitive therapy (catching, challenging, and changing our faulty thought processes) are key to successful therapy—as well as in everyday life.

   Research also finds that having a positive view of the future and an optimistic, attributional style are major contributors to mental health (Kleiman et al., 2017; Roepke & Seligman, 2016; Sachsenweger et al., 2015). Depressed people often suffer from a *depressive attribution style* of thinking, which means that they typically attribute negative events to internal, stable, and global causes. For example, "I failed because I'm unlucky, I have been throughout my life, and it affects all parts of my life." The good news is that social connections with others, which we discuss later in this list, can reduce this type of thinking and improve overall cognitive functioning (Bourassa et al., 2017; Cruwys et al., 2015).

   In addition, there is a wealth of research on the power of meditation in recognizing and gaining control of your thought processes. As discussed in Chapter 3, *mindfulness-based stress reduction (MBSR)* is linked with positive brain changes, as well as numerous health benefits, from better concentration and physical health to improved mental well-being (Hatchard et al., 2017; Shapiro & Carlson, 2017; Thomas et al., 2016).

2. **Acknowledge and express your feelings.** Although we all have negative emotions and conflicts that often need to be acknowledged and resolved, as a general rule, recognizing and expressing your *positive* emotions, particularly feelings of *gratitude*, can be a major avenue to mental health (see again Chapter 12). Noting what you're thankful for—from your significant other to catching the bus or subway before the doors close—will definitely improve your ability to cope with life's challenges. Being grateful also tends to increase your self-esteem and overall well-being (Drążkowski et al., 2017; Morgan et al., 2017; Yu et al., 2016).

   Interestingly, **well-being therapy (WBT)**, which focuses on personal growth and on noticing and savoring the positive aspects of our lives, has been successful in promoting overall mental health, as well as in increasing resilience and sustained recovery from several psychological disorders (Nierenberg et al., 2016; Ruini & Fava, 2014).

**Well-being therapy (WBT)** A newer form of psychotherapy aimed at enhancing psychological well-being by focusing on personal growth and the positive aspects of life.

Empathy is also critical to mental health (Andreychik & Lewis, 2017; Levy-Gigi & Shamay-Tsoory, 2017). As you recall from our earlier discussion of Rogers's client-centered therapy, empathy involves being a sensitive listener who understands and shares another's inner experience. The good news is that when you're being empathic, you're improving not only another person's self-acceptance and mental health, but also your own. In short, compassionate sharing of feelings and experiences benefits both parties—perhaps because it helps all of us to feel more accepted and less alone during life's inevitable ups and downs.

Finally, *love for yourself* may be the most significant emotional key to protecting your mental health. Self-care and self-compassion are not "selfish"! Self-compassion refers to a kind and nurturing attitude toward yourself, and research shows that it is positively linked with psychological flexibility and well-being (Homan, 2016; Marshall & Brockman, 2016; Stephenson et al., 2017). In other words, prioritize your well-being. When you're feeling frustrated and overwhelmed, allow yourself to say "no." Along with all the resources for coping mentioned in Chapter 3, keep in mind that "no" is a complete sentence. You don't have to explain your reasons for taking care of and loving yourself.

3. **Recognize and change your behaviors.** As discussed in several chapters of this text, "simply" eating the right food, getting enough exercise and sleep, and spending time in nature are all essential to our well-being and may help protect our mental health (Song et al., 2016; Wassing et al., 2016; White & Eyber, 2017). Surprisingly, research finds that even moderate exercise—20 to 30 minutes of walking a day—can prevent episodes of depression in the long term (Mammen & Faulkerner, 2013). Other research suggests that moderate exercise may be as helpful as psychotherapy or antidepressants (Ku et al., 2017; Kvam et al., 2016).

A second behavioral change that increases psychological health is to make someone else feel good. Studies show that volunteering and expressing kindness to others has a cyclical effect—doing a good deed for others makes them happier, which in turns makes you happier (Anik et al., 2011; Raposa et al., 2016; Xi et al., 2016)! As mentioned, spending time in nature is important to mental health, but it also unexpectedly increases our willingness to help. In a very simple field experiment, confederates (people who were part of the experiment) accidentally dropped a glove while walking in an urban green park filled with large trees, lawns, and flowers (Guéguen & Stefan, 2016). Researchers found that passersby who saw the dropping of the glove after walking through the park were far more likely to help by picking up the glove than those who had not yet entered the park.

Perhaps the best action you can take to protect your mental health is to enjoy and maintain your social connections (see the photo). Recent research shows that people who feel more connected to others have lower rates of anxiety and depression (Bourassa et al., 2017; McLeigh, 2015). For this and many other reasons, we need to remind ourselves to spend as much time as possible with our friends and loved ones, whether it's going on vacation or just watching a movie together.

One final tip for mental health—*try writing*! J. K. Rowling discovered the power of writing as a therapeutic tool in her struggles with depression. Like many successful figures, Rowling found that it provided structure for her daily life while helping her to get out of her own head. Empirical research finds that writing about stressful events in your life not only reduces their emotional impact but also may improve your overall physical and mental health—in short, your general well-being (Alexander, 2017; Carpenter, 2001; Pulverman et al., 2017).

*. . . the idea of just wandering off to a cafe with a notebook and writing and seeing where that takes me for awhile is just bliss.*
—J. K. Rowling

Blend Images - Ariel Skelley/Getty Images

## Retrieval Practice 15.4 | Psychotherapy in Perspective

Completing this self-test and the connections section, and then checking your answers by clicking on the answer button or by looking in Appendix B, will provide immediate feedback and helpful practice for exams.

### Self-Test

1. Discuss eclectic psychotherapy.

2. A(n) _____ group does not have a professional leader, and members assist each other in coping with a specific problem.

   **a.** self-help      **b.** encounter

   **c.** peer      **d.** behavior

3. _____ treats the family as a unit, and members work together to solve problems.

   **a.** Aversion therapy      **b.** An encounter group

   **c.** A self-help group      **d.** Family therapy

4. Which of the following is *not* a culturally universal feature of therapy?

   **a.** Naming the problem

   **b.** Demonstrating the right qualities

   **c.** Establishing rapport among family members

   **d.** Placing the problem in a familiar framework

5. A Japanese therapy designed to help clients discover personal guilt for having been ungrateful and troublesome to others and to develop gratitude toward those who have helped them is known as _____.

   **a.** Kyoto therapy      **b.** Okado therapy

   **c.** Naikan therapy      **d.** Nissan therapy

### Connections—Chapter to Chapter

Answering the following question will help you "look back and look ahead" to see the important connections among the subfields of psychology and chapters within this text.

In Chapter 1 (Introduction and Research Methods), you studied research methods, including the *experiment*. In this chapter, you learned that research supports the effectiveness of therapy in reducing symptoms of mental illness. Imagine that you are a researcher who wants to compare the relative effectiveness of two types of therapy to treat major depression. How would you go about designing an experiment to do that?

---

**Study Tip**

*The WileyPLUS program that accompanies this text provides for each chapter a* Media Challenge, Critical Thinking Exercise, *and* Application Quiz. *This set of study materials provides additional, invaluable study opportunities. Be sure to check it out!*

---

# Chapter Summary

## 15.1 Talk Therapies 496

- **Psychotherapy** refers to techniques employed to help people improve their overall psychological functioning and adjustment to life and to assist people suffering from psychological disorders. There are three general approaches to therapy—*talk, behavior,* and *biomedical.*

- In **psychoanalysis**, the therapist seeks to Identify the patient's unconscious conflicts and to help the patient resolve them. The five major techniques of psychoanalysis are **free association, dream analysis**, analysis of **resistance**, analysis of **transference**, and **interpretation**.

- In modern **psychodynamic therapy**, treatment is briefer, and the therapist takes a more directive approach (and puts less emphasis on unconscious childhood memories) than in traditional psychoanalysis.

- **Humanistic therapy** seeks to maximize personal growth, encouraging people to actualize their potential and relate to others in genuine ways.

- Rogers's client-centered therapy emphasizes **empathy, unconditional positive regard, genuineness**, and **active listening**.

- **Cognitive therapy** focuses on faulty thought processes and beliefs in treating problem behaviors. Through insight into negative self-talk (the unrealistic things people say to themselves), the therapist can use **cognitive restructuring** to challenge and change destructive thoughts or inappropriate behaviors.

- Ellis's **rational-emotive behavior therapy (REBT)** focuses on eliminating negative emotional reactions through logic, confrontation, and examination of irrational beliefs. In comparison, Beck's **cognitive-behavior therapy (CBT)** combines cognitive therapy (including changing faulty thinking) with behavior therapy (changing maladaptive behaviors).

- In **mindfulness-based cognitive therapy (MBCT)**, therapists help clients a state of consciousness that attends to ongoing events in a receptive and nonjudgmental way.

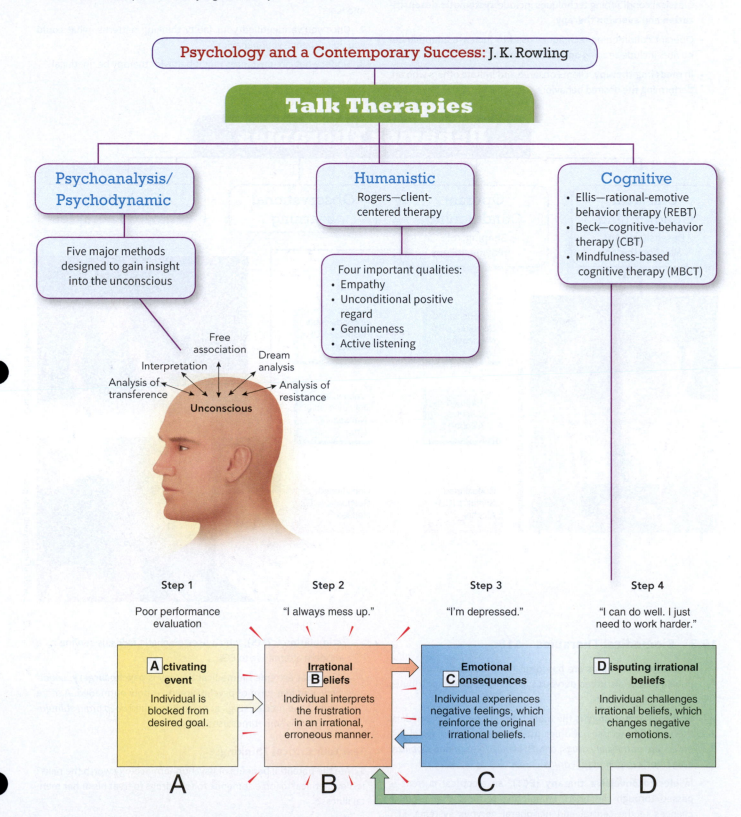

Psychology and a Contemporary Success: J. K. Rowling

## Talk Therapies

### Psychoanalysis/ Psychodynamic

Five major methods designed to gain insight into the unconscious

Free association

Interpretation

Dream analysis

Analysis of transference

Analysis of resistance

**Unconscious**

### Humanistic

Rogers—client-centered therapy

Four important qualities:
- Empathy
- Unconditional positive regard
- Genuineness
- Active listening

### Cognitive

- Ellis—rational-emotive behavior therapy (REBT)
- Beck—cognitive-behavior therapy (CBT)
- Mindfulness-based cognitive therapy (MBCT)

**Step 1**

Poor performance evaluation

**A**ctivating event

Individual is blocked from desired goal.

**A**

**Step 2**

"I always mess up."

Irrational **B**eliefs

Individual interprets the frustration in an irrational, erroneous manner.

**B**

**Step 3**

"I'm depressed."

Emotional **C**onsequences

Individual experiences negative feelings, which reinforce the original irrational beliefs.

**C**

**Step 4**

"I can do well. I just need to work harder."

**D**isputing irrational beliefs

Individual challenges irrational beliefs, which changes negative emotions.

**D**

## 15.2 Behavior Therapies 505

- In **behavior therapy**, the focus is on the problem behavior itself rather than on any underlying causes. The therapist uses learning principles to change behavior.
- Classical conditioning techniques include **systematic desensitization** and **aversion therapy**.
- Operant conditioning techniques used to increase adaptive behaviors include *shaping* and *reinforcement*.
- In **modeling therapy**, clients observe and imitate others who are performing the desired behaviors.

### Test Your Critical Thinking

**1.** Imagine that you were going to use the principles of cognitive-behavior therapy to change some aspect of your own thinking and behavior. If you'd like to quit smoking, or be more organized, how would you identify the faulty thinking perpetuating these behaviors and fears?

**2.** Once you've identified your faulty thinking patterns, what could you do to change your behavior?

**3.** Under what circumstances might behavior therapy be unethical?

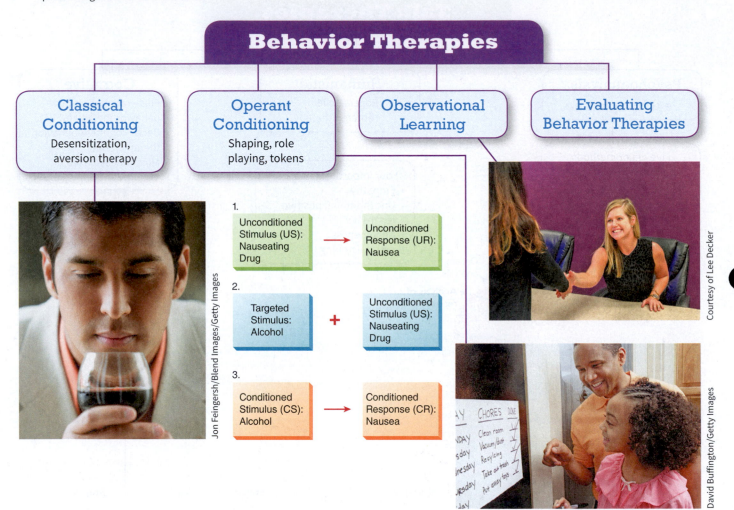

## 15.3 Biomedical Therapies 510

- **Biomedical therapies** are based on the premise that chemical imbalances or disturbed nervous system functioning contributes to problem behaviors.
- **Psychopharmacology** is the most common form of biomedical therapy. Major classes of drugs used to treat psychological disorders are *antianxiety drugs, antipsychotic drugs, mood stabilizer drugs,* and *antidepressant drugs.*
- In **electroconvulsive therapy (ECT)**, an electrical current is passed through the brain, stimulating seizures that produce changes in the central and peripheral nervous systems. ECT is used primarily in cases of severe depression that do not respond to other treatments. **Repetitive transcranial magnetic**

**stimulation (rTMS)**, which uses magnetic fields, is serving as a modern alternative to ECT.

- The most extreme biomedical therapy is **psychosurgery**. *Lobotomy*, an older form of psychosurgery, is now outmoded. A more limited and precise surgical procedure called *deep brain stimulation (DBS)* is sometimes used today.

### Test Your Critical Thinking

**1.** Are the potential benefits of psychopharmacology worth the risks? Is it ever ethical to force someone to take drugs to treat his or her mental illness?

**2.** If you or someone you loved were seriously depressed, would you be in favor of ECT? Why or why not?

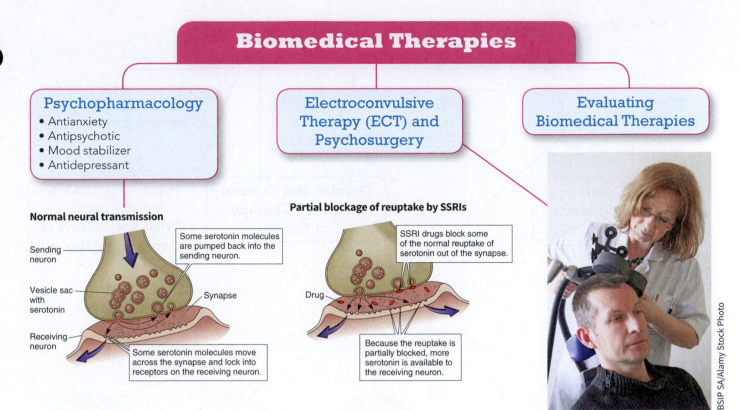

# Biomedical Therapies

## Psychopharmacology
- Antianxiety
- Antipsychotic
- Mood stabilizer
- Antidepressant

## Electroconvulsive Therapy (ECT) and Psychosurgery

## Evaluating Biomedical Therapies

**Normal neural transmission**

Sending neuron

Some serotonin molecules are pumped back into the sending neuron.

Vesicle sac with serotonin

Synapse

Receiving neuron

Some serotonin molecules move across the synapse and lock into receptors on the receiving neuron.

**Partial blockage of reuptake by SSRIs**

SSRI drugs block some of the normal reuptake of serotonin out of the synapse.

Drug

Because the reuptake is partially blocked, more serotonin is available to the receiving neuron.

BSIP SA/Alamy Stock Photo

## 15.4 Psychotherapy in Perspective 516

- All major forms of therapy are designed to address disturbed thoughts, disturbed emotions, disturbed behaviors, interpersonal and life situation difficulties, and biomedical disturbances. Many therapists take an **eclectic approach** and combine techniques from various therapies. Research indicates that, overall, therapy does work.

- In **group therapy**, multiple people meet together to work toward therapeutic goals. A variation is the **self-help group**, which is not guided by a professional. In marital and family therapy, the aim is to change maladaptive patterns of interaction.

- Telehealth/electronic therapy allows clinicians to reach more clients and provide greater access to information. But there are concerns about licensing, regulations, and abuses.

- Under specific circumstances, people can be involuntarily committed to mental hospitals for diagnosis and treatment. Problems with involuntary commitment led to deinstitutionalization—discharging as many patients as possible and discouraging admissions. Community services such as community mental health (CMH) centers help offset problems with deinstitutionalization.

- Therapies in all cultures share some common features, as well as core differences. Therapists must be sensitive and responsive to possible gender issues and cultural differences in order to build trust with clients and effect behavioral change.

### Test Your Critical Thinking

**1.** Which of the universal characteristics of therapists do you believe is the most important? Why?

**2.** If a friend were having marital problems, how would you convince him or her to go to a marriage or family therapist, using information you've gained from reading this chapter?

# Psychotherapy in Perspective

**Therapy Goals and Effectiveness**

**Therapy Formats**
Group, Family and Marital, Telehealth/Electronic

**Institutionalization**

**Research Challenge: Can Watching Movies Prevent Divorce?**

**Gender and Cultural Diversity: Therapy in Action**

**Psychology and Your Personal Success:** What Are the Keys to Good Mental Health?

**Therapy**
attempts to change

**Disturbed thoughts**

Therapists work to change faulty or destructive thoughts, provide new ideas or information, and guide individuals toward finding solutions to problems.

**Disturbed emotions**

Therapists help clients understand and control their emotions and relieve their emotional discomfort.

**Disturbed behaviors**

Therapists help clients eliminate troublesome behaviors and guide them toward more productive lives.

**Interpersonal and life situation difficulties**

Therapists help clients improve their relationships with others and avoid or minimize sources of stress in their lives.

**Biomedical disturbances**

Therapists work to relieve biological disruptions that directly cause or contribute to psychological difficulties (e.g., chemical imbalances that lead to depression).

# Key Terms

**Retrieval Practice**   *Write a definition for each term before turning back to the referenced page to check your answer.*

- active listening   500
- aversion therapy   507
- behavior therapies   505
- biomedical therapies   510
- client-centered therapy   499
- cognitive restructuring   501
- cognitive therapies   500
- cognitive-behavior therapy (CBT)   503
- dream analysis   497
- eclectic approach   517
- electroconvulsive therapy (ECT)   513
- empathy   499
- evidence-based practice in psychology (EBPP)   519

- free association   497
- genuineness   500
- group therapies   519
- humanistic therapies   499
- interpretation   498
- lobotomy   513
- mindfulness-based cognitive therapy (MBCT)   503
- modeling therapy   508
- psychoanalysis   497
- psychodynamic therapies   498
- psychopharmacology   510
- psychosurgery   513
- psychotherapy   497

- rational-emotive behavior therapy (REBT)   501
- repetitive transcranial magnetic stimulation (rTMS)   514
- resistance   498
- self-help group   519
- systematic desensitization   505
- therapeutic alliance   519
- token economy   507
- transference   498
- unconditional positive regard   499
- well-being therapy (WBT)   525

© alexxl66/iStockphoto

# Social Psychology

## ❖ Psychology and a Contemporary Success | Sonia Sotomayor

MCT via Getty Images

Sonia Sotomayor (1954–) was born in the Bronx borough of New York City as the elder of two children to immigrant parents with a very modest income. When Sonia's father died in 1963, she turned to books to escape her family's sadness, while her mother worked six days a week at two jobs to support Sonia and her brother. Sonia recalls that her mother pushed both of her children to become fluent in English and that she had an "almost fanatical emphasis" on higher education (Biography.com, n.d.; Shashkevich, 2017).

Sonia's and her mother's hard work and dedication obviously paid off. Despite developing diabetes when she was eight, dealing with her father's alcoholism, losing her father when she was nine, and growing up poor in a low-income housing project, Sonia graduated summa cum laude from Princeton University in 1976. She then attended Yale Law School, where she became an editor of the prestigious *Yale Law Journal*.

After earning her law degree in 1979, Sonia went on to serve in several high positions, including as an assistant district attorney in New York and as a judge on the United States Court of Appeals. During these years, she worked on cases involving numerous high-profile members of organized crime, child pornographers, and murderers. She was even threatened to the point of needing bodyguards (Sonia Sotomayor, 2014; Sonia Sotomayor Fast Facts, n.d.).

In 2009, Sonia Sotomayor was nominated and confirmed as an associate justice of the Supreme Court of the United States (see the photo), with the distinction of being the first justice of Hispanic heritage, the first Latina, and the third female justice (Sonia Sotomayor, n.d.). Her nomination by President Obama to the court was said to match his campaign promise. "We need somebody who's got the heart, the empathy, to recognize what its like to be a young teenage mom," Obama said. "The empathy to understand what it's like to be poor, or African-American, or gay, or disabled, or old" (Rosen, 2010).

*If you want to change someone's mind, you must understand what need shapes his or her opinion. To prevail, you must first listen.* —Sonia Sotomayor

## Chapter Overview

Why did we choose Justice Sotomayor as our famous figure for this final chapter? In addition to her obvious *growth mindset* and *grit*, she also epitomizes what we, as faculty, want for you, our dear reader and student of psychology. During her own college years, Sotomayor took a broad range of introductory courses, including psychology, economics, philosophy, and religious studies, before narrowing her interests to Latin American history. In her speech to graduates at Stanford University in 2017, Justice Sotomayor encouraged today's students to do the same. "I figured out first how to be a generally informed citizen before I tried to be a specialist in anything else. And that's the advice I would give all of you who are experiencing college. Take courses in areas that don't particularly interest you, but might make you a more knowledgeable person. . . . Curious people go further" (Shashkevich, 2017).

For many students and psychologists, your authors included, this chapter on *social psychology* is the most exciting of all because we're all born as social animals and almost everything we do is *social!* Unlike earlier chapters that focused on individual processes, like sensation and perception, memory, or personality, this chapter studies how large social forces, such as groups, social roles, and norms, bring out the best and worst in all of us. It is organized around three central themes: *social cognition, social influence,* and *social relations.*

We begin with social cognition and the study of attributions, attitudes, and prejudice. Then we look at social influence, with the subtopics of conformity, obedience, and group processes. We close with an examination of social relations, which includes aggression, altruism, and interpersonal attraction. Before reading on, check the misconceptions you may have about these topics in the following **Myth Busters**.

---

## Myth Busters

### True or False?

_____ **1.** Reading Harry Potter books can reduce prejudice.

_____ **2.** Taking a pain pill can change your attitudes.

_____ **3.** Flirting is a powerful way to increase your attractiveness to a potential mate.

_____ **4.** People wearing masks are more likely than unmasked individuals to engage in aggressive acts.

_____ **5.** Emphasizing gender differences may create and perpetuate prejudice.

_____ **6.** Substance abuse (particularly alcohol abuse) is a major factor in aggression.

_____ **7.** When people are alone, they are less likely to help another individual than when they are in a group.

_____ **8.** Looks are the primary factor in our initial feelings of attraction, liking, and love.

_____ **9.** Opposites attract.

_____ **10.** Romantic love generally starts to fade after 6 to 30 months.

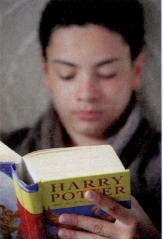

Godong/Alamy Stock Photo

**Answers:** Two of these statements are false. You'll find the answers within this chapter.

---

**16.1** # Social Cognition

### LEARNING OBJECTIVES

**Retrieval Practice**    While reading the upcoming sections, respond to each Learning Objective in your own words.

**Review the field of social psychology and its largest subfield, social cognition.**

- **Define** social psychology and social cognition.

- **Discuss** the attributional process and its errors, biases, and cultural factors.
- **Identify** attitudes and their three components.
- **Summarize** how attitudes are formed and changed.
- **Discuss** prejudice, its three components, and the factors that increase or decrease it.

---

**Social psychology**, one of the largest branches in the field of psychology, focuses on how other people influence our thoughts, feelings, and actions. In turn, one of its largest and most important subfields, *social cognition*, examines the way we think about and interpret ourselves and others. Interestingly, we now know that several areas of the prefrontal cortex are most active when we're thinking and behaving socially and that these areas are much larger in the human brain than in other animals (**Figure 16.1**). In this section, we will look at three of the key topics in social cognition—*attributions, attitudes*, and *prejudice*.

**Social psychology**    The branch of psychology that studies how others influence our thoughts, feelings, and actions.

## Attributions

Have you ever been in a serious argument with a loved one—perhaps a parent, close friend, or romantic partner? If so, how did you react? Were you overwhelmed with feelings of anger? Did you attribute the fight to the other person's ugly, mean temper and consider ending the

**Human**

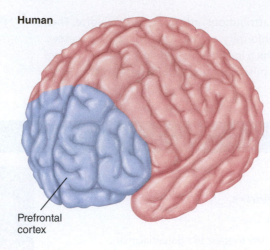

Prefrontal
cortex

**Rhesus
monkey**

**Cat**

Prefrontal
cortex

Prefrontal
cortex

**FIGURE 16.1** **Across the species** The prefrontal cortex of human beings is proportionately larger than that of other animals. In addition, it is very active during social behavior, suggesting that it plays an important role in human social functioning.

**Attribution** The explanations we make about the causes of behaviors or events.

**Fundamental attribution error (FAE)** A bias toward giving undue weight to personal, dispositional factors when explaining other people's behavior and underestimating the impact of external, situational factors; also known as the correspondence bias (CB).

**Saliency bias** A type of attributional bias in which people tend to focus on the most noticeable (salient) factors when explaining the causes of behavior.

**FIGURE 16.2** **Attribution in action** Do you see how studying this text and taking your college psychology course enriches your study of the "real world"? Now you have a deeper understanding of the joke behind this cartoon, as well as a label to apply to it— the FAE.

Loren Fishman/www.CartoonStock.com

relationship? Or did you calm yourself with thoughts of how he or she is normally a rational person and therefore must be unusually upset by something that happened at work or elsewhere?

Can you see how these two alternative explanations, or **attributions**, for the causes of behavior or events can either destroy or maintain relationships? The study of attributions is a major topic in social cognition and social psychology. Everyone wants to understand and explain why people behave as they do and why events occur as they do. Humans are known to be the only reason-seeking animals! But social psychologists have discovered another explanation: Developing logical attributions for behavior makes us feel safer and more in control (Heider, 1958; Lindsay et al., 2015). Unfortunately, our attributions are frequently marred by several attributional biases and errors.

## Attributional Errors and Biases

Think back to the example above. Do you recognize how attributing the fight to the bad character of the other person without considering possible situational factors could result from misguided biases in thinking? Suppose a new student joins your class and seems distant, cold, and uninterested in interaction. It's easy to conclude that she's unfriendly, and maybe even "stuck-up"—a dispositional (personality) attribution. If you later observed her in a one-to-one interaction with close friends, you might be surprised to find that she is very warm and friendly. In other words, her behavior apparently depends on the situation—a possibility you initially overlooked.

Along the same lines, a recent study found that math and science instructors at one public university who said that the greatest barriers to student learning were the internal deficiencies of the students were also the ones who used fewer effective teaching methods (Wieman & Welsh, 2016). Can you see how these instructors' belief that students were responsible for their own difficulties may have caused them to overlook possible situational factors, such as teaching methods, to explain poor student performance? Clearly, we're dealing here with a common problem. Indeed, the bias toward personal, dispositional factors rather than external, situational factors in our explanations for others' behavior is so common that it is called the **fundamental attribution error (FAE)** (Hopthrow et al., 2017; Jouffre & Croizet, 2016; Ross, 1977).

One reason for the FAE is that human personalities and behaviors are more salient or noticeable than situational factors. This **saliency bias** helps explain why people sometimes suggest that homeless people begging for money "should just go out and get a job"—a phenomenon also called "blaming the victim." (See **Figure 16.2**.)

Unlike the FAE, which commonly occurs when we're explaining others' behaviors, the

| Actor | | Observer |
| --- | --- | --- |
| **Situational attribution** | | **Dispositional attribution** |
| Focuses attention on external factors | | Focuses on the personal disposition of the actor |
| "I don't even like drinking beer, but it's the best way to meet women." | Courtesy of Richard Hosey | "He seems to always have a beer in his hand; he must have a drinking problem." |

**FIGURE 16.3   The actor–observer effect**   We tend to explain our own behavior in terms of external factors (situational attributions) and others' behavior in terms of their internal characteristics (dispositional attributions).

**self-serving bias** applies to attributions (explanations) we make for our own behavior. In this case, we tend to favor internal (dispositional) attributions for our successes and external (situational) attributions for our failures. This bias is motivated by our desire to maintain positive self-esteem and a good public image (Kalish & Luria, 2016; Lilly & Wipawayangkool, 2017). As you may have observed, students often take personal credit for doing well on an exam. If they fail a test, however, they tend to blame the instructor, the textbook, or the "tricky" questions. Similarly, elite Olympic athletes more often attribute their wins to internal (personal) causes, such as their skill and effort, while attributing their losses to external (situational) causes, such as bad equipment or poor officiating (Aldridge & Islam, 2012; Mackinnon et al., 2015).

How do we explain the discrepancy between the attributions we make for ourselves and those we make for others? According to the **actor–observer effect** (Jones & Nisbett, 1971), when examining our own behaviors, we are the *actors* in the situation and know more about our own intentions and behaviors. It's therefore easier for us to see when situational factors come into play: "I didn't tip the waiter because I got really bad service." In contrast, when explaining the behavior of others, we are *observing* the actors and tend to blame the person, using an internal, personal attribution: "She didn't tip the waiter because she's cheap" (**Figure 16.3**).

**Self-serving bias**   The tendency to credit one's own success to internal, dispositional factors, while blaming failure on external, situational factors.

**Actor–observer effect**   The tendency to attribute other people's behavior to dispositional actors, while seeing our own behavior as caused by the situation.

**Culture and Attributional Biases**   Both the fundamental attribution error and the self-serving bias may depend in part on cultural factors (Hu et al., 2017; Kreitler & Dyson, 2016; Lakshman & Estay, 2016). In highly individualistic cultures, like the United States, people are defined and understood as individual selves, largely responsible for their own successes and failures. In contrast, people in collectivistic cultures, like China and Japan, are primarily defined as members of their social network, responsible for doing as others expect. Accordingly, they tend to be more aware of situational constraints on behavior, making the FAE less likely (Bond, 2015; Iselin et al., 2016; Tang et al., 2014).

The self-serving bias is also much less common in collectivistic cultures because self-esteem is related not to doing better than others but to fitting in with the group. In Japan, for instance, the ideal person is aware of his or her shortcomings and continually works to overcome them rather than thinking highly of himself or herself (Heine & Renshaw, 2002; Shand, 2013). For specific tips on reducing your own attributional biases, see the following discussion.

❖ **Psychology and Your Personal Success** | How Can We Reduce Attributional Biases?

The key to making more accurate attributions begins with determining whether a given action stems mainly from personal factors or from the external situation. To do this, it helps to ask yourself the following four questions:

1. *Is the behavior unique or shared by others*? If a large, or increasing, number of people are engaging in the same behavior, such as rioting or homelessness, it's most likely the result of external, situational factors.

2. *Is the behavior stable or unstable?* If someone's behavior is relatively enduring and permanent, it may be correct to make a personal, dispositional attribution. However, before giving up on a friend who is often quick-tempered and volatile, we may want to consider his or her entire body of personality traits. If he or she is also generous, kind, and incredibly devoted, we could overlook these imperfections.

3. *Was the cause of the behavior controllable or uncontrollable?* Innocent victims of crime, like rape or robbery, are too often blamed for their misfortune because they were careless and lacked good judgment. They should not have "been in that part of town," "walking alone," and/or "dressed in expensive clothes." Obviously, these are inaccurate and unfair personal attributions, as well as destructive examples of "blaming the victim."

4. *What would I do in the same situation?* Given our natural tendency toward *self-serving biases* and the *actor-observer effect,* if we conclude that we would behave in the same way, the behavior is most likely the result of external, situational factors.

If you're concerned that these four questions take too much time, just save them for significant events, such as when considering ending a relationship due to your friend's or romantic partner's behaviors. In addition, given our natural tendency to make internal, personal attributions, we can improve our judgments of others by simply erring in the opposite direction—looking first for external causes. This is simply "giving others the benefit of the doubt," which is known to improve relationships, while also helping us avoid attributional errors.

## Attitudes

The second major area of social cognition concerns the formation and changing of *attitudes*. When we observe and respond to the world around us, we are seldom completely neutral. Rather, our responses toward subjects as diverse as pizza, gun control, and the latest Academy Award winning movie reflect our **attitudes**, which are *learned* predispositions to respond positively or negatively to a particular object, person, or event. Social psychologists generally agree that most attitudes have three ABC components: *affect* (feelings), *behavior* (actions), and *cognitions* (thoughts and beliefs) (**Figure 16.4**).

**Attitude** The learned predisposition to respond positively or negatively to a particular object, person, or event.

**Attitude Formation** As mentioned, we tend to learn our attitudes, and this learning generally occurs through direct instruction, personal experience, or watching others. In some

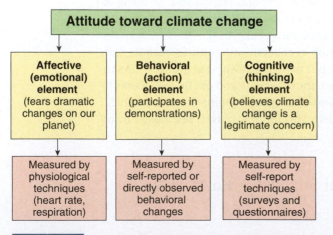

**Attitude toward climate change**

| Affective (emotional) element | Behavioral (action) element | Cognitive (thinking) element |
|---|---|---|
| (fears dramatic changes on our planet) | (participates in demonstrations) | (believes climate change is a legitimate concern) |
| Measured by physiological techniques (heart rate, respiration) | Measured by self-reported or directly observed behavioral changes | Measured by self-report techniques (surveys and questionnaires) |

Lauren Rinder/Shutterstock

**FIGURE 16.4** **The ABCs of attitudes** When social psychologists study attitudes, they measure each of the three ABC components: affect, behavior, and cognitions.

cases, these sources may differ, depending on our gender. For example, researchers have found that teenage boys are more likely to learn sexual attitudes from media representations of sexual behavior, whereas teenage girls tend to learn their sexual attitudes from their mothers, as long as they feel close to their mothers (Vandenbosch & Eggermont, 2011).

### Attitude Change

Although attitudes begin to form in early childhood, they're obviously not permanent, a fact that advertisers and politicians know and exploit. As shown in **Figure 16.5**, experiments have shown that even changing the photos in ads can change attitudes. However, a much more common method is to make direct, persuasive appeals, such as in ads that say, "Friends Don't Let Friends Drive Drunk!"

### Cognitive Dissonance

Surprisingly, psychologists have identified an even more efficient strategy than persuasion. The strongest personal change comes when we notice contradictions between our thoughts, feelings, and actions—the three components of all attitudes. Such contradictions typically lead to a state of unpleasant psychological tension, known as **cognitive dissonance**. According to Leon Festinger's (1957) *cognitive disonance theory*, we all share a strong need for consistency among our thoughts, feelings, and actions, and when we notice inconsistencies we experience unpleasant feelings of psychological tension, known as "dissonance."

To relieve this discomfort, we are highly motivated to change one or more of the three ABC components of our attitudes. For instance, a young woman who is engaged to be married might notice a feeling of attraction to someone other than her intended spouse and then might experience unpleasant tension from the contradiction (cognitive dissonance) between her feelings of attraction and her belief that she should be attracted only to her husband-to-be. To relieve the discomfort, she could break off the engagement or, more appropriately, change her beliefs to include the idea that feelings of attraction to others is normal and to be expected both before and after marriage.

A clever experiment focusing on the discomfort caused by cognitive dissonance found that taking a simple painkiller, acetaminophen, reduced the amount of attitude change among participants required to perform a potentially dissonance-producing task (DeWall et al., 2015). The acetominophen reduced overall pain, including the pain caused by cognitive dissonance. As a result, participants who took the painkiller were less motivated to change their attitudes than participants who took placebos!

Upon hearing about this study, one of our clever students declared that he now understands why everyone likes parties with lots of alcohol. Like the acetaminophen, alcohol reduces the pain caused by the cognitive dissonance associated with sex in a casual, hookup environment. What do you think? Do you agree?

Given that cognitive dissonance is often an effective approach to attitude change in all our lives, it's important to fully understand it. Let's closely examine the classic study by Leon Festinger and J. Merrill Carlsmith (1959). These experimenters asked college students to perform several very boring tasks, such as turning wooden pegs or sorting spools into trays. They were then paid either $1 or $20 to lie to *new* research participants by telling them that the boring tasks were actually very enjoyable. Surprisingly, those who were paid just $1 to lie subsequently changed their minds about the task, and actually reported more positive attitudes toward it, than those who were paid $20.

Why was there more attitude change among those who were paid only $1? All participants who lied to other participants presumably recognized the discrepancy between their initial beliefs and feelings (the task was boring)

**Cognitive dissonance** The unpleasant psychological tension we experience after noticing contradictions between our thoughts, feelings, and/or actions.

JM5 WENN Photos/NewsCom

Agencia el Universal/El Universal de Mexico/NewsCom

**FIGURE 16.5** **Using photos to change attitudes** Considering the high prevalence of very thin women and lean, "ripped" men displayed in magazines, on TV, and in movies, it's easy to see why many people in our Western culture develop a shared preference for a certain, limited body type. Thankfully, research finds that just showing women photographs of plus-size models (with a minimum clothing size of 16 and a BMI between 36 and 42) caused them to change their initial attitudes, which had been to prefer the thin ideal (Boothroyd et al., 2012). Can you see how ads that offer more realistic images (like the photo on the left), as well as the devastating effects of anorexia (like the photo on the right), might improve the overall health and self-image of both men and women? Sadly, the model in the photo on the right, Isabelle Caro, died of anorexia in 2010 at age 28.

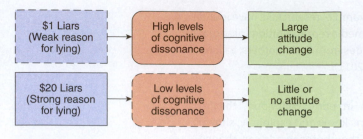

**FIGURE 16.6** **Why cheap lies hurt more** Note how lying for $20 creates less cognitive dissonance and less attitude change than lying for $1.

and their behavior (telling others it was fun). However, as you can see in **Figure 16.6**, the participants who were given insufficient monetary justification for lying (the $1 liars) apparently experienced greater *cognitive dissonance*. Therefore, to reduce their discomfort, they expressed more liking for the dull task. By comparison, those who received sufficient monetary justification (the $20 liars) had little or no motivation to change their attitude—they lied for the money! (Note that in 1959, when the experiment was conducted, $20 would have been the economic equivalent of about $200 today.)

Do you see the potential danger in how easily some participants in this classic study changed their thoughts and feelings about the boring task in order to match their behavior? Consider how cognitive dissonance might help explain why military leaders keep sending troops to a seemingly endless war. They obviously can't change the actions that led to the initial loss of lives, so they may reduce their cognitive dissonance by becoming even more committed to a belief that the war is justified. Given the importance of this theory to your everyday life, be sure to carefully study **Step-by-Step Diagram 16.1**.

**Culture and Cognitive Dissonance**  The experience of cognitive dissonance may depend on a distinctly Western way of thinking about and evaluating the self. As we mentioned earlier, people in Eastern cultures tend not to define themselves in terms of their individual accomplishments. For this reason, making a bad decision may not pose the same threat to self-esteem that it would in more individualistic cultures, such as the United States (Frazer et al., 2017; Kokkoris & Kühnen, 2013; Na & Chan, 2015).

## Prejudice

**Prejudice**, which literally means *prejudgment*, is a learned, unjustified negative attitude toward members of a particular group. Like all other attitudes, it's composed of three ABC elements: *affect* (emotions about the group), *behavior* (**discrimination**—an unjustifiable, negative action directed toward members of a group), and *cognitions* (**stereotypes**—overgeneralized beliefs about members of a group).

When we use the term *prejudice* here, we are referring to all three of these components. Note, though, that in everyday usage, *prejudice* often refers primarily to thoughts and feelings, while *discrimination* is used to describe actions. When the terms are used in this way, they do not overlap completely, as shown in **Figure 16.7**.

**Prejudice**  A learned, unjustified negative attitude toward members of a particular group; it includes thoughts (stereotypes), feelings, and behavioral tendencies (discrimination).

**Discrimination**  An unjustifiable, negative action directed toward members of a group; also the behavioral component of prejudice.

**Stereotype**  An overgeneralized belief about members of a group; also the cognitive component of prejudice.

**FIGURE 16.7** **Prejudice versus discrimination** Prejudice and discrimination are closely related, but either condition can exist without the other. The only situation without prejudice or discrimination in this example occurs when a person of color is given a job simply because he or she is the best candidate.

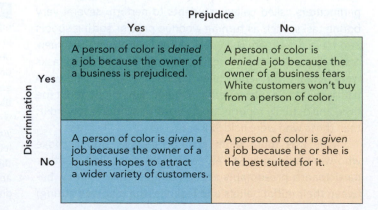

## STEP-BY-STEP DIAGRAM 16.1    **Understanding Cognitive Dissonance**

**STOP!** This Step-by-Step Diagram contains essential information NOT found elsewhere in the text, which is likely to appear on quizzes and exams. Be sure to study it CAREFULLY!

We've all noticed that people often say one thing, but do another. For example, why do some health professionals, who obviously know the dangers of smoking, continue to smoke?

**1** When inconsistencies or conflicts exist between our thoughts, feelings, and actions, they can lead to strong feelings of psychological discomfort (*cognitive dissonance*).

REGIONAL CANCER CENTER

"I smoke cigarettes."

"I know smoking cigarettes leads to cancer."

INSIDE PATIO ONLY

Spencer Grant/PhotoEdit

**Change actions**

**2** To reduce this cognitive dissonance, we are motivated to change our thoughts, feelings, and/or actions.

**Change thoughts and/or feelings**

**3a** Changing actions, such as quitting smoking, can be hard to do.

"I don't smoke cigarettes any more."

**3b** If unable or unwilling to change their actions, individuals can use one or more of the four methods shown here to change their thoughts and/or feelings.

**Change perceived importance of one of the conflicting cognitions:** "Experiments showing that smoking causes cancer have only been done on animals."

**Modify one or both of the conflicting cognitions or feelings:** "I don't smoke that much." "I don't care if I die earlier. I love smoking!"

**Add additional cognitions:** "I only eat healthy foods, so I'm better protected from cancer."

**Deny conflicting cognitions are related:** "There's no real evidence linking cigarettes and cancer."

### Overall Summary

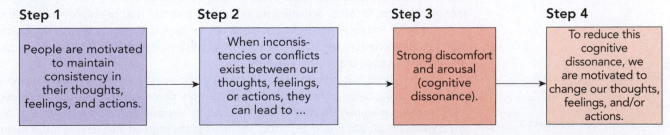

**Step 1**

People are motivated to maintain consistency in their thoughts, feelings, and actions.

**Step 2**

When inconsistencies or conflicts exist between our thoughts, feelings, or actions, they can lead to ...

**Step 3**

Strong discomfort and arousal (cognitive dissonance).

**Step 4**

To reduce this cognitive dissonance, we are motivated to change our thoughts, feelings, and/or actions.

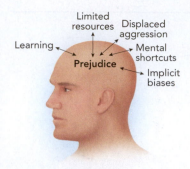

**FIGURE 16.8** **Which source best explains your own prejudices?**

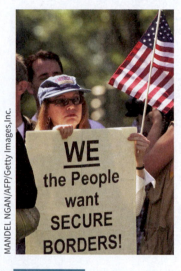

**FIGURE 16.9** **Prejudice and immigration** Can you identify which of the four sources of prejudice best explains this behavior?

**Ingroup favoritism** The tendency to judge members of the ingroup more positively than members of an outgroup.

**Outgroup homogeneity effect** The tendency to judge members of an outgroup as more alike and less diverse than members of the ingroup.

## Common Sources of Prejudice

How does prejudice originate? Five commonly cited sources are *learning*, *limited resources*, *displaced aggression*, *mental shortcuts*, and *implicit biases* (**Figure 16.8**).

1. **Learning** People learn prejudice the same way they learn other attitudes—primarily through *classical conditioning* and *observational learning* (Chapter 6). For example, a form of classical conditioning and observational learning occurs after repeated exposure to negative, stereotypical portrayals of people of color and women in movies, magazines, TV, and the Internet. This type of repeated pairing of negative images with particular groups of people builds viewers' prejudice against those groups (Brown et al., 2017; Killen et al., 2015; Sigalow & Fox, 2014). Similarly, hearing parents, friends, and public figures express their prejudices creates and reinforces prejudice (Koike et al., 2017; Miklikowska, 2017). *Ethnocentrism*, believing our own culture represents the norm or is superior to others, is another form of a classically conditioned or observationally learned prejudice.

   We also develop prejudice through operant conditioning. As a case in point, when people make prejudicial remarks or "jokes," they often gain attention and even approval from others. Sadly, denigrating others is also reinforcing because it boosts group cohesion among the initiators, while simultaneously fostering a negative disposition toward the targeted group (Fein & Spencer, 1997; Ford, 2015; Ho & O'Donohoe, 2014). Furthermore, once someone has one or more negative interactions or experiences with members of a specific group, he or she may generalize the resulting bad feelings and prejudice to all members of that group.

2. **Limited resources** A second source of prejudice is that when resources are limited, prejudice pays off! Most of us understand that prejudice and discrimination exact a high price on their victims, but few appreciate the significant economic and political advantages they offer to the dominant group (Bonilla-Silva, 2016; Dreu et al., 2015; Wilkins et al., 2015). The stereotype that people of color are inferior to Whites, for example, helps justify and perpetuate a social order in the United States in which White Americans hold disproportionate power and resources. Can you see why it's critical to recognize the power and economic advantages of prejudice for the dominant group? One of the core beliefs in psychology is that *behavior does not persist if it's not reinforced*.

3. **Displaced aggression** As a child, did you ever feel like hitting a sibling who was tormenting you? Frustration sometimes leads people to attack the perceived cause of that frustration. But, as history has shown, when the source is ambiguous, or too powerful and capable of retaliation, people often redirect their aggression toward an alternate, innocent target, known as a scapegoat (Gangloff et al., 2016; Ralph et al., 2016; Shigemura & Chhem, 2016). Blacks, Jews, Native Americans, and other less empowered groups have a long and tragic history of being scapegoated. Examples include blaming gay men in the 1980s for the AIDS epidemic or attributing the housing and banking collapse of 2008 to people of color or members of the working class for buying houses they could not afford. Similarly, some politicians campaigning for the U.S. presidential nomination in 2016 used immigrant, ethnic, and religious groups as scapegoats for the nation's problems (**Figure 16.9**).

4. **Mental shortcuts** The fourth source of prejudice comes from everyday *mental shortcuts* that we create to simplify our complex social world (McFarlane, 2014; Prati et al., 2015). Stereotypes allow us to make quick, helpful judgments about others, thereby freeing up mental resources for other activities. However, they also can lead to unforeseen negative outcomes. For instance, people use stereotypes as mental shortcuts when they create ingroups and outgroups. An *ingroup* is any category to which people see themselves as belonging; an *outgroup* is any other category.

   Research finds that ingroup members judge themselves more positively (as being more attractive, having better personalities, and being more deserving of resources) compared with outgroup members—a phenomenon known as **ingroup favoritism** (Hughes et al., 2017; Wilkins et al., 2017; Yu et al., 2016). Members of the ingroup also tend to judge members of the outgroup as more alike and less diverse than members of their own group, a phenomenon aptly known as the **outgroup homogeneity effect** (Brewer, 2015; Kenny et al., 2015; Ratner & Amodio, 2013). One of the many dangers of this erroneous belief is that when members of specific groups are not recognized as varied and complex individuals, it's easier to treat them in discriminatory ways.

A sad example of the outgroup homogeneity effect occurs during wars and international conflicts. Viewing people on the other side as simply faceless enemies makes it easier to kill large numbers of soldiers and civilians. This type of dehumanization and facelessness is almost always the first step toward justifying violence against others (Greenwald & Pettigrew, 2014; Haslam, 2015; Lee et al., 2014).

5. **Implicit biases**   Some believe that, like all attitudes, prejudice can operate even without a person's conscious awareness or control—a process known as automatic bias, or **implicit bias** (Hagiwara et al., 2017; Kubota & Phelps, 2016; Schmid & Amodio, 2017). As you recall from Chapter 8, we naturally put things into groups or categories to help us make sense of the world around us. Unfortunately, the prototypes and hierarchies we develop are sometimes based on incorrect stereotypes of various groups that later lead to implicit biases.

For example, researchers in one observational study found that Uber and Lyft drivers took longer to accept ride requests from Black travelers than from White travelers, that women were more often taken on significantly longer rides than men, and that taxis were significantly more likely to drive past Black travelers than White travelers (Ge et al., 2016). Similarly, consumers more often choose a company or a product based on a message read in a standard American English accent than either a Mandarin Chinese or a French accent (Livingston et al., 2017).

In addition, a 2015 study (Lavy & Sand) found that teachers grade boys higher than girls (when names are known) on math tests, even when the girls outscore the boys when the tests are graded anonymously. Unfortunately, these teachers are underestimating girls' ability in math and overestimating boys' ability. Comparable gender differences aren't seen for tests in other subjects, such as English and foreign languages. Finally, a study of NFL games found that Black quarterbacks are more likely to be benched after making a mistake than White quarterbacks (Volz, 2016).

How do we identify our hidden, implicit biases? A common method is the *Implicit Association Test (IAT)*. You can test yourself by going to https://implicit.harvard.edu/implicit.

*I'm going to assume I'm a racist when I'm talking about a race that isn't mine because I don't know what that experience is like.*

—Stephen Colbert (American Comedian, TV Host, Author)

### The Price of Prejudice

Before going on, it's important to note several tragic examples of our long, sad global history of prejudice (**Figure 16.10**). The atrocities committed against the Jews and other groups during the Holocaust, as well as the current crises in the Middle East and Africa, offer stark reminders of the cost of human hatred. Within the United States, our history of slavery; the current racial and gender disparities in employment, wealth, education, and health care; the current immigration controversy; and the stigma associated with mental illness (Chapters 14 and 15) all provide troubling evidence of the ongoing costs of prejudice (Glaser, 2015; Koike et al., 2017; Saridi et al., 2017).

**Implicit bias**   A hidden, automatic attitude that may guide behaviors independent of a person's awareness or control.

**FIGURE 16.10**   **The high price of prejudice**   If pictures truly are "worth a thousand words," these photos speak volumes about the atrocities associated with prejudice: (a) the Holocaust, when millions of Jews, as well as members of other groups, were exterminated by the Nazis, (b) slavery in the United States, where millions of Africans were bought and sold as slaves, and (c) the 2016 nightclub shooting in Orlando, Florida, which left 49 people dead and 53 wounded and serves as a painful reminder of the ongoing dangers members of the LGBT community still face in modern America.

©AP/Wide World Photos
a.

© North Wind Picture Archives/ The Image Works
b.

Orlando Sentinel/Getty Images
c.

**FIGURE 16.11** **How can we reduce prejudice?** On February 5, 2017, one man noticed some Nazi graffiti on the New York City subway and asked if anyone had any hand sanitizer to remove it. Virtually everyone in the train car joined in the removal effort (Bromwich, 2017). Do you recognize how the five approaches to combating prejudice are at work in this situation? Similarly, how might large changes in social policy, such as school busing, integrated housing, and increased civil rights legislation, gradually change attitudes and eventually lead to decreased prejudice and discrimination?

**Reducing Prejudice** What can we do to reduce and combat prejudice and discrimination? Five major approaches have been suggested: *cooperation with common goals*, *intergroup contact*, *cognitive retraining*, *cognitive dissonance*, and *empathy induction* (**Figure 16.11**).

1. **Cooperation with common goals** Research shows that one of the best ways to combat prejudice and discrimination is to encourage *cooperation* rather than *competition* (Kuchenbrandt et al., 2013; Price et al., 2013). Muzafer Sherif and his colleagues (1966, 1998) conducted an ingenious study to show the role of competition in promoting prejudice. The researchers artificially created strong feelings of ingroup and outgroup identification in a group of 11- and 12-year-old boys at a summer camp. They did this by physically separating the boys into different cabins and assigning different projects to each group, such as building a diving board or cooking out in the woods.

    Once each group developed strong feelings of group identity and allegiance, the researchers set up a series of competitive games, including tug-of-war and touch football. They awarded desirable prizes to the winning teams. Because of this treatment, the groups began to pick fights, call each other names, and raid each other's camps. Researchers pointed to these behaviors as evidence of the experimentally produced prejudice.

    The good news is that after using competition to create prejudice between the two groups, the researchers created "mini-crises" and tasks that required expertise, labor, and cooperation from both groups. Prizes were awarded to all, and prejudice between the groups slowly began to dissipate. By the end of the camp, the earlier hostilities and *ingroup favoritism* had vanished. Sherif's study showed not only the importance of cooperation as opposed to competition but also the importance of *superordinate goals* (the "mini-crises") in reducing prejudice. Modern research agrees with Sherif's findings regarding the value of cooperation and common goals (Rutland & Killen, 2015; Sierksma et al., 2015; Zhang, 2015).

2. **Intergroup contact** A second approach to reducing prejudice is to increase contact and positive experiences between groups (Dickter et al., 2015; Vedder et al., 2017). Surprisingly, even just imagined contact with other groups can reduce prejudice (West et al., 2017). However, as you just discovered with Sherif's study of the boys at the summer camp, contact can sometimes increase prejudice. Increasing contact works best under certain conditions that provide for *close interaction*, *interdependence* (superordinate goals that require cooperation), and *equal status*.

3. **Cognitive retraining** Even in modern times movies, television, and commercials still tend to emphasize gender differences—young boys are typically portrayed playing sports or computer games, whereas girls are more often shown putting on makeup or playing with dolls. Do you see how these repeated portrayals might increase and perpetuate gender stereotypes? Cognitive retraining can help reduce this effect. Researchers in one study played specific tones while participants viewed counter-stereotypes, such as the word "math" paired with a female face (Hu et al., 2015). Then, while the participants took a 90-minute nap, the researchers played the tones again to remind participants of these new pairings. This simple exercise led to lower rates of racial and sexual prejudice that lasted at least a week.

    We can also use cognitive retraining to reduce prejudice by encouraging people to selectively pay attention to *similarities* rather than *differences* between individuals and groups (Gaertner & Dovidio, 2014; Phillips & Ziller, 1997; West et al., 2014). Can you imagine what might happen if we didn't divide people into groups, such as people of color versus White (colorless?), Christian versus Muslim, or men versus women?

    In fact, one assumption behind cognitive retraining, known as *racial colorblindness*, suggests that we should simply ignore racial and ethnic differences. In other words, just treat everyone as an individual. But others believe avoiding or ignoring racial/ethnic categories discounts serious inequalities and thereby preserves the status quo (Babbitt et al., 2016; Bonilla-Silva, 2016). What do you think?

4. **Cognitive dissonance** As you may recall from the section on attitudes, one of the most efficient methods to change an attitude is with *cognitive dissonance*, and prejudice is an attitude.

    Each time we meet someone who does not conform to our prejudiced views, we experience dissonance—"I thought all gay men were effeminate. This guy is a deep-voiced professional athlete. I'm confused." To resolve the dissonance, we can maintain our stereotypes by saying, "This gay man is an exception to the rule." However, if we continue our contact with a large variety of gay men, or when the media portray numerous instances of nonstereotypical gay individuals, this "exception to the rule" defense eventually breaks down, the need for cognitive consistency rises, and attitude change (prejudice reduction) is likely to happen (Armstrong et al., 2017; Gawronski et al., 2012; Papageorgiou, 2013). See **Figure 16.12**.

5. **Empathy induction**  We've saved the best for last! Very surprising—and very encouraging—research has shown that we can successfully reduce prejudice by simply taking another's perspective—as demonstrated in the following **Research Challenge** (Boag & Carnelley, 2016;

**FIGURE 16.12**  **Breaking the "Gay barrier"**  Michael Sam (pictured here accepting the Arthur Ashe Courage Award) became the first openly gay National Football League draftee in 2014. In 2015, Sam signed a two-year contract with the Montreal Alouettes of the Canadian Football League—the first openly gay player in the CFL's history.

© Kevin Winter/Getty Images

## Research Challenge

### Can a 10-Minute Conversation Reduce Prejudice?

As we all know, advertising campaigns rarely, if ever, persuade people to change their attitudes—especially on sensitive topics like politics or prejudice. Even talking directly to people generally has little effect. However, a recent study found one method of persuasion that worked.

The researchers sent letters to 35,550 homes in the Miami area asking individuals to participate in a study for a small reward, which resulted in 1,825 volunteer participants (Broockman & Kalla, 2016). The researchers then sent 56 canvassers—some transgender, others not—to knock on the doors of 501 of these participants to have a 10-minute conversation. Half of the canvassers talked about being transgender. The other canvassers talked about recycling. In both cases, participants completed a survey before and after the conversation to measure their attitudes regarding transgender people. The effects were really remarkable. A 10-minute conversation with a random stranger led to decreases in *transphobia* greater than Americans' average decrease in homophobia from 1998 to 2012! And these effects lasted at least 3 months. Surprisingly, it didn't matter whether the interviewer was transgender or not.

What did matter, and why these researchers succeeded where most others have failed, is that they trained the canvassers in a new technique called "deep canvassing." Rather than just presenting facts and talking "to" someone, the canvassers asked participants to recall and discuss their own personal experiences with judgment or prejudice. Afterward, they were encouraged to think about how their story related to those of transgender people. In short, this deep-canvassing technique is another form of *empathy induction*— encouraging active perspective taking—which, in turn, leads to reduced prejudice.

Can you see why this research has been widely cited in scientific journals and the mass media as being "groundbreaking" and "monumentally important"? And why it may lead to a new field of research on prejudice reduction (Bohannon, 2016; Resnick, 2016)? It's because deeply held attitudes like prejudice are notoriously difficult to change. And if this method can work on something like transphobia, it might also be used to change public opinion about

gay marriage, climate change, immigration, and other significant topics. How can you use this in your own life if you want to change your own or others' attitudes? The first step is to recall a similar personal experience and

sturti/Getty Images

the accompanying painful emotions and reactions. Then encourage yourself and others to try to imagine the suffering of another group—such as that of gay and transgender people. As we've noted throughout this text, *empathy*, placing ourselves in the shoes of another, is key to better social relations in almost all parts of life.

**Test Yourself**

1. Based on the information provided, did this study (Broockman & Kalla, 2016) use descriptive, correlational, and/or experimental research?

2. If you chose:
   - *descriptive research*, is this a naturalistic observation, survey/interview, case study, and/or archival research?
   - *correlational research*, is this a positive, negative, or zero correlation?
   - *experimental research*, label the IV, DV, experimental group(s), and control group. (Note: If participants were not randomly assigned to groups, list it as a *quasi-experimental design*.)
   - both *descriptive* and *correlational*, answer the corresponding questions for both.

**Check your answers by clicking on the answer button or by looking in Appendix B.**

**Note:** The information provided in this study is admittedly limited, but the level of detail is similar to what is presented in most textbooks and public reports of research findings. Answering these questions, and then comparing your answers to those provided, will help you become a better critical thinker and consumer of scientific research.

Broockman & Kalla, 2016; Miklikowska, 2017). This type of *empathy induction* is further promoted by televised specials and Hollywood movies, like *42* and *Selma,* that help us understand and sympathize with the heroic struggles of Blacks to gain equal rights. Surprisingly, even just reading *Harry Potter* books appears to make people more tolerant. A clever study found that high school students who had read more books in the *Harry Potter* series had more positive feelings toward gay people and showed lower levels of prejudice toward immigrants (Vezzali et al., 2015).

## ❖ Psychology and Your Professional Success | The Power of Affirmative Action

In Chapter 17 (Industrial/Organizational Psychology), an optional chapter that accompanies this text, we discuss how job satisfaction is one of the greatest boosts to overall employee productivity. We also point out that employee turnover and absenteeism are two of the largest expenses for business owners. A recent report suggests that it costs approximately $8,000 to replace a $40,000 manager and about $213,000 to replace a $100,000 executive (Center for Nonprofit Management, 2017). Given that employees who experience prejudice in the workplace are less likely to be satisfied at work, and more likely to leave and/or miss work, it makes simple economic sense that prejudice costs money and that reducing prejudice will benefit both the employee and employer (Burns, 2012; Hebl et al., 2016).

On a higher moral ground, our entire society benefits if every person is given an equal opportunity to succeed. Consider our famous figure for this chapter, Justice Sonia Sotomayor. Despite being born to immigrant parents and an alcoholic father and being raised in a public housing project, she attended two of our nation's finest universities—thanks to affirmative action! Sotomayor proudly states: "I am the perfect affirmative action baby. My test scores were not comparable to my colleagues at Princeton and Yale…[but] I came to accept during my freshman year that many of the gaps in my knowledge and understanding were simply limits of class and cultural background, not lack of aptitude or application as I'd feared." She has noted on several occasions that the central purpose of affirmative action was "to create conditions whereby students from disadvantaged backgrounds could be brought to the starting line of a race many were unaware was even being run" (Sotomayor, 2014, p. 135). Can you see how this response also addresses the unfortunate belief that "disadvantaged people just make bad choices"? As Justice Sotomayor might say, people can't make choices they don't even know they have.

© Billy R. Ray/ Wiley

## Retrieval Practice 16.1 | Social Cognition

Completing this self-test and the connections section, and then checking your answers by clicking on the answer button or by looking in Appendix B, will provide immediate feedback and helpful practice for exams.

**Self-Test**

1. Discuss how prejudice relates to discrimination.

2. The two major attribution mistakes we make are the _____ and the _____.
   a. fundamental attribution error; self-serving bias
   b. situational attribution; dispositional attribution
   c. actor bias; observer bias
   d. stereotype; bias

**3.** Label the three components of attitudes.

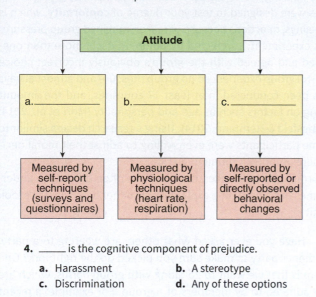

**4.** _____ is the cognitive component of prejudice.

   **a.** Harassment       **b.** A stereotype

   **c.** Discrimination      **d.** Any of these options

**5.** Which of the following is an example of the outgroup homogeneity effect?

   **a.** "You're not one of us."

   **b.** "We are all alike."

   **c.** "You can't tell those people apart."

   **d.** All of these options

**Connections—Chapter to Chapter**

Answering the following question will help you "look back and look ahead" to see the important connections among the subfields of psychology and chapters within this text.

Although this is the final chapter in the textbook, you may still look ahead to applying the concepts from this class to your future coursework, career, and personal life. In this chapter, you learned about attributions and how we explain the causes of behavior or events. What behavioral changes have you made (or do you plan to make) that you would attribute to having taken this course in psychology?

## 16.2    Social Influence

### LEARNING OBJECTIVES

**Retrieval Practice**    While reading the upcoming sections, respond to each Learning Objective in your own words.

**Review the main types of social influence.**

• **Define** social influence.

• **Discuss** conformity and the factors that contribute to it.

• **Describe** obedience and the situational factors that increase it.

• **Explain** how group membership affects our behaviors and decision making.

In the previous section, we explored the way we think about and interpret ourselves and others through _social cognition_. We now focus on _social influence:_ how situational factors and other people affect us. In this section, we explore three major topics—_conformity_, _obedience_, and _group processes_.

## Conformity

Imagine that you have volunteered for a psychology experiment on visual perception. All participants are shown two cards. The first card has only a single vertical line on it, while the second card has three vertical lines of varying lengths. Your task is to determine which of the three lines on the second card (marked A, B, or C) is the same length as the single line on the first card (marked X).

You are seated around a table with six other people, and everyone is called on in order. Because you are seated to the left of the seventh participant, you are always next to last to provide your answers. On the first two trials, everyone agrees on the correct line. However, on the third trial, your group is shown two cards like those in **Figure 16.13**. The first participant chooses line A as the closest in length to line X, an obviously wrong answer! When the second, third, fourth, and fifth participants also say line A, you really start to wonder: "What's going on here? Are they wrong, or am I?"

What do you think you would do at this point in the experiment? Would you stick with your convictions and say line B, regardless of what the others have answered? Or would you go along with the group? What you don't know is that the other six participants are actually _confederates_

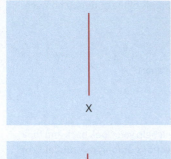

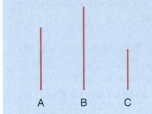

**FIGURE 16.13** **Solomon Asch's study of conformity** Which line (A, B, or C) is most like line X? Could anyone convince you otherwise?

**Conformity** A change in thoughts, feelings, or actions because of real or imagined group pressure.

**Normative social influence** A type of conforming based on the need to be liked, accepted, and approved of by others.

of the experimenter (that is, they're working with the experimenter and purposely giving wrong answers). Their incorrect responses were designed to test your degree of **conformity**, which is defined as a change in thoughts, feelings, or actions because of real or imagined group pressure.

In the original version of this experiment, conducted by Solomon Asch, more than one-third of the participants conformed and agreed with the group's obviously incorrect choice (Asch, 1951). (Participants in a control group experienced no group pressure and almost always chose correctly.) Asch's study has been conducted in at least 17 countries, and the amount of conformity has varied depending on factors such as age and personality (Mori et al., 2014; Tennen et al., 2013; Trautmann-Lengsfeld & Hermann, 2014). Using a research design similar to Asch's, researchers found that some participants were even willing to adjust their moral decisions when faced with social pressure (Kundu & Cummins, 2013).

Why are we so likely to conform? To the onlooker, conformity is often difficult to understand. Even the conformer sometimes has a hard time explaining his or her behavior. Let's look at three factors that drive conformity:

- **Normative social influence** Have you ever asked what others are wearing to a party, or copied your neighbor at a dinner party to make sure you picked up the right fork? One of the first reasons we conform is that we want to go along with group *norms*, which are expected behaviors generally adhered to by members of a group. For example, a recent study of Twitter found that tweeters are more likely to share a tweet if it already has a high number of retweets (Lee & Oh, 2017).

We usually submit to this type of **normative social influence** out of our need for approval and acceptance by the group (Feeney et al., 2017; Shang et al., 2017). Conforming to group norms makes us feel good, and it's often more adaptive to conform. However, on some occasions, this type of conformity can be harmful. One study found that normative social influence was a strong predictor of the intention to use tanning beds despite clear evidence that they're associated with increased risk of skin cancer (Carcioppolo et al., 2017; McWhirter & Hoffman-Goetz, 2015). (For an interesting example of everyday cultural norms, see the following **Gender and Cultural Diversity**.)

## Gender and Cultural Diversity

### How Does Culture Affect Personal Space?

Culture and socialization have a lot to do with shaping norms for personal space. If someone invades the invisible "personal bubble" around our bodies, we generally feel very uncomfortable. This may help explain why some people from the United States feel awkward when traveling to Mediterranean and Latin American countries where people generally maintain smaller interpersonal distances (Axtell, 2007; Fadel & Garcia-Navarro, 2013). As you can see in this photo, these Middle Eastern men are apparently comfortable with a small personal space and with showing male-to-male affection.

Children in our own Western culture also tend to stand very close to others until they are socialized to recognize and maintain greater personal distance. Furthermore, friends stand closer than strangers, women tend to stand closer than men, individuals with autism spectrum disorder tend to have a smaller personal space than others, and violent prisoners prefer approximately three times as much personal space as nonviolent prisoners (Andersen, 2014; Asada et al., 2016; Iachini et al., 2016).

If you'd like to experience the Western culture's norm for personal space, try this informal *norm violation* exercise. Approach a fellow student on campus and ask for directions to the bookstore, library, or some other landmark. As you are talking, move toward the person until you invade his or her personal space. You should be close

enough to almost touch toes. How does the person respond? How do you feel? Now repeat the process with another student. This time try standing 5 to 6 feet away while asking directions. Which procedure was most difficult for you? Most people think this will be a fun assignment. However, they often find it extremely difficult to willingly break unwritten cultural norms for personal space.

arabianEye/Getty Images

#### Test Your Critical Thinking

1. How might cultural differences in personal space help explain why U.S. travelers abroad are sometimes seen as being "too loud and brassy"?

2. Given that men and women have different norms for personal space, what effect might this have on their relationships?

- **Informational social influence**   Have you ever bought a product simply because of a friend's recommendation? In this case, you probably conformed not to gain your friend's approval, an example of normative social influence, but because you assumed that he or she had more information than you did, a case of **informational social influence**. Given that participants in Asch's experiment observed all the other participants giving unanimous decisions on the length of the lines, can you see how they may have conformed because they believed the others had more information than they did?

- **Reference groups**   The third major factor in conformity is the power of **reference groups**—the people we most admire, like, and want to resemble. Attractive actors and popular sports stars are paid millions of dollars to endorse products because advertisers know that we want to be as cool as LeBron James or as beautiful as Natalie Portman (Arsena et al., 2014; Isacco & Wade, 2017; Schulz, 2015). Of course, we also have more important reference groups in our lives—parents, friends, family members, teachers, religious leaders, and classmates—all of whom affect our willingness to conform.

  Interestingly, research shows that specific people (called "social referents") can have an outsized influence over others' attitudes and behaviors. One study found that by encouraging a small set of popular high school students to take a public stance against typical forms of conflict, such as bullying, overall levels of conflict were reduced by an estimated 30% (Paluck et al., 2016). Similarly, popular high school students' attitudes about alcohol use have been shown to have a substantial influence on alcohol consumption by other students in their school (Teunissen et al., 2012). Surprisingly, popular peers who had *negative* attitudes toward alcohol use were even more influential in determining rates of teenage drinking than those with positive attitudes!

**Informational social influence**  A type of conforming based on the need for information and direction.

**Reference groups**  Any groups that individuals use as a standard for evaluating themselves.

## Obedience

As we've seen, conformity means going along with the group. A second form of social influence, **obedience**, involves going along with direct commands, usually from someone in a position of authority. From very early childhood, we're socialized to respect and obey our parents, teachers, and other authority figures.

Conformity and obedience aren't always bad (**Figure 16.14**). In fact, we conform and obey most of the time because it's in our own best interests (and everyone else's) to do so. Like most people, we stand in line at a movie theatre instead of pushing ahead of others. This allows an orderly purchasing of tickets. Conformity and obedience allow social life to proceed with safety, order, and predictability.

However, on some occasions, it is important not to conform or obey. We don't want teenagers (or adults) engaging in risky sex or drug use just to be part of the crowd. And we don't want soldiers (or anyone else) mindlessly following orders just because they were told to do so by an authority figure. Recognizing and resisting destructive forms of obedience are essential to our society—and to social psychology. Let's start with an examination of a classic series of studies on obedience by Stanley Milgram (1963, 1974).

*Imagine that you have responded to a newspaper ad seeking volunteers for a study on memory. At the Yale University laboratory, an experimenter explains to you and another participant that he is studying the effects of punishment on learning and memory. You are selected to play the role of the "teacher." The experimenter leads you into a room, where he straps the other participant—the "learner"—into a chair. He applies electrode paste to the learner's wrist "to avoid blisters and burns" and attaches an electrode that is connected to a shock generator.*

*Next, you're led into an adjacent room and told to sit in front of this same shock generator, which is wired through the wall to the chair of the learner. (The setup for the experiment is illustrated in* **Figure 16.15**.*) The shock machine consists of 30 switches representing successively higher levels of shock, from 15 volts to 450 volts. Written labels appear below each group of switches,*

**Obedience**  The act of following direct commands, usually from an authority figure.

**FIGURE 16.14  When is it good to conform and obey?**   These people willingly obey the firefighters who order them to evacuate a building, and many lives are saved. What would happen to our everyday functioning if most people did not go along with the crowd or generally did not obey orders?

David McNew/Staff/Getty Images

**FIGURE 16.15** **Milgram's study on obedience** Under orders from an experimenter, would you, as "teacher," use this shock generator to shock a man (the "learner") who is screaming and begging to be released? Few people believe they would, but research shows otherwise.

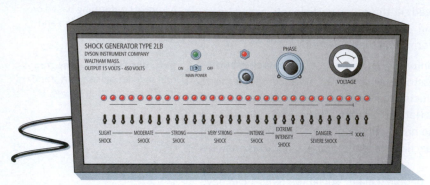

**a. Milgram's shock generator**

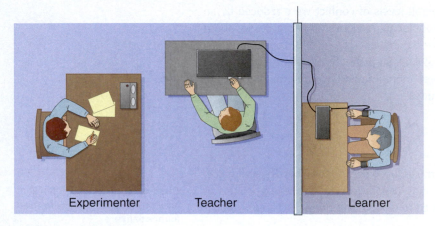

**b. Experimental setup**

*ranging from "Slight Shock" to "Danger: Severe Shock," all the way to "XXX." The experimenter explains that it is your job to teach the learner a list of word pairs and to punish any errors by administering a shock. With each wrong answer, you are to increase the shock by one level.*

*You begin teaching the word pairs, but the learner's responses are often wrong. Before long, you are inflicting shocks that you can only assume must be extremely painful. After you administer 150 volts, the learner begins to protest: "Get me out of here . . . I refuse to go on."*

*You hesitate, and the experimenter tells you to continue. He insists that even if the learner refuses to answer, you must keep increasing the shock levels. But the other person is obviously in pain. What will you do?*

The psychologist who designed this study, Stanley Milgram, was actually investigating not punishment and learning but obedience to authority: Would participants obey the experimenter's prompts and commands to shock another human being? In Milgram's public survey, fewer than 25% thought they would go beyond 150 volts. And no respondents predicted that they would go past the 300-volt level. Yet 65% of the teacher-participants in this series of studies obeyed completely—going all the way to the end of the scale (450 volts), even beyond the point when the "learner" (Milgram's confederate) stopped responding altogether.

Even Milgram was surprised by his results. Before the study began, he polled a group of psychiatrists, and they predicted that most people would refuse to go beyond 150 volts and that fewer than 1% of those tested would "go all the way." But, as Milgram discovered, 65% of his participants—men and women of all ages and from all walks of life—administered the highest voltage. Versions of Milgram's study have been partially replicated many times and in many countries (Dambrun & Valentiné, 2010; Doliński et al., 2017; Haslam et al., 2016). For example, a recent replication in Poland, with only slight modifications to improve the ethics of the procedure, found that 90% of people were willing to deliver the highest level of shock (Dolinski et al., 2017). The participants were also quite willing to shock women serving as learners—although at somewhat lower rates than when men were the learners.

Note that this research has been heavily criticized, and Milgram's full original setup could never be undertaken today due to ethical and moral considerations (Baumrind, 2015; Gibson, 2017; Griggs, 2017). Deception is a necessary part of some research, but the degree of it in Milgram's research and the discomfort of the participants would never be allowed under today's research standards. Follow-up studies have also revealed that Milgram did not adequately debrief some participants and did not use a standard procedure for all participants—two research requirements discussed in Chapter 1. These findings raise serious concerns about the validity of Milgram's findings and the ethical treatment of his participants.

One final reminder: The *"learner" was an accomplice of the experimenter and only pretended to be shocked.* Milgram provided specific scripts that the "learners" followed at every stage of the experiment. In contrast, the "teachers" were true volunteers who believed they were administering real shocks. Although they suffered and protested, in the final analysis, most still obeyed.

**Understanding Destructive Obedience**   Why did the teachers in Milgram's study obey the orders to shock a fellow participant, despite their moral objections? Are there specific circumstances that increase or decrease obedience? In a series of follow-up studies, Milgram found several key factors that influenced obedience: *legitimacy and closeness of the authority figure, remoteness of the victim, assignment of responsibility*, and *modeling or imitation of others*. See **Figure 16.16**. In addition to these four factors, researchers have discovered other deciding factors in obedience, including the following:

- **Socialization**   Can you see how socialization might help explain many instances of mindless and sometimes destructive obedience? From an early age, we're all taught to listen to and respect people in positions of authority. In this case, participants in Milgram's study came into the research lab with a lifetime of socialization toward the value of scientific research and respect for the experimenter's authority. They couldn't suddenly step outside themselves and question the morality of this particular experimenter and his orders.

- **The foot-in-the-door technique**   The step-wise actions in many obedience situations may help explain why so many people were willing to give the maximum shock in Milgram's study. The initial mild level of shock may have worked as a **foot-in-the-door technique**, in which a first, small request is used to set up later, larger requests. Once Milgram's participants complied with the initial request, they might have felt obligated to continue.

- **Adherence to ideologies**   Some film critics and political commentators have suggested that popular movies like *American Sniper,* with their heavy emphasis on unwavering obedience to authority, might be encouraging a military ideology that justifies the wartime killing of others (e.g., Frangicetto, 2015). In support of this position, archival research on Milgram's original study (Haslam et al., 2015b) found that the "teachers" were actually happy to participate—in spite of the emotional stress. Why? The participants believed they were contributing to a valuable enterprise with virtuous goals. Do you agree with archival researchers who suggest that the major ethical problem with Milgram's study lies not with the stress generated for the "teachers," but with the ideology used to justify harming others?

**Foot-in-the-door technique**   A process in which an initial, small request is used as a setup for a later, larger request.

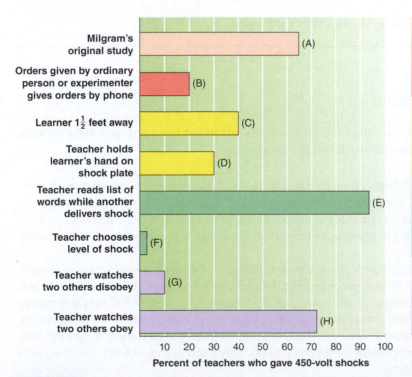

**1. Legitimacy and closeness of the authority figure**
In the original study, orders came from an experimenter assumed to have authority. When orders came from an ordinary person, or when the experimenter left the room and gave orders by phone, only of the teachers gave the full 450-volt shock. (Bar B on graph.)

**2. Remoteness of the victim**
When the learner was only $1\frac{1}{2}$ feet away from the teacher, rather than in another room, 40% of the teachers gave the highest level of shock. Surprisingly, when the teacher had to actually hold the learner's hand on the shock plate, obedience was still 30%. (Bars C and D on graph.)

**3. Assignment of responsibility**
When the teacher simply read the list of words, while another delivered the shock, obedience jumped to almost 94%. However, when the teacher was responsible for choosing the level of shock, rather than being told what level to deliver, only 3% obeyed. (Bars E and F on graph.)

**4. Modeling or imitating others**
When teachers watched two other teachers refuse to shock the learner, only 10% gave the full 450-volt shock. However, when they watched two other teachers obey, their obedience jumped to over 70% (Milgram, 1963, 1974). (Bars G and H on graph.)

**FIGURE 16.16**   **Four factors that affect why we obey**   The first bar on the graph represents Milgram's original study, in which 65% of the participants gave the learner the full 450-volt level of shock. The color coding on the other bars (dark pink, yellow, green, and blue) corresponds to the four major conditions that either increased or decreased obedience to authority.

- **Relaxed moral guard** One common intellectual illusion that hinders critical thinking about obedience is the belief that only evil people do evil things, or that evil announces itself. The experimenter in Milgram's study looked and acted like a reasonable person who was simply carrying out a research project. Because he was not seen as personally corrupt and evil, the participants' normal moral guard was down, which can maximize obedience. As philosopher Hannah Arendt has suggested, the horrifying thing about the Nazis was not that they were so deviant but that they were so "terrifyingly normal."

The good news is that this type of destructive obedience can be reduced. See the following **Try This Yourself.**

---

## Try This Yourself

### Modeling Civil Disobedience

Although the forces underlying obedience can be loud and powerful, one quiet, courageous, dissenting voice can make a difference. Perhaps the most beautiful and historically significant example of just this type of bravery occurred in Alabama in 1955. Rosa Parks boarded a bus and, as expected in those times, obediently sat in the back section marked "Negroes." When the bus became crowded, the driver told her to give up her seat to a White man. Surprisingly for those days, Parks quietly but firmly refused and was eventually forced off the bus by police and arrested. This single act of disobedience was a major catalyst for the civil rights movement and the later repeal of Jim Crow laws in the South. Today, Rosa Parks's courageous stand also inspires the rest of us to carefully consider when it is appropriate and good to obey authorities and when we must resist unethical or dangerous demands.

Bettmann/Getty Images

#### Test Your Critical Thinking

1. What were the major social factors that contributed to Rosa Parks's willingness to stand up against the bus driver who ordered her to give her seat to a White man?

2. Does her model of disobedience encourage you to follow her example? Why or why not?

---

## Group Processes

Although we seldom recognize the power of group membership, social psychologists have identified several important ways that groups affect us.

**Group Membership** How do the roles that we play within groups affect our behavior? This question fascinated social psychologist Philip Zimbardo. In his famous study at Stanford University, 24 carefully screened, well-adjusted young college men were paid $15 a day for participating in a two-week simulation of prison life (Haney et al., 1978; Zimbardo, 1993).

The students were randomly assigned to the role of either prisoner or guard. Prisoners were "arrested," frisked, photographed, fingerprinted, and booked at the police station. They were then blindfolded and driven to the "Stanford Prison." There, they were given ID numbers, deloused, issued prison clothing (tight nylon caps, shapeless gowns, and no underwear), and locked in cells. Participants assigned to be guards were outfitted with official-looking uniforms, official police nightsticks ("billy clubs"), and whistles, and they were given complete control.

Not even Zimbardo foresaw how the study would turn out. Although some guards were nicer to the prisoners than others, they all engaged in some abuse of power. The slightest disobedience was punished with degrading tasks or the loss of "privileges" (such as eating, sleeping, and washing). As demands increased and abuses began, the prisoners became passive and depressed. One prisoner fought back with a hunger strike, which ended with a forced feeding by the guards.

Four prisoners had to be released within the first four days because of severe psychological reactions. The study was stopped after only six days because of the alarming psychological changes in the participants.

Note that this was not a true experiment in that it lacked a control group, an operational definition, and clear measurements of the dependent variable (Chapter 1). However, it did provide valuable insights into the potential effects of roles on individual behavior (**Figure 16.17**). According to interviews conducted after the study, the students became so absorbed in their roles that they forgot they were participants in a psychology study (Zimbardo et al., 1977).

Zimbardo's study also demonstrates **deindividuation**. To be deindividuated means that we feel less self-conscious, less inhibited, and less personally responsible as a member of a group than when we're alone. This is particularly true when we feel anonymous. One of the most compelling explanations for deindividuation is the fact that the presence of others tends to increase arousal and feelings of anonymity, which is a powerful disinhibitor. As you may have noticed when attending large parties with people wearing costumes and masks, deindividuation can sometimes be healthy and positive. The anonymity and disinhibition contribute to the fun of being part of a happy, celebratory crowd. However, it also helps explain why vandalism seems to increase on Halloween (when people commonly wear masks), why cyberbullying occurs on the Internet, and why most crimes and riots occur at night—under the cover of darkness (Bae, 2016; Mikal et al., 2016; Tang & Fox, 2016). Can you imagine your own behavior changing under such conditions?

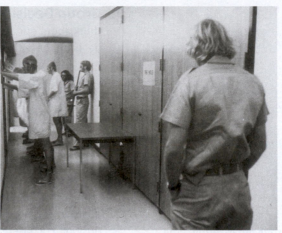

The Stanford Prison Experiment/Philip G. Zimbardo Professor Emeritus Stanford University

**FIGURE 16.17** **Power corrupts** Zimbardo's prison study showed how the power of roles and situations could produce dramatic changes in behavior in just a few days. Can you imagine what happens to prisoners during life imprisonment, six-year sentences, or even a few nights in jail?

**Deindividuation** The reduced self-consciousness, inhibition, and personal responsibility that sometimes occurs in a group, particularly when the members feel anonymous.

**Social facilitation** The tendency for an individual's performance on an easy task to improve due to the presence of others.

**Social loafing** The tendency for individuals to exert less effort in a group due to reduced accountability and risk of detection.

## Group and Individual Performance

Can the presence of others affect our performance? The answer is: "It depends." Sometimes having others around actually improves our performance—a phenomenon known as **social facilitation**. However, at other times, when people are observing us or when we're working in a group, our performance may be diminished, which is sometimes called *social impairment* (Kelly et al., 2013; Panagopoulos, 2017; Zajonc, 1965). How can both things be true? Think of times when you were assigned to work as a group for a class project or to give an individual presentation in class. If your group's task was simple or you had practiced your individual presentation many times, the presence of others probably increased your arousal and improved your performance—*social facilitation*. In contrast, if your group's task was difficult or you were not well prepared for your talk, the presence of others would likely lead to overarousal and impaired performance—*social impairment* (see **Figure 16.18**).

A second, and related, factor in group performance is the degree to which our performance is monitored and we're held personally responsible for the outcome. As you may have experienced when working in a group, it's easier for some people to slack off and do less than others. This phenomenon is called **social loafing** (Amichai-Hamburger, 2016; Kim et al., 2016; Latané, 1979). These same "loafers" will work harder when working alone because they realize they will be solely accountable for the outcome.

Given that social loafing is one of the major complaints about group assignments, how can we reduce this type of free riding on the efforts of others? Each individual's contributions can be made more identifiable, and all group members can be given the opportunity to anonymously assign points or grades to other group members. Teachers and supervisors should also work to increase team identification. When members of a group closely identify with other members and the team, they're more motivated to increase their efforts (e.g., Baumeister et al., 2016; De Cuyper et al., 2016).

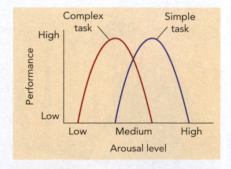

**FIGURE 16.18** **Social facilitation in action!** According to social facilitation theory (and the *Yerkes-Dodson law*, Chapter 12), we perform best at simple, well-learned tasks when our arousal is moderately high. But this same arousal leads to worse performance when the task is difficult and new.

**Group Decision Making** We've just seen how group membership affects the way we think about ourselves and our group or individual performance. But how do groups affect our decisions? Are two heads truly better than one?

Most people assume that group decisions are more conservative, cautious, and middle-of-the-road than individual decisions. But is this true? Initial investigations indicated that after discussing an issue, people in groups actually supported decisions that were riskier than the decisions they made as individuals before the discussion (Stoner, 1961). Subsequent research on this *risky-shift phenomenon*, however, shows that some groups support riskier decisions while others support more conservative decisions (Atanasov & Kunreuther, 2016; Liu & Latané, 1998; McGloin & Thomas, 2016).

How can we tell whether a given group's decision will be risky or conservative? A group's final decision depends primarily on its dominant *preexisting* tendencies. If the dominant initial position is risky, the final decision will be even riskier, and the reverse is true if the initial position is conservative—a process called **group polarization** (Davis & Mason, 2016; Keating et al., 2016; Mikulincer et al., 2015).

**Group polarization** The tendency for the decisions and opinions of group members to become more extreme (either riskier or more conservative), depending on the members' initial dominant tendency.

What causes group polarization? It appears that as individuals interact and share their opinions, they pick up new and more persuasive information that supports their original opinions, which may help explain why American politics have become so polarized in recent years (Gruzd & Roy, 2014; Suhay, 2015; Westfall et al., 2015). In addition, group polarization may explain how if we (1) interact only with like-minded people, (2) get our news only from sources that support our preexisting opinions, and (3) talk politics only with those who agree with us, we're likely to become even more polarized. An interesting study in Washington, DC, found that interns who worked in a partisan workplace became more polarized in their opinions than those who worked in less partisan environments (Jones, 2013).

Group polarization also occurs within the legal system. Imagine yourself as a member of a jury (**Figure 16.19**). In an ideal world, attorneys from both sides would present the essential facts of the case. Then, after careful deliberation, each individual juror would move from his or her initially neutral position toward the defendant to a more extreme position—either conviction or acquittal. In a not-so-ideal world, the quality of legal arguments from opposing sides may not be equal, you and the other members of the jury may not be neutral at the start, and group polarization may cause most jurors to make riskier or more conservative judgments than they would have on their own.

**Groupthink** The faulty decision making that occurs when maintaining group harmony becomes more important than making a good decision.

A related phenomenon is **groupthink**, which occurs when maintaining harmony among group members becomes more important than making a good decision (Brodbeck & Guillaume, 2015; Janis, 1972; Jones et al., 2016). As you can see in **Concept Organizer 16.1**, there are many factors that explain groupthink, but the two most influential might be the pressure for uniformity and the unwillingness to hear dissenting information. Many highly publicized tragedies—from our failure to anticipate the attack on Pearl Harbor in 1941 to the terrorist attacks of September 11 and the subsequent war in Iraq—have been blamed on groupthink. Groupthink might also help explain why so few coaches or other staff members responded to allegations of child abuse by Jerry Sandusky, former assistant football coach at Penn State University.

How can we prevent, or at least minimize, groupthink? As a critical thinker, first study the list of the antecedent conditions and symptoms of groupthink provided in Concept Organizer 16.1. Then try generating your own ideas for possible solutions. For example, you might suggest that group leaders either absent themselves from discussions or remain impartial and silent. Second, you might suggest that group members should avoid isolation, should be encouraged to voice their dissenting opinions, and should seek advice and input from outside experts. A third option is to suggest that members should generate as many alternatives as possible and that they should vote by secret ballot versus a show of hands. Finally, you might suggest that group members should be reminded that they will be held responsible for their decisions, which will help offset the illusion of invulnerability, collective rationalizations, stereotypes, and so on.

Exactostock/SuperStock

**FIGURE 16.19** **Juries and group polarization** When might group polarization be both a desirable and an undesirable part of jury deliberation?

| **CONCEPT ORGANIZER 16.1** | **How Groupthink Occurs** |
| --- | --- |

**STOP!** This Concept Organizer contains essential information NOT found elsewhere in the text, which is likely to appear on quizzes and exams. Be sure to study it CAREFULLY!

**a. The beginnings of groupthink**   The process of groupthink begins when group members feel a strong sense of cohesiveness and isolation from the judgments of qualified outsiders. Add a directive leader and little chance for debate, and we have the recipe for a potentially dangerous decision.

Blend Images—Jose Luis Pelaez Inc/Getty Images

**b. Marriage as an example of groupthink?**   Few people realize that the decision to marry can be a form of groupthink. (Remember that a "group" can have as few as two members.) When planning a marriage, a couple may show symptoms of groupthink such as an illusion of invulnerability ("We're different—we won't ever get divorced"), collective rationalizations ("Two can live more cheaply than one"), shared stereotypes of the outgroup ("Couples with problems just don't know how to communicate"), and pressure on dissenters ("If you don't support our decision to marry, we don't want you at the wedding").

## Groupthink

**Antecedent Conditions**

1  A highly cohesive group of decision makers
2  Insulation of the group from outside influences
3  A directive leader
4  Lack of procedures to ensure careful consideration of the pros and cons of alternative actions
5  High stress from external threats with little hope of finding a better solution than that favored by the leader

↓

Strong desire for group consensus—the groupthink tendency

↓

**Symptoms of Groupthink**

1  Illusion of invulnerability
2  Belief in the morality of the group
3  Collective rationalizations
4  Stereotypes of outgroups
5  Self-censorship of doubts and dissenting opinions
6  Illusion of unanimity
7  Direct pressure on dissenters

↓

**Symptoms of Poor Decision Making**

1  An incomplete survey of alternative courses of action
2  An incomplete survey of group objectives
3  Failure to examine risks of the preferred choice
4  Failure to reappraise rejected alternatives
5  Poor search for relevant information
6  Selective bias in processing information
7  Failure to develop contingency plans

↓

**Low probability of successful outcome**

---

Some of these recommendations for avoiding groupthink were carefully implemented in the decisions that led to the 2011 assassination raid on Osama bin Laden's compound. Before the final call, each member of President Obama's decision-making team was polled, and Vice President Joe Biden felt free to disagree (Landler, 2012). For an in-depth, fascinating look at groupthink, watch the classic 1957 film *Twelve Angry Men*.

On a final, more personal level, can you see how spending time on social media, like Facebook, might increase both group polarization and groupthink? It's because we generally "friend" or "follow" people on social media who share our values and attitudes. And research has found that this limited information pool creates a type of "political bubble," in which we're more likely to post and read one-sided news stories and comments that we and our friends favor (Bakshy et al., 2015). Furthermore, researchers have found that people tend to "unfriend" those with different political views (John & Dvir-Gvirsman, 2015). As you may have noticed, this type of unfriending can become particularly common during heated political times, such as before and after the 2016 U.S. elections. Does this research also help explain why people become so upset when their preferred presidential candidate loses? Our restricted "political bubble" has created a misperception that virtually "everyone I know voted for him or her!"

© Billy R. Ray/Wiley

## Retrieval Practice 16.2 | Social Influence

Completing this self-test and the connections section, and then checking your answers by clicking on the answer button or by looking in Appendix B, will provide immediate feedback and helpful practice for exams.

### Self-Test

1. Compare conformity with obedience.

2. What percentage of people in Milgram's original study were willing to give the highest level of shock (450 volts)?

   a. 45%          b. 90%
   c. 65%          d. 10%

3. Which of the following factors may contribute to destructive obedience?

   a. Remoteness of the victim
   b. Foot-in-the-door
   c. Socialization
   d. All these options

4. One of the most critical factors in deindividuation is _____ .

   a. loss of self-esteem      b. anonymity
   c. identity diffusion       d. group coagulation

5. Faulty decision making that occurs when maintaining group harmony becomes more important than making a good decision is known as _____ .

   a. the risky-shift          b. group polarization
   c. groupthink               d. destructive conformity

### Connections—Chapter to Chapter

Answering the following question will help you "look back and look ahead" to see the important connections among the subfields of psychology and chapters within this text.

In this chapter, you learned about the power of *reference groups* to influence conformity. Using Erikson's *psychosocial theory of development* (Chapter 10, Lifespan Development II), explain how reference groups may be especially important in the development of teens' attitudes toward drinking.

## 16.3  Social Relations

### LEARNING OBJECTIVES

**Retrieval Practice**   While reading the upcoming sections, respond to each Learning Objective in your own words.

**Summarize the influence of interpersonal relations.**
• **Define** social relations.

• **Discuss** aggression and the factors that increase and decrease it.
• **Describe** altruism and the factors that increase and decrease it.
• **Identify** interpersonal attraction and love, along with the factors that affect them.

Kurt Lewin (1890–1947), often considered the "father of social psychology," was among the first people to suggest that all behavior results from interactions between the individual and the environment. In this final section, on *social relations*, we explore how we develop and are affected by interpersonal relations, including aggression, altruism, and interpersonal attraction.

### Aggression

**Aggression**   Any behavior intended to cause psychological or physical harm to another individual.

Why do people act aggressively? What exactly is aggression? When we intentionally try to inflict psychological or physical harm on another, psychologists define it as **aggression**. In this section, we explore its multiple causes and possible ways to reduce it.

**Biological Factors**   Because aggression has such a long history and is found in all cultures, some scientists believe that humans are instinctively aggressive (Buss & Duntley, 2014; Holekamp & Strauss, 2016; Peper et al., 2015). Most social psychologists reject this "instinct" argument, but do accept the fact that biology plays a role. Studies suggest, for

example, that some individuals are genetically predisposed to have hostile, irritable tempera-
ments and to engage in aggressive acts (Chester et al., 2016; Eisner et al., 2017; Pappa et al.,
2016). Furthermore, studies have linked brain injuries, the hormone testosterone, and lowered
levels of some neurotransmitters with aggressive behavior (Angus et al., 2016; Cristofori et al.,
2016; Kimonis et al., 2017). Finally, substance abuse (particularly alcohol abuse) is a major factor
in aggression (Banks et al., 2017; Crane et al., 2017; Kose et al., 2015).

**Psychosocial Factors**    In addition to the various biological factors that lead to aggression, there are numerous psychological and social influences. For instance, aversive stimuli,
such as loud noise, heat, pain, bullying, insults, and foul odors, have been found to increase aggression (Anderson, 2001; DeWall et al., 2013; LaMotte et al., 2017). Researchers who examined
57,293 Major League Baseball games from 1952 through 2009 found that on hot days, baseball
pitchers were more likely to deliberately throw at and hit a batter in retaliation after a batter on
their own team had been hit by the opposing pitcher (Larrick et al., 2011)!

Aggression is also sometimes learned through observation, modeling, and reinforcement (Chapter 6). Social learning theory suggests that people raised in an aggressive culture
will develop more aggressive responses. As a case in point, the United States has a high rate
of violent crime, and U.S. media (TV, the Internet, movies, and video games) frequently portray violence, which may contribute to aggression in both children and adults (Behm-Morawitz
et al., 2016; Breuer et al., 2015; Krahé, 2016). Psychologist Bryan Gibson and his colleagues were
among the first to demonstrate experimentally that watching documentary-type reality TV shows
in which verbal and relational (e.g., bullying) aggression are prevalent increases viewer aggression more than watching violent crime drama (Gibson et al., 2016). In short, reality TV programs
are not just "harmless entertainment"—they may in fact increase physical aggression.

Keep in mind that some critics reject the conclusion that media violence increases aggression (e.g., Ferguson, 2010, 2015). However, several meta-analyses and a task force of experts
convened by the American Psychological Associaton (APA) all agree that media violence can
increase aggressive behavior, as well as aggressive thoughts, angry feelings, desensitization,
and overall physiological arousal (Bushman, 2016; Calvert et al., 2017).

**Reducing Aggression**    How can we control or eliminate aggression? Some people
suggest we should release aggressive impulses by engaging in harmless forms of aggression,
such as exercising vigorously, punching a pillow, or watching competitive sports. But studies
suggest that this type of *catharsis* doesn't really help and may actually increase aggressive feelings (Bushman, 2002; Kuperstok, 2008; Seebauer et al., 2014). Support also comes
from Darwin's (1872) theory of evolution, which proposed that freely expressing an emotion
intensifies it, whereas repression of emotions tends to soften them.

A more effective approach is to introduce *incompatible responses*. Because certain emotional responses, such as empathy and humor, are incompatible with aggression, purposely
making a joke or showing some sympathy for an opposing person's point of view can reduce
anger and frustration (Baumeister & Bushman, 2014; Gottman, 2015; Yip & Schweitzer, 2016).

In addition, the presence and use of guns greatly increases aggression, and firearm
violence affects everyone—particularly those targeted by hate and prejudice (Banks et al.,
2017; Frattaroli & Buggs, 2016; McDaniel & Belar, 2016). Given that the rate of gun homicides in
the United States remains substantially higher than in almost every other nation in the world,
the American Psychological Association (APA) commissioned a panel of experts to investigate
the best methods for preventing gun violence. Consider their three recommendations:

1. *Primary (or universal) prevention* involves promoting healthy development in the general
   population, such as teaching better social and communication skills to all ages.

2. *Secondary (or selective) prevention* consists of providing assistance for at-risk individuals,
   including mentoring programs and conflict-mediation services.

3. *Tertiary (or indicated) prevention* involves intensive services for individuals with a history of aggressive behavior to prevent a recurrence or escalation of aggression, such as
   programs that rehabilitate juvenile offenders (American Psychological Association, 2013).

Mark Pardew/AP Images

**FIGURE 16.20** **An example of true altruism?** A firefighter gives water to a koala during the devastating Black Saturday bushfires in Victoria, Australia, in 2009.

**Altruism** Prosocial behaviors designed to help or benefit others.

**Evolutionary theory of helping** A theory suggesting that altruism is an instinctual behavior that has evolved because it favors survival of the helper's genes.

**Egoistic model of helping** A proposed explanation for helping that suggests we help because of anticipated gain—later reciprocation, increased self-esteem, or avoidance of distress and guilt.

**Empathy–altruism hypothesis** A proposed explanation for helping that suggests we help because of empathy for someone in need.

# Altruism

After reading about all the problems with aggression, you will no doubt be relieved to discover that human beings also behave in positive ways. People help and support one another by donating blood, giving time and money to charities, aiding stranded motorists, and so on. **Altruism**, a form of *prosocial behavior*, consists of behaviors designed to help or benefit others (**Figure 16.20**).

**When and Why Do We Help?** There are three general approaches predicting when and why we help (**Figure 16.21**). The **evolutionary theory of helping** suggests that altruism is an instinctual behavior that has evolved because it favors survival of the helper's genes (Hackman et al., 2017; Vanderlaan et al., 2017; Wilson, 2015). By helping our own biological child, or other relative, we increase the odds of our own genes' survival.

Other research suggests that altruism may actually be self-interest in disguise. According to this **egoistic model of helping**, we help others only because we hope for later reciprocation, because it makes us feel virtuous, or because it helps us avoid feeling distressed or guilty (Dickert et al., 2015; Schroeder & Graziano, 2015).

Opposing the evolutionary and egoistic models is the **empathy–altruism hypothesis**, which suggests that simply seeing or hearing of another person's suffering can create *empathy*— a subjective grasp of that person's feelings or experiences (Humphrey & Adams, 2017; Lebowitz & Dovidio, 2015; Patil et al., 2017). And when we feel empathic toward another, we are motivated to help that person for his or her own sake. For example, middle school students who had been bullied were more likely to say that they would help another student who was being bullied (Batanova et al., 2014). The ability to empathize may even be innate. Research with newborn infants finds that they're more likely to cry and become distressed at the sound of another infant's cries or the cries of an infant chimpanzee than in response to tape recordings of their own cries (Geangu et al., 2010; Hay, 1994; Laible & Karahuta, 2014).

**Why Don't We Help?** In 1964, a young woman, Kitty Genovese, was brutally stabbed to death near her apartment building in New York City. The attack occurred about 3:00 A.M. and lasted for over half an hour. According to news reports at the time, 38 of her

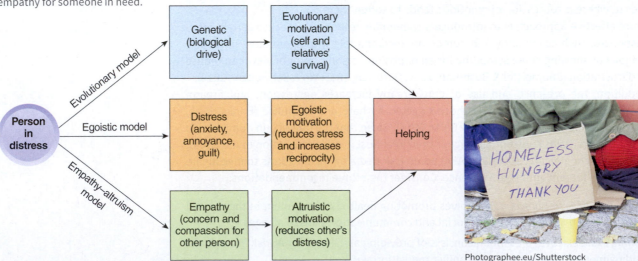

Photographee.eu/Shutterstock

**FIGURE 16.21** **Three models for helping altruism** Which of the three models for helping shown in this figure do you think provides the best explanation for why someone might give food or money to the man in this photo?

neighbors supposedly watched the repeated attacks and heard her screams for help—yet no one came to her aid. Finally, one neighbor called the police, but it was too late. Kitty Genovese had died.

The story of Kitty Genovese's murder gained national attention, with many people attributing her neighbors' alleged lack of responsiveness to the callousness of big city dwellers—New York City residents, in particular. It's important to note, however, that later investigations found the early news reports to be filled with errors (Griggs, 2015; Seedman & Hellman, 2014).

Despite the inaccuracies, this case inspired psychologists John Darley and Bibb Latané (1968) to conduct a large number of studies investigating exactly when, where, and why we do or don't help our fellow human beings. They found that whether or not someone helps depends on a series of interconnected events and decisions: the potential helper must notice what is happening, interpret the event as an emergency, accept personal responsibility for helping, decide how to help, and then actually initiate the helping behavior (**Step-by-Step Diagram 16.2**).

How does this sequence explain television news reports and "caught on tape" situations in which people are robbed or attacked, and no one comes to their aid? Potential helpers must first notice the incident and interpret it as an emergency (Steps 1 and 2). However, the breakdown in the decision to help generally comes at the third stage—*accepting personal responsibility for helping*. In follow-up interviews, most onlookers report that they failed to intervene and accept responsibility because they were certain that someone must already have called for "official" help, such as the police or an ambulance. This so-called **bystander effect** is a well-known problem that affects our helping behavior (Bennett et al., 2017; Brewster & Tucker, 2016; Casey et al., 2017).

Why are we less likely to help when others are around? According to the principle of **diffusion of responsibility**, we assume the responsibility for acting is shared, or diffused, among all onlookers (Brody & Vangelisti, 2016; Obermaier et al., 2016). In contrast, when we're the lone observer, we recognize that we have the sole responsibility for acting.

As a critical thinker, can you see how *informational social influence*, which we discussed earlier, may also play a role? Given that people in a group monitor the behavior of

**Bystander effect** A phenomenon in which the greater the number of bystanders, the less likely it is that any one individual will feel responsible for seeking help or giving aid to someone who is in need of help.

**Diffusion of responsibility** A phenomenon wherein a person is less likely to take responsibility for acting when others are present.

---

| STEP-BY-STEP DIAGRAM 16.2 | When and Why Don't We Help? |
| --- | --- |

**STOP!** This Step-by-step Diagram contains essential information NOT found elsewhere in the text, which is likely to appear on quizzes and exams. Be sure to study it CAREFULLY!

According to Latané and Darley's five-step decision process (1968), if our answer at each step is "yes," we will help someone who seems to need help. If our answer is "no" at any point, the helping process ends.

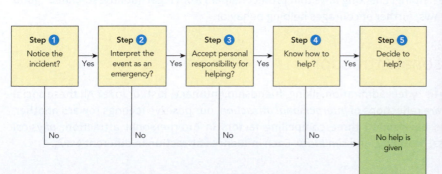

Sam Sarkis/Photodisc/Getty

others to determine how to behave, we often fail to act because we assume others have more information than we do. For a practical application of all these terms, see the following **Try This Yourself**.

---

## Try This Yourself

### Saving Your Own Life!

In one of the earliest studies of the failure to interpret a situation as an emergency, participants were asked to complete a questionnaire, either alone or with others. While they were working, a large amount of smoke was pumped into the room through a wall vent to simulate an emergency. As you might expect, most of the participants working alone, about 75%, quickly reported the smoke. In contrast, fewer than 40% reported smelling smoke when three other participants were in the room, and only 10% reported the smoke when they were with passive participants who ignored the smoke (Latané & Darley, 1968). Keep this study in mind when you're in a true emergency situation. Do not simply rely on others for information. Make your own quick decision to act. It may save your life!

© AndrewJohnson/iStockphoto

---

**How Can We Promote Helping?**   Considering what we've just learned about why we sometimes do and sometimes don't help (see again Step-by-Step Diagram 16.2), our first two steps for getting help from others are to have them "notice the event" and "interpret it as an emergency." Imagine that you're being viciously attacked in a public place. What should you do? You should begin by yelling and making a lot of noice to call attention your situation. Second, you need to clarify what's happening by screaming something like: "Help me! I'm being attacked." Then, to encourage others to take personal responsibility (step 3), try looking any bystander in the eye and say: "You in the red shirt, call 911!"

Do you see why the traditional advice most parents give to their children to prevent their abductions is problematic? Most parents only teach their children to yell and scream, but they forget that screaming children are often ignored because bystanders just assume they're misbehaving. Instead, children should be taught to make eye contact with an adult who may be watching and then to shout something like: "This isn't my parent. Help me!"

In reverse situations in which you are the bystander and not the victim, the first step is to notice the incident. Then, if it seems unclear whether someone needs help or not, simply ask: "Do you need help?" Note, however, that there are occasions when someone in desperate need of help can't verbally respond to questions, and we may need to take immediate action. For example, during the final stages of drowning (versus just distressed swimming), victims are trying so hard to inhale and stay afloat that they're unable to call or signal for help. (For more information on the *instinctive drowning response*, see http://mariovittone.com/2010/05/154/.)

In addition to these personal tips for increasing altruism, highly publicized television programs, like ABC's *What Would You Do?* and *CNN Heroes*, which honor and reward altruism, also increase helping. Enacting laws that protect helpers from legal liability, so-called "good Samaritan" laws, further encourages helping behavior.

## Interpersonal Attraction

What causes us to feel admiration, liking, friendship, intimacy, lust, or love? All these social experiences are reflections of *interpersonal attraction*, our positive feelings toward another. Psychologists have found three compelling factors in interpersonal attraction: *physical attractiveness*, *proximity*, and *similarity*. Each influences attraction in different ways.

**Physical Attractiveness**   The way people look—including facial characteristics, body size, and dress—is one of the most important factors in initial attraction (Buss, 2003, 2011; Fales et al., 2016; Olderbak et al., 2017). Attractive individuals are seen as more poised, interesting, cooperative, achieving, sociable, independent, intelligent, healthy, and sexually appealing (Kanazawa & Still, 2017; Sofer et al., 2015; Talamas et al., 2016). Recent studies even show that better-looking political candidates win more votes—particularly among low-knowledge voters (Ahler et al., 2017; Lev-On & Waismel-Manor, 2016).

Evolutionary psychologists have long argued that men prefer attractive women because youth and good looks generally indicate better health, sound genes, and high fertility. Women also feel attracted to healthy-looking men, along with reportedly preferring men with maturity and resources (e.g., Fales et al., 2016). According to evolutionary theorists, this preference reflects the fact that mature men with more resources would be better providers, and the responsibility of rearing and nurturing children has historically fallen primarily on women's shoulders (Buss, 1989, 2011; Souza et al., 2016; Valentine et al., 2014). However, a recent study of online dating found that perceptions of wealth did not affect men's or women's partner selections (Tskhay et al., 2017).

Consider, too, that beauty is in "the eye of the beholder" (**Figure 16.22**). What is judged as beautiful varies somewhat from era to era and culture to culture. For example, the Chinese once practiced foot binding because small feet were considered beautiful in women. All the toes except the big one were bent under a young girl's foot and into the sole. The incredible pain and physical distortion made it almost impossible for her to walk, and she also suffered chronic bleeding and frequent infections throughout her life (Dworkin, 1974).

Even in modern times, cultural demands for attractiveness encourage an increasing number of men and women to undergo strict, and sometimes dangerous, diets to reduce their body size, as well as expensive, and often painful, surgery to *increase* the size of their eyes, breasts, lips, chest, penis, or buttocks. At the same time, they also use surgery to *decrease* the size of their nose, ears, chin, waist, hips, and thighs (Azzarito et al., 2016; Jackson & Vares, 2015; Jeffreys, 2015). Sadly, but not surprisingly, when photos of actual college women were compared to a sample of Playboy Playmates and to imaginary women (e.g., cartoon and video-game characters), the college women were seen as the least attractive, and for both male and female raters, waist size was the most important determinant of female attractiveness (Lassek & Gaulin, 2016). Even more disturbing was the fact that the ideal, imaginary woman's measurements were nothing close to reality (see **Figure 16.23**).

Sandy Harvey

John Lander/Alamy Stock Photo

**FIGURE 16.22**   **Culture and attraction**   Which of these two women do you find most attractive? Both women are beautiful and appear healthy, but can you see how your cultural background might train you to prefer one look over the other?

Pictorial Press Ltd/Alamy Stock Photo

**FIGURE 16.23**   **Ideal female body?**   In the study mentioned in the text (Lassek & Gaulin, 2016), the average Playboy Playmate had a waist size of 23.5 inches, whereas the most popular imaginary woman, Jessica Rabbit—the cartoon character pictured here— was estimated to have a waist size of 10 inches. Can you see how these impossible and unrealistic images might contribute to some of the eating problems and disorders discussed in Chapter 12?

© Abel Mitja Varela/iStockphoto

**FIGURE 16.24** **Expert flirting tips** Although there are many ways to flirt, the two most universally successful ones for both sexes are *smiling* and *eye contact*.

❖ **Psychology and Your Personal Success** | Using Psychology to Increase Your Dating Appeal

So how do those of us who are not "superstar beautiful" manage to find mates? Researchers have found that past the initial meeting, a host of other factors, such as charisma, humor, personality, intelligence, and compassion become more important (Dillon et al., 2016; Talamas et al., 2016; Tornquist & Chiappe, 2015). Furthermore, research (and experience) shows that both sexes generally don't hold out for partners who are ideally attractive. Instead, according to the *matching hypothesis* and *mating intelligence* studies, we tend to select partners whose physical attractiveness approximately matches our own (Dillon et al., 2016; McClintock, 2014; Regan, 1998, 2011).

Among the least recognized but most effective ways to increase attractiveness is through flirting (see **Figure 16.24**). In addition, recent studies on body language conducted in the United States found that both men and women with "bigger postures"—outstretched arms and spread-apart legs—were judged more romantically appealing than those with limbs held tight (**Figure 16.25**).

Why is flirting so effective? It signals availability and romantic interest. Specifically, given that almost everyone fears rejection, flirting provides positive cues of your interest (Hall & Xing, 2015; Kurzban, 2014; Sprecher et al., 2015). Note, however, that if you're not truly interested or available for dating, flirting can be unfair and misleading. If you'd like more tips and information on flirting, try these semi-scientific websites:

- http://www.sirc.org/publik/flirt.pdf
- http://theweek. com/articles/448643/how-flirt-according-science

**Proximity** Attraction also depends on the two people being in the same place at the same time. Thus, *proximity*, or geographic nearness, is another major factor in attraction—(Finkel et al., 2015; Greenberg et al., 2015; Sprecher et al., 2015). One examination of over 300,000 Facebook users found that even though people can have relationships with people throughout the world, the likelihood of a friendship decreases as physical distance between people increases (Nguyen & Szymanski, 2012).

There is experimental evidence supporting a potentially causative link between proximity and attraction. For example, oxytocin, a naturally occurring bodily chemical, is known to be a major facilitator of interpersonal attraction and parental attachment (Goodson, 2013; Preckel et al., 2014; Weisman et al., 2012). In one very interesting experiment, the intranasal administration of oxytocin stimulated men in monogamous relationships, but not single ones, to keep a much greater distance between themselves and an attractive woman during a first encounter (Scheele et al., 2012). The researchers concluded that oxytocin may help men maintain their monogamous relationships by making them avoid close personal proximity to other women.

Why is proximity so important? It's largely due to *repeated exposure*. Just as familiar people become more physically attractive over time, repeated exposure also increases overall liking. This makes sense from an evolutionary point of view. Things we have seen before are less likely to pose a threat than novel stimuli (Kongthong et al., 2014; Monin, 2003; Yoshimoto et al., 2014). In addition,

Courtesy of Lee Decker

**FIGURE 16.25** **Body language and romantic attraction** Why are "bigger postures" more appealing? According to research, an expansive posture signals dominance, which is socially and culturally desirable in the United States, and thereby increases an individual's chance of being selected as a potential mate (Vacharkulksemsuk et al., 2016). Note that this research was conducted via speed-dating and smartphone-based dating applications. The results may not hold up past a second date!

repeated exposure explains why modern advertisers tend to run highly redundant ad campaigns with familiar faces and jingles. Again, repeated exposure generally increases liking!

Before going on, keep in mind that although proximity is a significant factor in initial attraction, there's also good evidence that many couples can create and maintain very successful long-distance relationships (see the **Research Challenge**).

**Similarity**    The major cementing factor for long-term relationships, whether liking or loving, is *similarity*. We tend to prefer and stay with, and even find more attractive, people who are most like us—those who share our ethnic background, social class, educational level, religion, interests, and attitudes (Brooks & Neville, 2017; Brown & Brown, 2015). One study found that people even

---

## Research Challenge

### Can Long-Distance Relationships Survive?

One of the key ingredients to satisfaction and happiness in romantic relationships is frequent physical contact. Yet up to 75% of college students report having been in a long-distance romantic relationship (LDR), and over 3 million American spouses successfully live apart for a variety of reasons (cited in Borelli et al., 2015).

How do couples, like the one in the photo, manage to survive (and even flourish) despite the relative lack of physical contact, reduced communication, and financial burdens associated with being separated by large geographical distances? The answer may be that they practice what's called *relational savoring*, meaning sharing an experience with another person in an emotionally close relationship (Borelli et al., 2014). *Savoring* itself has been defined as the process of attending to, intensifying, and prolonging the positive emotions attached to experiences (Bryant & Veroff, 2007). In other words, relational savoring means paying close attention to and relishing and delighting in experiences shared with our significant other.

Interested in the effects of relational savoring in LDR couples, researchers studied wives of military service members before and during their spouses' military deployment (Borelli et al., 2015). The researchers wondered whether relational savoring might result in better emotional states and protection against relationship threats in these couples. Participants were randomly assigned to one of three groups. Wives in the neutral condition were asked to think about and mentally replay their normal morning routine from the time they woke up until they left for work or school. In the *personal savoring* condition, the wives were asked to focus and reflect on a positive personal experience. In the *relational savoring* condition, the wives were prompted to think about a positive experience with their partner when they felt especially "cherished, protected, or accepted."

In all conditions, participating wives reported not only on the details surrounding the experience, but also on their thoughts and feelings. They were then asked to spend two minutes mentally reliving the event. Perhaps surprisingly, only the participants who engaged in relational savoring showed increases in their positive emotions, decreases in their negative emotions, and increases in relationship satisfaction following a simulated relationship stressor task.

What's the important takeaway? If a brief laboratory study prompting LDR participants to engage in relational savoring can

AvailableLight/Getty Images

have such positive effects, think about how it could be applied to your own life. While practicing the gratitude exercises mentioned in Chapter 12, remind yourself to stop and "savor" those moments and memories of times you felt particularly cherished, protected, or accepted by your romantic partner.

**Test Yourself**

1. Based on the information provided, did this study (Borelli et al., 2015) use descriptive, correlational, and/or experimental research?

2. If you chose:
   - *descriptive research*, is this a naturalistic observation, survey/interview, case study, and/or archival research?
   - *correlational research*, is this a positive, negative, or zero correlation?
   - *experimental research*, label the IV, DV, experimental group(s), and control group. (Note: If participants were not randomly assigned to groups, list it as a *quasi-experimental design*.)
   - both *descriptive* and *correlational* research, answer the corresponding questions for both

**Check your answers by clicking on the answer button or by looking in Appendix B.**

**Note:** The information provided in this study is admittedly limited, but the level of detail is similar to what is presented in most textbooks and public reports of research findings. Answering these questions, and then comparing your answers to those provided, will help you become a better critical thinker and consumer of scientific research.

judge others as less attractive if they hold a dissimilar political candidate preference (Nicholson et al., 2016). In other words, "birds of a feather flock together."

What about the old saying "opposites attract"? Although many people believe that couples need differences to "keep the spark alive," a recent large-scale study of over 47,000 participants found clear evidence for the importance of personality similarity between romantic partners and friends (Youyou et al., 2017). An attraction to a seemingly opposite person is more often based on the recognition that in one or two core personality traits, that person offers something we lack. In sum, lovers can enjoy some differences, but the more alike people are, the more both their loving and their liking endure. Unfortunately, initial attraction is most often guided by physical attractiveness and proximity, and we tend to ignore the importance of similarity in long-term relationships, which helps explain why there are so many breakups and divorces.

The following **Try This Yourself** feature offers a fun test of your understanding of the three factors in interpersonal attraction. Try it.

---

## Try This Yourself

### Understanding Interpersonal Attraction

Based on your reading of this section, can you explain Kvack's love for the wooden dummy?

**Answers:** Research shows that similarity is the best predictor of long-term relationships. As shown here, however, many people ignore dissimilarities and hope that their chosen partner will change over time.

---

**Triangular theory of love** Sternberg's theory that different stages and types of love result from three basic components—*intimacy*, *passion*, and *commitment*; Sternberg's consummate love is a combination of all three components.

## Loving Others
It's easy to see why interpersonal attraction is a fundamental building block of our feelings about others. But how do we make sense of love? Why do we love some people and not others? Many people find the subject to be alternately mysterious, exhilarating, comforting—and even maddening. In this section, we explore the *triangular theory of love* and the associated categories of *consummate love*, *romantic love*, and *companionate love*.

Robert Sternberg, a well-known researcher on creativity and intelligence (Chapter 8), proposed the **triangular theory of love** (Sternberg, 1986, 1988, 2006). As you can see in **Figure 16.26**, his theory suggests that different types and stages of love result from three basic components:

- **Intimacy**—emotional closeness and connectedness, mutual trust, friendship, warmth, self-disclosure, and forming of "love maps."

- **Passion**—sexual attraction and desirability, physical excitement, and a state of intense longing to be with the other.

- **Commitment**—permanence and stability, the decision to stay in the relationship for the long haul, and the feelings of security that go with this intention.

**FIGURE 16.26** **Sternberg's triangular theory of love** According to Sternberg, we all experience various forms and stages of love, six of which are seen as being on the outside of the triangle. He proposes that only true *consummate love* is inside the triangle because it includes a healthy balance of intimacy, passion, and commitment. Note that the balance among these three components naturally shifts and changes over the course of a relationship, but relationships based on only one or two of these elements are generally less fulfilling and less likely to survive.

For Sternberg, a healthy degree of all three components in both partners characterizes the fullest form of love, **consummate love**. Trouble occurs when one of the partners has a higher or lower need for one or more of the components. As expected, if one partner has a much higher need for intimacy and the other partner has a stronger interest in passion, this lack of compatibility can be fatal to the relationship—unless the partners are willing to compromise and strike a mutually satisfying balance (Sternberg, 2014).

When you think of romantic love, do you imagine falling in love, a magical experience that puts you on cloud nine? **Romantic love**, which is an intense feeling of attraction to another in an erotic context, has intrigued people throughout history (Fehr, 2015; Gottman, 2015; Vannier & O'Sullivan, 2017). Its intense joys and sorrows have inspired countless poems, novels, movies, and songs around the world. A cross-cultural study by anthropologists William Jankowiak and Edward Fischer found romantic love in 147 of the 166 societies they studied. They concluded that "romantic love constitutes a human universal or, at the least, a near universal" (1992, p. 154).

Romantic love may be almost universal, but even in the most devoted couples, the intense attraction and excitement of romantic love generally begin to fade 6 to 30 months after the relationship begins. Why? Romantic love is largely based on mystery and fantasy. People often fall in love with what they want another person to be—and these illusions usually fade with the realities of everyday living (Fletcher & Simpson, 2000; Levine, 2001). In contrast, **companionate love** is based on deep and lasting trust, caring, tolerance, and friendship, which slowly develops as couples grow and spend more time together. See the following two **Try This Yourself** features for more information.

> **Consummate love** Sternberg's strongest and most enduring type of love, based on a balanced combination of intimacy, passion, and commitment.
>
> **Romantic love** An intense feeling of attraction to another in an erotic context.
>
> **Companionate love** A type of strong and enduring love characterized by deep trust, caring, tolerance, and friendship.

## Try This Yourself

### Can You Find Lasting Love via Online Dating?

To test this question, researchers conducted an online survey of over 19,000 Americans (Cacioppo et al., 2013). Participants were asked if they were currently married, if they had ever been divorced, and if they met their current or former spouse online. Those who were married also completed a measure of relationship satisfaction.

Researchers then compared divorce rates and marital satisfaction for those who met their spouse online versus those who did not. Surprisingly, they found a higher level of marital satisfaction and a significantly lower divorce rate for those whose marriages started online. Can you think of topics from this or any other chapter in this text, or from your own life experiences, that might explain why relationships that start online may be longer lasting and more satisfying than those that start in more traditional ways?

© NetPhotos/Alamy Inc.

## Try This Yourself

### What Happens to Love over the Lifespan?

How can we keep romantic love alive? One of the most constructive ways is to recognize its fragile nature and nurture it with carefully planned surprises, flirting, flattery, and special dinners and celebrations. In the long run, however, romantic love's most valuable function might be to keep us attached long enough to move on to the deeper and more enduring companionate love.

As you can see in the figure, romantic love is high in the beginning of a relationship, but it tends to diminish over time, with periodic resurgences, or "spikes." In contrast, companionate love usually steadily increases over time. One reason may be that satisfaction grows as we come to recognize the lasting value of companionship and intimacy (Gottman, 2011, 2015; Jacobs Bao & Lyubomirsky, 2013; Regan, 2011). One tip for maximizing companionate love is to overlook each other's faults. People are more satisfied with relationships when they have a somewhat idealized perception of their partner (Barelds & Dijkstra, 2011; Morry et al., 2014; Regan, 2011). This makes sense in light of research on cognitive dissonance (discussed earlier). Idealizing our mates allows us to believe we have a good deal—and thereby avoid any cognitive dissonance that might arise when we see an attractive alternative. As Benjamin Franklin wisely said, "Keep your eyes wide open before marriage, and half shut afterwards."

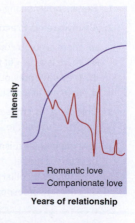

— Romantic love
— Companionate love

**Years of relationship**

Jason Stitt/Shutterstock

Ariel Skelley/Getty Images

moodboard/Getty Images

**Final Note** As the authors of this text, and your tour guides through the fascinating world of psychology, we hope you've enjoyed the journey. For us, the ultimate take-home message, which we hope you'll always remember, is that every human on this planet is an exclusive combination of a physical body, a complex system of mental processes, and a large context of sociocultural factors. Our deepest wish is that you'll make the most out of your own unique combination and foster your own growth mindset and grit—thereby improving your own life and the world around you.

Warmest regards,

*Karen R. Huffman*          *Katherine L. Dowdell*          *Cathrin A. Sanderson*

© Billy R. Ray/Wiley

## Retrieval Practice 16.3 | Social Relations

Completing this self-test and the connections section, and then checking your answers by clicking on the answer button or by looking in Appendix B, will provide immediate feedback and helpful practice for exams.

### Self-Test

1. Explain how making a joke might reduce aggression.

2. Altruism refers to actions designed to help others when _____ .
   a. there is no obvious benefit to oneself
   b. there is a benefit to the altruistic person
   c. they have previously helped you
   d. they are in a position to help you in the future

3. Onlookers to crimes sometimes fail to respond to cries for help because of the _____ phenomenon.
   a. empathy–altruism
   b. egoistic model
   c. inhumanity of large cities
   d. diffusion of responsibility

4. The positive feelings we have toward others is called _____ .
   a. affective relations
   b. interpersonal attraction
   c. interpersonal attitudes
   d. affective connections

5. A strong and lasting love characterized by deep trust, caring, tolerance, and friendship called _____ .
   a. companionate love
   b. intimate love
   c. passionate love
   d. all these options

### Connections—Chapter to Chapter

Answering the following question will help you "look back and look ahead" to see the important connections among the subfields of psychology and chapters within this text.

In Chapter 1 (Introduction and Research Methods) and throughout this text, you have learned to apply the biopsychosocial perspective to different aspects of behavior and mental processes. In this chapter, you discovered several factors involved in interpersonal attraction. Using the biopsychosocial model, explain why people are attracted to each other.

# Chapter Summary

## 16.1 Social Cognition   533

- **Social psychology** is the study of how other people influence our thoughts, feelings, and actions. The subfield of *social cognition* examines the way we think about and interpret ourselves and others.

- **Attributions** help us explain behaviors and events. However, these attributions are frequently marred by the **fundamental attribution error (FAE)**, the **self-serving bias**, and the **actor-observer effect**.

- **Attitudes** have three ABC components: *affect, behavior,* and *cognitions*. An efficient strategy for changing attitudes is to create **cognitive dissonance**.

- Like all other attitudes, **prejudice** includes three ABC components: *affect, behavior,* and *cognitions*. Five commonly cited sources of prejudice are *learning, limited resources, displaced aggression, mental shortcuts,* and *implicit biases*.

- How can we overcome prejudice? There are five general approaches: *cooperation with common goals, intergroup contact, cognitive retraining, cognitive dissonance,* and *empathy induction*.

**Test Your Critical Thinking**

**1.** Why do we tend to blame others for their misfortunes but deny responsibility for our own failures?

**2.** Have you ever changed a strongly held attitude? What caused you to do so?

**3.** Do you believe you are free of prejudice? After reading this chapter, which of the many factors that cause prejudice do you think is most important to change?

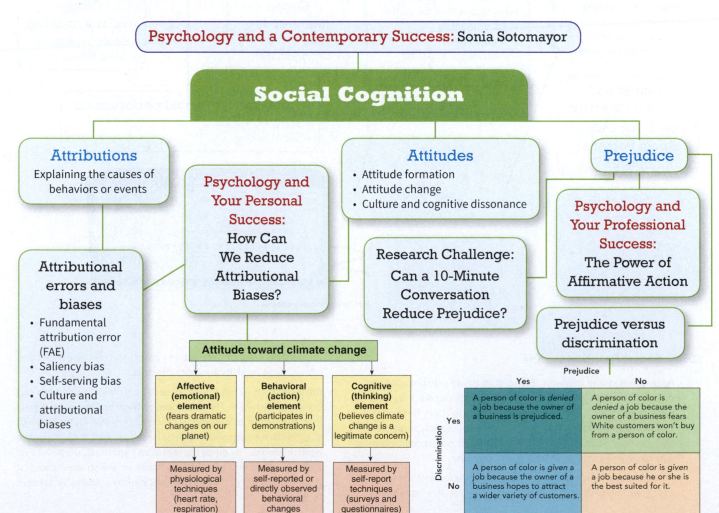

## 16.2 Social Influence   545

- **Conformity** involves changes in thoughts, feelings, or actions in response to real or imagined group pressure. People conform out of a desire for liking, acceptance, or approval (**normative social influence**), out of a need for more information and direction (**informational social influence**), and to match the behavior of those they like, admire, and want to be like (**reference group**).

- **Obedience** refers to following direct commands, usually from an authority figure. Milgram's study showed that a surprisingly large number of people obey orders even when they believe another human being is physically harmed. Milgram identified *legitimacy and closeness of the authority figure, remoteness of the victim, assignment of responsibility,* and *modeling or imitation of others* as the four major factors in obedience.

- Researchers have identified other important factors in obedience, including *socialization,* the *foot-in-the-door* technique, and a *relaxed moral guard.*

- The roles we play within groups strongly affect our behavior, as Zimbardo's Stanford Prison experiment showed. Zimbardo's study also demonstrated **deindividuation**. In addition, group performance is affected by **social facilitation** and **social loafing**. Furthermore, as we interact with others, **group polarization** and **groupthink** tend to occur. Both processes may hinder effective decision making.

### Test Your Critical Thinking

**1.** Explain how group membership has affected your own behavior and decision making.

**2.** How might Milgram's results relate to some aspects of modern warfare?

**3.** Have you ever done something wrong in a group that you would not have done if you had been alone? If so, what have you learned from this chapter that might help you avoid this behavior in the future?

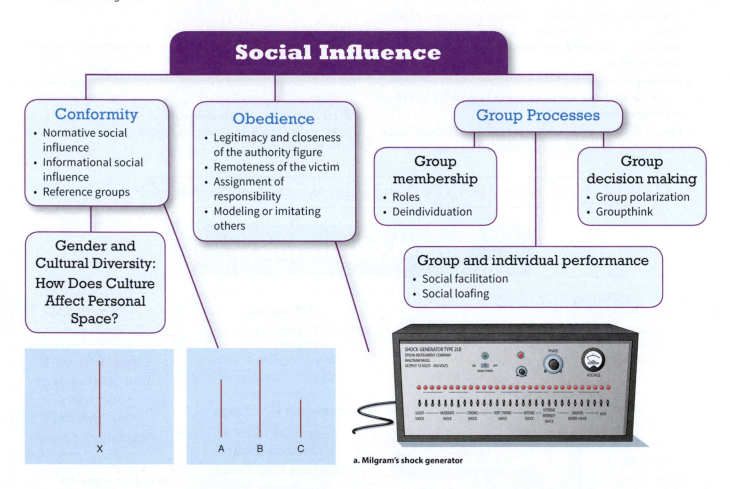

a. Milgram's shock generator

## 16.3 Social Relations   554

- **Aggression** is any behavior intended to cause psychological or physical harm to another. Several biological factors may help explain aggression, including genetic predisposition, hormones, and neurotransmitters. One psychosocial explanation for aggression is social learning—for example, through widespread exposure to violence on TV, the Internet, and so forth.

- Releasing aggressive feelings through engaging in harmless forms of aggression (catharsis) does not reduce aggression. Introducing incompatible responses (such as humor) and teaching social and communication skills are more effective.

- **Altruism** refers to actions designed to help others with no obvious benefit to the helper. The **evolutionary theory of helping** suggests that altruism is an evolved, instinctual behavior. Other research suggests that helping may actually be self-interest in disguise—the **egoistic model**. The **empathy–altruism hypothesis** proposes that although altruism is occasionally based on selfish motivations, it is sometimes truly selfless and motivated by empathy or concern for others.

- Latané and Darley found that in order for helping to occur, the potential helper must notice what is happening, interpret the event as an emergency, take personal responsibility for helping, know how to help, and then actually initiate the helping behavior.

- Psychologists have found at least three compelling factors in **interpersonal attraction:** physical attractiveness, proximity, and similarity.

- Sternberg proposed the **triangular theory of love**, which is based on the components of intimacy, passion, and commitment. In this system, **consummate love** depends on a healthy degree of all

three elements. **Romantic love** is an intense feeling of attraction to another in an erotic context, whereas **companionate love** is a strong, enduring love characterized by deep trust, caring, tolerance, and friendship.

**Test Your Critical Thinking**

**1.** Which of the major theories of aggression do you believe explains most acts of violence? Explain.

**2.** Which of the three major theories of helping do you find best explains why you tend to help others?

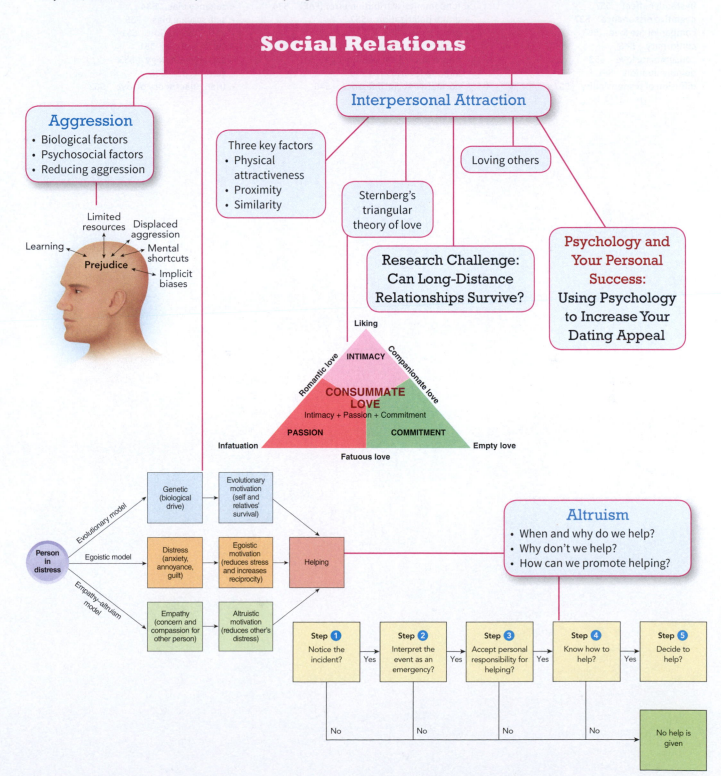

# Key Terms

**Retrieval Practice**  *Write a definition for each term before turning back to the referenced page to check your answer.*

- actor–observer effect  535
- aggression  554
- altruism  556
- attitude  536
- attribution  534
- bystander effect  557
- cognitive dissonance  537
- companionate love  563
- conformity  546
- consummate love  563
- deindividuation  551
- diffusion of responsibility  557

- discrimination  538
- egoistic model of helping  556
- empathy–altruism hypothesis  556
- evolutionary theory of helping  556
- foot-in-the-door technique  549
- fundamental attribution error (FAE)  534
- group polarization  552
- groupthink  552
- Implicit bias  541
- Informational social influence  547
- ingroup favoritism  540
- normative social influence  546

- obedience  547
- outgroup homogeneity effect  540
- prejudice  538
- reference groups  547
- romantic love  563
- saliency bias  534
- self-serving bias  535
- social facilitation  551
- social loafing  551
- social psychology  533
- stereotype  538
- triangular theory of love  562

# Statistics and Psychology

We are constantly bombarded by numbers: "On sale for 30 percent off," "70 percent chance of rain," "9 out of 10 doctors recommend," "Your scores on the SAT were in the 75th percentile." Businesses and advertisers use numbers to convince us to buy their products. College admission officers use SAT percentile scores to help them decide whom to admit to their programs. And, as you've seen throughout this text, psychologists use numbers to support or refute psychological theories and demonstrate that certain behaviors are indeed the result of specific causal factors.

When we use numbers in these ways, we're all using statistics. **Statistics** is a branch of applied mathematics that uses numbers to describe and analyze information on a subject. If you're considering a major in psychology, you may be surprised to learn that a full course in statistics is generally required for this major. Why? Statistics make it possible for psychologists to quantify the information we obtain in our studies. We can then critically analyze and evaluate this information. Statistical analysis is imperative for researchers to describe, predict, or explain behavior. As you'll recall from the so-called "Bobo doll" study in Chapters 6 and 16, Albert Bandura (1973) proposed that watching violence on television causes aggressive behavior in children. In carefully controlled experiments, he gathered numerical information and analyzed it according to specific statistical methods. The statistical analysis helped him substantiate that the aggression of his participants and the aggressive acts they had seen on television were related, and that the relationship was not mere coincidence.

Although statistics is a branch of applied mathematics, you don't have to be a math genius to understand it. Simple arithmetic is all we need for most of the calculations. For more complex statistics involving more complicated mathematics, computer programs are readily available. What is more important than learning the mathematical computations, however, is developing an understanding of when and why each type of statistic is used. The purpose of this appendix is to help you develop this understanding and to become a better consumer of the statistics that bombard us each day. In addition, we hope to increase your appreciation for the important role this form of math plays in the science of psychology.

**Statistics** The branch of applied mathematics that deals with the collection, calculation, analysis, interpretation, and presentation of numerical facts or data.

# Gathering and Organizing Data

Psychologists design their studies to facilitate gathering information about the factors they want to study. The information they obtain is known as *data* (data is plural; its singular is datum). When the data are gathered, they are generally in the form of numbers; if they aren't, they are converted to numbers. After they are gathered, the data must be organized in such a way that statistical analysis is possible. In the following section, we will examine the methods used to gather and organize information.

## Variables

When studying a behavior, psychologists normally focus on one particular factor to determine whether it has an effect on the behavior. This factor is known as a *variable*, which is, in effect, anything that can assume more than one value (see Chapter 1). Height, weight, sex, eye color, and scores on an IQ test or a video game are all factors that can assume more than one value and are therefore variables. Some will vary between people, such as eye color, or may even vary within one person, such as scores on a video game (the same person might get 10,000 points on one try and only 800 on another). In contrast to a variable, anything that remains the same and does not vary is called a *constant*. If researchers use only women in their research, then sex is a constant, not a variable.

In nonexperimental studies, variables can be factors that are merely observed through naturalistic observation or case studies, or they can be factors about which people are questioned in a test or survey. In experimental studies, the two major types of variables are independent and dependent variables.

*Independent variables* are those that are manipulated by the experimenter. For example, suppose we were to conduct a study to determine whether the sex of the debater influences the outcome of a debate. In this study, one group of participants watches a videotape of a debate between a man arguing the "pro" side and a woman arguing the "con"; another group watches the same debate, but with the pro and con roles reversed. Note that in both cases, the debaters follow a prepared "pro" or "con" script. Also note that the form of the presentation viewed by each group (whether "pro" is argued by a man or a woman) is the independent variable because the experimenter manipulates the form of presentation seen by each group.

Another example might be a study to determine whether a particular drug has any effect on a manual dexterity task. To study this question, we would administer the drug to one group and no drug to another. The independent variable would be the amount of drug given (some or none).

The *dependent variable* is a factor that results from, or depends on, the independent variable. It is a measure of some outcome or, most commonly, a measure of the participants' behavior. In the debate example, each participant's choice of the winner of the debate would be the dependent variable. In the drug experiment, the dependent variable would be each participant's score on the manual dexterity task.

## Frequency Distributions

After conducting a study and obtaining measures of the variable(s) being studied, psychologists need to organize the data in a meaningful way. **Table A.1** presents test scores from a Math Aptitude Test collected from 50 college students. This information is called *raw data* because there is no order to the numbers. They are presented as they were collected and are therefore "raw."

The lack of order in raw data makes them difficult to study. Thus, the first step in understanding the results of an experiment is to impose some order on the raw data. There are several ways to do this. One of the simplest is to create a *frequency distribution*, which shows the number of times a score or event occurs. Although frequency distributions are helpful in several ways, the major advantages are that they allow us to see the data in an organized manner and they make it easier to represent the data on a graph.

The simplest way to make a frequency distribution is to list all the possible test scores, then tally the number of people *(N)* who received those scores. **Table A.2** presents a frequency distribution using the raw data from Table A.1. As you can see, the data are now easier to read.

**TABLE A.1    Math Aptitude Test Scores for 50 College Students**

| | | | | |
|---|---|---|---|---|
| 73 | 57 | 63 | 59 | 50 |
| 72 | 66 | 50 | 67 | 51 |
| 63 | 59 | 65 | 62 | 65 |
| 62 | 72 | 64 | 73 | 66 |
| 61 | 68 | 62 | 68 | 63 |
| 59 | 61 | 72 | 63 | 52 |
| 59 | 58 | 57 | 68 | 57 |
| 64 | 56 | 65 | 59 | 60 |
| 50 | 62 | 68 | 54 | 63 |
| 52 | 62 | 70 | 60 | 68 |

**TABLE A.2** Frequency Distribution of 50 Students on Math Aptitude Test

| Score | Frequency | Score | Frequency |
|---|---|---|---|
| 73 | 2 | 61 | 2 |
| 72 | 3 | 60 | 2 |
| 71 | 0 | 59 | 5 |
| 70 | 1 | 58 | 1 |
| 69 | 0 | 57 | 3 |
| 68 | 5 | 56 | 1 |
| 67 | 1 | 55 | 0 |
| 66 | 2 | 54 | 1 |
| 65 | 3 | 53 | 0 |
| 64 | 2 | 52 | 2 |
| 63 | 5 | 51 | 1 |
| 62 | 5 | 50 | 3 |
| | | | Total 50 |

This type of frequency distribution is practical when the number of possible scores is 50 or fewer. However, when there are more than 10 possible scores it can be even harder to make sense out of the frequency distribution than the raw data. This can be seen in **Table A.3**, which presents the hypothetical Psychology Aptitude Test scores for 50 students. Even though there are only 50 actual scores in this table, the number of possible scores ranges from a high of 1390 to a low of 400. If we included zero frequencies there would be 100 entries in a frequency distribution of this data, making the frequency distribution much more difficult to understand than the raw data. If there are more than 20 possible scores, therefore, a *group frequency distribution* is normally used.

In a *group frequency distribution,* individual scores are represented as members of a group of scores or as a range of scores (see **Table A.4**). These groups are called *class intervals*. Grouping these scores makes it much easier to make sense out of the distribution, as you can see from the relative ease in understanding Table A.4 as compared to Table A.3. Group frequency distributions are also easier to represent on a graph.

When graphing data from frequency distributions, the class intervals are typically represented along the *abscissa* (the horizontal or *x* axis). The frequency is represented along the *ordinate* (the vertical or *y* axis). Information can be graphed in the form of a bar graph, called a *histogram*, or in the form of a point or line graph, called a *polygon*. **Figure A.1** shows a

**TABLE A.3** Psychology Aptitude Test Scores for 50 College Students

| | | | | |
|---|---|---|---|---|
| 1350 | 750 | 530 | 540 | 750 |
| 1120 | 410 | 780 | 1020 | 430 |
| 720 | 1080 | 1110 | 770 | 610 |
| 1130 | 620 | 510 | 1160 | 630 |
| 640 | 1220 | 920 | 650 | 870 |
| 930 | 660 | 480 | 940 | 670 |
| 1070 | 950 | 680 | 450 | 990 |
| 690 | 1010 | 800 | 660 | 500 |
| 860 | 520 | 540 | 880 | 1090 |
| 580 | 730 | 570 | 560 | 740 |

| TABLE A.4 | Group Frequency Distribution of Psychology Aptitude Test Scores for 50 College Students | |
|---|---|---|
| **Class Interval** | | **Frequency** |
| 1300–1390 | | 1 |
| 1200–1290 | | 1 |
| 1100–1190 | | 4 |
| 1000–1090 | | 5 |
| 900–990 | | 5 |
| 800–890 | | 4 |
| 700–790 | | 7 |
| 600–690 | | 10 |
| 500–590 | | 9 |
| 400–490 | | 4 |
| Total | | 50 |

histogram presenting the data from Table A.4. Note that the class intervals are represented along the bottom line of the graph (the *x* axis) and the height of the bars indicates the frequency in each class interval. Now look at **Figure A.2**. The information presented here is exactly the same as that in Figure A.1 but is represented in the form of a polygon rather than a histogram. Can you see how both graphs illustrate the same information? Even though graphs like these are quite common today, we have found that many students have never been formally taught how to read graphs, which is the topic of our next section.

## How to Read a Graph

Every graph has several major parts. The most important are the labels, the axes (the vertical and horizontal lines), and the points, lines, or bars. Find these parts in Figure A.1.

The first thing we should all notice when reading a graph is the labels because they tell what data are portrayed. Usually the data consist of the descriptive statistics, or the numbers used to measure the dependent variables. For example, in Figure A.1 the horizontal axis is labeled "Psychology Aptitude Test Scores," which is the dependent variable measure; the vertical axis is labeled "Frequency," which means the number of occurrences. If a graph is not labeled, as we sometimes see in TV commercials or magazine ads, it is useless and should be ignored. Even when a graph *is* labeled, the labels can be misleading. For example, if graph designers want to distort the information, they can elongate one of the axes. Thus, it is important to pay careful attention to the numbers as well as the words in graph labels.

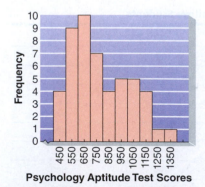

**FIGURE A.1** A histogram illustrating the information found in Table A4

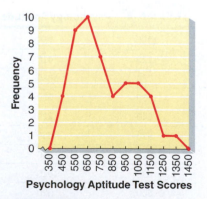

**FIGURE A.2** A polygon illustrating the information found in Table A4

Next, we need to focus on the bars, points, or lines on the graph. In the case of histograms like the one in Figure A.1, each bar represents the class interval. The width of the bar stands for the width of the class interval, whereas the height of the bar stands for the frequency in that interval. Look at the third bar from the left in Figure A.1. This bar represents the interval "600 to 690 Psychology Aptitude Scores," which has a frequency of 10. Can you see how this directly corresponds to the same class interval in Table A.4? Graphs and tables are both merely alternate ways of illustrating information.

Reading point or line graphs is the same as reading a histogram. In a point graph, each point represents two numbers, one found along the horizontal axis and the other found along the vertical axis. A polygon is identical to a point graph except that it has lines connecting the points. Figure A.2 is an example of a polygon, where each point represents a class interval and is placed at the center of the interval and at the height corresponding to the frequency of that interval. To make the graph easier to read, the points are connected by straight lines.

Displaying the data in a frequency distribution or in a graph is much more useful than merely presenting raw data and can be especially helpful when researchers are trying to find relations between certain factors. However, as we explained earlier, if psychologists want to make precise predictions or explanations, we need to perform specific mathematical computations on the data. How we use these computations, or statistics, is the topic of our next section.

# Uses of the Various Statistics

The statistics psychologists use in a study depend on whether they are trying to describe and predict behavior or explain it. When they use statistics to describe behavior, as in reporting the average score on the hypothetical Psychology Aptitude Test, they are using **descriptive statistics**. When they use them to explain behavior, as Bandura did in his study of children modeling aggressive behavior seen on TV, they are using **inferential statistics**.

## Descriptive Statistics

Descriptive statistics are the numbers used to describe the dependent variable. They can be used to describe characteristics of a *population* (an entire group, such as all people living in the United States) or a *sample* (a part of a group, such as a randomly selected group of 25 students from a given college or university). The major descriptive statistics include measures of central tendency (mean, median, and mode), measures of variation (variance and standard deviation), and correlation.

**Measures of Central Tendency**  Statistics indicating the center of the distribution are called *measures of central tendency,* which include the mean, median, and mode. They are all scores that are typical of the center of the distribution. The **mean** is the arithmetic average, and it is what most of us think of when we hear the word "average." The **median** is the middle score in a distribution—half the scores fall above it and half fall below it. The **mode** is the score that occurs most often.

**Mean**  What is your average exam score in your psychology class? What is the average yearly rainfall in your part of the country? What is the average reading test score in your city? When these types of questions ask for the average, they're generally asking for the "mean." The arithmetic *mean* is the weighted average of all the raw scores, which is computed by totaling all the raw scores and then dividing that total by the number of scores added together. In statistical computation, the mean is represented by an "X" with a bar above it ($\bar{X}$, pronounced "X bar"), each individual raw score by an "X," and the total number of scores by an "N." For example, if we wanted to compute the $\bar{X}$ of the raw statistics test scores in Table A.1, we would sum all the

**Descriptive statistics**  Mathematical methods used to describe and summarize sets of data in a meaningful way.

**Inferential statistics**  Mathematical procedures that provide a measure of confidence about how likely it is that a certain result appeared by chance.

**Mean**  The arithmetic average of a distribution, which is obtained by adding the values of all the scores and dividing by the number of scores (N).

**Median**  The halfway point in a set of data; half the scores fall above the median, and half fall below it.

**Mode**  The score that occurs most frequently in a data set.

**TABLE A.5**    **Computation of the Mean for 10 IQ Scores**

| IQ Scores X |
|:---:|
| 143 |
| 127 |
| 116 |
| 98 |
| 85 |
| 107 |
| 106 |
| 98 |
| 104 |
| 116 |
| $\Sigma X = 1100$ |

$$\text{Mean} = \overline{X} = \frac{\Sigma X}{N} = \frac{1{,}100}{10} = 110$$

$X$'s ($\Sigma$, with $\Sigma$ meaning sum) and divide by $N$ (number of scores). In Table A.1, the sum of all the scores is equal to 3100 and there are 50 scores. Therefore, the mean of these scores is

$$\overline{X} = \frac{3100}{50} = 62$$

**Table A.5** illustrates how to calculate the mean for 10 IQ scores.

**Median**   The *median* is the middle score in the distribution once all the scores have been arranged in rank order. If $N$ (the number of scores) is odd, then there actually is a middle score and that middle score is the median. When $N$ is even, there are two middle scores and the median is the mean of those two scores. **Table A.6** shows the computation of the median for two different sets of scores, one set with 15 scores and one with 10.

**Mode**   Of all the measures of central tendency, the easiest to compute is the *mode*, which is merely the most frequent score. It is computed by finding the score that occurs most often. Whereas there is always only one mean and only one median for each distribution, there can be more than one mode. **Table A.7** shows how to find the mode in a distribution with one mode (unimodal) and in a distribution with two modes (bimodal).
    There are several advantages to each of these measures of central tendency, but in psychological research the mean is used most often.

**Range**   A measure of the dispersion of scores between the highest and lowest scores.

**Standard deviation**   A computed measure of how much scores in a sample differ from the mean of the sample.

## Measures of Variation
When describing a distribution, it is not sufficient merely to give the central tendency; it is also necessary to give a *measure of variation*, which is a measure of the spread of the scores. By examining this **range**, or spread of scores, we can determine whether the scores are bunched around the middle or tend to extend away from the middle. **Figure A.3** shows three different distributions, all with the same mean but with different spreads of scores. You can see from this figure that, in order to describe these different distributions accurately, there must be some measures of the variation in their spread. The most widely used measure of variation is the **standard deviation**, which is represented by a lowercase s. The standard deviation is a standard measurement of how much the scores in a distribution deviate from the mean. The formula for the standard deviation is

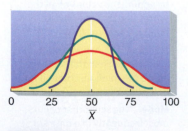

0    25    50    75    100
$\overline{X}$

**FIGURE A.3**   **Three distributions having the same mean but a different variability**

$$s = \sqrt{\frac{\Sigma(X - \overline{X})^2}{N}}$$

| TABLE A.6 | Computation of the Median for Odd and Even Numbers of IQ Scores | | TABLE A.7 | Finding the Mode for Two Different Distributions |
|---|---|---|---|---|

| IQ | IQ |
|---|---|
| 139 | 137 |
| 130 | 135 |
| 121 | 121 |
| 116 | 116 |
| 107 | 108 ← middle score |
| 101 | 106 ← middle score |
| 98 | 105 |
| 96 ← middle score | 101 |
| 84 | 98 |
| 83 | 97 |
| 82 | N = 10 |
| 75 | N is even |
| 75 | |
| 68 | |
| 65 | Median = $\dfrac{106 + 108}{2}$ = 107 |
| N = 15 | |
| N is odd | |

| IQ | IQ |
|---|---|
| 139 | 139 |
| 138 | 138 |
| 125 | 125 |
| 116 ← | 116 ← |
| 116 ← | 116 ← |
| 116 ← | 116 ← |
| 107 | 107 |
| 100 | 98 ← |
| 98 | 98 ← |
| 98 | 98 ← |
| Mode = most frequent score | Mode = 116 and 98 |
| Mode = 116 | |

**Table A.8** illustrates how to compute the standard deviation.

Most distributions of psychological data are bell-shaped. That is, most of the scores are grouped around the mean, and the farther the scores are from the mean in either direction, the fewer the scores. Notice the bell shape of the distribution in **Figure A.4**. Distributions such

| TABLE A.8 | Computation of the Standard Deviation for 10 IQ Scores | |
|---|---|---|
| IQ Scores $X$ | $X - \bar{X}$ | $(X - \bar{X})^2$ |
| 143 | 33 | 1089 |
| 127 | 17 | 289 |
| 116 | 6 | 36 |
| 98 | −12 | 144 |
| 85 | −25 | 625 |
| 107 | −3 | 9 |
| 106 | −4 | 16 |
| 98 | −12 | 144 |
| 104 | −6 | 36 |
| 116 | 6 | 36 |
| $\Sigma X = 1100$ | | $\Sigma(X - \bar{X})^2 = 2424$ |

Standard Deviation = s

$$= \sqrt{\frac{\Sigma(X - \bar{X})^2}{N}} = \sqrt{\frac{2424}{10}}$$

$$= \sqrt{242.4} = 15.569$$

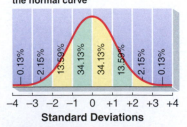

Percent of cases under portions of the normal curve

0.13% | 2.15% | 13.59% | 34.13% | 34.13% | 13.59% | 2.15% | 0.13%

−4  −3  −2  −1  0  +1  +2  +3  +4

**Standard Deviations**

**FIGURE A.4** **A normal distribution forms a bell-shaped curve** In a normal distribution, two-thirds of the scores lie between one standard deviation above and one standard deviation below the mean.

**Normal distribution** A symmetrical, bell-shaped curve that represents a set of data in which most scores occur in the middle of the possible range, with fewer and fewer scores near the extremes.

as this are called **normal distributions**. In normal distributions, as shown in Figure A.4, approximately two-thirds of the scores fall within a range that is one standard deviation below the mean to one standard deviation above the mean. For example, the Wechsler IQ tests (see Chapter 7) have a mean of 100 and a standard deviation of 15. This means that approximately two-thirds of the people taking these tests will have scores between 85 and 115.

## Correlation

Suppose for a moment that you are sitting in the student union with a friend. To pass the time, you and your friend decide to play a game in which you try to guess the height of the next man who enters the union. The winner, the one whose guess is closest to the person's actual height, gets a piece of pie paid for by the loser. When it is your turn, what do you guess? If you're like most people, you'll probably try to estimate the mean of all the men in the union and use that as your guess. The mean is almost always our best guess when we have no other information.

Now let's change the game a little and add a friend who stands outside the union and weighs the next man who enters the union. If your friend texts you with the information that this man weighs 125 pounds, without seeing him would you still predict that he's of average height? Probably not. You'd most likely guess that he's below the mean. Why? Because you intuitively understand that there is a *correlation* (Chapter 1), a relationship, between height and weight, with tall people usually weighing more than short people. Given that 125 pounds is less than the average weight for men, you'll probably guess a less-than-average height. The statistic used to measure this type of relationship between two variables is called a correlation coefficient.

### Correlation Coefficient

A *correlation coefficient* (Chapter 1) measures the relationship between two variables, such as height and weight or IQ and annual income. Given any two variables, there are three possible relationships between them: *positive, negative*, and *zero* (no relationship). A *positive relationship* exists when the two variables vary in the same direction (e.g., as height increases, weight normally also increases). A *negative relationship* occurs when the two variables vary in opposite directions (e.g., as temperatures go up, hot chocolate sales go down). There is a *zero* (no) *relationship* when the two variables vary totally independently of one another (e.g., there is no relationship between your height and the number of times you brush your teeth). **Figure A.5** illustrates these three types of correlations.

The computation and the formula for a correlation coefficient (correlation coefficient is delineated by the letter *"r"*) are shown in **Table A.9**. The correlation coefficient *(r)* always has a value between +1 and −1 (it is never greater than +1 and it is never smaller than −1). When *r* is close to +1, it signifies a high positive relationship between the two variables (as one variable goes up, the other variable also goes up). When *r* is close to −1, it signifies a high negative

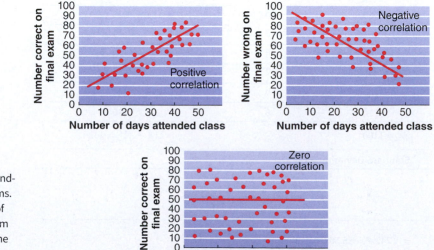

**FIGURE A.5** **Three types of correlation** Positive correlation (top left): as the number of days of class attendance increases, so does the number of correct exam items. Negative correlation (top right): as the number of days of class attendance increases, the number of incorrect exam items decreases. Zero correlation (bottom): the day of the month on which one is born has no relationship to the number of correct exam items.

| TABLE A.9 | Computation of Correlation Coefficient Between Height and Weight for 10 Men | | | |
|---|---|---|---|---|
| Height (inches) | | Weight (Pounds) | | |
| X | X² | Y | Y² | XY |
| 73 | 5,329 | 210 | 44,100 | 15,330 |
| 64 | 4,096 | 133 | 17,689 | 8,512 |
| 65 | 4,225 | 128 | 16,384 | 8,320 |
| 70 | 4,900 | 156 | 24,336 | 10,920 |
| 74 | 5,476 | 189 | 35,721 | 13,986 |
| 68 | 4,624 | 145 | 21,025 | 9,860 |
| 67 | 4,489 | 145 | 21,025 | 9,715 |
| 72 | 5,184 | 166 | 27,556 | 11,952 |
| 76 | 5,776 | 199 | 37,601 | 15,124 |
| 71 | 5,041 | 159 | 25,281 | 11,289 |
| Total = 700 | 49,140 | 1,630 | 272,718 | 115,008 |

$$r = \frac{N \cdot \Sigma XY - \Sigma X \cdot \Sigma Y}{\sqrt{[N \cdot \Sigma X^2 - (\Sigma X)^2]}\sqrt{[N \cdot \Sigma Y^2 - (\Sigma Y)^2]}}$$

$$r = \frac{10 \cdot 115,008 - 700 \cdot 1,630}{\sqrt{[10 \cdot 49,140 - 700^2]}\sqrt{[10 \cdot 272,718 - 1,630^2]}}$$

$$r = 0.92$$

relationship between the two variables (as one variable goes up, the other variable goes down). When r is 0, there is no linear relationship between the two variables being measured.

Correlation coefficients can be quite helpful in making predictions. Bear in mind, however, that predictions are just that: *predictions.* They will have some error as long as the correlation coefficients on which they are based are not perfect (+1 or −1). Also, correlations cannot reveal any information regarding causation. Merely because two factors are correlated, it does not mean that one factor causes the other. Consider, for example, ice cream consumption and swimming pool use. These two variables are positively correlated with one another, in that as ice cream consumption increases, so does swimming pool use. But nobody would suggest that eating ice cream *causes* swimming, or vice versa. Similarly, just because LeBron James eats Wheaties and can do a slam dunk it does not mean that you will be able to do one if you eat the same breakfast. The only way to determine the *cause* of behavior is to conduct an experiment and analyze the results by using inferential statistics.

## Inferential Statistics

Knowing the descriptive statistics associated with different distributions, such as the mean and standard deviation, can enable us to make comparisons between various distributions. By making these comparisons, we may be able to observe whether one variable is related to another or whether one variable has a causal effect on another. When we design an experiment specifically to measure causal effects between two or more variables, we use *inferential statistics* to analyze the data collected. Although there are many inferential statistics, the one we will discuss is the t-test, since it is the simplest.

*T-Test* Suppose we believe that drinking alcohol causes a person's reaction time to slow down. To test this hypothesis, we recruit 20 participants and separate them into two groups. We ask the participants in one group to drink a large glass of orange juice with one ounce of alcohol for every 100 pounds of body weight (e.g., a person weighing 150 pounds would get

| TABLE A.10 | Reaction Times in Milliseconds (MSEC) for Participants in Alcohol and no Alcohol Conditions and Computation of t | |
|---|---|---|
| **RT (MSEC) Alcohol $X_1$** | **RT (MSEC) No Alcohol $X_2$** | |
| 200 | 143 | |
| 210 | 137 | |
| 140 | 179 | |
| 160 | 184 | |
| 180 | 156 | |
| 187 | 132 | |
| 196 | 176 | |
| 198 | 148 | |
| 140 | 125 | |
| 159 | 120 | |
| $SX_1 = 1,770$ | $SX_2 = 1,500$ | |
| $N_1 = 10$ | $N_2 = 10$ | |
| $\bar{X}_1 = 177$ | $\bar{X}_2 = 150$ | |
| $s_1 = 24.25$ | $s_2 = 21.86$ | |

$$\Sigma_{\bar{X}1} = \frac{S}{\sqrt{N_1 - 1}} = 8.08 \qquad \Sigma_{\bar{X}2} = \frac{S}{\sqrt{N_2 - 1}} = 7.29$$

$$S_{\bar{X}1-\bar{X}2} = \sqrt{S_{\bar{X}1}^2 + S_{\bar{X}2}^2} = \sqrt{8.08^2 + 7.29^2} = 10.88$$

$$t = \frac{\bar{X}_1 - \bar{X}_2}{S_{\bar{X}1-\bar{X}2}} = \frac{177 - 150}{10.88} = 2.48$$

$$t = 2.48, p < .05$$

1.5 ounces of alcohol). We ask the control group to drink an equivalent amount of orange juice with no alcohol added. Fifteen minutes after the drinks, we have each participant perform a reaction time test that consists of pushing a button as soon as a light is flashed. (The reaction time is the time between the onset of the light and the pressing of the button.) **Table A.10** shows the data from this hypothetical experiment. It is clear from the data that there is definitely a difference in the reaction times of the two groups: There is an obvious difference between the means. However, it is possible that this difference is due merely to chance. To determine whether the difference is real or due to chance, we can conduct a t-test. We have run a sample t-test in Table A.10.

The logic behind a t-test is relatively simple. In our experiment we have two samples. If each of these samples is from the *same* population (e.g., the population of all people, whether drunk or sober), then any difference between the samples will be due to chance. On the other hand, if the two samples are from *different* populations (e.g., the population of drunk individuals *and* the population of sober individuals), then the difference is a significant difference and not due to chance.

If there is a significant difference between the two samples, then the independent variable must have caused that difference. In our example, there is a significant difference between the alcohol and the no alcohol groups. We can tell this because p (the probability that this t value will occur by chance) is less than .05. To obtain the p, we need only look up the t value in a statistical table, which is found in any statistics book. In our example, because there is a significant difference between the groups, we can reasonably conclude that the alcohol did cause a slower reaction time.

**A Final Word** In this brief Appendix A, we've discussed the major topics of how to gather and organize your data and the common uses of various statistics. For more information, consult a statistics textbook or an educational website, such as the following.

www.mathsisfun.com/dataonlinecourses.science.psu.edu/statprogram/review_of_basic_statistics www.wikihow.com/Understand-and-Use-Basic-Statisticsawuch

On the other hand, you may be feeling overwhelmed and may not want more information. You might also be overly anxious and very concerned knowing that psychology majors need to take one or more full courses in statistics. If so, don't panic! Learning statistics is much like learning another language. You begin with the basic rules of "grammar," which in the case of statistics involves the use of symbols and notation. Later, you'll advance on to practice with conversation, which in statistics means hours of homework.

We recognize that doing homework and learning another language may not sound appealing to you at this time. However, it's important to know that a basic understanding of statistics is essential to conducting or interpreting research—and to becoming an informed, everyday consumer. Furthermore, "fluency" in the language of statistics will make you much more employable and could even earn you a higher salary.

Note that if you truly panic at the thought of studying statistics, or suffer from serious "math anxiety," your psychology instructor or college counselor can provide specific guidance and advice. In addition, the following website offers immediate options and self-help techniques: http://www.mathpower.com/

# Answers to Self-tests, Connections, and Research Challenges

## Chapter 1   Introduction and Research Methods

**1.1 Introducing Psychology (p. 3) Self-Test**—1. d. 2. Critical thinking is defined as the process of objectively evaluating, comparing, analyzing, and synthesizing information. 3. c. 4. a. 5. d. **Connections**—1. Psychology is the scientific study of behavior and mental processes. Distinguishing fact from opinion is one of the most basic requirements of a science. Because behavior and mental processes are so complex, it is unlikely that a single perspective or theory would fully explain what we know about it. By welcoming divergent views, we are better able to consider

things we might overlook or take for granted (such as our own culture or gender). Finally, psychologists try to understand behavior and mental processes by synthesizing or combining various perspectives and scientific data into a meaningful and useful composite. 2. There are many reasons why a person might choose to help another. For an example, a behaviorist might say that I chose to help you because I have been rewarded for such behavior in the past. A humanistic psychologist might suggest that we help others because human nature is naturally positive and we are predisposed to do good deeds. According to a cognitive psychologist, helping behavior

could depend on whether I perceive that someone needs my help and whether I determine that I have the skills or means to help without harm to myself. **1.2 The Science of Psychology (p. 13) Self-Test**—1. Step 1 = Observation and literature review, Step 2 = Testable hypothesis, Step 3 = Research design, Step 4 = Data collection and analysis, Step 5 = Publication, Step 6 = Theory development. 2. d. 3. b. 4. Scientific theories are based on empirical evidence, rigorously tested, and are self-correcting. An opinion is simply the personal view of a single individual. A hunch" is just a best guess. 5. d. **Connections**—

| Scientific Method | Critical Thinking Components |
|---|---|
| Question and Literature review | Welcoming divergent views<br>Tolerating ambiguity<br>Thinking independently |
| Testable hypothesis | Employing precise terms<br>Applying knowledge to new situations<br>Define problems accurately |
| Research design | Synthesizing<br>Being eclectic<br>Employing metacognition |
| Data collection and analysis | Gathering information and delaying judgment<br>Analysis of data for value and content |
| Publication | Valuing truth above self-interest<br>Welcoming divergent views<br>Encouraging critical dialog |
| Theory development | Accepting change<br>Modifying judgments in light of new information<br>Synthesizing |

**1.3 Research Methods (p. 20) Self-Test**—1. b. 2. b. 3. c. 4. c. 5. b. **Connections**—1.

| Research Method | Examples |
|---|---|
| Naturalistic Observation | Researchers using naturalistic observation could stand behind a one-way mirror and observe if adding toy guns to a preschool classroom increases aggression. |
| Case Study | In a case study, a person with an unusual illness or injury might be studied at length to determine how the brain's structure or function might have been affected. For example, did the individual lose the ability to read or speak after the injury or illness? |
| Correlational Design | Researchers using a correlational design would compare the electrical recordings of the brain activity during a certain acvtivity (such as sleeping) in two different groups of people (such as those with depression and those without). This design would show whether there was a relationship or correlation between depression and brain wave activity during sleep. |
| Experiment | Scientists could lesion (damage or destroy) a small portion of the brain in an animal and compare the animal's functioning compared to an animal with an intact brain. Because the researchers manipulated or changed the individual's experience (destroying neurons), rather than observing animals in which that damage had already occurred, this is an experimental design. |

2. (Sample personal answer provided by your author KD) A stressor in my life is keeping track of the many, many obligations and appointments that I juggle as a teacher, wife, mother and hospice volunteer. I would *describe* the stress-related behavior as feeling anxious or overwhelmed when faced with all that needs to be remembered and accomplished. *Explaining* this stressor is probably fairly complex, but one answer could be an over-worked short–term memory! I simply have too many obligations to keep track of in my own head. Can I **predict** when this is most likely to occur? My work schedule has busy periods, such as the beginning, mid-term and end of a 16-week semester. These demanding times correspond to those of my son (a high school student) and my spouse (who works with colleges and universities). The stressor is less likely to occur during times when school is not in session. How can I *change* the impact of this stressor on my life? Well, quitting my job just isn't an option, so I have tried to make better use of the calendar app on my phone. At the beginning of each semester, I enter in all of the dates and events that I can, and connect all of my calendars (work, personal) to my phone app. Each Sunday, I check the entire upcoming week to see what's happening. These changes have helped me to feel less stressed (and to not miss meetings). **1.4 Tools for Student Success (p. 32) Self-Test—**1. c. 2. Survey, Question, Read, Recite, Review, and write. 3. a. 4. a. 5. d. **Connections—**A student who had a teacher who scolded or embarrassed him or her during or after an exam might develop test anxiety due to classical conditioning Similarly, a student who got a bad grade on a very important exam might develop test anxiety from operant conditioning. Finally, a student who watched another student become very anxious during an exam might develop test anxiety due to observational learning. **Research Challenge (p. 29)** Question 1: Experimental. Question 2: Two IV(s) = male or female participants were randomly assigned to one of two groups. Then one group completed the questionnaires hooked up to a supposed "polygraph machine" whereas the second completed questionnaires without being attached to the machine. Note that experiments, like this one, often have more than one IV, and in other cases they have more than one DV. DV = participants' reporting of particular behaviors. Experimental Group = participants supposedly hooked up to "lie detector." Control Group = participants not hooked up to "lie detector."

## Chapter 2    Neuroscience and Biological Foundations

**2.1 Neural and Hormonal Processes (p. 46) Self-Test—**1. Refer to Figure 2.1. 2. d. 3. c. 4. b. 5. c. **Connections—** When a neuron is activated, it triggers the terminal buttons at the axon's end to release neurotransmitters into the synapse. These chemicals move across the synaptic gap and attach to the membranes of the receiving neuron. Once these neurotransmitters have delivered their messages, they are released back into the synapse. In addition, the excess chemicals that do not adhere to a receiving neuron also remain in the synapse. The sending neuron then reabsorbs the excess in a process called 'reuptake.' SSRIs work by blocking the reuptake of serotonin by the sending neurons, which means that the chemical remains in the synapse for longer periods of time. And because the sending neuron cannot reabsorb as much serotonin, it will eventually begin to produce more of the neurotransmitter. Over time, both processes contribute to an increase in the levels of serotonin in the brain. **2.2 Nervous System Organization (p. 54) Self-Test—**1. Refer to Figure 2.4. 2. a. 3. d. 4. c. 5. d. **Connections—** Informed consent means that the participant is aware of the significant factors about the study that might influence their willingness to participate. This would be difficult for someone with a brain injury or other impairment that affects judgment and comprehension. Researchers must be thorough in explaining the risks and benefits in terms that the participant understands. If this is not possible, a guardian or family member with legal authority may give consent. The participant must understand that their involvement in the research study is voluntary, and can be withdrawn at any time with no negative consequences. A dependent person may have some fear that a failure to "cooperate" could endanger their care or relationships, so it is very important that this fear be directly addressed and the participant reassured that no harm will result if they want to quit. Researchers must be diligent about asking brain-injured or impaired participants if they want to continue with the study after it has begun. This should be done at each stage of the research, and/or at any sign of discomfort, pain or distress on the part of the participant. **2.3 A Tour Through the Brain (p. 61) Self-Test—**1. Refer to Figure 2.10. 2. b. 3. d. 4. c. 5. c. **Connections—** When meeting a stranger at a party, your limbic system might react in two different ways: (a) the amygdala might generate a fear response, prompting a desire to escape the situation

or (b) activation of the pleasure center of the limbic system could produce feelings of happiness. Which reaction is more typical of you? These different responses of the limbic system might have an influence on the formation of a shy or outgoing personality. **2.4 The Cerebral Cortex (p. 68) Self-Test—**1. Refer to Figure 2.16. 2. a (occipital). b (temporal). c (frontal). d (parietal). 3. d. 4. c. 5. The left hemisphere is generally considered our main language center, whereas the right hemisphere specializes in nonverbal information and spatial perception. **Connections—** (a) The frontal lobes are responsible for higher functioning, such as thinking, memory, initiative and reasoning. Deterioration of the frontal lobes would contribute to symptoms such as forgetting facts and life experiences, as well as difficulty with taking initiative and following through on an activity; (b) the temporal lobes are involved in hearing, language, memory and emotional control. Again, we see the relationship to memory, but add to it difficulty with using the correct word to identify objects that is often seen in Alzheimer's; (c) the occipital lobes are primarily involved in visual processing. This area of the brain seems relatively unaffected by Alzheimer's. Deterioration in the occipital lobes might contribute to the trouble that Alzheimer's patients have with recognizing familiar objects as the disease progresses; (d) damage to the parietal lobes could impair spatial perception and relationships, such as putting things together in an order or structure, and knowing where our body parts are in relation to each other. This could explain symptoms such as getting lost in a familiar area or forgetting the sequence of steps involved in getting dressed. **Research Challenge (pp. 66–67)** Question 1: Experimental. Question 2: IV = types of incentives, DV = brain activation. Experimental group = participants who were told that either overestimating or underestimating the amount of pennies in the jar would benefit them at their partner's expense, would benefit both of them, would benefit their partner at their own expense, or would only benefit one of them with no effect on the other. Control Group = participants who were told that aiming for the most accurate estimate would benefit both the participant and his or her partner. **Research Challenge (p. 71)** Question 1: Descriptive. Question 2: Case study.

## Chapter 3    Stress and Health Psychology

**3.1 Understanding Stress (p. 82) Self-Test—**1. d. 2. An approach–approach conflict is a forced choice between two options, both of which have equally desirable characteristics. An approach–avoidance conflict is a forced choice involving one option with equally desirable and undesirable characteristics. An avoidance–avoidance conflict is a forced choice between two options, both of which have equally undesirable characteristics. 3. c. 4. b. 5. c. **Connections**—The sympathetic and parasympathetic nervous systems work together to help us adapt. When an emergency exists, the sympathetic nervous system—fight-flight-freeze response—allows our bodies to respond to the perceived danger. When the danger passes, the parasympathetic nervous system returns our body to relaxed, normal functioning. Modern stressors (such as a difficult boss, a challenging college class schedule, or living in poverty) are often chronic and do not include the option to fight, flee, or freeze. As a result, our bodies may be stuck in the arousal stage for extended periods of time, which causes damage and impaired functioning. **3.2 Stress and Illness (p. 94) Self-Test**—1. Psychosomatic illness refers to a condition in which psychological factors, particularly stress and anxiety, influence the body to aggravate or complicate an existing illness. 2. d. 3. d. 4. b. 5. d. **Connections**—The hippocampus (a part of the limbic system) is involved in forming and retrieving memories. People with prolonged exposure to stress may develop PTSD, which may permanently damage the hippocampus. This damage, in turn, may result in difficulty with learning new information or recalling previously learned information. The hippocampus is also involved in shutting off the production of cortisol, a hormone involved in the body's response to prolonged stress. Damage to the hippocampus could impair its ability to reduce cortisol levels, resulting in further damage to the body. **3.3 Stress Management (p. 99) Self-Test**—1. Emotion-focused coping involves strategies we use to relieve or regulate our emotional reactions to a stressful situation. Problem-focused coping involves strategies we use to deal directly with a stressor 2. d. 3. b. 4. d. 5. d. **Connections**—1. How we experience and cope with stressors is strongly related to how we perceive and interpret them. Practicing CTCs can help us minimize the impact of stressors in several ways. *Empathizing:* Non-critical thinkers tend to be ego centric. They see everything in terms of themselves. (Sound like anyone you know?) It can lead to feeling isolated and/or blaming yourself for anything and everything that happens (increased stress). On the other hand, changing

your focus to understanding someone else's thoughts and feelings can help broaden your perspective, as well as strengthen the emotional connection you feel to others (decreased stress). *Accepting change:* Critical thinkers remain open to the need for adjustment and adaptation throughout their lives. Seeing change as an opportunity for growth and challenge decreases stress, whereas feeling threatened and fearful in the face of change increases stress. *Resisting overgeneralization:* Sometimes we fall into the temptation to say, "Oh this is just like last time. . . ." For example, you may have done poorly on your first quiz in a chemistry class. This may lead to overgeneralizing that experience to the rest of the course, making you feel more anxious and discouraged about your chances of success in the class—or even to college in general! Critical thinkers will try to avoid this 'tunnel vision' and catastrophizing. Instead they focus on each new situation with a view towards what can be changed or controlled. 2. Social interactions and relationships can increase our stress levels if they leave us feeling frustrated, angry or helpless. Some people and situations are difficult to deal with, but we may be stuck with them. Unfortunately though, when we are experiencing the negative emotions that go along with stress, we may hunker down and avoid social situations that might actually help us to cope. Taking a walk with your dog, calling a friend, or playing a game of basketball can help us cope with stress. This type of emotion-focused coping is very effective, especially when there is little when can do to change the stressor. We might also seek help or advice from a friend or family member to reduce or eliminate the stressor. **3.4 Health Psychology (p. 106) Self-Test**—1. Health psychology is a branch of psychology that studies how biological, psychological, and social (biopsychosocial) factors influence health, illness, and health-related behaviors. 2. a. 3. a. 4. d. 5. c. **Connections**—If you can answer this question, perhaps you should consider a career as a health psychologist! Changing unhealthy behaviors is very challenging, but not impossible. There are many possible motivators: rewards for short- and long-term goals, enlisting friends or others who share your goals for support and accountability, using visual/tangible reminders, etc. If you wanted to cut back on smoking, for example, you could start by keeping track of your cigarette use each day. That would provide a visual record of your progress. You might reward yourself by meeting your goals for the day, the week and/or the month

(as long as it's a reward that doesn't substitute one bad habit for another!). Joining a support group or just making a pact with a friend or partner can also help keep you on track. If you have a romantic partner, child, or grandchild keeping their photo handy to look at can remind you of why you want to quit smoking and help distract from the nicotine cravings too. A combination of motivational strategies will probably be more effective than just one. **Research Challenge (p. 93)** Question 1: Experimental. Question 2: First part of experiment IV = study practice versus retrieval practice. Second stage of experiment IV = Stressful task versus nonstressful task. DV = number of items remembered. Experimental group(s) = retrieval practice and stressful task. Control group(s) = study practice and nonstressful task. **Research Challenge (p. 109)** Question 1: Descriptive and correlational. Question 2: Archival research and negative correlation: increased success winning elections is associated with a decreased life expectancy.

### Chapter 4    Sensation and Perception

**4.1 Understanding Sensation (p. 117) Self-Test**—1. Bottom-up processing begins at the "bottom" sensory level and works "up." Top-down processing begins at the "top," higher-level cognitive processes, and works "down." 2. a. 3. c. 4. a. 5. b. **Connections**—During *transduction* and *coding*, receive is limited so that our brains are the amount of stimuli we not overwhelmed with unnecessary information. What would life be like if this filtering did not occur? If people with autism lack this same degree of filtering, it might explain common symptoms, such as the avoidance of touch or social interactions. And the desire for routine could be interpreted as an attempt to impose some stability and predictability on a chaotic world. It is important to emphasize that this is an exercise in empathy and critical thinking, rather than a scientific explanation for the symptoms of autism. **4.2 How We See and Hear (p. 123) Self-Test**—1. Refer to Process Diagram 4.1. 2. c. 3. b. 4. Refer to Process Diagram 4.2. 5. c. **Connections**—We inherit 23 pairs of chromosomes from our biological mother and father. One of these pairs determines our sex: XX for women, XY for men. Traits that show up mostly in men tend to be influenced by genes carried on the X chromosome. Women have two Xs, so any missing or defective gene on one X can be compensated for by a healthy gene on the other X. Men have only one X chromosome, and are more likely to show a trait influenced by a faulty or missing gene there. So men with color-deficient vision have inherited the condition from their mother, who is a carrier for the gene, but is generally not color-deficient herself. **4.3 Our Other Important Senses (p. 130) Self-Test—**1. c. 2. Smell and taste receptors are located near each other and closely interact since they both rely on chemoreceptors that are sensitive to certain chemical molecules. 3. d. 4. d. 5. b. **Connections—**(a) The olfactory bulb is key to processing smells; (b) the brain stem, thalamus, gustatory cortex, and somatosensory cortex process taste; (c) the parietal lobes contain the somatosensory cortices, which register the scratchy pain from the tag on your shirt and other body sensations. **4.4 Understanding Perception (p. 135) Self-Test—**1. Illusions are false or misleading perceptions shared by others in the same perceptual environment. Hallucinations are false sensory experiences that occur without external stimuli. Delusions are false beliefs, often of persecution or grandeur. 2. b. 3. a. 4. b. 5. b. **Connections—**1. A perceptual set is a readiness to perceive in a particular manner based on expectations. In other words, we see what we expect to see. Prejudice and discrimination could be created by perceptual sets that encourage negative associations, such as stereotypic media portrayals of ethnic minorities. 2. ESP is considered to be an example of pseudopsychology and studies claiming evidence of ESP have produced weak or controversial results. Remember, results in ESP research are notoriously "fragile" in that they do not hold up to scientific scrutiny.

Employing a variety of thinking processes means that critical thinkers are not bound to one way of thinking. They will use different strategies and dialectical thinking to analyze the strengths and weaknesses of opposing points of view. Analyzing data for value and content can be difficult when we lack the scientific training and statistical knowledge to fully evaluate the empirical evidence. But even nonscientists can be alert to recognizing appeals to emotion, unsupported assumptions and faulty logic that often accompany false claims or half-truths. Finally, employing metacognition–thinking about your own thinking–can help you understand how and why you think the way you do. **Research Challenge (p. 133)** Question 1: Experimental. Question 2: IV = background music. DV = participants' rating of how much they liked the beer's taste. Experimental groups = participants who

tasted the beer with background music. Control Group = participants who tasted the beer without background music. **Research Challenge (pp. 144–145)** Question 1: Both studies used experimental research techniques. Question 2: IV in both studies was the color of the shirt. DV (Study 1) = number of emails, DV (Study 2) = attractiveness and interest in dating/kissing/engaging in sexual activity. Experimental Group = participants wearing the color red. Control Group = participants wearing colors other than red.

## Chapter 5    States of Consciousness

**5.1 Understanding Consciousness (p. 153) Self-Test—**1. Consciousness is defined as our awareness of ourselves and our environment. 2. a. 3. d. 4. b. 5. d. **Connections—**In this chapter, levels of awareness was explained as existing on a continuum, ranging from high awareness and sharp, focused alertness at one extreme, to middle levels of awareness, to low awareness or even nonconsciousness and coma at the lowest extreme. In Chapter 13, Freud called the mind the "psyche" and asserted that it contains three levels of consciousness, or awareness, ranging from the *conscious* at the highest level of awareness, the *preconscious* at the middle level, and the *unconscious* at the very lowest. **5.2 Understanding Sleep and Dreams (p. 157) Self-Test—**1. Circadian rhythms are based on the internal, biological clock that governs bodily activities that occur on a 24- to 25-hour cycle. 2. c. 3. a. 4. a. 5. c. **Connections—**1. (a) The motor cortex in the frontal lobes would be most active if you were playing the piano; (b) if you were in a panic because you were late for your final exam, your limbic system would probably be highly involved; (c) the temporal lobes would most active in listening; (d) the cerebellum would provide the balance you would need to walk a tightrope. 2. The manifest content of your dream is what you remember happening. This is a sample dream provided by one of your authors (KD). In a recent dream, I was walking through a house, looking for my grandmother. I walked upstairs and through many rooms, but she was not there. What would Freud say about that? According to Freud, the latent content is the dream's unconscious, hidden meaning transformed into symbols within the dream's manifest content. In my dream, the house might represent myself or my psyche. Since the dream house was large and spacious, it might mean that I feel free and unrestricted in my life. To dream of looking for something in the house could symbolize

a need to find myself, or a recognition that something is missing from my sense of self. My grandmother could symbolize that I am looking for nurturing or reassurance. It's fun to think about, but most modern research finds little or no support for Freud's theory of dreams. **5.3 Psychoactive Drugs (p. 168) Self-Test—**1. a. 2. d. 3. Agonist drugs bind to a receptor and trigger a response that mimics or enhances a neurotransmitter's effect, whereas antagonist drugs trigger a response that blocks a neurotransmitter's effect. 4. a. 5. c. **Connections—**Symptoms of PTSD include flashbacks, sleep disturbances, emotional numbness, anxiety and being easily startled. Alcohol has a strong potential for abuse and dependence among those who suffer from PTSD because it helps them relax and forget for a time. However, it disrupts sleep, and reduces emotional and behavioral control. This disinhibition of control could be especially dangerous if the person with PTSD has a flashback while intoxicated. Excessive drinking also might make the person feel even more emotionally numb and further isolated from social relationships. In addition, alcohol distorts perception, which might make it more likely that the individual would interpret a neutral event in a harmful or hostile way. Finally, alcohol is a depressant, which could worsen symptoms such as guilt, depression, or hopelessness. **5.4 Meditation and Hypnosis (p. 176) Self-Test—**1. d. 2. Meditation is a group of techniques designed to focus attention, block out distractions, and produce an altered state of consciousness (ASC). Hypnosis is an ASC characterized by deep relaxation and a trance-like state of heightened suggestibility and intense focus. 3. b. 4. c. 5. b. **Connections—**If we can get the facts wrong when we are wide awake and alert, it seems likely that an ASC (such as hypnosis) would make us even more vulnerable to memory problems. In addition, when hypnotized, people are more likely to use their imaginations and to hallucinate. How can we be sure what was real versus imagined? Another potential problem is that people generally experience heightened suggestibility under hypnosis, and the hypnotist might inadvertently create a false memory. **Research Challenge (p. 155)** Question 1: Experimental. Question 2: IV = four driving conditions (driving alone, speaking to a passenger, driving alone while talking on a cell phone to a person in a remote condition, driving alone while talking on a cell phone to a remote person who shared the view of the driver and what the driver could see). DV = drivers' performance. Experimental

Group(s) = driving while speaking to a passenger alongside him or her in the simulator, driving alone while speaking on a hands-free cell phone to someone in a remote location, and driving alone while speaking on a hands-free cell phone to someone in a remote location, who could see the face of the driver and also observe the driving scene through a videophone. Control Group = driving alone.

### Chapter 6    Learning

**6.1 Classical Conditioning (p. 186) Self-Test**—1. c. 2. c. 3. d. 4. generalization. 5. b. **Connections**—The main ethical concern with using classical conditioning to change "unwanted" behaviors involves the issue of consent. Can a child or brain-damaged adult truly consent to this treatment? Probably not. Clearly, there is subjectivity and the potential for abuse involved in deciding which behaviors are "unwanted." Using classical conditioning for unwanted or self-injurious behaviors, usually involves applying pain, shocks or some other aversive consequences. Should a treatment applied to vulnerable individuals involve pain or shocks? These are controversial situations, but supporters of this approach typically emphasize that these are treatments of last resort, used only when no other options have proven effective. One might also argue that the treatment is less harmful than the behaviors it tries to eliminate. **6.2 Operant Conditioning (p. 194) Self-Test**—1. operant conditioning. 2. a. 3. c. 4. d. 5. c. **Connections**—If you are a parent, it's easy to come up with an example for this question. Parents are often frustrated when their kids don't seem to be motivated by punishments or rewards. Maybe you were that kid. What went wrong? One explanation is that the reinforcement or punishment wasn't enough to sway you from what you wanted to do. Imagine that your dad offered you $10 to cut the lawn. If you thought it was too little money for the job, and/or had something better to do, then you probably won't be motivated to do it. If dad then threatened a punishment to get you to cut the lawn, you would probably consider how inconvenient or aversive the punishment would be for you before making up your mind. Yet another factor to consider is whether you want to keep your dad happy. If that's important to you, then the reward/punishment he offered wouldn't be a big factor in your decision, and you would do it anyway. Clearly, the relationship between operant conditioning and motivation is more complicated than it first appears. **6.3 Cognitive–Social Learning (p. 206) Self-Test**—1.

Cognitive–social learning differs from classical conditioning and operant conditioning in that it emphasizes the interpretation or thinking that occurs within the organism: S–O–R (stimulus–organism–response). Also, according to this theory, humans have attitudes, beliefs, expectations, motivations, and emotions that affect learning more than the other two theories. 2. c. 3. c. 4. a. 5. b. **Connections**—The social-cognitive theory suggests that human attitudes, beliefs and expectations are largely learned through observation and imitation of others. In this era of 24/7 global connectivity, we can observe and learn from people and events all over the world. Unfortunately, much of what we see is scary. To keep people watching/clicking, media outlets need to keep us interested—and fear can do that. We can now worry about things we didn't even know about yesterday (and that will most likely never happen to us). So is the world more dangerous? It's a tough question to answer, but statistics suggest that the world is more peaceful today than at any other time in history. What is certain, though, is that most of us believe that there is much to fear. And for some of us, that may lead to an anxiety disorder. **6.4 Biology of Learning (p. 211) Self-Test**—1. c. 2. Mirror. 3. b. 4. d. 5. c. **Connections**—Altering the neurochemistry of your brain, in the absence of dysfunction or disease, is not something to take lightly. On the pro side, a drug that enhances learning could make some things much easier for you—acing that math requirement might sound like an excellent use for such a drug. On the other hand, all drugs have side effects. You have also learned that taking drugs that change brain chemistry tend to have long-lasting (or even permanent) effects on the brain's functioning. It would be difficult to know what the consequences might be on an unborn child or in later adulthood, which could be a significant disadvantage. **Research Challenge (p. 197)** Question 1: Experimental. Question 2: IV = presence of owner or bowl of treats. DV = dog's choice of owner or treats. (Note that there was no mention of random assignment, so this might qualify as a quasi-experimental design.) **Research Challenge (p. 210)** Question 1: Both descriptive and correlational. Question 2: Descriptive = survey/interview. Correlation = positive—greater media access lead to greater preferences for the thin ideal. (Note that this study also has many elements of an experiment, but it lacks random assignment, so it also could be considered a quasi-experimental design.)

### Chapter 7    Memory

**7.1 The Nature of Memory (p. 221) Self-Test**—1. Just as a computer translates keystrokes into its own electronic language, the human brain encodes sensory information into a neural code (language) it can understand and use. Once encoded, computer information is normally stored on a flash drive or hard drive, whereas human information is stored in the brain. To retrieve stored information in a computer we go to files on the hard drive, or to "files" in our brains. 2. d. 3. a. 4. b. 5. c. **Connections**—Chunking (grouping separate pieces of information a single unit) is quite similar to the Gestalt principles of organization because we often look for patterns when chunking. For example, phone numbers are usually presented in a sequence of three sets of numbers separated by hyphens. The principle of *proximity* influences us to naturally chunk the phone number into 3 groups rather than 10 separate numerals. When trying to remember what you might need to buy at the grocery store, you can chunk the items based on *similarity*–produce, dairy, paper goods, etc. You may use other Gestalt principles depending on what you are trying to remember. Using these principles to guide chunking may make the process more effective–and increase the likelihood that you get all of your groceries in one trip. **7.2 Forgetting (p. 233) Self-Test**—1. In *decay theory*, memory is processed and stored in a physical form. Therefore, connections between neurons probably deteriorate over time, leading to forgetting. 2. b. 3. c. 4. b. 5. c. **Connections**—The penny recognition problem can be attributed to an *encoding* failure. Without selectively attending to the features of a penny and making an effort to process its features, the relevant details don't get entered into LTM. For most people, encoding the fine details of a penny are not necessary or worth the time and effort to study. **7.3 Biological Bases of Memory (p. 238) Self-Test**—1. Long-term potentiation (LTP) is a long-lasting increase in neural sensitivity and/or a biological mechanism for learning and memory. 2. d. 3. d. 4. c. 5. c. **Connections**—1. There are several different ways to approach this research question. One method would be to use fMRI to record the brain activity of participants as they listen to several new pieces of music (song A, song B, song C). Then you might observe and record the brain areas that are most active during this initial exposure/learning phase. Next, participants' brains should be scanned again while they're listening to a set of music that includes one piece from the first set (song B, for example) amidst others they are hearing for the first time (song D, song E, song F). Finally, you would compare the brain activity during the familiar piece (song B) with the brain activity during the second set of new pieces of music. Is there a different area of the brain involved in listening to Song B? If so, you may have found an area of the brain involved in music memory. 2. In terms of our bodies, there is always a "sweet spot." Too much or too little of anything can cause problems. This seems to be true for the impact of emotional and even physical arousal on our ability to perform a task. Feeling too tired or too hyper may make it difficult to focus and could lead to encoding or retrieval failures. High levels of stress increase cortisol that, over time, can interfere with our memory functions. On the other hand, an optimal level of physical or emotional arousal may help keep us focused, and help us remember important details of what's happening at the time. Not only would that be evolutionarily advantageous, but it might help us remain engaged and effective at work and school too. **7.4 Memory Distortions and Improvement (p. 244) Self-Test—**1. We often shape, rearrange, or distort our memories due to our need for *logic* and *consistency*. We also edit, summarize, and augment new information and tie it to previously stored LTM memories for the sake of *efficiency*. 2. a. 3. c. 4. d. 5. d. **Connections—**Victims of childhood sexual abuse might unintentionally distort their memories because they may have failed to understand or recognize those behaviors as abuse until adulthood. Adults who abuse children also typically lie and distort their own abusive behaviors as a way of manipulating and confusing the child. Both child and adult victims of sexual assault might shape, rearrange, and distort their memories of the abuse in order to logically explain their past, their adult relationships, and current self-perceptions. **Research Challenge (p. 224)** Question 1: Experimental. Question 2: IV(s) = taking a general photograph, taking a zoomed-in photo, merely observing a museum object, DV = accuracy of memory for the object viewed or photographed. Experimental Group(s) = participants taking a general photograph, participants taking a zoomed-in photograph. Control Group = participants who simply observed the museum object.

## Chapter 8  Thinking, Language, and Intelligence

**8.1 Thinking (p. 258) Self-Test—**1. Cognition refers to the mental activities involved in acquiring, storing, retrieving, and using knowledge. 2. a. 3. b. 4. c. 5. d. **Connections—**Due to the *availability heuristic,* it's all too easy for many people to quickly come up with examples from recent current events or television shows about crimes committed by the mentally ill. The relative availability of such examples can influence our thoughts and feelings (attitudes) about the mentally ill as a group. This is especially unfortunate, given the fact that the vast majority of people with a psychiatric diagnosis are no more likely to commit crimes than anyone else. **8.2 Language (p. 266) Self-Test—**1. Language production begins when we first build words using *phonemes and morphemes,* and then we combine those words into sentences using rules of *grammar,* including *syntax* and *semantics.* 2. d. 3. c. 4. b. 5. d. **Connections—**1. Classical conditioning (CC) involves making associations between reflexive responses and environmental stimuli. CC might be used to teach the meaning of words such as "hot"—if a child reached toward a hot stove burner, the parent would most likely yell something like "No! Hot!" The child would then form an association between the word 'hot' and the loud scolding voice of the parent. Operant conditioning techniques include reinforcement and punishment to increase or decrease voluntary behaviors. Parents unknowingly use reinforcement and shaping when they smile and respond enthusiastically to their baby's attempts to speak (especially that first 'mama' or 'dada'). On the other hand, parents and older siblings may be dismayed to realize that toddlers often repeat inappropriate words learned through observational learning. **8.3 Intelligence (p. 272) Self-Test—**1. Intelligence is formally defined as the global capacity to think rationally, act purposefully, profit from experience, and deal effectively with the environment. 2. a. 3. b. 4. a. 5. b. **Connections—**As you've discovered throughout this text, we do not provide answers for the critical thinking questions because critical thinking is based on using your own critical faculties. In this case, write down your own definition of intelligence and use your critical thinking skills to evaluate if you've employed the CTC of employing precise terms. **8.4 Intelligence Controversies (p. 276) Self-Test—**1. Brain-imaging studies have found a significant correlation between brain size (adjusted for body size) and intelligence, but this is not always the case. Einstein's brain was only average in size. 2. b. 3. a. 4. d. 5. d. **Connections—**Intelligence testing and personality assessment are both criticized for potential cultural bias and diagnostic difficulties. However, intelligence test takers are far less likely than personality test takers to engage in deliberate deception and the social desirability bias. Few people who take IQ tests will want to fake their answers to appear less intelligent than they are, or will adjust their answers to appear more socially desirable. **Research Challenge (pp. 265–266)** Question 1: Descriptive. 2. Archival research.

## Chapter 9  Life Span Development I

**9.1 Studying Development (p. 290) Self-Test—**1. Developmental psychology studies age-related behavior and mental processes from conception to death. 2. d. 3. b. 4. a. 5. c. **Connections—**Using a cross-sectional design, you would select participants across the age range that you are interested in studying. For example, you could choose to study reaction time in groups of people who are 20, 30, 40 and 50 years of age. The study would occur within the same time period, such as during the month of May in 2018. Within this one month time period, you would compare the results for each age group to see if there were age-related differences in reaction time. In contrast, with a longitudinal design, you would start with a group of 20-year-old participants and measure their reaction times at that age. Then you would need to wait 10 years and again measure reaction times when the participants are 30 years old, and then repeat the process again when the participants were 40- and 50-years old. It would take 30 years to collect all of the data required to compare reaction times across the age span of 20 to 50 years using a longitudinal method. **9.2 Physical Development (p. 295) Self-Test—**1. Behavioral genetics is the study of the relative effects of heredity and the environment on behavior and mental processes. 2. b. 3. b. 4. c. 5. d. **Connections—**One example of dangerous risk-taking—riding a skateboard over barbed wire—could be explained in part by the slower maturing prefrontal cortex of the adolescent brain. In Ch. 2 you learned that the frontal lobes are responsible for higher functions like reasoning, initiative, motivation, impulse control, and emotional behavior. The relative lack of maturity in this brain region may make it more difficult for the adolescent to 'think through' the consequences of behaviors and therefore to act impulsively, which may lead to risky behaviors. **9.3 Cognitive Development (p. 306) Self-Test—**1. c. 2. Assimilation in Piaget's theory is the incorporation (assimilation) of new information into existing schemas. In contrast, accommodation is the process of adjusting (accommodating) existing schemas to incorporate new information. 3. b. 4. c. 5. d. **Connections**—During Piaget's first sensorimotor stage the child uses his or her senses and motor skills to explore and develop cognitively, which would involve the motor cortex of the frontal lobes and the somatosensory cortex of the parietal lobe. In addition to the involvement of the frontal lobes in generalized thinking, one of the chief developments during the preoperational stage is that of language, which is handled in Broca's area of the lower-left frontal lobe and Wernicke's area in the upper part of the left temporal lobe. Piaget's last two stages, concrete operational and formal operational, involve all parts of the brain, but primarily the frontal lobes. **9.4 Social-Emotional Development (p. 314) Self-Test**—1. a. 2. c. 3. c. 4. Mary = anxious/avoidant, Bob = anxious/ambivalent, Rashelle = securely attached. 5. In Baumrind's permissive-neglectful style, parents make few demands, with little structure or monitoring (low C). They also show little interest or emotional support and may be actively rejecting (low W). In the permissive-indulgent style, parents set few limits or demands (low C), but are highly involved and emotionally connected (high W). Parents with an authoritarian style are rigid and punitive (high C), but low on warmth and responsiveness (low W). Finally, parents who are authoritative generally set and enforce firm limits (high C), while being highly involved, tender, and emotionally supportive (high W). **Connections**—Both the permissive-neglectful and permissive-indulgent parent makes few demands and little or no monitoring of the child, so they're unlikely to use any punishments. However, in response to misbehavior (such as throwing a temper tantrum when a parent says 'No' to candy for dinner), the permissive-indulgent parent may give in to the child's demands simply to make the child happy. This would be an example of positive reinforcement of the child's misbehavior, so he or she is likely to act out again in the future. This parent has also been negatively reinforced because the child probably stopped his or her tantrum and is now happily eating candy for dinner. In contrast, the authoritative parent sets rules and expects age-appropriate behavior for the child. This parent is also warm and caring, and explains expectations to the child. In this same scenario, the authoritative parent may ignore the tantrum (neither reinforcement nor punishment) un-

til the child is calm or perhaps put the child in a time out (negative punishment—e.g., taking away social interaction or freedom). This parent might then hug the child (positive reinforcement for calming down) and explain why candy is not appropriate for dinner. The authoritative parent might later offer candy for dessert after the child eats all of his or her dinner (positive reinforcement). **Research Challenge (p. 291)** Question 1: Descriptive. Question 2: Case study.

## Chapter 10    Life Span Development II

**10.1 Moral Development (p. 325) Self-Test**—1. Morality is the ability to take the perspective of, or empathize with, others and to distinguish right from wrong. 2. The preconventional level. 3. c. 4. b. 5. c. **Connections**—Like Kohlberg's Stage 3 and the conventional level, in which morality is based on being nice and gaining approval, normative social influence is conforming out of a need to be liked, accepted, and approved of by others. In Kohlberg's Stage 4, morality is based on following societal laws, which is somewhat similar to people conforming due to informational social influence. In both cases, individuals look to others when they make moral decisions or conform out of their need for information and direction. In Kohlberg's postconventional level, individuals develop personal standards for right and wrong. In sharp contrast, people decide to conform to their reference groups because they like, admire, or want to be like them. **10.2 Personality Development (p. 328) Self-Test**—1. Temperament is generally defined as an individual's innate disposition or behavioral style and characteristic emotional response. 2. c. 3. c. 4. (a) Marcos=trust versus mistrust, (b) Ann=identity versus role confusion, (c) Teresa =initiative versus guilt, (d) George=ego integrity versus despair. **Connections**—1. *Nature or nurture:* The basis of personality, temperament, is a biological predisposition to behave and respond to the world in certain ways. These in-born tendencies interact with the child's experiences and environment (nurture) to shape personality development. *Stages or continuity:* Continuity of personality traits can be expected from the biological basis of temperament. Other than Erikson's eight psychosocial stages, there are no widely accepted stage theories of personality development. *Stability or change:* Having biologically-based temperamental characteristics are very likely to influence us throughout our lives, lending some continuity to certain personality traits. Life events though might have very dramatic effects on our personality development as well. A very shy child who

has a supportive family and lives in a benign environment may grow up to be very confident and comfortable in new situations. 2. Attachment theory and Erikson's psychosocial theory both seek to explain social and emotional development. The basis of each theory is trust between a caregiver and an infant. Successful resolution of both attachment and Erikson's Stage 1 depends on emotionally responsive individuals who support the child's need to explore the word while providing a secure base. Both theories emphasize the important of social relationships in healthy development and the continuity of positive early relationships into adult relationships. **10.3 Neurodevelopmental Disorders (p. 331) Self-Test**—1. c. 2. ADHD is characterized by a pattern of inattention and/or hyperactivity-impulsivity. 3. a. 4. b. 5. c. **Connections**—The criteria of *danger* is the least applicable to ADHD since sufferers are generally not a danger to themselves or others. The individual's inattention and hyperactivity-impulsivity are somewhat *deviant* from societal norms, but the best two criteria are probably *distress* and *dysfunction*. Individuals with ADHD typically suffer significant personal distress and their disorder generally interferes with their daily functioning. **10.4 Challenges of Adulthood (p. 335) Self-Test**—1. c. 2. b. 3. Many victims stay in abusive relationships because the abuse is cyclical and escalating. Second, abuse is difficult to identify and report. Third, the victim has mixed feelings. And, fourth, victims are often financially or physically dependent on the abuser. 4. b. 5. (a) bargaining, (b) denial, (c) acceptance, (d) anger, (e) depression. **Connections**—Victims might stay in abusive relationships due to groupthink's antecedent conditions, such as insulation of the group from outside influences, a directive leader (the abuser), and high stress from external threats (financial and physical insecurity). As in groupthink, they also might stay because they fail to survey alternative courses of action or to develop contingency plans. **Research Challenge (p. 341)** Question 1: Experimental. Question 2: IV(1) = age (younger versus older adults). IV(2) = photographs with positive and negative themes. DV=brain activity measured by fMRI scans. No mention of a control group. Also no mention of random assignment, which means it may be a quasi-experimental design.

## Chapter 11    Gender and Human Sexuality

**11.1 Studying Human Sexuality (p. 353) Self-Test**—1. During the Victorian Period, it was believed that masturbation led to blindness, impotence, acne, and insanity, whereas nocturnal emissions supposedly were linked to brain damage and death. 2. d. 3. d. 4. b. 5. c. **Connections**—One of the biggest potential drawbacks to survey data on sexuality is honesty. Participants may not want to disclose what they consider to be embarrassing, private or socially unacceptable behaviors or attitudes. The tendency to over-report "good behaviors" and to under-report "bad behaviors" is aptly named the *social desirability* response. Another possible concern is *sampling bias*. If the participants are not representative of the population as a whole, the data may not tell us much about normative sexual attitudes and behaviors. For example, if the survey participants are all traditional-aged college students, then we may get data that suggests certain sexual behaviors (such as short-term sexual encounters) are more commonly practiced than we might if the participant pool was selected from mid-day shoppers at a suburban mall. **11.2 Sexual Identity (p. 356) Self-Test**—1. The term *gender* refers to the sociocultural supposed differences between men and women, whereas *sex* refers to the biological differences between men and women, as well as physical activities such as masturbation and intercourse. 2. d. 3. b. 4. a. 5. c. **Connections**—Piaget's schemas can be considered 'mental blueprints' that help us to understand and organize our experiences. Gender schema theory suggests that children actively observe, interpret and judge the world around them. As children process this information, they create internal rules governing correct gender roles for boys and girls that form the basis for gender schemas for how they should act. **11.3 Sexual Behavior (p. 364) Self-Test**—1. a. 2. c. 3. c. 4. d. 5. Sexual prejudice is a negative attitude toward an individual because of her or his sexual orientation. The older, outdated term of *homophobia* is no longer recommended, in part, because it implies an individual pathology. In contrast, *sexual prejudice* reflects the fact that, like all forms of prejudice, it is socially constructed. **Connections**—People learn sexual prejudice like they do all attitudes, primarily through classical conditioning, operant conditioning, and observational learning. Sexual prejudice also helps justify and perpetuate a social order that benefits the heterosexual community—giving them more of the limited resources. Some people redirect their aggression toward members of the LGBTQ community making them convenient scapegoats. Sexual prejudice also serves as a convenient mental shortcut that

simplifies the complex social world by creating ingroups (heterosexuals) and outgroups (the LBGTQ community). **11.4 Sex Problems (p. 367) Self-Test**—1. A paraphilic disorder is any of a group of psychosexual disorders involving disturbing and repetitive sexual fantasies, urges, or behaviors that cause distress or impairment to the person and/orharm or risk of harm to others. 2. b. 3. d. 4. a. 5. c. **Connections**—Both operant conditioning and observational learning contribute to our understanding of what types of sexual behavior are expected of men and women. Our media is saturated with images of male-female sexuality (less so with same sex pairs) that provide us with models to observe all of the socially proscribed sexual scripts and the double-standard that encourages male sexuality while discouraging female sexuality. We may also observe through movies or television what happens to the person who fails to conform to society's expectations. Often this is the person who "doesn't get the girl (or guy)" and must transform themselves in order to gain a partner. Through operant conditioning and observational learning, we also internalize the expectations for our gender roles and act in ways that are most likely to be reinforced or rewarded by potential mates. Perhaps because there are fewer models of same sex behaviors, many same sex partners report greater equality and less stereotypical gender roles within those relationships. **11.5 Sex and Modern Life (p. 376) Self-Test**—1. Suggestions for counseling parents and other caregivers about avoiding child sexual abuse include: presenting sexual information to both male and female children in concrete terms and using age-appropriate language; teaching a child the difference between "okay" and "not okay" touches; and recognizing that abusers are most often family members, friends, or trusted people in positions of authority. 2. d. 3. c. 4. c. 5. b. **Connections**—Biologically women are subject to greater cyclical, hormonal changes than are men, which might contribute to the females' increased vulnerability to depression. Childbearing is another biological factor that carries with it not only physical, but psychosocial, challenges too. Psychosocial factors likely also contribute to higher depression in women. Examples might include increased risk for sexual violence, male/female differences in communication, traditional gender roles for women, sexual scripts and double standards that restrict freedom of expression, financial inequality, increased vulnerability to domestic violence and the

burdens of caregiving. **Research Challenge (pp. 357–358)** Question 1: Descriptive. Question 2: Archival. **Research Challenge (p. 372)** Question 1: Descriptive and correlational. Question 2: Survey/Interview. Positive correlation between political affiliation and sexual behavior.

## Chapter 12   Motivation and Emotion

**12.1 Theories of Motivation (p. 389) Self-Test**—1. Motivation is the set of factors that activate, direct, and maintain behavior, usually toward some goal. 2. d. 3. b. 4. d. 5. b. **Connections**—Answers will vary based on personal experience. **12.2 Motivation and Behavior (p. 394) Self-Test**—1. Biological factors (the stomach, biochemistry, the brain) and psychosocial factors (stimulus cues and cultural conditioning) both have significant effects on hunger and eating. 2. d. 3. a. 4. c. 5. c. **Connections**—At home and at school, most of us received our meals according to a schedule. Our awareness of this schedule developed over time and we came to associate a specific time of day (such as noon) with a meal. In classical conditioning terms, the hour of noon became a conditioned stimulus (CS) and triggered a conditioned response (CR)—feelings of hunger, thoughts about what to eat, and even salivation—that motivates us to get some lunch. **12.3 Components and Theories of Emotion (p. 403) Self-Test**—1. The three basic components of all emotions are *biological arousal* (e.g., heart pounding), *cognitive* (thoughts, values, and expectations), and *behavioral expressions* (e.g., smiles, frowns, running). 2. b. 3. a. 4. d. 5. a. **Connections**—Given that Botox injections inhibit the facial muscles involved in frowning, and that these same muscles are used for expressions of sadness, fear, surprise, disgust and anger, a therapist who has Botox injections might be less able to unconsciously imitate or pickup on the subtle facial expressions or sudden change of moods in their clients. This inhibition may, in turn, reduce the therapist's sensitive understanding and empathy for his or her clients. **12.4 Experiencing Emotions (p. 411) Self-Test**—1. c. 2. *Display rules* are a social group's informal norms that govern how, when, and where to express emotions. 3. d. 4. a. 5. d. **Connections**—Heuristics are simple rules or strategies that provide short cuts in decision-making. Emotions can serve as heuristics by providing us with a 'gut feeling' about which choice might make us happier. We don't need to go through all of the pros and cons of each option (although that might be more logical) if we experience strong emotion that guides us towards one of the choices over the other. Current moods can also influence our decisions. For example, we may be more likely to be generous and agree to a request for a charitable donation when in a good mood. **Research Challenge (p. 407)** Question 1: Experimental. Question 2: IV1 = photographs of women. IV2 = gender. IV3 = instructions vs. non-instruction. DV1 = sexual interest. DV2 = rape supportive attitude. Experimental group = half of the participants who were given instructions for nonverbal emotional cues. Control group = no instructions regarding nonverbal emotional cues. No mention of random assignment, which means it may be a quasi-experimental design.

## Chapter 13   Personality

**13.1    Psychoanalytic/Psychodynamic Theories (p. 423) Self-Test**—1. Personality is defined as a unique and relatively stable pattern of thoughts, feelings, and actions. 2. b. 3. d. 4. c. 5. c. **Connections**—Given that personality involves a unique and relatively stable pattern of thoughts, feelings, and actions it could be considered disordered or problematic when those patterns are inflexible or maladaptive. For example, a person who experiences severe instability in emotions, relationships, and self-image, along with impulsive and self-destructive behaviors (*borderline personality disorder*) is likely to have difficulties at home, school, work and in relationships with others. Similarly, someone with personality characteristics characterized by egocentrism and a lack of remorse or empathy for others (*antisocial personality disorder*) would also experience serious problems in their interpersonal relationships. **13.2 Trait Theories (p. 430) Self-Test**—1. Factor analysis is a statistical technique in which large arrays of data are grouped into more basic units (factors). 2. a. 3. d. 4. e. 5. c. **Connections**—The *Five Factor Model* (FFM) of personality includes Openness, Conscientiousness, Extraversion, Agreeableness, and Neuroticism. The characteristics of positive affect and optimism in Chapter 3 seem to share many of the same traits as the FFM traits of openness and agreeableness. The characteristic of locus of control in Chapter 3 is probably most closely aligned with the FFM trait of conscientiousness. Having an internal locus of control would probably mean someone is more organized, dependable, careful, and disciplined. **13.3 Humanistic Theories (p. 435) Self-Test**—1. Humanistic

approaches to personality focus on each person's internal feelings, thoughts, and sense of basic worth. 2. c. 3. c. 4. d. 5. c. **Connections**—According to Rogers, when an individual has experienced significant *conditional love* and acceptance, that person has learned that some aspects of their core being are unacceptable or unlovable. An atmosphere of *unconditional positive regard* would be one in which the individual comes to realize that their actions are separate from their inner selves. A client-centered therapist can help the client understand and recognize this, while encouraging the client to control their behavior so that they can develop a healthy self-concept and healthy relationships with others. The therapist would avoid making evaluative statements such as "You did the right thing" that imply that the client is being judged or needs the therapist's approval. When the client is treated with unconditional caring from the therapist, humanists believe that they become better able to value themselves in a similar way. **13.4 Social-Cognitive Theories (p. 438) Self-Test**—1. Bandura believed that our feelings of self-efficacy, or learned expectations of success in a given situation, play an important role in determining whether or not we succeed and reach our goals. It's basically another term for self-confidence. 2. d. 3. b. 4. b. 5. c. **Connections**—Interaction is central to Bandura's concept of *reciprocal determinism*, which suggests personal factors, the environment, and the individual's behavior all work as interacting reciprocal determinants. Interaction is also at the heart of *rational-emotive behavior therapy* (REBT). Ellis believed that personal factors (irrational beliefs) interact with activating events in the environment, and the emotional consequences. His REBT focuses on eliminating these irrational beliefs through logic, confrontation, and direct examination. **13.5 Biological Theories (p. 442) Self-Test**—1. Hans Eysenck, was one of the first trait theorist to propose that personality traits are biologically based—at least in part. 2. d. 3. a. 4. d. 5. b. **Connections**—Research has found a consistent relationship between sensation seeking and neurochemicals such as monoamine oxidase, an enzyme that regulates levels of neurotransmitters such as dopamine. Research suggests that dopamine is correlated with novelty seeking, impulsivity and drug abuse. According to the arousal theory, behaviors that arouse and activate the pleasure (dopamine) pathways in the brain may make sensation seeking

more likely in people with lower thresholds of these neurochemicals. **13.6 Personality Assessment (p. 444) Self-Test**—1. During the 1800s, phrenologists identified personality traits by measuring the bumps on someone's skull, and then compare those measurements with a chart that associated certain bumps with specific personality characteristics. 2. a. 3. a. 4. d. 5. b. **Connections**—Both intelligence and personality are most often measured with objective tests, like the Stanford-Binet and Wechsler Adult Intelligence Scale (WAIS) to measure intelligence, and the Minnesota Multiphasic Personality Inventory (MMPI) to measure personality. Intelligence tests are primarily different from personality assessment because they rely almost exclusively on objective tests, whereas personality testing can be done with interviews/observations and projective tests, as well as objective tests. **Research Challenge (p. 433)** Question 1: Descriptive and correlational. Question 2: Descriptive = naturalistic observation. Correlational = positive (gorilla life expectancy was positively correlated with the personality trait of extraversion).

## Chapter 14   Psychological Disorders

**14.1 Studying Psychological Disorders (p. 458) Self-Test**—1. The *Diagnostic and Statistical Manual of Mental Disorders (DSM)* provides detailed descriptions and classifications of psychological disorders. It is used for standardized diagnosis and improved communication among professionals and between professionals and patients. 2. a. 3. b. 4. Refer to Figure 14.3. 5. d. **Connections**—Answers will vary. If you chose medication, some factors to consider include cost, availability, effectiveness, and side effects. In contrast, with psychological treatments you might consider availability, cost, time commitment, and effectiveness. **14.2 Anxiety Disorders (p. 467) Self-Test**—1. Refer to Figure 14. 5. 2. a. 3. c. 4. b. 5. c. **Connections**—Child abductions by strangers are relatively rare, yet many parents still experience considerable anxiety over the possibility of it happening to their child. Social learning through the media may be the most likely culprit for this exaggerated fear. When child abductions do occur, they are headline news on all forms of media, 24 hours a day. Follow-up stories on prevention and rehashing of very old cases also fill the news channels. This near constant focus on the topic may create an unrealistic fear in parents about the probability that this could happen to their own child.

**14.3 Depressive and Bipolar Disorders (p. 472) Self-Test**—1. Depressive disorders involve a long lasting depressed mood without a clear trigger. In contrast, bipolar disorder refers to individuals who alternate between periods of depression and mania (characterized by hyperactivity and poor judgment). 2. b. 3. a. 4. d. 5. c. **Connections**— An internal locus of control means that you believe you can influence or control things that happen in your life. Someone with an internal locus of control is likely to keep trying in the face of challenges. When previous experiences with negative events have shown individuals that they do not have control, they may develop a learned sense of helplessness and may fail to act to escape. Due to their learned experiences of lack of control, people with learned helplessness may not develop an internal locus of control. Because they have learned that their efforts will have little or no impact, these individuals may be especially vulnerable to stress and depression when negative events happen in their lives. **14.4 Schizophrenia (p. 476) Self-Test**—1. Schizophrenia is a group of disorders, each characterized by a disturbance in perception (including hallucinations), language, thought (including delusions), emotions, and/or behavior. 2. b. 3. c. 4. a. 5. b. **Connections**—People with schizophrenia may have difficulty with the filtering and selection of incoming sensory information. They may focus too much on some sensations and too little on others. Thus, sensory information is jumbled and distorted, creating confusion about what is really happening. Disruptions in sensation may explain why people with schizophrenia experience hallucinations— false sensory perceptions that occur without external stimuli, such as hearing voices or feeling as if there are bugs under the skin. **14.5 Other Disorders (p. 480) Self-Test**—1. Obsessive-compulsive disorder (OCD) involves persistent, unwanted, fearful thoughts (obsessions) and/or irresistible urges to perform an act or repeated rituals (compulsions), which help relieve the anxiety created by the obsession. 2. a. 3. d. 4. b. 5. c. **Connections**—As discussed in Chapter 7, false memories are well-established phenomena that are relatively common and easy to create, whereas repressed memories (especially of childhood sexual abuse) is a complex and controversial topic. False memories also play a role in this chapter because some experts believe many cases of dissociative identity disorder (DID), which involves the presence of two or more

distinct personality systems in the same individual, are faked or result from false memories, and/or an unconscious need to please a therapist. **14.6 Gender and Cultural Effects (p. 484) Self-Test**—1. Men and women differ in their rates and experiences of depression. Women tend to obsess and ruminate on their depressive thoughts and emotions, whereas men tend to suppress their depressive thoughts and emotions. 2. d. 3. a. 4. b. 5. b. **Connections**—As discussed in Chapter 1, ethnocentrism may occur in general research when experimenters assume that behaviors typical of their own culture are shared in all cultures, and this bias can skew their research results. Because most research on psychological disorders (this chapter) originate and are conducted primarily in Western cultures, this type of restricted sampling can lead to a limited and ethnocentric understanding of psychological disorders. **Research Challenge (p. 474)** Question 1: Experimental. Question 2: IV = brain injections to induce injuries. DV = length of time to solve the maze. Experimental Group = rats who received the brain injections. Control Group = rats who did not receive the brain injections. **Research Challenge (p. 485)** Question 1: Descriptive. Question 2: Survey/Interview.

## Chapter 15 Therapy

**15.1 Talk Therapies (p. 496) Self-Test**— 1. These therapies differ significantly, yet they're often grouped together as "talk therapies" because they emphasize communication between the therapist and client, as opposed to the behavioral and biomedical therapies. 2. c. 3. d. 4. d. 5. b. **Connections**—Both theories focus on the interpretation of an event as the guiding influence on the emotion experienced. Although the two-factor theory of emotion also includes physiological arousal as a part of the process, the key to determining the label applied to that arousal is the person's expectations and interpretations of what is happening. In REBT, the theory goes further in labeling the interpretations as potentially faulty or irrational and incorporates a way to challenge the interpretation and ultimately change the emotion experienced. **15.2 Behavior Therapies (p. 505) Self-Test**—1. Behavior therapists believe that psychological disorders are primarily caused by inappropriate conditioning and learning. Therefore, their major goals are to reduce or eliminate those maladaptive behaviors and to increase adaptive ones. 2. c. 3. d. 4. b. 5. d. **Connections**—Two of the main ethical

concerns with using behavior therapies to change "maladaptive" behaviors are *voluntary participation* and *informed consent*. Can a deeply depressed or suicidal person volunteer or truly consent to this treatment? Probably not, but if someone is so deeply depressed that he or she is considering suicide, treatment without voluntary participation or informed consent is probably far less harmful than possible ethical violations. Furthermore, aversion therapy in classical conditioning for unwanted or self-injurious behaviors, usually involves applying pain, shocks or some other aversive consequences. Is this ethical? In sum, behavior therapies include several ethical considerations, but supporters typically emphasize that aversion therapies are generally treatments of last resort, used only when no other options have proven effective. **15.3 Biomedical Therapies (p. 510) Self-Test**—1. Psychiatrists are generally the only professionals who use biomedical (biological) therapies. However, in some states, licensed psychologists can prescribe certain medications, and they often work with clients receiving biomedical therapies. 2. b. 3. b. 4. c. 5. d. **Connections**—Stereotypes about biomedical therapies develop in much the same way as other stereotypes. For example, characters with mental illnesses portrayed in television shows or movies are often shown as helpless victims forced to take drugs or to submit to barbaric treatments, such as ECT and psychosurgery. Because the general public is constantly exposed to these distorted portrayals and may not have the opportunity to personally observe biomedical treatments, or to take a course in psychology, these stereotypes persist. **15.4 Psychotherapy in Perspective (p. 516) Self-Test**—1. Clinicians who use eclectic psychotherapy regularly borrow freely from various therapies to best suit their clients and the situation. 2. a. 3. d. 4. c. 5. c. **Connections**—Answers will vary. But here is an example. The experiment involves comparing two forms of therapy for the treatment of major depression. Participants will be adults between the ages of 25-40 who meet DSM criteria for major depressive disorder (MDD). Participants will be randomly assigned to weekly therapy sessions (either psychodynamic or cognitive-behavioral) with licensed psychologists who specialize in that form of therapy. At each session, participants will report their level of depressive symptoms using a standard depression inventory. At the end of 4 months of weekly therapy sessions, depressive symptom levels between the two treatment groups will be compared to see if one form of therapy was more effective at reducing symptoms of MDD. The independent variable (IV) is the type of therapy received; the dependent variable (DV) is depressive symptoms. **Research Challenge (p. 518)** Question 1: Experimental. Question 2: IV = varying amounts of training or instructions, including how to watch movies. DV = divorce rate after 3 years. Experimental Group(s) = the three "intervention" groups. Control Group = couples who received no training or instructions.

## Chapter 16    Social Psychology

**16.1 Social Cognition (p. 533) Self-Test—** 1. Prejudice is a learned, unjustified negative attitude toward members of a particular group, and it's composed of three ABC components—affective, behavioral, and cognitive. Discrimination is part of the behavioral component because it involves actions toward members of a group. 2. a. 3. Affect (feelings), Behavior (actions), and Cognitions (thoughts/beliefs). 4. b. 5. c. **Connections**—Answers will vary. But we sincerely hope there are many behavioral changes and concepts, ideas and topics from this course that you will find useful and applicable in your own life—and that you might attribute to your first psychology course! That's what *Psychology in Action* is all about. **16.2 Social Influence (p. 545) Self-Test—**1. Conformity is defined as a

change in thoughts, feelings, or actions because of real or imagined group pressure. In contrast, obedience involves going along with direct commands, usually from someone in a position of authority. 2. c. 3. d. 4. b. 5. c. **Connections**—Teenagers would be in Erikson's Identity stage, in which they are trying out and committing to different aspects of who they are. As part of that process, teens often take on different attitudes and perspectives than those of their parents and begin to identify more with peers. This makes peers—especially 'popular' teens–an important and influential reference group in this stage of development. Research suggests that if popular teens have a positive or negative attitude towards drinking, other teens in that school will tend to have a matching attitude. **16.3 Social Relations (p. 554) Self-Test—**1. Making a joke or even just showing sympathy for an opponent are both effective ways to reduce aggression because they introduce incompatible responses. It's difficult to laugh or feel sympathy for someone and still be aggressive. 2. a. 3. d. 4. b. 5. a. **Connections**—There are several examples of how the BPS model helps explain interpersonal attraction. From the biological perspective, evolution suggests that we are attracted to characteristics that indicate better health, genes, and fertility. Another biological factor, the body chemical oxytocin, is known to be important in forming both parental and romantic attachments. Next, looking at

it from a psychological perspective, we're most attracted to people who are similar to us—who share our interested and attitudes, as well as social and ethnic backgrounds. In short, we like people who think, feel, and behave like us (to a certain extent, anyway!). Finally, from a social approach, there are numerous cultural differences in certain aspects of what is considered attractive (for example, preferences for body size and shape). In addition, proximity (a major factor in attraction) is also socially influenced—where we live, work and go to school all have an impact on whom we meet and see frequently. **Research Challenge (p. 543)** Question 1: Experimental. Question 2: IV = conversations using deep-canvassing technique about being transgender or recycling, DV = reduction in transphobia. Experimental Group = those that discussed transgender issues. Control Group = those that discussed recycling. **Research Challenge (p. 561)** Question 1: Experimental. Question 2: IV = normal morning routine versus savoring (personal or relational), DV = emotional states and relationship satisfaction. Experimental Group(s) = wives who were asked to personally savor and wives who were asked to relationally savor. Control Group = wives who were asked to think about and mentally replay their normal morning routine.

**Abnormal behavior** Patterns of behaviors, thoughts, or emotions considered pathological (diseased or disordered) for one or more of these four reasons: deviance, dysfunction, distress, and/or danger.

**Absolute threshold** The minimum amount of stimulation necessary to consciously detect a stimulus 50% of the time.

**Accommodation (in developmental psychology)** According to Piaget, the process of adjusting (accommodating) existing schemas to incorporate new information.

**Accommodation (in sensation and perception)** The process by which the eye's ciliary muscles change the shape (thickness) of the lens so that light is focused on the retina; adjustment of the eye's lens permitting focusing on near and distant objects.

**Acculturative stress** The stress resulting from the many changes and pressures of adapting to a new culture; also known as "culture shock."

**Achievement motivation** The desire to excel, especially in competition with others.

**Acquisition (in classical conditioning)** The process by which learning occurs (is acquired) when an organism involuntarily links a neutral stimulus (NS) with an unconditioned stimulus (US), which in turn elicits the conditioned response (CR).

**Acquisition (in operant conditioning)** The process by which learning occurs (is acquired) when an organism voluntarily links a response with a consequence, such as a reward.

**Action potential** A neural impulse, or brief electrical charge, that carries information along the axon of a neuron; movement is generated when positively charged ions move in and out through channels in the axon's membrane.

**Activation–synthesis theory of dreams** The theory that dreams are a by-product of random, spontaneous stimulation of brain cells during sleep, which the brain combines (synthesizes) into coherent patterns, known as dreams.

**Active listening** A communication technique that requires listening with total attention to what another is saying; techniques include reflecting, paraphrasing, and clarifying what the person says and means.

**Activity theory of aging** A theory holding that successful aging is fostered by a full and active commitment to life.

**Actor–observer effect** The tendency to attribute other people's behavior to dispositional factors, while seeing our own behavior as caused by the situation.

**Acute stress** A short-term state of arousal in response to a perceived threat or challenge that has a definite endpoint.

**Adaptation-level phenomenon** A tendency to judge a new situation or stimulus relative to a neutral, "normal" level based on our previous experiences; we then adapt to this new level, and it becomes the new "normal."

**Adaptation/protection theory of sleep** The theory that sleep evolved to conserve energy and provide protection from predators.

**Addiction** A broad term that describes a compulsive craving for a substance, thing, or activity despite harmful consequences.

**Ageism** A form of prejudice or discrimination based on physical age; similar to racism and sexism in its negative stereotypes.

**Age-related positivity effect** The preference in older adults for positive over negative information and events in attention and memory.

**Aggression** Any behavior intended to cause psychological or physical harm to another individual.

**Agonist** A molecule that binds to a receptor and triggers a response that mimics or enhances a neurotransmitter's effect.

**AIDS (acquired immunodeficiency syndrome)** A disease in which the human immunodeficiency virus (HIV) destroys the immune system's ability to fight other diseases, thus leaving the body vulnerable to a variety of opportunistic infections and cancers.

**Algorithm** A logical, step-by-step procedure that, if followed correctly, will always eventually solve the problem.

**All-or-nothing principle** The principle that a neuron's response to a stimulus is either to fire with a full-strength response or not to fire at all; also known as the all-or-none law.

**Altered state of consciousness (ASC)** A temporary mental state, other than ordinary waking consciousness, that occurs during sleep, dreaming, psychoactive drug use, and hypnosis.

**Altruism** Prosocial behaviors designed to help or benefit others.

**Amygdala** A brain structure near the hippocampus that controls emotions, especially aggression and fear, and the formation of emotional memory; part of the limbic system.

**Androgyny [an-DRAH-juh-nee]** A combination of masculine and feminine characteristics and traits; from the Greek *andro* for "male" and *gyn* for "female."

**Anorexia nervosa** An eating disorder characterized by an obsessive fear of obesity, a need for control, self-imposed starvation, and a severe loss of weight.

**Antagonist** A molecule that binds to a receptor and triggers a response that blocks a neurotransmitter's effect.

**Anterograde amnesia** The inability to form new memories; forward-acting amnesia.

**Antisocial personality disorder (ASPD)** A personality disorder characterized by egocentrism and a lack of conscience, remorse, or empathy for others.

**Anxiety disorder** One of a group of psychological disorders characterized by disabling (uncontrollable and disruptive) fear or anxiety, accompanied by physiological arousal and related behavioral disturbances.

**Applied research** A type of research primarily conducted to solve practical, real-world problems; generally conducted outside the laboratory.

**Approach–approach conflict** A forced choice between two options, both of which have equally desirable characteristics.

**Approach–avoidance conflict** A forced choice involving one option with equally desirable and undesirable characteristics.

**Archetypes** Jung's term for the collective, universal images and patterns, residing in the unconscious, that have symbolic meaning for all people.

**Archival research** A descriptive research technique that studies existing data to find answers to research questions.

**Artificial intelligence (AI)** The scientific field concerned with creating machines that can simulate human thought processes and performance.

**Assertiveness** The behavior of confidently and directly standing up for your rights, or putting forward your views, without infringing on the rights or views of others; striking a balance between passivity and aggression.

**Assimilation** In Piaget's theory, the incorporation (assimilation) of new information into existing schemas.

**Association areas** The "quiet" areas in the cerebral cortex involved in interpreting, integrating, and acting on information processed by other parts of the brain.

**Associative learning** Learning that two events occur or happen together.

**Attachment** A strong emotional bond with special others that endures over time.

**Attention-deficit/hyperactivity disorder (ADHD)** A common developmental disorder characterized by a pattern of inattention and/or hyperactivity-impulsivity.

**Attitude** The learned predisposition to respond positively or negatively to a particular object, person, or event.

**Attribution** The explanations we make about the causes of behaviors or events.

**Audition** The sense or act of hearing.

**Autism spectrum disorder (ASD)** A developmental disorder that begins in early childhood and involves problems with social communication and social interaction, as well as restricted, repetitive patterns of behavior, interests, or activities.

**Automatic processes** Mental activities that require minimal attention and generally have little impact on other activities.

**Autonomic nervous system (ANS)** The subdivision of the peripheral nervous system (PNS) that controls the body's involuntary motor responses; it connects the sensory receptors to the central nervous system (CNS) and the CNS to the smooth muscle, cardiac muscle, and glands.

**Availability heuristic** A cognitive strategy (or shortcut) that estimates the frequency or likelihood of an event based on information that is readily available in our memory.

**Aversion therapy** A type of behavior therapy that pairs an aversive (unpleasant) stimulus with a maladaptive behavior in order to elicit a negative reaction to the target stimulus.

**Avoidance–avoidance conflict** A forced choice between two options, both of which have equally undesirable characteristics.

**Axon** A long, tube-like structure that conveys impulses away from a neuron's cell body toward other neurons or to muscles or glands.

**Basic anxiety** According to Horney, feelings of helplessness and insecurity that adults experience because as children they felt alone and isolated in a hostile environment.

**Basic research** A type of research primarily conducted to advance core scientific knowledge; most often conducted in universities and research laboratories.

**Behavioral genetics** The study of the relative effects of heredity and the environment on behavior and mental processes.

**Behavioral perspective** A modern approach to psychology that emphasizes objective, observable, environmental influences on overt behavior.

**Behavior therapies** A group of therapies that uses learning principles to reduce or eliminate maladaptive behaviors; techniques are based on classical and operant conditioning, along with observational learning.

**Binge-eating disorder (BED)** An eating disorder characterized by recurrent episodes of consuming large amounts of food (bingeing), not followed by purge behaviors.

**Binocular cues** Visual input from two eyes, which allows perception of depth or distance.

**Biological perspective** A modern approach to psychology that focuses on genetics and biological processes.

**Biological preparedness** The built-in (innate) readiness to form associations between certain stimuli and responses.

**Biomedical therapies** A group of therapies designed to alter brain functioning with biological or physical techniques, such as drugs, electroconvulsive therapy, and psychosurgery; also known as biological therapy.

**Biopsychosocial model** An integrative, unifying theme of modern psychology that sees biological, psychological, and social processes as interrelated and interacting influences.

**Bipolar disorder** A psychological disorder characterized by repeated episodes of mania (unreasonable elation, often with hyperactivity) alternating with depression.

**Blind spot** The point at which the optic nerve leaves the eye, which contains no receptor cells for vision—thus creating a "blind spot."

**Borderline personality disorder (BPD)** A psychological disorder characterized by severe instability in emotions, relationships, and self-image, along with impulsive and self-destructive behaviors.

**Bottom-up processing** A type of information processing that starts at the "bottom" with an analysis of smaller features, and then builds on them to create complete perceptions; data-driven processing that moves from the parts to the whole.

**Brainstem** A diffuse, stem-shaped area of the brain, including much of the midbrain, pons, and medulla; responsible for automatic survival functions, such as respiration and heartbeat.

**Bulimia nervosa** An eating disorder characterized by recurrent episodes of consuming large quantities of food (bingeing), followed by self-induced vomiting or laxative use (purging).

**Burnout** A state of physical, mental, and emotional exhaustion resulting from chronic exposure to high levels of stress, with little personal control.

**Bystander effect** A phenomenon in which the greater the number of bystanders, the less likely it is that any one individual will feel responsible for seeking help or giving aid to someone who is in need of help.

**Cannon-Bard theory** A theory proposing that emotions and physiological changes occur simultaneously ("I'm crying and feeling sad at the same time"); in this view, all emotions are physiologically similar.

**Case study** A descriptive research technique involving an in-depth study of a single research participant or a small group of individuals.

**Cataclysmic event** A stressful occurrence that happens suddenly and generally affects many people simultaneously.

**Cell body** The part of a neuron that contains the cell nucleus and other structures that help the neuron carry out its functions; also known as the soma.

**Central nervous system (CNS)** The part of the nervous system consisting of the brain and spinal cord.

**Cerebellum** The hindbrain structure responsible for coordinating fine muscle movement, balance, and some perception and cognition.

**Cerebral cortex** The thin surface layer on the cerebral hemispheres that regulates most complex behavior, including sensations, motor control, and higher mental processes.

**Character** Value judgments about an individual's morals, values, and ethical behaviors.

**Child sexual abuse (CSA)** A sexual act with a child that is intended to provide sexual gratification for the perpetrator; it includes both physical acts and noncontact exploitation.

**Chromosome** A threadlike molecule of DNA (deoxyribonucleic acid) that carries genetic information.

**Chronic pain** Continuous or recurrent pain over a period of six months or longer.

**Chronic stress** A continuous state of arousal in which demands are perceived as greater than the inner and outer resources available for dealing with them.

**Chunking** A memory technique involving grouping separate pieces of information into larger, more manageable units (or chunks).

**Circadian rhythm** The internal biological clock governing bodily activities, such as the sleep/wake cycle, that occur on a 24- to 25-hour cycle. (*Circa* means "about," and *dies* means "day.")

**Classical conditioning** Learning that develops through involuntarily paired associations; a previously neutral stimulus (NS) is paired (associated) with an unconditioned stimulus (US) to elicit a conditioned response (CR).

**Client-centered therapy** A form of talk therapy, developed by Carl Rogers, that provides a warm, supportive atmosphere that encourages self-actualization and improves the client's self-concept; techniques include empathy, unconditional positive regard, genuineness, and active listening.

**Cochlea [KOK-lee-uh]** The fluid-filled, coiled tube in the inner ear that contains the receptors for hearing.

**Coding** The process in which neural impulses travel by different routes to different parts of the brain; it allows us to detect various physical stimuli as distinct sensations.

**Cognition** The mental activities involved in acquiring, storing, retrieving, and using knowledge.

**Cognitive-behavior therapy (CBT)** A type of therapy, developed by Aaron Beck, that combines cognitive therapy (changing faulty thinking) with behavior therapy (changing maladaptive behaviors).

**Cognitive dissonance** The unpleasant psychological tension we experience after noticing contradictions between our thoughts, feelings, and/or actions.

**Cognitive map** A mental image of a three-dimensional space that an organism has navigated.

**Cognitive offloading** The use of external resources to reduce the information processing requirements of a task in order to reduce the cognitive demand.

**Cognitive perspective** A modern approach to psychology that focuses on the mental processes used in thinking, knowing, remembering, and communicating.

**Cognitive restructuring** A therapeutic process of learning to identify, dispute, and replace irrational or maladaptive thoughts with more realistic and positive beliefs.

**Cognitive–social learning theory** A theory that emphasizes the roles of thinking and social learning.

**Cognitive therapies** A group of talk therapies that focuses on changing faulty, distorted thoughts (cognitions); based on the assumption that thoughts intervene between events and reactions.

**Cognitive view of dreams** The perspective that dreaming is a type of information processing that helps us organize and interpret our everyday experiences.

**Collective unconscious** Jung's name for the deepest layer of the unconscious, which contains universal memories and archetypes shared by all people due to our common ancestral past.

**Comorbidity** The co-occurrence of two or more disorders in the same person at the same time, as when a person suffers from both depression and alcoholism.

**Concrete operational stage** Piaget's third stage of cognitive development (roughly ages 7 to 11), in which the child can think logically about concrete, tangible objects and events.

**Conditioned emotional response (CER)** An emotion, such as fear, that becomes a learned, conditioned response to a previously neutral stimulus (NS), such as a loud noise.

**Conditioned response (CR)** A learned reaction to a conditioned stimulus (CS) that occurs after previous repeated pairings with an unconditioned stimulus (US).

**Conditioned stimulus (CS)** A previously neutral stimulus (NS) that, after repeated pairings with an unconditioned stimulus (US), comes to elicit a conditioned response (CR).

**Conditioned taste aversion** A classically conditioned dislike for, and avoidance of, a specific taste when followed by nausea; normally occurs after only one association.

**Conduction hearing loss** A type of hearing loss that results from damage to the mechanical system that conducts sound waves to the cochlea; also called conduction deafness.

**Cones** Retinal receptor cells with high sensitivity to color and detail, but low sensitivity in dim light.

**Confirmation bias** The tendency to prefer information that confirms our preexisting positions or beliefs and to ignore or discount contradictory evidence; also known as remembering the "hits" and ignoring the "misses."

**Conflict** A forced choice between two or more incompatible goals or impulses.

**Conformity** A change in thoughts, feelings, or actions because of real or imagined group pressure.

**Confounding variable** An extraneous factor or variable that, if not controlled, could confuse, or confound, the effects of the independent variable (IV) and contaminate the results of an experiment; also known as the third-variable problem in correlational research.

**Conscious** In Freudian terms, thoughts or motives that a person is currently aware of.

**Consciousness** Our awareness of ourselves and our environment.

**Conservation** According to Piaget, the understanding that certain physical characteristics (such as volume) remain unchanged, even though appearances may change; a hallmark of Piaget's concrete operational stage.

**Consolidation** The process by which LTM memories become stable in the brain; neural changes that take place when a memory is formed.

**Constructive process** The process of organizing and shaping information during encoding, storage, and retrieval of memories.

**Consummate love** Sternberg's strongest and most enduring type of love, based on a balanced combination of intimacy, passion, and commitment.

**Continuous reinforcement** Reinforcement in which every correct response is reinforced.

**Control group** Participants in an experiment who do NOT receive the treatment under study—that is, those who are NOT exposed to the independent variable (IV).

**Controlled processes** Mental activities that require focused attention and generally interfere with other ongoing activities.

**Conventional morality** Kohlberg's second level of moral development, in which moral judgments are based on compliance with the rules and values of society.

**Convergence** A binocular depth cue in which the eyes turn inward (or converge) to fixate on an object.

**Convergent thinking** A type of thinking that seeks the single best solution to a problem.

**Corpus callosum** A bundle of neural fibers that connects the brain's two hemispheres.

**Correlational research** A type of research that examines whether and how two or more variables change together; designed to meet the goal of *prediction*.

**Correlation coefficient** A number from −1.00 to +1.00 that indicates the direction and strength of the relationship between two variables.

**Creativity** The ability to produce original, appropriate, and valued outcomes in a novel way; consists of three characteristics—originality, fluency, and flexibility.

**Critical period** A specific time during which an organism must experience certain stimuli in order to develop properly in the future.

**Critical thinking** The process of objectively evaluating, comparing, analyzing, and synthesizing information.

**Cross-sectional design** In developmental psychology, a research technique that measures individuals of various ages at one point in time and provides information about age differences.

**Crystallized intelligence (gc)** The store of knowledge and skills gained through experience and education; gc tends to increase over the life span.

**Debriefing** A discussion procedure conducted at the end of an experiment or study; participants are informed of the study's design and purpose, possible misconceptions are clarified, questions are answered, and explanations are provided for any possible deception.

**Defense mechanisms** Freud's term for the strategies the ego uses to reduce anxiety by unconsciously distorting reality.

**Deindividuation** The reduced self-consciousness, inhibition, and personal responsibility that sometimes occurs in a group, particularly when the members feel anonymous.

**Delusion** A false, imaginary belief that persists despite clear evidence to the contrary, such as delusions of grandeur; a symptom associated with psychosis.

**Dendrites** The branching fibers of neurons that receive neural impulses from other neurons and convey impulses toward the cell body.

**Dependent variable (DV)** The variable that is observed and measured for possible change; the factor that is affected by (or dependent on) the independent variable.

**Depressant** A drug that decreases bodily processes and overall responsiveness.

**Depressive disorders** A group of psychological disorders characterized profound and persistent sadness, despair, and/or decreased interest in things that were once pleasurable; moods severe enough to interfere with the ability to function.

**Depth perception** The ability to perceive three-dimensional space and to accurately judge distance.

**Descriptive research** A type of research that systematically observes and records behavior and mental processes without manipulating variables; designed to meet the goal of description.

**Developmental psychology** The study of age-related behavior and mental processes from conception to death.

**Diagnostic and Statistical Manual of Mental Disorders (DSM)** A manual developed by the American Psychiatric Association that is used primarily to classify psychological disorders.

**Diathesis-stress model** An explanation for the cause of certain disorders, such as schizophrenia, which suggests that people inherit a predisposition (or "diathesis") that increases their risk for psychological disorders when exposed to environmental or emotional stress; also known as the stress-vulnerability model.

**Difference threshold** The smallest physical difference between two stimuli that is consciously detectable 50% of the time; also called the *just noticeable difference* (JND).

**Diffusion of responsibility** A phenomenon wherein a person is less likely to take responsibility for acting when others are present.

**Discrimination** An unjustifiable, negative action directed toward members of a group; also the behavioral component of prejudice.

**Discrimination (in classical conditioning)** A learned ability to distinguish (discriminate) between similar stimuli so as NOT to involuntarily respond to a new stimulus as if it were the previously conditioned stimulus (CS); the opposite of generalization.

**Discrimination (in operant conditioning)** A learned ability to distinguish (discriminate) between similar stimuli based on whether responses to the stimuli are reinforced or punished and then to voluntarily respond accordingly; the opposite of generalization.

**Disengagement theory of aging** A theory holding that successful aging is characterized by mutual withdrawal between older people and society.

**Display rules** A set of informal cultural norms that control when, where, and how emotions should be expressed.

**Dissociative disorder** One of a group of psychological disorders characterized by a sudden break (*dissociation*) in conscious awareness, self-identity, and/or memory.

**Dissociative identity disorder (DID)** A psychological disorder characterized by the presence of two or more distinct personality systems (or identities) in the same individual; previously known as multiple personality disorder (MPD).

**Distress** The unpleasant, undesirable stress caused by aversive conditions.

**Distributed practice** A learning strategy in which studying or practice is broken up into a number of short sessions over a period of time; also known as spaced repetition.

**Divergent thinking** A type of thinking that produces many solutions to the same problem.

**DNA** The main constituent of chromosomes found in all living organisms, which transmits hereditary characteristics from parents to children; short for *deoxyribonucleic acid*.

**Double-blind study** An experimental technique in which both the researcher and the participants are unaware of (blind to) who is in the experimental group and who is in the control group.

**Double standard** The beliefs, values, and norms that subtly encourage male sexuality and discourage female sexuality.

**Dream analysis** In psychoanalysis, interpretation of the underlying true meaning of dreams to reveal unconscious processes.

**Drive-reduction theory** The theory that motivation begins with a physiological need (a lack or deficiency) that elicits a drive toward behavior that will satisfy the original need; once the need is met, a state of balance (homeostasis) is restored, and motivation decreases.

**Drug abuse** A type of drug taking that causes emotional or physical harm to the drug user or others.

**Eclectic approach** A treatment approach that draws from various therapies to best suit the client and the situation; also known as integrative therapy.

**Ego** In Freud's view, the somewhat conscious personality structure that develops out of the need to deal with demands of the real world; it operates on the reality principle.

**Egocentrism** In cognitive development, the inability to take the perspective of another person; a hallmark of Piaget's preoperational stage.

**Egoistic model of helping** A proposed explanation for helping that suggests we help because of anticipated gain—later reciprocation, increased self-esteem, or avoidance of distress and guilt.

**Elaborative rehearsal** A memory improvement method that makes the information more meaningful, and thereby transfers information from STM into LTM.

**Electroconvulsive therapy (ECT)** A biomedical therapy based on passing electrical current through the brain; it is used almost exclusively to treat serious depression when drugs and psychotherapy have failed.

**Embodied cognition** The theory that cognitive processes are influenced by bodily sensations and interactions with the environment.

**Embryonic period** The second stage of prenatal development, which begins after uterine implantation and lasts through the eighth week.

**Emerging adulthood** The age period from approximately 18–25 in which individuals in modern cultures have left the dependency of childhood but not yet assumed adult responsibilities.

**Emotion** A complex pattern of feelings that includes three components: biological (arousal), cognitive (thinking), and behavioral (expressions).

**Emotional intelligence (EI)** The ability to perceive, understand, manage, and utilize emotions accurately and appropriately.

**Emotion-focused coping** The strategies we use to relieve or regulate our emotional reactions to a stressful situation.

**Empathy–altruism hypothesis** A proposed explanation for helping that suggests we help because of empathy for someone in need.

**Empathy** In Rogerian terms, a sensitive understanding and sharing of another's inner experience.

**Encoding** The first step of the ESR memory model; process of moving sensory information into memory storage.

**Encoding-specificity principle** The principle that retrieval of information is improved if cues received at the time of recall are consistent with those present at the time of encoding.

**Encoding, storage, and retrieval (ESR) model** A memory model that involves three processes: *encoding* (getting information in), *storage* (retaining information for future use), and *retrieval* (recovering information).

**Endocrine system** A network of glands located throughout the body that manufacture and secrete hormones into the bloodstream.

**Endorphin** A chemical substance in the nervous system similar in structure and action to opiates; involved in pain control, pleasure, and memory.

**Epigenetics** The study of how nongenetic factors, such as age, environment, lifestyle, and disease, affect how (and if) genes are expressed; "epi" means "above" or "outside of."

**Episodic memory** A subsystem of long-term memory (LTM) that stores autobiographical events and the contexts in which they occurred; a mental diary of a person's life.

**Ethnocentrism** The belief that one's culture is typical of all cultures; also, viewing one's own ethnic group (or culture) as central and "correct" and judging others according to this standard.

**Eustress** The pleasant, desirable stress that arouses us to persevere and accomplish challenging goals.

**Evidence-based practice in psychology (EBPP)** A newer approach to therapy that integrates the best available evidence with the clinician's expertise, along with the client's characteristics, culture, and preferences.

**Evolutionary perspective** A modern approach to psychology that stresses natural selection, adaptation, and reproduction.

**Evolutionary theory of helping** A theory suggesting that altruism is an instinctual behavior that has evolved because it favors survival of the helper's genes.

**Excitement phase** The first stage of the sexual response cycle, characterized by increasing levels of arousal and engorgement of the genitals.

**Executive functions (EFs)** A set of higher-order cognitive processes controlled by the frontal lobes.

**Experiment** A careful manipulation of one or more variables (independent variables) to measure the effect on some behaviors or mental processes (the dependent variable).

**Experimental group** Participants in an experiment who receive the treatment under study—that is, those who are exposed to the independent variable (IV).

**Experimental research** A type of research that involves the manipulation and control of variables to determine cause and effect; designed to meet the goal of *explanation*.

**Experimenter bias** A bias that occurs when a researcher influences research results in the expected direction.

**Explicit/declarative memory** A subsystem of long-term memory (LTM) that involves conscious, easily described (declared) memories; consists of semantic memories (facts) and episodic memories (personal experiences).

**External locus of control** The belief that chance or outside forces beyond our control determine our fate.

**Extinction (in classical conditioning)** The gradual diminishing of a conditioned response (CR) when the unconditioned stimulus (US) is no longer paired with the conditioned stimulus (CS).

**Extinction (in operant conditioning)** The gradual diminishing of a conditioned response when it is no longer reinforced.

**Extrasensory perception (ESP)** Perceptual, so-called "psychic," abilities that supposedly go beyond the known senses (for example, telepathy, clairvoyance, and precognition).

**Extrinsic motivation** A type of motivation for a task or activity based on external incentives, such as rewards and punishments.

**Facial-feedback hypothesis** The hypothesis that movements of the facial muscles produce and/or intensify our subjective experience of emotion.

**Feature detectors** Neurons in the brain's visual system that respond to specific characteristics of stimuli, such as shape, angle, or movement.

**Fetal period** The third, and final, stage of prenatal development (eight weeks to birth).

**Five-factor model (FFM)** A model of personality traits that includes five basic dimensions: openness, conscientiousness, extraversion, agreeableness, and neuroticism; informally called the Big Five.

**Fixed interval (FI) schedule** Schedule in which a reinforcer is delivered for the first response made after a fixed period of has elapsed.

**Fixed ratio (FR) schedule** Schedule in which a reinforcer is delivered for the first response made after a fixed number of responses.

**Flashbulb memory (FBM)** A vivid, detailed, and near-permanent memory of an emotionally significant moment or event; memory resulting from a form of automatic encoding, storage, and later retrieval.

**Fluid intelligence (*gf*)** The ability to think speedily and abstractly and to solve novel problems; *gf* tends to decrease over the life span.

**Foot-in-the-door technique** A process in which an initial, small request is used as a setup for a later, larger request.

**Forebrain** A collection of upper-level brain structures including the cerebral cortex, limbic system, thalamus, and hypothalamus.

**Formal operational stage** Piaget's fourth stage of cognitive development (around age 11 and beyond), characterized by abstract and hypothetical thinking.

**Fovea** A tiny pit in the center of the retina that is densely filled with cones; it is responsible for sharp vision.

**Free association** In psychoanalysis, reporting whatever comes to mind without monitoring its contents.

**Frequency theory for hearing** The theory that pitch perception depends on how often the auditory nerve fires.

**Frontal lobes** The two lobes at the front of the brain involved in higher cognitive processes, speech production, and voluntary motor control.

**Frustration** The unpleasant tension, anxiety, and heightened sympathetic activity resulting from a blocked goal.

**Functional fixedness** A barrier to problem solving that comes from thinking about objects as functioning only in their usual or customary way.

**Functionalism** Early psychological approach associated with William James that explored how the mind functions to enable organisms to adapt to their environment.

**Fundamental attribution error (FAE)** A bias toward giving undue weight to personal, dispositional factors when explaining other people's behavior and underestimating the impact of external, situational factors; also known as the correspondence bias (CB).

**Gate-control theory of pain** The theory that pain sensations are processed and altered by certain cells in the spinal cord, which act as gates to interrupt and block some pain signals while sending others on to the brain.

**Gender** The psychological and sociocultural traits typically associated with one sex.

**Gender identity** One's sense of self-identification as belonging to the male or female sex.

**Gender roles** The culturally and socially defined prescriptions and expectations about the thoughts, feelings, and actions of men and women.

**Gender stereotypes** Gender role prescriptions and beliefs that are overly generalized and applied to all men and women.

**Gene** A segment of DNA (deoxyribonucleic acid) that occupies a specific place on a particular chromosome and carries the code for hereditary transmission.

**General adaptation syndrome (GAS)** Selye's three-stage (alarm, resistance, exhaustion) reaction to chronic stress; a pattern of nonspecific, adaptational responses to a continuing stressor.

**General intelligence (g)** Spearman's term for a common skill set that underlies all intellectual behavior.

**Generalization (in classical conditioning)** The process by which a conditioned response (CR) spreads (generalizes) and comes to be involuntarily elicited not only by the conditioned stimulus (CS), but also by stimuli similar to the CS; the opposite of discrimination.

**Generalization (in operant conditioning)** Voluntarily responding to a new stimulus as if it were the original, previously conditioned stimulus (CS); the opposite of discrimination.

**Generalized anxiety disorder (GAD)** An anxiety disorder characterized by persistent, uncontrollable, and free-floating, nonspecified anxiety.

**Genuineness** In Rogerian terms, being personally authentic and sincere; the awareness of one's true inner thoughts and feelings and the ability to share them honestly with others.

**Germinal period** The first stage of prenatal development, beginning with ovulation and followed by conception and implantation in the uterus; the first two weeks of pregnancy.

**Gestalt psychology** An early school of thought that emphasized our tendency to organize our perceptions into meaningful patterns and whole figures.

**Glial cells** The cells that provide structural, nutritional, and other functions for neurons; also called glia or neuroglia.

**Grammar** The set of rules (syntax and semantics) governing the use and structure of language.

**Grit** A psychological term referring to perseverance and passion in the pursuit of long-term goals.

**Group polarization** The tendency for the decisions and opinions of group members to become more extreme (either riskier or more conservative), depending on the members' initial dominant tendency.

**Group therapies** A form of therapy in which a number of people with similar concerns meet together to work toward therapeutic goals.

**Groupthink** The faulty decision making that occurs when maintaining group harmony becomes more important than making a good decision.

**Growth/development theory of sleep** The theory that deep sleep (Stage 3) is correlated with physical development, including changes in the structure and organization of the brain; infants spend far more time in Stage 3 sleep than adults.

**Growth mindset** A psychological term referring to a self-perception or a set of beliefs about one's personal abilities and the potential for change and improvement with effort.

**Gustation** The sense or act of tasting; receptors are located in the tongue's taste buds.

**Habituation** The brain's learned tendency to ignore or stop responding to unchanging information; an example of top-down processing.

**Hallucination** A false, imaginary sensory perception that occurs without an external, objective source, such as hearing voices that others do not hear; a symptom associated with psychosis.

**Hallucinogen** A drug that produces sensory or perceptual distortions.

**Hassles** The small problems of daily living that may accumulate and become a major source of stress.

**Health psychology** A branch of psychology that studies how biological, psychological, and social (biopsychosocial) factors influence health, illness, and health-related behaviors.

**Heuristic** An educated guess, or "rule of thumb," often used as a shortcut for problem solving; does not guarantee a solution to a problem but does narrow the alternatives.

**Hierarchy of needs** Maslow's view that basic human motives form a hierarchy; the lower motives (such as physiological and safety needs) must be met before advancing to higher needs (such as belonging and self-actualization).

**Higher-order conditioning** The process by which a new conditioned stimulus (CS) is created by pairing it with a previously conditioned stimulus (CS); also known as second-order conditioning.

**Hindbrain** The lower or hind region of the brain; collection of structures including the medulla, pons, and cerebellum.

**Hippocampus** The seahorse-shaped part of the limbic system involved in forming and retrieving memories.

**HIV positive** The state of being infected by the human immunodeficiency virus (HIV).

**Homeostasis** Our body's tendency to maintain equilibrium, or a steady state of internal balance, such as a constant internal temperature.

**Hormone** Chemical messengers manufactured and secreted by the endocrine glands, which circulate in the bloodstream to produce bodily changes or maintain normal bodily functions.

**HPA axis** Our body's delayed stress response, involving the hypothalamus, pituitary, and adrenal cortex; called the hypothalamic–pituitary–adrenocortical (HPA) axis.

**Humanistic perspective** A modern approach to psychology that perceives human nature as naturally positive and growth seeking; it emphasizes free will and self-actualization.

**Humanistic therapies** A group of talk therapies that emphasize maximizing a client's inherent capacity for self-actualization by providing a nonjudgmental, accepting atmosphere.

**Hypnosis** An altered state of consciousness (ASC) characterized by deep relaxation and a trance-like state of heightened suggestibility and intense focus.

**Hypothalamus** The small brain structure beneath the thalamus that helps govern drives (hunger, thirst, sex, and aggression) and hormones.

**Hypothesis** A tentative and testable explanation (or "educated guess") about the relationship between two or more variables; a testable prediction or question.

**Id** In Freud's view, the personality structure that is present at birth, completely unconscious, and strives to satisfy basic drives, such as hunger, sex, and aggression; it operates on the pleasure principle.

**Illusion** A false or misleading perception shared by others in the same perceptual environment.

**Illusory correlation** A mistaken perception that a relationship exists between variables when no statistical relationship actually exists.

**Implicit bias** A hidden, automatic attitude that may guide behaviors independent of a person's awareness or control.

**Implicit/nondeclarative memory** A subsystem within long-term memory (LTM) that contains memories independent of conscious recall; consists of procedural motor skills, priming, and simple classically conditioned responses.

**Imprinting** The process by which attachments are formed during critical periods in early life.

**Inattentional blindness** The failure to notice a fully visible, but unexpected, stimulus when our attention is directed elsewhere; also known as perceptual blindness.

**Incentive theory** The theory that motivation results from external stimuli that "pull" an organism in certain directions.

**Independent variable (IV)** The variable that is manipulated by the experimenter to determine its causal effect on the dependent variable; also called the treatment variable.

**Inferiority complex** Adler's idea that feelings of inferiority develop from early childhood experiences of helplessness and incompetence.

**Informational social influence** A type of conforming based on the need for information and direction.

**Informed consent** A participant's agreement to take part in a study after being told what to expect.

**Ingroup favoritism** The tendency to judge members of the ingroup more positively than members of an outgroup.

**Inner ear** The semicircular canals, vestibular sacs, and cochlea, which generate neural signals that are sent to the brain.

**Insanity** The legal (not clinical) designation for a situation in which an individual cannot be held responsible for his or her actions or is incompetent to manage his or her own affairs because of mental illness.

**Insight learning** A sudden understanding or realization of how a problem can be solved.

**Insomnia** A sleep disorder characterized by persistent problems in falling or staying asleep, or awakening too early.

**Instinctive drift** The tendency for conditioned responses to revert (drift back) to innate response patterns.

**Instinct** The fixed, unlearned response patterns found in almost all members of a species.

**Intelligence quotient (IQ)** An index of intelligence derived from standardized tests; originally computed by dividing mental age (MA) by chronological age (CA) and then multiplying by 100 but now derived by comparing individual scores with the scores of others of the same age.

**Intelligence** The global capacity to think rationally, act purposefully, profit from experience, and deal effectively with the environment.

**Internal locus of control** The belief that we control our own fate.

**Interpretation** A psychoanalyst's explanation of a client's free associations, dreams, resistance, and transference; more generally, any statement by a therapist that presents a problem in a new way.

**Intrinsic motivation** A type of motivation for a task or activity based on internal incentives, such as enjoyment and personal satisfaction.

**James-Lange theory** A theory of emotion suggesting that the subjective experience of emotion results from physiological arousal, rather than being its cause ("I feel sad because I'm crying"); in this view, each emotion is physiologically distinct.

**Kinesthesis** The sense that provides information about the location, orientation, and movement of individual body parts relative to each other; receptors are located in muscles, joints, and tendons.

**Language** A form of communication using sounds or symbols combined according to specified rules.

**Language acquisition device (LAD)** According to Chomsky, an innate mechanism within the brain that enables a child to analyze language and extract the basic rules of grammar.

**Latent content of dreams** According to Freud, a dream's unconscious, hidden meaning, which is transformed into symbols within the dream's manifest content (story line).

**Latent learning** Hidden learning that exists without behavioral signs; also known as implicit learning.

**Law of effect** Thorndike's rule that any behavior followed by pleasant consequences is likely to be repeated, whereas any behavior followed by unpleasant consequences is likely to be stopped.

**Learned helplessness** Seligman's term for a state of helplessness, or resignation, in which human or nonhuman animals fail to act to escape from a situation due to a history of repeated failures.

**Learning** A relatively permanent change in behavior or mental processes caused by experience.

**Learning/memory theory of sleep** The theory that sleep is important for learning and for the consolidation, storage, and maintenance of memories.

**Levels of processing model** A model of memory bases on a continuum of memory processing ranging from shallow to intermediate to deep, with deeper processing leading to improved encoding, storage, and retrieval.

**Limbic system** The interconnected group of forebrain structures involved with emotions, drives, and memory; its two most important structures are the hippocampus and amygdala.

**Lobotomy** An outmoded neurosurgical procedure for mental disorders that involved cutting nerve pathways between the frontal lobes and the thalamus and hypothalamus.

**Longitudinal design** In developmental psychology, a research design that measures individuals over an extended period and gives information about age changes.

**Long-term memory (LTM)** The third stage of memory, which stores information for long periods of time; the capacity is virtually limitless, and the duration is relatively permanent.

**Long-term potentiation (LTP)** A long-lasting increase in neural sensitivity; a biological mechanism for learning and memory.

**Maintenance rehearsal** The act of repeating information over and over to maintain it in short-term memory (STM).

**Major depressive disorder (MDD)** A psychological disorder characterized by significant symptoms of depression that occur nearly every day and last for two weeks or more.

**Mania** A state of abnormally elevated mood (either euphoric or irritable); also characterized by mental and physical hyperactivity, insomnia, and poor judgment.

**Manifest content of dreams** In Freudian dream analysis, the "surface," or remembered, story line, which contains symbols that mask the dream's latent content (the true meaning).

**Massed practice** A study technique in which time spent learning is grouped (or massed) into long, unbroken intervals; also called cramming.

**Meditation** A group of techniques generally designed to focus attention, block out distractions, and produce an altered state of consciousness (ASC); it's believed to enhance self-knowledge and well-being through reduced self-awareness.

**Medulla** The hindbrain structure responsible for vital, automatic functions, such as respiration and heartbeat.

**Memory** The persistence of learning over time; process by which information is encoded, stored, and retrieved.

**Mental age (MA)** An individual's level of mental development relative to that of others; mental age was initially used in comparison to chronological age (CA) to calculate IQ.

**Mental set** A fixed-thinking approach to problem solving that only sees solutions that have worked in the past.

**Meta-analysis** A statistical technique for combining and analyzing data from many studies in order to determine overall trends.

**Midbrain** The collection of structures in the middle of the brain responsible for coordinating movement patterns, sleep, and arousal.

**Middle ear** The hammer, anvil, and stirrup structures of the ear, which concentrate eardrum vibrations onto the cochlea's oval window.

**Mindfulness-based cognitive therapy (MBCT)** A therapy based on developing a state of consciousness that attends to ongoing thoughts, feelings, and events in a receptive and nonjudgmental way.

**Mindfulness-based stress reduction (MBSR)** A stress reduction strategy based on developing a state of consciousness that attends to ongoing events in a receptive and nonjudgmental way.

**Minnesota Multiphasic Personality Inventory (MMPI)** The most widely researched and clinically used self-report method of personality assessment; originally designed to reveal abnormal personality traits and behaviors, it's also used for various screening purposes.

**Mirror neurons** Neurons that fire (or are activated) when an action is performed, as well as when the actions or emotions of another are observed; believed to be responsible for empathy, imitation, language, and the deficits of some mental disorders.

**Misinformation effect** A memory error resulting from misleading information presented after an event, which alters memories of the event itself.

**Mnemonic** A strategy device that uses familiar information during the encoding of new information to enhance later recall.

**Modeling therapy** A type of therapy characterized by watching and imitating models who demonstrate desirable behaviors.

**Monocular cues** Visual input from a single eye alone that contributes to perception of depth or distance.

**Morality** The ability to take the perspective of, or empathize with, others and to distinguish right from wrong.

**Morpheme** The smallest meaningful unit of language; formed from a combination of phonemes.

**Motivation** A set of factors that activate, direct, and maintain behavior, usually toward some goal.

**Motor cortex** A region at the back of the frontal lobes responsible for voluntary movement.

**Myelin sheath** The layer of fatty insulation wrapped around the axon of some neurons that increases the rate at which neural impulses travel along the axon.

**Narcolepsy** A sleep order characterized by uncontrollable sleep attacks. (*Narco* means "numbness," and *lepsy* means "seizure.")

**Naturalistic observation** A descriptive research technique that observes and records behavior and mental processes in a natural, real-world setting.

**Natural selection** Darwin's principle of an evolutionary process in which heritable traits that increase an organism's chances of survival or reproduction are more likely to be passed on to succeeding generations.

**Nature–nurture controversy** An ongoing dispute about the relative contributions of nature (heredity) and nurture (environment) in determining the development of behavior and mental processes.

**Negative punishment** A process by which taking away (or removing) a stimulus following a response decreases the likelihood that the response will be repeated.

**Negative reinforcement** A process by which taking away (or removing) a stimulus following a response increases the likelihood that the response will be repeated.

**Nervous system** The electrochemical communication system that carries information to and from all parts of the body.

**Neurodevelopmental disorders** A group of disorders that usually begin in early life, causing problems with communication, cognitive abilities, social relationships, and/or behavior.

**Neurogenesis** The formation (generation) of new neurons.

**Neuron** The basic building block (nerve cell) of the nervous system; responsible for receiving, processing, and transmitting electrochemical information.

**Neuroplasticity** The brain's lifelong ability to reorganize and change its structure and function by forming new neural connections.

**Neurosis** A condition in which a person does not have signs of brain abnormalities and does not display grossly irrational thinking or violate basic norms but does experience subjective distress; no longer included in the DSM.

**Neurotransmitter** A chemical messenger released by neurons that travels across the synapse and allows neurons to communicate with one another.

**Neutral stimulus (NS)** A stimulus that, before conditioning, does not naturally bring about the response of interest.

**Nightmares** Anxiety-arousing dreams that generally occur near the end of the sleep cycle, during REM sleep.

**Non-rapid-eye-movement (NREM) sleep** The sleep stages (1 through 3) during which a sleeper does not show rapid eye movements.

**Nonsuicidal self-injury (NSSI)** A serious behavior problem in which people deliberately harm themselves without lethal intent.

**Normal distribution** A statistical term used to describe how traits are distributed within a population; IQ scores usually form a symmetrical, bell-shaped curve, with most scores falling near the average and fewer scores near the extremes.

**Normative social influence** A type of conforming based on the need to be liked, accepted, and approved of by others.

**Obedience** The act of following direct commands, usually from an authority figure.

**Obesity** An eating problem involving a body mass index of 30 or above, based on height and weight.

**Object permanence** According to Piaget, an understanding that objects continue to exist even when they cannot be seen, heard, or touched directly; a hallmark of Piaget's preoperational stage.

**Observational learning** The learning of new behaviors or information by watching and imitating others (also known as social learning or modeling).

**Obsessive-compulsive disorder (OCD)** A psychological disorder characterized by persistent, unwanted, fearful thoughts (obsessions) and/or irresistible urges to perform repetitive and/or ritualized behaviors (compulsions).

**Occipital lobes** The two lobes at the back of the brain that are primarily responsible for vision and visual perception.

**Oedipus complex** According to Freud, a young boy's development, during the phallic stage (ages 3 to 6 years), of sexual attraction to his mother and rivalry with his father.

**Olfaction** The sense or act of smelling; receptors are located in the nose's nasal cavity.

**Operant conditioning** A form of associative learning in which behavior increases if followed by reinforcement and decreases if followed by punishment; also known as instrumental conditioning.

**Operational definition** A precise description of how the variables in a study will be observed and measured.

**Opiate/opioid** A drug derived from opium that numbs the senses and relieves pain.

**Opponent-process theory of color** The theory that all color perception is based on three systems, each of which contains two color opposites (red versus green, blue versus yellow, and black versus white).

**Optimal-arousal theory** The theory that organisms are motivated to achieve and maintain an optimal level of arousal, which maximizes their performance.

**Optimism** A tendency to expect the best and to see the best in all things.

**Orgasm phase** The third stage of the sexual response cycle, when pleasurable sensations peak and orgasm occurs.

**Outer ear** The pinna, auditory canal, and eardrum structures, which funnel sound waves to the middle ear.

**Outgroup homogeneity effect** The tendency to judge members of an outgroup as more alike and less diverse than members of the ingroup.

**Pair bonding** The formation of enduring relationships between adult mates.

**Panic disorder** An anxiety disorder characterized by sudden onsets of intense terror and inexplicable panic attacks.

**Parallel distributed processing (PDP) model** The theory that memory is stored throughout the brain in web-like connections among interacting processing units operating simultaneously, rather than sequentially; also known as connectionism.

**Paraphilic disorder** Any of a group of psychosexual disorders involving disturbing and repetitive sexual fantasies, urges, or behaviors that cause distress or impairment to the person and/or harm or risk of harm to others.

**Parapsychology** The study of paranormal phenomena, such as ESP, ghosts, and psychokinesis, that are inexplicable by science.

**Parasympathetic nervous system** The subdivision of the autonomic nervous system (ANS) that is responsible for calming the body and conserving energy.

**Parietal lobes** The two lobes at the top of the brain in which bodily sensations are received and interpreted.

**Partial (intermittent) reinforcement** Reinforcement in which some, but not all, correct responses are reinforced.

**Participant bias** A bias that occurs when a research participant contaminates research results.

**Perception** The process of selecting, organizing, and interpreting sensory information into meaningful objects and events.

**Perceptual constancy** The tendency to perceive the environment as stable, despite changes in the sensory input.

**Perceptual set** The readiness to perceive in a particular manner based on expectations.

**Performance anxiety** The fear of being judged in connection with sexual activities.

**Peripheral nervous system (PNS)** The part of the nervous system composed of the nerves and neurons connecting the central nervous system (CNS) to the rest of the body.

**Personality** Our unique and relatively stable pattern of thoughts, feelings, and actions.

**Personality disorder** A psychological disorder characterized by chronic, inflexible, maladaptive personality traits, which cause significant impairment of social and occupational functioning.

**Pheromones [FARE-oh-mones]** Chemical signals released by organisms that trigger certain responses, such as aggression or sexual mating, in other members of the same species.

**Phobia** A persistent and intense, irrational fear and avoidance of a specific object, activity, or situation.

**Phoneme** The smallest basic unit of speech or sound in any given language.

**Physical dependence** The changes in bodily processes that make a drug necessary for minimal functioning.

**Placebo** An inactive substance or fake treatment used as a control technique in experiments; often used in drug research.

**Placebo effect** A change that occurs when a participant's expectations or beliefs, rather than the actual drug or treatment, cause a particular experimental outcome.

**Place theory for hearing** The theory that pitch perception is linked to the particular spot on the cochlea's basilar membrane that is most stimulated.

**Plateau phase** The second stage of the sexual response cycle; period of sexual excitement prior to orgasm.

**Polygraph** An instrument that measures physiological indicators (heart rate, respiration rate, blood pressure, and skin conductivity) to detect emotional arousal, which in turn supposedly reflects lying.

**Pons** The hindbrain structure involved in respiration, movement, waking, sleep, and dreaming.

**Positive affect** The experience or expression of positive feelings (affect), including happiness, joy, enthusiasm, and contentment.

**Positive psychology** The study of optimal human functioning; emphasizes positive emotions, traits, and institutions.

**Positive punishment** A process by which adding (or presenting) a stimulus following a response decreases the likelihood that the response will be repeated.

**Positive reinforcement** A process by which adding (or presenting) a stimulus following a response increases the likelihood that the response will be repeated.

**Postconventional morality** Kohlberg's third and highest level of moral development, in which individuals develop personal standards for right and wrong, and define morality in terms of abstract principles and values that apply to all situations

**Posttraumatic stress disorder (PTSD)** A long-lasting, trauma- and stressor-related disorder that overwhelms an individual's ability to cope.

**Preconscious** Freud's term for thoughts, motives, or memories that exist just beneath the surface of awareness and can be called to consciousness when necessary.

**Preconventional morality** Kohlberg's first level of moral development, in which morality is based on rewards, punishment, and exchange of favors.

**Prejudice** A learned, unjustified negative attitude toward members of a particular group; it includes thoughts (stereotypes), feelings, and behavioral tendencies (discrimination).

**Preoperational stage** Piaget's second stage of cognitive development (roughly ages 2 to 7); it is characterized by significant language, but the child lacks operations (reversible mental processes), and thinking is egocentric and animistic.

**Primary punisher** Any unlearned, innate stimulus, such as hunger or thirst, that punishes a response and thus decreases the probability that it will recur.

**Primary reinforcer** Any unlearned, innate stimulus (like food, water, or sex) that reinforces a response and thus increases the probability that it will recur.

**Priming** An exposure (often unconscious) to previously stored information that predisposes (or *primes*) our response to related stimuli.

**Proactive interference** A memory problem that occurs when old information disrupts (*interferes* with) the recall of new information; forward-acting interference.

**Problem-focused coping** The strategies we use to deal directly with a stressor to eventually decrease or eliminate it.

**Projective test** A method of personality assessment that uses a standardized set of ambiguous stimuli, such as inkblots or abstract drawings, which allow test takers to "project" their underlying motives, conflicts, and personality traits onto the test materials.

**Prototype** A mental image or best example that embodies the most typical features of a concept or category.

**Psychiatry** The branch of medicine that deals with the diagnosis, treatment, and prevention of mental disorders.

**Psychoactive drug** A chemical that changes mental processes, such as conscious awareness, mood, and perception.

**Psychoanalysis** A type of talk therapy, originated by Sigmund Freud, that emphasizes analysis and bringing unconscious thoughts and conflicts into conscious awareness.

**Psychoanalytic perspective** An earlier approach to psychology developed by Sigmund Freud, which focuses on unconscious processes, unresolved conflicts, and past experiences.

**Psychodynamic perspective** A modern approach to psychology that emphasizes unconscious dynamics, motives, conflicts, and past experiences; based on the psychoanalytic approach, but focuses more on social and cultural factors, and less on sexual drives.

**Psychodynamic therapies** A group of talk therapies that focus on conscious processes and current problems; briefer, more directive, and more modern forms of psychoanalysis.

**Psychological dependence** The psychological desire or craving to achieve a drug's effect.

**Psychological disorder** A clinically significant collection of symptoms (a syndrome) characterized by serious disruptions in an individual's thoughts, feelings, and/or actions.

**Psychology** The scientific study of behavior and mental processes.

**Psychology student syndrome (PSSS)** A condition often seen in psychology students concerned that they are experiencing the symptoms of a psychological disorder they're studying; also, using what is learned in a psychology class to "diagnose" someone of a psychological condition without full knowledge or proper certification.

**Psychoneuroimmunology** The interdisciplinary field that studies the effects of psychological and other factors on the immune system.

**Psychopharmacology** The use of drugs to relieve or control the major symptoms of psychological disorders.

**Psychophysics** The study of the link between the physical characteristics of stimuli and the psychological experience of them.

**Psychosexual stages** In Freudian theory, five developmental periods (oral, anal, phallic, latency, and genital) during which particular kinds of pleasures must be gratified if personality development is to proceed normally.

**Psychosis** A serious psychological condition in which thoughts and perceptions are so impaired that the individual loses contact with external reality.

**Psychosocial stages** Erikson's stages of development, each involving a psychosocial task that must be successfully resolved at a particular place in the life span.

**Psychosurgery** A form of biomedical therapy that involves alteration of the brain to bring about desirable behavioral, cognitive, or emotional changes; it is generally used when clients have not responded to other forms of treatment.

**Psychotherapy** Any of a group of therapies used to treat psychological disorders and to improve psychological functioning and adjustment to life.

**Puberty** The biological changes during adolescence that lead to sexual maturation and the ability to reproduce.

**Punishment** A process by which adding or removing a stimulus following a response decreases the likelihood that the response will be repeated.

**Random assignment** A research technique for assigning participants to experimental or control conditions so that each participant has an equal chance of being in either group; minimizes the possibility of biases or preexisting differences within or between the groups.

**Rape** The unlawful act of engaging in oral, anal, or vaginal penetration with a person through force or threat of force and without consent or with a person incapable of giving consent (due to age or physical or mental incapacity).

**Rapid-eye-movement (REM) sleep** The fourth stage of sleep, marked by rapid eye movements, irregular breathing, high-frequency brain waves, paralysis of large muscles, and often dreaming.

**Rational-emotive behavior therapy (REBT)** A form of talk therapy, developed by Albert Ellis, that focuses on eliminating negative emotional reactions through logic, confrontation, and examination of irrational beliefs.

**Reciprocal determinism** Bandura's belief that internal personal factors, the environment, and the individual's behavior all work as interacting (reciprocal) determinants of each other.

**Reference groups** Any groups that individuals use as a standard for evaluating themselves.

**Reflex** An innate, automatic response to a stimulus that has biological relevance for an organism (e.g., the knee-jerk reflex).

**Refractory period** A period of time following orgasm, during which further orgasm is considered physiologically rare for men.

**Reinforcement** A process by which adding or removing a stimulus following a response increases the likelihood that the response will be repeated.

**Reliability** The degree to which a test produces similar scores each time it is used; stability or consistency of the scores produced by an instrument.

**Repair/restoration theory of sleep** The theory that sleep allows organisms to repair their bodies or recuperate from depleting daily waking activities.

**Repetitive transcranial magnetic stimulation (rTMS)** A biomedical treatment that uses repeated magnetic field pulses targeted at specific areas of the brain.

**Representativeness heuristic** A cognitive strategy (or shortcut) that involves making judgments based on how well something matches (represents) an existing prototype or stereotype.

**Representative sample** A selected sample of participants whose demographics and characteristics accurately reflect the entire population of interest.

**Repression** According to Freud's psychoanalytic theory, a basic coping or defense mechanism that prevents anxiety-provoking thoughts, feelings and memories from reaching consciousness.

**Resilience** The ability to recover from or adapt effectively in the face of adversity.

**Resistance** A psychoanalytic therapy technique that examines a client's inability or unwillingness to confront unpleasant or fearful unconscious conflicts.

**Resolution phase** The fourth, and final, stage of the sexual response cycle, when the body returns to its unaroused state.

**Reticular formation (RF)** A diffuse set of neurons that helps screen incoming information and helps control arousal.

**Retinal disparity** The binocular cue of distance in which the separation of the eyes causes different images to fall on the two retinas.

**Retina** The light-sensitive inner surface of the back of the eye, which contains the receptor cells for vision (rods and cones).

**Retrieval cues** A prompt or stimulus that aids recall or retrieval of a stored piece of information from long-term memory (LTM).

**Retrieval** The third step of the ESR memory model; recovery of information from memory storage.

**Retroactive interference** A memory problem that occurs when new information disrupts (*interferes* with) the recall of old, "retro" information; backward-acting interference.

**Retrograde amnesia** The inability to retrieve information from the past; backward-acting amnesia.

**Rods** Retinal receptor cells with high sensitivity in dim light, but low sensitivity to details and color.

**Romantic love** An intense feeling of attraction to another in an erotic context.

**Rorschach Inkblot Test** The most widely used projective personality test, which is based on test takers' projections onto 10 inkblots.

**Saliency bias** A type of attributional bias in which people tend to focus on the most noticeable (salient) factors when explaining the causes of behavior.

**Sample bias** A bias that may occur when research participants are unrepresentative of the larger population.

**SAM system** Our body's initial, rapid-acting stress response, involving the sympathetic nervous system and the adrenal medulla; called the sympatho–adreno–medullary (SAM) system.

**Schedules of reinforcement** Specific patterns of reinforcement (either fixed or variable) that determine when a behavior will be reinforced.

**Schema** A Piagetian term for a cognitive framework, or "blueprint," formed through interaction with an object or event.

**Schizophrenia** A group of severe psychological disorders involving major disturbances in perception, language, thought, emotion, and/or behavior.

**Scientific method** The cyclical and cumulative research process used for gathering and interpreting objective information in a way that minimizes error and yields dependable results.

**Secondary punisher** Any learned stimulus, such as poor grades or a parking ticket, that punishes a response and thus decreases the probability that it will recur.

**Secondary reinforcer** Any learned stimulus (like money, praise, or attention) that reinforces a response and thus increases the probability that it will recur.

**Selective attention** The process of focusing conscious awareness onto a specific stimulus, while filtering out a range of other stimuli occurring simultaneously.

**Self-actualization** The humanistic term for the inborn drive to realize our full potential and to develop all our talents and capabilities.

**Self-concept** The image of oneself that develops from interactions with significant others and life experiences.

**Self-efficacy** Bandura's term for a person's learned expectation of success in a given situation; another term for self-confidence.

**Self-help group** A leaderless or non–professionally guided group in which members assist each other with a specific problem, as in Alcoholics Anonymous.

**Self-serving bias** The tendency to credit one's own success to internal, dispositional factors, while blaming failure on external, situational factors.

**Semantic memory** A subsystem of long-term memory (LTM) that stores general knowledge; a mental encyclopedia or dictionary.

**Sensation** The process of detecting, converting, and transmitting raw sensory information from the external and internal environments to the brain.

**Sensorimotor stage** Piaget's first stage of cognitive development (birth to approximately age 2), in which schemas are developed through sensory and motor activities.

**Sensorineural hearing loss** A type of hearing loss resulting from damage to cochlea's receptor (hair) hearing cells or to the auditory nerve; also called nerve deafness.

**Sensory adaptation** The sensory receptors' innate tendency to fatigue and stop responding to unchanging stimuli; an example of bottom-up processing.

**Sensory memory** The initial memory stage, which holds sensory information; it has relatively large capacity, but the duration is only a few seconds.

**Serial-position effect** A characteristic of memory retrieval in which information at the beginning and end of a series is remembered better than material in the middle.

**Sex** The state of being biologically male or female

**Sexual dysfunction** A difficulty in sexual functioning; a significant disturbance in a person's ability to respond sexually or to experience sexual pleasure.

**Sexuality** The ways in which we experience and express ourselves as sexual beings; includes sexual arousal, orientation, and behaviors.

**Sexually transmitted infection (STI)** An infection generally transmitted by vaginal, oral, or anal sex.

**Sexual orientation** A primary erotic attraction toward members of the same sex (homosexual, gay, lesbian), both sexes (bisexual), or the other sex (heterosexual).

**Sexual prejudice** A negative attitude toward an individual because of her or his sexual orientation.

**Sexual response cycle** Masters and Johnson's model of the typical human sexual response, consisting of four stages—excitement, plateau, orgasm, and resolution.

**Sexual scripts** The learned, socially constructed guidelines for our sexual interactions.

**Shaping** Delivering reinforcement following successive approximations of the desired response.

**Short-term memory (STM)** The second memory stage, which temporarily stores sensory information and transmits information to and from long-term memory (LTM); its capacity is limited to five to nine items, and it has a duration of about 30 seconds.

**Single-blind study** An experimental technique in which only the participants are unaware of (blind to) who is in the experimental group and who is in the control group.

**Sleep apnea** A disorder of the upper respiratory system that causes a repeated interruption of breathing during sleep; it also leads to loud snoring, poor-quality sleep, and excessive daytime sleepiness.

**Sleep terrors** Abrupt awakenings from NREM (non-rapid-eye-movement) sleep accompanied by intense physiological arousal and feelings of panic.

**Social facilitation** The tendency for an individual's performance on an easy task to improve due to the presence of others.

**Social loafing** The tendency for individuals to exert less effort in a group due to reduced accountability and risk of detection.

**Social psychology** The branch of psychology that studies how others influence our thoughts, feelings, and actions.

**Sociocultural perspective** A modern approach to psychology that emphasizes social interaction and the cultural determinants of behavior and mental processes.

**Socioemotional selectivity theory of aging** A theory holding that a natural decline in social contact occurs as older adults become more selective with their time.

**Somatic nervous system (SNS)** The subdivision of the peripheral nervous system (PNS) that connects the central nervous system (CNS) to sensory receptors and controls skeletal muscles.

**Somatosensory cortex** A region in the parietal lobes responsible for processing information from bodily sensations, such as touch and temperature.

**Source amnesia** A memory error caused by forgetting the origin of a previously stored memory; also called source confusion or source misattribution.

**Split-brain surgery** The cutting of the corpus callosum to separate the brain's two hemispheres; used medically to treat severe epilepsy; also provides information on the functions of the two hemispheres.

**Spontaneous recovery** The reappearance of a previously extinguished conditioned response (CR).

**SQ4R method** A study technique based on six steps: Survey, Question, Read, Recite, Review, and wRite.

**Standardization** A set of uniform procedures for administering and scoring a test; also, establishing norms by comparison with scores of a pretested group.

**Statistical significance** A statistical statement of how likely it is that a study's result occurred merely by chance.

**Stem cells** Immature (uncommitted) cells that have the potential to develop into almost any type of cell, depending on the chemical signals they receive.

**Stereotype** An overgeneralized belief about members of a group; also the cognitive component of prejudice.

**Stereotype threat** The awareness of a negative stereotype directed toward a group, which leads members of that group to respond in a self-fulfilling way that impairs their performance.

**Stimulant** A drug that increases overall activity and general responsiveness.

**Storage** The second step of the ESR memory model; retention of encoded information over time.

**Stress** The interpretation of specific events, called *stressors*, as threatening or challenging; the physical and psychological reactions to stress, known as the *stress response*.

**Stressor** A trigger or stimulus that induces stress.

**Structuralism** Early psychological approach promoted by Wundt and Titchener that used introspection to study the basic elements (or structures) of the mind.

**Subliminal perception** The detection of stimuli below the absolute threshold for conscious awareness.

**Superego** In Freud's view, the personality structure that develops as the center of morality, providing internalized ideals and standards for judgment; often referred to as the "conscience."

**Suprachiasmatic nucleus (SCN)** A set of cells within the hypothalamus that respond to light and control the circadian rhythm.

**Survey/interview** A descriptive research technique that questions a large sample of people to assess their behaviors and mental processes.

**Sympathetic nervous system** The subdivision of the autonomic nervous system (ANS) that is responsible for arousing the body and mobilizing its energy during times of stress; also called the "fight-flight-freeze" system.

**Synapse** The gap between the axon tip of the sending neuron and the dendrite and/or cell body of the receiving neuron; during an action potential, neurotransmitters are released and flow across the synapse.

**Systematic desensitization** A behavior therapy technique in which a client is first asked to create a hierarchy of ordered fears and then taught to relax while gradually confronting the feared stimulus.

**Technostress** A feeling of anxiety or mental pressure from overexposure or involvement with technology; stress caused by an inability to cope with modern technology.

**Temperament** An individual's innate disposition or behavioral style and characteristic emotional response.

**Temporal lobes** The two lobes on the sides of the brain above the ears that are involved in hearing, language comprehension, memory, and some emotional control.

**Teratogen** Any factor that causes damage or fetal death during prenatal development.

**Thalamus** The forebrain structure at the top of the brainstem that relays sensory messages to and from the cerebral cortex.

**Thanatology** [than-uh-TAHL-uh-gee] The study of death and dying; the term comes from *thanatus*, the Greek name for a mythical personification of death, and was borrowed by Freud to represent the death instinct.

**Thematic Apperception Test (TAT)** A projective personality test based on the stories test takers make up about ambiguous scenes.

**Theory** A well-substantiated explanation for a phenomenon or a group of facts that have been repeatedly confirmed by previous research.

**Theory of mind (ToM)** The understanding that other people don't have the same thoughts and feelings that we do, which generally develops during early childhood.

**Therapeutic alliance** A bond between the therapist and client based on mutual trust, respect, understanding, and cooperation; an essential factor in successful therapy.

**Third-variable problem** A situation in which a variable that has not been measured accounts for a relationship between two or more other variables; third variables are also known as confounding variables in experiments.

**Three-stage memory model** A memory model based on the passage of information through three stages: sensory, short-term, and long-term memory; also known as the Atkinson-Shiffrin theory.

**Tip-of-the-tongue (TOT) phenomenon** A strong, confident feeling of knowing something, while not being able to retrieve it at the moment.

**Token economy** A form of behavior therapy involving awarding "tokens" for desired behavior that can be exchanged later for rewards.

**Tolerance** The bodily adjustment to continued use of a drug in which the drug user requires greater dosages to achieve the same effect.

**Top-down processing** A type of information processing that starts at the "top" with higher-level analysis (prior knowledge and expectations), and then works "down" to recognize individual features as a unified whole; conceptually driven processing that moves from the whole to the parts.

**Trait** A relatively stable personality characteristic that describes a pattern of thinking, feeling, and acting.

**Transduction** The process of converting sensory stimuli into neural impulses that are sent along to the brain (for example, transforming light waves into neural impulses).

**Transference** A psychoanalytic therapy technique that explores situations in which a client attaches (transfers) to the therapist emotional reactions related to someone else in the client's life.

**Transgender** The state of having a gender identity that does not match one's biological sex; being born with the biological characteristics of one sex but feeling psychologically as if belonging to the other gender.

**Triangular theory of love** Sternberg's theory that different stages and types of love result from three basic components—*intimacy*, *passion*, and *commitment*; Sternberg's consummate love is a combination of all three components.

**Triarchic theory of intelligence** Sternberg's theory that intelligence involves three forms: analytical, creative, and practical.

**Trichromatic theory of color** The theory that color perception results from three types of cones in the retina, each most sensitive to either red, green, or blue; other colors result from a mixture of these three.

**Two-factor theory** Schachter and Singer's theory that emotion depends upon two factors—physiological arousal and cognitive labeling of that arousal.

**Unconditional positive regard** Rogers's term for love and acceptance with no "strings" (conditions) attached.

**Unconditioned response (UR)** An unlearned reaction to an unconditioned stimulus (US) that occurs without previous conditioning.

**Unconditioned stimulus (US)** A stimulus that elicits an unconditioned response (UR) without previous conditioning.

**Unconscious** Freud's term for the reservoir of largely unacceptable thoughts, feelings, memories, and other information that lies beneath conscious awareness; in modern terms, subliminal processing that lies beneath the absolute threshold (Chapter 4).

**Validity** The degree to which a test measures what it is intended to measure.

**Variable interval (VI) schedule** Schedule in which a reinforcer is delivered for the first response made after a variable period of time has elapsed.

**Variable ratio (VR) schedule** Schedule in which a reinforcer is delivered for the first response made after a variable number of responses.

**Vestibular sense** The sense that provides information about balance and movement; receptors are located in the inner ear.

**Volley principle for hearing** An explanation for pitch perception suggesting that clusters of neurons take turns firing in a sequence of rhythmic volleys, and that pitch depends on the frequency of these volleys.

**Well-being therapy (WBT)** A newer form of psychotherapy aimed at enhancing psychological well-being by focusing on personal growth and noticing and savoring the positive aspects of life.

**Wish-fulfillment view of dreams** The Freudian belief that dreams provide an outlet for unacceptable desires.

**Withdrawal** The discomfort and distress, including physical pain and intense cravings, experienced after stopping the use of an addictive drug.

**Working memory** A newer understanding of short-term memory (STM) that emphasizes the active processing of information.

**Yerkes-Dodson law** The law stating that maximum performance is related to levels of arousal; complex tasks require a relatively low level of arousal, whereas simple tasks require a relatively high arousal level.

**Zone of proximal development (ZPD)** Vygotsky's concept of the difference between what children can accomplish on their own and what they can accomplish with the help of others who are more competent.

**A Guide to Worldwide Pet Ownership.** (2017, January 3). *Pet Secure*. Retrieved from: http://www.petsecure.com.au/pet-care/a-guide-to-worldwide-pet-ownership/

**Abraham Lincoln Biography.** (n.d.). Abraham Lincoln Biography. *Biography online*. Retrieved from http://www.biographyonline.net/politicians/american/abraham-lincon.html

**Achenbaum, W. A., & Bengtson, V. L.** (1994). Re-engaging the disengagement theory of aging: On the history and assessment of theory development in gerontology. *Gerontologist, 34,* 756–763.

**Acierno, R., Gros, D. F., Ruggiero, K. J., Hernandez-Tejada, M. A., Knapp, R. G., Lejuez, C. W., . . . Tuerk, P. W.** (2016). Behavioral activation and therapeutic exposure for posttraumatic stress disorder: A noninferiority trial of treatment delivered in person versus home-based telehealth. *Depression and Anxiety, 33,* 415–423. http://dx.doi.org/10.1002/da.22476

**Acierno, R., Knapp, R., Tuerk, P., Gilmore, A. K., Lejuez, C., Ruggiero, K., . . . Foa, E. B.** (2017). A non-inferiority trial of Prolonged Exposure for posttraumatic stress disorder: In person versus home-based telehealth. *Behaviour Research and Therapy, 89,* 57–65. http://dx.doi.org/10.1016/j.brat.2016.11.009

**Adachi, T., Fujino, H., Nakae, A., Mashimo, T., & Sasaki, J.** (2014). A meta-analysis of hypnosis for chronic pain problems: A comparison between hypnosis, standard care, and other psychological interventions. *International Journal of Clinical and Experimental Hypnosis, 62,* 1–28. http://dx.doi.org/10.1080/00207144.2013.841471

**Adams, L. Y.** (2015). *Workplace mental health: Manual for nurse managers.* New York, NY: Springer.

**Adams, M. J., Majolo, B., Ostner, J., Schülke, O., De Marco, A., Thierry, B., . . . Weiss, A.** (2015). Personality structure and social style in macaques. *Journal of Personality and Social Psychology, 109,* 338–353. http://dx.doi.org/10.1037/pspp0000041

**Adams, R. B., Jr., & Nelson, A., J.** (2016). Eye behavior and gaze. In D. Matsumoto, H. C. Hwang, & M. G. Frank (Eds.), *APA handbook of nonverbal communication* (pp. 335–362). Washington, DC: American Psychological Association. http://dx.doi.org/:10.1037/14669-013

**Addis, D. R., Leclerc, C. M., Muscatell, K., & Kensinger, E. A.** (2010). There are age-related changes in neural connectivity during the encoding of positive, but not negative, information. *Cortex, 46,* 425–433. http://dx.doi.org/10.1016/j.cortex.2009.04.011

**Adele Diamond.** (n.d.). *Wikipedia.* Retrieved January 11, 2017 from https://en.wikipedia.org/wiki/Adele_Diamond

**Adelmann, P. K., & Zajonc, R. B.** (1989). Facial efference and the experience of emotion. *Annual Review of Psychology, 40,* 249–280.

**Adi-Japha, E., & Karni, A.** (2016). Time for considering constraints on procedural memory consolidation processes: Comment on Pan and Rickard (2015) with specific reference to developmental changes. *Psychological Bulletin, 142,* 568–571. http://dx.doi.org/10.1037/bul0000048

**Adler, A.** (1927/1954). *Understanding human nature.* New York: NY: Greenburg.

**Adolph, K. E., & Berger, S. E.** (2012). Physical and motor development. In M. H. Bornstein & M. E. Lamb (Eds.), *Cognitive development: An advanced textbook* (pp. 257–318). New York, NY: Psychology Press.

**Adolph, K. E., Dretch, K. S., & LoBue, V.** (2014). Fear of heights in infants? *Current Directions in Psychological Science, 23,* 60–66.

**Ahlbeck Bergendahl, I., Salvanes, A. G. V., & Braithwaite, V. A.** (2016). Determining the effects of duration and recency of exposure to environmental enrichment. *Applied Animal Behaviour Science, 176,* 163–169. http://dx.doi.org/10.1016/j.applanim.2015.11.002

**Ahler, D. J., Citrin, J., Dougal, M. C., & Lenz, G. S.** (2017). Face value? Experimental evidence that candidate appearance influences electoral choice. *Political Behavior, 39*(1), 77–102. http://dx.doi.org/10.1007/s11109-016-9348-6

**Ahlsén, E.** (2008). Embodiment in communication— Aphasia, apraxia, and the possible role of mirroring and imitation. *Clinical Linguistics & Phonetics, 22,* 311–315.

**Ahmetoglu, G., & Chamorro-Premuzic, T.** (2013). *Psych 101. Personality 101.* New York: NY: Springer.

**Ainsworth, M. D. S.** (1967). *Infancy in Uganda: Infant care and the growth of love.* Baltimore, MD: Johns Hopkins University Press.

**Ainsworth, M. D. S.** (2010). Security and attachment. In R. Volpe (Ed.), *The secure child: Timeless lessons in parenting and childhood education* (pp. 43–53). Charlotte, NC: Information Age.

**Ainsworth, M. D. S., Blehar, M., Waters, E., & Wall, S.** (1978). *Patterns of attachment: Observations in the strange situation and at home.* Hillsdale, NJ: Erlbaum.

**Aizer, A. A., Chen, M. H., McCarthy, E. P., Mendu, M. L., Koo, S., Wilhite, T. J., Nguyen, P. L.** (2013). Marital status and survival in patients with cancer. *Journal of Clinical Oncology, 31,* 3869–3876. http://dx.doi.org/10.1200/JCO.2013.49.6489.

**Akhter, S., Marcus, M., Kerber, R.A., Kong, M., & Taylor, K. C.** (2016). The impact of periconceptional maternal stress on fecundability. *Annals of Epidemiology, 26,* 710–716. http://dx.doi.org/10.1016/j.annepidem.2016.07.015

**Aknin, L. B., Mayraz, G., & Helliwell, J. F.** (2017). The emotional consequences of donation opportunities. *The Journal of Positive Psychology, 12,* 169–177. http://dx.doi.org/10.1080/17439760.2016.1163409

**Akyeampong, E., Hill, A. G., & Kleinman, A.** (Eds.). (2015). *The culture of mental illness and psychiatric practice in Africa.* Bloomington, IN: Indiana University Press.

**Alaerts, K., Geerlings, F., Herremans, L., Swinnen, S. P., Verhoeven, J., Sunaert, S., & Wenderoth, N.** (2015). Functional organization of the action observation network in autism: A graph theory approach. *PLoS ONE, 10*(8): e0137020. http://dx.doi.org/10.e0137020.

**Albert Einstein - Questions and Answers.** (n. d.). *Nobelprize.org.* Retrieved from http://www.nobelprize.org/nobel_prizes/physics/laureates/1921/einstein-faq.html

**Alberti, R. E., & Emmons, M. L.** (2008). *Your perfect right: Assertiveness and equality in your life and relationships.* Waupaca, WI: Impact Publications.

**Albert, M. A., & Dahling, J. J.** (2016). Learning goal orientation and locus of control interact to predict academic self-concept and academic performance in college students. *Personality and Individual Differences, 97,* 245–248. http://dx.doi.org/10.1016/j.paid.2016.03.074

**Albright, T. D.** (2015). Perceiving. *Daedalus, 144,* 22–41. http://dx.doi.org/10.1162/DAED_a_00315

**Albuquerque, D., Stice, E., Rodríguez-López, R., Manco, L., & Nóbrega, C.** (2015). Current review of genetics of human obesity: From molecular mechanisms to an evolutionary perspective. *Molecular Genetics and Genomics, 6,* 1–31. http://dx.doi.org/10.1007/s00438-015-1015-9

**Aldrich, D. P., & Meyer, M. A.** (2015). Social capital and community resilience. *American Behavioral Scientist, 59,* 254–269. http://dx.doi.org/10.1177/0002764214550299

**Aldridge, L. J., & Islam, M. R.** (2012). Cultural differences in athlete attributions for success and failure: The sports pages revisited. *International Journal of Psychology, 47,* 67–75.

**Alexander, J.** (2017). *Using writing as a therapy for eating disorders: The diary healer.* New York, NY: Routledge/Taylor & Francis Group.

**Al-Issa, I.** (2000). Culture and mental illness in Algeria. In I. Al-Issa (Ed.), *Al-Junun: Mental illness in the Islamic world* (pp. 101–119). Madison, CT: International Universities Press.

**Al Khatib, H. K., Harding, S. V., Darzi, J., & Pot, G. K.** (2017). The effects of partial sleep deprivation on energy balance: A systematic review and meta-analysis. *European Journal of Clinical Nutrition, 71*(5), 614–624. http://dx.doi.org/10.1038/ejcn.2016.201

**Alkozei, A., Smith, R., & Killgore, W. D. S.** (2017). Gratitude and subjective wellbeing: A proposal of two causal frameworks. *Journal of Happiness Studies.* No Pagination Specified. http://dx.doi.org/10.1007/s10902-017-9870-1

**Alladin, A.** (2016). *Integrative CBT for anxiety disorders: An evidence-based approach to enhancing cognitive behavioural therapy with mindfulness and hypnotherapy.* Hoboken, NJ: Wiley. http://dx.doi.org/10.1002/9781118509869

**Allam, M. D.-E., Soussignan, R., Patris, B., Marlier, L., & Schaal, B.** (2010). Long-lasting memory for an odor acquired at the mother's breast. *Developmental Science, 13,* 849–863.

**Allan, J. L., McMinn, D., & Daly, M.** (2016). A bidirectional relationship between executive function and health behavior: Evidence, implications, and future directions. *Frontiers in Neuroscience,* 10:386. http://dx.doi.org/10.3389/fnins

**Allan, N. P., Oglesby, M. E., Short, N. A., & Schmidt, N. B.** (2016). Examining the panic attack specifier in social anxiety disorder. *Cognitive Behaviour Therapy, 45,* 177–181. http://dx.doi.org/10.1080/16506073.2015.1124447

**Allday, E.** (2016, June 29). The streets' sickest, costliest: The mentally ill. *San Francisco Chronicle.*

Retrieved from http://projects.sfchronicle.com/sf-homeless/mental-health/

**Allison, R.** (2016). Gendered jocks or equal players? Athletic affiliation and hooking up among college students. *Sociological Spectrum, 36,* 255–270. http://dx.doi.org/i:10.1080/02732173.2015.1123127

**Allport, G. W.** (1937). *Personality: A psychological interpretation.* New York, NY: Holt, Rinehart and Winston.

**Allport, G. W., & Odbert, H. S.** (1936). Trait-names: A psycho-lexical study. *Psychological Monographs: General and Applied, 47,* 1–21.

**Almiron-Roig, E., Tsiountsioura, M., Lewis, H. B., Wu, J., Solis-Trapala, I., & Jebb, S. A.** (2015). Large portion sizes increase bite size and eating rate in overweight women. *Physiology & Behavior, 139,* 297–302. http://dx.doi.org/10.1016/j.physbeh.2014.11.041

**Alpár, A., Di Marzo, V., & Harkany, T.** (2016). At the tip of an iceberg: Prenatal marijuana and its possible relation to neuropsychiatric outcome in the offspring. *Biological Psychiatry, 79,* e33–e45. http://dx.doi.org/10.1016/j.biopsych.2015.09.009

**Al-Sharfi, M., Pfeffer, K., & Miller, K. A.** (2016). The effects of polygamy on children and adolescents: A systematic review. *Journal of Family Studies, 22,* 272–286. http://dx.doi.org/10.1080/13229400.2015.1086405

**Alvarez, A. N., Liang, C. T. H., & Neville, H. A.** (Eds.). (2016). *The cost of racism for people of color: Contextualizing experiences of discrimination.* Washington, DC: American Psychological Association. http://dx.doi.org/10.1037/14852-000

**Amadeo, K.** (2016). What are the odds of winning the lottery? *The Balance.* Retrieved June 9, 2017 from https://www.thebalance.com/what-are-the-odds-of-winning-the-lottery-3306232

**American Academy of Pediatrics.** (1999). Circumcision policy statement. *Pediatrics, 103,* 686–693.

**American Academy of Pediatrics.** (2005). Policy statement: AAP publications retired and reaffirmed. *Pediatrics,* 116, 796.

**American Academy of Pediatrics.** (2012). Circumcision policy statement. *Pediatrics,* 30, 585–586. http://dx.doi.org/10.1542/peds.2012-1989

**American Association of Suicidology (AAS)** (2016). *Myths about suicide.* Retrieved from http://www.suicidology.org/about-aas/national-suicide-prevention-week/myth-fact

**American Heart Association.** (2013). *Statistical fact sheet: 2013 update.* Retrieved from: http://www.heart.org/idc/groups/heart-public/@wcm/@sop/@smd/documents/downloadable/ucm_319588.pdf

**American Psychiatric Association.** (2013). *DSM: Diagnostic and statistical manual of mental disorders* (5th ed.). Washington, DC: American Psychiatric Association.

**American Psychological Association (APA).** (2009). Committee on Animal Research and Ethics (CARE) Annual Report 2009. From http://www.apa.org/science/leadership/care/2009-report.aspx

**American Psychological Association.** (2013). Gun violence: Prediction, prevention, and policy. *Public and Member Communications, Public Affairs Office.* Washington, DC: American Psychological Association. http://dx.doi.org/10.1-37/e647302013-001

**American Psychological Association.** (2016). *Resolution on data about sexual orientation and gender identity.* Retrieved from: http://www.apa.org/about/policy/data-sexual-orientation. aspx

**Amianto, F., Ottone, L., Abbate Daga, G., & Fassino, S.** (2015). Binge-eating disorder diagnosis and treatment: A recap in front of DSM-5. *BMC Psychiatry, 15,* Article ID 70.

**Amichai-Hamburger, Y., Gazit, T., Bar-Ilan, J., Perez, O., Aharony, N., Bronstein, J., & Sarah Dyne, T.** (2016). Psychological factors behind the lack of participation in online discussions. *Computers in Human Behavior, 55*(Part A), 268–277. http://dx.doi.org/10.1016/j.chb.2015.09.009

**Andersen, P. A.** (2014). Nonverbal immediacy in interpersonal communication. In A. W. Siegman & S. Feldman (Eds.), *Multichannel integrations of nonverbal behavior* (pp. 1–36). New York, NY: Psychology Press.

**Anderson, C. A.** (2001). Heat and violence. *Current Directions in Psychological Science, 10,* 33–38.

**Anderson, M. C., Ochsner, K. N., Kuhl, B., Cooper, J., Robertson, E., Gabrieli, S. W., . . . Gabrieli, J. D. E.** (2004). Neural systems underlying the suppression of unwanted memories. *Science, 303,* 232–235. http://dx.doi.org/10.1126/science.1089504

**Andics, A., Gábor, A., Gácsi, M., Faragó, T., Szabó, D., & Miklósi, Á.** (2016). Neural mechanisms for lexical processing in dogs. *Science, 353*(6303), 1030–1032. http://dx.doi.org/10.1126/science.aaf3777

**Ando, J., Fujisawa, K. K., Shikishima, C., Hiraishi, K., Nozaki, M., Yamagata, S., . . . Ooki, S.** (2013). Two cohort and three independent anonymous twin projects at the Keio Twin Research Center (KoTReC). *Twin Research & Human Genetics, 16,* 202–216. http://dx.doi. org/10.1017/thg.2012.13

**Andrade, C., Arumugham, S. S., & Thirthalli, J.** (2016). Adverse effects of electroconvulsive therapy. *Psychiatric Clinics of North America, 39,* 513–530. http://dx.doi.org/10.1016/j.psc.2016.04.004

**Andreychik, M. R., & Lewis, E.** (2017). Will you help me to suffer less? How about to feel more joy? Positive and negative empathy are associated with different other-oriented motivations. *Personality and Individual Differences, 105,* 139–149. http://dx.doi.org/10.1016/j.paid.2016.09.038

**Anestis, M. D., Khazem, L. R., Law, K. C., Houtsma, C., LeTard, R., Moberg, F., & Martin, R.** (2015). The association between state laws regulating handgun ownership and statewide suicide rates. *American Journal of Public Health, 105,* 2059–2067. http://dx.doi.org/10.2105/AJPH.2014.302465

**Angermeyer, M. C., Millier, A., Rémuzat, C., Refaï, T., Schomerus, G., & Toumi, M.** (2015). Continuum beliefs and attitudes towards people with mental illness: Results from a national survey in France. *International Journal of Social Psychiatry, 61*(3), 297–303. http://dx.doi.org/10.1177/0020764014543312

**Angus, D. J., Schutter, D. J. L. G., Terburg, D., van Honk, J., & Harmon-Jones, E.** (2016). A review of social neuroscience research on anger and aggression. In E. Harmon-Jones & M. Inzlicht (Eds.), *Social neuroscience: Biological approaches to social psychology* (pp. 223–246). New York, NY: Routledge/Taylor & Francis Group.

**Anicich, E. M., Swaab, R. I., & Galinsky, A. D.** (2015). Hierarchical cultural values predict success and mortality in high-stakes teams. *Proceedings of the National Academy of Sciences of the United States of America, 112,* 1338–1343. http://dx.doi.org/10.1073/pnas.1408800112

**Anik, L., Aknin, L. B., Norton, M. I., & Dunn, E. W.** (2011). Feeling good about giving: The benefits (and costs) of self-interested charitable behavior. In D. M. Oppenheimer & C. Y. Olivola (Eds.), *The science of giving: Experimental approaches to the study of charity* (pp. 3–13). New York, NY: Psychology Press.

**Anisman, H.** (2016). *Health psychology.* Thousand Oaks, CA: Sage.

**Antes, A. L.** (2016). Navigating the gray areas of scientific work: Questionable research practices and training in the responsible conduct of research. In A. Dade, L. Olafson, & S. M. DiBella (Eds.), *Implementing a comprehensive research compliance program: A handbook for research officers* (pp. 145–180). New York, NY: Springer.

**Anthenien, A. M., Lembo, J., & Neighbors, C.** (2017). Drinking motives and alcohol outcome expectancies as mediators of the association between negative urgency and alcohol consumption. *Addictive Behaviors, 66,* 101–107. http://dx.doi.org/10.1016/j.addbeh.2016.11.009

**Antonaccio, O., Botchkovar, E. V., & Hughes, L. A.** (2017). Ecological determinants of situated choice in situational action theory: Does neighborhood matter? *Journal of Research in Crime and Delinquency, 54*(2), 208–243. http://dx.doi.org/10.1177/0022427816678908

**Antoni, M. H., Bouchard, L. C., Jacobs, J. M., Lechner, S. C., Jutagir, D. R., Gudenkauf, L. M., . . . Blomberg, B. B.** (2016). Stress management, leukocyte transcriptional changes and breast cancer recurrence in a randomized trial: An exploratory analysis. *Psychoneuroendocrinology, 74,* 269–277. http://dx.doi.org/10.1016/j.psyneuen.2016.09.012

**Antunes, H. K., Leite, G. S., Lee, K. S., Barreto, A. T., Santos, R. V., Souza, H. S., . . . de Mello, M. T.** (2016). Exercise deprivation increases negative mood in exercise-addicted subjects and modifies their biochemical markers. *Physiology & Behavior, 156,* 182–190. http://dx.doi.org/10.1016/j.physbeh.2016.01.028

**Antypa, N., Souery, D., Tomasini, M., Albani, D., Fusco, F., Mendlewicz, J., & Serretti, A.** (2016). Clinical and genetic factors associated with suicide in mood disorder patients. *European Archives of Psychiatry and Clinical Neuroscience, 266,* 181–193. http://dx.doi.org/10.1007/s00406-015-0658-1

**APA Congressional Briefing.** (2015). APA congressional briefing highlights role of animal research in understanding human development. *Psychological Science Agenda, 29.* No Pagination Specified. http://dx.doi.org/10.1037/e525222015-003

**APA Presidential Task Force on Evidence-Based Practice.** (2006). Evidence-based practice in psychology. *American Psychologist, 61*(4), 271–285. http://dx.doi.org/10.1037/0003-066X.61.4.271

**APA's Press Release.** (2017, February 22). APA's survey finds constantly checking electronic devices linked to significant stress for most Americans. *APA.* Retrieved from http://dx.doi.org/10.1037/e501052017-001

**Apicella, C. L., Crittenden, A. N., & Tobolsky, V. A.** (2017). Hunter-gatherer males are more risk-seeking than females, even in late childhood. *Evolution and Human Behavior*. No Pagination Specified. http://dx.doi.org/10.1016/j.evolhumbehav.2017.01.003

**Applewhite, A.** (2016, September 3). You're how old? We'll be in touch. *New York Times.* Retrieved from https://www.nytimes.com/2016/09/04/opinion/sunday/youre-how-old-well-be-in-touch.html

**Aragona, M.** (2015). Rethinking received views on the history of psychiatric nosology: Minor shifts, major continuities. In P. Zachar, D. S. Stoyanov, M. Aragona, & A. Jablensky (Eds.), *International perspectives in philosophy and psychiatry. Alternative perspectives on psychiatric validation* (pp. 27–46). New York, NY: Oxford University Press.

**Arkowitz, H., & Lilienfeld, S. O.** (2017). *Facts and fictions in mental health.* Hoboken, NJ: Wiley-Blackwell.

**Armstrong, M., Morris, C., Abraham, C., & Tarrant, M.** (2017). Interventions utilizing contact with people with disabilities to improve children's attitudes toward disability: A systematic review and meta-analysis. *Disability and Health Journal, 10*(1), 11–22. http://dx.doi.org/10.1016/j.dhjo.2016.10.003

**Armstrong, T. A., Boutwell, B. B., Flores, S., Symonds, M., Keller, S., & Gangitano, D. A.** (2014). Monoamine oxidase A genotype, childhood adversity, and criminal behavior in an incarcerated sample. *Psychiatric Genetics, 24,* 164–171. http://dx.doi.org/10.1097/YPG.0000000000000033

**Arnal, P. J., Drogou, C., Sauvet, F., Regnauld, J., Dispersyn, G., Faraut, B., . . . Chennaoui, M.** (2016). Effect of sleep extension on the subsequent testosterone, cortisol and prolactin responses to total sleep deprivation and recovery. *Journal of Neuroendocrinology, 28,* 1–9. http://dx.doi.org/10.1111/jne.12346

**Arnedo, J., Svrakic, D. M., del Val, C., Romero-Zaliz, R., Hernández-Cuervo, H., Fanous, A. H., . . . Molecular Genetics of Schizophrenia Consortium.** (2015). Uncovering the hidden risk architecture of the schizophrenias: Confirmation in three independent genome-wide association studies. *The American Journal of Psychiatry, 172,* 139–153. http://dx.doi.org/10.1176/appi.ajp2014.14040435

**Arnett, J. J.** (2000). Emerging adulthood: A theory of development from the late teens through the twenties. *American Psychologist, 55,* 469–480.

**Arnett, J. J.** (2015). Identity development from adolescence to emerging adulthood: What we know and (especially) don't know. In K. C. McLean & M. Sved (Eds.), *The Oxford handbook of identity development* (pp. 53–64). New York, NY: Oxford University Press.

**Arntz, A.** (2015). Borderline personality disorder. In A. T. Beck, D. D. Davis, & A. Freeman (Eds.), *Cognitive therapy of personality disorders* (3rd ed., pp. 366–390). New York, NY: Guilford.

**Aronson, J., Jannone, S., McGlone, M., & Johnson-Campbell, T.** (2009). The Obama effect: An experimental test. *Journal of Experimental Social Psychology, 45,* 957–960. http://dx.doi.org/10.1016/j. jesp.2009.05.006

**Arora, P., Pössel, P., Barnard, A. D., Terjesen, M., Lai, B. S., Ehrlich, C. J., . . . Gogos, A. K.** (2015). Cognitive interventions. In R. Flanagan, K. Allen, & E. Levine (Eds.), *Cognitive and behavioral interventions in the schools: Integrating theory and research into practice* (pp. 221–248). New York, NY: Springer. http://dx.doi.org/10.1007/978-1-4939-1972-7

**Arsena, A., Silvera, D. H., & Pandelaere, M.** (2014). Brand trait transference: When celebrity endorsers acquire brand personality traits. *Journal of Business Research, 67,* 1537–1543. http://dx.doi.org/10.1016/j.jbusres.2014.01.011

**Arslan, G.** (2017). Psychological maltreatment, social acceptance, social connectedness, and subjective well-being in adolescents. *Journal of Happiness Studies.* No Pagination Specified. http://dx.doi.org/10.1007/s10902-017-9856-z

**Aruguete, M. S., & Hardy, P. M.** (2016). Performance attributions of African American and White college students. *North American Journal of Psychology, 18,* 257–268.

**Asada, K., Tojo, Y., Osanai, H., Saito, A., Hasegawa, T., & Kumagaya, S.** (2016). Reduced personal space in individuals with autism spectrum disorder. *PLoS ONE, 11*(1), Article e0146306.

**Ascherio, A., & Schwarzschild, M. A.** (2016). The epidemiology of Parkinson's disease: Risk factors and prevention. *The Lancet Neurology, 15*(12), 1257–1272. http://dx.doi.org/10.1016/S1474-4422(16)30230-7

**Asch, S. E.** (1951). Effects of group pressure upon the modification and distortion of judgment. In H. Guetzkow (Ed.), *Groups, leadership, and men: Research in human relations* (pp. 170–190). Pittsburgh, PA: Carnegie Press.

**Ashrafioun, L., Pigeon, W. R., Conner, K. R., Leong, S. H., & Oslin, D. W.** (2016). Prevalence and correlates of suicidal ideation and suicide attempts among veterans in primary care referred for a mental health evaluation. *Journal of Affective Disorders, 189,* 344–350. http://dx.doi.org/10.1016/j.jad.2015.09.014

**Ashton, J.** (2013, January 29). 10 cures for technostress. *Remodelista.* Retrieved from https://www.remodelista.com/posts/10-cures-for-technostress/

**Askenasy, J. J.** (2016). Low facing dreams. *Abnormal and Behavioral Psychology, 2,* 109. http://dx.doi.org/10.4172/abp.1000109

**Askew, C., Reynolds, G., Fielding-Smith, S., & Field, A. P.** (2016). Inhibition of vicariously learned fear in children using positive modeling and prior exposure. *Journal of Abnormal Psychology, 125,* 279–291. http://dx.doi.org/10.1037/abn0000131

**Asl, S. S., Saifi, B., Sakhaie, A., Zargooshnia, S., & Mehdizadeh, M.** (2015). Attenuation of ecstasy-induced neurotoxicity by N-acetylcysteine. *Metabolic Brain Disease, 30,* 171–181. http://dx.doi.org/10.1007/s11011-014-9598-0

**Atanasov, P. D., & Kunreuther, H.** (2015). Cautious defection: Group representatives cooperate and risk less than individuals. *Journal of Behavioral Decision Making, 29,* 372–380. http://dx.doi.org/10.1002/bdm.1880

**Atkinson, R. C., & Shiffrin, R. M.** (1968). Human memory: A proposed system and its control processes. In K. W. Spence & J. T. Spence (Eds.), *The psychology of learning and motivation* (Vol. 2, pp. 90–91). New York, NY: Academic Press.

**Atwood, J. D.** (2015). Sexual disorders and sex therapy. In J. L. Wetchler & L. L. Hecker (Eds.), *An introduction to marriage and family therapy* (2nd ed., pp. 431–467). New York, NY: Routledge/Taylor & Francis Group.

**Aucouturier, J. -J., Johansson, P., Hall, L., Segnini, R., Mercadié, L., & Watanabe, K.** (2016). Covert digital manipulation of vocal emotion alter speakers' emotional states in a congruent direction. *Proceedings of the National Academy of Sciences of the United States of America, 113,* 948–953. http://dx.doi.org/10.1073/pnas.1506552113

**Au, E. W. M.** (2015). Locus of control, self-efficacy, and the mediating effect of outcome control: Predicting course-level and global outcomes in an academic context. *Anxiety, Stress & Coping: An International Journal, 28,* 425–444. http://dx.doi.org/10.1080/10615806.2014.976761

**Augenstein, S.** (2016). Murder conviction, based solely on eyewitness testimony, reversed after 25 years. *Forensic Magazine.* Retrieved from http://www.forensicmag.com/news/2016/03/murder-conviction-based-solely-eyewitness-testimony-reversed-after-25-years

**Auger, A. P.** (2016). Genetic, epigenetic and gene-environment interactions: Impact on the pathogenesis of mental illnesses in women. In D. J. Castle & K. M. Abel (Eds.), *Comprehensive women's mental health* (pp. 45–54). New York, NY: Cambridge University Press.

**Augustinack, J. C., van der Kouwe, A. J. W., Salat, D. H., Benner, T., Stevens, A. A., Annese, J., . . . Corkin, S.** (2014). H.M.'s contributions to neuroscience: A review and autopsy studies. *Hippocampus, 24,* 1267–1286. http://dx.doi.org/10.1002/hipo.22354

**Avieli, H., Ben-David, S., & Levy, I.** (2016). Predicting professional quality of life among professional and volunteer caregivers. *Psychological Trauma: Theory, Research, Practice, and Policy, 8,* 80–87. http://dx.doi.org/10.1037/tra0000066

**Awasthi, A., & Mandal, M. K.** (2015). Facial expressions of emotions: Research perspectives. In M. K. Mandal & A. Awasthi (Eds.), *Understanding facial expressions in communication: Cross-cultural and multidisciplinary perspectives* (pp. 1–18). New York, NY: Springer. http://dx.doi.org/10.1007/978-81-322-1934-7_1

**Axtell, R. E.** (2007). *Essential do's and taboos: The complete guide to international business and leisure travel.* Hoboken, NJ: Wiley.

**Azzarito, L., Simon, M., & Marttinen, R.** (2016). "Stop photoshopping!": A visual participatory inquiry into students' responses to a body curriculum. *Journal of Teaching in Physical Education, 35*(1), 54–69. http://dx.doi.org/10.1123/jtpe.2014-0166

**Babbitt, L. G., Toosi, N. R., & Sommers, S. R.** (2016). A broad and insidious appeal: Unpacking the reasons for endorsing racial color blindness. In H. A. Neville, M. E. Gallardo, & D. W. Sue (Eds.), *The myth of racial color blindness: Manifestations, dynamics, and impact* (pp. 53–68). Washington, DC: American Psychological Association. http://dx.doi.org/10.1037/14754-004

**Babel, P.** (2016). Memory of pain induced by physical exercise. *Memory, 24,* 548–559. http://dx.doi.org/10.1080/09658211.2015.1023809.

**Bachmann, C. H., Wijlaars, L. P., Kalverdijk, L. J., Burcu, M., Glaeske, G., Schuiling-Veninga, C. C. M., . . . Zito, J. M. (2017).** Trends in ADHD medication use in children and adolescents in five western countries, 2005 –2012. *European Neuropsychopharmacology, 27*(5), 484–493. http://dx.doi.org/10.1016/j.euroneuro.2017.03.002

**Baddeley, A. D.** (1992). Working memory. *Science, 255,* 556–559. http://dx.doi.org/10.1126/science.1736359

**Baddeley, A. D.** (2007). *Working memory, thought, and action. Oxford psychology series.* New York, NY: Oxford University Press.

**Baddeley, A. D., Eysenck, M. W., & Anderson, M. C.** (2015). *Memory.* New York, NY: Psychology Press.

**Bae, M.** (2016). The effects of anonymity on computer-mediated communication: The case of independent versus interdependent self-construal influence. *Computers in Human Behavior, 55*(Part A), 300–309. http://dx.doi.org/10.1016/j.chb.2015.09.026

**Bagheri, B., Meshkini, F., Dinarvand, K., Alikhani, Z., Haysom, M., & Rasouli, M.** (2016). Life psychosocial stresses and coronary artery disease. *International Journal of Preventive Medicine, 7, 106.* http://dx.doi.org/10.4103/2008-7802.190598

**Bagot, K. S., & Kaminer, Y.** (2014). Efficacy of stimulants for cognitive enhancement in non-attention deficit hyperactivity disorder youth: A systematic review. *Addiction, 109,* 547–557. http://dx.doi.org/10.1111/add.12460

**Bailey, D. P., Smith, L. R., Chrismas, B. C., Taylor, L., Stensel, D. J., Deighton, K., . . . Kerr, C. J.** (2015). Appetite and gut hormone responses to moderate-intensity continuous exercise versus high-intensity interval exercise, in normoxic and hypoxic conditions. *Appetite, 89,* 237–245. http://dx.doi.org/10.1016/j.appet.2015.02.019

**Bailey, J. M., Vasey, P. L., Diamond, L M., Breedlove, S. M., Vilain, E., & Epprecht, M.** (2016). Sexual orientation, controversy, and science. *Psychological Science in the Public Interest, 17,* 45–101. http://dx.doi. org/10.1177/1529100616637616

**Baillargeon, R. & DeVos, J.** (1991). Object permanence in young infants: Further evidence. *Child Development, 62,* 1227–1246. http://dx.doi.org/10.2307/1130803

**Baines, L., Jones, A., & Christiansen, P.** (2016). Hopelessness and alcohol use: The mediating role of drinking motives and outcome expectancies. *Addictive Behaviors Reports, 4,* 65–69. http://dx.doi.org/10.1016/j.abrep.2016.11.001

**Bajwa, N. M., Halavi, S., Hamer, M., Semple, B. D., Noble-Haeusslein, L. J., Baghchechi, M., . . . Obenaus, A.** (2016). Mild concussion, but not moderate traumatic brain injury, is associated with long-term depression-like phenotype in mice. *PLoS ONE, 11*(1): e0146886. http://dx.doi.org/10.1371/journal.pone.0146886

**Baker, S.** (2015, January 3). Breaking the taboo: It's time to talk about mental health. *CNN Vital Signs.* http://www.cnn.com/search/?text=breaking+the+taboo+it%27s+time+to+talk+about+mental+health+baker

**Bakker, B. N., Klemmensen, R., Nørgaard, A. A., & Schumacher, G.** (2016). Stay loyal or exit the party? How openness to experience and extroversion explain vote switching. *Political Psychology, 37,* 419–429. http://dx.doi.org/10.1111/pops.12257

**Bakker, N., Shahab, S., Giacobbe, P., Blumberger, D. M., Daskalakis, Z. J., Kennedy, S. H., & Downar, J.** (2015). rTMS of the dorsomedial prefrontal cortex for major depression: Safety, tolerability, effectiveness, and outcome predictors for 10 Hz versus intermittent theta-burst stimulation. *Brain Stimulation,* 8, 208–215. http://dx.doi.org/10.1016/j.brs.2014.11.002

**Bakou, A., Margiotoudi, K., Kouroupa, A., & Vatakis, A.** (2014). Temporal and sensory experiences in the dreams of sighted and congenital blind individuals. *Procedia-Social and Behavioral Sciences, 126,* 188–189. http://dx.doi.org/10.1016/j.sbspro.2014.02.364

**Bakshy, E., Messing, S., & Adamic, L. A.** (2015). Exposure to ideologically diverse news and opinion on Facebook. *Science, 348,* 1130–1132. http://dx.doi.org/10.1126/science.aaa1160

**Bak, T. H., Long, M. R., Vega-Mendoza, M., & Sorace, A.** (2016). Novelty, challenge, and practice: The impact of intensive language learning on attentional functions. *Plos One, 11,* e0153485. http://dx.doi.org/10.1371/journal.pone.0153485.

**Balon, R.** (2015). Paraphilic disorders. In L. W. Roberts & A. K. Louie (Eds.), *Study guide to DSM-5®* (pp. 441–458). Arlington, VA: American Psychiatric Publishing.

**Balon, R.** (Ed.). (2016). *Practical guide to paraphilia and paraphilic disorders.* Cham, CH: Springer International Publishing. http://dx.doi.org/10.1007/978-3-319-42650-1

**Bandura, A.** (1969). *Principles of behavior modification.* New York, NY: Holt, Rinehart & Winston.

**Bandura, A.** (1986). *Social foundations of thought and action: A social cognitive theory.* Englewood Cliffs, NJ: Prentice Hall.

**Bandura, A.** (1989). Social cognitive theory. In R. Vasta (Ed.), *Annals of child development Vol. 6. Six theories of child development* (pp. 1–60). Greenwich, CT: JAI Press.

**Bandura, A.** (1997). *Self-efficacy: The exercise of control.* New York: NY: Freeman.

**Bandura A.** (2008). Reconstrual of "free will" from the agentic perspective of social cognitive theory. In J. Baer, J. C. Kaufman, & R. F. Baumeister (Eds.), *Are we free? Psychology and free will* (pp. 89–127). New York, NY: Oxford University Press.

**Bandura, A.** (2011). But what about that gigantic elephant in the room? In R. M. Arkin (Ed.), *Most underappreciated: 50 prominent social psychologists describe their most unloved work* (pp. 51–59). New York, NY: Oxford University Press.

**Bandura, A.** (2011). Social cognitive theory. In P. A. M. Van Lange, A. W. Kruglanski, & E. T. Higgins (Eds.), *Handbook of theories of social psychology* (Vol. 1, pp. 349–373). Thousand Oaks, CA: Sage.

**Bandura, A., Ross, D., & Ross, S.** (1961). Transmission of aggression through imitation of aggressive models. *Journal of Abnormal & Social Psychology, 63,* 575–582. http://dx.doi.org/10.1037/h0045925

**Bandura, A., & Walters, R. H.** (1963). *Social learning and personality development.* New York, NY: Holt, Rinehart and Winston.

**Banerjee, S. C., Greene, K., Yanovitzky, I., Bagdasarov, Z., Choi, S. Y., & Magsamen-Conrad, K.** (2015). Adolescent egocentrism and indoor tanning: Is the relationship direct or mediated? *Journal of Youth Studies, 18,* 357–375. http://dx.doi.org/10.1080/13676261.2014.963536

**Bankó, É. M., & Vidnyánszky, Z.** (2010). Retention interval affects visual short-term memory encoding. *Journal of Neurophysiology, 103,* 1425–1430. http://dx.doi.org/10.1152/jn.00868.2009

**Banks, G., Hadenfeldt, K., Janoch, M., Manning, C., Ramos, K., & Patterson Silver Wolf, D. A.** (2017). Gun violence and substance abuse. *Aggression and Violent Behavior, 34,* 113–116. http://dx.doi.org/10.1016/j.avb.2017.02.002

**Banks, J. B., Tartar, J. L., & Tamayo, B. A.** (2015). Examining factors involved in stress-related working memory impairments: Independent or conditional effects? *Emotion, 15,* 827–836. http://dx.doi.org/10.1037/emo0000096

**Baptista, J., Derakhshani, M., & Tressoldi, P. E.** (2015). Explicit anomalous cognition: A review of the best evidence in ganzfeld, forced choice, remote viewing and dream studies. In E. Cardeña, J. Palmer, & D. Marcusson-Clavertz (Eds.), *Parapsychology: A handbook for the 21st century* (pp. 192–214). Jefferson, NC: McFarland & Co.

**Barber, J. P., & Solomonov, N.** (2016). Psychodynamic theories. In J. C. Norcross, G. R. VandenBos, D. K. Freedheim, & B. O. Olantunji (Eds.), *APA handbook of clinical psychology: Theory and research* (Vol. 2, pp. 53–77). Washington, DC: American Psychological Association. http://dx.doi.org/10.1037/14773-003

**Barber, L. K., & Budnick, C. J.** (2015). Turning molehills into mountains: Sleepiness increases workplace interpretive bias. *Journal of Organizational Behavior, 36*(3), 360–381.

**Barceló, J.** (2017). The association between agreeableness, extraversion, and support for secessionist movements: Evidence from a large survey of more than 33,000 respondents in Catalonia. *Personality and Individual Differences, 107,* 102–107. http://dx.doi.org/10.1016/j.paid.2016.11.029

**Bardi, L., Regolin, L., & Simion, F.** (2014). The first time ever I saw your feet: Inversion effect in newborns' sensitivity to biological motion. *Developmental Psychology, 50,* 986–993. http://dx.doi.org/10.1037/a0034678

**Bareket-Bojmel, L., Hochman, G., & Ariely, D.** (2017). It's (not) all about the Jacksons: Testing different types of short-term bonuses in the field. *Journal of Management, 43,* 534–554. http://dx.doi.org/10.1177/0149206314535441

**Barelds, D. P. H., & Dijkstra, P.** (2011). Positive illusions about a partner's personality and relationship quality. *Journal of Research in Personality, 45,* 37–43.

**Bargh, J. A.** (2014). Our unconscious mind. *Scientific American, 310,* 30–37.

**Barkley, R. A.** (2017). *When an adult you love has ADHD: Professional advice for parents, partners, and siblings.* Washington, DC: American Psychological Association. http://dx.doi.org/10.1037/15963-004

**Barling, J., Barnes, C. M., Carleton, E., & Wagner, D. T.** (2016). *Work and sleep research insights for the workplace.* New York, NY: Oxford University Press.

**Barnes, J. C., Boutwell, B. B., & Beaver, K. M.** (2014). Genetic and nonshared environmental factors predict handgun ownership in early adulthood. *Death Studies, 38,* 156–164. http://dx.doi.org/10.1080/07481187.2012.738769

**Barnow, S., & Balkir, N.** (Eds.). (2013). *Cultural variations in psychopathology: From research to practice.* Cambridge, MA: Hogrefe.

**Barnum, S. E., Woody, M. L., & Gibb, B. E.** (2013). Predicting changes in depressive symptoms from pregnancy to postpartum: The role of brooding rumination and negative inferential styles. *Cognitive Therapy and Research, 37,* 71–77.

Barrett, D., Sogolow, Z., Oh, A., Panton, J., Grayson, M., & Justiniano, M. (2014). Content of dreams from WWII POWs. *Imagination, Cognition and Personality, 33,* 193–204. http://dx.doi.org/10.2190/IC.33.1–2.

Barton, A. L., & Hirsch, J. K. (2016). Permissive parenting and mental health in college students: Mediating effects of academic entitlement. *Journal of American College Health, 64,* 1–8. http://dx.doi.org/10.1080/07448481.2015.1060597

Basch, C. H., Kernan, W. D., & Menafro, A. (2016). Presence of candy and snack food at checkout in chain stores: Results of a pilot study. *Journal of Community Health, 41,* 1090–1093. http://dx.doi.org/10.1007/s10900-016-0193-7

Bas-Hoogendam, J. M., Blackford, J. U., Brühl, A. B., Blair, K. S., van der Wee, N. J. A., & Westenberg, P. M. (2016). Neurobiological candidate endophenotypes of social anxiety disorder. *Neuroscience and Biobehavioral Reviews, 71,* 362–378. http://dx.doi.org/10.1016/j.neubiorev.2016.08.040

Baskin-Sommers, A., Stuppy-Sullivan, A. M., & Buckholtz, J. W. (2016). Psychopathic individuals exhibit but do not avoid regret during counterfactual decision making. *Proceedings of the National Academy of Sciences of the United States of America, 113*(50), 14438–14443. http://dx.doi.org/10.1073/pnas.1609985113

Batanova, M., Espelage, D. L., & Rao, M. A. (2014). Early adolescents' willingness to intervene: What roles do attributions, affect, coping, and self-reported victimization play? *Journal of School Psychology, 52,* 279–293. *http://dx.doi.org/10.1016/j.jsp.2014.02.001*

Bateganya, M. H., Amanyeiwe, U., Roxo, U., & Dong, M. (2015). Impact of support groups for people living with HIV on clinical outcomes: A systematic review of the literature. *Journal of Acquired Immune Deficiency Syndromes, 68,* S368–S374. http://dx.doi.org/10.1097/QAI.0000000000000519

Bateman, A. W., & Fonagy, P. (2016). The role of mentalization in treatments for personality disorder. In W. J. Livesley, G. Dimaggio, & J. F. Clarkin (Eds.), *Integrated treatment for personality disorder: A modular approach* (pp. 148–172). New York, NY: Guilford Press.

Bates, J. E., Schermerhorn, A. C., & Petersen, I. T. (2014). Temperament concepts in developmental psychopathology. In M. Lewis & K. Rudolph (Eds.), *Handbook of developmental psychopathology* (pp. 311–329). New York, NY: Springer.

Batty, G. D, Russ, T. C., MacBeath, M., Starnatakis, E., & Kivimäki, M. (2017). Psychological distress in relation to site specific cancer mortality: Pooling of unpublished data from 16 prospective cohort studies. *British Medical Journal, 356,* j108. https://dx.doi.org/10.1136/bmj.j108

Baucom, B. R., Dickenson, J. A., Atkins, D. C., Baucom, D. H., Fischer, M. S., Weusthoff, S., ... Zimmermann, T. (2015). The interpersonal process model of demand/withdraw behavior. *Journal of Family Psychology, 29,* 80–90. http://dx.doi.org/10.1037/ fam0000044.

Bauer, G., & Hämmig, O. (Eds.). (2014). *Bridging occupational, organizational, and public health: A transdisciplinary approach.* New York, NY: Springer.

Bauer, P. J., & Larkina, M. (2014). Childhood amnesia in the making: Different distributions of autobiographical memories in children and adults. *Journal of Experimental Psychology: General, 143,* 597–611. http://dx.doi.org/10.1037/a0033307

Baugh, C. M., Kiernan, P. T., Kroshus, E., Daneshvar, D. H., Montenigro, P. H., McKee, A. C., & Stern, R. A. (2015). Frequency of head-impact-related outcomes by position in NCAA Division 1 collegiate football players. *Journal of Neurotrauma, 32,* 314–326. http://dx.doi.org/10.1089/neu.2014.3582

Baumeister, J. C., Papa, G., & Foroni, F. (2016). Deeper than skin deep – The effect of botulinum toxin-A on emotion processing. *Toxicon, 118,* 86. http://dx.doi.org/10.1016/j.toxicon.2016.04.044

Baumeister, J. C., Rumiati, R. I., & Foroni, F. (2015). When the mask falls: The role of facial motor resonance in memory for emotional language. *Acta Psychologica, 155,* 29. http://dx.doi.org/10.1016/j.actpsy.2014.11.012

Baumeister, R. F., Ainsworth, S. E., & Vohs, K. D. (2016). Are groups more or less than the sum of their members? The moderating role of individual identification. *Behavioral and Brain Sciences, 39:* e137. http://dx.doi.org/10.1017/S0140525X15000618

Baumeister, R. F., & Bushman, B. (2014). *Social psychology and human nature* (3rd ed.). Boston, MA: Cengage.

Baum, M. J., & Cherry, J. A. (2015). Processing by the main olfactory system of chemosignals that facilitate mammalian reproduction. *Hormones and Behavior, 68,* 53–64. http://dx.doi.org/10.1016/j.yhbeh.2014.06.003

Baumrind, D. (1980). New directions in socialization research. *American Psychologist, 35,* 639–652.

Baumrind, D. (2013). Authoritative parenting revisited: History and current status. In R. E. Larzelere, A. S. Morris, & A.W. Harrist (Eds.), *Authoritative parenting: Synthesizing nurturance and discipline for optimal child development* (pp. 11–34). Washington, DC: American Psychological Association.

Baumrind, D. (2015). When subjects become objects: The lies behind the Milgram legend. *Theory & Psychology, 25*(5), 690–696. http://dx.doi.org/10.1177/0959354315592062

Beach, F. A. (1977). *Human sexuality in four perspectives.* Baltimore, MD: The Johns Hopkins University Press.

Beail, N. (2016). Psychodynamic psychotherapy. In C. Hemmings & N. Bouras (Eds.), *Psychiatric and behavioral disorders in intellectual and developmental disabilities* (3rd ed., pp. 151–160). New York, NY: Cambridge University Press.

Bechtold, J., Hipwell, A., Lewis, D. A., Loeber, R., & Pardini, D. (2016). Concurrent and sustained cumulative effects of adolescent marijuana use on subclinical psychotic symptoms. *American Journal of Psychiatry, 173*(8), 781–789. http://dx.doi.org/10.1176/appi.ajp.2016.15070878

Beck, A. T. (1976). *Cognitive therapy and the emotional disorders.* New York, NY: International Universities Press.

Beck, A. T. (2000). *Prisoners of hate.* New York, NY: Harper Perennial.

Beck, A. T., & Bredemeier, K. (2016). A unified model of depression: Integrating clinical, cognitive, biological, and evolutionary perspectives. *Clinical Psychological Science, 4,* 596–619. http://dx.doi.org/10.1177/2167702616628523

Beck, A. T., Freeman, A., & Davis, D. D. (2015). General principles and specialized techniques in cognitive therapy of personality disorders. In A. T. Beck, D. D. Davis, & A. Freeman (Eds.), *Cognitive therapy of personality disorders* (3rd ed., pp. 97–124). New York, NY: Guilford.

Beck, A. T., Haigh, E. A. P., & Baber, K. F. (2012). Biological underpinnings of the cognitive model of depression: A prototype for psychoanalytic research. *Psychoanalytic Review, 99,* 515–537.

Beebe, K. R. (2014). Hypnotherapy for labor and birth. *Nursing for Women's Health, 18,* 48–59. http://dx.doi.org/10.1111/1751-486X.12093

Behen, M. E., & Chugani, H. T. (2015). Functional and structural correlates of early severe social deprivation. In R. K. Schutt, L. J. Seidman, & M. Keshavan (Eds.), *Social neuroscience: Brain, mind, and society* (pp. 280–319). Boston, MA: Harvard University Press. https://doi.org/10.4159/9780674286719-012

Behm-Morawitz, E., Lewallen, J., & Miller, B. (2016). Real mean girls? Reality television viewing, social aggression, and gender-related beliefs among female emerging adults. *Psychology of Popular Media Culture, 5*(4), 340–355. http://dx.doi.org/10.1037/ppm0000074

Beilin, H. (1992). Piaget's enduring contribution to developmental psychology. *Developmental Psychology, 28,* 191–204.

Belkind-Gerson, J., Hotta, R., Whalen, M., Nayyar, N., Nagy, N., Cheng, L., ... Dietrich, J. (2016). Engraftment of enteric neural progenitor cells into the injured adult brain. *BMC Neuroscience, 17,* Article 5. http://dx.doi.org/10.1186/s12868-016-0238-y

Bell, C. C. (2016). Gun violence, urban youth, and mental illness. In L. H. Gold & R. I. Simon (Eds.), *Gun violence and mental illness* (pp. 49–79). Arlington, VA: American Psychiatric Association.

Belli, R. (Ed.). (2012). *True and false recovered memories: Toward a reconciliation of the debate.* New York, NY: Springer. http://dx.doi.org/10.1007/978-1-4614-1195-6

Bell, S. L., Phoenix, C., Lovell, R., & Wheeler, B. W. (2015). Seeking everyday wellbeing: The coast as a therapeutic landscape. *Social Science & Medicine, 142,* 56–67. http://dx.doi.org/10.1016/j.socscimed.2015.08.011

Bem, S. L. (1974). The measurement of psychological androgyny. *Journal of Consulting and Clinical Psychology, 42,* 155–162. http://dx.doi.org/10.1037/h0036215

Bem, S. L. (1981). Gender schema theory: A cognitive account of sex typing. *Psychological Review, 88,* 354–364. http://dx.doi.org/10.1037/0033-295X.88.4.354

Bem, S. L. (1993). *The lenses of gender: Transforming the debate on sexual inequality.* New Haven, CT: Yale University Press.

Benjamin, L. T., Cavell, T. A., & Shallenberger, W. R. (1984). Staying with initial answers on objective tests: Is it a myth? *Teaching of Psychology, 11,* 133–141.

Bennet, J. (2015). We need an energy miracle. *The Atlantic.* Retrieved from https://www.theatlantic.com/magazine/archive/2015/11/we-need-an-energy-miracle/407881/

Bennett, J. (2013, May 15). How JK Rowling beat depression. *How I Beat Depression.* Retrieved March 16, 2017 from http://www.howibeatdepression.com/how-jk-rowling-beat-depression/#comment-38579

Bennett, N., & O'Donohue, W. T. (2016). Child abuser's threats and grooming techniques. In W. T. O'Donohue & M. Fanetti (Eds.), *Forensic interviews regarding child sexual abuse: A guide to evidence-based practice* (pp. 307–316). Cham, CH: Springer International Publishing. http://dx. doi. org/10.1007/978-3-319-21097-1_1.

Bennett, S., Banyard, V. L., & Edwards, K. M. (2017). The impact of the bystander's relationship with the victim and the perpetrator on intent to help in situations involving sexual violence. *Journal of Interpersonal Violence, 32*(5), 682–702. http://dx.doi.org/10.1177/0886260515586373

Bennett, S. M. (2016). Treatment of contamination obsessive-compulsive disorder. In E. A. Storch & A. B. Lewin (Eds.), *Clinical handbook of obsessive-compulsive and related disorders: A case-based approach to treating pediatric and adult populations* (pp. 5–21). Cham, CH: Springer International Publishing. http://dx.doi.org/10.1007/978-3-319-17139-5_2

Bennion, K. A., Steinmetz, K. R. M., Kensinger, E. A., & Payne, J. D. (2015). Sleep and cortisol interact to support memory consolidation. *Cerebral Cortex, 25,* 646–657. http://dx.doi.org/10.1093/cercor/bht255

Ben-Porath, Y. S. (2013). Self-report inventories: Assessing personality and psychopathology. In J. R. Graham, J. A. Naglieri, & I. B. Weiner (Eds.), *Handbook of psychology, Vol. 10. Assessment psychology* (2nd ed., pp. 622–644). Hoboken, NJ: Wiley.

Bentall, R. P., Wickham, S., Shevlin, M., & Varese, F. (2012). Do specific early-life adversities lead to specific symptoms of psychosis? A study from the 2007 The Adult Psychiatric Morbidity Survey. *Schizophrenia Bulletin, 38,* 734–740.

Beny, Y., & Kimchi, T. (2016). Conditioned odor aversion induces social anxiety towards females in wild-type and TrpC2 knockout male mice. *Genes, Brain and Behavior, 15,* 722–732. http://dx.doi.org/10.1111/gbb.12320

Ben-Zeév, A. (2014). Why a lover's touch is so powerful. *Psychology Today.* Retrieved from https://www.psychologytoday.com/blog/in-the-name-love/201405/why-lovers-touch-is-so-powerful

Beran, M. J., Parrish, A. E., Perdue, B. M., & Washburn, D. A. (2014). Comparative cognition: Past, present, and future. *International Journal of Comparative Psychology, 27,* 3–30.

Berger, J. (2015). *Personality* (9th ed.). Stamford, CT: Cengage Learning.

Berger, K. S. (2015). *Developing person through childhood and adolescence* (10th ed.). New York, NY: Worth.

Berlyne, D. E. (1970). Novelty, complexity, and hedonic value. *Perception and Psychophysics, 8,* 279–286.

Berman, J., & Prudic, J. (2013). Electroconvulsive therapy. In J. J. Mann, P. J. McGrath, & S. P. Roose (Eds.), *Clinical handbook for the management of mood disorders* (pp. 311–324). New York, NY: Cambridge University Press. http://dx.doi.org/10.1017/CBO9781139175869.024

Berman, N. C., Elliott, C. M., & Wilhelm, S. (2016). Cognitive behavioral therapy for obsessive-compulsive disorder: Theory, assessment, and treatment. In T. J. Petersen, S. E. Sprich, & S. Wilhelm (Eds.), *The Massachusetts General Hospital handbook of cognitive behavioral therapy. Current clinical psychiatry* (pp. 105–

115). Totowa, NJ: Humana Press. http://dx.doi.org/10.1007/978-1-4939-2605-3_8

Berman, S. M., Paz-Filho, G., Wong, M.-L., Kohno, M., Licinio, J., & London, E. D. (2013). Effects of leptin deficiency and replacement on cerebellar response to food-related cues. *The Cerebellum, 12,* 59–67. http://dx.doi.org/10.1007/s12311-012-0360-z

Bernard, L. L. (1924). *Instinct.* New York, NY: Holt.

Bernard, S., Clément, F., & Mercier, H. (2016). Wishful thinking in preschoolers. *Journal of Experimental Child Psychology, 141,* 267–274. http://dx.doi.org/10.1016/j.jecp.2015.07.018

Bernet, W., & Ash, D. R. (2007). *Children of divorce: A practical guide for parents, therapists, attorneys, and judges* (2nd ed.). Malabar, FL: Krieger.

Berns, G. S., Blaine, K., Prietula, M. J., & Pye, B. E. (2013). Short- and long-term effects of a novel on connectivity in the brain. *Brain Connectivity, 3,* 590–600. http://dx.doi.org/10.1089/brain.2013.0166

Berns, G. S., Brooks, A. M., & Spivak, M. (2015). Scent of the familiar: An fMRI study of canine brain responses to familiar and unfamiliar human and dog odors. *Behavioural Processes, 110,* 37–46. http://dx.doi.org/10.1016/j.beproc.2014.02.011

Berreman, G. (1971). *Anthropology today.* Del Mar, CA: CRM.

Berry, J., Poortinga, Y., Breugelmans, S., Chasiotis, A., & Sam, D. (2011). *Cross-cultural psychology: Research and applications* (3rd ed.). Cambridge, UK: Cambridge University Press.

Berry, J. W., & Ataca, B. (2010). Cultural factors in stress. In G. Fink (Ed.), *Stress consequences: Mental, neuropsychological and socioeconomic* (pp. 640–645). San Diego, CA: Elsevier Academic Press.

Berry, J. W., Kim, U., Minde, T., & Mok, D. (1987). Comparative studies of acculturative stress. *International Migration Review, 21,* 491–511. http://dx.doi.org/10.2307/2546607

Besemer, S., Loeber, R., Hinshaw, S. P., & Pardini, D. A. (2016). Bidirectional associations between externalizing behavior problems and maladaptive parenting within parent-son dyads across childhood. *Journal of Abnormal Child Psychology, 44,* 1387–1398. http://dx.doi.org/10.1007/s10802-015-0124-6

Best, D. L., & Bush, C. D. (2016). Gender roles in childhood and adolescence. In U. P. Gielen & J. L. Roopnarine (Eds.), *Childhood and adolescence: Cross-cultural perspectives and applications* (2nd ed., pp. 209–239). Santa Barbara, CA: Praeger.

Best, M., Lawrence, N. S., Logan, G. D., McLaren, I. P. L., & Verbruggen, F. (2016). Should I stop or should I go? The role of associations and expectancies. *Journal of Experimental Psychology: Human Perception and Performance, 42,* 115–137. http://dx.doi.org/10.1037/xhp0000116

Bevan, J. L., Gomez, R., & Sparks, L. (2014). Disclosures about important life events on Facebook: Relationships with stress and quality of life. *Computers in Human Behavior, 39,* 246–253. http://dx.doi.org/10.1016/j.chb.2014.07.021

Beyens, I., Frison, E., & Eggermont, S. (2016). "I don't want to miss a thing": Adolescents' fear of missing out and its relationship to adolescents' social needs, Facebook use, and Facebook related stress. *Computers in Human Behavior, 64,* 1–8. http://dx.doi.org/10.1016/j.chb.2016.05.083

Bhatnagar, K. A. C., Wisniewski, L., Solomon, M., & Heinberg, L. (2013). Effectiveness and feasibility of a cognitive-behavioral group interven-

tion for body image disturbance in women with eating disorders. *Journal of Clinical Psychology, 69,* 1–13.

Bianchi, E. C. (2014). Entering adulthood in a recession tempers later narcissism. *Psychological Science, 25,* 1429–1437. http://dx.doi.org/10.1177/0956797614532818

Bianchi, E. C. (2015). Assessing the robustness of the relationship between entering adulthood in a recession and narcissism. *Psychological Science, 26,* 537–538. http://dx.doi.org/10.1177/0956797614568157

Bianchi, M. (Ed.). (2014). *Sleep deprivation and disease: Effects on the body, brain and behavior.* New York, NY: Springer.

Biasibetti, R., Dos Santos, J. P. A., Rodrigues, L., Wartchow, K. M., Suardi, L. Z., Nardin, P., . . . Gonçalves, C. A. (2017). Hippocampal changes in STZ-model of Alzheimer's disease are dependent on sex. *Behavioural Brain Research, 316,* 205–214.

Bichescu-Burian, D., Steyer, J., Steinert, T., Grieb, B., & Tschöke, S. (2017). Trauma-related dissociation: Psychological features and psychophysiological responses to script-driven imagery in borderline personality disorder. *Psychophysiology, 54*(3), 452–461. http://dx.doi.org/10.1111/psyp.12795

Bick, J., Nguyen, V., Leng, L., Piecychna, M., Crowley, M. J., Bucala, R., . . . Grigorenko, E. L. (2015). Preliminary associations between childhood neglect, MIF, and cortisol: Potential pathways to long-term disease risk. *Developmental Psychobiology, 57,* 131–139. http://dx.doi.org/10.1002/dev.21265

Biering, K., Andersen, J. H., Lund, T., & Hjøllund, N. H. (2015). Psychosocial working environment and risk of adverse cardiac events in patients treated for coronary heart disease. *Journal of Occupational Rehabilitation, 25,* 770–775. http://dx.doi.org/10.1007/s10926-015-9585-2

Bilder, G. F. (2016). *Human biological aging: From macromolecules to organ systems.* Malden, MA: Wiley-Blackwell.

Bilimoria, K. Y., Chung, J. W., Hedges, L. V., Dahlke, A. R., Love, R., Cohen, M. E., . . . Mahvi, D. M. (2016). National cluster-randomized trial of duty-hour flexibility in surgical training. *New England Journal of Medicine, 374*(8), 713–727.

Bill Gates Biography. (n.d.). Bill Gates biography: Business leader, entrepreneur, philanthropist (1955). *Bio.com.* Retrieved from http://www.biography.com/people/bill-gates-9307520

Biography. (2017). Albert Einstein biography. *Biography.com.* Retrieved from http://www.biography.com/people/albert-einstein-9285408

Biography.com Editors. (n.d.). Ellen DeGeneres biography. *Biography.com.* Retrieved February 14, 2017 from http://www.biography.com/people/ellen-degeneres-9542420

Biography.com. (n.d.). J. K. Rowling Biography. *The Biography.com.* Retrieved March 17, 2017 from http://www.biography.com/people/jk-rowling-40998

Biography.com. (n.d.). Sonia Sotomayor biography. *Biography.com.* Retrieved March 22, 2017 from http://www.biography.com/people/sonia-sotomayor-453906

Biography of Nelson Mandela. (n.d.). *The Nelson Mandela Foundation (ZA).* Retrieved February 9, 2017 from https://www.nelsonmandela.org/content/page/biography

Birditt, K. S., & Newton, N. J. (2016). Theories of social support and aging. In N. A. Pachana (Ed.), *Encyclopedia of gerontology* (pp. 1–7).New York, NY: Springer.

Birmaher, B., & Brent, D. A. (2016). Depressive and disruptive mood dysregulation disorders. In M. K. Dulcan (Ed.), *Dulcan's textbook of child and adolescent psychiatry* (pp. 245–276). Arlington, VA: American Psychiatric Publishing.

Bissinger, B. (2015). Caitlyn Jenner: The full story. *Vanity Fair.* Retrieved from http://www.vanityfair.com/hollywood/2015/06/caitlyn-jenner-bruce-cover-annie-leibovitz

Bjälkebring, P., Västfjäll, D., Dickert, S., & Slovic, P. (2016). Greater emotional gain from giving in older adults: Age-related positivity bias in charitable giving. *Frontiers in Psychology, 7,* 846. http://doi.org/10.3389/fpsyg.2016.00846

Blacha, C., Schmid, M. M., Gahr, M., Freudenmann, R. W., Plener, P. L., Finter, F., . . . Schönfeldt-Lecuona, C. (2013). Self-inflicted testicular amputation in first lysergic acid diethylamide use. *Journal of Addiction Medicine, 7,* 83–84.

Black, C. N., Bot, M., Scheffer, P. G., & Penninx, B. W. J. H. (2017). Oxidative stress in major depressive and anxiety disorders, and the association with antidepressant use; results from a large adult cohort. *Psychological Medicine, 47*(5), 936–948. http://dx.doi.org/10.1017/S0033291716002828 17l

Black, J., & Barnes, J. L. (2015). Fiction and social cognition: The effect of viewing award-winning television dramas on theory of mind. *Psychology of Aesthetics, Creativity, and the Arts, 9,* 423–429. http://dx.doi.org/10.1037/aca0000031

Blecha, P. (2004). *Taboo tunes: A history of banned bands and censored songs.* San Francisco, CA: Backbeat.

Blekesaune, M. (2017). Is cohabitation as good as marriage for people's subjective well-being? Longitudinal evidence on happiness and life satisfaction in the british household panel survey. *Journal of Happiness Studies.* No Pagination Specified. http://dx.doi.org/10.1007/s10902-016-9834-x

Bloch, L., Haase, C. M., & Levenson, R. W. (2014). Emotion regulation predicts marital satisfaction: More than a wives' tale. *Emotion, 14,* 130–144. http://dx.doi.org/10.1037/a0034272

Blumberg, M. S. (2015). Developing sensorimotor systems in our sleep. *Current Directions in Psychological Science, 24,* 32–37. http://dx.doi.org/10.1177/0963721414551362

Blumberg, N. (2017). Malala Yousafzai: Pakistani activist. *Encyclopedia Britannica.* Retrieved from https://www.britannica.com/biography/Malala-Yousafzai

Blum, K., Oscar-Berman, M., Barh, D., Giordano, J., & Gold, M. S. (2013). Dopamine genetics and function in food and substance abuse. *Journal of Genetic Syndromes & Gene Therapy, 4:* 1000121.

Blunden, S., & Galland, B. (2014). The complexities of defining optimal sleep: Empirical and theoretical considerations with a special emphasis on children. *Sleep Medicine Reviews, 18,* 371–378. http://dx.doi.org/10.1016/j.smrv.2014.01.002

Boag, E. M., & Carnelley, K. B. (2016). Attachment and prejudice: The mediating role of empathy. *British Journal of Social Psychology, 55,* 337–356. http://dx.doi.org/10.1111/bjso.12132

Boag, S. (2012). *Freudian repression, the unconscious, and the dynamics of inhibition.* London, UK: Karnac.

Boag, S. (2015). Repression, defence, and the psychology of science. In S. Boag, L. A. W. Brakel, & V. Talvitie (Eds.), *Philosophy, science, and psychoanalysis: A critical* meeting (pp. 247–268). London, UK: Karnac Books.

Bodell, L. P., Brown, T. A., & Keel, P. K. (2017). Weight suppression predicts bulimic symptoms at 20-year follow-up: The mediating role of drive for thinness. *Journal of Abnormal Psychology, 126,* 32–37. http://dx.doi.org/10.1037/abn0000217

Boergers, J., Gable, C. J., & Owens, J. A. (2014). Later school start time is associated with improved sleep and daytime functioning in adolescents. *Journal of Developmental & Behavioral Pediatrics, 35,* 11–17. http://dx.doi.org/10.1097/DBP.0000000000000018

Bogaard, G., Meijer, E. H., Vrij, A., & Merckelbach, H. (2016) Strong, but wrong: Lay people's and police officers' beliefs about verbal and nonverbal cues to deception. *PLoS ONE,* 11(6): e0156615. http://dx.doi.org/10.1371/journal.pone.0156615

Bohannon, J. (2016, April 7). For real this time: Talking to people about gay and transgender issues can change their prejudices. *Science.* http://dx.doi.org/10.1126/science.aaf9890

Bohon, C. (2015). Feeding and eating disorders. In L. W. Roberts & A. K. Louie (Eds.), *Study guide to DSM-5*® (pp. 233–250). Arlington, VA: American Psychiatric Publishing.

Bonanno, G. A. (2012). Uses and abuses of the resilience construct: Loss, trauma, and health-related adversities. *Social Science & Medicine, 74,* 753–756. http://dx.doi.org/10.1016/j.socscimed.2011.11.022

Bond, M. H. (Ed.). (2015). *Oxford handbook of Chinese psychology.* New York, NY: Oxford University Press.

Bongers, P., & Jansen, A. (2017). Emotional eating and Pavlovian learning: Evidence for conditioned appetitive responding to negative emotional states. *Cognition and Emotion, 31*(2), 284–297. http://dx.doi.org/10.1080/02699931.2015.1108903

Bonilla-Silva, E. (2016). Down the rabbit hole: Color-blind racism in Obamerica. In H. A. Neville, M. E. Gallardo, & D. W. Sue (Eds.), *The myth of racial color blindness: Manifestations, dynamics, and impact* (pp. 25–38). Washington, DC: American Psychological Association. http://dx.doi.org/10.1037/14754-002

Bonnan-White, J., Yep, J., & Hetzel-Riggin, M. D. (2016). Voices from the past: Mental and physical outcomes described by American Civil War amputees. *Journal of Trauma & Dissociation, 17,* 13–34. http://dx.doi.org/10.1080/15299732.2015.1041070

Bonnet, M. H., & Arand, D. L. (2017). Pathophysiology of insomnia. In H. P. Attarian (Ed.), *Clinical handbook of insomnia* (pp. 41–57). Cham, CH: Springer International Publishing. http://dx.doi.org/10.1007/978-3-319-41400-3_4

Bonomi, C. (2015). *The cut and the building of psychoanalysis, Volume 1: Sigmund Freud and Emma Eckstein.* London, UK, New York, NY: Routledge.

Boothroyd, L.G., Jucker, J. L., Thornborrow, T., Jamieson, M. A., Burt, D. M., Barton, R. A., . . . Tovée, M. J. (2016). Television exposure predicts body size ideals in rural Nicaragua. *British Journal of Psychology,* 107, 752–767. http://dx.doi.org/10.1111/bjop.12184

Boothroyd, L. G., Tovee, M. T., & Pollett, T. (2012). Mechanisms of change in body size preferences. *PLoS ONE, 7:* e48691.

Bootzin, R. R., Blank, E., & Peck, T. (2015). Sleeping well. In S J. Lynn, W. T. O'Donohue, & S. O. Lilienfeld (Eds.), *Health, happiness, and well-being: Better living through psychological science* (pp. 168–194). Thousand Oaks, CA: Sage.

Borelli, J. L., Rasmussen, H. F., Burkhart, M. L., & Sbarra, D. A. (2015). Relational savoring in long-distance romantic relationships. *Journal of Social and Personal Relationships, 32,* 1083–1108. http://dx.doi.org/10.1177/0265407514558960

Borelli, J. L., Sbarra, D. A., Snavely, J. E., McMakin, D. L., Covey, J. K., Ruiz, S. K., . . . Chung, S. Y. (2014). With or without you: Attachment avoidance predicts non-deployed spouses' reactions to relationship challenges during deployment. *Professional Psychology: Research and Practice, 45,* 478–487. http://dx.doi.org/10.1037/a0037780

Borghans, L., Golsteyn, B. H. H., Heckman, J., & Humphries, J. E. (2011). Identification problems in personality psychology. *Personality and Individual Differences, 51*(3), 315–320. http://doi.org/10.1016/j.paid.2011.03.029

Bornstein, M. H., Arterberry, M. E., & Lamb, M. E. (2014). *Development in infancy: A contemporary introduction* (5th ed.). New York, NY: Psychology Press.

Bornstein, R. F. (2015). From surface to depth: Toward a more psychodynamically informed DSM-6. *Psychoanalytic Inquiry, 35,* 45–59. http://dx.doi.org/10.1080/07351690.2015.987592

Bornstein, R. F., & Huprich, S. K. (2015). Prologue: Toward an empirically informed 21st-century psychoanalysis: Challenges and opportunities. *Psychoanalytic Inquiry, 35*(Suppl1), 2–4. http://dx.doi.org/10.1080/07351690.2014.987589

Bottesi, G., Ghisi, M., Sica, C., & Freeston, M. H. (2017). Intolerance of uncertainty, not just right experiences, and compulsive checking: Test of a moderated mediation model on a non-clinical sample. *Comprehensive Psychiatry, 73,* 111–119. http://dx.doi.org/10.1016/j.comppsych.2016.11.014

Bouazzaoui, B., Follenfant, A., Ric, F., Fay, S., Croizet, J.-C., Atzeni, T., & Taconnat, L. (2016). Ageing-related stereotypes in memory: When the beliefs come true. *Memory, 24,* 659–668. http://dx.doi.org/10.1080/09658211.2015.1040802

Bouchard Jr., T. J. (2016). Genes and behavior: Nature via nurture. In R. J. Sternberg, S. T. Fiske, & D. J. Foss (Eds.), *Scientists making a difference: One hundred eminent behavioral and brain scientists talk about their most important contributions* (pp. 73–76). New York, NY: Cambridge University Press.

Bouchard, T. J., Jr. (1997). The genetics of personality. In K. Blum & E. P. Noble (Eds.), *Handbook of psychiatric genetics* (pp. 273–296). Boca Raton, FL: CRC Press.

Bouchard, T. J., Jr. (2013). Genetic influence on human psychological traits. In S. M. Downes & E. Machery (Eds.), *Arguing about human nature: Contemporary debates. Arguing about philosophy* (pp. 139–144). New York: NY: Routledge/Taylor & Francis Group.

Bouchard, T. J., Jr., & McGue, M. (1981). Familial studies of intelligence: A review. *Science,*

*212*, 1055–1059. http://dx.doi.org/10.1126/science.7195071

**Boucher, K. L., Rydell, R. J., & Murphy, M. C.** (2015). Forecasting the experience of stereotype threat for others. *Journal of Experimental Social Psychology, 58*, 56–62. http://dx.doi.org/10.1016/j.jesp.2015.01.002

**Bougard, C., Davenne, D., Espie, S., Moussay, S., & Léger, D.** (2016). Sleepiness, attention and risk of accidents in powered two-wheelers. *Sleep Medicine Reviews, 25*, 40–51. http://dx.doi.org/10.1016/j.smrv.2015.01.006

**Boulos L. J., Darcq E., & Kieffer B. L.** (2017). Translating the habenula-from rodents to humans. *Biological Psychiatry, 81*, 296–305. http://dx.doi.org/10.1016/j.biopsych.2016.06.003

**Boundy, E. O., Dastjerdi, R., Spiegelman, D., Fawzi, W. W., Missmer, S. A., Lieberman, E., . . . Chan, G. J.** (2016). Kangaroo mother care and neonatal outcomes: A meta-analysis. *Pediatrics, 137*, 1–16. http://dx.doi.org/10.1542/peds.2015-2238

**Bourassa, K. J., Memel, M., Woolverton, C., & Sbarra, D. A.** (2017). Social participation predicts cognitive functioning in aging adults over time: Comparisons with physical health, depression, and physical activity. *Aging & Mental Health, 21*(2), 133–146. http://dx.doi.org/10.1080/13607863.2015.1081152

**Bourne, L. E., Dominowski, R. L., & Loftus, E. F.** (1979). *Cognitive processes.* Englewood Cliff s, NJ: Prentice Hall.

**Bouton, M. E., & Todd, T. P.** (2014). A fundamental role for context in instrumental learning and extinction. *Behavioural Processes, 104*, 13–19. http://dx.doi.org/10.1016/j.beproc.2014.02.012

**Bouvet, R., & Bonnefon, J.-F.** (2015). Non-reflective thinkers are predisposed to attribute supernatural causation to uncanny experiences. *Personality and Social Psychology Bulletin, 41*, 955–961. http://dx.doi.org/10.1177/0146167215585728

**Bowlby, J.** (1969). *Attachment and loss: Vol. 1. Attachment.* New York, NY: Basic Books.

**Bowlby, J.** (1989). *Secure attachment.* New York, NY: Basic Books.

**Bowlby, J.** (1994). Pathological mourning and childhood mourning. In R. V. Frankiel (Ed.), *Essential papers on object loss* (pp. 185–221). New York, NY: New York University Press.

**Bowlby, J.** (2000). *Attachment.* New York, NY: Basic Books.

**Boxer, P., Huesmann, L. R., Dubow, E. F., Landau, S. F., Gvirsman, S. D., Shikahi, K., & Ginges, J.** (2013). Exposure to violence across the social ecosystem and the development of aggression: A test of ecological theory in the Israeli–Palestinian conflict. *Child Development, 84*, 163–177. http://dx.doi.org/10.1111/j.1467-8624.2012.01848.x

**Boyce, C. J., Wood, A. M., Daly, M., & Sedikides, C.** (2015). Personality change following unemployment. *Journal of Applied Psychology, 100*, 991–1011. http://dx.doi.org/10.1037/a0038647

**Boyle, G. J., Stankov, L., Martin, N. G., Petrides, K. V., Eysenck, M. W., & Ortet, G.** (2016). Hans J. Eysenck and Raymond B. Cattell on intelligence and personality. *Personality and Individual Differences, 103*, 40–47. http://dx.doi.org/10.1016/j.paid.2016.04.029

**Braakmann, D.** (2015). Historical paths in psychotherapy research. In O. C. G. Gelo, A. Pritz, & B. Rieken (Eds.), *Psychotherapy research: Foundations, process, and outcome* (pp. 39–65). Vienna, AT: Springer-Verlag Wien. http://dx.doi.org/10.1007/978-3-7091-1382-0

**Bradshaw, D. H., Chapman, C. R., Jacobson, R. C., & Donaldson, G. W.** (2012). Effects of music engagement on responses to painful stimulation. *Clinical Journal of Pain, 28*, 418–427.

**Brady, R. O., Jr., Tandon, N., Masters, G. A., Margolis, A., Cohen, B. M., Keshavan, M., & Öngür, D.** (2017). Differential brain network activity across mood states in bipolar disorder. *Journal of Affective Disorders, 207*, 367–376. http://dx.doi.org/10.1016/j.jad.2016.09.041

**Braithwaite, S. R., Doxey, R. A., Dowdle, K. K., & Fincham, F. D.** (2016). The unique influences of parental divorce and parental conflict on emerging adults in romantic relationships. *Journal of Adult Development, 23*, 214–225. http://dx.doi.org/10.1007/s10804-016-9237-6

**Branco, L. D., Cotrena, C., Pereira, N., Kochhann, R., & Fonseca, R. P.** (2014). Verbal and visuospatial executive functions in healthy elderly: The impact of education and frequency of reading and writing. *Dementia & Neuropsychologia, 8*, 155–161.

**Brand, B. L., Vissia, E. M., Chalavi, S., Nijenhuis, E. R. S., Webermann, A. R., Draijer, N., & Reinders, A. A. T. S.** (2016). DID is trauma based: Further evidence supporting the trauma model of DID. *Acta Psychiatrica Scandinavica, 134*(6), 560–563. http://dx.doi.org/10.1111/acps.12653

**Brandell, J. R., & Brown, S.** (2015). The new "bridge to adulthood": Searching for meaning and cohesion in the nexus of "hook-ups," Internet porn, and instant messages. *Smith College Studies in Social Work, 85*, 387–408. http://dx.doi.org/10.1080/00377317.2015.1089676

**Brannon, L.** (2016). *Gender: Psychological perspectives* (6th ed.). New York, NY: Psychology Press.

**Brannon, T. N., Markus, H. R., & Taylor, V. J.** (2015). "Two souls, two thoughts," two self-schemas: Double consciousness can have positive academic consequences for African Americans. *Journal of Personality and Social Psychology, 108*, 586–609. http://dx.doi.org/10.1037/a0038992

**Brassard, A., Dupuy, E., Bergeron, S., & Shaver, P. R.** (2015). Attachment insecurities and women's sexual function and satisfaction: The mediating roles of sexual self-esteem, sexual anxiety, and sexual assertiveness. *Journal of Sex Research, 52*, 110–119. http://dx.doi.org/10.1080/00224499.2013.838744.

**Bredesen, D. E.** (2014). Reversal of cognitive decline: A novel therapeutic program. *Aging, 6*, 707–717. PMCID:PMC4221920

**Bredie, W. L. P., Tan, H. S. G., & Wendin, K.** (2014). A comparative study on facially expressed emotions in response to basic tastes. *Chemosensory Perception, 7*, 1–9. http://dx.doi.org/10.1007/s12078-014-9163-6

**Breedlove, S. M.** (2017). Prenatal influences on human sexual orientation: Expectations versus data. *Archives of Sexual Behavior.* No Pagination Specified. http://dx.doi.org/10.1007/s10508-016-0904-2

**Breger, L.** (2014). Psychopathia sexualis: Sexuality in old and new psychoanalysis. *Journal of Clinical Psychology, 70*, 147–159. http://dx.doi.org/10.1002/jclp.22066

**Breland, K., & Breland, M.** (1961). The misbehavior of organisms. *American Psychologist, 16*, 681–684. http://dx.doi.org/10.1037/h0040090

**Brem, M. J., Florimbio, A. R., Elmquist, J., Shorey, R. C., & Stuart, G. L.** (2017). Antisocial traits, distress tolerance, and alcohol problems as predictors of intimate partner violence in men arrested for domestic violence. *Psychology of Violence.* No Pagination Specified. http://dx.doi.org/10.1037/vio0000088

**Bresin, K., Kling, L., & Verona, E.** (2017). The effect of acute physical pain on subsequent negative emotional affect: A meta-analysis. *Personality Disorders: Theory, Research, and Treatment.* No Pagination Specified. http://dx.doi.org/10.1037/per0000248

**Breuer, J., Scharkow, M., & Quandt, T.** (2015). Sore losers? A reexamination of the frustration-aggression hypothesis for colocated video game play. *Psychology of Popular Media Culture, 4*, 126–137. *http://dx.doi.org/10.1016/j.iheduc.2015.01.001*

**Brewer, M. B.** (2015). Motivated entitativity: When we'd rather see the forest than the trees. In S. J. Stroessner & J. W. Sherman (Eds.), *Social perception from individuals to groups* (pp. 161–176). New York, NY: Psychology Press.

**Brewer, N., Weber, N., Wootton, D., & Lindsay, D. D.** (2012). Identifying the bad guy in a lineup using confidence judgments under deadline pressure. *Psychological Science, 23*, 1208–1214. http://dx.doi.org/10.1177/0956797612441217

**Brewerton, T. D., & Dennis, A. B.** (2016). Perpetuating factors in severe and enduring anorexia nervosa. In S. Touyz, D. Le Grange, J. H. Lacey, & P. Hay (Eds.), *Managing severe and enduring anorexia nervosa: A clinician's guide* (pp. 28–63). New York, NY: Routledge/Taylor & Francis Group.

**Brewster, M., & Tucker, J. M.** (2016). Understanding bystander behavior: The influence of and interaction between bystander characteristics and situational factors. *Victims & Offenders, 11*(3), 455–481. http://dx.doi.org/10.1080/15564886.2015.1009593

**Brislin, R. W.** (2000). *Understanding culture's influence on behavior* (3rd ed.). Ft. Worth, TX: Harcourt.

**Brodbeck, F. C., & Guillaume, Y. R.** (2015). Effective decision making and problem solving in projects. In E. Bendoly, W. Van Wezel, & D. Bachrach (Eds.), *Applied psychology for project managers* (pp. 37–52). Berlin, DE: Springer.

**Brodsky, S. L., & Gutheil, T. G.** (2016). *The expert expert witness: More maxims and guidelines for testifying in court* (2nd ed.). Washington, DC: American Psychological Association. http://dx.doi.org/10.1037/14732-047

**Brodsky, S. L. & Gutheil, T. G.** (Eds.). (2016). *The expert expert witness: More maxims and guidelines for testifying in court* (2nd ed., pp. 156–159). Washington, DC: American Psychological Association. http://dx.doi.org/10.1037/14732-038

**Brody, G. H., Yu, T., Chen, E., Beach, S. R. H., & Miller, G. E.** (2016). Family-centered prevention ameliorates the longitudinal association between risky family processes and epigenetic aging. *Journal of Child Psychology and Psychiatry, 57*, 566–574. http://dx.doi.org/10.1111/jcpp.12495

**Brody, N., & Vangelisti, A. L.** (2016). Bystander intervention in cyberbullying. *Communication Monographs, 83*(1), 94–119. http://dx.doi.org/10.1080/03637751.2015.1044256

Broer, L., Codd, V., Nyholt, D., Deelen, J., Mangino, M., Willemsen, G., . . . Boomsma, D. I. (2013). Meta-analysis of telomere length in 19,713 subjects reveals high heritability, stronger maternal inheritance and a paternal age effect. *European Journal of Human Genetics, 21,* 1163–1168. http://dx.doi.org/10.1038/ejhg.2012.303

Bromwich, J. E. (2017, February 5). Subway riders scrub anti-semitic graffiti, as 'decent human beings.' *New York Times.* Retrieved February 5, 2017 from https://www.nytimes.com/2017/02/05/nyregion/swastika-nyc-subways.html

Broockman, D., & Kalla, J. (2016). Durably reducing transphobia: A field experiment on door-to-door canvassing. *Science, 353,* 220–224. http://dx.doi.org/10.1126/science.aad9713

Brooks, J. E., & Neville, H. A. (2017). Interracial attraction among college men: The influence of ideologies, familiarity, and similarity. *Journal of Social and Personal Relationships, 34*(2), 166–183. http://dx.doi.org/10.1177/0265407515627508

Brooks, S. (2015). Does personal social media usage affect efficiency and well-being? *Computers in Human Behavior, 46,* 26–37. http://dx.doi.org/10.1016/j.chb.2014.12.053

Broshek, D. K., DeMarco, A. P., & Freeman, J. R. (2015). A review of post-concussion syndrome and psychological factors associated with concussion. *Brain Injury, 29*(2), 228–237. http://dx.doi.org/10.3109/02699052.2014.974674.

Brown, A. S., & Lau, F. S. (2016). A review of the epidemiology of schizophrenia. In M. V. Pletnikov & J. Waddington (Eds.), *Modeling the psychopathological dimensions of schizophrenia: From molecules to behavior* (pp. 17–30). San Diego, CA: Elsevier Academic Press. http://dx.doi.org/10.1016/B978-0-12-800981-9.00002-X

Brown, C. S., Ali, H., Stone, E. A., & Jewell, J. A. (2017). U.S. children's stereotypes and prejudicial attitudes toward Arab Muslims. *Analyses of Social Issues and Public Policy (ASAP).* No Pagination Specified. http://dx.doi.org/10.1111/asap.12129

Brown, E., Gonzalez-Liencres, C., Tas, C., & Brüne, M. (2016). Reward modulates the mirror neuron system in schizophrenia: A study into the mu rhythm suppression, empathy, and mental state attribution. *Social Neuroscience, 11,* 175–186. http://dx.doi.org/10.1080/17470919.2015.1053982

Brown, M. A., & Brown, J. D. (2015). Self-enhancement biases, self-esteem, and ideal mate preferences. *Personality and Individual Differences, 74,* 61–65. http://dx.doi.org/10.1016/j.paid.2014.09.039

Brown, R., & Kulik, J. (1977). Flashbulb memories. *Cognition, 5,* 73–99. http://dx.doi.org/10.1016/0010-0277(77)90018-X

Brown, W. A. (2013). *The placebo effect in clinical practice.* New York, NY: Oxford University Press.

Bruine de Bruin, W., Lefevre, C. E., Taylor, A. L., Dessai, S., Fischhoff, B., & Kovats, S. (2016). Promoting protection against a threat that evokes positive affect: The case of heat waves in the United Kingdom. *Journal of Experimental Psychology: Applied, 22,* 261–271. http://dx.doi.org/10.1037/xap0000083

Bruning, R. H., & Kauffman, D. F. (2016). Self-efficacy beliefs and motivation in writing development. In C. A. MacArthur, S. Graham, & J. Fitzgerald (Eds.), *Handbook of writing research* (2nd ed., pp. 160–173). New York: NY: Guilford Press.

Brunoni, A. R., Valiengo, L., Baccaro, A., Zanāo, T. A., de Oliveira, J. F., Goulart, A., . . . Fregni, F. (2013). The sertraline vs electrical current therapy for treating depression clinical study: Results from a factorial, randomized, controlled trial. *JAMA Psychiatry, 70,* 383–391.

Brunyé, T., Burte, H., Houck, L. A., & Taylor, H. A. (2015). The map in our head is not oriented north: Evidence from a real-world environment. *PLoS ONE, 10*(9): e0135803. http://dx.doi.org/10.e0135803.

Brussoni, M., Gibbons, R., Gray, C., Ishikawa, T., Sandseter, E. B. H., Bienenstock, A., . . . Tremblay, M. S. (2015). What is the relationship between risky outdoor play and health in children? A systematic review. *International Journal of Environmental Research and Public Health, 12,* 6423–6454. http://dx.doi.org/10.3390/ijerph120606423

Bryant, F. B., & Veroff, J. (2007). *Savoring: A new model of positive experience.* Mahwah, NJ: Lawrence Erlbaum.

Bryant, N. B., & Gómez, R. L. (2015). The teen sleep loss epidemic: What can be done? *Translational Issues in Psychological Science, 1,* 116–125. http://dx.doi.org/10.1037/tps0000020

Buchholz, K. R., Bohnert, K. M., Sripada, R. K., Rauch, S. A., Epstein-Ngo, Q. M., & Chermack, S. T. (2017). Associations between PTSD and intimate partner and non-partner aggression among substance using veterans in specialty mental health. *Addictive Behaviors, 64,* 194–199. http://dx.doi.org/10.1016/j.addbeh.2016.08.039

Buckingham, G., & MacDonald, A. (2016). The weight of expectation: Implicit, rather than explicit, prior expectations drive the size–weight illusion. *The Quarterly Journal of Experimental Psychology, 69,* 1831–1841. http://dx.doi.org/10.1080/17470218.2015.1100642

Buckley, T., Soo Hoo, S. Y., Fethney, J., Shaw, E., Hanson, P. S., & Tofler, G. H. (2015). Triggering of acute coronary occlusion by episodes of anger. *European Heart Journal: Acute Cardiovascular Care, 4,* 493–498. http://doi.org/10.1177/2048872615568969

Buckner, J. D., & Terlecki, M. A. (2016). Social anxiety and alcohol-related impairment: The mediational impact of solitary drinking. *Addictive Behaviors, 58,* 7–11. http://dx.doi.org/10.1016/j.addbeh.2016.02.006

Buehler, S. (2014). *What every mental health professional needs to know about sex.* New York, NY: Springer.

Buglass, S. L., Binder, J. F., Betts, L. R., & Underwood, J. D. (2017). Motivators of online vulnerability: The impact of social network site use and FOMO. *Computers in Human Behavior, 66,* 248–255. http://dx.doi.org/10.1016/j.chb.2016.09.055

Bui, D. C., & McDaniel, M. A. (2015). Enhancing learning during lecture note-taking using outlines and illustrative diagrams. *Journal of Applied Research in Memory and Cognition, 4,* 129–135. http://dx.doi.org/10.1016/j.jarmac.2015.03.002

Bullis, J. R., & Hofmann, S. G. (2016). Adult anxiety and related disorders. In C. M. Nezu & A. M. Nezu (Eds.), *The Oxford handbook of cognitive and behavioral therapies* (pp. 291–311). New York, NY: Oxford University Press.

Bull, L. E., Oliver, C., & Woodcock, K. A. (2017). Signalling changes to individuals who show resistance to change can reduce challenging behaviour. *Journal of Behavior Therapy and Experimental Psychiatry, 54,* 58–70.http://dx.doi.org/10.1016/j.jbtep.2016.06.006

Burke-Aaronson, A. C. (2015). Skin-to-skin care and breast-feeding in the perioperative suite. *MCN: The American Journal of Maternal/Child Nursing, 40,* 105–109. http://dx.doi.org/10.1097/NMC.0000000000000113

Burnett, L. B., Roldan, C. J., & Adler, J. (2016). Cocaine toxicity. *Medscape.* Retrieved from http://emedicine.medscape.com/article/813959-overview#a4

Burns, C. (2012). The costly business of discrimination. *Center for American Progress.* Retrieved from https://www.americanprogress.org/wp-content/uploads/.../lgbt_biz_discrimination.pdf

Burns, J. K., Tomita, A., & Kapadia, S. (2014). Income inequality and schizophrenia: Increased schizophrenia incidence in countries with high levels of income inequality. *International Journal of Social Psychiatry, 60,* 185–196. http://dx.doi.org/10.1177/0020764013481426

Busch, F. (2014). *Creating a psychoanalytic mind: A psychoanalytic method and theory.* New York, NY: Routledge/Taylor & Francis Group.

Busch, F. (2015). Our vital profession. *The International Journal of Psychoanalysis, 96,* 553–568. http://dx.doi.org/10.1111/1745-8315.12349

Bushman, B. J. (2002). Does venting anger feed or extinguish the flame? Catharsis, rumination, distraction, anger and aggressive responding. *Personality & Social Psychology Bulletin, 28,* 724–731.

Bushman, B. J. (2016). *Aggression and violence: A social psychological perspective.* New York, NY: Psychology Press.

Bushman, B. J. (2016). Violent media and hostile appraisals: A meta-analytic review. *Aggressive Behavior, 42*(6), 605–613. http://dx.doi.org/10.1002/ab.21655

Buss, D. M. (1989). Sex differences in human mate preferences: Evolutionary hypotheses tested in 37 cultures. *Behavioral and Brain Sciences, 12,* 1–49.

Buss, D. M. (2003). *The evolution of desire: Strategies of human mating.* New York, NY: Basic.

Buss, D. M. (2008). *The evolution of desire: Strategies of human mating* (4th ed.). New York: NY: Basic Books.

Buss, D. M. (2011). *Evolutionary psychology: The new science of the mind* (4th ed.). Upper Saddle River, NJ: Prentice-Hall.

Buss, D. M. (2015). *The handbook of evolutionary psychology, applications.* Hoboken, NJ: Wiley.

Buss, D. M., Abbott, M., Angleitner, A., Asherian, A., Biaggio, A., Blanco-Villasenor, A., . . . Yang, K.-S. (1990). International preferences in selecting mates: A study of 37 cultures. *Journal of Cross-Cultural Psychology, 21,* 5–47. http://dx.doi.org/10.1177/0022022190211001

Buss, D. M., & Duntley, J. D. (2014). Intimate partner violence in evolutionary perspective. In T. K. Shackelford & R. D. Hansen (Eds.), *The evolution of violence* (pp. 1–21). New York, NY: Springer.

Butcher, J. N. (2000). Revising psychological tests: Lessons learned from the revision of the MMPI. *Psychological Assessment, 12,* 263–271.

Butcher, J. N. (2011). *A beginner's guide to the MMPI-2* (3rd ed.). Washington, DC: American Psychological Association.

Butler, M. G. (2017). Clinical and genetic aspects of the 15q11.2 BP1–BP2 microdeletion disorder. *Journal of Intellectual Disability Research, 61*(6), 568–579. http://dx.doi.org/10.1111/jir.12382

Bylund, E., & Athanasopoulos, P. (2015). Televised Whorf: Cognitive restructuring in advanced foreign language learners as a function of audiovisual media exposure. *Modern Language Journal, 99,* 123–137. http://dx.doi.org/10.1111/j.1540-4781.2015.12182.x

Byrne, C., Freil, L., Starner, T., & Jackson, M. M. (2017). A method to evaluate haptic interfaces for working dogs. *International Journal of Human-Computer Studies, 98,* 196–207. http://dx.doi.org/10.1016/j.ijhcs.2016.04.004

Cacciatore, J., & Rubin, J. B. (2016). The last of human desire: Grief, death, and mindfulness. In E. Shonin, W. Van Gordon, & M. D. Griffiths (Eds.), *Mindfulness and Buddhist-derived approaches in mental health and addiction* (pp. 247–257). Cham, CH: Springer International Publishing. http://dx.doi.org/10.1007/978-3-319-22255-4_12

Cacioppo, J. T., Cacioppo, S., Gonzaga, G. C., Ogburn, E. L., & VanderWeele, T. J. (2013). Marital satisfaction and break-ups differ across online and off-line meeting venues. *Proceedings of the National Academy of Sciences of the United States of America, 110,* 10135–10140.

Cacioppo, S., Bianchi-Demicheli, F., Frum, C., Pfaus, J. G., & Lewis, J. W. (2012). The common neural bases between sexual desire and love: A multilevel kernel density fMRI analysis. *The Journal of Sexual Medicine, 9,* 1048–1054.

Cahn, D. D. (2013). *Intimates in conflict: A communication perspective.* Hillsdale, NJ: Erlbaum.

Cain, D. J., Keenan, K., & Rubin, S. (Eds.). (2016). *Humanistic psychotherapies: Handbook of research and practice* (2nd ed.). Washington, DC: American Psychological Association.

Cain, M. S., Leonard, J. A., Gabrieli, J. D., & Finn, A. S. (2016). Media multitasking in adolescence. *Psychonomic Bulletin & Review, 23*(6), 1932–1941. http://dx.doi.org/10.3758/s13423-016-1036-3

Cain, S. (2016). *Quiet power: Growing up as an introvert in a world that can't stop talking.* New York, NY: Penguin.

Calati, R., & Courtet, P. (2016). Is psychotherapy effective for reducing suicide attempt and non-suicidal self-injury rates? Meta-analysis and meta-regression of literature data. *Journal of Psychiatric Research, 79,* 8–20. http://dx.doi.org/10.1016/j.jpsychires.2016.04.003

Calderwood, C., & Ackerman, P. L. (2016). The relative salience of daily and enduring influences on off-job reactions to work stress. *Stress and Health, 32*(5), 587–596. http://dx.doi.org/10.1002/smi.2665

Caine, R. N., Caine, G., McClintic, C., & Klimek, K. J. (2016). *12 brain/mind learning principles in action: Teach for the development of higher-order thinking and executive function* (3rd ed.). Thousand Oaks, CA: Corwin Press.

Caleza, C., Yáñez-Vico, R. M., Mendoza, A., & Iglesias-Linares, A. (2016). Childhood obesity and delayed gratification behavior: A systematic review of experimental studies. *The Journal of Pediatrics, 169,* 201–207. http://dx.doi.org/10.1016/j.jpeds.2015.10.008

Calkins, A. W., Park, J. M., Wilhelm, S., & Sprich, S. (2016). Basic principles and practice of cognitive behavioral therapy. In T. J. Petersen, S. Sprich, & S. Wilhelm (Eds.), *The Massachusetts*

*General Hospital handbook of cognitive behavioral therapy* (pp. 5–14). New York, NY: Springer. http://dx.doi.org/10.1007/978-1-4939-2605-3_2

Calvert, S. L., Appelbaum, M., Dodge, K. A., Graham, S., Nagayama Hall, G. C., Hamby, S., & Hedges, L. V. (2017). The American Psychological Association Task Force assessment of violent video games: Science in the service of public interest. *American Psychologist, 72*(2), 126–143. http://dx.doi.org/10.1037/a0040413

Camera, D., Coleman, H. A., Parkington, H. C., Jenkins, T. A., Pow, D. V., Boase, N., . . . Poronnik, P. (2016). Learning, memory and long-term potentiation are altered in Nedd4 heterozygous mice. *Behavioural Brain Research, 303,* 176–181. http://dx.doi.org/10.1016/j.bbr.2016.01.054

Cameron, D. S., Bertenshaw, E. J., & Sheeran, P. (2015). The impact of positive affect on health cognitions and behaviours: A meta-analysis of the experimental evidence. *Health Psychology Review, 9,* 345–365. http://dx.doi.org/10.1080/17437199.2014.923164

Campbell, J. R., & Feng, A. X. (2011). Comparing adult productivity of American mathematics, physics, and chemistry Olympians with Terman's longitudinal study. *Roeper Review: A Journal on Gifted Education, 33,* 18–25. http://dx.doi.org/10.1080/02783193.2011.530203

Campbell, L. F., Norcross, J. C., Vasquez, M. J. T., & Kaslow, N. J. (2013). Recognition of psychotherapy effectiveness: The APA resolution. *Psychotherapy, 50,* 98–101. http://dx.doi.org/10.1037/a0031817

Campbell, M. M., Sibeko, G., Mall, S., Baldinger, A., Nagdee, M., Susser, E., & Stein, D. J. (2017). The content of delusions in a sample of South African Xhosa people with schizophrenia. *BMC Psychiatry, 17,* Article 41.

Campbell, S. N., Zhang, C., Monte, L., Roe, A. D., Rice, K. C., Tach., Y., . . . Rissman, R. A. (2015). Increased tau phosphorylation and aggregation in the hippocampus of mice overexpressing corticotropin-releasing factor. *Journal of Alzheimer's Disease, 43,* 967–976. http://dx.doi.org/10.3233/JAD-141281.

Cannon, W. B., & Washburn, A. (1912). An explanation of hunger. *American Journal of Physiology, 29,* 441–454.

Cantio, C., Jepsen, J. R. M., Madsen, G. F., Bilenberg, N., & White, S. J. (2016). Exploring 'the autisms' at a cognitive level. *Autism Research, 9*(12), 1328–1339. http://dx.doi.org/10.1002/aur.1630

Cantisani, A., Koenig, T., Stegmayer, K., Federspiel, A., Horn, H., Müller, T. J., . . . Walther, S. (2016). EEG marker of inhibitory brain activity correlates with resting-state cerebral blood flow in the reward system in major depression. *European Archives of Psychiatry and Clinical Neuroscience, 266*(8), 755–764. http://dx.doi.org/10.1007/s00406-015-0652-7

Carcioppolo, N., Dunleavy, V. O., & Yang, Q. (2017). How do perceived descriptive norms influence indoor tanning intentions? An application of the theory of normative social behavior. *Health Communication, 32*(2), 230–239. http://dx.doi.org/10.1080/10410236.2015.1120697

Carducci, B. J. (2015). *Psychology of personality: Viewpoints, research, and applications* (3rd ed.). Hoboken, NJ: Wiley.

Carey, B. (2008, September 14). Training young brains to behave. *New York Times.* Retrieved from http://www.nytimes.com/2008/09/15/

health/healthspecial2/15brain.html?em&mtr-ref=sharpbrains.com&gwh=A11ACD95E332EEB-0B75C17DE0ABE80A4&gwt=pay

Carey, B. (2014, January 27). The older mind may just be a fuller mind. *New York Times.* Retrieved from http://newoldage.blogs.nytimes.com/2014/01/27/the-oldermind-may-just-be-a-fuller-mind/?action=click&contentCollection=U.S.&module=MostEmailed&version=Full&region=Marginalia&src=me&pgtype=article

Carey, B. (2016, November 3). When it comes to success, age really is just a number. *New York Times.* Retrieved from https://www.nytimes.com/2016/11/04/science/stem-careers-success-achievement.html?_r=0

Carey, K. B., Durney, S. E., Shepardson, R. L., & Carey, M. P. (2015). Precollege predictors of incapacitated rape among female students in their first year of college. *Journal of Studies on Alcohol and Drugs, 76,* 829–837. http://dx.doi.org/10.15288/jsad.2015.76.829

Carlo, G., Knight, G. P., Roesch, S. C., Opal, D., & Davis, A. (2014). Personality across cultures: A critical analysis of Big Five research and current directions. In F. T. L. Leong, L. Comas-Díaz, G. C. Nagayama Hall, V. C. McLoyd, & J. E. Trimble (Eds.), *APA handbook of multicultural psychology, Vol. 1. Theory and research* (pp. 285–298). Washington, DC: American Psychological Association. http://dx.doi.org/10.1037/14189-015

Carlson, J. D., & Englar-Carlson, M. (2013). Adlerian therapy. In J. Frew & M. D. Spiegler (Eds.), *Contemporary psychotherapies for a diverse world* (1st rev. ed., pp. 87–129). New York: NY: Routledge.

Carlson, J. M., Rubin, D., & Mujica-Parodi, L. R. (2017). Lost emotion: Disrupted brain-based tracking of dynamic affective episodes in anxiety and depression. *Psychiatry Research: Neuroimaging, 260,* 37–48. http://dx.doi.org/10.1016/j.pscychresns.2016.12.002

Carlson, N., & Birkett, M. (2017). *Physiology of behavior* (12th ed.). Upper Saddle River, NJ: Pearson.

Carney, C., Harland, K. K., & McGehee, D. V. (2016). Using event-triggered naturalistic data to examine the prevalence of teen driver distractions in rear-end crashes. *Journal of Safety Research, 57,* 47–52. http://dx.doi.org/10.1016/j.jsr.2016.03.010

Carothers, B. J., & Reis, H. T. (2013). Men and women are from Earth: Examining the latent structure of gender. *Journal of Personality and Social Psychology, 104,* 385–407. http://dx.doi.org/10.1037/a0030437

Carpenter, G. S. J., Carpenter, T. P., Kimbrel, N. A., Flynn, E. J., Pennington, M. L., Cammarata, C., . . . Gulliver, S. B. (2015). Social support, stress, and suicidal ideation in professional firefighters. *American Journal of Health Behavior, 39,* 191–196. http://dx.doi.org/10.5993/AJHB.39.2.5

Carpenter, S. (2001). A new reason for keeping a diary. *Monitor on Psychology, 32*(8), 68. http://www.apa.org/monitor/sep01/keepdiary.aspx p.

Carpenter, S. K., & Yeung, K. L. (2017). The role of mediator strength in learning from retrieval. *Journal of Memory and Language, 92,* 128–141.

Carroll, J. (2016). *Sexuality now: Embracing diversity* (5th ed.). Boston, MA: Cengage Learning.

Carskadon, M. A., Wolfson, A. R., Acebo, C., Tzischinsky, O., & Seifer, R. (1998). Adolescent sleep patterns, circadian timing, and sleepiness at a transition to early school days. *Sleep, 21,* 871–881.

Carstensen, L. L. (1993). Motivation for social contact across the life span: A theory of socioemotional selectivity. In J. E. Jacobs (Ed.), *Nebraska symposium on motivation, 1992: Developmental perspectives on motivation* (pp. 209–254). Lincoln, NE: University of Nebraska Press.

Carstensen, L. L. (1995). Evidence for a life-span theory of socioemotional selectivity. *Current Directions in Psychological Science, 4*(5), 151–156. http://doi.org/10.1111/1467-8721.ep11512261

Carstensen, L. L. (2006). The influence of a sense of time on human development. *Science, 312,* 1913–1915. http://dx.doi.org/10.1126/science.1127488

Carstensen, L. L., Turan, B., Scheibe, S., Ram, N., Ersner-Hershfield, H., Samanez-Larkin, G. R., . . . Nesselroade, J. R. (2011). Emotional experience improves with age: Evidence based on over 10 years of experience sampling. *Psychology and Aging, 26,* 21–33.

Carter, K. A., Hathaway, N. E., & Lettieri, C. F. (2014). Common sleep disorders in children. *American Family Physician, 89,* 368–377.

Cartwright, S., & Cooper, C. (2014). Towards organizational health: Stress, positive organizational behavior, and employee well-being. In G. F. Bauer & O. Hämmig (Eds.), *Bridging occupational, organizational, and public health: A transdisciplinary approach* (pp. 29–42). New York, NY: Springer.

Carvalho, F. R., Velasco, C., van Ee, R., Leboeuf, Y., & Spence, C. (2016). Music influences hedonic and taste ratings in beer. *Frontiers in Psychology, 7,* 636. https://doi.org/10.3389/fpsyg.2016.00636

Case, A., & Deaton, A. (2015). Rising morbidity and mortality in midlife among white non-Hispanic Americans in the 21st century. *Proceedings of the National Academy of Sciences of the United States of America, 112*(49), 15078–15083. Http://dx.doi.org/10.1073/pnas.1518393112

Casey, B. J., Kosofsky, B. E., & Bhide, P. G. (2014). Teenage brains: Think different? *Developmental Neuroscience, 36.* http://dx.doi.org/10.1159/isbn.978-3-318-02676-4

Casey, E. A., Lindhorst, T., & Storer, H. L. (2017). The situational-cognitive model of adolescent bystander behavior: Modeling bystander decision-making in the context of bullying and teen dating violence. *Psychology of Violence, 7*(1), 33–44. http://dx.doi.org/10.1037/vio0000033

Cashel, M. L. (2016). What counselors should know about personality assessments. In I. Marini & M. A. Stebnicki (Eds.), *The professional counselor's desk reference* (2nd ed., pp. 299–303). New York, NY: Springer.

Castaldelli-Maia, J. M., Ventriglio, A., & Bhugra, D. (2016). Tobacco smoking: From 'glamour' to 'stigma.' A comprehensive review. *Psychiatry and Clinical Neurosciences, 70,* 24–33. doi.org/10.1111/pcn.12365

Castillo, D. T., Chee, C. L., Nason, E., Keller, J., C'de Baca, J., Qualls, C., Fallon, S. K., . . . Keane, T. M. (2016). Group-delivered cognitive/exposure therapy for PTSD in women veterans: A randomized controlled trial. *Psychological Trauma: Theory, Research, Practice, and Policy, 8,* 404–412. http://dx.doi.org/10.1037/tra0000111

Castle, D. J., & Buckley, P. F. (2015). *Oxford psychiatry library. Schizophrenia* (2nd ed., rev. and updated). New York, NY: Oxford University Press.

Cattell, R. B. (1950). *Personality: A systematic, theoretical, and factual study.* New York: NY: McGraw-Hill.

Cattell, R. B. (1963). Theory of fluid and crystallized intelligence: A critical experiment. *Journal of Educational Psychology, 54,* 1–22.

Cattell, R. B. (1971). *Abilities: Their structure, growth, and action.* Boston, MA: Houghton Mifflin.

Cattell, R. B. (1990). Advances in Cattellian personality theory. In L. A. Pervin (Ed.), *Handbook of personality: Theory and research* (pp. 101–110). New York: NY: Guilford.

Cavanaugh, J., & Blanchard-Fields, F. (2015). *Adult development and aging.* Stamford, CT: Cengage Learning.

CDC. (2016, February 18). 1 in 3 adults don't get enough sleep. *CDC Newsroom.* Retrieved from http://www.cdc.gov/media/releases/2016/p0215-enough-sleep.html

Cea, N. F., & Barnes, G. E. (2015). The development of addiction-prone personality traits in biological and adoptive families. *Personality and Individual Differences, 82,* 107–113. http://dx.doi.org/10.1016/j.paid.2015.02.035

Cechnicki, A., Hanuszkiewicz, I., Polczyk, R., & Bielańska, A. (2011). Prognostic value of duration of untreated psychosis in long-term outcome of schizophrenia. *Medical Science Monitor: International Medical Journal of Experimental and Clinical Research, 17*(5), CR277–CR283. http://dx.doi.org/10.12659/MSM.881768

Çelikel, A., Demirkiran, D. S., Özsoy, S., Zeren, C., & Arslan, M. M. (2015). Factors associated with PTSD in cases of sexual assault. *Journal of Psychiatry, 18,* 1881.

Çelik, M., Kalenderoğlu, A., Almiş, H., & Turgut, M. (2016). TV programı sonrası gelişen Ölüm Kastı Olmayan Taklit İntiharlar: Beş Yaşında İki Olgu. / Copycat suicides without an intention to die after watching TV programs: Two cases at five years of age. *Nöropsikiyatri Arşivi/Archives of Neuropsychiatry, 53*(1), 83–84.

Center for Nonprofit Management. (2017). The true cost of employee turnover. *CNM.* Retrieved from https://cnmsocal.org/featured/true-cost-of-employee-turnover/

Centers for Disease Control. (2017). *Healthy weight—it's not a diet, it's a lifestyle!* Retrieved from: http://www.cdc.gov/healthyweight/assessing/bmi/adult_bmi/english_bmi_calculator/bmi_calculator.html

Centers for Disease Control and Prevention (CDC). (2015). The national intimate partner and sexual violence survey. *Injury Prevention and Control.* Retrieved September 4, 2015 from http://www.cdc.gov/violencePrevention/NISVS/index.html

Centers for Disease Control and Prevention (CDC). (2016). Mortality in the United States, 2015. *CDC.* Retrieved from https://www.cdc.gov/nchs/products/databriefs/db267.htm

Centers for Disease Control and Prevention (CDC). (2016). Smoking and tobacco use. *CDC.* Retrieved from http://www.cdc.gov/tobacco/data_statistics/fact_sheets/fast_facts/

Centers for Disease Control (CDC). (2016). A to Z: Before and during pregnancy. *Centers for Disease Control.* Retrieved from http://www.cdc.gov/ncbddd/index.html

Centers for Disease Control (CDC). (2016). TBI: Get the facts. *Centers for Disease Control and Prevention.* Retrieved from http://www.cdc.gov/traumaticbraininjury/get_the_facts.html

Cesario, J. (2014). Priming, replication, and the hardest science. *Perspectives on Psychological Science, 9,* 40–48. http://dx.doi.org/10.1177/1745691613513470

Chaby, L. E., Cavigelli, S. A., Hirrlinger, A. M., Caruso, M. J., & Braithwaite, V. A. (2015). Chronic unpredictable stress during adolescence causes long-term anxiety. *Behavioural Brain Research, 278,* 492–495. http://dx.doi.org/10.1016/j.bbr.2014.09.003

Chambers, A. M., & Payne, J. D. (2015). The memory function of sleep. In D. R. Addis, M. Barense, & A. Duarte (Eds.), *The Wiley handbook on the cognitive neuroscience of memory* (pp. 218–243). Hoboken, NJ: Wiley. http://dx.doi.org/10.1002/9781118332634.ch11

Chamorro, J., Bernardi, S., Potenza, M. N., Grant, J. E., Marsh, R., Wang, S., & Blanco, C. (2012). Impulsivity in the general population: A national study. *Journal of Psychiatric Research, 46,* 994–1001. http://dx.doi.org/10.1016/j.jpsychires.2012.04.023

Chamorro-Premuzic, T. (2011). *Personality and individual differences.* Malden, MA: Blackwell.

Chang, A., Le, C. P., Walker, A. K., Creed, S. J., Pon, C. K., Albold, S., . . . Ferrari, D. (2016). β 2-adrenoceptors on tumor cells play a critical role in stress-enhanced metastasis in a mouse model of breast cancer. *Brain, Behavior, and Immunity, 57,* 106–115. http://dx.doi.org/10.1016/j.bbi.2016.06.011

Chang, A.-M., Aeschbach, D., Duffy, J. F., & Czeisler, C. A. (2015). Evening use of light-emitting eReaders negatively affects sleep, circadian timing, and next-morning alertness. *Proceedings of the National Academy of Sciences of the United States of America, 112,* 1232–1237. http://dx.doi.org/10.1073/pnas.1418490112

Chang, H. Y., Keyes, K. M., Mok, Y., Jung, K. J., Shin, Y.-J., & Jee, S. H. (2015). Depression as a risk factor for overall and hormone-related cancer: The Korean cancer prevention study. *Journal of Affective Disorders, 173,* 1–8. http://dx.doi.org/10.1016/j.jad.2014.10.064

Chaplin, T. M. (2015). Gender and emotion expression: A developmental contextual perspective. *Emotion Review, 7,* 14–21.

Chapman, B., Fiscella, K., Duberstein, P., Kawachi, I., & Muennig, P. (2014). Measurement confounding affects the extent to which verbal IQ explains social gradients in mortality. *Journal of Epidemiology and Community Health, 68,* 728–733. http://dx.doi.org/10.1136/jech-2013-203741

Chaput, J. P., & Dutil, C. (2016). Lack of sleep as a contributor to obesity in adolescents: impacts on eating and activity behaviors. *International Journal of Behavioral Nutrition and Physical Activity, 13*(1), 103. http://dx.doi.org/10.1186/s12966-016-0428-0

Charles, L. E., Fekedulegn, D., Landsbergis, P., Burchfiel, C. M., Baron, S., Kaufman, J. D., . . . Roux, A. V. D. (2014). Associations of work hours, job strain, and occupation with endothelial function: The Multi-Ethnic Study of Atherosclerosis (MESA). *Journal of Occupational and*

*Environmental Medicine, 56,* 1153–1160. http://dx.doi.org/10.1097/JOM.0000000000000311

**Chen, A. C. H., Chang, R. Y-H., Besherat, A., & Baack, D. W.** (2013). Who benefits from multiple brand celebrity endorsements? An experimental investigation. *Psychology & Marketing, 30,* 850–860. http://dx.doi.org/10.1002/mar.20650

**Cheng, J., Niles, A. N., & Craske, M. G.** (2017). Exposure reduces negative bias in self-rated performance in public speaking fearful participants. *Journal of Behavior Therapy and Experimental Psychiatry, 54,* 101–107. http://dx.doi.org/10.1016/j.jbtep.2016.07.006

**Cheng, J. T., Tracy, J. L., Ho, S., & Henrich, J.** (2016). Listen, follow me: Dynamic vocal signals of dominance predict emergent social rank in humans. *Journal of Experimental Psychology: General, 145,* 536–547. http://dx.doi.org/10.1037/xge0000166

**Cheng, W., Rolls, E. T., Gu, H., Zhang, J., & Feng, J.** (2015). Autism: Reduced connectivity between cortical areas involved in face expression, theory of mind, and the sense of self. *Brain: A Journal of Neurology, 138*(5), 1382–1393. http://dx.doi.org/10.1093/brain/awv051

**Chen, M.-H., Su, T.-P., Chen, Y.-S., Hsu, J.-W., Huang, K.-L., Chang, W.-H., . . . Bai, Y.-M.** (2014). Higher risk of mood disorders among adolescents with ADHD and asthma: A nationwide prospective study. *Journal of Affective Disorders, 156,* 232–235. http://dx.doi.org/10.1016/j.jad.2013.10.053

**Chen, S., Yao, N., Qian, M., & Lin, M.** (2016). Attentional biases in high social anxiety using a flanker task. *Journal of Behavior Therapy and Experimental Psychiatry, 51,* 27–34. http://dx.doi.org/10.1016/j.jbtep.2015.12.002

**Chen, P., Chavez, O., Ong, D. C., & Gunderson, B.** (2017). Strategic resource for learning: A self-administered intervention that guides self-reflection on effective resource use enhances academic performance. *Psychological Science.* No Pagination Specified. http://dx.doi.org/10.1177/0956797617696456

**Chesin, M. S., Galfavy, H., Sonmez, C. C., Wong, A., Oquendo, M. A., Mann, J. J., & Stanley, B.** (2017). Nonsuicidal self-injury is predictive of suicide attempts among individuals with mood disorders. *Suicide and Life-Threatening Behavior.* No Pagination Specified. http://dx.doi.org/10.1111/sltb.12331

**Chester, D. S., DeWall, C. N., Derefinko, K. J., Estus, S., Lynam, D. R., Peters, J. R., & Jianga, Y.** (2016). Looking for reward in all the wrong places: Dopamine receptor gene polymorphisms indirectly affect aggression through sensation-seeking. *Social Neuroscience, 11*(5), 487–494. http://dx.doi.org/10.1080/17470919.2015.1119191

**Cheung, F., van de Vijver, F., & Leong, F.** (2011). Toward a new approach to the study of personality in culture. *American Psychologist, 66,* 593–603. http://dx.doi.org/10.1037/a0022389

**Chiau, H. Y., Muggleton, N. G., & Juan, C. H.** (2017). Exploring the contributions of the supplementary eye field to subliminal inhibition using double-pulse transcranial magnetic stimulation. *Human Brain Mapping, 38*(1), 339–351. http://dx.doi.org/10.1002/hbm.23364

**Chiesa, J. J., Duhart, J. M., Casiraghi, L. P., Paladino, N., Bussi, I. L., & Golombek, D. A.** (2015). Effects of circadian disruption on physiology and pathology: From bench to clinic (and

back). In R. Aguilar-Roblero, M. Díaz-Muñoz, & M. L. Fanjul-Moles (Eds.), *Mechanisms of circadian systems in animals and their clinical relevance* (pp. 289–320). New York, NY: Springer. http://dx.doi.org/10.1007/978-3-319-08945-4_15

**Chiou, K. S., Genova, H. M., & Chiaravalloti, N. D.** (2016). Structural white matter differences underlying heterogeneous learning abilities after TBI. *Brain Imaging and Behavior, 10*(4), 1274–1279. http://dx.doi.org/10.1007/s11682-015-9497-y

**Chmielewski, M., Zhu, J., Burchett, D., Bury, A. S., & Bagby, R. M.** (2017). The comparative capacity of the Minnesota Multiphasic Personality Inventory–2 (MMPI–2) and MMPI–2 Restructured Form (MMPI-2-RF) validity scales to detect suspected malingering in a disability claimant sample. *Psychological Assessment, 29,* 199–208. http://dx.doi.org/10.1037/pas0000328

**Cho, K., Barnes, C. M., & Guanara, C. L.** (2017). Sleepy punishers are harsh punishers: Daylight saving time and legal sentences. *Psychological Science, 28*(2), 242–247. http://dx.doi.org/10.1177/0956797616678437

**Cho, K. I. K., Shenton, M. E., Kubicki, M., Jung, W. H., Lee, T. Y., Yun, J. Y., . . . Kwon, J. S.** (2016). Altered thalamo-cortical white matter connectivity: Probabilistic tractography study in clinical-high risk for psychosis and first-episode psychosis. *Schizophrenia Bulletin, 42*(3), 723–731. http://dx.doi.org/10.1093/schbul/sbv169

**Choi, D.-H., & Shin, D.-H.** (2017). Exploring political compromise in the new media environment: The interaction effects of social media use and the Big Five personality traits. *Personality and Individual Differences, 106,* 163–171. http://dx.doi.org/10.1016/j.paid.2016.11.022

**Chomsky, N.** (1968). *Language and mind.* New York, NY: Harcourt, Brace, World.

**Chomsky, N.** (1980). *Rules and representations.* New York, NY: Columbia University Press.

**Christian, J. B., Bourgeois, N. E., & Lowe, K. A.** (2015). Cholesterol screening in US adults and awareness of high cholesterol among individuals with severe hypertriglyceridemia: National Health and Nutrition Examination Surveys 2001–2008. *Journal of Cardiovascular Nursing, 30,* 26–34. http://dx.doi.org/10.1097/JCN.0000000000000101

**Chrysikou, E. G., Motyka, K., Nigro, C., Yang, S.-I., & Thompson-Schill, S. L.** (2016). Functional fixedness in creative thinking tasks depends on stimulus modality. *Psychology of Aesthetics, Creativity, and the Arts, 10*(4), 425–435. http://dx.doi.org/10.1037/aca000005

**Chua, A., & Rubenfeld, J.** (2014). What drives success? *New York Times.* Retrieved from http://www.nytimes.com/2014/01/26/opinion/sunday/what-drives-success.html

**Chun, S.-Y., Jang, S.-Y., Choi, J.-W., Shin, J., & Park, E.-C.** (2016). Long-term effects of parental divorce timing on depression: A population-based longitudinal study. *International Journal of Social Psychiatry, 62,* 645–650. http://dx.doi.org/10.1177/0020764016667756

**Cicchetti, D.** (2016). Socioemotional, personality, and biological development: Illustrations from a multilevel developmental psychopathology perspective on child maltreatment. *Annual Review of Psychology, 67,* 187–211. http://dx.doi.org/10.1146/annurev-psych-122414-033259

**Clark, D. A.** (2016). Finding the self in a cognitive behavioral perspective. In M. Kyrios, R. Moulding, G. Doron, S. S. Bhar, M. Nedeljkovic, & M. Mikulincer (Eds.), *The self in understanding and treating psychological disorders* (pp. 40–49). New York, NY: Cambridge University Press.

**Clark, K. D., Quigley, N. R., & Stumpf, S. A.** (2014). The influence of decision frames and vision priming on decision outcomes in work groups: Motivating stakeholder considerations. *Journal of Business Ethics, 120,* 27–38. http://dx.doi.org/10.1007/s10551-013-1648-8

**Clarke, M. J., Marks, A. D. G., & Lykins, A. D.** (2015). Effect of normative masculinity on males' dysfunctional sexual beliefs, sexual attitudes, and perceptions of sexual functioning. *Journal of Sex Research, 52,* 327–337. http://dx.doi.org/10.1080/00224499.2013.860072

**Claro, S., Paunesku, D., & Dweck, C. S.** (2016). Growth mindset tempers the effects of poverty on academic achievement. *Proceedings of the National Academy of Sciences of the United States of America, 113*(31), 8664–8668. http://doi.org/10.1073/pnas.1608207113

**Cohen, A. B.** (Ed.). (2014). *Culture reexamined: Broadening our understanding of social and evolutionary influences.* Washington, DC: American Psychological Association. http://dx.doi.org/10.1037/14274-000

**Cohen, A., & Israel, M.** (2015). Exogenous control processes: Controlled and automatic. In J. G. W. Raaijmakers, A. H. Criss, R. L. Goldstone, R. M. Nosofsky, & M. Steyvers (Eds.), *Psychology Press festschrifts. Cognitive modeling in perception and memory: A festschrift for Richard M. Shiffrin* (pp. 16–34). New York, NY: Psychology Press.

**Cohen, C., Janicki-Deverts, D., Doyle, W. J., Miller, G. E., Frank, E., Rabin, B. S., & Turner, R. B.** (2012). Chronic stress, glucocorticoid receptor resistance, inflammation, and disease risk. *Proceedings of the National Academy of Sciences of the United States of America, 109,* 5995–5999. http://dx.doi.org/10.1073/pnas.1118355109

**Cohen, N., Margulies, D. S., Ashkenazi, S., Schaefer, A., Taubert, M., Henik, A., . . . Okon-Singer, H.** (2016). Using executive control training to suppress amygdala reactivity to aversive information. *NeuroImage, 125,* 1022–1031. http://dx.doi.org/10.1016/j.neuroimage.2015.10.069

**Cohen, R. A.** (2014). Mutual constraint of memory and attention. In R. A. Cohen (Ed.), *The neuropsychology of attention* (pp. 763–777). New York, NY: Springer. http://dx.doi.org/10.1007/978-0-38772639-7_24

**Cohen, S., Doyle, W. J., Turner, R. B., Alper, C. M., & Skoner, D. P.** (2003). Sociability and susceptibility to the common cold. *Psychological Science, 14,* 389–395. http://dx.doi.org/10.1111/1467-9280.01452

**Cohen, S., Janicki-Deverts, D., Turner, R. B., & Doyle, W. J.** (2015). Does hugging provide stress-buffering social support? A study of susceptibility to upper respiratory infection and illness. *Psychological Science, 26,* 135–147. http://doi.org/10.1177/0956797614559284

**Colapinto, J.** (2004, June 3). Gender gap: What were the real reasons behind David Reimer's suicide? *Slate.* Retrieved from http://www.slate.com/articles/health_and_science/medical_examiner/2004/06/gender_gap.html

**Cole, D. L.** (1982). Psychology as a liberating art. *Teaching of Psychology, 9,* 23–26.

Cole, M., Gray, J., Glick, J. A., & Sharp, D. W. (1971). *The cultural context of learning and thinking.* New York, NY: Basic Books.

Cole, P. M., & Moore, G. A. (2015). About face! Infant facial expression of emotion. *Emotion Review, 7,* 116–120. http://dx.doi.org/10.1177/1754073914554786

Colgrove, M., Bloomfield, H. H., & McWilliams, P. (1991). *How to survive the loss of a love.* Peabody, MA: Prelude Press.

Colizzi, M., Costa, R., & Todarello, O. (2014). Transsexual patients' psychiatric comorbidity and positive effect of cross-sex hormonal treatment on mental health: Results from a longitudinal study. *Psychoneuroendocrinology, 39,* 65–73. http://dx.doi.org/10.1016/j.psyneuen.2013.09.029

Collins, E. K., Mccabe, J. A., Hauptman, A. J., Meyers-Orr, B. M., & Stern, B. Z. (2014, August). Does picture generation enhance keyword mnemonic learning? Presented at American Psychological Association (APA) Annual Convention, Washington, DC. http://dx.doi.org/10.1037/e544392014-001

Collomp, K., Baillot, A., Forget, H., Coquerel, A., Rieth, N., & Vibarel-Rebot, N. (2016). Altered diurnal pattern of steroid hormones in relation to various behaviors, external factors and pathologies: A review. *Physiology & Behavior, 164,* 68–85. http://dx.doi.org/10.1016/j.physbeh.2016.05.039

Colman, I., Jones, P. B., Kuh, D., Weeks, M., Naicker, K., Richards, M., & Croudace, T. J. (2014). Early development, stress and depression across the life course: Pathways to depression in a national British birth cohort. *Psychological Medicine, 44,* 2845–2854. http://dx.doi.org/10.1017/S0033291714000385

Cona, F., Lacanna, M., & Ursino, M. (2014). A thalamo-cortical neural mass model for the simulation of brain rhythms during sleep. *Journal of Computational Neuroscience, 37,* 125–148. http://dx.doi.org/10.1007/s10827-013-0493-1

Conger, A. J., Dygdon, J. A., & Rollock, D. (2012). Conditioned emotional responses in racial prejudice. *Ethnic and Racial Studies, 35*(2), 298–319.

Connelly, B. S., & Hülsheger, U. R. (2012). A narrower scope or a clearer lens of personality? Examining sources of observers' advantages over self-reports for predicting performance. *Journal of Personality, 80,* 603–631. http://dx.doi.org/10.1111/j.14676494.2011.00744.x

Connelly, B. S., & Ones, D. S. (2010). Another perspective on personality: Meta-analytic integration of observers' accuracy and predictive validity. *Psychological Bulletin, 136,* 1092–1122. http://dx.doi.org/10.1037/a0021212

Connor, M., Wells, A., & Fisher, P. L. (2016). The nature of depression. In A. Wells & P. Fisher (Eds.), *Treating depression: MCT, CBT and third wave therapies* (pp. 3–23). Hoboken, NJ: Wiley-Blackwell.

Considering a Career. (2011). Becoming a health psychologist. *APA Division 38.* Retrieved from http://www.health-psych.org/AboutHowtoBecome.cfm

Constantino, M. J., Morrison, N, R., Coyne, A. E., & Howard, T. (2017). Exploring therapeutic alliance training in clinical and counseling psychology graduate programs. T*raining and Education in Professional Psychology.* No Pagination Specified. http://dx.doi.org/10.1037/tep0000157

Conte, H. R., Weiner, M. B., & Plutchik, R. (1982). Measuring death anxiety: Conceptual, psychometric, and factor-analytic aspects. *Journal of Personality and Social Psychology, 43,* 775–785.

Conway, M. (2015). *Flashbulb memories.* New York, NY: Psychology Press.

Cook, P. F., Brooks, A., Spivak, M., & Berns, G. S. (2015). Regional brain activity in awake unrestrained dogs. *Journal of Veterinary Behavior: Clinical Applications and Research, 16, 104–112. http://dx.doi.org/10.1016/j.jveb.2015.12.003*

Cook, P. F., Prichard, A., Spivak, M., & Berns, G. S. (2016). Awake canine fMRI predicts dogs' preference for praise versus food. *Social Cognitive and Affective Neuroscience, 11*(12), 1853–1862. http://dx.doi.org/10.1101/062703

Cooper, C. (2015). *Intelligence and human abilities: Structure, origins and applications* (2nd ed.). New York, NY: Routledge.

Coplan, R. J., & Bullock, A. (2012). Temperament and peer relationships. In M. Zentner & R. L. Shiner (Eds.), *Handbook of temperament* (pp. 442–461). New York, NY: Guilford Press.

Cordeira, J. W., Felsted, J. A.,Teillon, S., Daftary, S., Panessiti, M., Wirth, J., . . . Rios, M. (2014). Hypothalamic dysfunction of the thrombospondin receptor α2δ-1 underlies the overeating and obesity triggered by brain-derived neurotrophic factor deficiency. *Journal of Neuroscience, 34,* 554–565. http://dx.doi.org/10.1523/JNEUROSCI.1572-13.2014

Corkin, S. (2013). *Permanent present tense: The unforgettable life of the amnesic patient, H. M.* New York, NY: Basic Books.

Corona, R., Rodríguez, V. M., McDonald, S. E., Velazquez, E., Rodríguez, A., & Fuentes, V. E. (2017). Associations between cultural stressors, cultural values, and Latina/o college students' mental health. *Journal of Youth and Adolescence, 46,* 63–77. http://dx.doi.org/10.1007/s10964-016-0600-5

Corr, C. A. (2015). Let's stop "staging" persons who are coping with loss. *Illness, Crisis, & Loss, 23,* 226–241. http://dx.doi.org/10.1177/1054137315585423

Corr, C. A., Nabe, C. M., & Corr, D. M. (2009). *Death and dying: Life and living* (6th ed.). Belmont, CA: Wadsworth.

Correia, S. S., & Goosens, K. A. (2016). Input-specific contributions to valence processing in the amygdala. *Learning & Memory, 23*(10), 534–543. http://dx.doi.org/10.1101/lm.037887.114

Correll, J., Park, B., Judd, C. M., & Wittenbrink, B. (2002). The police officer's dilemma: Using ethnicity to disambiguate potentially threatening individuals. *Journal of Personality & Social Psychology, 83,* 1314–1329.

Corr, P. J., & Cooper, A. J. (2016). The Reinforcement Sensitivity Theory of Personality Questionnaire (RST-PQ): Development and validation. *Psychological Assessment, 28*(11), 1427–1440. http://dx.doi.org/10.1037/pas0000273

Costa, A. L., Sophia, E. C., Sanches, C., Tavares, H., & Zilberman, M. L. (2015). Pathological jealousy: Romantic relationship characteristics, emotional and personality aspects, and social adjustment. *Journal of Affective Disorders, 174,* 38–44. http://dx.doi.org/10.1016/j.jad.2014.11.017

Costa, P. T., Jr., & McCrae, R. R. (2011). The five-factor model, five-factor theory, and interpersonal psychology. In L. M. Horowitz & S. Strack (Eds.), *Handbook of interpersonal psychology: Theory, research, assessment, and therapeutic interventions* (pp. 91–104). Hoboken, NJ: Wiley.

Cote, J., Clobert, J., Brodin, T., Fogarty, S., & Sih, A. (2014). Personality traits and spatial ecology in nonhuman animals. In P. J. Rentfrow (Ed.), *Geographical psychology: Exploring the interaction of environment and behavior* (pp. 89–112). Washington, DC: American Psychological Association. http://dx.doi.org/10.1037/14272-006

Courage, M. L., & Adams, R. J. (1990). Visual acuity assessment from birth to three years using the acuity card procedures: Cross-sectional and longitudinal samples. *Optometry and Vision Science, 67,* 713–718.

Coutrot, A., Binetti, N., Harrison, C., Mareschal, I., & Johnston, A. (2016). Face exploration dynamics differentiate men and women. *Journal of Vision, 6*(14): 16. http://dx.doi.org/10.1167/16.14.16.

Coviello, L., Sohn, Y., Kramer, A. D. I., Marlow, C., Franceschetti, M., Christakis, N. A., & Fowler, J. H. (2014). Detecting emotional contagion in massive social networks. *PLoS ONE, 9*(3):e90315. http://dx.doi.org/10.1371/journal.pone.0090315

Covington, M. V., & Müeller, K. J. (2001). Intrinsic versus extrinsic motivation: An approach/avoidance reformulation. *Educational Psychology Review, 132,* 157–176.

Coyne, J. C., & Tennen, H. (2010). Positive psychology in cancer care: Bad science, exaggerated claims, and unproven medicine. *Annals of Behavioral Medicine, 39,* 16–26. http://dx.doi.org/10.1007/s12160-009-9154-z

Craig, A. R., Lattal, K. A., & Hall, E. G. (2014). Pausing as an operant: Choice and discriminated responding. *Journal of the Experimental Analysis of Behavior, 101,* 230–245. http://dx.doi.org/10.1002/jeab.73

Craik, F. I., & Lockhart, R. S. (1972). Levels of processing: A framework for memory research. *Journal of Verbal Learning and Verbal Behavior, 11,* 671–684. http://dx.doi.org/10.1016/S0022-5371(72)80001-X

Craik, F. I., & Tulving, E. (1975). Depth of processing and the retention of words in episodic memory. *Journal of Experimental Psychology: General, 104,* 268–294. http://dx.doi.org/10.1037/0096-3445.104.3.268

Crane, C. A., Godleski, S. A., Przybyla, S. M., Schlauch, R. C., & Testa, M. (2016). The proximal effects of acute alcohol consumption on male-to-female aggression: A meta-analytic review of the experimental literature. *Trauma, Violence, & Abuse, 17*(5), 520–531. http://dx.doi.org/10.1177/1524838015584374

Crane, C. A., Licata, M. L., Schlauch, R. C., Testa, M., & Easton, C. J. (2017). The proximal effects of acute alcohol use on female aggression: A meta-analytic review of the experimental literature. *Psychology of Addictive Behaviors, 31*(1), 21–26. http://dx.doi.org/10.1037/adb0000244

Cranley, N. M., Cunningham, C. J. L., & Panda, M. (2016). Understanding time use, stress and recovery practices among early career physicians: An exploratory study. *Psychology, Health & Medicine, 21,* 362–367. http://dx.doi.org/10.1080/13548506.2015.1061675

Craske, M. G. (2017). *Cognitive-behavior therapy* (2nd ed.). Washington, DC: American Psychological Association.

Crego, C., & Widiger, T. A. (2016). Personality disorders. In J. E. Maddux & B. A. Winstead (Eds.),

*Psychopathology: Foundations for a contemporary understanding* (4th ed., pp. 218–236). New York, NY: Routledge/Taylor & Francis Group.

**Crescentini, C., Chittaro, L., Capurso, V., Sioni, R., & Fabbro, F.** (2016). Psychological and physiological responses to stressful situations in immersive virtual reality: Differences between users who practice mindfulness meditation and controls. *Computers in Human Behavior, 59*, 304–316. http://dx.doi.org/10.1016/j.chb.2016.02.031

**Creswell, J. D., Taren, A. A., Lindsay, E. K., Greco, C. M., Gianaros, P. J., Fairgrieve, A., . . . Gerris, J. L.** (2016). Alterations in resting-state functional connectivity link mindfulness meditation with reduced Interleukin-6: A randomized controlled trial. *Biological Psychiatry, 80*(1), 53–61. https://doi.org/10.1016/j.biopsych.2016.01.008

**Crilly, R.** (2015). The ten most expensive paintings in history. *The Telegraph*. Retrieved (January 22, 2017) from http://www.telegraph.co.uk/news/worldnews/northamerica/usa/11596376/The-ten-most-expensive-paintings-in-history.html

**Cristea, I. A., Stefan, S., Karyotaki, E., David, D., Hollon, S. D., & Cuijpers, P.** (2017). The effects of cognitive behavioral therapy are not systematically falling: A revision of Johnsen and Friborg (2015). *Psychological Bulletin, 143*(3), 326–340. http://dx.doi.org/10.1037/bul0000062

**Cristofori, I., Zhong, W., Mandoske, V., Chau, A., Krueger, F., Strenziok, M., & Grafman, J.** (2016). Brain regions influencing implicit violent attitudes: A lesion-mapping study. *The Journal of Neuroscience, 36*, 2757–2768. http://dx.doi.org/10.1523/JNEUROSCI.2975-15.2016

**Crooks, R., & Baur, K.** (2016). *Our sexuality* (13th ed.). Independence, KY: Cengage.

**Crosson-Tower, C.** (2015). *Confronting child and adolescent sexual abuse.* Thousand Oaks, CA: Sage Publications.

**Cruwys, T., South, E. I., Greenaway, K. H., & Haslam, S. A.** (2015). Social identity reduces depression by fostering positive attributions. *Social Psychological and Personality Science, 6*, 65–74. http://dx.doi.org/10.1177/1948550614543309

**Csordas, T. J.** (2014). Afterword: Moral experience in anthropology. *Ethos, 42*, 139–152. http://dx.doi.org/10.1111/etho.12043

**Cuijpers, P.** (2017). Four decades of outcome research on psychotherapies for adult depression: An overview of a series of meta-analyses. *Canadian Psychology/Psychologie Canadienne,58*(1),7–19.http://dx.doi.org/10.1037/cap0000096

**Cullen, D., & Gotell, L.** (2002). From orgasms to organizations: Maslow, women's sexuality and the gendered foundations of the needs hierarchy. *Gender, Work & Organization, 9*, 537–555.

**Cummings, E., & Henry, W. E.** (1961). *Growing old: The process of disengagement.* New York, NY: Basic Books.

**Cummings, M. A.** (2015). The neurobiology of psychopathy: Recent developments and new directions in research and treatment. *CNS Spectrums, 20*, 200–206. http://dx.doi.org/10.1017/S1092852914000741.

**Curtiss, S.** (1977). *Genie: A psycholinguistic study of a modern-day "wild child."* New York, NY: Academic Press.

**Cusack, K., Jonas, D. E., Forneris, C. A., Wines, C., Sonis, J., Middleton, J. C., . . . Gaynes, B. N.** (2016). Psychological treatments for adults with posttraumatic stress disorder: A systematic review and meta-analysis. *Clinical Psychology Review, 43*, 128–141. http://dx.doi.org/10.1016/j.cpr.2015.10.003

**Cussen, V. A., & Mench, J. A.** (2014). Personality predicts cognitive bias in captive psittacines, Amazona amazonica. *Animal Behaviour, 89*, 123–130. http://dx.doi.org/10.1016/j.anbehav.2013.12.022

**Cutler, D. M., & Lleras-Muney, A.** (2006). Education and health: Evaluating theories and evidence. *National Bureau of Economic Research.* Retrieved from http://www.nber.org/papers/w12352

**D'Aconti, A.** (2013, December 19). A lesson from Jennifer Lawrence on social anxiety. *Healthy Place*. Retrieved from http://www.healthyplace.com/blogs/anxiety-schmanxiety/2013/12/a-lesson-from-jennifer-lawrence-on-social-anxiety/

**Dale, A., Lortie-Lussier, M., Wong, C., & De Koninck, J.** (2016). Dreams of Canadian students: Norms, gender differences, and comparison with American norms. *Journal of Cross-Cultural Psychology, 47*(7), 941–955. http://dx.doi.org/10.1177/0022022116655788

**D'Ambrosio, C., & Redline, S.** (2014). Sleep across the lifespan. In S. Redline & N. Berger (Eds.), *Impact of sleep and sleep disturbances on obesity and cancer* (pp. 1–23). New York, NY: Springer.

**Dambrun, M., & Valentiné, E.** (2010). Reopening the study of extreme social behaviors: Obedience to authority within an immersive video environment. *European Journal of Social Psychology, 40*(5), 760–773.

**Dana, R. H.** (2014). Personality tests and psychological science: Instruments, populations, practice. In F. T. L. Leong, L. Comas-Díaz, G. C. Nagayama Hall, V. C. McLoyd, & J. E. Trimble (Eds.), *APA handbooks in psychology. APA handbook of multicultural psychology, Vol. 2. Applications and training* (pp. 181–196). Washington, DC: American Psychological Association. http://dx.doi.org/10.1037/14187-011

**Dan, B.** (2017). Gap junctions in epilepsy: For better or worse. *Developmental Medicine & Child Neurology, 59*(1), 4. http://dx.doi.org/10.1111/dmcn.13290

**Daniluk, J. C., Koert, E., & Breckon, E.** (2014). Sexuality and infertility. In Y. Binik & K. Hall (Eds.), *Principles and practice of sex therapy* (pp. 419–435). New York, NY: Guilford.

**Danner, F., & Phillips, B.** (2008). Adolescent sleep, school start times, and teen motor vehicle crashes. *Journal of Clinical Sleep Medicine, 4*, 533–535.

**Dargis, M., Newman, J., & Koenigs, M.** (2016). Clarifying the link between childhood abuse history and psychopathic traits in adult criminal offenders. *Personality Disorders: Theory, Research, and Treatment, 7*, 221–228. http://dx.doi.org/10.1037/per0000147

**Darley, J. M., & Latané, B.** (1968). Bystander intervention in emergencies: Diffusion of responsibility. *Journal of Personality and Social Psychology, 8*, 377–383.

**Darwin, C.** (1859). The origin of species by means of natural selection; or the preservation of favoured races in the struggle for life. *Nature, 5*, 318–319. http://dx.doi.org/10.1038/005318a0

**Darwin, C.** (1872). *The expression of emotions in animals and man.* London, UK: Murray. http://dx.doi.org/10.1037/10001-000

**Darwin, C.** (1872). *The expression of emotions in man and animals.* New York, NY: Appleton & Company.

**Data-Franco, J., Singh, A., Popovic, D., Ashton, M., Berk, M., Vieta, E., . . . Dean, O. M.** (2017). Beyond the therapeutic shackles of the monoamines: New mechanisms in bipolar disorder biology. *Progress in Neuro-Psychopharmacology & Biological Psychiatry, 72*, 73–86. http://dx.doi.org/10.1016/j.pnpbp.2016.09.004

**Datta, A., Tschantz, M. C., & Datta, A.** (2015). Automated experiments on ad privacy settings: A tale of opacity, choice, and discrimination. *Proceedings on Privacy Enhancing Technologies, 2015*, 92–112. http://dx.doi.org/10.1515/popets-2015-0007

**Datu, J. A. D., Yuen, M., & Chen, G.** (2016). Grit and determination: A review of literature with implications for theory and research. *Journal of Psychologists and Counsellors in Schools*, 1–9. http://dx.doi.org/10.1017/jgc.2016.2

**Davidson, P., Carlsson, I., Jönsson, P., & Johansson, M.** (2016). Sleep and the generalization of fear learning. *Journal of Sleep Research, 25*, 88–95. http://dx.doi.org/10.1111/jsr.12339

**Davies, M. S., Strickland, T. L., & Cao, M.** (2014). Neuropsychological evaluation of culturally diverse populations. In F. T. L. Leong, L. Comas-Díaz, G. C. Nagayama Hall, V. C. McLoyd, & J. E. Trimble (Eds.), *APA handbook of multicultural psychology, Vol. 2: Applications and training* (pp. 231–251). Washington, DC: American Psychological Association. http://dx.doi.org/10.1037/14187-014

**Davis, N. T., & Mason, L.** (2016). Sorting and the split-ticket: Evidence from presidential and subpresidential elections. *Political Behavior, 38*, 337–354. http://dx.doi.org/10.1007/s11109-015-9315-7

**Dawkins, R.** (2016). *The selfish gene: 40th anniversary edition.* New York, NY: Oxford University Press.

**Dawson, K. M., O'Brien, K. E., & Beehr, T. A.** (2016). The role of hindrance stressors in the job demand–control–support model of occupational stress: A proposed theory revision. *Journal of Organizational Behavior, 37*, 397–415. http://dx.doi.org/10.1002/job.2049

**Day, M. A.** (2016). The application of mindfulness-based cognitive therapy for chronic pain. In S. J. Eisendrath (Ed.), *Mindfulness-based cognitive therapy: Innovative applications* (pp. 65–74). Cham, CH: Springer International Publishing. http://dx.doi.org/10.1007/978-3-319-29866-5_6

**Day, M. V., & Ross, M.** (2014). Predicting confidence in flashbulb memories. *Memory, 22*, 232–242. http://dx.doi.org/10.1080/09658211.2013.778290

**Dean, J.** (2015). The most common mental health problem is "contagious." *PsyBlog*. Retrieved from http://www.spring.org.uk/2015/05/the-most-common-mental-health-problem-is-contagious.php

**Deblinger, E., Mannarino, A. P., Cohen, J. A., Runyon, M. K., & Heflin, A. H.** (2015). *Child sexual abuse: A primer for treating children, adolescents, and their non-offending parents* (2nd ed.). New York, NY: Oxford University Press.

**DeBord, K. A., Fischer, A. R., Bieschke, K. J., & Perez, R. M.** (Eds.). (2017). *Handbook of sexual orientation and gender diversity in counseling and psychotherapy.* Washington, DC: American Psychological Association.

De Castella, K., & Byrne, D. (2015, February 13). My intelligence may be more malleable than yours: The revised implicit theories of intelligence (self-theory) scale is a better predictor of achievement, motivation, and student disengagement. *European Journal of Psychology of Education, 30*, 245–267. http://dx.doi.org/10.1007/s10212-015-0244-y

Decety, J., & Yoder, K. J. (2017). The emerging social neuroscience of justice motivation. *Trends in Cognitive Sciences, 21*(1), 6–14. http://dx.doi.org/10.1016/j.tics.2016.10.008

Deci, E. L., & Moller, A. C. (2005). The concept of competence: A starting place for understanding intrinsic motivation and self-determined extrinsic motivation. In A. J. Elliot & C. S. Dweck (Eds.), *Handbook of competence and motivation* (pp. 579–597). New York, NY: Guilford.

Deci, E. L., & Ryan, R. M. (1985). *Intrinsic motivation and self-determination in human behavior.* New York, NY: Plenum.

Deci, E. L., & Ryan, R. M. (2012). Self-determination theory. In P. A. M. Van Lange, A. W. Kruglanski, & E. T. Higgins (Eds.), *Handbook of theories of social psychology* (Vol. 1, pp. 416–436). Thousand Oaks, CA: Sage.

Deconinck, F. J. A., Smorenburg, A. R. P., Benham, A., Ledebt, A., Feltham, M. G., & Savelsbergh, G. J. P. (2015). Reflections on mirror therapy: A systematic review of the effect of mirror visual feedback on the brain. *Neurorehabilitation and Neural Repair, 29*, 349–361. http://dx.doi.org/10.1177/1545968314546134

De Cuyper, B., Boen, F., Van Beirendonck, C., Vanbeselaere, N., & Fransen, K. (2016). When do elite cyclists go the extra mile? Team identification mediates the relationship between perceived leadership qualities of the captain and social laboring. *International Journal of Sport Psychology, 47*(4), 355–372.

Deeb, R., Judge, P., Peterson, E., Lin, J. C., & Yaremchuk, K. (2014). Snoring and carotid artery intima-media thickness. *The Laryngoscope, 124*, 1486–1491. http://dx.doi.org/10.1002/lary.24527

de Gelder, B., & Huis in't Veld, E. (2016). Cultural differences in emotional expressions and body language. In J. Y. Chiao, S.-C. Li, R. Seligman, & R. Turner (Eds.), *The Oxford handbook of cultural neuroscience* (pp. 223–234). New York, NY: Oxford University Press.

de Jonge, P., Roest, A. M., Lim, C. C. W., Florescu, S. E., Bromet, E. J., Stein, D. J., . . . Scott, K. M. (2016). Cross-national epidemiology of panic disorder and panic attacks in the world mental health surveys. *Depression and Anxiety, 33*, 1155–1177. http://dx.doi.org/10.1002/da.22572

Dekel, S., & Farber, B. A. (2012). Models of intimacy of securely and avoidantly attached young adults. *The Journal of Nervous and Mental Disease, 200*, 156–162. http://dx.doi.org/10.1097/NMD.0b013e3182439702

Delahaij, R., & van Dam, K. (2016). Coping style development: The role of learning goal orientation and metacognitive awareness. *Personality and Individual Differences, 92*, 57–62. http://dx.doi.org/10.1016/j.paid.2015.12.012

Delmonico, D. L., & Griffin, E. J. (2014). Possession of child pornography: A case study. In W. T. O'Donohue (Ed.), *Case studies in sexual deviance: Toward evidence-based practice* (pp. 195–228). New York, NY: Routledge/Taylor & Francis Group.

Del Río, F. J., Cabello, F., & Fernández, I. (2015). Influence of substance use on the erectile response in a sample of drug users. *International Journal of Clinical and Health Psychology, 15*, 37–43.

Dement, W. C., & Wolpert, E. (1958). The relation of eye movements, bodily motility, and external stimuli to dream content. *Journal of Experimental Psychology, 53*, 543–553. http://dx.doi.org/10.1037/h0040031

Demos, K. E., Hart, C. N., Sweet, L. H., Mailloux, K. A., Trautvetter, J., Williams, S. E., . . . McCaffery, J. M. (2016). Partial sleep deprivation impacts impulsive action but not impulsive decision-making. *Physiology & Behavior, 164*, 214–219. http://dx.doi.org/10.1016/j.physbeh.2016.06.003

Denmark, T., Atkinson, J., Campbell, R., & Swettenham, J. (2014). How do typically developing deaf children and deaf children with autism spectrum disorder use the face when comprehending emotional facial expressions in British sign language? *Journal of Autism and Developmental Disorders, 44*, 2584–2592. http://dx.doi.org/10.1007/s10803-014-2130-x

Denny, B. T., Fan, J., Liu, X., Guerreri, S., Mayson, S. J., Rimsky, L., . . . Koenigsberg, H. W. (2016). Brain structural anomalies in borderline and avoidant personality disorder patients and their associations with disorder-specific symptoms. *Journal of Affective Disorders, 200*, 266–274. http://dx.doi.org/10.1016/j.jad.2016.04.053

Denovan, A., & Macaskill, A. (2017). Stress and subjective well-being among first year UK undergraduate students. *Journal of Happiness Studies, 18*(2), 505–525. http://dx.doi.org/10.1007/s10902-016-9736-y

Depp, C. A., Moore, R. C., Dev, S. I., Mausbach, B. T., Eyler, L. T., & Granholm, E. L. (2016). The temporal course and clinical correlates of subjective impulsivity in bipolar disorder as revealed through ecological momentary assessment. *Journal of Affective Disorders, 193*, 145–150. http://dx.doi.org/10.1016/j.jad.2015.12.016

Depression the Second Time Around. (n.d.). Warning signs of severe depression. *WebMD.* Retrieved from http://www.webmd.com/depression/second-time-12/warning-signs?page=1

De Putter, L. M. S., Van Yper, L., & Koster, E. H. W. (2017). Obsessions and compulsions in the lab: A meta-analysis of procedures to induce symptoms of obsessive-compulsive disorder. *Clinical Psychology Review, 52*, 137–147. http://dx.doi.org/10.1016/j.cpr.2017.01.001

DeRosse, P., Nitzburg, G. C., Ikuta, T., Peters, B. D., Malhotra, A. K., & Szeszko, P. R. (2015). Evidence from structural and diffusion tensor imaging for frontotemporal deficits in psychometric schizotypy. *Schizophrenia Bulletin, 41*, 104–114. http://dx.doi.org/10.1093/schbul/sbu150

DeRosse, P., Nitzburg, G. C., Kompancaril, B., & Malhotra, A. K. (2014). The relation between childhood maltreatment and psychosis in patients with schizophrenia and nonpsychiatric controls. *Schizophrenia Research, 155*, 66–71. http://dx.doi.org/10.1016/j.schres.2014.03.009

DeSoto, K. A., & Roediger, H. L. (2014). Positive and negative correlations between confidence and accuracy for the same events in recognition of categorized lists. *Psychological Science, 25*, 781–788. http://dx.doi.org/10.1177/0956797613516149

Desrosiers, A., Sipsma, H., Callands, T., Hansen, N., Divney, A., Magriples, U., & Kershaw, T. (2014). "Love hurts": Romantic attachment and depressive symptoms in pregnant adolescent and young adult couples. *Journal of Clinical Psychology, 70*, 95–106. http://dx.doi.org/10.1002/jclp.21979

de Tychey, C., Vandelet, E., Laurent, M., Lighezzolo-Alnot, J., Prudent, C., & Evrard, R. (2016). Child sexual abuse, baby gender, and intergenerational psychic transmission: An exploratory, projective psychoanalytic approach. *Psychoanalytic Review, 103*, 221–250. http://dx.doi.org/10.1521/prev.2016.103.2.221

Developmental Cognitive Neuroscience. (n.d.). *Lab of Adele Diamond.* Retrieved January 11, 2017 from http://www.devcogneuro.com/AdeleDiamond.html

DeWall, C. N., Anderson, C. A., & Bushman, B. J. (2013). Aggression. In H. Tennen, J. Suls, & I. B. Weiner (Eds.), *Handbook of psychology, Vol. 5. Personality and social psychology* (2nd ed., pp. 449–466). Hoboken, NJ: Wiley.

DeWall, C. N., Chester, D. S., & White, D. S. (2015). Can acetaminophen reduce the pain of decision-making? *Journal of Experimental Social Psychology, 56*, 117–120. http://dx.doi.org/10.1016/j.jesp.2014.09.006

Dewar, M., Alber, J., Butler, C., Cowan, N., & Della Sala, S. (2012). Brief wakeful resting boosts new memories over the long term. *Psychological Science, 23*, 955–960. http://dx.doi.org/10.1177/0956797612441220

Deweese, M. M., Robinson, J. D., Cinciripini, P. M., & Versace, F. (2016). Conditioned cortical reactivity to cues predicting cigarette-related or pleasant images. *International Journal of Psychophysiology, 101*, 59–68. http://dx.doi.org/10.1016/j.ijpsycho.2016.01.007

Dhamija, D., Tuvblad, C., & Baker, L. A. (2016). Behavioral genetics of the externalizing spectrum. In T. P. Beauchaine & S. P. Hinshaw (Eds.), *The Oxford handbook of externalizing spectrum disorders* (pp. 105–124). New York, NY: Oxford University Press.

Diamond, A. (2013). Executive functions. *Annual Review of Psychology, 64*, 135–168. http://dx.doi.org/10.1146/annurev-psych-113011-143750

Diamond, A. (2016). Why improving and assessing executive functions early in life is critical. In J. A. Griffin, P. McCardle, & L. S. Freund (Eds.), *Executive function in preschool-age children: Integrating measurement, neurodevelopment, and translational research* (pp. 11–43). Washington, DC: American Psychological Association. http://dx.doi.org/10.1037/14797-002

Diaz, K. M., Boothill, J. N., Seals, S. R., Hooker, S. P., Sims, M., Dubbert, P. M. . . . Shimbo, D. (2016). Sedentary behavior and subclinical atherosclerosis in African Americans: cross-sectional analysis of the Jackson heart study. *International Journal of Behavioral Nutrition and Physical Activity, 13*, 31. http://dx.doi.org/10.1186/s12966-016-0349-y

Diaz Vickery, K., Guzman-Corrales, L., Owen, R., Soderlund, D., Shimotsu, S., Clifford, P., & Linzer, M. (2016). Medicaid expansion and mental health: A Minnesota case study. *Families, Systems, & Health, 34*(1), 58–63. http://dx.doi.org/10.1037/fsh0000186

Dibbets, P., & Meesters, C. (2017). The influence of stimulus valence on confirmation bias in children. *Journal of Behavior Therapy and*

*Experimental Psychiatry, 54,* 88–92. http://dx.doi.org/10.1016/j.jbtep.2016.07.007

**Dibbets, P., van den Broek, A., & Evers, E. A. T.** (2015). Fear conditioning and extinction in anxiety- and depression-prone persons. *Memory, 23,* 350–364. http://dx.doi.org/10.1080/09658211.2014.88670

**Dickert, S., Västfjäll, D., & Slovic, P.** (2015). Neuroeconomics and dual information processes underlying charitable giving. In E. A. Wilhelms & V. F. Reyna (Eds.), *Neuroeconomics, judgment, and decision making* (pp. 181–199). New York, NY: Psychology Press.

**Dickter, C. L., Gagnon, K. T., Gyurovski, I. I., & Brewington, B. S.** (2015). Close contact with racial outgroup members moderates attentional allocation towards outgroup versus ingroup faces. *Group Processes & Intergroup Relations, 18,* 76–88. http://dx.doi.org/10.1177/1368430214527854

**Diefenbach, S., Hassenzahl, M., Eckoldt, K., Hartung, L., Lenz, E., & Laschke, M.** (2017). Designing for well-being: A case study of keeping small secrets. *The Journal of Positive Psychology, 12*(2), 151–158. http://dx.doi.org/10.1080/17439760.2016.1163405

**Diego, M. A., & Jones, N. A.** (2007). Neonatal antecedents for empathy. In T. Farrow & P. Woodruff (Eds.), *Empathy in mental illness* (pp. 145–167). New York, NY: Cambridge University Press.

**Dieleman, G. C., Huizink, A. C., Tulen, J. H. M., Utens, E. M. W. J., & Tiemeier, H.** (2016). Stress reactivity predicts symptom improvement in children with anxiety disorders. *Journal of Affective Disorders, 196,* 190–199. http://dx.doi.org/10.1016/j.jad.2016.02.022

**Diener, E.** (2016). Happiness is a virtue—Good for you and good for the world! In R. J. Sternberg, S. T. Fiske, & D. J. Foss (Eds.), *Scientists making a difference: One hundred eminent behavioral and brain scientists talk about their most important contributions* (pp. 345–348). New York, NY: Cambridge University Press.

**Diener, E., & Biswas-Diener, R.** (2002). Will money increase subjective well-being? A literature review and guide to needed research. *Social Indicators Research, 57,* 119–169.

**Diener, E., & Biswas-Diener, R.** (2008). *Happiness: Unlocking the mysteries of psychological wealth.* Hoboken, NJ: Blackwell Publishing. http://dx.doi.org/10.1002/9781444305159

**Diener, E., & Tay, L.** (2015). Subjective well-being and human welfare around the world as reflected in the Gallup World Poll. *International Journal of Psychology, 50,* 135–149. http://dx.doi.org/10.1002/ijop.12136

**Diering, G. H., Nirujogi, R. S., Roth, R. H., Worley, P. F., Pandey, A., & Huganir, R. L.** (2017). Homenr1a drives homeostatic scaling-down of excitatory synapses during sleep. *Science, 344*(6324), 511–515. http://dx.doi.org/10.1126/science.aai8355

**Dietrich, J., Viljaranta, J., Moeller, J., & Kracke, B.** (2017). Situational expectancies and task values: Associations with students' effort. *Learning and Instruction, 47,* 53–64. http://dx.doi.org/10.1016/j.learninstruc.2016.10.009

**DiFeliceantonio, A. G., Mabrouk, O. S., Kennedy, R. T., & Berridge, K. C.** (2012). Enkephalin surges in dorsal neostriatum as a signal to eat. *Current Biology, 22,* 1918–1924. http://dx.doi.org/10.1016/j.cub.2012.08.014

**DiFeo, G., & Shors, T. J.** (2017). Mental and physical skill training increases neurogenesis via cell survival in the adolescent hippocampus. *Brain Research, 1654,* 95–101. http://dx.doi.org/10.1016/j.brainres.2016.08.015

**Digdon, N.** (2017). The Little Albert controversy: Intuition, confirmation bias, and logic. *History of Psychology.* No Pagination Specified. http://dx.doi.org/10.1037/hop0000055

**DiGrazia, J., McKelvey, K., Bollen, J., & Rojas, F.** (2013). More tweets, more votes: Social media as a quantitative indicator of political behavior. *PLoS ONE, 8,* e79449. http://dx.doi.org/10.1371/journal.pone.0079449

**Dill, K. E., & Thill, K. P.** (2007). Video game characters and the socialization of gender roles: Young people's perceptions mirror sexist media depictions. *Sex Roles, 57,* 851–864. http://dx.doi.org/10.1007/s11199-007-9278-1

**Dillon, H. M., Adair, L. E., Geher, G., Wang, Z., & Strouts, P. H.** (2016). Playing smart: The mating game and mating intelligence. *Current Psychology: A Journal for Diverse Perspectives on Diverse Psychological Issues, 35*(3), 414–420. http://dx.doi.org/10.1007/s12144-015-9309-y

**Dillon, S.** (2009, January 22). Study sees an Obama effect as lifting Black test-takers. *New York Times.* Retrieved from http://www.nytimes.com/2009/01/23/education/23gap.html

**Dimaggio, G., Salvatore, G., MacBeth, A., Ottavi, P., Buonocore, L., & Popolo, R.** (2017). Metacognitive interpersonal therapy for personality disorders: A case study series. *Journal of Contemporary Psychotherapy, 47*(1), 11–21. http://dx.doi.org/10.1007/s10879-016-9342-7

**Dimberg, U., & Thunberg, M.** (1998). Rapid facial reactions to emotion facial expressions. *Scandinavian Journal of Psychology, 39*(1), 39–46.

**Dimberg, U., Thunberg, M., & Elmehed, K.** (2000). Unconscious facial reactions to emotional facial expressions. *Psychological Science, 11*(1), 86–89.

**Dimidjian, S., Goodman, S. H., Felder, J. N., Gallop, R., Brown, A. P., & Beck, A.** (2016). Staying well during pregnancy and the postpartum: A pilot randomized trial of mindfulness-based cognitive therapy for the prevention of depressive relapse/recurrence. *Journal of Consulting and Clinical Psychology, 84,* 134–145. http://dx.doi.org/10.1037/ccp0000068

**Dingus, T. A., Guo, F., Lee, S., Antin, J. F., Perez, M., Buchanan-King, M., & Hankey, J.** (2016). Driver crash risk factors and prevalence evaluation using naturalistic driving data. *Proceedings of the National Academy of Sciences of the United States of America, 113,* 2636–2641. http://dx.doi.org/10.1073/pnas.1513271113

**Ding, Y. H., Xu, X., Wang, Z. Y., Li, H. R., & Wang, W. P.** (2014). The relation of infant attachment to attachment and cognitive and behavioural outcomes in early childhood. *Early Human Development, 90,* 459–464. http://dx.doi.org/10.1016/j.earlhumdev.2014.06.004.

**Dinsmore, D. L., & Alexander, P. A.** (2016). A multi dimensional investigation of deep-level and surface-level processing. *Journal of Experimental Education, 84,* 213–244. http://dx.doi.org/10.1080/00220973.2014.979126

**Dirkes, J., Hughes, T., Ramirez-Valles, J., Johnson, T., & Bostwick, W.** (2016). Sexual identity development: Relationship with lifetime suicidal ideation in sexual minority women. *Journal of Clinical Nursing, 25,* 3545–3556. http://dx.doi.org/10.1111/jocn.13313

**Dirks-Linhorst, P. A.** (2013). An analysis of Missouri's insanity acquittee population, 1980–2009: Differences within African American insanity acquittees. *Journal of Ethnicity in Criminal Justice, 11,* 44–70.

**Dixon, R. W., Youssef, G. J., Hasking, P., Yücel, M., Jackson, A. C., & Dowling, N. A.** (2016). The relationship between gambling attitudes, involvement, and problems in adolescence: Examining the moderating role of coping strategies and parenting styles. *Addictive Behaviors, 58,* 42–46. http://dx.doi.org/10.1016/j.addbeh.2016.02.011

**Dobrow, S., Ganzach, Y., & Liu, Y.** (2016). Time and job satisfaction: A longitudinal study of the differential roles of age and tenure. *Journal of Management.* http://dx.doi.org/10.1177/0149206315624962

**Dobson, K. S.** (2016). The efficacy of cognitive-behavioral therapy for depression: Reflections on a critical discussion. *Clinical Psychology: Science and Practice, 23,* 123–125. http://dx.doi.org/10.1111/cpsp.12151

**Dodge, E.** (2016). Forty years of eating disorder–focused family therapy—The legacy of 'psychosomatic families'. *Advances in Eating Disorders, 4,* 219–227. http://dx.doi.org/10.1080/21662630.2015.1099452

**Dolev-Cohen, M., & Barak, A.** (2013). Adolescents' use of instant messaging as a means of emotional relief. *Computers in Human Behavior, 29,* 58–63. http://dx.doi.org/10.1016/j.chb.2012.07.016

**Dolezal, B. A., Neufeld, E. V., Boland, D. M., Martin, J. L., & Cooper, C. B.** (2017). Interrelationship between sleep and exercise: A systematic review. *Advances in Preventive Medicine, Article ID:*1364387. http://dx.org/10.1155/2017/1364387

**Doliński, D., Grzyb, T., Folwarczny, M., Grzybała, P., Krzyszycha, K., Martynowska, K., & Trojanowski, J.** (2017). Would you deliver an electric shock in 2015? Obedience in the experimental paradigm developed by Stanley Milgram in the 50 years following the original studies. *Social Psychological and Personality Science.* http://dx.doi.org/10.1177/1948550617693060

**Dombrowski, S. C.** (2015). *Psychoeducational assessment and report writing.* New York, NY: Springer. http://dx.doi.org/10.1007/978-1-4939-1911-6

**Domhoff, G. W.** (2003). *The scientific study of dreams: Neural networks, cognitive development, and content analysis.* Washington, DC: American Psychological Association.

**Domhoff, G. W.** (2010). Dream content is continuous with waking thought, based on preoccupations, concerns, and interests. *Sleep Medicine Clinics, 5,* 203–215.

**Domhoff, G. W.** (2017). *Dreams have psychological meaning and cultural uses, but no known adaptive function.* Dreamresearch.net. Retrieved from http://www2.ucsc.edu/dreams/Library/purpose.html

**Domhoff, G. W., & Fox, K. C.** (2015). Dreaming and the default network: A review, synthesis, and counterintuitive research proposal. *Consciousness and Cognition, 33,* 342–353. http://dx.doi.org/10.1016/j.concog.2015.01.019

**D'Onofrio, B. M., Rickert, M. E., Frans, E., Kuja-Halkola, R., Almqvist, C., Sjolander, A., . . . Lichtenstein, P.** (2014). Paternal age at childbearing and offspring psychiatric and academic morbidity. *JAMA Psychiatry, 71,* 432–438. http://dx.doi.org/10.1001/jamapsychiatry.2013.4525

Doran, J. M., Safran, J. D., & Muran J. C. (2017). An investigation of the relationship between the alliance negotiation scale and psychotherapy process and outcome. *Journal of Clinical Psychology, 73*(4), 449–465. http://dx.doi.org/10.1002/jclp.22340

dos Santos, R. G., Osório , F. L., Crippa, J. A. S., Riba, J., Zuardi, A. W., & Hallak, J. E. C. (2016). Antidepressive, anxiolytic, and antiaddictive effects of ayahuasca, psilocybin and lysergic acid diethylamide (LSD): A systematic review of clinical trials published in the last 25 years. *Therapeutic Advances in Psychopharmacology, 6,* 193–213. http://dx.doi.org/10.1177/2045125316638008

Doty, R. L., Tourbier, I., Ng, V., Neff , J., Armstrong, D., Battistini, M., . . . Sondheimer, S. J. (2015). Influences of hormone replacement therapy on olfactory and cognitive function in postmenopausal women. *Neurobiology of Aging, 36,* 2053–2059. http://dx.doi.org/10.1016/j.neurobiolaging.2015.02.028

Doulatram, G., Raj, T. D., & Govindaraj, R. (2015). Pregnancy and substance abuse. In A. Kaye, N. Vadivelu, & R. Urman (Eds.), *Substance abuse* (pp. 453–494). New York, NY: Springer.

Dovey, T. M., Boyland, E. J., Trayner, P., Miller, J., Rarmoul-Bouhadjar, A., Cole, J., & Halford, J. C. (2016). Alterations in taste perception due to recreational drug use are due to smoking a substance rather than ingesting it. *Appetite, 107,* 1–8. http://dx.doi.org/10.1016/j.appet.2016.07.016

Draganich, C., & Erdal, K. (2014). Placebo sleep affects cognitive functioning. *Journal of Experimental Psychology: Learning, Memory, and Cognition, 40,* 857–864. http://dx.doi.org/10.1037/a0035546

Drake, E. C., Sladek, M. R., & Doane, L. D. (2016). Daily cortisol activity, loneliness, and coping efficacy in late adolescence: A longitudinal study of the transition to college. *International Journal of Behavioral Development, 40,* 334–345. http://dx.doi.org/10.1177/0165025415581914

Drane, C. F., Modecki, K. L., & Barber, B. L. (2017). Disentangling development of sensation seeking, risky peer affiliation, and binge drinking in adolescent sport. *Addictive Behaviors, 66,* 60–65. http://dx.doi.org/10.1016/j.addbeh.2016.11.001

Drążkowski, D., Kaczmarek, L. D., & Kashdan, T. B. (2017). Gratitude pays: A weekly gratitude intervention influences monetary decisions, physiological responses, and emotional experiences during a trust-related social interaction. *Personality and Individual Differences, 110,* 148–153. http://dx.doi.org/10.1016/j.paid.2017.01.043

Dreu, C. K. W. D., Aaldering, H., & Saygi, Ö. (2015). Conflict and negotiation within and between groups. In M. Mikulincer, P. R. Shaver, J. F. Dovidio, & J. A. Simpson (Eds.), *APA handbook of personality and social psychology, Vol. 2. Group processes* (pp. 151–176). Washington, DC: American Psychological Association. http://dx.doi.org/10.1037/14342-006

Drew, L. (2013). What is the point of sleep? *New Scientist, 217,* 38–39.

Drexler, S. M., Merz, C. J., Hamacher-Dang, T. C., Tegenthoff, M., & Wolf, O. T. (2015). Effects of cortisol on reconsolidation of reactivated fear memories. *Neuropsychopharmacology, 40,* 3036–3043. http://dx.doi.org/10.1038/npp.2015.160.

Driessen, E., Van, H. L., Peen, J., Don, F. J., Kool, S., Westra, D., . . . Dekker, J. J. M. (2015). Therapist-rated outcomes in a randomized clinical trial comparing cognitive behavioral therapy and psychodynamic therapy for major depression. *Journal of Affective Disorders, 170,* 112–118. http://dx.doi.org/10.1016/j.jad.2014.08.023

Drigotas, S. M., Whitney, G. A., & Rusbult, C. E. (1995). On the peculiarities of loyalty: A diary study of responses to dissatisfaction in everyday life. *Personality and Social Psychology Bulletin, 21,* 596–609.

D'Souza, J., & Gurin, M. (2016). The universal significance of Maslow's concept of self-actualization. *The Humanistic Psychologist, 44,* 210–214. http://dx.doi.org/10.1037/hum0000027

Duarte-Guterman, P., Yagi, S., Chow, C., & Galea, L. A. (2015). Hippocampal learning, memory, and neurogenesis: Effects of sex and estrogens across the lifespan in adults. *Hormones & Behavior, 74,* 37–52.

Dubois, L., Diasparra, M., Bogl, L. -H., Fontaine-Bisson, B., Bédard, B., Tremblay, R. E., . . . Boivin, M. (2016). Dietary intake at 9 years and subsequent body mass index in adolescent boys and girls: A study of monozygotic twin pairs. *Twin Research and Human Genetics, 19,* 47–59. http://dx.doi.org/10.1017/thg.2015.97

Duckworth, A. (2016). *Grit: The power of passion and perseverance.* New York, NY: Scribner/Simon & Schuster.

Duits, P., Cath, D. C., Lissek, S., Hox, J. J., Hamm, A. O., Engelhard, I. M., . . . Baas, J. M. P. (2015). Updated meta-analysis of classical fear conditioning in the anxiety disorders. *Depression and Anxiety, 32,* 239–253. http://dx.doi.org/10.1002/da.22353

Duniec, E., & Raz, M. (2011). Vitamins for the soul: John Bowlby's thesis of maternal deprivation, biomedical metaphors and the deficiency model of disease. *History of Psychiatry, 22,* 93–107.

Dunlosky, J., Rawson, K. A., Marsh, E. J., Nathan, M. J., & Willingham, D. T. (2013). Improving students' learning with effective learning techniques: Promising directions from cognitive and educational psychology. *Psychological Science in the Public Interest, 14,* 4–58. http://dx.doi.org/10.1177/1529100612453266

Dunne, F. J., Jaffar, K., & Hashmi, S. (2015). Legal highs—NOT so new and still growing in popularity. *British Journal of Medical Practitioners, 8,* a801.

Dupuis, K., Pichora-Fuller, M. K., Chasteen, A. L., Marchuk, V., Singh, G., & Smith, S. L. (2015). Effects of hearing and vision impairments on the Montreal Cognitive Assessment. *Aging, Neuropsychology, and Cognition, 22,* 413–437. http://dx.doi.org/10.1016/j.neurobiolaging.2015.02.028

Dutton, J. (2014). ADHD parenting advice from Michael Phelps' Mom. *ADDitude.* Retrieved from http://www.additudemag.com/adhd/article/1998.html

Dweck, C. (2007). *Mindset: The new psychology of success.* New York, NY: Ballantine.

Dweck, C. S. (2006). *Mindset: The new psychology of success.* New York: NY: Random House.

Dweck, C. S. (2012). *Mindset: How you can fulfill your potential.* Boston, MA: Little, Brown.

Dweck, C. S. (2012). Mindsets and human nature: Promoting change in the Middle East, the

schoolyard, the racial divide, and willpower. *American Psychologist, 67,* 614–622. http://dx.doi.org/10.1037/a0029783

Dworkin, A. (1974). *Woman hating.* New York, NY: Dutton.

Dye, C. D., & Foley, C. A. (2017). Interpreting the data: Scientific inference. In M. Blume & B. C. Lust (Eds.), *Research methods in language acquisition: Principles, procedures, and practices* (pp. 211–225). Washington, DC: American Psychological Association. http://dx.doi.org/10.1037/15968-012

Eade, S., & Heaton, T. (2016, April 9). Dementia's links to minor trauma found in most contact sports. *Stuff.co.nz.* Retrieved from http://www.stuff.co.nz/sport/78615910/dementias-links-to-minor-trauma-found-in-most-contact-sports

Eagly, A. H. (2015). On comparing men and women. In V. Burr (Ed.), *Gender and psychology (Vol. I). Critical concepts in psychology* (pp. 168–176). New York, NY: Routledge/Taylor & Francis Group.

Earp, B. D. (2015). Do the benefits of male circumcision outweigh the risks? A critique of the proposed CDC guidelines. *Frontiers in Pediatrics, 3,* 18. http://dx.doi.org/10.3389/fped.2015.00018

Eaton, N. R., Keyes, K. M., Krueger, R. F., Balsis, S., Skodol, A. E., Markon, K. E., . . . Hasin, D. S. (2012). An invariant dimensional liability model of gender differences in mental disorder prevalence: Evidence from a national sample. *Journal of Abnormal Psychology, 121,* 282–288.

Ebbinghaus, H. (1885). *Memory: A contribution to experimental psychology.* New York, NY: Dover Publications.

Eddy, K. T., Murray, H. B., & Le Grange, D. (2016). Eating and feeding disorders. In M. K. Dulcan (Ed.), *Dulcan's textbook of child and adolescent psychiatry* (2nd ed., pp. 435–460). Arlington, VA: American Psychiatric Publishing, Inc.

Edel, M.-A., Raaff, V., Dimaggio, G., Buchheim, A., & Brüne, M. (2017). Exploring the effectiveness of combined mentalization-based group therapy and dialectical behaviour therapy for inpatients with borderline personality disorder—A pilot study. *British Journal of Clinical Psychology, 56*(1), 1–15. http://dx.doi.org/10.1111/bjc.12123

Edelson, L. R., Mokdad, C., & Martin, N. (2016). Prompts to eat novel and familiar fruits and vegetables in families with 1-3 year-old children: Relationships with food acceptance and intake. *Appetite, 99,* 138–148. http://dx.doi.org/10.1016/j.appet.2016.01.015

Edwards, K. M., Neal, A. M., & Rodenhizer-Stämpfli, K. A. (2017). Domestic violence prevention. In B. Teasdale & M. S. Bradley (Eds.), *Preventing crime and violence* (pp. 215–227). Cham, CH: Springer International Publishing. http://dx.doi.org/10.1007/978-3-319-44124-5_19

Effects of Marriage. (2017, February 3). Effects of marriage on physical health. *Marripedia.* Retrieved from http://marripedia.org/

Eggermont, J. J. (2015). The auditory cortex and tinnitus—A review of animal and human studies. *European Journal of Neuroscience, 41,* 665–676. http://dx.doi.org/10.1111/ejn.12759

Eguchi, H., Wada, K., & Smith, D. R. (2016). Recognition, compensation, and prevention of Karoshi, or death due to overwork. *Journal of Occupational and Environmental Medicine, 58,* e313–e314. http://dx.doi.org/10.1097/JOM.0000000000000797

Ehrlich, K. B., Miller, G. E., Rohleder, N., & Adam, E. K. (2016). Trajectories of relationship stress and inflammatory processes in adolescence. *Development and Psychopathology, 28,* 127–138. http://dx.doi.org/10.1017/S0954579415000334

Eichenbaum, H. (2013). Memory systems. In R. J. Nelson, S. J. Y. Mizumori, & I. B. Weiner (Eds.), *Handbook of psychology, Vol. 3. Behavioral neuroscience* (2nd ed., pp. 551–573). Hoboken, NJ: Wiley.

Eisner, P., Klasen, M., Wolf, D., Zerres, K., Eggermann, T., Eisert, A., & Mathiak, K. (2017). Cortico-limbic connectivity in MAOA-L carriers is vulnerable to acute tryptophan depletion. *Human Brain Mapping, 38*(3), 1622–1635. http://dx.doi.org/10.1002/hbm.23475

Ekman, P. (1993). Facial expression and emotion. *American Psychologist, 48,* 384–392.

Ekman, P. (2004). *Emotions revealed: Recognizing faces and feelings to improve communication and emotional life.* Thousand Oaks, CA: Owl.

Ekman, P., & Keltner, D. (1997). Universal facial expressions of emotion: An old controversy and new findings. In U. C. Segerstrale & P. Molnar (Eds.), *Nonverbal communication: Where nature meets culture* (pp. 27–46). Mahwah, NJ: Erlbaum.

El-Bar, N., Laufer, O., Yoran-Hegesh, R., & Paz, R. (2017). Over-generalization in youth with anxiety disorders. *Social Neuroscience, 12*(1), 76–85. http://dx.doi.org/10.1080/17470919.2016.1167123

Elder, A. B. (2016). Experiences of older transgender and gender nonconforming adults in psychotherapy: A qualitative study. *Psychology of Sexual Orientation and Gender Diversity, 3,* 180–186. http://dx.doi.org/10.1037/ sgd0000154

Eldred, S. M., & Eligon, J. (2016, May 10). Prince's doctor arrived with test results only him dead. *New York Times.* Retrieved from http://www.nytimes.com/2016/05/11/arts/music/princes-doctor-arrived-with-test-results-only-to-find-him-dead.html

Eley, T. C., McAdams, T. A., Rijsdijk, F. V., Lichtenstein, P., Narustye, J., Reiss, D., . . . Neiderhiser, J. M. (2015). The intergenerational transmission of anxiety: A children-of-twins study. *The American Journal of Psychiatry, 172,* 630–637. http://dx.doi.org/10.1176/appi.ajp.2015.14070818

Eligon, J., Kovaleski, S. F., & Coscarelli, J. (2016, May 4). Prince's addiction and an intervention too late. *New York Times.* Retrieved from http://www.nytimes.com/2016/05/05/arts/music/friends-sought-help-for-princes-addiction-lawyer-says.html?_r=0

Elison, J., & McGonigle, C. (2004). *Liberating losses: When death brings relief.* Boston, MA: Da Capo Press.

Elkind, D. (1967). Egocentrism in adolescence. *Child Development, 38,* 1025–1034.

Elkind, D. (2007). *The hurried child: Growing up too fast too soon* (25th anniversary ed.). Cambridge, MA: Da Capo.

Elliot, A. J., Neista Kayser, D. Greitemeyer, T., Lichtenfeld, S., Gramzow, R. H., Maier, M. A., & Liu, H. (2010). Red, rank, and romance in women viewing men. *Journal of Experimental Psychology: General, 139,* 399–417. http://dx.doi.org/10.1037/a0019689

Elliott, A., & J. Prager (Eds.) (2016). *The Routledge handbook of psychoanalysis in the social*

sciences and humanities. New York, NY: Taylor & Francis.

Ellis, A., & Ellis, D. J. (2011). *Rational emotive behavior therapy.* Washington, DC: American Psychological Association.

Ellis, A., & Ellis, D. J. (2014). Rational emotive behavior therapy. In G. R. VandenBos, E. Meidenbauer, & J. Frank-McNeil (Eds.), *Psychotherapy theories and techniques: A reader* (pp. 289–298). Washington, DC: American Psychological Association. http://dx.doi.org/10.1037/14295-031

Emilien, G., & Durlach, C. (2015). *Memory: Neuropsychological, imaging and psychopharmacological perspectives.* New York, NY: Psychology Press.

Emmons, R. A., & McCullough, M. E. (2003). Counting blessings versus burdens: An experimental investigation of gratitude and subjective well-being in daily life. *Journal of Personality and Social Psychology, 84,* 377–389. http://dx.doi.org/10.1037/0022-3514.84.2.377

Emslie, G. J., Croarkin, P., Chapman, M. R., & Mayes, T. L. (2016). Antidepressants. In M. K. Dulcan (Ed), *Dulcan's textbook of child and adolescent psychiatry* (2nd ed., pp. 737–768). Arlington, VA: American Psychiatric Publishing, Inc.

Endicott, K. L., & Endicott, K. M. (2014). Batek childrearing and morality. In D. Narvaez, K. Valentino, A. Fuentes, J. J. McKenna, & P. Gray (Eds.), *Ancestral landscapes in human evolution: Culture, childrearing and social wellbeing* (pp. 108–125). New York, NY: Oxford University Press.

English, T., & Carstensen, L. L. (2014). Selective narrowing of social networks across adulthood is associated with improved emotional experience in daily life. *International Journal of Behavioral Development, 38,* 195–202. http://dx.doi.org/10.1177/0165025413515404

Enright, R. D., & Fitzgibbons, R. P. (2015). *Forgiveness therapy: An empirical guide for resolving anger and restoring hope.* Washington, DC: American Psychological Association. http://dx.doi.org/10.1037/14526-000

Epley, N., & Schroeder, J. (2014). Mistakenly seeking solitude. *Journal of Experimental Psychology: General, 143,* 1980–1999. http://dx.doi.org/10.1037/a0037323

Erekson, D. M., & Lambert, M. J. (2015). Client-centered therapy. *The Encyclopedia of Clinical Psychology, 1–5.* http://dx.doi.org/10.1002/9781118625392.wbecp073

Erikson, E. (1950). *Childhood and society.* New York, NY: Norton.

Erlings, E. I. J. (2016). The law and practices of ritual male circumcision: Time for review. In S. Deb (Ed.), *Child safety, welfare and well-being: Issues and challenges* (pp. 95–113). New York, NY: Springer Science + Business Media. http://dx.doi.org/10.1007/978-81-322-2425-9_8

Erviti, M., Semal, C., Wright, B. A., Amestoy, A., Bouvard, M. P., & Demany, L. (2015). A late emerging auditory deficit in autism. *Neuropsychology, 29,* 454–462. http://dx.doi.org/10.1037/neu0000162

Esch, T. (2014). The neurobiology of meditation and mindfulness. In S. Schmidt & H. Walach (Eds.), *Meditation—neuroscientific approaches and philosophical implications* (pp. 153–173). New York, NY: Springer. http://dx.doi.org/10.1007/978-3-319-01634-4_9

Eskreis-Winkler, L., Shulman, E. P., Young, V., Tsukayama, E., Brunwasser, S. M., & Duck-

worth, A. L. (2016). Using wise interventions to motivate deliberate practice. *Journal of Personality and Social Psychology, 111,* 728–744. http://dx.doi.org/10.1037/pspp0000074

Espinosa-Hernández, G., Vasilenko, S. A., & Bámaca-Colbert, M. Y. (2016). Sexual behaviors in Mexico: The role of values and gender across adolescence. *Journal of Research on Adolescence, 26,* 603–609. http://dx.doi.org/10.1111/jora.12209

Esposito, G., Manian, N., Truzzi, A., & Bornstein, M. H. (2017). Response to infant cry in clinically depressed and non-depressed mothers. *PLoS ONE, 12*(1): e0169066. http://dx.doi.org/10.1371/journal.pone.0169066

Ethical Principles of Psychologists and Code of Conduct. (2016). In A.E. Kazdin (Ed.), *Methodological issues and strategies in clinical research* (4th ed., 495–512). Washington, DC: American Psychological Association. http://dx.doi.org/10.1037/14805-030

Evans, E. H., Adamson, A. J., Basterfield, L., Le Couteur, A., Reilly, J. K., Reilly, J. J., & Parkinson, K. N. (2017). Risk factors for eating disorder symptoms at 12 years of age: A 6-year longitudinal cohort study. *Appetite, 108,* 12–20. http://doi.org/10.1016/j.appet.2016.09.005

Everett, C., & Everett, S. V. (1994). *Healthy divorce.* San Francisco, CA: Jossey-Bass.

Eyo, U. B., Murugan, M., & Wu, L. J. (2017). Microglia–neuron communication in epilepsy. *Glia, 65*(1), 5–18. http://dx.doi.org/10.1002/glia.23006

Eysenck, H. J. (1967). *The biological basis of personality.* Springfield, IL: Thomas.

Eysenck, H. J. (1990). Biological dimensions of personality. In L. A. Pervin (Ed.), *Handbook of personality: Theory and research* (pp. 244–276). New York: NY: Guilford.

Faddiman, A. (1997). *The spirit catches you and you fall down.* New York, NY: Straus & Giroux.

Fadel, L., & Garcia-Navarro, L. (2013). How different cultures handle personal space. *NPR.* Retrieved from http://www.npr.org/sections/codeswitch/2013/05/05/181126380/how-different-cultures-handle-personal-space

Fagelson, M., & Baguley, D. M. (2016). Influences of amplified music. In D. M. Baguley & M. Fagelson (Eds.), *Tinnitus: Clinical and research perspectives* (pp. 129–143). San Diego, CA: Plural Publishing.

Fahnehjelm, K. T., Törnquist, A. L., Olsson, M., Bäckström, I., Grönlund, M. A., & Winiarski, J. (2016). Cataract after allogeneic hematopoietic stem cell transplantation in childhood. *Acta Paediatrica, 105,* 82–89. http://dx.doi.org/10.1111/apa.13173

Fairbairn, C. E., & Bresin, K. (2017). The effects of contextual familiarity on alcohol expectancies. *Experimental and Clinical Psychopharmacology, 25,* 13–23. http://dx.doi.org/10.1037/pha0000103

Fales, M. R., Frederick, D. A., Garcia, J. R., Gildersleeve, K. A., Haselton, M. G., & Fisher, H. E. (2016). Mating markets and bargaining hands: Mate preferences for attractiveness and resources in two national U.S. studies. *Personality and Individual Differences, 88,* 78–87. http://dx.doi.org/10.1016/j.paid.2015.08.041

Famous People. (n.d.). Ellen DeGeneres biography. *The Famous People.* Retrieved February 13, 2017 from http://www.thefamouspeople.com/profiles/ellen-degeneres-1329.php#YpmPWDOVpYrJIOAP.99

Fan, H., Li, T.-F., Gong, N., & Wang, Y.-X. (2016). Shanzhiside methylester, the principle effective iridoid glycoside from the analgesic herb Lamiophlomis rotata, reduces neuropathic pain by stimulating spinal microglial β-endorphin expression. *Neuropharmacology, 101,* 98–109. http://dx.doi.org/10.1016/j.neuropharm.2015.09.010

**Fan, S. P., Liberman, Z., Keysar, B., & Kinzler, K. D.** (2015). Early exposure to multilingual environment promotes effective communication. *Psychological Science, 26,* 1090–1097.http://dx.doi.org/10.1177/0956797615574699

**Fang, J., Prybutok, V., & Wen, C.** (2016). Shirking behavior and socially desirable responding in online surveys: A cross-cultural study comparing Chinese and American samples. *Computers in Human Behavior, 54,* 310–317. http://dx.doi.org/10.1016/j.chb.2015.08.019

**Fang, Z., Sergeeva, V., Ray, L. B., Viczko, J., Owen, A. M., & Fogel, S. M.** (2017). Sleep spindles and intellectual ability: Epiphenomenon or directly related? *Journal of Cognitive Neuroscience, 29(1),* 162–182. http://dx.doi.org/10.1162/jocn_a_01034

**Farah, M. J., Hutchinson, J. B., Phelps, E. A., & Wagner, A. D.** (2014). Functional MRI-based lie detection: Scientific and societal challenges. *Nature Reviews Neuroscience, 15,* 123–131. http://dx.doi.org/10.1038/nrn3665

**Fast, L. C., Harman, J. J., Maertens, J. A., Burnette, J. L., & Dreith, F.** (2015). Creating a measure of portion control self-efficacy. *Eating Behaviors, 16,* 23–30. http://dx.doi.org/10.1016/j.eatbeh.2014.10.009

**Feeney, J. R., Pliner, P., Polivy, J., & Herman, C. P.** (2017). The persistence of and resistance to social norms regarding the appropriate amount to eat: A preliminary investigation. *Appetite, 109,* 93–99. http://dx.doi.org/10.1016/j.appet.2016.11.031

**Fehr, B.** (2015). Love: Conceptualization and experience. In M. Mikulincer, P. R. Shaver, J. A. Simpson, & J. F. Dovidio (Eds.), *APA handbook of personality and social psychology, Vol. 3. Interpersonal relations* (pp. 495–522). Washington, DC: American Psychological Association. http://dx.doi.org/10.1037/14344-018

**Feinle-Bisset, C.** (2016). Upper gastrointestinal sensitivity to meal-related signals in adult humans—relevance to appetite regulation and gut symptoms in health, obesity and functional dyspepsia. *Physiology & Behavior, 162,* 69–82. http://dx.doi.org/10.1016/j.physbeh.2016.03.021

**Fein, S., & Spencer, S. J.** (1997). Prejudice as self-image maintenance: Affirming the self through derogating others. *Journal of Personality and Social Psychology, 73,* 31–44.

**Feldman, S.** (2014). *Development across a lifetime* (7th ed.). Essex, UK: Pearson.

**Felleman, B. I., Stewart, D. G., Simpson, T. L., Heppner, P. S., & Kearney, D. J.** (2016). Predictors of depression and PTSD treatment response among veterans participating in mindfulness-based stress reduction. *Mindfulness, 7(4),* 886–895. http://dx.doi.org/10.1007/s12671-016-0527-7

**Felson, J.** (2014). What can we learn from twin studies? A comprehensive evaluation of the equal environments assumption. *Social Science Research, 43,* 184–199. http://dx.doi.org/10.1016/j.ssresearch.2013.10.004

**Ferguson, C. J.** (2010). Violent crime research: An introduction. In C. J. Ferguson (Ed.), *Violent crime: Clinical and social impli-*
cations (pp. 3–18). Thousand Oaks, CA: Sage.

**Ferguson, C. J.** (2015). Does movie or video game violence predict societal violence? It depends on what you look at and when—Revised. *Journal of Communication, 65,* 193–212. http://dx.doi.org/10.1111/ jcom.12142

**Ferguson, K. T., & Casasola, M.** (2015). Are you an animal too? US and Malawian infants' categorization of plastic and wooden animal replicas. *Infancy, 20,* 189–207. http://dx.doi.org/10.1111/infa.12069

**Ferrari, P. F., Rozzi, S., & Fogassi, L.** (2005). Mirror neurons responding to observation of actions made with tools in monkey ventral pre-motor cortex. *Journal of Cognitive Neuroscience, 17,* 212–226. http://dx.doi.org/10.1162/0898929053124910

**Ferraro, A. J., Malespin, T., Oehme, K., Bruker, M., & Opel, A.** (2016). Advancing co-parenting education: Toward a foundation for supporting positive post-divorce adjustment. *Child & Adolescent Social Work Journal, 33,* 407–415. http://dx.doi.org/10.1007/s10560-016-0440-x

**Ferrie, A.** (2015, April 4). Source amnesia and advertising. *The Consumer Psychologist.* Retrieved from http://www.theconsumerpsychologist.com/2015/04/04/sourceamnesia-and-advertising/

**Festinger, L.** (1957). *A theory of cognitive dissonance.* Stanford, CA: Stanford University Press.

**Festinger, L. A., & Carlsmith, J. M.** (1959). Cognitive consequences of forced compliance. *Journal of Abnormal and Social Psychology, 58,* 203–210.

**Fielder, R. L., Carey, K. B., & Carey, M. P.** (2013). Are hookups replacing romantic relationships? A longitudinal study of first-year f emale college students. *The Journal of Adolescent Health, 52,* 657–659. http://dx.doi.org/10.1016/j.jadohealth.2012.09.001

**Field, K. M., Woodson, R., Greenberg, R., & Cohen, D.** (1982). Discrimination and imitation of facial expressions by neonates. *Science, 218,* 179–181. http://dx.doi.org/10.1016/S0163-6383(83)90316-8

**Fields, A., & Cochran, S.** (2011). Men and depression: Current perspectives for health care professionals. *American Journal of Lifestyle Medicine, 5,* 92–100.

**Fields, J. A.** (2015). Effects of deep brain stimulation in movement disorders on cognition and behavior. In A. I. Tröster (Ed.), *Clinical neuropsychology and cognitive neurology of Parkinson's disease and other movement disorders* (pp. 332–375). New York, NY: Oxford University Press.

**Fildes, A., van Jaarsveld, C. H., Llewellyn, C. H., Fisher, A., Cooke, L., & Wardle, J.** (2014). Nature and nurture in children's food preferences. *The American Journal of Clinical Nutrition, 99,* 911–917. http://dx.doi.org/10.3945/ajcn.113.077867

**Finegersh, A., Rompala, G. R., Martin, D. I. K., & Homanics, G. E.** (2015). Drinking beyond a lifetime: New and emerging insights into paternal alcohol exposure on subsequent generations. *Alcohol, 49,* 461–470. http://dx.doi.org/10.1016/j.alcohol.2015.02.008

**Finkel, E. J., Norton, M. I., Reis, H. T., Ariely, D., Caprariello, P. A., Eastwick, P. W., . . . Maniaci, M. R.** (2015). When does familiarity promote versus undermine interpersonal attraction? A proposed integrative model from erstwhile adversaries. *Perspectives on Psycho-*
logical Science, 10, 3–19. http://dx.doi.org/10.1177/1745691614561682

**Finkelhor, D.** (2012). *Characteristics of crimes against juveniles.* Durham, NH: Crimes against Children Research Center.

**Finkenauer, C., Buyukcan-Tetik, A., Baumeister, R. F., Schoemaker, K., Bartels, M., & Vohs, K. D.** (2015). Out of control: Identifying the role of self-control strength in family violence. *Current Directions in Psychological Science, 24,* 261–266. http://dx.doi.org/10.1177/0963721415570730

**Finley, E. P., Bollinger, M., Noël, P. H., Amuan, M. E., Copeland, L. A., Pugh, J., . . . Pugh, M. J. V.** (2015). A national cohort study of the association between the Polytrauma Clinical Triad and suicide-related behavior among US veterans who served in Iraq and Afghanistan. *American Journal of Public Health, 105,* 380–387. http://dx.doi.org/10.2105/AJPH.2014.301957

**Finzi, E., & Rosenthal, N. E.** (2014). Treatment of depression with on abotulinumtoxin A: A randomized, double-blind, placebo controlled trial. *Journal of Psychiatric Research, 52,* 1–6. http://dx.doi.org/10.1016/j.jpsychires.2013.11.006

**Firmin, M. W., Pugh, K. C., Sohn, V. A., Voss, A., & Chuang, Y. R.** (2016). Potential implications of legalized marijuana. *Psychology and Education: An Interdisciplinary Journal, 53*(3–4), 23–35.

**Fisher, M. A.** (2016). *Confidentiality limits in psychotherapy: Ethics checklists for mental health professionals.* Washington, DC: American Psychological Association.

**Fisher, T. D.** (2013). Gender roles and pressure to be truthful: The bogus pipeline modifies gender differences in sexual but not nonsexual behavior. *Sex Roles, 68,* 401–414. http://dx.doi.org/10.1007/s11199-013-0266-3

**Fishman, I., & Ng, R.** (2013). Error-related brain activity in extraverts: Evidence for altered response monitoring in social context. *Biological Psychology, 93,* 225–230. http://dx.doi.org/10.1016/j.biopsycho.2013.02.010

**Flamez, B. N., Ordway, A. M., Vela, J. C., & Hicks, J. F.** (2016). Generativity, death, dying, and bereavement. In D. Capuzzi & M. D. Stauffer (Eds.), *Human growth and development across the lifespan: Applications for counselors* (pp. 575–608). Hoboken, NJ: Wiley.

**Flannery, J. E., Beauchamp, K. G., & Fisher, P. A.** (2017). The role of social buffering on chronic disruptions in quality of care: Evidence from caregiver-based interventions in foster children. *Social Neuroscience, 12*(1), 86–91. http://dx.doi.org/10.1080/17470919.2016.1170725

**Fleet, T., Stashi, E., Zhu, B., Rajapakshe, K., Marcelo, K. L., Kettner, N. M., . . . York, B.** (2016). Genetic and environmental models of circadian disruption link SRC-2 function to hepatic pathology. *Journal of Biological Rhythms, 31*(5), 443–460. http://dx.doi.org/10.1177/0748730416657921

**Flegal, K. M., Kruszon-Moran, D., Carroll, M. D., Fryar, C. D., & Ogden, C. L.** (2016). Trends in obesity among adults in the United States, 2005 to 2014. *Journal of the American Medical Association, 315,* 2284–2291. http://dx.doi.org/10.1001/jama.2016.6458

**Fletcher, B. R., & Rapp, P. R.** (2013). Normal neurocognitive aging. In R. J. Nelson, S. J. Y. Mizumori, & I. B. Weiner (Eds.), *Handbook of psychology, Vol. 3. Behavioral neuroscience* (2nd ed., pp. 643–663). Hoboken, NJ: Wiley.

Fletcher, G. J. O., & Simpson, J. A. (2000). Ideal standards in close relationships: Their structure and functions. *Current Directions in Psychological Science, 9,* 102–105.

Flett, G. L., Goldstein, A. L., Pechenkov, I. G., Nepon, T., & Wekerle, C. (2016). Antecedents, correlates, and consequences of feeling like you don't matter: Associations with maltreatment, loneliness, social anxiety, and the five-factor model. *Personality and Individual Differences, 92,* 52–56. http://dx.doi.org/10.1016/j.paid.2015.12.014

Fligelman, B., Pham, T., Bryson, E. O., Majeske, M., & Kellner, C. H. (2016). Resolution of acute suicidality after a single right unilateral electroconvulsive therapy. *The Journal of ECT, 32,* 71–72. http://dx.doi.org/10.1097/YCT.0000000000000258

Flora, J., & Segrin, C. (2015). Family conflict and communication. In L. Turner & R. West (Eds.), *The SAGE handbook of family communication* (pp. 91–106). Thousand Oaks, CA: Sage Publishing.

Flores, A. R., Herman, J. L., Gates, G. J., & Brown, T. N. T. (2016). How many adults identify as transgender in the United States? *The Williams Institute.* Retrieved from http://williamsinstitute.law.ucla.edu/wp-content/uploads/How-Many-Adults-Identify-as-Transgender-in-the-United-States.pdf

Flores, G., Flores-Gómez, G. D., & de Jesús Gomez-Villalobos, M. (2016). Neuronal changes after chronic high blood pressure in animal models and its implication for vascular dementia. *Synapse, 70,* 198–205. http://dx.doi.org/10.1002/syn.21887

Flynn, J. R. (1987). Massive IQ gains in 14 nations: What IQ tests really measure. *Psychological Bulletin, 101,* 171–191. http://dx.doi.org/10.1037/0033-2909.101.2.171

Flynn, J. R. (2010). Problems with IQ gains: The huge vocabulary gap. *Journal of Psychoeducational Assessment, 28,* 412–433. http://dx.doi.org/10.1177/0734282910373342

Flynn, J., te Nijenhuis, J., & Metzen, D. (2014). The g beyond Spearman's g: Flynn's paradoxes resolved using four exploratory meta-analyses. *Intelligence, 44,* 1–10. http://dx.doi.org/10.1016/j.intell.2014.01.009

Foell, J., Bekrater-Bodmann, R., Diers, M., & Flor, H. (2014). Mirror therapy for phantom limb pain: Brain changes and the role of body representation. *European Journal of Pain, 18,* 729–739. http://dx.doi.org/10.1002/j.1532-2149.2013.00433.x

Foerde, K., & Shohamy, D. (2011). The role of the basal ganglia in learning and memory: Insight from Parkinson's disease. *Neurobiology of Learning and Memory, 96,* 624–636. http://dx.doi.org/10.1016/j.nlm.2011.08.006.

Foerde, K., Steinglass, J., Shohamy, D., & Walsh, B. T. (2015). Neural mechanisms supporting maladaptive food choices in anorexia nervosa. *Nature Neuroscience, 18,* 1571–1573. http://dx.doi.org/10.1038/nn.4136

Folkvord, F., Anschütz, D. J., & Buijzen, M. (2016). The association between BMI development among young children and (un)healthy food choices in response to food advertisements: A longitudinal study. *The International Journal of Behavioral Nutrition and Physical Activity, 13,* Article 16. http://dx.doi.org/10.1186/s12966-016-0340-7

Ford, R. (2013). Oscars: Ellen DeGeneres' hosting history. *The Hollywood Reporter.* Retrieved from http://www.hollywoodreporter.com/news/oscars-ellen-degeneres-hosting-history-598767

Ford, T. E. (2015). The social consequences of disparagement humor: Introduction and over-view. *Humor, 28,* 163–169. http://dx.doi.org/10.1515/humor-2015-0016

Forgas, J. P., & Eich, E. (2013). Affective influences on cognition: Mood congruence, mood dependence, and mood effects on processing strategies. In A. F. Healy, R. W. Proctor, & I. B. Weiner (Eds.), *Handbook of psychology, Vol. 4. Experimental psychology* (2nd ed., pp. 61–82). Hoboken, NJ: Wiley.

Forgasz, H., Leder, G., Mittelberg, D., Tan, H., & Murimo, A. (2015). Affect and gender. In B. Pepin & B. Roesken-Winter (Eds.), *Advances in mathematics education. From beliefs to dynamic affect systems in mathematics education: Exploring a mosaic of relationships and interactions* (pp. 245–268). New York, NY: Springer. http://dx.doi.org/10.1007/978-3-319-06808-4_12

Forkmann, T., Brakemeir, E.-L., Teismann, T., Schramm, E., & Michalak, J. (2016). The effects of mindfulness-based cognitive therapy and cognitive behavioral analysis system of psychotherapy added to treatment as usual on suicidal ideation in chronic depression: Results of a randomized-clinical trial. *Journal of Affective Disorders, 200,* 51–57. http://dx.doi.org/10.1016/j.jad.2016.01.047

Forster, M., Gower, A. L., Borowsky, I. W., & McMorris, B. J. (2017). Associations between adverse childhood experiences, student-teacher relationships, and non-medical use of prescription medications among adolescents. *Addictive Behaviors, 68,* 30–34. http://dx.doi.org/10.1016/j.addbeh.2017.01.004

Fortuna, L. R., & Vallejo, Z. (2015). *Treating co-occurring adolescent PTSD and addiction: Mindfulness-based cognitive therapy for adolescents with trauma and substance-abuse disorders.* Oakland, CA: Context Press/New Harbinger Publications.

Foulkes, D. (1993). Children's dreaming. In D. Foulkes & C. Cavallero (Eds.), *Dreaming as cognition* (pp. 114–132). New York, NY: Harvester Wheatsheaf.

Foulkes, D. (1999). *Children's dreaming and the development of consciousness.* Cambridge, MA: Harvard University Press.

Fowler, S. P. G. (2016). Low-calorie sweetener use and energy balance: Results from experimental studies in animals, and large-scale prospective studies in humans. *Physiology & Behavior, 164(Part B),* 517–523. http://dx.doi.org/10.1016/j.physbeh.2016.04.047

Fox, N. A., Bakermans-Kranenburg, M. J., Yoo, K. H., Bowman, L. C., Cannon, E. N., Vanderwert, R. E., . . . van IJzendoorn, M. H. (2016). Assessing human mirror activity with EEG mu rhythm: A meta-analysis. *Psychological Bulletin, 142,* 291–313. http://dx.doi.org/10.1037/bul0000031

Fraley, R. C., & Roisman, G. I. (2015). Early attachment experiences and romantic functioning: Developmental pathways, emerging issues, and future directions. In J. A. Simpson & W. S. Rholes (Eds.), *Attachment theory and research: New directions and emerging themes* (pp. 9–38). New York, NY: Guilford.

Fraley, R. C., & Shaver, P. R. (1997). Adult attachment and the suppression of unwanted thoughts. *Journal of Personality and Social Psychology, 73,* 1080–1091.

Francis, G. (2012). Too good to be true: Publication bias in two prominent studies from experimental psychology. *Psychonomic Bulletin & Review, 19,* 151–156. http://dx.doi.org/10.3758/s13423-012-0227-9

François, M., Barde, S., Achamrah, N., Breton, J., do Rego, J. -C., Coëffier, M., . . . Fetissov, S. O. (2015). The number of pre-proghrelin mRNA expressing cells is increased in mice with activity-based anorexia. *Neuropeptides, 51,* 17–23. http://dx.doi.org/10.1016/j.npep.2015.04.003

Franconeri, S. L., Alvarez, G. A., & Cavanagh, P. (2013). Flexible cognitive resources: Competitive content maps for attention and memory. *Trends in Cognitive Sciences, 17,* 134–141. http://dx.doi.org/10.1016/j.tics.2013.01.010

Frangicetto, T. (2015, May 22). American Sniper and the warrior cult. *Buck County Courier Times,* p. A9. Retrieved from http://www.buckscountycouriertimes.com/opinion/op-ed/american-sniper-and-the-warrior-cult/article_c9ec7de8-5f18-59dd-9300-c8f78603052f.html

Franz, J., & LaForge, S. (2016). The use of music-thanatology with palliative and end-of-life populations in healthcare settings. In P. D. Lambert (Ed.), *Managing arts programs in healthcare* (pp. 202–212). New York, NY: Routledge/Taylor & Francis Group.

Frattaroli, S., & Buggs, S. A. L. (2016). Decreasing gun violence: Social and public health interventions. In L. H. Gold & R. I. Simon (Eds.), *Gun violence and mental illness* (pp. 381–406). Arlington, VA: American Psychiatric Association.

Frau, R., Abbiati, F., Bini, V., Casti, A., Caruso, D., Devoto, P., & Bortolato, M. (2015). Targeting neurosteroid synthesis as a therapy for schizophrenia-related alterations induced by early psychosocial stress. *Schizophrenia Research, 168,* 640-658. http://dx.doi.org/10.1016/j.schres.2015.04.044

Frazer, A. L., Rubens, S., Johnson-Motoyama, M., DiPierro, M., & Fite, P. J. (2017). Acculturation dissonance, acculturation strategy, depressive symptoms, and delinquency in Latina/o adolescents. *Child & Youth Care Forum, 46(1),* 19–33. http://dx.doi.org/10.1007/s10566-016-9367-9

Freberg, L. A. (2016). *Neuroscience: An introduction to biological psychology* (3rd ed.). Boston, MA: Cengage Learning.

Frech, A., Lynch, J. L., & Barr, P. (2016). Health consequences of same and opposite-sex unions: Partnership, parenthood, and cardiovascular risk among young adults. *Journal of Behavioral Medicine, 39,* 13–27. http://dx.doi.org/10.1007/s10865-015-9673-y

Freedheim, D. K., & Weiner, I. B. (Eds.) (2013). *Handbook of psychology, Volume 1, History of psychology, 2nd Edition.* Hoboken, NJ: Wiley.

Freidin, E., Carballo, F., & Bentosela, M. (2017). Direct reciprocity in animals: The roles of bonding and affective processes. *International Journal of Psychology, 52(2),* 163–170. http://dx.doi.org/10.1002/ijop.12215

French, A. S., Sellier, M.-J., Moutaz, A. A., Guigue, A., Chabaud, M.-A., Reeb, P. D., . . . Marion-Poll, F. (2015). Dual mechanism for bitter avoidance in Drosophila. *The Journal of Neuroscience, 35,* 3990–4004. http://dx.doi.org/10.1523/JNEUROSCI.1312-14.2015

Frenda, S. J., Patihis, L., Loftus, E. F., Lewis, H. C., & Fenn, K. M. (2014). Sleep deprivation and false memories. *Psychological Science, 25,* 1674–1681. http://dx.doi.org/10.1177/0956797614534694.

Freund, A. M., & Ritter, J. O. (2009). Midlife crisis: A debate. *Gerontology, 55,* 582–591.

Friedman, E. M., Ruini, C., Foy, R., Jaros, L., Sampson, H., & Ryff, C. D. (2017). Lighten UP! A community-based group intervention to promote psychological well-being in older adults. *Aging & Mental Health, 21*(2), 199–205. http://dx.doi.org/10.1080/13607863.2015.1093605

Friedman, M. J. (2015). The human stress response. In N. C. Bernardy & M. J. Friedman (Eds.), *A practical guide to PTSD treatment: Pharmacological and psychotherapeutic approaches* (pp. 9–19). Washington, DC: American Psychological Association. http://dx.doi.org/10.1037/14522-002

Friesdorf, R., Conway, P., & Gawronski, B. (2015). Gender differences in responses to moral dilemmas: A process dissociation analysis. *Personality and Social Psychology Bulletin, 41,* 696–713. http://dx.doi.org/10.1177/0146167215575731

Friesen, M. D., Horwood, L. J., Fergusson, D. M., & Woodward, L. J. (2017). Exposure to parental separation in childhood and later parenting quality as an adult: Evidence from a 30-year longitudinal study. *Journal of Child Psychology and Psychiatry, 58,* 30–37. http://dx.doi.org/10.1111/jcpp.12610

Frisch, M., Aigrain, Y., Barauskas, V., Bjarnason, R., Boddy, S.-A., Czauderna, P., . . . Wijnen, R. (2013). Cultural bias in the AAP's 2012 technical report and policy statement on male circumcision. *Pediatrics.* Retrieved from http://pediatrics.aappublications.org/content/early/2013/03/12/peds.2012-2896.http://dx.doi.org/10.1542/peds.2012-2986

Frith, U. (2016, December 30). Theory of mind. *Serious Science.* Retrieved from http://serious-science.org/theory-of-mind-7939

Frodl, T., Janowitz, D., Schmaal, L., Tozzi, L., Dobrowolny, H., Stein, D. J., . . . Grabe, H. J. (2017). Childhood adversity impacts on brain subcortical structures relevant to depression. *Journal of Psychiatric Research, 86,* 58–65. http://dx.doi.org/10.1016/j.jpsychires.2016.11.010

Fu, C. Y., Moyle, W., & Cooke, M. (2013). A randomised controlled trial of the use of aromatherapy and hand massage to reduce disruptive behaviour in people with dementia. *BMC Complementary and Alternative Medicine, 13,* Article 165. http://dx.doi.org/10.1155/2013/790792

Fuhrmann, D., Knoll, L. J., & Blakemore, S.-J. (2015). Adolescence as a sensitive period of brain development. *Trends in Cognitive Sciences, 19,*558–566.http://dx.doi.org/10.1016/j.tics.2015.07.008

Furguson, E., Chamorro-Premuzic, T., Pickering, A., & Weiss, A. (2011). Five into one does go: A critique of the general factor of personality. In T. Chamorro-Premuzic, S. von Stumm, & A. Furnam (Eds.), *Wiley-Blackwell handbook of individual differences* (pp. 162–186). Chichester, UK: Wiley-Blackwell.

Furman, E. (1990, November). Plant a potato, learn about life (and death). *Young Children, 46*(1), 15–20.

Furuya, Y., Matsumoto, J., Hori, E., Boas, C. V., Tran, A. H., Shimada, Y., . . . Nishijo, H. (2014). Place-related neuronal activity in the monkey parahippocampal gyrus and hippocampal formation during virtual navigation. *Hippocampus, 24,* 113–130. http://dx.doi.org/10.1002/hipo.22209

Fyhri, A., & Phillips, R. O. (2013). Emotional reactions to cycle helmet use. *Accident Analysis and Prevention, 50,* 59–63. http://dx.doi.org/10.1016/j.aap.2012.03.027.

Gaertner, S. L., & Dovidio, J. F. (2014). *Reducing intergroup bias: The common ingroup identity model.* New York, NY: Routledge.

Gage, S. H., Hickman, M., & Zammit, S. (2016). Association between cannabis and psychosis: epidemiologic evidence. *Biological Psychiatry, 79*(7), 549–556. http://dx.doi.org/10.1016/j.biopsych.2015.08.001.

Gagnepain, P., Henson, R. N., & Anderson, M. C. (2014). Suppressing unwanted memories reduces their unconscious influence via targeted cortical inhibition. *Proceedings of the National Academy of Sciences of the United States of America, 111,* E1310–E1319. http://dx.doi.org/10.1073/pnas.1311468111

Gagnon, J. H. (1990). The explicit and implicit use of the scripting perspective in sex research. *Annual Review of Sex Research, 1,* 1–43.

Gaither, J. R., Leventhal, J. M., Ryan, S. A., & Camenga, D. R. (2016). National trends in hospitalizations for opioid poisonings among children and adolescents, 1997 to 2012. *JAMA Pediatrics, 170*(12), 1195. http://dx.doi.org/10.1001/jamapediatrics.2016.2154

Galinha, I. C., Garcia-Martín, M. A., Gomes, C., & Oishi, S. (2016). Criteria for happiness among people living in extreme poverty in Maputo, Mozambique. *International Perspectives in Psychology: Research, Practice, Consultation, 5,* 67–90. http://dx.doi.org/10.1037/ipp0000053

Galinha, I. C., Oishi, S., Pereira, C. R., Wirtz, D., & Esteves, F. (2014). Adult attachment, love styles, relationship experiences and subjective well-being: Cross-cultural and gender comparison between Americans, Portuguese, and Mozambicans. *Social Indicators Research, 119,* 823–852. http://dx.doi.org/10.1007/s11205-013-0512-7

Gallagher, B. J. III, & Jones, B. J. (2016). Neglect and hereditary risk: Their relative contribution to schizophrenia with negative symptomatology. *International Journal of Social Psychiatry,62,*235–242.http://dx.doi.org/10.1177/0020764015623974

Gallart-Palau, X., Lee, B. S., Adav, S. S., Qian, J., Serra, A., Park, J. E., . . . Sze, S. K. (2016). Gender differences in white matter pathology and mitochondrial dysfunction in Alzheimer's disease with cerebrovascular disease. *Molecular Brain, 9*(1), 27.

Gamble, T., & Walker, I. (2016). Wearing a bicycle helmet can increase risk taking and sensation seeking in adults. *Psychological Science, 27,* 289–294. http://dx.doi.org/10.1177/0956797615620784

Gana, K., Broc, G., Saada, Y., Amieva, H., & Quintard, B. (2016). Subjective wellbeing and longevity: Findings from a 22-year cohort study. *Journal of Psychosomatic Research, 85,* 28–34. http://dx.doi.org/10.1016/j.jpsychores.2016.04.004

Gander, F., Proyer, R. T., & Ruch, W. (2017). The subjective assessment of accomplishment and positive relationships: Initial validation and correlative and experimental evidence for their association with well-being. *Journal of Happiness Studies, 18*(3), 743–764. http://dx.doi.org/10.1007/s10902-016-9751-z

Gangloff, K. A., Connelly, B. L., & Shook, C. L. (2016). Of scapegoats and signals: Investor reactions to CEO succession in the aftermath of wrongdoing. *Journal of Management, 42*(6), 1614–1634. http://dx.doi.org/10.1177/0149206313515521

Gangwisch, J. E., Hale, L., Garcia, L., Malaspina, D., Opler, M. G., Payne, M. E., . . . Lane, D. (2015). High glycemic index diet as a risk factor for depression: Analyses from the Women's Health Initiative. *American Journal of Clinical Nutrition, 102,* 454–463. http://dx.doi.org/10.3945/ajcn.114.103846

Ganimian, A. J., & Murnane, R. J. (2016). Improving education in developing countries: Lessons from rigorous impact evaluations. *Review of Educational Research, 86,* 719–755. http://dx.doi.org/10.3102/0034654315627499

Ganzer, F., Bröning, S., Kraft, S., Sack, P.-M., & Thomasius, R. (2016). Weighing the evidence: A systematic review on long-term neurocognitive effects of cannabis use in abstinent adolescents and adults. *Neuropsychology Review, 26*(2), 186–222. http://dx.doi.org/10.1007/s11065-016-9316-2

Gao, Y., Bai, C., Zheng, D., Li, C., Zhang, W., Li, M., . . . Ma, Y. (2016). Combination of melatonin and Wnt-4 promotes neural cell differentiation in bovine amniotic epithelial cells and recovery from spinal cord injury. *Journal of Pineal Research: Molecular, Biological, Physiological and Clinical Aspects of Melatonin, 60,* 303–312. http://dx.doi.org/10.1111/jpi.12311

Gao, Z., Gao, Q., Tang, N., Shui, R., & Shen, M. (2016). Organization principles in visual working memory: Evidence from sequential stimulus display. *Cognition, 146,* 277–288. http://dx.doi.org/10.1016/j.cognition.2015.10.005

Garcia, J., & Koelling, R. A. (1966). Relation of cue to consequence in avoidance learning. *Psychonomic Science, 4,* 123–124. http://dx.doi.org/10.3758/BF03342209

Gardner, B., Phillips, L. A., & Judah, G. (2016). Habitual instigation and habitual execution: Definition, measurement, and effects on behaviour frequency. *British Journal of Health Psychology, 21,* 613–630. http://dx.doi.org/10.1111/bjhp.12189

Gardner, H. (1983). *Frames of mind.* New York, NY: Basic.

Gardner, H. (2008). Who owns intelligence? *The Jossey-Bass reader on the brain and learning* (pp. 120–132). San Francisco, CA: Jossey-Bass.

Gardner, R. A., & Gardner, B. T. (1969). Teaching sign language to a chimpanzee. *Science, 165,* 664–672.

Gardstrom, S., & Sorel, S. (2015). Music therapy methods. In B. Wheeler (Ed.), *Music therapy handbook* (p. 116–128). New York, NY: Guilford.

Garg, R., Levin, E., & Tremblay, L. (2016). Emotional intelligence: Impact on postsecondary academic achievement. *Social Psychology of Education, 19*(3), 627–642. http://dx.doi.org/10.1007/s11218-016-9338-x

Garland, T. S., Branch, K. A., & Grimes, M. (2016). Blurring the lines: Reinforcing rape myths in comic books. *Feminist Criminology, 11,* 48–68. http://dx.doi.org/10.1177/1557085115576386

Garnier, Y. M., Lepers, R., Stapley, P. J., Papaxanthis, C., & Paizis, C. (2017). Changes in cortico-spinal excitability following uphill versus downhill treadmill exercise. *Behavioural Brain Research, 317,* 242–250. http://dx.doi.org/10.1016/j.bbr.2016.09.051

**Garrett, B.** (2015). *Brain and behavior: An introduction to biological psychology* (4th ed.). Thousand Oaks, CA: Sage.

**Garrett, N., Lazzaro, S. C., Ariely, D., & Sharot, T.** (2016). The brain adapts to dishonesty. *Nature Neuroscience, 19,* 1727–1732. http://dx.doi.org/10.1038/nn.4426

**Gaspar, J. G., Street, W. N., Windsor, M. B., Carbonari, R., Kaczmarski, H., Kramer, A. F., & Mathewson, K. E.** (2014). Providing views of the driving scene to drivers' conversation partners mitigates cell-phone-related distraction. *Psychological Science, 25,* 2136–2146. http://dx.doi.org/10.1177/0956797614549774

**Gaudiano, B. A., Dalrymple, K. L., Weinstock, L. M., & Lohr, J. M.** (2015). The science of psychotherapy: Developing, testing, and promoting evidence-based treatments. In S. O. Lilienfeld, S. J. Lynn, & J. M. Lohr (Eds.), *Science and pseudoscience in clinical psychology* (2nd ed., pp. 155–190). New York, NY: Guilford.

**Gaudreau, P., Morinville, A., Gareau, A., Verner-Filion, J., Green-Demers, I., & Franche, V.** (2016). Autonomy support from parents and coaches: Synergistic or compensatory effects on sport-related outcomes of adolescent-athletes? *Psychology of Sport and Exercise, 25,* 89–99. http://dx.doi.org/10.1016/j.psychsport.2016.04.006

**Gawronski, B., Brochu, P. M., Sritharan, R., & Strack, F.** (2012). Cognitive consistency in prejudice-related belief systems: Integrating old-fashioned, modern, aversive, and implicit forms of prejudice. In B. Gawronski & F. Strack (Eds.), *Cognitive consistency: A fundamental principle in social cognition* (pp. 369–389). New York, NY: Guilford Press.

**Gazes, Y., Bowman, F. D., Razlighi, Q. R., O'Shea, D., Stern, Y., & Habeck, C.** (2016). White matter tract covariance patterns predict age-declining cognitive abilities. *NeuroImage, 125,* 53–60. http://dx.doi.org/10.1016/j.neuroimage.2015.10.016

**Gazzaniga, M. S.** (2009). The fictional self. In D. J. H. Mathews, H. Bok, & P. V. Rabins (Eds.), *Personal identity and fractured selves: Perspectives from philosophy, ethics, and neuroscience* (pp. 174–185). Baltimore, MD: Johns Hopkins University Press.

**Geangu, E., Benga, O., Stahl, D., & Striano, T.** (2010). Contagious crying beyond the first days of life. *Infant Behavior and Development, 33,* 279–288.

**Gebhardt, J. A.** (2016). Quagmires for clinical psychology and executive coaching? Ethical considerations and practice challenges. *American Psychologist, 71,* 216–235. http://dx.doi.org/10.1037/a0039806

**Geher, G., & Kaufman, S. B.** (2013). *Mating intelligence unleashed: The role of the mind in sex, dating, and love.* Oxford, UK: Oxford University Press.

**Geisinger, K. F., & McCormick, C.** (2013). Testing and assessment in cross-cultural psychology. In J. R. Graham, J. A. Naglieri, & I. B. Weiner (Eds.), *Handbook of psychology, Vol. 10: Assessment psychology* (2nd ed., pp. 114–139). Hoboken, NJ: Wiley.

**Gelder, B. D., Meeren, H. K., Righart, R., Stock, J. V., van de Riet, W. A., & Tamietto, M.** (2006). Beyond the face: Exploring rapid

influences of context on face processing. *Progress in Brain Research, 155,* 37–48.

**Gendron, M., Roberson, D., van der Vyver, J. M., & Barrett, L. F.** (2014). Perceptions of emotion from facial expressions are not culturally universal: Evidence from a remote culture. *Emotion, 14,* 251–262. http://dx.doi.org/10.1037/a0036052

**Geronazzo, M., Bedin, A., Brayda, L., Campus, C., & Avanzini, F.** (2016). Interactive spatial sonification for non-visual exploration of virtual maps. *International Journal of Human-Computer Studies, 85,* 4–15. http://dx.doi.org/10.1016/j.ijhcs.2015.08.004

**Gerring, J. P., & Vasa, R. A.** (2016). The Oxford handbook of head injury and externalizing behavior. In T. P. Beauchaine & S. P. Hinshaw (Eds), *The Oxford handbook of externalizing spectrum disorders* (pp. 403–415). New York, NY: Oxford University Press.

**Gerson, S. A., & Woodward, A. L.** (2014). Learning from their own actions: The unique effect of producing actions on infants' action understanding. *Child Development, 85,* 264–277. http://dx.doi.org/10.1111/cdev.12115

**Gerstorf, D., Hü lü r, G., Drewelies, J., Eibich, P., Duezel, S., Demuth, I., . . . Lindenberger, U.** (2015). Secular changes in late-life cognition and well-being: Towards a long bright future with a short brisk ending? *Psychology and Aging, 30,* 301–310. http://dx.doi.org/10.1037/pag0000016

**Geschwind, D. H., & State, M. W.** (2015). Gene hunting in autism spectrum disorder: On the path to precision medicine. *The Lancet Neurology, 14,* 1109–1120. http://dx.doi.org/10.1016/S1474-4422(15)00044-7

**Ge, Y., Knittel, C. R., MacKenzie, D., & Zoepf, S.** (2016). Racial and gender discrimination in transportation network companies. *National Bureau of Economic Research, Working Paper* No. 22776. Retrieved from http://www.nber.org/papers/w22776

**Ghabrial, M. A.** (2017). "Trying to figure out where we belong": Narratives of racialized sexual minorities on community, identity, discrimination, and health. *Sexuality Research & Social Policy, 14,* 42-55. http://dx.doi.org/10.1007/s13178-016-0229-x

**Gherasim, L. R., Brumariu, L. E., & Alim, C. L.** (2016). Parenting style and children's life satisfaction and depressive symptoms: Preliminary findings from Romania, France, and Russia. *Journal of Happiness Studies.* No Pagination Specified. http://dx.doi.org/10.1007/s10902-016-9754-9

**Giammarco, E. A.** (2016). The measurement of individual differences in morality. *Personality and Individual Differences, 88,* 26–34. http://dx.doi.org/10.1016/j.paid.2015.08.039

**Gianettoni, L., & Guilley, E.** (2016). Sexism and the gendering of professional aspirations. In K. Faniko, F. Lorenzi-Cioldi, O. Sarrasin, & E. Mayor (Eds.), *Gender and social hierarchies: Perspectives from social psychology* (pp. 11–25). New York, NY: Routledge/Taylor & Francis.

**Gibbons, S W., & Hickling, E. J.** (2016). Risk and resilience factors in combat military health care providers. In S. MacDermith Wadsworth, & D. S. Riggs (Eds.), *War and family life. Risk and resilience in military and veteran families* (pp. 181–193). Cham, CH: Springer International Publishing. http://dx.doi.org/10.1007/978-3-319-21488-7_10

**Gibbs, J. C.** (2014). *Moral development and real-*

*ity: Beyond the theories of Kohlberg, Hoffman, and Haidt* (3rd ed.). New York, NY: Oxford University Press.

**Gibbs, N.** (1995, October 2). The EQ factor. *Time,* 60–68.

**Gibbs, S.** (2014, May 14). Women in technology: No progress on inequality for 10 years. *The Guardian.* Retrieved from http://www.theguardian.com/technology/2014/may/14/women-technology-inequality-10-years-female

**Gibson, B., Thompson, J., Hou, B., & Bushman, B. J.** (2016). Just harmless entertainment? Effects of surveillance reality TV on physical aggression. *Psychology of Popular Media Culture, 5,* 66–73. http://dx.doi.org/10.1037/ppm0000040

**Gibson, E. J., & Walk, R. D.** (1960). The visual cliff. *Scientific American, 202,* 67–71.

**Gibson, S.** (2017). Developing psychology's archival sensibilities: Revisiting Milgram's 'obedience' experiments. *Qualitative Psychology, 4*(1), 73–89. http://dx.doi.org/10.1037/qup0000040

**Gilani, A. I., Chohan, M. O., Inan, M., Schobel, S. A., Chaudhury, N. H., Paskewitz, S., . . . Moore, H.** (2014). Interneuron precursor transplants in adult hippocampus reverse psychosis-relevant features in a mouse model of hippocampal disinhibition. *Proceedings of the National Academy of Sciences of the United States of America, 111,* 7450–7455. http://dx.doi.org/10.1073/pnas.1316488111

**Gilbert, A. C., Boucher, V. J., & Jemel, B.** (2015). The perceptual chunking of speech: A demonstration using ERPs. *Brain Research, 1603,* 101–113. http://dx.doi.org/10.1016/j.brainres.2015.01.032

**Gilberti, M.** (2016). Mental illness is no laughing matter. *U.S. News.* Retrieved from http://www.usnews.com/opinion/blogs/policy-dose/articles/2016-03-08/bernie-sanders-mentalhealth-joke-about-the-gop-isnt-funny

**Gilbert, S. J.** (2015). Strategic offloading of delayed intentions into the external environment. The *Quarterly Journal of Experimental Psychology, 68*(5), 971–992. http://dx.doi.org/10.1080/17470218.2014.972963

**Gilligan, C.** (1977). In a different voice: Women's conception of morality. *Harvard Educational Review, 47*(4), 481–517.

**Gilligan, C.** (1990). Teaching Shakespeare's sister. In C. Gilligan, N. Lyons, & T. Hanmer (Eds.), *Mapping the moral domain* (pp. 73–86). Cambridge, MA: Harvard University Press.

**Gilligan, C.** (1993). Adolescent development reconsidered. In A. Garrod (Ed.), *Approaches to moral development: New research and emerging themes* (pp103–132). New York, NY: Teachers College Press.

**Gilligan, C.** (2011). *Joining the resistance.* Oxford, UK: Polity Press.

**Gillihan, S. J., & Foa, E. B.** (2016). Exposure-based interventions for adult anxiety disorders, obsessive-compulsive disorder, and posttraumatic stress disorder. In C. M. Nezu & A. M. Nezu (Eds.), *The Oxford handbook of cognitive and behavioral therapies* (pp. 96–117). New York, NY: Oxford University Press.

**Gilmore, A. K., & Bountress, K. E.** (2016). Reducing drinking to cope among heavy episodic drinking college women: Secondary outcomes of a web-based combined alcohol use and sexual assault risk reduction intervention. *Addictive Behaviors, 61,* 104–111. http://dx.doi.org/10.1016/j.addbeh.2016.05.007

**Gil-Rivas, V., & Kilmer, R. P.** (2016). Building community capacity and fostering disaster resilience. *Journal of Clinical Psychology, 72*(12), 1318–1332. http://dx.doi.org/10.1002/jclp.22281

**Ginton, A.** (2017). Examining different types of comparison questions in a field study of cqt polygraph technique: Theoretical and practical implications. *Journal of Investigative Psychology and Offender Profiling.* No Pagination Specified. http://dx.doi.org/10.1002/jip.1475

**Ginzburg, H. M., & Bateman, D. J.** (2008). New Orleans medical students post-Katrina—An assessment of psychopathology and anticipatory transference of resilience. *Psychiatric Annals, 38,* 145–156. http://dx.doi.org/10.3928/00485713-20080201-01

**Glaser, J.** (2015). *Suspect race: Causes and consequences of racial profiling.* New York, NY: Oxford University Press.

**Goel, A., Chhabra, G., Weijma, R., Solari, M., Thornton, S., Achondo, B., . . . Kalra, O. P.** (2014). End-of-life care attitudes, values, and practices among health care workers. *American Journal of Hospice & Palliative Medicine, 31,* 139–147. http://dx.doi.org/10.1177/1049909113479440

**Goh, G. H., Mark, P. J., & Maloney, S. K.** (2016). Altered energy intake and the amplitude of the body temperature rhythm are associated with changes in phase, but not amplitude, of clock gene expression in the rat suprachiasmatic nucleus in vivo. *Chronobiology International, 33,* 85–97. http://dx.doi.org/10.3109/07420528.2015.1112395

**Goldberg, S., Werbeloff, N., Shelef, L., Fruchter, E., & Weiser, M.** (2015). Risk of suicide among female adolescents with eating disorders: A longitudinal population-based study. *Eating and Weight Disorders—Studies on Anorexia, Bulimia and Obesity, 30,* 295–300. http://dx.doi.org/10.1007/s40519-015-0176-1

**Goldfinch, A.** (2015). *Rethinking evolutionary psychology.* New York, NY: Palgrave Macmillan.

**Goldman, L.** (2014). *Life and loss: A guide to help grieving children* (3rd ed.). New York, NY: Routledge/Taylor & Francis Group.

**Goldstein, A. M., Morse, S. J., & Packer, I. K.** (2013). Evaluation of criminal responsibility. In R. K. Otto & I. B. Weiner (Eds.), *Handbook of psychology, Vol. 11. Forensic psychology* (2nd ed., pp. 440–472). Hoboken, NJ: Wiley.

**Goldstein, B.** (2015). *Cognitive psychology: Connecting mind, research, and everyday experience* (4th ed.). Stamford, CT: Cengage Learning.

**Goldstein, E. B.** (2014). *Sensation and perception* (9th ed.). Belmont, CA: Cengage.

**Goldstein, E. G.** (2014). *Cognitive psychology: Connecting mind, research, and everyday experience* (4th ed.). Belmont, CA: Cengage.

**Goldstein, R. B., Smith, S. M., Chou, S. P., Saha, T. D., Jung, J., Zhang, H., . . . Grant, B. F.** (2016). The epidemiology of dsm-5 posttraumatic stress disorder in the united states: Results from the national epidemiologic survey on alcohol and related conditions-iii. *Social Psychiatry and Psychiatric Epidemiology, 51*(8), 1137–1148. http://dx.doi.org/10.1007/s00127-016-1208-5

**Goldstein, S., Princiotta, D., & Naglieri, J. A.** (Eds.). (2015). *Handbook of intelligence: Evolutionary theory, historical perspective, and current concepts.* New York, NY: Springer. http://dx.doi.org/10.1007/978-1-4939-1562-0

**Goldstone, D.** (2017). Cognitive-behavioural therapy versus psychodynamic psychotherapy for the treatment of depression: A critical review of evidence and current issues. *South African Journal of Psychology, 47*(1), 84–96. http://dx.doi.org/10.1177/0081246316653360

**Goleman, D.** (1980, February). 1,528 little geniuses and how they grew. *Psychology Today,* 28–53.

**Goleman, D.** (1995). *Emotional intelligence: Why it can matter more than IQ.* New York, NY: Bantam.

**Goleman, D.** (2000). *Working with emotional intelligence.* New York, NY: Bantam Doubleday.

**Goleman, D.** (2008). Leading resonant teams. In F. Hesselbein & A. Shrader (Eds.), *Leader to leader 2: Enduring insights on leadership from the Leader to Leader Institute's award-winning journal* (pp. 186–195). San Francisco, CA: Jossey-Bass.

**Gonçalves, A. M. N., Dantas, C. D., & Banzato, C. E. M.** (2016). Values and DSM-5: Looking at the debate on attenuated psychosis syndrome. *BMC Medical Ethics, 17,* Article 7.

**Gonçalves, M., Amici, R., Lucas, R., Åkerstedt, T., Cirignotta, F., Horne, J., . . . Grote, L.** (2015). Sleepiness at the wheel across Europe: A survey of 19 countries. *Journal of Sleep Research, 24,* 242–253. http://dx.doi.org/10.1111/jsr.12267

**Gonyea, D., & Montanaro, D.** (2015, June 19). Predictably, Democrats, Republicans don't agree on Charleston causes, solutions. *NPR.* Retrieved from http://www. npr.org/sections/itsallpolitics/2015/06/19/415747034/predictably-democratsrepublicans-dont-agree-on-charleston-causes-solutions

**Gonzales-Backen, M. A., Dumka, L. E., Millsap, R. E., Yoo, H. C., Schwartz, S. J., Zamboanga, B. L., . . . Vazsonyi, A. T.** (2015). The role of social and personal identities in self-esteem among ethnic minority college students. *Identity: An International Journal of Theory and Research, 15,* 202–220. http://dx.doi.org/10.1080/15283488.2015.1055532

**González, V. V., Navarro, V., Miguez, G., Betancourt, R., & Laborda, M. A.** (2016). Preventing the recovery of extinguished ethanol tolerance. *Behavioural Processes, 124,* 141–148. http://dx.doi.org/10.1016/j.beproc.2016.01.004

**Goodall, J.** (1990). *Through a window: My thirty years with the chimpanzees of Gombe.* Boston, MA: Houghton-Mifflin.

**Goodchild, M., Nargis, N., Tursan d'Espaignet, E.** (2017). Global economic cost of smoking-attributable diseases. *British Medical Journal: Tobacco Control.* No Pagination Specified. http://dx.org/10.1136/tobaccocontrol-2016-053305

**Goodell, J.** (2014, March 13). Bill Gates: The Rolling Stone interview. *Rolling Stone.* Retrieved from http://www.rollingstone.com/culture/news/bill-gates-the-rolling-stone-interview-20140313

**Goodmon, L. B., Smith, P. L., Ivancevich, D., & Lundberg, S.** (2014). Actions speak louder than personality: Effects of Facebook content on personality perceptions. *North American Journal of Psychology, 16*(1), 105.

**Goodson, J. L.** (2013). Deconstructing sociality, social evolution and relevant nonapeptide functions. *Psychoneuroendocrinology, 38,* 465–478.

**Goodwin, C. J.** (2012). *A history of modern psychology* (4th ed.). Hoboken, NJ: Wiley.

**Goodwin, D. K.** (2005). *Team of rivals: The political genius of Abraham Lincoln.* New York, NY: Simon & Schuster.

**Goodwin, J., & Goodwin, K.** (2013). *Research in psychology: Methods and design* (7th ed.). Hoboken, NJ: Wiley.

**Goodyer, I. M., Reynolds, S., Barrett, B., Byford, S., Dubicka, B., Hill, J., . . . Fonagy, P.** (2017). Cognitive behavioural therapy and short-term psychoanalytical psychotherapy versus a brief psychosocial intervention in adolescents with unipolar major depressive disorder (IMPACT): A multicentre, pragmatic, observer-blind, randomised controlled superiority trial. *The Lancet Psychiatry, 4*(2), 109–119. http://dx.doi.org/10.1016/S2215-0366(16)30378-9

**Gorges, J., & Göke, T.** (2015). How do I know what I can do? Anticipating expectancy of success regarding novel academic tasks. *British Journal of Educational Psychology, 85,* 75–90. http://dx.doi.org/10.1111/bjep.12064

**Gosling, S. D.** (2008). Personality in nonhuman animals. *Social and Personality Compass, 2,* 985–1001.

**Gosling, S. D., & John, O. P.** (1999). Personality dimensions in nonhuman animals: Across-species review. *Current Directions in Psychological Science, 8,* 69–75.

**Gosling, S. D., Kwan, V. S. Y., & John, O. P.** (2004). A dog's got personality: A cross-species comparative approach to personality judgments in dogs and humans. *Journal of Personality and Social Psychology, 85,* 1161–1169.

**Gosselin, J. T.** (2016). Sexual dysfunctions and paraphilic disorders. In J. E. Maddux & B. A. Winstead (Eds.), *Psychopathology: Foundations for a contemporary understanding* (4th ed., pp. 237–265). New York, NY: Routledge/Taylor & Francis Group.

**Gottesman, I. I.** (1991). *Schizophrenia genesis: The origins of madness.* New York, NY: Freeman.

**Göttken, T., White, L. O., Klein, A. M., & von Klitzing, K.** (2014). Short-term psychoanalytic child therapy for anxious children: A pilot study. *Psychotherapy, 51,* 148–158. http://dx.doi.org/10.1037/a0036026

**Gottman, J. M.** (2011). *The science of trust: Emotional attunement for couples.* New York, NY: W. W. Norton.

**Gottman, J. M.** (2015). *Principia amoris: The new science of love.* New York, NY: Routledge/Taylor & Francis Group.

**Gottman, J. M., & Silver, N.** (2012). *What makes love last: How to build trust and avoid betrayal.* New York, NY: Simon & Schuster.

**Gottman, J. S., & Gottman, J. M.** (2015). *10 principles for doing effective couples therapy.* New York, NY: W. W. Norton.

**Gould, R.** (1975). Adult life stages: Growth toward self-tolerance. *Psychology Today, 8*(9), 74–78.

**Gouveia, M. J., Carona, C., Canavarro, M. C., & Moreira, H.** (2016). Self-compassion and dispositional mindfulness are associated with parenting styles and parenting stress: The mediating role of mindful parenting. *Mindfulness, 7,* 700–712. http://dx.doi.org/10.1007/s12671-016-0507-y

**Goyal, M., Singh, S., Sibinga, E. M., Gould, N. F., Rowland-Seymour, A., Sharma, R., . . . Haythornthwaite, J. A.** (2014). Meditation programs for psychological stress and well-being: A systematic review and meta-analysis. *JAMA Internal Medicine, 174,* 357–368. http://dx.doi.org/10.1001/jamainternmed.2013.13018

**Graber, R., Turner, R., & Madill, A.** (2016). Best friends and better coping: Facilitating psychological resilience through boys' and girls' closest friendships. *British Journal of Psychology, 107,* 338–358. http://dx.doi.org/10.1111/bjop.12135

**Graduate Study in Psychology.** (2017). *Graduate study in psychology: American Psychological Association.* Washington, DC: American Psychological Association. http://www.apa.org/pubs/books/4270101.aspx

**Graf, W., Miller, G. E., Epstein, L. G., & Rapin, I.** (2017). The autism "epidemic": Ethical, legal, and social issues in a developmental spectrum disorder. *Neurology, 88*(14), 1371–1380. http://dx.doi.org/10.1212/WNL.0000000000003791

**Graham, J., Meindl, P., Beall, E., Johnson, K. M., & Zhang, L.** (2016). Cultural differences in moral judgment and behavior, across and within societies. *Current Opinion in Psychology, 8,* 125–130. http://dx.doi.org/10.1016/j.copsyc.2015.09.007

**Granader, Y., Wallace, G. L., Hardy, K. K., Yerys, B. E., Lawson, R. A., Rosenthal, M., . . . Kenworthy, L.** (2014). Characterizing the factor structure of parent reported executive function in autism spectrum disorders: The impact of cognitive inflexibility. *Journal of Autism and Developmental Disorders, 44,* 3056–3062. http://dx.doi.org/10.1007/s10803-014-2169-8

**Granger, N., Franklin, R. J., & Jeffery, N. D.** (2014). Cell therapy for spinal cord injuries: What is really going on? *The Neuroscientist, 20,* 623–638. http://dx.doi.org/10.1177/1073858413514635

**Granhag, P. A., Vrij, A., & Verschuere, B.** (Eds.). (2015). *Detecting deception: Current challenges and cognitive approaches.* Malden, MA: Wiley-Blackwell.

**Granillo, M. T., Perron, B. E., Jarman, C., & Gutowski, S. M.** (2013). Cognitive behavioral therapy with substance use disorders: Theory, evidence, and practice. In M. G. Vaughn & B. E. Perron (Eds.), *Social work practice in the addictions* (pp. 101–118). New York, NY: Springer.

**Gray, S. J., & Gallo, D. A.** (2106). Paranormal psychic believers and skeptics: A large-scale test of the cognitive differences hypothesis. *Memory & Cognition, 44,* 242–261. http://dx.doi.org/10.3758/s13421-015-0563-x

**Greenaway, K. H., Storrs, K. R., Philipp, M. C., Louis, W. R., Hornsey, M. J., & Vohs, K. D.** (2015). Loss of control stimulates approach motivation. *Journal of Experimental Social Psychology, 56,* 235–241. http://dx.doi.org/10.1016/j.jesp.2014.10.009

**Greenberg, D. L.** (2004). President Bush's false [flashbulb] memory of 9/11/01. *Applied Cognitive Psychology, 18,* 363–370. http://dx.doi.org/10.1002/acp.1016

**Greenberg, J., Schmader, T., Arndt, J., & Landau, M.** (2015). *Social psychology: The science of everyday life.* New York, NY: Worth.

**Greene, J.** (2017). *Thinking and language* (5th ed.). New York, NY: Routledge.

**Greenfield, P. M., & Quiroz, B.** (2013). Context and culture in the socialization and development of personal achievement values: Comparing Latino immigrant families, European American families, and elementary school teachers. *Journal of Applied Developmental Psychology, 34,* 108–118. http://dx.doi.org/10.1016/j.appdev.2012.11.002

**Greenwald, A. G., & Pettigrew, T. F.** (2014). With malice toward none and charity for some: Ingroup favoritism enables discrimination.

*American Psychologist, 69,* 669–684. http://dx.doi.org/10.1037/a0036056

**Gregersen, E.** (1996). *The world of human sexuality: Behaviors, customs, and beliefs.* New York, NY: Irvington.

**Gregory, S., Fytche, D., Simmons, A., Kumari, V., Howard, M., Hodgins, S., & Blackwood, N.** (2012). The antisocial brain: Psychopathy matters. *Archives of General Psychiatry, 69,* 962–972.

**Griggs, R. A.** (2015). Coverage of the Phineas Gage story in introductory psychology textbooks: Was Gage no longer Gage? *Teaching of Psychology, 42,* 195–202. http://dx.doi.org/10.1177/0098628315587614

**Griggs, R. A.** (2015). The Kitty Genovese story in introductory psychology textbooks: Fifty years later. *Teaching of Psychology, 42,* 149–152. http://dx.doi.org/10.1177/0098628315573138

**Griggs, R. A.** (2017). Milgram's obedience study: A contentious classic reinterpreted. *Teaching of Psychology, 44*(1), 32–37. http://dx.doi.org/10.1177/0098628316677644

**Grigsby, S.** (2017, April 2). A dire collapse of hope. *Daily Kos.* Retrieved April 5, 2017 from http://www.dailykos.com/story/2017/4/2/1648658/—A-dire-collapse-of-hope

**Groome, D., Brace, N., Edgar, G., Edgar, H., Eysenck, M., Manly, . . . Styles, E.** (2014). *An introduction to cognitive psychology: Processes and disorders* (3rd ed.). New York, NY: Psychology Press.

**Grover, S., & Ghosh, A.** (2014). Somatic symptom and related disorders in Asians and Asian Americans. *Asian Journal of Psychiatry, 7,* 77–79. http://dx.doi.org/10.1016/j.ajp.2013.11.014

**Grubin, D.** (2016). Polygraph testing of sex offenders. In D. R. Laws & W. O'Donohue (Eds.), *Treatment of sex offenders: Strengths and weaknesses in assessment and intervention* (pp. 133–156). Cham, CH: Springer International Publishing. http://dx.doi.org/10.1007/978-3-319-25868-3_6

**Grünbaum, A.** (2015). Critique of psychoanalysis. In S. Boag, L. A. W. Brakel, & V. Talvitie (Eds.), *Philosophy, science, and psychoanalysis: A critical meeting* (pp. 1–36). London, UK: Karnac Books.

**Gruzd, A., & Roy, J.** (2014). Investigating political polarization on Twitter: A Canadian perspective. *Policy & Internet, 6,* 28–45. http://dx.doi.org/10.1002/1944-2866.POI354

**Grzybowski, S. J., Wyczesany, M., & Kaiser, J.** (2014). The influence of context on the processing of emotional and neutral adjectives–An ERP study. *Biological Psychology, 99,* 137–149. http://dx.doi.org/10.1016/j.biopsycho.2014.01.002

**Guardino, C. M., Schetter, C. D., Saxbe, D. E., Adam, E. K., Ramey, S. L., Shalowitz, M. U., & Community Child Health Network** (2016). Diurnal salivary cortisol patterns prior to pregnancy predict infant birth weight. *Health Psychology, 35,* 625–633. http://dx.doi.org/10.1037/hea0000313

**Guastello, S. J., Guastello, D. D., & Craft, L. L.** (1989). Assessment of the Barnum effect in computer-based test interpretations. *Journal of Psychology: Interdisciplinary and Applied, 123,* 477–484. http://dx.doi.org/10.1080/00223980.1989.10543001

**Guedes, M. J. C.** (2017). Mirror, mirror on the wall, am I the greatest performer of all? Narcissism and self-reported and objective performance. *Personality and Individual Differences,*

*108,* 182–185. http://dx.doi.org/10.1016/j.paid.2016.12.030

**Guéguen, N., & Jacob, C.** (2014). Clothing color and tipping: Gentlemen patrons give more tips to waitresses with red clothes. *Journal of Hospitality & Tourism Research, 38,* 275–280. http://dx.doi.org/10.1177/1096348012442546

**Guéguen, N., & Stefan, J.** (2016). "Green altruism": Short immersion in natural green environments and helping behavior. *Environment and Behavior, 48,* 324–342. http://dx.doi.org/10.1177/0013916514536576

**Guekht, A.** (2016). Dementia. In M. Mula (Ed.), *Neuropsychiatric symptoms of epilepsy* (pp. 235–254). Cham, CH: Springer International Publishing. http://dx.doi.org/10.1007/978-3-319-22159-5_14

**Guelzow, B. T., Loya, F., & Hinshaw, S. P.** (2017). How persistent is ADHD into adulthood? Informant report and diagnostic thresholds in a female sample. *Journal of Abnormal Child Psychology, 45,* 301–312. http://dx.doi.org/10.1007/s10802-016-0174-4

**Guilford, J. P.** (1967). *The nature of human intelligence.* New York, NY: McGraw-Hill.

**Gumz, M. L. (Ed.).** (2016). *Circadian clocks: Role in health and disease.* New York, NY: Springer Science + Business Media. http://dx.doi.org/10.1007/978-1-4939-3450-8

**Gunderson, J. G., & Links, P.** (2014). *Handbook of good psychiatric management for borderline personality disorder.* Arlington, VA: American Psychiatric Publishing.

**Gunnery, S. D., & Ruben, M. A.** (2016). Perceptions of Duchenne and non-Duchenne smiles: A meta-analysis. *Cognition and Emotion, 30*(3), 501–515. http://dx.doi.org/10.1080/02699931.2015.1018817

**Gunn, W. B., Jr., Haley, J., Prouty, A. M., & Robertson, J.** (2015). Systemic approaches: Family therapy. In H. T. Prout & A. L. Fedewa (Eds.), *Counseling and psychotherapy with children and adolescents: Theory and practice for school and clinical settings* (5th ed., pp. 317–355). Hoboken, NJ: Wiley.

**Guo, F., & Garvey, W. T.** (2016). Cardiometabolic disease risk in metabolically healthy and unhealthy obesity: Stability of metabolic health status in adults. *Obesity, 24,* 516–525. http://dx.doi.org/10.1002/oby.21344

**Guo, F., Xu, Q., Salem, H. M. A., Yao, Y., Lou, J., & Huang, X.** (2016). The neuronal correlates of mirror therapy: A functional magnetic resonance imaging study on mirror-induced visual illusions of ankle movements. *Brain Research, 1639,* 186–193. http://dx.doi.org/10.1016/j.brainres.2016.03.002

**Guo, W., Song, Y., Liu, F., Zhang, Z., Zhang, J., Yu, M., . . . Zhao, J.** (2015). Dissociation of functional and anatomical brain abnormalities in unaffected siblings of schizophrenia patients. *Clinical Neurophysiology, 126,* 927–932. http://dx.doi.org/10.1016/j.clinph.2015.01.025

**Gur, R. E., & Gur, R. C.** (2016). Sex differences in brain and behavior in adolescence: Findings from the Philadelphia Neurodevelopmental Cohort. *Neuroscience & Biobehavioral Reviews, 70,* 159–170. http://dx.doi.org/10.1016/j.neubiorev.2016.07.035

**Gurven, M., von Rueden, C., Massenkoff, M., Kaplan, H., & Lero Vie, M.** (2013). How universal is the big five? Testing the five-factor model of personality variation among forager-farmers in the Bolivian Amazon. *Journal of Personality and Social Psychology, 104,* 354–370. http://dx.doi.org/10.1037/a0030841

**Guryan, J., Kim, J. S., & Park, K.** (2015). Motivation and incentives in education: Evidence from a summer reading experiment. *National Bureau of Economic Research,* Working Paper No. 20918.

**Gutchess, A., & Huff , S.** (2016). Cross-cultural differences in memory. In J. Y. Chiao, S. –C. Li, R. Seligman, & R. Turner (Eds), *The Oxford handbook of cultural neuroscience. Oxford library of psychology* (pp. 155–169). New York, NY: Oxford University Press.

**Guveli, H., Anuk, D., Oflaz, S., Guveli, M. E., Yildirim, N. K., Ozkan, M., & Ozkan, S.** (2015). Oncology staff: Burnout, job satisfaction and coping with stress. *Psycho-Oncology, 24,* 926–931. http://dx.doi.org/10.1002/pon.3743

**Haaken, J.** (2010). *Hard knocks: Domestic violence and the psychology of storytelling.* New York, NY: Routledge/Taylor & Francis Group.

**Haas, B. W., Ishak, A., Anderson, I. W., & Filkowski, M. M.** (2015). The tendency to trust is reflected in human brain structure. *NeuroImage, 107,* 175–181. http://dx.doi.org/10.1016/j.neuroimage.2014.11.060 *inking* (5th ed.).

**Hackley, C.** (2007). Marketing psychology and the hidden persuaders. *The Psychologist, 20,* 488–490.

**Hackman, J., Munira, S., Jasmin, K., & Hruschka, D.** (2017). Revisiting psychological mechanisms in the anthropology of altruism. *Human Nature, 28*(1), 76–91. http://dx.doi.org/10.1007/s12110-016-9278-3

**Haghighi, A., Melka, M. G., Bernard, M., Abrahamowicz, M., Leonard, G. T., Richer, L., . . . Pausova, Z.** (2014). Opioid receptor mu 1 gene, fat intake and obesity in adolescence. *Molecular Psychiatry, 19,* 63–68. http://dx.doi.org/10.1038/mp.2012.179

**Haghighi, A., Schwartz, D. H., Abrahamowicz, M., Leonard, G. T., Perron, M., Richer, L., . . . Pausova, Z.** (2013). Prenatal exposure to maternal cigarette smoking, amygdala volume, and fat intake in adolescence. *JAMA Psychiatry, 70,* 98–105.

**Hagiwara, N., Slatcher, R. B., Eggly, S., & Penner, L. A.** (2017). Physician racial bias and word use during racially discordant medical interactions. *Health Communication, 32*(4), 401–408. http://dx.doi.org/10.1080/10410236.2016.1138389

**Hagmann-von Arx, P., Gygi, J. T., Weidmann, R., & Grob, A.** (2016). Testing relations of crystallized and fluid intelligence and the incremental predictive validity of conscientiousness and its facets on career success in a small sample of German and Swiss workers. *Frontiers in Psychology, 7,* Article 500.

**Haidt, J.** (2001). The emotional dog and its rational tail. *Psychological Review, 108*(4), 814–834. http://dx.doi.org/10.1037/0033-295X.108.4.814

**Haidt, J.** (2012). *The righteous mind: Why good people are divided by politics and religion.* New York, NY: Pantheon.

**Hair, N. L., Hanson, J. L., Wolfe, B. L., & Pollak, S. D.** (2015). Association of child poverty, brain development, and academic achievement. *JAMA Pediatrics, 169,* 822–829. http://dx.doi.org/10.1001/jamapediatrics.2015.1475

**Haith, M. M., & Benson, J. B.** (1998). Infant cognition. In W. Damon (Series Ed.) & D. Kuhn & R. S.

Siegler (Vol. Eds.), *Handbook of child psychology: Vol. 2. Cognition, perception, and language* (5th ed., pp. 199–254). New York, NY: Wiley

**Hajak, G., Lemme, K., & Zisapel, N.** (2015). Lasting treatment effects in a postmarketing surveillance study of prolonged-release melatonin. *International Clinical Psychopharmacology, 30,* 36–42. http://dx.doi.org/10.1097/YIC.0000000000000046

**Hakvoort, E. M., Bos, H. M. W., Van Balen, F., & Hermanns, J. M. A.** (2011). Postdivorce relationships in families and children's psychosocial adjustment. *Journal of Divorce & Remarriage, 52,* 125–146.

**Hall, E. V., & Livingston, R. W.** (2012). The hubris penalty: Biased responses to "Celebration" displays of black football players. *Journal of Experimental Social Psychology, 48,* 899–904. http://dx.doi.org/10.1016/j.jesp.2012.02.004

**Hall, G. C. N., & Ibaraki, A. Y.** (2016). Multicultural issues in cognitive-behavioral therapy: Cultural adaptations and goodness of fit. In C. M. Nezu & A. M. Nezu (Eds.), *The Oxford handbook of cognitive and behavioral therapies* (pp. 465–481). New York, NY: Oxford University Press.

**Hall, H. I., Song, R., Szwarcwald, C. L., & Green, T.** (2015). Time from infection with the human immunodeficiency virus to diagnosis, United States. *Journal of Acquired Immune Deficiency Syndromes, 69,* 248–251. http://dx.doi.org/10.1097/QAI.0000000000000589

**Hall, J. A., & Xing, C.** (2015). The verbal and nonverbal correlates of the five flirting styles. *Journal of Nonverbal Behavior, 39,* 41–68. http://dx.doi.org/10.1007/s10919-014-0199-8

**Halpern, D. F.** (2014). *Thought and knowledge: An introduction to critical thinking* (5th ed.). New York, NY: Psychology Press.

**Halpern, D., Valenzuela, S., & Katz, J. E.** (2016). "Selfie-ists" or "Narci-selfiers"?: A cross-lagged panel analysis of selfie taking and narcissism. *Personality and Individual Differences, 97,* 98–101. http://dx.doi.org/10.1016/j.paid.2016.03.019

**Hamilton, J., Daleiden, E., & Youngstrom, E.** (2016). Evidence-based practice. In M. K. Dulcan (Ed.), *Dulcan's textbook of child and adolescent psychiatry* (2nd ed., pp. 523–537). Arlington, VA: American Psychiatric Publishing, Inc.

**Hamilton, L. D., & Julian, A. M.** (2014). The relationship between daily hassles and sexual function in men and women. *Journal of Sex & Marital Therapy, 40*(5), 379–395. http://dx.doi.org/10.1080/0092623X.2013.864364

**Handler, M., Honts, C. R., & Nelson, R.** (2013). Information gain of the directed lie screening test. *Polygraph, 42,* 192–202.

**Haney, C., Banks, C., & Zimbardo, P.** (1978). Interpersonal dynamics in a simulated prison. *International Journal of Criminology and Penology, 1,* 69–97.

**Hara, Y., Yuk, F., Puri, R., Janssen, W. G., Rapp, P. R., & Morrison, J. H.** (2014). Presynaptic mitochondrial morphology in monkey prefrontal cortex correlates with working memory and is improved with estrogen treatment. *Proceedings of the National Academy of Sciences of the United States of America, 111,* 486–491. http://dx.doi.org/10.1073/pnas.1311310110

**Harden, B. J., Buhler, A., & Parra, L. J.** (2016). Maltreatment in infancy: A developmental perspective on prevention and intervention. *Trauma, Violence, & Abuse, 17*(4), 366–386. http://dx.doi.org/10.1177/1524838016658878

**Harjunen, V. J., Spapé, M., Ahmed, I., Jacucci, G., & Ravaja, N.** (2017). Individual differences in affective touch: Behavioral inhibition and gender define how an interpersonal touch is perceived. *Personality and Individual Differences, 107,* 88–95. http://dx.doi.org/10.1016/j.paid.2016.11.047

**Harker, C. M., Ibañez, L. V., Nguyen, T. P., Messinger, D. S., & Stone, W. L.** (2016). The effect of parenting style on social smiling in infants at high and low risk for asd. *Journal of Autism and Developmental Disorders, 46,* 2399–2407. http://dx.doi.org/10.1007/s10803-016-2772-y

**Harley, A., Kumar, D., & Agarwal, A.** (2016). The common characteristics between infertility and recurrent pregnancy loss. In A. Bashiri, A. Harlev, & A. Agarwal (Eds.), *Recurrent pregnancy loss: Evidence-based evaluation, diagnosis and treatment* (pp. 143–152). New York, NY: Springer. http://dx.doi.org/10.1007/978-3-319-27452-2_10

**Harley, T. A.** (2014). *The psychology of language: From data to theory* (4th ed.). New York, NY: Psychology Press.

**Harlow, H. F., Harlow, M. K., & Meyer, D. R.** (1950). Learning motivated by a manipulation drive. *Journal of Experimental Psychology, 40,* 228–234.

**Harlow, H. F., Harlow, M. K., & Suomi, S. J.** (1971). From thought to therapy: Lessons from a primate laboratory. *American Scientist, 59,* 538–549.

**Harlow, J.** (1868). Recovery from the passage of an iron bar through the head. *Publications of the Massachusetts Medical Society, 2,* 237–246.

**Harris, E., McNamara, P., & Durso, R.** (2015). Novelty seeking in patients with right- versus left-onset Parkinson disease. *Cognitive and Behavioral Neurology, 28,* 11–16. http://dx.doi.org/10.1097/WNN.0000000000000047.

**Harris, S.** (2013, November 18). Jennifer Lawrence on her anxiety disorder. *abc News.* Retrieved from http://abcnews.go.com/blogs/entertainment/2013/11/jennifer-lawrence-on-her-anxiety-disorder/

**Harrity, R., & Martin, R. G.** (1962). *The three lives of Helen Keller.* Garden City, NY: Doubleday.

**Hart, J., Nailling, E., Bizer, G. Y., & Collins, C. K.** (2015). Attachment theory as a framework for explaining engagement with Facebook. *Personality and Individual Differences, 77,* 33–40. http://dx.doi.org/10.1016/j.paid.2014.12.016

**Hartmann, E., & Hartmann, T.** (2014). The impact of exposure to Internet-based information about the Rorschach and the MMPI-2 on psychiatric outpatients' ability to simulate mentally healthy test performance. *Journal of Personality Assessment, 99,* 432–444. http://dx.doi.org/10.1080/00223891.2014.882342

**Harwood, C. G., Keegan, R. J., Smith, J. M. J., & Raine, A. S.** (2015). A systematic review of the intrapersonal correlates of motivational climate perceptions in sport and physical activity. *Psychology of Sport and Exercise, 18,* 9–25. http://dx.doi.org/10.1016/j.psychsport.2014.11.005

**Haslam, N.** (2015). Dehumanization and intergroup relations. In M. Mikulincer, P. R. Shaver, J. F. Dovidio, & J. A. Simpson (Eds.), *APA handbook of personality and social psychology, Vol. 2. Group processes* (pp. 295–314). Washington, DC: American Psychological Association. http://dx.doi.org/10.1037/14342-011

**Haslam, S. A., Reicher, S. D., & Birney, M. E.** (2016). Questioning authority: New perspectives on Milgram's 'obedience' research and its implications for intergroup relations. *Current Opinion in Psychology, 11,* 6–9. http://dx.doi.org/10.1016/j.copsyc.2016.03.007

**Haslam, S. A., Reicher, S. D., Millard, K., & McDonald, R.** (2015). 'Happy to have been of service': The Yale archive as a window into the engaged followership of participants in Milgram's 'obedience' experiments. *British Journal of Social Psychology, 54,* 55–83. http://dx.doi.org/10.1111/bjso.12074

**Hatchard, T., Mioduszewski, O., Zambrana, A., O'Farrell, E., Caluyong, M., Poulin, P. A., & Smith, A. M.** (2017). Neural changes associated with mindfulness-based stress reduction (MBSR): Current knowledge, limitations, and future directions. *Psychology & Neuroscience, 10*(1), 41–56. http://dx.doi.org/10.1037/pne0000073

**Hatemi, P. K., Crabtree, C., & McDermott, R.** (2017). The relationship between sexual preferences and political orientations: Do positions in the bedroom affect positions in the ballot box? *Personality and Individual Differences, 105,* 318–325. http://dx.doi.org/10.1016/j.paid.2016.10.008

**Hauner, K. K., Mineka, S., Voss, J. L., & Paller, K. A.** (2012). Exposure therapy triggers lasting reorganization of neural fear processing. *Proceedings of the National Academy of Sciences of the United States of America, 109,* 9203–9208.

**Hayashi, M. T., Cesare, A. J., Riversa, T., & Karlseder, J.** (2015). Cell death during crisis is mediated by mitotic telomere deprotection. *Nature, 522,* 492–496. http://dx.doi.org/10.1038/nature14513

**Hay, D. F.** (1994). Prosocial development. *Journal of Child Psychology and Psychiatry, 35,* 29–71.

**Hayflick, L.** (1965). The limited in vitro lifetime of human diploid cell strains. *Experimental Cell Research, 37,* 614–636. http://dx.doi.org/10.1016/0014-4827(65)90211-9

**Hayflick, L.** (1996). *How and why we age.* New York, NY: Ballantine.

**Hays, P. A.** (2014). *Creating well-being: Four steps to a happier, healthier life.* Washington, DC: American Psychological Association.

**Hazan, C., & Shaver, P.** (1987). Romantic love conceptualized as an attachment process. *Journal of Personality and Social Psychology, 52,* 511–524.

**Head, B. F., Dean, E., Flanigan, T., Swicegood, J., & Keating, M. D.** (2016). Advertising for cognitive interviews: A comparison of Facebook, Craigslist, and snowball recruiting. *Social Science Computer Review, 34*(3), 360–377. http://dx.doi.org/10.1177/0894439315578240

**Head, L. M.** (2014). The effect of kangaroo care on neurodevelopmental outcomes in preterm infants. *The Journal of Perinatal & Neonatal Nursing, 28,* 290–299. http://dx.doi.org/10.1097/JPN.0000000000000062.

**Hébert, M., Tourigny, M., Cyr, M., McDuff, P., & Joly, J.** (2009). Prevalence of childhood sexual abuse and timing of disclosure in a representative sample of adults from Quebec. *The Canadian Journal of Psychiatry/La Revue Canadienne de Psychiatrie, 54,* 631–636.

**Hebl, M., Ruggs, E., Martinez, L., Trump-Steele, R., & Nittrouer, C.** (2016). Understanding and reducing interpersonal discrimination in the workplace. In T. D. Nelson (Ed.), *Handbook of prejudice, stereotyping, and discrimination* (2nd. ed., pp. 387–407). New York, NY: Psychology Press.

**Heeren, G. A., Icard, L. D., O'Leary, A., Jemmott III, J. B., Ngwane, Z., & Mtose, X.** (2014). Protective factors and HIV risk behavior among South African men. *AIDS and Behavior, 18,* 1991–1997. http://dx.doi.org/10.1007/s10461-014-0767-2

**Heffner, K. L., Crean, H. F., & Kemp, J. E.** (2016). Meditation programs for veterans with posttraumatic stress disorder: Aggregate findings from a multi-site evaluation. *Psychological Trauma: Theory, Research, Practice, and Policy, 18,* 365–374. http://dx.doi.org/10.1037/tra0000106

**Hegewisch, A., & DuMonthier, A.** (2016). The gender wage gap: 2015; earning differences by race and ethnicity. *Institute for Women's Policy Research (IWPR).* Retrieved from http://www.iwpr.org/publications/recent-publications

**Heider, F.** (1958). *The psychology of interpersonal relations.* Hoboken, NJ: Wiley.

**Heimann, M., & Meltzoff, A. N.** (1996). Deferred imitation in 9- and 14-month-old infants. *British Journal of Developmental Psychology, 14,* 55–64. http://dx.doi.org/10.1111/j.2044-835X.1996.tb00693.x

**Heine, S. J., & Renshaw, K.** (2002). Interjudge agreement, self-enhancement, and liking: Cross-cultural divergences. *Personality and Social Psychology Bulletin, 28,* 578–587.

**Helbig-Lang, S., Rusch, S., & Lincoln, T. M.** (2015). Emotion regulation difficulties in social anxiety disorder and their specific contributions to anxious responding. *Journal of Clinical Psychology, 71,* 241–249. http://dx.doi.org/10.1002/jclp.22135

**Helleberg, M., May, M. T., Ingle, S. M., Dabis, F., Reiss, P., Fätkenheuer, G., . . . & Obel, N.** (2015). Smoking and life expectancy among HIV-infected individuals on antiretroviral therapy in Europe and North America. *AIDS, 29,* 221–229. http://dx.doi.org/10.1097/QAD.0000000000000540.

**Helmes, E., & Ward, B. G.** (2017). Mindfulness-based cognitive therapy for anxiety symptoms in older adults in residential care. *Aging & Mental Health, 21*(3), 272–278. http://dx.doi.org/10.1080/13607863.2015.1111862

**Hendricks, P. S., Johnson, M. W., & Griffiths, R. R.** (2015b). Psilocybin, psychological distress, and suicidality. *Journal of Psychopharmacology, 29,* 1041–1043. http://dx.doi.org/10.1177/0269881115598338

**Hendricks, P. S., Thorne, C. B., Clark, C. B., Coombs, D. W., & Johnson, M. W.** (2015a). Classic psychedelic use is associated with reduced psychological distress and suicidality in the United States adult population. *Journal of Psychopharmacology, 29,* 280–288. http://dx.doi.org/10.1177/0269881114565653

**Henkel, L. A.** (2014). Point and shoot memories: The influence of taking photos on memory for a museum tour. *Psychological Science, 25,* 396–402.

**Henning, G., Lindwall, M., & Johansson, B.** (2016). Continuity in well-being in the transition to retirement. *GeroPsych: The Journal of Gerontopsychology and Geriatric Psychiatry, 29,* 225–237. http://dx.doi.org/10.1024/1662-9647/a000155

**Henwood, B. F., Derejko, K.-S., Couture, J., & Padgett, D. K.** (2014). Maslow and mental health recovery: A comparative study of homeless programs for adults with serious mental illness. *Administration and Policy in Mental Health and Mental Health Services Research, 42,* 220–228. http://dx.doi.org/10.1007/s10488-014-0542-8

**Herbst, R. S., Hobin, J. A., & Gritz, E. R.** (2014). AACR celebrates 50 years of tobacco research and policy. *Clinical Cancer Research, 20,* 1709–1718. http://dx.doi.org/10.1158/1078-0432.CCR-14-0427

**Herisson, F. M., Waas, J. R., Fredriksson, R., Schiöth, H. B., Levine, A. S., & Olszewski, P. K.** (2016). Oxytocin acting in the nucleus accumbens core decreases food intake. *Journal of Neuroendocrinology, 28*(4). http://doi.org/10.1111/jne.12381

**Herman, A. I., DeVito, E. E., Jensen, K. P., & Sofuoglu, M.** (2014). Pharmacogenetics of nicotine addiction: Role of dopamine. *Pharmacogenomics, 15,* 221–234. http://dx.doi.org/10.2217/pgs.13.246

**Herman, L. M., Richards, D. G., & Woltz, J. P.** (1984). Comprehension of sentences by bottle-nosed dolphins. *Cognition, 16,* 129–139. http://dx.doi.org/10.1016/0010-0277(84)90003-9

**Hernandez, R., Kershaw, K. N., Siddique, J., Boehm, J. K., Kubzansky, L. D., Diez-Roux, A., . . . Lloyd-Jones, D. M.** (2015). Optimism and cardiovascular health: Multi-ethnic study of atherosclerosis (MESA). *Health Behavior and Policy Review, 2,* 62–73. http://dx.doi.org/10.14485/HBPR.2.1.6

**Herrero-Hahn, R., Rojas, J. G., Ospina-Díaz, J. M., Montoya-Juárez, R., Restrepo-Medrano, J. C., & Hueso-Montoro, C.** (2017). Cultural adaptation and validation of the cultural self-efficacy scale for Colombian nursing professionals. *Journal of Transcultural Nursing, 28,* 195–202. http://dx.doi.org/10.1177/1043659615613419

**Herriot, P.** (2014). *Attributes of memory.* New York, NY: Psychology Press.

**Hertel, G., Rauschenbach, C., Thielgen, M. M., & Krumm, S.** (2015). Are older workers more active copers? Longitudinal effects of age-contingent coping on strain at work. *Journal of Organizational Behavior, 36,* 514–537. http://dx.doi.org/10.1002/job.1995

**Hess, M. E., & Brüning, J. C.** (2014). The fat mass and obesity-associated (FTO) gene: Obesity and beyond? *Biochimica etBiophysica Acta (BBA)—Molecular Basis of Disease, 1842,* 2039–2047. http://dx.doi.org/10.1016/j.bbadis.2014.01.017

**Hilgard, E. R.** (1978). Hypnosis and consciousness. *Human Nature, 1,* 42–51.

**Hilgard, E. R.** (1992). Divided consciousness and dissociation. *Consciousness and Cognition, 1,* 16–31.

**Hillier, S. M., & Barrow, G. M.** (2011). *Aging, the individual, and society* (9th ed.). Belmont, CA: Cengage.

**Hing, N., Lamont, M., Vitartas, P., & Fink, E.** (2015). Sports bettors' responses to sports-embedded gambling promotions: Implications for compulsive consumption. *Journal of Business Research, 68,* 2057–2066. http://dx.doi.org/10.1016/j.jbusres.2015.03.003

**Hirsh-Pasek, K., Adamson, L., Bakeman, R., Golinkoff, R. M., Pace, A., Yust, P., & Suma, K.** (2015). The contribution of early communication to low-income children's language success. *Psychological Science, 26,* 1071–1083.

**Hirst, W., Phelps, E. A., Meksin, R., Vaidya, C. J., Johnson, M. K., Mitchell, K. J., . . . Olsson, A.** (2015). A ten-year follow-up of a study of memory for the attack of September 11, 2001: Flashbulb memories and memories for flashbulb events. *Journal of Experimental Psychology: General, 144,* 604–623. http://dx.doi.org/10.1037/xge0000055

Hively, K., & El-Alayli, A. (2014). "You throw like a girl": The effect of stereotype threat on women's athletic performance and gender stereotypes. *Psychology of Sport and Exercise, 15,* 48–55. http://dx.doi.org/10.1016/j.psychsport.2013.09.001

Ho, M., & O'Donohoe, S. (2014). Volunteer stereotypes, stigma, and relational identity projects. *European Journal of Marketing, 48,* 854–877. http://dx.doi.org/10.1108/EJM-11-2011-0637

Hobbs, W. R., Burke, M., Christakis, N. A., & Fowler, J. H. (2016). Online social integration is associated with reduced mortality risk. *Proceedings of the National Academy of Sciences of the United States of America, 113*(46), 12980–12984. http://dx.doi.org/10.1073/pnas.1605554113

Hobson, J. A. (1999). *Dreaming as delirium: How the brain goes out of its mind.* Cambridge, MA: MIT Press.

Hobson, J. A. (2005). In bed with Mark Solms? What a nightmare! A reply to Domhoff. *Dreaming, 15,* 21–29.

Hobson, J. A. (2015). Dreams and consciousness: Response to Colace and Boag. *Contemporary Psychoanalysis, 51*(1), 126–131. http://dx.doi.org/10.1080/00107530.2014.958048

Hobson, J. A., & McCarley, R. W. (1977). The brain as a dream state generator: An activation-synthesis hypothesis of the dream process. *American Journal of Psychiatry, 134,* 1335–1348.

Hobson, J. A., Sangsanguan, S., Arantes, H., & Kahn, D. (2011). Dream logic—The inferential reasoning paradigm. *Dreaming, 21,* 1–15.

Hoeschele, M., & Fitch, W. T. (2016). Phonological perception by birds: Budgerigars can perceive lexical stress. *Animal Cognition, 19,* 643–654. http://dx.doi.org/10.1007/s10071-016-0968-3

Hofman, M. A. (2015). Evolution of the human brain: From matter to mind. In S. Goldstein, D. Princiotta, & J. A. Naglieri (Eds.), *Handbook of intelligence: Evolutionary theory, historical perspective, and current concepts* (pp. 65–82). New York, NY: Springer. http://dx.doi.org/10.1007/978-1-4939-1562-0

Hofmann, K., Lamberz, C., Piotrowitz, K., Offermann, N., But, D., Scheller, A., . . . Kuerschner, L. (2017a). Tanycytes and a differential fatty acid metabolism in the hypothalamus. *Glia, 65,* 231–249. http://dx.doi.org/10.1002/glia.23088

Hofmann, T., Elbelt, U., Haas, V., Ahnis, A., Klapp, B. F., Rose, M., & Stengel, A. (2017b). Plasma kisspeptin and ghrelin levels are independently correlated with physical activity in patients with anorexia nervosa. *Appetite, 108,* 141–150. http://dx.doi.org/10.1016/j.appet.2016.09.032

Hofstede, G. J., Dignum, F., Prada, R., Student, J., & Vanhée, L. (2015). Gender differences: The role of nature, nurture, social identity and self-organization. In *Multi-Agent-Based Simulation XV* (pp. 72–87). Cham, CH: Springer International Publishing.

Hogan, T. P. (2013). *Psychological testing: A practical introduction* (3rd ed.). Hoboken, NJ: Wiley.

Holder, S. M., Warren, C., Rogers, K., Griffeth, B., Peterson, E., Blackhurst, D., & Ochonma, C. (2017). Involuntary processes: Knowledge base of health care professionals in a tertiary medical center in upstate South Carolina. *Community Mental Health Journal.* No Pagination Specified. http://dx.doi.org/10.1007/s10597-017-0115-x

Hole, J., Hirsch, M., Ball, E., & Meads, C. (2015). Music as an aid for postoperative recovery in adults: A systematic review and meta-analysis. *The Lancet, 386,* 1659–1671. http://dx.doi.org/10.1016/S0140-6736(15)60169-6

Holekamp, K. E., & Strauss, E. D. (2016). Aggression and dominance: An interdisciplinary overview. *Current Opinion in Behavioral Sciences, 12,* 44–51. http://dx.doi.org/10.1016/j.cobeha.2016.08.005

Holland, J. L. (1985). *Making vocational choices: A theory of vocational personalities and work environments* (2nd ed.). Englewood Cliffs, NJ: Prentice Hall.

Holland, J. L. (1994). *Self-directed search form R.* Lutz, FL: Psychological Assessment Resources.

Holman, E. A., Garfin, D. R., & Silver, R. C. (2014). Media's role in broadcasting acute stress following Boston Marathon bombings. *Proceedings of the National Academy of Sciences of the United States of America, 111,* 93–98. http://dx.doi.org/10.1073/pnas.1316265110

Holmes, L. (2016, December 29). A reminder that Carrie Fisher was an O.G. Mental Health Hero. *The Huffington Post.* Retrieved from http://www.huffingtonpost.com/entry/carrie-fisher-mental-health-princess-leia_us_562795dbe4b0bce347031e34

Holmes, R. M., Romeo, L., Ciraola, S., & Grushko, M. (2015). The relationship between creativity, social play, and children's language abilities. *Early Child Development and Care, 185,* 1180–1197. http://dx.doi.org/10.1080/03004430.2014.983916

Holmes, T. H., & Rahe, R. H. (1967). The Social Readjustment Rating Scale. *Journal of Psychosomatic Research, 11,* 213–218. http://dx.doi.org/10.1016/0022-3999(67)90010-4

Holshausen, K., Bowie, C. R., & Harkness, K. L. (2016). The relation of childhood maltreatment to psychotic symptoms in adolescents and young adults with depression. *Journal of Clinical Child and Adolescent Psychology, 45,* 241–247. http://dx.doi.org/10.1080/15374416.2014.952010

Homan, K. J. (2016). Self-compassion and psychological well-being in older adults. *Journal of Adult Development, 23,* 111–119. http://dx.doi.org/10.1007/s10804-016-9227-8

Hong, C., Chen, Z., & Li, C. (2017). "Liking" and being "liked": How are personality traits and demographics associated with giving and receiving "likes" on Facebook? *Computers in Human Behavior, 68,* 292–299. http://dx.doi.org/10.1016/j.chb.2016.11.048

Hong, F.-Y., & Chiu, S.-L. (2016). Factors influencing Facebook usage and Facebook addictive tendency in university students: The role of online psychological and Facebook usage motivation. *Stress and Health, 32,* 117–127. http://dx.doi.org/10.1002/smi.2585

Hong, S. L., Estrada-Sánchez, A. M., Barton, S. J., & Rebec, G. V. (2016). Early exposure to dynamic environments alters patterns of motor exploration throughout the lifespan. *Behavioural Brain Research, 302,* 81–87. http://dx.doi.org/10.1016/j.bbr.2016.01.007

Hooghe, A., Rosenblatt, P. C., & Rober, P. (2017). "We hardly ever talk about it": Emotional responsive attunement in couples after a child's death. *Family Process.* No Pagination Specified. http://dx.doi.org/10.1111/famp.12274

Hope, A. E., & Sugarman, L. I. (2015). Orienting hypnosis. *American Journal of Clinical Hypnosis, 57,* 212–229. http://dx.doi.org/10.1080/00029157.2014.976787

Hopthrow, T., Hooper, N., Mahmood, L., Meier, B. P., & Weger, U. (2017). Mindfulness reduces the correspondence bias. *The Quarterly Journal of Experimental Psychology, 70*(3), 351–360. http://dx.doi.org/10.1080/17470218.2016.1149498

Hori, H., Koga, N., Hidese, S., Nagashima, A., Kim, Y., Higuchi, T., & Kunugi, H. (2016). 24-h activity rhythm and sleep in depressed outpatients. *Journal of Psychiatric Research, 77,* 27–34. http://dx.doi.org/10.1016/j.jpsychires.2016.02.022

Horigian, V. E., & Szapocznik, J. (2015). Brief strategic family therapy: Thirty-five years of interplay among theory, research, and practice in adolescent behavior problems. In L. M. Scheier (Ed.), *Handbook of adolescent drug use prevention: Research, intervention strategies, and practice* (pp. 249–265). Washington, DC: American Psychological Association. http://dx.doi.org/10.1037/14550-015

Horney, K. (1939). *New ways in psychoanalysis.* New York: NY: International Universities Press.

Horney, K. (1945). *Our inner conflicts: A constructive theory of neurosis.* New York: NY: Norton.

Horta, B. L., de Mola, C. L., & Victora, C. G. (2015). Breastfeeding and intelligence: A systematic review and meta-analysis. *Acta Paediatrica, 104,* 14–19. http://dx.doi.org/10.1111/apa.13139

Horwath, E., & Gould, F. (2011). Epidemiology of anxiety disorders. In M. Tsuang, M. Tohen, & P. Jones (Eds.), *Textbook in psychiatric epidemiology* (3rd ed., pp. 311–328). Hoboken, NJ: Wiley.

Hosie, J., Gilbert, F., Simpson, K., & Daffern, M. (2014). An examination of the relationship between personality and aggression using the general aggression and five factor models. *Aggressive Behavior, 40,* 189–196. http://dx.doi.org/10.1002/ab.21510

Hosokawa, R., & Katsura, T. (2017). Marital relationship, parenting practices, and social skills development in preschool children. *Child and Adolescent Psychiatry and Mental Health, 11,* Article 2. http://dx.doi.org/10.1186/s13034-016-0139-y

How Many Paintings. (2017). How many paintings did Van Gogh sell during his lifetime? *Reference.* Retrieved January 22, 2017 from https://www.reference.com/art-literature/many-paintings-did-van-gogh-sell-during-his-lifetime-de765430bad3cf19

Howard, M. E., Jackson, M. L., Berlowitz, D., O'Donoghue, F., Swann, P., Westlake, J., . . . Pierce, R. J. (2014). Specific sleepiness symptoms are indicators of performance impairment during sleep deprivation. *Accident Analysis and Prevention, 62,* 1–8. http://dx.doi.org/10.1016/j.aap.2013.09.003

Howe, M. L., & Knott, L. M. (2015). The fallibility of memory in judicial processes: Lessons from the past and their modern consequences. *Memory, 23,* 633–656. http://dx.doi.org/10.1080/09658211.2015.1010709

Howell, J. A., McEvoy, P. M., Grafton, B., Macleod, C., Kane, R. T., Anderson, R. A., & Egan, S. J. (2016). Selective attention in perfectionism: Dissociating valence from perfectionism-relevance. *Journal of Behavior Therapy and Experimental Psychiatry, 51,* 100–108. http://dx.doi.org/10.1016/j.jbtep.2016.01.004

**Howes, M. B., & O'Shea, G.** (2014). *Human memory: A constructivist view.* San Diego, CA: Elsevier.

**Howes, O. D., McCutcheon, R., Owen, M. J., & Murray, R. M.** (2017). The role of genes, stress, and dopamine in the development of schizophrenia. *Biological Psychiatry, l81*(1), 9–20. http://dx.doi.org/10.1016/j.biopsych.2016.07.014

**Howes, O., McCutcheon, R., & Stone, J.** (2015). Glutamate and dopamine in schizophrenia: An update for the 21st century. *Journal of Psychopharmacology, 29,* 97–115. http://dx.doi.org/10.1177/0269881114563634

**Hsu, S.** (2016). Motivation and emotions: What guides our behavior? In C. Tien-Lun Sun (Ed.), *Psychology in Asia: An introduction* (pp. 211–249). Boston, MA: Cengage Learning.

**Hsu, S.** (2016). Psychological disorders. In C. Tien-Lun Sun (Ed.), *Psychology in Asia: An introduction* (pp. 349–394). Boston, MA: Cengage.

**Hsu, T. M., Suarez, A. N., & Kanoski, S. E.** (2016). Ghrelin: A link between memory and ingestive behavior. *Physiology & Behavior, 162,* 10–17. http://dx.doi.org/10.1016/j.physbeh.2016.03.039

**Hu, C. S., Wang, Q., Han, T., Weare, E., & Fu, G.** (2017). Differential emotion attribution to neutral faces of own and other races. *Cognition and Emotion, 31*(2), 360–368. http://dx.doi.org/10.1080/02699931.2015.1092419

**Hu, X., Antony, J. W., Creery, J. D., Vargas, I. M., Bodenhausen, G. V., & Paller, K. A.** (2015). Unlearning implicit social biases during sleep. *Science, 348,* 1013–1015. http://dx.doi.org/10.1126/science.aaa3841

**Huang, W., & Zhou, Y.** (2013). Effects of education on cognition at older ages: Evidence from China's Great Famine. *Social Science & Medicine, 98,* 54–62. http://dx.doi.org/10.1016/j.socscimed.2013.08.021

**Huang, Y., Xu, S., Hua, J., Zhu, D., Liu, C., Hu, Y., . . . Xu, D.** (2015). Association between job strain and risk of incident stroke: A meta-analysis. *Neurology, 85,* 1648–1654. http://dx.doi.org/10.1212/WNL.0000000000002098

**Huber, A., Lui, F., Duzzi, D., Pagnoni, G., & Porro, C. A.** (2014). Structural and functional cerebral correlates of hypnotic suggestibility. *PLoS ONE, 9,* 1–6. http://dx.doi.org/10.1371/journal.pone.0093187

**Huber, D., & Klug, G.** (2016). Münchner Psychotherapiestudie./Munich psychotherapy study. *Psychotherapeut, 61*(6), 462–467. http://dx.doi.org/10.1007/s00278-016-0139-7

**Hudson, H. M., Gallant-Shean, M. B., & Hirsch, A. R.** (2015). Chemesthesis, thermogenesis, and nutrition. In A. Hirsch (Ed.), *Nutrition and sensation* (pp. 175–192). Boca Raton, FL: Taylor & Francis.

**Hudson, N. W., & Fraley, R. C.** (2015). Volitional personality trait change: Can people choose to change their personality traits? *Journal of Personality and Social Psychology, 109,* 490–507.

**Hughes, J. M., Alo, J., Krieger, K., & O'Leary, L. M.** (2016). Emergence of internal and external motivations to respond without prejudice in White children. *Group Processes & Intergroup Relations, 19,* 202–216. http://dx.doi.org/10.1177/1368430215603457

**Hughes, S., Barnes-Holmes, D., & Smyth, S.** (2017). Implicit cross-community biases revisited: Evidence for ingroup favoritism in the absence of outgroup derogation in Northern Ireland. *The Psychological Record, 67*(1), 97–107. http://dx.doi.org/10.1007/s40732-016-0210-3

**Hull, C.** (1952). *A behavior system.* New Haven, CT: Yale University Press.

**Humes, K., & Hogan, H.** (2015). Do current race and ethnicity concepts reflect a changing America? In R. Bangs & L. E. Davis (Eds.), *Race and social problems: Restructuring inequality* (pp. 15–38). New York, NY: Springer. http://dx.doi.org/10.1007/978-1-4939-0863-9_2

**Humphrey, R. H., & Adams, L. L.** (2017). Heroic empathy: The heart of leadership. In S. T. Allison, G. R. Goethals, & R. M. Kramer (Eds.), *Handbook of heroism and heroic leadership* (pp. 459–475). New York, NY: Routledge/Taylor & Francis Group.

**Hundt, N. E., Barrera, T. L., Arney, J., & Stanley, M. A.** (2017). "It's worth it in the end": Veterans' experiences in prolonged exposure and cognitive processing therapy. *Cognitive and Behavioral Practice, 24*(1), 50–57. http://dx.doi.org/10.1016/j.cbpra.2016.02.003

**Hundt, N. E., Calleo, J. S., Williams, W., & Cully, J. A.** (2016). Does using cognitive-behavioural therapy skills predict improvements in depression? *Psychology and Psychotherapy: Theory, Research, and Practice, 89,* 235–238. http://dx.doi.org/10.1111/papt.12065

**Hunsley, J., Lee, C. M., Wood, J. M., & Taylor, W.** (2015). Controversial and questionable assessment techniques. In S. O. Lilienfeld, S. J. Gould, & J. M. Lohr (Eds.), *Science and pseudoscience in clinical psychology* (2nd ed., pp. 42–82). New York: NY: Guilford.

**Hunt, E., Bornovalova, M. A., & Patrick, C. J.** (2015). Genetic and environmental overlap between borderline personality disorder traits and psychopathy: Evidence for promotive effects of factor 2 and protective effects of factor 1. *Psychological Medicine, 45,* 1471–1481. http://dx.doi.org/10.1017/S003329171400260

**Huntjens, R. J. C., Wessel, I., Ostafin, B. D., Boelen, P. A., Behrens, F., & van Minnen, A.** (2016). Trauma-related self-defining memories and future goals in Dissociative Identity Disorder. *Behaviour Research and Therapy, 87,* 216–224. http://dx.doi.org/10.1016/j.brat.2016.10.002

**Hunt, P. S., & Barnet, R. C.** (2016). Adolescent and adult rats differ in the amnesic effects of acute ethanol in two hippocampus-dependent tasks: Trace and contextual fear conditioning. *Behavioural Brain Research, 298*(Part A), 78–87. http://dx.doi.org/10.1016/j.bbr.2015.06.046

**Husain, M.** (2013, October 7). Malala: The girl who was shot for going to school. *BBC News.* Retrieved from http://www.bbc.com/news/magazine-24379018

**Hussain, D., Shams, W. M., & Brake, W. G.** (2014). Estrogen and memory system bias in females across the lifespan. *Translational Neuroscience, 5,* 35–50. http://dx.doi.org/10.2478/s13380-014-0209-7

**Hutchins, T. L., & Prelock, P. A.** (2015). Beyond the theory of mind hypothesis: Using a causal model to understand the nature and treatment of multiple deficits in autism spectrum disorder. In R. H. Bahr & E. R. Silliman (Eds), *Routledge handbook of communication disorders* (pp. 247–257). New York, NY: Routledge/Taylor & Francis Group.

**Hutteman, R., Nestler, S., Wagner, J., Egloff, B., & Back, M. D.** (2015). Wherever I may roam: Processes of self-esteem development from adolescence to emerging adulthood in the context of international student exchange. *Journal of Personality and Social Psychology, 108,* 767–783.

**Hutton, J. S., Horowitz-Kraus, T., Mendelsohn, A. L., DeWitt, T., Holland, S. K., & the C-MIND Authorship Consortium.** (2015). Home reading environment and brain activation in preschool children listening to stories. *Pediatrics, 136,* 466–478. http://dx.doi.org/10.1542/peds.2015-0359

**Hwang, H. C., & Matsumoto, D.** (2016). Facial expressions. In D. Matsumoto, H. C. Hwang, & M. G. Frank (Eds.), *APA handbook of nonverbal communication* (pp. 257–287). Washington, DC: American Psychological Association. http://dx.doi.org/10.1037/14669-010

**Hwang, H., & Matsumoto, D.** (2015). Evidence for the universality of facial expressions of emotion. In M. K. Mandal & A. Awasthi (Eds.), *Understanding facial expressions in communication: Cross-cultural and multidisciplinary perspectives* (pp. 41–56). New York, NY: Springer. http://dx.doi.org/10.1007/978-81-322-1934-7_3

**Hyde, J. S.** (2014). Gender similarities and differences. *Annual Review of Psychology, 65,* 373–398. http://dx.doi.org/10.1146/annurev-psych-010213-115057

**Hyde, J. S.** (2016). Sex and cognition: gender and cognitive functions. *Current Opinion in Neurobiology, 38,* 53–56. http://dx.doi.org/10.1016/j.conb.2016.02.007

**Hyman, R.** (1981). Cold reading: How to convince strangers that you know all about them. In K. Fraizer (Ed.), *Paranormal borderlands of science* (pp. 232–244). Buffalo, NY: Prometheus.

**Hyman, R.** (1996). The evidence for psychic functioning: Claims vs. reality. *Skeptical Inquirer, 20,* 24–26.

**Iachini, T., Coello, Y., Frassinetti, F., Senese, V. P., Galante, F., & Ruggiero, G.** (2016). Peripersonal and interpersonal space in virtual and real environments: Effects of gender and age. *Journal of Environmental Psychology, 45,* 154–164. http://dx.doi.org/10.1016/j.jenvp.2016.01.004

**Iakoubov, L., Mossakowska, M., Szwed, M., & Puzianowska-Kuznicka, M.** (2015). A common copy number variation polymorphism in the CNTNAP2 gene: Sexual dimorphism in association with healthy aging and disease. *Gerontology, 61,* 24–31. http://dx.doi.org/10.1159/000363320

**Iglesias, A., & Iglesias, A.** (2014). Hypnosis aided fixed role therapy for social phobia: A case report. *American Journal of Clinical Hypnosis, 56,* 405–412. http://dx.doi.org/10.1080/00029157.2013.808166

**Iglesias, C., Sáiz, P. A., García-Portilla, P., & Bobes, J.** (2016). Antipsychotics. In P. Courtet (Ed.), *Understanding suicide: From diagnosis to personalized treatment* (pp. 313–327). Cham, CH: Springer International Publishing.

**Iheanacho, T., Kapadia, D., Ezeanolue, C. O., Osuji, A. A., Ogidi, A. G., Ike, . . . Ezeanolue, E. E.** (2016). Attitudes and beliefs about mental illness among church-based lay health workers: Experience from a prevention of mother-to-child HIV transmission trial in Nigeria. *International Journal of Culture and Mental Health, 9*(1), 1–13. http://dx.doi.org/10.1080/17542863.2015.1074260

**Iliff, J. J., Wang, M., Liao, Y., Plogg, B. A., Peng, W., Gundersen, G. A., . . . Nedergaard, M.** (2012). A paravascular pathway facilitates CSF flow through the brain parenchyma and the clearance of interstitial solutes, including amyloid β. *Science Translational Medicine, 4,* 147ra111. http://dx.doi.org/10.1126/scitranslmed.3003748

**Innocence Project.** (2016). Eyewitness misidentification. Retrieved from http://www.innocenceproject.org/causes/eyewitness-misidentification/

**Institute for Laboratory Animal Research** (ILAR). (2009). Retrieved from http://dels.nas.edu/ilar_n/ilarhome/

**Isacco, A. J., & Wade, J. C.** (2017). A review of selected theoretical perspectives and research in the psychology of men and masculinities. In R. F. Levant & Y. J. Wong (Eds.), *The psychology of men and masculinities* (pp. 139–168). Washington, DC: American Psychological Association. http://dx.doi.org/10.1037/0000023-006

**Iselin, A. -M. R., Mcvey, A. A., & Ehatt, C. M.** (2015). Externalizing behaviors and attribution biases. In T. P. Beauchaine & S. P. Hinshaw (Eds.), *The Oxford handbook of externalizing spectrum disorders* (pp. 347–359). New York, NY: Oxford University Press. http://dx.doi.org/10.1093/oxfordhb/9780199324675.013.12

**Israel, S., Moffitt, T. E., Belsky, D. W., Hancox, R. J., Poulton, R., Roberts, B., . . . Caspi, A.** (2014). Translating personality psychology to help personalize preventive medicine for young adult patients. *Journal of Personality and Social Psychology, 106,* 484–498. http://dx.doi.org/10.1037/a0035687

**Israel-Cohen, Y., & Kaplan, O.** (2015). Traumatic stress during population-wide exposure to trauma in Israel: Gender as a moderator of the effects of marital status and social support. *Stress and Health, 32,* 636–640. http://dx.doi.org/10.1002/smi.2647

**Itoh, K., & Hikasa, M.** (2014). Focusing and Naikan, a uniquely Japanese way of therapy. In G. Madison (Ed.), *Emerging practice in focusing-oriented psychotherapy: Innovative theory and applications* (pp. 112–125). London, UK: Jessica Kingsley.

**Ivanenko, A., & Johnson, K. P.** (2016). Sleep disorders. In M. K. Dulcan (Ed.), *Dulcan's textbook of child and adolescent psychiatry* (2nd ed., pp. 495–519). Arlington, VA: American Psychiatric Publishing. http://dx.doi.org/10.1176/appi.books.9781615370306.md23

**Iwanicki, S., & Lehmann, J.** (2015). Behavioral and trait rating assessments of personality in common marmosets (*Callithrix jacchus*). *Journal of Comparative Psychology, 129,* 205–217. http://dx.doi.org/10.1037/a0039318

**Izadpanah, S., Schumacher, M., & Barnow, S.** (2017). Anger rumination mediates the relationship between reinforcement sensitivity and psychopathology: Results of a 5-year longitudinal study. *Personality and Individual Differences, 110,* 49–54. http://dx.doi.org/10.1016/j.paid.2017.01.023

**Jack, R. E., Sun, W., Delis, I., Garrod, O. G. B., & Schyns, P. G.** (2016). Four not six: Revealing culturally common facial expressions of emotion. *Journal of Experimental Psychology: General, 145,* 708–730. http://dx.doi.org/10.1037/xge0000162

**Jackson, S.** (2016). *Research methods and statistics: A critical thinking approach* (5th ed.).Boston, MA: Cengage.

**Jackson, S., & Vares, T.** (2015). 'Perfect skin', 'pretty skinny': Girls' embodied identities and post-feminist popular culture. *Journal of Gender Studies, 24*(3), 347–360. http://dx.doi.org/10.1080/09589236.2013.841573

**Jacob, K. S.** (2014). DSM-5 and culture: The need to move towards a shared model of care within a more equal patient–physician partnership. *Asian Journal of Psychiatry, 7,* 89–91. http://dx.doi.org/10.1016/j.ajp.2013.11.012

**Jacobs Bao, K., & Lyubomirsky, S.** (2013). Making it last: Combating hedonic adaptation in romantic relationships. *The Journal of Positive Psychology, 8,* 196–206.

**Jacobs, R. H., Orr, J. L., Gowins, J. R., Forbes, E. E., & Langenecker, S. A.** (2015). Biomarkers of intergenerational risk for depression: A review of mechanisms in longitudinal high-risk (LHR) studies. *Journal of Affective Disorders, 175,* 494–506. http://dx.doi.org/10.1016/j.jad.2015.01.038

**Jacques, R.** (2013, September 25). 16 wildly successful people who overcame huge obstacles to get there. *The Huffington Post.* Retrieved from http://www.huffingtonpost.com/2013/09/25/successful-people-obstacles_n_3964459.html

**Jaekel, K. S., & Kortegast, C. A.** (2016). *Community college students.* In W. K. Killam, S. Degges-White, & R. E. Michel (Eds.), *Career counseling interventions: Practice with diverse clients* (pp. 9–15). New York, NY: Springer.

**Jafari-Sabet, M., Khodadadnejad, M. A., Ghoraba, S., & Ataee, R.** (2014). Nitric oxide in the dorsal hippocampal area is involved on muscimol state-dependent memory in the step-down passive avoidance test. *Pharmacology Biochemistry and Behavior, 117,* 137–143. http://dx.doi.org/10.1016/j.pbb.2013.12.010

**Jain, A., Marshall, J., Buikema, A., Bancroft, T., Kelly, J. P., & Newschaffer, C. J.** (2015). Autism occurrence by MMR vaccine status among US children with older siblings with and without autism. *Journal of the American Medical Association, 313*(15), 1534–1540. http://dx.doi.org/10.1001/jama.2015.3077

**James, S. D.** (2008, May 7). Wild child speechless after tortured life. *ABC News.* Retrieved from http://abcnews.go.com/Health/story?id54864490&page51

**James, W.** (1890). *The principles of psychology* (Vol. 2). New York, NY: Holt.

**Jandt, F.** (2016). *An introduction to intercultural communication: Identities in a global community* (8th ed.). Thousand Oaks, CA: Sage.

**Jang, Y., Koo, J. H., Kwon, I., Kang, E. B., Um, H. S., Soya, H., . . . Cho, J. Y.** (2017). Neuroprotective effects of endurance exercise against neuroinflammation in MPTP-induced Parkinson's disease mice. *Brain Research, 1655,* 186–193. http://dx.doi.org/10.1016/j.brainres.2016.10.029

**Jani, S., Johnson, R. S., Banu, S., & Shah, P.** (2016). Cross-cultural bias in the diagnosis of borderline personality disorder. *Bulletin of the Menninger Clinic, 80*(2), 146–165. http://dx.doi.org/10.1521/bumc.2016.80.2.146

**Janis, I. L.** (1972). *Victims of groupthink: A psychological study of foreign-policy decisions and fiascoes.* Boston, MA: Houghton Mifflin.

**Jankowiak, W., & Fischer, E.** (1992). Cross-cultural perspective on romantic love. *Ethnology, 31,* 149–155.

**Jankowiak, W. R., Volsche, S. L., & Garcia, J. R.** (2015). Is the romantic–sexual kiss a near human universal? *American Anthropologist, 117,* 535–539. http://dx.doi.org/10.1111/aman.12286

**Jaremka, L. M., Glaser, R., Loving, T. J., Malarkey, W. B., Stowell, J. R., & Kiecolt-Glaser, J. K.** (2013). Attachment anxiety is linked to alterations in cortisol production and cellular immunity. *Psychological Science, 24,* 272–279. http://dx.doi.org/10.1177/0956797612452571

**Jarvis, J.** (2014). Auditory and neuronal fetal environment factors impacting early learning development. *International Journal of Childbirth Education, 29,* 27–31.

**Jaul, E., Meiron, O., & Menczel, J.** (2016). The effect of pressure ulcers on the survival in patients with advanced dementia and comorbidities. *Experimental Aging Research, 42*(4), 382–389. http://dx.doi.org/10.1080/0361073X.2016.1191863

**Jean-Richard-Dit-Bressel, P., & McNally, G. P.** (2015). The role of the basolateral amygdala in punishment. *Learning & Memory, 22,* 128–137. http://dx.doi.org/10.1101/lm.035907.114

**Jee, C.** (2017, April 11). Six times AI has beaten humans in competitions: AlphaGo, Chinook, IBM Watson, and more: Computers vs humans. *Techworld.* Retrieved from http://www.techworld.com/picture-gallery/big-data/six-times-ai-has-beaten-humans-in-competitions-3636755/

**Jeffreys, S.** (2015). *Beauty and misogyny: Harmful cultural practices in the West, 2nd ed.* New York, NY: Routledge/Taylor & Francis Group.

**Jennifer Lawrence Biography.** (n.d.). Jennifer Lawrence Biography. *Biography.com.* Retrieved March 8, 2017 from http://www.biography.com/people/jennifer-lawrence-20939797

**Jennifer Lawrence.** (n.d.). Jennifer Lawrence. *Wikipedia.* Retrieved March 5, 2017 from https://en.wikipedia.org/wiki/Jennifer_Lawrence

**Jensen, M. P., Barber, J., Romano, J. M., Hanley, M. A., Raichle, K. A., Molton, I. R., . . . Patterson, D. R.** (2009). Effects of self-hypnosis training and EMG biofeedback relaxation training on chronic pain in persons with spinal-cord injury. *International Journal of Clinical and Experimental Hypnosis, 57*(3), 239–268. http://dx.doi.org/10.1080/00207140902881007

**Jessen, S., & Grossmann, T.** (2015). Neural signatures of conscious and unconscious emotional face processing in human infants. *Cortex, 64,* 260–270. http://dx.doi.org/10.1016/j.cortex.2014.11.007

**Ji, G., Yan, L., Liu, W., Qu, J., & Gu, A.** (2013). OGG1 Ser326Cys polymorphism interacts with cigarette smoking to increase oxidative DNA damage in human sperm and the risk of male infertility. *Toxicology Letters, 218,* 144–149. http://dx.doi.org/10.1016/j.toxlet.2013.01.017

**Jiang, W., Liao, J., Liu, H., Huang, R., Li, Y., & Wang, W.** (2015). [Brain structure analysis for patients with antisocial personality disorder by MRI]. Zhong nan da xue xue bao. Yi xue ban=Journal of Central South University. *Medical Sciences, 40,* 123–128. http://dx.doi.org/10.11817/j.issn.1672-7347.2015.02.002

**Jiang, W., Liu, H., Zeng, L., Liao, J., Shen, H., Luo, A., . . . Wang, W.** (2015). Decoding the processing of lying using functional connectivity MRI. *Behavioral and Brain Functions: BBF, 11*:1. http://dx.doi.org/10.1186/s12993-014-0046-4

**Jiang, W., Zhao, F., Guderley, N., & Manchaiah, V.** (2016). Daily music exposure dose and hearing problems using personal listening devices in adolescents and young adults: A systematic review. *International Journal of Audiology, 55,* 197–205. http://dx.doi.org/10.3109/14992027.2015.1122237

**Jiménez-Fernández, S., Gurpegui, M., Díaz-Atienza, F., Pérez-Costillas, L., Gerstenberg, M., & Correll, C. U.** (2015). Oxidative stress and antioxidant parameters in patients with major depressive disorder compared to healthy controls before and after antidepressant treatment: Results from a meta-analysis. *Journal of Clinical Psychiatry, 76*(12), 1658–1667. http://dx.doi.org/10.4088/JCP.14r09179

Jobin, J., Wrosch, C., & Scheier, M. F. (2014). Associations between dispositional optimism and diurnal cortisol in a community sample: When stress is perceived as higher than normal. *Health Psychology, 33,* 382–391. http://dx.doi.org/10.1037/a0032736.

Joeng, J. R., Turner, S. L., & Lee, K. H. (2013). South Korean college students' Holland Types and career compromise processes. *The Career Development Quarterly, 61,* 64–73. http://dx.doi.org/10.1002/j.2161-0045.2013.00036.x

Johansen, P. -O., & Krebs, T. S. (2015). Psychedelics not linked to mental health problems or suicidal behavior: A population study. *Journal of Psychopharmacology, 29,* 270–279. http://dx.doi.org/10.1177/0269881114568039

John, N. A., & Dvir-Gvirsman, S. (2015). "I don't like you any more": Facebook unfriending by Israelis during the Israel–Gaza conflict of 2014. *Journal of Communication, 65,* 953–974. http://dx.doi.org/10.1111/jcom.12188

John, P., & Pineño, O. (2015). Biological significance in human causal learning. *Psi Chi Journal of Psychological Research, 20,* 65–72.

Johns, B., & Jones, M. N. (2015). Generating structure from experience: A retrieval-based model of language processing. *Canadian Journal of Experimental Psychology/Revue canadienne de psychologieexperimentale, 69,* 233–251. http://dx.doi.org/10.1037/cep0000053

Johnson-Baker, K. A., Markham, C., Baumler, E., Swain, H., & Emery, S. (2016). Rap music use, perceived peer behavior, and sexual initiation among ethnic minority youth. *Journal of Adolescent Health, 58,* 317–322. http://dx.doi.org/10.1016/j.jadohealth.2015.11.003

Johnston, M. E., Sherman, A., & Grusec, J. E. (2013). Predicting moral outrage and religiosity with an implicit measure of moral identity. *Journal of Research in Personality, 47,* 209–217. http://dx.doi.org/10.1016/j.jrp.2013.01.006

Jones, A., Lankshear, A., & Kelly, D. (2016). Giving voice to quality and safety matters at board level: A qualitative study of the experiences of executive nurses working in England and Wales. *International Journal of Nursing Studies, 59,* 169–176. http://dx.doi.org/10.1016/j.ijnurstu.2016.04.007

Jones, D. A. (2013). The polarizing effect of a partisan workplace. *PS: Political Science and Politics, 46,* 67–73. http://dx.doi.org/10.1017/S1049096512001254

Jones, E. E., & Nisbett, R. E. (1971). *The actor and the observer: Divergent perceptions of the causes of behavior.* Morristown, NJ: General Learning.

Jones, J. D., & Comer, S. D. (2016). The epidemiology of pain and opioid abuse. In A. M. Matthews & J. C. Fellers (Eds.), *Treating comorbid opioid use disorder in chronic pain* (pp. 13–24). Cham, CH: Springer International Publishing. http://dx.doi.org/10.1007/978-3-319-29863-4_2

Jones, S. G., & Benca, R. M. (2013). Sleep and biological rhythms. In R. J. Nelson, S. J. Y. Mizumori, & I. B. Weiner (Eds.), *Handbook of psychology, Vol. 3. Behavioral neuroscience* (2nd ed., pp. 365–394). Hoboken, NJ: Wiley.

Joo, Y. J., Lim, K. Y., & Kim, N. H. (2016). The effects of secondary teachers' technostress on the intention to use technology in South Korea. *Computers & Education, 95,* 114–122. http://dx.doi.org/10.1016/j.compedu.2015.12.004

Jordan, C., Reid, A. M., Guzick, A. G., Simmons, J., & Sulkowski, M. L. (2017). When exposures go right: Effective exposure-based treatment for obsessive–compulsive disorder. *Journal of Contemporary Psychotherapy, 47*(1), 31–39. http://dx.doi.org/10.1007/s10879-016-9339-2

Jouffre, S. (2015). Power modulates over-reliance on false cardiac arousal when judging target attractiveness: The powerful are more centered on their own false arousal than the powerless. *Personality and Social Psychology Bulletin, 41,* 116–126. http://dx.doi.org/10.1177/0146167214559718

Jouffre, S., & Croizet, J.-C. (2016). Empowering and legitimizing the fundamental attribution error: Power and legitimization exacerbate the translation of role-constrained behaviors into ability differences. *European Journal of Social Psychology, 46*(5), 621–631. http://dx.doi.org/10.1002/ejsp.2191

Jouhanneau, M., Cornilleau, F., & Keller, M. (2014). Peripubertal exposure to male odors influences female puberty and adult expression of male-directed odor preference in mice. *Hormones and Behavior, 65,* 128–133. http://dx.doi.org/10.1016/j.yhbeh.2013.12.006

Jowett Hirst, E. S., Dozier, C. L., & Payne, S. W. (2016). Efficacy of and preference for reinforcement and response cost in token economies. *Journal of Applied Behavior Analysis, 49,* 329–345. http://dx.doi.org/10.1002/jaba.294

Jung, C. G. (1933). *Modern man in search of a soul.* New York: NY: Harcourt Brace.

Jung, C. G. (1936/1969). The concept of collective unconscious. In *Collected Works* (Vol. 9, Part 1). Princeton, NJ: Princeton University Press. (Original work published 1936).

Jung, R. E., & Haier, R. J. (2007). The Parieto-Frontal Integration Theory (P-FIT) of intelligence: Converging neuroimaging evidence. *Behavioral and Brain Sciences, 30,* 135–154. http://dx.doi.org/10.1017/S0140525X07001185

Junger, M., Montoya, L., & Overink, F. -J. (2017). Priming and warnings are not effective to prevent social engineering attacks. *Computers in Human Behavior, 66,* 75–87. http://dx.doi.org/10.1016/j.chb.2016.09.012

Junque, C. (2015). Structural and functional neuroimaging of cognition and emotion in Parkinson's disease. In A. I. Tröster (Ed.), *Clinical neuropsychology and cognitive neurology of Parkinson's disease and other movement disorders* (pp. 148–178). New York, NY: Oxford.

Juslin, P. N., Barradas, G. T, Ovsiannikow, M., Limmo, J., & Thompson, W. F. (2016). Prevalence of emotions, mechanisms, and motives in music listening: A comparison of individualist and collectivist cultures. *Psychomusicology: Music, Mind, and Brain, 26,* 293–326. http://dx.doi.org/10.1037/pmu0000161

Kalish, Y., & Luria, G. (2016). Leadership emergence over time in short-lived groups: Integrating expectations states theory with temporal person-perception and self-serving bias. *Journal of Applied Psychology, 101*(10), 1474–1486. http://dx.doi.org/10.1037/apl0000126

Kalokerinos, E.K., von Hippel, W., Henry, J. D., & Trivers, R. (2014). The aging positivity effect and immune function: Positivity in recall predicts higher CD4 counts and lower CD4 activation. *Psychology and Aging, 29,* 636–641. http://dx.doi.org/10.1037/a0037452

Kaminer, D., & Eagle, G. T. (2017). Interventions for posttraumatic stress disorder: A review of the evidence base. *South African Journal of Psychology, 47*(1), 7–22. http://dx.doi.org/10.1177/0081246316646950

Kammrath, L. K., & Dweck, C. (2006). Voicing conflict: Preferred conflict strategies among incremental and entity theorists. *Personality and Social Psychology Bulletin, 32,* 1497–1508. http://dx.doi.org/10.1177/0146167206291476

Kanazawa, S., & Still, M. C. (2017). Is there really a beauty premium or an ugliness penalty on earnings? *Journal of Business and Psychology.* No Pagination Specified. http://dx.doi.org/10.1007/s10869-017-9489-6

Kanbur, N., & Harrison, A. (2016). Co-occurrence of substance use and eating disorders: An approach to the adolescent patient in the context of family centered care. A literature review. *Substance Use & Misuse, 51,* 853–860. http://dx.doi.org/10.3109/10826084.2016.1155614

Kandler, C., Kornadt, A. E., Hagemeyer, B., & Neyer, F. J. (2015). Patterns and sources of personality development in old age. *Journal of Personality and Social Psychology, 109,* 175–191. http://dx.doi.org/10.1037/pspp0000028

Kapexhiu, K. (2015). Repetition and content implications in advertising wear out: A practitioner's view. *Advances in Social Sciences Research Journal, 2,* 204–209. http://dx. doi:10.14738/assrj.210.1513

Kaplan, R. L., Van Damme, I., Levine, L. J., & Loftus, E. F. (2016). Emotion and false memory. *Emotion Review, 8,* 8–13. http://dx.doi.org/10.1177/1754073915601228

Karakurt, G., & Silver, K. E. (2014). Therapy for childhood sexual abuse survivors using attachment and family systems theory orientations. *The American Journal of Family Therapy, 42,* 79–91. http://dx.doi.org/10.1080/01926187.2013.772872

Karanian, J. M., & Slotnick, S. D. (2015). Memory for shape reactivates the lateral occipital complex. *Brain Research, 1603,* 124–132. http://dx.doi.org/10.1016/j.brainres.2015.01.024

Karasik, L. B., Adolph, K. E., Tamis-LeMonda, C. S., & Bornstein, M. H. (2010). WEIRD walking: Cross-cultural research on motor development. *Behavioral and Brain Sciences, 33,* 95–96. http://dx.doi.org/10.1017/S0140525X10000117

Kasl-Godley, J. E., King, D. A., & Quill, T. E. (2014). Opportunities for psychologists in palliative care: Working with patients and families across the disease continuum. *American Psychologist, 69,* 364–376. http://dx.doi.org/10.1037/a0036735

Kaste, M. (2015, January 2). Trial of polygraph critic renews debate over tests' accuracy. *NPR.* Retrieved from http://www.npr.org/2015/01/02/371925732/trialof-polygraph-critic-renews-debate-over-tests-accuracy

Kastenbaum, R. J. (2012). *Death, society, and human experience* (11th ed.). Upper Saddle River, NJ: Prentice Hall.

Kato, T., & Kanba, S. (2016). Boundless syndromes in modern society: An interconnected world producing novel psychopathology in the 21st century. *Psychiatry and Clinical Neurosciences, 70,* 1–2. http://dx.doi.org/10.1111/pcn.12368

Katz, J. (2017, April 14). You draw it: Just how bad is the drug overdose epidemic. *NYTimes.* Retrieved April 24, 2017 from https://www.nytimes.com/interactive/2017/04/14/upshot/drug-overdose-epidemic-you-draw-it.html

Kaufman, S. B., Kozbelt, A., Silvia, P., Kaufman, J. C., Ramesh, S., & Feist, G. J. (2016). Who finds Bill Gates sexy? Creative mate preferences as a function of cognitive ability, personality, and creative achievement. *The Journal of Creative Behavior, 50,* 294–307. http://dx.doi.org/10.1002/jocb.78

Kaye, L. K., & Pennington, C. R. (2016). "Girls can't play": The effects of stereotype threat on females' gaming performance. *Computers in Human Behavior, 59,* 202–209. http://dx.doi.org/10.1016/j.chb.2016.02.020

Keating, J., Van Boven, L., & Judd, C. M. (2016). Partisan underestimation of the polarizing influence of group discussion. *Journal of Experimental Social Psychology, 65,* 52–58. http://dx.doi.org/10.1016/j.jesp.2016.03.002

Keatley, D. A., Allom, V., & Mullan, B. (2017). The effects of implicit and explicit self-control on self-reported aggression. *Personality and Individual Differences, 107,* 154-158. http://dx.doi.org/10.1016/j.paid.2016.11.046

Keats, D. M. (1982). Cultural bases of concepts of intelligence: A Chinese versus Australian comparison. In P. Sukontasarp, N. Yongsiri, P. Intasuwan, N. Jotiban, & C. Suvannathat (Eds.), *Proceedings of the second Asian workshop on child and adolescent development* (pp. 67–75). Bangkok, TH: Burapasilpa Press.

Keith, N., Unger, J. M., Rauch, A., & Frese, M. (2016). Informal learning and entrepreneurial success: A longitudinal study of deliberate practice among small business owners. *Applied Psychology: An International Review, 65,* 515–540. http://dx.doi.org/10.1111/apps.12054

Keles, S., Idsøe, T., Friborg, O., Sirin, S., & Oppedal, B. (2016). The longitudinal relation between daily hassles and depressive symptoms among unaccompanied refugees in Norway. *Journal of Abnormal Child Psychology,* 1–15. http://dx.doi.org/10.1007/s10802-016-0251-8

Keller, H. A. (1902). *The story of my life.* New York, NY: Grosset & Dunlap.

Keller, S. M., & Tuerk, P. W. (2016). Evidence-based psychotherapy (EBP) non-initiation among veterans offered an EBP for posttraumatic stress disorder. *Psychological Services, 13,* 42–48. http://dx.doi.org/10.1037/ser0000064

Kellner, C. H., Kaicher, D. C., Banerjee, H., Knapp, R. G., Shapiro, R. J., Briggs, M. C., . . . Liebman, L. S. (2015). Depression severity in electroconvulsive therapy (ECT) versus pharmacotherapy trials. *The Journal of ECT, 31,* 31–33. http://dx.doi.org/10.1097/YCT.0000000000000135

Kelly, D. L., Rowland, L. M., Patchan, K. M., Sullivan, K., Earl, A., Raley, H., . . . McMahon, R. P. (2016). Schizophrenia clinical symptom differences in women vs. men with and without a history of childhood physical abuse. *Child and Adolescent Psychiatry and Mental Health, 10,* Article 5. http://dx.doi.org/10.1186/s13034-016-0092-9

Kelly, J. R., McCarty, M. K., & Iannone, N. E. (2013). Interaction in small groups. In J. DeLamater & A. Ward (Eds.), *Handbook of social psychology* (2nd ed., pp. 413–438). New York, NY:

Springer Science + Business Media. http://dx.doi.org/10.1007/978-94-007-6772-0_14

Keltner, D., Kogan, A., Piff, P. K., & Saturn, S. R. (2014). The sociocultural appraisals, values, and emotions (SAVE) framework of prosociality: Core processes from gene to meme. *Annual Review of Psychology, 65,* 425–460. http://dx.doi.org/10.1146/annurevpsych-010213-115054

Kendra, M. S., Weingardt, K. R., Cucciare, M. A., & Timko, C. (2015). Satisfaction with substance use treatment and 12-step groups predicts outcomes. *Addictive Behaviors, 40,* 27–32. http://dx.doi.org/10.1016/j. addbeh.2014.08.003

Kennard, B. D., Emslie, G. J., Mayes, T. L., Nakonezny, P. A., Jones, J. M., Foxwell, A. A., & King, J. (2014). Sequential treatment with fluoxetine and relapse-prevention CBT to improve outcomes in pediatric depression. *The American Journal of Psychiatry, 171,* 1083–1090.

Kenny, D. A., Gomes, S. B., & Kowal, C. (2015). The Intergroup Social Relations Model: ISRM. *Group Dynamics: Theory, Research, and Practice, 19*(3), 152–165.

Kepner, T. (2016, May 23). Tony Gwynn's family sues tobacco industry, seeking recourse over fatal habit. *New York Times.* Retrieved from http://www.nytimes.com/2016/05/24/sports/baseball/tony-gwynn-family-sues-tobacco-altria-death.html

Kern, M. L., Eichstaedt, J. C., Schwartz, H. A., Park, G., Ungar, L. H., Stillwell, D. J., . . . Seligman, M. E. P. (2014). From "Sooo excited!!!" to "So proud": Using language to study development. *Developmental Psychology, 50,* 178–188. http://dx.doi.org/10.1037/a0035048

Kerns, R. D., Sellinger, J., & Goodin, B. R. (2011). Psychological treatment of chronic pain. *Annual Review of Clinical Psychology, 7,* 411–434. http://dx.doi.org/10.1146/annurev-clinpsy-090310-120430

Kerr, D. C. R., Washburn, I. J., Morris, M. K., Lewis, K. A. G., & Tiberio, S. S. (2015). Event-level associations of marijuana and heavy alcohol use with intercourse and condom use. *Journal of Studies on Alcohol and Drugs, 76,* 733–737.

Kershaw, K. N., Lewis, T. T.; Roux, A. V. D., Jenny, N. S., Liu, K., Penedo, F. J., & Carnethon, M. R. (2016). Self-reported experiences of discrimination and inflammation among men and women: The multi-ethnic study of atherosclerosis. *Health Psychology, 35,* 343–350. http://dx.doi.org/10.1037/hea0000331

Ketter, T. A., & Miller, S. (2015). Bipolar and related disorders. In L. W. Roberts & A. K. Louie (Eds.), *Study guide to DSM-5®* (pp. 99–111). Arlington, VA: American Psychiatric Publishing.

Keynan, J. N., Meir-Hasson, Y., Gilam, G., Cohen, A., Jackont, G., Kinreich, S., . . . Hendler, T. (2016). Limbic activity modulation guided by functional magnetic resonance imaging–inspired electroencephalography improves implicit emotion regulation. *Biological Psychiatry, 80*(6), 490–496. http://dx.doi.org/10.1016/j.biopsych.2015.12.024

Khan, M. Z., & He, L. (2015). The role of polyunsaturated fatty acids and GPR40 receptor in brain. *Neuropharmacology, 113,* 639–651. http://dx.doi.org/10.1016/j.neuropharm.2015.05.013

Khan, R., Brewer, G., Kim, S., & Centifanti, L. C. M. (2017). Students, sex, and psychopathy: Borderline and psychopathy personality traits

are differently related to women and men's use of sexual coercion, partner poaching, and promiscuity. *Personality and Individual Differences, 107,* 72–77. http://dx.doi.org/10.1016/j.paid.2016.11.027

Killen, M., & Hart, D. (1999). *Morality in everyday life: Developmental perspectives.* New York: NY. Cambridge University Press.

Killen, M., Hitti, A., & Mulvey, K. L. (2015). Social development and intergroup relations. In M. Mikulincer, P. R. Shaver, J. F. Dovidio, & J. A. Simpson (Eds.), *APA handbook of personality and social psychology, Vol. 2. Group processes* (pp. 177–201). Washington, DC: American Psychological Association. http://dx.doi.org/10.1037/14342-007

Kilpatrick, L. A., Suyenobu, B. Y., Smith, S. R., Bueller, J. A., Goodman, T., Creswell, J. D., . . . Naliboff, B. D. (2011). Impact of mindfulness-based stress reduction training on intrinsic brain connectivity. *NeuroImage, 56,* 290–298.

Kim, A., Kim, Y., Han, K., Jackson, S. E., & Ployhart, R. E. (2017a). Multilevel influences on voluntary workplace green behavior: Individual differences, leader behavior, and coworker advocacy. *Journal of Management, 43*(5), 1335–1358. http://dx.doi.org/10.1177/0149206314547386

Kim, D. S., Burt, A. A., Ranchalis, J. E., Wilmot, B., Smith, J. D., Patterson, K. E., . . . Jarvik, G. P. (2017b). Sequencing of sporadic Attention-Deficit Hyperactivity Disorder (ADHD) identifies novel and potentially pathogenic de novo variants and excludes overlap with genes associated with autism spectrum disorder. *American Journal of Medical Genetics Part B: Neuropsychiatric Genetics, 174*(4), 381–389. http://dx.doi.org/10.1002/ajmg.b.32527

Kim, E. S., Hagan, K. A., Grodstein, F., DeMeo, D. L., De Vivo, I., & Kubzansky, L. D. (2017). Optimism and cause-specific mortality: A prospective cohort study. *American Journal of Epidemiology, 185*(1), 21–29. http://dx.doi.org/https://doi.org/10.1093/aje/kww182

Kim, K., del Carmen Triana, M., Chung, K., & Oh, N. (2016). When do employees cyberloaf? An interactionist perspective examining personality, justice, and empowerment. *Human Resource Management, 55*(6), 1041–1058. http://dx.doi.org/10.1002/hrm.21699

Kim, S., Fernandez, S., & Terrier, L. (2017). Procrastination, personality traits, and academic performance: When active and passive procrastination tell a different story. *Personality and Individual Differences, 108,* 154–157. http://dx.doi.org/10.1016/j.paid.2016.12.021

Kim, Y.-K., Na, K.-S., Myint, A.-M., & Leonard, B. E. (2016). The role of pro-inflammatory cytokines in neuroinflammation, neurogenesis and the neuroendocrine system in major depression. *Progress in Neuro-Psychopharmacology & Biological Psychiatry, 64,* 277–284. http://dx.doi.org/10.1016/j.pnpbp.2015.06.008

Kim, Y., Morath, B., Hu, C., Byrne, L. K., Sutor, S. L., Frye, M. A., & Tye, S. J. (2016). Antidepressant actions of lateral habenula deep brain stimulation differentially correlate with CaMKII/GSK3/AMPK signaling locally and in the infralimbic cortex. *Behavioural Brain Research, 306,* 170–177. http://dx.doi.org/10.1016/j.bbr.2016.02.039

Kimonis, E. R., Goulter, N., Hawes, D. J., Wilbur, R. R., & Groer, M. W. (2017).

Neuroendocrine factors distinguish juvenile psychopathy variants. *Developmental Psychobiology, 59*(2), 161–173. http://dx.doi.org/10.1002/dev.21473

**King, B. M., & Regan, P.** (2015). *Human sexuality today* (8th ed.). Upper Saddle River, NJ: Pearson.

**King, D. B., & DeLongis, A.** (2013). Dyadic coping with stepfamily conflict: Demand and withdraw responses between husbands and wives. *Journal of Social and Personal Relationships, 30,* 198–206.

**Kingston, D. A.** (2016). Hypersexuality disorders and sexual offending. In A. Phenix & H. M. Hoberman (Eds.), *Sexual offending: Predisposing antecedents, assessments and management* (pp. 103–118). New York, NY: Springer Science + Business Media. http://dx.doi.org/10.1007/978-1-4939-2416-5_7

**Kinsey, A. C., Pomeroy, W. B., & Martin, C. E.** (1948). *Sexual behavior in the human male.* Oxford, UK: Saunders.

**Kinsey, A. C., Pomeroy, W. B., Martin, C. E., & Gebhard, P. H.** (1953). *Sexual behavior in the human female.* Oxford, UK: Saunders.

**Kirk, E., Gurney, D., Edwards, R., & Dodimead, C.** (2015). Handmade memories: The robustness of the gestural misinformation effect in children's eyewitness interviews. *Journal of Nonverbal Behavior, 39,* 259–273. http://dx.doi.org/10.1007/s10919-015-0210-z

**Kirkbride, J. B., Jones, P. B., Ullrich, S., & Coid, J. W.** (2014). Social deprivation, inequality, and the neighborhood-level incidence of psychotic syndromes in East London. *Schizophrenia Bulletin, 40,* 169–180. http://dx.doi.org/10.1093/schbul/sbs151

**Kishimoto, T., Chawla, J. M., Hagi, K., Zarate, C. A., Kane, J. M., Bauer, M., & Correll, C. U.** (2016). Single-dose infusion ketamine and non-ketamine n-methyl-d-aspartate receptor antagonists for unipolar and bipolar depression: A meta-analysis of efficacy, safety and time trajectories. *Psychological Medicine, 46,* 1459–1472. http://dx.doi.org/10.1017/S0033291716000064

**Kite, M. E.** (2013). Teaching about race and ethnicity. In D. S. Dunn, R. A. R. Gurung, K. Z. Naufel, & J. H. Wilson (Eds.), *Controversy in the psychology classroom: Using hot topics to foster critical thinking* (pp. 169–184). Washington, DC: American Psychological Association.

**Kivimäki, M., Nyberg, S. J., Batty, G. D., Fransson, E. I., Heikkila, K., Alfredsson, L., . . . Theorell, T.** (2012). Job strain as a risk factor for coronary heart disease: A collaborative metaanalysis of individual participant data. *Lancet, 380,* 1491–1497. http://dx.doi.org/10.1016/S0140-6736(12)60994-5

**Klahr, A. M., & Burt, S. A.** (2014). Elucidating the etiology of individual differences in parenting: A meta-analysis of behavioral genetic research. *Psychological Bulletin, 140,* 544–586. http://dx.doi.org/10.1037/a0034205

**Klapwijk, E. T., Aghajani, M., Colins, O. F., Marijnissen, G. M., Popma, A., Lang, N. D. J., . . . Vermeiren, R. R. J. M.** (2016). Different brain responses during empathy in autism spectrum disorders versus conduct disorder and callous-unemotional traits. *Journal of Child Psychology and Psychiatry, 57,* 737–747. http://dx.doi.org/10.1111/jcpp.12498

**Klauer, S. G., Guo, F., Simons-Morton, B. G., Quirnet, M. C., Lee, S. E., & Dingus, T. A.** (2014). Distracted driving and risk of road crashes among novice and experienced drivers. *The New England Journal of Medicine, 370,* 54–59. http://dx.doi.org/10.1056/NEJMsa1204142

**Kleiman, E. M., Chiara, A. M., Liu, R. T., Jager-Hyman, S. G., Choi, J. Y., & Alloy, L. B.** (2017). Optimism and well-being: A prospective multi-method and multi-dimensional examination of optimism as a resilience factor following the occurrence of stressful life events. *Cognition and Emotion, 31*(2), 269–283. http://dx.doi.org/10.1080/02699931.2015.1108284

**Klein, R. M., Dilchert, S., Ones, D. S., & Dages, K. D.** (2015). Cognitive predictors and age-based adverse impact among business executives. *Journal of Applied Psychology, 100,* 1497–1510. http://dx.doi.org/10.1037/a0038991

**Knapp, S. J., VandeCreek, L. D., & Fingerhut, R.** (2017). *Practical ethics for psychologists.* Washington, DC: American Psychologicaal Association.

**Kneeland, R. E., & Fatemi, S. H.** (2013). Viral infection, inflammation and schizophrenia. *Progress in Neuro-Psychopharmacology & Biological Psychiatry, 42,* 35–48. http://doi.org/10.1016/j.pnpbp.2012.02.001

**Knobloch-Fedders, L. M., Critcheld, K. L., Boisson, T., Woods, N., Bitman, R., & Durbin, C. E. References 5** (2014). Depression, relationship quality, and couples' demand/withdraw and demand/submit sequential interactions. *Journal of Counseling Psychology, 61,* 264–279. http://dx.doi.org/10.1037/a0035241

**Knoll, J. L., & Annas, G. D.** (2016). Mass shootings and mental illness. In L. H. Gold & R. I. Simon (Eds.), *Gun violence and mental illness* (pp. 81–104). Arlington, VA: American Psychiatric Association Publishing.

**Koch, C.** (2015, September 1). Will artificial intelligence surpass our own? *Scientific American.* Retrieved from https://www.scientificamerican.com/article/will-artificial-intelligence-surpass-our-own/

**Kohlberg, L.** (1964). Development of moral character and moral behavior. In L. W. Hoffman & M. L. Hoffman (Eds.), *Review of child development research (Vol. 1).* New York, NY: Sage.

**Kohlberg, L.** (1969). Stage and sequence: The cognitive-developmental approach to socialization. In D. A. Goslin (Ed.), *Handbook of socialization theory and research.* Chicago, IL: Rand McNally.

**Kohlberg, L.** (1984). *The psychology of moral development: Essays on moral development (Vol. 2).* San Francisco, CA: Harper & Row.

**Köhler, W.** (1925). *The mentality of apes.* New York, NY: Harcourt Brace Jovanovich.

**Koike, S., Yamaguchi, S., Ohta, K., Ojio, Y., Watanabe, K.-I., & Ando, S.** (2017). Mental-health-related stigma among Japanese children and their parents and impact of renaming of schizophrenia. *Psychiatry and Clinical Neurosciences, 71*(3), 170–179. http://dx.doi.org/10.1111/pcn.12423

**Kojima, T., Karino, S., Yumoto, M., & Funayama, M.** (2014). A stroke patient with impairment of auditory sensory (echoic) memory. *Neurocase, 20,* 133–143. http://dx.doi.org/10.1080/13554794.2012.732091

**Kokkoris, M. D., & Kühnen, U.** (2013). Choice and dissonance in a European cultural context: The case of Western and Eastern Europeans. *International Journal of Psychology, 48,* 1260–1266. http://dx.doi.org/10.1080/00207594.2013.766746

**Kongthong, N., Minami, T., & Nakauchi, S.** (2014). Gamma oscillations distinguish mere exposure from other likability effects. *Neuropsychologia, 54,* 129–138. http://dx.doi.org/10.1016/j.neuropsychologia.2013.12.021

**Konnikova, M.** (2014, Jan. 14). Goodnight. Sleep clean. *New York Times.* Retrieved from http://www.nytimes.com/2014/01/12/opinion/sunday/goodnight-sleep-clean.html?nl=todaysheadlines&emc=edit_th_20140112&_r=0

**Konnikova, M.** (2016, February 11). How people learn to become resilient. *The New Yorker.* Retrieved from http://www.newyorker.com/science/maria-konnikova/the-secret-formula-for-resilience

**Kono, M.** (2016). Effects of a reinforcement schedule controlling energy of pigeons' pecking response. *The Psychological Record, 1*–7. http://dx.doi.org/10.1007/s40732-016-0217-9

**Koo, C., Chung, N., & Nam, K.** (2015). Assessing the impact of intrinsic and extrinsic motivators on smart green IT device use: Reference group perspectives. *International Journal of Information Management, 35,* 64–79. http://dx.doi.org/10.1016/j.ijinfomgt.2014.10.001

**Koocher, G. P., McMann, M. R., Stout, A. O., & Norcross, J. C.** (2014). Discredited assessment and treatment methods used with children and adolescents: A Delphi Poll. *Journal of Clinical Child & Adolescent Psychology, 25,* 1–8. http://dx.doi.org/10.1080/15374416.2014.895941

**Kornmeier, J., Spitzer, M., & Sosic-Vasic, Z.** (2014). Very similar spacing-effect patterns in very different learning/practice domains. *PLoS ONE, 9,* 1–11. http://dx.doi.org/10.1371/journal.pone.0090656

**Korten, N. C. M., Comijs, H. C., Penninx, B. W. J. H., & Deeg, D. J. H.** (2017). Perceived stress and cognitive function in older adults: Which aspect of perceived stress is important? *International Journal of Geriatric Psychiatry, 32*(4), 439–445. http://dx.doi.org/10.1002/gps.4486

**Kose, S., Steinberg, J. L., Moeller, F. G., Gowin, J. L., Zuniga, E., Kamdar, Z. N., . . . Lane, S. D.** (2015). Neural correlates of impulsive aggressive behavior in subjects with a history of alcohol dependence. *Behavioral Neuroscience, 129,* 183–196. http://dx.doi.org/10.1037/bne0000038.

**Kosinski, M., Stillwell, D., & Graepel, T.** (2013). Private traits and attributes are predictable from digital records of human behavior. *Proceedings of the National Academy of Sciences of the United States of America, 110,* 5802–5805. http://dx.doi.org/10.1073/pnas.1218772110

**Kotowski, A.** (2012). Case study: A young male with auditory hallucinations in paranoid schizophrenia. *International Journal of Nursing Knowledge, 23,* 41–44.

**Kovas, Y., Garon-Carrier, G., Boivin, M., Petrill, S. A., Plomin, R., Malykh, S. B., . . . Vitaro, F.** (2015). Why children differ in motivation to learn: Insights from over 13,000 twins from 6 countries. *Personality and Individual Differences, 80,* 51–63. http://dx.doi.org/10.1016/j.paid.2015.02.006

**Kraft, T. L., & Pressman, S. D.** (2012). Grin and bear it: The influence of manipulated positive facial expression on the stress response. *Psychological Science, 23,* 1372–1378. http://dx.doi.org/10.1177/0956797612445312

**Krahé, B.** (2016). Violent media effects on aggression: A commentary from a cross-cultural perspective. *Analyses of Social Issues and Public Policy (ASAP), 16*(1), 439–442. http://dx.doi.org/10.1111/asap.12107

Kreager, D. A., Staff, J., Gauthier, R., Lefkowitz, E. S., & Feinberg, M. E. (2016). The double standard at sexual debut: Gender, sexual behavior and adolescent peer acceptance. *Sex Roles, 75,* 377–392. http://dx.doi.org/10.1007/s11199-016-0618-x

Kreger Silverman, L. (2013). *Psych 101: Giftedness 101.* New York, NY: Springer.

Kreitler, C. M., & Dyson, K. S. (2016). Cultural frame switching and emotion among Mexican Americans. *Journal of Latinos and Education, 15*(2), 91–96. http://dx.doi.org/10.1080/15348431.2015.1066251

Kreitz, C., Furley, P., Simons, D., & Memmert, D. (2016). Does working memory capacity predict cross-modally induced failures of awareness? *Consciousness and Cognition: An International Journal, 39,* 18–27. http://dx.doi.org/10.1016/j.concog.2015.11.010

Kress, T., Aviles, C., Taylor, C., & Winchell, M. (2011). Individual/collective human needs: (Re)theorizing Maslow using critical, sociocultural, feminist, and indigenous lenses. In C. Malott & B. Porfilio (Eds.), *Critical pedagogy in the twenty-first century: A new generation of scholars* (pp. 135–157). Charlotte, NC: Information Age.

Kring, A. M., Johnson, S. L., Davison, G. C., & Neale, J. M. (2010). *Abnormal psychology* (11th ed.). Hoboken, NJ: Wiley.

Kring, A. M., Johnson, S. L., Davison, G. C., & Neale, J. M. (2014). *Abnormal psychology* (13th ed.). Hoboken, NJ: Wiley.

Krippner, S. (2015). Finding gender differences in dream reports. In M. Kramer & M. Glucksman (Eds.), *Dream research: Contributions to clinical practice* (pp. 56–66). New York, NY: Routledge.

Krishna, G. (1999). *The dawn of a new science.* Los Angeles, CA: Institute for Consciousness Research.

Krizan, Z., & Herlache, A. D. (2016). Sleep disruption and aggression: Implications for violence and its prevention. *Psychology of Violence, 6*(4), 542–552. http://dx.doi.org/10.1037/vio0000018

Kroger, J. (2015). Identity development through adulthood: The move toward "wholeness." In K. C. McLean & M. Syed (Eds.), *The Oxford handbook of identity development* (pp. 65–80). New York, NY: Oxford University Press.

Kroll, M. E., Green, J., Beral, V., Sudlow, C. L. M., Brown, A., Kirichek, O., . . . For the Million Women Study Collaborators (2016). Adiposity and ischemic and hemorrhagic stroke: Prospective study in women and meta-analysis. *Neurology, 87,* 1473–1481. http://dx.doi.org/10.1212/WNL.0000000000003171

Krug, H. E., Bert, J. S., Dorman, C. W., Frizelle, S. P., Funkenbusch, S. C., & Mahowald, M. L. (2015). Substance p expression in the murine lumbar dorsal root ganglia: Effect of chronic inflammatory arthritis knee pain and treatment with IA vanilloids. *Osteoarthritis and Cartilage, 23,* A358–A359. http://dx.doi.org/10.1016/j.joca.2015.02.661

Krys, K., Hansen, K., Xing, C., Szarota, P., & Yang, M. M. (2014). Do only fools smile at strangers? Cultural differences in social perception of intelligence of smiling individuals. *Journal of Cross-Cultural Psychology, 45,* 314–321. http://dx.doi.org/10.1177/0022022113513922

Ksiazkiewicz, A., Ludeke, S., & Krueger, R. (2016). The role of cognitive style in the link between genes and political ideology. *Political Psychology, 37*(6), 761–776. http://dx.doi.org/10.1111/pops.12318

Ku, P.-W., Steptoe, A., & Chen, L.-J. (2017). Prospective associations of exercise and depressive symptoms in older adults: The role of apolipoprotein e4. *Quality of Life Research: An International Journal of Quality of Life Aspects of Treatment, Care & Rehabilitation, 26*(7), 1799–1808. http://dx.doi.org/10.1007/s11136-017-1537-1

Kübler-Ross, E. (1975). *Questions and answers on death and dying.* Oxford, UK: Macmillan.

Kübler-Ross, E. (1983). *On children and death.* New York, NY: Macmillan.

Kübler-Ross, E. (1997). *Death: The final stage of growth.* New York, NY: Simon & Schuster.

Kübler-Ross, E. (1999). *On death and dying.* New York, NY: Simon & Schuster.

Kubota, J. T., & Phelps, E. A. (2016). Insights from functional magnetic resonance imaging research on race. In T. D. Nelson (Ed.), *Handbook of prejudice, stereotyping, and discrimination* (2nd ed., pp. 299–312). New York, NY: Psychology Press.

Kuchenbrandt, D., Eyssel, F., & Seidel, S. K. (2013). Cooperation makes it happen: Imagined intergroup cooperation enhances the positive effects of imagined contact. *Group Processes & Intergroup Relations, 16,* 636–648. http://dx.doi.org/10.1177/1368430212470172

Kuczaj, S. A. (2017). Animal creativity and innovation. In J. Call, G. M. Burghardt, I. M. Pepperberg, C. T. Snowdon, & T. Zentall (Eds.), *APA handbook of comparative psychology: Perception, learning, and cognition, Vol. 2* (pp. 627–641). Washington, DC: American Psychological Association. http://dx.doi.org/10.1037/0000012-028

Kuczaj, S. A., Frick, E. E., Jones, B. L., Lea, J. S. E., Beecham, D., & Schnöller, F. (2015). Underwater observations of dolphin reactions to a distressed conspecific. *Learning & Behavior, 43,* 289–300. http://dx.doi.org/10.3758/s13420-015-0179-9

Kuehner, C. (2017). Why is depression more common among women than among men? *The Lancet Psychiatry, 4*(2), 146–158. http://dx.doi.org/10.1016/S2215-0366(16)30263-2

Kuhnert, R.-L., Begeer, S., Fink, E., & de Rosnay, M. (2017). Gender-differentiated effects of theory of mind, emotion understanding, and social preference on prosocial behavior development: A longitudinal study. *Journal of Experimental Child Psychology, 154,* 13–27. http://dx.doi.org/10.1016/j.jecp.2016.10.001

Kühn, S., Gleich, T., Lorenz, R. C., Lindenberger, U., & Gallinat, J. (2014). Playing Super Mario induces structural brain plasticity: Gray matter changes resulting from training with a commercial video game. *Molecular Psychiatry, 19,* 265–271. http://dx.doi.org/10.1038/mp.2013.120

Kuijper, S. J. M., Hartman, C. A., Bogaerds-Hazenberg, S. T. M., & Hendriks, P. (2017). Narrative production in children with autism spectrum disorder (ASD) and children with attention-deficit/hyperactivity disorder (ADHD): Similarities and differences. *Journal of Abnormal Psychology, 126,* 63–75. http://dx.doi.org/10.1037/abn0000231

Kuiper, N., Kirsh, G., & Maiolino, N. (2016). Identity and intimacy development, humor styles, and psychological well-being. *Identity: An International Journal of Theory and Research, 16,* 115–125. http://dx.doi.org/10.1080/15283488.2016.1159964

Kukucka, J., & Kassin, S. M. (2014). Do confessions taint perceptions of handwriting evidence? An empirical test of the forensic confirmation bias. *Law and Human Behavior, 38,* 256–270. http://dx.doi.org/10.1037/lhb0000066

Kulczynski, A., Ilicic, J., & Baxter, S. M. (2016). When your source is smiling, consumers may automatically smile with you: Investigating the source expressive display hypothesis. *Psychology & Marketing, 33,* 5–19. http://dx.doi.org/10.1002/mar.20857

Kumar, D. K. V., Choi, S. H., Washicosky, K. J., Eimer, W. A., Tucker, S., Ghofrani, J., . . . Moir, R. D. (2016). Amyloid-β peptide protects against microbial infection in mouse and worm models of Alzheimer's disease. *Science Translational Medicine, 8,* 340–372. http://doi.org/10.1126/scitranslmed.aaf1059

Kumari, V., Uddin, S., Premkumar, P., Young, S., Gudjonsson, G. H., Raghuvanshi, S., . . . Das, M. (2014). Lower anterior cingulate volume in seriously violent men with antisocial personality disorder or schizophrenia and a history of childhood abuse. *Australian and New Zealand Journal of Psychiatry, 48,* 153–161. http://dx.doi.org/10.1177/0004867413512690

Kumin, L. (2015). Intellectual disability. In M. R. Kerins (Ed.), *Child and adolescent communication disorders: Organic and neurogenic bases* (pp. 99–151). San Diego, CA: Plural.

Kundu, P., & Cummins, D. D. (2013). Morality and conformity: The Asch paradigm applied to moral decisions. *Social Influence, 8,* 268–279. http://dx.doi.org/10.1080/15534510.2012.727767

Kunze, A. E., Arntz, A., & Kindt, M. (2015). Fear conditioning with film clips: A complex associative learning paradigm. *Journal of Behavior Therapy and Experimental Psychiatry, 47,* 42–50. http://dx.doi.org/10.1016/j.jbtep.2014.11.007

Kuperstok, N. (2008). Effects of exposure to differentiated aggressive films, equated for levels of interest and excitation, and the vicarious hostility catharsis hypothesis. *Dissertation Abstracts International: Section B: The Sciences and Engineering, 68,* 4806.

Küpper-Tetzel, C. E. (2014). Understanding the distributed practice effect: Strong effects on weak theoretical grounds. *Zeitschrift für Psychologie, 222,* 71–81. http://dx.doi.org/10.1027/2151-2604/a000168

Kurth, F., MacKenzie-Graham, A., Toga, A. W., & Luders, E. (2014). Shifting brain asymmetry: The link between meditation and structural lateralization. *Social Cognitive and Affective Neuroscience, 10,* 55–61. http://dx.doi.org/10.1093/scan/nsu029

Kurzban, R. (2014). Covert sexual signaling: Human flirtation and implications for other social species. *Evolutionary Psychology, 12,* 549–569.

Kushlev, K., & Dunn, E. W. (2015). Checking email less frequently reduces stress. *Computers in Human Behavior, 43,* 220–228. http://dx.doi.org/10.1016/j.chb.2014.11.005

Kvam, S., Kleppe, C. L., Nordhus, I. H., & Hovland, A. (2016). Exercise as a treatment for depression: A meta-analysis. *Journal of Affective Disorders, 202,* 67–86. http://dx.doi.org/10.1016/j.jad.2016.03.063

Kyaga, S., Landén, M., Boman, M., Hultman, C. M., Långström, N., & Lichtenstein, P. (2012). Mental illness, suicide and creativity: 40-year prospective total population study. *Journal of Psychiatric Research, 47,* 83–90.

**Labouesse, M. A., Lassalle, O., Richetto, J., Iafrati, J., Weber-Stadlbauer, U., Notter, T., . . . Meyer, U.** (2017). Hypervulnerability of the adolescent prefrontal cortex to nutritional stress via reelin deficiency. *Molecular Psychiatry.* http://dx.doi.org/10.1038/mp.2016.193

**Labrum, T., & Solomon, P. L.** (2016). Factors associated with family violence by persons with psychiatric disorders. *Psychiatry Research, 244,* 171–178. http://dx.doi.org/10.1016/j.psychres.2016.07.026

**Lafleur, A., & Boucher, V. J.** (2015). The ecology of self-monitoring effects on memory of verbal productions: Does speaking to someone make a difference? *Consciousness and Cognition, 36,* 139–146. http://dx.doi.org/10.1016/j.concog.2015.06.015

**Lai, V. T., & Narasimhan, B.** (2015). Verb representation and thinking-for-speaking effects in Spanish-English bilinguals. In R. G. de Almeida & C. Manouilidou (Eds.), *Cognitive science perspectives on verb representation and processing* (pp. 235–256). Cham, CH: Springer. http://dx.doi.org/10.1007/978-3-319-10112-5_11

**Laible, D., & Karahuta, E.** (2014). Prosocial behaviors in early childhood. In L. M. Padilla-Walker & G. Carlo (Eds.), *Prosocial development: A multidimensional approach* (pp. 350–366). Oxford, UK: Oxford University Press.

**Laier, C., Schulte, F. P., & Brand, M.** (2013). Pornographic picture processing interferes with working memory performance. *Journal of Sex Research, 50,* 642–652. http://dx.doi.org/10.1080/00224499.2012.716873.

**Lake, E. M. R., Steffler, E. A., Rowley, C. D., Sehmbi, M., Minuzzi, L., Frey, B. N., & Bock, N. A.** (2016). Altered intracortical myelin staining in the dorsolateral prefrontal cortex in severe mental illness. *European Archives of Psychiatry and Clinical Neuroscience,* 1–8. https://doi.org/10.1007/s00406-016-0730-5

**Lakshman, C., & Estay, C.** (2016). Attributional complexity and leadership: Test of a process model in France and India. *International Journal of Cross Cultural Management, 16*(1), 53–76. http://dx.doi.org/10.1177/1470595815622653

**Lambert, F. R., & Lavenex, P. B.** (2017). The "when" and the "where" of single-trial allocentric spatial memory performance in young children: Insights into the development of episodic memory. *Developmental Psychobiology, 59*(2), 185–196. http://dx.doi.org/10.1002/dev.21479

**Lamer, S. A., Reeves, S. L., & Weisbuch, M.** (2015). The nonverbal environment of self-esteem: Interactive effects of facial-expression and eye-gaze on perceivers' self-evaluations. *Journal of Experimental Social Psychology, 56,* 130–138. http://dx.doi.org/10.1016/j.jesp.2014.09.010

**Lamont, P.** (2013). *Extraordinary beliefs: A historical approach to a psychological problem.* New York, NY: Cambridge University Press.

**LaMotte, A. D., Taft, C. T., Weatherill, R. P., Casement, M. D., Creech, S. K., Milberg, W. P., . . . McGlinchey, R. E.** (2017). Sleep problems and physical pain as moderators of the relationship between PTSD symptoms and aggression in returning veterans. *Psychological Trauma: Theory, Research, Practice, and Policy, 9*(1), 113–116. http://dx.doi.org/10.1037/tra0000178

**Lampinen, J. M., & Beike, D. R.** (2015). *Memory 101. The psych 101 series.* New York, NY: Springer.

**Lanciano, T., Curci, A., & Semin, G. R.** (2010). The emotional and reconstructive determinants of emotional memories: An experimental approach to flashbulb memory investigation. *Memory, 18,* 473–485.

**Landeira-Fernandez, J.** (2015). Participation of NMDA receptors in the lateral hypothalamus in gastric erosion induced by cold-water restraint. *Physiology & Behavior, 140,* 209–214. http://dx.doi.org/10.1016/j.physbeh.2014.12.038

**Landers, R. N., & Schmidt, G. B.** (2016). *Social media in employee selection and recruitment.* Cham, CH: Springer International Publishing.

**Landicho, L. C., Cabanig, M. C. A., Cortes, M. S. F., & Villamor, B. J. G.** (2014). Egocentrism and risk-taking among adolescents. *Asia Pacific Journal of Multidisciplinary Research, 2,* 132–142.

**Landler, M.** (2012). From Biden, a vivid account of Bin Laden decision. *New York Times.* Retrieved from http://thecaucus.blogs.nytimes.com/2012/01/30/from-biden-avivid-account-of-bin-laden-decision/

**Landsberg, L., Aronne, L. J., Beilin, L. J., Burke, V., Igel, L. I., Lloyd-Jones, D., & Sowers, J.** (2013). Obesity-related hypertension: Pathogenesis, cardiovascular risk, and treatment—A position paper of the Obesity Society and the American Society of Hypertension. *Obesity, 21,* 8–24. http://dx.doi.org/10.1002/oby.20181

**Laney, M. O.** (2013). *The introvert advantage: How to thrive in an extrovert world.* Prince Frederick, MD: Highbridge Company.

**Lange, B. P., & Euler, H. A.** (2014). Writers have groupies, too: High quality literature production and mating success. *Evolutionary Behavioral Sciences, 8,* 20–30. http://dx.doi.org/10.1037/h0097246

**Langmeyer, A., Guglhör-Rudan, A., & Tarnai, C.** (2012). What do music preferences reveal about personality? A cross-cultural replication using self-ratings and ratings of music samples. *Journal of Individual Differences, 33,* 119–130.

**Långström, N., Rahman, Q., Carlström, E., & Lichtenstein, P.** (2010). Genetic and environmental effects on same-sex sexual behavior: A population study of twins in Sweden. *Archives of Sexual Behavior, 39,* 75–80.

**Lapré, G., & Marsee, M. A.** (2016). The role of race in the association between corporal punishment and externalizing problems: Does punishment severity matter? *Journal of Child and Family Studies, 25,* 432–441. http://dx.doi.org/10.1007/s10826-015-0250-3

**Lariscy, R. A. W., & Tinkham, S. F.** (1999). The sleeper effect and negative political advertising. *Journal of Advertising, 28,* 13–30.

**La Roche, M. J., Davis, T. M., & D'Angelo, E.** (2015). Challenges in developing acultural evidence-based psychotherapy in the USA: Suggestions for international studies. *Australian Psychologist, 50,* 95–101. http://dx.doi.org/10.1111/ap.12085

**Larrick, R. P., Timmerman, T. A., Carton, A. M., & Abrevaya, J.** (2011). Temper, temperature, and temptation: Heat-related retaliation in baseball. *Psychological Science, 22,* 423–428. http://dx.doi.org/10.1177/0956797611399292

**Larzelere, M. M., & Campbell, J. S.** (2016). Disordered sleep. In M. A. Burg & O. Oyama (Eds.), *The behavioral health specialist in primary care: Skills for integrated practice* (pp. 161–183). New York, NY: Springer.

**Lasalvia, A., Penta, E., Sartorius, N., & Henderson, S.** (2015). Should the label "schizophrenia" be abandoned? *Schizophrenia Research, 162,* 276–284. http://dx.doi.org/10.1016/j.schres.2015.01.031

**Lasnier, G.** (2013). Popping the question is his job. *Newscenter.* Retrieved from http://news.ucsc.edu/2013/01/marriage-traditions.html

**Lassek, W. D., & Gaulin, S. J. C.** (2016). What makes Jessica rabbit sexy? Contrasting roles of waist and hip size. *Evolutionary Psychology, 14*(2), 1–16. http://dx.doi.org/10.1177/1474704916643459

**Latané, B., & Darley, J. M.** (1968). Group inhibition of bystander intervention in emergencies. *Journal of Personality and Social Psychology, 10,* 215–221.

**Latané, B., Williams, K., & Harkins, S.** (1979). Many hands make light the work: The causes and consequences of social loafing. *Journal of Personality and Social Psychology, 37*(6), 822–832. http://dx.doi.org/10.1037/0022-3514.37.6.822

**Latu, I., & Schmid Mast, M.** (2016). The effects of stereotypes of women's performance in male-dominated hierarchies: Stereotype threat activation and reduction through role models. In K. Faniko, F. Lorenzi-Cioldi, O. Sarrasin, & E. Mayor (Eds.), *Gender and social hierarchies: Perspectives from social psychology* (pp. 75–87). New York, NY: Routledge/Taylor & Francis.

**Latzman, R. D., Freeman, H. D., Schapiro, S. J., & Hopkins, W. D.** (2015). The contribution of genetics and early rearing experiences to hierarchical personality dimensions in chimpanzees (Pan troglodytes). *Journal of Personality and Social Psychology, 109,* 889–900. http://dx.doi.org/10.1037/pspp0000040

**Laumann, E., Gagnon, J., Michael, R., & Michaels, S.** (1994). *The social organization of sexuality: Sexual practices in the United States.* Chicago, IL: University of Chicago Press.

**Lavie, L.** (2015). Oxidative stress in obstructive sleep apnea and intermittent hypoxia—Revisited—The bad ugly and good: Implications to the heart and brain. *Sleep Medicine Reviews, 20,* 27–45. http://dx.doi.org/10.1016/j.smrv.2014.07.003

**Lavner, J. A., & Bradbury, T. N.** (2012). Why do even satisfied newlyweds eventually go on to divorce? *Journal of Family Psychology, 26,* 1–10. http://dx.doi.org/10.1037/a0025966

**LaVoie, N., Lee, Y.-C., & Parker, J.** (2016). Preliminary research developing a theory of cell phone distraction and social relationships. *Accident Analysis and Prevention, 86,* 155–160. http://dx.doi.org/10.1016/j.aap.2015.10.023

**Lavy, V., & Sand, E.** (2015). On the origins of gender human capital gaps: Short and long term consequences of teachers' stereotypical biases. *National Bureau of Economic Research, Working Paper No. 20909.*

**Lawrence, H. R., Nangle, D. W., Schwartz-Mette, R. A., & Erdley, C. A.** (2017). Medication for child and adolescent depression: Questions, answers, clarifications, and caveats. *Practice Innovations, 2*(1), 39–53. http://dx.doi.org/10.1037/pri0000042

**Layous, K., Nelson, S. K., Kurtz, J. L., & Lyubomirsky, S.** (2017). What triggers prosocial effort? A positive feedback loop between positive activities, kindness, and well-being. *The Journal of Positive Psychology, 12*(4), 385–398. http://dx.doi.org/10.1080/17439760.2016.1198924

**Lea, T., de Wit, J., & Reynolds, R.** (2014). Minority stress in lesbian, gay, and bisexual young adults in Australia: Associations with psychological distress, suicidality, and substance use. *Archives of Sexual Behavior, 43,* 1571–1578. http://dx.doi.org/10.1007/s10508-014-0266-6

**Leaming, M. R., & Dickinson, G. E.** (2011). *Understanding dying, death, and bereavement* (7th ed.). Belmont, CA: Cengage.

**Leaper, C.** (2013). Gender development during childhood. In P. D. Zelazo (Ed.), *Oxford hand- book of developmental psychology* (pp. 327– 377). New York, NY: Oxford University Press.

**Leaper, C.** (2015). Gender and social-cognitive development. In L. S. Liben, U. Müller, & R. M. Lerner (Eds.), *Handbook of child psychology and developmental science, Vol. 2: Cognitive processes* (7th ed., pp. 806–853). Hoboken, NJ: Wiley. http://dx.doi.org/10.1002/9781118963418.childpsy219

**Leaper, C., & Farkas, T.** (2015). The socialization of gender during childhood and adolescence. In J. E. Grusec & P. D. Hastings (Eds.), *Handbook of socialization: Theory and research* (2nd ed., pp. 541–565). New York, NY: Guilford Press.

**Lease, H., Hendrie, G. A., Poelman, A. A. M., Delahunty, C., & Cox, D. N.** (2016). A Sensory-Diet database: A tool to characterise the sensory qualities of diets. *Food Quality and Preference, 49,* 20–32. http://dx.doi.org/10.1016/j.foodqual.2015.11.010

**Leblond, M., Laisney, M., Lamidey, V., Egret, S., de La Sayette, V., Chételat, G., . . . Eustache, F.** (2016). Self-reference effect on memory in healthy aging, mild cognitive impairment and Alzheimer's disease: Influence of identity valence. *Cortex, 74,* 177–190. http://dx.doi.org/10.1016/j.cortex.2015.10.017

**Lebowitz, M. S., & Dovidio, J. F.** (2015). Implications of emotion regulation strategies for empathic concern, social attitudes, and helping behavior. *Emotion, 15,* 187–194. http://dx.doi.org/10.1037/a0038820

**LeDoux, J. E.** (1996). *The emotional brain: The mysterious underpinnings of emotional life.* New York, NY: Simon & Schuster.

**LeDoux, J. E.** (1998). *The emotional brain.* New York, NY: Simon & Schuster.

**LeDoux, J. E.** (2007). Emotional memory. *Scholarpedia, 2,* 180. http://dx.doi.org/10.4249/scholarpedia.1806

**LeDoux, J. E.** (2014). Coming to terms with fear. *Proceedings of the National Academy of Sciences of the United States of America, 111,* 2871–2878. http://dx.doi.org/10.1073/pnas.1400335111

**Lee, G. Y., & Kisilevsky, B. S.** (2014). Fetuses respond to father's voice but prefer mother's voice after birth. *Developmental Psychobiology, 56,* 1–11. http://dx.doi.org/10.1002/dev.21084

**Lee, H., & Oh, H. J.** (2017). Normative mechanism of rumor dissemination on Twitter. *Cyberpsychology, Behavior, and Social Networking, 20*(3), 164–171. http://dx.doi.org/10.1089/cyber.2016.0447

**Lee, H. S., Jung, H. S., & Sumner, A.** (2015). A cross-cultural analysis of perception on ageist attitudes between Korean and American social work students. *Korean Social Science Journal, 42,* 25–37. http://dx.doi.org/10.1007/s10591-015-9337-7

**Lee, K. E., Bryan, S. L., & LaPlant, J. T.** (2017). Game day meets election day: Sports records, election results, and the american south*. *Social Science Quarterly.* No Pagination Specified. http://dx.doi.org/10.1111/ssqu.12356

**Lee, M. L., Howard, M. E., Horrey, W. J., Liang, Y., Anderson, C., Shreeve, M. S., . . . Czeisler, C. A.** (2016a). High risk of near-crash driving events following night-shift work. *Proceedings of the National Academy of Sciences of the United States of America, 113,* 176–181. http://dx.doi.org/10.1073/pnas.1510383112

**Lee, P. C.** (2017). Maternal behavior. In J. Call, G. M. Burghardt, I. M. Pepperberg, C. T. Snowdon, & T. Zentall (Eds.), *APA handbook of comparative psychology: Basic concepts, methods, neural substrate, and behavior, Vol. 1* (pp. 723–741). Washington, DC: American Psychological Association. http://dx.doi.org/10.1037/0000011-035

**Lee, R. U., & Radin, J. M.** (2016). A population-based epidemiologic study of adult-onset narcolepsy incidence and associated risk factors, 2004–2013. *Journal of the Neurological Sciences, 370,* 29–34. http://dx.doi.org/10.1016/j.jns.2016.08.026

**Lee, T. L., Gelfand, M. J., & Kashima, Y.** (2014). The serial reproduction of conflict: Third parties escalate conflict through communication biases. *Journal of Experimental Social Psychology, 54,* 68–72. http://dx.doi.org/10.1016/j.jesp.2014.04.006

**Lee, Y., Syeda, K., Maruschak, N. A., Cha, D. S., Mansur, R. B., Wium-Andersen, I. K., . . . McIntyre, R. S.** (2016b). A new perspective on the anti-suicide effects with ketamine treatment: A procognitive effect. *Journal of Clinical Psychopharmacology, 36,* 50–56. http://dx.doi.org/10.1097/JCP.0000000000000441

**Legarreta, M., Graham, J., North, L., Bueler, C. E., McGlade, E., & Yurgelun-Todd, D.** (2015). DSM–5 posttraumatic stress disorder symptoms associated with suicide behaviors in veterans. *Psychological Trauma: Theory, Research, Practice, and Policy, 7,* 277–285. http://dx.doi.org/10.1037/tra0000026

**Lehr, D.** (2009). *The fence: A police cover-up along Boston's racial divide.* New York, NY: Harper Collins.

**Leichtman, M. D.** (2006). Cultural and maturational influences on long-term event memory. In L. Balter & C. S. Tamis-LeMonda (Eds.), *Child psychology: A handbook of contemporary issues* (2nd ed., pp. 565–589). New York, NY: Psychology Press.

**Leigh, H.** (2015). Affect, mood, emotions: Depressive disorders and bipolar and related disorders. In H. Leigh & J. Strltzer (Eds.), *Handbook of consultation-liaison psychiatry* (2nd ed., pp. 225–235). New York, NY: Springer. http://dx.doi.org/10.1007/978-3-319-11005-9

**Leising, K. J., Wong, J., & Blaisdell, A. P.** (2015). Extinction and spontaneous recovery of spatial behavior in pigeons. *Journal of Experimental Psychology: Animal Learning and Cognition, 41,* 371–377. http://dx.doi.org/10.1037/xan0000076

**Leiting, K. A., & Yeater, E. A.** (2017). A qualitative analysis of the effects of victimization history and sexual attitudes on women's hypothetical sexual assault scripts. *Violence Against Women, 23,* 46–66. http://dx.doi.org/10.1177/1077801216637472

**Lemley, J., Bazrafkan, S., & Corcoran, P.** (2017). Deep learning for consumer devices and services: Pushing the limits for machine learning, artificial intelligence, and computer vision. *IEEExplore.* Retrieved from http://ieeexplore.ieee.org/document/7879402/?reload=true

**Leone, R. M., Crane, C. A., Parrott, D. J., & Eckhardt, C. I.** (2016). Problematic drinking, impulsivity, and physical IPV perpetration: A dyadic analysis. *Psychology of Addictive Behaviors, 30,* 356–366. http://dx.doi.org/10.1037/adb0000159

**Lepper, M. R., Greene, D., & Nisbett, R. E.** (1973). Undermining children's intrinsic interest with extrinsic rewards: A test of the over-justification hypothesis. *Journal of Personality and Social Psychology, 28,* 129–137.

**Leslie, M.** (2000, July/August). The vexing legacy of Lewis Terman. *Stanford Magazine.* Retrieved from http://www.stanfordalumni.org/news/magazine/2000/julaug/articles/terman.html

**Levant, R. F., & Powell, W. A.** (2017). The gender role strain paradigm. In R. F. Levant & Y. J. Wong (Eds.), *The psychology of men and masculinities* (pp. 15–43). Washington, DC: American Psychological Association. http://dx.doi.org/10.1037/0000023-002

**Levant, R. F., & Wong, Y. J.** (2017). *The psychology of men and masculinities.* Washington, DC: American Psychological Association.

**LeVay, S.** (2003). Queer science: The use and abuse of research into homosexuality. *Archives of Sexual Behavior, 32,* 187–189.

**LeVay, S.** (2012). *Gay, straight, and the reason why: The science of sexual orientation.* New York, NY: Oxford University Press.

**Levenson, R. W.** (1992). Autonomic nervous system differences among emotions. *Psychological Science, 3,* 23–27.

**Levenson, R. W.** (2007). Emotion elicitation with neurological patients. In J. A. Coan & J. B. Allen (Eds.), *Handbook of emotion elicitation and assessment* (pp. 158–168). Oxford, UK: Oxford.

**Lev-On, A., & Waismel-Manor, I.** (2016). Looks that matter: The effect of physical attractiveness in low- and high-information elections. *American Behavioral Scientist, 60*(14), 1756–1771. http://dx.doi.org/10.1177/0002764216676249

**Levey, S.** (2014). *Introduction to language development.* San Diego, CA: Plural.

**Levi, B., Matzner, P., Goldfarb, Y., Sorski, L., Shaashua, L., Melamed, R., . . . Ben-Eliyahu, S.** (2016). Stress impairs the efficacy of immune stimulation by CpG-C: Potential neuroendocrine mediating mechanisms and significance to tumor metastasis and the perioperative period. *Brain, Behavior, and Immunity, 56,* 209–220. http://dx.doi.org/10.1016/j.bbi.2016.02.025

**Levine, J. R.** (2001). *Why do fools fall in love: Experiencing the magic, mystery, and meaning of successful relationships.* New York, NY: Jossey-Bass.

**Levine, L., & Munsch, J.** (2014). *Child development: An active learning approach.* Thousand Oaks, CA: Sage.

**Levine, P. A.** (2015). *Trauma and memory: Brain and body in a search for the living past.* New York, NY: North Atlantic.

**Levinson, D. J.** (1959). Role, personality, and social structure in the organizational setting. *The Journal of Abnormal and Social Psychology, 58,* 170–180.

**Levinson, D. J.** (1977). The mid-life transition: A period in adult psychosocial development. *Journal for the Study of Interpersonal Processes, 40,* 99–112.

Levinson, D. J. (1996). *The seasons of a woman's life.* New York, NY: Random House, Inc.

Levinthal, S. F. (2016). *Drugs, behavior, and modern society* (8th ed.). New York, NY: Pearson.

Levitan, R. D., Jansen, P., Wendland, B., Tiemeier, H., Jaddoe, V. W., Silveira, P. P., . . . Meaney, M. (2017). A DRD4 gene by maternal sensitivity interaction predicts risk for overweight or obesity in two independent cohorts of preschool children. *Journal of Child Psychology and Psychiatry, 58,* 180–188. http://dx.doi.org/10.1111/jcpp.12646

Levy-Gigi, E., & Shamay-Tsoory, S. G. (2017). Help me if you can: Evaluating the effectiveness of interpersonal compared to intrapersonal emotion regulation in reducing distress. *Journal of Behavior Therapy and Experimental Psychiatry, 55,* 33–40. http://dx.doi.org/10.1016/j.jbtep.2016.11.008

Lewicki, R. J., Polin, B., & Lount, R. B. Jr. (2016). An exploration of the structure of effective apologies. *Negotiation and Conflict Management Research, 9,* 177–196. http://dx.doi.org/101111/ncmr.12073

Lewis Rickert, J., Michels, V. J., & Herndon, C. (2015). Chronic pain. In M. A. Burg & O. Oyama (Eds.), *The behavioral health specialist in primary care: Skills for integrated practice* (pp. 131–159). New York, NY: Springer.

Li, C.-T., Chen, M.-H., Lin, W.-C., Hong, C.-J., Yang, B.-H., Liu, R-S., & Su, T.-P. (2016c). The effects of low-dose ketamine on the prefrontal cortex and amygdala in treatment-resistant depression: A randomized controlled study. *Human Brain Mapping, 37,* 1080–1090. http://dx.doi.org/10.1002/hbm.23085

Li, K., Simons-Morton, B., Gee, B., & Hingson, R. (2016b). Marijuana-, alcohol-, and drug-impaired driving among emerging adults: Changes from high school to one-year post-high school. *Journal of Safety Research, 58,* 15–20. http://dx.doi.org/10.1016/j.jsr.2016.05.003

Li, L., & Loo, B. P. Y. (2016). Mobility impairment, social engagement, and life satisfaction among the older population in China: A structural equation modeling analysis. *Quality of Life Research, 26*(5), 1273–1282. http://dx.doi.org/10.1007/s11136-016-1444-x

Li, S. H., & Graham, B. M. (2017). Why are women so vulnerable to anxiety, trauma-related and stress-related disorders? The potential role of sex hormones. *The Lancet Psychiatry, 4*(1), 73–82. http://dx.doi.org/10.1016/S2215-0366(16)30358-3

Li, W., Li, X., Huang, L., Kong, X., Yang, W., Wei, D., . . . Liu, J. (2015). Brain structure links trait creativity to openness to experience. *Social Cognitive and Affective Neuroscience, 10,* 191–198. http://dx.doi.org/10.1093/scan/nsu041

Li, W. O. (2016). Consciousness: How we perceive and become aware of our world. In C. Tien-Lun Sun (Ed.), *Psychology in Asia: An introduction* (pp. 127–173). Boston, MA: Cengage Learning.

Li, W. O. (2016). Learning and memory: How do we learn and retain new knowledge? In C. Tien-Lun Sun (Ed.), *Psychology in Asia: An introduction* (pp. 175–210). Boston, MA: Cengage.

Li, X., Semenova, S., D'Souza, M. S., Stoker, A. K., & Markou, A. (2014). Involvement of glutamatergic and GABAergic systems in nicotine dependence: Implications for novel pharmacotherapies for smoking cessation. *Neuropharmacology, 76,* 554–565. http://dx.doi.org/10.1016/j.neuropharm.2013.05.042

Li, X., Yan, X., Wu, J., Radwan, E., & Zhang, Y. (2016a). A rear-end collision risk assessment model based on drivers' collision avoidance process under influences of cell phone use and gender—A driving simulator based study. *Accident Analysis & Prevention, 97,* 1–18. http://dx.doi.org/10.1016/j.aap.2016.08.021

Liang, H.-L. (2015). Are you tired? Spillover and crossover effects of emotional exhaustion on the family domain. *Asian Journal of Social Psychology, 18,* 22–32. http://dx.doi.org/10.1111/ajsp.12075

Liao, L.-W., Zhu, M.-J., Shen, X.-T., Zhang, L., Li, W.-J., Tang, L-H., & Pan, G.-H. (2016). An open trial of modified Naikan therapy to patients with schizophrenia. *Chinese Journal of Clinical Psychology, 24*(1), 182–184.

Libero, L. E., Burge, W. L., Deshpande, H. D., Pestilli, F., & Kana, R. K. (2016). White matter diffusion of major fiber tracts implicated in autism spectrum disorder. *Brain Connectivity, 6*(9), 691–699. https://doi.org/10.1089/brain.2016.0442

Lien, J. W., & Yuan, J. (2015). The cross-sectional "Gambler's Fallacy": Set representativeness in lottery number choices. *Journal of Economic Behavior & Organization, 109,* 163–172. http://dx.doi.org/10.1016/j.jebo.2014.10.011

Lilienfeld, S. O., Lynn, S. J., & Ammirati, R. J. (2015). Science versus pseudoscience. *The Encyclopedia of Clinical Psychology,* 1–7. Hoboken, NJ: Wiley. http://dx.doi.org/10.1002/9781118625392.wbecp572

Lilienfeld, S. O., Lynn, S. J., Ruscio, J., & Beyerstein, B. L. (2010). *50 great myths of popular psychology: Shattering widespread misconceptions about human behavior.* Malden, MA: Wiley-Blackwell.

Lilliengren, P., Johansson, R., Lindqvist, K., Mechler, J., & Andersson, G. (2016). Efficacy of experiential dynamic therapy for psychiatric conditions: A meta-analysis of randomized controlled trials. *Psychotherapy, 53,* 90–104. http://dx.doi.org/10.1037/pst0000024

Lilly, J. D., & Wipawayangkool, K. (2017). When fair procedures don't work: A self-threat model of procedural justice. *Current Psychology: A Journal for Diverse Perspectives on Diverse Psychological Issues.* No Pagination Specified. http://dx.doi.org/10.1007/s12144-016-9555-7

Lima, A. S., Silva, K., Padovan, C. M., Almeida, S. S., & Hebihara Fukuda, M. T. (2014). Memory, learning, and participation of the cholinergic system in young rats exposed to environmental enrichment. *Behavioural Brain Research, 259,* 247–252. http://dx.doi.org/10.1016/j.bbr.2013.10.046

Lim, L., Chang, W., Yu, X., Chiu, H., Chong, M., & Kua, E. (2011). Depression in Chinese elderly populations. *Asia-Pacific Psychiatry, 3,* 46–53.

Lim, S., & Raymo, J. M. (2016). Marriage and women's health in Japan. *Journal of Marriage and Family, 78*(3), 780–796. http://dx.doi.org/10.1111/jomf.12298

Lin, C.-S., Hsieh, J.-C., Yeh, T.-C., Lee, S.-Y., & Niddam, D. M. (2013). Functional dissociation within insular cortex: The effect of pre-stimulus anxiety on pain. *Brain Research, 1493,* 40–47. http://dx.doi.org/10.1016/j.brainres.2012.11.035

Lin, H.-C., Manuel, J., McFatter, R., & Cech, C. (2016). Changes in empathy-related cry responding as a function of time: A time course study of adult's responses to infant crying. *Infant Behavior & Development, 42,* 45–59. http://dx.doi.org/10.1016/j.infbeh.2015.10.010

Lin, N., Pan, X.-D., Chen, A.-Q., Zhu, Y.-G., Wu, M., Zhang, J., & Chen, X.-C. (2014). Tripchlorolide improves age-associated cognitive deficits by reversing hippocampal synaptic plasticity impairment and NMDA receptor dysfunction in SAMP8 mice. *Behavioural Brain Research, 258,* 8–18. http://dx.doi.org/10.1016/j.bbr.2013.10.010

Lindeman, M., & Svedholm-Häkkinen, A. (2016). Does poor understanding of physical world predict religious and paranormal beliefs? *Applied Cognitive Psychology, 30*(5), 736–742. http://dx.doi.org/10.1002/acp.3248

Lindner, I., & Henkel, L. A. (2015). Confusing what you heard with what you did: False action memories from auditory cues. *Psychonomic Bulletin & Review, 22,* 1791–1797. http://dx.doi.org/10.3758/s13423-015-0837-0

Lindqvist, D., Dhabhar, F. S., James, S. J., Hough, C. M., Jain, F. A., Bersani, F. S., . . . Mellon, S. H. (2017). Oxidative stress, inflammation and treatment response in major depression. *Psychoneuroendocrinology, 76,* 197–205. http://dx.doi.org/10.1016/j.psyneuen.2016.11.031

Lindsay, D. S., Yonelinas, A. P., & Roediger, H. L., II. (Eds.). (2015). *Remembering: Attributions, processes, and control in human memory: Essays in honor of Larry Jacoby* (C. M. Kelley, Trans.). New York, NY: Psychology Press.

Lingle, S., & Riede, T. (2014). Deer mothers are sensitive to infant distress vocalizations of diverse mammalian species. *The American Naturalist, 184,* 510–522. http://dx.doi.org/10.1086/677677

Lingle, S., Wyman, M. T., Kotrba, R., Teichroeg, L. J., & Romanow, C. A. (2015). What makes a cry a cry? A review of infant distress vocalizations. *Zoology, 58,* 698–726. https://dx.doi.org/10.1093/czoolo/58.5.698

Lipowski, Z. J. (1986). Psychosomatic medicine: Past and present: I. Historical background. *The Canadian Journal of Psychiatry/La Revue canadienne de psychiatrie, 31*(1), 2–7.

Lippa, R. A. (2016). Biological influences on masculinity. In Y. J. Wong & S. R. Wester (Eds.), *APA handbook of men and masculinities* (pp. 187–209). Washington, DC: American Psychological Association. http://dx.doi.org/10.1037/14594-009

Lipsman, N., Giacobbe, P., & Lozano, A. M. (2015). Deep brain stimulation for the management of treatment-refractory major depressive disorder. In B. Sun & A. De Salles (Eds.), *Neurosurgical treatments for psychiatric disorders* (pp. 95–104). New York, NY: Springer. http://dx.doi.org/10.1007/978-94-017-9576-0

Littlewood, D. L., Gooding, P. A., Panagioti, M., & Kyle, S. D. (2016). Nightmares and suicide in posttraumatic stress disorder: The mediating role of defeat, entrapment, and hopelessness. *Journal of Clinical Sleep Medicine, 12,* 393–399. http://dx.doi.org/10.5664/jcsm.5592

Liu, C. S., Adibfar, A., Herrmann, N., Gallagher, D., & Lanctôt, K. L. (2017). Evidence for inflammation-associated depression. In R. Dantzer & L. Capuron (Eds.), *Inflammation-associated depression: Evidence, mechanisms and implications* (pp. 3–30). Cham, CH: Springer International Publishing.

**Liu, H.** (2009). Till death do us part: Marital status and US mortality trends, 1986–2000. *Journal of Marriage and Family, 71,* 1158–1173. http://dx.doi.org/10.1111/ j.1741–3737.2009.00661.x

**Liu, J. H., & Latané, B.** (1998). Extremitization of attitudes: Does thought-and discussion-induced polarization cumulate? *Basic and Applied Social Psychology, 20,* 103–110.

**Liu, L., Preotiuc-Pietro, D., Samani, Z. R., Moghaddam, M. E., & Ungar, L.** (2016). Analyzing personality through social media profile picture choice. *AAAI Digital Library.* Retrieved from https://sites.sas.upenn.edu/danielpr/publications/analyzing-personality-through-social-media-profile-picture-choice

**Liu, Z., Wu, D., Huang, J., Qian, D., Chen, F., Xu, J., . . . Wang, X.** (2016). Visual impairment, but not hearing impairment, is independently associated with lower subjective well-being among individuals over 95 years of age: A population-based study. *Archives of Gerontology and Geriatrics, 62,* 30–35. http://dx.doi.org/10.1016/j.archger.2015.10.011

**Livingston, B. A., Schilpzand, P., & Erez, A.** (2017). Not what you expected to hear: Accented messages and their effect on choice. *Journal of Management, 43*(3), 804–833. http://dx.doi.org/10.1177/0149206314541151

**Livingstone, K. M., & Isaacowitz, D. M.** (2016). Age differences in use and effectiveness of positivity in emotion regulation: The sample case of attention. In A. D. Ong & C. E. Löckenhoff (Eds.), *Emotion, aging, and health. Bronfenbrenner series on the ecology of human development* (pp. 31–48). Washington, DC: American Psychological Association. http://dx.doi.org/10.1037/14857-003

**LoBue, V.** (2013). What are we so afraid of? How early attention shapes our most common fears. *Child Development Perspectives, 7,* 38–42. http://dx.doi.org/10.1111/cdep.12012

**LoBue, V., & DeLoache, J. S.** (2008). Detecting the snake in the grass: Attention to fear-relevant stimuli by adults and young children. *Psychological Science, 19,* 284–289. http://dx.doi.org/10.1111/j.1467-9280.2008.02081.x

**Loebnitz, N., & Aschemann-Witzel, J.** (2016). Communicating organic food quality in China: Consumer perceptions of organic products and the effect of environmental value priming. *Food Quality and Preference, 50,* 102–108. http://dx.doi.org/10.1016/j.foodqual.2016.02.003

**Loflin, M., & Earleywine, M.** (2015). The case for medical marijuana: An issue of relief. *Drug and Alcohol Dependence, 149,* 293–297. http://dx.doi.org/10.1016/j.drugalcdep.2015.01.006

**Loftus, E.** (2002, May/June). My story: Dear mother. *Psychology Today,* 67–70.

**Loftus, E. F.** (1993). Psychologists in the eyewitness world. *American Psychologist, 48,* 550–552. http://dx.doi.org/10.1037/0003-066X.48.5.550

**Loftus, E. F.** (2002, May/June). My story: Dear Mother. *Psychology Today,* pp. 67–70.

**Loftus, E. F.** (2010). Afterword: Why parapsychology is not yet ready for prime time. Debating psychic experience: Human potential or human illusion? In S. Krippner & H. L. Friedman (Eds.), *Debating psychic experience: Human potential or human illusion?* (pp. 211–214). Santa Barbara, CA: Praeger/ABC-CLIO.

**Loftus, E. F.** (2013). 25 years of eyewitness science . . . finally pays off. *Perspectives on Psychological Science, 8,* 556–557. http://dx.doi.org/10.1177/1745691613500995

**Loftus, E. F., & Cahill, L.** (2007). Memory distortion from misattribution to rich false memory. In J. S. Nairne (Ed.), *The foundations of remembering: Essays in honor of Henry L. Roediger, III* (pp. 413–425). New York, NY: Psychology Press.

**Loftus, E.F., & Ketcham, K.** (1994). *The myth of repressed memory.* New York, NY: St. Martin's Press.

**Lohr, J. B., Palmer, B. W., Eidt, C. A., Aailabovina, S., Mausbach, B. T., Wolkowitz, O. M., . . . & Ieste, D. V.** (2015). Is post-traumatic stress disorder associated with premature senescence? A review of the literature. *The American Journal of Geriatric Psychiatry, 23,* 709–726. http://dx.doi.org/10.1016/j.jagp.2015.04.001

**Lohse, M., Garrido, L., Driver, J., Dolan, R. J., Duchaine, B. C., & Furl, N.** (2106). Effective connectivity from early visual cortex to posterior occipitotemporal face areas supports face selectivity and predicts developmental prosopagnosia. *The Journal of Neuroscience, 36,* 3821–3828. http://dx.doi.org/10.1523/JNEUROSCI.3621-15.2016

**Loonen, A. J., & Ivanova, S. A.** (2016). Circuits regulating pleasure and happiness—Mechanisms of depression. *Frontiers in Human Neuroscience, 10.*

**Lopez, S., Pedrotti, J., & Snyder, C.** (2015). *Positive psychology: The scientific and practical explorations of human strengths* (3rd ed.). Thousand Oaks, CA: Sage.

**López, S. R., & Guarnaccia, P. J.** (2016). Cultural dimensions of psychopathology: The social world's impact on mental disorders. In J. E. Maddux & B. A. Winstead (Eds.), *Psychopathology: Foundations for a contemporary understanding* (4th ed., pp. 59–75). New York, NY: Routledge/Taylor & Francis Group.

**Louie, A. K., & Roberts, L. W.** (2015). Anxiety disorders. In L. W. Roberts & A. K. Louie (Eds.), *Study guide to DSM-5®* (pp. 137–153). Arlington, VA: American Psychiatric Publishing.

**Loveland, J. L., & Fernald, R. D.** (2017). Differential activation of vasotocin neurons in contexts that elicit aggression and courtship. *Behavioural Brain Research, 317,* 188–203. http://dx.doi.org/10.1016/j.bbr.2016.09.008

**Loving, T. J., & Sbarra, D. A.** (2015). Relationships and health. In M. Mikulincer, P. R. Shaver, J. A. Simpson, & J. F. Dovidio (Eds.), *APA handbooks in psychology. APA handbook of personality and social psychology, Vol. 3. Interpersonal relations* (pp. 151–176). Washington, DC: American Psychological Association. http://dx.doi.org/10.1037/14344-006

**Low, S., Tiberio, S. S., Shortt, J. Wu, Capaldi, D. M., & Eddy, J. M.** (2017). Associations of couples' intimate partner violence in young adulthood and substance use: A dyadic approach. *Psychology of Violence, 7,* 120–127. http://dx.doi.org/10.1037/vio0000038

**Lu, C.-Q., Lu, J. J., Du, D.-Y., & Brough, P.** (2016). Crossover effects of work-family conflict among Chinese couples. *Journal of Managerial Psychology, 31,* 235–250. http://dx.doi.org/10.1108/JMP-09-2012-0283

**Lu, H.-C., & Mackie, K.** (2016). An introduction to the endogenous cannabinoid system. *Biological Psychiatry, 79,* 516–525. http://dx.doi.org/10.1016/j.biopsych.2015.07.028

**Lu, J. G., Quoidbach, J., Gino, F., Chakroff, A., Maddux, W. W., & Galinsky, A. D.** (2017). The dark side of going abroad: How broad foreign experiences increase immoral behavior. *Journal of Personality and Social Psychology, 112,* 1–16. http://dx.doi.org/10.1037/pspa0000068

**Lubar, J. F.** (2015). Optimal procedures in Z-score neurofeedback: Strategies for maximizing learning for surface and LORETA neurofeedback. In R. W. Thatcher & J. F. Lubar (Eds.), *Z score neurofeedback: Clinical applications* (pp. 41–58). San Diego, CA: Elsevier. http://dx.doi.org/10.1016/B978-0-12-801291-8.00003-0

**Luby, J. L., Belden, A. C., Whalen, D., Harms, M. P., & Barch, D. M.** (2016). Breastfeeding and childhood IQ: The mediating role of gray matter volume. *Journal of the American Academy of Child & Adolescent Psychiatry, 55,* 367–375. http://dx.doi.org/10.1016/j.jaac.2016.02.009

**Lucassen, E. A., Coomans, C. P., van Putten, M., de Kreij, S. R., van Genugten, J. H., Sutorius, R. P., . . . Löwik, C. W.** (2016). Environmental 24-hr cycles are essential for health. *Current Biology, 26*(14), 1843–1853.

**Luciani, J.** (2015). Why 80 percent of New Year's Resolutions fail. *U.S. News.* Retrieved from http://health.usnews.com/health-news/blogs/eat-run/articles/2015-12-29/why-80-percent-of-new-years-resolutions-fail

**Luginbuhl, P. J., McWhirter, E. H., & McWhirter, B. T.** (2016). Sociopolitical development, autonomous motivation, and education outcomes: Implications for low-income Latina/o adolescents. *Journal of Latina/o Psychology, 4,* 43–59. http://dx.doi.org/10.1037/lat0000041

**Luhrmann, T. M., Padmavati, R., Tharoor, H., & Osei, A.** (2015). Differences in voice-hearing experiences of people with psychosis in the USA, India and Ghana: Interview-based study. *The British Journal of Psychiatry, 206,* 41–44. http://dx.doi.org/10.1192/bjp.bp.113.139048

**Lunardo, R., & Livat, F.** (2016). Congruency between color and shape of the front labels of wine: effects on fluency and aroma and quality perceptions. *International Journal of Entrepreneurship and Small Business, 29*(4), 528–541.

**Luo, S., Monterosso, J. R., Sarpelleh, K., & Page, K. A.** (2015). Differential effects of fructose versus glucose on brain and appetitive responses to food cues and decisions for food rewards. *Proceedings of the National Academy of Sciences of the United States of America, 112,* 6509–6514. http://dx.doi.org/10.1073/pnas.1503358112

**Luria, A. R.** (1976). *Cognitive development: Its cultural and social foundations.* Cambridge, MA: Harvard University Press.

**Lynn, S. J., Krackow, E., Loftus, E. F., Locke, T. G., & Lillienfeld, S. O.** (2015). Constructing the past: Problematic memory recovery techniques in psychotherapy. In S. O. Lilienfeld, S. J. Lynn, & J. M. Lohr (Eds.), *Science and pseudoscience in clinical psychology* (2nd ed., pp. 210–244). New York, NY: Guilford.

**Lynn, S. J., Lilienfeld, S. O., Merckelbach, H., Maxwell, R., Baltman, J., & Giesbrecht, T.** (2016). Dissociative disorders. In J. E. Maddux & B. A. Winstead (Eds.), *Psychopathology: Foundations for a contemporary understanding* (4th ed., pp. 298–317). New York, NY: Routledge/Taylor & Francis Group.

**Lysiak, M.** (2015, June 19). Charleston massacre: Mental illness common thread for mass shootings. *Newsweek.* Retrieved from http://www.newsweek.com/charlestonmassacre-mental-illness-common-thread-mass-shootings-344789

Ma, C. L., Ma, X. T., Wang, J. J., Liu, H., Chen, Y. F., & Yang, Y. (2017). Physical exercise induces hippocampal neurogenesis and prevents cognitive decline. *Behavioural Brain Research, 317,* 332–339. http://dx.doi.org/10.1016/j.bbr.2016.09.067

Ma, Q., Jin, J., Meng, L., & Shen, Q. (2014). The dark side of monetary incentive: How does extrinsic reward crowd out intrinsic motivation. *Neuro Report: For Rapid Communication of Neuroscience Research, 25,* 194–198. http://dx.doi.org/10.1097/WNR.0000000000000113

Maack, D. J., Buchanan, E., & Young, J. (2015). Development and psychometric investigation of an inventory to assess fight, flight, freeze tendencies: The Fight, Flight, Freeze Questionnaire. *Cognitive Behaviour Therapy, 44,* 117–127. http://dx.doi.org/10.1080/16506073.2014.972443

Maasumi, K., Thompson, N. R., Kriegler, J. S., & Tepper, S. J. (2015). Effect of onabotulinumtoxinA injection on depression in chronic migraine. *Headache: The Journal of Head and Face Pain, 55*(9), 1218–1224.

Maasumi, K., Thompson, N. R., Kriegler, J. S., & Tepper, S. J. (2015). Effect of onabotulinumtoxin A injection on depression in chronic migraine. *Headache: The Journal of Head and Face Pain, 55*(9), 1218–1224.

Mabe, A. G., Forney, K. J., & Keel, P. K. (2014). Do you "like" my photo? Facebook use maintains eating disorder risk. *International Journal of Eating Disorders, 47,* 516–523. http://dx.doi.org/10.1002/eat.22254

Macey, P. M., Rieken, N. S., Kumar, R., Ogren, J. A., Middlekauff, H. R., Wu, P., . . . Harper, R. M. (2016). Sex differences in insular cortex gyri responses to the valsalva maneuver. *Frontiers in Neurology, 7.* http://dx.doi.org/10.3389/fneur.2016.00087

MacKenzie, J., Smith, T. W., Uchino, B., White, P. H., Light, K. C., & Grewen, K. M. (2014). Depressive symptoms, anger/hostility, and relationship quality in young couples. *Journal of Social and Clinical Psychology, 33,* 380–396. http://dx.doi.org/10.1521/ jscp.2014.33.4.380

Mackey, R. A., & O'Brien, B. A. (1998). Marital conflict management: Gender and ethnic differences. *Social Work, 43*(2), 128–141.

Mackinnon, S. P., Smith, S. M., & Carter-Rogers, K. (2015). Multidimensional self-esteem and test derogation after negative feedback. *Canadian Journal of Behavioural Science/ Revue Canadienne des Sciences du Comportement, 47,* 123–126. http://dx.doi.org/10.1037/a0038364

Macmillan, M. B. (2000). *An odd kind of fame: Stories of Phineas Gage.* Cambridge, MA: MIT Press.

Macmillan, M., & Lena, M. L. (2010). Rehabilitating Phineas Gage. *Neuropsychological Rehabilitation, 20,* 641–658. http://dx.doi.org/10.1080/09602011003760527

Madden, K., Middleton, P., Cyna, A. M., Matthewson, M., & Jones, L. (2012). Hypnosis for pain management during labour and childbirth. *Cochrane Database of Systematic Reviews, 11.* http://dx.doi.org/10.1002/14651858.CD009356

Madsen, H. B., & Kim, J. H. (2016). Ontogeny of memory: An update on 40 years of work on infantile amnesia. *Behavioural Brain Research, 298*(Part A), 4–14. http://dx.doi.org/10.1016/j.bbr.2015.07.030

Maggiolini, A., & Codecà, L. (2016). The typical contents of Freud's and Jung's dreams. *International Journal of Dream Research, 9*(1), 1–6.

Magid, M., Reichenberg, J. S., Poth, P. E., Robertson, H. T., LaViolette, A. K., Kruger, T. H., & Wollmer, M. A. (2014). Treatment of major depressive disorder using botulinum toxin A: A 24-week randomized, double-blind, placebo-controlled study. *Journal of Clinical Psychiatry, 115,* 71–79. http://dx.doi.org/10.4088/JCP.13m08845.

Magnavita, J. J., & Anchin, J. C. (2014). *Unifying psychotherapy: Principles, methods, and evidence from clinical science.* New York, NY: Springer.

Maher, J. P., & Conroy, D. E. (2016). A dual-process model of older adults' sedentary behavior. *Health Psychology, 35,* 262–272. http://dx.doi.org/10.1037/hea0000300

Mahn, H., & John-Steiner, V. (2013). Vygotsky and sociocultural approaches to teaching and learning. In W. M. Reynolds, G. E. Miller, & I. B. Weiner (Eds.), *Handbook of psychology, Vol. 7. Educational psychology* (2nd ed., pp. 117–145). Hoboken, NJ: Wiley.

Maier, C., Laumer, S., Weinert, C., & Weitzel, T. (2015). The effects of technostress and switching stress on discontinued use of social networking services: A study of Facebook use. *Information Systems Journal, 25,* 275–308. http://dx.doi.org/10.1111/isj.12068

Maier, S. F., & Seligman, M. E. (2016). Learned helplessness at fifty: Insights from neuroscience. *Psychological Review, 123*(4), 349–367.http://dx.doi.org/10.1037/rev0000033

Main, M., & Solomon, J. (1986). Discovery of an insecure-disorganized attachment pattern. In T. Brazelton & M. W. Yogman (Eds.), *Affective development in infancy* (pp. 95–124). Westport, CT: Ablex.

Main, M., & Solomon, J. (1990). Procedures for identifying infants as disorganized/disoriented during the Ainsworth Strange Situation. In M. T. Greenberg, D. Cicchetti, & E. M. Cummings (Eds.), *Attachment in the preschool years: Theory, research, and intervention, The John D. and Catherine T. MacArthur Foundation series on mental health and development* (pp. 121–160). Chicago, IL: University of Chicago Press.

Maisto, S. A., Galizio, M., & Connors, G. J. (2015). *Drug use and abuse* (7th ed.). Boston, MA: Cengage.

Major, B., Spencer, S., Schmader, T., Wolfe, C., & Crocker, J. (1998). Coping with negative stereotypes about intellectual performance: The role of psychological disengagement. *Personality & Social Psychology Bulletin, 24,* 34–50.

Major, R. J., Whelton, W. J., Schimel, J., & Sharpe, D. (2016). Older adults and the fear of death: The protective function of generativity. *Canadian Journal on Aging, 35,* 261–272. http://dx.doi.org/10.1017/S0714980816000143

Makinodan, M., Rosen, K. M., Ito, S., & Corfas, G. (2012). A critical period for social experience-dependent oligodendrocyte maturation and myelination. *Science, 337,* 1357–60. http://dx.doi.org/10.1126/science.1220845.

Malavé, S., Ramakrishna, J., Heylen, E., Bharat, S., & Ekstrand, M. L. (2014). Differences in testing, stigma, and perceived consequences of stigmatization among heterosexual men and women living with HIV in Bengaluru, India. *AIDS Care, 26,* 396–403. http://dx.doi.org/10.1080/09540121.2013.819409

Malgady, R. G., Castagno, R. M., & Cardinale, J. A. (2014). Clinical tests and assessment: Ethnocultural and linguistic bias in mental health evaluation of Latinos. In F. T. L. Leong, L. Comas-Díaz, G. C. Nagayama Hall, V. C. McLoyd, & J. E. Trimble (Eds.), *APA handbooks in psychology. APA handbook of multicultural psychology, Vol.2. Applications and training* (pp. 165–179). Washington, DC: American Psychological Association. http://dx.doi.org/10.1037/14187-010

Mallan, K. M., Lipp, O. V., & Cochrane, B. (2013). Slithering snakes, angry men and out-group members: What and whom are we evolved to fear? *Cognition and Emotion, 27,* 1168–1180. http://dx.doi.org/10.1080/02699931.2013.778195

Mallya, S., & Fiocco, A. J. (2016). Effects of mindfulness training on cognition and well-being in healthy older adults. *Mindfulness, 7,* 453–465. http://dx.doi.org/10.1007/s12671-015-0468-6

Maloney, E. A., Gunderson, E. A., Levine, S. C., & Beilock, S. L. (2015). Intergenerational effects of parents' math anxiety on children's math achievement and anxiety. *Psychological Science, 26,* 1480–1488. http://dx.doi.org/10.1177/0956797615592630.

Malooly, A. M., Flannery, K. M., & Ohannessian, C. M. (2017). Coping mediates the association between gender and depressive symptomatology in adolescence. *International Journal of Behavioral Development, 41*(2), 185–197. http://dx.doi.org/10.1177/0165025415616202

Mammen, G., & Faulkner, G. (2013). Physical activity and the prevention of depression: A systematic review of prospective studies. *American Journal of Preventive Medicine, 45,* 649–657. http://dx.doi.org/10.1016/j.amepre.2013.08.001.

Mancia, M., & Baggott, J. (2008). The early unrepressed unconscious in relation to Matte-Blanco's thought. *International Forum of Psychoanalysis, 17,* 201–212. http://dx.doi.org/10.1080/08037060701676359

Mancini, A. D., Littleton, H. L., & Grills, A. E. (2016). Can people benefit from acute stress? Social support, psychological improvement, and resilience after the Virginia Tech campus shootings. *Clinical Psychological Science, 4,* 401–417. http://dx.doi.org/10.1177/2167702615601001

Manczak, E. M., Mangelsdorf, S. C., McAdams, D. P., Wong, M. S., Schoppe-Sullivan, S., & Brown, G. L. (2016). Autobiographical memories of childhood and sources of subjectivity in parents' perceptions of infant temperament. *Infant Behavior & Development, 44,* 77–85. http://dx.doi.org/10.1016/j.infbeh.2016.06.001

Mandela, N. (1994). *Long walk to freedom.* New York, NY: Little, Brown.

Månsson, K. N., Salami, A., Carlbring, P., Boraxbekk, C. J., Andersson, G., & Furmark, T. (2017). Structural but not functional neuroplasticity one year after effective cognitive behaviour therapy for social anxiety disorder. *Behavioural Brain Research, 318,* 45–51. http://dx.doi.org/10.1016/j.bbr.2016.11.018

Many, M., Stepka, P., Celano, M., Petersen-Coleman, M. N., & Pate, L. (2014). Sexually abused children. In L. Grossman & S. Walfish (Eds.), *Translating psychological research into practice* (pp. 487–494). New York, NY: Springer.

**Maples-Keller, J. L., Berke, D. S., Few, L. R., & Miller, J. D.** (2016). A review of sensation seeking and its empirical correlates: Dark, bright, and neutral hues. In V. Zeigler-Hill & D. K. Marcus (Eds.), *The dark side of personality: Science and practice in social, personality, and clinical psychology* (pp. 137–156). Washington, DC: American Psychological Association. http://dx.doi.org/10.1037/14854-008

**Marchant, J.** (2016). *Cure: A journey into the science of mind over body.* New York, NY: Crown.

**Marcus Luttrell.** (n.d.). *AZQuotes.com.* Retrieved January 16, 2017, from AZQuotes.com Web site: http://www.azquotes.com/quote/1427672

**Marczinski, C. A.** (2014). *Drug use, misuse, and abuse.* Hoboken, NJ: Wiley.

**Marigold, D. C., & Anderson, J. E.** (2016). Shifting expectations of partners' responsiveness changes outcomes of conflict discussions. *Personal Relationships, 23*(3), 517–535. http://dx.doi.org/10.1111/pere.12141

**Market Opinion Research International** (MORI). (2005, January). *Use of animals in medical research for coalition for medical progress.* London, UK: Author.

**Mar, R. A., Tackett, J. L., & Moore, C.** (2010). Exposure to media and theory-of-mind development in preschoolers. *Cognitive Development, 25,* 69–78. http://dx.doi.org/10.1016/j.cogdev.2009.11.002

**Marshall, D. S.** (1971). Sexual behavior in Mangaia. In D. S. Marshall & R. C. Suggs (Eds.), *Human sexual behavior* (pp. 103–162). Englewood Cliffs, NJ: Prentice Hall.

**Marshall, E.-J., & Brockman, R. N.** (2016). The relationships between psychological flexibility, self-compassion, and emotional well-being. *Journal of Cognitive Psychotherapy, 30,* 60–72. http://dx.doi.org/10.1891/0889-8391.30.1.60

**Martey, R. M., Stromer-Galley, J., Banks, J., Wu, J., & Consalvo, M.** (2014). The strategic female: Gender-switching and player behavior in online games. *Information, Communication & Society, 17,* 286–300. http://dx.doi.org/10.1080/1369118X.2013.874493

**Martin, A. J., & Marsh, H. W.** (2006). Academic resilience and its psychological and educational correlates: A construct validity approach. *Psychology in the Schools, 43,* 267–281.

**Martínez-Hernáez, A., Carceller-Maicas, N., DiGiacomo, S. M., & Ariste, S.** (2016). Social support and gender differences in coping with depression among emerging adults: A mixed-methods study. *Child and Adolescent Psychiatry and Mental Health, 10,* Article 2. http://dx.doi.org/10.1186/s13034-015-0088-x

**Martinez-Murcia, F. J., Lai, M.-C., Górriz, J. M., Ramírez, J., Young, A. M. H., Deoni, S. C. L., . . . Suckling, J.** (2016). On the brain structure heterogeneity of autism: Parsing out acquisition site effects with significance-weighted principal component analysis. *Human Brain Mapping, 38,* 1208–1223. http://dx.doi.org/10.1002/hbm.23449

**Martin-Storey, A., Serbin, L. A., Stack, D. M., Ledingham, J. E., & Schwartzman, A. E.** (2012). Self and peer perceptions of childhood aggression, social withdrawal and likeability predict adult personality factors: A prospective longitudinal study. *Personality and Individual Differences, 53,* 843–848. http://dx.doi.org/10.1016/j.paid.2012.06.018

**Marx, D. M., Ko, S. J., & Friedman, R. A.** (2009). The "Obama effect": How a salient role model reduces race-based performance differences. *Journal of Experimental Social Psychology, 45,* 953–956. http://dx.doi.org/10.1016/j.jesp.2009.03.012

**Mase, A. S., Cho, H., & Prokopy, L. S.** (2015). Enhancing the Social Amplification of Risk Framework (SARF) by exploring trust, the availability heuristic, and agricultural advisors' belief in climate change. *Journal of Environmental Psychology, 41,* 166–176. http://dx.doi.org/10.1016/j.jenvp.2014.12.004

**Maslow, A. H.** (1954). *Motivation and personality.* New York, NY: Harper & Row.

**Maslow, A. H.** (1970). *Motivation and personality.* New York, NY: Harper & Row.

**Maslow, A. H.** (1999). *Toward a psychology of being* (3rd ed.). New York, NY: Wiley.

**Mason, S., & Zhou, F. C.** (2015). Editorial: Genetics and epigenetics of fetal alcohol spectrum disorders. *Frontiers in Genetics, 6,* 146. http://dx.doi.org/10.3389/fgene.2015.00146

**Massing-Schaffer, M., Liu, R. T., Kraines, M. A., Choi, J. Y., & Alloy, L. B.** (2015). Elucidating the relation between childhood emotional abuse and depressive symptoms in adulthood: The mediating role of maladaptive interpersonal processes. *Personality and Individual Differences, 74,* 106–111. http://dx.doi.org/10.1016/j.paid.2014.09.045

**Masten, A. S., & Coatsworth, J. D.** (1998). The development of competence in favorable and unfavorable environments: Lessons from research on successful children. *American Psychologist, 53,* 205–220. http://dx.doi.org/10.1037/0003-066X.53.2.205

**Master, A., Cheryan, S., & Meltzoff, A. N.** (2016). Computing whether she belongs: Stereotypes undermine girls' interest and sense of belonging in computer science. *Journal of Educational Psychology, 108,* 424–437. http://dx.doi.org/10.1037/edu0000061

**Masters, W. H., & Johnson, V. E.** (1961). Orgasm, anatomy of the female. In A. Ellis & A. Abarbonel (Eds.), *Encyclopedia of sexual behavior* (Vol. 2, pp. 792–805). New York, NY: Hawthorn.

**Masters, W. H., & Johnson, V. E.** (1966). *Human sexual response.* Boston, MA: Little, Brown.

**Masters, W. H., & Johnson, V. E.** (1970). *Human sexual inadequacy.* Boston, MA: Little, Brown.

**Mathes, J., Schredl, M., & Göritz, A. S.** (2014). Frequency of typical dream themes in most recent dreams: An online study. *Dreaming, 24,* 57–66. http://dx.doi.org/10.1037/a0035857

**Matlin, M. W., & Farmer, T. A.** (2016). *Cognition* (9th ed.). Hoboken, NJ: Wiley.

**Matsumoto, D.** (2000). *Culture and psychology: People around the world.* Belmont, CA: Cengage.

**Mauguière, F., & Corkin, S.** (2015). H.M. never again! An analysis of H. M.'s epilepsy and treatment. *Revue Neurologique, 171,* 273–281. http://dx.doi.org/10.1016/j.neurol.2015.01.002

**Maule, J., Witzel, C., & Franklin, A.** (2014). Getting the gist of multiple hues: Metric and categorical effects on ensemble perception of hue. *Journal of the Optical Society of America, 31,* A93–A102. http://dx.doi.org/10.1364/JOSAA.31.000A93

**Maunder, A.** (2016). *Victorian crime, madness, and sensation.* New York, NY: Routledge.

**May, A. C., Rudy, B. M., Davis, T. E., & Matson, J. L.** (2013). Evidence-based behavioral treatment of dog phobia with young children: Two case examples. *Behavior Modification, 37,* 143–160.

**May, M. T., Gompels, M., Delpech, V., Porter, K., Orkin, C., Kegg, S., . . . Sabin, C.** (2014). Impact on life expectancy of HIV-1 positive individuals of CD4· cell count and viral load response to antiretroviral therapy. *AIDS, 28,* 1193–1202. http://dx.doi.org/10.1097/QAD.0000000000000243

**Mayo Clinic.** (2017). Self-injury/cutting. *MayoClincic.org.* Retrieved February 22, 2017 from http://www.mayoclinic.org/diseases-conditions/self-injury/symptoms-causes/dxc-20165427

**Mayordomo-Rodríguez, T., Meléndez-Moral, J. C., Viguer-Segui, P., & Sales-Galán, A.** (2015). Coping strategies as predictors of well-being in youth adult. *Social Indicators Research, 122,* 479–489. http://dx.doi.org/10.1007/s11205-014-0689-4

**Ma, Y., Ratnasabapathy, R., & Gardiner, J.** (2017). Carbohydrate craving: Not everything is sweet. *Current Opinion in Clinical Nutrition & Metabolic Care, 20*(4), 261–265. http://doi.org/doi:10.1097/MCO.0000000000000374

**Mazandarani, A., Aguilar-Vafaie, M. E., & Domhoff, G.** (2013). Content analysis of Iranian college students' dreams: Comparison with American data. *Dreaming, 23,* 163–174. http://dx.doi.org/10.1037/a0032352

**McAnulty, R. D., & Milling, S.** (2015). *Sex therapy. The encyclopedia of clinical psychology.* Hoboken, NJ: Wiley. http://dx.doi.org/10.1002/9781118625392.wbecp291

**McCarthy, M. M., Arnold, A. P., Ball, G. F., Blaustein, J. D., & De Vries, G. J.** (2012). Sex differences in the brain: The not so inconvenient truth. *Journal of Neuroscience, 32,* 2241–2247. http://dx.doi.org/10.1523/JNEUROSCI.5372-11.2012

**McClelland, D. C.** (1958). Risk-taking in children with high and low need for achievement. In J. W. Atkinson (Ed.), *Motives in fantasy, action, and society* (pp. 306–321). Princeton, NJ: Van Nostrand.

**McClelland, D. C.** (1993). Intelligence is not the best predictor of job performance. *Current Directions in Psychological Science, 2,* 5–6.

**McClelland, J. L.** (2011). Memory as a constructive process: The parallel distributed processing approach. In S. Nalbantian, P. M. Matthews, & J. L. McClelland (Eds.), *The memory process: Neuroscientific and humanistic perspectives* (pp. 129–155). Cambridge, MA: MIT Press

**McClelland, J. L., Mirman, D., Folger, D. J., & Khaitan, P.** (2014). Interactive activation and mutual constraint satisfaction in perception and cognition. *Cognitive Science, 38*(6), 1139–1189. http://dx.doi.org/10.1111/cogs.12146

**McClintock, E. A.** (2014). Beauty and status: The illusion of exchange in partner selection? *American Sociological Review, 79,* 575–604. http://dx.doi.org/10.1177/0003122414536391.

**McClurg, J.** (2017, January 11). Rowling reigned over 2016 book sales, USA TODAY's annual list shows. *USA Today.* Retrieved March 16, 2017 from http://www.usatoday.com/story/life/books/2017/01/11/usa-today-2016-best-selling-book-trends-rowling-hawkins/96339968/

**McCormack, L., & Joseph, S.** (2014). Psychological growth in aging Vietnam veterans: Redefining shame and betrayal. *Journal of Humanistic Psychology, 54,* 336–355. http://dx.doi.org/10.1177/0022167813501393

**McCormick, D. A., McGinley, M. J., & Salkoff, D. B.** (2015). Brain state dependent activity in the cortex and thalamus. *Current Opinion in Neurobiology, 31,* 133–140. http://dx.doi.org/10.1016/j.conb.2014.10.003

**McCrae, R.** (2011). Cross-cultural research on the five-factor model of personality. *Online Readings in Psychology and Culture, Unit 4.* Retrieved from http://scholarworks.gvsu.edu/orpc/vol4/iss4/1

**McCrae, R. R.** (2015). A more nuanced view of reliability: Specificity in the trait hierarchy. *Personality and Social Psychology Review, 19,* 97–112. http://dx.doi.org/10.1177/1088868314541857

**McCrae, R. R., & Costa, P. T., Jr.** (2013). Introduction to the empirical and theoretical status of the five-factor model of personality traits. In T. A. Widiger & P. T. Costa, Jr. (Eds.), *Personality disorders and the five-factor model of personality* (3rd ed., pp. 15–27). Washington, DC: American Psychological Association.

**McCrae, R. R., Costa, P. T., Jr., Martin, T. A., Oryol, V. E., Rukavishnikov, A. A., Senin, I. G., . . . Urbánek, T.** (2004). Consensual validation of personality traits across cultures. *Journal of Research in Personality, 38,* 179–201.

**McCrae, R. R., Costa, P. T., Jr., Ostendorf, F., Angleitner, A., Hřebíčková, M., Avia, M. D., . . . Smith, P. B.** (2000). Nature over nurture: Temperament, personality, and life span development. *Journal of Personality and Social Psychology, 78,* 173–186. http://dx.doi.org/10.1037/0022-3514.78.1.173

**McCrae, R. R., Scally, M., Terracciano, A., Abecasis, G. R., & Costa P. T. Jr.** (2010). An alternative to the search for single polymorphisms: Toward molecular personality scales for the five-factor model. *Journal of Personality and Social Psychology, 99,* 1014–1024. http://dx.doi.org/10.1037/a0020964

**McDaniel, M. A., Cahill, M. J., Robbins, M., & Wiener, C.** (2014). Individual differences in learning and transfer: Stable tendencies for learning exemplars versus abstracting rules. *Journal of Experimental Psychology: General, 143,* 668–693. http://dx.doi.org/10.1037/a0032963

**McDaniel, S. H., & Belar, C. D.** (2016). Firearm violence prevention is a human rights issue. *APA Public Interest Directorate.* Retrieved from https://psychologybenefits.org/2016/06/27/firearm-violence-prevention-is-a-human-rights-issue/

**McDougall, W.** (1908). *Social psychology.* New York, NY: Putnam's Sons.

**McFarlane, D. A.** (2014). A positive theory of stereotyping and stereotypes: Is stereotyping useful? *Journal of Studies in Social Sciences, 8,* 140–163.

**McGeorge, C. R., Carlson, T. S., & Wetchler, J. L.** (2015). The history of marriage and family therapy. In J. L. Wetchler & L. L. Hecker (Eds.), *An introduction to marriage and family therapy* (2nd ed., pp. 3–42). New York, NY: Routledge/Taylor & Francis Group.

**McGillicuddy, N. B., Rychtarik, R. G., & Papandonatos, G. D.** (2015). Skill training versus 12-step facilitation for parents of substance-abusing teens. *Journal of Substance Abuse Treatment, 50,* 11–17. http://dx.doi.org/10.1016/j.jsat.2014.09.006

**McGloin, J. M., & Thomas, K. J.** (2016). Incentives for collective deviance: Group size and changes in perceived risk, cost, and reward. *Criminology, 54,* 459–486. http://dx.doi.org/10.1111/1745-9125.12111

**McGlone, M. S., & Pfiester, R. A.** (2015). Stereotype threat and the evaluative context of communication. *Journal of Language and Social Psychology, 34,* 111–137. http://dx.doi.org/10.1177/0261927X14562609

**McGrath, J. J., Petersen, L., Agerbo, E., Mors, O., Mortensen, P. B., & Pedersen, C. B.** (2014). A comprehensive assessment of parental age and psychiatric disorders. *JAMA Psychiatry, 71,* 301–309. http://dx.doi.org/10.1001/jamapsychiatry.2013.4081

**McGuinness, T. M.** (2015). Update on autism spectrum disorder: Vaccines, genomes, and social skills training. *Journal of Psychosocial Nursing and Mental Health Services, 53,* 27–30. http://dx.doi.org/10.3928/02793695-20150309-01

**McKellar, P.** (1972). Imagery from the standpoint of introspection. In P. W. Sheehan (Ed.), *The function and nature of imagery* (pp. 36–61). New York, NY: Academic Press.

**McKim, D. B., Niraula, A., Tarr, A. J., Wohleb, E. S., Sheridan, J. F., & Godbout, J. P.** (2016). Neuroinflammatory dynamics underlie memory impairments after repeated social defeat. *The Journal of Neuroscience, 36,* 2590–2604. *http://dx.doi.org/10.1523/JNEUROSCI.2394-15.2016*

**McKinnon, M. C., Palombo, D. J., Nazarov, A., Kumar, N., Khuu, W., & Levine, B.** (2015). Threat of death and autobiographical memory: A study of passengers from flight AT236. *Clinical Psychological Science, 3,* 487–502. http://dx.doi.org/10.1177/2167702614542280

**McLean, C. P., Su, Y. J., & Foa, E. B.** (2015). Mechanisms of symptom reduction in a combined treatment for comorbid posttraumatic stress disorder and alcohol dependence. *Journal of Consulting and Clinical Psychology, 83,* 655–661. http://dx.doi.org/10.1037/ccp0000024

**McLean, D., Thara, R., John, S., Barrett, R., Loa, P., McGrath, J., & Mowry, B.** (2014). DSM-IV "criterion A" schizophrenia symptoms across ethnically different populations: Evidence for differing psychotic symptom content or structural organization? *Culture, Medicine and Psychiatry, 38,* 406–426. http://dx.doi.org/10.1007/s11013-014-9385-8

**McLeigh, J. D.** (2015). Creating conditions that promote trust and participation by young people . . . And why it matters. *American Journal of Orthopsychiatry, 85,* S67–S69. http://dx.doi.org/10.1037/ort0000134

**McMurran, M., & Crawford, M. J.** (2016). Personality disorders. In C. M. Nezu & A. M. Nezu (Eds.), *The Oxford handbook of cognitive and behavioral therapies* (pp. 438–461). New York, NY: Oxford University Press.

**McNally, K.** (2016). A critical history of schizophrenia. London, UK: Palgrave Macmillan UK. http://dx.doi.org/10.1057/978-1-137-45681-6

**McNally, R. J.** (2012). Searching for repressed memory. *Nebraska Symposium on Motivation, 58,* 121–147. http://dx.doi.org/10.1007/978-1-4614-1195-6_4

**McNally, R. J., & Robinaugh, D. J.** (2015). Difficulties remembering the past and envisioning the future in people with trauma histories or complicated grief. In L. A. Watson & D. Bersten (Eds.), *Clinical perspectives on autobiographical memory* (pp. 242–264). New York, NY: Cambridge University Press. http://dx.doi.org/10.1017/CBO9781139626767.013

**McSweeney, F. K., & Murphy, E. S.** (2017). *The Wiley Blackwell handbook of operant and classical conditioning.* Hoboken, NJ: Wiley.

**McWhirter, J. E., & Hoffman-Goetz, L.** (2015). North American magazine coverage of skin cancer and recreational tanning before and after the WHO/IARC 2009 classification of indoor tanning devices as carcinogenic. *Journal of Cancer Education, 30*(3), 477–481. http://dx.doi.org/10.1007/s13187-014-0726-7

**Mead, W.** (2015). Cesar Millan biography. *The Biography.com.* Retrieved from http://www.biography.com/people/cesar-millan-082415

**Meaidi, A., Jennum, P., Ptito, M., & Kupers, R.** (2014). The sensory construction of dreams and nightmare frequency in congenitally blind and late blind individuals. *Sleep Medicine, 15,* 586–595. http://dx.doi.org/10.1016/j.sleep.2013.12.008

**Meaux, E., & Vuilleumier, P.** (2016). Facing mixed emotions: Analytic and holistic perception of facial emotion expressions engages separate brain networks. *NeuroImage, 141,* 154–173. http://dx.doi.org/10.1016/j.neuroimage.2016.07.004

**Mehrabian, A.** (1968). A relationship of attitude to seated posture orientation and distance. *Journal of Personality and Social Psychology, 10,* 26–30. http://dx.doi.org/10.1037/h0026384

**Mehrabian, A.** (1971). *Silent messages.* Belmont, CA: Cengage.

**Mehrabian, A.** (2007). *Nonverbal communication.* New Brunswick, NJ: Aldine Transaction.

**Mehra, R., & Strohl, K. P.** (2014). Pharmacology of sleep medicine. In K. Strohl (Ed.), *Competencies in sleep medicine* (pp. 27–44). New York, NY: Springer. http://dx.doi.org/10.1007/978-1-4614-9065-4_3

**Meier, M. H., Caspi, A., Cerdá, M., Hancox, R. J., Harrington, H., Houts, R., . . . Moffitt, T. E.** (2016). Associations between cannabis use and physical health problems in early midlife: A longitudinal comparison of persistent cannabis vs tobacco. *JAMA Psychiatry, 73*(7), 731–740. http://dx.doi.org/10.1001/jamapsychiatry.2016.0637

**Meijer, E. H., & Verschuere, B.** (2015). The polygraph: Current practice and new approaches. In P. A. Granhag, A. Vrij, & B. Verschuere (Eds.), *Detecting deception: Current challenges and cognitive approaches* (pp. 59–80). Hoboken, NJ: Wiley-Blackwell.

**Meirick, P. C., & Schartel Dunn, S.** (2015). Obama as exemplar: Debate exposure and implicit and explicit racial affect. *Howard Journal of Communications, 26,* 57–73. http://dx.doi.org/10.1080/10646175.2014.986312

**Meltzer, A. L., Makhavova, A., Hicks, L. L., French, J. E., McNulty, J. K., & Bradbury, T. N.** (2017). Quantifying the sexual afterglow: The lingering benefits of sex and their implications for pair-bonded relationships. *Psychological Science, 28*(5), 587-598. http://dx.doi.org/10.1177/0956797617691361

**Meltzoff, A. N., & Moore, M. K.** (1977). Imitation of facial and manual gestures by human neonates. *Science, 198,* 75–78. http://dx.doi.org/10.1126/science.198.4312.75

**Meltzoff, A. N., & Moore, M. K.** (1985). Cognitive foundations and social functions of imitation and intermodal representation in infancy. In J. Mehler & R. Fox (Eds.), *Neonate cognition: Beyond the blooming buzzing confusion* (pp. 139–156). Hillsdale, NJ: Erlbaum.

**Meltzoff, A. N., & Moore, M. K.** (1994). Imitation, memory, and the representation of persons. *Infant Behavior & Development, 17,* 83–99. http://dx.doi.org/10.1016/0163-6383(94)90024-8

Melzack, R. (1999). Pain and stress: A new perspective. In R. J. Gatchel & D. C. Turk (Eds.), *Psychosocial factors in pain: Critical perspectives* (pp. 89–106). New York, NY: Guilford.

Melzack, R., & Wall, P. D. (1965). Pain mechanisms: A new theory. *Science, 150,* 971–979.

Memili, E., Chang, E. P. C., Kellermanns, F. W., & Welsh, D. H. B. (2015). Role conflicts of family members in family firms. *European Journal of Work and Organizational Psychology, 24,* 143–151. http://dx.doi.org/10.1080/1359432X.2013.839549

Meng, Q., Zhuang, Y., Ying, Z., Agrawal, R., Yang, X., & Gomez-Pinilla, F. (2017). Traumatic brain injury induces genome-wide transcriptomic, methylomic, and network perturbations in brain and blood predicting neurological disorders. *EBioMedicine, 16,* 184. http://dx.doi.org/10.1016/j.ebiom.2017.01.04

Mentzel, T. Q., Lieverse, R., Bloemen, O., Viechtbauer, W., van Harten, P. N., & Genetic Risk and Outcome of Psychosis (GROUP) Investigators. (2017). High incidence and prevalence of drug-related movement disorders in young patients with psychotic disorders. *Journal of Clinical Psychopharmacology, 37*(2), 231–238. http://dx.doi.org/10.1097/JCP.0000000000000666

Mercadillo, R. E., Díaz, J. L., Pasaye, E. H., & Barrios, F. A. (2011). Perception of suffering and compassion experience: Brain gender disparities. *Brain and Cognition, 76,* 5–14. http://doi.org/10.1016/j.bandc.2011.03.019

Merckelbach, H., Lynn, S. J., & Lilienfeld, S. O. (2016). Vissia and co-workers claim that DID is trauma-based. But how strong is their evidence? *Acta Psychiatrica Scandinavica, 134*(6), 559–560. http://dx.doi.org/10.1111/acps.12642

Mermelshtine, R., & Barnes, J. (2016). Maternal responsive–didactic caregiving in play interactions with 10-month-olds and cognitive development at 18 months. *Infant and Child Development, 25,* 296–316. http://dx.doi.org/10.1002/icd.1961

Merrick, W. A. (2016). Changes in DSM-5 diagnostic criteria for paraphilic disorders. *Archives of Sexual Behavior, 45,* 2173–2179. http://dx.doi.org/10.1007/s10508-016-0845-9

Metcalf, P., & Huntington, R. (1991). *Celebrations of death: The anthropology of mortuary ritual* (2nd ed.). Cambridge, UK: Cambridge University Press.

Metgud, D., & Honap, R. (2015). Comparison of kangaroo mother care and tactile kinesthetic stimulation in low birth weight babies—An experimental study. *International Journal on Disability and Human Development, 14,* 147–150. http://dx.doi.org/10.1515/ijdhd-2014-0011

Mettler, E., Massey, C. M., & Kellman, P. J. (2016). A comparison of adaptive and fixed schedules of practice. *Journal of Experimental Psychology: General, 145,* 897–917. http://dx.doi.org/10.1037/xge0000170

Metz, K. (2016). *Careers in mental health: Opportunities in psychology, counseling, and social work.* Hoboken, NJ: Wiley.

Metzl, J., & MacLeish, K. T. (2015). Mental illness, mass shootings, and the politics of American firearms. *American Journal of Public Health, 105,* 240–249. http://dx.doi.org/10.2105/AJPH.2014.302242

Meyer, U. (2016). Rodent models of multiple environmental exposures with relevance to schizophrenia. In M. V. Pletnikov & J. Waddington (Eds.), *Modeling the psychopathological dimensions of schizophrenia: From molecules to behavior* (pp. 361–371). San Diego, CA: Elsevier Academic Press.

Miano, S. (2017). Circadian rhythm disorders in childhood. In S. Nevšímalová & O. Bruni (Eds.), *Sleep disorders in children* (pp. 253–280). Cham, CH: Springer International Publishing. http://dx.doi.org/10.1007/978-3-319-28640-2_12

Michael, R. B., & Garry, M. (2016). Ordered questions bias eyewitnesses and jurors. *Psychonomic Bulletin & Review, 23,* 601–608. http://dx.doi.org/10.3758/s13423-015-0933-1

Mikal, J. P., Rice, R. E., Kent, R. G., & Uchino, B. N. (2016). 100 million strong: A case study of group identification and deindividuation on Imgur.Com. *New Media & Society, 18*(11), 2485–2506.

Mikels, J. A., & Shuster, M. M. (2016). The interpretative lenses of older adults are not rose-colored—just less dark: Aging and the interpretation of ambiguous scenarios. *Emotion, 16,* 94–100. http://dx.doi.org/10.1037/emo0000104

Miklikowska, M. (2017). Development of anti-immigrant attitudes in adolescence: The role of parents, peers, intergroup friendships, and empathy. *British Journal of Psychology, 108*(3), 626–648. http://dx.doi.org/10.1111/bjop.12236

Mikulincer, M., Shaver, P. R., Dovidio, J. F., & Simpson, J. A. (Eds.). (2015). *APA handbook of personality and social psychology, Vol. 2. Group processes.* Washington, DC: American Psychological Association. http://dx.doi.org/10.1037/14342-000

Milgram, S. (1963). Behavioral study of obedience. *Journal of Abnormal and Social Psychology, 67,* 371–378. http://dx.doi.org/10.1037/h0040525

Milgram, S. (1974). *Obedience to authority: An experimental view.* New York, NY: Harper & Row.

Miller, A. A., & Spencer, S. J. (2014). Obesity and neuroinflammation: A pathway to cognitive impairment. *Brain, Behavior, and Immunity, 42,* 10–21. http://dx.doi.org/10.1016/j.bbi.2014.04.001

Miller, B. R., & Hen, R. (2015). The current state of the neurogenic theory of depression and anxiety. *Current Opinion in Neurobiology, 30,* 51–58. http://dx.doi.org/10.1007/978-94-017-9576-0

Miller, D. I., & Halpern, D. F. (2014). The new science of cognitive sex differences. *Trends in Cognitive Sciences, 18*(1), 37–45. http://dx.doi.org/10.1016/j.tics.2013.10.011

Miller, D. P., & Brooks-Gunn, J. (2015). Obesity. In T. P. Gullotta, R. W. Plant, & M. A. Evans (Eds.), *Handbook of adolescent behavioral problems: Evidence-based approaches to prevention and treatment* (2nd ed., pp. 287–304). New York, NY: Springer. http://dx.doi.org/10.1007/978-1-4899-7497-6_15

Miller, G. A. (1956). The magical number seven, plus or minus two: Some limits on our capacity for processing information. *Psychological Review, 63,* 81–97. http://dx.doi.org/10.1037/h0043158

Miller, J. G., & Bersoff, D. M. (1998). The role of liking in perceptions of the moral responsibility to help: A cultural perspective. *Journal of Experimental Social Psychology, 34,* 443–469.

Miller, J. L., Saklofske, D. H., Weiss, L. G., Drozdick, L., Llorente, A. M., Holdnack, J. A., & Prifitera, A. (2016). Issues related to the WISC-V assessment of cognitive functioning in clinical and special groups. In L. G. Weiss, D. H. Saklofske, J. A. Holdnack & A. Prifitera (Eds.), *WISC-V assessment and interpretation: Scientist-practitioner perspectives* (pp. 287–343). San Diego, CA: Elsevier Academic Press. http://dx.doi.org/10.1016/B978-0-12-404697-9.00010-8

Miller, K. B., Lund, E., & Weatherly, J. (2012). Applying operant learning to the stay-leave decision in domestic violence. *Behavior and Social Issues, 21,* 135–151. http://dx.doi.org/10.5210/bsi.v21i0.4015

Miller-Graff, L. E., & Cheng, P. (2017). Consequences of violence across the lifespan: Mental health and sleep quality in pregnant women. *Psychological Trauma: Theory, Research, Practice, and Policy.* No Pagination Specified. http://dx.doi.org/10.1037/tra0000252

Miller-Matero, L. R., Chipungu, K., Martinez, S., Eshelman, A., & Eisenstein, D. (2017). How do I cope with pain? Let me count the ways: Awareness of pain coping behaviors and relationships with depression and anxiety. *Psychology, Health & Medicine, 22,* 19–27. http://dx.doi.org/10.1080/13548506.2016.1191659

Millings, A., Walsh, J., Hepper, E., & O'Brien, M. (2013). Good partner, good parent: Responsiveness mediates the link between romantic attachment and parenting style. *Personality and Social Psychology Bulletin, 39,* 170–180. http://dx.doi.org/10.1177/0146167212468333

Mills, P. J., Redwine, L., Wilson, K., Pung, M. A., Chinh, K., Greenberg, B. H., . . . Chopra, D. (2015). The role of gratitude in spiritual well-being in asymptomatic heart failure patients. *Spirituality in Clinical Practice, 2*(1), 5–17. http://dx.doi.org/10.1037/scp0000050

Milojev, P., Osborne, D., & Sibley, C. G. (2014). Personality resilience following a natural disaster. *Social Psychological and Personality Science, 5,* 760–768.

Miltenberger, R. G. (2011). *Behavior modification: Principles and procedures* (5th ed.). Belmont, CA: Cengage.

Mindell, J. A., & Owens, J. A. (2015). *A clinical guide to pediatric sleep: Diagnosis and management of sleep problems* (3rd ed.). Alphen, NL: Wolters Kluwer.

Mineka, S., & Oehlberg, K. (2008). The relevance of recent developments in classical conditioning to understanding the etiology and maintenance of anxiety disorders. *Acta Psychologica, 127,* 567–580.

Mischel, W. (1966). Theory and research on the antecedents of self-imposed delay of reward. In B. A. Maher (Ed.), *Progress in experimental personality research* (pp. 85–131). New York: NY: Academic Press.

Mischel, W. (2014). *The marshmallow test: Mastering self-control.* New York, NY: Little, Brown, & Company.

Mischel, W., Ayduk, O., Berman, M. G., Casey, B. J., Gotlib, I. H., Jonides, J., . . . Shoda, Y. (2011). 'Willpower' over the life span: Decomposing self-regulation. *Social Cognitive and Affective Neuroscience, 6,* 252–256. http://dx.doi.org/10.1093/scan/nsq08

Mischel, W., & Ebbesen, E. B. (1970). Attention in delay of gratification. *Journal of Personality and Social Psychology, 16,* 329–337. http://dx.doi.org/10.1037/h0029815

Mitchell, B. A., & Wister, A. V. (2015). Midlife challenge or welcome departure? Cultural and family-related expectations of empty nest transitions. *The International Journal of Aging & Human Development, 81,* 260–280. http://dx.doi.org/10.1177/0091415015622790

Mitchell, J. M., O'Neil, J. P., Janabi, M., Marks, S. M., Jagust, W. J., & Fields, H. L. (2012). Alcohol consumption induces endogenous opioid release in the human orbitofrontal cortex and nucleus accumbens. *Science Translational Medicine, 4*: 116ra6. http://dx.doi.org/10.1126/scitranslmed.3002902

Mithoefer, M. C., Grob, C. S., & Brewerton, T. D. (2016). Novel psychopharmacological therapies for psychiatric disorders: Psilocybin and MDMA. T*he Lancet Psychiatry, 3*, 481–488.

Modecki, K. L., Hagan, M. J., Sandler, I., & Wolchik, S. A. (2015). Latent profiles of nonresidential father engagement six years after divorce predict long-term offspring outcomes. *Journal of Clinical Child & Adolescent Psychology, 44*(1), 123–136. http://dx.doi.org/10.1080/15374416.2013.865193

Mok, P. L. H., Webb, R. T., Appleby, L., & Pedersen, C. B. (2016). Full spectrum of mental disorders linked with childhood residential mobility. *Journal of Psychiatric Research, 78*, 57–64. http://dx.doi.org/10.1016/j.jpsychires.2016.03.011

Mokrova, I. L., O'Brien, M., Calkins, S. D., Leerkes, E. M., & Marcovitch, S. (2013). The role of persistence at preschool age in academic skills at kindergarten. *European Journal of Psychology of Education, 28*, 1495–1503. http://dx.doi.org/10.1007/s10212-013-0177-2

Mokrysz, C., Landy, R., Gage, S. H., Munafò, M. R., Roiser, J. P., & Curran, H. V. (2016). Are IQ and educational outcomes in teenagers related to their cannabis use? A prospective cohort study. *Journal of Psychopharmacology, 30*, 159–168. http://dx.doi.org/10.1177/0269881115622241

Moleiro, C., Ratinho, I., & Bernardes, S. (2017). Autonomy-connectedness in collectivistic cultures: An exploratory cross-cultural study among Portuguese natives, Cape-Verdean and Chinese people residing in Portugal. *Personality and Individual Differences, 104*, 23–28.

Molina, B. S., & Pelham, W. E., Jr. (2014). Attention-deficit/hyperactivity disorder and risk of substance use disorder: Developmental considerations, potential pathways, and opportunities for research. *Annual Review of Clinical Psychology, 10*, 607–639.

Møller, A. P., & Erritzøe, J. (2014). Predator–prey interactions, flight initiation distance and brain size. *Journal of Evolutionary Biology, 27*, 34–42. http://dx.doi.org/10.1111/jeb.12272

Monastra, V. J. (2014). Temperament may be inherited, but emotional control is learned. In V. J. Monastra (Ed.), *Parenting children with ADHD: 10 lessons that medicine cannot teach* (2nd ed., pp. 151–179). Washington, DC: American Psychological Association.

Money, J., Prakasam, K. S., & Joshi, V. N. (1991). Semen-conservation doctrine from ancient Ayurvedic to modern sexological theory. *American Journal of Psychotherapy, 45*, 9–13.

Monin, B. (2003). The warm glow heuristic: When liking leads to familiarity. *Journal of Personality and Social Psychology, 85*, 1035–1048.

Montangero, J., & Cavallero, C. (2015). What renders dreams more or less narrative? A microstructural study of REM-and Stage 2 dream reports upon morning awakening. *International Journal of Dream Research, 8*(2), 105–119.

Montenigro, P. H., Alosco, M. L., Martin, B. M., Daneshvar, D. H., Mez, J., Chaisson, C. E., . . . Tripodis, Y. (2017). Cumulative head impact exposure predicts later-life depression, apathy, executive dysfunction, and cognitive impairment in former high school and college football players. *Journal of Neurotrauma, 34*(2), 328–340. http://dx.doi.org/10.1089/neu.2016.4413

Moon, C., Lagercrantz, H., & Kuhl, P. K. (2013). Language experienced in utero affects vowel perception after birth: A two-country study. *ActaPaediatrica, 102*, 156–160. http://dx.doi.org/10.1111/apa.12098

Mooradian, T., Matzler, K., Uzelac, B., & Bauer, F. (2016). Perspiration and inspiration: Grit and innovativeness as antecedents of entrepreneurial success. *Journal of Economic Psychology, 56*, 232–243. http://dx.doi.org/10.1016/j.joep.2016.08.001

Moore, D. L. (2013). USA's Manteo Mitchell runs 4x400 relay on broken leg. *USA Today Sports.* Retrieved from http://usatoday30.usatoday.com/sports/olympics/london/track/story/2012–08–09/usa-man teo-mitchell-runs-4x400-relay-onbroken-leg/56915070/1

Moore, D. W. (2005). Three in four Americans believe in paranormal: Little change from similar results in 2001. *Americas.* Retrieved from http://www.gallup.com/poll/16915/threefour-americans-believe-paranormal.aspx

Morelli, S. A., Lee, I. A., Arnn, M. E., & Zaki, J. (2015). Emotional and instrumental support provision interact to predict well-being. *Emotion, 15*, 484–493. http://dx.doi.org/10.1037/ emo0000084

Morey, L. C. (2013). Measuring personality and psychopathology. In J. A. Schinka, W. F. Velicer, & I. B. Weiner (Eds.), *Handbook of psychology, Vol. 2. Research methods in psychology* (2nd ed., pp. 395–427). Hoboken, NJ: Wiley.

Morgan, B., Gulliford, L., & Kristjánsson, K. (2017). A new approach to measuring moral virtues: The Multi-Component Gratitude Measure. *Personality and Individual Differences, 107*, 179–189. http://dx.doi.org/10.1016/j.paid.2016.11.044

Morgan, C. A., & Southwick, S. (2014). Perspective: I believe what I remember, but it may not be true. *Neurobiology of Learning and Memory, 112*, 101–103. http://dx.doi.org/10.1016/j.nlm.2013.12.011

Morgan, C. A., Southwick, S., Steffian, G., Hazlett, G. A., & Loftus, E. F. (2013). Misinformation can influence memory for recently experienced, highly stressful events. *International Journal of Law and Psychiatry, 36*, 11–17. http://dx.doi.org/10.1016/j.ijlp.2012.11.002

Morgan, C. D., & Murray, H. A. (1935). A method of investigating fantasies. The Thematic Apperception Test. *Archives of Neurology and Psychiatry, 34*, 289–306.

Morgan, J. (2017). If other ways don't work, try the immune system? *The Lancet Neurology, 16*(2), 109. http://dx.doi.org/10.1016/S1474-4422(16)30307-6

Mori, K., Ito-Koyama, A., Arai, M., & Hanayama, A. (2014). Boys, be independent! Conformity development of Japanese children in the Asch experiment without using confederates. *Psychology, 5*, 617–623. http://dx.doi.org/10.4236/psych.2014.57073.

Morin-Major, J. K., Marin, M.-F., Durand, N., Wan, N., Juster, R.-P., & Lupien, S. J. (2016). Facebook behaviors associated with diurnal cortisol in adolescents: Is befriending stressful? *Psychoneuroendocrinology*, 63, 238–246. http://dx.doi.org/10.1016/j.psyneuen.2015.10.005

Morling, B. (2015). *Research methods in psychology: Evaluating a world of information* (2nd ed.). New York, NY: W.W. Norton & Company.

Morrison, A. B., Goolsarran, M., Rogers, S. L., & Jha, A. P. (2013). Taming a wandering attention: short-form mindfulness training in student Cohorts. *Frontiers in Human Neuroscience*, 7, 897. http://doi.org/10.3389/fnhum.2013.00897

Morrow, A. (2016, May 9). The four phases and the four tasks of grief. *Verywell.* Retrieved from https://www.verywell.com/the-four-phases-and-tasks-of-grief-1132550

Morry, M. M., Kito, M., & Dunphy, L. (2014). How do I see you? Partner enhancement in dating couples. *Canadian Journal of Behavioural Science, 46*, 356–365. http://dx.doi.org/10.1037/a0033167

Mortazavi, N, S., & Yarolahi, N. (2015). Meta-analysis of the relationship between resilience and mental health. *Journal of Fundamentals of Mental Health, 17*(3), 103–108. https://pdfs.semanticscholar.org/654b/1218c1e3e39bbebb-bae6479bf5dde413bde1.pdf

Mosher, C., & Akins, S. (2014). *Drugs and drug policy* (2nd ed.). Thousand Oaks, CA: Sage.

Moss-Racusin, C. A., Dovidio, J. F., Brescoll, V. L., Graham, M. J., & Handelsman, J. (2012). Science faculty's subtle gender biases favor male students. *Proceedings of the National Academy of Sciences of the United States of America, 109*, 16474–16479. http://dx.doi.org/10.1073/pnas.1211286109

Mouilso, E. R., & Calhoun, K. S. (2016). Personality and perpetration: Narcissism among college sexual assault perpetrators. *Violence Against Women, 22*, 1228–1242. http://dx.doi.org/10.1177/1077801215622575

Moulding, N. (2016). *Gendered violence, mental health and recovery in everyday lives: Beyond trauma.* London, UK: Taylor & Francis.

Moutinho, A., Pereira, A., & Jorge, G. (2011). Biology of homosexuality. *European Psychiatry, 26*, 1741–1753.

Moutsiana, C., Johnstone, T., Murray, L., Fearon, P., Cooper, P. J., Pliatsikas, C., . . . Halligan, S. L. (2015). Insecure attachment during infancy predicts greater amygdala volumes in early adulthood. *Journal of Child Psychology and Psychiatry, 56*, 540–548. http://dx.doi.org/10.1111/jcpp.12317

Mrazek, M. D., Franklin, M. S., Phillips, D. T., Baird, B., & Schooler, J. W. (2013). Mindfulness training improves working memory capacity and GRE performance while reducing mind wandering. *Psychological Science, 24*, 776–781. http://dx.doi.org/10.1177/0956797612459659

Mueller, P. A., & Oppenheimer, D. M. (2014) The pen is mightier than the keyboard: Advantages of longhand over laptop note taking. *Psychological Science*, 25, 1159–1168. http://dx.doi.org/10.1177/0956797614524581

Muise, A., Schimmack, U., & Impett, E. A. (2016). Sexual frequency predicts greater well-being, but more is not always better. *Social Psychological and Personality Science, 7*, 295–302. http://dx.doi.org/10.1177/1948550615616462

Mullen, N. W., Maxwell, H., & Bédard, M. (2015). Decreasing driver speeding with feedback and a token economy. *Transportation Research Part F: Traffic Psychology and Behaviour, 28*, 77–85. http://dx.doi.org/10.1016/j.trf.2014.11.008

Muller, C. A., Schmitt, K., Barber, A. L. A., & Hubert, L. (2015). Dogs can discriminate emotional expressions of human faces. *Current Biology, 5,* 601–605. doi.org/10.1016/j.cub.2014.12.055

**Müller, C. P., & Homberg, J. R.** (2015). The role of serotonin in drug use and addiction. *Behavioural Brain Research, 277,* 146–192. http://dx.doi.org/10.1016/j.bbr.2014.04.007

**Müller, S., Mychajliw, C., Hautzinger, M., Fallgatter, A. J., Saur, R., & Leyhe, T.** (2014). Memory for past public events depends on retrieval frequency but not memory age in Alzheimer's disease. *Journal of Alzheimer's Disease, 38,* 379–390. http://dx.doi.org/10.3233/JAD-130923

**Mullins, E. N., Miller, A. L., Cherian, S. S., Lumeng, J. C., Wright, K. P., Kurth, S., & Lebourgeois, M. K.** (2016). Acute sleep restriction increases dietary intake in preschool-age children. *Journal of Sleep Research, 26*(1), 48–54. http://dx.doi.org/10.1111/jsr.12450

**Munoz, L., & Anastassiou-Hadjicharalambous, X.** (2011). Disinhibited behaviors in young children: Relations with impulsivity and autonomic psychophysiology. *Biological Psychology, 86,* 349–359.

**Munsey, C.** (2006). Emerging adults: The in-between age. *Monitor on Psychology, 37,* 68. Retrieved from http://www.apa.org/monitor/jun06/emerging.aspx

**Murdock, K. K.** (2013). Texting while stressed: Implications for students' burnout, sleep, and well-being. *Psychology of Popular Media Culture, 2,* 207–221. http://dx.doi.org/10.1037/ppm0000012

**Murray, C. E., Lundgren, K., Olson, L. N., & Hunnicutt, G.** (2016). Practice update: What professionals who are not brain injury specialists need to know about intimate partner violence–related traumatic brain injury. *Trauma, Violence, & Abuse, 17,* 298–305. http://dx.doi.org/10.1177/1524838015584364

**Mustelin, L., Latvala, A., Raevuori, A., Rose, R. J., Kaprio, J., & Keski-Rahkonen, A.** (2016). Risky drinking behaviors among women with eating disorders—A longitudinal community-based study. *International Journal of Eating Disorders, 49,* 563–571. http://dx.doi.org/10.1002/eat.22526

**Myers, A.** (2015). Neonatal male circumcision, if not already commonplace, would be plainly unacceptable by modern ethical standards. *The American Journal of Bioethics, 15,* 54–55. http://dx.doi.org/10.1080/15265161.2014.990166

**Nagasawa, M., Mitsui, S., En, S., Ohtani, N., Ohta, M., Sakuma, Y., . . . Kikusui, T.** (2015). Social evolution. Oxytocin-gaze positive loop and the coevolution of human-dog bonds. *Science, 348,* 333–336. http://dx.doi.org/10.1126/science.1261022.

**Naghavi, M., Wang, H., Lozano, R., Davis, A., Liang, X., Zhou, M., . . . & Murray, C. J.** (2015). Global, regional, and national age–sex specific all-cause and cause-specific mortality for 240 causes of death, 1990–2013: A systematic analysis for the Global Burden of Disease Study 2013. *The Lancet, 385,* 117–171.

**Nairne, J. S., & Neath, I.** (2013). Sensory and working memory. In A. F. Healy, R. W. Proctor, & I. B. Weiner (Eds.), *Handbook of psychology, Vol. 4. Experimental psychology* (2nd ed., pp. 419–445). Hoboken, NJ: Wiley.

**Na, J., & Chan, M. Y.** (2015). Culture, cognition, and intercultural relations. In J. E. Warnick & D. Landis (Eds.), *Neuroscience in inter-*cultural contexts (pp. 49–71). New York, NY: Springer Science + Business Media. http://dx.doi.org/10.1007/978-1-4939-2260-4_3

**Naneix, F., Darlot, F., Coutureau, E., & Cador, M.** (2016). Long-lasting deficits in hedonic and nucleus accumbens reactivity to sweet rewards by sugar overconsumption during adolescence. *European Journal of Neuroscience, 43,* 671–680. http://dx.doi.org/10.1111/ejn.13149

**Nascimento, H., Vieira, E., Coimbra, S., Catarino, C., Costa, E., Bronze-da-Rocha, E., . . . Belo, L.** (2016). Adipokine gene single-nucleotide polymorphisms in Portuguese obese adolescents: Associations with plasma concentrations of adiponectin, resistin, IL-6, IL-1β, and TNF-α. *Childhood Obesity, 12,* 300–313. http://dx.doi.org/10.1089/chi.2015.0235

**Nash, R. A., Nash, A., Morris, A., & Smith, S. L.** (2016). Does rapport-building boost the eyewitness eye closure effect in closed questioning? *Legal and Criminological Psychology, 21*(2), 305–318. http://dx.doi.org/10.1111/lcrp.12073

**National Academies of Sciences, Engineering, and Medicine** (2017). *The health effects of cannabis and cannabinoids: The current state of evidence and recommendations for research.* Washington, DC: The National Academies Press. https://doi.org/10.17226/24625.

**National Alliance on Mental Health.** (2015). People with mental illness enrich our lives. *National Alliance on Mental Illness.* Retrieved May 24, 2015 from http://www2.nami.org/Template.cfm?Section=Helpline1&template=/ContentManagement/ContentDisplay.cfm&ContentID=4858

**National Alliance on Mental Illness (NAMI).** (n.d.). Mental health by the numbers. *NAMI.* Retrieved March 16, 2017 from http://www.nami.org/Learn-More/Mental-Health-By-the-Numbers

**National Institute of Mental Health (NIMH).** (2014). Post-traumatic stress disorder. *NIH.gov.* Retrieved from http://www.nimh.nih.gov/health/publications/post-traumatic-stress-disorder-ptsd/index.shtml

**National Institute of Mental Health (NIMH).** (2016). Major depression among adults. *NIH.gov.* Retrieved from https://www.nimh.nih.gov/health/statistics/prevalence/major-depression-among-adults.shtml

**National Institute of Mental Health (NIMH).** (2017). Any anxiety disorder among adults. *NIMH.* Retrieved February 16, 2017 from https://www.nimh.nih.gov/health/statistics/prevalence/any-anxiety-disorder-among-adults.shtml

**National Institutes of Health (NIH).** (2016). Infant and newborn development. *National Institutes of Health.* Retrieved from https://www.nlm.nih.gov/medlineplus/infantandnewborndevelopment.html

**National Sleep Foundation.** (2012). *National sleep foundation sleepiness test.* Retrieved from https://sleepfoundation.org/quiz/national-sleep-foundation-sleepiness-test

**National Sleep Foundation.** (2017). *How sleep works.* Retrieved (January 5, 2017) from https://sleepfoundation.org/how-sleep-works

**National Veterans Foundation.** (2016, August 12). Suicide among veterans, it's our obligation to help. *Lifeline for Vets.* Retrieved from https://nvf.org/suicide-among-veterans-obligation-help/

**Navarra, R. J., Gottman, J. M., & Gottman, J. S.** (2016). Sound relationship house theory and relationship and marriage education. In J. J. Ponzetti, Jr. (Ed.), *Evidence-based approaches to relationship and marriage education* (pp. 93–107). New York, NY: Routledge/Taylor & Francis Group.

**Navarro, P., & Hurtado, I.** (2015). Corporality and trauma. In M. Sáenz-Herrero (Ed.), *Psychopathology in women: Incorporating gender perspective into descriptive psychopathology* (pp. 161–183). Cham, CH: Springer. http://dx.doi.org/10.1007/978-3-319-05870-2

**Neal, D. T., & Chartrand, T. L.** (2011). Embodied emotion perception. *Social Psychological and Personality Science, 2*(6), 673–678. http://dx.doi.org/10.1177/1948550611406138

**Neale, J. M., Oltmanns, T. F., & Winters, K. C.** (1983). Recent developments in the assessment and conceptualization of schizophrenia. *Behavioral Assessment, 5,* 33–54.

**Neher, A.** (1991). Maslow's theory of motivation: A critique. *Journal of Humanistic Psychology, 31,* 89–112. http://dx.doi.org/10.1177/0022167891313010

**Neimeyer, R. A.** (2014). The changing face of grief: Contemporary directions in theory, research, and practice. *Progress in Palliative Care, 22,* 125–130. http://dx.doi.org/10.1179/1743291X13Y.0000000075

**Neimeyer, R. A., & Kosminsky, P.** (2014). Bereavement. In L. Grossman & S. Walfish (Eds.), *Translating psychological research into practice* (pp. 133–139). New York, NY: Springer.

**Neisser, U.** (1967). *Cognitive psychology.* New York, NY: Appleton-Century-Crofts.

**Nelsen, D. R., Kelln, W., & Hayes, W. K.** (2014). Poke but don't pinch: Risk assessment and venom metering in the western black widow spider, *Latrodectus Hesperus. Animal Behaviour, 89,* 107–114.

**Nelson Mandela.** (n.d.). *Wikipedia.* Retrieved February 9, 2017 from https://en.wikipedia.org/wiki/Nelson_Mandela

**Nelson, S. K., Layous, K., Cole, S. W., & Lyubomirsky, S.** (2016). Do unto others or treat yourself? The effects of prosocial and self-focused behavior on psychological flourishing. *Emotion, 16,* 850–861. http://dx.doi.org/10.1037/emo0000178

**Ness, R. B.** (2015). Promoting innovative thinking. *American Journal of Public Health, 105,* S114–S118. http://dx.doi.org/10.2105/AJPH.2014.302365

**Neubauer, A. C., Grabner, R. H., Freudenthaler, H. H., Beckmann, J. F., & Guthke, J.** (2004). Intelligence and individual differences in becoming neurally efficient. *ActaPsychologica, 116,* 55–74. http://dx.doi.org/10.1016/j.actpsy.2003.11.005

**Neumann, A., & Walter, S.** (2015). Depression as an adaptation: The infection–defense hypothesis and cytokine mechanisms. In T. Breyer (Ed.), *Epistemological dimensions of evolutionary psychology* (pp. 175–196). New York, NY: Springer. http://dx.doi.org/10.1007/978-1-4939-1387-9_9

**New, J. J., & German, T. C.** (2015). Spiders at the cocktail party: An ancestral threat that surmounts inattentional blindness. *Evolution and Human Behavior, 36,* 165–173. http://dx.doi.org/10.1016/j.evolhumbehav.2014.08.004

**Newcorn, J. H., Ivanov, I., Chacko, A., & Javdani, S.** (2016). Aggression and violence. In M. K. Dulcan (Ed.), *Dulcan's textbook*

*of child and adolescent psychiatry* (2nd. ed., pp. 603–620). Arlington, VA: American Psychiatric Publishing.

**Newman, B. W., & Newman, P. R.** (2015). *Theories of human development* (2nd ed.). New York, NY: Psychology Press.

**Newman, K. M.** (2016). Five science-backed strategies to build resilience. *Greater Good*. Retrieved from http://greatergood.berkeley.edu/article/item/five_science_backed_strategies_to_build_resilience?utm_source=GG+Newsletter+Nov+16%2C+2016&utm_campaign=GG+Newsletter+Nov+16+2016&utm_medium=email

**Newman, S. D.** (2016). Differences in cognitive ability and apparent sex differences in corpus callosum size. *Psychological Research, 80*(5), 853–859. http://dx.doi.org/10.1007/s00426-015-0688-3

**Ng, A. M., Chong, C. L. Y., Ching, J. Y. X., Beh, J. L., & Lim, P. P. F.** (2015). A critical comparison of the psychoanalytic and humanistic theory. *Academia.edu*. Retrieved from http://www.academia.edu/7304762/A_Critical_Comparison_of_the_Psychoanalytic_and_Humanistic_Theory

**Ng, H. B., Kao, K. L., Chan, Y. C., Chew, E., Chuang, K. H., & Chen, S. H.** (2016). Modality specificity in the cerebro-cerebellar neurocircuitry during working memory. *Behavioural Brain Research, 305*, 164–173. http://dx.doi.org/10.1016/j.bbr.2016.02.027

**Ng, T. H., Chung, K.-F., Ho, F. Y.-Y., Yeung, W.-F., Yung, K.-P., & Lam, T.-H.** (2015). Sleep-wake disturbance in interepisode bipolar disorder and high-risk individuals: A systematic review and meta-analysis. *Sleep Medicine Reviews, 20*, 46–58. http://dx.doi.org/10.1016/j.smrv.2014.06.006

**Nguyen, T. P., Karney, B. R., & Bradbury, T. N.** (2016). Childhood abuse and late marital outcomes: Do partner characteristics moderate the association? *Journal of Family Psychology, 31*(1), 82-92. http://dx.doi.org/10.1037/fam0000208

**Nguyen, T., & Szymanski, B.** (2012). Using location-based social networks to validate human mobility and relationships models. *Proceedings of the 2012 IEEE/ACM International Conference on Advances in Social Networks Analysis and Mining*, pp. 1247–1253.

**Nicassio, P. M., & Azizoddin, D. R.** (2016). The nature, efficacy, and future of behavioral treatments for arthritis. In P. M. Nicassio (Ed.), *Psychosocial factors in arthritis: Perspectives on adjustment and management* (pp. 273–288). Cham, CH: Springer International Publishing. http://dx.doi.org/10.1007/978-3-319-22858-7_16

**Nichols, D. C.** (2013, January 7). Review: Abraham Lincoln ponders his legacy in "Two Miles a Penny." *Los Angeles Times*. Retrieved from http://articles.latimes.com/2013/jan/07/entertainment/la-et-cm-abraham-lincoln-two-miles-a-penny-ruby-theater-20130107

**Nichols, D. E.** (2016). Psychedelics. *Pharmacological Reviews, 68*, 264–355. http://dx.doi.org/10.1124/pr.115.011478

**Nicholson, S. P., Coe, C. M., Emory, J., & Song, A. V.** (2016). The politics of beauty: The effects of partisan bias on physical attractiveness. *Political Behavior, 38*(4), 883–898. http://dx.doi.org/10.1007/s11109-016-9339-7

**Nickerson, R.** (1998). Confirmation bias: A ubiquitous phenomenon in many guises. *Review of General Psychology, 2*, 175–220. http://dx.doi.org/10.1037/1089-2680.2.2.175

**Nicklaus, S.** (2016). The role of food experiences during early childhood in food pleasure learning. *Appetite, 104*, 3-9. http://dx.doi.org/10.1016/j.appet.2015.08.022

**Nicolaides, N. C., Kyratzi, E., Lamprokostopoulou, A., Chrousos, G. P., & Charmandari, E.** (2015). Stress, the stress system and the role of glucocorticoids. *Neuroimmunomodulation, 22*, 6–19. http://dx.doi.org/10.1159/000362736

**NIDA.** (2016, May 14). Club drugs. *National Institute of Drug Abuse (NIDA)*. Retrieved from https://www.drugabuse.gov/drugs-abuse/club-drugs

**Nielsen, T., O'Reilly, C., Carr, M., Dumel, G., Godin, L., Solomonova, E., . . . Paquette, T.** (2015). Overnight improvements in two REM sleep-sensitive tasks are associated with both REM and NREM sleep changes, sleep spindle features, and awakenings for dream recall. *Neurobiology of Learning and Memory, 122*, 88–97. http://dx.doi.org/10.1016/j.nlm.2014.09.007

**Nierenberg, B., Mayersohn, G., Serpa, S., Holovatyk, A., Smith, E., & Cooper, S.** (2016). Application of well-being therapy to people with disability and chronic illness. *Rehabilitation Psychology, 61*, 32–43. http://dx.doi.org/10.1037/rep0000060

**Nishimoto, R.** (1988). A cross-cultural analysis of psychiatric symptom expression using Langer's twenty-two item index. *Journal of Sociology and Social Welfare, 15*, 45–62.

**Nishitani, S., Miyamura, T., Tagawa, M., Sumi, M., Takase, R., Doi, H., . . . Shinohara, K.** (2009). The calming effect of a maternal breast milk odor on the human newborn infant. *Neuroscience Research, 63*, 66–71. http://dx.doi.org/10.1016/j.neures.2008.10.007

**Nishiyama, K., & Johnson, J. V.** (1997). Karoshi—Death from overwork: Occupational health consequences of Japanese production management. *International Journal of Health Services, 27*, 625–641. http://dx.doi.org/10.2190/1JPC-679V-DYNT-HJ6G

**Nitschke, K., Köstering, L., Finkel, L., Weiller, C., & Kaller, C. P.** (2017). A meta-analysis on the neural basis of planning: Activation likelihood estimation of functional brain imaging results in the Tower of London task. *Human Brain Mapping, 38*, 396–413. http://dx.doi.org/10.1002/hbm.23368

**Nobel lecture** (1967). *Physics 1901–1921*. San Diego, CA: Elsevier Publishing.

**Noble, K. G., Houston, S. M., Brito, N. H., Bartsch, H., Kan, E., Kuperman, J. M., . . . Sowell, E. R.** (2015). Family income, parental education and brain structure in children and adolescents. *Nature Neuroscience, 18*, 773–778. http://dx.doi.org/10.1038/nn.3983

**Nobre, P.** (2014). Male sexual dysfunctions. In S. G. Hofmann, D. J. A. Dozois, W. Rief, & J. A. J. Smits (Eds.), *The Wiley handbook of cognitive behavioral therapy* (Vols. 1–3, pp. 645–671). Hoboken, NJ: Wiley-Blackwell.

**Noel, M., Beals-Erickson, S. E., Law, E. F., Alberts, N. M., & Palermo, T. M.** (2016). Characterizing the pain narratives of parents of youth with chronic pain. *The Clinical Journal of Pain, 32*(10), 849–858. http://dx.doi.org/10.1097/AJP.0000000000000346

**Nokia, M. S., Lensu, S., Ahtianen, J. P., Johansson, P. P., Koch, L. G., Britton, S. L., & Kainulainen, H.** (2016). Physical exercise increases adult hippocampal neurogenesis in male rats provided it is aerobic and sustained. *The Journal of Physiology, 594*(7), 1855–1873. http://dx.doi.org/10.1113/JP271552

**Nolan, D., & Amico, C.** (2016, February 23). How bad is the opiod epidemic? *Frontline*. Retrieved from http://www.pbs.org/wgbh/frontline/article/how-bad-is-the-opioid-epidemic/

**Nolan, P.** (2012). *Therapist and client: A relational approach to psychotherapy*. Malden, MA: Wiley-Blackwell.

**Norbury, A., & Husain, M.** (2015). Sensation-seeking: Dopaminergic modulation and risk for psychopathology. *Behavioural Brain Research, 288*, 79–93. http://dx.doi.org/10.1016/j.bbr.2015.04.015

**Normandin, L., Ensink, K., & Kernberg, O. F.** (2015). Transference-focused psychotherapy for borderline adolescents: A neurobiologically informed psychodynamic psychotherapy. *Journal of Infant, Child & Adolescent Psychotherapy, 14*, 98–110. http://dx.doi.org/10.1080/15289168.2015.1006008

**North, A. C., Sheridan, L. P., & Areni, C. S.** (2016). Music congruity effects on product memory, perception, and choice. *Journal of Retailing, 92*, 83–95. http://dx.doi.org/10.1016/j.jretai.2015.06.001

**Nowicki, S.** (2016). *Choice or chance: Understanding your locus of control and why it matters*. New York: NY: Prometheus Books.

**Obermaier, M., Fawzi, N., & Koch, T.** (2016). Bystanding or standing by? How the number of bystanders affects the intention to intervene in cyberbullying. *New Media & Society, 18*(8), 1491–1507. http://dx.doi.org/10.1177/1461444814563519

**O'Brien, F., Bible, J., Liu, D., & Simons-Morton, B. G.** (2017). Do young drivers become safer after being involved in a collision? *Psychological Science, 28*(4), 407–413. http://dx.doi.org/10.1177/0956797616688118

**Obschonka, M., Schmitt-Rodermund, E., Silbereisen, R. K., Gosling, S. D., & Potter, J.** (2013). The regional distribution and correlates of an entrepreneurship-prone personality profile in the United States, Germany, and the United Kingdom: A socioecological perspective. *Journal of Personality and Social Psychology, 105*, 104–122. http://dx.doi.org/10.1037/a0032275

**Ockerman, E.** (2016, June 22). 'Infant trackers' help parents keep tables on their babies. *Time*. Retrieved from http://time.com/4376283/quantified-self-parents-apps/

**O'Connell, B. H., O'Shea, D., & Gallagher, S.** (2016). Enhancing social relationships through positive psychology activities: A randomised controlled trial. *Journal of Positive Psychology, 11*, 149–162. http://dx.doi.org/10.1080/17439760.2015.1037860

**O'Farrell, K., & Harkin, A.** (2017). Stress-related regulation of the kynurenine pathway: Relevance to neuropsychiatric and degenerative disorders. *Neuropharmacology, 112*, 307–323. http://dx.doi.org/10.1016/j.neuropharm.2015.12.004

**O'Farrell, T. J., Schumm, J. A., Dunlap, L. J., Murphy, M. M., & Muchowski, P.** (2016). A randomized clinical trial of group versus standard behavioral couples therapy plus individually based treatment for patients with alcohol dependence. *Journal of Consulting and Clinical Psychology, 84*, 497–510. http://dx.doi.org/10.1037/ccp0000089

**Oglesby, M. E., Raines, A. M., Short, N. A., Capron, D. W., & Schmidt, N. B.** (2016).

Interpretation bias for uncertain threat: A replication and extension. *Journal of Behavior Therapy and Experimental Psychiatry, 51*, 35–42. http://dx.doi.org/10.1016/j.jbtep.2015.12.006

**Ohtomo, S.** (2017). Exposure to diet priming images as cues to reduce the influence of unhealthy eating habits. *Appetite, 109*, 83-92. http://dx.doi.org/10.1016/j.appet.2016.11.022

**Olderbak, S. G., Malter, F., Wolf, P. S. A., Jones, D. N., & Figueredo, A. J.** (2017). Predicting romantic interest at zero acquaintance: Evidence of sex differences in trait perception but not in predictors of interest. *European Journal of Personality, 31*, 42–62. http://dx.doi.org/10.1002/per.2087

**Olds, J., & Milner, P. M.** (1954). Positive reinforcement produced by electrical stimulation of septal area and other regions of rat brains. *Journal of Comparative and Physiological Psychology, 47*, 419–427.

**Olenski, A. R., Abola, M. V., & Jena, A. B.** (2015). Do heads of government age more quickly? Observational study comparing mortality between elected leaders and runners-up in national elections of 17 countries. *British Medical Journal, 351*:h6424. http://dx.doi.org/10.1136/bmj.h6424

**Olivennes, H.** (2017, April 17). Prince Harry says he sought counseling over his mother's death. *NYTimes*. Retrieved from https://www.nytimes.com/2017/04/17/world/europe/uk-prince-harry-death-princess-diana.html?_r=1

**Oller, J. W., Jr., Oller, S. D., & Oller, S. N.** (2014). *Milestones: Normal speech and language development across the life span* (2nd ed.). San Diego, CA: Plural.

**Ollmann, T., Péczely, L., László, K., Kovács, A., Gálosi, R., Berente, E., . . . Zoltán, L. L.** (2015). Positive reinforcing effect of neurotensin microinjection into the ventralpallidum in conditioned place preference test. *Behavioural Brain Research, 278*, 470–475. http://dx.doi.org/10.1016/j.bbr.2014.10.021

**Olmstead, S. B., Roberson, P. N. E., Pasley, K., & Fincham, F. D.** (2015). Hooking up and risk behaviors among first semester college men: What is the role of precollege experience? *Journal of Sex Research, 52*, 186–198. http://dx.doi.org/10.1080/00224499.2013.843147

**Olson, K. R., Durwood, L., DeMeules, M., & McLaughlin, K. A.** (2016). Mental health of transgender children who are supported in their identities. *Pediatrics, 137*, 1–8. http://doi.org/10.1542/peds.2015-3223

**Olson, K. R., Key, A. C., & Eaton, N. R.** (2015). Gender cognition in transgender children. *Psychological Science, 26*, 467–474. http://dx.doi.org/10.1177/0956797614568156

**Olulade, O. A., Jamal, N. I., Koo, D. S., Perfetti, C. A., LaSasso, C., & Eden, G. F.** (2016). Neuroanatomical evidence in support of the bilingual advantage theory. *Cerebral Cortex, 26*, 3196–3204. http://dx.doi.org/10.1093/cercor/bhv152

**O'Neil, J. M.** (2015). *Men's gender role conflict: Psychological costs, consequences, and an agenda for change.* Washington, DC: American Psychological Association. http://dx.doi.org/10.1037/14501-000

**Ophir, E., Nass, C., & Wagner, A. D.** (2009). Cognitive control in media multitaskers. *Proceedings of the National Academy of Sciences of the United States of America, 106*(37), 15583 -15587. http://doi.org/10.1073/pnas.0903620106

**Ophuis, R. H., Lokkerbol, J., Heemskerk, S. C. M., van Balkom, A. J. L. M., Hiligsmann, M., & Evers, S. M. A. A.** (2017). Cost-effectiveness of interventions for treating anxiety disorders: A systematic review. *Journal of Affective Disorders, 210*, 1–13. http://dx.doi.org/10.1016/j.jad.2016.12.005

**Oppenheim, M.** (2016, May 29). JK Rowling reaches out to a fan who suffers from depression and has had suicidal thoughts. *Independent*. Retrieved March 17, 2017 from http://www.independent.co.uk/news/people/jk-rowling-reaches-out-to-a-fan-who-suffers-from-depression-and-has-had-suicidal-thoughts-a7055161.html

**Oppezzo, M., & Schwartz, D. L.** (2014). Give your ideas some legs: The positive effect of walking on creative thinking. *Journal of Experimental Psychology: Learning, Memory, and Cognition, 40*, 1142–1152. http://dx.doi.org/10.1037/a0036577

**Oprah Winfrey Net Worth.** (n. d.). Oprah Winfrey net worth—from abused little girl to a powerful woman. *Net Worth City*. Retrieved from http://networthcity.com/oprah-winfrey-net-worth/

**Oram, S., Khalifeh, H., & Howard, L. M.** (2017). Violence against women and mental health. *The Lancet Psychiatry, 4*(2), 158–170. http://dx.doi.org/10.1016/S2215-0366(16)30261-9

**Oram, S., Trevillion, K., Feder, G., & Howard, L. M.** (2013). Prevalence of experiences of domestic violence among psychiatric patients: Systematic review. *The British Journal of Psychiatry, 202*, 94–99.

**Ormerod, T. C., & Dando, C. J.** (2015). Finding a needle in a haystack: Toward a psychologically informed method for aviation security screening. *Journal of Experimental Psychology: General, 144*, 76–84. http://dx.doi.org/10.1037/xge0000030

**Orrells, D.** (2015). *Sex: Antiquity and its legacy.* New York, NY: Oxford University Press.

**Orth-Gomér, K., Schneiderman, N., Vaccarino, V., & Deter, H.-C.** (Eds.). (2015). *Psychosocial stress and cardiovascular disease in women: Concepts, findings, future perspectives.* Washington, DC: American Psychological Association. http://dx.doi.org/10.1007/978-3-319-09241-6

**Oswald, B.** (2010, January 26). Yes, she's queen of all media, but to Discovery, she's life itself. *Winnipeg Free Press*. Retrieved from http://www.winnipegfreepress.com/opinion/columnists/yes-shes-queen-of-all-media-but-to-discovery-shes-life-itself-82678662.html

**Ottavi, P., Passarella, T., Pasinetti, M., Salvatore, G., & Dimaggio, G.** (2016). Adapting mindfulness for treating personality disorder. In W. J. Livesley, G. Dimaggio, & J. F. Clarkin (Eds.), *Integrated treatment for personality disorder: A modular approach* (pp. 282–302). New York, NY: Guilford.

**Ottaviano, G., Marioni, G., Frasson, G., Zuccarello, D., Marchese-Ragona, R., Staffieri, C., . . . Staffieri, A.** (2015). Olfactory threshold for bourgeonal and sexual desire in young adult males. *Medical Hypotheses, 84*, 437–441. http://dx.doi.org/10.1016/j.mehy.2015.01.035

**Oudekerk, B. A., Allen, J. P., Hessel, E. T., & Molloy, L. E.** (2015). The cascading development of autonomy and relatedness from adolescence to adulthood. *Child Development, 86*, 472–485. http://dx.doi.org/10.1111/cdev.12313

**Owens, C.** (2016). "Hotspots" and "copycats": A plea for more thoughtful language about suicide. *The Lancet Psychiatry, 3*(1), 19–20. http://dx.doi.org/10.1016/S2215-0366(15)00492-7

**Ozturk, O., Shayan, S., Liszkowski, U., & Majid, A.** (2013). Language is not necessary for color categories. *Developmental Science, 16*, 111–115.

**Pacek, L. R., Mauro, P. M., & Martins, S. S.** (2015). Perceived risk of regular cannabis use in the United States from 2002 to 2012: Differences by sex, age, and race/ethnicity. *Drug and Alcohol Dependence, 149*, 232–244.

**Pack, A. A.** (2015). Experimental studies of dolphin cognitive abilities. In D. L. Herzing & C. M. Johnson (Eds.), *Dolphin communication and cognition: Past, present, and future* (pp. 175–200). Cambridge, MA: MIT Press.

**Pagano, M. E., Wang, A. R., Rowles, B. M., Lee, M. T., & Johnson, B. R.** (2015). Social anxiety and peer helping in adolescent addiction treatment. *Alcoholism: Clinical and Experimental Research, 39*, 887–895. http://dx.doi.org/10.1111/acer.12691

**Pagano, M. E., White, W. L., Kelly, J. F., Stout, R. L., & Tonigan, J. S.** (2013). The 10-year course of AA participation and long-term outcomes: A follow-up study of outpatient subjects in Project MATCH. *Substance Abuse, 31*, 51–59. http://doi.org/10.1080/08897077.2012.691450

**Paiva, T., Gaspar, T., & Matos, M. G.** (2015). Sleep deprivation in adolescents: Correlations with health complaints and health-related quality of life. *Sleep Medicine, 16*, 521–527. http://dx.doi.org/10.1016/j.sleep.2014.10.010

**Paivio, A.** (1995). *Mental representations: A dual coding approach.* New York, NY: Oxford University Press.

**Palermo, T. M., Law, E. F., Fales, J., Bromberg, M. H., Jessen-Fiddick, T., & Tai, G.** (2016). Internet delivered cognitive-behavioral treatment for adolescents with chronic pain and their parents: A randomized controlled multicenter trial. *Pain, 157*, 174–185. http://dx.doi.org/10.1097/j.pain.0000000000000348.

**Palgi, S., Klein, E., & Shamay-Tsoory, S. G.** (2015). Intranasal administration of oxytocin increases compassion toward women. *Social Cognitive and Affective Neuroscience, 10*, 311–317. http://dx.doi.org/10.1093/scan/nsu040

**Palmiero, M., Di Giacomo, D., & Passafiume, D.** (2016). Can creativity predict cognitive reserve? *The Journal of Creative Behavior, 50*, 7–23. http://dx.doi.org/10.1002/jocb.62

**Paluck, E. L., Shepherd, H., & Aronow, P. M.** (2016). Changing climates of conflict: A social network experiment in 56 schools. *Proceedings of the National Academy of Sciences of the United States of America, 113*, 566–571. http://dx.doi.org/10.1073/pnas.1514483113

**Panagopoulos, C.** (2017). Evaluation potential and task performance: Evidence from two randomized field experiments in election administration. *Political Psychology*. No Pagination Specified. http://dx.doi.org/10.1111/pops.12425

**Pandolfo, G., Gugliandolo, A., Gangemi, C., Arrigo, R., Currò, M., La Ciura, G., . . . Caccamo, D.** (2015). Association of the COMT synonymous polymorphism Leu136Leu and missense variant Val158Met with mood disorders. *Journal of Affective Disorders, 177*, 108–113. http://dx.doi.org/10.1016/j.jad.2015.02.016

**Panja, D., & Bramham, C. R.** (2014). BDNF mechanisms in late LTP formation: A synthesis and breakdown. *Neuropharmacology, 76,* 664–676. http://dx.doi.org/10.1016/j.neuropharm.2013.06.024

**Panksepp, J.** (2017). Instinctual foundations of animal minds: Comparative perspectives on the evolved affective neural substrate of emotions and learned behaviors. In J. Call, G. M. Burghardt, I. M. Pepperberg, C. T. Snowdon, & T. Zentall (Eds.), *APA handbook of comparative psychology: Basic concepts, methods, neural substrate, and behavior, Vol. 1* (pp. 475–500). Washington, DC: American Psychological Association. http://dx.doi.org/10.1037/0000011-023

**Panova, T., & Lleras, A.** (2016). Avoidance or boredom: Negative mental health outcomes associated with use of information and communication technologies depend on users' motivations. *Computers in Human Behavior, 58,* 249–258. http://dx.doi.org/10.1016/j.chb.2015.12.062

**Panza, G. A., Taylor, B. A., & Thompson, P. D.** (2017). Physical activity intensity and subjective well-being in healthy adults. *Journal of Health Psychology.* No Pagination Specified. http://journals.sagepub.com/doi/10.1177/1359105317691589

**Papageorgiou, C.** (2013). Mental health promotion and prejudices. *Psychiatriki, 24,* 166–167.

**Papathanasiou, I. V., Tsaras, K., Neroliatsiou, A., & Roupa, A.** (2015). Stress: Concepts, theoretical models and nursing interventions. *American Journal of Nursing, 4,* 45–50. http://dx.doi.org/10.11648/j.ajns.s.2015040201.19

**Pappa, I., St Pourcain, B., Benke, K., Cavadino, A., Hakulinen, C., Nivard, M. G., . . . Tiemeier, H.** (2016). A genome-wide approach to children's aggressive behavior: The EAGLE consortium. *American Journal of Medical Genetics Part B: Neuropsychiatric Genetics, 171*(5), 562–572. http://dx.doi.org/10.1002/ajmg.b.32333

**Park, A.** (2016, April 11). 40% of former NFL players had brain injuries. *Time.* Retrieved from http://time.com/4289745/nfl-concussion-symptoms-treatment/

**Parker, G., & Graham, R.** (2016). More than man's best friend: Diagnostic dogs in psychiatry. *Australasian Psychiatry, 24,* 398–399. https://doi.org/10.1177/1039856216638780

**Parkes, C. M.** (1972). *Bereavement: Studies of grief in adult life.* New York, NY: International Universities Press.

**Parkes, C. M.** (2015). Responding to grief and trauma in the aftermath of disaster. In J. M. Stillion & T. Attig (Eds.), *Death, dying, and bereavement: Contemporary perspectives, institutions, and practices* (pp. 363–377). New York, NY: Springer Publishing Co.

**Parks, K. A., Frone, M. R., Muraven, M., & Boyd, C.** (2017). Nonmedical use of prescription drugs and related negative sexual events: Prevalence estimates and correlates in college students. *Addictive Behaviors, 65,* 258–263. http://dx.doi.org/10.1016/j.addbeh.2016.08.018

**Paterson, H. M., Kemp, R. I., & Ng, J. R.** (2011). Combating co-witness contamination: Attempting to decrease the negative effects of discussion on eyewitness memory. *Applied Cognitive Psychology, 25,* 43–52. http://dx.doi.org/10.1002/acp.1640

**Pathman, T., & Bauer, P. J.** (2013). Beyond initial encoding: Measures of the postencoding status of memory traces predict long-term recall during infancy. *Journal of Experimental Child Psychology,* *114,* 321–338. http://dx.doi.org/10.1016/j.jecp.2012.10.004

**Patihis, L., Ho, L. Y., Tingen, I. W., Lilienfeld, S. O., & Loftus, E. F.** (2014). Are the "memory wars" over? A scientist-practitioner gap in beliefs about repressed memory. *Psychological Science, 25,* 519–530. http://dx.doi.org/10.1177/0956797613510718

**Patil, I., Zanon, M., Novembre, G., Zangrando, N., Chittaro, L., & Silani, G.** (2017). Neuroanatomical basis of concern-based altruism in virtual environment. *Neuropsychologia.* No Pagination Specified. http://dx.doi.org/10.1016/j.neuropsychologia.2017.02.015

**Patra, B. N., & Balhara, Y. P.** (2012). Creativity and mental disorder. *British Journal of Psychiatry, 200,* 346.

**Patterson, F., & Linden, E.** (1981).*The education of Koko.* New York, NY: Holt, Rinehart and Winston.

**Pauen, S., & Hoehl, S.** (2015). Preparedness to learn about the world: Evidence from infant research. In T. Breyer (Ed.), *Epistemological dimensions of evolutionary psychology* (pp. 159–173). New York, NY: Springer Science + Business Media. http://dx.doi.org/10.1007/978-1-4939-1387-9_8

**Paul, M. A., Love, R. J., Hawton, A., Brett, K., McCreary, D. R., & Arendt, J.** (2015). Sleep deficits in the high Arctic summer in relation to light exposure and behaviour: Use of melatonin as a countermeasure. *Sleep Medicine, 16,* 406–413. http://dx.doi.org/10.1016/j.sleep.2014.12.012

**Paul, M., Lech, R. K., Scheil, J., Dierolf, A. M., Suchan, B., & Wolf, O. T.** (2016). Acute stress influences the discrimination of complex scenes and complex faces in young healthy men. *Psychoneuroendocrinology, 66,* 125–129. http://dx.doi.org/10.1016/j.psyneuen.2016.01.007

**Pawling, R., Kirkham, A. J., Hayes, A. E., & Tipper, S. P.** (2017). Incidental retrieval of prior emotion mimicry. *Experimental Brain Research, 235*(4), 1173–1184. http://dx.doi.org/10.1007/s00221-017-4882-y

**Paynter, A., & Leaper, C.** (2016). Heterosexual dating double standards in undergraduate women and men. *Sex Roles, 75*(7), 393-406. http://dx.doi.org/10.1007/s11199-016-0628-8

**Peacock, B. N., Scheiderer, D. J., & Kellermann, G. H.** (2017). Biomolecular aspects of depression: A retrospective analysis. *Comprehensive Psychiatry, 73,* 168–180. http://dx.doi.org/10.1016/j.comppsych.2016.11.002

**Pearce, N., Gallo, V., & McElvenny, D.** (2015). Head trauma in sport and neurodegenerative disease: An issue whose time has come? *Neurobiology of Aging, 36,* 1383–1389. http://dx.doi.org/10.1016/j.neurobiolaging.2014.12.024

**Pear, J. J.** (2016). *The science of learning* (2nd ed.). New York, NY: Psychology Press.

**Pearson, C. M., Wonderlich, S. A., & Smith, G. T.** (2015). A risk and maintenance model for bulimia nervosa: From impulsive action to compulsive behavior. *Psychological Review, 122,* 516–535. http://dx.doi.org/10.1037/a0039268

**Pedram, P., Zhai, G., Gulliver, W., Zhang, H., & Sun, G.** (2017). Two novel candidate genes identified in adults from the newfoundland population with addictive tendencies towards food. *Appetite, 115,* 71–79 http://dx.doi.org/10.1016/j.appet.2017.01.004

**Peleg, G., Katzir, G., Peleg, O., Kamara, M., Brodsky, L., Hel-Or, H., . . . Nevo, E.** (2006). Hereditary family signature of facial expression. *Proceedings of the National Academy of Sciences of the United States of America, 103,* 15921–15926. http://dx.doi.org/10.1073/pnas.0607551103

**Peleg, O., & Eviatar, Z.** (2017). Controlled semantic processes within and between the two cerebral hemispheres. *Laterality: Asymmetries of Body, Brain and Cognition, 22*(1), 1–16. http://dx.doi.org/10.1080/1357650X.2015.1092547

**Peltier, M. J.** (2007). *Cesar's way: The natural, everyday guide to understanding and correcting common dog problems.* New York, NY: Three Rivers Press.

**Pennebaker, J. W., Gosling, S. D., & Ferrell, J. D.** (2013). Daily online testing in large classes: Boosting college performance while reducing achievement gaps. *PLoS ONE, 8* (11), e79774. http://dx.doi.org/10.1371/journal.pone.0079774

**Peper, J. S., de Reus, M. A., van den Heuvel, M. P., & Schutter, D. J. L. G.** (2015). Short fused? Associations between white matter connections, sex steroids, and aggression across adolescence. *Human Brain Mapping, 36,* 1043–1052. http://dx.doi.org/10.1002/hbm.22684

**Perego, G., Caputi, M., & Ogliari, A.** (2016). Neurobiological correlates of psychosocial deprivation in children: A systematic review of neuroscientific contributions. *Child & Youth Care Forum, 45*(3), 329–352. http://dx.doi.org/10.1007/s10566-015-9340-z

**Perelman, M. A.** (2014). The history of sexual medicine. In D. L. Tolman, L. M. Diamond, J. A. Bauermeister, W. H. George, J. G. Pfaus, & L. M. Ward (Eds.), *APA handbook of sexuality and psychology: Vol. 2. Contextual approaches* (pp. 137–179). Washington, DC: American Psychological Association. http://dx.doi.org/10.1037/14194-005

**Pérez, P., & Gaviña, J.** (2015). Affective disorders. In M. Sáenz-Herrero (Ed.), *Psychopathology in women: Incorporating gender perspective into descriptive psychopathology* (pp. 527–559). Cham, CH: Springer. http://dx.doi.org/10.1007/978-3-319-05870-2

**Pérusse, L., Rice, T. K., & Bouchard, C.** (2014). Genetic component to obesity. In G. Bray & C. Bouchard (Eds.), *Handbook of obesity: Epidemiology, etiology, and physiopathology* (pp. 91–101). Boca Raton, FL: Taylor & Francis Group.

**Peter, C. J., Fischer, L. K., Kundakovic, M., Garg, P., Jakovcevski, M., Dincer, A., . . . . Akbarian, S.** (2016). DNA methylation signatures of early childhood malnutrition associated with impairments in attention and cognition. *Biological Psychiatry, 80*(10), 765–774. http://dx.doi.org/10.1016/j.biopsych.2016.03.2100

**Peterman, J. S., Carper, M. M., Elkins, R. M., Comer, J. S., Pincus, D. B., & Kendall, P. C.** (2016). The effects of cognitive-behavioral therapy for youth anxiety on sleep problems. *Journal of Anxiety Disorders, 37,* 78–88. http://dx.doi.org/10.1016/j.janxdis.2015.11.006

**Peteros, R. G., & Maleyeff, J.** (2015). Using Lean Six Sigma to improve investment behavior. *International Journal of Lean Six Sigma, 6,* 59–72. http://dx.doi.org/10.1108/IJLSS-03-2014-0007

**Peterson, C. C., Wellman, H. M., & Slaughter, V.** (2012). The mind behind the message: Advancing theory-of-mind scales for typically developing children, and those with deafness, autism, or asperger syndrome. *Child Development, 83*(2), 469–485.

**Petrocchi, N., & Couyoumdjian, A.** (2016). The impact of gratitude on depression and anxiety: The mediating role of criticizing, attacking, and reassuring the self. *Self and Identity, 15,* 191–205. http://dx.doi.org/10.1080/15298868.2015.1095794

**Petrosini, L., Cutuli, D., & De Bartolo, P.** (2013). Environmental influences on development of the nervous system. In R. J. Nelson, S. J. Y. Mizumori, & I. B. Weiner (Eds.), *Handbook of psychology, Vol. 3. Behavioral neuroscience* (2nd ed., pp. 461–479). Hoboken, NJ: Wiley.

**Pettit, M., & Hegarty, P.** (2014). Psychology and sexuality in historical time. In D. L. Tolman, L. M. Diamond, J. A. Bauermeister, W. H. George, J. G. Pfaus, & L. M. Ward (Eds.), *APA handbook of sexuality and psychology: Vol. 1. Person-based approaches* (pp. 63–78). Washington, DC: American Psychological Association. http://dx.doi.org/10.1037/14193-003

**Pew Research Center**. (2016, May 12). Changing attitudes on gay marriage. Retrieved from http://www.pewforum.org/2016/05/12/changing-attitudes-on-gay-marriage/

**Phan, H. P., & Ngu, B. H.** (2016). Sources of self-efficacy in academic contexts: A longitudinal perspective. *School Psychology Quarterly, 31*(4), 548–564. http://dx.doi.org/10.1037/spq0000151

**Phillip, A.** (2015, February 25). For Chris Kyle's killer, Eddie Ray Routh, life in prison may make jail an asylum. *The Washington Post.* Retrieved from http://www.washingtonpost.com/news/morning-mix/wp/2015/02/25/for-chris-kyles-killer-life-in-prison-may-make-prison-an-asylum/

**Phillips, R. O., Fyhri, A., & Sagberg, F.** (2011). Risk compensation and bicycle helmets. *Risk Analysis, 31,* 1187–1195. http://dx.doi.org/10.1111/j.1539-6924.2011.01589.x

**Phillips, S. T., & Ziller, R. C.** (1997). Toward a theory and measure of the nature of nonprejudice. *Journal of Personality and Social Psychology, 72,* 420–434.

**Piaget, J.** (1952). *The origins of intelligence in children.* New York, NY: Oxford University Press.

**Picker, I.** (2016). The effects of education on health. *National Bureau of Economic Research.* Retrieved from http://www.nber.org/digest/mar07/w12352.html

**Pill, N., Day, A., & Mildred, H.** (2017). Trauma responses to intimate partner violence: A review of current knowledge. *Aggression and Violent Behavior, 34,* 178–184. http://dx.doi.org/10.1016/j.avb.2017.01.014

**Pines, A.** (2014). Surgical menopause and cognitive decline. *Climacteric, 17,* 580–582. http://dx.doi.org/10.3109/13697137.2014.883244

**Piomelli, D.** (2015). Neurobiology of marijuana. In M. Galanter, H. D. Kleber, & K. T. Brady (Eds.), *The American Psychiatric Publishing textbook of substance abuse treatment* (5th ed., pp. 335–350). Arlington, VA: American Psychiatric Publishing.

**Pitzer, M., Esser, G., Schmidt, M. H., Hohm, E., Banaschewski, T., & Laucht, M.** (2017). Child regulative temperament as a mediator of parenting in the development of depressive symptoms: A longitudinal study from early childhood to preadolescence. *Journal of Neural Transmission, 124*(5), 631–641. http://dx.doi.org/10.1007/s00702-017-1682-2

**Planas-Sitjà, I., Deneubourg, J.-L., Gibon, C., & Sempo, G.** (2015). Group personality during collective decision-making: A multi-level approach. *Proceedings of the Royal Society B, 282.* http://dx.doi.org/10.1098/rspb.2014.2515.

**Plassmann, H., O'Doherty, J., Shiv, B., & Rangel, A.** (2008). Marketing actions can modulate neural representations of experienced pleasantness. *Proceedings of the National Academy of Sciences of the United States of America, 105,* 1050–1054.

**Platt, S. P., Bates, L., & Keyes, K.** (2016). Unequal depression for equal work? How the wage gap explains gendered disparities in mood disorders. *Social Science & Medicine, 149,* 1–8. http://dx.doi.org/10.1016/j.socscimed.2015.11.056

**Plattner, F., Hernández, A., Kistler, T. M., Pozo, K., Zhong, P., Yuen, E. Y., . . . Bibb, J. A.** (2014). Memory enhancement by targeting Cdk5 regulation of NR2B. *Neuron, 81,* 1070–1083. http://dx.doi.org/10.1016/j.neuron.2014.01.022

**Plomin, R., & Deary, I. J.** (2015). Genetics and intelligence differences: Five special findings. *Molecular Psychiatry, 20,* 98–108. http://dx.doi.org/10.1038/mp.2014.105

**Plomin, R., DeFries, J. C., Knopik, V. S., & Neiderhiser, J. M.** (2016). Top 10 replicated findings from behavioral genetics. *Perspectives on Psychological Science, 11,* 3–23. http://dx.doi.org/10.1177/1745691615617439

**Plucker, J. A., & Esping, A.** (2014). *The psych 101 series: Intelligence 101.* New York, NY: Springer.

**Plush, K., Hughes, P., Herde, P., & van Wettere, W.** (2016). A synthetic olfactory agonist reduces aggression when sows are mixed into small groups. *Applied Animal Behaviour Science, 185,* 45–51. http://dx.doi.org/10.1016/j.applanim.2016.09.011

**Pohl, R. F., Erdfelder, E., Hilbig, B. E., Liebke, L., & Stahlberg, D.** (2013). Effort reduction after self-control depletion: The role of cognitive resources in use of simple heuristics. *Journal of Cognitive Psychology, 25,* 267–276. http://dx.doi.org/10.1080/20445911.2012.758101

**Pokhrel, P., Herzog, T. A., Black, D. S., Zaman, A., Riggs, N. R., & Sussman, S.** (2013). Adolescent neurocognitive development, self-regulation, and school-based drug use prevention. *Prevention Science, 14,* 218–228. http://dx.doi.org/10.1007/s11121-012-0345-7

**Polanco-Roman, L., Gomez, J., Miranda, R., & Jeglic, E.** (2016). Stress-related symptoms and suicidal ideation: The roles of rumination and depressive symptoms vary by gender. *Cognitive Therapy and Research, 40*(5), 606–616. http://dx.doi.org/10.1007/s10608-016-9782-0

**Polito, V., Barnier, A. J., Woody, E. Z., & Connors, M. H.** (2014). Measuring agency change across the domain of hypnosis. *Psychology of Consciousness: Theory, Research, and Practice, 1,* 3–19. http://dx.doi.org/10.1037/cns0000010

**Polk, S. E., Schulte, E. M., Furman, C. R., & Gearhardt, A. N.** (2016). Wanting and liking: Separable components in problematic eating behavior? *Appetite, 115,* 45–53. http://dx.doi.org/10.1016/j.appet.2016.11.015

**Pollock, N. C., Noser, A. E., Holden, C. J., & Zeigler-Hill, V.** (2016). Do orientations to happiness mediate the associations between personality traits and subjective well-being? *Journal of Happiness Studies, 17,* 713–729. http://dx.doi.org/10.1007/s10902-015-9617-9

**Pomerantz, E. M., & Kempner, S. G.** (2013). Mothers' daily person and process praise: Implications for children's theory of intelligence and motivation. *Developmental Psychology, 49,* 2040–2046. http://dx.doi.org/10.1037/a0031840

**Pomponio, A. T.** (2002). *Psychological consequences of terror.* Hoboken, NJ: Wiley.

**Pope, C. N., Bell, T. R., & Stavrinos, D.** (2017). Mechanisms behind distracted driving behavior: The role of age and executive function in the engagement of distracted driving. *Accident Analysis & Prevention, 98,* 123–129. http://dx.doi.org/10.1016/j.aap.2016.09.030

**Pope, K. S., & Vasquez, M. J. T.** (2011). *Ethics in psychotherapy and counseling: A practical guide* (4th ed.). Hoboken, NJ: Wiley.

**Porritt, F., Shapiro, M., Waggoner, P., Mitchell, E., Thomson, T., Nicklin, S., & Kacelnik, A.** (2015). Performance decline by search dogs in repetitive tasks, and mitigation strategies. *Applied Animal Behaviour Science, 166,* 112–122. http://dx.doi.org/10.1016/j.applanim.2015.02.013

**Portrat, S., Guida, A., Phénix, T., & Lemaire, B.** (2016). Promoting the experimental dialogue between working memory and chunking: Behavioral data and simulation. *Memory & Cognition, 44,* 420–434. http://dx.doi.org/10.3758/s13421-015-0572-9

**Possemato, K., Bergen-Cico, D., Treatman, S., Allen, C., Wade, M., & Pigeon, W.** (2016). A randomized clinical trial of primary care brief mindfulness training for veterans with PTSD. *Journal of Clinical Psychology, 72,* 179–193. http://dx.doi.org/10.1002/jclp.22241

**Posthuma, D., de Geus, E. J. C., & Boomsma, D. I.** (2001). Perceptual speed and IQ are associated through common genetic factors. *Behavior Genetics, 31,* 593–602. http://dx.doi.org/10.1023/A:1013349512683

**Post, R. M., Altshuler, L. L., Kupka, R., McElroy, S. L., Frye, M. A., Rowe, M., . . . Nolen, W. A.** (2017). More childhood onset bipolar disorder in the United States than Canada or Europe: Implications for treatment and prevention. *Neuroscience and Biobehavioral Reviews, 74*(Part A), 204–213. http://dx.doi.org/10.1016/j.neubiorev.2017.01.022

**Poulin, M. J., Holman, E. A., & Buffone, A.** (2012). The neurogenetics of nice: Receptor genes for oxytocin and vasopressin interact with threat to predict prosocial behavior. *Psychological Science, 23,* 446–452. http://dx.doi.org/10.1177/0956797611428471

**Pozzulo, J.** (2017). *The young eyewitness: How well do children and adolescents describe and identify perpetrators?* Washington, DC: American Psychological Association. http://dx.doi.org/10.1037/14956-009

**Praszkier, R.** (2016). Empathy, mirror neurons and SYNC. *Mind & Society, 15*(1), 1–25. http://dx.doi.org/10.1007/s11299-014-0160-x

**Prather, A. A., Janicki-Deverts, D., Hall, M. H., & Cohen, S.** (2015). Behaviorally assessed sleep and susceptibility to the common cold. *Sleep, 38,* 1353–1959. http://dx.doi.org/10.5665/sleep.4968.

**Prati, F., Vasiljevic, M., Crisp, R. J., & Rubini, M.** (2015). Some extended psychological benefits of challenging social stereotypes: Decreased dehumanization and a reduced reliance on heuristic thinking. *Group Processes & Intergroup Relations, 18,* 801–816. http://dx.doi.org/10.1177/1368430214567762

Preckel, K., Scheele, D., Kendrick, K. M., Maier, W., & Hurlemann, R. (2014). Oxytocin facilitates social approach behavior in women. *Frontiers in Behavioral Neuroscience, 8,* Article ID 191. http://dx.doi.org/10.3389/fnbeh.2014.00191

Prenderville, J. A., Kennedy, P. J., Dinan, T. G., & Cryan, J. F. (2015). Adding fuel to the fire: The impact of stress on the ageing brain. *Trends in Neurosciences, 38,* 13–25. http://dx.doi.org/10.1016/j.tins.2014.11.001

Prestage, G., Bavinton, B., Grierson, J., Down, I., Keen, P., Bradley, J., & Duncan, D. (2015). Online dating among Australian gay and bisexual men: Romance or hooking up? *AIDS and Behavior, 19,* 1905–1913. http://dx.doi.org/10.1007/s10461-015-1032-z

Presti, D. E. (2016). *Foundational concepts in neuroscience: A brain-mind odyssey. The Norton series on interpersonal neurobiology.* New York, NY: W. W. Norton.

Price, J., Lefgren, L., & Tappen, H. (2013). Interracial workplace cooperation: Evidence from the NBA. *Economic Inquiry, 51,* 1026–1034. http://dx.doi.org/10.1111/j.1465-7295.2011.00438.x

Price, T. J., & Prescott, S. A. (2015). Inhibitory regulation of the pain gate and how its failure causes pathological pain. *Pain, 156,* 789–792. http://dx.doi.org/10.1097/j.pain.0000000000000139

Primeau, M., & O'Hara, R. (2015). Sleep-wake disorders. In L. W. Roberts & A. K. Louie (Eds.), *Study guide to DSM-5®* (pp. 267–290). Arlington, VA: American Psychiatric Publishing.

Proctor, C., Tweed, R., & Morris, D. (2016). The Rogerian fully functioning person: A positive psychology perspective. *Journal of Humanistic Psychology, 56,* 503–529. http://dx.doi.org/10.1177/0022167815605936

Prot, S., Gentile, D. A., Anderson, C. A., Suzuki, K., Swing, E., Lim, K. M., . . . Lam, B. C. (2014). Long-term relations among prosocial-media use, empathy, and prosocial behavior. *Psychological Science, 25,* 358–368. http://dx.doi.org/10.1177/0956797613503854.

Proulx, C., & Helms, H. (2008). Mothers' and fathers' perceptions of change and continuity in their relationships with young adult sons and daughters. *Journal of Family Issues, 29,* 234–261. http://dx.doi.org/10.1177/0192513X07307855

Proyer, R. T., Ruch, W., & Buschor, C. (2013). Testing strengths-based interventions: A preliminary study on the effectiveness of a program targeting curiosity, gratitude, hope, humor, and zest for enhancing life satisfaction. *Journal of Happiness Studies, 14,* 275–292. http://dx.doi.org/10.1007/s10902-012-9331-9

Przybylski, A. K., & Weinstein, N. (2013). Can you connect with me now? How the presence of mobile communication technology influences face-to-face conversation quality. *Journal of Social and Personal Relationships, 30,* 237–246. http://dx.doi.org/.10.1177/0265407512453827

Psychology Matters. (2006, June 30). Pushing buttons. Retrieved from http://www.psychology-matters.org/pushbutton.

Pullum, G. K. (1991). *The great Eskimo vocabulary hoax and other irreverent essays on the study of language.* Chicago, IL: University of Chicago Press.

Pultarova, T. (2017, April 25). Psychedelic drugs really do trigger a "higher" state of consciousness. *LiveScience.* Retrieved from http://www. livescience.com/58834-psychedelic-drugs-trigger-higher-state-of-consciousness.html?utm_source=ls-newsletter&utm_medium=email&utm_campaign=20170426-ls

Pulverman, C. S., Boyd, R. L., Stanton, A. M., & Meston, C. M. (2017). Changes in the sexual self-schema of women with a history of childhood sexual abuse following expressive writing treatment. *Psychological Trauma: Theory, Research, Practice, and Policy, 9*(2), 181–188. http://dx.doi.org/10.1037/tra0000163

Putnam, A. L., Sungkhasettee, V. W., & Roediger, H. L. (2016). Optimizing learning in college: Tips from cognitive psychology. *Perspectives on Psychological Science, 11,* 652–660. http://dx.doi.org/10.1177/1745691616645770

Putwain, D., & Remedios, R. (2014). The scare tactic: Do fear appeals predict motivation and exam scores? *School Psychology Quarterly, 29,* 503–516. http://dx.doi.org/10.1037/spq0000048

Qin, S., Young, C. B., Duan, X., Chen, T., Supekar, K., & Menon, V. (2014). Amygdala subregional structure and intrinsic functional connectivity predicts individual differences in anxiety during early childhood. *Biological Psychiatry, 75,* 892–901. http://dx.doi.org/10.1016/j.biopsych.2013.10.006.

Quas, J. A., Rush, E. B., Yim, I. S., Edelstein, R. S., Otgaar, H., & Smeets, T. (2016). Stress and emotional valence effects on children's versus adolescents' true and false memory. *Memory, 24,* 696–707. http://dx.doi.org/10.1080/09658211.2015.1045909

Quiano, K. (2016, March 21). Living in chains: In Indonesia, mentally ill kept shackled in filthy cells. *CNN World.* Retrieved from http://www.cnn.com/2016/03/20/asia/indonesia-mental-health/

Quinn, M. (2016). Here's how much your New Year's Resolution will cost you. *GoBankingRates.* Retrieved from https://www.gobankingrates.com/personal-finance/heres-much-new-years-resolution-cost

Quintana, D. S., Outhred, T., Westlye, L. T., Malhi, G. S., & Andreassen, O. A. (2016). The impact of oxytocin administration on brain activity: A systematic review and meta-analysis protocol. *Systematic Reviews, 5,* 205. http://dx.doi.org/10.1186/s13643-016-0386-2

Raaska, H., Elovainio, M., Sinkkonen, J., Stolt, S., Jalonen, I., Matomaki, J., . . . Lapinleimu, H. (2013). Adopted children's language difficulties and their relation to symptoms of reactive attachment disorder: FinAdo study. *Journal of Applied Developmental Psychology, 34,* 152–160. http://dx.doi.org/10.1016/j.appdev.2012.12.003

Rabellino, D., Densmore, M., Frewen, P. A., Théberge, J., & Lanius, R. A. (2016). The innate alarm circuit in post-traumatic stress disorder: Conscious and subconscious processing of fear- and trauma-related cues. *Psychiatry Research: Neuroimaging, 248,* 142–150. http://dx.doi.org/10.1016/j.pscychresns.2015.12.005

Radhika, P., Murthy, P., Sarin, A., & Jain, S. (2015). Psychological symptoms and medical responses in nineteenth-century India. *History of Psychiatry, 26,* 88–97. http://dx.doi.org/10.1177/0957154X14530815

Radvansky, G. A., & Ashcraft, M. H. (2016). *Cognition* (6th ed.). Upper Saddle River, NJ: Pearson.

Raffin, E., Richard, N., Giraux, P., & Reilly, K. T. (2016). Primary motor cortex changes after amputation correlate with phantom limb pain and the ability to move the phantom limb. *NeuroImage, 130,* 134–144. http://dx.doi.org/10.1016/j.neuroimage.2016.01.063

Rahafar, A., Maghsudloo, M., Farhangnia, S., Vollmer, C., & Randler, C. (2016). The role of chronotype, gender, test anxiety, and conscientiousness in academic achievement of high school students. *Chronobiology International, 33,* 1–9. http://dx.doi.org/10.3109/07420528.2015.1107084

Raine, J. (2016, August 30). Why it's so hard to ignore a baby's cry, according to science. *Time Magazine.* Retrieved from http://theconversation.com/why-its-so-hard-to-ignore-a-babys-cry-according-to-science-63245

Rajkumar, R. P., & Kumaran, A. K. (2015). Depression and anxiety in men with sexual dysfunction: A retrospective study. *Comprehensive Psychiatry, 60,* 114–118. http://dx.doi.org/10.1016/j.comppsych.2015.03.001

Ralph, S., Capewell, C., & Bonnett, E. (2016). Disability hate crime: Persecuted for difference. *British Journal of Special Education, 43*(3), 215–232. http://dx.doi.org/10.1111/1467-8578.12139

Ramakers, G. G. J., Kraaijenga, V. J. C., Cattani, G., van Zanten, G. A., & Grolman, W. (2016). Effectiveness of earplugs in preventing recreational noise–induced hearing loss: A randomized clinical trial. *JAMA Otolaryngology - Head & Neck Surgery, 142,* 551–558. http://dx.doi.org/10.1001/jamaoto.2016.0225

Ramchand, R., Ayer, L., Geyer, L., & Kofner, A. (2016). Factors that influence chaplains' suicide intervention behavior in the army. *Suicide and Life-Threatening Behavior, 46,* 35–45. http://dx.doi.org/10.1111/sltb.12170

Ramler, T. R., Tennison, L R., Lynch, J., & Murphy, P. (2016). Mindfulness and the college transition: The efficacy of an adapted mindfulness-based stress reduction intervention in fostering adjustment among first-year students. *Mindfulness, 7,* 179–188. http://dx.doi.org/10.1007/s12671-015-0398-3

Ramsay, C. E., Stewart, T., & Compton, M. T. (2012). Unemployment among patients with newly diagnosed first-episode psychosis: Prevalence and clinical correlates in a US sample. *Social Psychiatry and Psychiatric Epidemiology, 47,* 797–803. http://dx.doi.org/10.1007/s00127-011-0386-4

Ramscar, M., Hendrix, P., Shaoul, C., Milin, P., & Baayen H. (2014). The myth of cognitive decline: Non-linear dynamics of lifelong learning. *Topics in Cognitive Science, 6,* 5–42. http://dx.doi.org/10.1111/tops.12078

Randi, J. (2014, January 7). It's not a contest. James Randi Educational Foundation. Retrieved from http://www.randi.org/site/index.php/swift-blog/2304-its-not-a-contest.html

Raposa, E. B., Laws, H. B., & Ansell, E. B. (2016). Prosocial behavior mitigates the negative effects of stress in everyday life. *Clinical Psychological Science, 4*(4), 691–698. http://dx.doi.org/10.1177/2167702615611073

Rass, O., Ahn, W.-Y., & O'Donnell, B. F. (2016). Resting-state EEG, impulsiveness, and personality in daily and nondaily smokers. *Clinical Neurophysiology, 127,* 409–418. http://dx.doi.org/10.1016/j.clinph.2015.05.007

Ratner, K. G., & Amodio, D. M. (2013). Seeing "us vs. them": Minimal group effects on the neural encoding of faces. *Journal of Experimental Social Psychology, 49,* 298–301.

**Rattan, A., Savani, K., Chugh, D., & Dweck, C. S.** (2015). Leveraging mindsets to promote academic achievement: Policy recommendations. *Perspectives on Psychological Science, 10,* 721–726. http://dx.doi.org/10.1177/1745691615599383

**Rau, J.** (2016, February 2). Study suggests surgical residents can safely work longer shifts. *Health News from NPR.* Retrieved from http://www.npr.org/sections/health-shots/2016/02/02/465248609/study-suggests-surgical-residents-can-safely-work-longer-shifts

**Ravizza, S. M., Uitvlugt, M. G., & Fenn, K. M.** (2017). Logged in and zoned out: How laptop Internet use relates to classroom learning. *Psychological Science, 28*(2), 171–180. http://dx.doi.org/10.1177/0956797616677314

**Ray, A. L., Ullmann, R., & Francis, M. C.** (2015). Pain as a perceptual experience. In T. R. Deer, M. S. Leong, & A. L. Ray (Eds.), *Treatment of chronic pain by integrative approaches: The American Academy of Pain Medicine textbook on patient management* (pp. 1–13). New York, NY: Springer-Verlag. http://dx.doi.org/10.1007/978-1-4939-1821-8_1

**Ray, D. C., & Jayne, K. M.** (2016). Humanistic psychotherapy with children. In D. J. Cain, K. Keenan, & S. Rubin (Eds.), *Humanistic psychotherapies: Handbook of research and practice* (2nd ed., pp. 387–417). Washington, DC: American Psychological Association. http://dx.doi.org/10.1037/14775-013

**Raynald, Li, Y., Yu, H., Huang, H., Guo, M., Hua, R., . . . An, Y.** (2016). The heterotransplantation of human bone marrow stromal cells carried by hydrogel unexpectedly demonstrates a significant role in the functional recovery in the injured spinal cord of rats. *Brain Research, 1634,* 21–33. http://dx.doi.org/10.1016/j.brainres.2015.10.038

**Ray, W. J.** (2015). *Abnormal psychology: Neuroscience perspectives on human behavior and experience.* Thousand Oaks, CA: Sage.

**Reade, N.** (2015). The surprising truth about older workers. *AARP.* Retrieved from http://www.aarp.org/work/job-hunting/info-07-2013/older-workers-more-valuable.html

**Reardon, S.** (2015). Rave drug tested against depression: Companies and clinicians turn to ketamine to treat mental-health disorder as pipeline of new drugs dries up. *Nature, 517,* 130–131. http://dx.doi.org/10.1038/517130a

**Reble, E., Castellani, C. A., Melka, M. G., O'Reilly, R., & Singh, S. M.** (2017). VarScan2 analysis of de novo variants in monozygotic twins discordant for schizophrenia. *Psychiatric Genetics, 27*(2), 62–70. http://dx.doi.org/10.1097/YPG.0000000000000162

**Redondo, M. T., Beltrán-Brotóns, J. L., Reales, J. M., & Ballesteros, S.** (2015). Word-stem priming and recognition in type 2 diabetes mellitus, Alzheimer's disease patients and healthy older adults. *Experimental Brain Research, 233,* 3163–3174. http://dx.doi.org/10.1007/s00221-015-4385-7

**Reed, M.** (2015). Obesity. In R. M. McCarron, G. L. Xiong, C. R. Keenan, & H. A. Nasrallah (Eds.), *Preventive medical care in psychiatry: A practical guide for clinicians* (pp. 143–160). Arlington, VA: American Psychiatric Publishing.

**Rees, C. S., Breen, L. J., Cusack, L., & Hegney, D.** (2015). Understanding individual resilience in the workplace: The international collaboration of workforce resilience (icwr) model. *Frontiers in Psychology, 6,* 73. http://dx.doi.org/10.3389/fpsyg.2015.00073

**Regan, P.** (1998). What if you can't get what you want? Willingness to compromise ideal mate selection standards as a function of sex, mate value, and relationship context. *Personality and Social Psychology Bulletin, 24,* 1294–1303.

**Regan, P.** (2011). *Close relationships.* New York, NY: Routledge/Taylor & Francis Group.

**Rentfrow, P. J.** (2014). Geographical differences in personality. In P. J. Rentfrow (Ed.), *Geographical psychology: Exploring the interaction of environment and behavior* (pp. 115–137). Washington, DC: American Psychological Association. http://dx.doi.org/10.1037/14272-007

**Rentfrow, P. J., Gosling, S. D., & Potter, J.** (2008). A theory of the emergence, persistence, and expression of geographic variation in psychological characteristics. *Perspectives on Psychological Science, 3,* 339–369. http://dx.doi.org/10.1111/j.1745-6924.2008.00084.x

**Resnick, B.** (2016, April 8). These scientists can prove it's possible to reduce prejudice. *Vox: Science & Health.* Retrieved from http://www.vox.com/2016/4/7/11380974/reduce-prejudice-science-transgender

**Rest, J., Narvaez, D., Bebeau, M., & Thoma, S.** (1999). A neo-Kohlbergian approach: The DIT and schema theory. *Educational Psychology Review, 11*(4), 291–324.

**Reuter, T. R., Newcomb, M. E., Whitton, S. W., & Mustanski, B.** (2017). Intimate partner violence victimization in LGBT young adults: Demographic differences and associations with health behaviors. *Psychology of Violence, 7,* 101–109. http://dx.doi.org/10.1037/vio0000031

**Reyes-Rodríguez, M. L., Gulisano, M., Silva, Y., Pivarunas, B., Luna-Reyes, K. L., & Bulik, C. M.** (2016). "Las penas con pan duelen menos": The role of food and culture in Latinas with disordered eating behaviors. *Appetite, 100,* 102–109. http://dx.doi.org/10.1016/j.appet.2016.02.029

**Reynolds, F.** (2017). The contribution of qualitative research to understanding people's resilience and resourcefulness for maintaining well-being in the context of ill-health. *The Journal of Positive Psychology, 12*(3), 313–314. http://dx.doi.org/10.1080/17439760.2016.1262620

**Rhudy, J. L.** (2016). Emotional modulation of pain. In M. al'Absi & M. A. Flaten (Eds.), *The neuroscience of pain, stress, and emotion: Psychological and clinical implications* (pp. 51–75). San Diego, CA: Elsevier Academic Press. http://dx.doi.org/10.1016/B978-0-12-800538-5.00003-0

**Ricci, M. C., & Lee, M.** (2016). *Mindsets for parents: Strategies to encourage growth mindsets in kids.* Waco, TX: Prufrock Press.

**Rice, S. M., Fallon, B. J., Aucote, H. M., Möller-Leimkühler, A., Treeby, M. S., & Amminger, G. P.** (2014). Longitudinal sex differences of externalising and internalising depression symptom trajectories: Implications for assessment of depression in men from an online study. *International Journal of Social Psychiatry, 61,* 236–240. http://dx.doi.org/10.1177/0020764014540149

**Richardson, S. S.** (2015). *Sex itself: The search for male and female in the human genome.* Chicago, IL: University of Chicago Press.

**Riecher-Rössler, A.** (2017). Oestrogens, prolactin, hypothalamic-pituitary-gonadal axis, and schizophrenic psychoses. *The Lancet Psychiatry,* 4(1), 63–72. http://dx.doi.org/10.1016/S2215-0366(16)30379-0

**Riediger, M., & Luong, G.** (2016). Happy to be unhappy? Pro-and contrahedonic motivations from adolescence to old age. In A. D. Ong & C. E. Löckenhoff (Eds.), *Emotion, aging, and health. Bronfenbrenner series on the ecology of human development* (pp. 97–118). Washington, DC: American Psychological Association. http://dx.doi.org/10.1037/14857-006

**Riem, M. M. E., Bakermans-Kranenburg, M. J., Pieper, S., Tops, M., Boksem, M. A. S., Vermeiren, R. R. J. M., ... Rombouts, S. A. R. B.** (2011). Oxytocin modulates amygdala, insula, and inferior frontal gyrus responses to infant crying: A randomized controlled trial. *Biological Psychiatry, 70,* 291–297. http://dx.doi.org/10.1016/j.biopsych.2011.02.006

**Rimmele, U., Davachi, L., & Phelps, E. A.** (2012). Memory for time and place contributes to enhanced confidence in memories for emotional events. *Emotion, 12,* 834–846. http://dx.doi.org/10.1037/a0028003

**Rinehart, S. J., & Espelage, D. L.** (2016). A multilevel analysis of school climate, homophobic name-calling, and sexual harassment victimization/perpetration among middle school youth. *Psychology of Violence, 6,* 213–222. http://dx.doi.org/10.1037/a0039095

**Risal, A., Manandhar, K., Linde, M., Steiner, T. J., & Holen, A.** (2016). Anxiety and depression in Nepal: Prevalence, comorbidity and associations. *BMC Psychiatry, 16,* Article 102. http://dx.doi.org/10.1186/s12888-016-0810-0

**Risman, B. J., & Davis, G.** (2013). From sex roles to gender structure. *Current Sociology, 61,* 733–755. http://dx.doi. org/10.1177/0011392113479315

**Ritchwood, T. D., DeCoster, J.. Metzger, I. W., Bolland, J. M., & Danielson, C. K.** (2016). Does it really matter which drug you choose? An examination of the influence of type of drug on type of risky sexual behavior. *Addictive Behaviors, 60,* 97–102. http://dx.doi.org/10.1016/j. addbeh.2016.03.022

**Rizvi, S. L., Hughes, C. D., Hittman, A. D., & Vieira Oliveira, P.** (2017). Can trainees effectively deliver dialectical behavior therapy for individuals with borderline personality disorder? Outcomes from a training clinic. *Journal of Clinical Psychology.* No Pagination Specified. http://dx.doi.org/10.1002/jclp.22467

**Rizvi, S. L., & Salters-Pedneault, K.** (2013). Borderline personality disorder. In W. O'Donohue & S. O. Lilienfeld (Eds.), *Case studies in clinical psychological science: Bridging the gap from science to practice* (pp. 301–322). New York, NY: Oxford University Press.

**Rizzolatti, G.** (2014). Confounding the origin and function of mirror neurons. *Behavioral and Brain Sciences, 37,* 218–219. http://dx.doi.org/10.1017/S0140525X13002471

**Rizzolatti, G., Fadiga L., Fogassi L., & Gallese V.** (1996). Premotor cortex and the recognition of motor actions. *Cognitive Brain Research, 3,* 131–141. http://dx.doi.org/10.1016/0926-6410(95)00038-0

**Rizzolatti, G., Sinigaglia, C., & Anderson, F.** (2008). *Mirrors in the brain: How our minds share actions and emotions.* New York, NY: Oxford University Press.

**Robbins, L.** (2013). Neuralstem's stem cells give spinal injury patients hope. Retrieved from http://www.gazette.net/article/20130114/NEWS/130119667/neuralstemx2019-s-stem-cells-give-spinal-injury-patients-hope & template=gazette

**Robbins, S. P.** (1996). *Organizational behavior: Concepts, controversies, and applications.* Englewood Cliffs, NJ: Prentice Hall.

**Robehmed, N.** (2015, August 2015). The world's highest-paid actresses 2015: Jennifer Lawrence leads with $52 million. *Forbes.* Retrieved March 8, 2017 from https://www.forbes.com/sites/natalierobehmed/2015/08/20/the-worlds-highest-paid-actresses-2015-jennifer-lawrence-leads-with-52-million

**Robin, F., Dominguez, J, & Tilford, M.** (2009). *Your money or your life: 9 steps to transforming your relationship with money and achieving financial independence.* New York, NY: Penguin Books.

**Robins, S. K.** (2016). Misremembering. *Philosophical Psychology, 29,* 432–447. http://dx.doi.org/10.1080/09515089.2015.1113245

**Robinson, F. P.** (1970). *Effective study* (4th ed.). New York, NY: Harper & Row.

**Robinson, K. J., Hoplock, L. B., & Cameron, J. J.** (2015). When in doubt, reach out: Touch is a covert but effective mode of soliciting and providing social support. *Social Psychological and Personality Science, 6,* 831–839. http://dx.doi.org/10.1177/1948550615584197

**Robinson, O.** (2016). Emerging adulthood, early adulthood, and quarter-life crisis: Updating Erikson for the twenty-first century. In R. Žukauskienė (Ed.), *Emerging adulthood in a European context* (pp. 17–30). New York, NY: Routledge/Taylor & Francis Group.

**Robison, L. S., Ananth, M., Hadjiargyrou, M., Komatsu, D. E., & Panayotis, K. T.** (2017). Chronic oral methylphenidate treatment reversibly increases striatal dopamine transporter and dopamine type 1 receptor binding in rats. *Journal of Neural Transmission, 124*(5), 655-667. http://doi.org/10.1007/s00702-017-1680-4

**Robnett, R. D., & Leaper, C.** (2013). "Girls don't propose! Ew.": A mixed-methods examination of marriage tradition preferences and benevolent sexism in emerging adults. *Journal of Adolescent Research, 28,* 96–121. http://dx.doi.org/10.1177/0743558412447871

**Rode, L., Nordestgaard, B. G., & Bojesen, S. E.** (2015). Peripheral blood leukocyte telomere length and mortality among 64,637 individuals from the general population. *Journal of the National Cancer Institute, 107,* djv074. http://dx.doi.org/10.1093/jnci/djv074

**Rodkey, E. N., & Riddell, R. P.** (2013). The infancy of infant pain research: The experimental origins of infant pain denial. *The Journal of Pain, 14,* 338–350. http://dx.doi.org/10.1016/j.jpain.2012.12.017

**Rodriguez, C. M., Tucker, M. C., & Palmer, K.** (2015). Emotion regulation in relation to emerging adults' mental health and delinquency: A multi-informant approach. *Journal of Child and Family Studies, 25,* 1916–1925. http://dx.doi.org/10.1007/s10826-015-0349-6

**Roediger III, H. L.** (2017). Psychologists in university departments of psychology or psychological science. In R. J. Sternberg (Ed.), *Career paths in psychology: Where your degree can take you* (3rd ed., pp. 9–31). Washington, DC: American Psychological Association.

**Roepke, A. M., & Seligman, M. E. P.** (2016). Depression and prospection. *British Journal of Clinical Psychology, 55,* 23–48. http://dx.doi.org/10.1111/bjc.12087

**Rogers, C. R.** (1961). *On becoming a person.* Boston, MA: Houghton Mifflin.

**Rogers, C. R.** (1980). *A way of being.* Boston, MA: Houghton Mifflin.

**Rogers, P., Fisk, J. E., & Lowrie, E.** (2016). Paranormal believers' susceptibility to confirmatory versus disconfirmatory conjunctions. *Applied Cognitive Psychology, 30,* 628–634. http://dx.doi.org/10.1002/acp.3222

**Rogge, R. D., Cobb, R. J., Lawrence, E., Johnson, M. D., & Bradbury, T. N.** (2013). Is skills training necessary for the primary prevention of marital distress and dissolution? A 3-year experimental study of three interventions. *Journal of Consulting and Clinical Psychology, 81,* 949–961. http://dx.doi.org/10.1037/a0034209

**Rohlfs Domínguez, P.** (2014). Promoting our understanding of neural plasticity by exploring developmental plasticity in early and adult life. *Brain Research Bulletin, 107,* 31–36. http://dx.doi.org/10.1016/j.brainresbull.2014.05.006

**Rokke, P. D., & Lystad, C. M.** (2014). Mood-specific effects in the allocation of attention across time. *Cognition & Emotion, 29,* 27–50. http://dx.doi.org/10.1080/02699931.2014.893865

**Romeo, R. D.** (2017). The impact of stress on the structure of the adolescent brain: Implications for adolescent mental health. *Brain Research, 1654,* 185–191. http://dx.doi.org/10.1016/j.brainres.2016.03.021

**Romero, C., Master, A., Paunesku, D., Dweck, C. S., & Gross, J. J.** (2014). Academic and emotional functioning in middle school: The role of implicit theories. *Emotion, 14,* 227–234. http://dx.doi.org/10.1037/a0035490

**Rood, L., Roelofs, J., Bögels, S. M., & Meesters, C.** (2012). Stress-reactive rumination, negative cognitive style, and stressors in relationship to depressive symptoms in non-clinical youth. *Journal of Youth and Adolescence, 41,* 414–425. http://dx.doi.org/10.1007/s10964-011-9657-3

**Roozen, S., Peters, G. J., Kok, G., Townend, D., Nijhuis, J., & Curfs, L.** (2016). Worldwide prevalence of fetal alcohol spectrum disorders: A systematic literature review including meta-analysis. *Alcoholism, Clinical and Experimental Research, 40,* 18–32. http://dx.doi.org/10.1111/acer.12939

**Rosch, E.** (1978). *Principles of categorization.* In E. Rosch & B. B. Lloyd (Eds.), *Cognition and categorization* (pp. 27–48). Hillsdale, NJ: Erlbaum.

**Rosch, E. H.** (1973). Natural categories. *Cognitive Psychology, 4,* 328–350. http://dx.doi.org/10.1016/0010-0285(73)90017-0

**Rosen, J.** (2010, February 21). Supreme Court Justice Barack Obama? *Washington Post.* Retrieved from http://www.washingtonpost.com/wp-dyn/content/article/2010/02/18/AR2010021803275.html

**Rosenberg, A., Enos, F., & Hirschberg, J.** (2106). Measuring the voice. In D. Matsumoto, H. C. Hwang, & M. G. Frank (Eds.), *APA handbook of nonverbal communication* (pp. 459–498). Washington, DC: American Psychological Association. http://dx.doi.org/10.1037/14669-018

**Rosenhan, D. L.** (1973). On being sane in insane places. *Science, 179,* 250–258. http://dx.doi.org/10.1126/science.179.4070.250

**Rosenström, T., Ystrom, E., Torvik, F. A., Czajkowski, N. O., Gillespie, N. A., Aggen, S. H., . . . Reichborn-Kjennerud, T.** (2017). Genetic and environmental structure of dsm-iv criteria for antisocial personality disorder: A twin study. *Behavior Genetics, 47*(3), 265–277. http://dx.doi.org/10.1007/s10519-016-9833-z

**Rosenthal, R.** (1965). *Clever Hans: A case study of scientific method, introduction to Clever Hans.* New York, NY: Holt, Rinehart & Winston.

**Rosenthal, S. R., Buka, S. L., Marshall, B. D., Carey, K. B., & Clark, M. A.** (2016). Negative experiences on Facebook and depressive symptoms among young adults. *Journal of Adolescent Health, 59*(5), 510–516. http://dx.doi.org/10.1016/j.jadohealth.2016.06.023

**Rosenzweig, M. R., Bennett, E. L., & Diamond, M. C.** (1972). Brain changes in response to experience. *Scientific American, 226,* 22–29. http://dx.doi.org/10.1038/scientificamerican0272-22

**Rosner, T. M., D'Angelo, M. C., MacLellan, E., & Milliken, B.** (2015). Selective attention and recognition: Effects of congruency on episodic learning. *Psychological Research, 79,* 411–424. http://dx.doi.org/10.1007/s00426-014-0572-6

**Ross, B. M., & Millson, C.** (1970). Repeated memory of oral prose in Ghana and New York. *International Journal of Psychology, 5,* 173–181.

**Ross, L.** (1977). The intuitive psychologist and his shortcomings: Distortions in the attribution process. In L. Berkowitz (Ed.), *Advances in Experimental Social Psychology* (Vol. 10, pp. 173–220). New York, NY: Academic Press.

**Rothbaum, F., Kakinuma, M., Nagaoka, R., & Azuma, H.** (2007). Attachment and amae: Parent-child closeness in the United States and Japan. *Journal of Cross-Cultural Psychology, 38,* 465–486. http://dx.doi.org/10.1177/0022022107302315

**Rothenberg, A.** (2014). *Flight from wonder: An investigation of scientific creativity.* New York, NY: Oxford University Press.

**Rothgerber, H., & Wolsiefer, K.** (2014). A naturalistic study of stereotype threat in young female chess players. *Group Processes & Intergroup Relations, 17,* 79–90. http://dx.doi.org/10.1177/1368430213490212

**Roth, G., Kanat-Maymon, Y., & Assor, A.** (2016). The role of unconditional parental regard in autonomy-supportive parenting. *Journal of Personality, 84,* 716–725. http://dx.doi.org/10.1111/jopy.12194

**Rotter, J. B.** (1954). *Social learning and clinical psychology.* Englewood Cliffs, NJ: Prentice Hall.

**Rotter, J. B.** (1966). Generalized expectancies for internal versus external control of reinforcement. *Psychological Monographs: General & Applied, 80*(1), 1–28. http://dx.doi.org/10.1037/a0032736.

**Rotter, J. B.** (1990). Internal versus external control of reinforcement: A case history of a variable. *American Psychologist, 45,* 489–493.

**Rottinghaus, B., & Vaughn, J.** (2015, February 16). New ranking of U.S. presidents puts Lincoln at no. 1, Obama at 18, Kennedy judged most overrated. *Washington Post.* Retrieved from https://www.washingtonpost.com/news/monkey-cage/wp/2015/02/16/new-ranking-of-u-s-presidents-puts-lincoln-1-obama-18-kennedy-judged-most-over-rated/?utm_term=.d80ee3244e7c

**Rouder, J. N., Morey, R. D., & Province, J. M.** (2013). A Bayes factor meta-analysis of recent extrasensory perception experiments: Comment on Storm, Tressoldi, and Di Risio (2010). *Psychological Bulletin, 139,* 241–247.

**Routledge, C., Abeyta, A. A., & Roylance, C.** (2017). We are not alone: The meaning motive, religiosity, and belief in extraterrestrial intelligence. *Motivation and Emotion, 41(2)*, 35–146. http://dx.doi.org/10.1007/s11031-017-9605-y

**Rowling, J. K.** (2016). J. K. Rowling. *J. K. Website.com*. Retrieved March 17, 2017 from https://www.jkrowling.com/about/

**Rowling, J. K.** (n.d.) J. K. Rowling. *Wikipedia*. Retrieved March 16, 2017 from https://en.wikipedia.org/wiki/J._K._Rowling

**Roy, L., Crocker, A. G., Nicholls, T. L., Latimer, E., & Isaak, C. A.** (2016). Predictors of criminal justice system trajectories of homeless adults living with mental illness. *International Journal of Law and Psychiatry, 49(Part A)*, 75–83. http://dx.doi.org/10.1016/j.ijlp.2016.05.013

**Rubin, L. H., Wu, M., Sundermann, E. E., Meyer, V. J., Smith, R., Weber, K. M., . . . Maki, P. M.** (2016). Elevated stress is associated with prefrontal cortex dysfunction during a verbal memory task in women with HIV. *Journal of Neurology, 22*(6), 840–851. http://dx.doi.org/10.1007/s13365-016-0446-3

**Rucklidge, J. J., Downs-Woolley, M., Taylor, M., Brown, J. A., & Harrow, S.-E.** (2016). Psychiatric comorbidities in a New Zealand sample of adults with ADHD. *Journal of Attention Disorders, 20*, 1030–1038. http://dx.doi.org/10.1177/1087054714529457

**Ruffman, T., O'Brien, K. S., Taumoepeau, M., Latner, J. D., & Hunter, J. A.** (2016). Toddlers' bias to look at average versus obese figures relates to maternal anti-fat prejudice. *Journal of Experimental Child Psychology, 142*, 195–202. http://dx.doi.org/10.1016/j.jecp.2015.10.008

**Ruini, C., & Fava, G. A.** (2014). Increasing happiness by well-being therapy. In K. M. Sheldon & R. E. Lucas (Eds.), *Stability of happiness: Theories and evidence on whether happiness can change* (pp. 147–166). San Diego, CA: Elsevier Academic Press.

**Ruiz-Aranda, D., Extremera, N., & Pineda-Galan, C.** (2014). Emotional intelligence, life satisfaction and subjective happiness in female student health professionals: The mediating effect of perceived stress. *Journal of Psychiatric and Mental Health Nursing, 21*, 106–113. http://dx.doi.org/10.1111/jpm.12052

**Rumbaugh, D. M., von Glasersfeld, E. C., Warner, H., Pisani, P., & Gill, T. V.** (1974). Lana (chimpanzee) learning language: A progress report. *Brain and Language, 1*, 205–212. http://dx.doi.org/ 10.1016/0093-934X(74)90035-2

**Ruocco, A. C., Amirthavasagam, S., Choi-Kain, L. W., & McMain, S. F.** (2013). Neural correlates of negative emotionality in borderline personality disorder: An activation-likelihood-estimation meta-analysis. *Biological Psychiatry, 73*, 153–160.

**Rusbult, C. E., & Zembrodt, I. M.** (1983). Responses to dissatisfaction in romantic involvements: A multidimensional scaling analysis. *Journal of Experimental Social Psychology, 19*, 274–293.

**Rusbult, C. E., Zembrodt, I. M., & Gunn, L. K.** (1982). Exit, voice, loyalty, and neglect: Responses to dissatisfaction in romantic involvements. *Journal of Personality and Social Psychology, 43*, 1230–1242.

**Rushton, J. P., & Jensen, A. R.** (2010). Race and IQ: A theory-based review of the research in Richard Nisbett's Intelligence and how to get it. *The Open Psychology Journal, 3*, Article 9-35. http://dx.doi.org/10.2174/1874350101003010009

**Russ, S., & Wallace, C. E.** (2013). Pretend play and creative processes. *American Journal of Play, 6*, 136–148.

**Russell, V. A., Zigmond, M. J., Dimatelis, J. J., Daniels, W. M. U., & Mabandla, M. V.** (2014). The interaction between stress and exercise, and its impact on brain function. *Metabolic Brain Disease, 29*, 255–260. http://dx.doi.org/10.1007/s11011-013-9479-y

**Rutland, A., & Killen, M.** (2015). A developmental science approach to reducing prejudice and social exclusion: Intergroup processes, social-cognitive development, and moral reasoning. *Social Issues and Policy Review, 9*, 121–154. http://dx.doi.org/10.1111/sipr.12012

**Ryan, C. J., & Callaghan, S.** (2017). The impact on clinical practice of the 2015 reforms to the New South Wales Mental Health Act. *Australasian Psychiatry, 25*(1), 43–47. http://dx.doi.org/10.1177/1039856216663738

**Ryan, R. M., & Deci, E. L.** (2013). Toward a social psychology of assimilation: Self-determination theory in cognitive development and education. In B. W. Sokol, F. M. E. Grouzet, & U. Muller (Eds.), *Self-regulation and autonomy: Social and developmental dimensions of human conduct* (pp. 191–207). Cambridge, UK: Cambridge University Press. http://dx.doi.org/10.1017/cbo9781139152198.014

**Rydé, K., & Hjelm, K.** (2016). How to support patients who are crying in palliative home care: An interview study from the nurses' perspective. *Primary Health Care Research and Development, 17*(5), 479–488. http://dx.doi.org/10.1017/S1463423616000037

**Rymer, R.** (1993). *Genie: An abused child's first flight from silence*. New York, NY: HarperCollins.

**Saadat, S.** (2015). A review on paraphilias. *International Journal of Medical Reviews, 1*. Retrieved from http://journals.bmsu.ac.ir/ijmr/index.php/ijmr/article/view/83

**Sacco, R., Gabriele, S., & Persico, A. M.** (2015). Head circumference and brain size in autism spectrum disorder: A systematic review and meta-analysis. *Psychiatry Research, 234*(2), 239–251. http://doi.org/10.1016/j.pscychresns.2015.08.016.

**Sachsenweger, M. A., Fletcher, R. B., & Clarke, D.** (2015). Pessimism and homework in CBT for depression. *Journal of Clinical Psychology, 71*, 1153–1172. http://dx.doi.org/10.1002/jclp.22227

**Sacks, O.** (2015). *On the move: A life*. New York, NY: Knopf.

**Sáenz Herrero, M.** (2015). *Psychopathology in women: Incorporating gender perspective into descriptive psychopathology*. New York, NY: Springer.

**Safer, M. A., Murphy, R. P., Wise, R. A., Bussey, L., Millett, C., & Holfeld, B.** (2016). Educating jurors about eyewitness testimony in criminal cases with circumstantial and forensic evidence. *International Journal of Law and Psychiatry, 47*, 86–92. http://dx.doi.org/10.1016/j.ijlp.2016.02.041

**Sagong, B., Bae, J. W., Rhyu, M. R., Kim, U. K., & Ye, M. K.** (2014). Multiplex minisequencing screening for PTC genotype associated with bitter taste perception. *Molecular Biology Reports, 41*, 1563–1567. http://dx.doi.org/10.1007/s11033-013-3002-8

**Salk, R. H., Hyde, J. S., & Abramson, L. Y.** (2017). Gender differences in depression in representative national samples: Meta-analyses of diagnoses and symptoms. *Psychological* http://dx.doi.org/10.1037/bul0000102

**Salovey, P., & Mayer, J. D.** (1990). Emotional intelligence. *Imagination, Cognition, and Personality, 9*, 185–211.

**Salvi, C., Bricolo, E., Kounios, J., Bowden, E., & Beeman, M.** (2016). Insight solutions are correct more often than analytic solutions. *Thinking and Reasoning, 22*(4), 443–460. http://dx.doi.org/10.1080/13546783.2016.1141798

**Salzman, J. P., Kunzendorf, R. G., Saunders, E., & Hulihan, D.** (2014). The Primary Attachment Style Questionnaire: A brief measure for assessing six primary attachment styles before and after age twelve. *Imagination, Cognition and Personality, 33*, 113–149.

**Sample, I.** (2016, November 17). 'We can't let the bullies win': Elizabeth Loftus awarded 2016 John Maddox prize. *The Guardian*. Retrieved from https://www.theguardian.com/science/2016/nov/17/we-cant-let-the-bullies-win-elizabeth-loftus-awarded-2016-john-maddox-prize-false-memory.

**Samuels, B. A., Mendez-David, I., Faye, C., David, S. A., Pierz, K. A., Gardier, A. M., . . . David, D. J.** (2016). Serotonin 1A and serotonin 4 receptors: Essential mediators of the neurogenic and behavioral actions of antidepressants. *The Neuroscientist, 22*, 26–45. http://dx.doi.org/10.1177/1073858414561303

**Sánchez-Villegas, A., Toledo, E., de Irala, J., Ruiz-Canela, M., Pla-Vidal, J., & Martínez-González, M. A.** (2011). Fast-food and commercial baked goods consumption and the risk of depression. *Public Health Nutrition, 15*, 424–432.

**Sand, R. S.** (2014). *Dialog-on-Freud series. The unconscious without Freud*. Lanham, MD: Rowman & Littlefield.

**Sandberg, L.** (2016). In lust we trust? Masculinity and sexual desire in later life. *Men and Masculinities, 19*, 192–208. http://dx.doi.org/10.1177/1097184X15606948

**Sanders, A. R., Martin, E. R., Beecham, G. W., Guo, S., Dawood, K., Rieger, G., . . . Bailey, J. M.** (2015). Genome-wide scan demonstrates significant linkage for male sexual orientation. *Psychological Medicine, 45*, 1379–1388. http://dx.doi.org/10.1017/S0033291714002451

**Sanderson, C. A.** (2013). *Health psychology* (2nd ed.). Hoboken, NJ: Wiley.

**Sandner, B., Prang, P., Blesch, A., & Weidner, N.** (2015). Stem cell-based therapies for spinal cord regeneration. In H. Kuhn & A. Eisch (Eds.), *Neural stem cells in development, adulthood and disease* (pp. 155–174). New York, NY: Springer.

**Sándor, P., Szakadát, S., & Bódizs, R.** (2014). Ontogeny of dreaming: A review of empirical studies. *Sleep Medicine Reviews, 18*, 435–449. http://dx.doi.org/10.1016/j.smrv.2014.02.001

**Sanjuán, P., & Magallares, A.** (2014). Coping strategies as mediating variables between self-serving attributional bias and subjective well-being. *Journal of Happiness Studies, 15*, 443–453. http://dx.doi.org/10.1007/s10902-013-9430-2

**Sankar, A., Scott, J., Paszkiewicz, A., Giampietro, V. P., Steiner, H., & Fu, C. H. Y.** (2015). Neural effects of cognitive–behavioural therapy on dysfunctional attitudes in depression. *Psychological Medicine, 45*, 1425–1433. http://dx.doi.org/10.1017/S0033291714002529

**Santos, T. O.** (2016). Cognitive changes in aging: Implications for discourse processing. In L. S. Carozza (Ed), *Communication and aging: Creative approaches to improving the quality of life* (pp. 25–65). San Diego, CA: Plural Publishing.

**Sarafino, E. P., & Smith, T. W.** (2016). *Health psychology: Biopsychosocial interactions* (9th ed.). Hoboken, NJ: Wiley.

**Saraswat, A., Weinand, J. D., & Safer, J. D.** (2015). Evidence supporting the biologic nature of gender identity. *Endocrine Practice, 21,* 199–204. http://dx.doi.org/10.4158/EP14351.RA.

**Sargent, J. D., Tanski, S., & Stoolmiller, M.** (2012). Influence of motion picture rating on adolescent response to movie smoking. *Pediatrics, 130,* 228–236. http://dx.doi.org/10.1542/peds.2011-1787

**Saridi, M., Kordosi, A., Toska, A., Peppou, L. E., Economou, M., & Souliotis, K.** (2017). Attitudes of health professionals towards the stigma surrounding depression in times of economic crisis. *International Journal of Social Psychiatry, 63*(2), 115–125. http://dx.doi.org/10.1177/0020764016685348

**Sarkova, M., Bacikova-Sleskova, M., Orosova, O., Madarasova Geckova, A., Katreniakova, Z., Klein, D., . . . Dijk, J. P.** (2013). Associations between assertiveness, psychological well-being, and self-esteem in adolescents. *Journal of Applied Social Psychology, 43,* 147–154.

**Sassenberg, K., Moskowitz, G. B., Fetterman, A., & Kessler, T.** (2017). Priming creativity as a strategy to increase creative performance by facilitating the activation and use of remote associations. *Journal of Experimental Social Psychology, 68,* 128–138. http://dx.doi.org/10.1016/j.jesp.2016.06.010

**Satterly, M. V., & Anitescu, M.** (2015). Opioids and substance abuse. In A. D. Kaye, N. Vadivelu, & R. D. Urman (Eds.), *Substance abuse: Inpatient and outpatient management for every clinician* (pp. 179–192). New York, NY: Springer.

**Saucier, G., Kenner, J., Iurino, K., Malham, P. B., Chen, Z., Thalmayer, A. G., . . . Altschul, C.** (2015). Cross-cultural differences in a global "Survey of World Views." *Journal of Cross-Cultural Psychology, 46,* 53–70. http://dx.doi.org/10.1177/0022022114551791

**Savage-Rumbaugh, E. S.** (1990). Language acquisition in a nonhuman species: Implications for the innateness debate. *Developmental Psychobiology, 23,* 599–620. http://dx.doi.org/10.1002/dev.420230706

**Saxon, S. V., Etten, M. J., & Perkins, E. A.** (2014). *Physical change and aging: A guide for the helping professions* (6th ed.). New York, NY: Springer.

**Sayal, K., Heron, J., Maughan, B., Rowe, R., & Ramchandani, P.** (2014). Infant temperament and childhood psychiatric disorder: Longitudinal study. *Child: Care, Health and Development, 40,* 292–297. http://dx.doi.org/10.1111/cch.12054

**Schachter, S., & Singer, J. E.** (1962). Cognitive, social, and physiological determinants of emotional state. *Psychological Review, 69,* 379–399.

**Schaeffer, E. L., Cerulli, F. G., Souza, H. O. X., Catanozi, S., & Gattaz, W. F.** (2014). Synergistic and additive effects of enriched environment and lithium on the generation of new cells in adult mouse hippocampus. *Journal of Neural Transmission, 121,* 695–706. http://dx.doi.org/10.1007/s00702-014-1175-5

**Schäfer, M., & Quiring, O.** (2015). The press coverage of celebrity suicide and the development of suicide frequencies in Germany. *Health Communication, 30*(11), 1149–1158. http://dx.doi.org/10.1080/10410236.2014.923273

**Schalet, A. T.** (2011). *Not under my roof: Parents, teens, and the culture of sex.* Chicago, IL: University of Chicago Press.

**Schare, M. L., Wyatt, K. P., Skolnick, R. B., Terjesen, M., Haak Bohnenkamp, J., Lai, B. S., . . . Ehrlich, C. J.** (2015). Cognitive and behavioral interventions. In R. Flanagan, K. Allen, & E. Levine (Eds.), *Cognitive and behavioral interventions in the schools: Integrating theory and research into practice* (pp. 249–283). New York, NY: Springer. http://dx.doi.org/10.1007/978-1-4939-1972-7

**Scharfman, H. E., & MacLusky, N. J.** (2017). Sex differences in hippocampal area CA3 pyramidal cells. *Journal of Neuroscience Research, 95,* 563–575. http://dx.doi.org/10.1002/jnr.23927

**Scharrer, E., & Ramasubramanian, S.** (2015). Intervening in the media's influence on stereotypes of race and ethnicity: The role of media literacy education. *Journal of Social Issues, 71,* 171–185. http://dx.doi.org/10.1111/josi.12103

**Schartner, M. M., Carhart-Harris, R. L., Barrett, A. B., Seth, A. K., & Muthukumaraswamy, S. D.** (2017). Increased spontaneous MEG signal diversity for psychoactive doses of ketamine, LSD and psilocybin. *Scientific Reports,* 7: 4642.1 http://dx.doi.org/10.1038/srep46421

**Scheele, D., Striepens, N., Güntürkün, O., Deutschländer, S., Maier, W., Kendrick, K. M., & Hurlemann, R.** (2012). Oxytocin modulates social distance between males and females. *The Journal of Neuroscience, 32,* 16074–16079.

**Scheele, D., Wille, A., Kendrick, K. M., Stoffel-Wagner, B., Becker, B., Güntürkün, O., . . . Hurlemann, R.** (2013). Oxytocin enhances brain reward system responses in men viewing the face of their female partner. *Proceedings of the National Academy of Science of the United States of America, 110,* 20308–20313. http://dx.doi.org/10.1073/pnas.1314190110

**Scherman, D.** (2014). *Advanced textbook on gene transfer, gene therapy and genetic pharmacology: Principles, delivery and pharmacological and biomedical applications of nucleotide-based therapies.* London, UK: Imperial College Press.

**Schick, T., Jr., & Vaughn, L.** (2014). *How to think about weird things: Critical thinking for a new age* (7th ed.). New York, NY: McGraw-Hill.

**Schiffer, B., Pawliczek, C., Müller, B., Forsting, M., Gizewski, E., Leygraf, N., & Hodgins, S.** (2014). Neural mechanisms underlying cognitive control of men with lifelong antisocial behavior. *Psychiatry Research: Neuroimaging, 222,* 43–51. http://dx.doi.org/10.1016/j.pscychresns.2014.01.008

**Schilling, C., Kühn, S., Sander, T., & Gallinat, J.** (2014). Association between dopamine D4 receptor genotype and trait impulsiveness. *Psychiatric Genetics, 24,* 82. http://dx.doi.org/10.1097/YPG.0000000000000005

**Schimmel, P.** (2014). *Sigmund Freud's discovery of psychoanalysis: Conquistador and thinker.* New York: NY: Routledge/Taylor & Francis Group.

**Schim, S. M., Briller, S. H., Thurston, C. S., & Meert, K. L.** (2007). Life as death scholars: Passion, personality, and professional perspectives. *Death Studies, 31,* 165–172.

**Schindler, B., Vriends, N., Margraf, J., & Stieglitz, R.-D.** (2016). Ways of acquiring flying phobia. *Depression and Anxiety, 33*(2), 136–142. http://dx.doi.org/10.1002/da.22447

**Schlegel, A., & Barry, H.** (2017). Pain, fear, and circumcision in boys' adolescent initiation ceremonies. *Cross-Cultural Research.* No Pagination Specified. http://dx.doi.org/10.1177/1069397116685780

**Schlichting, M. L., & Preston, A. R.** (2014). Memory reactivation during rest supports upcoming learning of related content. *Proceedings of the National Academy of Sciences of the United States of America, 111,* 15845–15850. http://dx.doi.org/10.1073/pnas.1404396111

**Schmid, P. C., & Amodio, D. M.** (2017). Power effects on implicit prejudice and stereotyping: The role of intergroup face processing. *Social Neuroscience, 12*(2), 218–231. http://dx.doi.org/10.1080/17470919.2016.1144647

**Schmidt, F., & Fleming, R. W.** (2016). Visual perception of complex shape-transforming processes. *Cognitive Psychology, 90,* 48–70. http://dx.doi.org/10.1016/j.cogpsych.2016.08.002

**Schmidt, S. R.** (2012). *Essays in cognitive psychology. Extraordinary memories for exceptional events.* New York, NY: Psychology Press.

**Schmitgen, M. M., Walter, H., Drost, S., Rückl, S., & Schnell, K.** (2016). Stimulus-dependent amygdala involvement in affective theory of mind generation. *NeuroImage, 129,* 450–459. http://dx.doi.org/10.1016/j.neuroimage.2016.01.029

**Schmitt, D. P.** (2015). *The evolution of sexuality.* Cham, CH: Springer International Publishing.

**Schnack, H. G., Nieuwenhuis, M., Haren, N. E., Abramovic, L., Scheewe, T. W., Brouwer, R. M., . . . Kahn, R. S.** (2014). Can structural MRI aid in clinical classification? A machine learning study in two independent samples of patients with schizophrenia, bipolar disorder and healthy subjects. *NeuroImage, 84,* 299–306. http://dx.doi.org/10.1016/j.neuroimage.2013.08.05

**Schnall, P. L., Dobson, M., & Landsbergis, P.** (2016). Globalization, work, and cardiovascular disease. *International Journal of Health Services, 46,* 656–692. http://dx.doi.org/10.1177/0020731416664687

**Schneider, K., Fraser Pierson, J., & Bugental, J.** (Eds.). (2015). *The handbook of humanistic psychology.* Thousand Oaks, CA: Sage.

**Schneidman, E. S.** (1969). Suicide, lethality and the psychological autopsy. *International Psychiatry Clinics, 6,* 225–250.

**Schoenmaker, C., Juffer, F., van IJzendoorn, M. H., van den Dries, L., Linting, M., Vander voort, A., & Bakermans-Kranenburg, M. J.** (2015). Cognitive and health-related outcomes after exposure to early malnutrition: The Leiden longitudinal study of international adoptees. *Children and Youth Services Review, 48,* 80–86. http://dx.doi.org/10.1016/j.childyouth.2014.12.010

**Schomerus, G., Angermeyer, M. C., Baumeister, S. E., Stolzenburg, S., Link, B. G., & Phelan, J. C.** (2016). An online intervention using information on the mental health-mental illness continuum to reduce stigma. *European Psychiatry, 32,* 21–27. http://dx.doi.org/10.1016/j.eurpsy.2015.11.006

**Schonert-Reichl, K. A., Oberle, E., Lawlor, M. S., Abbott, D., Thomson, K., Oberlander, T. F., & Diamond, A.** (2015). Enhancing cognitive and social–emotional development through a simple-to-administer mindfulness-based school program for elementary school children: A randomized controlled trial. *Developmental Psychology, 51,* 52–66. http://doi.org/10.1037/a0038454

**Schroder, H. S., Yalch, M. M., Dawood, S., Callahan, C. P., Brent Donnellan, M., & Moser, J. S.** (2017). Growth mindset of anxiety buffers the link between stressful life events and psychological distress and coping strategies. *Personality and Individual Differences, 110,* 23–26. http://dx.doi.org/10.1016/j.paid.2017.01.016

**Schröder, J., Jelinek, L., & Moritz, S.** (2017). A randomized controlled trial of a transdiagnostic internet intervention for individuals with panic and phobias – one size fits all. *Journal of Behavior Therapy and Experimental Psychiatry, 54,* 17–24. http://dx.doi.org/10.1016/j.jbtep.2016.05.002

**Schroeder, D. A., & Graziano, W. G.** (Eds.). (2015). *The Oxford handbook of prosocial behavior.* Oxford, UK: Oxford University Press.

**Schroers, W.** (2014). Memory improvement—spaced repetition. *Field-theory.org.* Retrieved from http://www.field-theory.org/articles/memory/spaced_repetition.html

**Schug, J., Yoo, S. H., & Atreya, G.** (2017). Norms regulating emotional expressions relate to national level generalized trust. *Evolutionary Behavioral Sciences, 11,* 23–35. http://dx.doi.org/10.1037/ebs0000068

**Schulze, L., Schmahl, C., & Niedtfeld, I.** (2016). Neural correlates of disturbed emotion processing in borderline personality disorder: A multimodal meta-analysis. *Biological Psychiatry, 79,* 97–106. http://dx.doi.org/10.1016/j.biopsych.2015.03.027

**Schulz, H. M.** (2015). Reference group influence in consumer role rehearsal narratives. *Qualitative Market Research: An International Journal, 18,* 210–229. http://dx.doi.org/10.1108/QMR-02-2012-0009

**Schunk, D. H., & Zimmerman, B. J.** (2013). Self-regulation and learning. In W. M. Reynolds, G. E. Miller, & I. B. Weiner (Eds.), *Handbook of psychology, Vol. 7. Educational psychology* (2nd ed., pp. 45–68). Hoboken, NJ: Wiley.

**Schüz, B., Bower, J., & Ferguson, S. G.** (2015). Stimulus control and affect in dietary behaviours. An intensive longitudinal study. *Appetite, 87,* 310–317. http://dx.doi.org/10.1016/j.appet.2015.01.002

**Schwartz, A. J., Boduroglu, A., & Gutchess, A. H.** (2014). Cross-cultural differences in categorical memory errors. *Cognitive Science, 38,* 997–1007.

**Schwartz, B., & Krantz, J.** (2016). *Sensation and perception.* Thousand Oaks, CA: Sage.

**Schwartz, N. G., Rattner, A., Schwartz, A. R., Mokhlesi, B., Gilman, R. H., Bernabe-Ortiz, A., . . . CRONICAS Cohort Study Group.** (2015). Sleep disordered breathing in four resource-limited settings in Peru: Prevalence, risk factors, and association with chronic diseases. *Sleep, 38*(9), 1451–1459.

**Schwartz, P., & Kempner, M.** (2015). *50 great myths of human sexuality.* Chichester, UK: Wiley-Blackwell.

**Schwartz, S. J., Zamboanga, B. L., Luyckx, K., Meca, A., & Ritchie, R.** (2016). Identity in emerging adulthood: Reviewing the field and looking forward. In J. J. Arnett (Ed.), *The Oxford handbook of emerging adulthood* (pp. 401–420). New York, NY: Oxford University Press.

**Schwarz, A.** (2013, May 1). Attention-deficit drugs face new campus rules. *New York Times.* Retrieved from http://www.nytimes.com/2013/05/01/us/colleges-tackle-illicit-use-of-adhd-pills.html

**Scoboria, A., Wade, K. A., Lindsay, D. S., Azad, T., Strange, D., Ost, J., & Hyman, I. E.** (2017). A mega-analysis of memory reports from eight peer-reviewed false memory implantation studies. *Journal of Memory, 25,* 146–163. http://dx.doi.org/10.1080/09658211.2016.1260747

**Scott, C.** (2015). *Learn to teach: Teach to learn.* New York, NY: Cambridge University Press.

**Scott-Phillips, T. C.** (2015). Nonhuman primate communication, pragmatics, and the origins of language. *Current Anthropology, 56,* 56–80.

**Scribner, S.** (1977). Modes of thinking and ways of speaking: Culture and logic reconsidered. In P. N. Johnson-Laird & P. C. Wason (Eds.), *Thinking: Readings in cognitive science* (pp. 324–339). New York, NY: Cambridge University Press.

**Sdrulla, A. D., Chen, G., & Mauer, K.** (2015). Definition and demographics of addiction. In A. Kaye, N. Vadivelu, & R. Urman (Eds.), *Substance abuse* (pp. 1–15). New York, NY: Springer.

**Seay, T. A., & Sun, C. T. L.** (2016). Psychotherapies: What can be done when the mind is unwell? In C. Tien-Lun Sun (Ed.), *Psychology in Asia: An introduction* (pp. 395–422). Boston, MA: Cengage Learning.

**Sebelius, K.** (2014). *The health consequences of smoking—50 years of progress: A report of the Surgeon General.* Atlanta, GA: US Department of Health and Human Services, Centers for Disease Control and Prevention, National Center for Chronic Disease Prevention and Health Promotion, Office on Smoking and Health. Retrieved from http://www.surgeongeneral.gov/library/reports/50-years-of-progress/execsummary.Pdf

**Sedikides, C., & Alicke, M. D.** (2012). Self-enhancement and self-protection motives. In R. M. Ryan (Ed.), *The Oxford handbook of human motivation. Oxford library of psychology* (pp. 303–322). New York: NY: Oxford University Press.

**Seebauer, L., Froß, S., Dubaschny, L., Schönberger, M., & Jacob, G. A.** (2014). Is it dangerous to fantasize revenge in imagery exercises? An experimental study. *Journal of Behavior Therapy and Experimental Psychiatry, 45,* 20–25.

**Seedat, S., Scott, K. M., Angermeyer, M. C., Berglund, P., Bromet, E. J., Brugha, T. S., . . . Kessler, R. C.** (2009). Cross-national associations between gender and mental disorders in the World Health Organization World Mental Health Surveys. *Archives of General Psychiatry, 66,* 785–795.

**Seedman, A. A., & Hellman, P.** (2014). *Fifty years after Kitty Genovese: Inside the case that rocked our faith in each other.* New York, NY: The Experiment.

**Seeley, R. J., & Berridge, K. C.** (2015). The hunger games. *Cell, 16,* 805–806. http://dx.doi.org/10.1016/j.cell.2015.02.028

**Segarra-Echebarría, R., Fernández-Pérez, I., García-Moncho, J. M., & Delarze-Carrillo, L.** (2015). Psychosexual development and sexual dysfunctions. In M. Sáenz-Herrero (Ed.), *Psychopathology in women: Incorporating gender perspective into descriptive psychopathology* (pp. 25–51). Cham, CH: Springer International Publishing. http://dx.doi.org/10.1007/978-3-319-05870-2

**Sehgal, P.** (2015, December 1). The profound emptiness of "resilience." *The New York Times Magazine.* Retrieved from http://www.nytimes.com/2015/12/06/magazine/the-profound-emptiness-of-resilience.html?_r=1

**Seifer, R., Dickstein, S., Parade, S., Hayden, L. C., Magee, K. D., & Schiller, M.** (2014). Mothers' appraisal of goodness of fit and children's social development. *International Journal of Behavioral Development, 38,* 86–97. http://dx.doi.org/10.1177/0165025413507172

**Sekiguchi, A., Kotozaki, Y., Sugiura, M., Nouchi, R., Takeuchi, H., Hanawa, S., . . . Kawashima, R.** (2014). Long-term effects of postearthquake distress on brain microstructural changes. *BioMed Research International, Volume 2014,* Article ID 180468. http://doi.org/10.1155/2014/180468

**Sell, C., Möller, H., & Taubner, S.** (2017). Effectiveness of integrative imagery and trance-based psychodynamic therapies: Guided imagery psychotherapy and hypnopsychotherapy. *Journal of Psychotherapy Integration.* No Pagination Specified. http://dx.doi.org/10.1037/int0000073

**Seligman, M. E. P.** (1975). *Helplessness: On depression, development, and death.* San Francisco, CA: Freeman.

**Seligman, M. E. P.** (2003). The past and future of positive psychology. In C. L. M. Keyes & J. Daidt (Eds.), *Flourishing: Positive psychology and the life well-lived* (pp. xi–xx). Washington, DC: American Psychological Association.

**Seligman, M. E. P.** (2007). Coaching and positive psychology. *Australian Psychologist, 42,* 266–267.

**Seligman, M. E. P.** (2012). *Flourish: A visionary new understanding of happiness and well being.* Riverside, NJ: Atria.

**Seligman, M. E. P.** (2015). Chris Peterson's unfinished masterwork: The real mental illnesses. *The Journal of Positive Psychology, 10,* 3–6. http://dx.doi.org/10.1080/17439760.2014.888582

**Seligman, M. E. P., & Maier, S. F.** (1967). Failure to escape traumatic shock. *Journal of Experimental Psychology, 74,* 1–9. http://dx.doi.org/10.1037/h0024514

**Sella, F., Berteletti, I., Lucangeli, D., & Zorzi, M.** (2017). Preschool children use space, rather than counting, to infer the numerical magnitude of digits: Evidence for a spatial mapping principle. *Cognition, 158,* 56–67. http://dx.doi.org/10.1016/j.cognition.2016.10.010

**Selye, H.** (1936). A syndrome produced by diverse nocuous agents. *Nature, 138,* 32. http://dx.doi.org/10.1038/138032a0

**Selye, H.** (1974). *Stress without distress.* Philadelphia, PA: Saunders.

**Selye, H.** (1983). The stress concept: Past, present, and future. In C. L. Cooper (Ed.), *Stress research* (pp. 1–20). New York, NY: Wiley.

**Semlyen, J., King, M., Varney, J., & Hagger-Johnson, G.** (2016). Sexual orientation and symptoms of common mental disorder or low wellbeing: Combined meta-analysis of 12 UK population health surveys. *BMC Psychiatry, 16,* Article 67.

**Sénécal, V., Deblois, G., Beauseigle, D., Schneider, R., Brandenburg, J., Newcombe, J., . . . Arbour, N. G.** (2016). Production of IL-27 in multiple sclerosis lesions by astrocytes and myeloid cells: Modulation of local immune responses. *Glia, 64,* 553–569. http://dx.doi.org/10.1002/glia.22948

**Seo, H.-S., & Hummel, T.** (2015). Influence of auditory cues on chemosensory perception. In B. Guthrie, J. Beauchamp, A. Buettner, & B. K. Lavine

(Eds.), *The Chemical Sensory Informatics of Food: Measurement, Analysis, Integration* (Vol. 1191, pp. 41–56). Columbus, OH: American Chemical Society. http://dx.doi.org/10.1021/bk-2015-1191.ch004

**Shackelford, T. K., & Hansen, R. D.** (Eds.). (2015). *Evolutionary psychology. The evolution of sexuality.* Cham, CH: Springer International Publishing. http://dx.doi.org/10.1007/978-3-319-09384-0

**Shafer, K., Jensen, T. M., & Holmes, E. K.** (2016). Divorce stress, stepfamily stress, and depression among emerging adult stepchildren. *Journal of Child and Family Studies, 26,* 851–862. http://dx.doi.org/10.1007/s10826-016-0617-0

**Shaked, A., & Clore, G. L.** (2017). Breaking the world to make it whole again: Attribution in the construction of emotion. *Emotion Review, 9,* 27–35. http://dx.doi.org/10.1177/1754073916658250

**Shakya, A., Soni, U. K., Rai, G., Chatterjee, S. S., & Kumar, V.** (2015). Gastro-protective and anti-stress efficacies of monomethyl fumarate and a fumaria indica extract in chronically stressed rats. *Cellular and Molecular Neurobiology, 36,* 621–635. http://dx.doi.org/10.1007/s10571-015-0243-1

**Shand, G.** (2013). Culture and the self: A comparison of attitudes to study among English and Japanese students in state secondary education. *Compare: A Journal of Comparative and International Education, 43,* 857–858. http://dx.doi.org/10.1080/03057925.2012.752623

**Shang, S. S. C., Wu, Y.-L., & Sie, Y.-J.** (2017). Generating consumer resonance for purchase intention on social network sites. *Computers in Human Behavior, 69,* 18–28. http://dx.doi.org/10.1016/j.chb.2016.12.014

**Shannon, P. J., Wieling, E., McCleary, J. S., & Becher, E.** (2015). Exploring the mental health effects of political trauma with newly arrived refugees. *Qualitative Health Research, 25,* 443–457. http://dx.doi.org/10.1177/1049732314549475

**Shapiro, S. L., & Carlson, L. E.** (2017). *The art and science of meditation: Integrating mindfulness into psychology and the helping professions* (2ʳᵈ ed.). Washington, DC: American Psychological Association.

**Sharma, A., Tiwari, S., & Singaravel, M.** (2016). Circadian rhythm disruption: Health consequences. *Biological Rhythm Research, 47*(2), 191–213. http://dx.doi.org/10.1080/09291016.2015.1103942

**Sharma, V. K., Rango, J., Connaughton, A. J., Lombardo, D. J., & Sabesan, V. J.** (2015). The current state of head and neck injuries in extreme sports. *Orthopaedic Journal of Sports Medicine, 3.* http://dx.doi.org/10.1177/2325967114564358

**Shashkevich, A.** (2017, March 10). Supreme Court Justice Sonia Sotomayor emphasizes importance of broad education, empathy in her talk at Stanford. *Stanford News.* Retrieved from http://news.stanford.edu/2017/03/10/justice-sonia-sotomayor-speaks-stanford/

**Shaw, A. M., Timpano, K. R., Tran, T. B., & Joormann, J.** (2015). Correlates of Facebook usage patterns: The relationship between passive Facebook use, social anxiety symptoms, and brooding. *Computers in Human Behavior, 48,* 575–580. http://dx.doi.org/10.1016/j.chb.2015.02.003

**Shaw, J., & Porter, S.** (2015). Constructing rich false memories of committing crime. *Psychological Science, 26,* 291–301. http://dx.doi.org/10.1177/0956797614562862

**Shaw, N. D., Butler, J. P., McKinney, S. M., Nelson, S. A., Ellenbogen, J. M., & Hall, J. E.** (2012). Insights into puberty: The relationship between sleep stages and pulsatile LH secretion. *Journal of Clinical Endocrinology & Metabolism, 97,* E2055–E2062. http://dx.doi.org/10.1210/jc.2012-2692

**Sheehy, G.** (1976). *Passages: Predictable crises of adult life.* New York, NY: Bantam.

**Shenk, J. W.** (2005). Lincoln's great depression. *The Atlantic.* Retrieved from https://www.theatlantic.com/magazine/archive/2005/10/lincolns-great-depression/304247/

**Shenkman, R.** (2016). *Political animals: How our Stone-Age brain gets in the way of smart politics.* New York, NY: Basic Books.

**Shepherd, S. V.** (2017). *The Wiley handbook of evolutionary neuroscience.* Hoboken, NJ; Wiley-Blackwell.

**Sher, L., & Braswell, K.** (2011, July 1). Most infamous convicted and alleged mommy murderers in history. *abcNews.* Retrieved from http://abcnews.go.com/2020/infamous-convicted-alleged-mommy-murderers-infamous-cases-andrea/story?id=13956527

**Sher, L., Fisher, A. M., Kelliher, C. H., Penner, J. D., Goodman, M., Koenigsberg, H. W., . . . Hazlett, E. A.** (2016). Clinical features and psychiatric comorbidities of borderline personality disorder patients with versus without a history of suicide attempt. *Psychiatry Research, 246,* 261–266. http://dx.doi.org/10.1016/j.psychres.2016.10.003

**Sherif, M.** (1966). *In common predicament: Social psychology of intergroup conflict and cooperation.* Boston, MA: Houghton Mifflin.

**Sherif, M.** (1998). Experiments in group conflict. In J. M. Jenkins, K. Oatley, & N. L. Stein (Eds.), *Human emotions: A reader* (pp. 245–252). Malden, MA: Blackwell.

**Sherman, R. A., Rauthmann, J. F., Brown, N. A., Serfass, D. G., & Jones, A. B.** (2015). The independent effects of personality and situations on real-time expressions of behavior and emotion. *Journal of Personality and Social Psychology, 109,* 872–888.

**Shigemura, J., & Chhem, R. K.** (Eds.) (2016). *Mental health and social issues following a nuclear accident: The case of Fukushima.* Tokyo, JP: Springer. http://dx.doi.org/10.1007/978-4-431-55699-2

**Shin, J., Seo, E., & Hwang, H.** (2016). The effects of social supports on changes in students' perceived instrumentality of schoolwork for future goal attainment. *Educational Psychology, 36,* 1024–1043. http://dx.doi.org/10.1080/01443410.2015.1072135

**Shiraev, E.** (2015). *A history of psychology: A global perspective* (2nd ed.). Thousand Oaks, CA: Sage.

**Short, F., & Thomas, P.** (2015). *Core approaches in counselling and psychotherapy.* New York, NY: Routledge/Taylor & Francis Group.

**Shweder, R. A.** (2011). Commentary: Ontogenetic cultural psychology. In L. A. Jensen (Ed.), *Bridging cultural and developmental approaches to psychology: New syntheses in theory, research, and policy* (pp. 303–310). New York, NY: Oxford University Press.

**Siegel, A. B.** (2010). Dream interpretation in clinical practice: A century after Freud. *Sleep Medicine*

*Clinics, 5,* 299–313. http://dx.doi.org/10.1016/j.jsmc.2010.01.001

**Siegel, J. M.** (2000, January). Narcolepsy. *Scientific American,* 76–81. http://dx.doi.org/10.1038/scientificamerican0100-76.

**Sierksma, J., Thijs, J., & Verkuyten, M.** (2015). In-group bias in children's intention to help can be overpowered by inducing empathy. *British Journal of Developmental Psychology, 33,* 45–56. http://dx.doi.org/10.1111/bjdp.12065

**Sievert, L., Morrison, L. A., Reza, A. M., Brown, D. E., Kalua, E., & Tefft, H. T.** (2007). Age-related differences in health complaints: The Hilo women's health study. *Women & Health, 45,* 31–51. http://dx.doi.org/10.1300/J013v45n03-03

**Sifferlin, A.** (2017). Eleven surprising uses for Botox. *Time.* http://time.com/4501839/botox-inection-wrinkles-migraine-depression/?xid=newsletter-brief

**Sigalow, E., & Fox, N. S.** (2014). Perpetuating stereotypes: A study of gender, family, and religious life in Jewish children's books. *Journal for the Scientific Study of Religion, 53,* 416–431. http://dx.doi.org/10.1111/jssr.12112

**Sigmundsson, H., Loras, H. W., & Haga, M.** (2017). Exploring task-specific independent standing in 3- to 5- month-old infants. *Frontiers in Psychology.* No Pagination Specified. https://doi.org/10.3389/fpsyg.2017.00657

**Signorielli, N.** (2014). Television's gender-role images and contributions to stereotyping: Past, present, future. In D. G. Singer & J. L. Singer (Eds.), *Handbook of children and the media* (2nd ed., pp. 321–339). Thousand Oaks, CA: Sage.

**Silber, K.** (2014). *Schizophrenia.* Basingstoke, UK: Palgrave Macmillan.

**Silverstein, M. L.** (2013). *Personality and clinical psychology. Personality assessment in depth: A casebook.* New York: NY: Routledge.

**Silvia, P. J., Delaney, P. F., & Marcovitch, S.** (2017). *What psychology majors could (and should) be doing: A guide to research experience, professional skills, and your options after college* (2nd ed.). Washington, DC: American Psychological Association.

**Simm, A., & Klotz, L.-O.** (2015). Stress and biological aging: A double-edged sword. *Zeitschrift für Gerontologie und Geriatrie, 48,* 505–510. http://dx.doi.org/10.1007/s00391-015-0928-6

**Simons, D. J., & Chabris, C. F.** (1999). Gorillas in our midst: Sustained inattentional blindness for dynamic events. *Perception, 28,* 1059–1074. http://dx.doi.org/10.1068/p2952

**Simons, L. G., Wickrama, K. A. S., Lee, T. K., Landers-Potts, M., Cutrona, C., & Conger, R. D.** (2016). Testing family stress and family investment explanations for conduct problems among African American adolescents. *Journal of Marriage and Family, 78,* 498–515. http://dx.doi.org/10.1111/jomf.12278

**Sinatra, R., Wang, D., Deville, P., Song, C., & Barabási, A.-L.** (2016). Quantifying the evolution of individual scientific impact. *Science, 354*(6312). http://dx.doi.org/10.1126/science.aaf5239

**Siniscalchi, A., Bonci, A., Biagio Mercuri, N., De Siena, A., De Sarro, G., Malferrari, G., . . . Gallelli, L.** (2015). Cocaine dependence and stroke: Pathogenesis and management. *Current Neurovascular Research, 12,* 163–172. http://dx.doi.org/10.2174/1567202612666615030511014

**Sin, N. L., Kumar, A. D., Gehi, A. K., & Whooley, M. A.** (2016). Direction of association between depressive symptoms and lifestyle behaviors in patients with coronary heart disease: The Heart and Soul Study. *Annals of Behavioral Medicine, 50*(4), 523–532. http://dx.doi.org/10.1007/s12160-016-9777-9

**Sissa Medialab.** (2016, May 12). Emotions in the age of Botox. *ScienceDaily.* Retrieved from www.sciencedaily.com/releases/2016/05/160512085113.htm

**Skinner, B. F.** (1956). A case history in the scientific method. *American Psychologist, 11,* 221–233. http://dx.doi.org/10.1037/h0047662

**Skinner, B. F.** (1958). Diagramming schedules of reinforcement. *Journal of the Experimental Analysis of Behavior, 1,* 67–68. http://dx.doi.org/10.1901/jeab.1958.1-67

**Slane, J. D., Klump, K. L., McGue, M., & Iacono, G.** (2014). Genetic and environmental factors underlying comorbid bulimic behaviours and alcohol use disorders: A moderating role for the dysregulated personality cluster? *European Eating Disorders Review, 22,* 159–169. http://dx.doi.org/10.1002/erv.2284

**Smalheiser, N. R., Zhang, H., & Dwivedi, Y.** (2014). Enoxacin elevates microRNA levels in rat frontal cortex and prevents learned helplessness. *Frontiers in Psychiatry, 5,* 6. http://dx.doi.org/10.3389/fpsyt.2014.00006

**Smart, R., & Tsong, Y.** (2014). Weight, body dissatisfaction, and disordered eating: Asian American women's perspectives. *Asian American Journal of Psychology, 5,* 344–352. http://dx.doi.org/10.1037/a0035599

**Smiley, P. A., Tan, S. J., Goldstein, A., & Sweda, J.** (2016). Mother emotion, child temperament, and young children's helpless responses to failure. *Social Development, 25,* 285–303. http://dx.doi.org/10.1111/sode.12153

**Smith, A. M., Floerke, V. A., & Thomas, A. K.** (2016). Retrieval practice protects memory against acute stress. *Science, 354,* 1046–1048. http://dx.doi.org/10.1126/science.aah5067

**Smith, C. E., & Warneken, F.** (2014). Does it always feel good to get what you want? Young children differentiate between material and wicked desires. *British Journal of Developmental Psychology, 32,* 3–16. http://dx.doi.org/10.1111/bjdp.12018

**Smith, D., Smith, R., & Misquitta, D.** (2016). Neuroimaging and violence. *Psychiatric Clinics of North America, 39*(4), 579–597. http://dx.doi.org/10.1016/j.psc.2016.07.006

**Smith, K. Z., Smith, P. H., Cercone, S. A., McKee, S. A., & Homish, G. G.** (2016). Past year non-medical opioid use and abuse and PTSD diagnosis: Interactions with sex and associations with symptom clusters. *Addictive Behaviors, 58,* 167–174. http://dx.doi.org/10.1016/j.addbeh.2016.02.019

**Smith, L. E., Bernal, D. R., Schwartz, B. S., Whitt, C. L., Christman, S. T., Donnelly, S., . . . Kobetz, E.** (2014). Coping with vicarious trauma in the aftermath of a natural disaster. *Journal of Multicultural Counseling and Development, 42,* 2–12. http://dx.doi.org/10.1002/j.2161-1912.2014.00040.x

**Smith, L. S.** (2016). Family-based therapy for parent-child reunification. *Journal of Clinical Psychology, 72,* 498–512. http://dx.doi.org/10.1002/jclp.22259

**Smith, M., Robinson, L., & Segal, R.** (2012). How much sleep do you need? Sleep cycles and stages, lack of sleep, and getting the hours you need. *HelpGuide.Org.* Retrieved from http://helpguide.org/life/ sleeping.htm

**Smith, M. L., & Glass, G. V.** (1977). Meta-analysis of psychotherapy outcome studies. *American Psychologist, 32,* 752–760. http://dx.doi.org/10.1037/0003-066X.32.9.752

**Smith, M. L., Glass, G. V., & Miller, T. I.** (1980). *The benefits of psychotherapy.* Baltimore, MD: Johns Hopkins University Press.

**Smith, N. K., Madeira, J., & Millard, H. R.** (2015). Sexual function and fertility quality of life in women using in vitro fertilization. *Journal of Sexual Medicine, 12,* 985–993. http://dx.doi.org/10.1111/jsm.1282

**Smith, R. L. (Ed.).** (2015). *Treatment strategies for substance and process addictions.* Alexandria, VA: American Counseling Association.

**Smith, T. B., & Trimble, J. E.** (2016). The association of received racism with the well-being of people of color: A meta-analytic review. In T. B. Smith & J. E. Trimble (Eds.), *Foundations of multicultural psychology: Research to inform effective practice* (pp. 167–180). Washington, DC: American Psychological Association. http://dx.doi.org/10.1037/14733-009

**Snider, S. E., Quisenberry, A. J., & Bickel, W. K.** (2016). Order in the absence of an effect: Identifying rate-dependent relationships. *Behavioural Processes, 127,* 18–24. http://dx.doi.org/10.1016/j.beproc.2016.03.012

**Sobral, M., Pestana, M. H., & Constança, P.** (2015). The impact of cognitive reserve on neuropsychological and functional abilities in Alzheimer's disease patients. *Psychology & Neuroscience, 8,* 39–55. http://dx.doi.org/10.1037/h0101022

**Sofer, C., Dotsch, R., Wigboldus, D. H. J., & Todorov, A.** (2015). What is typical is good: The influence of face typicality on perceived trustworthiness. *Psychological Science, 26,* 39–47. http://dx.doi.org/10.1177/0956797614554955

**Soh, D. W.** (2017, April 25). Cross-cultural evidence for the genetics of homosexuality. *Scientific American.* Retrieved from https://www.scientificamerican.com/article/cross-cultural-evidence-for-the-genetics-of-homosexuality/

**Solms, M.** (1997). *The neuropsychology of dreams.* Hillsdale, NJ: Erlbaum.

**Solnit, R.** (2009). *A paradise built in hell: The extraordinary communities that arise in disaster.* New York, NY: Penguin.

**Soloff, P. H., Abraham, K., Burgess, A., Ramaseshan, K., Chowdury, A., & Diwadkar, V. A.** (2017). Impulsivity and aggression mediate regional brain responses in Borderline Personality Disorder: An fMRI study. *Psychiatry Research: Neuroimaging, 260,* 76–85. http://dx.doi.org/10.1016/j.pscychresns.2016.12.009

**Solomon, G. S., & Zuckerman, S. L.** (2015). Chronic traumatic encephalopathy in professional sports: Retrospective and prospective views. *Brain Injury, 29,* 164–170. http://dx.doi.org/10.3109/02699052.2014.965205

**Song, A., Severini, T., & Allada, R.** (2016). How jet lag impairs Major League Baseball performance. *Proceedings of the National Academy of Sciences of the United States of America, 114*(6), 1407–1412. http://dx.doi.org/10.1073/pnas.1608847114

**Song, M. J., & Bharti, K.** (2016). Looking into the future: Using induced pluripotent stem cells to build two and three dimensional ocular tissue for cell therapy and disease modeling. *Brain Research, 1638(Pt A),* 2–14. http://dx.doi.org/10.1016/j.brainres.2015.12.011

**Song, T. M., An, J. -Y., Hayman, L. L., Woo, J. -M., & Yom, Y. -H.** (2016). Stress, depression, and lifestyle behaviors in Korean adults: A latent means and multi-group analysis on the Korea health panel data. *Behavioral Medicine, 42,* 72–81. http://dx.doi.org/10.1080/08964289.2014.943688

**Sonia Sotomayor.** (2014). *My beloved world.* New York, NY: Vintage.

**Sonia Sotomayor Fast Facts.** (n.d.). Sonia Sotomayor fast facts: CNN library. *CNN.* Retrieved March 21, 2017 from http://www.cnn.com/2013/03/08/us/sonia-sotomayor-fast-facts/

**Sonia Sotomayor.** (n.d.). Sonia Sotomayor. *Wikipedia.* Retrieved March 22, 2017 from https://en.wikipedia.org/wiki/Sonia_Sotomayor

**Sori, C. F., & Biank, N.** (2016). Talking to children about death. In C. F. Sori, L. L. Hecker, & M. E. Bachenberg (Eds.), *The therapist's notebook for children and adolescents: Homework, handouts, and activities for use in psychotherapy, 2nd ed.* (pp. 244–247). New York, NY: Routledge/Taylor & Francis Group.

**Soto-Escageda, J. A., Estañol-Vidal, B., Vidal-Victoria, C. A., Michel-Chávez, A., Sierra-Beltran, M. A., & Bourges-Rodríguez, H.** (2016). Does salt addiction exist? *Salud Mental, 39*(3), 175–181. http://dx.doi.org/10.17711/SM.0185-3325.2016.016

**Southwick, S., & Watson, P.** (2015). The emerging scientific and clinical literature on resilience and psychological first aid. In N. C. Bernardy & M. J. Friedman (Eds.), *A practical guide to PTSD treatment: Pharmacological and psychotherapeutic approaches* (pp. 21–33). Washington, DC: American Psychological Association. http://dx.doi.org/10.1037/14522-003

**Souza, A. L., Conroy-Beam, D., & Buss, D. M.** (2016). Mate preferences in Brazil: Evolved desires and cultural evolution over three decades. *Personality and Individual Differences, 95,* 45–49. http://dx.doi.org/10.1016/j.paid.2016.01.053

**Spearman, C.** (1923). *The nature of "intelligence" and the principles of cognition.* London, UK: Macmillan.

**Spence, C.** (2016). Sound–the forgotten flavour sense. In B. Piqueras-Fiszman & C. Spence (Eds.), *Multisensory flavor perception: From fundamental neuroscience through to the marketplace* (pp. 81–105). Duxford, UK: Elsevier.

**Sperling, G.** (1960). The information available in brief visual presentations. *Psychological Monographs, 74,* 1–29. http://dx.doi.org/10.1037/h0093759

**Spiegel, D.** (2015). Hypnosis and pain control. In T. R. Deer, M. S. Leong, & A. L. Ray (Eds.), *Treatment of chronic pain by integrative approaches: The American Academy of Pain Medicine textbook on patient management* (pp. 115–122). New York, NY: Springer. http://dx.doi.org/10.1007/978-1-4939-1821-8

**Spiegel, D., Lewis-Fernández, R., Lanius, R., Vermetten, E., Simeon, D., & Friedman, M.** (2013). Dissociative disorders in DSM-5. *Annual Review of Clinical Psychology, 9,* 299–326. http://dx.doi.org/10.1146/annurev-clinpsy-050212-185531

**Spiegler, M.** (2016). *Contemporary behavior therapy* (6th ed.). Boston, MA: Cengage Learning.

**Spinazzola, J., Hodghon, H., Liang, L. J., Ford, J. D., Layne, C. M., Pynoos, R. S., . . . Kisiel, C.** (2014). Unseen wounds: The contribution of psychological maltreatment to child and adolescent mental health and risk outcomes. *Psychological*

*Trauma: Theory, Research, Practice, and Policy, 6,* S18–S28. http://dx.doi.org/10.1037/a0037766

**Sprecher, S., & Fehr, B.** (2011). Dispositional attachment and relationship-specific attachment as predictors of compassionate love for a partner. *Journal of Social and Personal Relationships, 28,* 558–574. http://dx.doi.org/10.1177/0265407510386190

**Sprecher, S., Felmlee, D., Metts, S., & Cupach, W.** (2015). Relationship initiation and development. In M. Mikulincer, P. R. Shaver, J. A. Simpson, & J. F. Dovidio (Eds.), *APA handbook of personality and social psychology, Vol. 3. Interpersonal relations* (pp. 211–245). Washington, DC: American Psychological Association. http://dx.doi.org/10.1037/14344-008

**Sriwilai, K., & Charoensukmongkol, P.** (2016). Face it, don't Facebook it: Impacts of social media addiction on mindfulness, coping strategies and the consequence on emotional exhaustion. *Stress and Health: Journal of the International Society for the Investigation of Stress, 32*(4), 427–434. http://dx.doi.org/10.1002/smi.2637

**Stack, L.** (2016, November 16). Ellen DeGeneres and Kareem Abdul-Jabbar among 2016 Presidential Medal of Freedom recipients. *New York Times.* Retrieved from https://www.nytimes.com/2016/11/17/us/politics/obama-2016-presidential-medal-of-freedom.html?rref=collection%2Ftimestopic%2FDegeneres%2C%20Ellen&action=click&contentCollection=timestopics&region=stream&module=stream_unit&version=latest&contentPlacement=2&pgtype=collection&_r=0

**Stadler, M., Aust, M., Becker, N., Niepel, C., & Greiff, S.** (2017). Choosing between what you want now and what you want most: Self-control explains academic achievement beyond cognitive ability. *Personality and Individual Differences, 94,* 168–172. http://dx.doi.org/10.1016/j.paid.2016.01.029

**Stamatakis, A. M., Van Swieten, M., Basiri, M. L., Blair, G. A., Kantak, P., & Stuber, G. D.** (2016). Lateral hypothalamic area glutamatergic neurons and their projections to the lateral habenula regulate feeding and reward. *The Journal of Neuroscience, 36,* 302–311. http://dx.doi.org/10.1523/JNEUROSCI.1202-15.2016

**Stange, M., Graydon, C., & Dixon, M. J.** (2016). "I was that close": Investigating players' reactions to losses, wins, and near-misses on scratch cards. *Journal of Gambling Studies, 32,* 187–203. http://dx.doi.org/10.1007/s10899-015-9538-x

**Stanley, I. H., Hom, M. A., & Joiner, T. E.** (2016). A systematic review of suicidal thoughts and behaviors among police officers, firefighters, EMTs, and paramedics. *Clinical Psychology Review, 44,* 25–44. http://dx.doi.org/10.1016/j.cpr.2015.12.002

**Stanovich, K. E.** (2015). Rational and irrational thought: The thinking that IQ tests miss. *Scientific American, 23,* 12–17. http://dx.doi.org/10.1038/scientificamericangenius0115-12

**Starr, C. R., & Zurbriggen, E. L.** (2017). Sandra Bem's gender schema theory after 34 years: A review of its reach and impact. *Sex Roles, 76*(9), 566–578. http://dx.doi.org/10.1007/s11199-016-0591-4

**Starr, P.** (2015, November 3). A shocking rise in White death rates in midlife—and what it says about American society. *The American Prospect.* Retrieved May 3, 2017 from http://prospect.org/article/shocking-rise-white-death-rates-midlife-and-what-it-says-about-american-society

**Steele, C. M., & Aronson, J.** (1995). Stereotype threat and the intellectual test performance of African Americans. *Journal of Personality and Social Psychology, 69,* 797–811.

**Steers, M-L N., Wickham, R. E., & Acitelli, L. K.** (2014). Seeing everyone else's highlight reels: How Facebook usage is linked to depressive symptoms. *Journal of Social and Clinical Psychology, 33,* 701–731. http://dx.doi.org/10.1521/jscp.2014.33.8.701

**Stefanek, E., Strohmeier, D., Fandrem, H., & Spiel, C.** (2012). Depressive symptoms in native and immigrant adolescents: The role of critical life events and daily hassles. *Anxiety, Stress and Coping: An International Journal, 25,* 201–217. http://dx.doi.org/10.1080/10615806.2011.605879

**Stefanovics, E. A., He, H., Cavalcanti, M., Neto, H., Ofori-Atta, A., Leddy, M., Ighodaro, A., & Rosenheck, R.** (2016). Witchcraft and biopsychosocial causes of mental illness: Attitudes and beliefs about mental illness among health professionals in five countries. *Journal of Nervous and Mental Disease, 204*(3), 169–174. http://dx.doi.org/10.1097/NMD.0000000000000422

**Steger, I.** (2016, October 7). People are working themselves to death in Japan and the government is finally taking it seriously. *Quartz.* Retrieved from https://qz.com/803424/people-are-working-themselves-to-death-in-japan-and-the-government-is-finally-taking-it-seriously/

**Stein, S. J., & Deonarine, J. M.** (2015). Current concepts in the assessment of emotional intelligence. In S. Goldstein, D. Princiotta, & J. A. Naglieri (Eds.), *Handbook of intelligence: Evolutionary theory, historical perspective, and current concepts* (pp. 381–402). New York, NY: Springer. http://dx.doi.org/10.1007/978-1-4939-1562-0_24

**Steiner, K. L., Pillemer, D. B., Thomsen, D. K., & Minigan, A. P.** (2014). The reminiscence bump in older adults' life story transitions. *Memory, 22,* 1002–1009. http://dx.doi.org/10.1080/09658211.2013.86335

**Steinmayr, R., & Kessels, U.** (2017). Good at school=successful on the job? Explaining gender differences in scholastic and vocational success. *Personality and Individual Differences, 105,* 107–115. http://dx.doi.org/10.1016/j.paid.2016.09.032

**Stephenson, E., Watson, P. J., Chen, Z. J., & Morris, R. J.** (2017). Self-compassion, self-esteem, and irrational beliefs. *Current Psychology: A Journal for Diverse Perspectives on Diverse Psychological Issues.* No Pagination Specified. http://dx.doi.org/10.1007/s12144-017-9563-2

**Steptoe, A., Kivimäki, M., Lowe, G., Rumley, A., & Hamer, M.** (2016). Blood pressure and fibrinogen responses to mental stress as predictors of incident hypertension over an 8-year period. *Annals of Behavioral Medicine, 50*(6), 898–906. http://dx.doi.org/10.1007/s12160-016-9817-5

**Sternberg, K.** (2014). *Psychology of love 101.* New York, NY: Springer.

**Sternberg, R. J.** (1985). *Beyond IQ: A triarchic theory of human intelligence.* New York, NY: Cambridge University Press.

**Sternberg, R. J.** (1986). A triangular theory of love. *Psychological Review, 93,* 119–135.

**Sternberg, R. J.** (1988). *The triangle of love.* New York, NY: Basic Books.

**Sternberg, R. J.** (2006). A duplex theory of love. In R. J. Sternberg & K. Weis (Eds.), *The new psychology of love* (pp. 184–199). New Haven, CT: Yale University Press.

**Sternberg, R. J.** (2014). Teaching about the nature of intelligence. *Intelligence, 42,* 176–179. http://dx.doi.org/10.1016/j.intell.2013.08.010

**Sternberg, R. J.** (2015). Multiple intelligences in the new age of thinking. In S. Goldstein, D. Princiotta, & J. A. Naglieri (Eds.), *Handbook of intelligence: Evolutionary theory, historical perspective, and current concepts* (pp. 229–241). New York, NY: Springer. http://dx.doi.org/10.1007/978-1-4939-1562-0_16

**Sternberg, R. J.** (2017). *Career paths in psychology: Where your dreams can take you* (3rd ed.). Washington, DC: American Psychological Association.

**Sternberg, R. J.** (Ed.). (2017). *Career paths in psychology: Where your degree can take you* (3rd ed.). Washington, DC: American Psychological Association.

**Steverman, B.** (2016, May 13). 'I'll never retire': Americans break record for working past 65. *Bloomberg.* Retrieved from https://www.bloomberg.com/news/articles/2016-05-13/-i-ll-never-retire-americans-break-record-for-working-past-65

**Stiglitz, J. E.** (2015, December 7). When inequality kills. *Project Syndicate.* Retrieved May 3, 2017 from https://www.project-syndicate.org/commentary/lower-life-expectancy-white-americans-by-joseph-e—stiglitz-2015-12?barrier=accessreg

**Stiles, N. R. B., Zheng, Y., & Shimojo, S.** (2015). Length and orientation constancy learning in 2-dimensions with auditory sensory substitution: The importance of self-initiated movement. *Frontiers in Psychology, 6,* Article 842.

**Stoll, J. L., & Brooks, J.** (2015). Behavior therapy. In F. Chan, N. L. Berven, & K. R. Thomas (Eds.), *Counseling theories and techniques for rehabilitation and mental health professionals* (2nd ed., pp. 133–155). New York, NY: Springer.

**Stone, M. H.** (2014). The spectrum of borderline personality disorder: A neurophysiological view. *Current Topics in Behavioral Neurosciences, 21,* 23–46. http://dx.doi.org/10.1007/7854_2014_308

**Stoner, J. A.** (1961). A comparison of individual and group decisions involving risk. Unpublished master's thesis, School of Industrial Management, MIT, Cambridge, MA.

**Stopper, C. M., & Floresco, S. B.** (2015). Dopaminergic circuitry and risk/reward decision making: Implications for schizophrenia. *Schizophrenia Bulletin, 41,* 9–14. http://dx.doi.org/10.1093/schbul/sbu165

**Storm, B. C., Stone, S. M., & Benjamin, A. S.** (2017). Using the Internet to access information inflates future use of the Internet to access other information. *Memory, 25*(6), 717–723. http://dx.doi.org/10.1080/09658211.2016.1210171

**Stover, C. S., & Lent, K.** (2014). Training and certification for domestic violence service providers: The need for a national standard curriculum and training approach. *Psychology of Violence, 4,* 117–127. http://dx.doi.org/10.1037/a0036022

**Strachan, E., Duncan, G., Horn, E., & Turkheimer, E.** (2017). Neighborhood deprivation and depression in adult twins: Genetics and gene×environment interaction. *Psychological*

*Medicine, 47*(4), 627–638. http://dx.doi.org/10.1017/S0033291716002622

**Strack, F., Martin, L. L., & Stepper, S.** (1988). Inhibiting and facilitating conditions of the human smile: A nonobstrusive test of the facial feedback hypothesis. *Journal of Personality and Social Psychology, 54,* 768–777.

**Strain, J. F., Didehbani, N., Spence, J., Conover, H., Bartz, E. K., Mansinghani, S., . . . Womack, K. B.** (2017). White matter changes and confrontation naming in retired aging National Football League athletes. *Journal of Neurotrauma, 34*(2), 372–379. http://dx.doi.org/10.1089/neu.2016.4446

**Strassberg, D. S., Mackaronis, J. E., & Perelman, M. A.** (2015). Sexual dysfunctions. In P. H. Blaney, R. F. Krueger, & T. Millon (Eds.), *Oxford textbook of psychopathology* (3rd ed., pp. 421–462). New York, NY: Oxford University Press.

**Stratton, G. M.** (1896). Some preliminary experiments on vision without inversion of the retinal image. *Psychological Review, 3,* 611–617. http://dx.doi.org/10.1037/h0072918

**Straub, R. O.** (2014). *Health psychology* (4th ed.). New York, NY: Worth.

**Strauss, B. M., Shapiro, D. A., Barkham, M., Parry, G., & Machado, P. P. P.** (2015). "The times they are a-changin": 25 years of psychotherapy research—A European and Latin American perspective. *Psychotherapy Research, 25,* 294–308. http://dx.doi.org/10.1080/10503307.2014.1002439

**Stricker, L. J., & Rock, D. A.** (2015). An "Obama effect" on the GRE General Test? *Social Influence, 10,* 11–18. http://dx.doi.org/10.1080/15534510.2013.878665

**Stroebe, W.** (2016). Firearm availability and violent death: The need for a culture change in attitudes toward guns. *Analyses of Social Issues and Public Policy (ASAP), 16*(1), 7–35. http://dx.doi.org/10.1111/asap.12100

**Sue, D., Sue, D., Sue, S., & Sue, D.** (2016). *Understanding abnormal behavior* (11th ed.). Stamford, CT: Cengage.

**Suerken, C. K., Reboussin, B. A., Egan, K. L., Sutfin, E. L., Wagoner, K. G., Spangler, J., & Wolfson, M.** (2016). Marijuana use trajectories and academic outcomes among college students. *Drug and Alcohol Dependence, 162,* 137–145. http://dx.doi.org/10.1016/j.drugalcdep.2016.02.041

**Sugar, J. A., Riekse, R. J., Holstege, H., & Faber, M. A.** (2014). *Introduction to aging: A positive, interdisciplinary approach.* New York, NY: Springer.

**Sugarman, H., Impey, C., Buxner, S., & Antonellis, J.** (2011). Astrology beliefs among undergraduate students. *Astronomy Education Review, 10.* http://dx.doi.org/10.3847/AER2010040

**Suh, S., Chang, Y., & Kim, N.** (2015). Quantitative exponential modelling of copycat suicides: Association with mass media effect in South Korea. *Epidemiology and Psychiatric Sciences, 24*(2), 150–157. http://dx.doi.org/10.1017/S204579601400002X

**Suhay, E.** (2015). Explaining group influence: The role of identity and emotion in political conformity and polarization. *Political Behavior, 37,* 221–251. http://dx.doi.org/10.1007/s11109-014-9269-1

**Suher, J., Raj R., & Hoyer, W.** (2016). Eating healthy or feeling empty? How the "Healthy = Less Filling" intuition influences satiety. *The*

*Journal of the Association for Consumer Research, 1,* 26–40. https://doi.org/10.1086/684393

**Suicide Basic Facts.** (2015). Suicide: 2015 facts and figures. *American Foundation for Suicide Prevention.* Retrieved from http://www.afsp.org/news-events/in-the-news/suicide-2015-facts-and-figures-infographic

**Suissa, A. J.** (2015). Cyber addictions: Toward a psychosocial perspective. *Addictive Behaviors, 43,* 28–32. http://dx.doi.org/10.1016/j.addbeh.2014.09.020

**Suizzo, M-A., Rackley, K. R., Robbins, P. A., Jackson, K. M., Rarick, J. R. D., & McClain, S.** (2017). The unique effects of fathers' warmth on adolescents' positive beliefs and behaviors: Pathways to resilience in low-income families. *Sex Roles, 77*(1), 46–58. http://dx.doi.org/10.1007/s11199-016-0696-9

**Sullivan, T. A.** (2014). Greedy institutions, overwork, and work-life balance. *Sociological Inquiry, 84,* 1–15. http://dx.doi.org/10.1111/soin.12029

**Sundstrom, E. D., Lounsbury, J. W., Gibson, L. W., & Huang, J. L.** (2016). Personality traits and career satisfaction in training and development occupations: Toward a distinctive T&D personality profile. *Human Resource Development Quarterly, 27,* 13–40. http://dx.doi.org/10.1002/hrdq.21223

**Sun, H., Liu, Z., & Ma, X.** (2016). Interactions between astrocytes and neurons in the brainstem involved in restraint water immersion stress-induced gastric mucosal damage. *NeuroReport: For Rapid Communication of Neuroscience Research, 27,* 151–159. http://dx.doi.org/10.1097/WNR.0000000000000515.

**Super, C., & Harkness, S.** (2015). Charting infant development: Milestones along the way. In L. A. Jensen (Ed.), *The Oxford handbook of human development and culture: An interdisciplinary perspective* (pp. 79–93). New York, NY: Oxford University Press.

**Suso-Ribera, C., & Gallardo-Pujol, D.** (2016). Personality and health in chronic pain: Have we failed to appreciate a relationship? *Personality and Individual Differences, 96,* 7–11. http://dx.doi.org/10.1016/j.paid.2016.02.063

**Sussman, T. J., Szekely, A., Hajcak, G., & Mohanty, A.** (2016). It's all in the anticipation: How perception of threat is enhanced in anxiety. *Emotion, 16,* 320–327. http://dx.doi.org/10.1037/emo0000098

**Sutin, A. R., Stephan, Y., Carretta, H., & Terracciano, A.** (2015). Perceived discrimination and physical, cognitive, and emotional health in older adulthood. *The American Journal of Geriatric Psychiatry, 23,* 171–179. http://dx.doi.org/10.1016/j.jagp.2014.03.007

**Sutin, A. R., Terracciano, A., Milaneschi, Y., An, Y., Ferrucci, L., & Zonderman, A. B.** (2013). Cohort effect on well-being: The legacy of economic hard times. *Psychological Science, 24*(3), 379–385. http://doi.org/10.1177/0956797612459658

**Suwabe, K., Hyodo, K., Byun, K., Ochi, G., Yassa, M. A., & Soya, H.** (2017). Acute moderate exercise improves mnemonic discrimination in young adults. *Hippocampus, 27*(3), 229–234. http://dx.doi.org/10.1002/hipo.22695

**Suzuk, Y., Tamesue, D., Asahi, K., & Ishikawa, Y.** (2015). Grit and work engagement: A cross-sectional study. *PLoS ONE, 10* (9), Article e0137501.

**Suzuki, L. A., Naqvi, S., & Hill, J. S.** (2014). Assessing intelligence in a cultural context. In F. T. L.

Leong, L. Comas-Díaz, G. C. Nagayama Hall, V. C. McLoyd, & J. E. Trimble (Eds.), *APA handbook of multicultural psychology, Vol. 1: Theory and research* (pp. 247–266). Washington, DC: American Psychological Association. http://dx.doi.org/10.1037/14189-013

**Svetkey, B.** (2017, January 26). Panic attacks and phobias on the way to the Oscars. *The Hollywood Reporter.* Retrieved from http://www.hollywoodreporter.com/features/emma-stones-battle-shyness-panic-attacks-phobias-way-oscars-968543

**Swaab, D. F.** (2014). *We are our brains: A neurobiography of the brain, from the womb to Alzheimer's.* (J. Hedley-Prôle, Trans.). New York, NY: Spiegel & Grau/Random House.

**Swain, J. E., & Ho, S. S.** (2012). What's in a baby-cry? Locationist and constructionist frameworks in parental brain responses. *Behavior and Brain Sciences, 35,* 167–168. http://dx.doi.org/10.1017/S0140525X11001762

**Swanson, A.** (2016, April 6). Who gets divorced in America, in 7 charts. *The Washington Post.* Retrieved from https://www.washingtonpost.com/news/wonk/wp/2016/04/06/who-gets-divorced-in-america-in-7-charts/?utm_term=.f1bd14f6cd24

**Sweeney, S., Air, T., Zannettino, L., & Galletly, C.** (2015). Gender differences in the physical and psychological manifestation of childhood trauma and/or adversity in people with psychosis. *Frontiers in Psychology, 6,* Article 1768.

**Sylvestre, A., & Mérette, C.** (2010). Language delay in severely neglected children: A cumulative or specific effect of risk factors? *Child Abuse & Neglect, 34,* 414–428. http://dx.doi.org/10.1016/j.chiabu.2009.10.003

**Szkodny, L. E., & Newman, M. G.** (2014). Generalized anxiety disorder. In S. G. Hofmann, D. J. A. Dozois, W. Rief, & J. A. J. Smits (Eds.), *The Wiley handbook of cognitive behavioral therapy* (Vols. 1–3, pp. 1001–1022). Malden, MA: Wiley-Blackwell.

**Takarangi, M. K. T., & Loftus, E. F.** (2016). Suggestion, placebos, and false memories. In A. Raz & C. S. Harris (Eds.), *Placebo talks: Modern perspectives on placebos in society* (pp. 204–226). New York, NY: Oxford University Press.

**Takashima, A., & Bakker, I.** (2017). Memory consolidation. In H.-J. Schmid (Ed.), *Entrenchment and the psychology of language learning: How we reorganize and adapt linguistic knowledge* (pp. 177–200). Boston, MA: De Gruyter Mouton. http://dx.doi.org/10.1037/15969-009

**Talamas, S. N., Mavor, K. I., & Perrett, D. I.** (2016). The influence of intelligence on the endorsement of the intelligence-attractiveness halo. *Personality and Individual Differences, 95,* 162–167. http://dx.doi.org/10.1016/j.paid.2016.02.053

**Tallinen, T., Chung, J. Y., Biggins, J. S., & Mahadevan, L.** (2014). Gyrification from constrained cortical expansion. *Proceedings of the National Academy of Sciences of the United States of America, 111*(35), 12667–12672. http://dx.doi.org/10.1073/pnas.1406015111

**Tamir, M., Bigman, Y. E., Rhodes, E., Salerno, J., & Schreier, J.** (2015). An expectancy-value model of emotion regulation: Implications for motivation, emotional experience, and decision making. *Emotion, 15,* 90–103. http://dx.doi.org/10.1037/emo0000021

**Tan, G., Rintala, D. H., Jensen, M. P., Fukui, T., Smith, D., & Williams, W.** (2015b). A randomized controlled trial of hypnosis compared with biofeedback for adults with chronic low back pain. *European Journal of Pain, 19,* 271–280. http://dx.doi.org/10.1002/ejp.545

Tan, H. S. G., Fischer, A. R., Tinchan, P., Stieger, M., Steenbekkers, L. P. A., & van Trijp, H. C. (2015). Insects as food: Exploring cultural exposure and individual experience as determinants of acceptance. *Food Quality and Preference, 42,* 78–89. http://dx.doi.org/10.1016/j.foodqual.2015.01.013

Tan, X., Alén, M., Cheng, S. M., Mikkola, T. M., Tenhunen, J., Lyytikäinen, A., . . . Cheng, S. (2015a). Associations of disordered sleep with body fat distribution, physical activity and diet among overweight middle-aged men. *Journal of Sleep Research, 24,* 414–424. http://dx.doi.org/10.1111/jsr.12283

Tang, W. Y., & Fox, J. (2016). Men's harassment behavior in online video games: Personality traits and game factors. *Aggressive Behavior, 42*(6), 513–521. http://dx.doi.org/10.1002/ab.21646

Tang, Y., Newman, L. S., & Huang, L. (2014). How people react to social-psychological accounts of wrongdoing: The moderating effects of culture. *Journal of Cross-Cultural Psychology, 45,* 752–763. http://dx.doi.org/10.1177/0022022114527343

Tang, Y. Y., Posner, M. I., & Rothbart, M. K. (2014). Meditation improves self-regulation over the life span. *Annals of the New York Academy of Sciences, 1307,* 104–111. http://dx.doi.org/10.1111/nyas.12227

Tannen, D. (1990). *You just don't understand: Women and men in conversation.* New York, NY: HarperCollins.

Tannen, D. (2007). Power maneuvers and connection maneuvers in family interaction. In D. Tannen, S. Kendall & C. Gordon (Eds.), *Family talk: Discourse and identity in four American families* (pp. 27–48). Oxford, UK: Oxford University Press.

Tannen, D. (2011). Turn-taking and intercultural discourse and communication. In C. B. Paulston, S. Kiesling, & E. Rangel (Eds.), *The handbook of intercultural discourse and communication* (pp. 133–157). Hoboken, NJ: Wiley.

Tanzer, M., Freud, E., Ganel, T., & Avidan, G. (2014). General holistic impairment in congenital prosopagnosia: Evidence from Garner's speeded-classification task. *Cognitive Neuropsychology, 30,* 429–445. http://dx.doi.org/10.1080/02643294.2013.873715

Tarafdar, M., Tu, Q., & Ragu-Nathan, T. S. (2010). Impact of technostress on end-user satisfaction and performance. *Journal of Management Information Systems, 27,* 303–334. http://dx.doi.org/10.2753/MIS0742-1222270311

Tarr, B., Launay, J., & Dunbar, R. I.M. (2016). Silent disco: Dancing in synchrony leads to elevated pain thresholds and social closeness. *Evolution and Human Behavior, 37,* 343–349. http://dx.doi.org/10.1016/j.evolhumbehav.2016.02.004

Tarrant, D. (2016, August 10). Marcus Luttrell has a twin brother and he's a neuroscientist. *The Dallas Morning News.* Retrieved from http://taskandpurpose.com/marcus-luttrell-twin-brother-hes-neuroscientist/

Tartakovsky, M. (2013). 7 persistent myths about introverts & extroverts. *Psych Central.*

Retrieved on February 28, 2017, from https://psychcentral.com/blog/archives/2013/09/11/7-persistent-myths-about-introverts-extroverts/

Taub, E. (2004). Harnessing brain plasticity through behavioral techniques to produce new treatments in neurorehabilitation. *American Psychologist, 59,* 692–704. http://dx.doi.org/10.1037/0003-066X.59.8.692

Taub, E., Uswatte, G., & Mark, V. W. (2014). The functional significance of cortical reorganization and the parallel development of CI therapy. *Frontiers in Human Neuroscience, 8,* Article 396.

Tavassolie, T., Dudding, S., Madigan, A. L., Thorvardarson, E., & Winsler, A. (2016). Differences in perceived parenting style between mothers and fathers: Implications for child outcomes and marital conflict. *Journal of Child and Family Studies, 25,* 2055–2068. http://dx.doi.org/10.1007/s10826-016-0376-y

Tavernier, R., Choo, S. B., Grant, K., & Adam, E. K. (2016). Daily affective experiences predict objective sleep outcomes among adolescents. *Journal of Sleep Research, 25,* 62–69. http://dx.doi.org/10.1111/jsr.12338

Tay, L., & Diener, E. (2011). Needs and subjective well-being around the world. *Journal of Personality and Social Psychology, 101,* 354–365. http://dx.doi.org/10.1037/a0023779

Tayama, J., Li, J., & Munakata, M. (2016). Working long hours is associated with higher prevalence of diabetes in urban male Chinese workers: The Rosai Karoshi study. *Stress and Health, 32,* 84–87. http://dx.doi.org/10.1002/smi.2580

Taylor, D. J., Zimmerman, M. R., Gardner, C. E., Williams, J. M., Grieser, E. A., Tatum, J. I., . . . Ruggero, C. (2014). A pilot randomized controlled trial of the effects of cognitive-behavioral therapy for insomnia on sleep and daytime functioning in college sudents. *Behavior Therapy, 45,* 376–389. http://dx.doi.org/10.1016/j.beth.2013.12.010

Taylor-Clift, A., Holmgreen, L., Hobfoll, S. E., Gerhart, J. I., Richardson, D., Calvin, J. E., & Powell, L. H. (2016). Traumatic stress and cardiopulmonary disease burden among low-income, urban heart failure patients. *Journal of Affective Disorders, 190,* 227–234. http://dx.doi.org/10.1016/j.jad.2015.09.023

Taylor, K. N., & Abba, N. (2015). Mindfulness meditation in cognitive-behavioral therapy for psychosis. In B. A. Gaudiano (Ed.), *Incorporating acceptance and mindfulness into the treatment of psychosis: Current trends and future directions* (pp. 170–200). New York, NY: Oxford University Press.

Taylor, L., Chrismas, B. C. R., Dascombe, B., Chamari, K., & Fowler, P. M. (2016). Sleep medication and athletic performance—The evidence for practitioners and future research directions. *Frontiers in Physiology, 7,* 83. http://doi.org/10.3389/fphys.2016.00083

Taylor, S. E. (2006). Tend and befriend: Biobehavioral bases of affiliation under stress. *Current Directions in Psychological Science, 15,* 273–277. http://dx.doi.org/10.1111/j.1467-8721.2006.00451.x

Taylor, S. E. (2012). Tend and befriend theory. (2012). In P. A. M. Van Lange, A. W. Kruglanski, & E. T. Higgins (Eds.), *Handbook of theories of social psychology* (Vol 1., pp. 32–49). Thousand Oaks, CA: Sage.

Tebbe, E. A., & Moradi, B. (2016). Suicide risk in trans populations: An application of mi-

nority stress theory. *Journal of Counseling Psychology, 63*(5), 520–533. http://dx.doi.org/10.1037/cou0000152

Tedeschi, R. G., & Blevins, C. L. (2015). From mindfulness to meaning: Implications for the theory of posttraumatic growth. *Psychological Inquiry, 26,* 373–376. http://dx.doi.org/10.1080/1047840X.2015.1075354

Tei, S., Becker, C., Sugihara, G., Kawada, R., Fujino, J., Sozu, T., . . . Takahashi, H. (2015). Sense of meaning in work and risk of burnout among medical professionals. *Psychiatry and Clinical Neurosciences, 69,* 123–124. http://dx.doi.org/10.1111/pcn.12217

Teicher, M. H., & Samson, J. A. (2016). Annual research review: Enduring neurobiological effects of childhood abuse and neglect. *Journal of Child Psychology and Psychiatry, 57,* 241–266. http://dx.doi.org/10.1111/jcpp.12507

Tekgol Uzuner, G., & Uzuner, N. (2017). Cerebrovascular reactivity and neurovascular coupling in patients with obstructive sleep apnea. *International Journal of Neuroscience, 127*(1), 59–65. http://dx.doi.org/10.3109/00207454.2016.1139581

Tellegen, A. (1985). Structures of mood and personality and their relevance to assessing anxiety with an emphasis on self-report. In A. H. Tuma & J. D. Maser (Eds.), *Anxiety and the anxiety disorders* (pp. 681–706). Hillsdale, NJ: Erlbaum.

Templeton, J. A., Dixon, M. J., Harrigan, K. A., & Fugelsang, J. A. (2015). Upping the reinforcement rate by playing the maximum lines in multi-line slot machine play. *Journal of Gambling Studies, 31,* 949–964. http://dx.doi.org/10.1007/s10899-014-9446-5

Tennen, H., Suls, J., & Weiner, I. B. (Eds.). (2013). *Handbook of psychology, Vol. 5. Personality and social psychology* (2nd ed.). Hoboken, NJ: Wiley.

Teo, A. R., Choi, H., & Valenstein, M. (2013). Social relationships and depression: Ten-year follow-up from a nationally representative study. *PLoS ONE, 8*(4), e62396. http://dx.doi.org/10.1371/journal.pone.0062396

Terman, L. M. (1916). *The measurement of intelligence.* Boston, MA: Houghton Mifflin.

Terman, L. M. (1925). *Genetic studies of genius: Vol. 1. Mental and physical traits of a thousand gifted children.* Palo Alto, CA: Stanford University Press.

Terman, L. M. (1954). Scientists and nonscientists in a group of 800 gifted men. *Psychological Monographs, 68,* 1–44.

Terrace, H. S. (1979, November). How Nim Chimpsky changed my mind. *Psychology Today,* 65–76.

Tesarz, J., Schuster, A. K., Hartmann, M., Gerhardt, A., & Eich, W. (2012). Pain perception in athletes compared to normally active controls: A systematic review with meta-analysis. *Pain, 153,* 1253–1262.

Tetrick, L. E., & Peiró, J. M. (2016). Health and safety: Prevention and promotion. In M. J. Grawitch & D. W. Ballard (Eds.), *The psychologically healthy workplace: Building a win-win environment for organizations and employees* (pp. 199–229). Washington, DC: American Psychological Association. http://dx.doi.org/10.1037/14731-010

Teunissen, H. A., Spijkerman, R., Prinstein, M. G., Cohen, G. L., Engles, R. C., & Scholte, R. H. (2012). Adolescents' conformity to their peers' pro-alcohol and anti-alcohol norms: The power of popularity. *Alcoholism: Clinical and Experimental Research, 36,* 1257–1267.

**Thames, A. D., Arbid, N., & Sayegh, P.** (2014). Cannabis use and neurocognitive functioning in a non-clinical sample of users. *Addictive Behaviors, 39,* 994–999. http://dx.doi.org/10.1016/j.addbeh.2014.01.019

**Thapar, A., & Cooper, M.** (2016). Attention deficit hyperactivity disorder. *The Lancet, 387(10024),* 1240–1250. http://dx.doi.org/10.1016/S0140-6736(15)00238-X

**The Amazing Meeting.** (2011). The amazing one: James Randi. Retrieved from http://www.amazingmeeting.com/speakers#randi

**The Gender Wage Gap** (2016, April 1). *Institute for Women's Policy Research.* Retrieved from http://www.iwpr.org/publications/recent-publications

**The State of Mental Health in America.** (2017). The state of mental health in America, 2017. *MentalHealthAmerica.net.* Retrieved from http://www.mentalhealthamerica.net/issues/state-mental-health-america

**Thieme, H., Morkisch, N., Rietz, C., Dohle, C., & Borgetto, B.** (2016). The efficacy of movement representation techniques for treatment of limb pain—A systematic review and meta-analysis. *The Journal of Pain, 17,* 167–180. http://dx.doi.org/10.1016/j.jpain.2015.10.015

**Thomas, A., & Chess, S.** (1977). *Temperament and development.* New York, NY: Brunner/Mazel.

**Thomas, A., & Chess, S.** (1987). Roundtable: What is temperament: Four approaches. *Child Development, 58,* 505–529.

**Thomas, A., & Chess, S.** (1991). Temperament in adolescence and its functional significance. In R. M. Lerner, A. C. Petersen, & J. Brooks-Gunn (Eds.), *Encyclopedia of adolescence* (Vol. 2). New York, NY: Garland.

**Thomas, J., Raynor, M., & Bahussain, E.** (2016). Stress reactivity, depressive symptoms, and mindfulness: A Gulf Arab perspective. *International Perspectives in Psychology: Research, Practice, Consultation, 5,* 156–166. http://dx.doi.org/10.1037/ipp0000055

**Thomason, T.** (2014). Issues in the diagnosis of Native American culture-bound syndromes. *Arizona Counseling Journal.* Retrieved from http://works.bepress.com/cgi/viewcontent.cgi?article=1181&context=timothy_thomason

**Thomassin, K., Guérin Marion, C., Venasse, M., & Shaffer, A.** (2017). Specific coping strategies moderate the link between emotion expression deficits and nonsuicidal self-injury in an inpatient sample of adolescents. *Child and Adolescent Psychiatry and Mental Health, 11,* 21. http://doi.org/10.1186/s13034-017-0158-3

**Thompson, D.** (1997, March 24). A boy without a penis. *Time,* 83.

**Thompson, E.** (2015). *Waking, dreaming, being: Self and consciousness in neuroscience, meditation, and philosophy.* New York, NY: Columbia University Press.

**Thompson, G.** (2003). *Who was Helen Keller?* New York, NY: Penguin Press.

**Thorn, R.** (2013). 12 tips for surviving personal crisis. *Huffington Post.* Retrieved from http://www.huffingtonpost.com/rayanne-thorn/mindfulness-practice_b_4026593.html

**Thorndike, E. L.** (1898). Animal intelligence. *Psychological Review Monograph, 2*(8).

**Thorndike, E. L.** (1911). *Animal intelligence.* New York, NY: Macmillan.

**Thrailkill, E. A., & Bouton, M. E.** (2015). Contextual control of instrumental actions and habits. *Journal of Experimental Psychology: Animal Learning and Cognition, 41,* 69–80. http://dx.doi.org/10.1037/xan0000045

**Thurstone, L. L.** (1938). *Primary mental abilities.* Chicago, IL: University of Chicago Press.

**Tips for Coping with Crisis.** (2015). Northeastern University. University Health and Counseling Services. Retrieved June 10, 2015 from http://www.northeastern.edu/uhcs/health-and-wellness/tips-coping-crisis-traumatic-events/

**Todd, P. M., & Gigerenzer, G.** (2000). Precis of simple heuristics that make us smart. *Behavioral and Brain Sciences, 23,* 727–741. http://dx.doi.org/10.1017/S0140525X00003447

**Toepfer, S. M., & Walker, K.** (2009). Letters of gratitude: Improving well-being through expressive writing. *Journal of Writing Research, 1,* 181–198.

**Tolman, D. L., Diamond, L. M., Bauermeister, J. A., George, W. H., Pfaus, J. G., & Ward, L. M.** (Eds.). (2014). *APA handbook of sexuality and psychology: Vol. 1. Person-based approaches.* Washington, DC: American Psychological Association. http://dx.doi.org/10.1037/14193-000

**Tolman, E. C., & Honzik, C. H.** (1930). Introduction and removal of reward and maze performance in rats. *University of California Publications in Psychology, 4,* 257–275.

**Tomash, J. J., & Reed, P.** (2013). The generalization of a conditioned response to deception across the public/private barrier. *Learning and Motivation, 44,* 196–203. http://dx.doi.org/10.1016/j.lmot.2012.12.001

**Topham, G. L., Hubbs-Tait, L., Rutledge, J. M., Page, M. C., Kennedy, T. S., Shriver, L. H., & Harrist, A. W.** (2011). Parenting styles, parental response to child emotion, and family emotional responsiveness are related to child emotional eating. *Appetite, 56,* 261–264.

**Topper, M., Emmelkamp, P. M. G., Watkins, E., & Ehring, T.** (2017). Prevention of anxiety disorders and depression by targeting excessive worry and rumination in adolescents and young adults: A randomized controlled trial. *Behaviour Research and Therapy, 90,* 123–136. http://dx.doi.org/10.1016/j.brat.2016.12.015

**Tornquist, M., & Chiappe, D.** (2015). Effects of humor production, humor receptivity, and physical attractiveness on partner desirability. *Evolutionary Psychology, 13*(4), 1–13. http://dx.doi.org/10.1177/1474704915608744

**Torrens, M., & Rossi, P.** (2015). Mood disorders and addiction. In G. Dom & F. Moggi (Eds.), *Co-occurring addictive and psychiatric disorders: A practice-based handbook from a European perspective* (pp. 103–117). New York, NY: Springer-Verlag. http://dx.doi.org/10.1007/978-3-642-45375-5_8

**Tosh, J.** (2016). *Psychology and gender dysphoria: Feminist and transgender perspective.* New York, NY: Routledge.

**Tousseyn, T., Bajsarowicz, K., Sánchez, H., Gheyara, A., Oehler, A., Geschwind, M., . . . DeArmond, S. J.** (2015). Prion disease induces Alzheimer disease—Like neuropathologic changes. *Journal of Neuropathology and Experimental Neurology, 74,* 873–888. http://dx.doi.org/10.1097/NEN.0000000000000228

**Tovel, H., & Carmel, S.** (2014). Maintaining successful aging: The role of coping patterns and resources. *Journal of Happiness Studies, 15,* 255–270. http://dx.doi.org/10.1007/s10902-013-9420-4

**Trail, S. M.** (2015). Sexual disorders. In L. Sperry, J. Carlson, J. D. Sauerheber, & J. Sperry (Eds.), *Psychopathology and psychotherapy: DSM-5 diagnosis, case conceptualization, and treatment* (3rd ed., pp. 265–283). New York, NY: Routledge/Taylor & Francis Group.

**Tran, D. M., & Westbrook, R. F.** (2015). Rats fed a diet rich in fats and sugars are impaired in the use of spatial geometry. *Psychological Science, 26,* 1947–1957. http://dx.doi.org/10.1177/0956797615608240

**Trautmann-Lengsfeld, S. A., & Herrmann, C. S.** (2014). Virtually simulated social pressure influences early visual processing more in low compared to high autonomous participants. *Psychophysiology, 51,* 124–135. http://dx.doi.org/10.1111/psyp.12161

**Travers, K. M., Creed, P. A., & Morrissey, S.** (2015). The development and initial validation of a new scale to measure explanatory style. *Personality and Individual Differences, 81,* 1–6. http://dx.doi.org/10.1016/j.paid.2015.01.045

**Treat, T. A., Church, E. K., & Viken, R. J.** (2017). Effects of gender, rape-supportive attitudes, and explicit instruction on perceptions of women's momentary sexual interest. *Psychonomic Bulletin & Review, 24*(3), 979–986. http://dx.doi.org/10.3758/s13423-016-1176-5

**Treffert, D. A.** (2014). Savant syndrome: Realities, myths and misconceptions. *Journal of Autism and Developmental Disorders, 44,* 564–571. http://dx.doi.org/10.1007/s10803-013-1906-8

**Trofimova, I., & Robbins, T. W.** (2016). Temperament and arousal systems: A new synthesis of differential psychology and functional neurochemistry. *Neuroscience and Biobehavioral Reviews, 64,* 382–402. http://dx.doi.org/10.1016/j.neubiorev.2016.03.008

**Troll, L. E., Miller, S. J., & Atchley, R. C.** (1979). *Families in later life.* Belmont, CA: Wadsworth.

**Trumbo, M. C., Leiting, K. A., McDaniel, M. A., & Hodge, G. K.** (2016). Effects of reinforcement on test-enhanced learning in a large, diverse introductory college psychology course. *Journal of Experimental Psychology: Applied, 22*(2), 148–160. http://dx.doi.org/10.1037/xap0000082

**Tsai, K. C.** (2015). All work and no play makes an adult a dull learner. *Journal of Education and Training, 2,* 184–191. http://dx.doi.org/10.5296/jet.v2i1.6979

**Tsai, Y., Lu, B., Ljubimov, A. V., Girman, S., Ross-Cisneros, F. N., Sadun, A. A., . . . Wang, S.** (2014). Ocular changes in TgF344-AD rat model of Alzheimer's disease. *Investigative Ophthalmology & Visual Science, 55,* 521–534. http://dx.doi.org/10.1167/iovs.13-12888

**Tseng, Y.-F., Chen, C.-H., & Wang, H.-H.** (2014). Taiwanese women's process of recovery from stillbirth: A qualitative descriptive study. *Research in Nursing & Health, 37,* 219–228. http://dx.doi.org/10.1002/nur.21594

**Tsien, J. Z.** (2000, April). Building a brainier mouse. *Scientific American, 282,* 62–68. http://dx.doi.org/10.10789248

**Tskhay, K. O., Clout, J. M., & Rule, N. O.** (2017). The impact of health, wealth, and attractiveness on romantic evaluation from photographs of faces. *Archives of Sexual Behavior.* No

Pagination Specified. http://dx.doi.org/10.1007/s10508-017-0963-z

**Tsoukalas, I.** (2012). The origin of REM sleep: A hypothesis. *Dreaming, 22,* 253–283.

**Tucker, S., Pek, S., Morrish, J., & Ruf, M.** (2015). Prevalence of texting while driving and other risky driving behaviors among young people in Ontario, Canada: Evidence from 2012 and 2014. *Accident Analysis and Prevention, 84,* 144–152. http://dx.doi.org/10.1016/j.aap.2015.07.011

**Tulving, E., & Thompson, D. M.** (1973). Encoding specificity and retrieval processes in episodic memory. *Psychological Review, 80,* 352–373. http://dx.doi.org/10.1037/h0020071

**Tummala-Narra, P.** (2016). A historical overview and critique of the psychoanalytic approach to culture and context. In P. Tummala-Narra (Ed.), *Psychoanalytic theory and cultural competence in psychotherapy* (pp. 7–29). Washington, DC: American Psychological Association. http://dx.doi.org/10.1037/14800-002

**Tunçel, Ö. K., Akbaş, S., & Bilgici, B.** (2016). Increased ghrelin levels and unchanged adipocytokine levels in major depressive disorder. *Journal of Child and Adolescent Psychopharmacology, 26,* 733–739. http://dx.doi.org/10.1089/cap.2015.0149

**Turkheimer, E., Pettersson, E., & Horn, E. E.** (2014). A phenotypic null hypothesis for the genetics of personality. *Annual Review of Psychology, 65,* 515–540. http://dx.doi.org/10.1146/annurev-psych-113011-143752

**Turner, M. J.** (2016). Rational Emotive Behavior Therapy (REBT), irrational and rational beliefs, and the mental health of athletes. *Frontiers in Psychology, 7,* Article 1423.

**Turnwald, B. P., Boles, D. Z., & Crum, A. J.** (2017). Association between indulgent descriptions and vegetable consumption: Twisted carrots and dynamite beets. *JAMA Internal Medicine.* No Pagination Specified. http://jamanetwork.com/journals/jamainternalmedicine/fullarticle/2630753

**Tversky, A., & Kahneman, D.** (1974). Judgment under uncertainty: Heuristics and biases. *Science, 185,* 1124–1131. http://dx.doi.org/10.1126/science.185.4157.1124

**Tversky, A., & Kahneman, D.** (1993). Probabilistic reasoning. In A. I. Goldman (Ed.), *Readings in philosophy and cognitive science* (pp. 43–68). Cambridge, MA: MIT Press.

**Tweedie, D., Rachmany, L., Rubovitch, V., Li, Y., Holloway, H. W., Lehrmann, E., . . . Pick, C. G.** (2016). Blast traumatic brain injury–induced cognitive deficits are attenuated by preinjury or postinjury treatment with the glucagon-like peptide-1 receptor agonist, exendin-4. *Alzheimer's & Dementia, 12*(1), 34–48. http://dx.doi.org/10.1016/j.jalz.2015.07.489

**Tyner, S., Brewer, A., Helman, M., Leon, Y., Pritchard, J., & Schlund, M.** (2016). Nice doggie! Contact desensitization plus reinforcement decreases dog phobias for children with autism. *Behavior Analysis in Practice, 9*(1), 54–57. http://dx.doi.org/10.1007/s40617-016-0113-4

**Uehara, I.** (2015). Developmental changes in memory-related linguistic skills and their relationship to episodic recall in children. *PLoS ONE, 10*(9), Article e0137220.

**Ulrich, R. E., Stachnik, T. J., & Stainton, N. R.** (1963). Student acceptance of generalized personality interpretations. *Psychological Reports, 13,* 831–834. http://dx.doi.org/10.2466/pr0.1963.13.3.831

**Underwood, E.** (2013). Sleep: The brain's housekeeper? *Science, 342,* 301. http://dx.doi.org/10.1126/science.342.6156.301

**Underwood, M. K., & Ehrenreich, S. E.** (2017). The power and pain of adolescents' digital communication: Cyber victimization and the perils of lurking. *American Psychologist, 72*(2), 144–158. http://www.americanpsychologist-digital.org/americanpsychologist/20170203?folio=144&pg=74#pg74

**University of California - Los Angeles.** (2017, March 6). Head injuries can alter hundreds of genes and lead to serious brain diseases. *ScienceDaily.* Retrieved March 9, 2017 from http://www.sciencedaily.com/releases/2017/03/170306134233.htm

**Unsworth, N., Spillers, G. J., & Brewer, G. A.** (2012). Dynamics of context-dependent recall: An examination of internal and external context change. *Journal of Memory and Language, 66,* 1–16. http://dx.doi.org/10.1016/j.jml.2011.05.001

**Urban, L. A.** (2016). Alternative treatments. In A. M. Matthews & J. C. Fellers (Eds.), *Treating comorbid opioid use disorder in chronic pain* (pp. 25–33). Cham, CH: Springer International Publishing. http://dx.doi.org/10.1007/978-3-319-29863-4_3

**Urbanová, L., Vyhnánková, V., Krisová, Š., Pacík, D., & Nečas, A.** (2015). Intensive training technique utilizing the dog's olfactory abilities to diagnose prostate cancer in men. *Acta Veterinaria Brno, 84,* 77–82. http://dx.doi.org/10.2754/avb201585010077

**Urriza, J., Arranz-Arranz, B., Ulkatan, S., Téllez, M. J., & Deletis, V.** (2016). Integrative action of axonal membrane explored by trains of subthreshold stimuli applied to the peripheral nerve. *Clinical Neurophysiology, 127,* 1707–1709. http://dx.doi.org/10.1016/j.clinph.2015.07.024

**Urzúa, A., Ferrer, R., Canales Gaete, V., Núñez Aragón, D., Ravanal Labraña, I., & Tabilo Poblete, B.** (2017). The influence of acculturation strategies in quality of life by immigrants in Northern Chile. *Quality of Life Research: An International Journal of Quality of Life Aspects of Treatment, Care & Rehabilitation, 6*(3), 717–726. http://dx.doi.org/10.1007/s11136-016-1470-8

**U.S. Bureau of Labor Statistics** (2016). Household data annual averages. *Bureau of Labor Statistics.* Retrieved from http://www.bls.gov/cps/cpsaat37.pdf

**U.S. Bureau of Labor Statistics** (2017). *Occupational outlook handbook.* Washington, DC: U.S. Department of Labor. https://www.bls.gov/ooh/

**Uvnäs-Moberg, K., Handlin, L., & Petersson, M.** (2015). Self-soothing behaviors with particular reference to oxytocin release induced by non-noxious sensory stimulation. *Frontiers in Psychology, 5,* Article 1529.

**Vacharkulksemsuk, T., Reit, E., Khambatta, P., Eastwick, P. W., Finkel, E. J., & Carney, D. R.** (2016). Dominant, open nonverbal displays are attractive at zero-acquaintance. *Proceedings of the National Academy of Sciences of the United States of America, 113,* 4009–4014. http://dx.doi.org/10.1073/pnas.1508932113

**Vaillant, G. E.** (2012). *Triumphs of experience: The men of the Harvard Grant Study.* Cambridge, MA: Harvard University Press.

**Valchev, V. H., van de Vijver, F. J. R., Meiring, D., Nel, J. A., Hill, C., Laher, S., & Adams, B. G.** (2014). Beyond agreeableness: Social–relational personality concepts from an indigenous and cross-cultural perspective. *Journal of Research in Personality, 48,* 17–32. http://dx.doi.org/10.1016/j.jrp.2013.10.003

**Valentine, K. A., Li, N. P., Penke, L., & Perrett, D. I.** (2014). Judging a man by the width of his face: The role of facial ratios and dominance in mate choice at speed-dating events. *Psychological Science, 25,* 806–811. http://dx.doi.org/10.1177/0956797613511823

**Vallejo-Medina, P., & Sierra, J. C.** (2013). Effect of drug use and influence of abstinence on sexual functioning in a Spanish male drug-dependent sample: A multisite study. *The Journal of Sexual Medicine, 10,* 333–341. http://dx.doi.org/10.1111/j.1743-6109.2012.02977.x.

**Vallejo-Torres, L., Castilla, I., González, N., Hunter, R., Serrano-Pérez, P., & Perestelo-Pérez, L.** (2015). Cost-effectiveness of electroconvulsive therapy compared to repetitive transcranial magnetic stimulation for treatment-resistant severe depression: A decision model. *Psychological Medicine, 45,* 1459–1470. http://dx.doi.org/10.1017/S0033291714002554

**van Avesaat, M., Troost, F. J., Ripken, D., Hendriks, H. F., & Masclee, A. A. M.** (2015). Ileal brake activation: Macronutrient-specific effects on eating behavior? *International Journal of Obesity, 39,* 235–243. http://dx.doi.org/10.1038/ijo.2014.112

**Van Belle, G., Lefèvre, P., & Rossion, B.** (2015). Face inversion and acquired prosopagnosia reduce the size of the perceptual field of view. *Cognition, 136,* 403–408. http://dx.doi.org/10.1016/j.cognition.2014.11.037

**Van de Carr, F. R., & Lehrer, M.** (1997). *While you are expecting: Your own prenatal classroom.* New York, NY: Humanics.

**van de Kamp, M.-T., Admiraal, W., van Drie, J., & Rijlaarsdam, G.** (2015). Enhancing divergent thinking in visual arts education: Effects of explicit instruction of metacognition. *British Journal of Educational Psychology, 85,* 47–58. http://dx.doi.org/10.1111/bjep.12061

**van den Akker, K., Havermans, R. C., & Jansen, A.** (2015). Effects of occasional reinforced trials during extinction on the reacquisition of conditioned responses to food cues. *Journal of Behavior Therapy and Experimental Psychiatry, 48,* 50–58. http://dx.doi.org/10.1016/j.jbtep.2015.02.001

**van den Berg, S. M., de Moor, M. H. M., Verweij, K. J. H., Krueger, R. F., Luciano, M., Arias Vasquez, A., . . . Boomsma, D. I.** (2016). Meta-analysis of genome-wide association studies for extraversion: Findings from the genetics of personality consortium. *Behavior Genetics, 46,* 170–182. http://dx.doi.org/10.1007/s10519-015-9735-5

**Vandenbosch, L., & Eggermont, S.** (2011). Temptation Island, The Bachelor, Joe Millionaire: A prospective cohort study on the role of romantically themed reality television in adolescents' sexual development. *Journal of Broadcasting & Electronic Media, 56,* 563–580.

**VanderLaan, D. P., Petterson, L. J., & Vasey, P. L.** (2017). Elevated kin-directed altruism emerges in childhood and is linked to feminine gender expression in samoan fa'afafine: A retrospective study. *Archives of Sexual Behavior, 46,* 95–108. http://dx.doi.org/10.1007/s10508-016-0884-2

**van der Lely, S., Frey, S., Garbazza, C., Wirz-Justice, A., Jenni, O. G., Steiner,**

R., . . . **Schmidt, C.** (2015). Blue blocker glasses as a countermeasure for alerting effects of evening light-emitting diode screen exposure in male teenagers. *Journal of Adolescent Health, 56,* 113–119. http://dx.doi.org/10.1016/j.jadohealth.2014.08.002

**van der Pligt, J., & Vliek, M.** (2016). *The psychology of influence.* New York, NY: Psychology Press.

**van der Weiden, A., Prikken, M., & van Haren, N. E. M.** (2015). Self-other integration and distinction in schizophrenia: A theoretical analysis and a review of the evidence. *Neuroscience and Biobehavioral Reviews, 57,* 220–237. http://dx.doi.org/10.1016/j.neubiorev.2015.09.004

**van Dijk, S. J., Molloy, P. L., Varinli, H., Morrison, J. L., Muhlhausler, B. S., Buckley, M., . . . Tellam, R. L.** (2015). Epigenetics and human obesity. *International Journal of Obesity, 39,* 85–97. http://dx.doi.org/10.1038/ijo.2014.34

**van Dongen, J., Willemsen, G., Heijmans, B. T., Neuteboom, J., Kluft, C., Jansen, R., . . . Boomsma, D. I.** (2015). Longitudinal weight differences, gene expression and blood biomarkers in BMI-discordant identical twins. *International Journal of Obesity, 39,* 899–909. http://dx.doi.org/10.1038/ijo.2015.24

**van IJzendoorn, M. H., & Bakermans-Kranenburg, M. J.** (2010). Invariance of adult attachment across gender, age, culture, and socioeconomic status? *Journal of Social and Personal Relationships, 27,* 200–208. http://dx.doi.org/10.1177/0265407509360908

**van Lenthe, F. J., Jansen, T., & Kamphuis, C.** (2015). Understanding socio-economic in equalities in food choice behaviour: Can Maslow's pyramid help? *British Journal of Nutrition, 113,* 1139–1147. http://dx.doi.org/10.1017/S0007114515000288

**van Meurs, B., Wiggert, N., Wicker, I., & Lissek, S.** (2014). Maladaptive behavioral consequences of conditioned fear-generalization: A pronounced, yet sparsely studied, feature of anxiety pathology. *Behaviour Research and Therapy, 57,* 29–37. http://dx.doi.org/10.1016/j.brat.2014.03.009

**van Name, M., Giannini, C., Santoro, N., Jastreboff , A. M., Kubat, J., Li, F., . . . Caprio, S.** (2015). Blunted suppression of Acyl-Ghrelin in response to fructose ingestion in obese adolescents: The role of insulin resistance. *Obesity, 23,* 653–661. http://dx.doi.org/10.1002/oby.21019

**van Ommen, M. M., van Beilen, M., Cornelissen, F. W., Smid, H. G. O. M., Knegtering, H., Aleman, A., . . . GROUP Investigators** (2016). The prevalence of visual hallucinations in non-affective psychosis, and the role of perception and attention. *Psychological Medicine, 46,* 1735–1747. http://dx.doi.org/10.1017/S0033291716000246

**van Paaschen, F.** (2017, January 16). The human brain vs. computers. *Thrive Global.* Retrieved from https://journal.thriveglobal.com/the-human-brain-vs-computers-5880cb156541

**van Passel, B., Danner, U., Dingemans, A., van Furth, E., Sternheim, L., van Elburg, A., . . . Cath, D.** (2016). Cognitive remediation therapy (CRT) as a treatment enhancer of eating disorders and obsessive compulsive disorders: Study protocol for a randomized controlled trial. *BMC Psychiatry, 16,* Article 393.

**Vannier, S. A., & O'Sullivan, L. F.** (2017). Passion, connection, and destiny: How romantic expecta-

tions help predict satisfaction and commitment in young adults' dating relationships. *Journal of Social and Personal Relationships, 34*(2), 235–257. http://dx.doi.org/10.1177/0265407516631156

**Vassoler, F. M., Byrnes, E. M., & Pierce, R. C.** (2014). The impact of exposure to addictive drugs on future generations: Physiological and behavioral effects. *Neuropharmacology, 76,* 269–275. http://dx.doi.org/10.1016/j.neuropharm.2013.06.016

**Vecchione, M., Dentale, F., Alessandri, G., Imbesi, M. T., Barbaranelli, C., & Schnabel, K.** (2016). On the applicability of the big five implicit association test in organizational settings. *Current Psychology.* No Pagination Specified. http://dx.doi.org/10.1007/s12144-016-9455-x

**Vedder, P., Wenink, E., & van Geel, M.** (2017). Intergroup contact and prejudice between Dutch majority and Muslim minority youth in The Netherlands. *Cultural Diversity and Ethnic Minority Psychology.* No Pagination Specified. http://dx.doi.org/10.1037/cdp0000150

**Vélez, C. E., Wolchik, S. A., Tein, J.-Y., & Sandler, I.** (2011). Protecting children from the consequences of divorce: A longitudinal study of the effects of parenting on children's coping processes. *Child Development, 82,* 244–257. http://doi.org/10.1111/j.1467-8624.2010.01553.x

**Venables, P. H., & Raine, A.** (2016). The impact of malnutrition on intelligence at 3 and 11 years of age: The mediating role of temperament. *Developmental Psychology, 52,* 205–220. http://dx.doi.org/10.1037/dev0000046

**Ventriglio, A., Ayonrinde, O., & Bhugra, D.** (2016). Relevance of culture-bound syndromes in the 21st century. *Psychiatry and Clinical Neurosciences, 70,* 3–6. http://dx.doi.org/10.1111/pcn.12359

**Ventriglio, A., Mari, M., Bellomo, A., & Bhugra, D.** (2015). Homelessness and mental health: A challenge. *International Journal of Social Psychiatry, 61*(7), 621–622. http://dx.doi.org/10.1177/0020764015585680

**Vezzali, L., Stathi, S., Giovannini, D., Capozza, D., & Trifiletti, E.** (2015). The greatest magic of Harry Potter: Reducing prejudice. *Journal of Applied Social Psychology, 45,* 105–121. http://dx.doi.org/10.1111/jasp.12279

**Vinall, J., & Grunau, R. E.** (2014). Impact of repeated procedural pain-related stress in infants born very preterm. *Pediatric Research, 75,* 584–587. http://dx.doi.org/10.1038/pr.2014.16

**Virring, A., Lambek, R., Thomsen, P. H., Møller, L. R., & Jennum, P. J.** (2016). Disturbed sleep in attention-deficit hyperactivity disorder (ADHD) is not a question of psychiatric comorbidity or ADHD presentation. *Journal of Sleep Research, 25*(3), 333–340. http://dx.doi.org/10.1111/jsr.12377

**Visintin, E., De Panfilis, C., Amore, M., Balestrieri, M., Wolf, R. C., & Sambataro, F.** (2016). Mapping the brain correlates of borderline personality disorder: A functional neuroimaging meta-analysis of resting state studies. *Journal of Affective Disorders, 204,* 262–269. http://dx.doi.org/10.1016/j.jad.2016.07.025

**Visser, S. N., Danielson, M. L., Bitsko, R. H., Holbrook, J. R., Kogan, M. D., Ghandour, R. M., . . . Blumberg, S. J.** (2014). Trends in the parent-report of health care provider-diagnosed and medicated attention-deficit/hyperactivity disorder: United States, 2003–2011. *Journal of the American Academy of Child & Adolescent Psychiatry, 53,* 34–46.

**Vissia, E. M., Giesen, M. E., Chalavi, S., Nijenhuis, E. R. S., Draijer, N., Brand, B. L., & Reinders, A. A. T. S.** (2016). Is it Trauma- or Fantasy-based? Comparing dissociative identity disorder, post-traumatic stress disorder, simulators, and controls. *Acta Psychiatrica Scandinavica, 134,* 111–128. http://dx.doi.org/10.1111/acps.12590

**Viviani, R., Nagl, M., & Buchheim, A.** (2015). Psychotherapy outcome research and neuroimaging. In O. C. G. Gelo, A. Pritz, & B. Rieken (Eds.), *Psychotherapy research: Foundations, process, and outcome* (pp. 611–634). New York, NY: Springer. http://dx.doi.org/10.1007/978-3-7091-1382-0_30

**Vlaeyen, J. W., Morley, S., & Crombez, G.** (2016). The experimental analysis of the interruptive, interfering, and identity-distorting effects of chronic pain. *Behaviour Research and Therapy, 86,* 23–34. http://dx.doi.org/10.1016/j.brat.2016.08.016

**Vliegenthart, J., Noppe, G., van Rossum, E. F. C., Koper, J. W., Raat, H., & van den Akker, E. L. T.** (2016). Socioeconomic status in children is associated with hair cortisol levels as a biological measure of chronic stress. *Psychoneuroendocrinology, 65,* 9–14. http://dx.doi.org/10.1016/j.psyneuen.2015.11.022

**Vokey, J. R., & Read, J. D.** (1985). Subliminal messages: Between the devil and the media. *American Psychologist, 40,* 1231–1239.

**Volz, B. D.** (2016). Race and quarterback survival in the National Football League. *Journal of Sports Economics.* No Pagination Specified.

**von Dawans, B., Fischbacher, U., Kirschbaum, C., Fehr, E., & Heinrichs, M.** (2012). The social dimension of stress reactivity: Acute stress increases prosocial behavior in humans. *Psychological Science, 23,* 651–660. http://dx.doi.org/10.1177/0956797611431576

**von der Embse, N. P., Schultz, B. K., & Draughn, J. D.** (2015). Readying students to test: The influence of fear and efficacy appeals on anxiety and test performance. *School Psychology International, 36,* 620–637. http://dx.doi.org/10.1177/0143034315609094

**Von Drehle, D.** (2017, February 17). Barack Obama ranked 12th best U.S. president ever in major survey of historians. *Time.* Retrieved from http://time.com/4674300/cspan-presidents-rank-2017/

**von Hofsten, C.** (2013). Action in infancy: A foundation for cognitive development. In W. Prinz, M. Beisert, & A. Herwig (Eds.), *Action science foundation of an emerging discipline* (pp. 255–280). New York, NY: Oxford University Press.

**Von Stumm, S., & Plomin, R.** (2015). Socioeconomic status and the growth of intelligence from infancy through adolescence. *Intelligence, 48,* 30–36. http://dx.doi.org/10.1016/j.intell.2014.10.002

**Vonmoos, M., Hulka, L. M., Preller, K. H., Minder, F., Baumgartner, M. R., & Quednow, B. B.** (2014). Cognitive impairment in cocaine users is drug-induced but partially reversible: Evidence from a longitudinal study. *Neuropsychopharmacology, 39,* 2200–2210. http://dx.doi.org/10.1038/npp.2014.71

**Vorster, A. P., & Born, J.** (2015). Sleep and memory in mammals, birds and invertebrates. *Neuroscience and Biobehavioral Reviews, 50,* 103–119. http://dx.doi.org/10.1016/j.neubiorev.2014.09.020

**Vrij, A., & Fisher, R. P.** (2016). Which lie detection tools are ready for use in the criminal justice system? *Journal of Applied Research in Memory and Cognition, 5,* 302–307. http://dx.doi.org/10.1016/j.jarmac.2016.06.014

**Vygotsky, L. S.** (1962). *Thought and language.* Cambridge, MA: MIT Press.

**Wagner, D. A.** (1982). Ontogeny in the study of culture and cognition. In D. A. Wagner & H. W. Stevenson (Eds.), *Cultural perspectives on child development* (pp. 105–123). San Francisco, CA: Freeman.

**Wagner, F. L., Rammsayer, T. H., Schweizer, K., & Troche, S. J.** (2014). Relations between the attentional blink and aspects of psychometric intelligence: A fixed-links modeling approach. *Personality and Individual Differences, 58,* 122–127. http://dx.doi.org/10.1016/j.paid.2013.10.023

**Waldron, J. C., Wilson, L. C., Patriquin, M. A., & Scarpa, A.** (2015). Sexual victimization history, depression, and task physiology as predictors of sexual revictimization: Results from a 6-month prospective pilot study. *Journal of Interpersonal Violence, 30,* 622–639. http://dx.doi.org/10.1177/0886260514535258

**Walker, A. K., Rivera, P. D., Wang, Q., Chuang, J. C., Tran, S., Osborne-Lawrence, S., . . . Zigman, J. M.** (2015). The P7C3 class of neuroprotective compounds exerts antidepressant efficacy in mice by increasing hippocampal neurogenesis. *Molecular Psychiatry, 20,* 500–508. http://dx.doi.org/10.1038/mp.2014.34

**Walker, H. M., & Gresham, F. M.** (2016). *Handbook of evidence-based practices for emotional and behavioral disorders* (Reprint edition). New York, NY: Guilford Press.

**Walker, J. V., III, & Lampropoulos, G. K.** (2014). A comparison of self-help (homework) activities for mood enhancement: Results from a brief randomized controlled trial. *Journal of Psychotherapy Integration, 24,* 46–64. http://dx.doi.org/10.1037/a0036145

**Wallack, L., & Thornburg, K.** (2016). Developmental origins, epigenetics, and equity: Moving upstream. *Maternal and Child Health Journal, 20,* 935–940. http://dx.doi.org/10.1007/s10995-016-1970-8

**Walsh, K., & Cross, W.** (2013). Depression: Classification, culture and the westernisation of mental illness. In N. Kocabasoglu (Ed.), *Mood disorders.* Retrieved from http://cdn.intechopen.com/pdfs/42233/InTech-Depression_classification_culture_and_the_westernisation_of_mental_illness.pdf

**Walsh, K., Zwi, K., Woolfenden, S., & Shlonsky, A.** (2015). School-based education programmes for the prevention of child sexual abuse. *Cochrane Database of Systematic Reviews,* Issue 4. http://dx.doi.org/10.1002/14651858.CD004380.pub3

**Walton, G. M., & Cohen, G. L.** (2011). A brief social-belonging intervention improves academic and health outcomes of minority students. *Science, 331,* 1447–1451. http://dx.doi.org/10.1126/science.1198364

**Wamsley, E. J., & Stickgold, R.** (2010). Dreaming and offline memory processing. *Current Biology, 20,* 1010–1013. http://dx.doi.org/10.1016/j.cub.2010.10.045

**Wan, L., Crookes, K., Dawel, A., Pidcock, M., Hall, A., & McKone, E.** (2017). Face-blind for other-race faces: Individual differences in other-race recognition impairments. *Journal of Experimental Psychology: General, 146,* 102–122. http://dx.doi.org/10.1037/xge0000249

**Wang, C. C., Shih, H. C., Shyu, B. C., & Huang, A. C. W.** (2017). Effects of thalamic hemorrhagic lesions on explicit and implicit learning during the acquisition and retrieval phases in an animal model of central post-stroke pain. *Behavioural Brain Research, 317,* 251–262. http://dx.doi.org/10.1016/j.bbr.2016.09.053

**Wang, L., Luo, P., Zhang, F., Zhang, Y., Wang, X., Chang, F., . . . Xia, Z.** (2017). Toll-like receptor 4 protects against stress-induced ulcers via regulation of glucocorticoid production in mice. *Stress: The International Journal on the Biology of Stress, 20*(1), 2–9. http://dx.doi.org/10.1080/10253890.2016.1224843

**Wang, M.-T., & Kenny, S.** (2014). Longitudinal links between fathers' and mothers' harsh verbal discipline and adolescents' conduct problems and depressive symptoms. *Child Development, 85,* 908–923. http://dx.doi.org/10.1111/cdev.12143

**Wang, Q.** (2011). Autobiographical memory and culture. *Online readings in psychology and culture, 5.* http://dx.doi.org/10.9707/2307-0919.1047

**Wang, R., Liu, H., Jiang, J., & Song, Y.** (2017). Will materialism lead to happiness? A longitudinal analysis of the mediating role of psychological needs satisfaction. *Personality and Individual Differences, 105,* 312–317. http://dx.doi.org/10.1016/j.paid.2016.10.014

**Wang, Y., Zhang, L., Kong, X., Hong, Y., Cheon, B., & Liu, J.** (2016). Pathway to neural resilience: Self-esteem buffers against deleterious effects of poverty on the hippocampus. *Human Brain Mapping, 37*(11), 3757–3766. http://dx.doi.org/10.1002/hbm.23273

**Wansink, B., & van Ittersum, K.** (2012). Fast food restaurant lighting and music can reduce calorie intake and increase satisfaction. *Psychological Reports, 111*(1), 228–232. http://dx.doi.org/10.2466/01.PR0.111.4.228-232

**Washington, M. C., Williams, K., & Sayegh, A. I.** (2016). The feeding responses evoked by endogenous cholecystokinin are regulated by different gastrointestinal sites. *Hormones and Behavior, 78,* 79–85. http://dx.doi.org/10.1016/j.yhbeh.2015.10.019

**Wassing, R., Benjamins, J. S., Dekker K., Moens, S., Spiegelhalder, K., Feige, B., . . . Van Someren, E. J. W.** (2016). Slow dissolving of emotional distress contributes to hyperarousal. *Proceedings of the National Academy of Sciences of the United States of America, 113,* 2538–2543. http://dx.doi.org/10.1073/pnas.1522520113

**Watkins, C. E., Jr.** (2016). Listening, learning, and development in psychoanalytic supervision: A self psychology perspective. *Psychoanalytic Psychology, 33,* 437–471. http://dx.doi.org/10.1037/a0038168

**Watsky, R. E., Ludovici Pollard, K., Greenstein, D., Shora, L., Dillard-Broadnax, D., Gochman, P., . . . Ordóñez, A. E.** (2016). Severity of cortical thinning correlates with schizophrenia spectrum symptoms. *Journal of the American Academy of Child & Adolescent Psychiatry, 55,* 130–136. http://dx.doi.org/10.1016/j.jaac.2015.11.008

**Watson, J. B.** (1913). Psychology as the behaviorist views it. *Psychological Review, 20,* 158–177. http://dx.doi.org/10.1037/h0074428

**Watson, J. B., & Rayner, R.** (1920). Conditioned emotional reactions. *Journal of Experimental Psychology, 3,* 1–14. http://dx.doi.org/10.1037/h0069608

**Watson, J. C., & Greenberg, L. S.** (2017). Working with worry: Anxiety splits. In J. C. Watson & L. S. Greenberg (Eds.), *Emotion-focused therapy for generalized anxiety* (pp. 135–163). Washington, DC: American Psychological Association. http://dx.doi.org/10.1037/0000018-007

**Watts, B. V., Zayed, M. H., Llewellyn-Thomas, H., & Schnurr, P. P.** (2016). Understanding and meeting information needs for patients with posttraumatic stress disorder. *BMC Psychiatry, 16,* Article 21. http://dx.doi.org/10.1186/s12888-016-0724-x

**Weaver, M. F., Hopper, J. A., & Gunderson, E. W.** (2015). Designer drugs 2015: Assessment and management. *Addiction Science and Clinical Practice, 10,* 1–9. http://dx.doi.org/10.1186/s13722-015-0024-7

**Webb, B., Hine, A. C., & Bailey, P. E.** (2016). Difficulty in differentiating trustworthiness from untrustworthiness in older age. *Developmental Psychology, 52,* 985–995. http://dx.doi.org/10.1037/dev0000126

**Webb, S.** (2016). Schizophrenia. In A. Breland-Noble, C. S. Al-Mateen, & N. N. Singh (Eds.), *Handbook of mental health in African American youth. Springer series on child and family* studies (pp. 249–259). Cham, CH: Springer International Publishing. http://dx.doi.org/10.1007/978-3-319-25501-9_15

**Wechsler, D.** (1944). *The measurement of adult intelligence* (3rd ed.). Baltimore, MD: Williams & Wilkins.

**Wechsler, D.** (1977). *Manual for the Wechsler Intelligence Scale for Children* (Rev.). New York, NY: Psychological Corporation.

**Weeks, B. E., & Garrett, R. K.** (2014). Electoral consequences of political rumors: Motivated reasoning, candidate rumors, and vote choice during the 2008 US presidential election. *International Journal of Public Opinion Research, 26,* 401–422. http://dx.doi.org/10.1093/ijpor/edu005

**Weems, C. F., Scott, B. G., Banks, D. M., & Graham, R. A.** (2012). Is TV traumatic for all youths? The role of preexisting posttraumatic stress symptoms in the link between disaster coverage and stress. *Psychological Science, 23,* 1293–1297. http://dx.doi.org/10.1177/0956797612446952

**Wegmann, E., & Brand, M.** (2016). Internet-communication disorder: It's a matter of social aspects, coping, and Internet-use expectancies. *Frontiers in Psychology, 7*:1747.

**Weiler, L. M., Lyness, K. P., Haddock, S. A., & Zimmerman, T. S.** (2015). Contextual issues in couple and family therapy: Gender, sexual orientation, culture, and spirituality. In J. L. Wetchler & L. L. Hecker (Eds.), *An introduction to marriage and family therapy* (2nd ed., pp. 65–116). New York, NY: Routledge/Taylor & Francis Group.

**Weimer, A. A., Dowds, S. J. P., Fabricius, W. V., Schwanenflugel, P. J., & Suh, G. W.** (2017). Development of constructivist theory of mind from middle childhood to early adulthood and its relation to social cognition and behavior. *Journal of Experimental Child Psychology, 154,* 28–45. http://dx.doi.org/10.1016/j.jecp.2016.10.002

**Weiner, B.** (1972). *Theories of motivation.* Chicago, IL: Rand-McNally.

**Weiner, B.** (2015). On the cross-cultural trail, searching for (non)-replication. *International Journal of Psychology, 50,* 303–307. http://dx.doi.org/10.1002/ijop.12156

**Weinstein, D., Launay, J., Pearce, E., Dunbar, R. I. M., & Stewart, L.** (2016). Singing and social bonding: Changes in connectivity and pain threshold as a function of group size. *Evolution and Human Behavior, 37,* 152–158. http://dx.doi:10.1016/j.evolhumbehav.2015.10.002

**Weinstein, N., Ryan, W. S., DeHaan, C. R., Przybylski, A. K., Legate, N., & Ryan, R. M.** (2012). Parental autonomy support and discrepancies between implicit and explicit sexual identities: Dynamics of self-acceptance and defense. *Journal of Personality and Social Psychology, 102,* 815–832. http://dx.doi.org/10.1037/a0026854

**Weinstein, Y., Nunes, L. D., & Karpicke, J. D.** (2016). On the placement of practice questions during study. *Journal of Experimental Psychology: Applied, 22,* 72–84. http://dx.doi.org/10.1037/xap0000071

**Weintraub, K.** (2016). Young and sleep deprived. *Monitor on Psychology, 47,* 46. Retrieved from http://www.apa.org/monitor/2016/02/sleep-deprived.aspx

**Weir, K.** (2014, October). Mind games. *Monitor on Psychology, 45.* No Pagination Specified. http://dx.doi.org/10.1037/e577942014-009

**Weir, K.** (2017). (Dis)Connected. *American Psychological Association.* Retrieved from http://www.apa.org/monitor/2017/03/cover-disconnected.aspx

**Weisman, O., Zagoory-Sharon, O., & Feldman, R.** (2012). Oxytocin administration to parent enhances infant physiological and behavioral readiness for social engagement. *Biological Psychiatry, 72,* 982–989.

**Weiss, A., Gartner, M. C., Gold, K. C., & Stoinski, T. S.** (2013). Extraversion predicts longer survival in gorillas: An 18-year longitudinal study. *Proceedings of the Royal Society B-Biological Sciences, 280,* 1–5. http://dx.doi.org/10.1098/rspb.2012.2231

**Weiss, A., Staes, N., Pereboom, J. J., Inoue-Murayama, M., Stevens, J. M., & Eens, M.** (2015). Personality in bonobos. *Psychological Science, 26,* 1430–1439. http://dx.doi.org/10.1177/0956797615589933.

**Weisz, J. R., Kuppens, S., Ng, M. Y., Eckshtain, D., Ugueto, A. M., Vaughn-Coaxum, R., . . . Fordwood, S. R.** (2017). Overall effectiveness. What five decades of research tells us about the effects of youth psychological therapy: A multilevel meta-analysis and implications for science and practice. *American Psychologist, 72*(2), 79–117. http://dx.doi.org/10.1037/a0040360

**Weitlauf, J. C., Cervone, D., Smith, R. E., & Wright, P. M.** (2001). Assessing generalization in perceived self-efficacy: Multidomain and global assessments of the effects of self-defense training for women. *Personality and Social Psychology Bulletin, 27,* 1683–1691. http://dx.doi.org/10.1177/01461672012712011

**Wergård, E.-M., Westlund, K., Spångberg, M., Fredlund, H., & Forkman, B.** (2016). Training success in group-housed long-tailed macaques (Macaca fascicularis) is better explained by personality than by social rank. *Applied Animal Behaviour Science, 177,* 52–58. http://dx.doi.org/10.1016/j.applanim.2016.01.017

**Werner, K. H., Roberts, N. A., Rosen, H. J., Dean, D. L., Kramer, J. H., Weiner, M. W., . . . Levenson, R. W.** (2007). Emotional reactivity and emotion recognition in frontotemporal lobar degeneration. *Neurology, 69,* 148–155.

**Werner, S., & Roth, D.** (2014). Stigma in the field of intellectual disabilities: Impact and initiatives for change. In P. W. Corrigan (Ed.), *The stigma of disease and disability: Understanding causes and overcoming injustices* (pp. 73–91). Washington, DC: American Psychological Association. http://dx.doi.org/10.1037/14297-005

**West, K., Hotchin, V., & Wood, C.** (2017). Imagined contact can be more effective for participants with stronger initial prejudices. *Journal of Applied Social Psychology, 47*(5), 282–292. http://dx.doi.org/10.1111/jasp.12437

**West, T. V., Magee, J. C., Gordon, S. H., & Gullett, L.** (2014). A little similarity goes a long way: The effects of peripheral but self-revealing similarities on improving and sustaining interracial relationships. *Journal of Personality and Social Psychology, 107,* 81–100. http://dx.doi.org/10.1037/a0036556

**Westfall, J., Van Boven, L., Chambers, J. R., & Judd, C. M.** (2015). Perceiving political polarization in the United States: Party identity strength and attitude extremity exacerbate the perceived partisan divide. *Perspectives on Psychological Science, 10,* 145–158. http://dx.doi.org/10.1177/1745691615569849

**Weyandt, L. L., Oster, D. R., Gudmundsdottir, B. G., DuPaul, G. J., & Anastopoulos, A. D.** (2017). Neuropsychological functioning in college students with and without ADHD. *Neuropsychology, 31,* 160–172. http://dx.doi.org/10.1037/neu0000326

**Whealin, J., & Barnett, E.** (2014). Child sexual abuse. *National Center for Post Traumatic Stress Disorder, U.S. Department of Veterans Affairs.* Retrieved from http://www.ptsd.va.gov/professional/trauma/other/child_sexual_abuse.asp

**Whillans, A. V., Weidman, A. C., & Dunn, E. W.** (2016). Valuing time over money is associated with greater happiness. *Social Psychological and Personality Science, 7,* 213–222. http://dx.doi.org/10.1177/1948550615623842

**Whitbourne, S. K., & Mathews, M. J.** (2009). Pathways in Adulthood: A counterpoint to the midlife crisis myth. *American Psychological Association Annual Convention.* Toronto, Ontario, Canada.

**Whitbourne, S. K., & Whitbourne, S. B.** (2014). *Adult development and aging: Biological perspectives* (5th ed.). Hoboken, NJ: Wiley.

**White, S. C., & Eyber, C.** (2017). Positive mental health and wellbeing. In R. G. White, S. Jain, D. M. R. Orr, & U. M. Read (Eds.), *The Palgrave handbook of sociocultural perspectives on global mental health* (pp. 129–150). New York, NY: Palgrave Macmillan. http://dx.doi.org/10.1057/978-1-137-39510-8_7

**White, T., Andreasen, N. C., & Nopoulos, P.** (2002). Brain volumes and surface morphology in monozygotic twins. *Cerebral Cortex, 12,* 486–493. http://dx.doi.org/10.1093/cercor/12.5.486

**Whorf, B. L.** (1956). *Language, thought, and reality.* New York, NY: Wiley.

**Wieczorek, J., Blazejczyk, K., & Morita, T.** (2016). Changes in melatonin secretion in tourists after rapid movement to another lighting zone without transition of time zone. *Chronobiology International, 33*(2), 220–233. http://dx.doi.org/10.3109/07420528.2015.1130050

**Wieman, C., & Welsh, A.** (2016). The connection between teaching methods and attribution errors. *Educational Psychology Review, 28*(3),

645–648. http://dx.doi.org/10.1007/s10648-015-9317-3

**Wiemer, J., & Pauli, P.** (2016). Fear-relevant illusory correlations in different fears and anxiety disorders: A review of the literature. *Journal of Anxiety Disorders, 42,* 113–128. http://dx.doi.org/10.1016/j.janxdis.2016.07.003

**Wild, J., & Clark, D. M.** (2015). Experiential exercises and imagery rescripting in social anxiety disorder: New perspectives on changing beliefs. In N. C. Thoma & D. McKay (Eds.), *Working with emotion in cognitive-behavioral therapy: Techniques for clinical practice* (pp. 216–236). New York, NY: Guilford.

**Wilkie, G., Sakr, B., & Rizack, T.** (2016). Medical marijuana use in oncology: A review. *JAMA Oncology, 2,* 670–675. http://dx.doi.org/10.1001/jamaoncol.2016.0155.

**Wilkins, C. L., Wellman, J. D., Babbitt, L. G., Toosi, N. R., & Schad, K. D.** (2015). You can win but I can't lose: Bias against high-status groups increases their zero-sum beliefs about discrimination. *Journal of Experimental Social Psychology, 57,* 1–14. http://dx.doi.org/10.1016/j.jesp.2014.10.008

**Wilkins, C. L., Wellman, J. D., Flavin, E. L., & Manrique, J. A.** (2017). When men perceive anti-male bias: Status-legitimizing beliefs increase discrimination against women. *Psychology of Men & Masculinity.* No Pagination Specified. http://dx.doi.org/10.1037/men0000097

**Wilkinson, J., & Spargo, C.** (2016, September 1). Killer mom Andrea Yates. *Daily Mail.com.* Retrieved from http://www.dailymail.co.uk/news/article-3769609/Andrea-Yates-grieves-day-five-children-drowned-tub-15-years-ago-likely-never-leave-Texas-mental-hospital.html

**Wilkinson, T. L.** (2017, February 9). The girl who gave Malala a voice. *Billionaire.* Retrieved from http://www.billionaire.com/philanthropy/charities/2718/thegirl-who-gave-malala-a-voice

**Willen, R. M., Mutwill, A., MacDonald, L. J., Schiml, P. A., & Hennessy, M.B.** (2017). Factors determining the effects of human interaction on the cortisol levels of shelter dogs. *Applied Animal Behaviour Science, 186,* 41–48. http://dx.doi.org/10.1016/j.applanim.2016.11.002

**Williams, C. L., & Lally, S. J.** (2016). MMPI-2, MMPI-2-RF, and MMPI-A administrations (2007–2014): Any evidence of a "new standard?" *Professional Psychology: Research and Practice.* No Pagination Specified. http://dx.doi.org/10.1037/pro0000088

**Williams, D. L.** (2014). Neural integration of satiation and food reward: Role of GLP-1 and orexin pathways. *Physiology & Behavior, 136,* 194–199. http://dx.doi.org/10.1016/j.physbeh.2014.03.013

**Williams, D. R., Priest, N., & Anderson, N. B.** (2016). Understanding associations among race, socioeconomic status, and health: Patterns and prospects. *Health Psychology, 35,* 407–411. http://dx.doi.org/10.1037/hea0000242

**Williams, R. S., Biel, A. L., Dyson, B. J., & Spaniol, J.** (2017). Age differences in gain- and loss-motivated attention. *Brain and Cognition, 111,* 171–181. http://dx.doi.org/10.1016/j.bandc.2016.12.003

**Williams, S. C. P.** (2013, July 15). Obesity gene linked to hunger hormone. *Science NOW.* Retrieved from http://news.sciencemag.org/sciencenow/2013/07/obesitygene-linkedtohunger-ho.html? ref=em#.UeTHLsf3tP0.email

Williams, S. S. (2001). Sexual lying among college students in close and casual relationships. *Journal of Applied Social Psychology, 31*(11), 2322–2338.

Williamson, J. N., & Williamson, D. G. (2015). Sleep-wake disorders. In L. Sperry, J. Carlson, J. D. Sauerheber, & J. Sperry (Eds.), *Psychopathology and psychotherapy: DSM-5 diagnosis, case conceptualization, and treatment* (3rd ed., pp. 243–264). New York, NY: Routledge/Taylor & Francis Group.

Willyard, C. (2011). Men: A growing minority. *grad-PSYCH, 9,* 40–44. http://dx.doi.org/10.1037/e669902010-010

Wilson, D. S. (2015a). *Does altruism exist? Culture, genes, and the welfare of others.* New Haven, CT: Yale University Press.

Wilson, E. O. (1975). *Sociobiology: The new synthesis.* Cambridge, MA: Harvard University Press.

Wilson, E. O. (1978). *On human nature.* Cambridge, MA: Harvard University Press.

Wilson, E. O. (2013). *The social conquest of earth.* New York, NY: Liveright.

Wilson, M. (2015b, June 5). A Manhattan fortune teller cost him fortune after fortune. *New York Times.* http://www.nytimes.com/2015/06/06/nyregion/he-went-to-thefortuneteller-now-his-fortune-is-gone.html?

Wimmer, H., & Perner, J. (1983). Beliefs about beliefs: Representation and constraining function of wrong beliefs in young children's understanding of deception. *Cognition, 13,* 103–128.

Wineburg, S., & McGrew, S. (2016, November 1). Why students can't Google their way to the truth. *Education Week.* Retrieved May 1, 2017 from http://www.edweek.org/ew/articles/2016/11/02/why-students-cant-google-their-way-to.html

Winston, C. N., Maher, H., & Easvaradoss, V. (2017). Needs and values: An exploration. *The Humanistic Psychologist.* No Pagination Specified. http://dx.doi.org/10.1037/hum0000054

Witelson, S. F., Kigar, D. L., & Harvey, T. (1999). The exceptional brain of Albert Einstein. *The Lancet, 353,* 2149–2153. http://dx.doi.org/10.1016/S0140-6736(05)70590-0

Witt, W. P., Mandell, K. C., Wisk, L. E., Cheng, E. R., Chatterjee, D., Wakeel, F., . . . Zarak, D. (2016). Infant birthweight in the US: The role of preconception stressful life events and substance use. *Archives of Women's Mental Health, 19*(3), 529–542. http://dx.doi.org/10.1007/s00737-015-0595-z

Wixted, J. T., Mickes, L., Clark, S. E., Gronlund, S. D., & Roediger, H. L. III. (2015). Initial eyewitness confidence reliably predicts eyewitness identification accuracy. *American Psychologist, 70,* 515–526. http://dx.doi.org/10.1037/a0039510

Wolkow, A., Aisbett, B., Reynolds, J., Ferguson, S. A., & Main, L. C. (2016). Acute psychophysiological relationships between mood, inflammatory and cortisol changes in response to simulated physical firefighting work and sleep restriction. *Applied Psychophysiology and Biofeedback, 41*(2), 165–180. http://dx.doi.org/10.1007/s10484-015-9329-2

Wollan, M. (2015). How to beat a polygraph test. *The New York Times Magazine.* Retrieved from http://www.nytimes.com/2015/04/12/magazine/how-to-beat-apolygraph-test.html?_r=0

Wolpe, J., & Plaud, J. J. (1997). Pavlov's contributions to behavior therapy. *American Psychologist, 52,* 966–972.

Wong, Y. J., Ho, M.-H. R., Wang, S.-Y., & Miller, I. S. K. (2017). Meta-analyses of the relationship between conformity to masculine norms and mental health-related outcomes. *Journal of Counseling Psychology, 64*(1), 80–93. http://dx.doi.org/10.1037/cou0000176

Wood, A., Lupyan, G., Sherrin, S., & Niedenthal, P. (2016). Altering sensorimotor feedback disrupts visual discrimination of facial expressions. *Psychonomic Bulletin & Review, 23*(4), 1150–1156. http://dx.doi.org/10.3758/s13423-015-0974-5

Wood, J. T., & Fixmer-Oraiz, N. (2016). *Gendered lives: Communication, gender, and culture.* Boston, MA: Cengage.

Woodley of Menie, M. A., & Madison, G. (2015). The association between g and K in a sample of 4246 Swedish twins: A behavior genetic analysis. *Personality and Individual Differences, 74,* 270–274. http://dx.doi.org/10.1016/j.paid.2014.10.027

Woodley of Menie, M. A., Peñaherrera, M. A., Fernandes, H. B. F., Becker, D., & Flynn, J. R. (2016). It's getting bigger all the time: Estimating the Flynn effect from secular brain mass increases in Britain and Germany. *Learning and Individual Differences, 45,* 95–100. http://dx.doi.org/10.1016/j.lindif.2015.11.004

Woodward, N. D., & Heckers, S. (2015). Brain structure in neuropsychologically defined subgroups of schizophrenia and psychotic bipolar disorder. *Schizophrenia Bulletin, 41,* 1349–1359. http://dx.doi.org/10.1093/schbul/sbv048

Woodward, N. D., & Heckers, S. (2016). Mapping thalamocortical functional connectivity in chronic and early stages of psychotic disorders. *Biological Psychiatry, 79*(12), 1016–1025. http://dx.doi.org/10.1016/j.biopsych.2015.06.026

Workman, L., & Reader, W. (2014). *Evolutionary psychology: An introduction* (3rd ed.). New York, NY: Cambridge University Press.

World Facts (2016). Top ten leading causes of death in the world. *Worldatlas.* Retrieved from http://www.worldatlas.com/articles/top-ten-leading-causes-of-death-in-the-world.html

World Health Organization (WHO). (2011). Depression. *World Health Organization.* Retrieved from February 12, 2011 from http://www.who.int/topics/depression/en/

World Health Organization (WHO). (2017a). Mental health. *World Health Organization.* Retrieved February 27, 2017 from http://www.who.int/mental_health/prevention/genderwomen/en/

World Health Organization (WHO). (2017b). Suicide fact sheet. *World Health Organization.* Retrieved February 27, 2017 from http://www.who.int/mediacentre/factsheets/fs398/en/

Worthington, E. L., Jr., Berry, J. W., Hook, J. N., Davis, D. E., Scherer, M., Griffin, B. J., . . . Campana, K. L. (2015). Forgiveness-reconciliation and communication-conflict-resolution interventions versus retested controls in early married couples. *Journal of Counseling Psychology, 62,* 14–27. http://dx.doi.org/10.1037/cou0000045

Wright, H., Li, X., Fallon, N. B., Crookall, R., Giesbrecht, T., Thomas, A., . . . Stancak, A. (2016). Differential effects of hunger and satiety on insular cortex and hypothalamic functional connectivity. *European Journal of Neuroscience,* *43*(9), 1181–1189. http://dx.doi.org/10.1111/ejn.13182

Wright, P. J., & Bae, S. (2016). Pornography and male socialization. In Y. J. Wong & S. R. Wester (Eds.), *APA handbook of men and masculinities* (pp. 551–568). Washington, DC: American Psychological Association. http://dx.doi.org/10.1037/14594-025

Wright, T. (2016). *Gender and sexuality in male-dominated occupations: Women working in construction and transport.* New York, NY: Palgrave Macmillan.

Wright, T. J., Boot, W. R., & Brockmole, J. R. (2015). Functional fixedness: The functional significance of delayed disengagement based on attention set. *Journal of Experimental Psychology: Human Perception and Performance, 41,* 17–21. http://dx.doi.org/10.1037/xhp0000016

Wrzesniewski, A., Schwartz, B., Cong, X., Kane, M., Omar, A., & Kolditz, T. (2014). Multiple types of motives don't multiply the motivation of West Point cadets. *Proceedings of the National Academy of Sciences of the United States of America, 111,* 10990–10995. http://dx.doi.org/10.1073/pnas.1405298111

Wu, J., Perry, D. C., Bupp, J. E., Jiang, F., Polgar, W. E., Toll, L., & Zaveri, N. T. (2014). [125I] AT-1012, a new high affinity radioligand for the α3β4 nicotinic acetylcholine receptors. *Neuropharmacology, 77,* 193–199. http://dx.doi.org/10.1016/j.neuropharm.2013.09.023

Wu, X. N., Zhang, T., Qian, N. S., Guo, X. D., Yang, H. J., Huang, K. B., . . . Pan, S. Y. (2015). Antinociceptive effects of endomorphin-2: Suppression of substance P release in the inflammatory pain model rat. *Neurochemistry international, 82,* 1–9. http://dx.doi.org/10.1016/j.neuint.2015.01.004

Wyman, A. J., & Vyse, S. (2008). Science versus the stars: A double-blind test of the validity of the NEO Five Factor Inventory and computer-generated astrological natal charts. *Journal of General Psychology, 135,* 287–300.

Xi, J., Lee, M., LeSuer, W., Barr, P., Newton, K., & Poloma, M. (2016). Altruism and existential wellbeing. *Applied Research in Quality of Life, 12*(1), 67–88. http://dx.doi.org/10.1007/s11482-016-9453-z

Xiao, K., & Yamauchi, T. (2016). Subliminal semantic priming in near absence of attention: A cursor motion study. *Consciousness and Cognition, 38,* 88–98. http://dx.doi.org/10.1016/j.concog.2015.09.013

Xie, L., Kang, H., Xu, Q., Chen, M. J., Liao, Y., Thiyagarajan, M., . . . Nedergaard, M. (2013). Sleep drives metabolite clearance from the human brain. *Science, 342,* 373–377. http://dx.doi.org/10.1126/science.1241224

Xu, H., & Tracey, T. J. G. (2016). Cultural congruence with psychotherapy efficacy: A network meta-analytic examination in China. *Journal of Counseling Psychology, 63*(3), 359–365. http://dx.doi.org/10.1037/cou0000145

Xue, S. W., Tang, Y. Y., Tang, R., & Posner, M. I. (2014). Short-term meditation induces changes in brain resting EEG theta networks. *Brain and Cognition, 87,* 1–6. http://dx.doi.org/10.1016/j.bandc.2014.02.008

Yadollahpour, A., Hosseini, S. A., & Shakeri, A. (2016). Rtms for the treatment of depression: A comprehensive review of effective protocols on right dlpfc. *International Journal of Mental*

*Health and Addiction, 14,* 539–549. http://dx.doi.org/10.1007/s11469-016-9669-z

**Yamada, H.** (1997). *Different games, different rules: Why Americans and Japanese misunderstand each other.* London, UK: Oxford University Press.

**Yamaguchi, K., Inoue, Y., Ohki, N., Satoya, N., Inoue, F., Maeda, Y., . . . Nagai, A.** (2014). Gender-specific impacts of apnea, age, and BMI on parasympathetic nerve dysfunction during sleep in patients with obstructive sleep apnea. *PLoS ONE, 9,* 1–11. http://dx.doi.org/10.1371/journal.pone.0092808

**Yamazaki, T., Nagao, S., Lennon, W., & Tanaka, S.** (2015). Modeling memory consolidation during posttraining periods in cerebellovestibular learning. *Proceedings of the National Academy of Sciences of the United States of America, 112,* 3541–3546. http://dx.doi.org/10.1073/pnas.1413798112

**Yang, J., Hou, X., Wei, D., Wang, K., Li, Y., & Qiu, J.** (2016). Only-child and non-only-child exhibit differences in creativity and agreeableness: Evidence from behavioral and anatomical structural studies. *Brain Imaging and Behavior, 11*(2), 493–502. http://dx.doi.org/10.1007/s11682-016-9530-9

**Yang, J., Watanabe, J., Kanazawa, S., Nishida, S. Y., & Yamaguchi, M. K.** (2015). Infants' visual system nonretinotopically integrates color signals along a motion trajectory. *Journal of Vision, 15,* Article ID 25. http://dx.doi.org/10.1167/15.1.25

**Yang, T.** (2016). Image schemas in verb–particle constructions: Evidence from a behavioral experiment. *Journal of Psycholinguistic Research, 45,* 379–393. http://dx.doi.org/10.1007/s10936- 015-9354-6

**Yannis, G., Laiou, A., Papantoniou, P., & Gkartzonikas, C.** (2016). Simulation of texting impact on young drivers' behavior and safety on motorways. *Transportation Research Part F: Traffic Psychology and Behaviour, 41,* 10–18. http://dx.doi.org/10.1016/j.trf.2016.06.003

**Yapko, M. D.** (2015). *Essentials of hypnosis* (2nd ed.). New York, NY: Routledge/Taylor & Francis Group.

**Yasnitsky, A.** (2015). *Vygotsky: An intellectual biography.* Boca Raton, FL: Taylor & Francis Group.

**Yeager, D. S., Romero, C., Paunesku, D., Hulleman, C. S., Schneider, B., Hinojosa, C., . . . Dweck, C. S.** (2016). Using design thinking to improve psychological interventions: The case of the growth mindset during the transition to high school. *Journal of Educational Psychology, 108*(3), 374–391. http://doi.org/10.1037/edu0000098

**Yetish, G., Kaplan, H., Gurven, M., Wood, B., Pontzer, H., Manger, P. R., . . . Siegel, J. M.** (2015). Natural sleep and its seasonal variations in three pre-industrial societies. *Current Biology, 25,* 2862–2868. http://dx.doi.org/10.1016/j.cub.2015.09.046

**Yin, H., Pantazatos, S. P., Galfalvy, H., Huang, Y.-Y., Rosoklija, G. B., Dwork, A. J., . . . Mann, J. J.** (2016). A pilot integrative genomics study of GABA and glutamate neurotransmitter systems in suicide, suicidal behavior, and major depressive disorder. *American Journal of Medical Genetics Part B: Neuropsychiatric Genetics, 171,* 414–426. http://dx.doi.org/10.1002/ajmg.b.32423

**Yip, J. A., & Schweitzer, M. E.** (2016). Mad and misleading: Incidental anger promotes

deception. *Organizational Behavior and Human Decision Processes, 137,* 207–217. http://dx.doi.org/10.1016/j.obhdp.2016.09.006

**Yoshimoto, S., Imai, H., Kashino, M., & Takeuchi, T.** (2014). Pupil response and the subliminal mere exposure effect. *PLoS ONE, 9,* e90670. http://dx.doi.org/10.1371/journal. pone.0090670

**Yoshimura, S. M., & Berzins, K.** (2017). Grateful experiences and expressions: The role of gratitude expressions in the link between gratitude experiences and well-being. *Review of Communication, 17,* 106–118. http://dx.doi.org/10.1080/15358593.2017.1293836

**You, S., Lim, S. A., & Kim, E. K.** (2017). Relationships between social support, internal assets, and life satisfaction in Korean adolescents. *Journal of Happiness Studies.* No Pagination Specified. http://dx.doi.org/10.1007/s10902-017-9844-3

**Young, A., & Wimmer, R. D.** (2017). Implications for the thalamic reticular nucleus in impaired attention and sleep in schizophrenia. *Schizophrenia Research, 180,* 44–47. http://dx.doi.org/10.1016/j.schres.2016.07.011

**Young, K. S.** (2017). The evolution of Internet addiction. *Addictive Behaviors, 64,* 229–230. https://doi.org/10.1016/j.addbeh.2015.05.016

**Young, S. G., Brown, C. M., & Ambady, N.** (2012). Priming a natural or human-made environment directs attention to context-congruent threatening stimuli. *Cognition & Emotion, 26,* 927–933. http://dx.doi.org/10.1080/02699931.2011.625399

**Young, T.** (1802). On the theory of light and colours. *Philosophical Transactions of the Royal Society, 92,* 12–48.

**Youyou, W., Kosinski, M., & Stillwell, D.** (2015). Computer-based personality judgments are more accurate than those made by humans. *Proceedings of the National Academy of Sciences of the United States of America, 112,* 1036–1040. http://dx.doi.org/10.1073/pnas. 1418680112

**Youyou, W., Stillwell, D., Schwartz, H. A., & Kosinski, M.** (2017). Birds of a feather do flock together. *Psychological Science, 28*(3), 276–284. http://dx.doi.org/10.1177/0956797616678187

**Yu, C. K.-C.** (2012). Dream motif scale. *Dreaming, 22,* 18–52. http://dx.doi.org/10.1037/a0026171

**Yu, H., Cai, Q., Shen, B., Gao, X., & Zhou, X.** (2017). Neural substrates and social consequences of interpersonal gratitude: Intention matters. *Emotion, 17*(4), 589–601. http://dx.doi.org/10.1037/emo0000258

**Yu, J., Zhu, L., & Leslie, A. M.** (2016). Children's sharing behavior in mini-dictator games: The role of in-group favoritism and theory of mind. *Child Development, 87*(6), 1747–1757. http://dx.doi.org/10.1111/cdev.12635

**Zagorksi, N.** (2005). Profile of Elizabeth F. Loftus. *Proceedings of the National Academy of Sciences of the United States of America, 102,* 13721–13723. http://dx.doi.org/10.1073/pnas.0506223102

**Zaitsu, W.** (2016). External validity of Concealed Information Test experiment: Comparison of respiration, skin conductance, and heart rate between experimental and field card tests. *Psychophysiology, 53,* 1100–1107. http://dx.doi.org/10.1111/psyp.12650

**Zajonc, R. B.** (1965). Social facilitation. *Science, 149* (Whole No. 3681), 269–274. http://dx.doi.org/10.1126/science.149.3681.269

**Zarrindast, M. R., Ownegh, V., Rezayof, A., & Ownegh, F.** (2014). The involvement of dorsal

hippocampus in dextromethorphan-induced state-dependent learning in mice. *Pharmacology Biochemistry and Behavior, 116,* 90–95. http://dx.doi.org/10.1016/j.pbb.2013.11.015

**Zeanah, C. H., & Gleason, M. M.** (2015). Annual research review: Attachment disorders in early childhood—clinical presentation, causes, correlates, and treatment. *Journal of Child Psychology and Psychiatry, 56,* 207–222. http://dx.doi.org/10.1111/jcpp.12347

**Zerbe Enns, C., Rice, J. K., & Nutt, R. L.** (Eds.). (2015). *Psychological practice with women: Guidelines, diversity, empowerment.* Washington, DC: American Psychological Association. http://dx.doi.org/10.1037/14460-008

**Zerwas, S., Larsen, J. T., Petersen, L., Thornton, L. M., Mortensen, P. B., & Bulik, C. M.** (2015). The incidence of eating disorders in a Danish Nationwide Register Study: Associations with suicide risk and mortality. *Journal of Psychiatric Research, 65,* 16–22. http://dx.doi.org/10.1016/j.jpsychires.2015.03.003

**Zhang, B., Tian, D., Yu, C., Zhang, J., Tian, X., von Deenen, K. M., . . . Liu, Y.** (2015). Altered baseline brain activities before food intake in obese men: A resting state fMRI study. *Neuroscience Letters, 584,* 156–161.

**Zhang, H.** (2015). Moderate tolerance promotes tag-mediated cooperation in spatial Prisoner's dilemma game. *Physica A: Statistical Mechanics and its Applications, 424,* 52–61. http://dx.doi.org/10.1016/j.physa.2015.01.005

**Zhang, M. W., Harris, K. M., & Ho, R. C.** (2016). Is off -label repeat prescription of ketamine as a rapid antidepressant safe? Controversies, ethical concerns, and legal implications. *BMC Medical Ethics, 17,* Article 4. http://dx.doi.org/10.1186/s12910-016-0087-3

**Zhang, Q.-F., Yuan, Y.-T., Ren, Q.-T., & Lu, Y.-Z.** (2014). A randomized single-blind controlled trial of combination of Naikan and Morita therapy (NMT) in patients with generalized anxiety. *Chinese Mental Health Journal, 28,* 651–656.

**Zhang, W., Liu, H., Jiang, X., Wu, D., & Tian, Y.** (2014). A longitudinal study of posttraumatic stress disorder symptoms and its relationship with coping skill and locus of control in adolescents after an earthquake in China. *PLoS ONE, 9,* e88263. http://dx.doi.org/10.1371/journal.pone.0088263

**Zhang, Y., & Han, B.** (2016). Positive affect and mortality risk in older adults: A meta-analysis. *Psych Journal, 5*(2), 125–138. http://dx.doi.org/10.1002/pchj.129

**Zhang, Y., Lin, C. -H., Zhang, D., & Choi, Y.** (2017). Motivation, strategy, and English as a foreign language vocabulary learning: A structural equation modelling study. *British Journal of Educational Psychology, 87,* 57–74. http://dx.doi.org/10.1111/bjep.12135

**Zhang, Y. Q., Zhu, D., Zhou, X. Y., Liu, Y. Y., Qin, B., Ren, G. P., & Xie, P.** (2015). Bilateral repetitive transcranial magnetic stimulation for treatment-resistant depression: A systematic review and meta-analysis of randomized controlled trials. *Brazilian Journal of Medical and Biological Research, 48,* 198–206. http://dx.doi.org/10.1590/1414-431X20144270

**Zhao, J., & Wood, J. N.** (2015). Glycine at the gate—from model to mechanism. *Neuron, 85,* 152–1154. http://dx.doi.org/10.1016/j.neuron.2015.03.012

**Zhong, W., Li, Y., Li, P., Xu, G., & Mo, L.** (2015). Short-term trained lexical categories produce preattentive categorical perception of color: Evidence from ERPs. *Psychophysiology, 52,* 98–106. http://dx.doi.org/10.1111/psyp.12294

**Zhou, B., Gao, W., Lv, J., Yu, C., Wang, S., Liao, C., . . . Li, L.** (2015). Genetic and environmental influences on obesity-related phenotypes in Chinese twins reared apart and together. *Behavior Genetics, 45,* 427–437. http://dx.doi.org/10.1007/s10519-015-9711-0

**Zhou, X., Hu, X., Zhang, C., Wang, H., Zhu, X., Xu, L., . . . Yu, Y.** (2016). Aberrant functional connectivity and structural atrophy in subcortical vascular cognitive impairment: Relationship with cognitive impairments. *Frontiers in Aging Neuroscience, 8,* Article 14. http://dx.doi.org/10.3389/fnagi.2016.00014

**Zhou, X., & Wu, X.** (2016). The relationship between rumination, posttraumatic stress disorder, and posttraumatic growth among Chinese adolescents after earthquake: A longitudinal study. *Journal of Affective Disorders, 193,* 242–248. http://dx.doi.org/10.1016/j.jad.2015.12.076

**Zhu, B., Chen, C., Loftus, E. F., He, Q., Chen, C., Lei, D., . . . Dong, Q.** (2012). Brief exposure to misinformation can lead to long-term false memories. *Applied Cognitive Psychology, 26,* 301–307. http://dx.doi.org/10.1002/acp.1825

**Zilcha-Mano, S., Muran, J. C., Hungr, C., Eubanks, C. F., Saftran, J. D., & Winston, A.** (2016). The relationship between alliance and outcome: Analysis of a two-person perspective on alliance and session outcome. *Journal of Consulting and Clinical Psychology, 84*(6), 484–496. http://dx.doi.org/10.1037/ccp0000058

**Zilioli, S., Slatcher, R. B., Chi, P., Li, X., Zhao, J., & Zhao, G.** (2017). The impact of daily and trait loneliness on diurnal cortisol and sleep among children affected by parental HIV/AIDS. *Psychoneuroendocrinology, 75,* 64–71. http://dx.doi.org/10.1016/j.psyneuen.2016.10.012

**Zimbardo, P. G.** (1993). Stanford prison experiment: A 20-year retrospective. Invited presentation at the meeting of the Western Psychological Association, Phoenix, AZ.

**Zimbardo, P. G., Ebbeson, E. B., & Maslach, C.** (1977). *Influencing attitudes and changing behavior.* Reading, MA: Addison-Wesley.

**Zimmer, C.** (2017, February 2). The purpose of sleep? To forget, scientists say. *New York Times.* Retrieved from https://www.nytimes.com/2017/02/02/science/sleep-memory-brain-forgetting.html

**Zinbarg, R. E., Anand, D., Lee, J. K., Kendall, A. D., & Nuñez, M.** (2015). Generalized anxiety disorder, panic disorder, social anxiety disorder, and specific phobias. In P. H. Blaney, R. F. Krueger, & T. Millon (Eds.), *Oxford textbook of psychopathology* (3rd ed., pp. 133–162). New York, NY: Oxford University Press.

**Zinik, G., & Padilla, J.** (2016). Rape and paraphilic coercive disorders. In A. Phenix & H. M. Hoberman (Eds.), *Sexual offending: Predisposing antecedents, assessments and management* (pp. 45–66). New York, NY: Springer Science + Business Media. http://dx.doi.org/10.1007/978-1-4939-2416-5_4

**Zorrilla, I., López-Zurbano, S., Cano, A. I., & González-Pinto, A.** (2015). Schizophrenia and gender. In M. Sáenz-Herrero (Ed.), *Psychopathology in women: Incorporating gender perspective into descriptive psychopathology* (pp. 621–639). Cham, CH: Springer. http://dx.doi.org/10.1007/978-3-319-05870-2

**Zuberbühler, K.** (2015). Linguistic capacity of non-human animals. *WIREs Cognitive Science, 6,* 313–321. http://dx.doi.org/10.1002/wcs.1338

**Zuckerman, M.** (1978, February). The search for high sensation. *Psychology Today,* 38–46.

**Zuckerman, M.** (1979). *Sensation seeking: Beyond the optimal level of arousal.* Hillsdale, NJ: Erlbaum.

**Zuckerman, M.** (1994). *Behavioral expressions and biosocial bases of sensation seeking.* New York: NY: Cambridge University Press.

**Zuckerman, M.** (2004). The shaping of personality: Genes, environments, and chance encounters. *Journal of Personality Assessment, 82,* 11–22.

**Zuckerman, M.** (2014). Sensation seeking, impulsivity and the balance between behavioral approach and inhibition. *Personality and Individual Differences, 60,* S4. http://dx.doi.org/10.1016/j.paid.2013.07.150

**Zuckerman, M., & Aluja, A.** (2015). Measures of sensation seeking. In G. J. Boyle, D. H. Saklofske, & G. Matthews (Eds.), *Measures of personality and social psychological constructs* (pp. 352–380). San Diego, CA: Elsevier Academic Press. http://dx.doi.org/10.1016/B978-0-12-386915-9.00013-9

**Zvolensky, M. J., Jardin, C., Garey, L., Robles, Z., & Sharp, C.** (2016). Acculturative stress and experiential avoidance: Relations to depression, suicide, and anxiety symptoms among minority college students. *Cognitive Behaviour Therapy, 45,* 501–517. http://dx.doi.org/10.1080/16506073.2016.1205658

**Zysberg, L., Orenshtein, C., Gimmon, E., & Robinson, R.** (2017). Emotional intelligence, personality, stress, and burnout among educators. *International Journal of Stress Management, 24*(Suppl 1), 122–136. http://dx.doi.org/10.1037/str0000028

Constantino, M. J., 519
Conway, M., 240
Cook, P. F., 197
Cooper, A. J., 89
Cooper, C., 108, 273
Cooper, M., 333
Coplan, R. J., 330
Copernicus, N., 16
Cordeira, J. W., 67
Corkin, S., 243
Corona, R., 87
Corr, C. A., 345, 346
Corr, D. M., 345
Corr, P. J., 89
Correia, S. S., 212
Correll, J., 144
Corwyn, R. F., 319
Costa, A. L., 317
Costa, P. T., Jr., 431
Cote, J., 433
Courage, M. L., 302
Courtet, P., 483
Coutrot, A., 362
Couyoumdjian, A., 416
Coviello, L., 413
Covington, M. V., 401
Coyne, J. C., 96
Craig, A. R., 202
Craik, F. I., 223, 224
Crane, C. A., 17, 172, 272, 555
Cranley, N. M., 84
Craske, M. G., 6, 500
Crawford, M. J., 483
Crego, C., 483
Crescentini, C., 177
Creswell, J. D., 103, 177
Cristea, I. A., 503
Cristofori, I., 555
Croizet, J.-C., 534
Crooks, R., 355, 368, 369, 378, 379
Cross, W., 487
Crosson-Tower, C., 376
Cruwys, T., 524
Csikszentmihaly, M., 156
Csordas, T. J., 328
Cuijpers, P., 517
Cullen, D., 393
Cummings, E., 340
Cummins, D. D., 546
Curtiss, S., 292
Cusack, K., 508
Cussen, V. A., 433

**D**

D'Aconti, A., 469
Dahling, J. J., 440
Dahmer, Jeffrey, 482
Dale, A., 164
D'Ambrosio, C., 303
Dambrun, M., 548
Dan, B., 46
Dana, R. H., 445
Dando, C. J., 406
Daniluk, J. C., 370
Danner, F., 158
Dargis, M., 483
Darley, J. M., 557, 558
Darwin, C., 8, 269, 413, 555
Data-Franco, J., 475
Datta, A., 357
Datu, J. A. D., 2, 38, 400
Davidson, P., 192
DaVinci, L., 162

Davies, M. S., 281
Davis, N. T., 552
Dawkins, R., 8
Dawson, K. M., 108
Day, M. A., 96
Day, M. V., 241
De Castella, K., 281
De Cuyper, B., 551
DeGeneres, E., 352, 366
de Jonge, P., 404
de Klerk, F. W., 325
De Putter, L. M. S., 481
de Tychey, C., 429
Dean, J., 470
Deary, I. J., 280
Deblinger, E., 376
DeBord, K. A., 364, 524
Decety, J., 326
Deci, E. L., 401
Deconinck, F. J. A., 122
Deeb, R., 167
Dekel, S., 318
Del Río, F. J., 372
Delahaij, R., 100
Delgado Gaitan, C., 295
Delmonico, D. L., 376
DeLoache, J. S., 214
DeLongis, A., 381
Dement, W. C., 162
Demos, K. E., 158, 159
Denholm, R., 298
Denmark, T., 413
Dennis, A. B., 399
Denny, B. T., 483
Denovan, A., 103
Deonarine, J. M., 278
Depp, C. A., 473
DeRosse, P., 70, 479
DeSoto, K. A., 245
Desrosiers, A., 317
DeVos, J., 309
DeWall, C. N., 537, 555
Deweese, M. M., 189
Dhamija, D., 482, 483
Diamond, A., 69, 72, 104
Diamond, Adele, 45, 69
Diaz, K. M., 97
Diaz, Vickery, K., 522
Dibbets, P., 262, 449, 467
Dickert, S., 556
Dickinson, G. E., 345
Dickter, C. L., 542
Diego, M. A., 312
Dieleman, G. C., 89
Diener, E., 7, 8, 104, 415, 437
Diering, G. H., 163
Dietrich, J., 392
DiFeliceantonio, A. G., 52
DiFeo, G., 57
Digdon, N., 449
DiGrazia, J., 22
Dijkstra, P., 563
Dill, K. E., 209
Dillon, H. M., 560
Dillon, S., 282
Dimaggio, G., 498, 503
Dimidjian, S., 503
Dimberg, U., 410
Ding, Y. H., 315
Dingus, T. A., 155, 156
Dinsmore, D. L., 224
Dirkes, J., 366
Dirks-Linhorst, P. A., 462

Dixon, M. J., 202
Dixon, R. W., 100
Dobrow, S., 22
Dobson, K. S., 503
Dodge, E., 520
Dolev-Cohen, M., 100
Doliński, D., 548
Dombrowski, S. C., 274
Domhoff, G., 164, 165
Domhoff, G. W., 162, 163, 164, 165
D'Onofrio, B. M., 300
Doran, J. M., 519
dos Santos, R. G., 513
Doty, R. L., 304
Doulatram, G., 25, 298, 299
Dovey, T. M., 133
Dovidio, J. F., 542, 556
Dowdell, K., 12
Draganich, C., 30
Drake, E. C., 90
Drane, C. F., 391
Drążkowski, D., 524
Dreu, C. K. W. D., 540
Drew, L., 162
Driessen, E., 498
Drigotas, S. M., 380
D'Souza, J., 393, 437
Duarte-Guterman, P., 63
Dubois, L., 398
Duckworth, A., 283
Duits, P., 470
DuMonthier, A., 357
Duniec, E., 315
Dunlosky, J., 34, 236, 249
Dunn, E. W., 84, 341, 415, 525
Dunn, T. L., 261
Dunne, F. J., 175
Duntley, J. D., 554
Dupuis, K., 305
Durlach, C., 239, 240
Dutil, C., 158
Dutton, J., 334
Dvir-Gvirsman, S., 553
Dweck, C. S., 2, 38, 276, 281, 283, 380, 400, 440
Dworkin, A., 559
Dye, C. D., 144
Dyson, K. S., 535

**E**

Eade, S., 56
Eagle, G. T., 519
Eagly, A. H., 362
Earleywine, M., 175
Eaton, N. R., 486
Ebbesen, E. B., 440, 551
Ebbeson, E. B., 551
Ebbinghaus, H., 233, 252
Eddy, K. T., 398
Edel, M.-A., 483
Edelson, L. R., 208
Edwards, K. M., 339
Eggermont, J. J., 129
Eggermont, S., 537
Eguchi, H., 108
Ehrenreich, S. E., 84
Ehrlich, K. B., 83
Eich, E., 231
Eichenbaum, H., 225, 228
Eienstein, A., 152, 162, 177, 279, 435, 437
Eisner, P., 555

Ekman, P., 413
El-Alayli, A., 282
El-Bar, N., 6, 192
Elder, A. B., 366
Eldred, S. M., 174
Eley, T. C., 470
Eligon, J., 174
Elison, J., 344
Elkind, D., 311
Elliot, A. J., 144, 145
Elliott, A., 424
Ellis, A., 501–502
Ellis, H., 354
Emilien, G., 239, 240
Emmons, M. L., 382
Emmons, R. A., 416
Emslie, G. J., 481
Endicott, K. L., 328
Endicott, K. M., 328
Englar-Carlson, M., 428
English, T., 341
Enright, R. D., 382
Epley, N., 415
Erdal, K., 30
Erekson, D. M., 500
Ericsson, K. A., 283
Erikson, E., 330–332
Erritzøe, J., 279
Erviti, M., 226
Esch, T., 177
Escher, M. C., 176
Eskreis-Winkler, L., 283
Espelage, D. L., 360
Esping, A., 273, 276
Espinosa-Hernández, G., 354
Esposito, G., 269
Essau, C. A., 467
Estay, C., 535
Euler, H. A., 264
Evans, E. H., 398
Everett, C., 338
Everett, S. V., 338
Eviatar, Z., 154
Eyber, C., 525
Eyo, U. B., 45, 46, 57
Eysenck, H. J., 431

**F**

Faddiman, A., 484
Fadel, L., 546
Fagelson, M., 129
Fahnehjelm, K. T., 57
Fales, J., 504
Fales, M. R., 559
Fan, H., 51, 122
Fan, S. P., 268
Fang, J., 9
Fang, Z., 158
Fantz, R. L., 302
Farah, M. J., 415
Farber, B. A., 318
Farkas, T., 356
Farmer, T. A., 108
Fast, L. C., 397
Fatemi, S. H., 479
Faulkner, G., 525
Fava, G. A., 525
Fehr, B., 317, 563
Fein, S., 540
Feinle-Bisset, C., 395
Feldman, S., 229
Felleman, B. I., 103
Felson, J., 280

Riecher-Rössler, A., 478
Riede, T., 269
Riediger, M., 341
Rimmele, U., 241
Rinehart, S. J., 360
Risal, A., 404
Risko, E. F., 261
Ritter, J. O., 343
Rizvi, S. L., 483
Rizzolatti, G., 213
Robbins, L., 57
Robbins, T. W., 442
Robehmed, N., 457
Roberts, L. W., 468
Robin, F., 416
Robinaugh, D. J., 377
Robins, S. K., 222
Robinson, F. P., 34
Robinson, K. J., 316
Robinson, O., 332
Robison, L. S., 334
Robnett, R. D., 359
Rock, D. A., 282
Rode, L., 305
Rodkey, E. N., 302
Rodriguez, C. M., 318
Roediger, H. L., II, 23, 33, 36, 37, 230, 245, 249, 534
Roepke, A. M., 524
Rogers, C., 6, 99, 436–437, 438, 466, 499, 500
Rogers, P., 145
Rogge, R. D., 518
Rohlfs Domínguez, P., 212
Roisman, G. I., 317
Rokke, P. D., 231
Romeo, R. D., 83
Romero, C., 281
Rood, L., 100
Roof, Dylann, 464
Rooseve H. E., 437
Roozen, S., 25, 298, 299
Rorschach, H., 446
Rosch, E., 259
Rosch, E. H., 268
Rosen, J., 532
Rosenberg, A., 270
Rosenhan, D. L., 462
Rosenström, T., 482, 483
Rosenthal, N. E., 409
Rosenthal, R., 29
Rosenthal, S. R., 84
Rosenzweig, M. R., 239
Rosner, T. M., 137
Ross, B. M., 237
Ross, L., 534
Ross, M., 241
Rossi, P., 107
Roth, D., 275
Roth, G., 436
Rothbaum, F., 316
Rothenberg, A., 265
Rothgerber, H., 282
Rotter, J. B., 102, 440
Rottinghaus, B., 422
Rouder, J. N., 145
Roulette, J. W., 295
Routh, E. R., 262
Routledge, C., 145
Rowling, J. K., 495, 499, 502, 525
Roy, J., 552
Roy, L., 522
Ruben, M. A., 405

Rubenfeld, J., 283
Rubin, J. B., 344
Rubin, L. H., 91
Rucklidge, J. J., 333
Ruffman, T., 208
Ruini, C., 525
Ruiz-Aranda, D., 278
Rumbaugh, D. M., 271
Ruocco, A. C., 483
Rusbult, C. E., 380, 381
Rushton, J. P., 279
Russell, V. A., 89
Rutland, A., 542
Ryan, C. J., 522
Ryan, R. M., 401
Rycholowska, M., 270, 271
Rymer, R., 292

**S**

Saadat, S., 368
Sacco, R., 335
Sachsenweger, M. A., 524
Sacks, O., 142
Sáenz-Herrero, M., 523
Safer, M. A., 245
Sagong, B., 132
Saks, Elyn, 458
Salk, R. H., 485
Salovey, P., 278
Salters-Pedneault, K., 483
Salvi, C., 259
Sam, Michael, 543
Sample, I., 221
Samson, J. A., 376
Samuels, B. A., 512
Sánchez-Villegas, A., 473
Sand, E., 541
Sand, R. S., 429
Sandberg, L., 354
Sanders, A. R., 364
Sanderson, C. A., 2, 3, 82, 179, 240, 295–296, 441, 564
Sandner, B., 57
Sándor, P., 164
Sanjuán, P., 449
Sankar, A., 504
Santos, T. O., 273
Sarafino, E. P., 108
Saraswat, A., 360
Sargent, J. D., 107
Saridi, M., 541
Sarkova, M., 382
Sassenberg, K., 120
Satir, V., 302
Satterly, M. V., 174
Saucier, G., 9
Savage-Rumbaugh, E. S., 272
Saxon, S. V., 304
Sbarra, D. A., 84, 524, 525, 561
Schachter, S., 408
Schaeffer, E. L., 212
Schäfer, M., 465
Schalet, A. T., 354
Schare, M. L., 506
Scharfman, H. E., 63
Scharrer, E., 209
Schartel Dunn, S., 282
Schartner, M. M., 174
Scheele, D., 53, 560
Scherman, D., 297
Schick, T., Jr., 145
Schilling, C., 442
Schim, S. M., 345

Schimmel, P., 429
Schindler, B., 470
Schlegel, A., 355
Schlichting, M. L., 230
Schmid, P. C., 541
Schmid Mast, M., 362
Schmidt, F., 142
Schmidt, G. B., 170
Schmidt, S. R., 241
Schmitgen, M. M., 258
Schmitt, D. P., 362
Schnall, P. L., 108
Schneider, K., 436, 437, 499
Schneidman, E. S., 465
Schoenmaker, C., 280
Schomerus, G., 459
Schonert-Reichl, K. A., 104
Schroder, H. S., 489
Schröder, J., 521
Schroeder, D. A., 556
Schroeder, J., 415
Schroers, W., 236
Schug, J., 413
Schulz, H. M., 547
Schulze, L., 410
Schunk, D. H., 400
Schüz, B., 396
Schwartz, A. J., 237
Schwartz, B., 119, 132, 401
Schwartz, D. L., 258, 264
Schwartz, N. G., 167
Schwartz, P., 378
Schwartz, S. J., 332
Schwarz, A., 334
Schwarzschild, M. A., 45, 56
Schweitzer, M. E., 555
Scoboria, A., 246, 247
Scott, C., 313
Scott-Phillips, T. C., 271
Scribner, S., 237, 312
Sdrulla, A. D., 168
Seau, Junior, 474
Seay, T. A., 496, 523
Sebelius, K., 107
Sedikides, C., 449
Seebauer, L., 555
Seedat, S., 486
Seedman, A. A., 557
Seeley, R. J., 395
Segarra-Echebarría, R., 368
Segrin, C., 381, 382
Sehgal, P., 489
Seifer, R., 330
Sekiguchi, A., 86
Seligman, M. E., 200
Seligman, M. E. P., 7, 8, 103, 200, 474, 524
Sell, C., 498
Sella, F., 144
Selye, H., 82, 88–89, 92
Semlyen, J., 366
Sénécal, V., 46
Seo, H.-S., 133
Shackelford, T. K., 368
Shafer, K., 338
Shaked, A., 409
Shakya, A., 95
Shamay-Tsoory, S. G., 89, 525
Shand, G., 535
Shannon, P. J., 487
Shapiro, S. L., 524
Sharma, A., 158
Sharma, V. K., 69

Shashkevich, A., 532
Shaver, P. R., 318
Shaw, A. M., 84
Shaw, N. D., 303
Sheehy, G., 343
Shenk, J. W., 423
Shenkman, R., 390
Shepherd, S. V., 214
Sher, L., 461, 483
Sherif, M., 542
Sherman, R. A., 440
Shiffrin, R. M., 225
Shigemura, J., 540
Shin, D.-H., 432, 445
Shin, J., 283
Shiraev, E., 460
Shohamy, D., 240, 398
Shors, T. J., 57
Short, F., 474, 498
Shuster, M. M., 341
Shweder, R. A., 312
Siegel, A. B., 163, 293
Siegel, J. M., 165, 166
Sierksma, J., 542
Sierra, J. C., 372
Sievert, L., 304
Sifferlin, A., 258, 409
Signorielli, N., 359
Silber, K., 476
Silver, K. E., 376
Silver, N., 381
Silverstein, M. L., 446
Silvia, P. J., 522
Silvia, P. J., 11
Simm, A., 89
Simons, D. J., 154
Simons, L. G., 83
Simpson, J. A., 563
Sin, N. L., 97
Sinatra, R., 306
Singer, J. E., 408
Siniscalchi, A., 173
Sissa Medialab, 410
Skinner, B. F., 6, 195–196, 199, 201, 202, 203
Slane, J. D., 398
Slotnick, S. D., 222
Smalheiser, N. R., 475
Smart, R., 399
Smiley, P. A., 330
Smith, A. M., 16, 97, 524
Smith, C. E., 326
Smith, D. R., 108
Smith, K. Z., 84, 93
Smith, L. S., 520
Smith, M., 159
Smith, M. L., 517
Smith, N. K., 175, 370
Smith, R., 91, 340, 482
Smith, S. M., 97, 535
Sobral, M., 305
Sofer, C., 559
Solms, M., 162
Solnit, R., 93
Soloff, P. H., 483
Solomon, G. S., 241
Solomon, J., 317
Solomon, P. L., 339
Solomonov, N., 429, 497, 498
Solotaroff, L., 140
Song, A., 158
Song, M. J., 57
Song, T. M., 525

# Subject Index

*Note:* Page numbers followed by an "f" indicates the entry is in a figure, and a page number followed by a "t" indicates the entry is in a table.

## A

Abnormal behavior, 459–460, 459f. *See also* Psychological disorders
Absolute threshold, 119, 119t, 120f
Abuse, domestic violence and, 338–339
Academic success, poverty and, 92
Accommodation, 141, 306, 307f
  depth perception and, 140
  aging and, 303
Acculturative stress, 86–87
Acetylcholine, 52t
Achievement measurement, 400
Achievement motivation, 399–400
Acquisition
  classical conditioning and, 192, 191t, 191f, 193f, 204t
  operant conditioning and, 201, 201f. 204t
Acronyms, 232
Action potential, 48
Activation-synthesis theory of dreams, 163
Active listening, 500
Active reading, 33–34
Activity theory of aging, 339
Actor-observer effect, 535, 535f
Acute stress, 83–84
Adaptation-level phenomenon, 417
Adaption/protection theory of sleep, 162
Adderall, 333
Addiction, 168
  addictive disorders, 463t
  career costs of, 170
  different cultures and, 174
  psychoactive drugs and, 168
Adler, Alfred, 428
Adolescent development
  brain changes and, 302, 302f
  growth spurts and, 301, 302f
  physical development, 301–302
  puberty and, 301–302
  secondary sex characteristics and, 302, 302f
  sleep and, 302
  teenage brain and, 302, 302f
Adolescent egocentrism, 310, 310f, 311
Adolescent narcissism, 310, 310f
Adoption studies, personality and, 443, 443f
Adrenal glands, 52t, 53, 84, 96
Adrenaline (epinephrine), 52t, 53, 96
Adult development
  ageism and, 304–305
  brain in late adulthood, 304
  cellular-clock theory, 304
  emerging/young adulthood, 303
  Hayflick limit and, 304
  late adulthood, 303–304
  male climacteric and, 303
  menopause and, 303
  middle adulthood, 303
  physical development, 303–305
  secondary aging and, 304
  wear-and-tear theory and, 304
Adulthood
  aging and, 339–340
  attachment styles in, 316–317
  challenges of, 335–341
  divorce and, 336

domestic violence and, 338–339
empty-nest syndrome and, 342, 342f
enduring love and, 336–338
grief, death, and dying, 342–345
midlife crises and, 342
relationships and, 335–339
Advertising, 190, 190f
Aerial perspective, 141
Age-related positivity effect, 340
Ageism, 304–305
Aggression, 554–555
  biological factors and, 554–555
  conflicts and, 382
  psychosocial factors and, 555
  reduction of, 555
Aging
  activity theory of aging, 339
  age-related positivity effect, 340
  brain differences and, 341
  challenges of, 339–340
  disengagement theory and, 339, 340f
  happiness and, 340-341
  hearing and, 129, 129f
  sleep cycle and, 163, 163f
  socioemotional selectivity theory and, 340
  theories of, 339–340
  work and retirement and, 339
Agonist drugs, 51, 168, 168f
Agoraphobia, 469
Agreeableness, 431-432, 431f
AIDS (acquired immunodeficiency virus), 374
Ainsworth, Mary, 315
Ainsworth's levels of attachment, 315
Alcohol intake, 171–172
  behavioral effects and, 172, 172t, 172f
  binge drinking and, 172, 172t, 172f
  fetal alcohol syndrome (FAS) and, 298, 298f
  rape and, 172, 172f
  sexual effects of, 372t
Alcoholics Anonymous, 520
Algorithms, problem solving and, 260
All-or-nothing principle, 48
All-or-nothing thinking, 504
Altered state of consciousness (ASC), 153. *See also* Sleep and dreams
Altruism, 556–558
  bystander effect and, 557
  diffusion of responsibility and, 557
  egoistic model of helping and, 556
  empathy-altruism hypothesis, 556
  evolutionary theory of helping and, 556
  Kitty Genovese case and, 556–557
  models for, 556, 556f
  process diagram and, 557, 557f
  promoting helping and, 558
Alzheimer's disease (AD), 243, 243f, 304
American Crowbar Case, 71, 71f
American Psychological Association (APA), 9, 11, 17
American Sign Language (ASL), 271, 271f, 272f
Amnesia, 242–243, 242f
  anterograde amnesia, 242–243, 242f
  consolidation and, 242
  retrograde amnesia, 242–243, 242f
  source amnesia, 236, 236f

Amok, 462
Amphetamine, 170, 171t
  psychosis and, 170, 461
  sexual effects of, 372t
Amplitude, 123
Amygdala, 65, 66f, 404, 404f
Amyotrophic lateral sclerosis (ALS), 56, 56f
Anal-expulsive personality, 427
Anal-retentive personality, 427
Anal stage, psychosexual, 427
Analytical psychology, 428
Androgyny, 358–359
Andropause, 303
Animism, 308
Anorexia nervosa, 399t
Antagonist drugs, 51, 168, 169f
Anterograde amnesia, 242–243, 242f
Antianxiety drugs, 511t
Antidepressant drugs, 511–512, 511t, 512f
Antipsychotic drugs, 511t
Antisocial personality disorder (ASPD), 482–483
Anxiety disorders, 463t, 467–471
  biological factors and, 470–471
  faulty cognitive processes and, 469
  generalized anxiety disorder, 467–468, 468f
  major categories of, 467, 468f
  maladaptive learning and, 470
  panic disorder, 468
  phobias, 468–469
  psychological factors and, 469–470, 469f
  sex hormones and, 471
  sociocultural factors and, 471
Anxious/ambivalent attachment, 315, 316, 316f
Anxious/avoidant attachment, 315, 316, 316f
Apes, language research and, 271–272, 271f, 272f
Applied research, 13–14, 14f
Approach-approach conflict, 84
Approach-avoidance conflict, 84
Archetypes, 428, 428f
Archival research, 22
Artificial concepts, 259
Artificial intelligence (AI), 258
Asch, Solomon, 546, 546f
Assertiveness, conflicts and, 382
Assimilation, cognitive development and, 306, 307f
Association areas, brain, 73
Association for Psychological Science (APS), 11, 17
Associative learning, 194
Asylums, 460
Attachment, 314–317
  adulthood and, 316–317
  Ainsworth's levels of, 315, 316f
  infants and, 315, 316f
  romantic attachment styles, 317
  touch and, 314–315, 314f, 315f
Attention, observational learning and, 209, 209f
Attention-deficit/hyperactivity disorder (ADHD), 332–333
Attention narrowing, 240
Attitudes, 536–538
  changes and, 537–538, 537f